WORLD TRADE ORGANIZATION

Dispute Settlement Reports

2005

Volume XXIII

Pages 11003-11752

CAMBRIDGE
UNIVERSITY PRESS

CAMBRIDGE
UNIVERSITY PRESS

Shaftesbury Road, Cambridge CB2 8EA, United Kingdom

One Liberty Plaza, 20th Floor, New York, NY 10006, USA

477 Williamstown Road, Port Melbourne, VIC 3207, Australia

314–321, 3rd Floor, Plot 3, Splendor Forum, Jasola District Centre, New Delhi – 110025, India

103 Penang Road, #05–06/07, Visioncrest Commercial, Singapore 238467

Cambridge University Press is part of Cambridge University Press & Assessment, a department of the University of Cambridge.

We share the University's mission to contribute to society through the pursuit of education, learning and research at the highest international levels of excellence.

www.cambridge.org
Information on this title: www.cambridge.org/9780521886031

First published 2007

A catalogue record for this publication is available from the British Library

ISBN 978-0521-88603-1 Hardback

THE WTO DISPUTE SETTLEMENT REPORTS

The *Dispute Settlement Reports* of the World Trade Organization (the "WTO") include panel and Appellate Body reports, as well as arbitration awards, in disputes concerning the rights and obligations of WTO Members under the provisions of the *Marrakesh Agreement Establishing the World Trade Organization.* The *Dispute Settlement Reports* are available in English. Volumes comprising one or more complete cases contain a cumulative list of published disputes. The cumulative list for cases that cover more than one volume is to be found in the first volume for that case.

This volume may be cited as DSR 2005:XXIII

TABLE OF CONTENTS

MEXICO – DEFINITIVE ANTI-DUMPING MEASURES ON BEEF AND RICE

COMPLAINT WITH RESPECT TO RICE

Report of the Panel

WT/DS295/R

Adopted by the Dispute Settlement Body
on 20 December 2005
as Modified by the Appellate Body Report

TABLE OF CONTENTS

TABLE OF ANNEXES

ANNEX A

RESPONSES OF THE UNITED STATES TO MEXICO'S REQUEST OF A PRELIMINARY RULING

ANNEX B

PARTIES' AND THIRD PARTIES' RESPONSES TO QUESTIONS POSED IN THE CONTEXT OF THE FIRST SUBSTANTIVE MEETING OF THE PANEL

ANNEX C

PARTIES' RESPONSES TO QUESTIONS POSED IN THE CONTEXT OF THE SECOND SUBSTANTIVE MEETING OF THE PANEL

ANNEX D

REQUEST FOR CONSULTATIONS AND REQUEST FOR THE ESTABLISHMENT OF A PANEL

TABLE OF CASES CITED IN THIS REPORT

Short Title	Full Case Title and Citation
Argentina – Footwear (EC)	Appellate Body Report, *Argentina – Safeguard Measures on Imports of Footwear*, WT/DS121/AB/R, adopted 12 January 2000, DSR 2000:I, 515
Argentina – Poultry Anti-Dumping Duties	Panel Report, *Argentina – Definitive Anti-Dumping Duties on Poultry from Brazil*, WT/DS241/R, adopted 19 May 2003
Brazil – Aircraft	Appellate Body Report, *Brazil – Export Financing Programme for Aircraft*, WT/DS46/AB/R, adopted 20 August 1999, DSR 1999:III, 1161
Brazil – Aircraft	Panel Report, *Brazil – Export Financing Programme for Aircraft*, WT/DS46/R, adopted 20 August 1999, as modified by the Appellate Body Report, WT/DS46/AB/R, DSR 1999:III, 1221
Canada – Wheat Exports and Grain Imports	Panel Report, *Canada – Measures Relating to Exports of Wheat and Treatment of Imported Grain*, WT/DS276/R, adopted 27 September 2004, as upheld by the Appellate Body Report, WT/DS276/AB/R
EC – Bananas III	Appellate Body Report, *European Communities – Regime for the Importation, Sale and Distribution of Bananas*, WT/DS27/AB/R, adopted 25 September 1997, DSR 1997:II, 591
EC – Bed Linen	Appellate Body Report, *European Communities – Anti-Dumping Duties on Imports of Cotton-Type Bed Linen from India*, WT/DS141/AB/R, adopted 12 March 2001, DSR 2001:V, 2049
EC – Bed Linen (Article 21.5 – India)	Appellate Body Report, *European Communities – Anti-Dumping Duties on Imports of Cotton-Type Bed Linen from India – Recourse to Article 21.5 of the DSU by India*, WT/DS141/AB/RW, adopted 24 April 2003
Guatemala – Cement II	Panel Report, *Guatemala – Definitive Anti-Dumping Measures on Grey Portland Cement from Mexico*, WT/DS156/R, adopted 17 November 2000, DSR 2000:XI, 5295

Short Title	Full Case Title and Citation
Japan – Agricultural Products II	Panel Report, *Japan – Measures Affecting Agricultural Products*, WT/DS76/R, adopted 19 March 1999, as modified by the Appellate Body Report, WT/DS76/AB/R, DSR 1999:I, 315
Japan – Film	Panel Report, *Japan – Measures Affecting Consumer Photographic Film and Paper*, WT/DS44/R, adopted 22 April 1998, DSR 1998:IV, 1179
Korea – Dairy	Appellate Body Report, *Korea – Definitive Safeguard Measure on Imports of Certain Dairy Products*, WT/DS98/AB/R, adopted 12 January 2000, DSR 2000:I, 3
Mexico – Corn Syrup	Panel Report, *Mexico – Anti-Dumping Investigation of High Fructose Corn Syrup (HFCS) from the United States*, WT/DS132/R and Corr.1, adopted 24 February 2000, DSR 2000:III, 1345
Mexico – Corn Syrup (Article 21.5 – US)	Appellate Body Report, *Mexico – Anti-Dumping Investigation of High Fructose Corn Syrup (HFCS) from the United States – Recourse to Article 21.5 of the DSU by the United States*, WT/DS132/AB/RW, adopted 21 November 2001, DSR 2001:XIII, 6675
Thailand – H-Beams	Appellate Body Report, *Thailand – Anti-Dumping Duties on Angles, Shapes and Sections of Iron or Non-Alloy Steel and H-Beams from Poland*, WT/DS122/AB/R, adopted 5 April 2001, DSR 2001:VII, 2701
Thailand – H-Beams	Panel Report, *Thailand – Anti-Dumping Duties on Angles, Shapes and Sections of Iron or Non-Alloy Steel and H-Beams from Poland*, WT/DS122/R, adopted 5 April 2001, as modified by the Appellate Body Report, WT/DS122/AB/R, DSR 2001:VII, 2741
US – 1916 Act	Appellate Body Report, *United States – Anti-Dumping Act of 1916*, WT/DS136/AB/R, WT/DS162/AB/R, adopted 26 September 2000, DSR 2000:X, 4793
US – Carbon Steel	Appellate Body Report, *United States – Countervailing Duties on Certain Corrosion-Resistant Carbon Steel Flat Products from Germany*, WT/DS213/AB/R and Corr.1, adopted 19 December 2002

Short Title	Full Case Title and Citation
US – Corrosion-Resistant Steel Sunset Review	Appellate Body Report, *United States – Sunset Review of Anti-Dumping Duties on Corrosion-Resistant Carbon Steel Flat Products from Japan*, WT/DS244/AB/R, adopted 9 January 2004
US – DRAMS	Panel Report, *United States – Anti-Dumping Duty on Dynamic Random Access Memory Semiconductors (DRAMS) of One Megabit or Above from Korea*, WT/DS99/R, adopted 19 March 1999, DSR 1999:II, 521
US – Gasoline	Appellate Body Report, *United States – Standards for Reformulated and Conventional Gasoline*, WT/DS2/AB/R, adopted 20 May 1996, DSR 1996:I, 3
US – Hot-Rolled Steel	Appellate Body Report, *United States – Anti-Dumping Measures on Certain Hot-Rolled Steel Products from Japan*, WT/DS184/AB/R, adopted 23 August 2001, DSR 2001:X, 4697
US – Malt Beverages	GATT Panel Report, *United States – Measures Affecting Alcoholic and Malt Beverages*, adopted 19 June 1992, BISD 39S/206.
US – Offset Act (Byrd Amendment)	Appellate Body Report, *United States – Continued Dumping and Subsidy Offset Act of 2000*, WT/DS217/AB/R, WT/DS234/AB/R, adopted 27 January 2003
US – Softwood Lumber IV	Panel Report, *United States – Final Countervailing Duty Determination with Respect to Certain Softwood Lumber from Canada*, WT/DS257/R and Corr.1, adopted 17 February 2004, as modified by the Appellate Body Report, WT/DS257/AB/R
US – Wheat Gluten	Appellate Body Report, *United States – Definitive Safeguard Measures on Imports of Wheat Gluten from the European Communities*, WT/DS166/AB/R, adopted 19 January 2001, DSR 2001:II, 717
US – Wool Shirts and Blouses	Appellate Body Report, *United States – Measure Affecting Imports of Woven Wool Shirts and Blouses from India*, WT/DS33/AB/R and Corr.1, adopted 23 May 1997, DSR 1997:I, 323

I. INTRODUCTION

1.1 On 16 June 2003, the Government of United States requested consultations with the Government of Mexico pursuant to Article 4 of the *Understanding on Rules and Procedures Governing the Settlement of* Disputes ("DSU"), Article XXII:1 of the *General Agreement on Tariffs and Trade 1994* ("GATT 1994"), Article 17.3 of the *Agreement on Implementation of Article VI of the General Agreement on Tariffs and Trade 1994* ("AD Agreement"), and Article 30 of the *Agreement on Subsidies and Countervailing Measures* ("SCM Agreement"), with respect to Mexico's definitive anti-dumping measures on beef and long-grain white rice, published in the *Diario Oficial* on 28 April 2000 and 5 June 2002 respectively, as well as any amendments thereto or extensions thereof and any related measures and also with respect to certain provisions of Mexico's Foreign Trade Act and its Federal Code of Civil Procedure.[1] Mexico and the United States held consultations on 31 July and 1 August 2003, but failed to settle the dispute.

1.2 On 19 September 2003, the United States requested the establishment of a panel[2] pursuant to Article 6 of the DSU, Article 17.4 of the AD Agreement, and Article 30 of the SCM Agreement. At its meeting on 7 November 2003, the Dispute Settlement Body (the "DSB") established a Panel in accordance with Article 6 of the DSU to examine the matter referred to the DSB by United States in document WT/DS295/2.[3] At that meeting, the parties to the dispute also agreed that the Panel should have standard terms of reference. The terms of reference are, therefore, the following:

> "To examine, in the light of the relevant provisions of the covered agreements cited by the United States in document WT/DS295/2, the matter referred to the DSB by the United States in that document, and to make such findings as will assist the DSB in making the recommendations or in giving the rulings provided for in those agreements".

1.3 On 4 February 2004, the United States requested the Director-General to determine the composition of the Panel, pursuant to paragraph 7 of Article 8 of the DSU. This paragraph provides:

> "If there is no agreement on the panelists within 20 days after the date of the establishment of a Panel, at the request of either party, the Director-General, in consultation with the Chairman of the DSB and the Chairman of the relevant Council or Committee, shall determine the composition of the panel by appointing the panelists whom the Director-General considers most appropriate in accordance with any relevant special or additional rules or procedures of the covered agreement or covered agreements which are at issue in

---

[1] WT/DS295/1, G/L/631, G/ADP/D50/1,G/SCM/D54/1.

[2] WT/DS295/2. The United States did not include claims with respect to the anti-dumping measure on beef in its request for the establishment of a Panel.

[3] WT/DS295/3.

the dispute, after consulting with the parties to the dispute. The Chairman of the DSB shall inform the Members of the composition of the panel thus formed no later than 10 days after the date the Chairman receives such a request".

1.4 On 13 February 2004, the Director-General accordingly composed the Panel as follows:

Chairman: Mr. Crawford Falconer

Members: Ms. Marta Calmon Lemme

Ms. Enie Neri de Ross

1.5 China, the European Communities, and Turkey reserved their rights to participate in the Panel proceedings as third parties.

1.6 The Panel met with the parties on 17-18 May 2004 and on 3 August 2004. It met with the third parties on 18 May 2004.

1.7 The Panel submitted its interim report to the parties on 11 March 2005. The Panel submitted its final report to the parties on 25 May 2005.

II. FACTUAL ASPECTS

2.1 This dispute concerns the imposition of definitive anti-dumping duties by Mexico on imports of "long-grain white rice" from the United States. The United States also challenges a number of provisions of Mexico's Foreign Trade Act and a provision of its Federal Code of Civil Procedure on an "as such" basis.

2.2 On 2 June 2000, the Mexican Rice Council (Consejo Mexicano del Arroz, A.C. or "CMA") filed a petition with the Secretariat of Commerce and Industrial Development ("SECOFI"), the administrator of Mexico's anti-dumping law at that time[4].

2.3 The initiation of the investigation was published in the *Diario Oficial de la Federación* dated 11 December 2000. The investigated product was defined as "long-grain white rice". "Long-grain white rice" is produced from *paddy rice* or whole rice. After drying and cleaning (and storing), *paddy rice* is ground to produce whole rice with the layers of bran that still cover the grain. Later, the whole rice is further ground with machines to extract the bran layers through abrasion. After the bran layers have been taken away from the grain, the rice is called regular ground white rice. Machines will then separate the whole grains from the broken ones, and sort them out by size, thus producing various types of rice including the "long-grain white rice".[5]

---

[4] Due to a name change, the investigation was completed by the current administrator of Mexico's anti-dumping law, the Ministry of Economy (Secretaria de Economía or "Economía").

[5] Final Determination (Exhibit MEX-11, US-6 and US-7), paras.5 and 161. More precisely, Economia has defined it as having the following characteristics: a) It is a graminaceous plant, of the genus Olyza, and the species Sativa; b) Of a white crystalline color; c) With proportions Length: Width greater than 2.1; d) With characteristic culinary uses. (Final Determination, para.5)

2.4 The period of investigation for the purpose of the dumping determination covered the period of 1 March to 31 August 1999. For the purpose of injury examination, the Ministry of Economy (SECOFI's successor agency that administers the Mexican anti-dumping laws) analyzed data for the same period of 1 March to 31 August for the years 1997, 1998 and 1999[6]. The Ministry of Economy ("Economía") notified the initiation of the anti-dumping investigation to the petitioners, to the Government of the United States and to the two exporters that were specifically identified as the "exporters" in the petition, Producers Rice Mill Inc. ("Producers Rice") and Riceland Foods Inc. ("Riceland"), providing them with a copy of the petition and its attachments, as well as of the official questionnaire of the investigation.

2.5 Subsequent to initiation and prior to the preliminary determination, two additional exporters came forward to ask for copies of the questionnaire: The Rice Company("Rice Company")[7] and Farmers Rice Milling Company ("Farmers Rice"). Both companies, together with Producers Rice and Riceland, submitted questionnaire responses to Economía on 22 February 2001 and 6 March 2001. In addition to the questionnaire responses, Producers Rice, Riceland, Rice Company, Farmers Rice, and the USA Rice Federation (a trade association based in the United States) made a submission commenting upon and contesting various aspects of the petition and notice of initiation.

2.6 Economía published its preliminary determination on 18 July 2001. In it, Economía determined that Riceland, Rice Company, and Farmers Rice were not dumping. As to the fourth exporter, Producers Rice, Economía preliminarily determined that it made no sales of subject rice to Mexico during the POI. Economía's preliminary determination also found that there was no evidence of injury to the domestic industry.

2.7 On 5 June 2002, Economía published its final determination. In it, Economía found no evidence of dumping regarding Farmers Rice and Riceland and imposed a zero per cent duty to these exporters. For the Rice Company, Economía found a 3.93 per cent margin of dumping and imposed a duty of 3.93 per cent. For the imports from the remaining US exporters, Economía imposed a duty of 10.18 per cent based on the facts available.

III. PARTIES' REQUESTS FOR FINDINGS AND RECOMMENDATIONS

A. United States

3.1 The United States requests that the Panel make the following findings[8]:

---

[6] The data gathered by Economía, however, seemed to have covered the full 3-year period of the investigation.

[7] This company is also referred to in the Final Determination as "The Rice Corporation".

[8] United States' first written submission, para. 291. In its oral statement at the first substantive meeting (para. 8) as well as in its second written submission (paras. 16 and 18), the United States also made a claim on Article VI:6(a) of GATT 1994.

(a) Economía's use of a POI that ended more than fifteen months prior to the initiation of the anti-dumping investigation and nearly three years prior to the final determination is inconsistent with Mexico's obligations under Article VI:2 of GATT 1994 and Articles 1, 3.1, 3.2, 3.4, and 3.5 of the AD Agreement;

(b) Economía's limitation of its injury analysis to only six months of 1997, 1998, and 1999 is inconsistent with Mexico's obligations under Articles 1, 3.1, 3.5, and 6.2 of the AD Agreement;

(c) Economía's failure to collect the evidence on price effects and volumes that it needed to conduct its injury analysis in an objective manner is inconsistent with Mexico's obligations under Articles 3.1, 3.2, and 6.8 and Annex II of the AD Agreement;

(d) Economía's failure to objectively consider whether there was a significant increase in the volume of dumped imports or whether the dumped imports had a significant effect on prices is inconsistent with Mexico's obligations under Articles 3.1 and 3.2 of the AD Agreement;

(e) Economía's failure to conduct an objective analysis of the relevant economic factors is inconsistent with Mexico's obligations under Articles 3.1 and 3.4 of the AD Agreement;

(f) Economía's inclusion of non-dumped imports in its evaluation of volume, price effects, and the impact of the dumped imports on the domestic industry is inconsistent with Mexico's obligations under Articles 3.1, 3.2, and 3.5 of the AD Agreement;

(g) Economía's failure to provide in sufficient detail the findings and conclusions reached on all issues of fact and law with respect to its determination of injury is inconsistent with Mexico's obligations under Article 12.2 of the AD Agreement;

(h) Economía's failure to exclude firms with anti-dumping margins of zero per cent from the anti-dumping measure is inconsistent with Mexico's obligations under Article 5.8 of the AD Agreement;

(i) Economía's application of an adverse facts available-based dumping margin to the non-shipping exporter Producers Rice is inconsistent with Mexico's obligations under Articles 6.2, 6.4, 6.8, 9.4, and 9.5 of the AD Agreement and Paragraphs 3, 5, 6, and 7 of Annex II;

(j) Economía's application of an adverse facts available-based dumping margin to the US producers and exporters that it did not investigate is inconsistent with Mexico's obligations under Articles 6.1, 6.6, 6.8, 6.10, 9.4, 9.5, and 12.1 of the AD Agreement and paragraphs 1 and 7 of Annex II;

(k) Economía's failure to provide sufficient information on the findings and conclusions of fact and law and the reasons that led to the imposition of the adverse facts available-based margin on Producers Rice and the unexamined US exporters and producers is inconsistent with Mexico's obligations under Article 12.2 of the AD Agreement;

(l) Economía's application of an adverse facts available-based margin to Producers Rice and the unexamined US exporters and producers is inconsistent with Mexico's obligations under Articles 1 and 9.3 of the AD Agreement;

(m) Economía's levying of an anti-dumping duty greater than the margin of dumping is inconsistent with Mexico's obligations under Article VI:2 of GATT 1994;

(n) Article 53 of Mexico's Foreign Trade Act is inconsistent "as such" with Article 6.1.1 of the AD Agreement and Article 12.1.1 of the SCM Agreement;

(o) Article 64 of Mexico's Foreign Trade Act is inconsistent "as such" with Articles 6.8, 9.3, 9.4, and 9.5 of the AD Agreement, paragraphs 1, 3, 5, and 7 of Annex II of the AD Agreement, and Articles 12.7 and 19.3 of the SCM Agreement;

(p) Article 68 of Mexico's Foreign Trade Act is inconsistent "as such" with Articles 5.8, 9.3, and 11.2 of the AD Agreement and Articles 11.9 and 21.2 of the SCM Agreement;

(q) Article 89D of Mexico's Foreign Trade Act is inconsistent "as such" with Article 9.5 of the AD Agreement and Article 19.3 of the SCM Agreement;

(r) Article 93V of Mexico's Foreign Trade Act is inconsistent "as such" with Article 18.1 of the AD Agreement and Article 32.1 of the SCM Agreement; and

(s) Articles 68 and 97 of Mexico's Foreign Trade Act, and Section 366 of Mexico's Federal Code of Civil Procedure ("FCCP"), are inconsistent "as such" with Articles 9.3, 9.5, and 11.2 of the AD Agreement, and Articles 19.3 and 21.2 of the SCM Agreement.

3.2 The United States requests that, based on the above findings, the Panel recommend that Mexico bring its measures into conformity with its obligations under the AD Agreement, the SCM Agreement, and GATT 1994.

B. Mexico

3.3 As a preliminary matter, Mexico requests that the Panel issue a preliminary ruling on the deficiencies of the United States' panel request and decline to rule on the complaints raised in breach of Article 4.5, 4.7 and 6.2 of the DSU or Article 17.4 of the AD Agreement. Specifically, Mexico claims as follows[9]:

(a) The United States' panel request exhibits three basic deficiencies, i.e.:

---

[9] Mexico's first written submission, para. 309.

(i) it does not present the problem clearly;

(ii) it does not identify a specific measure at issue; and

(iii) it raises complaints regarding matters that were not the subject of consultations.

(b) The above is contrary to DSU Articles 6.2, 4.5 and 4.7 and AD Agreement Article 17.4.

(c) Consequently, the United States' request was filed in a manner inconsistent with AD Agreement Article 17.5.

3.4 On the merits, Mexico requests that the Panel make the following determinations[10]:

(a) In regard to the challenge raised against the measures imposed on dumped imports of long-grain white rice:

(i) Mexico established its period of investigation without breaching its obligations under Article VI:2 of the GATT 1994 and Articles 1, 3.1, 3.2, 3.4 and 3.5 of the AD Agreement;

(ii) Mexico, in limiting its injury analysis to the months of March to August of 1997, 1998 and 1999, did not contravene its obligations under Articles 1, 3.1, 3.5, and 6.2 of the AD Agreement;

(iii) Mexico conducted its injury analysis in an objective manner by carrying out an objective examination based on positive evidence of price effects and volumes, without violating its obligations under Articles 3.1, 3.2 and 6.8 and Annex II to the AD Agreement;

(iv) Mexico objectively considered whether there was a significant increase in the volume of dumped imports and whether the dumped imports had a significant effect on prices, thus acting in a manner consistent with its obligations under Articles 3.1 and 3.2 of the AD Agreement;

(v) Mexico conducted an objective analysis of the relevant economic factors, thus meeting its obligations under Articles 3.1 and 3.4 of the AD Agreement;

(vi) Mexico did not violate its obligations under Articles 3.1, 3.2 and 3.5 of the AD Agreement;

(vii) Mexico provided in sufficient detail the findings and conclusions reached on all issues of fact and law with respect to its determination of injury, thus meeting its obligations under Article 12.2 of the AD Agreement;

10 Mexico's first written submission, para. 310.

(viii) Mexico, in imposing an anti-dumping measure of zero per cent, did not contravene its obligations under Article 5.8 of the AD Agreement;

(ix) Mexico, in applying a facts available-based dumping margin, did not act in a manner inconsistent with its obligations under Articles 6.2, 6.4, 6.8, 9.4 and 9.5 of the AD Agreement and paragraphs 3, 5, 6, and 7 of Annex II to the AD Agreement;

(x) Mexico, in applying a facts available-based dumping margin to the US producers and exporters that it did not investigate, did not violate its obligations under Articles 6.1, 6.6, 6.8, 6.10, 9.4, 9.5 and 12.1 of the AD Agreement and paragraphs 1 and 7 of Annex II to the AD Agreement;

(xi) Mexico provided sufficient information on its findings and conclusions of fact and law and the reasons that led the investigating authority to impose the facts available-based margin on *Producers Rice* and the unexamined US exporters and producers, without contravening its obligations under Article 12.2 of the AD Agreement;

(xii) Mexico, in applying a facts available-based margin to *Producers Rice* and the unexamined US exporters and producers, did not violate its obligations under Articles 1 and 9.3 of the AD Agreement; and

(xiii) Mexico did not levy an anti-dumping duty greater than the margin of dumping calculated and hence did not contravene its obligations under Article VI:2 of the GATT 1994;

(b) In regard to the challenge raised against the revision of the Foreign Trade Act:

(i) Article 53 of Mexico's Foreign Trade Act is consistent as such with Article 6.1.1 of the AD Agreement and Article 12.1.1 of the SCM Agreement;

(ii) Article 64 of Mexico's Foreign Trade Act is consistent as such with Articles 6.8, 9.3, 9.4 and 9.5 and paragraphs 1, 3, 5 and 7 of Annex II to the AD Agreement, and Articles 12.7 and 19.3 of the SCM Agreement;

(iii) Article 68 of Mexico's Foreign Trade Act is consistent as such with Articles 5.8, 9.3 and 11.2 of the AD Agreement and Articles 11.9 and 21.2 of the SCM Agreement;

(iv) Article 89D of Mexico's Foreign Trade Act is consistent as such with Article 9.5 of the AD Agreement and Article 19.3 of the SCM Agreement;

(v) Article 93.V of Mexico's Foreign Trade Act is consistent as such with Article 18.1 of the AD Agreement and Article 32.1 of the SCM Agreement; and

(vi) Articles 68 and 97 of Mexico's Foreign Trade Act and Article 366 of Mexico's Federal Code of Civil Procedure are consistent as such with Articles 9.3, 9.5 and 11.2 of the AD Agreement and Articles 19.3 and 21.2 of the SCM Agreement.

3.5 In view of the foregoing, Mexico requests that the Panel conclude that the definitive anti-dumping measures adopted in respect of imports of long-grain white rice from the United States and the amendment of the Foreign Trade Act are consistent with Mexico's obligations under the AD Agreement, in particular Articles 1, 3, 5, 6, 9, 12, 18 and Annex II; the SCM Agreement, in particular Articles 11, 12, 19, 21 and 32; and the GATT 1994, in particular Article VI.

IV. ARGUMENTS OF THE PARTIES

4.1 The arguments of the parties are set forth in their written and oral submissions to the Panel, and in their answers to questions. The parties' arguments as presented in their submissions are summarised in this section. The summaries are based on the executive summaries submitted by the parties.[11] The response of the United States to Mexico's request for a preliminary ruling as well as parties' written answers to questions from the Panel are set forth in the Annexes. (*See* list of annexes at page xi.)

A. First Written Submission of the United States

4.2 The following are the United States' arguments in its first written submission:

1. The imposition of anti-dumping duties on US long-grain white rice

(a) Economía's Use of a Stale Period of Investigation Breached Articles VI:2 of GATT 1994 and Articles 1, 3.1, 3.2, 3.4, and 3.5 of the AD Agreement

4.3 The purpose of an anti-dumping measure is not to punish exporters for past dumping practices. Rather, it is to "offset or prevent" dumping that is presently causing or threatening to cause material injury to a domestic industry in the importing country. A Member is not offsetting or preventing injurious dumping if the dumping or injury has completely ceased or never existed. Thus, in order to impose an anti-dumping measure, the investigating authority must examine, as part of its initial investigation pursuant to Article 5 of the AD Agreement, a period of time that is as close to the date of initiation as practicable.

11 All the footnotes in sections IV:A – IV:H are original footnotes of the parties.

4.4 In the present case, the petitioning industry selected the POI that it wanted Economía to examine for the dumping investigation and the evaluation of injury, and Economía accepted its request over the objection of the US exporters and the importers. As a consequence, there was more than a fifteen-month gap between the end of the POI (August 1999) and the initiation of the investigation (December 2000). Economía did not even collect, much less examine, any data for that fifteen-month period. By the time Economía issued its final determination on 5 June 2002, this gap had stretched to nearly three years.

4.5 These periods were so remote in time that the information collected by the investigating authority was incapable of providing a basis for an objective finding of dumping, injury, and causation (as those terms are defined and used in the AD Agreement) or a determination based on positive evidence. For example, the more than fifteen-month gap between the end of the POI and the date of initiation (and the nearly three-year gap between the end of the POI and the final determination) means:

- Economía's examination of volume and price effects was not objective or based on positive evidence as required by Articles 3.1 and 3.2 of the AD Agreement;
- Economía's examination of "all relevant economic factors" having a bearing on the state of the domestic industry was not objective or based on positive evidence as required by Articles 3.1 and 3.4 of the AD Agreement; and
- Economía's determination that the dumped imports were "causing" injury to the domestic industry was not objective or based on positive evidence as required by Articles 3.1 and 3.5 of the AD Agreement.

4.6 Economía also lacked the information it needed to determine that the subject imports *are* being dumped, and that they *are* the cause of *present* material injury (or threat) to the domestic industry producing the like product.

4.7 Thus, the imposition of an anti-dumping measure on long-grain white rice from the United States breached Articles 1, 3.1, 3.2, 3.4, and 3.5 of the AD Agreement and Article VI:2 of the GATT 1994.

(b) Economía Breached Articles 1, 3.1, 3.5, and 6.2 of the AD Agreement by Limiting Its Examination of Injury to Only Six Months of 1997, 1998, and 1999

4.8 The petitioner in the rice investigation asked Economía to examine only the March to August time period, because this period allegedly reflected the main import activity of the product under investigation. Economía agreed that imports were concentrated during that period, and consequently limited its injury analysis to the data for March - August of each of the years at issue in its investigation (1997, 1998, 1999). Economía's decision to conduct its analysis in this manner resulted in breaches of Articles 1, 3.1, 3.5, and 6.2 of the AD Agreement.

4.9 *First*, Economía's investigation of injury was not based on "positive evidence." As the Appellate Body stated in *United States - Hot-Rolled Steel*, the term "positive evidence" relates to "the quality of the evidence that authorities may rely upon in making a determination... [T]he evidence must be of an affirmative, objective and verifiable character, and...it must be credible." Economía's investigation of injury was not based on "positive evidence" for the simple reason that it failed even to *examine* the evidence pertaining to half of the period of injury analysis.

4.10 *Second*, Economía's decision to focus its investigation on only March to August of each year also prevented its examination from being objective. To examine only those parts of the year when imports levels are high may overlook positive developments in other parts of the year, and thus give a misleading impression of the data relating to the condition of the industry as a whole. But this is exactly what Economía did.

4.11 These actions contravened Articles 1, 3.1, 3.5, and 6.2 of the AD Agreement.

(c) Economía's Conduct of its Injury Analysis Breached Articles 3.1, 3.2, 3.4, 3.5, 6.8, 12.2, and Annex II of the AD Agreement

4.12 Separate and apart from the breaches arising from Economía's choice of a POI, Economía's conduct of its injury analysis was inconsistent with WTO rules.

4.13 *First*, Article 3.1 of the AD Agreement states that injury determinations must be based on "positive evidence" and must involve an "objective examination" of the volume of the dumped imports and their effect on prices in the domestic market for like products, and the consequent impact of the imports on domestic producers of such products. By failing to actively seek out information pertinent to these matters, Economía did not make it possible to conduct an objective examination of the injury factors, and consequently did not base its determination on positive evidence. Economía then compounded its error by basing its determination on the facts available, contrary to Article 6.8 and Annex II.

4.14 *Second*, Article 3.2 of the AD Agreement requires investigating authorities to consider "whether there has been a *significant* increase in the *dumped* imports, either in absolute terms or relative to production or consumption in the importing Member." Nothing in the discussion of this issue indicates that Economía actually considered whether there were *significant* absolute or relative increases in the volume of the *dumped* imports. Economía's failure to conduct a proper examination of this issue breached Articles 3.1 and 3.2 of the AD Agreement.

4.15 *Third*, Economía breached Articles 3.1 and 3.4 of the AD Agreement by failing to conduct an objective analysis of certain "relevant economic factors" that it was required to evaluate under Article 3.4.

4.16 *Fourth*, Economía breached Articles 3.1, 3.2, and 3.5 of the AD Agreement by focusing its injury analysis on *all* imports of the investigated product from the United States, irrespective of whether the imports were dumped, instead of conducting an objective examination of the effect of the *dumped* imports alone.

4.17 *Finally*, Economía failed to explain sufficiently the findings and conclusions it reached on all issues of law, and thus breached 12.2 of the AD Agreement.

(d) Economía's Failure to Exclude Firms with Anti-dumping Margins of Zero per cent from the Anti-dumping Measure is Inconsistent with Article 5.8 of the AD Agreement

4.18 Economía also breached WTO rules by failing to exclude two of the firms it examined – Farmers Rice and Riceland – from the anti-dumping measure. Farmers Rice and Riceland each had dumping margins of zero per cent. Since neither firm was dumping, neither firm was causing any injury to the Mexican rice industry through the "effects of dumping." Nevertheless, Economía applied the anti-dumping measure to both firms, and each firm remains subject to future review and the possible application of anti-dumping duties. By treating Farmers Rice and Riceland in this manner, Economía breached Article 5.8 of the AD Agreement.

(e) Economía's Application of an Adverse "Facts Available" Dumping Margin to Producers Rice and to US Producers and Exporters that It Did Not Examine Is Inconsistent with Article VI:2 of the GATT 1994, Articles 1, 6.1, 6.2, 6.6, 6.8, 6.10, 9.3, 9.4, 9.5, 12.1, and 12.2 of the AD Agreement, and Paragraphs 1, 3, 5, 6, and 7 of Annex II of the AD Agreement

4.19 A basic principle underlying the AD Agreement, embodied in Article 1, is that anti-dumping measures shall be applied "only...pursuant to investigations initiated and conducted in accordance with the provisions of this Agreement." The Agreement provides for conducting investigations based on the actual data of individual interested parties, and Article 6.10 of the AD Agreement requires "as a rule" that the authorities "shall determine an individual margin of dumping for each known exporter or producer concerned of the product under investigation."

4.20 The sole exception provided to this rule, set forth in the second sentence of Article 6.10, arises when the sheer number of potential interested parties is so large that making an individual determination for each exporter or producer would be "impracticable." In such cases, authorities may limit their examination, either by using statistically valid samples or by examining the largest percentage of the volume of the exports which can reasonably be investigated. The Agreement then provides for the "residual" margin (i.e., the margin assigned to the uninvestigated firms) to be based on the calculation method set out in Article 9.4 of the AD Agreement for determining the ceiling for the "all others" rate.

4.21 Economía's conduct of the rice investigation breached these rules. Specifically, Economía improperly:

- sent its anti-dumping questionnaire to only two companies that were listed in the petition but claimed to be investigating every producer or exporter in the United States;
- calculated individual margins of dumping for one of those companies and two others that came forward on their own initiative and asked to be included in the investigation, but assigned an adverse "facts available" margin taken from the petition to Producers Rice, even though that firm demonstrated that it had no exports to Mexico during the POI; and
- treated all other exporters and producers in the United States as "uncooperative" respondents, and assigned them an adverse facts available margin taken from the petition, even though Economía never sent any of the affected companies a copy of the questionnaire or informed them of the consequences that would flow from not providing the information that it never requested them to provide.

(i) Analysis of Articles 6.1, 6.8, 6.10, and 9.4 of the AD Agreement, and Paragraph 1 of Annex II of the AD Agreement

4.22 The core legal provisions implicated by this issue are Articles 6.10 and 9.4 of the AD Agreement, Articles 6.1 and 6.8 of the AD Agreement, and paragraph 1 of Annex II. These provisions require investigating authorities to either individually examine and then calculate an individual margin of dumping for every producer or exporter of the product in the country under investigation, or else, if the authorities limit their examination to a subset of exporters or producers, to assign a neutral "all others" rate to those producers and exporters that are not individually examined. An investigating authority is not permitted to do what Economía did in the rice investigation – which was to individually investigate just a few exporters, and then assign an adverse facts available-based margin to everyone else.

4.23 This conclusion flows from the text of Article 6.10, which requires, "as a rule," that individual dumping margins be established for *each* producer or exporter. The rule is subject to a single exception, when the number of exporters or producers is so large that the determination of individual margins for each producer or exporter would be impracticable. In such cases, and only in such cases, an investigating authority may limit its examination to a subset of producers or exporters. Article 6.10 does not permit an investigating authority to announce the initiation of an anti-dumping investigation, send its questionnaire to a few producers or exporters, deem every other producer or exporter in the country as also being investigated, and apply a dumping margin based on the "facts available" to any company that does not "appear."

4.24 Articles 1, 5, 6.1, 6.5, 6.6, 6.8, and 9.4 of the AD Agreement, and paragraph 1 of Annex II, provide contextual support for the conclusion that Article 6.10 does not permit investigating authorities to take such a passive approach to their investigations.

4.25 *First*, Articles 6.1 and 6.8 of the AD Agreement, and paragraph 1 of Annex II, provide that an investigating authority must make known to the exporters or producers the information that is required of them. This informs the nature of the examination to be undertaken by authorities under Article 6.10 in determining margins: an investigating authority cannot simply wait for exporters or producers to respond to a general notice and then apply the facts available to any firms that do not appear; rather, the authorities must actively seek to identify individual exporters and producers, inform them of the information that is needed, and ensure they understand the consequences of not supplying the requested information.

4.26 *Second*, Article 9.4 requires investigating authorities to assign a neutral "all others" rate to producers and exporters that they do not individually examine. The Appellate Body has described this rate as a "maximum limit, or ceiling" that investigating authorities "shall not exceed."[12] Inasmuch as the calculation method in Article 9.4 does not allow the resulting margin to contain *any* element of the facts available, there is no basis for an interpretation of Article 6.10 that would permit investigating authorities to routinely assign total "facts available" margins to firms that they do not individually investigate.

4.27 *Third*, Articles 1, 5, 6.5, and 6.6 of the AD Agreement provide context for confirming that Articles 6.1, 6.8, 6.10, 9.4, and paragraph 1 of Annex II, require an investigating authority to (1) actively determine the universe of potential respondents; (2) actively send questionnaires to those producers or exporters from which it is seeking information; and (3) either take active steps to investigate every known producer and exporter, or else examine a representative sample and assign a neutral "all others" margin that is *not* based on the facts available to everyone else.

(ii) Economía's Application of an Adverse "Facts Available" Dumping Margin to Producers Rice Breached Articles 6.8, 9.4, and 9.5, and Paragraphs 3, 5, 6, and 7 of Annex II of the AD Agreement

4.28 Given these requirements, Economía breached its WTO obligations by applying a margin based on adverse "facts available" to Producers Rice. Producers Rice was named in the petition and in the Initiation Notice. The record demonstrates that Producers Rice was an "appearing party" that, with other respondent parties, established a domicile for legal purposes in Mexico in order to par-

[12] Report of the Appellate Body, *US – Hot-Rolled Steel*, para. 116.

ticipate in the investigation, requested an extension of time to respond to Economía's questionnaire, provided a timely response to that questionnaire, including arguments regarding flaws in the petition, requested and attended a technical information meeting, participated through its representative at the public hearing, offered post-hearing final allegations, and filed "additional remarks." Economía, however, disregarded all of these facts, and only took into account that Producers Rice did not export to Mexico during the six-month POI.

4.29 Under Article 17.6(i) of the AD Agreement, a panel that is assessing the facts of a matter before it must determine whether the authority's establishment of the facts was proper and whether its evaluation of those facts was unbiased and objective. An unbiased and objective investigating authority would not have concluded that Producers Rice had failed to appear in the rice investigation, or that the necessary prerequisites for assigning an adverse facts available margin to Producers Rice were met. Economía's decision to apply adverse facts available to Producers Rice in the absence of any legitimate grounds to do so was inconsistent with Articles 6.2, 6.8, 9.4, and 9.5 of the AD Agreement, paragraphs 3, 5, 6, and 7 of Annex II of the AD Agreement.

4.30 In addition, Economía breached Articles 6.2 and 6.4 of the AD Agreement by failing to disclose to Producers Rice (and Farmers Rice, Riceland, and Rice Company) the Export Price information that the petitioner used in calculating the adverse facts available margin in the petition.

(iii) Economía's Application of an Adverse "Facts Available" Dumping Margin to the US Producers and Exporters that It Did Not Examine Breached Articles 6.1, 6.2, 6.6, 6.8, 6.10, 9.4, 9.5, 12.1, and Paragraphs 1 and 7 of Annex II of the AD Agreement

4.31 Economía breached Articles 6.1, 6.2, 6.6, 6.8, 6.10, 9.4, 9.5, and 12.1 of the AD Agreement, and paragraphs 1 and 7 of Annex II of the AD Agreement, by individually examining only three exporters or producers in the rice investigation and assigning an adverse facts available margin to every other producer and exporter in the United States.

4.32 For example, Economía made no effort to investigate each exporter or producer of the subject merchandise, choosing instead to (i) send its questionnaire to just the two firms officially designated as exporters in the petition, (ii) investigate only those firms and two other firms that came forward on their own, and (iii) apply an adverse, facts available-based margin to every other producer and exporter in the United States. An objective and unbiased investigating authority would not have concluded that there were only two exporters or producers of long-grain white rice in the United States. Economía's establishment of the facts with respect to this matter was improper, and that by conducting its investigation in this manner, Economía breached Article 6.10.

4.33 Similarly, Article 6.6 of the AD Agreement requires that authorities "satisfy themselves as to the accuracy of the information supplied by interested parties upon which their findings are based." The petition identified only two US exporters of long-grain white rice, and Economía apparently accepted that listing at face value (even though the petition itself relied upon data from another major exporter). Once again, an objective and unbiased investigating authority would not have reached such a conclusion, and Economía's establishment of the facts with respect to this matter was improper.

4.34 Furthermore, in *US – Hot-Rolled Steel*, the Appellate Body found that the calculation method set forth in Article 9.4 for determining the ceiling for the "all others" rate precludes the use of any margins which are calculated, *even in part*, using facts available. The rate applied by Economía to US rice exporters was not based *in part* on facts available, as was the case in *US – Hot-Rolled Steel*. It was based *entirely* on facts available. Not only that, but the 10.18 per cent rate was *adverse* facts available – a clear breach of Mexico's WTO obligations.

4.35 Economía also breached Article 6.8 and paragraph 7 of Annex II of the AD Agreement, by using the petition margin without corroborating the underlying information that the petitioner used to calculate the margin. As was the case with respect to Producers Rice, there is no evidence on the record of the rice investigation to suggest that the unexamined exporters and producers – which were never sent a copy of Economía's anti-dumping questionnaire – were uncooperative in any way. Moreover, as previously explained, Economía failed to check the presumptions embodied in the petition against independent data available during the investigation, much less to exercise "special circumspection" in its application of the petition information to the unexamined producers and exporters.

4.36 Finally, Economía's efforts to identify and obtain contact information for interested parties other than those listed in the petition were inadequate. Economía failed to examine the accuracy and adequacy of the CMA's list of only two "known" exporters, a list that did not even include a third exporter, the Rice Company, whose website, the content of which was attached to the petition as Annex H, describes it as "one of the largest US exporters as regards paddy rice and white milled rice." In this manner, Economía breached Article 12.1 of the AD Agreement, which requires authorities to notify interested parties about the initiation of an investigation.

(iv) Economía's Failure to Provide Sufficient Information on the Findings and Conclusions of Fact and Law and the Reasons that Led to the Imposition of the Adverse Facts Available-Based Margin on Producers Rice and the Unexamined Exporters and Producers Breached Article 12.2 of the AD Agreement

4.37 Article 12.2 of the AD Agreement requires that the public notice of any preliminary or final anti-dumping determination "shall set forth, or otherwise make available through a separate report, in sufficient detail the findings and conclusions reached on all issues of fact and law considered material by the investigating authorities." Despite this requirement, Economía provided only the most summary rationale for its decision to base the margin for Producers Rice and the unexamined exporters and producers on adverse facts available. Furthermore, Economía's references to Article 54 of the Mexican Foreign Trade Act as a supposed basis for its decision to apply a facts available margin to these firms were unfounded.

(v) Economía's Application of an Adverse Facts Available-Based Margin to Producers Rice and the Unexamined Exporters and Producers Breached Articles 1 and 9.3 of the AD Agreement and Article VI:2 of GATT 1994

4.38 Article 9.3 of the AD Agreement states that "[t]he amount of anti-dumping duty shall not exceed the margin of dumping as established under Article 2." Because Economía failed to calculate the residual margin on the basis of the neutral formula set forth in Article 9.4, the amount of the margin it assigned to Producers Rice and the unexamined exporters and producers exceeded the margin of dumping established under Article 2, and thus breached Article 9.3.

4.39 Article 1 of the AD Agreement provides that an anti-dumping measure shall be applied only under the circumstances provided for in Article VI of GATT 1994 and pursuant to investigations initiated and conducted in accordance with the provisions of this Agreement. Because Economía's conduct of the rice investigation breached numerous other provisions of the AD Agreement, Economía also breached Article 1.

4.40 Finally, as a result of the adverse assumptions made in assigning an adverse margin to non-shipper Producers Rice and to the other non-examined companies in the rice investigation, the anti-dumping duty levied on their products was "greater in amount than the margin of dumping in respect of such products" which could permissibly have been calculated in accordance with the provisions of the AD Agreement. Because the duties Mexico levied on these "all others" companies was, and continues to be, greater in amount than the appropriate margin of dumping, Mexico violated Article VI:2 of GATT 1994.

2. *Mexico's Foreign Trade Act and its FCCP – Articles 53, 64, 68, 89D, 93V, and 97 of Mexico's Foreign Trade Act, and Section 366 of Mexico's FCCP, are inconsistent "as such" with several of Mexico's obligations under the AD and SCM Agreements*

4.41 Various provisions of Mexico's Foreign Trade Act and its FCCP are inconsistent with Mexico's WTO obligations.

4.42 *First*, Article 53 of the Foreign Trade Act requires interested parties to present arguments, information, and evidence to the investigating authorities within 28 days of the day after publication of the initiation notice. This provision breaches Articles 6.1.1 and 12.1.1 of the AD and SCM Agreements, respectively, by counting the time to respond from the date of initiation instead of the date of receipt, and by preventing the investigating authorities from considering and granting extension requests.

4.43 *Second*, Article 64 of the Foreign Trade Act is the provision of Mexican law that applies to the calculation of individual anti-dumping and countervailing duty margins and the application of margins to exporters and producers that are not individually examined and that do not receive individual margins. The provision does not, however, provide for the application of a neutral "all others" margin to the unexamined firms. Rather, Article 64 requires the investigating authorities to apply a margin based on adverse facts available – specifically, the *highest* margin obtained from the facts available – to any firm that does not receive an individual margin. Article 64 requires this outcome even for a firm, like Producers Rice, that participates in the investigation and demonstrates that it had no exports during the period of investigation. By requiring the investigating authorities to assign rates in this manner, Article 64 is inconsistent "as such" with Mexico's obligations under Articles 6.8, 9.3, 9.4, and 9.5 of the AD Agreement, paragraphs 1, 3, 5, and 7 of Annex II of the AD Agreement, and Articles 12.7 and 19.3 of the SCM Agreement.

4.44 *Third*, Article 68 of the Foreign Trade Act is the provision of Mexican law that applies to the review of final anti-dumping and countervailing duty margins determined in investigations. By requiring investigating authorities to conduct reviews of producers that were found not to be dumping or receiving countervailable subsidies during the original investigation, Article 68 is inconsistent with Mexico's obligations under Article 5.8 of the AD Agreement and Article 11.9 of the SCM Agreement.

4.45 In addition, Article 68 of the Foreign Trade Act also requires producers and exporters seeking reviews of their own anti-dumping or countervailing duty margins to demonstrate that their sales during the review period were "representative." The imposition of this "representativeness" requirement is inconsistent as such with Articles 9.3 and 11.2 of the AD Agreement, and with Article 21.2 of the SCM Agreement.

4.46 *Fourth*, Article 89D of the Foreign Trade Act is the provision of Mexican law that implements the expedited review provisions of the AD and SCM Agreements. By impermissibly restricting the ability of parties to obtain such reviews, Article 89D breaches Mexico's obligations under Article 9.5 of the AD Agreement and Article 19.3 of the SCM Agreement.

4.47 *Fifth*, Article 93V of the Foreign Trade Act provides for the application of fines on importers that enter products subject to anti-dumping and countervailing duty investigations while such investigations are underway. This provision constitutes a non-permissible specific action against dumping or a subsidy that is inconsistent with Mexico's obligations under Article 18.1 of the AD Agreement and Article 32.1 of the SCM Agreement.

4.48 *Finally*, Article 366 of Mexico's FCCP and Articles 68 and 97 of Mexico's Foreign Trade Act preclude Mexican authorities from conducting reviews of anti-dumping and countervailing duties while a judicial review of the underlying anti-dumping or countervailing duty measure is ongoing, including a "binational panel" review under Chapter Nineteen of the *North American Free Trade Agreement*. By requiring the Mexican authorities to reject requests for such reviews, Articles 366, 68, and 97 breach Articles 9.3, 9.5, and 11.2 of the AD Agreement, and Articles 19.3 and 21.2 of the SCM Agreement.

4.49 Article 64 of the Foreign Trade Act exacerbates the harm caused by the fact that Articles 366, 68 and 97 preclude the Mexican authorities from conducting the reviews that WTO rules require. As previously discussed, Article 64 requires Economía to apply an adverse, facts available-based anti-dumping or countervailing duty margin to *every* producer or exporter in the country subject to the investigation, other than those few that receive individual rates, even if the firms subject to the adverse, facts available-based margins demonstrate that they had no shipments during the period of review or were never even sent a questionnaire. These firms lose twice: Economía first assigns them an adverse (often petition-based) margin that has no relation to reality but effectively locks them out of the Mexican market, and it then denies them any review, and thus any opportunity to obtain an individual rate, over the course of a judicial challenge that may take years.

B. First Written Submission of Mexico

4.50 The following are Mexico's arguments in its first written submission:

1. Request for a preliminary ruling

(a) Introduction

4.51 Throughout these proceedings, the United States has not shown the slightest respect for the formal requirements governing the terms of reference of the Panel, affecting the latter's capacity to settle this dispute and Mexico's rights to due process. The request for the establishment of a panel does not fulfil the requirements laid down in Articles 4.5, 4.7 and 6.2 of the DSU, nor has the United States duly complied with Article 17.4 and 17.5 of the AD Agreement. Mexico's capacity for rebuttal was also impaired by the fact that Mexico did not receive the Spanish version of the United States' first written submission until 16 April 2004.

(b) Requirements for the request for establishment of a Panel

4.52 The Appellate Body has clarified the elements of the matter referred to the DSB,[13] specifying that flaws in a request for the establishment of a panel

---

[13] *US – Carbon Steel*, Report of the Appellate Body, para. 125.

cannot be subsequently be cured.[14] Concepts such as "specific measures at issue" and "legal basis" are essential for an understanding of the nature of the matter referred to the DSB. Article 6.2 lays down the minimum requirements for a definition of a panel's terms of reference and the precise procedural stage at which this should be done. Under Article 6.2 of the DSU, "[i]t is not enough ... that 'the legal basis of the complaint' is summarily identified; the identification must 'present the problem clearly'".[15] In addition, a responding party is entitled to know what case it has to answer so that it can begin preparing its defence.[16]

(c) Deficiencies in the request for the establishment of a Panel submitted by the United States

(i) Ambiguous and vague complaints which do not present the problem clearly

4.53 First of all, the United States submits that Mexico violated Article VI of the GATT 1994;[17] this is as ambiguous as to assert a violation of the AD and SCM Agreements as a whole. Second, the United States alleges violations of Article 4.1 of the AD Agreement[18] defining the "domestic industry", to which the facts referred to bear no relation. Third, the United States argues that Mexico breached the AD Agreement by applying the facts available to a US rice exporter,[19] whereas the provisions on which the United States relies do NOT refer to the case in question. Fifth, the United States is equally mistaken in saying that Mexico applied the facts available in establishing the anti-dumping margins assigned to US exporters that were not individually investigated.[20] The United States attempted to correct the omission in paragraph 40 of its first written submission.

(ii) Failure to identify a specific measure at issue

4.54 In paragraph 3 of the request for the establishment of a panel, the United States goes as far as to claim that Mexico breached a number of Articles of the AD and SCM Agreements, on the basis of "conversations" with a number of Mexican officials. It has been made clear that such conversations cannot be deemed to be a measure.[21] Consequently, the affirmation in the United States' request for the establishment of a panel clearly fails to identify a specific measure at issue

14 *EC – Bananas III*, Report of the Appellate Body, para. 143.
15 *Korea – Dairy*, Report of the Appellate Body, para. 120.
16 *Thailand – H-Beams*, Report of the Appellate Body, para. 88.
17 Request for the establishment of a panel (WT/DS295/2), para. 1(a).
18 *Ibid.*
19 *Ibid.*, section 1(f). The provisions in question are Articles 6.6, 6.8 and 6.10, 9.3, 9.4 and 9.5 and paras. 1, 3, 5, 6 and 7 of Annex II of the Anti-Dumping Agreement.
20 *Ibid.*, section 1(g).
21 *Japan – Film*, Report of the Panel, para. 10.43. *US – Corrosion-Resistant Steel Sunset Review*, Report of the Appellate Body, para. 87.

4.55 If, *arguendo*, the above were to constitute a measure, the manner in which the United States presents its argument would clearly constitute a failure to comply with Article 6.2 of the DSU since the problem would be far from being presented clearly, thus denying Mexico any basis for rebuttal.

(iii) Complaints which were at no time included by the United States in its consultations with Mexico, but which it nevertheless presents in its panel request

4.56 Pursuant to Article 4.5 of the DSU, WTO Members are under the obligation to attempt to achieve a solution in the course of the consultations, and failure to settle the dispute during the consultations is a precondition for entitlement to request the establishment of a panel under Article 4.7 of the DSU. In other words, the United States is required to request consultations on all matters included in the panel request. Article 17.4 of the AD Agreement confirms such a requirement and, according to the Appellate Body, consultations "... provide the parties an opportunity to define and delimit the scope of the dispute between them ...".[22] Thus, matters left outside the scope of the consultations could not be taken up in the panel request submitted by the United States; the provisions at issue are the following:

Provisions invoked	Paragraphs in the request for the establishment of a panel not included in the consultations
AD Article 1	Paragraphs 1(a), 1(g)
AD Article 4.1	Paragraph 1(a)
AD Article 11.2	Paragraph 2(c)
AD Article 18.1	Paragraph 2(e)
Paragraph 1 of Annex II	Paragraph 2(b)
Paragraph 3 of Annex II	Paragraph 2(b)
Paragraph 5 of Annex II	Paragraph 2(b)
Paragraph 6 of Annex II	Paragraph 2(b)
Paragraph 7 of Annex II	Paragraph 2(b)
SCM Article 12.5	Paragraph 2(b)
SCM Article 21.2	Paragraph 2(c)
SCM Article 32.1	Paragraph 2(e)
Article VI:2 of the GATT	Paragraph 1(i)

4.57 Even the United States claim in paragraph 1(a) of the panel request was not the subject of consultations with Mexico except in relation to the anti-dumping investigation on beef, as is expressly noted in the third paragraph of the request for consultations.

22 *Mexico – Corn Syrup (Article 21.5 – US)*, Report of the Appellate Body, para. 54.

4.58 Mexico had already brought up these irregularities at the DSB meeting of 2 October 2003.[23]

(d) Conclusion

4.59 As the responding party, Mexico has a right to due process. The request for the establishment of a panel exhibits fundamental flaws that prevent Mexico from preparing its defence. In view of the foregoing, Mexico requests the Panel to issue a preliminary ruling on the deficiencies in the panel request submitted by the United States and to refrain from ruling on claims brought in contravention of Articles 4.5, 4.7 and 6.2 of the DSU and Article 17.4 and 17.5 of the AD Agreement.

2. Legal arguments

(a) Economía complied with Article VI:2 of the GATT 1994 and Articles 1, 3.1, 3.2, 3.4 and 3.5 of the AD Agreement with regard to the establishment of the Period of Investigation

4.60 Economía complied with Articles 1, 3.1, 3.2, 3.4 and 3.5 of the AD Agreement and VI:2 of the GATT, by correctly establishing the periods of investigation (for dumping purposes) and analysis (for determination of injury) in the anti-dumping investigation on imports of long-grain white rice originating in the United States, as a result of an objective examination based on positive evidence.

4.61 The United States argues that the examination of volume and effects on prices, the examination of "all relevant economic factors and indices" and the determination that the dumped imports caused injury were neither objective nor based on positive evidence because of the obsolescence of the information used. There is no provision in the AD Agreement which indicates how remote a period of investigation should be. Consequently, Mexico did not breach Article 3.2 of the Agreement.

4.62 Economía complied with Article 3.1, 3.2 and 3.4 of the AD Agreement by conducting an objective examination, based on positive evidence, of the volume of the imports, their effect on prices, and all relevant economic factors and indices. Moreover, the final determination notes that the *dumped* imports caused injury to the domestic industry during the period of analysis, so that there are no grounds for alleging lack of information for the purposes of such a determination.

23 Minutes of the DSB meeting of 2 October 2003.

(b) Economía complied with Articles 1, 3.1, 3.5 and 6.2 of the AD Agreement with regard to the establishment of the Period of Analysis

4.63 The United States argues that Economía violated Articles 1, 3.1, 3.5 and 6.2 of the AD Agreement in allowing the petitioner to set the period of investigation as March to August 1999 and in establishing the months of March to August 1997, 1998 and 1999 as the period of analysis.

4.64 The periods of investigation and analysis were established correctly and Economía carried out an objective examination based on positive evidence, making sure that the parties had an opportunity to defend their interests in accordance with Article 6.2. of the AD Agreement.

4.65 The AD Agreement does not specify in detail how the period of analysis should be included in an anti-dumping investigation. In order to prevent distortions stemming from seasonal market fluctuations, a comparison was made between AD Agreement Article 3.4 indicators for similar periods in 1997, 1998 and 1999. The Economía did not violate the AD Agreement in setting the period of analysis inasmuch as the Agreement does not prohibit the comparison of periods equivalent to the period of investigation for the purposes of injury determination.

4.66 The United States indicates that the spring/summer (S/S) (October to December) season yield of paddy rice is greater than the fall/winter (F/W) (June-July) yield and, consequently, domestic production of long-grain white rice is greater during the S/S season than during the F/W season. Hence, the United States argues that, by setting the period of analysis as March to August of each year, Economía acted in a manner inconsistent with the AD Agreement because it failed to analyse the S/S harvest period, which is that during which, according to the United States, imports decline. The reason for setting the period of analysis as March to August 1997, 1998 and 1999 was to maintain the objectivity of the analysis. The argument that there were increases in domestic production and falls in imports of long-grain white rice during the S/S season is without foundation insofar as domestic production of this product does not depend on domestic production of paddy rice; indeed, when there is a drop in the latter domestic producers of long-grain white rice rely on imported paddy rice. Domestic production of long-grain white rice therefore remains virtually constant throughout the year – as was the case in 1997, 1998 and 1999.

4.67 Furthermore, the domestic producers only proposed March to August 1999 as the period of investigation and, having found this period to be reasonable, Economía established it as such, without violating the AD Agreement. As stated in paragraph 68 of the preliminary determination, moreover, the exporters provided no evidence of the convenience to select another period of investigation.

4.68 The investigating authority established the period of analysis on the basis of previous periods comparable to the period of investigation, which does not contravene the AD Agreement. The investigating authority's examination was objective and based on positive evidence, since it used comparable information concerning the same seasonal segments.

4.69 The United States argues that, in setting the period of analysis, Economía acted inconsistently with the AD Agreement because it did not examine "all relevant evidence" as required by Article 3.5 of the AD Agreement and because, in disregarding the claims of exporters and importers concerning the exclusion of information pertaining to the periods from September to February and the remoteness in time of the period analysed, Economía did not provide an opportunity to the parties to defend their interests, thereby infringing Article 6.2 of the AD Agreement.

4.70 The period of analysis was established without contravening the AD Agreement and all relevant evidence was examined in the injury analysis. Since there was no infringement of Article 3.5 of the AD Agreement, it cannot be argued that Article 6.2 was violated as a result of a breach of Article 3.5.

4.71 The investigating authority complied with Article 6.2 of the AD Agreement in giving the parties attending the public hearing an opportunity to meet with other parties having adverse interests, and the exporting companies had a full *opportunity* to present their arguments in relation to the hearing, which they did.

(c) Economía conducted its injury analysis in accordance with Articles 3.1, 3.2, 3.4, 3.5, 6.8 and 12.2 and Annex II of the AD Agreement

4.72 Economía based its injury determination on positive evidence and on an objective examination of the effect on prices, the volume of imports, the impact on domestic prices and relevant economic factors, properly using the best information available and giving sufficient detail of its findings and conclusions on issues of fact and law. It thus complied with Articles 3.1, 3.2, 3.4, 3.5, 6.8 and 12.2 and Annex II of the AD Agreement.

4.73 The United States argues that Economía did not carry out an objective examination of the effect on prices inasmuch as it based its analysis on information selected by the petitioner and "did not send questionnaires to any purchasers". In addition, it submits that Economía did not examine the import declarations (*pedimentos de importación*). The United States says that Economía made no effort to identify exporters and importers other than those mentioned by the petitioner and thereby contravened the AD Agreement.

4.74 An investigating authority complies with the standard laid down in Article 3.1 of the AD Agreement when: (a) It bases itself on affirmative, objective, verifiable and credible evidence; and (b) it gathers and evaluates that evidence in good faith and fundamental fairness. Economía fulfilled those conditions by carrying out an objective examination, based on positive evidence, of the volume of imports, their effect on prices for like products and the impact on the domestic industry.

4.75 The AD Agreement does not require any particular methodology for making price comparisons and evaluating effects on prices, but the analysis must be objective and based on positive evidence. In the absence of specific guidelines, an investigating authority may conduct its analysis in the manner it deems appropriate provided that it bases itself on positive evidence and makes an objective examination.

4.76 The United States argues that Economía based its analysis on information sources selected by the petitioner in the investigation, in breach of the AD Agreement. As the Appellate Body determined in *US – Wool Shirts and Blouses*, the United States failed to discharge its burden of proof in not putting forward a clear and detailed allegation or any supporting evidence. Notwithstanding the foregoing, Mexico submits that it did not infringe the AD Agreement.

4.77 As regards the fact that no questionnaires were sent to the purchasers, the AD Agreement contains no provision requiring such steps to be taken in an investigation, so that it is wrong to maintain that Mexico failed to act in compliance with the AD Agreement.

4.78 As to the *pedimentos*, these are not available to the investigating authority nor were they supplied by the petitioner. The investigating authority has "lists of *pedimentos*", which provide a variety of information but do not show the names or domiciles of the exporting firms.

4.79 The United States further argues that Economía's collection of information for the purposes of considering absolute and relative volumes of production and consumption was not objective and that Economía failed to conduct an objective evaluation of volume in using neither the *pedimentos* nor accurate information on the importers' import volumes. Mexico repeats that although the AD Agreement does not lay down any particular methodology for analysing the volume of imports and does not require the investigating authority to obtain more information than that supplied by the parties, the analysis must be carried out objectively, on the basis of positive evidence. Moreover, Economía requested information from the exporters and importers but did not obtain an adequate response. Mexico holds that it carried out an objective examination based on positive evidence, in accordance with the AD Agreement.

4.80 Mexico did not use the information supplied by *The Rice Company* because, despite being asked to do so, the firm failed to provide data for 1997 and 1998. Therefore, the information it supplied for 1999 was disregarded for reasons of procedural fairness, since other appearing parties did submit data for the entire period of analysis.

4.81 The United States indicates that Economía used the methodology proposed by the petitioners, even though it could only identify the long-grain white rice imports corresponding to the investigated period and cannot be extrapolated to the previous similar periods, in breach of Article 3.2. of the AD Agreement. Mexico repeats that Article 3.2 contains no guideline whatsoever as to whether use of the methodology proposed by the petitioner constitutes a violation of the AD Agreement. This methodology was used from the outset, in the preliminary determination, and no objection or better proposal was made. Consequently, the investigating authority requested further information from the exporters and the latter either did not respond or failed to supply the relevant information.

4.82 The United States asserts that Economía violated Article 6.8 and paragraphs 1 and 7 of Annex II of the AD Agreement by basing its injury analysis on the best information available, arguing that the reason for this is that Economía lacked accurate information on import volumes and value because it did not send questionnaires to all exporters, importers and purchasers and failed to consult the *pedimentos*. In the opinion of the United States, the investigating authority did not make the necessary effort to obtain information from the interested parties, nor did it notify them pursuant to paragraph 1 of Annex II relating to the use of the best information available. The United States accordingly concludes that none of the requirements of Article 6.8 of the AD Agreement was met for the purposes of applying the "adverse facts available".

4.83 There is no obligation to send questionnaires to all exporters, importers and purchasers, nor does the AD Agreement contain any provision requiring the investigating authority actively to seek information in an anti-dumping investigation, so that the above-mentioned argument is unfounded.

4.84 According to Article 6.1.1 of the AD Agreement, an investigating authority has the option to send questionnaires to producers and foreign exporters but is under no obligation to do so, much less in respect of all of them. In the case of purchasers, the possibility is not even contemplated in the AD Agreement, and so there is no obligation to send questionnaires to them. Mexico complied with its obligations, moreover, by transmitting to the United States authorities the public notice of initiation, the text of the application for initiation of an investigation and the annexes thereto, and the questionnaire for exporters and foreign producers.

4.85 In compliance with paragraph 1 of Annex II to the AD Agreement, the third paragraph of the introduction on the questionnaire provided to *Producers Rice* and *Riceland*, as well as to the United States' Embassy in Mexico, specified that if the required information was not supplied, Economía's determination would be based on the facts available. Accordingly, the United States' allegation that these points were not notified to the exporters is without foundation.

4.86 The United States argues that Economía violated Article 3.1 and 3.2 of the AD Agreement by failing to objectively consider whether there had been a significant increase in the volume (in absolute or relative terms) of dumped imports or significant effects on prices. Mexico rejects this argument.

4.87 According to the Panel's finding in *Thailand – H-Beams*, Mexico is under no obligation to make an explicit finding as to whether the increase in dumped imports is "significant". Mexico contends that the examination relating to the increase in total imports and dumped imports and the analysis of significant effects on prices is dealt with, albeit not explicitly, in the final determination.

4.88 The United States submits that Economía violated Article 3.1 and 3.4 of the AD Agreement in failing to conduct an objective analysis of the relevant economic factors. It also argues that the investigating authority did not properly evaluate inventories or market share, nor did it evaluate factors affecting domestic prices. For the purposes of its injury analysis, Economía carried out an objective examination in accordance with Article 3.4 of the AD Agreement. As detailed in the final determination, the analysis was properly conducted and covered the inventories, the objective assessment of market share, the factors affecting domestic prices and their impact on the domestic industry. All the factors listed in Article 3.4 were reviewed in the anti-dumping investigation and, as a result of this overall evaluation, Economía arrived at the conclusion set forth in the final determination.

4.89 The United States argues that Economía violated Article 3.1, 3.2 and 3.5 of the AD Agreement by including non-dumped imports in its evaluation of volume, effects on prices and the impact of dumped imports on the domestic industry.

4.90 The final determination shows that both the "volume of imports" and the "volume of dumped imports" were analysed and that the latter were the cause of the injury suffered by the domestic industry.

4.91 The United States also submits that Economía contravened Article 12.2 of the AD Agreement by failing to include in sufficient detail in its final determination the findings and conclusions reached on issues of law.

4.92 Economía considers that the final determination sets out in ample and sufficient detail the findings and conclusions reached on issues of fact and law relating to dumping, injury and causal relationship which it deemed relevant, as well as the reasons which led the investigating authority to impose definitive measures.

(d) Article 5.8 of the AD Agreement is not applicable to firms with dumping margins of zero per cent

4.93 The United States argues that Economía failed to exclude firms with dumping margins equivalent to zero per cent from the measures imposed in the final determination, contending that the investigation should have been terminated immediately. Furthermore, it submits that, inasmuch as these firms were not excluded from the anti-dumping measures, they remain subject to future administrative review and the possible imposition of anti-dumping duties, which is inconsistent with Article 5.8 of the AD Agreement.

4.94 Mexico contends that Article 5.8 of the AD Agreement does not apply because the investigation resulted in a determination of dumping, injury and causal link between the two. This led Economía to impose definitive anti-dumping measures by issuing a public notice of termination, whereby the anti-dumping investigation was concluded. Furthermore, a zero per cent duty does not de facto constitute an anti-dumping duty as it causes no prejudice to the exporter. As no anti-dumping duty is being charged, it cannot be considered that a *de minimis* margin exists or that an anti-dumping duty in excess of the dumping margin is being charged.

4.95 As to the claim that US exporters will be subject to review and the possible application of a definitive measure, Mexico would point out that, if those exporters do not engage in dumping, such reviews will not lead to the application of any measure. The AD Agreement *does not prohibit* a review of exporters for which a zero per cent dumping margin has been calculated. If the negotiators of the Agreement had determined that such exporters should not be subject to review, they would have done so explicitly.

4.96 Consequently, Mexico reiterates that it did not violate Article 5.8 of the AD Agreement and that this provision does not apply in this specific instance, given that the anti-dumping investigation ended with the publication in the Official Journal (DOF) of the official notice of termination and a zero per cent duty cannot actually be regarded as an anti-dumping duty.

(e) Mexico applied the facts available to *Producers Rice* and to the US producers and exporters that were not investigated in a manner consistent with the AD Agreement

4.97 The United States is wrong in claiming that Economía applied the "adverse facts available" to *Producers Rice* and to the producers and exporters which it did not examine, and that this is inconsistent with the WTO Agreements.

4.98 This argument is entirely unfounded. The United States is seeking to impose on Mexico obligations that are not derived from the AD Agreement or, contrary to Article 17.6 of the AD Agreement, it rejects *a priori* Mexico's permissible interpretation of the provisions of the Agreement.

4.99 Mexico is *not* obliged to determine an individual dumping margin for *all* exporters or producers inasmuch as Article 6.10 of the AD Agreement establishes the obligation to do so solely in respect of *known* exporters, which is what Economía did. Mexico complied with the AD Agreement by issuing the public notice of initiation and by notifying the known exporters and the United States' Embassy in Mexico.

4.100 Moreover, Mexico did not limit its examination to a reasonable number of exporters and was therefore under no obligation to calculate a margin of dumping in conformity with Article 9.4 of the AD Agreement for exporters or producers that were not included in the examination.

4.101 In the case of US exporters that were not investigated individually and were not included in the investigation and/or did not provide the information needed to calculate a margin of dumping, Economía was obliged to apply the facts available, in accordance with Article 6.8 of the AD Agreement. Mexico complied with its obligations in providing the United States' authorities with the public notice of initiation of the investigation, the text of the application for initiation and the annexes thereto and the questionnaire for exporters and foreign producers, and in convening all natural or legal persons that had an interest in the investigation, through the publication of the public notice of initiation.

4.102 Likewise, Economía acted consistently with Article 6.8 of the AD Agreement in applying to *Producers Rice* the facts available, because if an interested party does not participate in the investigation or has no exports during the period of investigation, it must be considered that it *did not provide* the information needed to calculate a dumping margin.

4.103 Regarding the United States' claim that Mexico acted in a manner inconsistent with Annex II to the AD Agreement, Mexico would make the following comments:

(a) Mexico acted consistently with paragraph 3 of Annex II to the AD Agreement by applying Article 6.8 of the Agreement to the exporting firm *Producers Rice*, as this firm did not provide the information needed and there was thus no information to be taken into account.

(b) The investigating authority acted consistently with paragraph 5 of Annex II to the AD Agreement, as the exporting firm *Producers Rice* did not provide information that was ideal in any respect for the purposes of calculating a dumping margin. Economía therefore was under no obligation to take this information into account.

(c) In addition, Mexico acted consistently with paragraph 6 of Annex II to the AD Agreement because Economía did not reject any evidence or information provided by *Producers Rice.* but *accepted* that information and acted in accordance with the provisions of the AD Agreement in calculating the dumping margin applicable.

4.104 Contrary to the United States' claim, the determinations of Economía amply and sufficiently reflect the findings and conclusions reached by the investigating authority on the questions of dumping, injury and their causal relationship, and include all the issues of fact and law considered relevant by Economía. Consequently, there was no violation of the AD Agreement in that respect.

4.105 Mexico did not levy anti-dumping duties in excess of the dumping margins. The margins were correctly calculated by Economía and the duties levied are consistent with those margins. Mexico thus acted consistently with the GATT 1994.

(f) Complaints by the United States regarding the Foreign Trade Act

4.106 The United States challenges, as such, a number of provisions of the Foreign Trade Act and of other legal instruments as well. Its complaints are without merit for the following reasons:

- There is no *prima facie* case of violation of these provisions, as such;
- the United States bases itself on misinterpretations of the Foreign Trade Act and disregards the meaning and scope of the provisions challenged; and
- it relies on the rice investigation, which ended before the challenged provisions came into effect, to support its claims.

4.107 According to the report of the Appellate Body in *US– Carbon Steel*, where the consistency of a Member's law as such with a WTO Agreement is being challenged, the country's legislation is presumed to be consistent *until proven otherwise*. Thus, the burden of establishing *prima facie* that there has been a violation as such of the WTO Agreements rests with the complaining party. The United States consequently bears the burden of proving *prima facie* that Mexican legislation infringes the WTO Agreements, but has not done so.

4.108 The United States also claims that the Mexican law is "mandatory", without analysing the relationship between this legislation and international agreements. According to the Appellate Body report in *US – Corrosion-Resistant Steel Sunset Review*, in the event of claims brought against legislation "as such" the distinction between mandatory and discretionary legislation should be analysed on a case-specific basis and should not be applied in a "mechanistic" fashion.

4.109 **Article 53 of the Foreign Trade Act** is consistent as such with Articles 6.1.1 of the AD Agreement and 12.1.1 of the SCM Agreement, which specify that "[e]xporters or foreign producers *receiving questionnaires* ... shall be given at least 30 days for reply ...". Mexico is therefore not required to grant this time-limit to exporters that *were not sent a questionnaire*. This is confirmed in the final report of the Panel in *Argentina – Poultry Anti-dumping Duties*.

4.110 If the 30-day period were granted to any interested party that presented itself after the initiation of the investigation, the ensuing delay would lead to infringement of the time-limits laid down in Articles 5.10 of the AD Agreement and 11.11 of the SCM Agreement.

4.111 On the subject of extensions, Mexico rejects the United States' argument on the grounds that Article 53 of the Foreign Trade Act does not in any way prohibit the granting of extensions, and even in administrative procedures extensions have been granted on request. The United States has thus failed to make a *prima facie* case that this Foreign Trade Act provision is inconsistent as such with the AD and SCM Agreements.

4.112 **Article 64 of the Foreign Trade Act** is consistent with Articles 6.8 of the AD Agreement and 12.7 of the SCM Agreement inasmuch as, if an interested party does not participate in the investigation or had no exports during the period of investigation and consequently the exporter in question *does not provide* the necessary information, the investigating authority may calculate its margin of dumping or subsidization on the basis of the facts available, pursuant to Articles 6.8 of the AD Agreement and 12.7 of the SCM Agreement.

4.113 The United States mistakenly alleges that Article 64 of the Foreign Trade Act is inconsistent with the AD Agreement because it mandates the investigating authority to impose on exporters that had no exports during the period of investigation, or did not participate in the investigation, a margin of dumping other than that determined in accordance with Article 9.4 of the AD Agreement, and that imposition of an anti-dumping duty in excess of the dumping margin therefore constitutes a violation of Article 9.3 of the AD Agreement.

4.114 It should be pointed out that Article 9.4 of the AD Agreement only applies where the investigating authority has limited its examination to a reasonable number of interested parties, in accordance with Article 6.10 of the AD Agreement. The calculation method set out in Article 9.4 does not apply to exporters or foreign producers which have not provided the necessary information or have not participated in the investigation. The dumping margin for such exporters and foreign producers must be calculated on the basis of the facts available, pursuant to Article 6.8 of the AD Agreement. Consequently, a violation of Article 9.3 cannot be alleged where Article 9.4 does not apply.

4.115 Article 64 of the Foreign Trade Act is consistent with paragraph 3 of Annex II to the AD Agreement because it requires the investigating authority to consider all *verifiable information.* If an exporter fails to provide the necessary information – normal value and export price in the case at hand – then there is no verifiable information to consider.

4.116 Paragraph 5 of Annex II to the AD Agreement stipulates that the investigating authority may not disregard the information provided by the exporter even if it is not ideal *in all respects*. In other words, if it is to be taken into consideration, the information must be ideal in at least one respect. Mexico repeats that if an exporter fails to provide the information – namely normal value and export price data – needed to determine its margin of dumping, then there is no minimum amount of information to be considered.

4.117 Mexico rejects the United States' argument concerning paragraphs 1 and 7 of Annex II to the AD Agreement, inasmuch as paragraph 1 specifies that if the interested party fails to provide the information required, the investigating authority will be free to make determinations on the basis of the facts available, including those contained in the application for the initiation of an investigation, and the last sentence of paragraph 7 of the Annex provides that if an interested party does not cooperate and fails to provide the investigating authority with relevant information, this situation may lead to *a result which is less favourable* to the interested party than if the party did cooperate.

4.118 **Article 68 of the Foreign Trade Act** is consistent "as such" with Articles 5.8, 9.3 and 11.2 of the AD Agreement and 11.9 and 21.1 of the SCM Agreement. Articles 5 of the AD Agreement and 11 of the SCM Agreement apply solely to investigations and not to reviews. If in the course of the investigation sufficient evidence of dumping or subsidization is found to exist, there is no obligation whatsoever under these Articles to refrain from conducting subsequent proceedings (such as administrative reviews), because once the definitive measure has been imposed, Articles 5.8 of the AD Agreement and 11.9 of the SCM Agreement cease to apply.

4.119 Moreover, the fact of subjecting to review exporters to which no positive margin of dumping or subsidization was assigned in the investigation does not cause them prejudice of any kind, since it does not entail any payment of duty. In any case, reviews carried out in respect of exporters with no positive dumping margin are similar to those provided for in Article 9.3.1 of the AD Agreement.

4.120 The United States' interpretation of Article 68 of the Foreign Trade Act is wrong inasmuch as this provision does not impose a "representativeness" requirement as a condition for the investigating authority to conduct reviews such as those provided for in Articles 21.2 of the SCM Agreement and 9.3 and 11.2 of the AD Agreement. The United States will therefore have to prove, *prima facie*, that the Foreign Trade Act is inconsistent with the WTO Agreements.

4.121 As has already been recognized in the submissions circulated in the course of the proceedings of the WTO Negotiating Group on Rules,[24] there *are no* clear provisions in the Agreements as to how to conduct administrative review and new shipper procedures, and the authorities of WTO Members therefore have discretion to establish the rules that they deem appropriate.

4.122 **Article 89D of the Foreign Trade Act** is consistent as such with Articles 9.5 of the AD Agreement and 19.3 of the SCM Agreement. The United States basically puts forward two arguments: This Article applies only to producers and not to exporters; and it requires producers to demonstrate that their exports were representative.

4.123 The first claim of the United States is without foundation because the provisions of the Foreign Trade Act – as stipulated in Article 2 of the Act – must be applied in a manner consistent with those of the international treaties to which Mexico is party. Mexico accordingly confines itself to applying anti-dumping and countervailing duties as provided for in Article VI of the GATT 1994 and in the AD and SCM Agreements.

4.124 The second claim of the United States is also without foundation because, although Articles 9.5 of the AD Agreement and 19.3 of the SCM Agreement do not expressly so provide, in view of their context, object and purpose, it is both natural and logical to request that a new shipper's volume of exports during the review period be representative. If such were not the case, it would be impossible for the investigating authority to make a proper price comparison, and it would be unable to meet its obligation to determine an individual margin of dumping if the new shipper were to export one single unit of the product under investigation.

4.125 The United States is wrong in claiming that **Article 93.V of the Foreign Trade Act** requires the Mexican investigating authority to impose fines on importers that import goods that are like or identical to goods subject to an anti-dumping or countervailing duty investigation and that this constitutes a non-permissible specific action against dumping or a subsidy, prompting it to contend that Article 93.V is inconsistent as such with Articles 18.1 of the AD Agreement and 32.1 of the SCM Agreement.

4.126 First, Mexico repeats that insofar as the United States has failed to prove that Article 93.V of the Foreign Trade Act is inconsistent with the AD Agreement or the SCM Agreement, Article 93.V should be deemed to be consistent

---

[24] *Submission From Canada Respecting the Agreement On Implementation of Article VI of the GATT 1994 (The Anti-Dumping Agreement)*, TN/RL/W/47, presented to the Negotiating Group on Rules on 27 January 2003 and circulated to Members the following day.

with Mexico's WTO obligations, as determined by the Appellate Body in its report on *US – Carbon Steel*.

4.127 Second, even if the United States had produced the relevant evidence, Mexico will demonstrate that there is no inconsistency of any kind between Article 93.V of the Foreign Trade Act and the WTO Agreements inasmuch as Article 2 of the Foreign Trade Act stipulates that all provisions of the Foreign Trade Act must be applied in accordance with the provisions of international treaties to which Mexico is party.

4.128 Furthermore, Article 93.V of the Foreign Trade Act does not require the investigating authority to apply its provisions but gives it discretion to impose fines. This is proved by the fact that Mexico has never imposed such fines on WTO Members, even though this possibility has existed in the Foreign Trade Act since 1994.

Article 366 of the Federal Code of Civil Procedure and Articles 68 and 97 of the Foreign Trade Act do not, as such, violate Articles 9.3, 9.5 and 11.2 of the AD Agreement or 19.3 and 21.2 of the SCM Agreement

4.129 The United States mistakenly argues that **Articles 68 and 97 of the Foreign Trade Act and 366 of the Federal Code of Civil Procedure** (FCCP) preclude the investigating authority from conducting reviews while a judicial review is under way, and that this violates Articles 9.3, 9.5 and 11.2 of the AD Agreement and 19.3 and 21.2 of the SCM Agreement.

4.130 With regard to Article 366 of the FCCP, the United States has failed to satisfy the burden of proof required of the claimant. This allegation should therefore not be considered further by the Panel. Indeed, the supporting evidence adduced by the United States (Exhibit US-20) contains no reference to this Article, and the United States has not put forward a clear and detailed allegation or produced any evidence of its assertion.

4.131 Moreover, Articles 68 and 97 of the Foreign Trade Act, by considering as definitive only anti-dumping or countervailing duties that have not been challenged under any procedure, provide legal certainty by ensuring that there are no contradictory rulings. Mexico considers that legal certainty affords a guarantee for exporters, who do not even have to pay any anti-dumping or countervailing duties while the challenge procedure is under way.

4.132 Articles 68 and 97 of the Foreign Trade Act do not infringe Article 9.3.2 of the AD Agreement inasmuch as they do not prohibit the reimbursement of duties paid in excess or state that such duties will not be refunded, and the refund is made promptly within the time-frame specified in the AD Agreement, once the proceedings in question have come to an end.

4.133 Moreover, Articles 68 and 97 of the Foreign Trade Act are not in breach of Articles 9.5 of the AD Agreement and 19.3 of the SCM Agreement. The provisions of the Foreign Trade Act neither preclude nor prohibit such a procedure. The United States is seeking to attribute to Mexico obligations that are not to be found in the WTO Agreements, given that the AD and SCM Agreements do not require a new shipper review to be *initiated* immediately after an application for such a review has been made, but specify that a new shipper review, once initiated, should be carried out promptly/expeditiously. The United States will have to prove its assertions by establishing a *prima facie* case in this respect.

C. First Oral Statement of the United States

4.134 The following summarizes the United States' arguments in its first oral opening and closing statements:

1. Opening statement

4.135 Authorities conducting AD investigations must conduct their examinations in an objective and unbiased manner. The authority must investigate the domestic industry, and the effects of dumped imports, in an unbiased manner, without favouring the interests of any party in the investigation. Authorities "are not entitled to conduct their investigation in such a way that it becomes more likely that, as a result of the fact-finding or evaluation process, they will determine that the domestic industry is injured."

4.136 Mexico did not conduct its rice investigation in an objective and unbiased manner. It allowed the petitioner to decide which exporters and producers should be sent the anti-dumping questionnaire, and to choose which part of the year should be examined for dumping and injury. When the US firm Producers Rice demonstrated that it had no shipments of rice to Mexico during the POI, Mexico rejected its information and based its margin on adverse facts available. And Mexico failed even to collect, much less examine, more than a year's worth of data that preceded the initiation of the investigation. The AD Agreement places obligations on Mexico, and Mexico has failed to rebut the United States' *prima facie* case that it has breached them.

(a) Mexico's use of a stale POI

4.137 With the exception of Mexico, all of the parties in this dispute agree that a Member's discretion in setting a POI is not boundless. The period investigated cannot be so remote in time that the information that the authority collects is incapable of providing a basis for an objective finding of dumping, injury, and causation. The fifteen month gap in the present case (and the three year gap between the end of the POI and the final determination) is inconsistent with numerous provisions of the AD Agreement and the GATT 1994.

4.138 Mexico argues that the AD Agreement creates no obligations with respect to the age of the data that a Member may use in reaching its determinations, and that it has complete freedom to do whatever it wants. This is not correct. The POI should end as close to the initiation date as practicable. Mexico has pointed to nothing justifying its decision to ignore 15 months worth of recent data, let alone the three years of data by the time of the final determination. The only rationale that Mexico provided in its notice was that it selected the POI the petitioner wanted.

(b) Mexico limited its injury analysis to only six months of 1997, 1998, and 1999

4.139 An authority conducting an analysis of injury and causation must conduct an objective examination, and it must base its determinations on positive evidence. Mexico's limitation of its investigation to only half of each of the years at issue failed to meet either of these requirements.

4.140 Mexico argues that the AD Agreement creates no obligations on this matter, that it is "entirely free" to do whatever it wants, and that therefore its approach was objective and based on positive evidence. Mexico is wrong. For example, the text of Article 3.5 of the AD Agreement plainly states that an authority must examine "all relevant evidence" that is before it. Mexico has failed to explain why the evidence for half of the POI was not "relevant."

4.141 Mexico's approach created distortion, because focusing an injury and causation analysis on the period when import presence is highest cannot but create a misleading picture of the state of the domestic industry. Mexico has *no idea* what the state of the industry was over the course of the *entire* POI, because Mexico did not examine the data for half of that period.

(c) Mexico's conduct of its injury analysis

4.142 Mexico's examination of the injury data was flawed in four ways. The first flaw arises from Mexico's failure to collect the evidence on price effects and volumes that it needed to conduct its analysis in an objective manner, and its improper use of the facts available. Mexico argues that the AD Agreement creates no relevant obligations. It fails, however, to explain *why* the approach that it chose was objective and based on positive evidence, as Article 3.1 requires.

4.143 For example, if Mexico had sought information from purchasers of long-grain white rice, it would have been able to directly compare the prices the purchasers paid for the domestic product and the prices they paid for the imported product. Similarly, Mexico could have obtained data from the *pedimentos.* Furthermore, Mexico rejected accurate data that The Rice Company submitted for the year 1999, in favour of using inaccurate data from the petitioner. In addition, Article 6.8 and Annex II do not permit an authority to base its analysis of injury on the facts available without first making an effort to obtain the data from the interested parties, or to use that data without first seeking to corroborate it against independent data sources.

4.144 The second flaw arises from Mexico's failure to objectively consider whether there was a significant increase in the volume of dumped imports or significant price effects. Only four paragraphs of its determination were relevant to the examination of the dumped imports, and they show that the *volume* of the dumped imports *declined* during the three-year period of the injury analysis. And none of those paragraphs even mention significant *price* effects.

4.145 The third flaw arises from Mexico's failure to conduct an objective analysis of certain "relevant economic factors." Mexico's examination of inventories and market share was not objective, and it did not even examine "other factors affecting domestic prices." The final flaw in Mexico's analysis of the injury data is that it included non-dumped imports in its evaluation of volume, price effects, and the impact of the dumped imports on the domestic industry.

(d) Mexico's failure to exclude firms with AD margins of zero from the measure

4.146 Mexico ignores that the second and third sentences of Article 5.8 refer to the "margin" of dumping being *de minimis*. The term "margin" refers to the "individual margin of dumping determined for each of the investigated exporters and producers" of the investigated product. When Article 5.8 refers to terminating when the "margin" is *de minimis*, it is referring to termination for individual firms. The fourth sentence of Article 5.8 provides contextual support for this interpretation. That sentence demonstrates that the "volume" analysis may be done on a country-wide basis. There is no such language addressing the dumping analysis.

(e) Mexico's application of an adverse "facts available" margin to Producers Rice and to US producers and exporters that it did not examine

4.147 Mexico investigated only the two exporters that the petitioner named in the petition and two other firms that came forward on their own, and it applied an adverse, facts-available margin to Producers Rice and every other exporter and producer in the United States. Mexico argues that the AD Agreement contains no obligations with respect to this topic and that it has total freedom to apply the facts available to such firms, including "less favourable" facts available from the petition. Mexico's argument is illogical, inconsistent with the text of the AD Agreement, and contradictory to the findings of the Appellate Body on this topic.

4.148 Mexico's argument is inconsistent with the text of the AD Agreement because Mexico bases its entire argument on a flawed interpretive approach that relies on partial citations of Articles 6.8 and 6.10, viewed in isolation, and divorced from the broader context of the overall Agreement. Its argument is contrary to the findings of the Appellate Body because the Appellate Body found in *EC Bed Linen 21.5* that Article 6.10 of the AD Agreement "requires, 'as a rule', that individual dumping margins be established for *each* producer or exporter." Its interpretation is illogical because the drafters established a detailed set of rules that were meant to ensure that unexamined firms are not unfairly prejudiced if they are not included in an AD investigation. The idea that the drafters would have created detailed rules to protect "known" firms, and left "unknown" firms subject to the application of adverse facts available, is implausible at best.

4.149 The AD Agreement protects both known firms *and* unknown firms. It does this by requiring authorities to send their questionnaire to firms that are included "in the investigation," and by restricting the application of margins based on the facts available to cases where a firm *is* sent the questionnaire, is warned about the consequences of not responding, but nevertheless fails to provide the necessary information. If an authority does not take these steps, then it cannot claim to be including the firm "in the investigation," and the firm is entitled to a neutral all other's rate calculated in accordance with Article 9.4 of the AD Agreement.

4.150 Mexico argues that Article 9.4 only applies when the authority limits its investigation to a subset of exporters. But Mexico *did* limit its investigation by choosing not to send its questionnaire to The Rice Company. It also did so by failing to consult the *pedimento* data held by Mexican Customs, when it chose not to reference public data that would have identified every producer of the subject product in the United States, and when it chose not to ask the petitioner whether the two firms listed as "known" exporters in the petition were truly the *only* exporters or producers that the petitioner knew of. Mexico's submission does not contest several of the United States' claims addressing its treatment of Producers Rice and the unexamined firms.

(f) Claims Regarding the Foreign Trade Act and Article 366 of the FCCP

4.151 Mexico argues that treaties are self-executing under Mexican law and that it must apply its laws in a way that is consistent with its treaties. This is beside the point if Mexico's laws *mandate* WTO-inconsistent action.

4.152 The first statutory provision at issue is Article 53 of the Foreign Trade Act, which sets a mandatory deadline of 28 working days for interested parties to respond to Mexico's AD questionnaire, and counts the 28 days from the date of publication of the initiation notice. Mexico argues that it would be "illogical" to provide the full 30 days to interested parties that are not initially sent the questionnaire. The issue for the Panel is quite clear: Is Mexico correct that Articles 6.1.1 and 12.1.1 only apply when an authority "sends" the questionnaire to an interested party? Or is the proper interpretation that both provisions count the 30 day deadline from the date of *receipt*?

4.153 The second statutory provision at issue in this dispute is Article 64 of the Foreign Trade Act. Article 64 *requires* Mexico to apply the *highest* level of facts available to firms that do not export during the POI or that do not "appear" in its investigation. Mexico argues that Article 6.8 of the AD Agreement permits a Member to apply the facts available to a party that fails to provide necessary information, and Mexico is therefore justified in applying the facts available to firms that have no shipments during the POI or that do not "appear" in the investigation. Mexico's argument is based on a partial citation of a portion of Article 6.8 without reference to any of the other provisions of the AD Agreement, including Article 6.1 and paragraph 1 of Annex II.

4.154 Mexico argues that Article 64 is not inconsistent with Article 9.4 of the AD Agreement because Article 9.4 requires Members to exclude margins that are based on the facts available. Mexico misses the point. Article 64 is inconsistent with Article 9.4 of the AD Agreement, because Article 64 requires Mexico to *apply* facts available-based margins to firms that *should have* received a neutral "all others" margin calculated in accordance with Article 9.4.

4.155 Mexico's argument with respect to paragraph 1 of Annex II ignores that an authority must "specify in detail the information required" and "ensure that the party is aware" of the consequences of not providing the information, before it may apply the facts available. Its argument that paragraph 7 of Annex II permits a "less favourable" result if a firm refuses to cooperate ignores that by requiring Mexico to *always* apply the *highest* level of facts available, Article 64 precludes taking cooperation into account. It does not contest that Article 64 of the Foreign Trade Act breaches Article 9.5 of the AD Agreement or Article 19.3 of the SCM Agreement.

4.156 The third provision at issue is Article 68 of the Foreign Trade Act, which mandates a breach of WTO rules for two reasons: *first*, it requires Mexico to review firms that were found not to be dumping or receiving subsidies; and *second*, it mandates that Mexico require firms seeking reviews to demonstrate that the volume of their exports was "representative."

4.157 Articles 5.8 of the AD Agreement and 11.9 of the SCM Agreement require authorities to exclude firms from AD and CVD measures if the authorities find that the firms are not dumping or receiving subsidies. If a firm is excluded from the measure, then there is no basis to subject the firm to a review. Yet Article 68 requires such reviews. Therefore, it breaches Articles 5.8 and 11.9. Moreover, a proper textual analysis of Articles 9.3 and 11.2 of the AD Agreement, and Article 21.2 of the SCM Agreement demonstrates that a firm that meets the criteria in those provisions has a *right* to obtain a review. Since those conditions do not include showing that import volumes were "representative," Article 68 of the Foreign Trade Act – by imposing that condition – breaches Articles 9.3, 11.2, and 21.2.

4.158 The fourth provision at issue is Article 89D of the Foreign Trade Act, which mandates that firms seeking expedited reviews demonstrate that the volume of their exports was representative. The ordinary meaning of the *text* of the provisions demonstrates that a firm that meets the criteria in those provisions has a *right* to obtain an expedited review. Those conditions do not include showing that import volumes were "representative." And Article 89D breaches Article 9.5 of the AD Agreement and Article 19.3 of the SCM Agreement because it only allows producers (and not non-producing exporters) to obtain reviews.

4.159 The fifth provision is Article 93V of the Foreign Trade Act, which requires Mexico to impose fines on importers that import certain goods subject to an AD or CVD investigation. Article 93V is inconsistent with Articles 18.1 of the AD Agreement and 32.1 of the SCM Agreement because it is a non-permissible specific action against dumping. Mexico has not contested that Article 93V is "specific" to dumping or subsidization; "against" dumping or subsidization; and not "in accordance with the provisions of GATT 1994," as interpreted by the AD and SCM Agreements. Mexico's only defence is to argue that it has discretion not to impose the fine. But, although Article 93V gives Mexico discretion to determine whether the factual predicates for applying a fine exist, it *mandates* the application of a fine if they do.

4.160 The final set of provisions at issue are Article 366 of the FCCP and Articles 68 and 97 of the Foreign Trade Act. They are inconsistent "as such" with the AD and SCM Agreements because they preclude the Mexican authorities from conducting reviews of AD and CVD measures during judicial proceedings. Article 366 states that a proceeding "shall be suspended" pending resolution of another matter. By precluding Mexico from conducting reviews in this manner, Article 366 is inconsistent with Articles 9.3, 9.5, and 11.2 of the AD Agreement, and Articles 19.3 and 21.2 of the SCM Agreement.

4.161 Mexico's submission does not even address the United States' claim that Articles 68 and 97 of the Foreign Trade Act breach Article 11.2 of the AD Agreement and Article 21.2 of the SCM Agreement. As for the fact that Articles 68 and 97 breach Article 9.5 of the AD Agreement and Article 19.3 of the SCM Agreement, Mexico asserts that those provisions allow a Member to wait as long as it likes before initiating an expedited review, if it conducts the review promptly once it initiates. Mexico's argument contradicts the text of Articles 9.5 and 19.3.

4.162 Mexico does not contest that Articles 68 and 97 of the Foreign Trade Act preclude Mexico from conducting reviews of measures under Article 9.3.2 of the AD Agreement while judicial reviews of the measures are underway. It argues instead that its approach is permissible because the duties are not "definitive" until the judicial review is complete. Mexico is wrong on the facts.

2. *Closing statement*

4.163 As the United States noted in its oral statement, Mexico's submission had failed to rebut the United States' *prima facie* case that Mexico has breached its WTO obligations in numerous ways. Mexico's oral statement yesterday was quite similar to its written submission, and also did not rebut the United States' *prima facie* case.

4.164 Because the United States' oral statement addressed the content of Mexico's written submission, and because Mexico's oral statement was quite similar to its written submission, it has only a few additional comments to make today.

4.165 The first point pertains to Mexico's request for a preliminary ruling. The United States addressed all of the points that Mexico raised yesterday, in the United States' written response. The United States filed that response on 7 May. The United States would like to make one additional point, however, pertaining to Mexico's argument that it was prejudiced because it only received the Spanish-language version of the United States' written submission on 16 April, a week before its written submission was due. If there were merit to this claim, one might have expected that Mexico's oral statement would have set out the new arguments that Mexico did not have time to include in its written submission. Mexico has had the Spanish-language version of the submission of the United States for at least a month. The fact that Mexico's oral statement did not differ much from its written submission suggests that it was not prejudiced by the date it received the translation of the submission of the United States.

4.166 The second point pertains to Mexico's use of the facts available in assigning an anti-dumping margin to Producers Rice. Mexico argued yesterday that its application of the facts available was justified because Producers Rice had what Mexico described as an "obligation" to present the information that Mexico needed to conduct a margin. But Producers Rice demonstrated to Mexico that it had no shipments during the POI. There was nothing more that Producers Rice could have given to Mexico. It is not objective or unbiased for an authority to apply an adverse anti-dumping margin to a firm that was unable to provide information that does not exist.

4.167 The United States would also like to address Mexico's comment yesterday that Articles 68 and 89D of the Foreign Trade Act do not require firms seeking reviews to demonstrate that the volume of their sales was representative. The United States is confused by Mexico's argument. Article 68 reads: "[t]he Party requesting a review shall satisfy Economía that the volume of exports to Mexico during the review period is representative." Article 89D contains virtually identical text. The provisions speak for themselves.

4.168 On the issue of Article 93V of the Foreign Trade Act, Mexico argued that the application of fines is discretionary, and that proof of this fact is that it has never, in fact, applied such a fine. This proves nothing, because Mexico has not pointed to any case where it found that the conditions for imposing a fine were met, and yet it decided not to impose one. The text of the provision itself is mandatory.

4.169 Finally, the United States will comment further on the Panel's questions about the mandatory/discretionary issue, and the relevance of that issue to Mexico's laws, in its response to the Panel's questions and in the United States' second written submission.

D. First Oral Statement of Mexico

4.170 The following summarizes Mexico's arguments in its first oral statements:

1. Preliminary ruling

(a) Ambiguities of the United States

4.171 Firstly, the fact that Mexico did not, at the preliminary stage, contest certain claims by the United States does not mean that Mexico accepts that the United States met the formal requirements.

4.172 Mexico notes that the United States asserts that Mexico confuses what is a claim (*reclamación*) with what is an argument (*argumento*). This is not correct. The United States' claims were not set out clearly or simply refer to irrelevant provisions. Mexico did not suggest that the United States should have put forward arguments in its request for the establishment of a panel.

4.173 The United States' request is ambiguous in at least three instances. Firstly, the United States is highly ambiguous when it alleges a violation of Article VI of the GATT 1994 as it does not specifically indicate to which paragraphs it is referring and proposes unrealistic methods to make good the omission. Secondly, the United States refers to Article 4.1 of the AD Agreement, even though this is in no way related to the rest of the claim. Thirdly, the "narrative description" given by the United States in sections 1(g) and 1(f) of the request for the establishment of a panel has no relevance to the legal bases claimed.

(b) Damage requirement in procedural violations

4.174 The United States wrongly argues that at the current stage of the proceedings (i.e. the panel stage), Mexico has not shown how the violations caused by ambiguity have affected it. Firstly, there is no provision laying down such a requirement. Secondly, *arguendo* that such a requirement existed, at the present procedural stage it is impossible to determine the effect. Thirdly, also *arguendo* that a requirement existed, the combination of factors including the ambiguities and the long delay in translating the first written submission of the United States, had an impact on Mexico's defence.

(c) Identification of the measure

4.175 Article 366 of the Federal Code of Civil Procedure may be considered a measure. Nevertheless, the United States does not understand the relationship among the Articles of various Mexican laws and endeavours to remedy this by citing statements by "Mexican officials". Article 366 is a measure that bears no relation to the anti-dumping proceedings and the United States tries to make good this error by using statements by "Mexican officials".

4.176 Alternatively, as Mexico indicated in its written submission, in the event that the Panel rejects its arguments the United States did not provide a brief summary of the legal bases of the complaint sufficient to present the problem clearly.

(d) Legal bases not included in the consultations

4.177 In its request for the establishment of a panel, the United States improperly added 13 new legal bases that were not included in its request for consultations. This is contrary to the provisions of Article 4.5 and 4.7 of the DSU and Article 17.4 and 17.5 of the AD Agreement. The United States argued that the wording of Article 4.4 of the DSU allowed it to omit almost anything. A proper reading of Articles 4.4 and 6.2 of the DSU, however, indicates that the legal bases of the complaint must be the same in the request for consultations and in the request for a panel; the only thing that changes is the level of specificity, not the legal basis. Following the United States' criterion would lead to absurd cases.

2. *Legal arguments regarding the anti-dumping investigation into imports of United States' long-grain white rice*

4.178 Mexico emphasizes that the United States' arguments are not substantiated by the AD Agreement and considers that the United States is trying to impose on Mexico obligations that are not covered by the Agreement, thus violating Article 17.6 of the AD Agreement by dismissing *a priori* the permissible interpretation of those provisions by Mexico.

(a) Economía complied with Article VI:2 of the GATT 1994 and with Articles 1, 3.1, 3.2, 3.4 and 3.5 of the AD Agreement with regard to the establishment of the Period of Investigation

4.179 Economía complied with Articles 1, 3.1, 3.2, 3.4 and 3.5 of the AD Agreement and Article VI:2 of the GATT in the anti-dumping investigation into imports of long-grain white rice from the United States by correctly establishing the periods of investigation (for dumping purposes) and analysis (for determination of injury), as a result of an objective examination based on positive evidence.

4.180 In the request for the establishment of a panel, the United States set out arguments on Articles 1 of the AD Agreement and VI:2 of the GATT 1994 that were not the subject of consultations, violating Articles 4.5 and 4.7 of the DSU and 17.4 of the AD Agreement; therefore, its claims should be dismissed.

4.181 With regard to determination of the period of investigation, the AD Agreement does not contain any provision establishing how remote that period should be. Since it is impossible to violate an obligation that does not exist, Mexico did not contravene Article 3.2 of the AD Agreement in fixing that period. Furthermore, in the course of the investigation, no exporter put forward objections or evidence sufficient to change it.

4.182 Economía complied with Article 3.1, 3.2 and 3.4 of the AD Agreement by conducting an objective examination, based on positive evidence of the volume of the imports, their effect on prices, and relevant economic factors and indices. Moreover, the final determination indicates that during the period analysed dumped imports caused injury to the domestic industry.

(b) Economía complied with Articles 1, 3.1, 3.5 and 6.2 of the AD Agreement with regard to the establishment of the period analysed

4.183 In the request for the establishment of a panel, the United States included arguments on Articles 1 of the AD Agreement and VI of the GATT 1994 that were not the subject of consultations, thus violating Articles 4.5 and 4.7 of the DSU and 17.4 of the AD Agreement.

4.184 The periods of investigation and analysis were established correctly and Economía carried out an objective examination based on positive evidence, making sure that the parties had an opportunity to defend their interests in accordance with Article 6.2 of the AD Agreement.

4.185 The AD Agreement does not indicate how the period of analysis should be included in an anti-dumping investigation, therefore Economía did not violate the AD Agreement, which does not prohibit the comparison of periods equivalent to the period of investigation in order to determine injury. In this particular case and in order to prevent distortion, the factors listed in Article 3.4 of the AD Agreement that related to the period of investigation were compared to similar periods in 1997 and 1998, and this is not inconsistent with the AD Agreement.

4.186 The United States indicates that the spring/summer (October-December) season yield of paddy rice is greater than the fall/winter (June – July) yield and, consequently, domestic production of long-grain white rice is greater in the former than in the latter.

4.187 Mexico set the period of analysis as March to August 1997, 1998 and 1999, in order to maintain the objectivity of the analysis. When there is a drop in domestic production of paddy rice, domestic producers of long-grain white rice rely on imported paddy rice, so the domestic production of the product investigated remained virtually constant in 1997, 1998 and 1999. The United States' argument is therefore without foundation inasmuch as domestic production of this product does *not* depend on domestic production of paddy rice.

4.188 In the analysis of injury and the causal relationship with dumping, all relevant evidence was examined and, therefore, there was no breach of Article 3.5 of the AD Agreement. Consequently, it cannot be argued that, as a result of this violation, Article 6.2 of the AD Agreement was also violated. In compliance with Article 6.2 of the AD Agreement, a public hearing was held and interested parties were given the opportunity to meet with parties having adverse interests; moreover, the exporting companies subsequently presented their arguments in relation to what occurred during the hearing.

(c) Economía conducted its injury analysis in accordance with Articles 3.1, 3.2, 3.4, 3.5, 6.8 and 12.2 and Annex II of the AD Agreement

4.189 In its request for the establishment of a panel, the United States included arguments on paragraphs 1, 3, 5, 6 and 7 of Annex II to the AD Agreement that were not the subject of consultations, thus violating Articles 4.5 and 4.7 of the DSU and 17.4 of the AD Agreement.

4.190 Economía based its injury determination on positive evidence and on an objective examination of the effect on prices, the volume of imports, the impact on domestic prices and relevant economic factors, properly using the best information available and giving sufficient detail of its findings and conclusions on issues of fact and law. It thus complied with Articles 3.1, 3.2, 3.4, 3.5, 6.8 and 12.2 and Annex II of the AD Agreement.

4.191 The investigating authority of a WTO Member complies with Article 3.1 of the AD Agreement when: (a) It bases itself on affirmative, objective, verifiable and credible evidence; and (b) it gathers and evaluates that evidence in good faith and fundamental fairness. Economía fulfilled those conditions by carrying out an objective examination, based on positive evidence, of the volume of imports, their effect on prices for like products and the impact on the domestic industry.

4.192 The AD Agreement does not require any particular methodology for making price comparisons and evaluating effects on prices, and this was recognized by the United States in paragraph 90 of its first submission. An investigating authority may, therefore, conduct its analysis in the manner it deems appropriate provided that it bases itself on positive evidence and makes an objective examination, as Mexico did.

4.193 The United States does not put forward a clear and detailed allegation or any supporting evidence regarding the information sources used by Economía to carry out its analysis, thus failing to discharge its burden of proof, as determined by the Appellate Body in *US – Wool Shirts and Blouses*. Furthermore, it is sufficient to state that, in its analysis, Mexico did not violate the AD Agreement.

4.194 In addition, the AD Agreement does not establish an obligation to send questionnaires to purchasers, and the investigating authority did not consider it necessary to do so. It is therefore wrong to maintain that Mexico failed to act in compliance with the Agreement.

4.195 With regard to the import declarations (*pedimentos*), it should be emphasized that these are *not* available to the investigating authority. The investigating authority only has "list of *pedimentos*", which do *not* show the names or domiciles of exporters.

4.196 Mexico also reiterates that the AD Agreement does not lay down any particular methodology for analysing the volume of imports nor does it require the investigating authority to obtain more information than that supplied by the parties. In this connection, Economía did request information from exporters and importers on this particular point but did not obtain an adequate response[25], as can be seen in Exhibit MEX-4 to the first written submission.

4.197 Mexico repeats that Article 3.2 of the AD Agreement does not say that use of the methodology proposed by the petitioner constitutes a breach of the AD Agreement. This methodology was used from the outset and no objection was raised by the exporters. Once the preliminary determination had been issued, no objection or better or alternative proposal was made.

4.198 Furthermore, Mexico submits that there is no obligation to send questionnaires to *all* exporters, importers and purchasers. Pursuant to Article 6.1.1 of the AD Agreement, an investigating authority may send questionnaires to foreign producers and exporters, but is not obliged to send them to all. Mexico complied with its obligations by transmitting to the United States' authorities the public notice of initiation, the text of the application for initiation of an investigation and the annexes thereto, and the questionnaire for exporters and foreign producers.

4.199 Moreover, in compliance with paragraph 1 of Annex II to the AD Agreement, as indicated in the third paragraph of the introduction on the investigation questionnaire, Mexico did inform the interested parties that, if the information required in the questionnaire was not provided, Economía's determination would

---

[25] Official communications UPCI.310.01.0623, UPCI.310.01.0631 and UPCI.310.01.0632 of 23 March 2001 (Exhibit MEX-4).

be based on the facts available. Accordingly, the United States' allegation that these points were not notified to the exporters is without foundation.

4.200 Regarding an objective analysis of the relevant economic factors, Economía made an objective examination in accordance with Article 3.4 of the AD Agreement. The final determination contains an analysis of all these factors; consequently, the United States' allegation in this respect is without foundation.

4.201 Furthermore, it is wrong to assert that Mexico included non-dumped imports in its evaluation of volume, effect on prices and the impact of dumped imports on the domestic industry. The final determination shows that both the "total volume of imports" and the "volume of dumped imports" were analysed and that the latter were the cause of the injury suffered by the domestic industry.

4.202 Regarding the content of the final determination, Economía considers that it sets out in ample and sufficient detail the findings and conclusions reached on issues of fact and law relating to dumping, injury and the causal relationship which it deemed relevant, as well as the reasons which led the investigating authority to impose definitive measures; consequently, Mexico asserts that it did not violate any provision of the AD Agreement.

(d) Article 5.8 of the AD Agreement is not applicable to firms with dumping margins of zero per cent

4.203 Article 5.8 of the AD Agreement cannot be used in support of the argument that firms with dumping margins of zero per cent should be excluded from the measure because the investigation resulted in a determination of dumping, injury and their causal relationship, which led Economía to impose definitive anti-dumping measures. Furthermore, a zero per cent duty does not constitute a de facto anti-dumping duty as it causes no prejudice to the exporter. Since no anti-dumping duty is being charged, it cannot be considered that a *de minimis* margin exists or that an anti-dumping duty in excess of the dumping margin is being charged, as argued by the United States.

4.204 As to the claim that US exporters will be subject to review and the possible application of a definitive measure, if those exporters do not engage in dumping, such reviews will not lead to the application of any measure. The AD Agreement *does not prohibit* a review of exporters with a zero per cent dumping margin. If the negotiators of the Agreement had determined that such exporters should not be subject to review, they would have done so explicitly.

(e) Mexico applied the facts available to Producers Rice and to the US producers and exporters that were not investigated in a manner consistent with the AD Agreement

4.205 In the request for the establishment of a panel, the United States put forward arguments concerning Articles 1 and 9.3 and paragraphs 1, 3, 5, 6 and 7 of Annex II of the AD Agreement and Article VI:2 of the GATT 1994 that were not the subject of consultations, thus violating Articles 4.5 and 4.7 of the DSU and 17.4 of the AD Agreement.

4.206 The United States' argument concerning the application of a dumping margin to US exporters on the basis of the facts available is not substantiated by the AD Agreement. Mexico considers that the United States is trying to impose obligations on Mexico that are not to be found in the AD Agreement; or, contrary to Article 17.6 of the AD Agreement, it rejects *a priori* Mexico's permissible interpretation of the provisions of the Agreement.

4.207 Mexico is *not* obliged to determine an individual dumping margin for *all* exporters or producers inasmuch as Article 6.10 of the AD Agreement establishes the obligation to do so only in respect of *known* exporters, which is what Economía did.

4.208 Moreover, Article 9.4 of the AD Agreement only applies when the investigating authority limits its examination to a reasonable number of exporters or producers. Mexico did not limit its examination to a reasonable number of exporters or producers; therefore, this Article does not apply when a dumping margin is calculated for exporters that did not export or did not participate in the investigation.

4.209 In the case of US exporters that were not investigated individually and were never included in the investigation and/or did not provide the necessary information, Economía was obliged to apply the facts available, in accordance with Article 6.8 of the AD Agreement. Mexico acted consistently with the AD Agreement in applying the facts available to *Producers Rice*, because if an interested party does not participate in the investigation or has no exports during the period of investigation, it must be considered that it *did not provide* the information needed to calculate a dumping margin. Article 6.8 of the AD Agreement allows a dumping margin to be calculated on the basis of the facts available.

4.210 Mexico acted in a manner consistent with Annex II to the AD Agreement, as can be seen from the following considerations:

(a) Mexico acted consistently with paragraph 3 of Annex II to the Agreement by applying Article 6.8 of the AD Agreement to *Producers Rice* as the firm did not provide the information needed to calculate a dumping margin and there was thus no information from the exporter to be taken into account.

(b) Economía acted consistently with paragraph 5 of Annex II to the AD Agreement, as *Producers Rice* did not provide information that was ideal in at least one respect for the calculation of a dumping margin.

(c) In addition, Economía acted consistently with paragraph 6 of Annex II to the AD Agreement because it did not reject any of the information provided by *Producers Rice* but *accepted* it and acted in accordance with the provisions of the AD Agreement in calculating the dumping margin applicable.

4.211 Furthermore, contrary to the United States' claim, the determinations of Economía amply and sufficiently reflect the findings and conclusions reached on the dumping, injury and their causal relationship, and include all the issues of fact and law considered relevant by Economía. Consequently, there was no violation of the AD Agreement in that respect.

4.212 Mexico did not levy anti-dumping duties in excess of the dumping margins. The margins were correctly calculated by Economía and the duties levied are consistent with those margins. Mexico thus acted consistently with the GATT 1994 and the AD Agreement.

3. *Complaints by the United States regarding the Foreign Trade Act*

4.213 According to the report of the Appellate Body in *US – Carbon Steel*, it is presumed that a Member's legislation is consistent as such with the WTO Agreements *until proven otherwise*. Thus, the burden of establishing *prima facie* that there has been a violation in this respect rests with the complaining party. The United States bears the burden of proving *prima facie* that the Foreign Trade Act violates the WTO Agreements, but has not done so.

4.214 The United States asserts that the Foreign Trade Act is "mandatory", without taking into account the relationship between this legislation and international agreements. According to the Appellate Body report in *US – Corrosion-Resistant Steel Sunset Review*, in the event of claims brought against legislation "as such" the distinction between mandatory and discretionary legislation should be analysed on a case specific basis and should not be applied in a "mechanistic" fashion.

4.215 **Article 53 of the Foreign Trade Act** is consistent as such with Articles 6.1.1 of the AD Agreement and 12.1.1 of the SCM Agreement, which provide that "[e]xporters or foreign producers *receiving questionnaires* ... shall be given at least 30 days for reply ... ". Mexico is therefore not required to grant this time-limit to exporters *that were not sent a questionnaire*. This is confirmed in the final report of the Panel in *Argentina – Poultry Anti-Dumping Duties*. On the subject of extensions, Article 53 of the Foreign Trade Act does *not* in any way prohibit the granting of extensions, and in administrative procedures US exporters have been granted extensions when they so requested.

4.216 **Article 64 of the Foreign Trade Act** is consistent with Articles 6.8 of the AD Agreement and 12.7 of the SCM Agreement inasmuch as if a party does not participate in the investigation or had no exports during the period of investigation, and consequently *does not provide* the necessary normal value and export price information, the investigating authority may calculate the relevant margin on the basis of the facts available.

4.217 Likewise, Article 9.4 of the AD Agreement only applies where the investigating authority limits its examination to a reasonable number of interested parties, in accordance with Article 6.10 of the AD Agreement. The calculation method set out therein does not apply to exporters or foreign producers that have not provided the necessary information or have not participated in the investigation. It cannot therefore be claimed — as the United States does — that applying Article 64 of the Foreign Trade Act means imposing an anti-dumping duty in excess of the dumping margin, in violation of Article 9.3 of the AD Agreement.

4.218 Article 64 of the Foreign Trade Act is consistent with paragraph 3 of Annex II to the AD Agreement as it requires the investigating authority to consider all *verifiable information*. Thus, if an exporter fails to provide the necessary information on the normal value and export price, then there is no verifiable information to consider. Paragraph 5 of the Annex provides that the investigating authority should not disregard the information provided by the exporter even if it is not ideal *in all respects*. In other words, if it is to be taken into consideration, the information must be ideal in at least one respect; therefore, if no information on the normal value and export price is provided, it cannot be taken into account.

4.219 Mexico rejects the United States' argument concerning paragraphs 1 and 7 of Annex II to the AD Agreement inasmuch as paragraph 1 specifies that if the interested party fails to provide the information required, the investigating authority will be free to make determinations on the basis of the facts available, including those contained in the application for the initiation of the investigation, and the last sentence of paragraph 7 of the Annex provides that if an interested party does not cooperate and fails to provide the investigating authority with relevant information, this could lead to *a result which is less favourable* to for the interested party than if the party did cooperate. This would occur after the said information had been compared with that available from independent sources.

4.220 **Article 68 of the Foreign Trade Act** is consistent "as such" with Articles 5.8, 9.3 and 11.2 of the AD Agreement and 11.9 and 21.1 of the SCM Agreement. Articles 5 of the AD Agreement and 11 of the SCM Agreement apply solely to investigations and not to reviews. Once the definitive measure has been imposed, Articles 5.8 of the AD Agreement and 11.9 of the SCM Agreement cease to apply. In any case, reviews carried out in respect of exporters with no positive dumping margin are similar to those provided in Article 9.3.1 of the AD Agreement.

4.221 The United States' interpretation of Article 68 of the Mexican Foreign Trade Act is wrong inasmuch as this provision does not impose a "representativeness" requirement as a condition for the investigating authority to conduct reviews such as those provided for in Articles 21.2 of the SCM Agreement and 9.3 and 11.2 of the AD Agreement.

4.222 **Article 89D of the Foreign Trade Act** is consistent as such with Articles 9.5 of the AD Agreement and 19.3 of the SCM Agreement. The United States basically puts forward two arguments: this Article applies only to producers and not to exporters; and it requires foreign producers to demonstrate that their exports were representative.

4.223 Mexico reiterates that the provisions of the Foreign Trade Act must be applied in a manner consistent with those of the international treaties to which Mexico is party, as stipulated in Article 2 of the Foreign Trade Act. Thus, Mexico confines itself to applying anti-dumping and countervailing duties as provided for in Article VI of the GATT 1994 and in the AD and SCM Agreements.

4.224 Although Articles 9.5 of the AD Agreement and 19.3 of the SCM Agreement do not expressly so provide, in view of their context, object and purpose, it is both natural and logical to request that a new exporter's volume of exports during the review period be representative. If such were not the case, it would be impossible for the investigating authority to make a proper price comparison, and it would be unable to meet its obligation to determine an individual margin of dumping if the new exporter were to export one single unit of the product investigated.

4.225 **Article 93.V of the Foreign Trade Act** is consistent as such with Articles 18.1 of the AD Agreement and 32.1 of the SCM Agreement. The United States has failed to prove that Article 93.V of the Foreign Trade Act is inconsistent with the AD Agreement or the SCM Agreement. Even if the United States had produced the relevant evidence, Mexico holds that there is no inconsistency of any kind between Article 93.V of the Mexican law and the WTO Agreements inasmuch as Article 2 of the Foreign Trade Act stipulates that all of the provisions of the Foreign Trade Act must be applied in accordance with the provisions of international treaties to which Mexico is party. Furthermore, Article 93.V of the Foreign Trade Act does *not* require the investigating authority to apply its provisions but gives Economía discretion to impose fines. This is proved by the fact that Mexico has never imposed such fines on Members of the WTO, even though this possibility has existed in the Foreign Trade Act since 1994.

4.226 **Articles 68 and 97 of the Foreign Trade Act and 366 of the Federal Code of Civil Procedure** (FCCP) do not violate Articles 9.3, 9.5 and 11.2 of the AD Agreement and 19.3 and 21.2 of the SCM Agreement.

4.227 With regard to Article 366 of the FCCP, the United States has failed to make a *prima facie* case of violation as such of this Article; therefore, its allegation should not be considered further by the Panel. Even in its Exhibit US-20 there is no proof that Article 366 of the FCCP was applied.

4.228 Articles 68 and 97 of the Foreign Trade Act, by considering as definitive only anti-dumping or countervailing duties that have not been challenged under any procedure, give interested parties legal certainty. On the one hand, the Foreign Trade Act allows them to guarantee the amount of the anti-dumping duties fixed in the final determination that is subject to challenge; and on the other, it ensures that there are no contradictory rulings by the authorities. Such legal certainty affords a guarantee for exporters, who are not required to pay any duties while the challenge procedure is under way. Where the ruling is in their favour, the security is annulled or the amounts already paid are refunded with interest.

4.229 Articles 68 and 97 of the Foreign Trade Act are not inconsistent with Article 9.3.2 of the AD Agreement inasmuch as they do not prohibit the reimbursement of duties paid in excess. The refund is made promptly within the timeframe specified in the AD Agreement, once the proceedings in question have come to an end.

4.230 Moreover, Articles 68 and 97 of the Foreign Trade Act are not in breach of Articles 9.5 of the AD Agreement and 19.3 of the SCM Agreement on the new exporter procedure inasmuch as none of the provisions of the Foreign Trade Act precludes or expressly prohibits such a procedure. The requirement in the AD Agreement is that a new exporter procedure, once initiated, should be carried out promptly (or expeditiously in the words of the SCM Agreement). There is *no* requirement to *initiate* the new exporter procedure immediately after an application for such a procedure has been made.

E. Second Written Submission of the United States

4.231 The following are the United States' arguments in its second written submission:

1. Introduction

4.232 Mexico's imposition of an anti-dumping measure on long-grain white rice from the United States breached numerous provisions of the AD Agreement and the GATT 1994. Several provisions of Mexico's Foreign Trade Act and its Federal Code of Civil Procedure ("FCCP") are inconsistent with provisions of the AD Agreement and the SCM Agreement.

4.233 Mexico's responses to the United States' claims have barely addressed the substance of the arguments of the United States. Instead, Mexico has mostly replied with broad assertions that the AD and SCM Agreements create no obligations with respect to the issues that the United States has raised, and that Mexico has freedom to do whatever it wants. Mexico is incorrect. The AD and SCM Agreements do place obligations on Mexico, and Mexico has failed to rebut the *prima facie* case of the United States that Mexico has breached these obligations.

2. Economía's use of a stale Period of Investigation

(a) Mexico is unable to justify Economía's use of a stale POI

4.234 The purpose of an anti-dumping investigation is to determine whether a domestic industry is *presently* injured (or threatened with injury) by dumping that is *presently* occurring. Therefore, an authority must seek to base its determinations of dumping and injury on a period that includes the most recent available information. If an authority chooses instead to examine information that does not include the most recent available information, it must be able to justify its approach and explain why its determinations are objective, unbiased, and based on positive evidence.

4.235 Mexico's response to the Panel's question 2(c) has confirmed that Economía had no justification for its decision to base its injury determination on stale data, except that it selected the POI that the petitioner asked it to examine. It took this approach even though the foreign respondents and the importers objected. Mexico has also confirmed that Economía did not seek to use a POI that ended as close to the initiation date as practicable.

4.236 Furthermore, Mexico has not contested that Economía took no steps to update the injury information after it initiated its investigation, with the result that its final determination of injury was based on data that was *three to five* years old.

4.237 Mexico's sole defence on this issue is that it interprets the AD Agreement as placing no limits on the age of the information that an authority may use in reaching its determinations of dumping and injury, and that Economía is under no obligation to obtain the most recent information available when it conducts its investigations. Mexico is wrong.

(b) An investigating authority must base its injury investigations on a period that includes the most recent available information

4.238 Numerous provisions in the AD Agreement and the GATT 1994 illustrate the need for authorities to base their injury investigations on a period that includes the most recent available information. For example, Article 3.7 of the AD Agreement requires an authority to base a threat determination:

> on facts, and not merely on allegation, conjecture or remote possibility. The change in circumstances which would create a situation in which the dumping would cause injury must be clearly foreseen and imminent.

4.239 If an authority fails to evaluate data that includes the most recent available data, it will not be in a position to make judgments about situations that *are* imminent; at most, it will be able to make predictions about situations that might have been imminent at some time in the past.[26] Thus, Article 3.7 of the AD Agreement presumes that the authority is making its determination based on data that *include* the most recent available information.

4.240 Similarly, Article 3.4 of the AD Agreement requires an authority to evaluate all relevant economic factors, including actual and *potential* decline in sales, profits, etc., and actual and *potential* negative effects on cash flow, inventories, etc. The term "potential" refers to the future, and implies that the authority is evaluating data that includes information that is as current as possible.

4.241 In addition, Article VI:1 of the GATT 1994 states that dumping "is to be condemned if it *causes or threatens* material injury," and Article VI:6(a) states that a contracting party may only levy an anti-dumping duty if it finds that the dumping is such as to *cause or threaten* material injury (emphasis added). Both of these provisions imply that the injury is occurring in the present (or threaten-

---

[26] Similarly, footnote 10 to Article 3.7 states that one situation that might support an affirmative finding of threat of material injury is where "there is convincing reason to believe that there will be, in the near future, substantially increased importation of the product at dumped prices." An authority will only be in a position to make predictions about the "near future" if it is basing those predictions on information that includes recent data.

ing to occur in the near future). An objective authority will only be in a position to make determinations about the present, or the near future, if it is examining a period that includes the most recent data available.

4.242 The necessity for an authority to consider events that happened in the past does not give an authority free rein to choose which part of the past to consider. In the rice investigation, Economía made no effort to collect information for the period between the end of the POI and the initiation of the anti-dumping investigation or to update its data thereafter. The fifteen-month gap between the end of the POI and the date of initiation and the nearly *three-year* gap between the end of the POI and the final determination means (1) Economía's examination of volume and price effects was not objective or based on positive evidence as required by Articles 3.1 and 3.2 of the AD Agreement; (2) Economía's examination of "all relevant economic factors" having a bearing on the state of the domestic industry was not objective or based on positive evidence as required by Articles 3.1 and 3.4 of the AD Agreement; and (3) Economía's determination that the dumped imports were "causing" injury to the domestic industry was not objective or based on positive evidence as required by Articles 3.1 and 3.5 of the AD Agreement.

3. Economía's limitation of its examination of injury

4.243 Economía's decision to allow the petitioners to set the POI for its dumping analysis as March - August 1999 and its focus on only March to August of 1997, 1998, and 1999 for its injury analysis resulted in breaches of Articles 1, 3.1, 3.5, and 6.2 of the AD Agreement.

4.244 *First*, the sole reason for Economía's decision to base its *dumping* analysis on the March to August time period was that the petitioner requested it to examine that period. Moreover, instead of using a neutral approach, Economía always assumes that the POI that the petitioner suggests is appropriate; if the foreign respondents disagree, it places the evidentiary burden on them to demonstrate that it should use another period instead. Moreover, when the respondents in the rice investigation *did* come forward and object to the POI, Economía summarily rejected their concerns.[27] Contrary to Mexico's assertion, footnote 4 of the AD Agreement is not relevant, because it merely addresses the determination of whether sales have been made below cost over an extended period of time.

4.245 *Second*, the sole reason for Economía's decision to base its *injury* analysis on the March to August time period was that the petitioner requested it to examine that period. Mexico's statement that Economía conducted its injury analysis on the basis of the "period selected by the petitioners" speaks volumes. The petitioner requested Economía to examine the March to August time period specifically because the petitioner believed imports were concentrated in that period, and Economía initiated the case on that basis. An objective and unbiased authority would not have done so.

---

[27] See, *e.g.*, Preliminary Determination, para. 66 (Exhibits US-14&15).

4.246 *Third*, Mexico has rejected the idea that Economía took "seasonality" into account in making this decision. Therefore, there are absolutely no grounds to conclude that concerns about seasonality justified the approach that Economía took.

4.247 *Fourth*, Economía did collect data for every month in the three-year injury POI; it simply chose not to examine half of that information. By contrast, a *proper* injury analysis looks at the evidence for the *entire* POI. The fact that the non-examined half of each of the three years reflects a large portion of domestic production makes it *vital* for an authority to examine evidence for the entire POI.

4.248 The Appellate Body made a similar point in *US – Hot-Rolled Steel*, when it found that an authority could not objectively examine a domestic industry if it focused on just one part of that industry. As the Appellate Body stated:

> Different parts of an industry may exhibit quite different economic performance during any given period. Some parts may be performing well, while others are performing poorly. To examine only the poorly performing parts of an industry...may give a misleading impression of the data relating to the industry as a whole, and may overlook positive developments in other parts of the industry. Such an examination may result in highlighting the negative data in the poorly performing part, without drawing attention to the positive data in other parts of the industry.

4.249 In sum, "an examination of only certain parts of a domestic industry does not ensure a proper evaluation of the state of the domestic industry as a whole, and does not, therefore, satisfy the requirements of 'objectiv[ity]' in Article 3.1 of the *Anti-Dumping Agreement*."

4.250 The Appellate Body's observations are equally valid with respect to the examination of the entirety of the injury data relating to an industry. The economic performance of a domestic industry may vary over the course of a year. To examine only one part of the year may overlook positive developments in other parts of the year, and thus give a misleading impression of the data relating to the condition of the industry as a whole. Yet this is exactly what Economía did.

4.251 Moreover, ignoring the evidence for half of each of the three years of the POI precluded Economía from conducting an objective examination of the causal relationship between the dumped imports and any injury to the domestic industry. Economía's approach ensured that its examination was not based on all relevant evidence before it, as Article 3.5 of the AD Agreement requires.

4. *Economía's conduct of its injury analysis*

4.252 Economía's injury analysis breached Articles 3.1, 3.2, 3.4, 3.5, 6.8, 12.2, and Annex II of the AD Agreement on at least four different grounds.

4.253 Mexico's response to the Panel's questions further demonstrates that Economía breached Articles 3.1, 3.2, and 6.8 of the AD Agreement, as well as Annex II, by failing to collect the information on price effects and volumes that it needed to conduct its injury analysis in an objective manner and to base its determinations on positive evidence.

4.254 To be specific, Mexico has confirmed that numerous types of non-subject rice entered during the POI under tariff heading 1006.30.01 of Mexico's tariff schedule, and its answers demonstrate that Economía failed properly to separate the subject imports from the non-subject imports before it conducted its injury analysis.

4.255 Mexico argues that Economía did separate the subject imports from the non-subject imports, and that it used several methodologies to do so. In actuality, however, the only methodology that Economía used was the flawed procedure supplied by the petitioner. The petitioner's methodology was based on a flawed statistical procedure that focused on isolating imports of short-grain and medium-grain rice using monthly *average* prices for those products in the *US* market, that arbitrarily assumed that any rice that entered Mexico above a certain price *had* to be short-grain or medium grain and *could not* be long-grain white rice, and that did not even address the question of how to separate imports of glazed rice and parboiled rice, which were also not part of the subject product.[28] Moreover, even that analysis is applied only to 1999. Economía simply guessed at import levels for 1997 and 1998.[29] Furthermore, Mexico is mistaken in claiming that Economía also sought to base its injury determination on information obtained from the exporters. In actuality, Economía only sought volume and value information from Farmers Rice, Riceland, The Rice Company, and Producers Rice.

4.256 Mexico is also mistaken in claiming that Economía sought to separate the subject imports from the non-subject imports using information on the total volume of imports from the United States. The fact that the import data contained both subject and non-subject merchandise in tariff heading 1006.30.01 is what created the need to separate the two in the first place.

4.257 Finally, Mexico has confirmed that Economía ignored one reliable and neutral method that *would* have allowed it to collect the information that it needed to conduct an objective examination of the injury factors, and to base its determination on positive evidence – namely, consulting the *pedimentos*.

4.258 Mexico confirms that the *pedimentos* identify the volume and value of each import. Thus, it is indisputable that Economía could have used the *pedimentos* to obtain volume and value data that would have been specific to the subject merchandise, and substantially more accurate than the information on which it relied.

4.259 Mexico argues that the description field in the *pedimentos* does not necessarily describe in sufficient detail the product being imported, and that Economía would have needed to consult the invoices in cases where the description was not sufficiently precise. The invoices, however, are attached to the *pedimentos*.

---

[28] In fact, paras. 229-232 of the final determination, setting out Economía's methodology, make no reference to any attempt to separate out glazed rice and parboiled rice.

[29] See Final Determination, para. 239 (Exhibits US-6&7).

Moreover, even if Economía had only used the *pedimentos* that specifically identified the imports as long-grain white rice, it still would have had a substantial amount of precise data on volumes and values that it could have used in its determinations.

4.260 Mexico also argues that it would have been "impractical" to consult each and every *pedimento*. Even if Economía had only consulted a representative sample, however, it still would have had better data that it could have used in performing its analyses.

4.261 In addition, Mexico confirmed that the *pedimentos* identified the exporter and importer for each shipment. Thus, if Economía had consulted the *pedimentos* and encountered questions about the content of a particular shipment, it could have consulted either party, confirmed the nature of the merchandise, and ensured that it had accurate information on volumes and values. Alternatively, since the *pedimentos* listed the names and addresses of the exporters and importers, Economía could have simply sent them its questionnaire, and asked *them* to provide the necessary information. Economía failed to do so.

4.262 Finally, the Panel may wish to keep in mind the evidence that the United States submitted in response to question 17 from the Panel, which demonstrates that Mexico has been willing to use the *pedimentos* to benefit domestic industries seeking the imposition of anti-dumping measures. Mexico has gone so far as to release actual *pedimentos* to its domestic industry, and has allowed them to use the *pedimentos* to support their allegations of dumping and injury.

5. Economía's failure to exclude Farmers Rice and Riceland from the measure

4.263 Article 5.8 of the AD Agreement requires Members to exclude from anti-dumping measures firms that are individually examined in an anti-dumping investigation and found not to be dumping. Mexico's failure to exclude Farmers Rice and Riceland from the anti-dumping measure on long-grain white rice breached Article 5.8.

4.264 Mexico will impose an anti-dumping measure on every producer and exporter in the investigated country as long as it finds at least *one* exporter to be dumping at more than *de minimis* levels. This includes applying the measure to producers that are investigated and found *not* to be dumping. Economía will not examine whether the weighted average margin of all exporters is greater than *de minimis* when it decides to impose an anti-dumping measure.

4.265 The outcome of the rice investigation illustrates the consequences of Mexico's approach. By "deeming" every exporter and producer in the investigated country as being included in the investigation and applying an adverse, facts available-based margin to the unexamined exporters and producers, Economía will almost certainly find at least one firm to be dumping in every anti-dumping investigation, and thus it will never find a basis to terminate an investigation due to "*de minimis*" dumping margins. Mexico's interpretation of Article 5.8 reads the *de minimis* dumping language out of the AD Agreement.

4.266 Mexico's interpretation of Article 5.8 fails to take into account that the second and third sentences of Article 5.8 refer to the "margin" of dumping being *de minimis*. The Appellate Body has interpreted the term "margin" in Article 9.4 of the AD Agreement as referring to the "individual margin of dumping determined for each of the investigated exporters and producers" of the investigated product. Nothing in the text of Article 5.8 of the AD Agreement suggests that the term "margin" should be interpreted differently in Article 5.8 than in Article 9.4.

4.267 The fourth sentence of Article 5.8 of the AD Agreement provides contextual support for the view of the United States. That sentence states that the "volume" analysis is normally done on a country-wide basis. The absence of similar language suggesting that the dumping analysis is to be done on a country-wide basis supports the conclusion that the *de minimis* standard is to be applied on a company-specific basis.

4.268 The EC claims that the term "country" is used in various places in the AD Agreement and the GATT 1994, and that the concept of dumping involves a "strong connotation of a country-wide assessment." In actuality, however, the concept of dumping involves a strong connotation of *firm-specific* assessment. Several provisions of the AD Agreement support this view.

4.269 Moreover, there is no "internal inconsistency" involved in terminating an anti-dumping investigation on a firm-specific basis, and no risk that doing so will lead to "parallel" investigations. Nor will interpreting Article 5.8 to require the exclusion of firms with zero margins of dumping require or lead to "several company specific cases or investigations." On the contrary, an authority can conduct a single investigation of multiple firms, and then terminate its investigation with respect to specific firms by excluding firms that were investigated and found not to be dumping from the measure.

6. *Economía's application of an adverse "Facts Available" dumping margin*

(a) Economía should have taken steps to investigate additional exporters

4.270 Mexico has confirmed that the *pedimentos* identify the exporters of the subject merchandise, and that Mexico therefore knew the identity of *every* exporter of the subject merchandise to Mexico during the POI. Economía's failure to review the *pedimentos* to obtain the contact information for the exporters or to take any other steps to investigate more than just the two exporters that the petitioner designated in the petition was neither objective nor unbiased.

4.271 *First*, Mexico's argument that examining the *pedimentos* would have caused a "significant delay" in the initiation of the investigation is not credible. Economía only investigated *dumping* for March to August 1999, so even under Mexico's theory, reviewing the *pedimentos* would have taken approximately two weeks at most. It took Economía *six months* to initiate the investigation; the need to spend two weeks to gather the information it needed to contact the "known" exporters would not have dissuaded an objective and unbiased authority.

4.272 *Second*, Economía could have chosen instead to take other steps to identify additional exporters. For example, if Economía had consulted the *Rice Journal*, it would have obtained the names, addresses, and phone numbers for *every* rice miller in the United States.

4.273 *Third*, Mexico mischaracterizes the arguments of the United States on this issue when it claims that it was under no obligation to identify *all* of the exporters of long-grain white rice in the United States. The United States agrees that there is no such obligation. On the contrary, the second sentence of Article 6.10 explicitly permits an authority to limit its investigation. Therefore, Economía only needed to identify enough exporters to allow it to take either approach. An objective and unbiased administering authority would have done so.

4.274 *Fourth*, Economía's failure to conduct a proper investigation of the known exporters was particularly biased and non-objective because of the consequences for the firms that it did not individually investigate. Economía treated *every* exporter or producer in the United States as being included in the investigation. It then applied an adverse, facts available-based margin taken from the petition to any firm that did not learn of the investigation on its own and appear at the clerk's office in Mexico City to obtain a copy of the questionnaire. Given the negligible consequences for the petitioner of a slight delay in initiation, an objective and unbiased authority would have taken the necessary time to ensure that the due process rights of the foreign respondents were adequately protected.

4.275 *Finally*, Economía did not satisfy itself as to the accuracy of the petitioner's listing of only two exporters, as Articles 5.3 and 6.6 of the AD Agreement require. Although Economía used the *listado* data to check the volume and value data that the petitioner submitted, it was not able to use that source to confirm the identity of the exporters, and it did not check the *pedimentos*.

(b) Mexico is misinterpreting the relevant requirements of the AD Agreement

4.276 Economía also breached the AD Agreement and the GATT 1994 by applying an adverse, facts available-based margin taken from the petition to Producers Rice and the unexamined exporters and producers. Mexico's only response to the claims of the United States has been to argue that the AD Agreement creates no obligations with respect to "unknown" exporters and producers, or exporters that had no shipments during the POI, and that Article 6.8 of the AD Agreement authorized it to apply adverse facts available to such firms. Mexico even claims that an authority only needs to consider the exporters that are "known" to the *petitioner*, and not those known to itself. Mexico's interpretation is incorrect.

4.277 The illogic of Mexico's interpretation can perhaps best be seen by considering the response that the *EC* provided to the Panel's question 1(A) to the EC. Like Mexico, the EC disclaims any need for an authority to take any steps to identify exporters other than those listed in the petition. The EC further argues that it would be permissible for an authority to initiate an anti-dumping investigation even if the petitioner only identifies the exporting country, and identifies *no* exporters or producers at all. The EC has also agreed with Mexico that an authority is under no obligations with respect to "unknown" exporters or producers, and that it is permissible to apply facts available-based margins to those firms.

4.278 Thus, taken to its logical conclusion, the EC's and Mexico's interpretation of Articles 6.10 and 9.4 and the facts available provisions would permit an authority to initiate an investigation on the basis of a petition that did not identify *any* "known" exporters, publish a notice of the initiation of an anti-dumping investigation in its official journal, and then send its questionnaire to *nobody*. Then, unless a firm learned of the investigation on its own, entered an appearance, and obtained a copy of the questionnaire, the authorities could apply the petition margin to the entire country without having to examine *anyone*. While this outcome might be expedient for the authority (and beneficial for the petitioner), it is not consistent with the terms of the AD Agreement.

4.279 As the United States has previously discussed, Mexico's interpretation is based on a flawed interpretive approach that relies on partial citations of Articles 6.8 and 6.10, viewed in isolation, and divorced from the broader context of the overall AD Agreement. Mexico's approach is wrong. A proper interpretive approach must take into account the *entirety* of the AD Agreement. This means Mexico must take into account all of the provisions that the United States has identified in its submissions and statements, and that Mexico has ignored to date.

4.280 Mexico must also explain how its interpretation is consistent with Article 9.5 of the AD Agreement, which permits certain exporters to receive an expedited review if they can demonstrate, among other conditions, that they are "not related to any of the exporters or producers in the exporting country *who are subject to the anti-dumping duties on the product*." (Emphasis added.) This provision applies *specifically* to exporters and producers who did not export the subject merchandise to the importing Member during the POI. Mexico includes *every* exporter or producer of the product in its investigations, and it applies the anti-dumping duties on the product to all of them (either because they receive an individual calculated rate or because they are assigned the adverse, facts available rate taken from the petition). Therefore, because Producers Rice and the unexamined exporters and producers are all "subject to the anti-dumping duties on the product," they do not qualify for an expedited review under Article 9.5 of the AD Agreement. Mexico's interpretation reads Article 9.5 out of the AD Agreement.

(c) An investigating authority may not apply a facts available margin to an exporter that was never even sent the questionnaire

4.281 The AD Agreement prohibits an authority from applying a margin based on the facts available to an exporter or producer that was never even sent the questionnaire. Article 6 and Annex II of the AD Agreement are the provisions most relevant to this point. The Appellate Body has described Article 6 as an article that:

"establishes a framework of procedural and due process obligations." Its provisions "set out evidentiary rules that apply *throughout* the course of the anti-dumping investigation, and provide also for due process rights that are enjoyed by 'interested parties' *throughout* such an investigation."

4.282 This "framework of procedural and due process obligations" includes Article 6.1 of the AD Agreement, which *requires* investigating authorities to give interested parties "in an anti-dumping investigation" notice of the information that they require and ample opportunity to present in writing all evidence which the interested parties consider relevant in respect of the investigation in question. Moreover, the Appellate Body has emphasized that Article 6.1 creates obligations with respect to *individual* exporters and producers.

4.283 Paragraph 1 of Annex II of the AD Agreement then reiterates this obligation by *requiring* investigating authorities to *ensure* that respondents receive *proper* notice of the rights of the investigating authorities to use the facts available. Although Article 6.8 permits investigating authorities to apply the facts available to firms that fail to provide necessary information, they "are *not* entitled to resort to best information available in a situation where a party does not provide certain information if the authorities failed to specify in detail the information which was required."

4.284 Given these requirements, Economía cannot simply publish a general notice in its *Diario Oficial* announcing the initiation of an anti-dumping investigation, purport to be investigating every producer and exporter in the subject country, and apply a facts available-based margin to any firms that do not come forward on their own and enter an appearance in the proceeding. Rather, it must observe the procedural and due process obligations that are contained in Article 6 and that it owes to interested parties *throughout* the investigation. This means that if Economía is including a particular exporter "in an anti-dumping investigation," it must give notice to that *individual* exporter by sending the exporter a copy of the questionnaire, asking it to respond, and *ensuring* that the exporter understands that a failure to respond may result in the application of a margin based on the facts available. If it fails to take these steps, then it cannot apply a facts available-based margin to that exporter.

4.285 Alternatively, an authority may choose to limit its investigation in accordance with Article 6.10 of the AD Agreement. In that case, however, it may only apply a neutral "all others" rate, calculated in accordance with Article 9.4 of the AD Agreement, to the unexamined exporters and producers. Regardless of the approach it chooses, an authority *cannot* apply a facts available-based margin to an exporter or producer that is never sent the questionnaire.

(d) Economía breached paragraph 7 of Annex II

4.286 Mexico concedes that it did not observe the requirements of paragraph 7 of Annex II when it applied the facts available to Producers Rice. Mexico claims that it was under no obligation to do so. It also failed to observe paragraph 7 with respect to the unexamined exporters and producers. Similarly, there is no evidence on the record of the rice investigation to suggest that Economía failed to take steps to check the presumptions embodied in the petition against independent data available during the investigation, or to exercise "special circumspection" in its application of the petition margin to Producers Rice and the unexamined producers and exporters.

7. *Mexico's Foreign Trade Act and its Federal Code of Civil Procedure*

4.287 Mexico has largely agreed with the United States' interpretation of the operation of the various articles of the Foreign Trade Act and the FCCP at issue in this dispute; it has focused its defence instead on the United States' interpretation of the relevant WTO obligations. For the most part, this defence has been composed of broad assertions that the AD and SCM Agreements create no obligations with respect to the matters addressed by the challenged provisions. Mexico's arguments are wrong.

4.288 Mexico has also argued that the United States' arguments on this issue have failed to take into account the interrelationship between the AD and SCM Agreements and Mexico's domestic law. The United States has previously explained why this argument is incorrect as well.

4.289 Mexico's replies to the Panel's questions have also failed to rebut the United States' *prima facie* case. In question 28, the Panel asks Mexico whether it would be required to amend a law in the event that the DSB adopted a panel report finding the law to be WTO-inconsistent. Mexico fails to respond directly to the question, stating only that it would be obligated to remove the inconsistency. It is not at all clear what this means. The important point, however, is that the stated scenario will only arise if the Panel finds the laws to be WTO-inconsistent. Mexico views each of the actions that the challenged provisions require as consistent with its WTO obligations; therefore, Mexico does not, as a matter of its municipal law, have any ability not to perform the actions the challenged provisions require.

4.290 Furthermore, because Mexico sees no conflict between its WTO obligations and the actions that the challenged provisions require, the scenario that the Panel sets out in question 29 can also arise, if at all, only if the Panel itself finds the laws to be WTO-inconsistent (and the Dispute Settlement Body adopts that finding). At that point, Mexico would be in the same position as any other Member whose laws are found to be inconsistent with WTO rules – it will need to determine what steps are necessary to remove the inconsistency.

4.291 Similarly, Mexico states that the WTO agreements would prevail over the Foreign Trade Act in the event that a certain provision of the law were found inconsistent with WTO rules. Again, even if this were true, the key point is that Economía is the administrator of the Foreign Trade Act, and Economía views each of the challenged provisions as consistent with WTO rules. Therefore, in Mexico's view, there is no conflict, and thus there is no basis in Mexico's municipal law for the WTO Agreement to override any of the challenged provisions.

4.292 In reply to the Panel's question 31, Mexico asserts that Article 68 of the Foreign Trade Act does not require an exporter to demonstrate that its volume of exports was "representative" as a sine qua non for the initiation of a review. It states that the exporter "should" make this demonstration during the course of the proceeding itself, however. As the United States demonstrated in its response to this same question, Economía does in fact require exporters seeking reviews to make such a demonstration; Economía addresses the issue in the initiation notice itself.

4.293 In any event, Mexico's argument seeks to elevate form over substance. Rejecting a review request in the course of a proceeding for a failure to demonstrate a "representative" volume of sales is tantamount to rejecting the review at the outset. In either event, Article 68 precludes firms from obtaining a review; therefore, it is inconsistent as such with Articles 9.3 and 11.2 of the AD Agreement, and with Article 21.2 of the SCM Agreement.[30]

4.294 Mexico's response to the Panel's question 33 attempts to defend Article 89D of the Foreign Trade Act by pointing to Article 47 of its regulations. The cited provision does nothing to rebut the United States' *prima facie* case that Article 89D is inconsistent "as such" with Article 9.5 of the AD Agreement and Article 19.3 of the SCM Agreement. Article 47 establishes rules for determining the costs of production for trading companies. It appears in the section of Mexico's anti-dumping regulations that sets out the methodologies that Economía is to apply in calculating anti-dumping margins. It has nothing to do with the question of who is entitled to obtain an expedited review, however. And even if it did, the hierarchy of laws in Mexico is such that the regulations are subordinate to the Foreign Trade Act; the decree that implemented Article 89D makes clear that the regulations continue in effect only insofar as they are not inconsistent with the provisions of the decree.

4.295 Finally, Mexico seeks to convince the Panel that no issue arises from the fact that Article 366 of Mexico's FCCP and Articles 68 and 97 of Mexico's Foreign Trade Act preclude Mexican authorities from conducting reviews of anti-dumping and countervailing duties while a judicial review of the underlying anti-dumping or countervailing duty measure is ongoing, because the interested parties may post a bond in lieu of paying the duties themselves while the litigation is underway. The ability to post a bond does not ameliorate the negative effects of the preclusion of reviews, or to remedy the WTO breaches that result therefrom.

4.296 The United States previously submitted to the Panel a letter from Economía to Sun Land, a US beef exporter that is subject to Mexico's anti-dumping measure on certain US beef products. That measure, imposed in July 2000, is being reviewed by a "binational panel" established under Chapter Nineteen of the North American Free Trade Agreement. Economía denied Sun Land's request for a review on the grounds that Articles 68 and 97 of the

[30] Mexico makes the same assertion with respect to Article 89D of the FTA in its response to the Panel's Question 32. As the United States demonstrated in its response to Panel Question 32, Mexico's arguments about Article 89D are similarly without merit, and the Panel should reject them as well.

Foreign Trade Act preclude it from conducting the review while the NAFTA litigation is underway. Although the binational panel recently remanded the beef determination to Economía for further proceedings, the litigation continues today.

4.297 Anti-dumping duties are assessed against the importers, not the exporters or producers. Thus, it is the importer, and not the exporter or producer, that has to decide whether it is willing to post a bond as security against potential anti-dumping duties. After Mexico refused to conduct a review of Sun Land while the NAFTA litigation was ongoing, Sun Land's importer informed Sun Land that it was not willing to post a bond with respect to any of Sun Land's beef products that are subject to the Mexican anti-dumping measure. In addition, Sun Land was unable to find another importer willing to post a bond. As a consequence of its inability to obtain a review and post a bond, Sun Land has been effectively locked out of the Mexican market for the products subject to the anti-dumping measure.

4.298 Thus, the preclusion of reviews causes real and substantial commercial harm to exporters that are subject to Mexican anti-dumping measures. It also presents exporters that are subject to Economía's adverse, facts available-based petition margins with two mutually exclusive choices: they can seek judicial review of the order itself, knowing that doing so will preclude them from obtaining an administrative review that might reduce their margin, thus guaranteeing their exclusion from the market for a period of years; or they can seek an administrative review in an effort to reduce their margin, and thus forfeit any chance to challenge the legitimacy of the order in court.[31] Neither the AD Agreement nor the SCM Agreement permits a Member to impose such a choice under its domestic law.

8. *Mexico has failed to contest numerous US claims*

4.299 Finally, Mexico has failed to date to contest – let alone rebut – numerous claims of the United States.

F. *Second Written Submission of Mexico*

4.300 The following are Mexico's arguments in its second written submission:

[31] In addition, if they forfeit their chance to seek judicial review and wait to seek an administrative review instead, they run the risk that a different firm will request judicial review in the meantime. In that case, they will find themselves with no remedy at all, because Mexico refuses to conduct administrative reviews of any firm if any other firm is seeking judicial review.

1. Complaints relating to the anti-dumping investigation on imports of long-grain white rice originating in the United States of America regardless of the country of provenance

(a) Introduction

4.301 Mexico hereby refutes the assertions made by the United States at the first substantive meeting of the Panel and reaffirms the arguments put forward by Mexico in its first written submission and its oral statement at that substantive meeting.

4.302 Mexico emphasizes that its first written submission, oral statement, replies to the questions posed by the Panel at the first substantive meeting and rebuttal submission should be considered as a whole. It also requests the Panel that, in view of their significance, the preliminary objections raised in its first written submission be treated on a par with the investigation itself. In this connection, the United States once again introduces a number of arguments based on Articles that were not the subject of consultations or included in its request for the establishment of a panel or its first submission. Mexico accordingly requests that these arguments be dismissed.

4.303 The United States puts a tendentious interpretation on Mexico's arguments and misrepresents them, while making claims based on *a priori* premises with no grounding in the AD Agreement and seeking to impose on Mexico its own administrative practice and its own interpretation of the AD Agreement, in breach of Article 17.6 of the Agreement.

4.304 The aforementioned points are clearly visible in the affirmations made by the United States in its *Opening Statement* at the first substantive meeting and in the document entitled *Answers of the United States to Questions of the Panel in Connection with its First Substantive Meeting* ("*Answers*").

4.305 In this document, Mexico responds to the assertions of the United States in its *Opening Statement* of 17 May 2004 and to a number of the replies contained in its *Answers*. Since many of the United States' arguments are a repetition of those set forth in its first submission, Mexico reiterates its position and makes cross-references to its own first written submission, indicating the paragraphs in which it has already responded to the questions raised by the United States.

4.306 The United States' arguments concerning the alleged inconsistency of the Foreign Trade Act with the WTO Agreements are based on a single premise, which is the supposedly mandatory nature of the Articles of the Foreign Trade Act at issue. *A contrario sensu*, this means that if the Articles in question are not mandatory, then they are not in any way inconsistent with the WTO Agreements.

4.307 The United States has not established a *prima facie* case of violation of the WTO Agreements. Mexico stresses that the provisions of the Foreign Trade Act are consistent with these Agreements, as its own arguments have demonstrated.

(b) Mexico complied with Articles 1, 3.1, 3.2, 3.4 and 3.5 of the AD Agreement and Articles VI:2 and VI:6(a) of the GATT 1994 with regard to the establishment of the period of investigation

4.308 Article VI:6(a) of the GATT 1994 was not cited in the request for consultations, the request for the establishment of a panel or the first submission of the United States. The United States' arguments in this respect should therefore be dismissed.

4.309 Mexico believes that a clear reading of the Article is important, because no violation of the GATT attributable to the Mexican investigating authority can be deduced from its wording since the authority applied an anti-dumping duty after it had determined that dumped exports from the United States were causing injury to Mexico's domestic industry, as explained in paragraph 398 of the final determination.

4.310 Mexico (as indeed any other WTO Member) does *not* have complete freedom to do whatever it wants and has never made any such claim. On the other hand, it *does* have discretion to establish the period of investigation that it deems most appropriate. As concerns the remoteness of the period investigated, the circumstances of each case will determine what timeframe is appropriate for the investigation.

4.311 Mexico takes the view that it is desirable for the period of investigation to be as close as practicable to the date of initiation of an anti-dumping investigation but observes that there is no provision establishing any obligation in that regard. If the period under investigation is remote and yet adequate for the anti-dumping investigation, it should not be rejected but should be evaluated and, as appropriate, used for the purposes of the relevant analysis.

4.312 Mexico stresses the biased emphasis, in footnote 4 in the United States' *Answers*, on the fact that it set as the period of investigation the months from March to August 1999 for two reasons: (a) because the petitioner so requested; and (b) because the imports of long-grain white rice were concentrated in that period. The United States attempts to make it appear as though Mexico acted in an arbitrary and non-objective manner.

4.313 The first part of the United States' claim reiterates the statement made in the United States' first submission, without referring to the arguments Mexico adduced in paragraphs 55, 56 and 67 of its first written submission to show that Mexico did not breach the AD Agreement in setting the period of investigation in the way that it did.

4.314 As regards the second part of the claim, although imports of long-grain white rice were indeed negligibly higher over the periods March to August of 1999 and 1998 than during the rest of each year, this was not the case in 1997, when imports from the United States were lower in that period than during the rest of the year. Thus, imports of white rice from the United States increased and the comparable periods differed slightly from the rest of each year in terms of imports. The United States' argument is therefore without substance.

4.315 Mexico observes that in paragraph 9 of its *Answers* the United States misrepresents Mexico's arguments and then directs the Panel to them as it sees fit.

4.316 As can be noted in paragraph 55 of its first written submission, Mexico did not establish the period of investigation in order to eliminate distortions but *used, as the period of injury analysis, previous periods comparable to the period investigated.* The period of investigation was not "selected" by the investigating authority but was suggested by the petitioner and, since *no one demonstrated* that it was inappropriate, the investigating authority had no objections.

4.317 The United States' assertion in paragraph 11 of its *Answers* should be dismissed because there is no line of reasoning to be derived therefrom. In any event, Mexico has already stated its reasons for setting the period of investigation in the way that it did. The United States has failed to establish *prima facie* that Mexico committed a violation in this regard.

4.318 In addition, as Mexico demonstrated in its first written submission and its response to question 13 posed by the Panel, there is no seasonality with respect to domestic production or the imports.

4.319 Furthermore, the United States did not respond to the Panel's *first* question regarding the use of events that happened in the past, nor did it offer any opinion as to whether a period of investigation covering 12-month-old data would be inconsistent with the AD Agreement. On the other hand, the United States emphasized that it was "not arguing that there is a specific length of time beyond which the POI becomes *per se* inconsistent with the AD Agreement", in contradiction to the argument developed in its first submission in respect of the remoteness of the period of investigation. The United States having changed its mind, it must be assumed that it is abandoning the argument set forth in its first submission. Mexico also refers to its response to question 2 posed by the Panel. The United States' reply to this question is that there is no consistent approach in Mexican practice with respect to the establishment of a period of investigation. Mexico stresses that, on average, there are about 10 months between periods of investigation and the initiation of its investigations.

4.320 In the investigations on partially hydrogenated fatty acid and triple-pressed stearic acid, the periods investigated used data that were 10 months old, which demonstrates the consistency with which Economía determines periods of investigation. On the other hand, the period did not necessarily have to be the same in both cases, since periods of investigation should be consistent with the circumstances of each case. When a petitioner suggests a period of investigation, the investigating authority therefore determines whether or not it is appropriate.

(c) Economía complied with Articles 1, 3.1, 3.5 and 6.2 of the AD Agreement regarding the establishment of the period of analysis

4.321 With regard to the comparable periods within the period of analysis, Mexico's comparison, for the purposes of injury analysis, between the periods March-August of 1997, 1998 and 1999 was carried out in an objective manner and on the basis of positive evidence. Mexico reiterates that (as any other

WTO Member) it does not have complete freedom to do whatever it wants, but it does have discretion to establish the period of analysis that it deems most appropriate, provided that it does so in a manner consistent with the AD Agreement.

4.322 The United States held that Mexico breached Article 3.5 of the AD Agreement because Mexico failed to consider half of the period of investigation and to explain why it was not relevant. Mexico finds no link between the period of investigation and Article 3.5 of the AD Agreement, given that this provision relates to the period of injury analysis. Moreover, Mexico did consider all the information relevant to the dumping analysis within the period of investigation.

4.323 Mexico submits that the use of comparable periods eliminated any distortions that might have occurred in the injury analysis.

4.324 Mexico fails to understand why the United States considers that Mexico had no idea what the state of the industry was over the course of the period of investigation, even though it examined all the information for the period investigated and compared it in its *entirety* with the data for previous comparable periods within the period of analysis. Now, if the United States is referring to the fact that Mexico had no knowledge of the state of the domestic industry because its injury analysis did not encompass all three years in question, Mexico directs the Panel to its replies to questions 3 and 4 of the Panel relating to the first substantive meeting.

4.325 Mexico repeats that it complied with Article 6.2 del AD Agreement, since it gave the parties every opportunity to defend their interests. The United States is seeking to place on Mexico the obligation to analyse information that was not part of the anti-dumping investigation.

(d) Economía conducted its injury analysis in a manner consistent with Articles 3.1, 3.2, 3.4, 3.5, 6.8 and 12.2 and Annex II of the AD Agreement

4.326 As regards the alleged breaches of Articles 3.1, 3.2, 3.4, 3.5, 6.8 and 12.2 and Annex II of the AD Agreement, Mexico examined the data for the entire period of investigation and not only half of the data, since the period investigated covered the period March to August 1999.

4.327 Turning to the United States' argument concerning the failure to collect evidence on price effects and volumes, Mexico refers to its reply on the subject in its first written submission and maintains that it did conduct its injury analysis in an objective manner, on the basis of positive evidence. So far, the United States has failed to prove the contrary.

4.328 Economía does not have physical possession of the *pedimentos*, which are brought to the knowledge of the investigating authority when petitioners produce them as evidence. The fact of requesting and awaiting the reception of such documents would delay the initiation of an investigation even further. Hence, the investigating authority relies on the list of *pedimentos*.

4.329 In respect of the claim in paragraph 51 of the United States' *Answers*, there are cases in which the *pedimentos* are produced by the petitioners, since there are agreements to that effect between certain chambers or associations and the Ministry of Finance and Public Credit, as provided for in Article 144, paragraph XXVI,[32] of Mexico's Customs Law. This does not mean that the Mexican Rice Council (CMA) concluded any such agreement or that it was under the obligation to do so.

4.330 The United States has not demonstrated why it contends that Economía's failure to seek information from the purchasers of the merchandise under investigation constitutes a breach of the AD Agreement. Moreover, it points out that it did not suggest that the questionnaire be sent to all purchasers; the opposite emerges from its first submission, however. The United States thus appears to be seeking to partly modify its argument, which should therefore be dismissed.

4.331 The United States argues in its *Opening Statement* that Article 6.1.1 of the AD Agreement refers only to the time frame for exporters to respond to questionnaires, and fails to mention that this time frame applies solely to exporters that have received the questionnaire. On this matter, Mexico directs the Panel to its first written submission.

4.332 The United States puts a tendentious interpretation on the AD Agreement, making only partial reference to it and establishing non-existent linkages between its provisions. Mexico did not say that its interpretation of AD Agreement Article 6.1.1 nullified the obligation laid down in AD Agreement Article 3.1. It established the regulatory scope of Article 6.1.1 and concluded that neither this provision nor Article 3.1 had been breached.

4.333 Concerning the analysis of the significant increase in the volume of dumped imports and significant price effects, Mexico refers the Panel to paragraphs 114 to 117 of its first written submission.

4.334 The United States alleges that Mexico did not conduct an objective analysis of certain factors listed in Article 3.4 of the AD Agreement. Mexico refers the Panel to its arguments in paragraphs 118 to 122 of its first submission. The United States also places on Mexico the non-existent obligation to collect data for the period subsequent to the period of investigation. In so doing, it makes yet another baseless allegation of violation of the AD Agreement.

4.335 As regards paragraph 37 of the United States' *Opening Statement*, Mexico refers the Panel to paragraph 124 of its first written submission.

4.336 In response to paragraph 10 of the United States' *Answers*, Mexico refers to its written replies to questions 3 and 4 of the Panel relating to the first substan-

[32] "Article 144. The Ministry [SHCP] shall, in addition to the powers conferred on it under the Tax Code of the Federation and other laws, have discretion to:

...

> XXVI.- Release the information contained in the pedimentos to Industrial Chambers and Industry Associations grouped in Confederations, as provided in the Law of Business Chambers and Confederations thereof, that participate with the Tax Administration Service in the Program on Customs and Tax Control by Industrial Sector. Similarly, it may release to taxpayers information in the pedimentos pertaining to any operations performed by them.
>
> ... ."

tive meeting, and repeats that Economía gathered data for each month between January 1997 and December 1999.

4.337 The United States asserts that Mexico gathered no additional injury data after initiating its investigation. According to Mexico, this is not inconsistent with the AD Agreement. In addition, this is an argument that was not raised in the consultations or included in the panel request or the first written submission of the United States, in violation of Articles 4.5 and 4.7 of the DSU and Article 17.4 of the AD Agreement. It should therefore be dismissed.

4.338 In paragraph 12 of its *Answers*, the United States contends that Economía did not act in an objective and impartial manner, because at least half of domestic production occurred during the September-February time frame, and yet Economía set the months of March to August as the period of investigation.

4.339 Firstly, the fact that at least half of domestic production occurred during the September to February period does not affect the impartiality and objectiveness of the injury analysis, since the analysis covered the same periods of each year. In other words, the comparison was not between half of domestic production and all imports for an entire year. Secondly, the domestic producers argued that the imports were concentrated over the months of March to August, but this occurred, to a negligible extent, only in the years 1998 and 1999 and consequently, Economía accepted that period. In addition, no one raised any objections or proposed any other time frame. Mexico refers the Panel to its first written submission, which explains in detail why use of the months of March to August of each year does not contravene the AD Agreement. The United States' argument is therefore entirely without basis.

4.340 The United States claims in its *Answers* that the problems arising from an examination of only partial year data "are particularly acute when the domestic industry has production during all 12 months of a year" and that in order to comply with Articles 3.1, 3.4 and 4.1 of the AD Agreement, the investigating authority must examine the impact of the dumping on the domestic industry over a full-year period. The United States bases its claim on Article 4.1 of the AD Agreement, which was not the subject of consultations or included in its panel request or its first submission, in breach of Articles 4.5 and 4.7 of the DSU and Article 17.4 of the AD Agreement. Mexico accordingly requests that the claim be dismissed.

4.341 Moreover, seasonality being irrelevant, one segment of a given year is identical in structure to any other segment of that same year. The selection of the period has no implications in terms of comparability. Even if seasonality were an issue, the structure would be the same for a comparison of the same periods of each year. Thus, Mexico holds that the claim set out in paragraph 13 of the United States' *Answers* is entirely without merit.

4.342 Furthermore, Mexico does not bear the burden of proving that Articles 3.2 and 3.4 of the AD Agreement explicitly permit it to take the action it did. It is for the United States to demonstrate that Mexico acted in a manner inconsistent with the AD Agreement. Since the United States has provided no evidence in support of its arguments nor has it made a *prima facie* case, Mexico requests that its claims in this regard be dismissed.

4.343 In paragraph 19 of its *Answers*, the United States says that Article 4.1 of the AD Agreement requires an investigating authority to examine the domestic industry "as a whole" or those producers that constitute a "major proportion of total domestic production", and that because Economía examined production for half of each year, there was no way for it to be certain that it was complying with Article 4.1. The United States once again introduces a claim that was not the subject of consultations or mentioned in any subsequent document, in violation of Articles 4.5 and 4.7 of the DSU and Article 17.4 of the AD Agreement. This claim should therefore be dismissed.

4.344 Firstly, Article 4.1 of the AD Agreement does not provide grounds for the United States' assertions. Article 4.1 specifies that the investigation should include every domestic producer but not that it should encompass production for all months of the year. Secondly, the United States loses sight of where the burden lies in asserting that there was no way for Economía to be certain that it was complying with Article 4.1. The United States ought to produce evidence of its assertion, rather than expect Mexico to prove that its argument is without merit. In addition to the United States' argument not being sufficient to establish a *prima facie* case that Mexico violated the AD Agreement, the fact that it was not raised in the consultations or included in any subsequent document gives Mexico cause to request that it be dismissed.

4.345 As to the United States' argument in paragraph 20 of its *Answers*, Mexico refers the Panel to its reasoning in paragraphs 84 to 88 of its first written submission.

4.346 Concerning paragraphs 21 to 23 of the United States' *Answers*, it should first be pointed out that the United States once again introduces new arguments based on Article 4.1 of the AD Agreement, which was not the subject of consultations or included in any subsequent document, in breach of Articles 4.5 and 4.7 of the DSU and Article 17.4 of the AD Agreement. Secondly, the United States makes bald assertions with no underlying reasons. Its complaint should therefore be dismissed. Thirdly, Mexico emphasizes that its injury analysis of economic factors and indices relating to the domestic industry involved a major proportion of the industry at all times. The reasons for not considering the same subset of producers in the analysis of each injury factor were that there were producers that failed to provide the appropriate data or verifiable information, or they were no longer in operation. This is not a violation of Article 4.1 or Article 3.1 of the AD Agreement and, as Mexico stated earlier, the United States does not adduce evidence in support of its claim.

4.347 With respect to the United States' claim in paragraph 27 of its *Answers* regarding the modification of tariff heading 1006.30.01, Mexico emphasizes that the United States yet again puts forward arguments that were included neither in its request for consultations nor in any subsequent document, which is contrary to Articles 4.5 and 4.7 of the DSU and Article 17.4 of the AD Agreement. They should therefore be dismissed.

4.348 Moreover, the modification introduced on 18 May 2001 applied as of that date and was not applicable to the earlier data. Since the information considered in the investigation on long-grain white rice pre-dated 18 May 2001, the modification had no impact on the data considered in the investigation.

4.349 Regarding paragraph 32 of the United States' *Answers*, Mexico refers the Panel to paragraphs 93 and 94 of its first written submission, in which it explains why it was unable to use the *pedimentos* and demonstrates that such action is not inconsistent with the WTO Agreements. In addition, it was impracticable to separate out the imports of long-grain white rice on the basis of the *pedimentos*.

4.350 It is odd that the United States should argue that, for the purpose of determining the volume of imports of long-grain white rice, it is necessary to separate out all types of rice other than long-grain white rice that come under the same tariff heading in order to ascertain, by process of elimination, the volume corresponding to the imports at issue. This is impractical, and Economía therefore considered that the best method of identifying the volumes corresponding to long-grain white rice was to do so directly and not by process of elimination, as stated in paragraph 231 of the determination. In view of the foregoing, Mexico holds that the United States' arguments are no more than idle speculation.

4.351 The United States contends that the table and arguments in paragraphs 60 to 62 of Mexico's first written submission were prepared for the purposes of this dispute. It is not true that the table does not appear in the administrative record. The data listed in the table were provided by the CMA in its application for the investigation, the responses to the notice issued by Economía and the replies to requests for information. Since that information was not challenged, Economía regarded it as valid. Consequently, Mexico repeats that the United States' assertions regarding the inclusion of the table in the administrative record are irrelevant.

4.352 As to the United States' argument regarding *Covadonga*'s prices and the fact that Economía failed to explain the causal relationship between the dumped imports from the United States and those prices, Mexico observes that the United States once again makes claims that were not part of the consultations or included in subsequent documents, which is contrary to Articles 4.5 and 4.7 of the DSU and Article 17.4 of the AD Agreement. Mexico accordingly requests the Panel to dismiss these claims. The above notwithstanding, Mexico emphasizes that *Covadonga* was the *only* enterprise in the entire domestic industry that *apparently* displayed "different" behaviour. As detailed in paragraph 286 of the final determination, however, the extent of the difference was practically negligible and the industry as a whole nevertheless recorded adverse performance.

4.353 Concerning paragraph 36 of the United States' *Answers*, Mexico responded that "... it is not said that even if all the *pedimentos* had been available it would have been possible to determine with certainty the total amount of imports of the subject product ... " and went on to develop a series of arguments in that respect. The United States' claim is therefore totally unfounded. In this connection, Mexico refers to its written reply to question 15 of the Panel in relation to the first substantive meeting.

4.354 The United States loses sight of certain aspects in its response to question 18 of the Panel asking it to provide more information on the *USA Rice Federation* and to indicate the number of producers it represents. The United States replied to both queries but in so doing added a further argument against Mexico that was not included in the request for consultations or in any subsequent document and should therefore be dismissed. The United States contends that Economía could have contacted the *USA Rice Federation* to obtain information on the US firms. Had Mexico taken such a course of action, it would have violated Article 5.5. of the AD Agreement. The United States' argument is therefore without merit.

4.355 The United States submits that Economía looked at all imports from the United States and not just the dumped imports in evaluating whether import levels had increased during the period of investigation, and that it based its conclusions only on data from the exporter *Farmers Rice*. Paragraph 217 of the final determination contains merely descriptive information, and it is therefore not valid to infer therefrom that the dumped imports were not taken into account. With regard to its having considered only data from *Farmers Rice*, Mexico refers the Panel to paragraphs 205, 228, 229 and 230 of the preliminary ruling and paragraph 270 of the final determination.

4.356 As to Economía having compared the fall in domestic prices to the fall in prices of all imports and not just of the dumped imports, including the prices of *Farmers Rice* and *Riceland*, Mexico refers the Panel to paragraph 269 of the final determination and paragraph 248 of the preliminary ruling.

4.357 While it is true that the share of the dumped imports did not increase in relative terms, this is not decisive evidence for concluding that there was no injury to the domestic industry, since the injury analysis should be comprehensive. Furthermore, although the dumped imports did not rise in terms of relative share, they *did* show an increase in absolute terms, as stated in paragraph 244 of the final determination.

(e) Article 5.8 of the AD Agreement is not applicable to firms with margins of dumping of zero per cent

4.358 With respect to the argument relating to Article 5.8 of the AD Agreement, Mexico refers the Panel to the considerations set out in paragraphs 131 to 137 of its first written submission.

4.359 In paragraph 41 of its *Opening Statement*, the United States observes that, as the WTO Appellate Body held in paragraph 118 of its report in *US – Hot-Rolled Steel*, the term "margin" refers to the "individual margin of dumping determined for each of the investigated exporters and producers". Thus, the United States argues that Article 5.8 of the AD Agreement refers to termination of the investigation for individual firms. The United States is mistaken in its interpretation. In *EC – Bed Linen*, which constitutes the basis for the Appellate Body's reasoning in paragraph 118 cited above, the Appellate Body refers to the fact that the term "margins" should reflect a comparison that is based upon examination of all of the relevant home market and export market transactions, and that it should be calculated for each individual firm. The Appellate Body thus describes only what the calculation of a margin of dumping should include, without referring to the scope of the term "margin" as it appears in Article 5.8 of the AD Agreement. On the other hand, Article 3.3 of the AD Agreement specifies that the basis for calculating margins of dumping in accordance with AD Agreement Article 5.8 applies to each country as a whole. Hence Article 5.8 does not establish that firms with *de minimis* margins of dumping should be excluded from the measure but that the investigation is to be terminated where the investigating authority concludes that the margin of dumping is *de minimis* – a determination that must be made for each country as a whole and not on a firm-specific basis.

4.360 In view of the foregoing, there are no grounds for the United States to assert that certain firms should not be subject to the measure and should be exempt from subsequent review.

(f) Mexico applied the facts available to US producers and exporters in a manner consistent with the AD Agreement

4.361 Turning to the claim in paragraph 44 of the United States' *Opening Statement*, Mexico emphasizes that it has never made the assertions attributed to it by the United States.

4.362 The statement in paragraph 46 of the United States' *Opening Statement* is an *a priori* premise without substance. Mexico refers the Panel to the response it gave in its first written submission concerning the Articles mentioned by the United States.

4.363 Mexico's first written submission already responds to the claim made by the United States in paragraph 47 of its *Opening Statement.*

4.364 The claim in paragraph 48 of the United States' *Opening Statement* relies on a partial citation of Article 6.10 of the AD Agreement. On this matter, Mexico refers the Panel to paragraph 141 of its first written submission.

4.365 The United States specifies what steps an investigating authority should supposedly take in order to calculate a dumping margin based on the facts available and submits that if these steps are not taken the margin should be calculated in accordance with Article 9.4 of the AD Agreement. Mexico is under no obligation to conduct its investigations in the manner indicated by the United States. On this matter, Mexico refers the Panel to paragraphs 138 to 181 of its first written submission.

4.366 The United States also alleges that Mexico did limit its examination to a reasonable number of interested parties and ought therefore to have applied an "all others" dumping margin calculated in accordance with Article 9.4 of the AD Agreement. The United States thus accepts by implication that Article 9.4 of the AD Agreement applies only where the examination is limited. Consequently, if the United States fails to demonstrate that Mexico limited its examination in accordance with Article 6.10 of the AD Agreement, its argument should be dismissed.

4.367 The United States advances a number of reasons in support of the foregoing. On this matter, Mexico refers the Panel to paragraphs 138 to 181 of its first written submission and emphasizes that none of these "reasons" affords valid grounds for the United States' claim. Thus, since it did not limit its examination, Mexico was under no obligation to calculate "all others" margins in conformity with Article 9.4 of the AD Agreement.

4.368 As to the claim in paragraph 53 of the United States' *Opening Statement*, Mexico refers the Panel to paragraphs 163, 164, 171 and 172 of its first written submission.

4.369 Lastly, in paragraph 54 of its *Opening Statement*, the United States submits that Mexico failed to respond to the following complaints:

(a) That Mexico's treatment of *Producers Rice* was inconsistent with paragraph 7 of Annex II of the AD Agreement. On this point, Mexico refers the Panel to paragraph 164 of its first written submission.

(b) That Mexico breached Article 6.6 of the AD Agreement by failing to satisfy itself that the list of known exporters was accurate and complete. On this point, Mexico refers the Panel to paragraph 152 of its first written submission.

(c) That Mexico breached Articles 6.2 and 6.4 of the AD Agreement by failing to provide the US exporters with the *pedimentos* that it gave to the Mexican industry. Mexico insists that its first written submission must be read as a whole. In addition, paragraphs 41 and 42 of the final determination show that information was sought from the petitioners, which sent a copy of *pedimento de importación* 3035 8000812 with the corresponding invoice. Thus, the United States' claim is unfounded since the documents it refers to are in the investigation file[33] and were available to the parties. This matter was dealt with in paragraphs 93 and 94 of Mexico's first written submission.

(d) That Mexico has not denied that the margin contained in the petition was "adverse". On this point, Mexico refers to its written answer to question 25 of the Panel in relation to the first substantive meeting, in which Mexico stated that whether or not *Producers Rice.* cooperated bears *no* relationship to the fact that a facts-available dumping margin was calculated for that firm, since Article 6.8 of the AD Agreement stipulates that its provisions apply when a party does not provide the necessary information. Economía therefore applied paragraph 1 of the Annex.

[33] Administrative file of the anti-dumping investigation concerning long-grain white rice 07/00, confidential version, Volume 20, Folio 0103882.

(e) That Mexico has not denied that it breached Article 12.1 of the AD Agreement by failing to give notice to the parties. On this point, Mexico refers the Panel to paragraphs 155 to 157 of its first written submission.

(f) That Mexico's determination is inconsistent with Article 12.2 of the AD Agreement. Mexico answered this claim in paragraph 177 of its first written submission. Mexico insists that it is for the United States to submit proof of its assertion in order to make a *prima facie* case, rather than expect Mexico to do so in its capacity as defendant.

4.370 In its *Answers*, the United States raised a number of arguments that have a bearing on the issues discussed here. Mexico responds to these arguments in the paragraphs below.

4.371 Concerning paragraphs 28 to 31 of the United States' *Answers*, it cannot be inferred from the petition that the prices taken by the petitioners to calculate the normal value correspond to rice with a higher price than that used in reckoning the export price. It is therefore incorrect to say that Economía's intent was to increase the margin of dumping. Moreover, Economía took the appropriate action since there were no objections to the calculations proposed by the petitioner.

4.372 With respect to paragraphs 38 to 41 of the United States' *Answers*, Mexico refers to its written answer to question 16(a) posed by the Panel in relation to the first substantive meeting.

4.373 In paragraph 39 of its *Answers*, the United States claims that there is no basis for limiting the obligation to send a copy of the petition only to those exporters known to the petitioner *if the investigating authority knows of other exporters*. Mexico submits that the investigating authority relies on exporters identified by the petitioners *and, if it knows no others*, must send the petition to those exporters alone.

4.374 In paragraph 41 of its *Answers*, the United States contends that China's interpretation (as indeed Mexico's interpretation of Article 6.10 of the AD Agreement) is illogical because it would create an incentive for petitioners to under-report the range of known exporters. In this connection, Article 6.1.3 of the AD Agreement seeks to avert such a situation in laying down an obligation for the investigating authority to send the petition *to the authorities of the exporting country*. For the above reasons, Mexico holds that the United States' interpretation is entirely unfounded.

4.375 According to paragraph 42 of the United States' *Answers*, the issue before the Panel is whether Mexico was bound under the AD Agreement to take certain steps in conducting its investigation and whether it failed to take them. The United States evades the Panel's question without explaining the practical effect of its assertions. The issue before the Panel is not that indicated by the United States. The issue to be addressed is whether the AD Agreement sets rules on the subject, whether or not the United States is right in its interpretation regarding the obligations of an investigating authority, whether its interpretation is the only permissible one and whether Mexico acted in a manner that cannot be treated as a permissible interpretation. Since the AD Agreement does not establish clear rules, its provisions have to be interpreted. The United States fails to explain why Mexico's practice "is unreasonable" and when the Panel draws its attention to the matter it merely skirts the question.

4.376 In response to the United States' arguments in paragraphs 43 to 49 of its *Answers*, Mexico stresses that the United States is seeking to impose on Mexico its administrative practice and its interpretation of various provisions of the AD Agreement, in breach of Article 17.6 of the AD Agreement.

4.377 The questionnaires can be obtained from Economía's web site, so the United States' claim in paragraph 45 of its *Answers* is unfounded. Mexico emphasizes that in various investigations US exporters have known of the investigation and have appeared before the Mexican authority. It is common practice for officials of the United States' Embassy to forward notices of initiation of an investigation to their exporters, which are not barred from participating in the investigation. The anti-dumping investigation concerning United States' exports of bovine meat and edible offal provided evidence of this.

4.378 As to paragraph 49 of the United States' *Answers,* Mexico refers the Panel to paragraph 112 of its first written submission, in which it explains why the United States' claim is unfounded.

2. *Complaints relating to the Foreign Trade Act and Article 366 of the Federal Code of Civil Procedure*

(a) Article 53

4.379 As demonstrated in paragraphs 218 to 221 of Mexico's first written submission, the time-limit set in Article 6.1.1 of the AD Agreement and Article 12.1.1 of the SCM Agreement applies only to foreign producers and/or exporters who have been sent the questionnaire, that is, those that are known.

4.380 Both the AD Agreement and the SCM Agreement establish a period of 37 days for exporters or foreign producers to reply to the questionnaires. Thus, the period allowed by the Foreign Trade Act is longer (28 working days) than that provided by the Agreements, meaning that the Foreign Trade Act affords greater opportunities for defence. This was demonstrated in paragraph 228 of Mexico's first written submission.

4.381 If the period of 37 days were granted to any interested party that presented itself after the initiation of the investigation, the ensuing delay would entail non-observance of the time-limits prescribed in Article 5.10 of the AD Agreement and Article 11.11 of the SCM Agreement. The above is in line with paragraph 33 of the report of the Appellate Body in *US – Hot-Rolled Steel.*

(b) Article 64

4.382 Most of the United States' arguments challenging the provision of the Foreign Trade Act in question are based on the allegation that Mexico has misconstrued the WTO provisions. That only goes to show that the United States has based its argument on mere suppositions that are devoid of substance.

4.383 The United States submits that Mexico cites only part of Article 6.8 of the AD Agreement without referring to Article 6.1 and paragraph 1 of Annex II of the AD Agreement. Mexico cited Article 6.8 of the AD Agreement properly and showed in paragraph 240 of its first written submission that Article 64 of the Foreign Trade Act is consistent with the AD Agreement for the following reasons (which apply equally to Article 12.7 of the SCM Agreement):

(a) It allows the investigating authority to calculate margins of dumping for parties that do not provide the necessary information, as upheld by the Appellate Body in paragraph 119 of its report on *US – Hot-Rolled Steel.*

(b) If an interested party does not appear in the investigation or had no exports during the period of investigation, then that exporter will *not provide* the necessary normal value and export price data.

(c) In such cases, the investigating authority may calculate the margin of dumping on the basis of the facts available.

(d) Article 64 of the Foreign Trade Act thus stipulates that margins of dumping are to be calculated on the basis of the facts available for parties that do not appear in the investigation or have no exports during the period of investigation.

4.384 Article 6.1 of the AD Agreement was not the subject of consultations, and Mexico therefore requests the Panel to disregard it. Furthermore, the United States has not explained why it deems Article 64 of the Foreign Trade Act to be inconsistent with Article 6.1 of the AD Agreement.

4.385 Article 64 of the Foreign Trade Act is not inconsistent with Annex II of the AD Agreement, as has already been demonstrated in paragraphs 246 to 252 of Mexico's first written submission.

4.386 The United States contends in paragraph 70 of its *Opening Statement* that Article 64 of the Foreign Trade Act is inconsistent with Article 9.4 of the AD Agreement because it requires Mexico to apply a margin calculated on the basis of the facts available to firms that should have received an "all others" margin. Mexico refers the Panel in this connection to paragraphs 241 to 245 of its first written submission.

4.387 As to the allegation that Article 64 is inconsistent with Article 9.5 of the AD Agreement and Article 19.3 of the SCM Agreement, the United States asserts that the investigating authority is required to apply the highest margin of dumping to firms with no shipments and that where such firms are "deemed to have been investigated", they are "subject to anti-dumping duties" and are not eligible for new shipper review. The interpretation the United States puts on the above-mentioned Articles of the AD Agreement and the SCM Agreement is absurd and contradicts its own administrative practice. If one were to accept the United States' assertion, an "all others" margin calculated in accordance with

Article 9.4 of the AD Agreement would likewise prevent firms with no shipments from applying for a new shipper review.

4.388 Article 64 of the Foreign Trade Act does not prevent foreign producers or exporters that made no shipments during the period of investigation from seeking a new shipper review, provided that they fulfil the requirements of Article 9.5 of the AD Agreement and Article 19.3 of the SCM Agreement. Indeed, on the request of a US exporter, after the revision of the Foreign Trade Act had taken effect, Mexico initiated a new shipper review.[34]

(c) Article 68 of the Foreign Trade Act

4.389 In paragraph 76 of its *Opening Statement*, the United States cites Article 5.8 of the AD Agreement and Article 11.9 of the SCM Agreement in alleging the inconsistency of Article 68 of the Foreign Trade Act with the WTO Agreements. With regard to the United States' interpretation of Article 5.8 of the AD Agreement – particularly the scope of the word "margin" – Mexico has the following comments. Article 5.8 of the AD Agreement does not establish that firms that are not dumping must be excluded from the measure. The Article says that the investigation must be terminated where the investigating authority determines that the margin of dumping is *de minimis*, and the margin is to be determined for the country as a whole and not firm by firm, pursuant to Article 3.3 of the AD Agreement and Article 15.3 of the SCM Agreement. There are thus no grounds for alleging that some firms should not be subject to the measure and are hence exempt from subsequent review.

4.390 As to the representative volumes required by Article 68 of the Foreign Trade Act, and in response to paragraphs 76 to 81 of the United States' *Answers*, Mexico affirms once again that representative export volumes are not a requirement for the initiation of a review, and refers the Panel to paragraphs 262 to 266 of its first written submission.

4.391 Mexico emphasizes that the United States interprets to suit its own ends the resolution that it offers as evidence, since nowhere does the text of the resolution[35] mention the representativeness of import volumes as a requirement for initiation of the review. What the resolution does contain is an analysis of import volumes derived from the fact that the review applicants supplied such informa-

---

[34] Resolution accepting the application of the interested party and declaring initiation of the new shipper procedure, pertaining to the final determination on imports of dessert apples of the varieties Red Delicious and its mutations and Golden Delicious, currently classified under heading 0808.10.01 of the Tariff established under the General Import and Export Duty Law, originating in the United States, regardless of the country of provenance. Published in the Official Journal of the Federation (DOF) of 21 October 2003 (Exhibit MEX-12).

[35] Resolution declaring initiation of the review of the definitive anti-dumping duties imposed on imports of dessert apples of the varieties Red Delicious and its mutations and Golden Delicious, currently classified under heading 0808.10.01 of the Tariff established under the General Import and Export Duty Law, originating in the United States, regardless of the country of provenance. Published on 21 October 2003 in the Official Journal of the Federation (DOF) (first section), page 16 (Exhibit MEX-13).

tion. The dumping analysis is to be found in paragraphs 46 and 47 of the resolution.

4.392 Moreover, there is no evidence in the resolution that the application for review was rejected because it did not fulfil the representativeness requirement. It was rejected for other reasons, which are detailed in paragraph 95 of the resolution.

(d) Article 89D of the Foreign Trade Act

4.393 According to paragraph 79 of the United States' *Opening Statement*, Mexico alleged that the WTO Agreements establish no obligation in respect of the requirement to show representativeness prescribed in Article 89D of the Foreign Trade Act – an argument that Mexico did not adduce. Furthermore, the United States repeats that Article 89D of the Foreign Trade Act applies only to foreign producers and not to exporters, and that producers are required to demonstrate that the exports were representative.

4.394 With regard to the first of those claims, in its *Opening Statement* the United States overlooks the argument in paragraphs 268 and 269 of Mexico's first written submission, which refers to Article 2 of the Foreign Trade Act and the fact that the Act must be considered as a whole and *not* in isolation when determining whether or not its provisions are inconsistent with the WTO Agreements. Mexico also indicates that in the case of unfair international trade practices by WTO Members, it applies anti-dumping and countervailing duties as provided for in Article VI of the GATT 1994 and in the AD and SCM Agreements.

4.395 In order to disprove the United States' allegation, Mexico refers the Panel to Article 47 of the Foreign Trade Act Regulations, which establishes how the buying cost is to be determined for exporters, i.e. trading enterprises.

4.396 Mexico has conducted new shipper reviews both for foreign producers and for exporters on the basis of Article 47 of the Foreign Trade Act Regulations, proof of which is the resolution initiating the new shipper procedure concerning imports of apples from the United States,[36] paragraph 19 of which establishes that the provisions of the Foreign Trade Act Regulations that govern ordinary procedures – which include Article 47 mentioned above – apply to the new shipper procedure. Thus, the provisions of the Foreign Trade Act Regulations that apply to new shipper reviews are those set forth in Titles IV and VI thereof. Furthermore, paragraphs 3 and 32 of the resolution show that a new shipper review was initiated at the request of an exporting firm, which invalidates the United States' claim.

4.397 With regard to the second claim, Mexico stresses that representativeness is a requirement not for initiating a new shipper review but for the determination of an individual margin of dumping or subsidy, this being for economic reasons. Thus, although Article 9.5 of the AD Agreement and Article 19.3 of the SCM Agreement do not expressly so provide, given the context and the object and

[36] *Ibid.* Supra footnote 21.

purpose of the Agreements it is natural and logical to request that a new shipper's volume of exports during the review period be representative.

4.398 Concerning paragraphs 82 to 84 of the United States' *Answers*, Mexico explains that paragraph 16 of the resolution initiating the above-mentioned new shipper procedure states that " ... *a review shall be carried out promptly to determine the individual margin of price discrimination for the exporters or producers* ... provided that the said exporters or producers demonstrate that they have carried out export operations in representative volumes ... " (emphasis added). Consequently, the representative volume requirement is for determining the individual margin of dumping and not for initiating of a new shipper review.

(e) Article 93.V of the Foreign Trade Act

4.399 The United States argues in paragraphs 82 and 83 of its *Opening Statement* that Article 93.V of the Foreign Trade Act is inconsistent with the WTO Agreements because it *requires* the investigating authority to apply the fines established therein. In rebuttal, Mexico refers the Panel to paragraphs 274 to 282 of its first written submission, which specifies that in interpreting the context of Article 93.V of the Foreign Trade Act account should be taken of Article 2 of the Foreign Trade Act, which stipulates that the Foreign Trade Act must be applied in a manner consistent with the international treaties to which Mexico is party.

4.400 In paragraph 84 of its *Opening Statement,* the United States asserts that the language of Article 93.V is enough to show that Mexico lacks the discretionary authority to impose the fines. Mexico refers the Panel in this connection to paragraphs 283 to 286 of its first written submission. It should likewise be pointed out that Article 93.V of the Foreign Trade Act establishes that the fines are to apply "when ... it is deemed probable that [the imports] undermine the remedial effect of the countervailing duty ... ". Thus, Economía has discretion as to whether or not the fines are to be applied.

(f) Article 366 of the FCCP and Articles 68 and 97 of the Foreign Trade Act

4.401 With regard to the United States' claim that Article 366 of the FCCP is inconsistent as such with the WTO Agreements, Mexico repeats what it said in paragraph 297 of its first written submission, i.e. that the Article does not apply directly to the subject-matter or the procedures regulated by the Foreign Trade Act. The United States notes in this context that the very fact of attaching the text of Article 366 of the FCCP to its first written submission is enough to demonstrate the scope and meaning of its provisions. On this point, Mexico refers the Panel to paragraphs 293 to 299 of Mexico's first written submission, and note in addition that the United States must prove its claim *prima facie.*

4.402 In paragraph 87 of its *Opening Statement*, the United States observes that Mexico did not contest the allegation that Articles 68 and 97 of the Foreign Trade Act breach Article 11.2 of the AD Agreement and Article 21.2 of the SCM Agreement. Mexico wishes to clarify that its rebuttal of this claim is to be found in paragraphs 300 to 303 of its first written submission. The United States misinterprets Mexico's arguments. Indeed, by waiting for the duties to be confirmed in order to carry out a review of them, Mexico is securing and safeguarding the interests of the parties, sparing them any possible injury. This is borne out by the fact that applicants that challenge the final determination are not required to pay any duties pending the resolution of their case, and are asked only for a surety to cover the duties, pursuant to Article 98.III of the Foreign Trade Act.

4.403 As to the United States' argument in paragraph 92 of its *Opening Statement*, Mexico emphasizes that although in its Semi-Annual Report Mexico reported the conclusion of an anti-dumping investigation concerning beef with the application of "definitive duties", this does *not* imply that the duties were confirmed. The US exporters brought challenge proceedings and accordingly provided sureties in respect of the imports they have effected in recent years, pursuant to Article 98 of the Foreign Trade Act.

4.404 Concerning the alleged inconsistency of Articles 68 and 97 of the Foreign Trade Act with Article 9.3.2 of the AD Agreement, Mexico reiterates what it said in paragraph 304 of its first written submission.

4.405 With respect to the alleged inconsistency of Articles 68 and 97 of the Foreign Trade Act with Article 9.5 of the AD Agreement and Article 19.3 of the SCM Agreement, Mexico is unaware of the grounds for the United States' claim, since none of the provisions of the Foreign Trade Act precludes or expressly prohibits a new shipper review from being carried out.

4.406 It should also be noted that the WTO Agreements require new shipper reviews to be carried out promptly (AD Agreement) and expeditiously (SCM Agreement). The United States is thus attempting to assign to Mexico obligations that are not to be found in the Agreements, since neither the AD Agreement nor the SCM Agreement lays down an obligation to *initiate* a new shipper review as soon as it has been applied for; what the Agreements do require is that, once initiated, the review must be carried out promptly and/or expeditiously.

4.407 As to paragraph 93 of the United States' *Opening Statement*, Articles 68 and 97 of the Foreign Trade Act provide certainty in law and preclude conflicting court rulings by treating as definitive only such anti-dumping or countervailing duties as have not been challenged in some procedure. Thus, once the dispute is settled the sureties posted by the exporters will be collected, or else it may determined that the original duty was unlawful, in which case the sureties will be returned.

G. Second Oral Statement of the United States

4.408 The following summarizes the United States' arguments in its second oral opening and closing statements:

1. *Opening statement*

(a) Mexico's use of a stale POI

4.409 Numerous provisions in the AD Agreement and the GATT 1994 illustrate the need for authorities to base their injury investigations on a period that includes the most recent available information. The panel report in *US – Softwood Lumber VI* also supports this conclusion.

4.410 The *US – Softwood Lumber VI* panel stated that it must be clear from an authority's determination of threat of material injury that the authority has evaluated "how the future will be different from the *immediate* past, such that the situation of no present material injury will change in the imminent future to a situation of material injury....". An authority that fails to examine data that includes the most recent available information will not be in a position to make judgments about the *immediate* past. The same can be said about findings of present injury. An authority can only make objective determinations about the present, or the imminent future, if it is examining a period that *includes* the most recent available information.

4.411 In its second submission, Mexico says it would be "preposterous" for a Member to base its findings on information that is ten years old. Thus, Mexico apparently now concedes that an authority's discretion in setting a POI is not without limit. According to Mexico, the appropriateness of a particular POI will depend on the facts of a particular case. The United States and Mexico apparently agree. However, Mexico has pointed to nothing to justify its decision to ignore 15 months worth of recent data, or its decision not to collect any additional injury data after the initiation of the investigation. Although Mexico baldly asserts in its second submission that the POI in the rice investigation yielded objective information on dumping and injury, it has provided no evidence in support of its claim.

(b) Economía limited its injury examination to six months of 1997, 1998, and 1999

4.412 Mexico claims not to understand the argument of the United States that Economía breached WTO rules by only examining injury information for half of the POI. To clarify, Mexico breached WTO rules by only examining half of the *injury* POI.

4.413 Mexico also seeks to rebut the United States' claims by introducing another new table. This new table allegedly contains information on imports from the United States to Mexico on a monthly basis from 1997 through 1999. The Panel should disregard Mexico's table.

4.414 First, the new table does not appear to be record evidence. Mexico has provided no citation to the record for this table, or a photocopy of the page in the record where it is contained. Second, Mexico has failed to identify the source of the data in the table. Economía lacked accurate data on imports of long-grain white rice from the United States. The petitioners' import data included unknown quantities of glazed and parboiled rice, as well as short-grain rice and medium-grain rice. Thus, if the information in the table is from the petitioners' data, there is no basis to conclude that it accurately reflects the true level of imports of long-grain white rice during the three-year injury POI. Third, the table directly contradicts Economía's findings that imports were concentrated in the March to August time period. Mexico's complete reversal of its own position demonstrates that there was no justification for Economía's decision to examine only half of the injury POI.

4.415 In any event, the United States is objecting *per se* to Economía's decision to limit its injury analysis to only half of the injury POI. Mexico has conceded that seasonality was not relevant, and it is indisputable that Economía failed to examine at least half of the domestic industry's production over the course of the entire injury POI. Thus, Economía's injury analysis would have been inconsistent with WTO rules even if imports had *not* been concentrated in the March to August time period.

4.416 Mexico's argument that it was acceptable to look at a "representative sample" of the data is unfounded. Nothing in Economía's published determinations indicates that it focused on the March to August time period because it believed that period was a "representative sample." Nor are there any findings or evidence demonstrating that the period was, in fact, representative of the year as a whole.

(c) Mexico's conduct of its injury analysis

4.417 Mexico argues that Economía does not have access to the *pedimentos*. In actuality, although Economía may not have *possession* of the *pedimentos*, it does have *access* to them. It simply does not request such access, because Economía believes the AD Agreement does not require it to do so, and because it would take too much time.

4.418 Second, Mexico notes that Economía collected information through December 1999. But even if this is so, the fact remains that it did not *consider* information for any period after August 1999.

4.419 Third, Economía failed to conduct an objective examination of the domestic industry as defined by Article 4.1 of the AD Agreement because it did not examine a consistent set of producers when it conducted its injury analysis. Mexico justifies Economía's approach on the grounds that not all of the domestic producers provided the requested information. This was the case with respect to production volumes, sales, installed capacity, employment data, wages, and financial performance.

4.420 These reporting failures were not minor. The missing data pertained to many of the most critical factors necessary for Economía's injury analysis. Economía's published determinations do not adequately explain why the domestic industry was unable to provide the requested data. Nor is there any indication that Economía took steps to ensure the objectivity of its injury analysis by making further efforts to obtain it. Economía seems to have simply used the data its industry was willing to provide. Economía's willingness to conduct its injury analysis in this way undermined the objectivity of its injury determination. An objective investigating authority would not permit its domestic producers to control the injury analysis by allowing them to self-select which information they are willing to provide. For in doing so, the authority makes it possible for the domestic industry to influence the outcome of its investigation, by having each individual producer only provide its data for factors that are indicative of injury. In this way, the industry can ensure that the aggregate data for the "industry" will reflect injury.

4.421 Mexico tries to cast doubt on Economía's findings about Covadonga by stating that Covadonga "apparently" exhibited different behaviour. But Economía made these factual findings. The alleged fall in the domestic industry's prices was one of the primary findings underlying Mexico's injury determination, but the evidence demonstrates that Covadonga's prices actually rose during the injury POI.

4.422 Mexico states that it would have breached Article 5.5 of the AD Agreement if it had contacted the Rice Federation to obtain information on the "known" exporters. Nothing in Article 5.5 prevented Economía from contacting the Rice Federation *after* it initiated the investigation.

4.423 Mexico argues that the dumped imports increased in absolute terms. But as paragraph 244 of the final determination makes clear, the dumped imports actually *fell* over the course of the entire injury POI. Thus, one of the primary factors underlying Economía's injury determination was wrong.

(d) Mexico's failure to exclude firms with AD margins of zero per cent

4.424 Mexico argues that Article 3.3 of the AD Agreement demonstrates that the Article 5.8 *de minimis* calculation applies to the country as a whole. Article 3.3 has nothing to do with the dumping determination. Article 3.3 is an injury provision that uses the definition of *de minimis* in Article 5.8 as a means to establish a threshold for determining which countries may be cumulated for injury purposes. The cumulation analysis is country-wide by its very nature.

4.425 Article 5.8 itself states that the margin of dumping is to be considered *de minimis* if the margin is less than two per cent, "expressed as a percentage of the export price." Export prices are inherently firm-specific. If the drafters had intended to require termination only if the *weighted average* margin of dumping for *all* of the investigated firms was *de minimis*, they could have said so. This is what they did in Article 9.4 of the AD Agreement, which requires authorities to calculate the all other's rate on the basis of the "weighted average margin of dumping" calculated for the selected exporters and producers.

4.426 Finally, if a company is investigated and found not to be dumping, there is simply no basis under Article 1 of the AD Agreement to apply the measure to that firm.

(e) Mexico's application of an adverse "facts available" dumping margin

4.427 Mexico's arguments on this issue ignore that Articles 6.1 and 6.8 of the AD Agreement, and paragraph 1 of Annex II, *prohibit* an authority from applying a margin based on the facts available to an exporter or producer that was never sent the questionnaire and asked to respond.

4.428 Mexico argues that a Member is only required to apply a neutral margin under Article 9.4 of the AD Agreement when it has investigated a sample of exporters and producers. In Mexico's view, Economía did not sample, so it is under no obligation to apply a neutral margin to the unexamined firms. But Articles 6.1 and 6.8, and paragraph 1 of Annex II, contain an *independent* set of obligations that a Member must *always* observe when it bases margins on the facts available. One of the key obligations is that an authority that includes a particular exporter "in an anti-dumping investigation" must give notice to that *individual* exporter, by sending the exporter a copy of the questionnaire, asking it to respond, and *ensuring* that the exporter understands that a failure to respond may result in the application of a margin based on the facts available. If an authority fails to take these steps with respect to an individual exporter or producer, then it *cannot* apply a margin based on the facts available.

4.429 Mexico also argues that it met the notice requirements of paragraph 1 of Annex II by sending its questionnaire to Producers Rice and Riceland, as well as to the Embassy of the United States. But the AD Agreement does not permit an authority to shift the burden for providing the requisite notice to the foreign respondents, or the foreign government. Economía did not send its questionnaire to the uninvestigated exporters and producers; therefore, it cannot apply facts available-based margins to them.

4.430 Mexico argues that it did not "limit" its investigation by only sending its questionnaire to the exporters and producers that the petitioners identified as such in the petition, and by not sending the questionnaire to the Rice Company, or to the exporters and producers identified in the *pedimentos,* or to the exporters or producers identified in public sources, such as the *Rice Journal*, because Article 6.10 only provides a single basis for limiting an investigation. But Mexico is only half right. The only *permissible* basis for limiting an investigation is where the number of exporters and producers is so large that calculating individual margins would be impracticable. Economía limited its investigation in an *impermissible* way, by remaining passive and taking no steps to conduct a proper examination of *all* of the known exporters and producers, or an examination of a representative sample, or the largest percentage of the exporters who could reasonably be investigated.

4.431 Mexico responds to the United States' demonstration that the petition margin was adverse by arguing that the petitioners did not inform it that the petition overstated the normal value, and thus overstated the dumping margin. But the petitioners' silence does not excuse Economía from its obligation to examine the accuracy of the information, as Articles 5.3 and 6.6 of the AD Agreement require, or its obligation to check the information in the petition against other independent sources, as paragraph 7 of Annex II of the AD Agreement requires. Nor does it change the fact that the petition margin *was* adverse.

4.432 Finally, with respect to the claim that Economía breached Articles 6.2 and 6.4, it has become apparent to the United States that it misunderstood the nature of the data taken from the *listados*. The United States had assumed that it was public information, because Mexico shared it with its domestic industry. But the United States now believes it must be confidential information. Articles 6.2 and 6.4 of the AD Agreement do not require a Member to disclose confidential information to interested parties. On the other hand, if the data *is* confidential, the United States does not understand how Mexico justifies sharing it with its domestic industry in the first place.

(f) Claims regarding the Foreign Trade Act and Article 366 of the FCCP

4.433 *Article 53*: Mexico has confirmed that Article 53 precludes Economía from providing exporters and producers who are not initially *sent* the questionnaire the full 30 day response time that Article 6.1.1 of the AD Agreement and 12.1.1 of the SCM Agreement require it to provide. The proper interpretation of the relevant WTO provisions is that *any* producer or exporter who receives the questionnaire is entitled to have 30 days to reply, and that the 30 days are counted from the date of *receipt*, not from the date the questionnaire is sent. Therefore, Article 53 of the Foreign Trade Act breaches WTO rules.

4.434 *Article 64*: Mexico argues in its second submission that the United States has not explained why Article 64 is inconsistent with Article 6.1 of the AD Agreement. Mexico is mistaken. Article 64 is inconsistent with Article 6.1 of the AD Agreement because it requires Economía to apply the highest facts available to firms that do not "appear" in the investigation, even when Economía has not complied with Article 6.1. Mexico also argues that Article 9.4 only applies when an authority investigates a sample of exporters or producers. But by its plain terms, Article 64 *always* requires Economía to apply the highest level of facts available to exporters and producers that have no exports during the POI or that do not "appear" in its investigations. Therefore, even if Economía were to overtly limit its investigation in accordance with Article 6.10, Article 64 would still *require* it to apply the highest facts available to those producers and exporters. But Article 9.4 requires an authority that has limited its investigation to apply the neutral margin to *all* of the exporters or producers that are not included in the examination.

4.435 *Articles 68 and 89D*: Mexico argues that it is both "natural and logical" to require an exporter seeking a review to have a representative amount of sales, because the authority would not otherwise be able to make a proper price comparison. But a small number of export sales, even the sale of a single unit, as long as it is a bona fide sale, is not an obstacle to calculating a margin. Moreover, Mexico concedes that a party must demonstrate a representative volume of sales to obtain an individual margin of dumping or subsidization under Article 89D. In addition, the United States supplied evidence in response to the Panel's question 31 which confirmed that Mexico requires firms seeking reviews under Article 68 to demonstrate a representative volume of sales. Whether one characterizes it as a requirement to initiate or conduct a review of the margin, or a requirement to obtain a new margin, Articles 68 and 89D require exporters and producers to demonstrate a representative volume of sales.

4.436 *Article 93*: Mexico has not contested the United States' demonstration that Article 93V is (1) "specific" to dumping or subsidization; (2) "against" dumping or subsidization; and (3) not "in accordance with the provisions of GATT 1994," as interpreted by the AD and SCM Agreements. Moreover, Mexico argues in its second submission that Article 93V is discretionary, because Economía allegedly has discretion to decide in a particular case whether the conditions for imposing a fine are met. But if Economía finds the conditions *are* met, it *must* impose a fine. Mexico also argues that Article 93V is discretionary because it merely states that it "shall be the responsibility" of Economía to punish the infringing activity. This is equivalent to saying that the law is discretionary because Economía may simply choose not to enforce it. As the panel stated in *United States – Measures Affecting Alcoholic and Malt Beverages*, the non-enforcement of a provision that mandates WTO-inconsistent action does not make the provision itself discretionary.

4.437 *Article 366 of the FCCP and Articles 68 and 97 of the Foreign Trade Act*: Mexico has argued that Article 366 of the FCCP does not *directly* apply to the subject matter or procedures of the Foreign Trade Act. Mexico seems to be implying that the provision is *indirectly* applicable. It is also telling that Mexico has made no effort to *explain* why Article 366 does not apply, directly or indirectly, to the Foreign Trade Act.

4.438 Turning next to Articles 68 and 97 of the Foreign Trade Act, Mexico appears to be distinguishing between duties that are "definitive" and duties that are "binding," and it seems to accept that a Member imposes "definitive duties" at the time that it issues the final determination. But Articles 11.2 of the AD Agreement and 21.2 of the SCM Agreement state that Members "shall" review the need for the continued imposition of the duty, "upon request," if a reasonable period of time has elapsed since the "imposition" of the "definitive duty." The term "imposition of the definitive duty" refers to the imposition of the AD or CVD measure itself. This can be seen, for example, in Article 11.1 of the AD Agreement. Neither Article 11.2 of the AD Agreement nor Article 21.2 of the SCM Agreement permits an authority to refuse a review on the grounds that the measure is not "binding" until the end of judicial review.

4.439 Mexico appears to argue that Articles 68 and 97 do not preclude expedited reviews under AD Agreement Article 9.5 and SCM Article 19.3. But Mexico stated during consultations that those Articles *did* preclude such reviews. Moreover, Article 89D of the Foreign Trade Act only permits an exporter to request a review if the good is subject to a "final" duty. But under Article 97, only determinations issued at the end of a judicial proceeding can be considered "final." Therefore, Article 97 does preclude expedited reviews.

(g) Conclusion

4.440 The United States has two final points. First, Mexico argues that the Panel should disregard any claims or arguments that do not appear in the United States' first written submission. But nothing in the DSU suggests that a Party's first written submission defines the scope of permissible claims and arguments that a Party may raise over the course of a dispute. On the contrary, as the Appellate Body found in *EC – Bananas III*:

> There is no requirement in the DSU or in GATT practice for arguments on all claims relating to the matter referred to the DSB to be set out in a complaining party's first written submission to the panel. It is the panel's terms of reference, governed by Article 7 of the DSU, which set out the claims of the complaining parties relating to the matter referred to the DSB.

4.441 All of the claims that the United States has raised in this dispute were in the panel request. So Mexico's claim that the United States did not set forth certain claims in its request is wrong.

4.442 Second, the United States feels compelled to comment on language that Mexico unfortunately chose to employ in its second written submission and the allegations of bad faith that Mexico made today. Its allegations are inaccurate, as even a cursory review of the United States' presentations demonstrates. But, that is not why the United States is raising this matter today. Rather, the United States' concern is with the use by one sovereign nation of derogatory language towards another sovereign nation. Language like this is completely inappropriate and has no place in WTO dispute settlement proceedings, as has been recognized in the past by panels and members of the Appellate Body.

2. *Closing statement*

4.443 The United States has presented a *prima facie* case with respect to its claims. Mexico has not rebutted that case. And all of the United States' claims are in the panel request, contrary to Mexico's assertions. For example, Mexico argued that the United States did not make a claim under Article 4.1 of the AD Agreement, but the claim is in the panel request, as part of the first set of claims. As is a claim under Article 1 of the AD Agreement. The United States urges the Panel to look to the papers filed in this dispute, and what they actually say, and not just to Mexico's arguments about them.

4.444 There was a long discussion today about the POIs that Mexico uses in its dumping cases. What seemed clear from the discussion is that Mexico normally lets the petitioners pick the POI and then puts the burden on the respondents to show why the suggested POI should not be used. The United States had some of the same questions as the Panel about Mexico's approach, so the United States did some research. The United States included information about eight or ten Mexican investigations in the previous responses to Panel questions. In all of those cases, in 2003, the United States found that Mexico accepted the petitioners' proposed POI. Moreover, the length of the POIs varied quite a bit – from six to eighteen months. The only reason the United States was able to find for this was that those were the lengths that the petitioners requested.

4.445 Regarding the *listados*, the United States believes Mexico could have done, and should have done, what the Panel put its finger on: *i.e.*, Mexico had the information before it on the importers' names and the *pedimento* numbers, and it should have looked at the information and used it to gather what it needed to be sure it had conducted a full, vigorous investigation with all of the facts. The authorities have an interest in a full investigation. They also could have sent injury questionnaires to the importers listed in the *listados* and obtained – and then used – better volume and value data than they did.

4.446 Regarding the Foreign Trade Act provisions, the United States is challenging these provisions of Mexico's law as such, not as applied, so the text is the relevant evidence. There is no need for the United States to provide examples of the application of the provisions, as Mexico suggested in its closing statement. If Mexico wishes to provide examples of the application of the provisions to disprove the United States' reading of the text, it can provide them, but there is no obligation on the part of the United States to do so to meet its *prima facie* case in this dispute.

4.447 Finally, regarding Mexico's continued arguments that the challenged legal provisions are discretionary, Mexico is using an odd formulation of the mandatory/discretionary principle. For example, Mexico is not claiming that, while its laws are WTO-inconsistent, Article 2 of the Foreign Trade Act provides it the discretion to apply the laws in a WTO-consistent manner. Rather, Mexico holds steadfast to its argument that its laws on their face are WTO-consistent. Thus, there is no conflict, in its view, between what its laws require and what its WTO obligations require. Therefore, there is no issue of discretion here.

4.448 In that respect, the Appellate Body's dicta that the mandatory/discretionary principle cannot be mechanistically applied in every dispute is relevant, because this principle is not relevant in this dispute. Mexico's so-called "discretionary" argument, if taken to its logical end, would mean that any WTO Member with a domestic law that says that it shall apply its laws in a WTO-consistent manner is essentially shielded from any and all claims that its laws are "as such" inconsistent with WTO rules, regardless of what the laws say. This conclusion is untenable.

H. Second Oral Statement of Mexico

4.449 The following summarizes Mexico's arguments in its second oral statements:

4.450 Mexico observes that the United States continues to act in bad faith, distorting Mexico's arguments and interpreting them with bias, and attempting to influence the Panel's view. It likewise persists in attempting to impose on Mexico its own administrative practice and interpretation of the AD Agreement, and to lay down and impose obligations not derived from that Agreement. Furthermore, it disregards Article 17.6 of the AD Agreement which allows that there may be more than one permissible interpretation of some of its provisions.

4.451 The United States is required to act in good faith, according to Article 3.10 of the DSU and the ruling set forth in the final report of the WTO Appellate Body in *US – Offset Act (Byrd Amendment)*, and as prescribed by the Panel that heard the case *Argentina – Poultry Anti-Dumping Duties*.

4.452 The United States' breaches go beyond the WTO Agreements: on numerous occasions the United States has acted inconsistently with Articles 4.5 and 4.7 of the DSU as well as Article 17.4 of the AD Agreement by introducing new arguments, attempting to influence the Panel through bias, capitalizing on its own disregard of the rules and leaving Mexico with no basis for defence. At the same time it has attributed to Mexico assertions the latter never made and has demonstrated that it can argue either way, depending on the end pursued – witness its proposal JOB(04)60 to the Negotiating Group on Rules. In that document it submits that a new shipper review should be denied to exporters failing to show that they have exported "in commercial quantity", which is precisely the objection it raises to Mexico's Foreign Trade Act although the latter makes no such provision. The Panel should accordingly dismiss the United States' claims and, above all, find that the United States has acted in breach of the principle of good faith embodied in Article 3.10 of the DSU.

1. Anti-dumping investigation on imports of long-grain white rice originating in the United States regardless of the country of provenance

(a) Mexico Complied with Articles 1, 3.1, 3.2, 3.4 and 3.5 of the AD Agreement and Articles VI:2 and VI:6(a) of the GATT 1994 with Regard to the Establishment of the Period of Investigation

4.453 In its first written submission the United States argues that the POI is inconsistent *per se* because of its remoteness. Then, in its "Answers", it denies making any such assertion only to reiterate it in its second written submission. This lack of inconsistency in the United States' position makes its claim unclear and leaves Mexico with no basis on which to mount a defence. Mexico therefore request the Panel to disregard these assertions.

4.454 With regard to the assertion that an anti-dumping investigation must determine whether or not a domestic industry is injured by dumping that is occurring presently, Mexico refers the Panel to its arguments in paragraphs 43 to 46 of its first written submission.

4.455 Mexico wishes to point out that the exporters and importers disagreed with the POI set by the investigating authority, but produced no convincing reasons for adopting some other POI. Nor did they propose a more suitable alternative period or submit any evidence warranting the selection of a different period by the investigating authority.

4.456 The United States continues to introduce claims that were not brought up in consultations or in its request for the establishment of a Panel. A case in point is Article 3.7 of the AD Agreement, relied on by the United States to "illustrate" the fact that the AD Agreement requires a more recent period for the investigation than the one used by Mexico. Nothing in that Article warrants such an assumption.

4.457 Mexico emphasizes that Article VI:6(a) was neither addressed in consultations nor included in the Panel request or the United States' first written submission. The United States' assertions in this connection must therefore be disregarded.

4.458 Contrary to the United States' assertion, an investigating authority is not bound to gather information between the end of the POI and the initiation of the anti-dumping investigation, or to update the information in the course of the investigation.

4.459 It is plain from the report of the Appellate Body in *EC – Bed linen (21.5 – India)*, cited as a precedent by the United States, that that case is immaterial to the present dispute since it concerns the selection of a method for determining injury and not the selection of a POI. The United States thus concludes its pleadings with unfounded assertions based on *a priori* premises all of which ought, in Mexico's opinion, to be dismissed by the Panel.

(b) Mexico Complied with Articles 1, 3.1, 3.5 and 6.2 of the AD Agreement with Regard to the Establishment of the Period of Investigation

4.460 In response to section III of the United States' second written submission, Mexico wishes to make the following points. *First*, in determining the POI, the investigating authority examined the petitioner's proposal and since none of the parties submitted any evidence of the need to set a different period, accepted it. This is not the same thing as allowing the petitioner to set the POI. *Secondly*, seasonality was *not* the element that prompted the authority to set the period examined in the way it did. *Thirdly*, for the injury analysis, in the interests of a fair comparison earlier periods comparable to the POI were set within the period examined (period considered for injury purposes, which covers three full years), so the petitioner did not select the period examined.

4.461 The United States cites the report of the Appellate Body in *US – Hot-Rolled Steel,* in which the Appellate Body found that the investigating authority cannot objectively examine a domestic industry by focusing on one part of that industry. The above-mentioned report refers to a case in which the authority based its injury analysis on a segment of the industry, which is not the case here. The rice investigation examined the entire domestic industry during comparable periods in each year of the period examined. Mexico accordingly deems that the United States' reasoning is unsound and that the United States fails to make a *prima facie* case of breach of the Agreement.

4.462 As to the United States' arguments concerning the use of comparable periods within the period examined, Mexico points out that for the injury analysis it compared the periods from March to August of 1997, 1998 and 1999 in an objective manner and on the basis of positive evidence. In Mexico's view, the use of comparable periods for injury analysis eliminates any distortions that might have occurred during the period examined.

4.463 For the foregoing reasons, Mexico is of the view that the United States' pleas of breach of Articles 1, 3.1, 3.5 and 6.2 of the AD Agreement should be rejected.

(c) Economía Conducted its Injury Analysis in a Manner Consistent with Articles 3.1, 3.2, 3.4, 3.5, 6.8, 12.2 and Annex II of the AD Agreement

4.464 With regard to the failure to collect evidence regarding price effect and volume, Mexico refers the Panel to its first written submission and underlines that it did carry out its injury analysis objectively and on the basis of positive evidence. The United States has failed to prove *prima facie* that Mexico's injury analysis lacked objectivity and was not based on positive evidence.

4.465 As to the United States contention that the investigating authority took into account non- dumped imports in evaluating volume, price effects and the impact of dumped imports on the domestic industry, and that the injury analysis included all imports, Mexico believes that a distinction must be drawn between "volume of imports" and "volume of dumped imports". The former comprises all imports into Mexico and the latter is the volume of dumped imports. In the final determination the entire section on injury analysis, particularly paragraphs 206 to 221, analyses this matter.

4.466 The United States alleges that the investigating authority's findings lacked sufficient detail. But the final determination gives the arguments of fact and of law that Economía took as a basis. The final determination thus meets the requirements of Article 12.2 of the AD Agreement.

4.467 Furthermore, it cannot be confirmed from Mexico's answers to questions 10, 12 and 15 of the Panel that different types of rice entered under the same tariff heading or that the authority did not separate the dumped imports from the others. The information analysed by Economía predates that modification of tariff heading 1006.30.99 (18 May 2001), and the modification applies as from the date of into entry into force, it does not apply to the information used in the rice investigation. It thus has no repercussions for the historical data considered in the rice investigation and there is no reason to believe that the changes of 18 May 2001 would make the rice investigation data any more precise.

4.468 According to the United States, Mexico stated that it used only one method and that Mexico's assertion that it used several methods is wrong. Paragraph 239 of the final determination indicates that *several methods were used* but the best was the petitioner's, and not that the petitioner's was the only method used. Mexico also points out that it did not guess the volume of imports but estimated it using the method indicated in paragraphs 229 and 230 of the final determination. It also wishes to clarify that in its reply to question 12 of the Panel, it stated not that it based its determination on information from exporters but that it took the method proposed by the latter into account in estimating the volume of imports of the subject product.

4.469 As required by the AD Agreement Economía sent questionnaires to known exporters and producers, and sent notice of the initiation of an investigation together with the questionnaire and the petition to the United States Embassy in Mexico.

4.470 The information supplied by two of the importers was disregarded because no public version of it was submitted and because it was not shown to be "confidential or restricted commercial information" as required, in breach of several provisions of the relevant law.

4.471 In its answer to question 17 of the Panel the United States gave incorrect information. Sometimes, petitioners submit *pedimentos* given that, under Article 144 section XXVI of the Customs Law, agreements on access to information may exist between Chambers or Associations of domestic producers and the Ministry of Finance and Public Credit. However, that does not mean that the individual domestic producers or every Chamber or Association have indeed concluded an agreement of that kind, nor that it is mandatory to conclude such agreements for those Chambers or Associations or for the Ministry of Finance and Public Credit.

4.472 As to the allegation that Economía could have identified imports of long-grain white rice by consulting the *pedimentos*, and its assertion concerning the way in which imports of different types of rice were separated out, Mexico refers the Panel to paragraphs 93 and 94 of its first written submission. Furthermore, contrary to what the United States asserts, *it is not possible to identify imports of long-grain white rice separately from the pedimentos.*

4.473 The conclusion the investigating authority reached on the injury analysis was the result of an overall evaluation of all the relevant economic factors referred to in Article 3.4 of the AD Agreement. The United States places on Mexico a non-existent obligation to gather information subsequent to the POI. Mexico finds it odd that the United States should suggest that in order to determine the volume of imports of long-grain white rice it is necessary to separate all the different types of long-grain white rice, which would be impracticable. The investigating authority took the view that the best method of separating the volumes of long-grain white rice was *directly and not by elimination.*

4.474 The United States also alleges that to determine whether there was any increase in import volumes during the POI, Economía took into account total imports from the United States and not only dumped imports and that, moreover, it based its conclusions on the information of a single exporter.

4.475 As to the allegation that Mexico looked at the information of only one exporter, paragraph 205 of the preliminary determination indicates that Economía requested information from all US exporters that appeared and that the only exporter to submit full information was *Farmers Rice.* Moreover, the others had thirty working days in which to enter any objections and supporting evidence but chose not to take up the opportunity. Economía accordingly decided to maintain its finding. Mexico therefore considers that the United States' argument is without merit.

(d) Article 5.8 of the AD Agreement Is Not Applicable to Firms with Margins of Dumping of Zero Per Cent

4.476 With regard to the United States' assertion concerning Article 5.8 of the AD Agreement, Mexico refers the Panel to paragraphs 131 to 137 of its first written submission and enlarges below on its answer to question 20 of the Panel.

4.477 In that answer Mexico explained that all exporters would be subject to the measure, meaning the final determination and not the application of positive anti-dumping duties. Thus, to impose duties Mexico must ascertain in its final determination the position of each individual exporter. This does not mean that anti-dumping duties will be imposed on every producer and exporter investigated where at least one has exports with a margin of dumping above *de minimis*. In the same answer Mexico noted: "*Each enterprise will be assigned the anti-dumping duty corresponding to its individual margin, provided that the total volume of imports from the country in question is above the de minimis level*", since it is logical to determine an individual margin of dumping for each enterprise that has supplied the requisite information during the investigation. An exporter that submits all the requisite information on normal value and export prices will not be subject to the application of facts available. The answer ends: "*Any exporter for which the IA finds a more than zero and below de minimis margin of dumping would receive a zero per cent duty*", which does not imply the imposition of an anti-dumping duty, and Mexico therefore takes the view that it cannot be regarded as such, strictly speaking, let alone as a breach of the AD Agreement.

4.478 The United States submits that in its reply to question 20 Mexico asserted that in deciding to impose an anti-dumping measure, Economía will not examine whether the weighted average margin of all exporters is greater than *de minimis*, so Mexico is obviously using a firm by firm approach. The United States is mistaken. Mexico never made such an assertion.

4.479 Furthermore, according to Article 3.3 of the AD Agreement, paragraph 118 of the report of the Appellate Body in *US – Hot-Rolled Steel* and paragraph 149 of the report of the Appellate Body in *US – Carbon Steel*, the determination of *de minimis* margins of dumping under Article 5.8 of the AD Agreement must be based on each country taken as a whole.

4.480 The United States relies on paragraph 118 of the report of the Appellate Body in *US – Hot-Rolled Steel* (which in turn refers to the report of the Appellate Body in *EC – Bed Linen*) to argue that the word "margin" in Article 9.4 of the AD Agreement refers to the individual margins of dumping for each exporter or producer. As a reading of that paragraph shows, the United States' interpretation is wrong. In *EC – Bed Linen*, the Appellate Body ruled that the term "margins" must reflect a comparison that is based upon an examination of all the relevant home market and export market transactions, and must be calculated for each individual firm. The Appellate Body states only what the calculation of a dumping margin is to include, but says nothing of the scope of the word "margin" as it appears in Article 5.8 of the AD Agreement.

4.481 Mexico points out that the provision in Article 5.8 of the AD Agreement that volume should be assessed on the basis of the country as a whole on no account implies that this is an exception to the rule or that the rule is a firm-by-firm approach.

4.482 It must be clearly understood that the anti-dumping investigation ends upon issuance of the final determination, a measure from which exporters not subjected to an anti-dumping duty cannot be excluded. The United States lacks clarity, in Mexico's view, in holding that Mexico should end the investigation in respect of exporters whose exports were found not to have been dumped, since Mexico decides in the final determination the anti-dumping duties that are to be imposed, and that determination likewise decrees the end of the investigation for all exporters. Any action taken after the final determination does not form part of the investigation, so Article 5.8 of the AD Agreement does not apply to any examination carried out after the final determination has been issued.

4.483 For the foregoing reasons, Mexico deems the United States' assertions to be unfounded.

(e) Mexico applied the facts available to *Producers Rice* and to the US Producers and Exporters That Were Not Investigated in a Manner Consistent with the AD Agreement

4.484 The United States puts forward the following new arguments:

(i) On the strength of Mexico's assertion that it would have taken 40 days to examine all the *pedimentos* from 1997 to 1999, the United States submits that it would have taken Mexico only two weeks to examine the *pedimentos* of 1999.

4.485 The United States' assertion is wrong. What Mexico said was that it would have taken about 40 days to *obtain* the *pedimentos* – not "examine" them. The time needed by Economía to examine them would have to be added to the 40 days.

(ii) The United States alleges that Mexico has not explained how its interpretation regarding the application of facts available is consistent with Article 9.5 of the AD Agreement, since if all firms are subjected to anti-dumping duties, there are no exporters able to apply for an expedited review.

4.486 The United states is mistaken. What Article 9.5 of the AD Agreement says is that there must be no relation with other exporters or producers which are subject to anti-dumping duties, which means that there must be no relation with exporters or producers examined individually and which are assigned a positive anti-dumping duty. Besides, if the United States' reading were correct, even if Mexico were to calculate an "all others" margin of dumping in accordance with Article 9.4 of the AD Agreement – as the United States claims it should have done – exporters not investigated individually would not qualify for an expedited review under Article 9.5. The United States' interpretation is at odds with its own argument and would prevent the holding of an expedited review.

(iii) The United States submits that Mexico's answer to question 17(c) of the Panel shows that Economía failed to satisfy itself as to the accuracy of the petitioner's list of exporters, as Articles 5.3 and 6.6 of the AD Agreement require.

4.487 What Article 5.3 of the AD Agreement requires is an examination of the accuracy and adequacy of the evidence provided in the application to determine whether there is sufficient evidence of *dumping, injury and a causal relationship*. It lays down no obligation to identify all existing exporters. Since Mexico used the best available information in respect of exporters that did not appear, Article 6.6 of the AD Agreement is immaterial.

(iv) The United States contends that by not sending a questionnaire to all exporters, Mexico limited its investigation to a reasonable number of exporters, and that it had a duty to identify a reasonable number or the largest percentage of them that could reasonably be investigated.

4.488 Mexico did not limit its examination to a reasonable number of exporters, but sent a questionnaire to known exporters and the United States Government. Furthermore, it published a notice summoning all exporters and interested persons. Nothing in the AD Agreement requires Mexico to act in the manner prescribed by the United States.

(v) According to the United States, Mexico claims that it need consider only exporters known to the petitioner and not those known to the investigating authority.

4.489 The United States is mistaken. Mexico never made such an assertion.

(vi) The United States says that " ... the EC's and Mexico's interpretation of ... would permit an authority to initiate an investigation on the basis of a petition that did not identify *any* "known" exporters, publish a notice of the initiation ... in its Official Journal, and ... send its questionnaire to *nobody*."

4.490 Since an investigating authority cannot know all exporters and producers of all products marketed in the world, to attempt to assign it such a task is illogical. By the same token it is logical that the investigating authority should notify and send questionnaires to the authorities of the exporting country and to *known* exporters and producers when it is able to draw on the information in the petition. It is likewise logical to assume that the authorities would forward those documents to their exporters and producers that were not notified individually. The role of the authority in the exporting country as set out in Article 6.1.3 of the AD Agreement supports Mexico's interpretation. The United States' assertions are therefore without merit.

(vii) The United States submits that nothing in the negotiating history of the AD Agreement suggests that the intent was to allow Members to ignore the requirements of Article 9.4 with respect to unexamined firms.

4.491 The United States bases that argument on a false assumption that Mexico limited its examination to a reasonable number of exporters. Regardless of the negotiating history, Article 9.4 applies only when the authority limits its examination. Since Mexico did not do so, Article 9.4 does not apply here.

4.492 The United States further submits that Mexico calculated margins of dumping for two exporters that came forward on their own. That assertion is wrong: the investigating authority calculated individual dumping margins for exporters that were sent the questionnaire and to *one exporter* that came forward spontaneously.

4.493 Economía was not bound to send the questionnaire to all United States producers and exporters, but only to those known to the investigating authority. Mexico would stress in this context that it is frequently the case that officials of the United States Diplomatic Representation in Mexico await notices of initiation of an investigation and forward them to their exporters, which are not barred from participating in the investigation.

4.494 Furthermore, the third paragraph of the introduction to the questionnaire sent to *Producers Rice* and *Riceland.* and to the US Embassy in Mexico shows that they were made aware, in accordance with paragraph 1 of Annex II of the AD Agreement, that if the requisite information was not provided, Economía would base its determination on facts available. The United States' claim is therefore unfounded.

4.495 Besides, the questionnaires for the investigation can be obtained from Economía's website, so the United States' contention that exporters had to go to the authority's offices in Mexico City is unfounded.

4.496 Mexico denies breaching Article 12.1 of the AD Agreement: it notified both the United States authorities and the exporters known to Economía individually.

4.497 Mexico complied with Article 6.8 and Annex II of the AD Agreement in calculating the margins of dumping on the basis of facts available.

4.498 Mexico has interpreted the AD Agreement as a whole, taking account of the full text of every material Article. The United States insists, citing the report of the Appellate Body in *US – Wheat Gluten*, that an investigating authority must not remain "passive". In that case the Appellate Body was ruling on the evaluation of factors to determine the existence of *material injury* in an investigation concerning *safeguards*, which is quite different from *identifying all exporters or producers* in an *anti-dumping* investigation. The argument is therefore without merit.

4.499 The United States' interpretations of the scope of rights of due process in fact go further even than the provisions of Article 6 of the AD Agreement, which is unacceptable.

4.500 The United States contends that the investigating authority acted inconsistently with paragraph 7 of Annex II of the AD Agreement. Whether or not *Producers Rice* cooperated bears *no* relation to the fact that the investigating authority calculated its margin of dumping on the basis of facts available, since Article 6.8 of the AD Agreement allows it to do so. The investigating authority applied not paragraph 7 but paragraph 1 of Annex II. The United States' allegation is therefore devoid of merit.

2. *Complaints relating to the Foreign Trade Act and article 366 of the Federal Code of Civil Procedure*

4.501 The United States' arguments concerning the alleged inconsistency, as such, of the Foreign Trade Act with the WTO Agreements are based on a single premise: the supposedly mandatory nature of the articles of the Foreign Trade Act at issue. This means, *contrario sensu*, that if the articles at issue are not mandatory – as Mexico has already demonstrated – then neither are they inconsistent with the WTO Agreements.

4.502 Furthermore, it is necessary to take into account Article 2 of the Foreign Trade Act and the fact that the Act must be considered as a whole and *not* in isolation when determining whether or not its provisions are inconsistent with the WTO Agreements.

4.503 The United States has failed to prove that Mexican legislation is inconsistent with WTO rules. In other words, it has not made a *prima facie* case of breach of those rules by Mexico. Accordingly, the Foreign Trade Act must be deemed consistent with the WTO Agreements.

4.504 As to the allegations concerning **Article 53 of the Foreign Trade Act**, the time-limit set in Article 6.1.1 of the AD Agreement and Article 12.1.1 of the SCM Agreement *applies only to foreign producers and/or exporters that were sent the questionnaire, i.e. known producers or exporters*. In this respect the Foreign Trade Act allows a longer period (38 days) than the Agreements, thus affording more opportunity for defence.

4.505 With regard to **Article 64 of the Foreign Trade Act**, it is consistent with the AD Agreement and the SCM Agreement, because if an interested party does not appear in the investigation and had no exports during the POI, then that exporter will *not provide* the requisite information on normal value and export price, and in that case the investigating authority may calculate its margin of dumping on the basis of facts available.

4.506 The United States further contends that Article 64 of the Foreign Trade Act is inconsistent with Article 9.4 of the AD Agreement because it requires Mexico to apply a margin based on facts available to firms that should have received an "all others" margin. Clearly, Article 9.4 should apply only where the investigating authority has limited its examination to a reasonable number of interested parties in accordance with Article 6.10 of the AD Agreement, which Economía did not do.

4.507 The United States submits that under Article 64 of the Foreign Trade Act, the investigating authority is required to apply the highest margin of dumping to firms with no shipments and that where such firms are "deemed to have been investigated" they are "subject to anti-dumping duties" and are therefore not eligible for new shipper review.

4.508 That interpretation contradicts even the United States' own practice. Were one to accept its assertion, an "all others" margin calculated in accordance with Article 9.4 of the AD Agreement would likewise prevent firms with no shipments from applying for a new shipper review. Mexico repeats that Article 64 of the Foreign Trade Act is not a bar to applying for a new shipper review. In fact, at the request of a United States exporter and after the revision of the Foreign Trade Act had taken effect, Mexico initiated a new shipper review, as can be seen from Exhibit MEX-12, submitted by Mexico as evidence.

4.509 With regard as to **Article 68 of the Foreign Trade Act**, the United States alleges that it is inconsistent with the WTO Agreements, citing Article 5.8 of the AD Agreement and Article 11.9 of the SCM Agreement. Article 5.8 of the AD Agreement does not require firms that are not dumping to be excluded from the measure. There are thus no grounds for alleging that some firms must not be subjected to the measure and are hence exempt from subsequent review.

4.510 As to the representative volumes required by Article 68 of the Foreign Trade Act, Mexico maintains that representative export volumes are not a requirement for initiation of a review.

4.511 Furthermore, nowhere does the resolution cited by the United States mention representative import volumes as a requirement for initiation of the review. Nor does it contain any evidence that the application for review was rejected because it did not fulfil the representativeness requirement. It was rejected in the case of some of the applicant firms for other reasons, which are detailed in paragraph 95 of the resolution.

4.512 The United States maintains its argument that **Article 89D** applies only to foreign producers and not to exporters, and that producers are required to demonstrate that their exports were representative.

4.513 As to the first of those assertions, Article 47 of the Foreign Trade Act Regulations expressly provides that "for trading companies, the buying cost shall be taken as the cost of production ... ", which includes exporters.

4.514 As to the second assertion, Mexico stresses that representativeness is a requirement not for initiating a new shipper review but for determining an individual margin of dumping or subsidy. Thus, although Article 9.5 of the AD Agreement and Article 19.3 of the SCM Agreement do not expressly so provide, it is natural and logical to demand of a new exporter that it make shipments in order for the latter to be reviewed. The United States' interpretation perhaps derives from the fact that the United States proposed making representativeness a requirement for initiation of a new shipper review in the Negotiating Group on Rules[37] at its meeting of 12 and 13 July 2004.

4.515 With regard to the United States argument concerning the hierarchy of laws in the Mexican legal system, Mexico points out that this subject is not among the issues covered by the Panel's terms of reference. Only Mexican courts have the authority to interpret the manner in which Mexico's local laws interact. Mexico accordingly deems that the United States' assertions must be dismissed.

4.516 The United States has failed to show that Article 89D of the Foreign Trade Act is inconsistent with the WTO provisions. Mexico, on the other hand, has conducted new shipper reviews for foreign producers and for exporters on the basis of Article 47 of the Foreign Trade Act Regulations, as shown in Exhibit MEX-12.

4.517 The United States further asserts that **Article 93.V of the Foreign Trade Act** is inconsistent with the WTO Agreements because it *requires* the investigating authority to apply the fines established therein. Mexico reiterates that account must be taken of Article 2 of the Foreign Trade Act, which stipulates that the Foreign Trade Act must be applied in a manner consistent with the international treaties to which Mexico is a party.

4.518 As is plain from Article 93.V, Economía has discretion to determine whether or not the fines must be applied. Further proof of this is that although this article has been in force since 1993, its provisions have never been applied to any Member of the WTO.

4.519 In response to the United States' claim that **Article 366 of the Federal Code of Civil Procedure (FCCP)** is inconsistent as such with the WTO Agreements, Mexico wishes to point out that US-20 – to which the United States alludes in its reply – does not refer to Article 366 of the FCCP. As already stated, Article 366 of the FCCP does not apply to the subject-matter or the procedures governed by the Foreign Trade Act. Mexico maintains that the United States fails to make a *prima facie* case and that its claim must be dismissed.

---

[37] New Shipper Reviews (ADA Article 9.5), informal paper JOB(04)/60 circulated on 25 May 2004/Formal document TN/RL/GEN/1 – TN/RL/W/156/Rev.1 circulated on 14 July 2004.

4.520 The United States asserts that Mexico failed to respond to the allegation that **Articles 68 and 97 of the Foreign Trade Act** offend against Article 11.2 of the AD Agreement and Article 21.2 of the SCM Agreement. Mexico's arguments on the matter are to be found in paragraphs 300 to 303 of its first submission. By waiting for the duties to be binding in order to carry out a review of them, Mexico is securing and safeguarding the interests of the parties, sparing them any possible injury.

4.521 As to the allegation that Articles 68 and 97 of the Foreign Trade Act are inconsistent with Article 9.3.2 of the AD Agreement, Mexico maintains what it said in paragraph 304 of its first written submission, in which it already established that the investigating authority will return any duties paid in excess upon conclusion of the relevant procedure. In no instance does Mexico breach the provisions of the AD Agreement.

4.522 As to the allegation that Article 68 and 97 of the Foreign Trade Act are inconsistent with Article 9.5 of the AD Agreement and Article 19.3 of the SCM Agreement, the United States lacks any basis for its claim since no provision of the Foreign Trade Act precludes or prohibits the holding of a new shipper review. Furthermore, the WTO Agreements require new shipper reviews, once initiated, to be carried out promptly, according to the AD Agreement and expeditiously, according to the SCM Agreement, but do not require a review to be *initiated* as soon as it is applied for.

4.523 Mexico wishes to point out to the Panel that the United States' allegation that Articles 68 and 97 of the Foreign Trade Act constitute a quantitative restriction to trade is quite mistaken, since never has there been any restriction, either *de jure* or *de facto*, on the normal conduct of the commercial transactions of *Sun Land Beef Company, Inc.* or any other foreign company.

V. ARGUMENTS OF THE THIRD PARTIES[38]

5.1 The arguments of the third parties are set forth in their written and oral submissions to the Panel, which are summarized below. The third parties' written answers to questions posed by the Panel are set forth in the Annexes to this report (*see* list of annexes at page xi).[39]

A. Third Party Written Submission of China

5.2 In its third party written submission, China made the following arguments:

[38] All the footnotes in sections V:A - V:F are original footnotes of the third parties.

[39] The Panel posed questions only to the European Communities. No other third party responded or commented on the questions.

1. *Issue 1: The closeness of the Period of Investigation to the Date of Initiation*

5.3 In the alleged anti-dumping investigation, Mexico's investigating authorities established a period of investigation ("POI") the ending of which was fifteen months earlier than the initiation of the investigation.

5.4 Although the AD Agreement itself does not establish any specific guidelines for determining an appropriate POI, the Anti-Dumping Committee has issued a recommendation to the effect that, as a general rule, POI shall be "ending as close to the date of initiation as is practicable". China does not consider that the time lag of fifteen months between the ending of POI and the date of initiation is in compliance with the spirit and substance of the recommendation of the Anti-Dumping Committee.

5.5 China believes that the evaluation of the closeness of the POI to the date of initiation should be considered in the context of its purpose and function under the AD Agreement.

5.6 The closeness of the POI is important for the investigation and the determination of the existence of injury and dumping margin. The data collected in a remote, non-proximate POI cannot prove that the dumped imports continue to exist at the present time, and that the level of such dumped imports "causes or threatens to cause material injury" to a domestic industry in the importing country. In order to ensure a fair and equitable investigation, the data collected within the POI shall meet the requirement of "objectivity" and "positive evidence", as such terms are defined in Article 3.1 of the AD Agreement. China agrees with the United States' assertion that the discretion of the investigating authorities to set the POI "is not boundless". As a general rule, the investigating authorities shall select the POI that is as close to the date of initiation of the investigation as practicable.

2. *Issue 2: The seasonality of the Period of Investigation*

5.7 The United States alleges that Mexico's investigating authorities examined only the March to August time period in each year of the POI for injury analysis. Such six-month period reflected the main import activity of the product under investigation when domestic production is at a seasonal low. Mexico's investigating authorities did not investigate the data in the September to February time period when domestic production is at a seasonal high and the import of the product under investigation is, conversely, relatively low. For the purpose of injury analysis, Mexico's investigating authorities did not compare the data of the seasonal high period with those of the seasonal low period. Instead, it only compared the data of the same season, on a year-to-year basis.

5.8 China takes no position as to whether or not the methodology adopted by Mexico in this dispute, which is to examine only an annual portion/season of the POI, as being inconsistent with its WTO obligations. Instead, China deems it appropriate to highlight the issue of the seasonal characteristic that is implicit in the POI stipulated for this investigation.

5.9 China believes that the investigating authorities have the discretion to consider seasonality when establishing the POI of a specific investigation. The Anti-Dumping Committee in its recommendation, did recognize the discretion of investigating authorities to "take account of the particular circumstances of a given investigation, to ensure that periods of data collection are appropriate in each case". Moreover, the Anti-Dumping Committee further recommended that "in establishing the specific periods of data collection in a particular investigation, investigating authorities may, if possible, consider the characteristics of the product in question, including *seasonality and cyclicality*" (emphasis added).

5.10 China also believes that the examination of a domestic industry by the investigating authorities from a seasonal perspective shall be conducted in an "objective" manner as required by Article 3.1 of the AD Agreement. The requirements of objectivity means that, where investigating authorities undertake an examination of a domestic industry in one season, they should, in principle, examine, in like manner, the same industry in all other seasons, as well as examine the industry for the whole year. Or, in the alternative, the investigating authorities should provide a satisfactory explanation as to why it is not necessary to examine certain seasons that have been excluded from examination.

3. Issue 3: Investigating authorities' obligations as to evidence collection

5.11 The United States alleged in the first written submission, that Mexico's "failure to investigate or attempt to gather data from readily available sources" breached Articles 3.1 and 3.2 of the AD Agreement because Mexico failed to "identify exporters and importers other than the handful of those mentioned in the petition"; failed to "send its anti-dumping questionnaire to exporters and importers other than the few designated as such in the petition, or to purchasers"; failed to "consult the customs declarations"; and failed to "seek to obtain accurate import volume information from importers".

5.12 The United States interpreted that the requirements of "objectivity" and "positive evidence" make it obligatory for the investigating authorities to "actively seek out information pertinent to" the investigation, and to "investigate or attempt to gather data from readily available sources". In other words, the United States asserts that the investigating authorities are obligated to actively collect evidence in order to fulfil the requirements of "objectivity" and "positive evidence". China offers a different interpretation than that of the United States with regard to the approach in order to meet the standard of "objectivity" and "positive evidence" as set forth in Articles 3.1 and 3.2 of the AD Agreement.

5.13 China believes that the obligations of the investigating authorities with regard to evidence collection are to give notice of information required to all interested parties and to provide ample opportunity to present in writing all evidence, rather than to actively collect evidence as asserted by the United States. Article 6.1 of the AD Agreement clearly described the obligations of the investigating authorities as the following: "[a]ll interested parties in an anti-dumping investigation shall be given notice of the information which the authorities require and ample opportunity to present in writing all evidence which they consider relevant in respect of the investigation in question."

5.14 The scope of the obligations of the investigating authorities as to the verification of the accuracy of the information provided by interested parties as defined in Article 6.6. of the AD Agreement is to "satisfy themselves as to the accuracy of the information ... upon which their findings are based."

5.15 The requirement that the investigating authorities shall "satisfy themselves as to the accuracy of the information provided by interested parties" was clearly described by the panel in *US – DRAMS.* The panel here stated that if the investigating authorities are obligated to actively seek evidence from all sources available, it is also likely that "anti-dumping investigations would, as a consequence, become totally unmanageable". China concurs with the panel's findings.

5.16 Only when the investigating authorities have to operate under "best information available" as described in Paragraph 7 of Annex II of the AD Agreement that the obligations to verify the accuracy of the information through independent sources arise "where practicable".

5.17 In sum, China does not find in the AD Agreement a solid legal basis to support the assertion of the United States that investigating authorities are obligated to actively seek evidence through independent sources except under very specific circumstances.

4. Issue 4: Known exporters

5.18 The United States alleged in this dispute, that Mexico's investigating authorities "improperly sent its anti-dumping questionnaire to only two companies that were listed in the petition" and "made no effort to identify exporters and importers other than the handful of those mentioned in the petition". The allegation raises the issue of the obligations of investigating authorities with respect to "known" exporters for the United States has asserted that Articles 5 and 6 of the AD Agreement "require an investigating authority to *actively determine the universe of potential respondents*" and to "*actively seek to identify individual exporters and producers*". China does not agree with such assertion and interpretation.

5.19 China believes that Article 5.2 of the AD Agreement expressly places the burden of identifying "known" exporters on the petitioners by stating that a petition shall include "the identity of each known exporter or foreign producer" of the product in question. In Article 6.1.3, the use of the definite article "the" before "known exporters" shows that the phrase "known exporters" has been used in the previous text of the AD Agreement. Given that both Article 5.2 and Article 6.1.3 use the same wording "known exporter", the "known exporters" under Article 6.1.3 refer to "each known exporter" under Article 5.2. Therefore, the AD Agreement suggests that investigating authorities shall rely on the petitioners to identify "known" exporters in their petition(s).

5.20 China would submit that at the outset of the investigation, the investigating authorities shall rely on the information in the petition to identify "known" exporters. The authorities are obligated to check the "accuracy and adequacy" of such information and if the authorities believe that such information is not accurate or adequate, it shall give reasonable time to the petitioners to provide further information or satisfactory explanation. There is no legal basis in the AD Agreement for the interpretation that the investigating authorities are obligated to actively seek to identify "known" exporters by themselves from available sources.

5. *Issue 5: Exporters that had no export during the POI*

5.21 The United States alleged that Mexico' investigating authorities improperly calculated dumping margin on the basis of adverse facts available for an exporter that had made no export sale during the POI but that had fully cooperated with the investigating authorities in the investigation. The United States asserts that a neutral "all other rate" shall be applied to such exporter because its full cooperation left no warrant to apply adverse facts available that are strictly confined in Article 6.8 of the AD Agreement. Furthermore, the United States stated that such exporter shall be entitled to the "new shipper" review as provided in Article 9.5 of the AD Agreement. China believes that the United States' interpretation that an exporter that made no export sales during the POI should have certain dumping margin applied to it (whether this is the neutral "all other rate", or the dumping margin based upon facts available) is in error.

5.22 China would base its position on the following: *firstly*, an exporter that made no export sales during the POI shall not be considered as having been dumping the products under investigation because no dumping margin can be calculated for such exporter due to the non-existence of an applicable export price. Article 2.1 of the AD Agreement provides that "a product is to be considered as being dumped, if the *export price* of the product exported from one country to another is less than the comparable price, in the ordinary course of trade, for the like product when destined for consumption in the exporting country" (emphasis added). An exporter that made no export sales during the POI had no export price that can be used to compare with the normal value to calculate dumping margin, therefore, the product under investigation of such exporter cannot "be considered as being dumped".

5.23 *Secondly*, Article 9.5 of the AD Agreement expressly requires that "no anti-dumping duties shall be levied on imports from such exporters or producers" "who have not exported the product to the importing Member during the period of investigation".

5.24 China believes that it is erroneous to impose any dumping margin on an exporter that made no export sales during the POI, whether this be the neutral "all other rate" or that based upon facts available.

B. *Third Party Written Submission of the European Communities*

5.25 In its third party written submission, the EC made the following arguments:

1. *Stale period of investigation*

5.26 Although the AD Agreement contains no express rule in the text concerning the selection of the period of investigation, an investigating authority's discretion in that respect is not boundless. Having regard to the context and purpose of the relevant provisions, particularly the use of the present tense, there is a limit on how long the period between the end of the period of investigation and the initiation of the original investigation can be. An excessive gap would not be representative and would not be consistent with the obligation contained in Article 3.1 AD Agreement to conduct an objective examination based on positive evidence.

2. *Use of March to August 1997, 1998 and 1999 for injury analysis*

5.27 Article 3.1 AD Agreement begins with the words "A determination of injury ..." (singular). From the wording of this provision it is clear that the AD Agreement requires an investigating authority to make one injury determination. An investigating authority cannot, without further reasonable explanation, make several discrete injury determinations relating, for example, to different companies forming part of the domestic industry, or relating to different time periods. Mexico defined the period at issue in its anti-dumping investigation as beginning on 1 March 1997 and ending on 30 August 1999. Thus, of its own accord, Mexico clearly identified that period as the relevant period for making its (one) injury determination. Having defined the period as it did, Mexico was bound to treat that period consistently thereafter in accordance with that definition. Thus, it follows, with respect to Article 3, including Articles 3.1 and 3.5, that Mexico had to make "a determination of injury" for that period – and not for the various segments of that period selected by Mexico. There is nothing in the AD Agreement that provides for an investigating authority to make more than one injury determination; to the contrary, all references to the making of an injury determination are references to a determination of injury. Having defined the period at issue as it did, Mexico could not subsequently take the position that some segments of that period were no longer relevant for the purposes of comparison or assessment. Mexico was not permitted to see the temporal characteristics of its injury investigation in one way for one purpose, and in another way for another. Mexico had become bound by its own logic.

3. *Injury analysis including non-dumped imports*

5.28 Even where the AD Agreement does not require any particular methodology for the determination of injury, the analysis conducted by an investigating authority must be objective and based on positive evidence. Imports from companies found not to have dumped cannot be included in the evaluation of volume, price effects and the impact of dumped imports on the domestic industry.

4. *De minimis dumping margin*

5.29 The wording of Article 5.8 AD Agreement contemplates the termination of the "investigation" in respect of the exporting country as a whole, not with respect to individual exporters. This interpretation is in line with the first sentence of Article 5.8 AD Agreement which requires that a complaint be rejected and the investigation be terminated promptly in case of lack of sufficient evidence to proceed with the case. Where the investigating authority determines a *de minimis* dumping margin for a specific exporter, Article 5.8 AD Agreement requires that no duty be imposed and collected from that exporter. It does not require the termination of the entire investigation (provided that the country-wide margin is above *de minimis*). In the opinion of the European Communities, both the method used by Mexico and the method suggested by the United States constitute permissible interpretations of the AD Agreement.

5. *All others rate, facts available*

(a) Irrelevance of Articles 9.4 and 10.6 of the AD Agreement

5.30 The provisions of Articles 6.10 (other than the first sentence) and 9.4 AD Agreement relate to the situation in which exporters are known and sampling techniques are used. Absent sampling, these provisions are irrelevant for the determination of an anti-dumping duty.

(b) An all others rate is permissible for unknown exporters

5.31 The AD Agreement does not contain any specific rule concerning the rate or amount of duty to be imposed on unknown exporters in the investigated country. An "all others" rate may be imposed on such exporters - a residual country specific rate. Article 6.10 AD Agreement, first sentence, refers to "known" exporters, and in any event contains the words "as a rule". Contextual support for such an interpretation may also be found in Article 2.1 AD Agreement, which defines dumping, and which refers to the product exported from "one country to another". Article 9.2 AD Agreement refers to the imposition of duties on imports "from all sources", and permits the authorities to name the supplying country if it is impractical to name the suppliers, as it would be if they are unknown. Furthermore, Article 9.3 AD Agreement contains rules concerning refunds. If an exporter did not appear during the original investigation, there is nothing on the face of Article 9.3 that would prevent such exporter from requesting a periodic review or a refund pursuant to those provisions. In any event, there being no dispute between the parties on this point, there is no need for the Panel to make any findings in this respect.

5.32 Unknown exporters, like known exporters, are interested parties within the meaning of Article 6.8 AD Agreement. If unknown exporters do not provide necessary information within a reasonable period, then, as in the case of known exporters, determinations may be made on the basis of the facts available. Unknown exporters choose, following the notice of initiation, not to appear and not to complete a questionnaire response. It necessarily follows that the "all others" rate may lawfully be based on the highest rate found in respect of a known exporter, whether or not on the basis of the facts available.

(c) Meaning of known and unknown exporters

5.33 Absent any contrary indication in the written record, the European Communities considers that exporters mentioned in the complaint or which respond to the notice of initiation may be considered to be known. That is a reasonable basis on which to proceed, which corresponds to a permissible interpretation of the AD Agreement. An investigating authority is not required by the AD Agreement to make further unilateral and autonomous enquiry.

(d) Application of an all others rate to unknown producers

5.34 The same analysis, mutatis mutandis, in respect of unknown (non-exporting) producers in the investigated country, would also be based on a permissible interpretation of the AD Agreement. Article 9.5 AD Agreement contains special rules in respect of so-called "newcomer" or "new shipper" reviews.

(e) Application of an all others rate to known producers

5.35 The AD Agreement also does not contain any specific rule concerning the rate or amount of duty to be imposed on (non-exporting) producers who are known. Producers Rice was a known producer which did not export during the investigation period. The imposition on Producers Rice of an "all others" rate based on the facts available was consistent with the AD Agreement, for all the reasons set out above. As explained above Articles 6.10 (other than the first sentence) and 9.4 AD Agreement relate to sampling and are irrelevant for this specific case. Producers Rice was not excluded from a sample. It simply had no exports. The absence of an export price precludes the calculation of a company specific dumping margin, but does not preclude the application of an "all others" rate. Article 9.5 AD Agreement contains special rules in respect of so-called "newcomer" or "new shipper" reviews in order to address the situation in which a producer without any exports and thus subject to the all others rate does have exports subsequent to the period of investigation. In all the circumstances, the imposition on Producers Rice of the same "all others" rate as that applicable to other unknown exporters and known producers, as the case may be based on the facts available, was a reasonable basis on which to proceed.

6. As such

5.36 Further to the Report of the Appellate Body in *US–Corrosion-Resistant Steel Sunset Review*, it is unnecessary for a measure to be "mandatory" as opposed to "discretionary" in order for such measure to be reviewed by a Panel for consistency with the AD Agreement.

C. Third Party Written Submission of Turkey

5.37 In its third party written submission, Turkey made the following arguments:

1. Selection of an investigation period that ended more than fifteen months prior to the date of initiation of the investigation

5.38 The United States submits that Mexico acted inconsistently with Article VI:2 of GATT 1994 and Articles 1, 3.1, 3.2, 3.4, and 3.5 of the AD Agreement by selecting a period for its dumping investigation that ended more than fifteen months prior to the date of initiation of the investigation. The United States, further contends that, those periods were so remote in time that the information collected by the investigating authority was incapable of providing a basis for an objective finding of dumping, injury and causation or a determination based on positive evidence.

5.39 Turkey submits that although the AD Agreement does not establish any specific period of investigation, the wording of both the AD Agreement and Article VI of GATT 1994 leads authorities to investigate the presence of dumping, injury and causation at the most recent time period. Thus, authorities should not be allowed to initiate a dumping investigation and examine any time period that they believe dumping was exercised for the sake of imposing anti-dumping duties.

5.40 In this respect, Article VI:1 of GATT 1994 states that dumping is to be condemned if it causes or threatens material injury to an established industry or materially retards the establishment of a domestic industry. The paragraph continues by the definition of dumping which is also in present tense. Likewise, Article VI:2 of GATT 1994 states that a contracting party may levy on any dumped product an anti-dumping duty not greater in amount than the margin of dumping to offset or prevent dumping. The other paragraphs of Article VI of GATT 1994 also follow the same trend and presents remedies for situations that took place in the near past.

5.41 Furthermore, Article 3.4 of the AD Agreement lists the relevant economic factors and indices having a bearing on the state of the industry that should be examined. Here one can easily notice that the required examination should be done as to the actual and potential position of the listed factors. Also in Article 3.5 it is clearly stated that the authorities should demonstrate that dumped imports are causing injury to the domestic industry.

5.42 In this respect, in light of the above cited clear obligations to examine actual and potential positions rather than past experiences, Turkey believes that even if the AD Agreement does not establish a certain time period, an unbiased and objective authority would not establish dumping margin on the basis of the past information that is not valid anymore.

5.43 In Turkey's view, the period of data collection for dumping investigations should end as close to the date of initiation as is practicable. This is also important for purposes of predictability and transparency of the investigations and credibility of the authority's actions.

2. *Limitation of inquiry*

5.44 The United States submits that Mexico's decision to allow the petitioners to set the POI for its dumping analysis as March-August 1999 and its subsequent decision to focus on only March to August of 1997, 1998 and 1999 for its injury analysis resulted in breaches of Articles 1, 3.1, 3.5 and 6.2 of the AD Agreement. The United States further contends that Economía's investigation of injury was not based on positive evidence for simple reason that it failed even to examine the evidence pertaining to half of the period of injury analysis. United States continued that Economía by taking this approach, made it more likely to determine that the domestic industry was injured."

5.45 In accordance with Article 17 of the AD Agreement, the panels are entitled to determine whether the authorities' establishment of the facts was proper and whether their evaluation of those facts was unbiased and objective. In this respect, the Panel may consider here if selection of those particular periods resulted in a solution different from what it would be if the whole one-year period were taken, in other words what an objective and unbiased authority would do in any given investigation. In addition, Turkey believes that seasonality is an important aspect of this investigation. The Panel may also focus on the seasonality of the subject product and its conformity with the practice of limiting the inquiry to certain parts of the year.

5.46 Turkey being a third party is not in a position to comment on if the results would be different if the whole one-year period was evaluated. Yet, what Turkey would like to emphasize is that in any such case if the authority is deviating from its normal practice it should provide the reasons for such deviation and invite the interested parties to submit rebuttal arguments if they would consider such practice not appropriate.

5.47 Turkey reckons that such arbitrary implementations should not be allowed as they would certainly place question marks as regards the objectivity of the authority and the outcomes of the investigation. In other words, authorities should not be allowed to manipulate the investigations as necessary.

3. *Application of "adverse facts available" to certain companies*

5.48 The United States considers that Economía's application of an adverse "facts available" dumping margin to Producers Rice and to US producers and exporters that it did not examine is inconsistent with Article VI:2 of the GATT 1994, Articles 1, 6.1, 6.2, 6.6, 6.8, 6.10, 9.3, 9.4, 9.5, 12.1 and 12.2 of the

AD Agreement and paragraphs 1, 3, 5, 6 and 7 of Annex II of the AD Agreement. The United States continues that an investigating authority is not permitted to examine individually just a few exporters and then assign an adverse facts available based margin to everyone else.

5.49 As regards the use of facts available, Article 6.8 clearly identifies the circumstances under which an investigating authority may resort to the "facts available". In accordance with this Article, only if an interested party "refuses access to" necessary information within a reasonable period, "otherwise does not provide" necessary information within a reasonable period, or "significantly impedes the investigation", the investigating authority may make determinations on the basis of the facts available.

5.50 Thus, the investigating authorities shall avoid the arbitrary implementation of "facts available" and for those companies who were not individually examined for reasons other than listed in Article 6.8 and the authority shall not calculate a margin based on facts available.

5.51 However, under certain circumstances the case may not be so straightforward. Assume a case where the investigating authority has acted to the best of its ability in reaching all the interested parties, that is to say he sent questionnaires to all the known exporters/producers, published a notice of initiation and notified the government of the exporting Member and requested assistance to reach unknown exporters/producers in the exporting Member. Some may here still argue that the authority did not notify all interested parties individually and those parties should not receive facts available based margins.

5.52 Assume that in the above scenario only one exporter/producer cooperated with the authority and responded to the questionnaire while all the other exporter/producers avoided cooperation. The only cooperating company received *de minimis* dumping margin. Here, would it be still rational to argue that those non-cooperating companies should receive the margin of the cooperating company or a neutral "all others rate" but not a dumping margin based on facts available?

5.53 In Turkey's view, application of facts available should be considered on a case by case basis. In any case the investigating authorities and interested parties should fulfil their respective requirements and bear the results of their relevant actions.

5.54 As regards the treatment of "new shippers", the only Article that is relevant with potential exporters of the product concerned in the AD Agreement is Article 9.5. The purpose of this Article is to eliminate the unfairness of punishing the newcomers with the residual duty of the original investigation for reasons beyond their control. The Article clearly states that to request a review those exporters or producers must show that they are not related to any of the exporters or producers in the exporting country who are subject to the anti-dumping duties on the product. This provision clarifies that the original investigation has already finished and the duties are in place, thus it does not recognize that new shippers can request an individual treatment during the investigation. Then the same Article continues that the review for those companies should be initiated and carried out on an accelerated basis and no anti-dumping duties shall be levied on imports of such exporters or producers while the review is being carried out. That is to say, regardless of the duty placed on the company they will not be subjected to that in the course of the investigation but may only be required to place guarantees or to withhold appraisement. In this respect, investigating authorities are not required by the AD Agreement to carry out individual investigations for those companies who did not export during the investigation period.

5.55 The United States further alleges that Economía failed to disclose to the exporters the export price information, which established the basis for the determination of the adverse facts available dumping margin. This information involved pedimento information obtained by the CMA from the Mexican Secretariat of Treasury. According to the United States, Economía did not include this information and the relevant documents in the public file of the investigation. Thus, the United States asserts that Economía, having acted as such, breached Article 6.2 and 6.4 of the AD Agreement.

5.56 Article 6.2 of the AD Agreement states that all interested parties shall have the right to defend their interests in the course of the investigation. Article 6.4 requires the authorities to provide "timely opportunities for all interested parties to see all information that is relevant to the presentation of their cases, that is not confidential (...), and that is used by the authorities in an anti-dumping investigation, (...)".

5.57 In view of the above requirements, Turkey believes that the authorities shall provide all interested parties access to non-confidential information that is relevant for the parties in making their cases so that the interested parties can use the opportunity to defend their rights, as stipulated under Article 6.2. The authorities' acting so will also render the investigation process more transparent and benefit all interested parties.

4. *Consistency of domestic legislation*

5.58 The United States alleges that various provisions of Mexico's Foreign Trade Act and its FCCP are inconsistent with Mexico's WTO obligations. The United States contends that particularly the provisions regarding time limit for responding questionnaires, facts available, reviews, new shipper reviews and application of fines are inconsistent with Articles 5.8, 6.1.1, 9.3, 9.5, 11.2, 12.1.1 and 18.1 of the AD Agreement and Articles 11.9, 19.3, 21.2 and 32.1 of the SCM Agreement.

5.59 Turkey submits that the Members being signatory to the Final Act of the Uruguay Round and the Agreement Establishing the WTO, commit themselves to be abide by the rules and procedures of the WTO Agreements. The presence of such commitment provides security and predictability to the multilateral trading system. Members should avoid impairing or nullifying benefits accruing to other Members by taking measures not allowed under the WTO Agreements.

5.60 In this respect, domestic Legislations of the Members designed to implement the WTO Agreements shall be compatible with the requirements of the relevant Agreements. Otherwise, the WTO Agreements and the multilateral system would prove unnecessary since Members might adopt Legislations with completely different obligations. This would inevitably result in chaos and unpredictability of the international environment.

5.61 As a matter of fact, Members are not precluded of having domestic Legislations. On the contrary, the WTO Agreements put forward general principles of application and they do not generally describe the procedures to be followed to act consistently with those principles. Thus, domestic Legislations are especially important in those instances where they help to describe procedures and rules that should be followed in order to be compatible with the Agreements. However, the balance should be set. The provisions of the domestic legislations should not create unnecessary burden for the respondents and they should not contradict or annul the provisions of the WTO Agreements.

5. Conclusion

5.62 Turkey has serious concerns in WTO Members' interpretation of the fulfilment of their obligations under the AD Agreement.

5.63 To this end, Turkey believes that among others, it is very essential for sake of transparency, fairness and appropriate functioning of this Agreement that the interested parties should not be deprived of their rights as specified in detail in the Agreement, the authorities should abide by the provisions of the Agreements in conducting an anti-dumping investigation in an unbiased and objective manner. Lastly, Turkey believes that the domestic Legislation of Members should be in compliance with the relevant WTO Agreements to preserve the implementation standards of measures in such areas as the area of anti-dumping and subsidies.

D. Third Party Oral Statement of China

5.64 China, in its oral statement, made the following arguments:

1. Issue 1: The closeness of the Period of Investigation to the Date of Initiation

5.65 In the alleged anti-dumping investigation, Mexico's investigating authorities established a period of investigation ("POI") the ending of which was fifteen months earlier than the initiation of the investigation.

5.66 Although the AD Agreement itself does not establish any specific guidelines for determining an appropriate POI, the Anti-Dumping Committee has issued a recommendation to the effect that, as a general rule, POI shall be "ending as close to the date of initiation as is practicable". China does not consider that the time lag of fifteen months between the ending of POI and the date of initiation is in compliance with the spirit and substance of the recommendation of the Anti-Dumping Committee.

5.67 China believes that the evaluation of the closeness of the POI to the date of initiation should be considered in the context of its purpose and function under the AD Agreement.

5.68 The closeness of the POI is important for the investigation and the determination of the existence of injury and dumping margin. The data collected in a remote, non-proximate POI cannot prove that the dumped imports continue to exist at the present time, and that the level of such dumped imports "causes or threatens to cause material injury" to a domestic industry in the importing country. In order to ensure a fair and equitable investigation, the data collected within the POI shall meet the requirement of "objectivity" and "positive evidence", as such terms are defined in Article 3.1 of the AD Agreement. China agrees with the United States' assertion that the discretion of the investigating authorities to set the POI "is not boundless". As a general rule, the investigating authorities shall select the POI that is as close to the date of initiation of the investigation as practicable.

2. *Issue 2: The seasonality of the Period of Investigation*

5.69 The United States alleges that Mexico's investigating authorities examined only the March to August time period in each year of the POI for injury analysis. Such six-month period reflected the main import activity of the product under investigation when domestic production is at a seasonal low. Mexico's investigating authorities did not investigate the data in the September to February time period when domestic production is at a seasonal high and the import of the product under investigation is, conversely, relatively low. For the purpose of injury analysis, Mexico's investigating authorities did not compare the data of the seasonal high period with those of the seasonal low period. Instead, it only compared the data of the same season, on a year-to-year basis.

5.70 China takes no position as to whether or not the methodology adopted by Mexico in this dispute, which is to examine only an annual portion/season of the POI, as being inconsistent with its WTO obligations. Instead, China deems it appropriate to highlight the issue of the seasonal characteristic that is implicit in the POI stipulated for this investigation.

5.71 China believes that the investigating authorities have the discretion to consider seasonality when establishing the POI of a specific investigation. The Anti-Dumping Committee in its recommendation did recognize the discretion of investigating authorities to "take account of the particular circumstances of a given investigation, to ensure that periods of data collection are appropriate in each case". Moreover, the Anti-Dumping Committee further recommended that "in establishing the specific periods of data collection in a particular investigation, investigating authorities may, if possible, consider the characteristics of the product in question, including *seasonality and cyclicality*" (emphasis added).

5.72 China also believes that the examination of a domestic industry by the investigating authorities from a seasonal perspective shall be conducted in an "objective" manner as required by Article 3.1 of the AD Agreement. The requirements of objectivity means that, where investigating authorities undertake an examination of a domestic industry in one season, they should, in principle, examine, in like manner, the same industry in all other seasons, as well as examine the industry for the whole year. Or, in the alternative, the investigating authorities should provide a satisfactory explanation as to why it is not necessary to examine certain seasons that have been excluded from examination.

3. *Issue 3: Investigating authorities' obligations as to evidence collection*

5.73 The United States alleged in the first written submission, that Mexico's "failure to investigate or attempt to gather data from readily available sources" breached Articles 3.1 and 3.2 of the AD Agreement because Mexico failed to "identify exporters and importers other than the handful of those mentioned in the petition"; failed to "send its anti-dumping questionnaire to exporters and importers other than the few designated as such in the petition, or to purchasers"; failed to "consult the customs declarations"; and failed to "seek to obtain accurate import volume information from importers".

5.74 The United States interpreted that the requirements of "objectivity" and "positive evidence" make it obligatory for the investigating authorities to "actively seek out information pertinent to" the investigation, and to "investigate or attempt to gather data from readily available sources". In other words, the United States asserts that the investigating authorities are obligated to actively collect evidence in order to fulfil the requirements of "objectivity" and "positive evidence". China offers a different interpretation than that of the United States with regard to the approach in order to meet the standard of "objectivity" and "positive evidence" as set forth in Articles 3.1 and 3.2 of the AD Agreement.

5.75 China believes that the obligations of the investigating authorities with regard to evidence collection are to give notice of information required to all interested parties and to provide ample opportunity to present in writing all evidence, rather than to actively collect evidence as asserted by the United States. Article 6.1 of the AD Agreement clearly described the obligations of the investigating authorities as the following: "[a]ll interested parties in an anti-dumping investigation shall be given notice of the information which the authorities require and ample opportunity to present in writing all evidence which they consider relevant in respect of the investigation in question."

5.76 The scope of the obligations of the investigating authorities as to the verification of the accuracy of the information provided by interested parties as defined in Article 6.6. of the AD Agreement is to "satisfy themselves as to the accuracy of the information … upon which their findings are based."

5.77 The requirement that the investigating authorities shall "satisfy themselves as to the accuracy of the information provided by interested parties" was clearly described by the panel in *US – DRAMS*. The panel here stated that if the investigating authorities are obligated to actively seek evidence from all sources available, it is also likely that "anti-dumping investigations would, as a consequence, become totally unmanageable". China concurs with the panel's findings.

5.78 Only when the investigating authorities have to operate under "best information available" as described in Paragraph 7 of Annex II of the AD Agreement that the obligations to verify the accuracy of the information through independent sources arise "where practicable".

5.79 In sum, China does not find in the AD Agreement a solid legal basis to support the assertion of the United States that investigating authorities are obligated to actively seek evidence through independent sources except under very specific circumstances.

4. Issue 4: Known exporters

5.80 The United States alleged in this dispute, that Mexico's investigating authorities "improperly sent its anti-dumping questionnaire to only two companies that were listed in the petition" and "made no effort to identify exporters and importers other than the handful of those mentioned in the petition". The allegation raises the issue of the obligations of investigating authorities with respect to "known" exporters for the United States has asserted that Articles 5 and 6 of the AD Agreement "require an investigating authority to *actively determine the universe of potential respondents*" and to "*actively seek to identify individual exporters and producers*". China does not agree with such assertion and interpretation.

5.81 China believes that Article 5.2 of the AD Agreement expressly places the burden of identifying "known" exporters on the petitioners by stating that a petition shall include "the identity of each known exporter or foreign producer" of the product in question. In Article 6.1.3, the use of the definite article "the" before "known exporters" shows that the phrase "known exporters" has been used in the previous text of the AD Agreement. Given that both Article 5.2 and Article 6.1.3 use the same wording "known exporter", the "known exporters" under Article 6.1.3 refer to "each known exporter" under Article 5.2. Therefore, the AD Agreement suggests that investigating authorities shall rely on the petitioners to identify "known" exporters in their petition(s).

5.82 China would submit that at the outset of the investigation, the investigating authorities shall rely on the information in the petition to identify "known" exporters. The authorities are obligated to check the "accuracy and adequacy" of such information and if the authorities believe that such information is not accurate or adequate, it shall give reasonable time to the petitioners to provide further information or satisfactory explanation. There is no legal basis in the AD Agreement for the interpretation that the investigating authorities are obligated to actively seek to identify "known" exporters by themselves from available sources.

5. Issue 5: Exporters that had no export during the POI

5.83 The United States alleged that Mexico' investigating authorities improperly calculated dumping margin on the basis of adverse facts available for a exporter that had made no export sale during the POI but that had fully cooperated with the investigating authorities in the investigation. The United States asserts that a neutral "all other rate" shall be applied to such exporter because its full cooperation left no warrant to apply adverse facts available that are strictly confined in Article 6.8 of the AD Agreement. Furthermore, the United States stated that such exporter shall be entitled to the "new shipper" review as provided in Article 9.5 of the AD Agreement. China believes that the United States' interpretation that an exporter that made no export sales during the POI should have certain dumping margin applied to it (whether this is the neutral "all other rate", or the dumping margin based upon facts available) is in error.

5.84 China would base its position on the following: *firstly*, an exporter that made no export sales during the POI shall not be considered as having been dumping the products under investigation because no dumping margin can be calculated for such exporter due to the non-existence of an applicable export price. Article 2.1 of the AD Agreement provides that "a product is to be considered as being dumped, if the *export price* of the product exported from one country to another is less than the comparable price, in the ordinary course of trade, for the like product when destined for consumption in the exporting country" (emphasis added). An exporter that made no export sales during the POI had no export price that can be used to compare with the normal value to calculate dumping margin, therefore, the product under investigation of such exporter cannot "be considered as being dumped".

5.85 *Secondly*, Article 9.5 of the AD Agreement expressly requires that "no anti-dumping duties shall be levied on imports from such exporters or producers" "who have not exported the product to the importing Member during the period of investigation".

5.86 China believes that it is erroneous to impose any dumping margin on an exporter that made no export sales during the POI, whether this be the neutral "all other rate" or that based upon facts available.

E. Third Party Oral Statement of the European Communities

5.87 EC, in its oral statement, made the following arguments:

1. Introduction

5.88 The European Communities makes this third party oral submission because of its systemic interest in the correct interpretation of the AD Agreement.

5.89 In this oral submission the European Communities, reacting to certain statements made by Mexico in its first written submission and by the other third parties, will comment on the following points:

(a) the use by Mexico of a stale period of investigation, ending more than 15 months before initiation of the investigation;

(b) the use by Mexico of three select segmented six month periods for its injury determination;

(c) the application of an "all others" rate based on the facts available to unknown and known exporters or producers; and

(d) Article 93V of the Mexican Foreign Trade Act.

2. *Stale period of investigation*

5.90 The European Communities would respectfully draw the Panel's attention to what is essentially consensus among the United States and all of the third parties: China; the European Communities; and Turkey. All agree that the AD Agreement is silent on the period of time that may elapse between the end of the investigation period and the initiation of the proceeding. There is no express rule in the text. Despite this, all agree, remarkably, that it is not a permissible interpretation of the AD Agreement to conclude that there is no limit to the period of time that may elapse. That proposition is based on context and purpose, rather than text.

5.91 It is a proposition derived from the fact that numerous provisions of GATT 1994, Article VI and the AD Agreement are in the present tense, or express a requirement of temporal proximity between the regulated behaviour (dumping causing injury) and its consequences (the measures that may be adopted under the AD Agreement); and from the numerous provisions of the AD Agreement that require an investigating authority to proceed in an objective manner, based on positive evidence.

5.92 The European Communities welcomes such an approach, it being one that validates in a balanced manner all the relevant rules of interpretation, giving fair weight to the overall logic of the Agreement, and the role of WTO dispute settlement. EC invites the Panel to embrace it.

3. *Use of March to August 1997, 1998 and 1999 for injury analysis*

5.93 On the question of the periods analysed for the purposes of the injury investigation, the European Communities also draws the attention of the Panel to the substantial degree of consensus between the United States and the third parties, both as to interpretative technique, and the conclusion to be drawn on this point.

5.94 The European Communities considers that the Panel need not consider whether or not there may be an issue of seasonality in this case, because that issue was not raised by or relied on by the investigating authority.

5.95 Rather, the European Communities considers that the Panel may and should make findings based on the general obligation of an investigating authority to adhere in its determinations to a coherent internal logic. This also results from the various provisions of the AD Agreement which require an investigating authority to proceed in an objective manner and base its findings on positive evidence. A determination that is internally contradictory cannot be, in all respects, objective and based on positive evidence. Some part of it must be non-objective and/or not based on positive evidence. The Appellate Body recently reiterated this basic requirement in the *EC–Bed Linen* case. It applies to an injury determination with just as much force as it applies to a dumping determination.

5.96 In this case, the Panel need do no more than find that Mexico determined it to be appropriate to assess injury over the three year period 1997, 1998 and 1999; that in principle Mexico was thus bound by its own logic to make its injury determinations on a consistent and objective basis in relation to that period; and that Mexico departed from the logic it had itself established by ignoring certain events relevant to injury assessment that took place during that three year period, without any explanation. Mexico thus acted inconsistently with the AD Agreement.

5.97 On the question of seasonality, the European Communities would not rule out the possibility that it may have a role to play when fixing the parameters of a single homogenous injury investigation period; or even that it should be taken into consideration within a period of injury investigation that extends over more than one season. That would not mean, however, that an investigating authority would be free to simply ignore certain events during the relevant period, without explanation.

5.98 For example, in determining whether or not the margin of dumping would be *de minimis* or the volume of imports negligible for the purposes of Article 3.3 of the AD Agreement, it is highly doubtful that an investigating authority could entirely ignore low season imports.

5.99 The same is true of the factors listed in Article 3.4 of the AD Agreement in relation to the examination of the impact of the dumped imports on the domestic industry, many of which by definition have a temporal aspect, and the measurement of which could therefore be severely distorted if arbitrarily restricted to certain sub-periods within the injury investigation period.

5.100 The same observation may be made in relation to the factors listed in Article 3.5 of the AD Agreement, those being factors causing injury other than dumped imports. Events relevant to the assessment of these factors cannot be simply ignored just because they happen to fall outside the particular sub-period or sub-periods arbitrarily selected by the investigating authority.

5.101 These observations are confirmed if it is recalled that seasonality may affect all Members to a greater or lesser extent. There may even be cases in which, in one season of the calendar year, Member A exports to Member B, whilst in another season of the calendar year, Member B exports the same product to Member A. In such a case, to look at only half the picture, could well result in a particularly distorted view of the situation.

4. All others rate, facts available

5.102 The European Communities recalls that there is no dispute between the parties as to whether a residual duty can be imposed on imports from unknown exporters or known non-exporting producers. Both parties agree that a residual duty can be imposed in both circumstances. Thus, contrary to what China suggests in its third party submission[40], the Panel is not asked to make any findings on this particular point. The parties disagree only on the question of how the residual duty should be established, that is, on whether or not such a duty can be based on facts available. This is therefore the specific issue on which the Panel is called upon to make findings in this case. The European Communities has pointed out that nothing in the AD Agreement precludes the residual duty from being based on facts available. In particular, Article 9.4 of the AD Agreement is irrelevant to this question, being limited to the specific circumstances in which sampling is used.

5. Fines imposed pursuant to Article 93V of the Foreign Trade Act

5.103 In so far as Article 93V of the Mexican Foreign Trade Act effectively requires the imposition of fines for dumped or subsidised imports from WTO Members, the European Communities would support the United States' claim that this is an impermissible specific action against dumping or subsidisation in violation of Article 18.1 of the AD Agreement and Article 32.1 of the SCM Agreement. The European Communities would also take this opportunity to recall that the United States has yet has to bring its own legislation into conformity with these specific obligations of the AD Agreement and the SCM Agreement by complying with the rulings in the *US–1916 Act* case and the *US–Offset Act (Byrd Amendment)* case.

F. Third Party Oral Statement of Turkey

5.104 Turkey, in its oral statement, made the following arguments:

5.105 Turkey has not made submissions with respect to all matters raised before this Panel. However, Turkey would like to remind that this should not be understood to imply that Turkey either agrees with or objects to such interpretations of the Agreement by the parties to the dispute.

5.106 Turkey presents the four issues that it had raised in its written submission:

(a) Selection of an investigation period that ended more than fifteen months prior to the date of initiation of the investigation;

(b) Limitation of inquiry to only certain months where imports were at their highest and domestic production was lowest;

(c) Application of "adverse facts available" to certain companies;

(d) Consistency of domestic Legislations with provisions of the AD Agreement and the Agreement on Subsidies and Countervailing Measures and obligations of Members.

5.107 As for the first issue, that is, Economía's selection of an investigation period that ended more than fifteen months prior to the date of initiation of the investigation, Turkey acknowledges that the AD Agreement does not establish any

[40] Third party written submission of China, paras. 32 to 35.

specific period of investigation. However, in Turkey's view, the wording of both the Agreement and Article VI of GATT 1994 leads the authorities to investigate the presence of dumping, injury and causation in the most recent time period. It is Turkey's opinion that the period of data collection for dumping investigations should end as close to the date of initiation as is practicable to display fair results. This is also important for purposes of predictability and transparency of the investigations and credibility of the authority's actions.

5.108 As for the second issue on the limitation of inquiry to only certain months where imports were at their highest and domestic production was lowest, Turkey would like to refer to Article 17 of the Agreement. In accordance with the said Article, the panels are entitled to determine whether the authorities' establishment of the facts was proper and whether their evaluation of those facts was unbiased and objective. In this respect, the Panel may consider here if selection of those particular periods resulted in a solution different from what it would be if the whole one-year period were taken, in other words what an objective and unbiased authority would do in any given investigation. In addition, Turkey thinks that seasonality is an important aspect of this investigation. The Panel may also focus on the seasonality of the subject product and its conformity with the practice of limiting the inquiry to certain parts of the year.

5.109 Turkey would also like to emphasize that in case the authority is deviating from its normal practice, it should provide the reasons for such deviation for purposes of transparency and predictability and invite the interested parties to submit rebuttal arguments if they would consider such practice inappropriate.

5.110 The third issue that Turkey would like to bring up is the application by Mexico of "adverse facts available" to certain US producer/exporters. As regards the use of facts available, Article 6.8 clearly identifies the circumstances under which an investigating authority may resort to the "facts available". In accordance with this Article, only if an interested party "refuses access to" necessary information within a reasonable period, or "otherwise does not provide" necessary information within a reasonable period, or "significantly impedes the investigation", the investigating authority may make determinations on the basis of the facts available.

5.111 However, under certain circumstances the case may not be so straightforward. Assume a case where the investigating authority has acted to the best of its ability in reaching all the interested parties, that is to say it sent questionnaires to all the known exporters/producers, published a notice of initiation and notified the government of the exporting Member and requested assistance to reach unknown exporters/producers in the exporting Member.

5.112 Assume that in the above scenario only one exporter/producer cooperated with the authority and responded to the questionnaire while all the other exporter/producers avoided cooperation. The only cooperating company received *de minimis* dumping margin. Here, Turkey does not think that those non-cooperating companies should receive the margin of the cooperating company or a neutral "all others rate". In such case, calculation of the dumping margin for the non-cooperating parties should be based on facts available.

5.113 In Turkey's view, application of facts available should be considered on a case by case basis. In any case the investigating authorities and interested parties should fulfil their respective requirements and bear the results of their relevant actions.

5.114 As regards the treatment of "new shippers", the only Article that is relevant with potential exporters of the product concerned in the Agreement is Article 9.5. The purpose of this Article is to eliminate the unfairness of punishing the newcomers with the residual duty of the original investigation for reasons beyond their control. The Article clearly states that to request a review those exporters or producers must show that they are not related to any of the exporters or producers in the exporting country which are subject to the anti-dumping duties on the product. This provision clarifies that the original investigation has already finished and the duties are in place, thus it does not recognize that new shippers can request an individual treatment during the investigation. Then the same Article continues that the review for those companies should be initiated and carried out on an accelerated basis and no anti-dumping duties shall be levied on imports of such exporters or producers while the review is being carried out. That is to say, regardless of the duty placed on the company they will not be subjected to that in the course of the investigation but may only be required to place guarantees or to withhold appraisement. In this respect, investigating authorities are not required by the Agreement to carry out individual investigations for those companies who did not export during the investigation period.

5.115 The last issue Turkey would like to raise is the consistency of domestic Legislations with the WTO Agreements and the WTO obligations of the Members. Turkey would like to remind that its written submission on this issue had been made before Turkey had the opportunity to examine Mexico's submission. Therefore, concerning this last issue, Turkey's submission did not include the views and approach that it would like to present after having examined Mexico's submission as well.

5.116 In this case, the United States refers to some provisions of the Mexican Foreign Trade Act that it considers to be inconsistent with the AD Agreement and the SCM Agreement. However, Mexico stated in its submission that the challenged Legislation entered into force several months after the termination of the investigation on imports of long-grain white rice originating in the United States. In other words, the reformed legislation subject to challenge by the United States was not in force during the time when the investigation was ongoing. Thus, Turkey believes that, even though the Mexican Foreign Trade Act involves some provisions allegedly inconsistent with the aforementioned Agreements, these were introduced after the termination of the subject investigation and should therefore be excluded from the scope of this panel and examined independently from this proceeding.

VI. INTERIM REVIEW

6.1 On 11 March 2005, the Panel issued its Interim Report to the parties. On 29 March 2005, the United States and Mexico requested the Panel to review precise aspects of the Interim Report, in accordance with Article 15.2 of the DSU. Mexico also requested the Panel to hold a further meeting with the parties pursuant to Article 15 of the DSU and paragraph 8 of the Panel's Working Procedures. The meeting was held on 25 April 2005.

6.2 We have briefly outlined our treatment of the parties' requests below. Where necessary, we have also made certain technical revisions to our Report.

A. Comments by the United States

6.3 In its comments on the Interim Report, the United States requests the Panel to make a number of technical and typographical corrections. Where appropriate, we made such corrections to our Report.

6.4 The United States requests the Panel to amend paragraph 7.62 of the Report relating to the Recommendation of the Committee on Anti-Dumping Practices in order to reflect that this Recommendation supports the interpretation of the Panel rather than providing "useful context" for the correct interpretation of the obligations. According to the United States, the Recommendation cannot be considered as "context" in the very particular sense in which that word has meaning under the Vienna Convention on the Law of Treaties, and this term should, therefore, be avoided. In its comment on the request of the United States, Mexico stated that the Recommendation is not binding and does not create new obligations for WTO Members. We note that the United States pointed out that this is also the reason why it would prefer to avoid the use of the term "context" in this paragraph. In order to avoid any misunderstanding, we amended our Report to state that this Recommendation provides "useful support" for our interpretation.

6.5 With respect to paragraph 7.223 of our Report, the United States requests the Panel to amend the Report to make sure that it is clear that the Panel findings address the consistency of Article 53 of the Act with both Article 6.1.1 of the AD Agreement and Article 12.1.1 of the SCM Agreement. We accept the request of the United States and have amended our Report accordingly.

6.6 The United States requests the Panel to reconsider its position set out in paragraph 7.299 that the United States failed to provide sufficient evidence that Article 97 of the Act deals with the expedited reviews that are provided for in Article 9.5 of the AD Agreement and Article 19.3 of the SCM Agreement. According to the United States, under Article 97 of the Act, only determinations issued at the end of a judicial proceeding can be considered "final". Since Article 89D of the Act only permits an exporter to request a review if the good in question is subject to a final duty, Article 97 of the Act, when read together with Article 89D of the Act does preclude expedited reviews and is, therefore, inconsistent with Article 9.5 of the AD Agreement and Article 19.3 of the SCM Agreement.

6.7 We consider that we sufficiently explain our position with regard to Article 97 of the Act in our Report. As the United States acknowledges, Article 89D of the Act is the relevant provision of the Act addressing expedited reviews. Article 97 of the Act does not, as such, deal with expedited reviews. Article 97 of the Act only becomes relevant due to the particular language used in Article 89D of the Act referring to a "final duty". In our view, the United States thus failed to adduce sufficient evidence that Article 97 of the Act, as such, is inconsistent with the obligations concerning expedited reviews set forth in Article 9.5 of the AD Agreement and Article 19.3 of the SCM Agreement. We do not consider that the US comments are of such nature as to require us to reconsider our position and to amend our report. We, therefore, reject the request of the United States in this respect.

6.8 The United States requests the Panel to amend footnote 202 of the Report dealing with Mexico's argument that the United States should have adduced evidence of the application of the challenged provisions of the Act. The United States requests the Panel to restate its rejection of this argument by Mexico. According to the United States, the question of Mexican law does not implicate WTO or general public international legal issues, but is a question of fact from the standpoint of WTO proceedings. In its comment on the request of the United States, Mexico states that it does not consider this to be a matter of fact and repeats its argument that the United States failed to make a *prima facie* case.

6.9 While we agree with the United States that the question of the meaning a WTO Member's law is a question of fact, we note that in this footnote we are responding to an argument made by Mexico that WTO jurisprudence required the complaining party to adduce particular evidence to prove this fact. As we explain in footnote 202, we do not agree with Mexico that this fact is necessarily to be demonstrated in a particular way. Neither has Mexico demonstrated that rules of general public international law provide for such a particular evidentiary requirement. In light of the comments received, and in order to clarify our position, we have slightly reworded this footnote.

B. Comments by Mexico

1. Observations concerning the section on the anti-dumping measure imposed on imports of long-grain white rice from the United States

6.10 Mexico requests the Panel to amend paragraph 7.52 and footnote 66 of the Report to reflect more fully Mexico's arguments as set forth in paragraphs 44 and 45 of Mexico's First Written Submission. We consider that for the purposes of our findings, paragraph 7.52 already accurately reflected Mexico's position. However, in order to avoid any misunderstanding, we changed the grammar of the paragraph's sentence relating to Mexico's view of the purpose of an anti-dumping measure so as to track Mexico's own wording as much as possible.

6.11 Mexico requests the Panel to clarify and complete the last part of paragraph 7.52 as Mexico considers that the last sentence of this paragraph is not clear and overlooks what was said in paragraph 67 of Mexico's First Written Submission. The United States considers that the Panel accurately reflected Mexico's statement in this respect and refers to footnote 71 of our Report. We note that the last part of paragraph 7.52 is taken almost verbatim from paragraph 35 of Mexico's Second Written Submission. In addition, we consider that the relevant part of the paragraph of Mexico's First Written Submission that Mexico wants the Panel to incorporate in the Final Report is already reflected in the penultimate sentence of paragraph 7.52 of our Report. We, therefore, reject Mexico's request to amend our Report.

6.12 Mexico requests the Panel to include a number of paragraphs of Mexico's Second Written Submission into paragraph 7.57 of the Report, which it considers to be incomplete and inaccurate. In addition, according to Mexico, what the Panel refers to as a position held by Mexico is not a submission of Mexico's but a comment on what was said by the United States in its Opening Statement at the first substantive meeting. We note that paragraph 7.57 is part of our analysis of the arguments of the parties which, as such, have been set forth in more detail in our Report, in "Section IV: Arguments of the Parties" and in the relevant part of "Section VII: Findings" dealing with the arguments of the parties. In paragraph 7.57, we highlight a particularly relevant statement by Mexico. We do not consider it necessary to include in this paragraph of our analysis a more elaborate explanation of Mexico's arguments which are fully reflected elsewhere in the Report. We, therefore, reject Mexico's request to amend our Report.

6.13 Mexico requests the Panel to amend paragraph 7.82 of the Report to reflect that it did not argue that taking a six month period was the *only* way of avoiding distortions. Mexico also requests the Panel to further amend paragraph 7.82 of the Report to reflect that Mexico did not state or give any indication that by "distortions" it was referring to "certain developments which occur in the remaining six months which perhaps undo part of the effect of the imports that entered the country during the six months that were examined", as Mexico considers is suggested in the Report. The United States considers that the Panel never claimed that Mexico made such a statement, but that the Panel was rather providing its own assessment of the facts in question.

6.14 We accept Mexico's comment that it did not say that applying a six month period was the *only* way of avoiding distortions, and we have amended our Report accordingly. We do not consider that we need to make the additional amendment to paragraph 7.82 of our Report as requested by Mexico. We note that paragraph 7.82 contains *our* analysis of Mexico's arguments in defence of the time period chosen, which has to be read in light of the fact that Mexico itself clearly indicated that seasonality was not an issue in adopting this six month period of investigation. This statement is thus our reflection of Mexico's explanations and not a summary of Mexico's argument, as Mexico seems to be suggesting. We consider that we sufficiently explained in our Report our position with respect to the failure to examine six months of each of the years of the period of investigation. We therefore reject Mexico's request to amend our Report.

6.15 Mexico requests the Panel to include the necessary details in footnote 78 of the Report to show that Mexico did not submit that "... its practise ... shows delays of sometimes six months, on other occasions 20 months between the end of the period of investigation and the date of initiation of the investigation, depending on the period of investigation the applicant is proposing". Mexico refers to a more complete description of its arguments in paragraphs 43 and 44 of its Second Written Submission. We acknowledge that, answering a question from the Panel, it was the United States, rather than Mexico, which presented an overview of the relevant practice of Mexico with respect to the choice of the period of investigations.[41] Mexico, in its Second Written Submission, however, did not contest the accuracy of these data, but rather confirmed that its practice reveals that on average there are about 10 months between the end of the period of investigation and the initiation of the investigation. In light of Mexico's request, we have slightly amended footnote 78 of our Report in order to clarify this point.

6.16 Mexico requests the Panel to amend paragraph 7.95 of the Report to more accurately reflect Mexico's position that it considers that an investigating authority is not required to send questionnaires to *all* the foreign producers and exporters. We accept Mexico's request and have amended our Report accordingly.

6.17 Mexico comments that on four occasions in the Report, the Panel refers to a "reasonable" investigating authority. Mexico requests the Panel to include an explanation of the term "reasonable". While we consider that a reasonable investigating authority is in the first place an authority which conducts an objective evaluation of the matter before it, in the sense given to the term "objective" by the Appellate Body in *inter alia* the case of *US – Hot-Rolled Steel,*[42] we decided that such a reference to a "reasonable" investigating authority in the paragraphs identified by Mexico was not necessary and we have amended our Report accordingly.

6.18 Mexico considers that paragraph 7.134 of the Report regarding Mexico's argument that it suffices for one exporter to be found to have been dumping above the *de minimis* level for all exporters to be included in the application of

---

[41] US First Answers to Questions, para. 5 (question 2). This was confirmed by the United States in its comments on the Mexican request for interim review.

[42] Appellate Body report, *US - Hot-Rolled Steel*, para. 193:

> "193. The term "objective examination" aims at a different aspect of the investigating authorities' determination. While the term "positive evidence" focuses on the facts underpinning and justifying the injury determination, the term "objective examination" is concerned with the investigative process itself. The word "examination" relates, in our view, to the way in which the evidence is gathered, inquired into and, subsequently, evaluated; that is, it relates to the conduct of the investigation generally. The word "objective", which qualifies the word "examination", indicates essentially that the "examination" process must conform to the dictates of the basic principles of good faith and fundamental fairness. In short, an "objective examination" requires that the domestic industry, and the effects of dumped imports, be investigated in an unbiased manner, without favouring the interests of any interested party, or group of interested parties, in the investigation. The duty of the investigating authorities to conduct an "objective examination" recognizes that the determination will be influenced by the objectivity, or any lack thereof, of the investigative process."

the measure, does not fully reflect Mexico's position. Mexico requests the Panel to include a reference to Mexico's argument set forth in its First Written Submission that if exporters do not engage in dumping, a review will not lead to the application of any measure - in the sense of the imposition of a duty - and such exporters will be able to continue enjoying their right to export without a dumping margin. The United States considers that the argument referred to by Mexico has nothing to do with the point the Panel is making in paragraph 7.134 of the Report. We are of the view that, in any case, such a reference as requested by Mexico is already contained in footnote 138 of our Report. We therefore reject Mexico's request to further amend our Report.

6.19 Mexico requests the Panel to clarify footnote 142 which provides that Mexico did *not* argue that an investigation has to be terminated if the country-wide dumping margin is below *de minimis*. Mexico fails to understand in what way the fact that Mexico did not make this argument may affect the analysis contained in the Panel's findings, given that it is not an issue in dispute. We note that footnote 142 implicitly refers to an argument made by the European Communities as a Third Party that the investigation is only to be terminated if the country-wide dumping margin is below *de minimis.* We consider it relevant, in light of this argument made by one of the Third Parties concerning the interpretation of Article 5.8 of the AD Agreement, to indicate that this possible argument was not one made by Mexico before us. While this fact does not alter our analysis, it completes our discussion of the arguments of the parties concerning the correct interpretation of Article 5.8 of the AD Agreement. We, therefore, reject Mexico's request to amend our Report.

6.20 Mexico considers that paragraph 7.143 of the Report which states that Mexico argues that termination of the investigation is only required when all of the margins of dumping for all exporters or producers are below *de minimis*, does not accurately reflect its position. Mexico requests the Panel to reflect the fact that Mexico asserted in its Answers to Questions from the Panel relating to the first substantive meeting that any exporter for which the authority finds a more than zero and below *de minimis* margin of dumping would receive a zero per cent duty. In addition, Mexico asserts that in its Second Written Submission it argued that the investigation is to be terminated where the investigating authority concludes that the margin of dumping is *de minimis* – a determination that must be made for each country as a whole and not on a firm-specific basis.

6.21 We note that paragraph 7.143 of the Report contains our analysis of the various arguments of the parties which are set forth in more detail elsewhere in the Report. We consider that the above statement that Mexico wants us to amend or delete is based on Mexico's argument, which it repeated in its comments on the Interim Report, that "it does suffice for one exporter to have been found to be dumping above the *de minimis* level for all exporters to be included in the application of the measure".[43] We, therefore, do not agree with Mexico that its position is not accurately reflected in paragraph 7.143 of the Report. We explain in this paragraph, and other relevant paragraphs, our interpretation of Article 5.8 of

[43] Mexico First Answers to Questions, question 20.

the AD Agreement. We conclude that Article 5.8 of the AD Agreement refers to exporter-specific margins of dumping. We wish to add that in paragraph 7.144 we address and reject Mexico's argument that the application of a zero per cent duty to an exporter does not constitute the application of a measure. We therefore see no reason to amend our Report as suggested by Mexico and reject Mexico's request in this respect.

6.22 Mexico considers that its position is not properly reflected in footnote 144 of the Report dealing with the alleged practical problem of an interpretation of Article 5.8 of the AD Agreement that could lead to parallel investigations against the same products from the same country. Mexico requests that part of the footnote referring to Mexico's position be deleted. In light of the fact that the argument of practicality was mainly one made by the European Communities in its Third Party Submission, we accept Mexico's request and have amended footnote 144 accordingly.

6.23 Mexico considers incorrect the statement of the Panel in paragraph 7.197 of the Report that "throughout the application the name of a third US exporter, the 'Rice Corporation' is referred to". Mexico points out that the only reference to that exporter in the application for initiation of an investigation is to be found in Annex H of the application. Mexico requests the Panel to amend the Report accordingly. In commenting on the Mexican request, the United States argues that the Panel is correct in stating that the name of this US exporter appeared throughout the application. We note that, as rightly pointed out by the United States, pages 23, 24 and 44 of the application and page 42 of part II of the application clearly refer to this US exporter. We therefore reject Mexico's request to amend our Report.

6.24 Mexico is of the view that paragraph 7.199 of the Report does not adequately reflect its position. According to Mexico, it did not acknowledge that it would have been possible to identify all US exporters by examining the so-called pedimentos. Mexico states that, while the pedimentos contain information on the names of the exporters, this does not necessarily mean that all the exporters of long-grain white rice can be identified. Mexico argues that the pedimentos would allow identification only of exporters of white rice, without any indication as to whether they exported short-grain, pre-cooked, etc. white rice, because the product description in the pedimentos serves only to ensure that the imported product corresponds to the tariff heading description, which covers many types of white rice. Mexico therefore requests the Panel to amend this paragraph to more accurately reflect its position. The United States considers that the Panel made a correct statement of fact concerning the information contained in the pedimentos.

6.25 We note that Mexico clearly stated that the pedimentos contain information not only on the volume and value of the imports, but also on the identity of the exporters.[44] We acknowledge Mexico's point that the pedimentos do not always distinguish between exporters of various types of white rice. This does not alter our view, which we have further clarified by adding a sentence to footnote

[44] Mexico First Answers to Questions, question 15.

193. Mexico's statement that the pedimentos included imports of *all* white rice, which is clearly inclusive of the subject *long grain* white rice, only confirms our view. We therefore reject to make the amendment requested by Mexico.

2. *Observations concerning the section concerning the Foreign Trade Act ("the Act")*

6.26 Mexico considers that footnote 202 of the Report does not accurately reflect Mexico's position. Mexico notes that the Panel concludes in this footnote that there is no basis for a requirement to adduce evidence in each of a party's "as such" claims of the application of the law, while Mexico had pointed to an Appellate Body report which came to the opposite conclusion. We note that Mexico's comments do not concern the presentation of Mexico's position, but rather that Mexico is commenting on the fact that we did not follow it in its argumentation. As becomes clear from the conclusion in this footnote, we do not consider that the Appellate Body report in *US – Carbon Steel* that Mexico has referred to actually supports Mexico's argument. The Appellate Body stated that such evidence of inconsistent legislation will typically be produced in the form of the text of the relevant legislation or legal instruments, "**which may be supported, as appropriate**, by evidence of consistent application of such laws, the pronouncements of domestic courts on the meaning of such laws, the opinions of legal experts and the writings of recognized scholars" (emphasis added). In our view, the Appellate Body was thus clearly not requiring that for an "as such" claim to be successful, evidence is to be adduced of the application of the law by the executive authorities and the domestic courts, in each case. We consider that our Report sufficiently explains the basis for our findings of inconsistency of several parts of the Act. We therefore reject Mexico's request to amend our Report.

6.27 Mexico considers that footnote 204 of the Report concerning the impact of the direct effect of WTO Agreements in Mexican law does not accurately reflect its position. In particular Mexico considers that reference should be made to its argument expressed in paragraph 206 of its First Written Submission that the Act has to be implemented as established in Article 2 of the Act in a manner congruent with the provisions of the Marrakesh Agreement and the Agreements it encompasses. Mexico requests the Panel to modify its findings so that they faithfully reflect the position held by Mexico in this dispute. We note that in footnote 204, which Mexico is referring to, as well as in paragraphs 7.224 and 7.225, we explain in detail why we do not follow Mexico's argument with regard to the impact for our review of Mexican law of the direct effect of the WTO Agreements in Mexican law. We consider that Mexico's position is accurately reflected both in paragraph 7.215 as well as in the above mentioned paragraphs. We, therefore, reject Mexico's request to amend our Report.

6.28 Mexico considers that its argument that the AD Agreement does not require the questionnaires to be sent to all exporters and foreign producers is not properly reflected in paragraph 7.232 of the Report as this paragraph refers to all *interested parties*. Mexico requests the Panel to amend its Report to reflect that

Mexico's statement was not about all interested parties, but only about all exporters and foreign producers. We accept Mexico's request and have amended our Report accordingly.

6.29 Mexico requests the Panel to clarify the meaning of the term "to obtain" an administrative review in paragraph 7.253 of the Report. As became clear during the interim review meeting, Mexico's comment seems to be that the Panel should make a distinction between the right to obtain the initiation of a review and the right to have the duties reviewed. We consider that in paragraph 7.253 of our Report we explain that we do not consider this to be a meaningful distinction and we reject Mexico's argument in clear terms. We are of the view that our Report is sufficiently clear on what is meant by the terms "to obtain a review". We, therefore, reject Mexico's request to amend our Report.

6.30 Mexico requests the Panel to amend paragraph 7.262 of the Report which discusses the scope of Article 89D of the Act, and refers to a recent case in which a new-shipper review was initiated for a trading house, "rather than a producer". Mexico considers that this last part of paragraph 7.262 gives the impression that the firm in question was involved both in exporting and in producing, and that exporting was its main activity, which is not the case. Mexico requests the Panel to delete from paragraph 7.262 the phrase "rather than a producer". We accept Mexico' s request and have amended our Report accordingly.

6.31 Mexico further considers that paragraphs 7.262 and 7.263 of the Report should reflect the fact that Mexico argued in its Second Written Submission that Article 47 of the Act's Regulations provides for new-shipper reviews for non-producing enterprises, i.e. enterprises devoted solely to exportation. We note that in these two paragraphs we describe Mexico's argument. Since it is correct that Mexico made this argument based on Article 47 of the Act's Regulations, we accept Mexico's request and have amended our Report accordingly. We note that in light of our findings on another aspect of Article 89D of the Act, we do not rule on the aspects of the claim that Mexico's comments relate to.

6.32 Mexico requests the Panel to specify in paragraph 7.67 of the Report that the argument of the United States which is reflected in that paragraph is based on data for paddy rice rather than long-grain white rice. We note that in paragraph 7.83 of the Report we explicitly state that these data concern imports of paddy rice and explain the importance we attach to these data. We therefore see no need to amend this paragraph 7.67 dealing with the arguments of the United States in respect of its claim.

6.33 Finally, Mexico requests the Panel to make certain clerical changes to the English and Spanish texts of the Report. We accept Mexico's request and have amended our Report accordingly.

VII. FINDINGS

7.1 This case concerns two sets of claims made by the United States regarding, on the one hand, the definitive anti-dumping measures imposed on imports of long-grain white rice from the United States, and on the other hand, a number of provisions of Mexico's Foreign Trade Act and its Federal Code of Civil Procedure.

A. General Issues

1. Standard of Review

7.2 In light of the claims and arguments made by the parties in the course of these Panel proceedings, we recall, at the outset of our examination, the standard of review we must apply to the matter before us.

7.3 Article 11 of the Understanding on Rules and Procedures Governing the Settlement of Disputes ("the DSU")[45], in isolation, sets forth the appropriate standard of review for panels for all covered agreements except the Anti-Dumping Agreement ("AD Agreement"). Article 11 imposes upon panels a comprehensive obligation to make an "objective assessment of the matter", an obligation which embraces all aspects of a panel's examination of the "matter", both factual and legal.

7.4 Article 17.6 of the AD Agreement sets forth the special standard of review applicable to anti-dumping disputes. It provides:

> "(i) in its assessment of the facts of the matter, the panel shall determine whether the authorities' establishment of the facts was proper and whether their evaluation of those facts was unbiased and objective. If the establishment of the facts was proper and the evaluation was unbiased and objective, even though the panel might have reached a different conclusion, the evaluation shall not be overturned;"
>
> "(ii) the panel shall interpret the relevant provisions of the Agreement in accordance with customary rules of interpretation of public international law. Where the panel finds that a relevant provision of the Agreement admits of more than one permissible interpretation, the panel shall find the authorities' measure to be in conformity with the Agreement if it rests upon one of those permissible interpretations."

7.5 Thus, together, Article 11 of the DSU and Article 17.6 of the AD Agreement set out the standard of review we must apply with respect to both the factual and legal aspects of our examination of the claims and arguments raised by the parties.[46]

7.6 In light of this standard of review, in examining the claims under the AD Agreement in the matter referred to us, we must evaluate whether Mexico's

---

[45] Article 11 of the DSU states: "The function of panels is to assist the DSB in discharging its responsibilities under this Understanding and the covered agreements. Accordingly, a panel should make an objective assessment of the matter before it, including an objective assessment of the facts of the case and the applicability of and conformity with the relevant covered agreements, and make such other findings as will assist the DSB in making the recommendations or in giving the rulings provided for in the covered agreements..."

[46] Appellate Body Report, *US – Hot-Rolled Steel*, paras. 54-62.

measures at issue are consistent with relevant provisions of the AD Agreement. If we find that the Mexican investigating authorities have properly established the facts and evaluated them in an unbiased and objective manner, and that the determinations rest upon a permissible interpretation of the relevant provisions, we will consider this measure to be consistent with the relevant provisions of the AD Agreement. Our task is not to perform a *de novo* review of the information and evidence on the record, nor to substitute our judgment for that of the Mexican authorities, even though we might have arrived at a different determination were we examining the record ourselves.

2. *Burden of Proof*

7.7 We recall that the general principles applicable to burden of proof in WTO dispute settlement require that a party claiming a violation of a provision of the WTO Agreement by another Member must assert and prove its claim.[47] In these Panel proceedings, the United States, which has challenged the consistency of the Mexican anti-dumping measure and of certain provisions of Mexico's law, thus bears the burden of demonstrating an inconsistency with the relevant provisions of the Agreement. We also note that it is generally for each party asserting a fact to provide proof thereof.[48] We also recall that a *prima facie* case is one which, in the absence of effective refutation by the other party, requires a panel, as a matter of law, to rule in favour of the party presenting the *prima facie* case.

B. *Mexico's Request For Preliminary Rulings*

7.8 In its first submission to the Panel of 26 April 2004, Mexico requested the Panel to issue a preliminary ruling that a number of claims made by the United States were outside the Panel's terms of reference. At the request of the Panel, the United States submitted its comments on Mexico's request on 7 May 2004.

7.9 We first summarize the arguments of the parties before making our findings with respect to Mexico's request for a preliminary ruling.

1. *Arguments of the Parties*

(a) Mexico

7.10 Mexico requests the Panel to issue a preliminary ruling concerning alleged deficiencies in the United States' request for establishment of a panel[49] (the "US request for establishment") and to abstain from entertaining those claims that are not consistent with Article 6.2 of the DSU or were not subject to prior consultations. In addition, Mexico considers that the US request for establishment is inconsistent with Article 17.5 (i) of the AD Agreement.

---

[47] Appellate Body Report, *US – Wool Shirts and Blouses*, p. 337.

[48] *Ibid.*

[49] WT/DS295/2

7.11 First, Mexico submits that the US request for establishment fails to comply with Article 6.2 of the DSU as it fails to provide a brief summary of the legal basis of the complaint sufficient to present the problem clearly. In addition, Mexico argues that one of the measures challenged by the United States was not properly identified in the request for establishment.

7.12 In particular, Mexico argues that the following claims set forth in the request for establishment are overly vague and unclear:

- the claim of violation of Article VI of the GATT 1994 which fails to specify which of the paragraphs of Article VI of the GATT 1994 are alleged to have been violated;
- the claim relating to Article 4.1 of the AD Agreement concerning the definition of the domestic industry as the United States merely refers to violations of Article 3 of the AD Agreement and fails to explain why it considers that Article 4.1 of the AD Agreement would have been violated;
- the claim relating to the use of facts available to a non-shipping exporter set forth in section 1(f) of the request for establishment, which refers to a large number of provisions of the AD Agreement which concern the acceptance and processing of information, and are unrelated to whether or not an exporter has effected any exports during a specific period and the legal consequences thereof;
- the claim relating to the use of facts available to non-appearing exporters set forth in section 1 (g) of the request for establishment as the United States again refers to a number of provisions of the AD Agreement which are unrelated to the situation of such exporters as well as the United States' failure to explain why it considers that certain decisions of the Mexican Authority in this regard were taken in an "improper manner".

7.13 In addition, in Mexico's view, the US request for establishment fails to identify Article 366 of the Federal Code of Civil Procedure ("FCCP") as one of the challenged measures. According to Mexico, the US request for establishment does not refer to Article 366 of the Code of Civil Procedure itself, but rather only to statements of Mexican officials concerning Article 366 of the FCCP and Articles 68 and 97 of the Foreign Trade Act ("the Act"). According to Mexico, the statements of certain officials, which are included in the request for establishment, are clearly not "measures" that may be challenged before the WTO.

7.14 Furthermore, Mexico asserts that the request for establishment contains a number of claims which were not part of the consultations in violation of Article 4.5 and 4.7 of the DSU. Mexico argues that these provisions as well as Article 17.4 of the AD Agreement require that the consultations form the basis for the request for establishment of a panel. Therefore, Mexico submits, those provisions on which no consultations were held should be discarded by the Panel.[50]

---

[50] Mexico lists these provisions in para. 34 of its First Submission.

7.15 In addition, Mexico argues that the claim concerning the alleged failure to examine all relevant factors in the injury analysis was only discussed in the consultations concerning the anti-dumping measures imposed on imports of beef, and was not discussed in the consultations relating to the imposition of anti-dumping duties on rice, the subject of the current dispute settlement proceedings. As no consultations were held on this claim, Mexico requests the Panel to discard it.

7.16 Finally, according to Mexico, as a consequence of the previously identified inconsistencies of the request for establishment with the DSU, the United States also failed to comply with the requirement of Article 17.5 of the AD Agreement to indicate how a benefit accruing to it has been nullified or impaired. The request for establishment is therefore in Mexico's view, also inconsistent with Article 17.5 of the AD Agreement.

7.17 Mexico claims that the prejudice it suffered from the lack of clarity in the US request for establishment was exacerbated by the fact that, as the US submission was made in English, additional time for the preparation of Mexico's defence was lost due to translation of the submission.

(b) United States

7.18 The United States considers that the US request for establishment of the Panel is fully consistent with the relevant provisions of the DSU and the AD Agreement, and submits that Mexico's request should therefore be rejected.

7.19 First, the United States argues that there is no requirement in Article 6.2 of the DSU that the request for establishment provide a summary of the specific legal arguments which will be developed in the submissions. Article 6.2 of the DSU requires that the claims must be included in the panel request, but not the arguments in support of these claims. The United States submits that its request lists the specific provision of the AD Agreement and the GATT 1994 alleged to be violated and provides, in addition, a brief textual explanation of the basis of the complaint. In particular,

- with regard to Article VI of the GATT 1994, the United States is of the view that the narrative description which accompanies the allegation leaves no doubt as to which of the paragraphs of Article VI of the GATT 1994 it considers to have been violated, as it focuses on the only two paragraphs that are relevant to this dispute, paragraphs 2 and 6(a);
- with regard to Article 4.1 of the AD Agreement, the United States is of the view that Mexico does not argue that the claim should be more specific, but that it is unable to understand which of the statements in the narrative description result in a breach of the Article invoked. The United States is of the view that Mexico's request should be rejected because Article 6.2 of the DSU does not require that the request contains the arguments to support the claim;

- with regard to the sections 1 (f) and (g) of the request, the United States considers that Mexico concedes that the United States request challenged the application of facts available to the non-shipping exporter, Producers Rice (subsection 1(f)) and to all other exporters that were not individually examined (subsection 1(g)), but that Mexico is of the view that the United States has not adequately explained how Mexico's use of facts available violated these provisions. The United States argues that Article 6.2 of the DSU requires that the claims must be made in the request for establishment, but that there is no similar requirement that the request set forth all the arguments in support of the claims.

7.20 In any case, the United States submits, Mexico failed to demonstrate that it was somehow prejudiced by this alleged failure to satisfy the requirements of Article 6.2 of the DSU. The United States submits that Mexico's assertion of prejudice is contradicted by the facts since Mexico's first written submission contains a lengthy response to each of the challenged US claims.

7.21 In addition, the United States argues that its request for establishment clearly indicates that Article 366 of the FCCP is the measure challenged, and not the statements of Mexican officials concerning the application of this provision. This, the United States submits, is clear from the second sentence of section 3 of the US request for establishment. There is, therefore, no basis for the Mexican argument that the United States failed to identify Article 366 of the FCCP as the "specific measure at issue".

7.22 Furthermore, the United States considers that Mexico's arguments pertaining to the alleged inadequacy of the consultations lack merit. The United States argues that there is no requirement in the DSU that a Member cannot include a claim in its request for establishment unless the particular claim was discussed during consultations. The United States is of the view that consultations are not "dress rehearsals" for the panel process requiring Members to have worked out all of their claims and positions in advance and presenting them in consultations for the other side to practice its prepared responses.

7.23 The United States further asserts that consultations were held in respect of the US claims concerning the examination of the injury factors by the investigating authority also in respect of the anti-dumping measures imposed on imports of rice, and not just in respect of the beef investigation. More importantly, however, the United States considers that the DSU does not contain a requirement as to the adequacy of the consultations. The United States notes that the United States and Mexico spent two days consulting at length on each of the specific measures at issue in this dispute, and there is therefore, no basis for Mexico's assertion that the United States acted inconsistently with Articles 4.5 and 4.7 of the DSU with respect to consultations over the disputed measures. The United States also rejects Mexico's argument of violation of Article 17.4 of the AD Agreement which in the United States' view only requires that the Member requesting the establishment of a panel "consider" that the consultations have failed to achieve a mutually agreed solution. Such was the case in this dispute, and the United States submits that Mexico's Article 17.4 of the AD Agreement claim is thus groundless.

7.24 Finally, the United States rejects Mexico's arguments of violation of Article 17.5 of the AD Agreement, as the United States is of the view that Article 17.5 of the AD Agreement does not impose an additional obligation on the complaining party.

2. *Analysis*

7.25 We consider that Mexico's request for a preliminary ruling raises three main issues concerning (i) Article 6.2 of the DSU and the extent of the obligation to provide a "brief summary of the legal basis of the complaint" in the request for establishment of a panel and to identify "the specific measure at issue"; (ii) the relationship between the request for establishment and the scope of the consultations; and (iii) the need to demonstrate nullification or impairment of interests in the request for establishment under Article 17.5 of the AD Agreement. We will address each of these issues in this order.

(a) Conformity of the Request for Establishment with Article 6.2 of the DSU

7.26 Article 6.2 of the DSU concerning the request for establishment of a panel provides as follows:

> "The request for the establishment of a panel shall be made in writing. It shall indicate whether consultations were held, identify the specific measures at issue and provide a brief summary of the legal basis of the complaint sufficient to present the problem clearly. In case the applicant requests the establishment of a panel with other than standard terms of reference, the written request shall include the proposed text of special terms of reference".

7.27 According to Article 6.2 of the DSU, therefore, the request for establishment must identify *the specific measures at issue and must provide a brief summary of the legal basis of the complaint sufficient to present the problem clearly.* Mexico's request concerning Article 6.2 of the DSU relates to the absence of a sufficient summary of the legal basis of the complaint with regard to alleged violations of Article VI of the GATT 1994, Article 4.1 of the AD Agreement and the use of facts available in the case of non-shipping exporters and exporters not individually investigated. In addition, Mexico argues that the request for establishment relating to Article 366 of the FCCP failed to properly identify the specific measure at issue.

7.28 The first question before us is thus whether the US request for establishment provided a brief summary of the claim sufficient to present the problem clearly. In other words, the question is whether the "brief summary" was such that Mexico knew what case it had to answer, enabling it to begin preparing its defence.[51] This in our view does not mean that the complainant is required, in its request for establishment, to set out the arguments in support of this claim. We consider that there is a significant difference between the claims identified in the request for the establishment of a panel, which establish the panel's terms of reference under Article 7 of the DSU, and the arguments supporting those claims, which are set out and progressively clarified in the first written submissions, the rebuttal submissions and the first and second panel meetings with the parties.[52] We recall that the purpose of the terms of reference, apart from defining the scope of the dispute, is to serve the due process objective of notifying the parties of the nature of the complainant's case.[53]

7.29 First, with respect to Mexico's arguments concerning the lack of specificity of the request with regard to the alleged violation of Article VI of the GATT 1994, we recall that the US request for establishment provides in relevant part as follows:

> "(1) On 5 June 2002, Mexico published in the *Diario Oficial* its definitive anti-dumping measure on long-grain white rice. This measure appears to be inconsistent with the following provisions of the AD Agreement and the GATT 1994:
>
> > (a) Article VI of the GATT 1994 and Articles 1, 3.1, 3.2, 3.4, 3.5, and 4.1 of the AD Agreement because Mexico based its injury and causation analyses on only six months of data for each of the years examined; failed to collect or examine recent data; failed to properly evaluate the relevant economic factors; failed to base its determination on a demonstration that the dumped imports are, through the effects of dumping, causing injury within the meaning of the AD Agreement; and failed to base its injury determinations on positive evidence or to conduct objective examinations of the volume of dumped imports, the effect of those imports on prices in the domestic market of like products, and the impact of the imports on domestic producers of those products;" (footnote omitted).

7.30 Mexico considers that it is not sufficiently clear from the request which of the many subparagraphs of Article VI of the GATT 1994 the United States is alleging to have been violated. We recall that, while it is so that sometimes even a mere listing of the provisions allegedly violated may suffice to comply with the requirement of Article 6.2 of the DSU to provide a brief summary of the legal basis of the complaint,[54] this is not always the case, and especially in case the provision alleged

---

[51] For a recent application of this approach, see Panel Report, *Canada – Wheat Exports and Grain Imports*, para. 6.10 (para. 30 of the Panel's preliminary ruling).

[52] We note that this was also the view held by the Appellate Body in the *EC – Bananas* case. See Appellate Body Report, *EC – Bananas*, para. 141.

[53] Appellate Body Report, *United States – Carbon Steel*, para. 126.

[54] Appellate Body Report, *Korea – Dairy*, para. 124:

"There may be situations where the simple listing of the articles of the agreement or agreements involved may, in the light of attendant circumstances, suffice to meet the standard of clarity in the

to have been violated, consist of various paragraphs and subparagraphs, further specification may be required to inform the parties of the scope of the claims in a sufficiently clear manner. In the end, what matters is whether the request provided a brief summary of the legal basis of the complaint sufficient to present the problem clearly. In case a complainant chooses to comply with this requirement by merely listing treaty provisions without any further narrative explanation of the problem, it is of course all important to know which of the paragraphs or subparagraphs the complainant is referring to in case the treaty provision consist of several of such paragraphs each dealing with slightly different issues. A general reference to such a multilayered treaty provision may in such circumstances not be enough to present the problem clearly. The facts before us are somewhat different, as the US request for establishment does more than simply listing the treaty provisions alleged to have been violated. The United States also provides a narrative in which it briefly explains the problem the United States has with the challenged measure. In our view, the question before us is thus whether, the reference to the provisions of the Agreement, *together with the narrative* which accompanied the listing of these provisions, were sufficient to present the problem clearly so that the defendant was able to understand the case against it.

7.31 While we consider that the US request for establishment could have been clearer in identifying precisely which of the paragraphs of Article VI of the GATT 1994 the United States claims to have been violated, we do not agree with Mexico that the request for establishment in this respect did not provide a brief summary of the legal basis of the claim sufficient to present the problem clearly. We consider that it is important when examining the consistency of part of the request for establishment with Article 6.2 of the DSU, not to examine parts of this request in isolation. Rather, in our view, the request must be considered as a whole, and the different claims in the request for establishment must be read in their context.[55] In our view, the accompanying narrative and the provisions of the AD Agreement also alleged to have been violated make it clear that the US claims in this respect concern the determination of injury caused by dumped imports. We agree with the United States that only a very limited number of paragraphs of Article VI of the GATT 1994, such as paragraphs 2 and 6 (a) are in fact relevant to this matter. We therefore reject Mexico's request in respect of Article VI of the GATT 1994.

7.32 Second, with respect to Mexico's arguments concerning Article 4.1 of the AD Agreement in section 1 (a) of the request for establishment, we note that Mexico stated that in its view the United States focuses its arguments on viola-

statement of the legal basis of the complaint. However, there may also be situations in which the circumstances are such that the mere listing of treaty articles would not satisfy the standard of Article 6.2. This may be the case, for instance, where the articles listed establish not one single, distinct obligation, but rather multiple obligations. In such a situation, the listing of articles of an agreement, in and of itself, may fall short of the standard of Article 6.2.".

[55] We find support for this view in statement of the Appellate Body in the *US – Carbon Steel* case:

> "Moreover, compliance with the requirements of Article 6.2 must be determined on the merits of each case, having considered the panel request as a whole, and in the light of attendant circumstances." Appellate Body Report, *US – Carbon Steel*, para. 127.

tions of various provisions of Article 3 of the AD Agreement and that Mexico is thus unable to determine specifically which of these facts may be considered a violation of any of the obligations provided for in Article 4.1 of the AD Agreement. We are of the view that the request for establishment clearly specifies the particular provision allegedly violated and explains in sufficient detail the legal basis of its claim. While Mexico may disagree with the United States and may well argue that Article 4.1 of the AD Agreement which sets forth a definition of the domestic industry is not applicable or is irrelevant in this case, this, we find, is a matter of substance and one which is to be addressed in the submissions to the Panel. We consider that the request for establishment provides a brief summary of the legal basis of the claim sufficient to present the problem clearly by, in addition to listing the legal basis of its claim, providing a narrative setting forth the US allegations concerning the failure to properly identify injury to the domestic industry. In our view, Mexico is really arguing that the United States should have provided more ample argument as to why it considered that the Mexican investigating authority acted inconsistently with Article 4.1 of the AD Agreement. As we stated earlier, the request for establishment is to set forth a brief summary of the legal basis of the claim, not to set out the arguments in support of this claim. We wish to emphasise that our views concerning the consistency of the request for establishment with Article 6.2 of the DSU in no way prejudge our findings as to the merits of the US claims, nor to the relevance or lack thereof of certain of the provisions invoked by the complainant.

7.33 Third, with regard to Mexico's arguments concerning sections 1 (f) and (g) of the US request and the use of facts available to a non-shipping exporter, and the exporters which were not individually investigated, we note that the US request for establishment provides as follows:

> "(f) Articles 6.6, 6.8, 6.10, 9.3, 9.4, and 9.5 of the AD Agreement, and paragraphs 1, 3, 5, 6, and 7 of Annex II of the AD Agreement, by applying the facts available to a US respondent rice exporter that was investigated and found to have no shipments during the period of investigation;
>
> (g) Articles 1, 6.1, 6.6, 6.8, 6.10, 9.3, 9.4, 9.5, 12.1, and 12.2 of the AD Agreement, and paragraphs 1, 3, 5, 6, and 7 of Annex II of the AD Agreement, by applying the facts available in establishing the anti-dumping margins that it assigned to US exporters that were not individually investigated, and by doing so in an improper manner;"

7.34 Mexico argues that it fails to see how such provisions relating to the acceptance and processing of information are relevant to the situation of these two categories of exporters. In our view, the United States request of establishment provides a sufficient summary of the legal basis of the US claims that facts available were applied to determine a margin of dumping for certain categories of exporters in a manner inconsistent with those provisions of the AD Agreement dealing with the use of best information available. Again, we consider that the United States is not required in its request for establishment to set forth the arguments in support of this claim. Whether the provisions alleged to have been violated are relevant and applicable is a question we do not need to decide when reviewing the consistency of the request for establishment with Article 6.2 of the DSU.

7.35 Finally, Mexico considers that section 3 of the request for establishment fails to identify Article 366 of the FCCP as the measure at issue. This section of the request for establishment reads as follows:

> "3. Mexican officials have asserted that Article 366 of Mexico's Federal Code of Civil Procedure and Articles 68 and 97 of the Act prevent Mexico from conducting reviews of anti-dumping or countervailing duty orders while a judicial review of the order is ongoing, including a "binational panel" review pursuant to Chapter Nineteen of the *North American Free Trade Agreement*. **These provisions appear to be inconsistent** with Articles 9.3, 9.5, and 11.2 of the AD Agreement, and Articles 19.3 and 21.2 of the SCM Agreement." (emphasis added)

7.36 In our view, the request for establishment clearly refers to Article 366 of the FCCP rather than to the statements of Mexican officials concerning its application, as the challenged measure in question. We consider the statements to have been referred to merely in support of the claim of inconsistency. We therefore find that section 3 of the request for establishment specifies clearly the specific measure at issue, and these measures are Article 366 of the FCCP and Article 68 and 97 of the Act.

7.37 In sum, we find that the request for establishment provides a summary of the legal basis of the complaint sufficient to present the problem clearly as required by Article 6.2 of the DSU with regard to the claims set forth in sections 1 (f) and (g) of the request, as well as with regard to the claim concerning Article VI of the GATT 1994 and Article 4.1 of the AD Agreement set forth in section 1 (a) of the request. Finally, we find that the request for establishment specifies clearly that Article 366 of the FCCP and Articles 68 and 97 of the Act are the specific measures at issue, and we thus reject Mexico's request in this respect.

(b) Lack of Identity between the Request for Consultations and the Request for Establishment

7.38 Mexico asserts that the request for establishment contains a number of violations of Agreement provisions which were not mentioned in the request for consultations and on which, it argues, no consultations were held. This aspect of Mexico's request for a preliminary ruling concerns the extent to which Articles 4.5 and 4.7 of the DSU as well as Article 17.4 of the AD Agreement provide that the permissible scope of the request for establishment is limited by the scope of the request for consultations.

7.39 Articles 4.5 and 4.7 of the DSU provide as follows:

Article 4

Consultations

> 5. In the course of consultations in accordance with the provisions of a covered agreement, before resorting to further action under this Understanding, Members should attempt to obtain satisfactory adjustment of the matter.
>
> [...]
>
> 7. If the consultations fail to settle a dispute within 60 days after the date of receipt of the request for consultations, the complaining party may request the establishment of a panel. The complaining party may request a panel during the 60-day period if the consulting parties jointly consider that consultations have failed to settle the dispute.

7.40 Article 17.4 of the AD Agreement provides:

> 17.4 If the Member that requested consultations considers that the consultations pursuant to paragraph 3 have failed to achieve a mutually agreed solution, and if final action has been taken by the administering authorities of the importing Member to levy definitive anti-dumping duties or to accept price undertakings, it may refer the matter to the Dispute Settlement Body ("DSB"). When a provisional measure has a significant impact and the Member that requested consultations considers that the measure was taken contrary to the provisions of paragraph 1 of Article 7, that Member may also refer such matter to the DSB.

7.41 In our view, these provisions do not in any way require a complete identity between the scope of the request for consultations and the request for establishment, nor do they, in our view, limit the scope of the request for establishment to the exact scope of the request for consultations. While we read these provisions to require that Members should attempt to find a mutually agreed solution on the "matter" in dispute through consultations, this, in our view, only requires that request for consultations relate to the same subject matter as the request for establishment of a panel.[56] In sum, and provided the request for establishment concerns a dispute on which consultations have been requested,

---

[56] We note that, in the past, both panels and the Appellate Body reached a similar conclusion that the scope of the request for establishment need not be identical to the scope of the request for consultations. See e.g. Panel Report, *Japan – Agricultural Products II*, para. 8.4 (i); Panel report, *Brazil – Aircraft*, para. 7.9. Appellate Body Report, *Brazil – Aircraft*, para. 132:

> "132. We do not believe, however, that Articles 4 and 6 of the DSU, or paragraphs 1 to 4 of Article 4 of the SCM Agreement, require a precise and exact identity between the specific measures that were the subject of consultations and the specific measures identified in the request for the establishment of a panel. As stated by the Panel, "[o]ne purpose of consultations, as set forth in Article 4.3 of the SCM Agreement, is to 'clarify the facts of the situation', and it can be expected that information obtained during the course of consultations may enable the complainant to focus the scope of the matter with respect to which it seeks establishment of a panel.[...]" (footnote omitted).

there is no need for the matter (i.e. the specific measures at issue and the legal basis of the complaint) as identified in the request for establishment to be identical to the matter on which consultations were requested.

7.42 Mexico argues that for certain of the measures challenged no consultations were held on a number of the provisions alleged to have been violated by these measures. In particular, Mexico argued that the following provisions were not covered by the consultations but were included in the request for establishment:

Provision invoked	Paragraph in the request for establishment of a Panel
AD Article 1	Paragraphs 1(a), 1(g)
AD Article 4.1	Paragraph 1(a)
AD Article 11.2	Paragraph 2(c)
AD Article 18.1	Paragraph 2(e)
Paragraph 1 of Annex II	Paragraph 2(b)
Paragraph 3 of Annex II	Paragraph 2(b)
Paragraph 5 of Annex II	Paragraph 2(b)
Paragraph 6 of Annex II	Paragraph 2(b)
Paragraph 7 of Annex II	Paragraph 2(b)
SCM Article 12.5	Paragraph 2(b)
SCM Article 21.2	Paragraph 2(c)
SCM Article 32.1	Paragraph 2(e)
Article VI:2 of the GATT 1994	Paragraph 1(i)

7.43 In light of our finding that there is no need for a complete identity between the request for establishment and the request for consultations, we do not consider that we would not be able to rule on the alleged violations of the provisions mentioned by Mexico in the above table simply because they were not mentioned in the request for consultations. In our view, the fact that certain provisions were added to the list of alleged violations in the request for establishment compared to the request for consultations is a consequence of the consultation process which serves the purpose of clarifying the facts of the situation enabling the complainant to focus the scope of the matter with respect to which it seeks the establishment of a panel. It does not mean that no consultations were held on the matter, as the only difference between the request for consultations and the request for establishment consists of the fact that a number of closely related legal provisions alleged to have been violated were added. The measures remained the same and so did the legal basis for the complaint, as is evident from the narrative provided in the request for establishment. In our view, consultations were thus held on the matter on which the establishment of a Panel was requested. We therefore reject Mexico's request in this respect.

7.44 Mexico also argues that one claim concerning the failure to examine all relevant factors affecting the domestic industry was part of the consultations concerning the investigation on imported beef, but was not part of the consultations that took place relating to the measures imposed on imports of rice, the matter before the panel in this case.

7.45 As a factual matter, Mexico is correct that the request for consultations limits the claim concerning the failure to evaluate all relevant factors of Article 3.4 to the beef investigation.[57] However, in our view, and for the same reasons as mentioned above, as long as the request for establishment concerns a matter on which consultations were requested, there is no requirement that all the specific provisions alleged to have been violated in the request for establishment were also part of the consultations. Since consultations took place in respect of the alleged inconsistency of the injury determination in the rice investigation with Article 3 of the AD Agreement, it seems that the United States was entitled to formulate its request for establishment on the basis of any combination or subset of the legal provisions and claims relevant to the rice investigation on which consultations were held. Moreover, we note that the request for establishment refers to the "failure to *properly* evaluate the relevant economic factors" which is slightly different from the "failure to evaluate all relevant economic factors" mentioned in the request for consultations for the beef investigation. The failure to properly evaluate all factors effectively relates to the failure "to base its injury determinations on positive evidence or to conduct objective examinations of [....] the impact of the imports on domestic producers of those products" which was explicitly part of the request for consultation both with regard to the rice and the beef investigation. We therefore reject Mexico's request in this respect.

(c) Nullification or Impairment of Benefits under Article 17.5 of the AD Agreement

7.46 Mexico argues that the US request for establishment was inconsistent with Article 17.5 (i) of the AD Agreement as it failed to indicate in which way the US interests were nullified or impaired by the alleged violations.

7.47 Article 17.5 (i) of the AD Agreement provides as follows:

> "17.5 The DSB shall, at the request of the complaining party, establish a panel to examine the matter based upon:
>
> (i) a written statement of the Member making the request indicating how a benefit accruing to it, directly or indirectly, under this

---

57 The Request for Consultations (DS 295/1) reads in pertinent part as follows:

> "In particular, the United States believes that the anti-dumping measures on beef and rice are inconsistent with at least the following provisions:
>
> Article 3 of the AD Agreement, because Mexico, *inter alia*, based its injury (or threat) and causation analyses on only six months of data for each of the years examined; failed to collect or examine recent data; **failed in the beef investigation to evaluate all relevant economic factors and indices having a bearing on the state of the industry**; and failed to base its injury determinations on positive evidence or to conduct objective examinations of the volume of dumped imports, the effect of those imports on prices in the domestic market of like products, and the impact of the imports on domestic producers of those products;" (emphasis added).

Agreement has been nullified or impaired, or that the achieving of the objectives of the Agreement is being impeded, and ..."

7.48 We consider that the US request for establishment contains allegations of violation of the AD Agreement which, if demonstrated, will constitute a *prima facie* case of nullification or impairment under Article 3.8 of the DSU. In our view, since the US request for establishment describes the factual and legal circumstances alleged to constitute the asserted violations of the cited provisions of the AD Agreement in some detail, such statements suffice to "indicate how" benefits accruing to the United States under the AD Agreement have been nullified or impaired, as required by Article 17.5(i) of the AD Agreement.[58] In any case, we understand Mexico to be arguing that, *as a consequence of* the alleged inconsistencies of the US request for establishment with Article 6.2 of the DSU and Articles 4.5 and 4.7 of the DSU, the request for establishment is also inconsistent with Article 17.5 (i) of the AD Agreement. In light of our findings rejecting Mexico's allegations of inconsistency, we also reject Mexico's consequential claim of violation of Article 17.5 (i) of the AD Agreement.

3. *Conclusion*

7.49 For the reasons set forth above, we reject Mexico's request for a preliminary ruling that the US request for establishment was inconsistent with Article 6.2 of the DSU, Articles 4.5 and 4.7 of the DSU, and Articles 17.4 and 17.5 of the AD Agreement.

C. *Claims Relating to the Anti-dumping Measure on Rice*

1. *Claims relating to the Injury determination*

(a) Claim 1: Economía[59]'s use of a period of investigation that ended more than fifteen months prior to the initiation of the anti-dumping investigation and nearly three years prior to the final determination is inconsistent with Mexico's obligations under Article VI:2 of GATT 1994 and Articles 1, 3.1, 3.2, 3.4, and 3.5 of the AD Agreement

---

[58] We find support for our view in the report of the Panel in the *Mexico – Corn Syrup* case: "In our view, a request for establishment that alleges violations of the AD Agreement which, if demonstrated, will constitute a prima facie case of nullification or impairment under Article 3.8 of the DSU, contains a sufficient allegation of nullification or impairment for purposes of Article 17.5(i). In addition, as noted above, the request must indicate how benefits accruing to the complaining Member are being nullified or impaired."

Panel Report, *Mexico – Corn Syrup*, para. 7.28.

[59] Economía is the Mexican investigating authority.

(i) Arguments of the Parties

United States

7.50 The United States submits that the Mexican investigating authority failed to satisfy the legal requirements for imposing an anti-dumping measure as the period of investigation used was so remote in time that the information collected by the investigating authority (Economía) was incapable of providing a basis for an objective finding based on positive evidence of injury and the causal link between dumped imports and the injury to the domestic industry. In particular, the United States claims that the more than fifteen-month gap between the end of the period of investigation and the initiation of the investigation implied that the investigating authority's examination of volume and price effects, its examination of all relevant economic factors having a bearing on the state of the industry and Economía's determination that the dumped imports were causing injury to the domestic industry was not objective nor based on positive evidence as required by Articles 3.1, 3.2, 3.4 and 3.5 of the AD Agreement respectively.[60] By imposing AD duties in violation of the provisions of the AD Agreement, the United States submits that Economía has also violated Article 1 of the AD Agreement.

7.51 According to the United States, the purpose of an anti-dumping measure is to offset or prevent dumping that is presently causing or threatening to cause material injury to a domestic industry.[61] Therefore, the United States argues, an investigating authority is to base its determinations of dumping and injury on a period that includes the most recent available information. The United States argues that Article VI of the GATT 1994, as well as the AD Agreement require that the period of investigation should end as closely as possible to the initiation of the investigation if it is to meaningfully inform the investigating authority of dumping currently causing injury. The United States is of the view that the use of the present tense in a number of provisions of the AD Agreement, such as Articles 2, 3.4, 3.5, 3.7, and 5.8 of the AD Agreement, as well as in Articles VI.1 and VI.6 (a) of the GATT 1994 support its claim that an investigating authority must examine a period of time that is as close to the date of initiation as practicable.[62] Therefore, the United States is of the view that a period of investigation which ends more than 15 months prior to the initiation of the investigation does not allow the investigating authority to make an objective determination based on positive evidence of dumping which is causing injury.[63] The United States asserts that the Mexican investigating authority did not provide any justification based on record evidence as to the choice of the particular period of investigation apart from the fact that this was the period of investigation suggested by the ap-

60 US First Submission, para. 61.

61 US First Submission, para. 57. US Second Submission, para. 9.

62 US First Submission, para. 56. The United States considers there is support for this view in the Recommendation Concerning the Periods of Data Collection for Anti-Dumping Investigations, G/ADP/6, adopted 5 May 2000 of the WTO Committee on Anti-Dumping Practices.

63 The period of investigation ended in August 1999, while the investigation was initiated only in December of the following year, 11 December 2000. The application had been filed in June 2000.

plicants, nor did it explain why it was not possible to use more recent data or to update the injury data during the course of the investigation.[64] The United States therefore requests the Panel to find that Economía's use of a stale period of investigation in its anti-dumping investigation of US long-grain white rice breached Articles 1, 3.1, 3.2, 3.4, 3.5 of the AD Agreement and Articles VI.2 and VI.6 (a) of the GATT 1994.[65]

Mexico

7.52 Mexico asserts that Economía complied with all the requirements of Articles 3.1, 3.2, 3.4, 3.5 of the AD Agreement and made an objective determination based on positive evidence of the volume and price effects of dumped imports, their overall impact on the domestic industry, and the causal relationship between the dumped imports and the injury to the domestic industry. Mexico considers that the AD Agreement does not impose any guidelines on the period of data collection to be used for the determination of dumping and injury. Mexico is of the view that the aim of an anti-dumping measure is to offset or prevent dumping - which does not necessarily have to occur in the present – that causes or threatens to cause injury to the domestic industry.[66] Mexico considers that the AD Agreement does not impose any limits on the remoteness of the period of investigation.[67] It is of the view that is desirable but not mandatory for the period of investigation to be as close as practicable to the date of initiation of an anti-dumping investigation.[68] According to Mexico, only the circumstances of the case can determine what period is appropriate for the investigation and in this particular instance, Mexico considers that the period used was suitable since it yielded objective data on dumping, injury and the causal link between the two.[69] Mexico emphasises that the period of investigation was not "selected" by the investigating authority, but rather that it was a period suggested by the applicant which complied with a number of criteria,[70] and that no one demonstrated that it would be incorrect to maintain this period. In Mexico's view, it was therefore not for the investigating authority to raise any such objections either.[71]

---

[64] US Answers to Questions from the Panel following the First Substantive Meeting with the Parties, ("First Answers to Questions"), paras. 3 and 7. The United States considers that the necessity for an investigating authority to consider events that happened in the past does not give an authority free rein to choose which past to consider. US First Answers to Questions, para. 4.

[65] US Second Submission, para. 18.

[66] Mexico First Submission, para. 44. Mexico's Answers to Questions from the Panel following the Second Substantive Meeting with the Parties ("Second Answers to Questions"), question 4.

[67] Mexico First Answers to Questions, question 2.

[68] Mexico Second Submission, para. 23.

[69] Mexico Second Submission, para. 22.

[70] In its Second Answers to Questions, Mexico clarified that the investigating authority examines whether the period suggested by the applicant a) covers at least 6 months; b) is accompanied by information and proof; c) is the same as the period for which information with regard to normal value and export price is provided by the applicant. Mexico Second Answers to Questions, Question 1.

[71] Mexico Second Submission, para. 35.

(ii) Analysis

7.53 We start our analysis by recalling the undisputed facts on the record. The Mexican investigating authority examined data for a period of investigation covering March to August 1999 for purposes of its dumping determination, and March to August 1997, 1998, and 1999 for purposes of its injury analysis. The investigation was initiated on 11 December 2000, 15 months after the end of the period of investigation. Final anti-dumping measures were imposed on 5 June 2002, a little less than three years after the end of the period of investigation. The United States claims that the use of a period of investigation by the Mexican investigating authority in this case ending 15 months prior to initiation is not consistent with the AD Agreement. The United States argues that such a "stale" period of investigation did not provide the investigating authority with positive evidence and did not allow the authority to make an objective determination of injury, as required by Articles 3.1, 3.2, 3.4 and 3.5 of the AD Agreement, as such outdated data are uninformative of the current state of the domestic industry. According to the United States, Mexico therefore also acted in a manner inconsistent with Article 1 of the AD Agreement and Article VI of the GATT 1994.

7.54 We start our analysis with Article 3.1 of the AD Agreement which sets forth the general requirement for making an injury determination. It provides as follows:

> 3.1 A determination of injury for purposes of Article VI of GATT 1994 shall be based on positive evidence and involve an objective examination of both (a) the volume of the dumped imports and the effect of the dumped imports on prices in the domestic market for like products, and (b) the consequent impact of these imports on domestic producers of such products.

7.55 Articles 3.1 of the AD Agreement thus requires that the injury determination be based on positive evidence and that it involve an objective examination. In our view, positive evidence is in the first place evidence which is material to the case at hand, in other words it is to be relevant and pertinent with respect to the issue to be decided. It is positive which make it "evidence" as opposed to unrelated facts. In addition, it must have the characteristics of being inherently reliable and creditworthy.[72] An objective examination, in turn, requires in our view that the investigative process establishing the facts be objective and unbiased. We agree with what the Appellate Body stated in this respect in the *US – Hot-Rolled Steel* case:

> "The term "objective examination" aims at a different aspect of the investigating authorities' determination. While the term "positive evidence" focuses on the facts underpinning and justifying the injury determination, the term "objective examination" is concerned with the investigative process itself. The word "examination" re-

[72] We note that in the *US – Hot-Rolled Steel* case, the Appellate Body stated that:

> "The word 'positive' means, to us, that the evidence must be of an *affirmative*, *objective* and *verifiable* character, and that it must be *credible*." Appellate Body Report, *US – Hot-rolled Steel*, para.192. (emphasis added).

> lates, in our view, to the way in which the evidence is gathered, inquired into and, subsequently, evaluated; that is, it relates to the conduct of the investigation generally. The word "objective", which qualifies the word "examination", indicates essentially that the "examination" process must conform to the dictates of the basic principles of good faith and fundamental fairness."[73]

7.56 The choice of the period of investigation is obviously crucial in this investigative process as it determines the data that will form the basis for the assessment of dumping, injury and the causal relationship between dumped imports and the injury to the domestic industry.

7.57 It is clear that the AD Agreement does not contain any specific and express rules concerning the period to be used for data collection in an anti-dumping investigation. As acknowledged by Mexico, this does not mean that the authorities' discretion in using a certain period of investigation is boundless. Mexico considers that it would be preposterous to suggest that measures may be imposed after an investigation which was based on data relating to a period of investigation which ended ten years ago, and accepts that it would be desirable that the period of investigation end as closely as practicable to the date of initiation of the investigation. While we do not need to decide in the abstract whether the period of investigation always has to end as close as practicable to the date of initiation of the investigation, we are of the view that there is necessarily an inherent real-time link between the investigation leading to the imposition of measures and the data on which the investigation is based. We find strong textual support for this view in Article VI of the GATT 1994, as well as a number of provisions of the AD Agreement:

Article VI.2 of the GATT 1994 provides that:

> "In order to offset or prevent dumping, a contracting party may levy on any dumped product an anti-dumping duty not greater in amount than the margin of dumping in respect of such product".

Article 11 of the AD Agreement similarly provides that:

> "An anti-dumping duty shall remain in force only as long as and to the extent necessary to counteract dumping which is causing injury".

In addition, Article 3.5 of the AD Agreement states that:

> "It must be demonstrated that the dumped imports *are*, through the effects of dumping, as set forth in paragraphs 2 and 4, *causing injury* within the meaning of this Agreement. [...]". (emphasis added)

7.58 We are of the view that these provisions are clear textual evidence that measures may be imposed to offset dumping presently causing injury. The terms "offset" and "counteract" connote the concept of a current reaction against a prevailing (i.e. existing and present) force. Thus, if an anti-dumping duty may be imposed only to "offset" dumping, and only for "as long as necessary" to "coun-

[73] Appellate Body Report, *US – Hot-Rolled Steel*, para. 193.

teract" dumping, it is clear that this is an entitlement to act that is itself strictly conditioned on the active presence of its reciprocal - in this case, injurious dumping that is taking place at that time. There is therefore an inherent real-time link between the imposition of the measure and the conditions for application of the measure, dumping causing injury. The use of the present tense in Article 3.5 of the AD Agreement is clear evidence of this temporal connection between what is investigated and what needs to be demonstrated in order to allow the imposition of measures, i.e. that dumped imports *are causing* injury. Of course, it is well established that the data on the basis of which this determination is made may be based on a past period, known as the period of investigation. Nevertheless, because this "historical" data is being used to draw conclusions about the current situation, it follows that the more recent data is likely to be inherently more relevant and thus especially important to the investigation. This, as a consequence, implies that the data considered concerning dumping, injury and the causal link should include, to the extent possible, the most recent information, taking into account the inevitable delay caused by the need for an investigation, as well as any practical problems of data collection in any particular case.

7.59 We find contextual support for this proposition in other provisions of the AD Agreement, such as Article 14 dealing with anti-dumping actions on behalf of a third country. Article 14.2 of the AD Agreement provides as follows:

> "14.2 Such an application [for an anti-dumping action on behalf of a third country] shall be supported by price information to show that the imports are being dumped and by detailed information to show that the alleged dumping *is causing injury* to the domestic industry concerned in the third country. The government of the third country shall afford all assistance to the authorities of the importing country to obtain any further information which the latter may require." (emphasis added)

7.60 In other words, Article 14.2 of the AD Agreement provides that the evidence in an application to start an anti-dumping action on behalf of a third country is offered to show that dumping is *presently causing injury* to the domestic industry of the requesting country. If such is the case in respect of applications for third country anti-dumping actions, it seems reasonable to conclude that a similar temporal requirement exists when the anti-dumping proceedings relate to injury being caused to a Member's own domestic industry.[74]

[74] We consider that further contextual support can be found in the Agreement on Safeguards, and Article 2.1 of the Agreement on Safeguards in particular. This provision allows for the imposition of safeguard measures if it has been determined that a product is being imported into the country's territory in such increased quantities and under such conditions as to cause or threaten to cause serious injury to the domestic industry. As the Appellate Body noted in the *Argentina – Footwear (EC)* case (para. 130):

> "[...] In our view, the use of the present tense of the verb phrase "is being imported" in both Article 2.1 of the *Agreement on Safeguards* and Article XIX:1(a) of the GATT 1994 indicates that it is necessary for the competent authorities to examine recent imports, and not simply trends in imports during the past five years – or, for that matter, during any other period of several years.[130] In our view, the phrase "is being imported" implies that the increase in imports must have been sudden and recent.

7.61 The AD Agreement allows Members to re-balance the injurious situation that is created by dumping. This implies that on the one side of the balance, there is injurious dumping, which is counter-balanced by the anti-dumping duty. It is therefore necessary to base a determination of dumping causing injury on data that is pertinent or relevant with regard to the current situation, taking into account the inevitable delay caused by the practical need to conduct an investigation. To impose anti-dumping duties without objectively examining relevant evidence on the dumping causing injury which is on one side of the balance would thus clearly run counter to the AD Agreement.

7.62 Finally, we note that the Committee on Anti-Dumping Practices adopted a Recommendation concerning the Periods of Data Collection for Anti-Dumping Investigations (G/ADP/6, adopted 5 May 2000) which sets forth guidelines for determining what period or periods of data collection may be appropriate for the examination of dumping and of injury. The Recommendation stipulates *inter alia* that the period of data collection should end as close to the initiation of the investigation as possible.[75] While we note that this Recommendation is a non-binding guide to the common understanding of Members on appropriate implementation of the AD Agreement, and does not add new obligations, nor detract from the existing obligations of Members under the Agreement[76], we do consider that this Recommendation provides useful support for the correct interpretation of the obligations found in the text of the AD Agreement.[77]

---

[130] The Panel, in footnote 530 to para. 8.166 of the Panel Report, recognizes that the present tense is being used, which it states "would seem to indicate that, whatever the starting-point of an investigation period, it has to *end* no later than the very recent past." (emphasis added) Here, we disagree with the Panel. We believe that the relevant investigation period should not only end in the very recent past, the investigation period should be the recent past."

We are of the view that while there are clear differences in the conditions for imposing measures under the AD Agreement and the Agreement on Safeguards, both anti-dumping and safeguard measures are based on an *investigation* which is to determine the existence of the conditions for application by using a certain period of investigation for which data will be collected. In our view, where Article 2.1 of the Safeguards Agreement explicitly provides that no measure may be imposed unless it has been demonstrated that a product is being imported in such quantities, Article VI:2 of the GATT 1994, read in conjunction with Article 2.1 and 3.5 of the AD Agreement similarly provides that no measure may be imposed unless it has been demonstrated that a product is being dumped and that these dumped imports *are causing injury* to the domestic industry.

[75] The Recommendation Concerning the Periods of Data Collection for Anti-Dumping Investigations (G/ADP/6, adopted 5 May 2000) provides in relevant part that:

"the Committee recommends that with respect to original investigations to determine the existence of dumping and consequent injury -

1. As a general rule:

(a) the period of data collection for dumping investigations normally should be twelve months, and in any case no less than six months, ending as close to the date of initiation as is practicable;" (footnote omitted).

[76] G/ADP/M/7 at para 40, G/ADP/AHG/R/7, para. 2

[77] We note that panels in the past have also referred to this Recommendation in their reasoning. See e.g. Panel report, *Guatemala – Cement II*, para. 8.266; Panel report, *US – Hot-Rolled Steel*, footnote 152; Panel report, *Argentina – Poultry Anti-Dumping Duties*, para. 7.287.

7.63 In sum, data of ten years old may well be reliable and creditworthy as to past dumping then causing injury but such data obviously are of much less relevance to the question whether that dumping is presently causing injury. Certainly, more recent data are more relevant to this question. As we discussed earlier, the AD Agreement requires that the conditions for imposing anti-dumping measures, that dumped imports are causing injury, have to be present at the time of imposition of the measure, to the extent practically possible. The requirement of a time-consuming and sometimes complicated investigation to demonstrate the existence of dumping and the ensuing injury poses a practical impediment to a complete identity in time between the imposition of the measure and the conditions for such imposition, i.e. dumping causing injury. Although this practical problem may lead to the situation in which any determination of dumping causing injury has by the time of the imposition of the measure become more of a proxy than a real time assessment of the current situation, it would, in our view, not be correct to be led by the practical necessity to examine the past to assess the present to accept that an investigating authority could justifiably base itself on old data to the exclusion of more recent data which was available and usable. To the contrary, the fact that an investigation of up to 12 months may have to be conducted to determine dumping, injury and the causal link magnifies the importance of having a period of data collection which ends as closely as possible to the date of initiation, as by the time of the possible imposition of the measure another 12 months may have passed. We established above the textual and contextual support in the GATT 1994 and the AD Agreement for this basic proposition.

7.64 In the investigation concerning imports of long-grain white rice from the United States, the period of investigation used by Mexico ended in August 1999. The application suggesting this particular period of investigation March – August 1999 was submitted by the domestic industry on 2 June 2000. The investigation was initiated only six months later, on 11 December 2000. The investigating authority accepted the period of investigation suggested by the applicants, even though at the time of initiation that period had ended more than 15 months earlier. During the investigation, no attempt was made to update any of the information obtained from the interested parties to reflect what had occurred in the 15 months between the end of the period of investigation in August 1999 and the start of the investigation in December 2000. Definitive anti-dumping measures were imposed on 5 June 2002, almost three years after the end of the period of investigation. We note that Mexico has not argued that practical problems necessitated this particular period of investigation, nor has Mexico ever argued that it was not possible for practical or other reasons to update the information to cover the 15 months or part thereof from the end of the period of investigation to the date of initiation of the investigation. As Mexico clearly stated, the applicants proposed this particular period of investigation, and it is Mexico's general practice to accept the proposed period of investigation.[78] Neither the investigating

[78] In response to the submission of data by the United States concerning Mexico's practice in this regard, Mexico explains that its practice shows delays of sometimes 6 months, on other occasions 20 months between the end of the period of investigation and the date of initiation of the investigation,

authority at the time of the investigation, nor Mexico in its arguments before us provided any other reason why more recent information was not sought. This fifteen month gap between the end of the period of investigation and the initiation of the investigation amounts to a relatively lengthy hiatus. A great deal could have happened – or changed – over a fifteen month period, and there is simply no evidence on record in respect of it. A hiatus of such a duration is, in our view, sufficiently long as to impugn the reliability of the period of investigation to deliver, for the purposes of a determination, evidence that has the requisite pertinence or relevance (see para. 7.55 *supra*). In other words, given the passage of time and the uncertainty about the factual situation in that relevant interim, the information lacks credibility and reliability, thereby failing to meet the criterion of "positive evidence" pursuant to Article 3.1 of the AD Agreement.

7.65 In light of all these considerations, we find that by choosing to base its determination of injury on a period of investigation which ended more than fifteen months before the initiation of the investigation, Mexico failed to comply with the obligation set forth in Article 3.1 of the AD Agreement to make a determination of injury which is based on positive evidence and which involves an objective examination of the volume and price effects of the alleged dumped imports or of the consequent impact of these imports on domestic producers of the like product at the time measures were imposed. We therefore find that Mexico acted in a manner which is inconsistent with Article 3.1 of the AD Agreement. As a consequence, and in light of our finding of violation of Article 3.1 of the AD Agreement which is an overarching provision that sets forth a Member's fundamental obligation with respect to injury determinations,[79] we find that Mexico acted in breach of Articles 3.2, 3.4 and 3.5 of the AD Agreement when considering the volume and price effects of the dumped imports, all relevant factors affecting the state of the industry and the causal relationship between dumped imports and the alleged injury to the domestic industry, respectively. In light of these findings, we do not consider it necessary in order to resolve this aspect of the dispute to examine the US claims of violation of Article 1of the AD Agreement and Article VI of the GATT 1994.

(b) Claim 2: Economía's limitation of its injury analysis to only six months of 1997, 1998, and 1999 is inconsistent with Mexico's obligations under Articles 1, 3.1, 3.5, and 6.2 of the AD Agreement

(i) Arguments of the Parties

United States

---

depending on the period of investigation the applicant is proposing. The data submitted by the United States, which were not contested by Mexico, show that, on average, the period of investigation ends 10 months before the date of initiation, which is also 8 months less than was the case in the rice investigation.

[79] See Appellate Body Report, *Thailand – H-Beams*, para. 106.

7.66 The United States argues that the selective use of data from only part of the year covering the peak period of import activity does not allow an investigating authority to make an objective determination based on positive evidence of injury caused by dumped imports, as required by Article 3.1 of the AD Agreement. According to the United States, if an authority only considers the evidence for half of the period of investigation for the injury analysis, there is simply no way for the authority to determine the true state of the domestic industry over the course of the entire period of investigation, and thus no way to conclude that the authority's examination is consistent with Article 3.1 of the AD Agreement.[80]

7.67 The United States submits that the information on which the determination is based which ignores half of each of the three years of the period of investigation does not constitute positive evidence. In addition, the United States submits, by ignoring the period September – February of each year, Economía disregarded the portion of the year when domestic production of milled rice was at its seasonal high, and import penetration at its seasonal low.[81] The United States submits that Economía agreed with the applicants that imports were concentrated during the period March to August and consequently limited its injury analysis to the data for March – August of each of the years at issue in the investigation.[82] In any case, and even if imports had not been concentrated in the March to August time period, the United States is of the view that by limiting its injury analysis to only half of the period of investigation, Economía's injury analysis is inconsistent with WTO rules.[83]

7.68 According to the United States, the determination cannot be objective because the period chosen covers only a very specific period of the year during which imports are at a high, and thus ignores the fact that the industry might fare better during the other period of the year. The United States argues that the requirement of making an "objective analysis" implies that "investigating authorities are not entitled to conduct their investigation in such a way that it becomes more likely that, as a result of the fact-finding or evaluation process, they will determine that the industry is injured".[84] According to the United States, to ex-

---

80 US First Answers to Questions, para. 20.

81 The United States asserts that Economía's findings with respect to at least two economic factors, market share and capacity utilization, serve to illustrate the inevitable and obvious distortions that resulted from this focussed approach. US First Submission, para. 71 – 72. The United States points to various paragraphs in Economía's published determinations in which the authority confirms that imports were concentrated in the March – August period. US First Answers to Questions, para. 15.

82 US First Submission, para. 67. According to the United States, this narrowed focus is evident throughout the preliminary and the final determinations. See US First Submission, footnote 68.

83 The United States thus emphasises that it is objecting *per se* to Economía's decision to limit the injury analysis to only half of the period of investigation, and not only to the fact that Economía limited its analysis to the period when imports were concentrated. US First Answers to Questions, para. 16 and US Oral Statement at the Second Substantive meeting of the Panel with the parties (the "Second Oral Statement"), para. 15.

84 US First Submission, para 76 quoting from Appellate Body Report, *US – Hot-Rolled Steel*, para. 196. The United States points to the analysis of capacity utilization and performance of the industry in terms of sales revenue as two examples of a flawed analysis. In the United States' view, the period not examined would likely have led to higher sales revenue, since the September – February period

amine only those parts of the year when import levels are high may overlook positive developments in other parts of the year, and thus give a misleading impression of the data relating to the condition of the industry as a whole, in breach of Article 3.1 of the AD Agreement.[85] The United States is of the view that the period of investigation for injury should include all months of the year in which there is domestic production, assuming the data is reasonably available.[86]

7.69 The United States further argues that Economía's disregard of six months worth of data for each of the three years of the period of investigation is inconsistent with the requirement of Article 3.5 of the AD Agreement to make a determination of causation based on "all relevant evidence" before the authorities. The United States submits that in the absence of an objective examination of all relevant evidence, and not just of a part of the evidence relating to the March - August period, the analysis of the causal link between the dumped imports and injury to the industry is inevitably flawed.

7.70 The United States further submits that Economía's dismissal of the concerns of exporters and importers that participated in the investigation concerning the flawed period of investigation, prevented them from pointing to evidence from the missing months that might have supported their views. This, the United States argues, is inconsistent with Article 6.2 of the AD Agreement. Finally, the United States argues that as a consequence of the breaches of Articles 3.1 and 3.5, Article 1 of the AD Agreement is also violated.

Mexico

7.71 Mexico argues that the AD Agreement does not provide for any rules on how the period of investigation for the injury analysis should be integrated in the anti-dumping investigation. Mexico asserts that Economía gathered all the information available over a period of three years ("the period analysed"), including the year covered by the "period of investigation" for dumping purposes, March – August 1999. It then limited its comparison to strictly comparable periods, i.e. the periods in the preceding two years that covered exactly the same months as those of the "period of investigation", thereby eliminating any possible distortions in the market under analysis.[87] In any case, Mexico argues that the

---

was the time in which import volumes were low and domestic sales volumes at their seasonal high. By ignoring these data, Economía was not able to consider whether any recovery of sales revenue from October through December offset or overcompensated any decline in sales revenue relating to June- July production and reflected in the March – August data. US First Submission, para. 80.

[85] The United States finds support for its argument in the Appellate Body Report in the *US – Hot-Rolled Steel* case in which the Appellate Body found that "an examination of only parts of a domestic industry does not ensure a proper evaluation of the state of the domestic industry as a whole, and does not, therefore, satisfy the requirements of 'objective[ity]' in Article 3.1 of the Anti-Dumping Agreement". Appellate Body Report, *US – Hot-Rolled Steel*, para. 206, quoted in US First Submission, para. 82.

[86] US First Answers to Questions, para. 13.

[87] Mexico, First Answers to Questions, answer to question 3. Mexico First Submission, para. 55. In its First Submission, Mexico argued that these differences could arise from the seasonal character of the product. In its First Answers to Questions, and its Second Submission, it clarified that seasonality was not an issue in the decision to base the determination on the March – August period of each of

AD Agreement does not stipulate anything on the choice of the period of investigation for injury, leaving the investigating authority with unfettered discretion to determine itself the appropriate period of investigation for the injury analysis.[88]

7.72 Mexico rejects the United States' assertion that the period March – August is the period of highest import penetration. According to Mexico, the production of long-grain white rice is more or less constant throughout the year, as it is independent of the production cycles of paddy rice. This is so because the long-grain white rice producers will simply import the paddy rice during certain parts of the year, but this does not affect their production levels.[89] The US argument that production is much higher, and imports much lower, during the second part of the year which was not examined by Economía is, therefore, in Mexico's view, baseless.[90]

7.73 In addition, in Mexico's view, since the period of investigation was not inconsistent with any provision of the AD Agreement, there is no basis for the US argument that the injury analysis failed to examine all relevant evidence as required by Article 3.5 of the AD Agreement or that the interested parties were not given an opportunity to defend their interests. Mexico points out that the interested parties were given an opportunity to meet with parties with an opposing interest[91] and they were all given every opportunity to present their views, in accordance with Article 6.2 of the AD Agreement. In the absence of a violation of any provision of the AD Agreement, there is also no basis for the US claim of a consequential violation of Article 1 of the AD Agreement.

(ii) Analysis

7.74 The claim of the United States concerns the choice of the period of investigation for the injury analysis and the data used by the investigating authority when examining injury. The United States argues that by ignoring part of these data, Mexico failed to base its injury analysis on positive evidence and did not conduct an objective examination of the state of the domestic industry, as required by Article 3.1 of the AD Agreement. Moreover, the United States submits, Mexico violated Article 3.5 of the AD Agreement, as its determination of the existence of a causal link between the dumped imports and the alleged injury to the domestic industry was not based on all relevant evidence as half of the relevant information was ignored. Mexico on the other hand submits that the AD Agreement does not contain any obligations with regard to the period of investigation for the determination of injury and asserts that it was necessary to examine these particular six months of every year instead of the full year in order to ensure that the period of the injury analysis paralleled the six month period chosen for the analysis of dumping, so as to avoid any distortions.

---

the three years of the injury analysis only. See Mexico First Answers to Questions, question 3; Mexico Second Submission, para. 39.

88 Mexico First Submission, para. 57.

89 Mexico includes a table which demonstrates that throughout each of the years examined the domestic production levels remained stable. Mexico First Submission, para. 60.

90 Mexico adds that none of the participating exporters presented convincing reasons why the period of investigation was to be changed.

91 Mexico asserts that a hearing took place on 18 January 2002.

7.75 We note that in its Preliminary Determination the Mexican investigating authority stated that "the investigated period is March – August 1999 and, therefore, the period for injury analysis is the one between March 1997 and August 1999".[92] In response to a question from the Panel, Mexico confirmed that "the investigating authority gathered all the information available over a period of three years, including the year covered by the 'period of investigation'; however, it limited its comparison to strictly comparable periods, i.e. the periods in the preceding two years that covered exactly the same months as those of the 'period of investigation'" [for dumping]."[93] In other words, for injury purposes, the investigating authority analysed data for the months of March – August of three consecutive years, 1997, 1998 and 1999, and data from the period September – February of each of these years were disregarded.

7.76 The United States asserts that by doing so, Mexico breached its obligations under Article 3.1 of the AD Agreement and 3.5 of the AD Agreement, which provide as follows:

> 3.1 A determination of injury for purposes of Article VI of GATT 1994 shall be based on positive evidence and involve an objective examination of both (a) the volume of the dumped imports and the effect of the dumped imports on prices in the domestic market for like products, and (b) the consequent impact of these imports on domestic producers of such products.
>
> 3.5 It must be demonstrated that the dumped imports are, through the effects of dumping, as set forth in paragraphs 2 and 4, causing injury within the meaning of this Agreement. The demonstration of a causal relationship between the dumped imports and the injury to the domestic industry shall be based on an examination of all relevant evidence before the authorities. The authorities shall also examine any known factors other than the dumped imports which at the same time are injuring the domestic industry, and the injuries caused by these other factors must not be attributed to the dumped imports. Factors which may be relevant in this respect include, *inter alia*, the volume and prices of imports not sold at dumping prices, contraction in demand or changes in the patterns of consumption, trade restrictive practices of and competition between the foreign and domestic producers, developments in technology and the export performance and productivity of the domestic industry.

7.77 We note, as we have done with regard to the previous claim, that the AD Agreement does not set forth any express requirement regarding the choice of the period of investigation for the purpose of conducting an injury analysis. We are of the view, however, that the requirement to base a determination of injury on positive evidence and pursuant to an objective examination nevertheless imposed certain obligations on the Mexican investigating authorities with regard to the

---

[92] Preliminary Determination, para. 69. Exhibits US-14 and US-15.

[93] Mexico, First Answers to Questions, question 3.

completeness of the data used as the basis for its determination. In this respect, we recall that in any case under the Panel's standard of review set forth in Article 17.6 of the AD Agreement, we are to assess whether the authority's establishment of the facts was proper, and its evaluation unbiased and objective.[94] The question before us is thus whether it was proper of the Mexican investigating authority in this particular case to base its injury determination on data covering only half of the three-year period (for which, as it happens, data were actually gathered), and whether such a limited data set enabled the authority to make an objective examination of injury.

7.78 We consider that an objective examination of the facts starts with an objective and unbiased investigative process. We agree with the following statement of the Appellate Body in the *US - Hot-Rolled Steel* case summing up the requirement to conduct an "objective examination":

> "In short, an "objective examination" requires that the domestic industry, and the effects of dumped imports, be investigated in an unbiased manner, without favouring the interests of any interested party, or group of interested parties, in the investigation. The duty of the investigating authorities to conduct an "objective examination" recognizes that the determination will be influenced by the objectivity, or any lack thereof, of the investigative process". (footnote omitted).[95]

7.79 As we stated earlier, the choice of the period of investigation is crucial in this process as it determines the data that will form the basis for the assessment of the impact of dumping. An examination or investigation can only be "objective" if it is based on data which provide an accurate and unbiased picture of what it is that one is examining.

7.80 In our view, an objective examination of the effects of dumping on the state of the domestic industry which enables the authority to conclude that dumped imports caused injury to the domestic industry involves an analysis of trends over time of the volume and price of imports and of the state of the domestic industry. It is only such an analysis which will enable the authority to objectively gauge the effects of the dumped imports on the domestic industry as required by Article 3.1 of the AD Agreement, and to assess whether the injury

---

[94] We note that the Appellate Body in the *EC – Bed Linen (Article 21.5 – India)* case also linked the objective examination requirement with the panel's standard of review that requires it to examine whether the authority's establishment of the facts was proper. The Appellate Body explained in a footnote:

> "These requirements of paragraphs 1 and 2 of Article 3, as well as the requirements of Article 17.6(i), that investigating authorities establish the facts of the matter *properly* and evaluate those facts in an *unbiased and objective* manner, are mutually supportive and reinforcing. In *US – Hot-Rolled Steel*, we explained in respect of Article 17.6(i) that:
>
> … panels must assess if the establishment of the facts by the investigating authorities was *proper* and if the evaluation of those facts by those authorities was *unbiased* and *objective*. (original italics)"

Appellate Body report, *EC – Bed Linen (Article 21.5 – India)*, footnote 141

[95] Appellate Body Report, *US – Hot-Rolled Steel*, para. 193.

found to exist is caused by the dumped imports as required by Article 3.5 of the AD Agreement.

7.81 For the purposes of examining the injury to the domestic industry, the Mexican investigating authority collected data for three years, 1997, 1998, and 1999. There does not appear to have been any problems in obtaining such data for this continuous period of three years. However, in its examination of that data, it decided not to use half of the information gathered. The authority thus based its determination on data relating to six months of each of the three years of the period of investigation, the months of March to August. In our view, and absent any proper justification for doing so, such an examination on the basis of an incomplete set of data cannot be objective, nor does the selective use of certain data for the injury analysis constitute a proper establishment of the facts on which to base the determination.[96]

7.82 We wish to note in this respect that our ruling should not be read as to imply that there could never be any convincing and valid reasons for examining only parts of years. Mexico has not however presented any convincing arguments to this effect, whether in its investigation or in its arguments before us. Mexico's only argument is that it was necessary to examine only data relating to the six months from March to August because this was also the six month period chosen for the analysis of the existence of dumping.[97] We see no *a priori* reason why a period of investigation on the injury analysis should be chosen to fit the period of investigation for the dumping analysis in case the latter period of investigation covers a period of less than 12 months. In our view, there is nothing in the AD Agreement that would require such an approach, quite to the contrary. Mexico submits that in order to avoid distortions due to the differences in volume of imports, sales or production during the other six months, it used for its injury analysis a similar six month period. We do not find this to constitute a proper justification for ignoring half of the data concerning the domestic industry. In fact, it seems that what Mexico refers to as distortions are certain developments which occur in the remaining six months which perhaps undo part of the effect of the imports that entered the country during the six months that were examined. This is precisely the kind of information we consider it is necessary to examine in order for the determination to be that of an objective and unbiased investigating authority.

7.83 In fact, we recall that the applicants suggested this particular six month period of March – August 1999 as it reflected the period of highest import penetration.[98] The Mexican investigating authority itself confirms this in the Preliminary Determination, stating that, in accordance with the information provided by

---

[96] Our finding in this respect is made independent of the question as to the biased nature of the choice for these specific six months chosen.

[97] In its First Submission, Mexico suggested that its choice of period of investigation was justified for reasons relating to the seasonality of the product concerned. Mexico has not, however further developed this argument and has subsequently clarified that seasonality was not an issue in this case. See Mexico First Answers to Questions, question 3; Mexico Second Submission, para. 39.

[98] Application for initiation of an anti-dumping investigation regarding imports of long-grain white rice from the United States, page 34. Exhibit US–8.

the applicant, "imports tend to be concentrated during the period from March to August every year, which corresponds to the investigated period proposed by the petitioner".[99] While we acknowledge that the authority was in this quote discussing the imports of paddy rice, the raw material for the production of the subject long-grain white rice, it clearly accepted the link made between production of paddy rice and the imports of the final product which the applicant points out is mainly imported in the period March – August. As the applicant claimed, during this period paddy rice is not harvested and for that reason this period adequately reflects the import activity.[100]

7.84 In our view, there are some similarities between the failure to examine part of the year for which data were collected, and the situation discussed by the Appellate Body in the *US – Hot-Rolled Steel* case involving an analysis of only a segment of the domestic industry, rather than the domestic industry as a whole. The Appellate Body found that an examination of only certain parts of a domestic industry does not ensure a proper evaluation of the state of the domestic industry as a whole, and does not, therefore, satisfy the requirements of "objectiv[ity]" in Article 3.1 of the Anti-Dumping Agreement.[101] We consider that the following reasoning of the Appellate Body leading to this conclusion is equally applicable to the situation before us in which an important part of the year in which the domestic industry was fully operational was disregarded in the injury analysis:

> "204. We have already stated that it may be highly pertinent for investigating authorities to examine a domestic industry by part, sector or segment. However, as with all other aspects of the evaluation of the domestic industry, Article 3.1 of the *Anti-Dumping Agreement* requires that such a sectoral examination be conducted in an "objective" manner. In our view, this requirement means that, where investigating authorities undertake an examination of one part of a domestic industry, they should, in principle, examine, in like manner, all of the other parts that make up the industry, as well as examine the industry as a whole. Or, in the alternative, the investigating authorities should provide a satisfactory explanation as to why it is not necessary to examine directly or specifically the other parts of the domestic industry. Different parts of an industry may exhibit quite different economic performance during any given period. Some parts may be performing well, while others are performing poorly. To examine only the poorly performing parts of an industry, even if coupled with an examination of the whole industry, may give a misleading impression of the data relating to the industry as a whole, and may overlook positive developments in other parts of the industry. Such an examination may result in highlighting the negative data in the poorly per-

[99] Preliminary Determination, para. 65. Exhibits US -14 and US-15.
[100] Preliminary Determination, para. 64. Exhibits US -14 and US-15.
[101] Appellate Body Report, *US – Hot-Rolled Steel*, para. 206.

> forming part, without drawing attention to the positive data in other parts of the industry. We note that the reverse may also be true – to examine only the parts of an industry which are performing well may lead to overlooking the significance of deteriorating performance in other parts of the industry."[102]

7.85 We find that the acceptance of a period of investigation proposed by the applicants because it allegedly represented the period of highest import penetration and would thus show the most negative side of the state of the domestic industry is not what can be expected of an objective and unbiased investigating authority. The question whether production was in fact lower during these months or not and whether the situation of the domestic industry was, in fact, worse during these six months or not is, in our view, irrelevant in this respect.

7.86 In sum, we find that the injury analysis of the Mexican investigating authority in the rice investigation which was based on data covering only six months of each of the three years examined, is inconsistent with Article 3.1 of the AD Agreement as it is not based on positive evidence and does not allow for an objective examination, as it necessarily, and without any proper justification, provides only a part of the picture of the situation. In addition, we find that the particular choice of the limited period of investigation in this case was not that of an unbiased and objective investigating authority as the authority was aware of, and accepted, the fact that the period chosen reflected the highest import penetration, thus ignoring data from a period in which it can be expected that the domestic industry was faring better.

7.87 As a consequence, we also find that Mexico acted inconsistently with Article 3.5 of the AD Agreement as it failed to base its determination of the existence of a causal relationship between the dumped imports and the alleged injury to the domestic industry on *all relevant evidence* before the authorities, as required by Article 3.5 of the AD Agreement.

7.88 In light of our findings on Article 3.1 and 3.5 of the AD Agreement, we do not find it necessary to address in this context the US claim under Article 1 of the AD Agreement and Article 6.2 of the AD Agreement. That is, having determined that the measure at issue is inconsistent with the cited Articles, and exercising the discretion implicit in the principle of judicial economy, we do not deem it necessary to examine whether the investigation which led to the inconsistent measure was consistent with the procedural rules on providing for all interested parties a full opportunity for the defence of their interests set forth in Article 6.2 of the AD Agreement. We do not consider that this would add anything to our findings or would be useful in the implementation of our ruling.

---

[102] Appellate Body Report, *US – Hot-Rolled Steel*, para. 204.

(c) Claim 3: Economía's failure to collect the evidence on price effects and volumes that it needed to conduct its injury analysis in an objective manner is inconsistent with Mexico's obligations under Articles 3.1, 3.2, 6.8 and Annex II of the AD Agreement

(i) Arguments of the Parties

United States

7.89 The United States submits that the injury determination in as far as it concerned the volume and price effects of the dumped imports on the domestic industry was not conducted in an objective manner, nor based on positive evidence, as required by Articles 3.1 and 3.2 of the AD Agreement. With regard to the volume of dumped imports, the United States argues that Economía failed to collect the data it needed to examine in an objective manner whether there had been a significant increase in dumped imports, as required by Article 3.2 of the AD Agreement. In particular, Economía did not use the customs declarations (the "pedimentos") or seek to obtain accurate import volume information from importers. In addition, Economía rejected information from the only company found to have been dumping (the Rice Company)[103], and drew inferences about volumes and prices of dumped imports from the data provided by another company for non-dumped imports.[104] Its determination of the volume of dumped imports was therefore not objective nor based on positive evidence, in violation of Article 3.1 and 3.2 of the AD Agreement.

7.90 With regard to the examination of the price effects of the alleged dumped imports on the domestic industry, the United States submits that Economía failed to even attempt to collect information it needed to conduct a proper price analysis as required by Article 3.2 of the AD Agreement. The United States argues that the analysis under Article 3.2 of the AD Agreement of the price effects of the dumped imports entails a comparison of data concerning prices for the dumped imports on the one hand, and data concerning prices for the domestic like product on the other hand. While the AD Agreement does not require any particular methodology for making price comparisons and evaluating price effects, the United States submits that Article 3.1 of the AD Agreement requires that this analysis consist of an objective examination based on positive evidence. According to the United States, Economía chose to rely instead on biased information sources that the applicants had selected, and thus compared the actual sales values reported by the domestic producers to fictitious unit values for the

103 According to the United States, the reasons given by Economía for rejecting the information was that such information covered only the year 1999 and not also 1997 and 1998. The United States points out that Economía did accept however less accurate estimates preferred by the applicants even though those estimates also pertained only to the 1999 period of analysis. US First Submission, para. 98.

104 US First Submission, para. 97.

dumped imports that it derived using a methodology proposed by the applicant.[105]

7.91 Finally, the United States submits that Economía used facts available to determine volume and price effects of the dumped imports and relied on secondary source information, without first having made an effort to obtain the data from the interested parties. In addition, it used such data without first seeking to corroborate them against independent sources, in breach of Article 6.8 and paragraphs 1 and 7 Annex II of the AD Agreement.

Mexico

7.92 Mexico submits that Economía made an objective determination based on positive evidence of the volume of dumped imports and the effect of the dumped imports on prices, in accordance with Articles 3.1 and 3.2 of the AD Agreement. Mexico fails to see on what basis the United States is arguing that because Economía based its analysis partly on information provided by the applicant, Economía violated the Agreement.

7.93 According to Mexico, the AD Agreement does not impose a particular methodology for conducting a volume or price analysis, nor does it impose an obligation on Economía to obtain more information than such as provided by the parties, as long as it makes an objective determination based on positive evidence.[106] Mexico rejects the United States' suggestion that Economía should have take the initiative to obtain and examine the pedimentos in which it could have found more ample information on prices and sales volumes. In any case, Mexico asserts that such pedimentos are kept by the Customs Office, and were therefore not at the disposal of Economía. As such documents were not provided by the applicant either, Economía could not rely on these documents for any price and volume information. Moreover, such pedimentos would not have enabled Economía to distinguish the subject imports from other imports coming in under the same tariff heading.

7.94 Mexico is of the view that the mere fact that Economía accepted the methodology proposed by the applicant for estimating import volumes is not inconsistent with Article 3.2 of the AD Agreement, especially since the exporters concerned failed to provide the information or did not respond at all.[107] Mexico submits that the information provided by the Rice Company was not accepted for reasons of procedural equality as it only related to one of the three years of the period of investigation, while others did provide information for all three years and similar information was requested from the Rice Company without success.

---

[105] According to the United States, Economía did not request data from a broad range of importers of the products, did not request sales information on the prices at which the importers made sales to their customers, nor did it seek information from purchasers to compare the prices paid for the dumped product with the prices paid for the domestic product. By not doing so, the United States asserts that Economía did not have accurate unit value data on the dumped imports.

[106] Mexico First Submission, para. 97.

[107] Mexico takes issue with the United States' suggestion that Economía accepted from the applicant information it rejected from the exporter. Mexico argues that Economía used the applicant information and methodology as the starting point but conducted further research.

Mexico thus asserts that the determination of the volume of dumped imports and their price effect was not inconsistent with Articles 3.1 and 3.2 of the AD Agreement.

7.95 With regard to the United States' assertion that Economía was not allowed to apply facts available as it did not send questionnaires to all exporters and did not consult the pedimentos, Mexico submits that it was not required to do so by the AD Agreement. Mexico argues that there is no provision in the AD Agreement which requires an investigating authority to actively go out and seek information as part of an anti-dumping investigation. Mexico argues that under Article 6.1 of the AD Agreement the investigating authority can, but is not obliged to send questionnaires to all the foreign producers and exporters. Mexico complied with its obligations under Article 6.1.3 of the AD Agreement by sending the notice of initiation and the forms for producers and exporters to the known exporters and to the US authorities, and published the notice of initiation. Mexico argues that the only customs document that the investigating authority had in its possession were the excerpts of the customs declarations, also known as the "listados". As these listados did not contain the names of exporters, no other exporters than those mentioned in the application were known to Economía. The forms sent to the known exporters and the US authorities clearly indicated that facts available could be used in case the required information was not provided. In Mexico's view, Economía thus complied with Article 6.8 of the AD Agreement.

(ii) Analysis

7.96 The United States claims that Mexico failed to base the part of its injury determination relating to the trends in the volume of dumped imports and the price effects of the dumped imports on positive evidence as it failed to collect the information required to make an objective examination of injury based on positive evidence, as required by Articles 3.1 and 3.2 of the AD Agreement. In addition the United States argues that the use of secondary source information without having sought to obtain the information from the interested parties is inconsistent with Article 6.8 of the AD Agreement and Annex II thereto.

7.97 Articles 3.1 and 3.2 of the AD Agreement provide as follows:

> 3.1 A determination of injury for purposes of Article VI of GATT 1994 shall be based on positive evidence and involve an objective examination of both (a) the volume of the dumped imports and the effect of the dumped imports on prices in the domestic market for like products, and (b) the consequent impact of these imports on domestic producers of such products.
>
> 3.2 With regard to the volume of the dumped imports, the investigating authorities shall consider whether there has been a significant increase in dumped imports, either in absolute terms or relative to production or consumption in the importing Member. With regard to the effect of the dumped imports on prices, the investigating authorities shall consider whether there has been a sig-

> nificant price undercutting by the dumped imports as compared with the price of a like product of the importing Member, or whether the effect of such imports is otherwise to depress prices to a significant degree or prevent price increases, which otherwise would have occurred, to a significant degree. No one or several of these factors can necessarily give decisive guidance.

7.98 Article 3.1 of the AD Agreement thus requires in relevant part that an injury determination is to be based on positive evidence and involve an objective examination of the volume of the dumped imports and the effect of the dumped imports on prices in the domestic market for like products. Article 3.2 of the AD Agreement elaborates on these requirements by requiring the authority to consider whether there has been a significant increase in dumped imports and whether there has been a significant price undercutting by the dumped imports as compared with the price of a like product of the importing Member, or whether the effect has been to depress prices or prevent price increases. It is clear from reading these two provisions in combination that the basis for any evaluation as to the volume of dumped imports or the price effects of such imports has to be positive evidence. We concur with the views expressed by the Appellate Body in the *US – Hot-Rolled Steel* case, that the word "positive" means that the evidence must be of an affirmative, objective and verifiable character, and that it must be credible.[108] We wish to emphasise that our task is not to perform a *de novo* review of the information and evidence on the record, nor to substitute our judgment for that of the Mexican authorities. Rather we examine what the evidence was on which the authorities based its examination and whether the determination made was the result of an objective examination based on positive evidence. In this respect, we consider it important to recall our standard of review under the AD Agreement as set forth in Article 17.6 (i) of the AD Agreement:

> "(i) in its assessment of the facts of the matter, the panel shall determine whether the authorities' establishment of the facts was proper and whether their evaluation of those facts was unbiased and objective. If the establishment of the facts was proper and the evaluation was unbiased and objective, even though the panel might have reached a different conclusion, the evaluation shall not be overturned;"

7.99 In other words, if we find that the Mexican investigating authorities have properly established the facts and evaluated them in an unbiased and objective manner, and that the determinations rest upon a permissible interpretation of the relevant provisions, we will consider this measure to be consistent with the relevant provisions of the AD Agreement.

7.100 The authority explains how it established the volume of dumped imports of the subject product into Mexico in its final determination.[109] The final determination shows that the authorities were confronted with the problem of distinguishing first the subject rice imports (i.e. "long-grain white rice") from imports

[108] Appellate Body Report, *US – Hot-Rolled Steel*, para. 192.
[109] Final Determination, (Exhibits US-6 and US-7) paras. 206 – 261.

of all types of rice, and second the imports of the subject product that were dumped into Mexico from those imports that entered Mexico at undumped prices. The first problem arose from the fact that the tariff line under which subject imports of long-grain white rice were imported, 1006.30.01, at the time of the investigation also covered other types of rice such as medium and short grain rice, as well as glazed or parboiled rice which were not part of the investigation.[110]

7.101 The investigating authority examined various methods of extracting from the total imports that entered the country under this tariff line, those imports relating to the subject product, long-grain white rice. The authority first examined the "method using the exporters' verifiable information". The authority had requested information about long-grain white rice exports from each of the four companies that participated in the investigation. One firm replied that it had not exported and it did not provide any information. Two other companies, the Rice Company and Riceland were found to have submitted proper information for the period of investigation for the dumping analysis (1999). However, for the rest of the period of investigation (years 1997 – 1998) the authority found that only information on exports to other countries were submitted (the case of the Rice Company), or only a copy of a worksheet in which the exports of the investigated product were not clearly itemized was submitted (the case of Riceland). In sum, the authority considered that the only company to provide correct information for the whole period of investigation was Farmers Rice, whose exports increased by 303.7 per cent in the 1998 March – August period compared to the previous corresponding period and by 12.3 per cent during the investigated period in 1999 in relation to the previous comparable period.[111] The authority considered that two of the three participating companies did not provide accurate information for the whole investigated period, and decided for that reason not to use the information submitted by these two companies. Instead, it established that the variation observed in the case of Farmers Rice was an acceptable indicator of the behaviour of the exports by the two other participating firms, Riceland and the Rice Company.

7.102 We consider it important to note at this juncture that the authority found no dumping margin for Farmers Rice, allegedly the only company that provided full information and of which the imports were used as an indicator of the volume of dumped imports. No dumping margin was found with respect to imports from Riceland either, a company whose exports the authority states represented

---

[110] As becomes clear from, for example, para. 7 of the Notice of Initiation (Exhibit US-2):

> "The petitioner also indicated that other types of white rice enter the country under tariff code 1006.30.01 of the Schedule in the General Import Tax Law and that these types have different characteristics from those of the product under investigation and are classified commercially in two groups: short grain rice and medium grain rice. However, the tariff description in the Schedule under the General Import Tax law is general and makes no reference to this type of classification. Thus, the customs declarations do not differentiate the type of rice that is entering the United Mexican States."

[111] Final Determination (Exhibits US-6 and US-7), paras. 226 – 227.

an important proportion of imports from the United States into Mexico under tariff line 1006.30.01.[112]

7.103 For determining the volume of imports from companies other than the four participating firms, the authority decided to use the methodology proposed by the applicant:

> "229. ... [T]he Ministry found that the petitioner submitted a method that intends to differentiate some products from others for the purpose of calculating the dumping margin. This method is based on the confidence interval analysis. For this, the behavior of long grain rice prices on the one hand and of the prices of short grain and medium grain rice on the other were observed in the United States of America during the investigated period. Thus, the medium grain and short grain rice group had a minimum price of $0.458 U.S. dollars per kilogram and a maximum price of $0.509 dollars per kilogram. Finally, the CMA indicated that, based on the above, presumably any importation made at a price above 0.458 dollars per kilogram would be of rices different from the investigated one, while those imports made at prices below such amount would correspond to long grain rice.
>
> 230. With this information as a starting point, and as was established at paragraph 221 of the preliminary determination, unquestioned by any of the interested parties, the Ministry calculated the volume of imports that would correspond to these price levels, and it subtracted the result from the total volume of imports from the United States of America that entered into the Mexican territory under tariff section 1006.30.01 of what was then the *Tarifa de la Ley del Impuesto General de Importación* during the investigated period. The above was carried out taking the *listado de pedimentos de importación* of the SIC-M, from which they eliminated those transactions with a price above $0.458 US dollars per kilogram. In this way, the Ministry considered that the rest of the imports could correspond to long grain white rice, which was not disproved during the investigation."[113]

7.104 In sum, the methodology proposed by the applicant was that rice imported below a certain price level was to be treated as the subject product, long-grain white rice, while rice imported above that price was not. The authority explained that it decided to use this methodology, even though it presented the important shortcoming that it failed to provide accurate information on the periods prior to the period of investigation used for dumping purposes, i.e. for the years 1997-1998.[114] While in the case of the exporting firms that participated in the investi-

---

[112] Final Determination (Exhibits US-6 and US-7), para. 228.

[113] Final Determination (Exhibits US-6 and US-7), paras. 229 – 230.

[114] The authority made the following statement in para. 232 of the Final Determination:

> "We have to point out that, when analyzing the information from which the above concepts are inferred, the Ministry found that the price of the long grain rice in the

gation, this failure to provide accurate information for the years 1997-1998 implied that they were assumed to all have behaved in the same manner as the one exporter that provided full and accurate data (Farmers Rice), in applying the applicant's method the authority overcame this problem of lack of accurate data for the years 1997 – 1998 by simply assuming that the level of imports of the subject product in the total imports of all types of rice during the years of 1997 and 1998 was the same as in the year 1999:

> "239. [T]he Ministry decided that the best methodology in order to make this estimate [on the volume of imports from the United States] was the one presented by the CMA [the petitioner]; however, such methodology, as noted in paragraph 232 of this determination, *could only identify long grain white rice imports corresponding to the investigated period [of 1999] and cannot be extrapolated to previous similar periods. Therefore, the Ministry decided it was appropriate to consider that the investigated imports, as they were estimated in paragraph 230 of this determination, maintained the same participation in the total imports coming from the United States of America.*[…]." (emphasis added)

7.105 On this basis the authority established that the investigated imports increased 8.6 per cent in the period March-August 1998 in relation to the same period in the previous year, and increased 3.4 per cent during the dumping investigation period in relation to the previous comparable period. We recall that with regard to the level of imports from the examined exporters, the authority found, on the basis of the assumption that all exporters behaved in a manner similar to Farmers Rice, that the exports to Mexico from the companies that appeared in the investigation increased 303.7 per cent and 12.3 per cent in the analyzed periods.[115]

7.106 The authority then addressed the second problem of separating the volume of dumped subject imports from non-dumped subject imports, and found as follows:

> "243. Article 3.2 of the Anti-dumping Agreement states that it shall be considered whether there has been a significant increase in dumped imports. In order to comply with this article the Ministry made two groups of imports:
>
> a) The imports that will be subject to a residual dumping margin, that is the group obtained from subtracting, from the investigated imports, which correspond solely to long grain white rice, the volume of exports made by the exporting companies that participated in the investigation, and

United States of America was not always below the price of the other types of rice, as is stated in paragraph 224 of the preliminary determination. Therefore the Ministry considers that this estimation method cannot be used consistently during the periods previous to the investigated one". Final Determination (Exhibits US-6 and US-7), para. 232.

[115] Final Determination (Exhibits US-6 and US-7) para. 241.

> b) The exports made by The Rice Corporation, for which a dumping margin of 3.93 per cent was established. *The sum of these two data groups corresponds to the dumped imports.*
>
> 244. Based on what is set forth in the above paragraph, the Ministry observed that these imports decreased 3.2 per cent in the period March-August 1998 in relation to the previous comparable period and increased 1.2 per cent in the investigated period in relation to the same period of the previous year. Thus, the Ministry concluded that the dumped imports increased in the investigated period, in terms of articles 64(I) of the Regulations of the Foreign Trade Act, and 3.2 of the Anti-dumping Agreement." [116] (emphasis added)

7.107 In other words, the authority took the total volume of imports of the subject product and subtracted from that amount the imports from the exporters that participated in the investigation and for which no dumping margin was found.

7.108 With regard to the analysis of the evolution of prices of the subject imports and their effects on domestic prices, the investigating authority first concluded that the prices of dumped imports were decreasing in the following manner:

> "[A]s the price of all kinds of rice decreased during the investigated period and as the export price of Farmers Rice Milling also decreased, it is reasonable to conclude that the prices of the remaining imports, including the dumped imports, decreased. This argument was not refuted by any of the parties during the proceeding."[117]

7.109 In examining the effects on domestic prices, the authority reasoned as follows:

> "285. The Ministry found that during the investigated period, dumped imports were 17.8 per cent below the domestic price of the previous comparable period, and 24.2 per cent below that which existed in the period March-August 1997.
>
> [...]
>
> 294. Based on the aforementioned, the Ministry observed a decline in the prices of the domestic products that coincided with a decrease in the prices of the imports from the United States of America, dumped or not – although the prices of the dumped imports were 6.5 per cent below the price of non-dumped imports -, as well as with the presence of the product from Argentina.
>
> 295. Consequently, the Ministry observed that the information that was available during the final stage of the investigation shows that the imports of the investigated product were priced below the

[116] Paras. 243 and 244 of the Final Determination (Exhibits US-6 and US-7).

[117] Final Determination (Exhibits US-6 and US-7), para. 270.

domestic product, except for the exports from Riceland Foods, Inc., which did not have a dumping margin.

296. Therefore, the Ministry determined that, during the investigated period, the dumped products were priced below the domestic product. It was also observed that the price of the dumped imports was lower than the prices of the domestic products in periods previous to the investigated period. Due to this, the Ministry determined that this situation provoked the decline in the prices of the domestic producers. Also, the Ministry considers that the entry during the investigated period of imports at reduced prices from Argentina and the decline, in the same period, of the price of non-dumped imports from the United States of America contributed to the decline in prices of the merchandise produced domestically. Thus, the Ministry determined that the dumped imports from the United States of America contributed to pressure the domestic producers to lower their prices in the investigated period."[118]

7.110 The question before us is thus whether the investigating authority based its determination on information which is affirmative, objective, verifiable and credible.[119] We are of the view that the way in which the investigating authority established the facts on the basis of which it was going to consider the trends in volume of dumped imports was not a proper establishment of the facts, for the following reasons.

7.111 As is clear from the authority's final determination, the volume analysis is not based on facts, but on assumption after assumption. The methodology of the applicant which the authority decided to use is based on the unsubstantiated assumption that rice sold below a certain price level must be long-grain white rice. Although the authority itself concludes that this was a flawed assumption[120], it decided to use this methodology. However, because the assumption apparently held true only for the investigated period of the year 1999, the authority had to make another unsubstantiated assumption, which was that in fact during the previous years the subject imports kept the same share in the total amount of imports of all types of rice from the United States. We recall that these assumptions were used in order to establish the trends in the volume of the imports of the subject product, long-grain white rice from the United States, without any distinction between the dumped and the non-dumped imports.

7.112 In parallel with the applicant's methodology for the determination of the volume trends of subject imports, the authority determined the trends in the volume of imports from the examined exporters. The authority first rejected the information provided by two of the three exporters examined, among which the

---

118 Final Determination (Exhibits US-6 and US-7), paras. 285 and 294 - 296.

119 Appellate Body Report, *US – Hot-Rolled Steel*, para. 192:

"The term 'positive evidence' relates, in our view, to the *quality* of the evidence that authorities may rely upon in making a determination. The word "positive" means, to us, that the evidence must be of an *affirmative, objective* and *verifiable* character, and that it must be *credible*." (emphasis added)

120 Final Determination (Exhibits US-6 and US-7), para. 232.

Rice Company, the only company of these three for which a positive margin of dumping was established, and again based its conclusion as to their volume of subject imports on an unsubstantiated assumption, i.e. the assumption that all examined firms' export volumes showed a similar trend to that of the exporter which provided full three year volume information, Farmers Rice. We note that no margin of dumping was established with regard of exports from this company, Farmers Rice. On the basis of all these assumptions, the authority then determined the volume of dumped imports by subtracting all imports from the three examined exporters from the total amount of assumed subject imports, and adding the imports from the one examined company for which a margin for dumping was found, the Rice Company. It is clear that the authority did not base itself on positive evidence, but on, in our view unjustified, assumptions, and the authority has therefore failed to properly establish the facts. We do not wish to imply by this that an authority is never allowed to complete its analysis by drawing certain inferences, provided it offers a well reasoned explanation. However, we are of the view that the investigating authority did not do this in this case. Actually, it appears that in making its assumptions, the investigating authority consistently chose to make assumptions which negatively affected the exporters' interests. In our view, the authority could just as readily have concluded the exact opposite from the facts on which it based its assumptions. For that reason as well, we consider that the Mexican authority failed to conduct an objective examination of the volume of the dumped imports.

7.113 With regard to the basis for the authority's finding on the price decrease of the dumped imports, we come to much the same conclusions. We consider that an investigating authority conducting an objective and unbiased investigation could not have reached the conclusion that prices of dumped imports were decreasing on the basis of the flawed analysis based on unsubstantiated assumptions made by the Mexican investigating authority. In the statement on price decreases quoted above, the authority compares three types of prices: (a) export price of all types of rice (both subject rice and non-subject rice), (b) export price of Farmers Rice, and (c) the export price of the "remaining imports, including the dumped imports". We recall that Farmers Rice is "the only exporter to present information related to the entire investigated period, although this company did not have a margin of dumping"[121]. Thus, the logic of Economía is that because the price of a broader category of rice – i.e. category (a) - declined, and because the prices of one participating exporter of the subject product, who was not found to have been dumping, decreased, the third category of rice – (c) or "dumped imports" - is a sub-set of the first category of rice, and this third category of rice must have declined also.[122] We do not consider this to be a warranted assumption on the basis of the evidence in this case. Let us assume, for arguments sake, that import of category (a) (or "all kinds of rice") represented

[121] Final Determination (Exhibits US-6 and US-7), para. 268.

[122] It goes without saying that one cannot *assume* that the price of dumped imports are *cheaper* than non-dumped imports (e.g. price of Farmers Rice). Thus, we fail to see, from the explanation given in the Final Determination (Exhibits US-6 and US-7), how the price of Farmers Rice (i.e .category (b)) fit into Economía's logic here.

100 tons, and its price declined by 7 per cent. Let us also assume that of that 100 tons, 10 tons represented "dumped imports". If the price of the latter increased 2 per cent while the price of the rest (i.e. 90 tons) decreased by 8 per cent, the price of "all kinds of rice" would still decrease by 7 per cent.[123] In our view, such flawed assumptions are clearly not "positive evidence" on which an examination of the price effects of dumped imports is to be based.

7.114 We are not convinced either that an objective and unbiased investigating authority had no choice but to base itself on the above unsubstantiated assumptions for lack of better information. The determination of dumping and injury are the result of an investigation to be conducted in an objective and unbiased manner. In our view, the Mexican investigating authority failed to comply with its obligation to determine the volume of dumped imports on the basis of positive evidence and to make an objective examination by failing to conduct a proper investigation. We consider that to conduct an "investigation" requires a proper degree of activity on the part of the competent authorities because authorities charged with conducting an inquiry or a study – to use the treaty language, an "investigation" – must actively seek out pertinent information.[124] As we will discuss later in respect of the use of facts available to unexamined exporters, we are of the view that the investigating authority failed to ensure that all interested parties were informed of the information required of them, as the authority sent questionnaires only to those exporters listed in the application and those that appeared subsequent to the initiation of the investigation. It is clear that had the authorities properly informed all interested parties the authority could reasonably be considered to have knowledge of and if it had sent questionnaires to a larger number of exporters, more, and more accurate information could have been gathered on the volume of the subject imports.

7.115 Moreover, it appears that very useful and valuable information which could have provided a more accurate basis for any assessment of the volume of the subject imports existed in the form of the pedimentos which contained all information on volume and value of the imports, the exporting enterprise, the importing enterprise, the duties and other taxes paid, the date of the transaction, the customs point of entry of the goods, the tariff line under which the transaction was conducted and so forth.[125] Even though it appears the field for entering the product description does not necessarily contain all the details of the product covered by the pedimento, and even accepting that even if all the pedimentos had been available it might not have been possible to determine with certainty the total amount of imports of the subject product, such data would in any case have constituted a more objective basis of evidence for making a reasonable estimate of the amount of dumped imports. In any case, from Mexico's answers to our questions with regard to the pedimentos, we conclude that in cases where the pedimento would have simply referred to white rice without distinguishing

---

[123] 10x(0.02)+90x(-0.08) = 100x(-0.07)

[124] We thus concur with the view expressed by the Appellate Body in the *US – Wheat Gluten* case. Appellate Body Report, *US – Wheat Gluten*, para. 53.

[125] Mexico First Answers to Questions, question 15.

whether the product imported was long-grain or other white rice, it would still be possible to find the precise product description by referring to additional documents such as the invoices issued by the exporter, bills of lading, and so forth. While we acknowledge that this would have required some additional work for the investigating authority we are of the view that the authority cannot have its cake and eat it at the same time. If an authority does not send out questionnaires to all exporters it could reasonably be expected to have knowledge of, and does not ensure that as many exporters as possible are otherwise informed of the information required by, for example, requesting the assistance of the authorities of the exporting country or known industry associations in the exporting country, then it cannot complain about the fact that it will have to become more active itself in gathering sufficient positive evidence on which to base its injury determination.

7.116 In sum, we find that the investigating authority's injury analysis with regard to the volume and price effects of dumped imports was inconsistent with the requirements of Articles 3.1 and 3.2 of the AD Agreement to conduct an objective examination based on positive evidence of the volume and price effects of the dumped imports.

7.117 In light of our findings on Articles 3.1 and 3.2 of the AD Agreement, we do not consider it necessary to continue our analysis of the US claim with regard to Article 6.8 and Annex II of the AD Agreement alleged to have been violated by the Mexican investigating authority's failure to base its determination of the volume and price effects of dumped imports on positive evidence, and make no findings in this respect.

(d) Claim 4: Economía's failure to objectively consider whether there was a *significant* increase in the volume of *dumped* imports or whether the dumped imports had a significant effect on prices is inconsistent with Mexico's obligations under Articles 3.1 and 3.2 of the AD Agreement

(i) Arguments of the Parties

United States

7.118 According to the United States, while Economía's injury analysis included a lot of discussion of the volume of imports, much of the discussion did not address the relevant dumped imports. Moreover, the United States submits, the data that reflect the calculated volumes of dumped imports show that those imports actually declined, both in absolute and relative terms during the selected three year period.[126] The United States submits that an objective and unbiased

[126] US First Submission, para. 104. The United States refers to paras. 244, 248, 254, and 259 of the Final Determination (Exhibits US-6 and US-7) which deal with dumped imports. According to the United States, these data show that the volume of dumped imports declined (para. 244), as did their share of apparent domestic consumption (para. 248) and internal consumption (para. 254). The vol-

investigating authority would not, in light of these facts have found that there was a significant increase in dumped imports, and Economía's findings in this case thus breached Article 3.2 of the AD Agreement.

7.119 The United States further argues that Economía evaluated the effect of imports on prices, but failed to consider whether their effect was "significant" as required by Article 3.2 of the AD Agreement. For that reason as well, the United States submits, Economía 's determination is inconsistent with Article 3.2 of the AD Agreement.

7.120 For these reasons, according to the United States, Economía's determination was not objective nor based on positive evidence and thus also inconsistent with Article 3.1 of the AD Agreement.

Mexico

7.121 Mexico rejects the United States' assertion that Economía failed to make an objective determination of a significant increase in the volume of imports and of the price effects of the dumped imports. Mexico argues that the significance of the increase is addressed in paragraphs 209-261 of the Final Determination, albeit in an implicit manner.[127]

(ii) Analysis

7.122 In the light of our earlier findings in respect of the authority's injury determination which we find not to have been based on positive evidence and not to have involved an objective examination, we do not find it necessary to address the US claim described above concerning the specific conclusions of the authority based on such flawed premises. That is, having determined that the authority's determination in respect of injury is inconsistent with the cited provision, and exercising the discretion implicit in the principle of judicial economy, we do not deem it necessary to examine whether certain of the conclusions of the authority gave rise to further inconsistencies in respect of that determination.

(e) Claim 5: Economía's failure to conduct an objective analysis of the relevant economic factors is inconsistent with Mexico's obligations under Articles 3.1 and 3.4 of the AD Agreement

(i) Arguments of the Parties

United States

7.123 The United States submits that Economía failed to examine "all" relevant economic factors affecting the industry, as required by Article 3.4 of the AD

---

ume of dumped imports in relation to domestic production remained flat (10.2–10.7–10.1) (para. 259). See US First Submission, paras. 105 – 109.

[127] Mexico First Submission, para. 116. By way of example, Mexico refers to para. 212 in which it was determined that total imports rose and para. 217 that showed that imports from the United States increased during the period.

Agreement. The United States refers in particular to the failure to examine the "factors affecting domestic prices", such as the quality differences or other factors affecting domestic prices such as brand reputation.

7.124 In addition, the United States submits that Economía's conclusions concerning some of the injury factors examined did not correspond with the facts on the record. In particular, Economía's conclusion that inventories increased, and market share declined are not supported by the facts on the record as found in the final determination. The United States submits that Economía's determination is therefore inconsistent with Article 3.4 of the AD Agreement, as well as Article 3.1, as it was neither objective nor based on positive evidence.

Mexico

7.125 Mexico submits that all relevant factors having a bearing on the industry were objectively examined in accordance with Articles 3.1 and 3.4 of the AD Agreement. Mexico emphasises that not one factor is determinative. With regard to the factor raised by the United States, inventories, Mexico submits that the Final Determination shows that there was a 7.3 per cent increase, even if this was preceded by a decrease.[128]

(ii) Analysis

7.126 In the light of our earlier findings in respect of the authority's injury determination which we find not to have been based on positive evidence and not to have involved an objective examination, we do not find it necessary to address the US claim described above concerning the specific aspects of this injury determination based on such flawed premises. That is, having determined that the authority's determination in respect of injury is inconsistent with the cited provision, and exercising the discretion implicit in the principle of judicial economy, we do not deem it necessary to examine whether certain aspects of the determination gave rise to further inconsistencies in respect of that determination.

(f) Claim 6: Economía's inclusion of non-dumped imports in its evaluation of volume, price effects, and the impact of the dumped imports on the domestic industry is inconsistent with Mexico's obligations under Articles 3.1, 3.2, and 3.5 of the AD Agreement

(i) Arguments of the Parties

United States

[128] Final determination (Exhibits US-6 and US-7), para. 318. Similarly, Mexico asserts, market participation was discussed in paras. 313 – 315 of the Final Determination, and the effects of imports on prices of the like product in paras. 271 -296. Mexico First Submission, para. 121.

7.127 The United States argues that Economía's injury and causation analysis examined the effects of all imports from the United States, both those that Economía acknowledged were not dumped and those that it alleged were dumped. The United States submits that Articles 3.1, 3.2 and 3.5 of the AD Agreement which govern the analysis of injury to the domestic industry caused by dumped imports, require an objective examination of the volume and effect of imports that are dumped to the exclusion of the volume and effect of imports that are not dumped.[129] Although Economía noted the data computed for the dumped imports alone, the United States argues that its examination and the final affirmative determination show that in reaching the determination, Economía considered the volume and price effects of all imports from the United States of long-grain white rice.[130] Therefore, the United States submits that Economía's failure to conduct an objective examination of the effect of the dumped imports alone is inconsistent with Articles 3.1, 3.2 and 3.5 of the AD Agreement.

Mexico

7.128 With regard to the United States' assertion that non-dumped imports were included in the assessment of the volume and price effects of imports, Mexico argues that a separate analysis is present throughout the determination of imports from the United States in general and dumped imports from the United States in particular.[131] Mexico recalls that Economía reached the conclusion that almost 75 per cent of all imports from the United States were dumped and that this was the percentage of imports that was causing injury.[132]

(ii) Analysis

7.129 In the light of our earlier findings in respect of the authority's injury determination which we find not to have been based on positive evidence and not to have involved an objective examination, we do not find it necessary to address the US claim described above concerning the specific aspects of this injury determination based on such flawed premises. That is, having determined that the authority's determination in respect of injury is inconsistent with the cited provision, and exercising the discretion implicit in the principle of judicial economy, we do not deem it necessary to examine whether certain aspects of the determination gave rise to further inconsistencies in respect of that determination.

(g) Claim 7: Economía's failure to provide in sufficient detail the findings and conclusions

[129] The United States finds support for its argument in Appellate Body Report, *EC – Bed Linen (Article 21.5 – India)*, para. 111 – 112.

[130] The United States considers that Economía's focus on all investigated imports, and not just the dumped imports, is most apparent in its discussion of the price effects. See US First Submission, paras. 120-123.

[131] Mexico refers to paras. 206 – 221 of the Final Determination (Exhibits US-6 and US-7).

[132] Mexico First Submission, para. 124.

reached on all issues of fact and law with respect to its determination of injury is inconsistent with Mexico's obligations under Article 12.2 of the AD Agreement

(i) Arguments of the Parties

United States

7.130 The United States submits that several findings in Economía's final injury determination belie an objective examination of volume, price effects, and impact, and are not adequately explained as Article 12.2 of the AD Agreement requires.[133]

Mexico

7.131 Mexico argues that the Final Determination sets forth in a detailed manner all considerations and findings on fact and law concerning dumping, injury and the causal link, in accordance with Article 12.2 of the AD Agreement.

(ii) Analysis

7.132 In light of our earlier findings pursuant to Article 3 of the AD Agreement, we do not find it necessary to address in this context the US claim under Article 12.2 of the AD Agreement. That is, having determined that the measure at issue is inconsistent with the cited Article, and exercising the discretion implicit in the principle of judicial economy, we do not deem it necessary to examine whether the investigation which led to the inconsistent measure was consistent with the procedural rules concerning notification in Article 12.2 of the AD Agreement. We do not consider that this would add anything to our findings or would be useful in the implementation of our ruling.

2. *Claims relating to the margin of dumping and the application of the measure*

(a) Claim 8: Economía's failure to exclude firms with anti-dumping margins of zero per cent from the anti-dumping measure is inconsistent with Mexico's obligations under Article 5.8 of the AD Agreement

(i) Arguments of the Parties

United States

133 The United States mentions four examples to illustrate its point. It refers by way of example *inter alia* to the failure to explain the effects of low-priced imports from Argentina which increased significantly during the period of investigation. US First Submission, para. 125.

7.133 The United States submits that Article 5.8 of the AD Agreement requires the termination of the investigation in case of a margin of dumping which is below *de minimis*. According to the United States, the term "margin" refers to the individual margin of dumping determined for each of the investigated exporters or producers.[134] The United States therefore argues that Article 5.8 of the AD Agreement requires that an investigation against an exporter is to be terminated in case the conclusion is that the exporter in question was not dumping. Economía found that two exporters, Farmers Rice and Riceland, had not been dumping during the period of investigation, but still included them in the anti-dumping measure. While a zero per cent anti-dumping duty was imposed with regard to these exporters, the United States emphasises that both exporters remain subject to subsequent reviews, and the possible application of duties in the future. The United States submits that the failure of Economía to terminate its investigation with respect to Farmers Rice and Riceland which it found not to have been dumping violates Article 5.8 of the AD Agreement.[135]

Mexico

7.134 Mexico is of the view that Article 5.8 of the AD Agreement has not been violated as the investigation demonstrated that imports from the United States had been dumped into Mexico above *de minimis* levels, and that injury was caused by such dumping. According to Mexico, Article 5.8 of the AD Agreement does not refer to the individual investigation of each exporter but to the investigation against imports from a particular country in general. Mexico considers that it suffices for one exporter to be found to have been dumping above *de minimis* level for all exporters to be included in the application of the measure, and each enterprise will be assigned the anti-dumping duty corresponding to its individual margin provided that the total volume of imports from a particular country is above the negligible level.[136] According to Mexico, Article 3.3 of the AD Agreement specifies that the basis for calculating margins of dumping in accordance with Article 5.8 applies to each country as a whole, and that Article 5.8 thus does not in any way establish that firms with *de minimis* margins of dumping should be excluded from the measure.[137] Moreover, Mexico is of the view that a zero per cent duty level does not *de facto* constitute an anti-dumping duty, as it cannot cause any disadvantage to the exporter concerned. Further, Mexico argues that there is nothing in the AD Agreement which prohibits that exporters be submitted to a review even if the exporters did not dump during the original period of investigation.[138] If the drafters had wanted to prohibit such reviews, they would have done so explicitly. Mexico therefore asserts that to

---

[134] The United States finds support for this definition in the Appellate Body report, *US – Hot – Rolled Steel*, para 118.

[135] The United States further notes that the investigating authority took no steps to examine whether the weighted average margin of all exporters was greater than *de minimis* when it decided to impose the anti-dumping measure. US First Answers to Questions, para. 62.

[136] Mexico First Answers to Questions, question 20.

[137] Mexico Second Submission, para. 138.

[138] Mexico asserts that in case a review demonstrates that there is no dumping, the exporter will continue to enjoy a 0 per cent duty level.

include Riceland and Farmers Rice in the anti-dumping measure in respect of long-grain white rice from the United States was not inconsistent with Article 5.8 of the AD Agreement.

(ii) Analysis

7.135 The United States claims that by not excluding from the definitive anti-dumping measure two US exporters which were found to have exported at un-dumped prices, Mexico violated Article 5.8 of the AD Agreement, which provides as follows:

> 5.8 An application under paragraph 1 shall be rejected and an investigation shall be terminated promptly as soon as the authorities concerned are satisfied that there is not sufficient evidence of either dumping or of injury to justify proceeding with the case. There shall be immediate termination in cases where the authorities determine that the margin of dumping is *de minimis*, or that the volume of dumped imports, actual or potential, or the injury, is negligible. The margin of dumping shall be considered to be *de minimis* if this margin is less than 2 per cent, expressed as a percentage of the export price. The volume of dumped imports shall normally be regarded as negligible if the volume of dumped imports from a particular country is found to account for less than 3 per cent of imports of the like product in the importing Member, unless countries which individually account for less than 3 per cent of the imports of the like product in the importing Member collectively account for more than 7 per cent of imports of the like product in the importing Member. [139]

7.136 The first sentence of Article 5.8 of the AD Agreement requires an authority to reject an application and terminate an investigation promptly as soon as the authorities are satisfied that there is not sufficient evidence of either dumping or injury. The second sentence requires the immediate termination (of the investigation) in cases where the authorities determine that the margin of dumping is *de*

[139] In French, Article 5.8 provides in relevant part as follows:

> "Une demande présentée au titre du paragraphe 1 sera rejetée et une enquête sera close dans les moindres délais dès que les autorités concernées seront convaincues que les éléments de preuve relatifs soit au dumping soit au dommage ne sont pas suffisants pour justifier la poursuite de la procédure. La clôture de l'enquête sera immédiate dans les cas où les autorités détermineront que la marge de dumping est *de minimis* ou que le volume des importations, effectives ou potentielles, faisant l'objet d'un dumping, ou le dommage, est négligeable.[...]"

In Spanish, Article 5.8 reads in relevant part:

> "La autoridad competente rechazará la solicitud presentada con arreglo al párrafo 1 y pondrá fin a la investigación sin demora en cuanto se haya cerciorado de que no existen pruebas suficientes del dumping o del daño que justifiquen la continuación del procedimiento relativo al caso. Cuando la autoridad determine que el margen de dumping es *de minimis*, o que el volumen de las importaciones reales o potenciales objeto de dumping o el daño son insignificantes, se pondrá inmediatamente fin a la investigación. [...]."

minimis or that the volume of dumped imports, actual or potential, or the injury is negligible. The third sentence then continues by explaining that the margin of dumping is *de minimis* if it is less than 2 per cent, expressed as a percentage of the export price. The fourth sentence provides that the volume of dumped imports is negligible if the volume of dumped imports from a particular country is found to account for less than 3 per cent of imports of the like product in the importing Member.

7.137 In our view, in the AD Agreement the term "margin of dumping" refers to the individual margin of dumping of an exporter or producer rather than to a country-wide margin of dumping. This is evidenced by Article 6.10 of the AD Agreement which provides that "the authorities shall, as a rule, determine an individual margin of dumping for each known exporter or producer concerned of the product under investigation".[140] As the text of Article 6.10 of the AD Agreement makes clear, this provision provides for the general rule of calculating an individual margin of dumping for each known exporter or producer. The exception to this rule is the case in which there are too many foreign producers or exporters so that an individual margin of dumping will only be calculated for a representative sample, while for the other non-sampled producers or exporters, Article 9.4 of the AD Agreement determines what the maximum amount of the duty is that can be applied to them. In sum, both the general rule and the exception to the rule provide for the calculation of individual margins of dumping, and do not envisage the calculation of a country-wide margin.

7.138 We examined the rest of the AD Agreement to see whether there is anything in the Agreement that contradicts this conclusion that the term margin of dumping in the AD Agreement is company-specific rather than country-wide. Article 8.1 of the AD Agreement concerning price undertakings as an alternative to the imposition of an anti-dumping duty provides that proceedings may be suspended or terminated without the imposition of provisional measures or anti-dumping duties upon receipt of satisfactory voluntary undertakings from any exporter to revise its prices, and stipulates that the price increases under such undertakings shall not be higher than necessary to eliminate the margin of dumping. It is clear that in this provision as well, the term margin of dumping referred to is exporter-specific, and does not refer to the average margin of dumping for all exports from all producers or exporters of a country.

7.139 Article 9.3 of the AD Agreement provides that the amount of the anti-dumping duty shall not exceed the margin of dumping as established under Article 2. Article 2 of the AD Agreement provides a definition of dumping and sets forth the manner in which a margin of dumping is to be established under the AD Agreement. A number of references to the "exporter or producer under investigation" in Article 2, for example in Article 2.2.1.1, 2.2.2, and 2.3 of the AD Agreement, make explicit the generally accepted understanding that Article 2 of

[140] If an individual margin cannot be determined for each known exporter for practical reasons, the Agreement allows the authorities to sample and calculate an individual margin for the sampled exporters.

the AD Agreement prescribes the manner in which an individual margin of dumping for an exporter or producer under investigation is to be determined.[141]

7.140 Article 9.5 of the AD Agreement requires the authorities to promptly carry out a review for the purpose of determining individual margins of dumping for any exporters or producers in the exporting country who have not exported the product to the importing Member during the period of investigation. This Article as well clearly refers to individual margins of dumping. Article 12.2.1 of the AD Agreement requires that the public notice of a preliminary or final determination include, *inter alia*, the "margins of dumping established and a full explanation of the reasons for the methodology used in the establishment and comparison of the export price and the normal value under Article 2". The term margins of dumping is in this context clearly used to refer to the margins of dumping calculated for each individual exporter, as required by Article 6.10 of the AD Agreement. In other words, whenever the Agreement refers to the determination of a margin of dumping, it refers to the margin of dumping determined for the individual exporter. In fact we note that Mexico does not appear to disagree with our understanding as it calculates individual margins of dumping for all exporters participating in the investigation, including even those that did not export during the period of investigation. Therefore, we are of the view that the investigation which is to be immediately terminated under the second sentence of Article 5.8 of the AD Agreement is the investigation in respect of the individual exporter for which a zero or *de minimis* margin was established.

7.141 We also consider relevant in this respect the fact the second sentence requires the immediate termination of the investigation in case the margin of dumping is *de minimis* or the *volume of dumped imports is negligible.* According to Article 5.8 of the AD Agreement, negligibility is to be determined in respect of the volume of dumped imports "*from a particular country*". In short, in Article 5.8 of the AD Agreement, the margin of dumping is juxtaposed to the volume of dumped imports. While it is expressly stipulated that the latter is to be examined on a country-wide basis, no such stipulation is made with regard to the margin of dumping. This further confirms our view that the reference to the margin of dumping in Article 5.8 of the AD Agreement is, as is the case in the other provisions of the AD Agreement referred to above, a reference to the individual margin of dumping which is to be determined on an exporter-specific basis.[142]

7.142 We further find support for our reading that Article 5.8 of the AD Agreement in relevant part requires the termination of the investigation in respect of an individual exporter in the Panel report in the *US – DRAMs* case which also reached the conclusion that the *de minimis* rule in Article 5.8 of the AD Agreement concerns the question whether an individual exporter will be subject to an anti-dumping order. The panel in that case concluded that the *de*

---

[141] We note that it is indeed the general practice among WTO Members, including Mexico, to calculate an individual margin of dumping, rather than country-wide margins of dumping.

[142] We note that in any case Mexico did not argue that an investigation has to be terminated if the country-wide dumping margin is below *de minimis*, but rather that such an investigation does not need to be terminated as soon as there is one exporter or producer found to have been dumping.

minimis rule of Article 5.8 did not apply in the context of the duty assessment procedure of Article 9.3 as had been argued by Korea in that case, and found that:

> "6.90 [...]As explained above, we consider that the text of Article 5.8, when read in its context, does not require that a Member apply the Article 5.8 *de minimis* test in an Article 9.3 duty assessment procedure. In any event, there are possible logical explanations for applying different *de minimis* standards in investigations and Article 9.3 duty assessment procedures. Article 5.8 requires the termination of investigations in cases where the margin of dumping is *de minimis. Thus, in the context of Article 5.8, the function of the de minimis test is to determine whether or not an exporter is subject to an anti-dumping order. In the context of Article 9.3 duty assessment procedures, however, the function of any de minimis test applied by Members is to determine whether or not an exporter should pay a duty.* A *de minimis* test in the context of an Article 9.3 duty assessment procedure will not remove an exporter from the scope of the order. Thus, the implications of the *de minimis* test required by Article 5.8, and any *de minimis* test that Members choose to apply in Article 9.3 duty assessment procedures, differ significantly. Accordingly, we are not convinced that Korea's policy argument requires us to abandon our conclusion that the text of Article 5.8, when read in its context, does not require that a Member apply the Article 5.8 *de minimis* test in an Article 9.3 duty assessment procedure." (underlining added)[143]

7.143 Mexico argues that termination of the investigation is only required when all of the margins of dumping for all exporters or producers are below *de minimis*. We do not find this argument convincing. If this had been the intention of the drafters of the Agreement, they would certainly have used the plural and would have required the immediate termination of the investigation in cases where the authorities determine that the margins of dumping **are** *de minimis*. They did not do so. It is clear, however, that if all of the margins of dumping are below *de minimis*, the overall investigation would have to be terminated and no measures could be imposed at all. But we do not consider it justified to deduce from that the conclusion that as long as there is *one* exporter found to have been dumping above *de minimis* levels, the investigation can continue against *all* exporters or producers concerned.

7.144 Mexico submits that, even if the panel were to agree with the United States on the interpretation of Article 5.8, Mexico's application of the AD order to the two exporters found not to have been dumping at a zero per cent duty rates, did not really constitute the application of a measure and was fully consistent with Article 9.3 of the AD Agreement. We understand Mexico to argue that as long as Economía respects the requirement of Article 9.3 that no duty in excess of the margin of dumping be imposed, there is nothing in the Agreement

[143] Panel Report, *US – DRAMs*, para. 6.90.

which prohibits the inclusion of non-dumping exporters in the Anti-dumping measure. We do not find these arguments convincing. Article 5 of the AD Agreement is entitled "Initiation and subsequent investigation" and concerns the investigation to determine whether or not an exporter or producer of the subject product may be subject to an anti-dumping order. We are of the view that in this context Article 5.8 of the AD Agreement requires the termination of the investigation, and thus the exclusion from the anti-dumping order of any exporter or producer with a below *de minimis* margin of dumping. This, in our opinion, is the essential difference between Article 5.8 of the AD Agreement and Article 9.3 of the AD Agreement which deals with the amount of the duty to be imposed and collected, after it has been established that a duty may be applied to the exporter or producer in question. To accept Mexico's argument that the application of a zero per cent duty does not really constitute the imposition of a measure as it complies with Article 9.3 of the AD Agreement would moreover render Article 5.8 of the AD Agreement meaningless. Indeed, it would not be a violation of Article 9.3 of the AD Agreement to impose a duty at 0.5 per cent if that was the margin of dumping for the exporter concerned, but doing so would clearly be inconsistent with the requirement of Article 5.8 of the AD Agreement to terminate the investigation in case of a *de minimis* dumping margin. As convincingly explained by the Panel in the *US – DRAMs* case, both provisions serve a different purpose and compliance with Article 9.3 of the AD Agreement does not equal compliance with Article 5.8 of the AD Agreement.[144]

7.145 In sum, we find that by not terminating the investigation against two US exporters which the authority found to have exported at undumped prices and by not excluding these two exporters from the application of the definitive anti-dumping measure, Mexico acted in a manner which is inconsistent with Article 5.8 of the AD Agreement.

[144] The EC, as a third party, argued that requiring an authority to terminate an investigation against those exporters found not to be dumping above *de minimis* levels and excluding them from the measure could lead to the need to have a parallel investigation against the same product from the same country soon after the application of the measure, as the excluded exporters could use the imposition of the duty to start dumping into the market if the investigating country. This would be so because no administrative or changed circumstances reviews would apply to such exporters, once they had been excluded from the application of the measure. We do not find this scenario to be very likely. If the exporters were able to compete in the market during the period of investigation without dumping, and this while others were engaging in dumping practices, we do not consider that it would be necessarily so that such exporters would start dumping their products, once an anti-dumping duty is in place, as this anti-dumping duty has indirectly also increased their competitive position. It thus seems that it could be argued that there is actually even less reason for them to engage in dumping than before the duty was in place. Be all that as it may, scoping out concerns about practical consequences – whether plausible or otherwise – does not in any event constitute a basis to go against the plain meaning of the text. An exporter whose dumping margin is found to be de minimis is, under the Agreement, effectively returned to precisely the same position as an exporter which is not dumping. The Agreement – otherwise drafted – could have provided for some differentiation of treatment as between these cases. But it does not in fact do so. It is not our place to read into the text provisions which invent distinctions that are not in fact there.

(b) Claim 9: Economía's application of an adverse facts available-based dumping margin to the non-shipping exporter Producers Rice is inconsistent with Mexico's obligations under Articles 6.2, 6.4, 6.8, 9.4, and 9.5 of the AD Agreement and Paragraphs 3, 5, 6, and 7 of Annex II

(i) Arguments of the Parties

United States

7.146 According to the United States, Economía 's decision to apply an adverse facts available margin to the US firm Producers Rice is inconsistent with Article 6.8 and Annex II of the AD Agreement since Economía acknowledged that this US firm, which did not export the subject product to Mexico during the period of investigation, fully cooperated with the authorities. As Producers Rice did not refuse access to, and did not otherwise fail to provide necessary information, nor significantly impeded the investigation, the application of a facts available margin was inconsistent with Article 6.8 of the AD Agreement. In addition, the United States considers that Economía failed to comply with a number of the requirements laid down in Annex II of the AD Agreement. In particular, the United States submits that, in breach of paragraph 3 of Annex II, Economía failed to take into account when making its determination that Producers Rice was a fully cooperative respondent. Moreover, the United States argues, it is clear from Annex II of the AD Agreement that Economía has to play an active role in informing the parties of the kind of information required, as well as of the consequences of not providing the information or of not cooperating. In the United States' view, Economía failed to inform Producers Rice of the fact that its questionnaire response or the explanations and evidence provided therein were in any way unacceptable, nor did Economía solicit any further explanations or evidence from this firm. In the absence of compliance by Economía with this duty to inform, the determination of a dumping margin based on facts available is inconsistent with Article 6.8 and paragraph 6 of Annex II. In addition, there was no evidence that this producer failed to act to the best of its ability and the application of facts available was thus also in violation of paragraph 5 of Annex II. Finally, and in the absence of any basis to conclude that the exporter in question failed to cooperate with Economía, the use of adverse facts available was clearly inconsistent with paragraph 7 of Annex II.[145] In addition, the United States claims that Economía breached paragraph 7 of Annex II also for another reason. According to the United States, because Economía failed to check the presumptions embodied in the application against independent data available during the investigation, much less to exercise "special circumspection" in its application of

[145] The United States argues that the margin of 10.18 per cent was adverse as it was almost triple the highest margin found for the three exporters examined and each component of the margin was based on flawed data and unsupported assumptions that served to increase the dumping margin. US First Submission, para. 159-164.

the information and presumptions therein, the Mexican investigating authority breached paragraph 7 of Annex II.[146]

7.147 In addition, the United States argues that by imposing a residual duty rate on this cooperative exporter which was completely based on adverse facts available, Economía acted in a manner which is inconsistent with Article 9.4 of the AD Agreement which requires that the neutral residual duty rate for non-investigated exporters be determined on the basis of the weighted average of the dumping margins found to exist but with the exclusion, *inter alia*, of margins based on facts available. In light of the fact that the residual duty rate applied to Producers Rice was on the contrary exclusively based on adverse facts available, the United States is of the view that Economía acted in a manner which is inconsistent with Article 9.4 of the AD Agreement.

7.148 Furthermore, the United States submits that the application of an anti-dumping duty based on adverse facts available to an exporter which did not export during the period of investigation is inconsistent with Article 9.5 of the AD Agreement which requires Economía to conduct an expedited review in order to determine an individual margin of dumping for exporters which did not export during the period of investigation, and which would otherwise be covered by the neutral residual duty that applied to the product. The United States argues that the firms seeking review under Article 9.5 of the AD Agreement when entering the export market would have previously been subject to an all-others dumping margin calculated under Article 9.4, and not as a "facts available" margin calculated under Article 6.8 of the AD Agreement.[147] The United States considers that the placement of Article 9.5 of the AD Agreement immediately after Article 9.4 of the AD Agreement as well as the textual link between Article 9.5 of the AD Agreement and the requirement of determining an individual margin of dumping provided for in Article 6.10 of the AD Agreement confirm its view. Moreover, the United States submits that by considering Producers Rice to have been investigated, assigning it a facts available-based margin, and considering it thus as an exporter subject to AD duties, Economía has precluded this firm from receiving a review under Article 9.5 of the AD Agreement, and thus breached that provision.

7.149 Finally, the United States submits that Economía breached Article 6.2 and 6.4 of the AD Agreement by failing to disclose to this exporter, Producers Rice, the export price information that was used in the calculation of the adverse facts available margin. According to the United States, under Article 6.4 of the AD Agreement, Economía should have made the abstract of the customs declaration ("listado"), on which the export price was based, available to Producers Rice. The United States submits that this was information which was obviously relevant to the presentation of this firm's case, was used by the authorities, and was

---

[146] According to the United States, Mexico conceded in its First Answers to Questions, answers to question 25, that it did not observe the requirements of paragraph 7 of Annex II, when it applied the facts available to Producers Rice, claiming that it was under no obligation to do so. US Second Submission, para. 83.

[147] US First Submission, para. 172.

not confidential. Economía's failure to provide the exporter an opportunity to prepare presentations on the basis of this information breached Article 6.4 of the AD Agreement and as a consequence Economía also acted in a manner inconsistent with Article 6.2 of the AD Agreement.

Mexico

7.150 With regard to the application of facts available to Producers Rice, Mexico submits that Article 6.8 of the AD Agreement clearly provides that in case information necessary for the calculation of the margin is not provided, the determination may be based on the facts available. According to Mexico, Producers Rice did not provide export price information which is necessary for the calculation of a dumping margin, and the authority was thus entitled under Article 6.8 of the AD Agreement to resort to the facts available for the calculation of the margin of dumping. Since Producers Rice failed to provide necessary information, its general cooperation in the investigation becomes irrelevant for the purpose of applying Article 6.8 of the AD Agreement.

7.151 Mexico further considers that paragraph 3 of Annex II of the AD Agreement dealing with the use of best information available was not violated either as no verifiable information on the export price, which under paragraph 3 is to be taken into account, was provided by Producers Rice. Economía's application of facts available was not inconsistent with paragraph 5 of Annex II of the AD Agreement either, as no information was provided. With regard to the obligation of paragraph 6 of Annex II of the AD Agreement to inform the party concerned that its information was not accepted, Mexico submits that no violation occurred as Economía did accept all the information, but the information submitted simply did not allow for the calculation of a margin.[148] Neither does Mexico consider Economía's use of facts available to have been inconsistent with paragraph 7 of Annex II as all it did was to calculate a duty based on the facts available including those contained in the application for initiation, in accordance with paragraph 1 of Annex II of the AD Agreement.

7.152 In addition, Mexico argues that there is no requirement to apply the neutral rate of Article 9.4 of the AD Agreement to the non-shipping exporter as Article 9.4 of the AD Agreement only applies in case the authorities have limited their investigation and have sampled certain exporters. That was not the case in the rice investigation. According to Mexico, the AD Agreement does not regulate how the anti-dumping duty should be calculated for exporters that have no exports during the period of the investigation.[149] Mexico rejects the US argument that a general obligation exists to calculate a neutral all others rate to the non-shipping exporters which could be deduced from Article 9.5 of the

[148] Mexico considers that Economía took account of the company's assertion that it had no exports of the subject product during the investigation, and thus did not reject any information from this company. According to Mexico, para. 6 of Annex II of the AD Agreement applies only in case the information provided is rejected by the authority, which was not the case in the rice investigation, as no information was provided in the first place.

[149] Mexico First Answers to Questions, question 24.

AD Agreement relating to new shipper reviews. The fact that Article 9.5 of the AD Agreement comes immediately after Article 9.4 of the AD Agreement cannot be read to imply that before a new shipper review under Article 9.5 of the AD Agreement is undertaken, the margin to be applied is to be calculated in accordance with the methodology set forth in Article 9.4 of the AD Agreement.

7.153 With regard to the US claims under Article 6.2 and 6.4 of the AD Agreement, Mexico argues that the information from the "listado" documents referred to by the United States was part of the investigation file and thus available to the parties.[150]

(ii) Analysis

7.154 The United States claims that the investigating authority's calculation of a margin of dumping based on the facts available for a US firm which did not export the subject product during the period of investigation was inconsistent with the AD Agreement, as this firm responded to the questionnaire and fully cooperated with the authority. According to the United States a "neutral" all others rate under Article 9.4 of the AD Agreement should have been calculated for this non-shipping exporter. Mexico submits that Article 9.4 of the AD Agreement is simply not relevant to this situation which did not involve the use of a sample by the investigating authority. Mexico argues that in case the authorities are not provided with the necessary information to calculate a dumping margin, facts available under Article 6.8 of the AD Agreement may be used. In the Final Determination itself, the Mexican authorities explicitly relied on Article 6.8 of the AD Agreement, and cited to this provision as the basis for their determination of a margin for Producers Rice.

7.155 We first deal with the United States claim that the residual duty for Producers Rice should have been determined on the basis of the methodology described in Article 9.4 of the AD Agreement.

7.156 Article 9.4 of the AD Agreement provides that:

> 9.4 When the authorities have limited their examination in accordance with the second sentence of paragraph 10 of Article 6, any anti-dumping duty applied to imports from exporters or producers not included in the examination shall not exceed:
>
> > (i) the weighted average margin of dumping established with respect to the selected exporters or producers or,
> >
> > (ii) where the liability for payment of anti-dumping duties is calculated on the basis of a prospective normal value, the difference between the weighted average normal value of the selected exporters or producers and the export prices of exporters or producers not individually examined,
>
> provided that the authorities shall disregard for the purpose of this paragraph any zero and *de minimis* margins and margins estab-

[150] Mexico, Second Submission, para. 165.

> lished under the circumstances referred to in paragraph 8 of Article 6. The authorities shall apply individual duties or normal values to imports from any exporter or producer not included in the examination who has provided the necessary information during the course of the investigation, as provided for in subparagraph 10.2 of Article 6.

7.157 We consider that Article 9.4 of the AD Agreement deals with the very specific and defined situation of the use of a sample by the investigating authority. As the first sentence sets forth, the limits imposed by the methodology provided for by Article 9.4 (i) and (ii) of the AD Agreement apply in case the authorities have limited their examination in accordance with the second sentence of paragraph 10 of Article 6.[151] The second sentence of Article 6.10 provides that:

> "[I]n cases where the number of exporters, producers, importers or types of products involved is so large as to make such a determination impracticable, the authorities may limit their examination either to a reasonable number of interested parties or products by using samples which are statistically valid on the basis of information available to the authorities at the time of the selection, or to the largest percentage of the volume of the exports from the country in question which can reasonably be investigated".

7.158 For this particular situation, Article 9.4 of the AD Agreement provides a specific methodology with regard to the calculation of the duty for those interested parties that did not form part of the sample. We see no requirement to apply that methodology in a case which does not involve sampling. In our view, Article 9.4 of the AD Agreement simply does not apply to any other situation.

---

[151] Article 6.10 of the AD Agreement reads as follows:

> 6.10 The authorities shall, as a rule, determine an individual margin of dumping for each known exporter or producer concerned of the product under investigation. In cases where the number of exporters, producers, importers or types of products involved is so large as to make such a determination impracticable, the authorities may limit their examination either to a reasonable number of interested parties or products by using samples which are statistically valid on the basis of information available to the authorities at the time of the selection, or to the largest percentage of the volume of the exports from the country in question which can reasonably be investigated.
>
> 6.10.1 Any selection of exporters, producers, importers or types of products made under this paragraph shall preferably be chosen in consultation with and with the consent of the exporters, producers or importers concerned.
>
> 6.10.2 In cases where the authorities have limited their examination, as provided for in this paragraph, they shall nevertheless determine an individual margin of dumping for any exporter or producer not initially selected who submits the necessary information in time for that information to be considered during the course of the investigation, except where the number of exporters or producers is so large that individual examinations would be unduly burdensome to the authorities and prevent the timely completion of the investigation. Voluntary responses shall not be discouraged.

7.159 The US argument that the placement of this provision immediately preceding Article 9.5 of the AD Agreement dealing with new shipper reviews implies that its rules also apply to non-shipping exporters is not convincing, as we do not find that anything can be deduced in and of itself from the sequence of provisions in the Agreement, particularly when the provision in question relates to an exceptional situation, while the subsequent provision does not. The United States also argues that the non-sampled interested parties and the new shippers dealt with by Article 9.5 are in a similar position and that by analogy the same Article 9.4 methodology for the calculation of a residual duty rate should apply.[152] We are not convinced that the text of the Agreement supports this view. In this respect, we find particularly relevant, the absence of any cross-referencing in Article 9.5 of the AD Agreement dealing with new shippers to the calculation methodology of Article 9.4 of the AD Agreement. This absence of cross-referencing is particularly conspicuous if one were to accept, *arguendo*, the analogous situation of non-sampled and non-shipping exporters. Indeed, especially in such a situation, one would expect the drafters to have explicitly referred to Article 9.4 of the AD Agreement. As on other occasions, where the drafters intended to see obligations apply in similar circumstances, they explicitly provided for such cross-referencing.[153] We recall in this respect that the Appellate Body also found that the absence of such cross-referencing to obligations contained in other provisions is revealing of the absence of such an obligation.[154] We find that Article 9.4 of the AD Agreement does not refer to non-shipping exporters outside a sampling situation, and that there was therefore no obligation for the Mexican authorities to calculate a residual duty margin for Producers Rice based on the "neutral" methodology set forth in Article 9.4 of the AD Agreement. We therefore reject the US claim in this respect.

7.160 The United States further claims that the Mexican investigating authority acted in breach of Article 6.8 of the AD Agreement when resorting to the use of facts available to calculate a duty rate for the non-shipping exporter, Producers Rice. The United States points in particular to the full co-operation offered by Producers Rice in responding to the questionnaire. Mexico asserts that the authority was entitled to base the calculation of a dumping margin for Producers Rice on the facts available provided by the applicant and that it complied with all

---

[152] The United States argues that both are in a similar position because the non-shipping exporter is in a way in the same situation as the non-sampled producers in the sense that it could not provide the information necessary to calculate a dumping margin, not because it was never asked to submit such information, as is the case with non-sampled exporters, but because it did not export. Such non-shipping exporters should thus similarly not be "punished" for the fact that it was not possible for the authority to establish an individual margin. Therefore, and rather than applying a facts available rate, a neutral residual rate should apply to them, one which as Article 9.4 requires, excludes all margins established on the basis of facts available.

[153] Examples of such cross-referencing of obligations in the AD Agreement can be found in Article 7.5 on provisional measures stating that the relevant provisions of Article 9 shall be followed; Article 11.4 dealing with reviews and cross-referencing to the provisions of Article 6 regarding evidence and procedure.

[154] See Appellate Body Report, *US – Carbon Steel*, para. 69.

the requirements concerning the use of the facts available under Article 6.8 of the AD Agreement when calculating a margin of dumping for Producers Rice.[155]

7.161 The Final Determination explains the treatment accorded to Producers Rice in the following manner:

> "Producers Rice Mill Inc. stated that it did not make any exports of the investigated product during the investigated period, due to which the Ministry qualified it according to the facts of which it had knowledge, which are described in paragraphs 138 to 157 of this determination"[156]

7.162 The Final Determination further provides the following explanation for the particular method used for the calculation of the dumping margin:

> "For the company Producers Rice Mill, Inc., in accordance with paragraph 62 of this determination, and the other companies that did not appear in this phase of the investigation, in accordance with articles 6.8 of the Anti-dumping Agreement and 54 of the Foreign Trade Statute, the ministry calculated the dumping margin applicable to long grain white rice based on the information submitted by the petitioner, and in accordance with the methodology that is described in the following paragraphs, and that corresponds to paragraphs 36 to 54 of the Initial determination of the anti-dumping investigation published in the Federation Official Gazette dated December 11 2000."[157]

7.163 It is clear therefore that the investigating authority considered that it was entitled under Article 6.8 of the AD Agreement to calculate a margin of dumping for Producers Rice on the basis of the facts available. We will therefore examine whether the investigating authority complied with the obligations set forth in Article 6.8 of the AD Agreement in this case.[158]

7.164 Article 6.8 of the AD Agreement provides as follows:

> 6.8 In cases in which any interested party refuses access to, or otherwise does not provide, necessary information within a reasonable period or significantly impedes the investigation, preliminary and final determinations, affirmative or negative, may be made on the basis of the facts available. The provisions of Annex II shall be observed in the application of this paragraph.

---

[155] We note that both parties agree that Producers Rice is an interested party in the investigation even if it has not exported during the period of investigation.

[156] Final Determination, para. 62. Exhibits US -6 and US-7.

[157] Final determination, para. 138. Exhibits US-6 and US-7.

[158] We are mindful of the fact that the AD Agreement does not expressly provide specific guidelines as to the way in which to deal with the calculation of the rate for new shippers, and that it could be argued that Article 6.8 of the AD Agreement actually does not govern the situation of the non-exporting party. However, in light of Mexico's position both at the time of the investigation, and in the proceedings before us that Article 6.8 of the AD Agreement does apply, and that the authority was complying with Article 6.8 of the AD Agreement when determining a margin of dumping for Producers Rice, we will examine the United States' claim on the assumption that Article 6.8 of the AD Agreement applies to this situation.

7.165 Paragraph 7 of Annex II provides as follows:

ANNEX II

BEST INFORMATION AVAILABLE IN TERMS OF PARAGRAPH 8 OF ARTICLE 6

> 7. If the authorities have to base their findings, including those with respect to normal value, on information from a secondary source, including the information supplied in the application for the initiation of the investigation, they should do so with special circumspection. In such cases, the authorities should, where practicable, check the information from other independent sources at their disposal, such as published price lists, official import statistics and customs returns, and from the information obtained from other interested parties during the investigation. It is clear, however, that if an interested party does not cooperate and thus relevant information is being withheld from the authorities, this situation could lead to a result which is less favourable to the party than if the party did cooperate.

7.166 Article 6.8 of the AD Agreement thus allows for determinations to be made on the basis of facts available, but only in case an interested party "refuses access" to necessary information within a reasonable period, or "otherwise does not provide" such information within a reasonable period, or when it "significantly impedes" the investigation. Article 6.8 of the AD Agreement further stipulates that when resorting to the use of facts available, the provisions of Annex II shall be observed. Annex II, entitled "Best Information Available in Terms of Paragraph 8 of Article 6" contains a number of obligations the investigating authority has to comply with in order for the use of facts available in a given case to be in accordance with Article 6.8 of the AD Agreement.[159] The use of the term "*best* information" means that information has to be not simply correct or useful *per se*, but the most fitting or "most appropriate"[160] information available in the case at hand. Determining that something is "best" inevitably requires, in our view, an evaluative, comparative assessment as the term "best" can only be properly applied where an unambiguously superlative status obtains. It means that, for the conditions of Article 6.8 of the AD Agreement and Annex II to be complied with, there can be no better information available to be used in the particular circumstances. Clearly, an investigating authority can only be in a position to make that judgement correctly if it has made an inherently comparative evaluation of the "evidence available". This is reinforced, in our view, by the requirement in paragraph 3 of Annex II that all information which is verifiable, which is

[159] Article 6.8 of the AD Agreement requires that the provisions of Annex II of the AD Agreement be observed in the use of facts available, and the use of facts available in a manner which is inconsistent with Annex II is thus also inconsistent with Article 6.8 of the AD Agreement.

[160] New Shorter Oxford Dictionary, p. 218.

appropriately submitted and supplied in a timely fashion is to be taken into account when determinations are made. In similar vein, paragraph 5 of Annex II does not allow an authority to disregard information, even though that information is not ideal in all respects, provided the interested party has acted to the best of its ability. Finally, and perhaps most importantly, such a conclusion is evident from the requirement set forth in paragraph 7 of Annex II that, in case the authorities have to base their findings on information from a secondary source they should do so with special circumspection, and check, where practicable, the information from other independent sources at their disposal, such as published price lists, official import statistics and customs returns and from the information obtained from other interested parties during the investigation.

7.167 We recall that the non-shipping exporter, Producers Rice was identified by the applicant as a "known exporter" in the application. The investigating authority sent a questionnaire to Producers Rice requesting it to provide necessary information on normal value and export price which would enable the authority to calculate a margin of dumping for this company. Producers Rice responded to the questionnaire, stating that during the period of investigation it had not exported the subject product to Mexico. Producers Rice did provide comments on the question of injury to the domestic industry. The investigating authority determined that a margin based on the facts available was to be calculated for Producers Rice due to the fact that it did not make any exports during the investigated period.[161] Assuming, *arguendo*, that an authority would be entitled to apply the facts available in the calculation of a margin of dumping in such a situation as this, we consider that the manner in which the facts available were used in this investigation with regard to Producers Rice was not in accordance with Article 6.8 and Annex II of the AD Agreement. The Final Determination demonstrates that the facts available margin was arrived at on the basis of the information contained in the application. In effect, the explanation provided for in the Final Determination as to the use of the applicant's information as the basis for calculating the 10.18 per cent facts available margin is exactly the same as that given in the Notice of Initiation.[162][163] We note that this margin is much higher than any margin calculated for the exporters that were individually examined.[164] In examining the record, we find no basis to consider that the authority made any attempt to check the applicant's information against information obtained from other interested parties or undertook the evaluative, comparative assessment that would have enabled the authority to assess whether the information provided by the applicant was indeed the *best* information available. Nor for that matter can it be said that it used the applicant's information with "special circumspection" as

---

[161] Final Determination, para. 62. Exhibits US-6 and US-7.

[162] Compare paras. 139 – 157 of the Final Determination (Exhibits US-6 and US-7) with paragraphs 36-54 of the Notice of Initiation (Exhibits US-1 and US-2). Paragraph 157 of the Final Determination explicitly acknowledges as much, by referring back to the above quoted para. 138 of the Final Determination.

[163] The authority discusses how it reached the facts available margin of 10.18 % in paras. 138-156 of the Final Determination (Exhibits US-6 and US-7).

[164] We note that for two exporters no dumping margin was found, while for a third exporter a margin of 3.93 per cent was calculated.

required by paragraph 7 of Annex II. From the record we conclude that the authority relied on data provided by the applicant in the application concerning normal value and export price, and that the record shows no attempt to examine the applicant's information to assess whether this information was the most fitting or appropriate for making determinations with regard to Producers Rice. In sum, it is clear from the record that the authority did not check the information obtained from other interested parties during the investigation, or used the information provided by the applicant with special circumspection, as required by paragraph 7 of Annex II.

7.168 For all these reasons, we find that the Mexican investigating authority calculated a margin of dumping on the basis of the facts available for Producers Rice in a manner which is not consistent with Article 6.8 of the AD Agreement, read in light of paragraph 7 of Annex II of the AD Agreement. In light of this finding we do not consider it necessary to consider the US claims under paragraphs 3, 5, and 6 of Annex II, and Article 9.5 of the AD Agreement. Nor do we consider it necessary for the resolution of the dispute to examine the US claims concerning Articles 6.2 and 6.4 of the AD Agreement. That is, having determined that the measure at issue is inconsistent with the cited provision, and exercising the discretion implicit in the principle of judicial economy, we do not deem it necessary to examine whether the investigation which led to the inconsistent measure was consistent with the procedural rules of Articles 6.2 and 6.4 of the AD Agreement.

(c) Claim 10: Economía's application of an adverse facts available-based dumping margin to the US producers and exporters that it did not investigate is inconsistent with Mexico's obligations under Articles 6.1, 6.6, 6.8, 6.10, 9.4, 9.5, and 12.1 of the AD Agreement and paragraphs 1 and 7 of Annex II

(i) Arguments of the Parties

United States

7.169 The United States considers that Mexico breached numerous provisions of the AD Agreement by individually examining only three exporters and applying an adverse facts available margin to all other non-investigated exporters. In particular, the United States argues that (a) Mexico failed to individually examine all known exporters and to determine an individual duty rate for all or to apply a neutral all-others rate in case it wished to limit the number of exporters examined; and (b) Mexico wrongly applied adverse facts available to non-examined American producers and exporters.

7.170 According to the United States, Article 6.10 of the AD Agreement requires "as a rule" that an investigating authority establish an individual margin of dumping for each known producer or exporter, unless the number of exporters or producers is so large that the determination of individual margins for each producer or exporter would be impracticable. In such a case, an investigating authority may limit its examination, and, under Article 9.4, apply a "neutral" all others rate to producers or exporters that were not individually examined. According to the United States, Economía never even made an effort to calculate an individual margin for each exporter or producer of the subject merchandise as required by Article 6.10 of the AD Agreement. Economía simply sent a questionnaire to only two exporters mentioned in the application and examined those two as well as two other exporters who voluntarily appeared, assuming a lack of co-operation from all other exporters. This, the United States submits, is a violation of Article 6.10 of the AD Agreement, as no objective and unbiased investigating authority would have concluded that there were only two exporters or producers of long-grain white rice in the United States. The United States submits that Article 6.10 of the AD Agreement does not permit investigating authorities to take a passive approach to their investigations, but must either take affirmative steps to investigate every producer or exporter or else take affirmative steps to limit their investigation by selecting a subset of such producers or exporters.[165]

7.171 Moreover, the United States considers that Economía failed to comply with Article 6.6 of the AD Agreement which requires Economía to satisfy itself as to the accuracy of the information supplied by the interested party upon which the determination is based. In the United States' view, Economía simply accepted at face value the information in the application which indicated that there were only two exporters of the product to Mexico, even though the application itself mentioned data relating to a third exporter. According to the United States, it would have sufficed for Economía to consult the customs declarations ("pedimentos") that the Mexican customs authorities collects from importers to have been able to identify every exporter from the United States.

7.172 In any case, the United States argues, where an investigating authority limits its investigation in accordance with Article 6.10 of the AD Agreement, the rate applicable to the producers and exporters which were not individually examined should be calculated in accordance with Article 9.4 of the AD Agreement, which does not allow the use of margins based on facts available. The United States considers that *de facto* the Mexican investigating authority limited its investigation by not sending questionnaires to an exporter mentioned in an annex to the application, not consulting the pedimentos and not using public data to identify all US exporters. As Economía applied a margin entirely based on facts available to the non-examined producers and exporters, it breached Article 9.4 of the AD Agreement. Finally, according to the United States, the assumption applied by Economía that all producers and exporters are considered to have been investigated implies that no exporter or producer will be eligible for an expedited review under Article 9.5 as this applies only to non-investigated producers and exporters. The United States submits that by acting in this manner, Economía has breached Article 9.5 of the AD Agreement by rendering it a nullity.

[165] US First Submission, para. 140 – 141.

7.173 In addition, the United States submits that by applying facts available to the unexamined firms when it never sent them a copy of the anti-dumping questionnaire or took any other steps to ensure that they had received the notice that the AD Agreement requires, Economía breached Articles 6.1, 6.2 and 6.8 of the AD Agreement and paragraph 1 of Annex II. The United States asserts that Mexico failed to provide the exporters and producers notice of the information which Economía required, as required by Article 6.1 of the AD Agreement. According to the United States, Article 6.1 of the AD Agreement establishes that an investigating authority that has decided to include a particular exporter or producer in the anti-dumping investigation cannot simply announce that it has initiated the investigation and place the burden on the producer or exporter to come forward and appear.[166] The United States further argues that Economía did not give all exporters and producers a "full opportunity" to defend their interests as required by Article 6.2 of the AD Agreement. Moreover, Mexico's application of facts available without having specified the information which was required and without providing proper notice to the interested parties of the rights of Economía to use facts available is a breach of Article 6.8 and paragraph 1 of Annex II of the AD Agreement.[167]

7.174 Furthermore, the United States considers that the use of adverse facts available for the unexamined firms in the absence of any evidence of uncooperative behaviour by any of such firms, is a breach of Article 6.8 and paragraph 7 of Annex II of the AD Agreement. Moreover, Economía failed to apply the information contained in the application with "special circumspection" as required by paragraph 7 Annex II.

7.175 Finally, the United States argues that Economía failed to ensure that all interested parties known to have an interest in the investigation were notified as required by Article 12.1 of the AD Agreement. The United States submits that the Mexican investigating authority failed to notify a third exporter mentioned in an Annex to the application, and did not notify other US exporters or producers which could have been identified by the authority on the basis of the customs record.

Mexico

7.176 Mexico argues that there is no obligation under Article 6.10 of the AD Agreement to calculate an individual margin for all exporters or producers, but only for those that are known to the authorities. According to Mexico, the known exporters are those that are made known to the authorities in the application, or

---

[166] US First Submission, para. 145.

[167] The United States argues that Articles 1, 5, 6.5 and 6.6 of the AD Agreement provide further context for confirming that Articles 6.1, 6.8, 6.10, 9.4 and para. 1 Annex II require an investigating authority to (1) actively determine the universe of potential respondents; (2) actively send questionnaires to those producers or exporters from which it is seeking information; and (3) either take active steps to investigate every known producer and exporter, or else examine a representative sample and assign a "neutral" all other margin that is not based on the facts available to everyone else. US First Submission, para. 151.

that appear subsequent to the initiation of the investigation.[168] Mexico complied with this obligation. Mexico argues that it did not limit its examination to a reasonable number of exporters, but assigned individual margins to all the exporters and producers that participated in the investigation and that therefore the methodology for the calculation of a neutral all others rate under Article 9.4 of the AD Agreement is not applicable. It emphasises in this respect that it never refused to accept the participation of any US exporter that wanted to participate in the investigation.[169] Mexico submits that inasmuch as it complied with the obligation to send questionnaires to the known exporters and to calculate an individual dumping margin for all the exporters that submitted the necessary information to the investigating authority, it was entitled to make final determinations for the remaining exporters on the basis of the facts available, in accordance with Article 6.8 and Annex II of the AD Agreement.[170] Mexico argues that it applied paragraph 1 of Annex II which establishes clearly that if a party does not provide the information requested, the latter will be free to make the determinations on the basis of the facts available, including those contained in the application for initiation.[171]

7.177 Mexico argues that it complied with all its obligations under Article 6 of the AD Agreement by providing the United States authorities in Mexico[172] and the two known exporters, Producers Rice[173] and Riceland[174], with the public notice of initiation of the investigation, the text of the application for initiation and the annexes thereto and the form for exporters and foreign producers. In addition, it convened hearings for all natural or legal persons interested in the investigation through the publication of the official notice of initiation published in the Official Journal (DOF) on 11 December 2000.[175] Mexico does not consider Article 6.6 of the AD Agreement to be applicable to the situation in which the margin was based on facts available. Neither does it consider that Article 5.3 of the AD Agreement required it to verify whether the names of the exporters mentioned in the application included all existing US exporters but simply whether the application mentions the names of the exporters known to the applicant and whether the firms mentioned were exporters of the subject product.[176]

7.178 With regard to the United States' assertion that it would have sufficed for the investigating authority to consult the customs declarations (pedimentos) in

---

[168] Mexico First Answers to Questions, question 16.
[169] Mexico Second Oral Statement, para. 70.
[170] Mexico First Submission, para. 159.
[171] Mexico asserts that the third paragraph of the introduction to the questionnaires clearly stated that such would be the case, thus complying with para. 1 of Annex II.
[172] Official communication UPCI.310.00.3082 of 8 November 2000 (Exhibit MEX-8). and official communication UPCI.310.00.3089 of 11 December 2000 (Exhibit MEX-9).
[173] Official communication UPCI.310.00.3296 of 11 December 2000 (Exhibit MEX-6).
[174] Official communication UPCI.310.00.3297 of 11 December 2000 (Exhibit MEX-7).
[175] Resolution accepting the interested party's application and initiating the anti-dumping investigation on imports of long-grain white rice, a product classified under heading 1006.30.01 of the Tariff established by the General Import and Export Duties Law, originating in the United States of America, regardless of the country of provenance, published in the Official Journal (DOF) of 11 December 2000 (Exhibit MEX-10).
[176] Mexico Second Oral Statement, para. 68-69.

order to have found the names of every exporter, Mexico argues that such pedimentos were not in the hands of the investigating authority but rather of the Ministry of Finance and Public Credit and that to request and receive such documents would have seriously delayed the proceedings (by approximately 40 days).[177] More importantly, Mexico considers that the AD Agreement does not require the authority to obtain such pedimentos and identify all exporters and the authority therefore did not attempt to obtain them.[178]

(ii) Analysis

7.179 We recall that the application filed by the Mexican domestic industry mentioned two US exporters, Producers Rice and Riceland. The Mexican investigating authority initiated the investigation and sent a notice of initiation as well as a questionnaire to the two exporters listed in the application as the exporters known to the applicant, and to the US embassy in Mexico City. The Notice of Initiation stated that a period of 30 days was given to any interested party to appear before the investigating authority to submit the official investigation form which could be obtained at the clerk's office of the International Trade Practices Unit in Mexico City.[179] Two US exporters, the Rice Company and Farmers Rice, as well as an industry association, the USA Rice Federation, came forward out of their own initiative, and received questionnaires. Individual margins of dumping were assigned to all four US exporters that "participated" in the investigation. For all other US exporters which did not come forward themselves, and did not provide information, a residual margin of dumping was calculated based on the facts available.

7.180 The United States claims that the investigating authority failed to abide by its obligation under Article 6.10 of the AD Agreement to determine an individual margin of dumping for each known exporter or producer as no efforts were undertaken by the authority to obtain knowledge of US exporters other than those two named in the application, and the two that came forward of their own initiative. The US submits that the authority failed to actively identify and inform interested parties of the investigation as required by Articles 6.1 and 12.1 of the AD Agreement. As a consequence, the US submits that the application of facts available to calculate a margin of dumping for these uninvestigated firms is therefore also inconsistent with Article 6.8 of the AD Agreement. Mexico on the other hand is of the view that Article 6.10 of the AD Agreement requires the calculation of an individual margin of dumping only with regard to the exporters that were known to the investigating authority. As the authority provided the required notification to, and calculated an individual margin of dumping for, the exporters made known to the authority by the applicants, as well as for those exporters that made themselves known to the authority, Mexico considers that it fully complied with Articles 6.1, 12.1 and 6.10 of the AD Agreement, and its use

[177] Mexico First Answers to Questions, question 17. Mexico Second Answers to Questions, questions 5 and 10.

[178] Mexico First Answers to Questions, question 17.

[179] Notice of initiation, paras. 152 – 153. Exhibits US-1 and US-2.

of facts available for the non-appearing firms is thus justified under Article 6.8 of the AD Agreement.

7.181 Article 6.10 of the AD Agreement provides as follows:

> 6.10 The authorities shall, as a rule, determine an individual margin of dumping for each known exporter or producer concerned of the product under investigation. In cases where the number of exporters, producers, importers or types of products involved is so large as to make such a determination impracticable, the authorities may limit their examination either to a reasonable number of interested parties or products by using samples which are statistically valid on the basis of information available to the authorities at the time of the selection, or to the largest percentage of the volume of the exports from the country in question which can reasonably be investigated.
>
> 6.10.1 Any selection of exporters, producers, importers or types of products made under this paragraph shall preferably be chosen in consultation with and with the consent of the exporters, producers or importers concerned.
>
> 6.10.2 In cases where the authorities have limited their examination, as provided for in this paragraph, they shall nevertheless determine an individual margin of dumping for any exporter or producer not initially selected who submits the necessary information in time for that information to be considered during the course of the investigation, except where the number of exporters or producers is so large that individual examinations would be unduly burdensome to the authorities and prevent the timely completion of the investigation. Voluntary responses shall not be discouraged.

7.182 Article 6.10 of the AD Agreement thus set forth the general rule that the authorities shall determine an individual margin of dumping for each known exporter or producer concerned of the product under investigation. The disagreement between the parties centres around the extent of active involvement required from the authorities in identifying the foreign exporters and producers for which it is to calculate an individual margin of dumping. In line with general rules of interpretation of customary international law, we will examine the terms of Article 6.10 of the AD Agreement in their ordinary meaning and in light of their context and taking into account the object and purpose of the Agreement.

7.183 The ordinary meaning of the term "known" is "learned, apprehended mentally; familiar, esp. familiar to all, generally known or recognized. Also, identified as such"[180]. In other words, "known" exporters or producers are those which the investigating authority has learned about or has knowledge of. As such, the ordinary meaning of the term does not tell us whether the authority is required to take any active steps to become aware of any foreign exporter or producer or whether, on the other hand, it suffices for an authority to rely on the applicant to

[180] New Shorter Oxford Dictionary, p. 1504.

identify the exporters and to expect the interested foreign exporters and producers to make themselves known to the authority. In order to answer this question we examine the obligations set forth in the AD Agreement which provide the necessary context in light of which the requirement to calculate an individual margin of dumping for each known exporter and producer has to be read.

7.184 This context is formed by the overarching obligation to conduct *an investigation* and by the specific obligations on the authority to ensure that all interested parties are informed of the information required of them and are given the opportunity to present all evidence to support their case.

7.185 The first important obligation is the requirement expressed in Article 1 of the AD Agreement that an anti-dumping measure shall only be applied pursuant to *investigations* initiated and conducted in accordance with the provisions of the AD Agreement. Among others, Article 5 of the AD Agreement entitled "Initiation and Subsequent Investigation" and Article 6 of the AD Agreement further elaborate on the specific requirements that an investigating authority has to comply with when conducting this investigation. The term "to investigate" means "to search or inquire into; examine a matter systematically or in detail; make an (official) inquiry into"[181] and an "investigator" is not surprisingly defined as "a researcher"[182]. In our view, an investigating authority required to conduct an investigation in an objective and unbiased manner has to play an active role in the search of the information it requires in order to make its determination. We thus concur with the view expressed by the Appellate Body, albeit in a different context, in the *US - Wheat Gluten* case that:

> "[T]he ordinary meaning of the word "investigation" suggests that the competent authorities should carry out a "systematic inquiry" or a "careful study" into the matter before them. The word, therefore, suggests a proper degree of activity on the part of the competent authorities because authorities charged with conducting an inquiry or a study – to use the treaty language, an "investigation" – must actively seek out pertinent information".[183]

7.186 While it is clear that the interested parties, including the applicants, play a very important role in the fact gathering process, the obligation of conducting an investigation and making a determination remains that of the investigating authority, and not that of the interested parties. This is evidenced, for example, by the requirement of Article 6.6 of the AD Agreement that the investigating authorities "during the course of an investigation satisfy themselves as to the accuracy of the information supplied by interested parties upon which its findings are based".[184]

---

181 New Shorter Oxford Dictionary, p. 1410.

182 *Ibid.*

183 Appellate Body Report, *US – Wheat Gluten*, para. 53.

184 Paragraph 7 of Annex II similarly requires in case secondary source information is to be used that such be done with "special circumspection" and that "In such cases, the authorities should, where practicable, check the information from other independent sources at their disposal, such as published

7.187 In sum, we are of the view that the term "known exporter or producer" in Article 6.10 of the AD Agreement refers to the exporters or producers that an unbiased and objective investigating authority properly establishing the facts would be reasonably expected to have become conversant with. Article 6.10 of the AD Agreement is a general requirement that the authority has to comply with, at the latest, at the end of the investigation when making the determinations. This implies that the exporters that are known to the authorities at that point are those that an objective and unbiased investigating authority properly establishing the facts and conducting an active investigation could have and should have reasonably been considered to have knowledge of.[185]

7.188 Clearly, the exporters that would be "known" to an investigating authority which makes little or no effort to inform itself will be far less than those "known" to an authority that has been reasonably active. Interpreted in its context, the term "known" cannot be construed in such an artificially contrived and solipsistic manner as to become a warrant for a passive investigative approach. To do so would be to effectively read out of the AD Agreement an important aspect of the obligation of an investigating authority regarding the conduct of an investigation.

7.189 We wish to emphasise that this does not imply that we are of the view that an investigating authority is required to go to the other extreme and actively identify each and every foreign exporter or producer of the subject product. In our view, such a reading would read the term "known" out of the Agreement's requirement to calculate an individual margin only for each "known" exporter or producer of the subject product.[186] What is reasonable to expect of the investigating authority as far as the identification of foreign exporters or producers goes

price lists, official import statistics and customs returns, and from the information obtained from other interested parties during the investigation".

[185] In this respect, there is an important difference with the context in which the term "known exporters" is used in Article 5.2 of the AD Agreement. In Article 5.2 (ii) of the AD Agreement, it is provided that the application shall contain such information as is reasonably available to the applicant on *inter alia* "the identity of each known exporter or foreign producer". This provision deals with the content requirements of an application and the "known" exporters are clearly those that *according to the information reasonably available to the applicant* are those exporters that are *known to the applicant*. In our view, as is the case for all the other information that under Article 5.2 of the AD Agreement the applicants should inform the authorities of, such as prices at which the product in question is sold or the volume of the allegedly dumped imports and the effects on prices, the investigating authority cannot simply accept this information as a basis for making its determinations, but is required through conducting an unbiased and objective investigation to establish and evaluate the facts. This is the whole purpose of the investigation, which as becomes clear from a number of provisions in the Agreement is the responsibility of the investigating authority. Especially in light of the important consequences that flow from the determination of the known exporters, it would render the requirement to conduct an "investigation" meaningless to leave this identification in the hands of one of the interested parties, the applicants.

[186] We recall that it is a generally accepted rule of treaty interpretation that an interpreter is to give full meaning to all the terms of the Agreement and not to adopt such an interpretation that reads certain terms out of the Agreement. See, e.g, Appellate Body Report, *US – Gasoline*, p. 23:

> "...One of the corollaries of the 'general rule of interpretation' in the *Vienna Convention* is that interpretation must give meaning and effect to all the terms of the treaty. An interpreter is not free to adopt a reading that would result in reducing whole clauses or paragraphs of a treaty to redundancy or inutility."

will depend on the circumstances of each case and the information provided by the interested parties that could assist the authority in identifying such foreign exporters or producers.[187]

7.190 In addition, the AD Agreement contains a number of express obligations on the investigating authorities to inform all interested parties of the initiation of the investigation and of the information that is required of them. Article 6.1 of the AD Agreement provides as follows:

> 6.1 All interested parties in an anti-dumping investigation shall be given notice of the information which the authorities require and ample opportunity to present in writing all evidence which they consider relevant in respect of the investigation in question.
>
> > 6.1.1 Exporters or foreign producers receiving questionnaires used in an anti-dumping investigation shall be given at least 30 days for reply. Due consideration should be given to any request for an extension of the 30-day period and, upon cause shown, such an extension should be granted whenever practicable.
> >
> > 6.1.2 Subject to the requirement to protect confidential information, evidence presented in writing by one interested party shall be made available promptly to other interested parties participating in the investigation.
> >
> > 6.1.3 As soon as an investigation has been initiated, the authorities shall provide the full text of the written applica-

[187] We note that the Panel in the *Argentina – Poultry Anti-Dumping Duties* case also rejected a similarly restrictive reading of the Agreement's requirement to notify all interested parties known to have an interest in the investigation under Article 12.1 of the AD Agreement. The slightly different yet similar situation before the panel in that case concerned certain exporters which were mentioned in an annex to the petition but without an address. The Argentine authorities were arguing that the address was not known to them and that they had asked the authorities of the country of export for assistance which was all that was required of them under the notification requirement of Article 12.1 of the AD Agreement. The Panel rejected this restrictive reading of the obligations incumbent on the investigating authorities to notify all known interested parties:

> "7.132 [...] We accept that there may be circumstances in which an investigating authority may not have sufficient information to allow it to notify all interested parties known to have an interest in an investigation. In this sense, the fact that an exporter is 'known' by the investigating authority to have an interest in an investigation does not necessarily mean that sufficient details concerning the exporter are 'known' to the investigating authority such that it may make the Article 12.1 notification. In other words, knowledge of an exporter's interest in an investigation does not necessarily imply knowledge of contact details regarding that exporter. In such circumstances, however, we consider that the nature of the Article 12.1 notification obligation is such that the investigating authority should make all reasonable efforts to obtain the requisite contact details. Sending a letter with only a very general request for assistance, without specifying the exporters for which contact details are required, does not satisfy the need to make all reasonable efforts"

Panel report, *Argentina – Poultry Anti-Dumping Duties*, para.7.132. The panel in that case also found that there was *prima facie* evidence that exporters mentioned in an annex to the petition are "known" to the authorities and should thus be notified. See Panel report, *Argentina – Poultry Anti-Dumping Duties*, para. 7.131.

> tion received under paragraph 1 of Article 5 to the known exporters and to the authorities of the exporting Member and shall make it available, upon request, to other interested parties involved. Due regard shall be paid to the requirement for the protection of confidential information, as provided for in paragraph 5. (footnotes omitted)

7.191 Article 6.1 of the AD Agreement thus requires that all interested parties be given notice of the information required, which under Article 6.1.3 AD Agreement includes at least that the full text of the application is to be provided to the known exporters. Article 12.1 AD Agreement similarly provides for a notification requirement with regard to all interested parties known to have an interest in the investigation:

> 12.1 When the authorities are satisfied that there is sufficient evidence to justify the initiation of an anti-dumping investigation pursuant to Article 5, the Member or Members the products of which are subject to such investigation and other *interested parties known to the investigating authorities to have an interest therein* shall be notified and a public notice shall be given.

7.192 Thus, the AD Agreement makes clear that the investigation concerns not just the exporters and producers made known to the authorities by the applicant, or that make themselves known, but relates to all interested parties. In our view, in order to comply with *inter alia* the requirement to ensure that all interested parties be given notice of the information required of them, the investigating authority when conducting an investigation cannot remain entirely passive in the identification of the interested parties. We consider highly relevant the fact that Article 6.1.3 of the AD Agreement and Article 12.1 of the AD Agreement require the authorities to provide the full text of the application to all known exporters as well as notify all interested parties known to have an interest in the investigation of the initiation of the investigation. In our view, an investigating authority complies with these obligations by informing those interested parties it can reasonably obtain knowledge of. It clearly does not suffice for the authority to inform only those exporters identified by the applicant, as the notification requirement applies to interested parties known to the authority, and not simply those known to the applicant, as in Article 5.2 of the AD Agreement. Nor would the authority in our view be complying with this crucial obligation by expecting the interested parties to make themselves known to the authorities. It seems that the latter approach is inherently problematic since it leaves unanswered the question how such exporters become aware of the investigation such that they would come forward and make themselves known to the authority and participate in the investigation if the authority does not first contact the interested parties and does not first inform all interested parties known to have an interest in the investigation of the initiation of the investigation.

7.193 We are of the view that the requirement of Article 6.1 of the AD Agreement is more than a matter of mere procedural rectitude, but is fundamental to a correct application of *inter alia* Article 6.8 of the AD Agreement which provides as follows:

> 6.8 In cases in which any interested party refuses access to, or otherwise does not provide, necessary information within a reasonable period or significantly impedes the investigation, preliminary and final determinations, affirmative or negative, may be made on the basis of the facts available. The provisions of Annex II shall be observed in the application of this paragraph.

7.194 We consider that in case an interested party has not been properly notified and informed of the information it is required to submit under Article 6.1 of the AD Agreement, it cannot be argued to have refused access to or to otherwise have withheld necessary information or to have significantly impeded the investigation. This is evidenced also by the requirement in paragraph 1 of Annex II of the AD Agreement which provides that:

> 1. As soon as possible after the initiation of the investigation, the investigating authorities should specify in detail the information required from any interested party, and the manner in which that information should be structured by the interested party in its response. The authorities should also ensure that the party is aware that if information is not supplied within a reasonable time, the authorities will be free to make determinations on the basis of the facts available, including those contained in the application for the initiation of the investigation by the domestic industry.

7.195 We note that Article 6.8 of the AD Agreement makes clear that the provisions of Annex II such as the above quoted paragraph 1 have to be observed by the authority when applying facts available to make its determinations.[188]

7.196 We will therefore now turn to the facts of this case in order to determine whether the Mexican investigating authority complied with the requirements of Articles 6.1, 6.8, 6.10 and 12.1 of the AD Agreement.

7.197 We recall that the application referred to two US exporters, Producers Rice, and Riceland. The Mexican authorities, upon initiation of the investigation, sent a copy of the application, together with the notice of initiation, to these two exporters as well as to the US authorities in Mexico City. Questionnaires were sent to the two US exporters mentioned in the application. The notice to the US authorities included a form by which interested parties could make themselves known. We note that throughout the application the name of a third US exporter, the "Rice Corporation"[189], is referred to as one of the largest US exporters. In spite of the fact that this important exporter's name appeared from time to time, no effort was made by the authorities to obtain more information on this exporter

---

[188] Apart from setting forth independent obligations, we consider that the above quoted provisions also provide further context in which to read the requirement of Article 6.10 of the AD Agreement to calculate an individual margin of dumping for "each known exporter or producer" of the subject product.

[189] The Final Determination (Exhibits US-6 and US-7) refers to the Rice Company by this name.

either from the applicants or from the US authorities.[190] However, this exporter, as well as fourth exporter not mentioned in the application, the Farmers Rice, came forward itself and an individual margin of dumping was calculated for these two exporters, as well as for the two exporters explicitly listed in the application.

7.198 The absence of these two exporters that came forward themselves, one of which actually appeared on several places in the application, revealed to the authority that the list of foreign exporters or producers was incomplete.[191] The incomplete listing in the application of the foreign exporters or producers was also evidenced by the fact that the application stated that the subject product is produced in six states of the United States,[192] while both exporters explicitly listed as exporters known to the applicants, come from one and the same state, Arkansas.

7.199 In addition, Annex M to the application refers to, and includes contact details for, two industry associations in the United States, the USA Rice Council and the Rice Millers Association, stating that the latter's members represent 97 per cent of all US milled production. As it is explicitly stated in Annex M, while these organizations are not themselves producers of rice, they can provide general and specific information about the rice industry in the United States. Mexico further acknowledges that it would have been possible to identify all US exporters by examining the so-called pedimentos,[193] but considers that it was under no obligation to consult these pedimentos which were being held by the Ministry of Finance and Public Credit. Mexico does not argue that it was impossible to obtain the pedimentos, but rather that requesting the pedimentos would have caused a delay of about 40 days.[194] Information on US exporters seems to have been available from a number of public sources as well such as a US magazine for the rice industry, the Rice Journal, a source mentioned in Annex S to the application.[195] This Rice Journal contains all the names and contact details of US producers.[196] While the investigating authority notified the US authorities of the initiation of the investigation as required by Article 6.1.3 and 12.1 of the AD Agreement, it did not request the assistance of the authorities in identifying US exporters or producers. We do not consider that an investigating authority is complying with its investigatory task by assuming that the authorities of the exporting country will inform the foreign producers and exporters of the initiation such that they can come forward and present their data. The government of the

[190] For example, Annex H to the Petition concerned information on "The Rice Company" – Exhibit US -8, p. 44.

[191] This does not necessarily mean that the information contained in the application was not sufficient to justify the initiation of the investigation, a question we are in any case not asked to rule on.

[192] These six States are Arkansas, California, Louisiana, Mississippi, Missouri, and Texas. See Petition, page 10 (Exhibit US-8); Annex M to petition, Exhibit US-17.

[193] This is clear from Mexico's statement that the pedimentos included imports of *all* white rice which is clearly inclusive of the subject merchandise, long grain white rice. For an example of a pedimento and the kind of information contained therein, see Exhibit US-12.

[194] Mexico First Answers to Questions, question 17.

[195] Annex S to petition, Rice Outlook 1999, p. 6, Exhibit US-9.

[196] Exhibit US -18.

exporting Member is to be notified because, according to Article 6.11 (ii) of the AD Agreement, it is an interested party in its own right, not because that government should do the work for the investigating authority. For all of these reasons we consider that an objective and unbiased investigating authority conducting an investigation in a reasonable manner should have made more of an effort to obtain knowledge of other US exporters. The authority knew that the listing in the application was far from complete, and it had sufficient information before it that would have enabled the authority to identify other US producers and exporters. It is, in our view, the task of the investigating authority and not of the interested parties to inform all interested parties of the information that is required and to conduct a proper investigation. We are of the view that the investigating authority is not allowed to rely on the initiative of the interested parties for the fulfilment of obligations which are really its own.

7.200 For the reason set out above, we find that the investigating authority failed to comply with Articles 6.1 and 12.1 of the AD Agreement as it failed to notify all interested parties known to have an interest in the investigation of the initiation of the investigation and of the information required of them. We are of the view that these violations are not to be viewed as some kind of minor or inconsequential procedural infringement as they have important implication(s) with regard to the use of facts available under Article 6.8 of the AD Agreement. As we stated earlier, in case the authorities do not properly notify and inform the interested parties, it is not permitted to apply the facts available to make determinations with regard to these interested parties. We thus conclude that by applying the facts available in the calculation of a margin of dumping for the US exporters or producers that were known or could reasonably have been known to the authority, Mexico acted in a manner which is inconsistent with Article 6.8 and paragraph 1 of Annex II of the AD Agreement. In light of this finding, we do not find it necessary to examine the US argument concerning the inconsistency of the Mexican measure with paragraph 7 of Annex II, and do not make any ruling with regard to this aspect of the US claim.

7.201 In addition, we find that Mexico acted in breach of Article 6.10 of the AD Agreement by remaining entirely passive in the identification of exporters or producers interested in the investigation, and by not calculating an individual margin for dumping for each exporter or producer that was known or should reasonably have been known to the investigating authority.

7.202 In light of our findings under Articles 6.1, 6.8, 6.10 and 12.1 of the AD Agreement, we do not consider it necessary for the resolution of the dispute to also examine the US claims concerning Articles 6.6, 9.4, and 9.5 of the AD Agreement, and do not make any findings in this respect.

(d) Claim 11: Economía's failure to provide sufficient information on the findings and conclusions of fact and law and the reasons that led to the imposition of the adverse facts available-based margin on Producers Rice and the unexamined US

exporters and producers is inconsistent with Mexico's obligations under Article 12.2 of the AD Agreement

(i) Arguments of the Parties

United States

7.203 The United States submits that Economía provided only the most summary rationale for its decision to base the margin of Producers Rice and the unexamined exporters and producers on adverse facts available. Economía thus failed to provide sufficiently detailed information on all issues of fact and law as required by Article 12.2 of the AD Agreement.

Mexico

7.204 Mexico submits that the Final Determination sets forth the findings on all issues of fact and law in a sufficiently detailed manner.

(ii) Analysis

7.205 In light of our findings on Articles 6.1, 6.8, 6.10 and 12.1 of the AD Agreement, we do not find it necessary to address in this context the US claim under Article 12.2 of the AD Agreement. That is, having determined that the measure at issue is inconsistent with the cited Articles, and exercising the discretion implicit in the principle of judicial economy, we do not deem it necessary to examine whether the investigation which led to the inconsistent measure was consistent with the procedural rules concerning notification in Article 12.2 of the AD Agreement. We do not consider that this would add anything to our findings or would be useful in the implementation of our ruling.

(e) Claim 12: Economía's application of an adverse facts available-based margin to Producers Rice and the unexamined US exporters and producers is inconsistent with Mexico's obligations under Articles 1 and 9.3 of the AD Agreement

(i) Arguments of the Parties

United States

7.206 The United States states that by failing to calculate the residual margin of dumping for the non-examined exporters and Producers Rice on the basis of the neutral formula set forth in Article 9.4, the amount of the margin assigned to those producers inevitable exceeded the margin of dumping established under Article 2, and thus breached Article 9.3 which provides that the amount of the duty shall not exceed the margin of dumping as established under Article 2.

7.207 In addition, by imposing duties in a manner inconsistent with the provisions of the Agreement, the United States argues, Economía also violated Article

1 which requires that measures be applied only after an investigation conducted in accordance with the provisions of the Agreement.

Mexico

7.208 Mexico argues that Article 9.4 of the AD Agreement is not applicable and that Article 9.3 of the AD Agreement has therefore not been violated either.

(ii) Analysis

7.209 In light of the finding made above concerning the inconsistency with Articles 6.1, 6.8, 6.10 and 12.1 of the AD Agreement, we do not find it necessary for the resolution of the dispute to address the US claims concerning the inconsistency of the use of facts available with Articles 9.3 and 1 of the AD Agreement. We therefore do not make any rulings in this respect.

(f) Claim 13: Economía's levying of an anti-dumping duty greater than the margin of dumping is inconsistent with Mexico's obligations under Article VI:2 of GATT 1994

(i) Arguments of the Parties

United States

7.210 The United States submits that, because the duties that Mexico levied on the "all others" companies was greater in amount than the appropriate margin of dumping, Mexico also violated Article VI:2 of the GATT 1994 which provides that a duty may be imposed which is not greater in amount than the margin of dumping in respect of such product.

Mexico

7.211 In Mexico's view, since the measures taken are consistent with the AD Agreement, there can be no consequent violation of Article VI: 2 of the GATT 1994.

(ii) Analysis

7.212 In light of the finding made above concerning the inconsistency of the dumping margin calculation with Articles 6.1, 6.8, 6.10 and 12.1 of the AD Agreement, we do not find it necessary for the resolution of the dispute to address this US claim concerning the inconsistency with Article VI:2 of the GATT 1994. We therefore do not make any rulings in this respect.

D. *Claims Concerning Mexico's Foreign Trade Act and Section 366 of Mexico's FCCP as such*

1. *Claim 14: Article 53 of Mexico's Foreign Trade Act is inconsistent "as such" with Article 6.1.1 of the AD Agreement and Article 12.1.1 of the SCM Agreement*

(a) Arguments of the Parties

(i) United States

7.213 The United States asserts that Article 53 of the Act requires interested parties to present arguments, information, and evidence to Economía within 28 days after publication of the initiation notice. The United States submits that Article 6.1.1 of the AD Agreement, and its SCM counterpart, Article 12.1.1 of the SCM Agreement, provide that interested parties are to be given at least 30 days to reply to questionnaires counting from the date of receipt of the questionnaire, and not counting from the date of publication of the notice of initiation. In addition, these provisions state that an authority should, after due consideration, grant extensions of this time period, upon cause shown, "whenever practicable". The United States asserts that Mexico only sends questionnaires to the producers or exporters named in the application, and listed in the notice of initiation. This implies, in the United States' view, that Article 53 of the Act will preclude Economía from providing other exporters or foreign producers which come forward following the initiation to ask for copies of the questionnaires 30 days to respond, since the time has started counting from the date of publication of the initiation notice and not from the time the questionnaires were sent to these interested parties that appeared after initiation. In addition, the United States submits that Article 53 of the Act prevents Economía from giving due consideration to extension requests, let alone granting such requests. The United States is thus of the view that Article 53 of the Act is inconsistent as such with Articles 6.1.1 of the AD Agreement and 12.1.1 of the SCM Agreement.

(ii) Mexico

7.214 Mexico submits that Article 6.1.1 of the AD Agreement and Article 12.1.1 of the SCM Agreement do not oblige Economía to provide for 30 days to respond to questionnaires with respect to exporters that were not sent a questionnaire. Mexico is of the view that if the 30-day period were granted to any interested party that presented itself after the initiation of the investigation, the ensuing delay would entail failure to observe the time-limits laid down in, and hence a violation of, Article 5.10 of the AD Agreement and 11.11 of the SCM Agreement. Second, Mexico asserts that according to Article 3 of the Act[197], the term 28 "days" in Article 53 of the Act has to be read as "working days". Given the fact that it is common practice in Mexico to send out the questionnaires the day following publication of the initiation, Mexico argues that Article 53 of the Act

---

[197] Article 3 of the Act provides as follows: "...where this Act refers to time-limits in days these shall be understood to mean working days and where it refers to months or years these shall be understood to mean calendar months or years".

thus actually provides for at least 38 calendar days, which is more than Article 6.1.1 of the AD Agreement and Article 12.1.1 of the SCM Agreement require.[198] Finally, Mexico submits that nothing in Article 53 of the Act prohibits Economía from authorizing extensions of the deadline, and several exporters have successfully requested such extensions.[199] In any case, and in the event the panel should consider that the United States has provided evidence of such an alleged prohibition based on the text of the Act, Mexico argues that Article 6.1.1 of the AD Agreement and 12.1.1 of the SCM Agreement apply congruently to Mexican anti-dumping and countervailing duty investigations, and the investigating authority may grant extensions on the basis of these Articles.

7.215 Finally, Mexico submits that, in any case, by virtue of Article 133 of its Constitution, treaties such as the WTO Agreements are self-executing and automatically applicable in Mexican law, and as Article 2 of the Act makes clear, the Act will be implemented in a manner which is congruent with the provisions of the WTO Agreements. According to Mexico, the Act thus does not mandate any WTO inconsistent action.

(b) Analysis

7.216 The United States claim concerns Article 53 of the Act which provides as follows:

> The interested parties shall submit their arguments, information and evidence in conformity with the applicable legislation, within a period of 28 days from the day following the publication of the initiating resolution.

7.217 According to the United States, by not starting to count the 28 days for replies to questionnaires from the date of receipt of such questionnaires but rather from the date of initiation, Article 53 of the Act fails to provide all interested parties an equal right to have 30 days to respond to questionnaires, as required by Article 6.1.1 of the AD Agreement, and its SCM counterpart, Article 12.1.1 of the SCM Agreement. Article 6.1.1 of the AD Agreement provides that[200]:

> 6.1.1 Exporters or foreign producers receiving questionnaires used in an anti-dumping investigation shall be given at least 30

[198] Mexico First Submission, para. 227.

[199] Mexico First Submission, para. 229. Mexico does not provide specific examples.

[200] Article 12.1.1 of the SCM Agreement similarly provides that:

> 12.1.1 Exporters, foreign producers or interested Members receiving questionnaires used in a countervailing duty investigation shall be given at least 30 days for reply.[40] Due consideration should be given to any request for an extension of the 30-day period and, upon cause shown, such an extension should be granted whenever practicable.
>
> [40] As a general rule, the time-limit for exporters shall be counted from the date of receipt of the questionnaire, which for this purpose shall be deemed to have been received one week from the date on which it was sent to the respondent or transmitted to the appropriate diplomatic representatives of the exporting Member or, in the case of a separate customs territory Member of the WTO, an official representative of the exporting territory.

> days for reply.[15] Due consideration should be given to any request for an extension of the 30-day period and, upon cause shown, such an extension should be granted whenever practicable.
>
> [15] As a general rule, the time-limit for exporters shall be counted from the date of receipt of the questionnaire, which for this purpose shall be deemed to have been received one week from the date on which it was sent to the respondent or transmitted to the appropriate diplomatic representative of the exporting Member or, in the case of a separate customs territory Member of the WTO, an official representative of the exporting territory.

7.218 We are of the view that the wording of Article 6.1.1 of the AD Agreement makes it very clear that any exporter or foreign producer which receives a questionnaire is to be given at least 30 days for reply. As footnote 15 adds, this time limit shall as a general rule be counted from the date of receipt of the questionnaire, which shall be deemed to have been received one week from the date on which it was sent. We do not understand the United States to consider inconsistent the fact that Article 53 of the Act provides for 28 days only, instead of the 30 days required by Article 6.1.1 of the AD Agreement as it seems to acknowledge that, by virtue of Article 3 of the Act, the days referred to in the Act refer to working days.[201] As Mexico's administrative practice is to send the questionnaires out the day following the publication of the initiation, the parties seem to be in agreement that exporters listed in the application and to which questionnaires are sent at the time of initiation would in fact have at least 30 calendar days to respond, as required by Article 6.1.1 of the AD Agreement.

7.219 The United States does challenge, however, the consistency of Article 53 of the Act with Article 6.1.1 of the AD Agreement with regard to exporters or foreign producers which were not listed in the application as being known to the applicant and which for that reason were not sent a questionnaire at initiation. Mexico is of the view that the 30-day period of Article 6.1.1 of the AD Agreement only applies to exporters or foreign producers to which a questionnaire was sent at initiation and not to those exporters or producers that appear later in the course of the investigation. According to Mexico Article 6.1.1 of the AD Agreement does not oblige Economía to provide for 30 days to respond to questionnaires with respect to exporters which received questionnaires only after such exporters had come forward and requested such questionnaires.

7.220 We consider that Article 6.1.1 of the AD Agreement clearly provides that any exporter or foreign producer receiving a questionnaire shall be given 30 days for reply. This 30-day rule does not make a distinction between those exporters that received a questionnaire at the time of initiation because they happened to be known to the applicant and were thus informed of the initiation, and those that make themselves known or the existence of which becomes known to the authorities and to which questionnaires are sent following initiation. In our view,

[201] Article 3 of the Mexican Foreign Trade Act (LCE) speaks of "días habiles". See Mexico's First Submission, para. 225.

by using the date of publication of the initiation notice as the starting point for the time period for questionnaire responses, Article 53 of the Act effectively prevents Mexico from giving each exporter or foreign producer receiving a questionnaire 30 days to respond. For that reason we consider Article 53 of the Act to be inconsistent with the unequivocal requirement in Article 6.1.1 of the AD Agreement to provide for 30 days to respond to questionnaires.[202]

7.221 The United States also argues that Article 53 of the Act is inconsistent with the second sentence of Article 6.1.1 of the AD Agreement because it prevents Economía from giving due consideration to extension requests, let alone granting such requests. Mexico submits that Article 53 of the Act does not have this effect.

7.222 Even assuming *arguendo* that we were to agree with Mexico that nothing in Article 53 of the Act prevents the authorities from granting extensions, when requested, this, in our view would not be able to cure the original failure to provide for 30 days to respond to questionnaires for all exporters or foreign producers. The first sentence of Article 6.1.1 of the AD Agreement is categorical in requiring that 30 days be given to respond to questionnaires. The second sentence of Article 6.1.1 of the AD Agreement dealing with extension requests, thus refers to requests to obtain more than the 30 days required. Exporters or foreign producers receiving questionnaires should not be forced to use the possibility of requesting extensions to obtain the time period of 30 days they are entitled to, without any showing of good cause. Article 6.1.1 of the AD Agreement requires Members, with regard to extension requests, to give "due consideration" to such request, and to grant them, "whenever practicable". The language of the first sentence of Article 6.1.1 of the AD Agreement relating to the 30 days rule does not contain such caveats and does not allow for any exceptions, and exporters or foreign producers should not be forced to hope to obtain by requesting extensions a time period for responding to questionnaires they are in any case entitled to.

7.223 In sum, we find that Article 53 of the Act is as such inconsistent with Article 6.1.1 of the AD Agreement. In addition, we consider that the requirement contained in Article 6.1.1 of the AD Agreement to provide for 30 days to respond to questionnaires is identical to that of Article 12.1.1 of the SCM Agreement. For the same reasons as set forth above, we therefore find that Article 53 of the Act is as such also inconsistent with Article 12.1.1 of the SCM Agreement.

---

[202] We note that Mexico has argued that the United States should have adduced evidence, in each of its claims concerning the law as such, of the application of the law by the executive authorities and its interpretation by the domestic courts. We find no basis for such a requirement in this case. These sources may become important in WTO jurisprudence or general public international law as the adjudicator may in certain circumstances need to consider the interpretation of the law by domestic courts and the application by the executive authority in order to determine the real scope and meaning of the text of the domestic law. In this case, where the United States as the complainant has made a *prima facie* case that the language of the domestic law in question is on its face manifestly WTO inconsistent, we do not consider that – absent anything more substantive and concrete than the counter-assertion by Mexico of its consistency – we would have to wait until a domestic law is applied and interpreted by the domestic courts before this law could be dealt with by a WTO panel.

7.224 We finally note that Mexico argues that in Mexican law, international agreements such as the WTO agreements are "self-executing" and automatically applicable in Mexico, and that any domestic law has to be applied in a manner which is compatible with Mexico's international obligations.[203] While we understand the important role given to Mexico's international commitments by providing for the direct effect of international agreements such as the WTO Agreements in Mexican law, we do not consider that for this reason, Mexico's laws would be shielded from any review of the consistency of these laws with the WTO Agreements or that such laws can never be found to be inconsistent with the WTO Agreements. The fact that provision is made for the direct effect of the WTO Agreements does not automatically and inevitably ensure a correct interpretation of the WTO Agreements, at least not in a situation where there is also a distinct domestic legal provision which manifestly conflicts with the terms of the Agreements. In our view, the direct effect of the WTO Agreements in Mexican law may prove important in case the domestic law leaves the authority with discretion to apply the law in a WTO consistent manner. However, in case the domestic law which implements Mexico's international commitments with regard to for example the AD Agreement and SCM Agreement, as does the Act, is clear and manifestly conflicts with and effectively impairs the enjoyment of the rights which the affected party is unconditionally entitled to under the WTO Agreement, as is the case here, then the direct effect of the WTO Agreements cannot shield the domestic law from such scrutiny by WTO panels.[204]

7.225 This is especially so in case the challenged provisions do not leave any room for interpretation but are clearly inconsistent with the WTO Agreement. Absent any contrary indication that the law does not mean what the text of the law indicates it means, the challenged provision of the law is inconsistent with the Agreement. In this case, Mexico has not provided any such evidence, quite to the contrary, it has vigorously defended its law as being consistent as such with the WTO Agreement, and has argued that the law does not provide for 30 days to respond to questionnaires in case such questionnaires are sent to exporters that appear after the initiation because this is not required by the AD Agreement. Since we find that the AD Agreement does provide for such a right to have 30 days to respond to questionnaires for all exporters receiving such questionnaires, we find this provision of the Act to be inconsistent as such with Articles 6.1.1 of the AD Agreement and 12.1.1 of the SCM Agreement.

---

[203] Mexico First Submission, paras. 202 - 206. Mexico asserts that this is set forth in Article 2 of the Act which provides as follows: "The provisions of this Act are public policy provisions that apply throughout the Republic, without prejudice to the provisions of the international treaties or agreements to which Mexico is party".

[204] While Mexico is right in saying that a Member's law is assumed to be a good faith implementation of its commitments until proven otherwise, it is therefore also correct to assume that by drafting the law the way it did, Mexico assumingly considered it was implementing its commitments in a WTO consistent manner, and it can thus be assumed that the executive authority will simply execute what the law requires it do without questioning the legal validity of such obligations in light of the WTO Agreement. In fact to find otherwise, and taking the Mexican argument to its logical conclusion, would imply that it does not matter at all what the law says since the WTO Agreements have direct effect and they prevail. Such a reading which renders the domestic legal provisions completely irrelevant cannot be correct.

2. *Claim 15: Article 64 of Mexico's Foreign Trade Act is inconsistent "as such" with Articles 6.8, 9.3, 9.4, and 9.5 of the AD Agreement, paragraphs 1, 3, 5, and 7 of Annex II of the AD Agreement, and Articles 12.7 and 19.3 of the SCM Agreement*

(a) Arguments of the Parties

(i) United States

7.226 The United States submits that Article 64 of the Act breaches Article 9.4 of the AD Agreement as it does not provide for the application of a neutral "all others " rate for unexamined exporters and producers. According to the United States, Article 64 of the Act requires the application of the highest margin obtained from the facts available to, *inter alia*, (a) firms which "failed to appear" at the investigation because they were not properly informed and never received a questionnaire; and (b) firms which cooperate but demonstrate that they did not export during the period of investigation. Therefore, the United States argues, at least with regard to these two categories of firms Article 64 of the Act is inconsistent as such with Article 9.4 of the AD Agreement.

7.227 In addition, the United States argues, Article 64 of the Act violates Articles 6.8 of the AD Agreement, and paras. 1, 3, 5 and 7 of Annex II of the AD Agreement, which limit the applicability of facts available to situations where information that was requested from individually examined firms was not provided within a reasonable period of time or in case of significant impediment of the investigation. Under Article 64 of the Act, the investigating authority is required to blindly apply the highest margin to firms even if such firms were never informed of the information that was required of them in violation of para. 1 of Annex II. Article 64 of the Act also applies in cases in which the firms acted to the best of their abilities as is the case for cooperative producers who did not export during the period of investigation, thereby violating paras. 3, 5 and 7 of Annex II. Finally by requiring the imposition of the highest margin, the Act precludes the investigating authority from using the secondary source information "with special circumspection" as required by paragraph 7 of Annex II, and this with regard to all categories of situations to which Article 64 of the Act applies.

7.228 For the same reasons, and because it deprives the investigating authority of all discretion to evaluate the appropriateness of using facts available for parties which were cooperative or not individually examined, the United States submits that Article 64 also violates Article 12.7 of the SCM Agreement. The United States submits that the Act also violates Article 19.3 of the SCM Agreement requiring that duties be levied "in appropriate amounts" in each case, as nothing in the SCM Agreement justifies a determination that the appropriate amounts of duties for parties that did not export or were not even sent a questionnaire is necessarily the highest margin suggested by the applicant.

7.229 Finally, the United States submits that Article 64 of the Act breaches the Articles 19.3 of the SCM Agreement and 9.5 of the AD Agreement concerning expedited reviews. Article 19.3 of the SCM Agreement provides for expedited reviews for exporters who were not actually investigated for reasons other than a refusal to cooperate. As uninformed producers and producers who simply did not export during the period of investigation are deemed to have been investigated, no producer will ever be able to claim the benefits of an expedited review and Article 64 of the Act thus renders Article 19.3 of the SCM Agreement a nullity. Similarly, Article 9.5 of the AD Agreement provides for expedited reviews if the producers which did not export during the period of investigation are not related to exporters subject to the duties on the product. The United States asserts that since under Article 64 of the Act, firms that did not export are deemed to have been investigated, such firms will never be able to request the benefit of an expedited review under Article 9.5 of the AD Agreement, as they are not just related to exporters subject to the duties, they are themselves subject to the duties. Article 64 of the Act thus breaches Article 9.5 of the AD Agreement as well.

7.230 Finally, the United States argues that, in light of the fact that Article 64 of the Act requires the application of the highest margin rather than the neutral all others rate, the Act also inevitably violates Article 9.3 of the AD Agreement as it will lead to the imposition of duties in excess of the margin of dumping established under Article 2 of the AD Agreement.

(ii) Mexico

7.231 Mexico asserts that Article 64 of the Act which stipulates that the margin of dumping or subsidization is to be calculated on the basis of the facts available for interested parties that do not appear in the investigation or have no exports during the period of investigation and have therefore not provided the necessary information is consistent with the provisions of the AD Agreement and the SCM Agreement. Mexico is of the view that Articles 6.8 of the AD Agreement and 12.7 of the SCM Agreement provide for the application of facts available in case information necessary for the determination of a margin is not provided. This is the case when exporters do not appear in the investigation or do not export during the period of investigation, as this implies that the exporters will not provide the normal value or export price information necessary for the calculation of a margin of dumping or subsidization.

7.232 In Mexico's view, Article 64 of the Act does not violate paragraphs 3 and 5 of Annex II of the AD Agreement either as these provisions contain obligations in case information was provided, while in the cases covered by Article 64 of the Act no information whatsoever has been received on one or more essential elements of a margin determination. In addition, Mexico is of the view that there is no obligation on the investigating authority to send questionnaires to all exporters and foreign producers and it is therefore justified to base a determination with regard to non-participating or non-exporting interested parties that do not provide the necessary information on the facts available, including the information contained in the application. For this reason, Article 64 of the Act is thus also consistent with paragraphs 1 and 7 of Annex II of the AD Agreement.

7.233 According to Mexico, Article 9.4 of the AD Agreement is only applicable in case the investigating authority has limited the number of exporters investigated to a sample and there does not exist any obligation in the AD Agreement to calculate a neutral all others rate for non-appearing or non-shipping exporters. Article 64 of the Act is thus not inconsistent with Article 9.4 of the AD Agreement either.

7.234 Furthermore, Mexico submits that Article 64 of the Act on no grounds prevents foreign producers or exporters that have made no shipments during the period of investigation from seeking a new shipper review, if they comply with the requirements of Article 9.5 of the AD Agreement and 19.3 of the SCM Agreement. Mexico refers to a request for a new shipper review granted by the authority after the revision of the Act had taken effect in support of its argument that Article 64 of the Act does not prohibit such reviews.[205]

7.235 Finally, Mexico submits that, in any case, by virtue of Article 133 of its Constitution, treaties such as the WTO Agreements are self-executing and automatically applicable in Mexican law, and as Article 2 of the Act makes clear, the Act will be implemented in a manner which is congruent with the provisions of the WTO Agreements. According to Mexico, the Act thus does not mandate any WTO inconsistent action.

(b) Analysis

7.236 The US claim concerns Article 64 of the Act which reads in pertinent part as follows:

> "... The Ministry shall determine a countervailing duty on the basis of the highest margin of price discrimination or subsidization obtained from the facts available, in the following cases:
>
> I. When the producers fail to appear at the investigation; or
>
> II. When the producers fail to provide the information in a proper and timely fashion, significantly impede the investigation, or supply information or evidence that is incomplete, incorrect or does not derive from their accounts, thus preventing the determination of an individual margin of price discrimination or subsidization; or
>
> III. When the producers have not exported the product subject to investigation during the investigation period.
>
> The facts available shall be understood to mean those substantiated by evidence and data provided by the interested parties or additional parties in a proper and timely fashion, and by the information gathered by the investigating authority."[206]

7.237 We first examine the US claim concerning the inconsistency of Article 64 of the Act with Article 6.8 and Annex II of the AD Agreement, and Article 12.7

[205] Mexico's Second Submission, para 213, footnote 12 –Exhibit MEX -12.

[206] We note that the term "countervailing duty" referred to throughout the Act is used to refer to both anti-dumping duties and countervailing duties.

of the SCM Agreement. We recall that Article 6.8 of the AD Agreement provides as follows:

> 6.8 In cases in which any interested party refuses access to, or otherwise does not provide, necessary information within a reasonable period or significantly impedes the investigation, preliminary and final determinations, affirmative or negative, may be made on the basis of the facts available. The provisions of Annex II shall be observed in the application of this paragraph.[207]

Article 6.8 of the AD Agreement thus allows for the use of facts available in case an interested party (i) refuses access to, or (ii) otherwise does not provide, necessary information within a reasonable period or (iii) significantly impedes the investigation. Article 64 of the Act on the other hand provides for the use of the highest margin based on the facts available with regard to producers that (i) fail to appear (Article 64.I of the Act); or (ii) fail to provide the information in a proper and timely fashion; or (iii) significantly impede the investigation; or (iv) supply information or evidence that is incomplete, incorrect or does not derive from their accounts (Article 64.II of the Act); or (v) that did not export the subject product during the period of investigation (Article 64.III of the Act). It is clear that the first and fifth category of situations covered by Article 64 of the Act are not expressly provided for in Article 6.8 of the AD Agreement which disciplines and restricts the use of facts available. We will therefore first consider the US arguments concerning Article 64.II of the Act and the use of the highest facts available margin to producers which fail to provide the information in a proper and timely fashion, significantly impede the investigation, or supply information or evidence that is incomplete, incorrect or does not derive from their accounts, thus preventing the determination of an individual margin of price discrimination or subsidization.

7.238 We recall that Article 6.8 of the AD Agreement provides that in certain situations in which access to necessary information is refused, such information is otherwise not provided within a reasonable period, or the investigation is significantly impeded, the authorities may make their determinations on the basis of the facts available. The fact gathering and evidentiary context in which Article 6.8 of the AD Agreement provides for this possibility clearly shows that Article 6.8 of the AD Agreement is there to allow authorities to continue with the investigation and make a determination, positive or negative, on the basis of the facts that are available. The Agreement expresses a clear preference for first-hand information, but does not allow any party to hold the authority hostage by not providing the necessary information, and thus provides that second-best information from secondary sources may be used in certain well-defined circumstances.

---

[207] Article 12.7 of the SCM Agreement similarly provides as follows:

> "In cases in which any interested Member or interested party refuses access to, or otherwise does not provide, necessary information within a reasonable period or significantly impedes the investigation, preliminary and final determinations, affirmative or negative, may be made on the basis of the facts available."

In light of the almost identical wording of Article 12.7 of the SCM Agreement, our analysis under Article 6.8 of the AD Agreement applies to Article 12.7 SCM of the Agreement as well.

The use of facts available under Article 6.8 of the AD Agreement is not however intended to operate as a punishment for those parties that do not provide such information. In fact, as paragraphs 1, 3, 5 and 7 of Annex II of the AD Agreement entitled "Best Information Available in Terms of Paragraph 8 of Article 6" clearly show, all the information provided by the parties, even if not ideal in all respects, should to the extent possible be used by the authorities, and in case secondary source information is to be used, the authorities should do so with special circumspection.[208] The final sentence of paragraph 7 of Annex II, in our view, only states the obvious that in case of non-co-operation, the result of such use of secondary source information could be less favourable to the party than if the party did cooperate. By making it a requirement to always use the highest margin based on the facts available Article 64 of the Act prohibits the authority from taking into account the specific circumstances of each individual case of non-provision of information. This effectively prevents the authority from being able to undertake the inherently comparative evaluation of this evidence available in a case at hand that is needed to meet the requirement that the facts available to be used are the "best" information that is available.[209] This, in our view, requires the authority to use those data which are most appropriate and best suited to replace the missing data. Since Article 64 of the Act effectively prevents the authorities from using the best information to replace the missing

---

[208] These paragraphs 1,3, 5 and 7 of Annex II provide as follows:

1. As soon as possible after the initiation of the investigation, the investigating authorities should specify in detail the information required from any interested party, and the manner in which that information should be structured by the interested party in its response. The authorities should also ensure that the party is aware that if information is not supplied within a reasonable time, the authorities will be free to make determinations on the basis of the facts available, including those contained in the application for the initiation of the investigation by the domestic industry.

3. All information which is verifiable, which is appropriately submitted so that it can be used in the investigation without undue difficulties, which is supplied in a timely fashion, and, where applicable, which is supplied in a medium or computer language requested by the authorities, should be taken into account when determinations are made. If a party does not respond in the preferred medium or computer language but the authorities find that the circumstances set out in paragraph 2 have been satisfied, the failure to respond in the preferred medium or computer language should not be considered to significantly impede the investigation.

5. Even though the information provided may not be ideal in all respects, this should not justify the authorities from disregarding it, provided the interested party has acted to the best of its ability.

7. If the authorities have to base their findings, including those with respect to normal value, on information from a secondary source, including the information supplied in the application for the initiation of the investigation, they should do so with special circumspection. In such cases, the authorities should, where practicable, check the information from other independent sources at their disposal, such as published price lists, official import statistics and customs returns, and from the information obtained from other interested parties during the investigation. It is clear, however, that if an interested party does not cooperate and thus relevant information is being withheld from the authorities, this situation could lead to a result which is less favourable to the party than if the party did cooperate.

[209] See para. 7.166 above.

data, we find that Article 64 of the Act is inconsistent with Article 6.8 and paragraphs 1, 3, 5 and 7 of Annex II of the AD Agreement.[210]

7.239 We will now address the US claim with regard to Article 64.I of the Act concerning the use of the highest facts available margin for producers which fail to appear. In similar vein, we consider that the use of facts available to make determinations with regard to exporters or producers that fail to appear could as such be permitted by Article 6.8 of the AD Agreement. We wish to emphasise that this will at least be the case if the investigating authority has first made a reasonable effort to ensure that all interested parties are informed of the information required, and if a copy of the application and a notice of the initiation has been sent to all exporters that an objective investigating authority can reasonably be considered to have knowledge of, as required by Article 6.1.3 and 12.1 of the AD Agreement.[211] Indeed, in case a party is informed of the initiation, is requested to provide information or is sent a questionnaire, but does not respond and does not take part in the investigation, we consider that Article 6.8 of the AD Agreement would clearly allow the authority to use the facts available. However, and for the same reasons as set forth above, we are of the view that a rule which provides for the use of the highest margin based on the facts available in each case of a failure to appear is not consistent with the requirement that the facts used to replace the missing data should be the best and most appropriate information available. To indiscriminately require the use of the highest margin even if completely unrelated to the exporter which failed to appear, does, in our view, not comply with this requirement. We thus find that Article 64.I of the Act is inconsistent with Article 6.8 and paragraphs 1, 3, 5 and 7 of Annex II of the AD Agreement.

7.240 Finally, Article 64.III of the Act requires the application of the highest margin based on the facts available to producers which did not export during the period of investigation.

---

[210] This is not, in our view, inconsistent with any view that it is conceivable that in a particular case, the "best information available" leads to use of the highest margin. What is however inconceivable is that this can be predetermined to be *always* the "best information available".

[211] We note that, in Mexico, the situation covered by the "failure to appear" in Article 64.I of the Act would seem to cover also that of any interested party which, even when not requested to provide information, fails to make itself known to the investigating authority so that it can be examined individually. We are mindful of the fact that Article 64 of the Act was revised following the conclusion of the rice investigation and that this investigation can thus not be considered as evidence of the application of Article 64 of the Act. Nevertheless, Mexico does not contest that the category of "producers that fail to appear" in Article 64.I of the Act is to be understood to cover all foreign producers or exporters that do not provide information, irrespective of the fact that no effort was undertaken by the authority to contact such exporters and to inform them of the information required for the determination. According to Mexico, the investigating authority is not required to take an active approach, and complies with all the obligations under the AD Agreement by providing questionnaires to the exporters or foreign producers listed in the application and to those that come forward out of their own initiative because they have learned about the initiation. As we stated earlier, we are of the view, that an investigating authority which fails to ensure that all interested parties are given notice of the information that is required of them and ample opportunity to present all evidence they consider relevant to their case, is not entitled to make determinations on the basis of the facts available. In our view, such exporters cannot be considered to have failed to provide necessary information, since they were never properly informed of the information they were requested to provide.

7.241 Once again, and assuming *arguendo* that a margin of dumping for non-shipping exporters is governed by the terms of Article 6.8 of the AD Agreement [212]we are of the view that the problem with Article 64.III of the Act consists of the indiscriminate requirement to use the highest margin based on the facts available rather than the margin that results from the use of the best information available. In effect, Article 64 of the Act does not simply provide for the use of facts available in order to calculate a margin of dumping for the non-shipping exporter. It rather requires that for all non-shipping exporters, regardless of the circumstances of the case, the highest margin found on the basis of the facts available is to be applied to such non-shipping exporters. For the reasons set forth above, we are of the view that such a rule that requires the authority to always apply the highest margin is inconsistent with Article 6.8 and paragraphs 1, 3, 5 and 7 of Annex II of the AD Agreement.

7.242 In sum, and for the reasons set forth above, we find that Article 64 of the Act which requires the authority to determine "a countervailing duty on the basis of the highest margin of price discrimination or subsidization" obtained from the facts available in the three situations described in Article 64 of the Act to be inconsistent with Article 6.8 of the AD Agreement and paragraphs 1, 3, 5 and 7 of Annex II of the AD Agreement, and Article 12.7 of the SCM Agreement.[213] In light of our findings, we do not consider it necessary for the resolution of this dispute to make any rulings on the US claims with regard to violations of Article 9.3, 9.4, 9.5 of the AD Agreement, and Article 19.3 of the SCM Agreement.

3. *Claim 16: Article 68 of Mexico's Foreign Trade Act is inconsistent "as such" with Articles 5.8, 9.3, and 11.2 of the AD Agreement and Articles 11.9 and 21.2 of the SCM Agreement*

(a) Arguments of the Parties

(i) United States

7.243 The United States argues that Article 68 of the Act requires the investigating authority to conduct reviews of final anti-dumping and countervailing measures with respect to companies that were found not to have been dumping or not to have received countervailable subsidies during the original period of investigation. The United States submits that this is clearly inconsistent with the explicit requirement of Article 5.8 of the AD Agreement and 11.9 of the SCM Agreement to terminate the investigation immediately in case no margin of dumping or countervailable subsidy was found to exist.

7.244 In addition, the United States argues that Article 68 of the Act is inconsistent with the AD and SCM Agreement as it requires exporters or producers requesting a review to demonstrate that the sales during the review period were

---

[212] See footnote 158.

[213] For the reasons given in paras. 7.224 and 7.225, we reject the Mexican defence on the basis of the direct effect of international agreements in Mexican law.

"representative", while no such additional requirement for obtaining a review exists in Articles 9.3 and 11.2 of the AD Agreement and 21.2 of the SCM Agreement. In the view of the United States, these provisions do not permit the introduction of such an additional requirement. The United States therefore submits that by requiring the authority to deny a review unless a party demonstrates that its exports were "representative", Article 68 of the Act is inconsistent as such with the AD Agreement and the SCM Agreement.

(ii) Mexico

7.245 Mexico rejects the US allegations of inconsistency of Article 68 of the Act with Articles 5.8, 9.3 and 11.2 of the AD Agreement and Articles 11.9 and 21.2 of the SCM Agreement. First, Mexico argues that Article 5.8 of the AD Agreement and 11.9 of the SCM Agreement do not apply to reviews but only to original investigations. Mexico therefore considers that the US argument that Article 68 of the Act violates Articles 5.8 of the AD Agreement and 11.9 of the SCM Agreement in subjecting to administrative reviews exporters for whom no margin of dumping or subsidization was determined is without merit since the allegedly infringed Articles do not even apply in the case of reviews. Furthermore, Mexico is of the view that Article 5.8 of the AD Agreement and Article 11.9 of the SCM Agreement do not require the exclusion of an exporter from the measure and therefore from being subjected to reviews simply because no margin of dumping was established in the original investigation. According to Mexico, Article 3.3 of the AD Agreement and 15.3 of the SCM Agreement clearly show that an investigation is only to be terminated in case the margin of dumping calculated on a country-wide basis rather than a firm-specific basis is below *de minimis*. In any case, Mexico is of the view that a review does not imply the imposition of a duty and thus does not negatively affect the exporters concerned. Such reviews are thus similar to those provided in Article 9.3.1 of the AD Agreement concerning the determination of final liability for payment of anti-dumping duties.

7.246 Mexico further submits that Article 68 of the Act does not impose a "representativeness" requirement as a condition for the investigating authority to conduct reviews such as those provided for in Article 21.2 of the SCM Agreement and Articles 9.3 and 11.2 of the AD Agreement. According to Mexico, there are no clear provisions in the AD Agreement or SCM Agreement as to the procedures for conducting administrative reviews and new exporter reviews, and the "representativeness" requirement of Article 68 of the Act is merely a means of ascertaining that the export volumes reported in administrative review or new shipper reviews reflect normal volumes that are representative of the sales policies of exporters seeking such reviews. Mexico asserts that an exporter is not required to show "representative volume of sales" in order to obtain the initiation of a review, but that an interested party will need to demonstrate such representativeness in order to be able to determine a margin of dumping for that party.[214] In

[214] Mexico First Answers to Questions, question 31.

any case, according to Mexico, the United States fails to demonstrate that such a requirement is a sine qua non requirement for the initiation of such reviews.[215]

7.247 Finally, Mexico submits that, in any case, by virtue of Article 133 of its Constitution, treaties such as the WTO Agreements are self-executing and automatically applicable in Mexican law, and as Article 2 of the Act makes clear, the Act will be implemented in a manner which is congruent with the provisions of the WTO Agreements. According to Mexico, the Act thus does not mandate any WTO inconsistent action.

(b) Analysis

7.248 The United States makes two claims concerning Article 68 of the Act. First, the United States argues that by subjecting exporters for which the original investigation showed a margin of dumping or subsidization below *de minimis* to administrative reviews, Article 68 of the Act is inconsistent with Article 5.8 of the AD Agreement and 11.9 of the SCM Agreement. Second, the United States submits that by requiring exporters requesting a review to show that their volume of sales during the review period was representative, Article 68 of the Act is in breach of Articles 9.3 and 11.2 of the AD Agreement and Article 21.2 of the SCM Agreement.

7.249 We will first examine the US claim of violation of Article 5.8 of the AD Agreement and Article 11.9 of the SCM Agreement. Article 5.8 of the AD Agreement provides as follows[216]:

> 5.8 An application under paragraph 1 shall be rejected and an investigation shall be terminated promptly as soon as the authorities concerned are satisfied that there is not sufficient evidence of either dumping or of injury to justify proceeding with the case. There shall be immediate termination in cases where the authorities determine that the margin of dumping is *de minimis*, or that the volume of dumped imports, actual or potential, or the injury, is negligible. The margin of dumping shall be considered to be *de minimis* if this margin is less than 2 per cent, expressed as a percentage of the export price. The volume of dumped imports shall normally be regarded as negligible if the volume of dumped imports from a particular country is found to account for less than 3 per cent of imports of the like product in the importing Member,

---

[215] Mexico asserts that this is clear from a recent review on imports of dessert apples from the United States (Exhibit MEX-13).

[216] Article 11.9 of the SCM Agreement provides as follows:

> 11.9 An application under para. 1 shall be rejected and an investigation shall be terminated promptly as soon as the authorities concerned are satisfied that there is not sufficient evidence of either subsidization or of injury to justify proceeding with the case. There shall be immediate termination in cases where the amount of a subsidy is *de minimis*, or where the volume of subsidized imports, actual or potential, or the injury, is negligible. For the purpose of this paragraph, the amount of the subsidy shall be considered to be *de minimis* if the subsidy is less than 1 per cent *ad valorem*.

> unless countries which individually account for less than 3 per cent of the imports of the like product in the importing Member collectively account for more than 7 per cent of imports of the like product in the importing Member.

7.250 In turn, Article 68 of the Act in pertinent part provides as follows:

> Final countervailing duties shall be reviewed annually at the request of a party or ex officio by the Ministry at any time, as shall imports from producers for whom no positive margin of price discrimination or subsidization was determined in the investigation...

7.251 Article 68 of the Act thus requires the review of producers for which during the original investigation it was determined that they had not been engaged in dumping practices or had not received any subsidies. In our view, and for the reasons set forth above when discussing the US claims concerning the inclusion in the Anti-dumping measures on rice of the two exporters found not to have been dumping during the period of investigation, we find that Article 5.8 of the AD Agreement requires the termination of the investigation with regard to such exporters found not to have been dumping above *de minimis* levels, and requires that such exporters be excluded from the measures imposed. The logical consequence of such an exclusion of producers found not to have been dumping is that they can not subsequently be subjected to administrative or changed circumstances reviews. While we agree with Mexico that the specific requirements concerning *de minimis* do not apply in the case of reviews of the duties imposed, this does not imply that Article 68 of the Act dealing with reviews cannot be inconsistent with Article 5.8 of the AD Agreement insofar as it imposes the review of measures with regard to producers to which such measures should not have been applied in the first place. The possibility of reviewing the zero per cent duty margin imposed on such non-dumping exporters also reveals the important meaning of the imposition of such a zero per cent duty which, in spite of its appearance, does not equal the termination of the investigation as required by Article 5.8 of the AD Agreement. We therefore find that Article 68 of the Act is as such inconsistent with Article 5.8 of the AD Agreement. For the same reasons, *mutatis mutandis*, Article 68 of the Act is in breach of Article 11.9 of the SCM Agreement.

7.252 The second claim of the United States with regard to Article 68 of the Act concerns the consistency with Article 9.3 and 11.2 of the AD Agreement and 21.2 of the SCM Agreement of the "representativeness" requirement which, according to the United States, is imposed by Article 68 of the Act. Article 68 of the Act in pertinent part reads as follows:

> The party requesting a review shall satisfy the Ministry that the volume of exports to Mexico during the review period is representative.[217]

---

[217] See *Mexico's 2003 WTO Notification* (G/ADP/N/1/MEX/1/Suppl.2), at page 9. The equivalent Spanish text reads: "La solicitante de una revisión deberá demostrar ante la Secretaría que el volumen

7.253 We consider that Article 68 of the Act clearly imposes as a requirement to obtain an administrative, i.e. duty assessment review, or a changed circumstances review a showing by the party requesting such reviews that its volume of exports to Mexico during the review period was representative. Article 68 of the Act, by using such mandatory wording that the party requesting such reviews "shall satisfy" the Ministry leaves little to be desired in terms of clarity of what is required of a party requesting reviews. In fact, Mexico confirmed as much in its answer to a question from the panel, when it stated that an exporter is not required to show a representative volume of sales in order to obtain the initiation of a review, but that "in the course of a review, an interested party will need to demonstrate such representativeness in order to be able to determine a margin of dumping for that party".[218] In other words, we understand Mexico to confirm that while a review may be initiated without a showing of representativeness, the duties will not be reviewed for any party that fails to satisfy the authority that the volume of exports during the review period was representative. We do not consider meaningful the distinction drawn by Mexico between the right to obtain the initiation of a review and the right to have the duties reviewed, as an initiation of review without chance of success because of a failure to demonstrate representative volume of exports is meaningless.

7.254 The question before us is thus whether such a requirement to show representative volume of exports is consistent with Article 9.3 and 11.2 of the AD Agreement and 21.2 of the SCM Agreement.

7.255 Article 9.3 of the AD Agreement provides as follows:

> 9.3 The amount of the anti-dumping duty shall not exceed the margin of dumping as established under Article 2.
>
> 9.3.1 When the amount of the anti-dumping duty is assessed on a retrospective basis, the determination of the final liability for payment of anti-dumping duties shall take place as soon as possible, normally within 12 months, and in no case more than 18 months, after the date on which a request for a final assessment of the amount of the anti-dumping duty has been made.[20] Any refund shall be made promptly and normally in not more than 90 days following the determination of final liability made pursuant to this sub-paragraph. In any case, where a refund is not made within 90 days, the authorities shall provide an explanation if so requested.
>
> 9.3.2 When the amount of the anti-dumping duty is assessed on a prospective basis, provision shall be made for a prompt refund, upon request, of any duty paid in excess of the margin of dumping. A refund of any such duty paid in excess of the actual margin of dumping shall normally take place within 12 months, and in no

de las exportaciones realizadas a México durante el período de revisión es representativo." *Ibid.* (Spanish) at page 10.

[218] Mexico First Answers to Questions, question 31.

> case more than 18 months, after the date on which a request for a refund, duly supported by evidence, has been made by an importer of the product subject to the anti-dumping duty. The refund authorized should normally be made within 90 days of the above-noted decision.
>
> 9.3.3 In determining whether and to what extent a reimbursement should be made when the export price is constructed in accordance with paragraph 3 of Article 2, authorities should take account of any change in normal value, any change in costs incurred between importation and resale, and any movement in the resale price which is duly reflected in subsequent selling prices, and should calculate the export price with no deduction for the amount of anti-dumping duties paid when conclusive evidence of the above is provided.
>
> [20] It is understood that the observance of the time-limits mentioned in this subparagraph and in subparagraph 3.2 may not be possible where the product in question is subject to judicial review proceedings.

7.256 Article 11.2 of the AD Agreement provides that:

> 11.2 The authorities shall review the need for the continued imposition of the duty, where warranted, on their own initiative or, provided that a reasonable period of time has elapsed since the imposition of the definitive anti-dumping duty, upon request by any interested party which submits positive information substantiating the need for a review.[21] Interested parties shall have the right to request the authorities to examine whether the continued imposition of the duty is necessary to offset dumping, whether the injury would be likely to continue or recur if the duty were removed or varied, or both. If, as a result of the review under this paragraph, the authorities determine that the anti-dumping duty is no longer warranted, it shall be terminated immediately.[219]
>
> [21] A determination of final liability for payment of anti-dumping duties, as provided for in paragraph 3 of Article 9, does not by itself constitute a review within the meaning of this Article.

---

[219] Article 21.2 of the SCM Agreement similarly provides as follows:

> 21.2 The authorities shall review the need for the continued imposition of the duty, where warranted, on their own initiative or, provided that a reasonable period of time has elapsed since the imposition of the definitive countervailing duty, upon request by any interested party which submits positive information substantiating the need for a review. Interested parties shall have the right to request the authorities to examine whether the continued imposition of the duty is necessary to offset subsidization, whether the injury would be likely to continue or recur if the duty were removed or varied, or both. If, as a result of the review under this paragraph, the authorities determine that the countervailing duty is no longer warranted, it shall be terminated immediately.

7.257 It is clear that these provisions do not as such require a showing of representativeness of sales volumes in order for a duty to be reviewed. With regard to duty assessment or administrative reviews Article 9.3 of the AD Agreement clearly states that the amount of the anti-dumping duty shall not exceed the margin of dumping as established under Article 2. Therefore, Article 9.3.2 states that provision shall be made for a prompt refund, upon request, of any duty paid in excess of the margin of dumping. The only condition imposed by Article 9.3.2 is that a request for refund shall be duly supported by evidence. In our view, the "evidence" referred to in this context of determining final liability for the product relates to the information required to determine a margin of dumping in line with Article 2 of the AD Agreement, i.e. normal value and export price information. Article 9.3 thus does not require the exporters concerned to first demonstrate that the sales made during the review period were "representative" in order for the authority to be obliged to review the duties and refund the duties paid in excess of the margin of dumping. Neither does Article 2 of the AD Agreement provide that the number of export sales of an exporter has to be "representative" for the authority to be able to determine a margin of dumping for this exporter. It would in our view be inconsistent with the Agreement to refuse to refund the duties paid in excess of the margin of dumping, because only a small number of such export sales were made. Article 9.3.2 of the AD Agreement requires that any duty paid in excess of the margin of dumping is to be refunded, and the number of export sales is thus completely irrelevant in this respect. We therefore conclude that no such requirement can be imposed on the exporter when it is requesting the refund of the duties paid in excess of the margin of dumping through an administrative review.

7.258 With regard to changed circumstances review, Article 9.3 and 11.2 of the AD Agreement similarly does not include a requirement of "representativeness" in order for the exporter to be entitled to request a changed circumstances review. The only requirements imposed by Article 11.2 of the AD Agreement on the request by an exporter for such a review are that a reasonable period of time has lapsed, and that the interested party requesting the review submits positive information substantiating the need for a review. As the second sentence of Article 11.2 of the AD Agreement makes clear, such positive information relates to whether the continued imposition of the duty is necessary to offset dumping, whether the injury would be likely to continue or recur if the duty were removed or varied, or both. If those conditions are met, Article 11.2 of the AD Agreement stipulates that the authorities shall review the need for the continued imposition of the duty. In our view, Article 11.2 of the AD Agreement thus requires an authority to review the need for the continued imposition of the duty in case these two requirements are met.

7.259 Article 68 of the Act requires *as a rule* that *each time* an interested party is unable to show that volume of exports during the review period was representative, such a review is to be denied. This in our view is inconsistent with the Agreement. Under a changed circumstances review of Article 11.2 of the AD Agreement, the authority examines whether there is continued need for the measure and whether the duty is to be varied or removed. A situation could be envisaged where the positive information substantiating the need for a review that the interested party is to adduce in support of its request relates only to its domestic sales and the normal value side of the dumping margin. A possible example could be a case where an exporter requests a review based on an important and dramatic drop in the normal value for the product due to a change in the cost structure of the company for example. This will have an obvious effect on the dumping margin and may thus warrant a review that leads to the duty being removed or varied. The change in circumstances is unrelated to export side of the equation. An interested party is entitled to a changed circumstances review under Article 11.2 of the AD Agreement and 21.2 of the SCM Agreement, if it submits positive information substantiating the need for a review. What such positive information relates to will depend from case to case, and such positive information does not, in our view, necessarily include that a representative number of exports sales were made. We consider that by requiring the authority to reject a review each time the volume of export sales was not representative, even in cases where the change in circumstances is unrelated to the export price, Article 68 of the Act requires the authority to reject reviews in a manner which is inconsistent with Article 11.2 of the AD Agreement.[220]

7.260 We therefore find that by imposing this additional requirement that interested parties requesting a review are required to always satisfy the authority that the volume of the export sales was representative, Article 68 of the Act is as such inconsistent with Articles 9.3 and 11.2 of the AD Agreement and, *mutatis mutandis*, Article 21.2 of the SCM Agreement.[221]

4. *Claim 17: Article 89D of Mexico's Foreign Trade Act is inconsistent "as such" with Article 9.5 of the AD Agreement and Article 19.3 of the SCM Agreement*

(a) Arguments of the Parties

(i) United States

7.261 The United States asserts that Article 89 D of the Act restricts the ability of interested parties to obtain expedited reviews in a manner which is inconsistent with Article 9.5 of the AD Agreement and Article 19.3 of the SCM Agreement. According to the United States, Article 89D of the Act requires a producer to demonstrate that the volume of exports during the review period was "representative", while no such requirement exists in Articles 9.5 of the AD Agreement and 19.3 of the SCM Agreement. In addition, under the Act such expedited reviews are available to producers only, while the AD Agreement and the SCM

220 We acknowledge that the representativeness of the export sales can in certain situations be a relevant factor in determining whether it is appropriate to remove or vary the duty. A showing of such representativeness may thus be requested as part of the "positive information substantiating the need for a review" which is to be submitted by the interested party requesting the review. Whether that is so will depend on the circumstances of each case. In our view, the rule of Article 68 of the Act fails to take these specific circumstances into account.

221 For the reasons set forth in paras. 7.224 and 7.225, we reject Mexico's defence based on the direct effect of international treaties in Mexican law.

Agreement provide for such reviews for both producing and non-producing exporters.

(ii) Mexico

7.262 Mexico argues that Article 89D of the Act is not inconsistent with Article 9.5 of the AD Agreement or Article 19.3 of the SCM Agreement. First, Mexico is of the view that even if Articles 9.5 of the AD Agreement and 19.3 of the SCM Agreement do not do so expressly, it is in light of the context and purpose of these provisions only logical that the authorities require that the review be based on a representative amount of exports, as only this will enable the authorities to conduct an adequate price comparison. Second, Mexico asserts that although Article 89D of the Act mentions only "producers", the text of Article 89D of the Act has to be read in combination with the WTO Agreements themselves. Mexico asserts that Article 89D of the Act confers a right to a new shipper review under certain circumstances to both producers and exporters as is evidenced by the resolution initiating the new shipper procedure concerning imports of apples from the United States, paragraphs 3 and 32 of which show that the new shipper review was initiated at the request of an exporting firm which was a trading enterprise.[222] Moreover, Mexico argues, Article 47 of the Act's Regulations also allows new shipper reviews for non-producing enterprises, i.e. enterprises devoted solely to exportation.

7.263 Finally, Mexico submits that, in any case, by virtue of Article 133 of its Constitution, treaties such as the WTO Agreements are self-executing and automatically applicable in Mexican law, and as Article 2 of the Act makes clear, the Act will be implemented in a manner which is congruent with the provisions of the WTO Agreements. According to Mexico, the Act thus does not mandate any WTO inconsistent action.

(b) Analysis

7.264 The US claim concerns Article 89D of the Act which provides as follows:

> Article 89D – Producers of goods subject to a final countervailing duty who exported no such goods during the period under investigation in the proceedings that gave rise to such duty may request the Ministry to initiate a procedure for new exporters with a view to assessing individual margins of price discrimination, provided that:
>
> I. Their exports to the national territory of the goods subject to countervailing duties were subsequent to the period under investigation in the proceedings that gave rise to the countervailing duty. **The requesting party shall satisfy the Ministry that the volume of exports during the period of review is representative**; and

[222] Mexico Second Submission, para. 230. Exhibit MEX – 12.

> II. They show that they are not related in any way to the producers or exporters in the exporting country determined to be subject to a specific countervailing duty. (emphasis added)

7.265 According to the United States Article 89D of the Act provides for a requirement of "representativeness" that is not provided for by Article 9.5 of the AD Agreement or 19.3 of the SCM Agreement. Article 9.5 of the AD Agreement provides as follows:

> If a product is subject to anti-dumping duties in an importing Member, the authorities shall promptly carry out a review for the purpose of determining individual margins of dumping for any exporters or producers in the exporting country in question who have not exported the product to the importing Member during the period of investigation, provided that these exporters or producers can show that they are not related to any of the exporters or producers in the exporting country who are subject to the anti-dumping duties on the product. Such a review shall be initiated and carried out on an accelerated basis, compared to normal duty assessment and review proceedings in the importing Member. No anti-dumping duties shall be levied on imports from such exporters or producers while the review is being carried out. The authorities may, however, withhold appraisement and/or request guarantees to ensure that, should such a review result in a determination of dumping in respect of such producers or exporters, anti-dumping duties can be levied retroactively to the date of the initiation of the review.

7.266 In our view, this provision clearly does not subject the right to an expedited new shipper review to a showing of a "representative" volume of export sales as does Article 89D of the Act. Article 9.5 of the AD Agreement provides that the authorities shall promptly carry out a review, provided that the exporters or producers who have not exported the product subject to a duty during the period of investigation can show that they are not related to any of the exporters or producers in the exporting country who are subject to the anti-dumping duties on the product. In sum, in case a producer or exporter which (i) has not exported the product to the country concerned during the period of investigation and (ii) is not related to an exporter or producer already subject to the duty requests a new shipper review, the authority is required to promptly carry out such a review. Article 89 D of the Act on the other hand provides that an exporter may request an expedited review in case it (i) has not exported during the period of investigation, (ii) is not related to an exporter or producer that is already subject to a duty, and (iii) can demonstrate that the volume of exports during the review period is representative. We consider that to the extent that Article 89 D of the Act subjects the entitlement to a prompt review to a showing of representative volumes of export sales, it is inconsistent with Article 9.5 of the AD Agreement, which does not allow an authority to deny a request for reasons other than the two mentioned above and explicitly set forth in Article 9.5 of the AD Agreement.

7.267 Article 19.3 of the SCM Agreement provides as follows:

> 19.3 When a countervailing duty is imposed in respect of any product, such countervailing duty shall be levied, in the appropriate amounts in each case, on a non-discriminatory basis on imports of such product from all sources found to be subsidized and causing injury, except as to imports from those sources which have renounced any subsidies in question or from which undertakings under the terms of this Agreement have been accepted. Any exporter whose exports are subject to a definitive countervailing duty but who was not actually investigated for reasons other than a refusal to cooperate, shall be entitled to an expedited review in order that the investigating authorities promptly establish an individual countervailing duty rate for that exporter.

7.268 Article 19.3 of the SCM Agreement thus similarly provides for the right to an expedited review of an exporter whose exports are subject to a definitive duty but who was not actually investigated for reasons other than a refusal to cooperate. Article 19.3 of the SCM Agreement does not subject this right to any other conditions than the fact that the exporter's product is subject to a definitive duty and that he was not actually investigated for reasons other than a refusal to cooperate. For reasons, similar to those expressed earlier, we consider that Article 89 D of the Act is inconsistent with Article 19.3 of the SCM Agreement as it imposes an additional requirement not provided for in Article 19.3 of the SCM Agreement for the exporters to be entitled to an expedited review. The mandatory language of Article 89 D of the Act inevitably implies that an authority will reject a request for an expedited review by an exporter whose product is subject to a countervailing duty but who was not actually investigated for a reason other than a refusal to cooperate in case no representative volume of export sales were made during the period of review which is inconsistent with the clear obligation in Article 19.3 of the SCM Agreement to provide for such reviews in such circumstances.

7.269 We therefore find that Article 89D of the Act is as such inconsistent with Article 9.5 of the AD Agreement and Article 19.3 of the SCM Agreement.[223] In light of our findings, we do not consider it necessary for the resolution of this dispute to consider the US arguments based on the fact that Article 89 D of the Act only talks about producers, while Article 9.5 of the AD Agreement entitles both exporters and producers to an expedited review. In any case, we note that Mexico clarified that it is of the view that the use of the term producers does not imply that exporters are not similarly entitled to such reviews.[224] [225]

[223] For the reasons set forth in paras. 7.224 and 7.225, we reject Mexico's defence based on the direct effect of international treaties in Mexican law.

[224] In support of its statement, Mexico submitted a resolution initiating the new shipper procedure concerning imports of apples from the United States, para. 3 and 32 of which show that the new shipper review was initiated at the request of an exporting firm which was a trading enterprise rather than a producer of the subject product. Mexico Second Submission, para. 230. Exhibit MEX – 12.

[225] Mexico First Answers to Questions, question 33.

5. *Claim 18: Article 93V of Mexico's Foreign Trade Act is inconsistent "as such" with Article 18.1 of the AD Agreement and Article 32.1 of the SCM Agreement*

(a) Arguments of the Parties

(i) United States

7.270 The United States argues that Article 93V of the Act provides for the imposition of fines for importers which enter products subject to anti-dumping or countervailing duty investigations while such investigations are underway. This, according to the United States, is a specific action against dumping or against subsidies which is not provided for by the AD or SCM Agreement and is therefore inconsistent with Articles 18.1 of the AD Agreement and 32.1 of the SCM Agreement. The United States submits that there is a "clear, direct and unavoidable connection" between the determination that the constituent elements of dumping or subsidization exist and the imposition of a fine under Article 93V of the Act. In the view of the United States, it is therefore a "specific action" relating to dumping or subsidization, which is "against" dumping/subsidization since it has an adverse bearing on dumping or subsidization and creates an incentive to terminate such practices. As the fines envisaged under Article 93 V of the Act constitute a "specific action against dumping/subsidization" which is not contemplated in the AD and SCM Agreement, as it does not take the form of a definitive anti-dumping duty, a provisional measure or price undertaking, Article 93V of the Act is inconsistent with Article 18.1 of the AD Agreement and Article 32.1 of the SCM Agreement.[226]

(ii) Mexico

7.271 Mexico submits that the United States failed to establish any violation with the AD Agreement or the SCM Agreement of this provision of the Mexican law which has to be read in light of Mexico's international obligations under the WTO Agreements. In addition, the United States failed to adduce evidence of the interpretation of this provision by the domestic courts and the doctrine, or its application by the authorities. In the absence of such proof, the law has to be assumed to be consistent with Mexico's obligations under the WTO Agreements. In addition, Mexico asserts that Article 93V of the Act does not oblige Economía to impose fines but merely authorises it to do so. Article 93V of the Act is therefore not as such inconsistent with Articles 18.1 of the AD Agreement and 32.1 of the SCM Agreement.

7.272 Finally, Mexico submits that, in any case, by virtue of Article 133 of its Constitution, treaties such as the WTO Agreements are self-executing and automatically applicable in Mexican law, and as Article 2 of the Act makes clear, the Act will be implemented in a manner which is congruent with the provisions of

---

[226] The United States refers to a detailed discussion of the meaning of a "specific action against dumping/subsidization" in the report of the Appellate Body in the *US – Offset Act (Byrd Amendment)* case, paras. 224 -269.

the WTO Agreements. According to Mexico, the Act thus does not mandate any WTO inconsistent action.

(b) Analysis

7.273 The US claim concerns the consistency of Article 93 V of the Act with Articles 18.1 of the AD Agreement and 32.1 of the SCM Agreement. Article 93V of the Act provides in pertinent part that:

> It shall be the responsibility of the Ministry to punish the following infringements:
>
> (V) Importation, once the investigation is under way, of identical or like goods in significant quantities, as compared to total imports and domestic production, within a relatively short period, when in the light of the timing and the volume of the imports and other circumstances such imports are considered likely to undermine the remedial effect of the countervailing duty: by a fine equivalent to the amount resulting from the application of the final countervailing duty to the imports entered for up to five months following the date of initiation of the investigation. This penalty shall only be applied once the Ministry has issued the resolution determining the final countervailing duties...

7.274 Article 18.1 of the AD Agreement in turn provides that:

> 18.1 No specific action against dumping of exports from another Member can be taken except in accordance with the provisions of GATT 1994, as interpreted by this Agreement.[24]
>
> [24] This is not intended to preclude action under other relevant provisions of GATT 1994, as appropriate.

7.275 Article 32.1 of the SCM Agreement similarly provides as follows:

> 32.1 No specific action against a subsidy of another Member can be taken except in accordance with the provisions of GATT 1994, as interpreted by this Agreement.[56]
>
> [56] This paragraph is not intended to preclude action under other relevant provisions of GATT 1994, where appropriate.

7.276 In our view, the only specific action against dumping that is in accordance with the provisions of the GATT 1994 as interpreted by the AD Agreement are those set forth in the AD Agreement and consist of definitive anti-dumping duties, provisional measures and price undertakings.[227] The same holds true for

[227] We find support for this view in the Appellate Body Report in the *US – 1916 Act* case in which the Appellate Body found that Article VI of the GATT 1994, in particular Article VI:2, read in conjunction with the AD Agreement, limits the permissible responses to dumping to definitive anti-dumping duties, provisional measures and price undertakings:

> "137. As we have concluded above, Article VI of the GATT 1994 and the Anti-Dumping Agreement apply to "specific action against dumping". Article VI, and, in particular, Article VI:2, read in conjunction with the Anti-Dumping Agreement,

specific action against a subsidy, for which the SCM Agreement provides as the only remedies the imposition of definitive countervailing duties, provisional measures or an undertaking. It is clear therefore that the imposition of a fine is not permitted in case it can be demonstrated that it is imposed as a specific action against dumping or subsidization.

7.277 The important question for us to answer remains whether Article 93V of the Act is a specific action against dumping or subsidization such that the imposition of fines would be inconsistent with Article 18.1 of the AD Agreement and 32.1 of the SCM Agreement. We concur with the following view expressed by the Appellate Body in the *US – CDSOA 2000* case:

> "Accordingly, a measure that may be taken only when the constituent elements of dumping or a subsidy are present, is a "specific action" in response to dumping within the meaning of Article 18.1 of the *Anti-Dumping Agreement* or a "specific action" in response to subsidization within the meaning of Article 32.1 of the *SCM Agreement*. In other words, the measure must be inextricably linked to, or have a strong correlation with, the constituent elements of dumping or of a subsidy. Such link or correlation may, as in the 1916 Act, be derived from the text of the measure itself."[228]

7.278 In our view, the imposition of fines under Article 93V of the Act is inextricably linked to, and strongly correlated with, a determination of dumping, as defined in Article VI:1 of the GATT 1994 and in the Anti-Dumping Agreement, or a determination of a subsidy, as defined in the SCM Agreement. Article 93V of the Act provides for the possibility to impose fines in case (i) a product identical or similar to the subject product is being imported; (ii) after the investigation has been initiated; (iii) in significant quantities within a relatively short period of time; and (iv) such imports are likely to undermine the remedial effect of the countervailing duty. The level of the fine is determined by the amount of the final duty. Such fines may only be imposed following a final determination and may be applied to imports that entered the country for up to five months following the date of initiation of the investigation. As the text of Article 93V of the Act clearly shows, importers may be fined only once anti-dumping duties or countervailing duties have been imposed, and the fines may be collected only pursuant to an anti-dumping duty order or countervailing duty order. In addition, and as an anti-dumping duty order or a countervailing duty order can be imposed

---

> limit the permissible responses to dumping to definitive anti-dumping duties, provisional measures and price undertakings. Therefore, the 1916 Act is inconsistent with Article VI:2 and the Anti-Dumping Agreement to the extent that it provides for "specific action against dumping" in the form of civil and criminal proceedings and penalties.
>
> 138. With the caveat that Article VI:2 must be read together with the relevant provisions of the Anti-Dumping Agreement, we, therefore, agree with the conclusion of the Panel that:
>
> ... by providing for the imposition of fines or imprisonment or for the recovery of treble damages, the 1916 Act violates Article VI:2 of the GATT 1994. "

Appellate Body Report, *US – 1916 Act*, paras. 137 – 138, footnote omitted.

[228] Appellate Body Report, *US – Offset Act (Byrd Amendment)*, para. 239.

only following a determination of dumping or subsidization respectively, we consider that there is a clear, direct and unavoidable connection between the determination of dumping and subsidization and the imposition of fines under Article 93 V of the Act. In sum, we consider that Article 93V of the Act fines may be imposed only following a determination that the constituent elements of dumping or subsidization are present, and such fines therefore constitute a "specific action" related to dumping or a subsidy within the meaning of Article 18.1 of the AD Agreement and of Article 32.1 of the SCM Agreement. In addition, we find that by threatening to impose fines on anyone importing the product subject to an anti-dumping investigation, Article 93V of the Act clearly provides for a specific action against dumping or subsidization which is not provided for in the AD or SCM Agreement.

7.279 In fact we note that Mexico does not appear to argue the contrary but submits that Article 93V of the Act does not require the authority to impose such fines but merely authorises it do so. We do not consider this argument to be convincing. When a law like the Act provides that it "shall be the responsibility of the Ministry to punish the following infringements",[229] it does more than just dividing competences among the government, but rather stipulates that fines are to be imposed in case the conditions of Article 93V of the Act are met and that it is up to the Ministry of Economy responsible also for the conduct of anti-dumping and countervailing duty investigations to impose such fines.

7.280 For the reasons set forth above, we conclude that Article 93V of the Act is inconsistent with Article 18.1 of the AD Agreement and 32.1 of the SCM Agreement.[230] [231]

---

[229] The Spanish original of the law reads: "*Corresponde a la Secretaría* sancionar las siguientes infracciones: ...".

[230] For the reasons set forth in paras. 7.224 and 7.225, we reject Mexico's defence based on the direct effect of international treaties in Mexican law.

[231] In fact we note that Article 93 V of the Act appears to be aiming to remedy a situation of injury which is difficult to repair caused by massive imports entering the country in a relatively short period of time following the initiation of the investigation but prior to the imposition of any measures. A very similar situation is addressed in Article 10.6 of the AD Agreement and Article 20.6 of the SCM Agreement which allow, under certain strict conditions, for the retroactive application of duties even prior to the application of provisional measures in such cases as an exception to the general rule of non-retroactive effect of duties. The retroactive application of duties is clearly a specific action against dumping as explicitly provided for in the AD Agreement and the SCM Agreement. In light of the fact that the fines of Article 93V of the Act operate in the same manner and its amount is limited to the amount of the duty, such fines are obviously also a specific action against dumping or subsidization, but one not provided for in the AD Agreement or the SCM Agreement, and therefore inconsistent with Article 18.1 of the AD Agreement and Article 32.1 of the SCM Agreement. In any case, and even assuming *arguendo* that there really is no practical difference between the retroactive application of anti-dumping or countervailing duties and the imposition of fines in an equal amount, it is clear that Article 93 V of the Act allows for the imposition of such fines without imposing the same requirements and conditions as are set forth in Article 10.6 of the AD Agreement and Article 20.6 of the SCM Agreement. However, as no claims were made before us with regard to Article 10.6 of the AD Agreement and Article 20.6 of the SCM Agreement, we do not need to make any rulings in this respect.

6. *Claim 19: Articles 68 and 97 of Mexico's Foreign Trade Act, and Section 366 of Mexico's FCCP, are inconsistent "as such" with Articles 9.3, 9.5, and 11.2 of the AD Agreement, and Articles 19.3 and 21.2 of the SCM Agreement*

(a) Arguments of the Parties

(i) United States

7.281 The United States submits that Articles 68 and 97 of the Act, and Section 366 of Mexico's FCCP preclude the authorities from conducting a review of anti-dumping or countervailing duties while a judicial review, either national or bi-national before a NAFTA panel is ongoing. This, the United States submits, is in clear violation of the entitlement to such reviews of the duties as set forth in Articles 9.3 of the AD Agreement on administrative reviews, 9.5 of the AD Agreement and 19.3 of the SCM Agreement on expedited reviews and 11.2 of the AD Agreement and 21.2 of the SCM Agreement on changed circumstances reviews.[232]

7.282 The United States asserts that the harm is being exacerbated by the fact that Article 64 of the Act requires Economía to impose the highest facts available margin on all exporters that did not receive an individual margin of dumping. This implies that exporters which requested that an individual margin of dumping be determined through an expedited review will not only have to wait until any possible judicial review has been finalized, but will in the meantime be confronted with duties determined on the basis of the highest facts available margin of dumping.

(ii) Mexico

7.283 Mexico considers that the United States failed to discharge its burden of proof by not adducing evidence on the alleged applicability of Section 366 of the FCCP to reviews of anti-dumping or countervailing duties.[233] Furthermore, Mexico considers that Articles 68 and 97 of the Act which provide that the duties only become definitive if no review is ongoing seek to ensure legal certainty. The rule that no reviews will be undertaken until all legal challenges are over thus provides a guarantee for exporters which are not obliged to pay any definitive duties until after such challenges are finalized, but may provide a guarantee of payment until such time as the duty becomes definitive.[234] With regard to the alleged inconsistency with Article 9.3.2 of the AD Agreement, Mexico asserts that the authority will refund any duties paid in excess once the relevant proceed-

---

[232] The United States submits as evidence of the operation of the challenged provisions of the Act a letter of the investigating authority to a US Beef exporter in which the authority rejects this exporter's request for a review of the duties on the basis of the fact that such duties were not considered definitive as the duties had been challenged before a bi-national NAFTA panel. Exhibit US-20.

[233] Mexico considers relevant the fact that the evidence introduced by the United States in support of its interpretation of the operation of the challenged provisions (Exhibit US-20) does not even mention Article 366 of the FCCP.

[234] Mexico First Submission, para. 302.

ings have been completed and the duties imposed in the investigation are regarded as being definitive, and nothing in the challenged provisions states otherwise.

7.284 As far as new shippers are concerned, Mexico is of the view that the challenged provisions do not preclude or expressly prohibit such new shipper reviews. In addition, Mexico considers that there is no obligation under the AD/SCM Agreement that prohibits a Member from not initiating such a procedure while challenge proceedings are under way. According to Mexico there is no obligation to immediately initiate such a procedure once an application has been made, but rather only to carry out such review promptly (in the AD Agreement) or expeditiously (in the SCM Agreement), once initiated. Therefore the provision that no review for new shippers will be initiated until after a legal challenge is over, is not inconsistent with the AD Agreement or the SCM Agreement.

7.285 Finally, Mexico submits that, in any case, by virtue of Article 133 of its Constitution, treaties such as the WTO Agreements are self-executing and automatically applicable in Mexican law, and as Article 2 of the Act makes clear, the Act will be implemented in a manner which is congruent with the provisions of the WTO Agreements. According to Mexico, the Act thus does not mandate any WTO inconsistent action.

(b) Analysis

7.286 The US claim concerns a challenge of Article 366 of the FCCP and Articles 68 and 97 of the Act. Article 366 of the FCCP provide as follows:

> The process will be suspended, when a decision cannot be reached until a resolution in another matter is made, and in any other special case determined by the Law.

7.287 We recall that Article 68 of the Act reads in pertinent part:

> Final countervailing duties shall be reviewed annually at the request of a party...as shall imports from producers for whom no positive margin of price discrimination or subsidization was determined in the investigation....

7.288 Article 97 of the Act reads:

> Any interested party may, in respect of the resolutions and actions referred to in Article 94, paragraph (V), choose to resort to the alternative dispute settlement mechanisms ... If such mechanisms are chosen:
>
> II. Only the resolution issued by the Ministry as a result of the decision emanating from the alternative mechanisms shall be considered final;

7.289 The United States argues that, in case a judicial review of the measure is requested, before a domestic or bi-national body, the challenged provisions require the authority to suspend all administrative, expedited and changed circumstances reviews. In essence Mexico confirms that the provisions operate in this manner, but argues that this does not constitute a violation of any of the provisions alleged to have been violated. Mexico mainly argues that as long as judicial review proceedings are ongoing, the duty has not become "definitive" and hence no reviews have to be undertaken, as such reviews all relate to products subject to "definitive" anti-dumping or countervailing duties. The fact that this is the way the Mexican system works is further evidenced by the letter of the investigating authority to a US exporter of beef which was requesting a review of the anti-dumping duties, in which the authority rejected such request and stated the following:

> "in conformity with Articles 68 of the FTA and 99, 100 and 101 of the Regulation, in order to be able to request a review it is required that the determination subject of the review be definitive, ...
>
> In this particular case, the final determination on bovine meat and edible offals, published in the Official Journal of 28 April 2000, is not of a definitive nature, as will be considered as final only the determination of the Secretaria which results from the decision taken by the mechanisms of alternative dispute resolution, in conformity with Article 97 II of the FTA".[235]

7.290 The question before us is thus whether a Member is permitted to reject request for reviews because of the fact that judicial review proceedings have been initiated and for as long as such proceedings have not been finalized. Article 68 of the Act deals with administrative as well as changed circumstances reviews. The obligations for Members with regard to such reviews are set forth in Articles 9.3 and 11.2 of the AD Agreement and Article 21.2 of the SCM Agreement.

7.291 Article 9.3 of the AD Agreement reads in pertinent part as follows:

> 9.3 The amount of anti-dumping duty shall not exceed the margin of dumping as established under Article 2.
>
>> 9.3.2 When the amount of the anti-dumping duty is assessed on a prospective basis, provision shall be made for a prompt refund, upon request, of any duty paid in excess of the margin of dumping. A refund of any such duty paid in excess of the actual margin of dumping shall normally take place within 12 months, and in no case more than 18 months, after the date on which a request for a refund, duly supported by evidence, has been made by an importer of the product subject to the anti-dumping duty. The refund authorized should normally be made within 90 days of the above-noted decision.

7.292 Article 11.2 of the AD Agreement reads as follows:

> The authorities shall review the need for the continued imposition of the duty, where warranted, on their own initiative or, provided that a reasonable period of time has elapsed since the imposition of

[235] We note that this translation is ours. Exhibit US-20.

> the definitive anti-dumping duty, upon request by any interested party which submits positive information substantiating the need for a review. Interested parties shall have the right to request the authorities to examine whether the continued imposition of the duty is necessary to offset dumping, whether the injury would be likely to continue or recur if the duty were removed or varied, or both. If, as a result, of the review under this paragraph, the authorities determine that the anti-dumping duty is no longer warranted, it shall be terminated immediately.

7.293 Article 21.2 of the SCM Agreement provides that:

> The authorities shall review the need for the continued imposition of the duty, where warranted, on their own initiative or, provided that a reasonable period of time has elapsed since the imposition of the definitive countervailing duty, upon request by any interested party which submits positive information substantiating the need for a review. Interested parties shall have the right to request the authorities to examine whether the continued imposition of the duty is necessary to offset subsidization, whether the injury would be likely to continue or recur if the duty were removed or varied, or both. If, as a result, of the review under this paragraph, the authorities determine that the countervailing duty is no longer warranted, it shall be terminated immediately.

7.294 In sum, these provisions all require the authorities, in case a product is subject to a duty, to review the amount of and/or need for continued imposition of such duties. Article 9.3.2 of the AD Agreement states that provision shall be made for a prompt refund, upon request, of any duty paid in excess of the margin of dumping, and that a refund of any such duty paid in excess of the actual margin of dumping shall normally take place within 12 months, and in no case more than 18 months, after the date on which a request for a refund, duly supported by evidence, has been made by an importer of the product subject to the anti-dumping duty. Article 11.2 of the AD Agreement in turn states in equally unequivocal terms that the authorities shall review the need for the continued imposition of the duty, where warranted, on their own initiative or, provided that a reasonable period of time has elapsed since the imposition of the definitive anti-dumping duty, upon request by any interested party which submits positive information substantiating the need for a review. If, as a result, of the review under this paragraph, the authorities determine that the anti-dumping duty is no longer warranted, it shall be terminated immediately.

7.295 We are of the view that a product is subject to a duty as soon as an investigation has been concluded and a final determination has been made deciding to impose anti-dumping or countervailing duties. The term "duty" in the context of Articles 9.3 and 11.2 of the AD Agreement and 21.2 of the SCM Agreement is a clear reference to the duty that Members may impose at the end of an investigation which has led to an affirmative determination of dumping /subsidization, injury and a causal link between the two. Article 9 of the AD Agreement, and

Article 19 of the SCM Agreement make a clear distinction between the imposition of the duty on the one hand and collection of the duty on the other. As Article 9.1 of the AD Agreement states, the decision whether to impose anti-dumping duties and the decision whether the amount of the duty to be imposed shall be the full margin of dumping or less, are decisions to be made by the authorities of the importing Member. Article 9.2 of the AD Agreement then deals with the next step following imposition of the duty, as it concerns the collection of the duty. Article 9.2 of the AD Agreement provides that when an anti-dumping duty is imposed in respect of any product, such anti-dumping duties shall be collected in the appropriate amounts in each case. Article 9.3 of the AD Agreement then follows up on what Article 9.2 of the AD Agreement had said about collection of the duty in the appropriate amounts, by stating that the amount of the anti-dumping duty shall not exceed the margin of dumping. Articles 9.3.1 and 9.3.2 then further specify how this requirement is to be met in a retrospective and a prospective system respectively. Such provisions thus deal with collection of the duty. We thus conclude that a product is subject to a duty once the decision under Article 9.1 of the AD Agreement to impose such a duty has been taken. Once this decision has been taken, the duty is necessarily a definitive duty in the sense of the AD Agreement. A similar analysis applies, *mutatis mutandis*, to Article 19 of the SCM Agreement.

7.296 We recall in this respect that the AD and SCM Agreement only provide for three permissible specific actions against dumping or subsidization, price undertakings, provisional measures, which may take the form of a provisional duty and which are taken for a limited period of time following a preliminary affirmative determination, and definitive duties. The duties imposed by an authority following an investigation which resulted in an affirmative final determination are final or definitive anti-dumping or countervailing duties, even if the authorities decides to collect such duties only provisionally, and conditional upon the results of the judicial review proceedings. We therefore do not agree with Mexico that as long as a judicial review is ongoing with regard to the final determination, the duties imposed are not really definitive duties but only guarantees and the product is thus not subject to a duty during this often lengthy judicial review period. It is not because the definitive duties are only provisionally collected that they are no longer definitive duties. [236]

7.297 We find that Articles 9.3.2 and 11.2 of the AD Agreement leave little to be desired for in terms of clarity and require the review of duties and their refund or the application of such duties in an amended amount when requested to do so, and in case certain well-defined conditions are met. In case the conditions are

---

[236] In fact, no duties would then ever be definitive as Article 9.3 of the AD Agreement provides for refunds in case duties have been paid in excess of the margin of dumping, which implies that the collection of the duty due is not definitive until after such a duty assessment review period. In the case of a retrospective system final liability is only determined through a duty assessment review covering a period following the date of the final determination and the imposition of the duty. Although the final liability remains open during that period of time, the duties are definitive from the date of imposition, and the product is subject to a duty as of the final determination of the authority and its decision to impose duties.

met, the authority is not allowed to reject such requests for reason that the judicial review of the measures in question is still ongoing. We therefore find that Article 68 of the Act in combination with Article 97 of the Act are inconsistent as such with Articles 9.3.2 and 11.2 of the AD Agreement and 21.2 of the SCM Agreement by requiring the authority to reject requests for reviews until after the conclusion of the judicial review proceedings.[237]

7.298 With regard to Article 366 of the FCCP, the provision of the Mexican Federal Code of Civil Procedure also challenged by the United States, we consider that the United States has failed to establish a *prima facie* case concerning the meaning and role of the provision in anti-dumping and countervailing duty investigations. We find that the United States has not sufficiently explained which "proceedings" this provision refers to and failed to provide sufficient arguments concerning the context of this provision the meaning and scope of which is not immediately clear to us. In our view, it does not suffice for a party to discharge itself of the burden of proof by simply stating that a provision of another Member's law has a certain effect without providing the proper context in which to read and understand this provision. While the United States may consider it telling that Mexico has made no effort to explain why Article 366 does not apply, directly or indirectly, to the Act[238], we consider that the United States, as the complaining party, is the first to have failed to provide sufficient evidence of the applicability to and role played by this provision in AD and CVD proceedings and reviews in Mexico.

7.299 We note that the United States has also challenged the consistency of these provisions of the Act with the requirement to perform expedited reviews set forth in Article 9.5 of the AD Agreement and 19.3 of the SCM Agreement. In our view, however, the United States has provided insufficient evidence that Article 68 of the Act,[239] or Articles 97 of the Act or 366 of the FCCP deal with such reviews. We therefore find that the United States has failed to establish a *prima facie* case of violation by these challenged provisions of the obligations with regard to expedited reviews set forth in Article 9.5 of the AD Agreement and Article 19.3 of the SCM Agreement.

VIII. CONCLUSIONS AND RECOMMENDATIONS

8.1 In the light of our findings above concerning the determination of injury by Economía in the investigation on imports of long-grain white rice from the United States, we conclude:

(a) that Mexico acted inconsistently with Articles 3.1, 3.2, 3.4 and 3.5 of the AD Agreement by choosing to base its injury determination on a period of investigation which ended more than fifteen months before the initiation of the investigation. We apply judicial econ-

[237] For the reasons set forth in paras. 7.224 and 7.225, we reject Mexico's defence based on the direct effect of international treaties in Mexican law.

[238] US Second Oral Statement, para. 58.

[239] We note that from the discussions concerning other claims in this case, it seems that it is Article 89D of the Act that actually deals with such expedited reviews.

omy and do not make any findings on the US claim of violation of Article VI:2 of GATT 1994 and Article 1 of the AD Agreement;

(b) that Mexico acted inconsistently with Articles 3.1 and 3.5 of the AD Agreement by limiting its injury analysis to only six months of the years 1997, 1998, and 1999. We apply judicial economy and do not make any findings on the US claims of violation of Articles 1 and 6.2 of the AD Agreement;

(c) that Mexico acted inconsistently with Article 3.1 and 3.2 of the AD Agreement by failing to conduct an objective examination based on positive evidence of the price effects and volume of dumped imports as part of its injury analysis. We apply judicial economy and do not make any findings on the US claims of violation of Article 6.8 and Annex II of the AD Agreement.

8.2 Having reached the conclusions set forth above that the injury determination is inconsistent with Articles 3.1, 3.2, 3.4 and 3.5 of the AD Agreement, we apply judicial economy and do not rule on the US claims that:

(a) Economía's failure to objectively consider whether there was a significant increase in the volume of dumped imports or whether the dumped imports had a significant effect on prices is inconsistent with Mexico's obligations under Articles 3.1 and 3.2 of the AD Agreement;

(b) Economía's failure to conduct an objective analysis of the relevant economic factors is inconsistent with Mexico's obligations under Articles 3.1 and 3.4 of the AD Agreement;

(c) Economía's inclusion of non-dumped imports in its evaluation of volume, price effects, and the impact of the dumped imports on the domestic industry is inconsistent with Mexico's obligations under Articles 3.1, 3.2, and 3.5 of the AD Agreement;

(d) Economía's failure to provide in sufficient detail the findings and conclusions reached on all issues of fact and law with respect to its determination of injury is inconsistent with Mexico's obligations under Article 12.2 of the AD Agreement.

8.3 In the light of the above findings concerning the dumping margin determination by Economía in the investigation on imports of long-grain white rice from the United States, we conclude:

(a) that Mexico acted inconsistently with Article 5.8 of the AD Agreement by not terminating the investigation on two US exporters which the authority found to have exported at undumped prices and by not excluding these two exporters from the application of the definitive anti-dumping measure;

(b) that Mexico acted inconsistently with Article 6.8 and paragraph 7 of Annex II of the AD Agreement in its application of a facts available-based dumping margin to the non-shipping exporter Producers Rice. We apply judicial economy and do not make any findings on the US claims of violation of Articles 6.2, 6.4, and 9.5 of the AD Agreement, and paragraphs 3, 5 and 6 of Annex II;

(c) that Mexico acted inconsistently with Articles 6.1, 6.8, paragraph 1 of Annex II, and Articles 6.10 and 12.1 of the AD Agreement in its application of a facts available-based dumping margin to the US producers and exporters that it did not investigate. We apply judicial economy and do not make any findings on the US claims of violation of Articles 6.6, 9.4, 9.5 and paragraph 7 of Annex II of the AD Agreement.

8.4 Having reached the conclusions set forth above that Economía's dumping margin determination is inconsistent with Articles 5.8, 6.1, 6.8, 6.10 and 12.1 of the AD Agreement, we apply judicial economy and do not rule on the US claims that:

(a) Economía's failure to provide sufficient information on the findings and conclusions of fact and law and the reasons that led to the imposition of the adverse facts available-based margin on Producers Rice and the unexamined US exporters and producers is inconsistent with Mexico's obligations under Article 12.2 of the AD Agreement;

(b) Economía's application of an adverse facts available-based margin to Producers Rice and the unexamined US exporters and producers is inconsistent with Mexico's obligations under Articles 1 and 9.3 of the AD Agreement;

(c) Economía's levying of an anti-dumping duty greater than the margin of dumping is inconsistent with Mexico's obligations under Article VI:2 of GATT 1994.

8.5 In light of our findings above on the US challenges against Mexico's law as such, we conclude:

(a) that Article 53 of Mexico's Foreign Trade Act is inconsistent as such with Article 6.1.1 of the AD Agreement and Article 12.1.1 of the SCM Agreement;

(b) that Article 64 of Mexico's Foreign Trade Act is inconsistent as such with Articles 6.8 and paragraphs 1, 3, 5 and 7 of Annex II of the AD Agreement, and 12.7 of the SCM Agreement. We apply judicial economy and do not make any findings on the US claims of violation of Articles 9.3, 9.4, and 9.5 of the AD Agreement, and Article 19.3 of the SCM Agreement;

(c) that Article 68 of Mexico's Foreign Trade Act is inconsistent as such with Articles 5.8, 9.3, and 11.2 of the AD Agreement and Articles 11.9 and 21.2 of the SCM Agreement;

(d) that Article 89D of Mexico's Foreign Trade Act is inconsistent as such with Article 9.5 of the AD Agreement and Article 19.3 of the SCM Agreement;

(e) that Article 93V of Mexico's Foreign Trade Act is inconsistent as such with Article 18.1 of the AD Agreement and Article 32.1 of the SCM Agreement; and

(f) that Articles 68 and 97 of Mexico's Foreign Trade Act are inconsistent as such with Articles 9.3, and 11.2 of the AD Agreement, and Article 21.2 of the SCM Agreement, but that the United States failed to make a *prima facie* case that Article 366 of the FCCP is inconsistent with Articles 9.3, 9.5 and 11.2 of the AD Agreement and 19.3 and 21.2 of the SCM Agreement, and also that the United States failed to make a *prima facie* case of violation by the challenged provisions of the Act of Articles 9.5 of the AD Agreement and 19.3 of the SCM Agreement.

8.6 Under Article 3.8 of the DSU, in cases where there is infringement of the obligations assumed under a covered agreement, the action is considered *prima facie* to constitute a case of nullification or impairment of benefits under that agreement. Accordingly, we conclude that to the extent Mexico has acted inconsistently with the provisions of the AD Agreement and the SCM Agreement, it has nullified or impaired benefits accruing to the United States under those Agreements.

8.7 We therefore recommend that the Dispute Settlement Body request Mexico to bring its measures into conformity with its obligations under the AD Agreement and the SCM Agreement.

ANNEX A

RESPONSES OF THE UNITED STATES TO MEXICO'S REQUEST FOR A PRELIMINARY RULING

Content	Page
Annex A-1 Responses of the United States	11263

ANNEX A-1

RESPONSES OF THE UNITED STATES
7 May 2004

TABLE OF CONTENTS

I. INTRODUCTION

1. Mexico offers no legitimate basis for its request for a preliminary ruling ("Mexico's Request") that the US panel request in this dispute fails to meet the requirements of Article 6.2 of the *Understanding on the Rules and Procedures*

Governing the Settlement of Disputes ("DSU"). To the contrary, as required by Article 6.2, the US panel request properly "identif[ies] the specific measures at issue and provide[s] a brief summary of the legal basis of the complaint sufficient to present the problem clearly".

2. Mexico is seeking to have this Panel read into Article 6.2 a requirement that is not there and that the Appellate Body has specifically rejected: namely, that the United States summarize the specific legal arguments to be presented in the first US submission. The Appellate Body in *EC Bananas*[1] has already rejected the suggestion that a complaining party must summarize its legal arguments in the panel request, and this Panel should do so as well.

3. Mexico is also seeking to have this Panel find that the US panel request does not "identify the specific measure" with respect to one of the measures at issue in this dispute, Article 366 of Mexico's Federal Code of Civil Procedure ("FCCP"). Inasmuch as Article 366 is specifically identified in the panel request, there is no basis for such a finding.

4. Mexico has also failed to provide any legitimate basis for its argument that the US panel request is inconsistent with Articles 4.5 and 4.7 of the DSU, or Articles 17.4 and 17.5 of the *Agreement on Implementation of Article VI of the General Agreement on Tariffs and Trade 1994* ("AD Agreement"). The gist of Mexico's argument is that the US panel request contains legal claims that were not the subject of consultations. Mexico fails to recognize that it is the panel request, and not the consultation request, that establishes the scope for this Panel's work.

II. STATEMENT OF FACTS

5. The United States requested formal dispute settlement consultations with Mexico on the definitive anti-dumping measures on beef and rice, and on various provisions of Mexico's Foreign Trade Act and Article 366 of the FCCP, on 16 June 2003.[2] The United States and Mexico held two days of consultations with respect to the measures in Mexico City, on 31 July and 1 August 2003, but failed to resolve the dispute.

6. Consequently, on 19 September 2003, the United States requested the establishment of a panel, specifically identifying the definitive anti-dumping measure on rice, Articles 53, 64, 68, 89D, 93V, and 97 of the Foreign Trade Act, and Article 366 of the FCCP as the specific measures at issue, and providing a

---

1 Appellate Body Report on *European Communities – Regime for the Importation, Sale and Distribution of Bananas*, WT/DS27/AB/R, adopted 25 September 1997, para. 141 ("*EC Bananas AB*").

2 *Mexico – Definitive Anti-Dumping Measures on Beef and Rice, Request for Consultations by the United States*, WT/DS295/1, G/L/631, G/ADP/D50/1, G/SCM/D54/1, circulated 23 June 2003 ("US Consultation Request").

brief summary of the legal basis of the complaint.[3] The Panel was established on 7 November 2003.[4]

III. THE REQUIREMENTS OF DSU ARTICLE 6.2

7. Article 6.2 of the DSU requires, in relevant part, that a request for the establishment of a panel "identify the specific measures at issue and provide a brief summary of the legal basis of the complaint sufficient to present the problem clearly".

8. Mexico's Request contains a number of quotations from Appellate Body reports that explain this provision and emphasize its role and importance in dispute settlement. It has entirely missed, however, one aspect of these reports that is critical to the issue now before this Panel: **the key distinction between *claims* – which must be included in the panel request – and the *arguments* in support of those claims – which need not be included. As the Appellate Body explained in *EC Bananas*:**

> In our view, there is a significant difference between the *claims* identified in the request for the establishment of a panel, which establish the panel's terms of reference under Article 7 of the DSU, and the *arguments* supporting those claims, which are set out and progressively clarified in the first written submissions, the rebuttal submissions and the first and second panel meetings with the parties.[5]

9. Furthermore, the Appellate Body in *EC Bananas* made clear that a panel request may in some cases adequately state a claim if the request simply cites the pertinent provision of the WTO agreement:

> We accept the Panel's view that it was sufficient for the Complaining Parties to list the provisions of the specific agreements alleged to have been violated *without setting out detailed arguments as to which specific aspects of the measures at issue relate to which specific provisions of those agreements.*[6]

10. Mexico also fails to note that – according to the Appellate Body – even in cases where simply citing the pertinent provisions would *not* satisfy the requirements of Article 6.2, the Panel is not automatically deprived of jurisdiction over the matter. Rather, the Appellate Body has found that a panel must examine, based on the "particular circumstances of the case", whether the defect has prejudiced the ability of the responding party to defend itself given the actual

---

3 *Mexico – Definitive Anti-Dumping Measures on Beef and Rice, Request for the Establishment of a Panel by the United States*, WT/DS295/2, circulated 22 September 2003 ("US Panel Request").

4 *Mexico – Definitive Anti-Dumping Measures on Beef and Rice, Constitution of the Panel Established at the Request of the United States, Note by the Secretariat*, WT/DS295/3 (19 February 2004).

5 *EC Bananas AB*, para. 141.

6 *Ibid.* (emphasis added).

course of the panel proceedings. As the Appellate Body explained in *Korea Dairy*:

> In assessing whether the European Communities' request met the requirements of Article 6.2 of the DSU, we consider that, in view of the particular circumstances of this case and in line with the letter and spirit of Article 6.2, the European Communities' request should have been more detailed. *However, Korea failed to demonstrate to us that the mere listing of the articles asserted to have been violated has prejudiced its ability to defend itself in the course of the Panel proceedings. Korea did assert that it had sustained prejudice, but offered no supporting particulars in its appellant's submission nor at the oral hearing.* We, therefore, deny Korea's appeal relating to the consistency of the European Communities' request for the establishment of a panel with Article 6.2 of the DSU.[7]

11. Therefore, in evaluating claims that a panel request fails to provide a brief summary of the legal basis of the complaint sufficient to present the problem clearly, as required by DSU Article 6.2, the Panel may consider the particular circumstances of the dispute, including whether the responding party has been prejudiced.

12. Mexico asserts that the US panel request (1) does not provide a brief summary of the legal basis of the complaint sufficient to present the problem clearly; and (2) does not identify the "specific measure at issue" with respect to Article 366 of the FCCP, and that Mexico has thereby been prejudiced. As detailed in the sections that follow, Mexico's objections are wrong on both counts.

IV. CONTRARY TO MEXICO'S ALLEGATIONS, THE US PANEL REQUEST PROVIDES A BRIEF SUMMARY OF THE LEGAL BASIS OF THE COMPLAINT SUFFICIENT TO PRESENT THE PROBLEM CLEARLY

13. The first of Mexico's complaints about the US panel request is that the request is too vague, and that it allegedly does not provide a brief summary of the legal basis of the complaint sufficient to present the problem clearly, as Article 6.2 requires. Mexico's complaint is groundless.

14. It is important to note at the outset that Mexico only challenges the sufficiency of the US panel request with respect to a few of the US claims.[8] Accordingly, the United States is proceeding under the assumption that Mexico consid-

---

[7] *Korea – Definitive Safeguard Measure on Imports of Certain Dairy Products*, WT/DS98/AB/R, adopted 12 January 2000, para 131 ("*Korea Dairy*") (emphasis added). The Appellate Body concluded in *Korea Dairy* that simply listing the articles of the agreement involved may not be sufficient if, for example, the articles listed established multiple obligations. *Ibid.*, para. 124.

[8] Specifically, Mexico questions the listing of Article VI of GATT 1994 and Article 4.1 of the AD Agreement in subsection 1(a) of the panel request, and it questions the articles listed in subsections 1(f) and (g) of the panel request. See Mexico's Request, paras. 14-19.

ers the other claims that it did not challenge in its preliminary ruling request as being sufficient for purposes of Article 6.2.[9]

15. With respect to the claims that Mexico does challenge, the US panel request does provide a brief summary of the legal basis of the complaint sufficient to present the problem clearly, as required by Article 6.2. It both lists the specific provisions of the AD Agreement and the *General Agreement on Tariffs and Trade 1994* ("GATT 1994") alleged to be violated, and provides, in addition, a brief textual explanation of the basis of the complaint.

16. Turning first to subsections 1(f) and (g) of the US panel request, the United States lists 15 specific provisions of the AD Agreement (including five specific paragraphs of Annex II of the AD Agreement). Mexico has failed to provide any reason as to why citing these specific provisions was insufficient under DSU Article 6.2. For example, Mexico has made no effort to explain why it was unclear from the US citation of Article 6.8 and Annex II (the "facts available" provisions) of the AD Agreement that the United States was challenging Mexico's use of the facts available in assigning anti-dumping margins to Producers Rice (in subsection 1(f)) and all of the rest of the exporters and producers in the United States that Mexico did not individually examine (in subsection 1(g)).

17. On the contrary, Mexico *concedes* that the US request in fact asserts that Mexico's application of the facts available to those entities breached the listed provisions. What it objects to is that it believes the United States has not adequately explained *how* Mexico's application of the facts available breached each of the provisions (in other words, the United States did not in its panel request provide arguments to support its claims).[10] As noted above, previous panels and the Appellate Body have been very careful to distinguish between the claims that must be made in a panel request under Article 6.2 – *i.e.*, the brief summary of the legal *basis* for the complaint sufficient to present the problem clearly – and the *arguments* supporting those claims. The claims must be set forth in the panel request. The arguments need not be.[11]

18. Mexico's challenge to the US claim that the injury and causation analyses breached Article 4.1 of the AD Agreement suffers from a similar flaw.[12] Mexico does not argue that the claim should have been more specific; the request cites clearly to the first paragraph of Article 4. Mexico even concedes that the United States included a narrative description that provided further information with

---

[9] Specifically, Mexico does not question five of the seven articles listed in subsection 1(a), any of the articles listed in subsections 1(b)-(e), (h), or (i), or any portion of subsections 2 or 3.

[10] *Ibid.*, paras. 17-18.

[11] See, *e.g.*, *EC Bananas AB*, para. 141; Appellate Body Report on *Thailand – Anti-Dumping Duties on Angles, Shapes and Sections of Iron or Non-Alloy Steel and H-Beams from Poland,* WT/DS122/AB/R, adopted 5 April 2001, at para. 88, n.36 (noting that there is a "significant difference between the *claims* identified in the request for the establishment of a panel, which establish the panel's terms of reference...and the *arguments* supporting those claims," and that the arguments are clarified in the first written submission and in subsequent documents.) While Mexico cited paragraph 88 of the *Thai Steel AB* report, it omitted reference to footnote 36, which is appended to that paragraph. See Mexico's Request, para. 11.

[12] *Ibid.*, paras. 15-16.

respect to the claim. It objects, however, that it is unable to understand which of the statements in the narrative description results in a breach of Article 4.1. Thus, its concern is with the US *arguments*, and not with the specificity of the claim itself.

19. Turning next to Mexico's objection to the US claim under Article VI of GATT 1994, it is true that Article VI has several paragraphs.[13] However, Mexico cannot argue that it was unable to understand which paragraphs were relevant to the matters in dispute. In the US panel request, the Article VI claim is accompanied by a lengthy narrative description that provides more than sufficient detail about the nature of the US claims and demonstrates that the majority of Article VI is simply not relevant. The plain facts underlie this conclusion. For example, the narrative description does not address the imposition of countervailing duties (which is the topic of paragraphs 3 and 5 of Article VI), because there is no Mexican countervailing duty measure on US rice. Similarly, the description does not mention either of the scenarios that are the subject of paragraphs 4 or 7 of Article VI, because the anti-dumping measure does not involve either issue. Rather, the narrative focuses on issues that are addressed by the only paragraphs of Article VI that are relevant to this dispute: paragraphs 2 and 6(a). As such, through the narrative description in the US panel request, the United States provided Mexico a brief summary of the legal basis of the complaint with respect to Article VI that is sufficient to present the problem clearly.

20. Furthermore, it is worth noting that in Mexico's panel request in *United States – Anti-Dumping Measures On Oil Country Tubular Goods From Mexico*, Mexico includes a claim under Article VI of GATT 1994, but fails to specify which paragraphs of Article VI are relevant.[14] Thus, it is apparent that Mexico itself believes a citation to Article VI as a whole is not inconsistent with Article 6.2 of the DSU.

21. In sum, Mexico has not presented any reasons why subsections 1(a), (f), and (g) of the US panel request should be found inconsistent with the requirements of Article 6.2 of the DSU.

V. THE US PANEL REQUEST DOES NOT PREJUDICE THE ABILITY OF MEXICO TO DEFEND ITSELF

22. Even if Mexico had succeeded in demonstrating that the US panel request does not meet the requirements of DSU Article 6.2, which it has not, Mexico has offered nothing to suggest that it has been prejudiced.

23. In *Korea Dairy*, the Appellate Body denied Korea's claim that the panel request had failed to provide a brief summary of the legal basis of the complaint sufficient to present the problem clearly, for the following reason: although Korea had asserted prejudice, it offered no supporting particulars and failed to dem-

---

[13] Mexico's Request, para. 14.

[14] See *United States – Anti-Dumping Measures On Oil Country Tubular Goods From Mexico, Request for the Establishment of a Panel by Mexico*, WT/DS282/2, circulated 29 July 2003.

onstrate that the panel request had prejudiced its ability to defend itself during the panel proceedings.[15] Mexico categorically asserts that it is prejudiced by the US panel request, but only in the vaguest and most conclusory manner.

24. Mexico's only explanation of how it has been prejudiced is its assertion that the alleged deficiencies in the panel request are impeding its ability to prepare a defence.[16] It has failed completely, however, to provide any supporting particulars as to why this is so. Moreover, its assertion is contradicted by the facts, since Mexico's first written submission contains a lengthy response to each of the challenged US claims.[17]

25. In light of the Appellate Body's reasoning in *Korea Dairy*, Mexico's mere assertion of prejudice is plainly insufficient to establish prejudice. As was the case for Korea in that dispute, Mexico has "offered no supporting particulars" and has "failed to demonstrate" that its ability to defend itself in the panel proceedings has been prejudiced.

VI. MEXICO'S ASSERTION THAT THE US PANEL REQUEST DOES NOT IDENTIFY ARTICLE 366 OF THE FEDERAL CODE OF CIVIL PROCEDURE AS A "SPECIFIC MEASURE AT ISSUE" IS INCORRECT

26. Mexico's second objection to the US panel request under Article 6.2 of the DSU is that the request allegedly failed to identify Article 366 of the FCCP as a "specific measure at issue". Mexico first made this assertion at the DSB meeting where the United States first requested the formation of a panel in this dispute. As the United States explained at that time, and as it further explained at the DSB meeting that established the panel, Mexico's assertion is groundless.

27. Section 3 of the US panel request states the following:

> Mexican officials have asserted that **Article 366 of Mexico's Federal Code of Civil Procedure and Articles 68 and 97 of the Foreign Trade Act** prevent Mexico from conducting reviews of anti-dumping or countervailing duty orders while a judicial review

---

[15] *Korea – Dairy*, para 131.

[16] Mexico's Request, para. 38. Mexico's only other assertion of prejudice relates to the date on which it received an English-language translation of the US first written submission. Mexico's Request, para. 5. It is not clear to the United States how the date that Mexico received the first written submission is relevant to determining whether Mexico was prejudiced by the panel request. The United States notes, however, that Mexico received five weeks to prepare its first written submission – which is two weeks longer than the maximum period proposed in Appendix 3 of the DSU. In addition, if any Party has been prejudiced by the "translation" issue, it is the United States, which has had to prepare and file this response to Mexico's Request *before* receiving the English-language translation. Although we have done our best to respond to Mexico's complaints in a comprehensive manner, we may need to supplement our response after we receive the English translation.

[17] In *United States – Lamb Meat*, the Panel found that the United States had not provided adequate "supporting particulars" in support of its claim of prejudice. It based its finding in part on the fact that the US first written submission contained a detailed rebuttal to the challenged claims. See Panel Report on *United States – Safeguard Measures on Imports of Fresh, Chilled or Frozen Lamb Meat from New Zealand and Australia*, WT/DS177/R, WT/DS178/R, adopted 16 May 2001, para. 5.51.

> of the order is ongoing, including a "binational panel" review pursuant to Chapter Nineteen of the *North American Free Trade Agreement*. These provisions appear to be inconsistent with Articles 9.3, 9.5, and 11.2 of the AD Agreement, and Articles 19.3 and 21.2 of the SCM Agreement.[18]

28. Mexico focuses solely on the first sentence, which refers to the assertions made by the Mexican officials. It ignores completely, however, the second sentence, which plainly states that it is the "provisions" themselves – including Article 366 of the FCCP – that the United States is challenging, and not the assertions of the Mexican officials. While it is barely credible that Mexico would take from the first sentence the understanding that the United States was challenging assertions rather than the provision, when the paragraph is viewed in its entirety, it is plain that Mexico's claims are groundless.[19]

29. Furthermore, the US representative specifically addressed this issue at the DSB meeting that established this Panel, after Mexico claimed not to understand which measure the United States was challenging:

> The United States wished to address briefly two erroneous statements that Mexico had made during [the first DSB meeting that considered the US panel request]. First, Mexico had mistakenly asserted that the United States had abandoned its claim addressing Article 366 of Mexico's Federal Code of Civil Procedure. In actuality, this claim appeared in section 3 of the panel request. Second, Mexico had asserted that the United States was claiming that certain statements of Mexican officials were "measures". As the request itself made clear, the United States was making no such claim. Rather, it had cited statements of Mexican officials with respect to certain provisions that *are* measures – namely, Article 366 of the Federal Code of Civil Procedure, and Articles 68 and 97 of the Foreign Trade Act.[20]

30. Accordingly, there is no doubt that Article 366 is a "specific measure at issue". Moreover, there is no need for the Panel to address Mexico's arguments that statements of Mexican officials cannot be considered "measures".[21] The

---

[18] US Panel Request, Section (3).

[19] The notion that the United States would be challenging the statements of the Mexican officials about Article 366, rather than Article 366 itself, is even more difficult to credit given discussions on this topic at consultations. The United States provided Mexico with a list of questions during consultations that specifically addressed Article 366. As an introduction to the questions, the United States noted, as it did in the US panel request, that Mexican officials had claimed in meetings with US officials that Article 366 of the FCCP precluded Mexico from conducting reviews while judicial review proceedings were ongoing. The seven questions that followed, however, were addressed to Article 366 itself, and not to the assertions of the Mexican officials. Thus, it was abundantly clear to Mexico that the measure in question was Article 366, and not the statements by the Mexican officials *about* Article 366.

[20] *Minutes of Meeting, Held in the Centre William Rappard on 2 October 2003*, WT/DSB/M/156, 10 November 2003, para. 45.

[21] Mexico's Request, paras. 22-26.

United States has made no arguments to the contrary. It is Article 366 – and not statements about Article 366 – that is the measure at issue.

31. For the foregoing reasons, there are no grounds for Mexico's assertion that the United States failed to identify Article 366 of the FCCP as a "specific measure at issue" in this dispute, and therefore no grounds to conclude that the US panel request does not meet the requirements of DSU Article 6.2 with respect to this measure.

VII. MEXICO'S CHALLENGES TO THE ADEQUACY OF CONSULTATIONS LACK MERIT

32. Mexico's final challenge to the US panel request pertains to the adequacy of the consultations with respect to the claims at issue. Mexico argues that a Member cannot include a legal claim in a panel request unless that claim was discussed during consultations.[22] It also complains about the adequacy of the consultations with respect to Mexico's evaluation of the injury factors in the rice investigation.[23] Neither objection has merit.

33. *First*, there is no basis for Mexico's contention that a Member cannot include a claim in its panel request unless the claim was discussed during consultations. A consultation request must provide an "identification of the measures at issue and an indication of the legal basis for the complaint".[24] However, nothing in the DSU requires that a Member must have ascertained all of the possible legal claims and relevant provisions of the WTO agreements *before* the Member can even request consultations. One of the purposes of consultations is to foster a better understanding of the relevant measures and concerns of the various Members in order to promote a satisfactory adjustment of the matter. Consultations are often the first time that the Member maintaining the measure provides a detailed description of the measure and relevant facts and legal documents. Consultations are not a "dress rehearsal" or "moot court" for the panel process requiring Members to have worked out all of their claims and positions in advance and presenting them in the consultations for the other side to practice its prepared responses.

34. The DSU reflects the difference between requests for panels and requests for consultations by using different terms for each. With respect to panels, the DSU requires that a request for the establishment of a panel provide a "brief summary of the legal basis of the complaint sufficient to present the problem clearly".[25] However, with respect to consultations, the DSU merely requires that requests for consultations give "an indication" of the legal basis for the complaint.[26] Moreover, previous panels have rejected the approach that Mexico is urging here – for example, the panel in *Japan – Agricultural Products* rejected

---

[22] Mexico's Request, paras. 33-34.
[23] *Ibid.*, para. 35.
[24] DSU Art. 4.4.
[25] *Ibid.*, Art. 6.2.
[26] *Ibid.*, Art. 4.4.

Japan's argument that the US panel request could not include a claim under Article 7 of the *Agreement on the Application of Sanitary and Phytosanitary Measures* if the claim was not included in the consultation request and no consultations were held on it.[27]

35. *Second*, Mexico's complaint about the alleged inadequacy of the consultations with respect to Mexico's evaluation of the injury factors is equally without merit. Contrary to Mexico's assertion, the consultations did address Mexico's evaluation of the injury factors in the rice investigation. More fundamentally, precisely to avoid litigation over what the parties did or did not say during consultations, the DSU only requires that the consultation request identify the measure that is the subject of the consultations; there is no requirement as to the adequacy of the consultations themselves. As the panel noted in *Korea – Taxes on Alcoholic Beverages*:

> The only requirement under the DSU is that consultations were in fact held, or were at least requested, and that a period of sixty days has elapsed from the time consultations were requested to the time a request for a panel was made. What takes place in those consultations is not the concern of a panel.[28]

36. In addition, the panel in *Bananas III* specifically rejected the contention that consultations must lead to an adequate explanation of the complainants' case:

> As to the EC argument that consultations must lead to an adequate explanation of the Complainants' case, we cannot agree. Consultations are the first step in the dispute settlement process. While one function of the consultations may be to clarify what the case is about, there is nothing in the DSU that provides that a complainant cannot request a panel unless its case is adequately explained in the consultations. The fulfilment of such a requirement would be difficult, if not impossible, for a complainant to demonstrate if a respondent chose to claim a lack of understanding of the case, a result which would undermine the automatic nature of panel establishment under the DSU. The only prerequisite for requesting a panel is that the consultations have "fail[ed] to settle a dispute within 60 days of receipt of the request for consultations ...". Ultimately, the function of providing notice to a respondent of a complainant's claims and arguments is served by the request for establishment of a panel and by the complainant's submissions to that panel.[29]

---

[27] Panel Report on *Japan – Measures Affecting Agricultural Products*, WT/DS76/R, adopted 19 March 1999, para. 8.4(i).

[28] Panel Report on *Korea – Taxes on Alcoholic Beverages*, WT/DS75/R, WT/DS84/R, adopted 17 February 1999, para. 10.19 (*citing* Panel Report on *European Communities – Regime for the Importation, Sale and Distribution of Bananas, Complaint by the United States*, WT/DS27/R/USA, adopted 25 September 1997, para. 7.19 ("*Bananas III*")).

[29] *Bananas III*, para. 7.20 (footnote omitted).

37. In the present case, the United States and Mexico spent two full days in Mexico City consulting at length on each of the specific measures at issue in this dispute. In addition, more than sixty days elapsed from the time the United States requested consultations to the time the request for the panel was made.[30] Therefore, there is no basis for Mexico's assertion that the United States has acted inconsistently with Articles 4.5 and 4.7 of the DSU with respect to consultations over the disputed measures.

38. Finally, Mexico also claims that the US panel request is inconsistent with Articles 17.4 and 17.5 of the AD Agreement. Neither claim has merit. *First*, to the extent that Article 17.4 creates any obligation with respect to consultations, it is that the requesting Member "consider" that the consultations have failed to achieve a mutually agreed solution. The United States so considered in this dispute. In the view of the United States, the consultations in this case have, in fact, failed to achieve a mutually satisfactory solution. Therefore, Mexico's Article 17.4 claim is groundless.

39. *Second*, Mexico's claim under Article 17.5 of the AD Agreement must fail because Article 17.5 imposes no obligation on the complaining party; rather, it establishes that the DSB shall, upon the request of the complaining party, establish a panel to examine the matter based on the panel request and the facts made available in conformity with appropriate domestic procedures to the authorities of the importing Member.

VIII. CONCLUSION

40. For the reasons stated above, Mexico's arguments in support of its request for a preliminary ruling that the US panel request does not meet the requirements of Articles 4.5, 4.7, and 6.2 of the DSU or Articles 17.4 or 17.5 of the AD Agreement are without merit. Accordingly, the Panel should reject that request.

---

[30] *Compare* US Consultation Request (demonstrating that the United States requested consultations on 16 June 2003) *to* US Panel Request (demonstrating that the United States requested the Panel on 19 September 2003).

ANNEX B

PARTIES' AND THIRD PARTIES' RESPONSES TO QUESTIONS POSED IN THE CONTEXT OF THE FIRST SUBSTANTIVE MEETING OF THE PANEL

ANNEX B-1

RESPONSES OF THE UNITED STATES

Questions concerning the period of investigation

1. The United States points (for example, in paragraph 57 of its first submission) to the use of the present tense in various provisions of the Anti-Dumping Agreement (the "AD Agreement") to support its claim that the POI must be as close to the date of initiation as practicable.

(a) Could the US elaborate on this view in light of the fact that it is inevitable that an investigation has to consider events that happened in the past. Does the US argue that there is any specific length of time beyond which the POI becomes inconsistent with the AD Agreement?

(b) For example, in view of the US, would a POI that ended 12 months prior to the initiation be inconsistent with the AD Agreement?

Answer:

1. The United States agrees that an investigation of dumping and injury must necessarily consider events that happened in the past. For this reason, we are not arguing that there is a specific length of time beyond which the POI becomes *per se* inconsistent with the AD Agreement. However, the purpose of an anti-dumping investigation is to determine whether a domestic industry is *presently* injured (or threatened with injury) by dumping that is *presently* occurring.[1] Therefore, an investigating authority must seek to base its determinations of dumping and injury on the most recent available information. If an investigating

[1] As the Panel notes, the United States pointed to numerous provisions in the AD Agreement supporting this conclusion in its first written submission. See US First Written Submission, para. 57.

authority chooses instead to base its analyses on information that is not the most recent available information, it must be able to justify its approach and explain why, despite its approach, its determinations are objective, unbiased, and based on positive evidence.

2. In the rice investigation, Economía provided *no* explanation for its decision to base its determinations on stale data, other than that the POI it selected was the one the petitioner asked for. For example, Economía provided no explanation of its decision to base its dumping analysis on data for March to August *1999*, when it did not even initiate its investigation until December *2000*.

3. Similarly, Economía provided no explanation for its decision to base its injury determination on data that was *already* fifteen months to three years old on the date of initiation, in lieu of collecting the most recent injury information that was available at that time. Economía also provided no explanation for its failure to update its injury data during the course of its investigation, with the consequence that the data was three to five years old at the time of the final determination. Economía also failed to explain how its injury analysis had any relevance to the situation of the domestic industry at the time of the final determination (or even at the time of initiation), given that the import volumes, price effects, and economic factors that it analyzed were for a period of time that was well before the initiation of the investigation, and years before the final injury determination.

4. The necessity for an investigating authority to consider events that happened in the past does not give an authority free rein to choose which part of the past to consider. Rather, the authority must evaluate the most recent information that is available.[2] Economía made no effort to collect information for September 1999 to December 2000, and it made no effort to update its data thereafter. As a consequence of its failure to collect recent information, Economía had no idea whether dumped imports were causing injury to the domestic industry as of the date that it *initiated* its investigation, much less on the date that it published its final determination.

2. Mexico argues that "there is no provision in the AD Agreement which indicates how remote an anti-dumping period of analysis must be" (para 49 of its first submission).

(a) In Mexico's view, is there no limit in the AD Agreement on how "old" the data can be on which the dumping and injury analysis may be based ? If Mexico is of the view that there are certain limits, please explain what, in Mexico's views, are the criteria for determining whether a POI is consistent with the AD Agreement or not?

2 *Compare* Appellate Body Report, *European Communities Anti-Dumping Duties on Imports of Cotton-Type Bed Linen from India, Recourse to Article 21.5 of the DSU by India*, WT/DS141/AB/R, adopted 24 April 2003, para. 113 ("*EC – Bed Linen 21.5 AB*") (stating that the absence of a specified methodology for calculating the volume of the "dumped imports" does not give an investigating authority unfettered discretion to "pick and choose whatever methodology they see fit...". Rather, the methodology must ensure that the determination is made on the basis of "positive evidence" and involves an "objective examination".).

(b) What is the Mexican practice in respect of the POI?

Answer:

5. In evaluating Mexico's response to this question, the Panel may wish to consider the following information relating to the anti-dumping investigations that **Economía** initiated on US products in 2003-2004:[3]

Investigation	Initiation Date	Length of POI	Gap Between End of POI and Initiation Date
Epoxidized Soybean Oil	17 May 2004	10 months (January to October 2003)	6.5 months
Crystal Polystyerene	13 January 2004	12 months (July 2002 to June 2003)	6.5 months
Newsprint	25 November 2003	12 months (January to December 2002)	11 months
Carbon Steel Line Pipe	29 August 2003	12 months (January to December 2001)	20 months
Hydrogen Peroxide	17 July 2003	12 months (January to December 2002)	6.5 months
Triple-Pressed Stearic Acid	11 June 2003	12 months (August 2001 to July 2002)	10 months
Fatty Acid	6 June 2003	19 months (January 2001 to July 2002)	10 months
Certain Pork Products	7 January 2003	6 months (April to September 2002)	3 months

6. The POIs that **Economía** established in these investigations suggests that it has no consistent approach with respect to the length of the POI it uses, other than that it uses the POI that the petitioners suggest in their petitions (even when, as in the rice investigation, the exporters object). It also suggests that Mexico often bases its determinations on stale data. Evidence of **Economía's willingness to allow the petitioner** to craft the POI can be seen in particular in the investigations of *Triple-Pressed Stearic Acid* and *Fatty Acid.* Although the two investigations were filed by the same Mexican producer (Quimic S.A. de C.V.) on the same day, and initiated within a few days of each other, the POIs in the two investigations differ substantially.

(c) Are there particular reasons why more recent data were not used in this case? Is Mexico of the view that the POI used in this case was the one closest to the initiation as far as "practicability" is concerned? If so, please elaborate.

---

3 The United States is attaching the relevant pages of each of the initiation notices as Exhibit US-21. The notices are in Spanish, as the United States does not have English-language translations.

Answer:

7. The only rationale that Economía provided in its published determinations for its decision to use stale data in conducting its analyses of dumping and injury was that the petitioner requested the March to August 1999 time period, and that imports were concentrated during that period.[4] Economía's decision to conduct its investigation in accordance with the petitioner's wishes, over the objections of the foreign exporters[5], belies any suggestion that Economía's choice of POI was objective or unbiased.

8. Furthermore, it is not factually accurate that the POI that Economía used in its investigation was the closest practicable to the date of initiation. By December 2000, dumping and injury data would have been available for all of 1999 and most of 2000. By the time of the final determination, injury data would have existed for all of 2000 and 2001 and possibly for 2002 as well.

3. Could Mexico explain the reason why it considered that the March - August 6 month period was appropriate for the injury analysis, including whether "seasonality" was one of the reasons.

Answer:

9. As the Panel will recall, Mexico clarified during the first panel meeting that "seasonality" was not a reason for its decision to limit its analysis to the March to August period. Furthermore, although Mexico argued in paragraph 55 of its first written submission that its choice of POI was designed in part to eliminate distortions in production levels, it argued in paragraph 60 of that same submission that production levels were constant throughout the year. Mexico's shifting rationales further confirm that Economía's choice of POI in this investigation was neither objective nor unbiased.

4. Could Mexico clarify whether the Panel is correct to understand that the investigating authority had the data necessary to perform an injury analysis for the full three year period, but chose not to use this data as it considered that the period should correspond to the period on which the analysis for dumping was made? Please elaborate.

---

[4] In particular, in paragraph 111 of the Notice of Initiation, Economía stated that, according to the petitioners:

> [T]he main importing activity of the finished product [milled rice] takes place in the period that goes from March thorough August in which there are no harvests of paddy rice and that for this reason such period adequately reflects importing activities.

Rice Initiation Notice, Exhibits US-1&2, para. 111. Economía repeated this statement in paragraph 64 of the Preliminary Determination and reached the conclusion that, according to the information provided by the petitioners:

> [I]mports tend to concentrate in the period from March through August of each year, which corresponds to the period of investigation proposed by the petitioners.

Exhibits US-14&15, para. 65.

[5] See, *e.g.*, Preliminary Determination, para. 66 (Exhibits US-14 & 15).

Answer:

10. The United States understands that Economía did in fact collect data for each month between March 1997 and August 1999, even though it only examined the data for the March to August time periods. However, Economía did not attempt to collect any data for the time period between September 1999 and December 2000, and it did not attempt to collect any additional injury data after it initiated the investigation.

5. Could Mexico explain why it considered that this particular 6 month period was adequate in terms of a dumping analysis. Was the fact that that was the period which the petitioners cited the sole reason?

Answer:

11. The United States has been able to find only two places in **Economía's** published determinations where it addresses its use of a six month period for the *dumping* analysis (other than the discussion of the concentration of imports in the March to August time period). First, **Economía** stated at paragraph 2 of its initiation notice that "the petitioner stated that during the period that includes March through August 1999 imports of long-grain milled rice, originating from the United States, were made at discriminatory prices, which caused injury to the domestic industry producing like goods". Second, Economía stated in paragraph 150 of the initiation notice that it had resolved to accept the petition and initiate an anti-dumping investigation on long-grain milled rice imports from the United States, "setting as the period of investigation the period encompassed from 1 March through 31 August 1999".

6. Is the United States of the view that an investigating authority is always precluded from choosing a POI for the injury analysis other than a full-year (12 months) period? If not, please explain specifically why the case at issue is not permissible.

Answer:

12. In the rice investigation, Economía's focus on the March-August time period was neither objective nor unbiased because at least half of domestic production occurred during the September-February time frame, and yet Economía focused on the March to August period because the petitioner argued that imports were concentrated in that period.

13. The problems arising from an examination of only partial year data are particularly acute when the domestic industry has production during all 12 months of a year. In order to comply with the requirements of Articles 3.1, 3.4, and 4.1 of the AD Agreement, the investigating authority must examine the impact of the dumped imports on the domestic producers as a whole. Therefore, the POI for injury should include all months of the year in which there is domestic production (assuming the data is reasonably available).

14. If the product under investigation is truly "seasonal" in character, an investigating authority might be justified in focusing its analysis on certain seasonal segments, provided that it does not fail to consider the other segments in the year. During the first panel meeting, however, Mexico denied that the production of long-grain milled white rice is seasonal, or that seasonality is relevant to this dispute.

7. The petitioners appear to have suggested this particular POI (March-August 6 month period), for reasons relating to the alleged seasonal character of the product, and as this period was representative of the increased import penetration. Precisely that, it seems, is the reason why the US objects to this period of investigation as it represents only that part of the year during which imports are at a high. In the US view, what are the facts on the record which demonstrate that imports of the subject product were concentrated in the March - August period, other than the petitioner's statement referred to in para. 65 of the preliminary determination? What other basis, if any, does the US have for its view that imports were at a high during this period?

Answer:

15. To be clear, the United States does not contest **Economía's** findings that imports were concentrated in the March to August time period. At least five paragraphs in **Economía's** published determinations, in addition to paragraph 65 of the preliminary determination, indicate that imports were in fact concentrated in this way:

- Paragraph 112 of the initiation notice states that "the petitioner indicated that major import activity in the finished product occurs in the period from March to August when there are no harvests of paddy rice and thus the period adequately reflects import activity."
- Paragraph 113 of the same notice states that "[f]or its part, the Secretariat noted that according to the information provided by the petitioner, the production of paddy rice is concentrated in early October and early February of each year and that imports tend to be concentrated in the period between March and August of each year, which corresponds to the period proposed for investigation by the petitioner."
- Paragraph 43(D) of the preliminary determination cites the petitioner's argument that "the main importing activity of white rice is carried out in the period in which there are not crops of "paddy" rice, therefore the period from March to August of each year reflects such activity...."
- Paragraph 64 of the preliminary determination repeats the discussion contained in paragraph 112 of the initiation notice.
- Paragraph 67 of the preliminary determination cites the petitioner's argument that "the chosen period is the one in which the paddy

rice harvests are not performed and therefore it is the one that reflects the import activity."

16. In any event, the United States is objecting *per se* to **Economía's** decision to limit its injury analysis to only half of the POI, and not only to the fact that **Economía** limited its analysis to the period when imports were concentrated. Mexico has conceded that seasonality was not relevant in this investigation, and it is indisputable that **Economía** failed to examine at least half of the domestic industry's production over the course of the entire POI. Thus, **Economía's** injury analysis would have been inconsistent with WTO rules even if imports had *not* been concentrated in the March to August time period.

17. *First*, Article 3.2 of the AD Agreement requires an investigating authority to consider whether there has been a significant increase in dumped imports or significant price effects. Nothing in Article 3.2 suggests that it is permissible for an investigating authority to conduct this analysis by considering evidence for only half of the three-year POI.

18. *Second*, Article 3.4 of the AD Agreement requires an investigating authority to evaluate *all* relevant economic factors and indices having a bearing on the state of the industry, and Article 3.5 of the AD Agreement requires an investigating authority to examine *all* relevant evidence before it. Neither provision permits an investigating authority to establish a three-year POI and then ignore the evidence for half of that period.

19. *Third*, Article 4.1 of the AD Agreement normally requires an investigating authority to examine the domestic producers "as a whole", or those producers whose collective output constitutes a "major proportion of total domestic production." In the rice investigation, domestic production of milled long-grain white rice spanned the entire year, yet **Economía** only examined the production for half of that period. If a Member only examines the evidence for half of the POI, there is no way to be certain that it is, in fact, meeting its obligations under Article 4.1.

20. *Finally*, Article 3.1 of the AD Agreement requires a determination of injury to be based on "positive evidence" and involve an "objective examination" of volume, price effects, and the impact of the dumped imports on the domestic producers of the like product. If an investigating authority only considers the evidence for half of the POI, there is simply no way for the authority to determine the true state of the domestic industry over the course of the *entire* POI, and thus no way to conclude that the authority's examination is consistent with Article 3.1.

Questions concerning the injury analysis

8. What, according to the parties, is the definition of the domestic industry allegedly injured by the dumped imports? Does the domestic industry considered in the injury analysis include producers of paddy rice or only of milled rice?

Answer:

21. The product under investigation was defined as long-grain milled rice. Therefore, the domestic industry should have been comprised of the "domestic producers as a whole" of long-grain milled rice (that is, the Mexican millers of paddy rice) or the domestic producers whose collective output of long-grain milled rice constituted a major proportion of the total domestic production of that product.[6]

22. In actuality, however, **Economía** failed to examine a consistent set of producers of long-grain milled rice when it conducted its injury analysis. To the contrary, **Economía** repeatedly shifted its analysis from one subset of producers to another, as it examined various factors. For example:

- **Economía** based its analysis of the effect of the imports on domestic prices on seven producers' data: IPACPA, Schettino, GEVSA, Mexicana de Arroz, Arrocera de Occidente, Arrocera del Bajio, and Covadonga.[7]
- **Economía** based its analysis of production volumes on eight producers' data: IPACPA, Schettino, GEVSA, Mexicana de Arroz, Arrocera de Occidente, Arrocera del Bajio, Industrias COREREPE, and Molino La Chontalpa.[8]
- **Economía** based its analysis of sales on eleven producers' data: IPACPA, Schettino, GEVSA, Mexicana de Arroz, Arrocera de Occidente, Arrocera del Bajio, Industrias COREREPE, Molino La Chontalpa, Champoton, Molino Trapiche de Labra, and Covadonga.[9]
- **Economía** based its analysis of inventories on six producers' data: IPACPA, Schettino, GEVSA, Mexicana de Arroz, Arrocera del Bajio, and Champoton.[10]
- **Economía** based its analysis of capacity utilization on three to five producers' data: IPACPA, Schettino, GEVSA, Champoton, and Industrias COREREPE.[11]
- **Economía** based its analysis of employment on seven producers' data (but not the same seven used for the analysis of prices): IPACPA, Schettino, GEVSA, Mexicana de Arroz, Arrocera del Bajio, Champoton, and Covadonga.[12]
- **Economía** based its analysis of wages on three producers' data: IPACPA, Schettino, and GEVSA.[13]

---

[6] AD Agreement, Art. 4.1.
[7] Final Determination, para. 278 (Exhibits US-6&7).
[8] *Ibid.*, para. 303.
[9] *Ibid.*, paras. 305, 307.
[10] *Ibid.*, para. 317.
[11] *Ibid.*, paras. 326, 328.
[12] *Ibid.*, para. 333.
[13] *Ibid.*, para. 334.

- **Economía** based its analysis of financial performance (in terms of profitability, return on investment, cash flow, and capacity to raise capital) on seven producers' data: IPACPA, Schettino, GEVSA, Mexicana de Arroz, Arrocera de Occidente, Arrocera del Bajio, and Covadonga.[14]

23. Thus, **Economía's** injury analysis did not constitute an "objective examination" of the domestic industry as defined in Article 4.1 of the AD Agreement, and its conclusions were not supported by the positive evidence that Article 3.1 requires.

9. Could Mexico clarify whether the import data also include data relating to imports of paddy rice or is the "rice" referred to in the Final Determination always "milled" rice? Are the terms "rice", "white rice" and "long grain white rice" as they appear throughout the Final Determination used as synonyms?

Answer:

24. Depending upon the issues involved, the public notices of the investigation make reference to imports of paddy rice, imports of milled rice, and imports of long-grain milled rice (the product under investigation). Even references to imports of "long grain white rice" should more properly refer to "imports *deemed to be* long grain white rice", however, given the absence of record data distinguishing between subject and non-subject merchandise. The United States discusses this point further in response to question 10 below.

10. Could Mexico clarify whether paddy rice also enters the Mexican market under tariff heading 1006.30.01? More in general, which categories of rice fall under this tariff heading?

Answer:

25. Under the Harmonized System, imports of paddy rice and imports of milled rice are classified under different tariff headings. At the time of initiation of the rice investigation, imports of paddy rice were classified under heading 1006.10.01 of the Mexican Tariff Schedule while imports of semi-milled and milled rice were classified under heading 1006.30.01.

26. Heading 1006.10.01 applies (and applied at the time) only to imports of paddy rice. In contrast, heading 1006.30.01 included semi-milled and milled rice, irrespective of the grain length and irrespective of whether the rice had been polished ("*pulido*"), glazed ("*glaseado*"), or parboiled ("*precocido*").[15] Inasmuch as the Customs classifications did not indicate which white rice imports were im-

---

[14] *Ibid.*, para. 338.

[15] See, *e.g.*, Notice of Initiation, para. 19 (Exhibits US-1&2); Preliminary Determination, paras. 9, 22 (Exhibits US-14&15).

ports of long-grain white rice, the data that **Economía** used for its determinations of dumping (prices) and injury (volumes and prices) were based on estimates.

27. On 18 May 2001, while the investigation was ongoing, heading 1006.30.01 was modified to apply only to imports of long-grain milled rice. Other imports previously classified under that heading were shifted to a new heading 1006.30.99.[16] This modification post-dated the August 1999 end of the POI, and the United States is not aware of any evidence suggesting that **Economía** took any steps to examine the new, more precise data.

11. Could the parties clarify whether the rice imported into Mexico under tariff heading 1006.30.01 covers rice in any or all of the 5 stages of processing mentioned in para.161 of the Final Determination and that, therefore, some of the rice imported under this tariff heading will need to undergo further processing in Mexico before entering the consumer market as a finished product?

Answer:

28. Paragraph 161 of the final determination references paddy rice, husked rice (rice with husk removed), milled rice, and broken rice. During the POI, paddy rice, husked rice, milled rice, and broken rice were classified, respectively, under headings 1006.10.01, 1006.20.01, 1006.30.01, and 1006.40.01 of the Mexican Tariff Schedule.

29. Broken rice is not rice at a particular "stage of processing", but rather a lower-value type of milled rice resulting from breakage of grains during the milling process. Product consisting entirely of broken rice entered under tariff heading 1006.40.01. The milled rice entered under tariff heading 1006.30.01, however, normally also contains some broken grains.[17] Milled rice containing higher percentages of broken grains corresponds to lower "grades" of milled rice, and sells for lower prices.[18]

30. The United States explained in its first written submission that the margin **Economía** took from the petition and applied to Producers Rice and the unexamined producers and exporters was adverse.[19] This "adverseness" was due in part to the fact that the petitioner compared an export price based on *all* imports designated as long grain white rice to a normal value based solely on prices for high grade rice with few broken grains, thus overstating the dumping margin.[20]

12. If it is correct that both subject and non-subject imports of rice from the United States entered the Mexican market under the above mentioned tariff heading, could Mexico explain the methodology that was used by the investigating authority to separate the subject imports of long grain white

---

16 Preliminary Determination, para. 23 (Exhibits US-14&15).

17 See US First Written Submission, footnotes 167-68.

18 *Ibid.*

19 *Ibid.*, paras. 159-165.

20 See *Ibid.*, paras. 163-64 and footnotes 166-68.

rice that came in under this heading from the non-subject imports of other types of rice (short grain, etc.)?

Answer:

31. As the United States explained in response to question 11, imports of paddy rice, husked rice, and broken rice were classified under headings other than 1006.30.01 (to be specific, headings 1006.10.01, 1006.20.01 and 1006.40.01, respectively). However, heading 1006.30.01 applied to both subject and non-subject imports (*i.e.,* semi-milled and milled rice, irrespective of the grain length and irrespective of whether the rice was polished, glazed or par-boiled).[21] Therefore, for purposes of its injury determination, **Economía** needed to separate imports of long-grain milled rice from imports of the other types of rice also classified under heading 1006.30.01.

32. The United States noted in its first written submission that **Economía** could have separately identified imports of long-grain milled rice on the basis of the information provided in the *pedimentos* for all the shipments that entered under heading 1006.30.01 during the POI. Instead, **Economía** relied on a flawed statistical procedure that focused on isolating imports of short-grain and medium-grain rice, and that did not even address the question of how to separate out imports of glazed rice and parboiled rice, which were also not part of the subject product. In fact, paragraphs 229-232 of the final determination, setting out **Economía's** methodology, make no reference to any attempt to separate out glazed rice and parboiled rice.[22]

13. Could Mexico clarify whether its statement that the domestic industry kept production of long grain white rice stable throughout the year by importing rice during the off-season, is a reference to the imports of paddy rice, or whether such imports are also of semi-processed rice?

Answer:

33. If the Panel is referring to paragraphs 60-62 of Mexico's first written submission, the United States notes again that Mexico has provided no citations to the administrative record of the rice investigation for the referenced table. To the contrary, Mexico's reference to "common knowledge" suggests that the table is a non-record document that Mexico prepared for purposes of this dispute.

---

21 The petitioners specifically defined the subject product as "long-grain milled rice." Initiation Notice, para. 1 (Exhibits US-1&2). Economía did not modify this definition in any way and it initiated the investigation with respect to "long-grain milled rice." *Ibid.*, para. 150. Moreover, the petitioners explicitly excluded glazed rice, parboiled rice, short-grain rice, and medium-grain rice from the scope of the investigation, on the grounds that these types of rice did not compete with domestic long-grain milled rice. *Ibid.*, paras. 10-15.

22 Paragraph 239 of the final determination indicates that Economía used the methodology described in paragraphs 229-232 for its analysis of 1999. For 1997 and 1998, Economía simply guessed that imports of long-grain white rice entered in proportions equal to all imports of white rice from the United States. See *Ibid.*

34. Furthermore, it is also important to reiterate **Economía's** finding in the investigation that Covadonga, one of the major Mexican producers, lowered its prices by mixing low-priced imports of *milled* rice from Argentina with its own production. The Argentine imports were priced below the prices of the US imports. **Economía** failed to explain in its published determinations how it could have found any causal relationship between the allegedly dumped imports from the United States and Covadonga's sales prices, given that Covadonga's sales prices *increased* when its imports from Argentina were excluded from the calculation.[23]

14. In para. 265 of the Final Determination, the Investigating Authority discusses the ex-factory price difference between Argentinian rice and US rice when exported to Mexico. Could Mexico indicate how high the Mexican import duty for rice from non-NAFTA countries like Argentina is? Was all the rice referred to as "rice imported from Argentina" fully processed long grain white rice ready for domestic consumption?

15. Could Mexico clarify whether the information contained in the "pedimentos" would have allowed the investigating authority to determine with certainty the precise amount of imports of the subject product, long grain white rice, from the United States and from other countries, without any need to apply a methodology to distinguish subject from non-subject imports?

Answer:

35. The United States explained in its first written submission that the *pedimentos* provide a wealth of information for each import shipment.[24] Moreover, Exhibit US-12 reproduces the format for the *pedimentos* that was applicable during 1999. As the instruction sheet for that document indicates (the instruction sheet is also set out in Exhibit US-12), there are 57 specific fields in the *pedimentos*, including fields for reporting a full description of the imported goods (field 32), the unit price of the goods (field 33), and the quantity of goods involved (field 53), as reported in the invoice. The instruction sheet also notes that field 32 should contain "the nature and the technical and commercial characteristics needed and sufficient for determining customs classification".

36. Therefore, if **Economía** had so chosen, it could have collected the *pedimentos* for the shipments of the subject product during the POI, and thus would have been in a position to separate the subject imports (imports of long-grain milled rice) from non-subject imports (imports of short-grain rice, medium-grain rice, glazed rice, and parboiled rice), and calculate precisely the price and the quantity of the subject imports.

---

23 See Final Determination, paras. 286 and 290 (Exhibits US-6&7); US First Written Submission, para. 125.

24 US First Written Submission, n. 25 and accompanying text.

37. The United States notes in its response to question 17 below that Mexico has shown a willingness to use the *pedimentos* where doing so will benefit domestic industries seeking the imposition of anti-dumping measures. It also explains that Mexican petitioners have used *pedimentos* released to them by the Mexican government to separate subject products from non-subject products imported under the same tariff heading.

16. (a) Could the parties comment on the following argument made by China in its oral statement (page 5):

"Given that both Article 5.2 and Article 6.1.3 use the same wording "known exporter", the "known exporters" under Article 6.1.3 refer to "each known exporter" under Article 5.2. Therefore, the AD Agreement suggests that investigating authorities shall rely on the petitioners to identify "known" exporters in their petition(s)".

Answer:

38. The United States does not agree with China's interpretation of Article 6.1.3 of the AD Agreement. Article 6.1.3 places obligations on the *investigating authority*, not on the petitioner. There is no textual link to Article 5.2 or any other language in the text of Article 6.1.3 suggesting that the authority is only required to send a copy of the petition to the exporters known to the petitioner, and not to the exporters known to itself. If the drafters of the AD Agreement had intended to limit the obligation in Article 6.1.3 in such a manner, they presumably would have said so.

39. The broader context of Article 6.1 supports the conclusion that the reference to "known" exporters in Article 6.1.3 is to those exporters known to the investigating authority. The first sentence of Article 6.1 states that "[a]ll interested parties in an anti-dumping investigation shall be given notice of the information which the authorities require and ample opportunity to present in writing all evidence which they consider relevant...." Given the requirement to notify "all" interested parties, there is no logical basis for limiting the obligation to send the petition to only those exporters known to the petitioner if the investigating authority knows of other exporters.

40. In addition, Article 6.2 of the AD Agreement states that "all" interested parties shall have a full opportunity for the defence of their interests, and Article 6.4 states that authorities shall provide opportunities for "all" interested parties to see relevant information. These provisions illustrate the emphasis that Article 6 places on ensuring that the interests of all interested parties involved in an anti-dumping investigation are protected, and militate against an interpretation of Article 6.1.3 that would lead to fewer parties receiving the information they need to defend themselves.

41. Finally, China's interpretation (like Mexico's interpretation of Article 6.10 and its overall approach to assigning margins to uninvestigated firms) is illogical, because it would create an incentive for petitioners to under-report the range

of exporters known to them, because doing so would allow them to manipulate the investigation to the detriment of the investigated parties.

(b) **Is it Mexico's view that the term "known" exporters in Article 6.1.3 AD Agreement, only relates to the exporters that are "made known" to it by the petitioner ?**

(c) **Could the US explain why it considers that it was so unreasonable of the authority to assume, given the nature of the industry, that by making its public initiation notification, by sending the questionnaires to the two known exporters and by notifying the US authorities in Mexico, all exporters would be informed of the initiation of the investigation and of the need to provide information? Is this not confirmed by the behaviour of the USA Rice Federation (see also question 18 below)?**

Answer:

42. The issue before the Panel is whether **Economía** was under an obligation with respect to the AD Agreement to take certain steps in the conduct of its investigation, and whether it failed to take those steps.

43. In order to act consistently with Mexico's WTO obligations, **Economía** could have, on one hand, investigated and made an effort to calculate an individual margin of dumping for each known exporter or producer. Taking this approach would have required **Economía** to send a copy of the anti-dumping questionnaire to each firm that was included in the investigation and to ensure that each firm understood the consequences of not replying before **Economía** could apply a facts available-based margin to it.[25] On the other hand, **Economía** could have limited its investigation to a subset of exporters and producers.[26] Taking this other approach would have required **Economía** to apply a neutral margin, calculated in accordance with Article 9.4 of the AD Agreement, to the unexamined firms.

44. However, **Economía** chose instead to take a third approach that is not consistent with the AD Agreement: it limited its investigation by only sending its anti-dumping questionnaire to the two firms that the petitioner designated as "known" exporters in the petition. Then, having made this decision, it applied an adverse, facts-available based margin, instead of a neutral margin, to the unexamined firms. **Economía's** approach served both to minimize the investigative burden on itself and to maximize the anti-dumping margins applied to the for-

[25] The Appellate Body noted in *United States – Japan Sunset AB* that Article 6.1 is one of several provisions in Article 6 that, either explicitly or by implication, create obligations with respect to each *individual* exporter or producer. Appellate Body Report, *United States – Sunset Review of Anti-Dumping Duties on Corrosion-Resistant Carbon Steel Flat Products from Japan*, DS/244/AB/R, adopted 9 January 2004, para. 152 ("*United States – Japan Sunset AB*").

[26] Specifically, a reasonable number of interested parties using statistically valid samples, or the largest percentage of the volume of the exports which could reasonably be investigated. AD Agreement, Art. 6.10, second sentence.

eign exporters and producers. But under the AD Agreement, **Economía** cannot have it both ways.

45. *First*, **Economía** limited its investigation by choosing to only send its questionnaire to the two exporters specifically identified as "known" exporters in the petition, and by failing to send its questionnaire to The Rice Company, a known exporter mentioned repeatedly in the petition and described in Annex H of the petition as "one of the largest US exporters as regards paddy rice and white milled rice".[27] It also limited its investigation by choosing not to consult the *pedimentos*, which were in the possession of the Mexican government and identified every exporter of the subject merchandise to Mexico during the POI, thus making them known to Mexico. **Economía** also limited its investigation by taking no steps to review publicly available information that would have provided names and contact information for every US producer in the United States.[28] Then, **Economía** increased the difficulty for any firm not identified by the petitioner to participate in the investigation by requiring it to appear in Mexico City to obtain a copy of the questionnaire.[29]

46. *Second*, **Economía** did not apply a neutral margin calculated in accordance with Article 9.4 of the AD Agreement to the unexamined producers and exporters. Rather, it applied an adverse, facts available-based margin to them. There are numerous provisions of the AD Agreement, however, that place limitations on the ability of a Member to apply margins based on the facts available. The United States discussed these provisions at length in its first written submission and in its oral statement at the first panel meeting.[30] **Economía** failed to comply with any of them.

47. *Third*, Article 12.1 of the AD Agreement requires an investigating authority initiating an anti-dumping investigation to give public notice *and* notify the interested parties known to the investigating authorities. Therefore, it is not enough for a Member to simply publish a notice of initiation of an investigation and thereby meet its obligations under Article 12.1. The fact that the USA Rice Federation (the "Federation") came forward and asked to participate in the investigation proves only that the Federation subsequently learned of the investigation. It does not prove that any other firm knew that it had been "deemed" included in the investigation, or that the Federation or any other firm was aware of **Economía's** plan to breach its WTO obligations by applying an adverse, facts available-based margin to firms that were never even sent a questionnaire. The initiation notice says nothing of the sort.

[27] Petition Annex H, at 2. (Exhibit US-10). **Economía**'s failure to send the questionnaire to The Rice Company demonstrates that it is not accurate to state that **Economía** sent its questionnaire to the "known" exporters.

[28] See Exhibits US-18 and 19 (excerpts from the industry publication *Rice Journal* for 1999 and 2000, respectively, providing contact information).

[29] Initiation Notice, para. 153. (Exhibits US-1&2). The Panel should also recall Mexico's argument that it would be "illogical" to provide such firms the full 30 days to respond to the questionnaire that the AD Agreement requires. See Mexico's First Written Submission, para. 220-21.

[30] See, *e.g.*, US First Written Submission, paras. 142-148, 174-183, 192-195; US oral statement at the first panel meeting, paras. 45-51.

48. The Panel's question suggests that **Economía** might have taken the approach that it did because of the "nature of the industry" that it was investigating. The United States is not aware of any evidence on the record of the rice investigation supporting this assumption. If anything, the record evidence suggests instead that **Economía's** approach reflected a conscious decision to favour the interests of the petitioner by ignoring readily available information, shifting the burden for providing the requisite notice from itself to the US exporters and producers, as well as to the US government, and ensuring that a prohibitive facts available-based anti-dumping margin would be applied to as many US exporters and producers as possible.

49. If **Economía** had not deemed *every* producer and exporter of the subject merchandise in the country to be "in the investigation" when it only sent its questionnaire to two of them, and if it had applied a neutral "all others" margin calculated in accordance with Article 9.4 to the uninvestigated exporters and producers, then **Economía's** failure to provide the unexamined exporters and producers the notice that Article 6.1 and paragraph 1 of Annex II require would not have been an issue. **Economía** did claim that it was investigating every US exporter and producer in the United States, however, and it applied an adverse, facts available-based margin taken from the petition to all but three of them. As the United States demonstrated in its first written submission, **Economía's** approach breached numerous provisions of the AD Agreement and the GATT 1994.

17. The US argues that all the Mexican investigating authority had to do was to look into the "pedimentos" to find out who the other US exporters were.

(a) Could Mexico indicate whether this assertion is correct, do the "pedimentos" identify all the exporters?

Answer:

50. Exhibit US-12 reproduces the format for the *pedimentos* that was applicable during 1999. As the United States noted in its first written submission, field 19 in the *pedimentos* requests the name of the foreign supplier involved, together with its business address.[31]

(b) Could Mexico clarify whether the investigating authority attempted to obtain the "pedimentos"? If so, what was the reason why such information was not obtained, or could not be used?

Answer:

51. In evaluating Mexico's response to the Panel's questions on the *pedimentos*, the Panel may wish to also take into account Mexico's willingness to use the *pedimentos* to benefit domestic industries seeking the imposition of anti-dumping measures. For example, on 17 May 2004 (the day of the first panel

[31] US First Written Submission, n. 25 (final sentence).

meeting in this dispute), **Economía** published an initiation notice in its anti-dumping investigation of *Epoxidized Soybean Oil from the United States.*[32] The notice indicates that Mexico's Ministry of the Treasury released actual *pedimentos* to the petitioners in that case and that the petitioners used data taken from the *pedimentos* to support their allegations of dumping and injury.[33]

52. Similarly, in **Economía's** anti-dumping investigation of *Crystal Polystyrene from the United States*, the petitioners obtained copies of *pedimentos* from the Mexican government and used them to support their allegations of dumping and injury.[34] Moreover, the petitioners in the *Crystal Polystyrene* investigation

---

[32] *Resolucion por la que se acepta la solicitud de parte interesada y se declara el inicio de la investigación antidumping sobre las importaciones de aceite epoxidado de soya, mercancía actualmente clasificada en la fracción arancelaria 1518.00.02 de la Tarifa de la Ley de los Impuestos Generales de Importación y de Exportación, originarias de los Estados Unidos de América, independientemente del país de procedencia*, Diario Oficial de la Federacion (segunda seccion) 11 (17 May 2004) ("*Soybean Oil Initiation Notice*") (Exhibit US-22). The attached exhibit is the Spanish-language original, because the United States does not have an English-language translation of the notice.

[33] In paragraph 16 of the initiation notice, Economía takes stock of all of the information that the petitioners submitted in their petition. Economía notes in particular that the petitioners provided:

> Customs declarations [*pedimentos*] from 2002 through October 2003 accompanied by their [corresponding] invoices, certificates of analysis and the translation of the latter.

Soybean Oil Initiation Notice, para. 16(C). Economía then notes in paragraph 24 that:

> To document the export price, the companies EIQSA and RYMSA [the two petitioners] provided customs declarations [*pedimentos*] which establish the price at which epoxidized soybean oil was exported from the United States of America to Mexico during the period of investigation. *The petitioners obtained this information from the Ministry of the Treasury through ANIQ.*

Ibid., para. 24 (ANIQ is the acronym for *Asociacion Nacional de la Industria Quimica* or the National Association of the Chemical Industry) (emphasis added). Finally, in assessing the petitioners' allegations of injury, the initiation notice states that:

> The petitioners obtained statistics of definitive imports corresponding to the tariff heading 1518.00.02 of Mexico's Import Tariff Schedule at the level of customs declarations provided by the General Customs Administration for the period of investigation.
>
> ... The petitioners stated that the customs declarations were obtained through ANIQ and that the totality of such declarations referred to epoxidized soybean oil.
>
> According to the foregoing, the petitioners presented an import database that refers exclusively to epoxidized soybean oil originating in the United States of America for the period under review.

Ibid., paras. 64(A), 64(C), 64(D).

[34] *Resolucion por la que se acepta la solicitud de parte interesada y se declara el inicio de la investigación antidumping sobre las importaciones de poliestireno cristal, mercancía actualmente clasificada en la fraccionnes arancelarias 3903.19.02 y 3903.19.99 de la Tarifa de la Ley de los Impuestos Generales de Importación y de Exportación, originarias de los Estados Unidos de América, independientemente del país de procedencia,* Diario Oficial de la Federacion (primera seccion) 25 (13 January 2004) ("Crystal Polystyrene Initiation Notice") (Exhibit US-23). The attached exhibit is the Spanish-language original, because the United States does not have an English-language translation of the notice.

used the *pedimentos* to separate out the imports of the subject product from other, non-subject merchandise imported under the same tariff heading.[35]

53. In sum, Mexico's willingness to allow petitioners to use the *pedimentos* to support dumping and injury claims in other investigations illustrates (1) that the *pedimentos* can be used to obtain value and volume information for products subject to anti-dumping investigations; and (2) that Economía's failure to use them in the investigation at issue to identify "known" exporters or to use them in its injury analyses was neither objective nor unbiased.[36]

(c) Could Mexico explain whether the Mexican investigating authority in its normal practice verifies the information provided by the petitioners concerning the exporters mentioned in the petition? If so, how does the authority go about checking this information?

Answer:

54. The United States has been unable to identify any evidence in **Economía's** initiation notice suggesting that **Economía** took any steps to verify the accuracy and adequacy of the information that the petitioner submitted with respect to the "known" exporters in the investigation at issue. For example, **Economía** did not question the petitioner's omission of The Rice Company as a known exporter, notwithstanding that the petitioner used information from The Rice Company's web site to support the petition.[37]

18. Could the United States provide more information on the "USA Rice Federation", which according to the Final Determination made itself known to the investigating authority. Which and how many producers does it represent?

---

[35] Economía noted at para. 29A of the Initiation Notice that:

> [Petitioners] obtained a representative sample of copies of pedimentos from the General Administration of Customs for the period of investigation and identified the type of product that each importer buys, *the terms of sale*, the means of transportation, and the presentation of the product (in bags or in bulk), inter-alia. *Subsequently, they eliminated the shipments that do not correspond to crystal polystyrene [the subject product]. The sample of pedimentos accounts for 73.6 per cent of the total volume imported under tariff headings 3903.19.02 and 3903.19.99 of the TIGIE [Schedule of the General Import Tax, which is the formal name for Mexico's Harmonized Tariff Schedule] during the period under investigation.*

Ibid., para. 29A (emphasis added) (Exhibit US-23).

[36] In addition, para. XXVI of Article 144 of Mexico's Customs Law provides that Mexico's Ministry of the Treasury shall:

> [r]elease the information contained in the *pedimentos* to Industrial Chambers and Industry Associations grouped in Confederations, as provided in the Law of Business Chambers and Confederations thereof, that participate with the Tax Administration Service [Mexico's IRS] in the Program on Customs and Tax Control by Industrial Sector....

This is yet another example of Mexico's willingness to allow its domestic industries to use *pedimento* data to support their cases in anti-dumping proceedings.

[37] See Initiation Notice, para. 28(y) (Exhibits US-1&2).

Answer:

55. The Federation is a rice industry organization that serves as a national advocate for all segments of the US rice industry. It conducts activities to influence government programs, develops and initiates programmes to increase worldwide demand for US rice, and provides other services to increase industry profitability for all industry segments. The Federation has three charter members: the US Rice Producers' Group, the Rice Millers' Association, and the USA Rice Council. Each of those organizations has a distinct identity and serves its own segment of the US rice industry.

56. The Federation was in existence when the petitioner filed its petition, and it was one source among many that the petitioner and **Economía** could have contacted to obtain publicly available information on the names and contact information of US producers and exporters of long-grain white rice. However, neither the petitioner nor **Economía** contacted the Federation.[38] In the context of this dispute, the AD Agreement required ***Economía*** to calculate a margin for each known exporter and producer, to send a copy of the anti-dumping questionnaire to each firm that was included in the investigation, and to ensure that each such firm understood the consequences of not replying before **Economía** could apply a facts available-based margin to it.[39] Mexico therefore cannot cite the fact that the Federation subsequently came forward on its own and asked to participate in the anti-dumping investigation as a means of relieving Mexico of its WTO obligations or of "curing" its failure to meet those obligations.

19. Could the US explain why it considers that the Mexican authority failed to separate the dumped from the non-dumped imports while the Final Determination on numerous occasions refers to dumped imports separately and explicitly?

Answer:

57. As the Appellate Body stated in *EC Bed Linen 21.5 AB*, Article 3.1 of the AD Agreement requires investigating authorities to ensure that their injury determinations are:

> made on the basis of "positive evidence" and an "objective examination" of the volume and effect of imports that *are dumped* – and

---

[38] For example, Economía did not send the Federation a copy of the petition or its anti-dumping questionnaire or otherwise ask it for assistance in identifying members of the US rice industry. The Federation obtained the questionnaire by coming forward on its own and appearing at Economía's offices in Mexico City.

[39] The Appellate Body noted in *United States – Japan Sunset AB* that Article 6.1 is one of several provisions in Article 6 that, either explicitly or by implication, create obligations with respect to each *individual* exporter or producer. Appellate Body Report, *United States – Sunset Review of Anti-Dumping Duties on Corrosion-Resistant Carbon Steel Flat Products from Japan*, DS/244/AB/R, adopted 9 January 2004, para. 152 ("*United States – Japan Sunset AB*").

to the exclusion of the volume and effect of imports that *are not dumped.*[40]

Thus, an investigating authority must focus its analysis on the dumped imports. **Economía**, by contrast, made its determinations on the basis of an examination of the volume and effect of *all* imports, including both the dumped and the non-dumped imports. The US first written submission lists several examples of this point.[41]

58. For example, **Economía** looked at *all* imports from the United States, and not just dumped imports, in determining whether import levels had increased during the period of investigation.[42] **Economía** examined the import levels for Riceland and Farmers Rice – two companies that were found not to be dumping – and based its overall conclusions on data for the non-dumping Farmers Rice.[43]

59. Similarly, **Economía** compared the fall in domestic prices to the fall in prices of *all* imports (including third country imports), and not just the dumped imports.[44] **Economía** specifically included in its analysis the prices of Farmers Rice and Riceland, neither of which were dumped, imports of non-subject merchandise, and imports from Argentina (which were priced below the dumped imports).[45]

60. Moreover, **Economía** stated that the "dumped imports" did not register an increase in their share of domestic consumption, and that they maintained their share of internal consumption.[46] These statements are only accurate, however, if they were based on data for *all* of the investigated imports, and not just the dumped imports. The data for the *dumped* imports actually showed that:

- The dumped imports' share of apparent domestic consumption actually *fell* – from 5.7 per cent in March – August 1997 to 4.8 per cent in March–August 1999.[47]
- Similarly, the dumped imports' share of internal consumption *fell* – from 6.9 per cent in March–August 1997 to 6.5 per cent in March–August 1999.[48]

---

40 *EC – Bed Linen 21.5 AB,* para. 111.

41 See US First Written Submission, paras. 120-124.

42 See, *e.g.*, Final Determination, para. 217 (Exhibit US-6&7).

43 *Ibid.*, para. 228.

44 *Ibid.*, paras. 262-296.

45 *Ibid.*, paras. 281-82, 291. As the United States noted in its first written submission, Mexico failed to explain how it could have found any causal relationship between the allegedly dumped imports from the United States and Covadonga's sales price, given that Covadonga's sales price *increased* when its sales of its imports from Argentina were excluded from the calculation. See *Ibid.*, paras. 286 and 290; US First Written Submission, para. 125.

46 Final Determination, para. 261 (Exhibit US-6&7).

47 *Ibid.*, para. 248. By comparison, the investigated imports as a whole constituted 6.6 per cent of apparent consumption in March to August 1997, and 6.5 per cent in March to August 1999. *Ibid.*, para. 247.

48 *Ibid.*, para. 254. By comparison, the investigated imports as a whole constituted 8.1 per cent of internal consumption in March to August 1997, and 8.7 per cent in March to August 1999. *Ibid.*, para. 247.

- Finally, the share of the dumped imports in comparison with domestic production *fell* – from 10.2 per cent in March–August 1997 to 10.1 per cent in March–August 1999.[49]

61. In sum, Articles 3.1., 3.2, and 3.5 of the AD Agreement required **Economía** to conduct an objective examination of the volume, price effects, and impact of the *dumped* imports, and **Economía** failed to do so.

Questions concerning Article 5.8 AD Agreement

20. In Mexico's view, does it suffice for one exporter to have been found to be dumping above *de minimis* levels for all other exporters to be included in the application of the measure under Article 5.8 AD Agreement or does Mexico consider that some sort of country-wide rate needs to be established and that, only if that country-wide rate is above *de minimis*, will all exporters from that country be covered by the measure? Could Mexico clarify whether an exporter for which a below *de minimis*, but more than zero margin of dumping was found, would receive a 0 per cent duty or would a duty be imposed on such an exporter equal to the *de minimis* margin?

Answer:

62. In the rice investigation, **Economía** did find only one company to be dumping. The other three exporters that **Economía** examined either had margins of zero (Farmers Rice and Riceland) or did not export to Mexico during the POI (Producers Rice).[50] Nevertheless, **Economía** applied the anti-dumping measure to every producer or exporter in the United States, including Farmers Rice and Riceland. **Economía** took no steps to examine whether the weighted average margin of all exporters was greater than *de minimis* when it decided to impose the anti-dumping measure.[51]

63. It is important to note that the consequence of (1) **Economía's** refusal to apply Article 5.8 on a firm-specific basis; (2) its practice of "deeming" every exporter and producer in the investigated country as being included in the investigation; and (3) its application of adverse, facts available-based margins to the unexamined exporters and producers, is that **Economía** will almost certainly find at least one firm to be dumping, and thus never find a basis to terminate an investigation due to "*de minimis*" dumping margins. The only case where the language will have meaning for Mexico is the exceedingly rare one where **Economía** individually investigates *every* exporter and producer of the subject product in the country under investigation and calculates a zero or *de minimis* margin of dumping for each of them. By effectively reading the *de minimis* dumping margins

---

[49] *Ibid.*, para. 259. By comparison, the share of the investigated imports as a whole was 11.8 per cent in March to August 1997, and 13.5 per cent in March to August 1999. *Ibid.*, para. 258.

[50] See Final Determination, para. 400 (Exhibits US-6&7).

[51] *Ibid.*, paras. 398-404.

language out of the AD Agreement, Mexico's interpretation of Article 5.8 breaches the principle of effectiveness of treaty interpretation.

21. Could Mexico clarify whether this is a correct understanding of the way in which the Mexican system operates: if an exporter was not dumping during the POI, but a dumping margin was found for other exporters of the product, this non-dumping exporter will be included in the measure, but a 0% duty will be imposed. If later the review shows that the exporter had since engaged in dumping, a duty will be imposed on him equivalent to the new margin of dumping.

(a) Is this a correct understanding of the system?

(b) Will a new injury analysis be required before such duties may be imposed?

22. Could the US please react to the European Communities suggestion (in para. 8 in fine of its written submission) that the US interpretation of Article 5.8 AD Agreement raises the practical problem of the possibility of two parallel proceedings against imports from the same country?

Answer:

64. It is not clear to the United States what the European Communities (EC) means when it suggests that the US interpretation of Article 5.8 may lead to "parallel" proceedings against imports from the same country, or how such an outcome would differ from the normal situation in an anti-dumping investigation. In a sense, the "dumping" side of an anti-dumping investigation is *always* a series of "parallel" investigations, because the investigating authority examines the export prices and normal values of each individual firm under investigation, and it determines an individual margin of dumping for each such firm. It is this very aspect of the dumping calculation that makes it possible for an investigating authority to exclude from the anti-dumping measure those individual firms that are investigated and found not to be dumping.

65. Furthermore, there is no reason to assume that a firm that is found not to be dumping in an investigation, and excluded from the measure, would subsequently begin to dump. Unlike a firm that is investigated and found to be dumping, a firm that is investigated and found *not* to be dumping has demonstrated that it is able to sell in the export market without engaging in such practices. If the firm is able to sell without dumping when there is no anti-dumping measure in place, it will presumably be able to continue doing so thereafter (particularly if its competitors are subject to the measure). Thus, there is no reason to assume that there would be any need for an investigating authority to conduct a new investigation.

66. Finally, the United States has excluded individual firms from anti-dumping measures in the past without encountering "practical problems" or "parallel proceedings".

67. In sum, if a firm is investigated during the investigation and found not to be dumping, there is no basis under the AD Agreement to apply the anti-dumping measure to that firm.

Questions concerning the use of facts available and the all others rate

23. In para. 176 of its submission, and para. 61. (c) of its oral statement, Mexico argues that para. 6 of Annex II was complied with as the information of the non-shipping exporter, Producers Rice, was "accepted".

(a) Could Mexico clarify what information this company provided which was accepted by the authority?

(b) Is Mexico of the view that para. 6 does not apply to situations in which the information is not provided, or is not provided within a reasonable period of time, but only to situations in which information which was provided is rejected?

24. Article 68 of the Foreign Trade Act mentions three categories of exporters to which the highest margin shall be applied. One of these categories seems to cover the situation provided for in Article 6.8 AD Agreement.

(a) Does Mexico consider that the two other categories (non-appearing exporters and non-shipping exporters) are not covered by the situation described in Article 6.8 AD Agreement?

(b) What is the view of the US on the relevance, if any, of the fact that Article 68 of the Foreign Trade Act provides for these three separate categories?

Answer:

68. Subparagraph II of Article 64 appears to address the application of the facts available in the situation set out in Article 6.8 of the AD Agreement. The fact that subparagraphs I and III require **Economía** to apply the facts available in two additional situations is evidence that Article 64 requires **Economía** to apply the facts available when the necessary prerequisites for doing so in accordance with Article 6.8 and Annex II of the AD Agreement are absent.

69. Furthermore, subparagraph II of Article 64 is also inconsistent with WTO rules. The United States noted this point, for example, in paragraphs 237-329 of its first written submission.

(c) Is Mexico of the view that the AD Agreement does not provide any rules on how to calculate an all others rate for non-appearing parties and non-shipping exporters, or is Mexico arguing that the maximum duty that can be imposed on such exporters under the Agreement is a facts available margin?

Answer:

70. Even if one were to interpret the AD Agreement as not providing rules on how to calculate an all others rate for non-appearing parties and non-shipping exporters, the fact remains that Articles 6.1 and 6.8 and Annex II of the AD Agreement do provide rules that Members must follow when applying margins based on the facts available. For the reasons set out in our first written submission[52], **Economía's** application of the facts available to Producers Rice and the unexamined exporters and producers breached these rules.

25. In Mexico's view, does para. 7 of Annex II allow for unfavourable results only in case of non-cooperative parties or in all cases in which the necessary information is not provided?

Questions concerning the challenge of the law as such

26. According to the parties, to what extent is the distinction mandatory / discretionary legislation still applicable in WTO law after the Appellate Body statement in para. 93 of its decision in the US - Corrosion Resistant Steel case (DS 244)?

Answer:

71. In paragraph 93 of the relevant report, the Appellate Body stated that it had not, "as yet, been required to pronounce generally upon the continuing relevance or significance of the mandatory/discretionary distinction. Nor do we consider that this appeal calls for us to undertake a comprehensive examination of this distinction."[53] Therefore, the Appellate Body's statements do not provide grounds to conclude that the doctrine is no longer applicable in WTO law.

72. As the United States discusses in greater detail in responding to question 27, Mexico has alleged that there is no conflict between its WTO obligations and the challenged Mexican legal provisions. Indeed, Mexico's enactment of the challenged provisions is premised upon its view that no such conflict exists. Therefore, the issue of whether Mexico has "discretion" to ignore an FTA provision that conflicts with the AD Agreement does not arise.

27. Could the US explain to what extent it considers the challenged Mexican legal provisions to be mandatory in nature in light of the argument by Mexico of the direct effect of the WTO Agreements in Mexican municipal law?

---

[52] US First Written Submission, paras. 174-183, 192-195.

[53] Appellate Body Report, *United States – Sunset Review of Anti-Dumping Duties on Corrosion-Resistant Carbon Steel Flat Products from Japan*, DS/244/AB/R, adopted January 9, 2004, para. 93 ("*United States – Japan Sunset AB*") (footnote omitted).

Answer:

73. The so-called "mandatory/discretionary" doctrine applies when a law is capable of being applied in both a WTO-consistent and a WTO-inconsistent manner. Each of the legal provisions at issue in this dispute, by contrast, *requires* **Economía** to act in a particular manner. For example, Article 64 of the FTA does not say that **Economía** *may* apply the highest facts available to firms that did not export to Mexico during the POI; it *requires* **Economía** to do so. Mexico has not alleged otherwise. Mexico's suggestion that it is required to apply its laws in a WTO-consistent manner cannot insulate those laws from challenge if the laws themselves grant **Economía** no discretion to apply them in a WTO-consistent manner.

74. Furthermore, **Economía** is the administrator of Mexico's anti-dumping laws, and **Economía** views each of the challenged provisions as in itself consistent with WTO rules, without any need to somehow override these laws through application of WTO rules under municipal law. Mexico has made this point repeatedly during this dispute. In other words, as a matter of Mexican municipal law, Mexico has been interpreting its WTO obligations as not precluding the challenged laws from requiring actions which are, in fact, WTO-inconsistent. Mexico has therefore not considered it necessary to test whether, under Mexican municipal law, the direct effect of the WTO Agreements could actually override a law which on its face mandates what is, in fact, WTO-inconsistent action. Moreover, given Mexico's view that, as a matter of Mexican municipal law, WTO rules do not preclude the challenged laws from operating as provided in the laws themselves, Mexico does not, as a matter of municipal law, have discretion to disregard their otherwise mandatory aspects.

75. Thus, the issue of "discretion" might only arise with respect to the challenged laws in the event that this Panel finds the laws to be inconsistent with Mexico's WTO obligations. At that point, it would fall to Mexico to explain in the implementation phase of the dispute what steps it would need to take to reconcile its WTO-inconsistent laws with its WTO obligations, just as it would for any other Member whose domestic law was found to be inconsistent on its face with WTO rules.

28. Could Mexico explain whether, in case the DSB were to adopt a panel report finding an inconsistency of a Mexican law with the WTO Agreements, it considers that it would be obliged to amend the law to bring the law into conformity with the WTO Agreement?

29. Could Mexico clarify whether private parties may be successful when they file a suit against the administration before the domestic courts of Mexico in case the administration failed to comply with a statutory obligation, even if this obligation is inconsistent with the WTO Agreement, requiring the administration to comply with such obligations?

30. Is it Mexico's view that if a certain provision is somehow found to be inconsistent with the WTO Agreements, that is, in case a conflict is found between the Foreign Trade Act and the WTO Agreements, then the WTO

Agreements would prevail by virtue of Article 133 of the Political Constitution and Article 2 of the Foreign Trade Act?

31. In para. 263 - 266 of its submission, Mexico argues that the "representativeness" requirement in Article 68 of the Foreign Trade Act is only a tool, and that the US is wrong in suggesting that it is a condition *sine qua non* for the initiation of a review.

(a) Could Mexico clarify whether a review may be initiated if the party concerned cannot demonstrate that its sales volume for the period was representative?

(b) What in the Mexican practice is considered to be a "representative" volume?

Answer:

76. The United States has noted previously that the plain language of Article 68 imposes a condition for exporters seeking reviews to demonstrate that the volume of exports of the subject merchandise during the review period was representative. In the event that Mexico contests this fact, the Panel may wish to refer to the attached initiation notice for a Mexican "Article 68" review that is currently ongoing, which demonstrates that Mexico does in fact require exporters seeking reviews to make such a demonstration.[54]

77. The review in question involves several exporters. According to the initiation notice, each exporter stated that "the volume exported in the period under investigation [the review period] was representative, given that its shipments were made in commercial volumes and in a regular fashion throughout such period", and provided supporting data on export sales to **Economía**.[55]

78. Furthermore, paragraphs 38-42 of the attached initiation notice are entitled "Legal Requirements for the Review". Paragraph 38 states that, according to Article 68 of the FTA and Article 99 of the Regulation, reviews of definitive anti-dumping duties are subject to the substantive and procedural rules set forth in those articles. Therefore, inasmuch as the "representative exports" requirement is set forth in Article 68, reviews are subject to that requirement.

79. Paragraph 47 of the initiation notice states that **Economía** applied two tests to determine whether the exports of the various firms during the review period were representative. First, **Economía** compared the export volumes of the

---

[54] *Resolucion por la que se declara el inicio de la revision de la cuota compensatoria definitiva impuesta a las importaciones de manzanas de mesa de las variedades Red Delicious y sus mutaciones y Golden Delicious, mercancia clasificada actualmente en la fraccion arancelaria 0808.10.01 de la Tarifa de la Ley de los Impuestos Generales de Importacion y de Exportacion, originarias de los Estados Unidos de America, independientemente del pais de prodedencia,* Diario Oficial de la Federacion (primera seccion) 16 (21 October 2003). (Exhibit US-24).

[55] *Ibid.* at paras. 11C and 12A (Chelan), 15B and 16A (Dovex), 17C and 18A (Holtzinger), 19D and 20A (L&M), 21B and 22A (Manson), 23B and 24A (Northern Fruit), 25C and 26A (Nuchief), 27F and 28A (Oneonta), 29C and 30A (PAC), 31C and 32A (Rainer Fruit), 33D and 34A (Sage), and 35C and 36A (Stemilt) (Exhibit US-24).

firms against the volumes of their domestic (US) sales. Second, **Economía** compared the export volumes of the firms against the average volume of exports for all of the companies that were involved in the original investigation. At paragraph 48 of the notice, **Economía** concludes that six of the firms passed both tests and, at paragraph 49, it concludes that the volume of exports during the review period by such firms was representative, "*in conformity with Article 68 of the Foreign Trade Law*" (emphasis added).[56]

80. Finally, paragraph 92A of the notice states that, "in conformity with Article 68 of the [FTA], the volume of exports made in the period that goes from January through July 2003 by [the companies qualifying for the review] was representative."

81. In sum, Mexico did require the exporters seeking the reviews to demonstrate that the volume of their exports of the subject merchandise during the review period was representative.

32. Is it the view of Mexico that, with regard to new shippers (Article 89 D of the Foreign Trade Act), the representativeness requirement is not inconsistent with the AD Agreement or the Subsidies and Countervailing Measures ("SCM") Agreement because it is the only logical and sensible way of ensuring that the Authority can make a proper price comparison for the establishment of an individual margin (as Mexico seems to be saying in para. 270 of its written submission) or is Mexico's arguments simply that it is not a condition *sine qua non*, and is this "requirement" for that reason not inconsistent with the AD and SCM Agreements (as paras. 263-266 of the written submission seem to suggest with regard to the similar requirement in Article 68 of the Foreign Trade Act)?

Answer:

82. The United States has noted previously that the plain language of Article 89D imposes a condition for exporters seeking reviews to demonstrate that the volume of exports of the subject merchandise during the review period was representative. In the event that Mexico contests this fact, the Panel may wish to refer to the attached initiation notice for a Mexican "new shipper" review that was initiated on the same date as the "Article 68" review discussed in response to question 31. Paragraph 16 of the initiation notice states as follows:

> In accordance with Article 89D of the FTL and Article 9.5 of the Anti-Dumping Agreement, an expedited review will be undertaken to determine an individual dumping margin for exporters or producers..., *provided that such exporters demonstrate that they have made export sales to Mexico of the subject merchandise, in repre-*

[56] Mexico rejected the requests of the other exporters on unrelated grounds.

sentative volumes, subsequent to the period of investigation in the proceeding that gave rise to the anti-dumping duty at issue ...[57]

83. The document also notes the exporter's assertion that it had exported a representative volume of the subject merchandise to Mexico after the imposition of the anti-dumping measure, and that the firm had provided evidence documenting its assertion.[58]

84. Thus, **Economía** did require the exporter seeking the review to demonstrate that the volume of its exports of the subject merchandise during the review period was representative.

33. In its submission and oral statement, Mexico does not directly reply to the US argument in para. 261 of the US submission that Article 89 D of the Foreign Trade Act only applies to producers, but clearly asserts that it will apply its laws in accordance with the Agreement. Could Mexico clarify whether Article 89 D of the Foreign Trade Act also applies to exporters?

34. Could Mexico clarify whether, pending a judicial review, no definitive duties will be imposed or collected as it seems to be arguing in paras. 301 - 302 of its written submission?

35. Could Mexico clarify whether the importation of "identical or like goods" on which fines may be imposed under certain circumstances in Article 93 V of the Foreign Trade Act also refers to imports of the products from third countries, i.e. from countries other than the one investigated in the anti-dumping investigation?

---

57 *Resolucion por la que se acepta la solicitud de parte interesada y se declara el inicio del procedimiento de nuevo exportador, en relacion con la resolucion definitiva sobre las importaciones de manzanas de mesa de las variedades Red Delicious y sus mutaciones y Golden Delicious, mercancia clasificada actualmente en la fraccion arancelaria 0808.10.01 de la Tarifa de la Ley de los Impuestos Generales de Importacion y de Exportacion, originarias de los Estados Unidos de America, independientemente del pais de prodedencia,* Diario Oficial de la Federacion (primera seccion) 29, at para. 16 (21 October 2003) (emphasis added). (Exhibit US-25).

58 *Ibid.*, paras. 13(C), 14(G).

ANNEX B-2

RESPONSES OF MEXICO

Questions concerning the period of investigation

1. UNITED STATES

2. Mexico argues that "there is no provision in the AD Agreement which indicates how remote an anti-dumping period of analysis must be" (para. 49 of its first submission).

(a) In Mexico's view, is there no limit in the AD Agreement on how "old" the data can be on which the dumping and injury analysis may be based? If Mexico is of the view that there are certain limits, please explain what, in Mexico's views, are the criteria for determining whether a POI is consistent with the AD Agreement or not?

Answer:

The AD Agreement establishes no limit regarding the remoteness of the period of investigation (POI).

(b) What is the Mexican practice in respect of the POI?

Answer:

The petitioners in an investigation suggest a POI in their application for initiation; the investigating authority analyses the information and evidence contained in the application and decides what POI it will use, which is reflected in the determination concerning the initiation of the investigation.

(c) Are there particular reasons why more recent data were not used in this case? Is Mexico of the view that the POI used in this case was the one closest to the initiation as far as "practicability" is concerned? If so, please elaborate.

Answer:

Mexico considers that an investigating authority is not required under the AD Agreement to gather the data that are most recent in relation to the initiation of the investigation. As regards agricultural products, Mexico notes that in its practice there may be an interval of several months between the end of the period of investigation and the initiation of the investigation.

3. Could Mexico explain the reason why it considered that the March - August 6 month period was appropriate for the injury analysis, including whether "seasonality" was one of the reasons.

Answer:

The basic idea behind the periods of comparison used in the injury analysis in the rice case was the following:

The petitioner in the anti-dumping investigation provided information on the unfair dumping practice for the period March-August 1999. The investigating authority ("IA") conducted an analysis to determine whether the unfair practice had had any effects during the period selected by the petitioners and hence whether it had had any impact on the economic and financial indicators for the domestic industry over the period in question. That six-month period was therefore defined as the "period of investigation".

In order to confirm the initial hypothesis, it was considered that the period in question should be distinct from previous periods in which the unfair practice either did not exist or had had no impact on industry indicators. The IA accordingly gathered all the information available over a period of three years ("period analysed"), including the year covered by the "period of investigation"; however, it limited its comparison to strictly comparable periods, i.e. the periods in the preceding two years that covered exactly the same months as those of the "period of investigation".

The "period of investigation" over which the adverse effects of the unfair practice were allegedly observed was thus compared with "comparable" periods in which the practice did not occur. The hypothetical expectation was that the domestic industry would be found to be healthy in the preceding comparable periods whereas unfavourable indicators would be observed in the "period of investigation".

The above approach was adopted to ensure strict comparability of the periods analysed; even if it had been necessary in the long-grain white rice investigation to consider the seasonality factor – which was not the case – comparing the "period of investigation" with previous comparable periods would eliminate any possible distortions in the market under analysis.

The March-August period in this case is not more appropriate in the strict sense than any other period that might have been selected. On the other hand, as has already been pointed out, it is the period for which the petitioners had information on the unfair practice and hence that which must be compared against similar periods.

4. Could Mexico clarify whether the Panel is correct to understand that the investigating authority had the data necessary to perform an injury analysis for the full three year period, but chose not to use this data as it considered that the period should correspond to the period on which the analysis for dumping was made? Please elaborate.

Answer:

Indeed, the IA had before it information covering the period January 1997 to December 1999 and, for the reasons explained in the preceding reply, the comparison was made between the "period of investigation" and similar periods over the preceding two years.

5. Could Mexico explain why it considered that this particular 6 month period was adequate in terms of a dumping analysis. Was the fact that that was the period which the petitioners cited the sole reason?

Answer:

Generally speaking, the IA considers that in principle the "period of investigation" proposed by a petitioner is adequate in terms of performing the dumping analysis and that it can serve as a basis for the injury analysis. However, the IA has authority to modify the initial "period of investigation" provided that it receives relevant arguments, accompanied by pertinent evidence, which lead it to consider that the period is not adequate. This is why a simple, unsubstantiated allegation cannot serve as a basis for modifying the period of investigation.

It is important to note that the AD Agreement stipulates in footnote 4 that "[t]he extended period of time should normally be one year but shall in no case be less than six months". The IA considered that the period of investigation suggested by the petitioner fulfilled that obligation, and hence accepted it for the purposes of initiating the investigation.

6. UNITED STATES

7. UNITED STATES

Questions concerning the injury analysis

8. What, according to the parties, is the definition of the domestic industry allegedly injured by the dumped imports? Does the domestic industry considered in the injury analysis include producers of paddy rice or only of milled rice?

Answer:

The domestic industry covers only producers of long-grain white rice. It does not include producers of paddy rice.

9. Could Mexico clarify whether the import data also include data relating to imports of paddy rice or is the "rice" referred to in the Final Deter-

mination always "milled" rice? Are the terms "rice", "white rice" and "long grain white rice" as they appear throughout the Final Determination used as synonyms?

Answer:

The entire injury analysis refers exclusively to long-grain white rice.

10. Could Mexico clarify whether paddy rice also enters the Mexican market under tariff heading 1006.30.01? More in general, which categories of rice fall under this tariff heading?

Answer:

No. Only polished white rice enters under tariff heading 1006.30.01. Paddy rice is imported under heading 1006.10.01 and husked rice under heading 1006.20.01. Over the period of investigation, several types of polished white rice in addition to long-grain white rice entered under the first tariff heading, i.e. glutinous short-grain rice, parboiled rice, etc.; however, all of these share the characteristics of white rice.

11. Could the parties clarify whether the rice imported into Mexico under tariff heading 1006.30.01 covers rice in any or all of the 5 stages of processing mentioned in para. 161 of the Final Determination and that, therefore, some of the rice imported under this tariff heading will need to undergo further processing in Mexico before entering the consumer market as a finished product?

Answer:

Rice is generally sold in large quantities and in bulk, and is transported by rail or ship over vast distances. It is therefore practically impossible to export semi-processed rice from the United States to Mexico – that is, in any of the five stages of processing – because in view of adverse climate conditions or possible pest contamination (weevils, insects, fungus, bacteria, etc.), the only forms in which rice can be imported are paddy rice, with its natural protective husk, and white or polished rice, which has already undergone all the stages of processing and from which the husk and bran (the part most susceptible to pests) have been removed.

12. If it is correct that both subject and non-subject imports of rice from the United States entered the Mexican market under the above mentioned tariff heading, could Mexico explain the methodology that was used by the investigating authority to separate the subject imports of long grain white rice that came in under this heading from the non-subject imports of other types of rice (short grain, etc.)?

Answer:

It was impossible to make an exact separation, and various methodologies (volume of imports from the United States, exporter/importer methodology, methodology based on verifiable exporter data and Mexican Rice Council (CMA) methodology) were therefore used to estimate the volume of imports of the product. The methodologies are explained in paragraphs 217 to 244 of the Final Determination.

13. Could Mexico clarify whether its statement that the domestic industry kept production of long grain white rice stable throughout the year by importing rice during the off-season, is a reference to the imports of paddy rice, or whether such imports are also of semi-processed rice?

Answer:

The domestic industry is able to keep up production throughout the year by importing paddy rice from the United States. As explained above, the importation of semi-processed rice is complicated.

14. In para. 265 of the Final Determination, the Investigating Authority discusses the ex-factory price difference between Argentinean rice and US rice when exported to Mexico. Could Mexico indicate how high the Mexican import duty for rice from non-NAFTA countries like Argentina is? Was all the rice referred to as "rice imported from Argentina" fully processed long grain white rice ready for domestic consumption?

Answer:

A 10 per cent duty is paid on white rice imported from Argentina and other countries with which Mexico has no trade treaty.

The reference in the Final Determination to imports from Argentina concerns long-grain white rice. As stated in paragraph 365 of the document, the product was purchased by a Mexican producer of white rice and mixed with its own production for marketing purposes.

15. Could Mexico clarify whether the information contained in the "pedimentos" would have allowed the investigating authority to determine with certainty the precise amount of imports of the subject product, long grain white rice, from the United States and from other countries, without any need to apply a methodology to distinguish subject from non-subject imports?

Answer:

The document known as the *pedimento de importación* (import declaration) includes various types of information such as the volume and value of the imports, the exporting enterprise, the importing enterprise, the duties and other taxes paid, the date of the transaction, the customs point of entry of the goods, the type of transport used to ship them to Mexico, the tariff heading under which the transaction was conducted, and so forth.

However, the field for entering the product description does not necessarily contain all the details of the product covered by the *pedimento*. Sometimes the imported product is simply described as "white rice", without any specification as to whether it is long grain, short grain or parboiled. Since the sole purpose of this field is to ensure that the product corresponds to its description in the tariff heading and the latter covers many types of white rice, any white rice will come under that heading.

The type of rice most extensively produced and sold in Mexico and the United States and common to both markets is long-grain white rice, so it may reasonably be assumed that the majority of imports concern this particular product. On the other hand, it is not said that even if all the *pedimentos* had been available it would have been possible to determine with certainty the total amount of imports of the subject product.

In addition, the rice trade involves a large number of operations. For example, 1,183 transactions were recorded in 1997, 1,088 in 1998 and 1,207 in 1999. It would have been impractical, therefore, to request access to every single *pedimento* under tariff heading 1006.30.01 for the three years covered by the "period analysed" and to single out the transactions that concerned long-grain white rice. Where a *pedimento* merely stated that white rice was being imported, without specifying whether it was long grain, short grain or of any other type, the investigation regarding that particular *pedimento* would have required referring to additional documents such as the invoices issued by the exporter, bills of lading, and so forth, in the hope that any of these would provide a precise description of the product.

This is why in such cases the IA relies on reasonable estimates of import volumes and prices of the subject product. It also asks the exporters themselves to provide specific data on their exports to Mexico. Replies from exporters are normally expected to cover the major share of estimated exports, thus ensuring the accuracy of the IA's calculations. In the long-grain white rice case, for instance, the data for the "period of investigation" received from the exporters cover 59.8 per cent of the estimated imports (as indicated in paragraph 207 of the Final Determination). Unfortunately, the exporters, despite having been requested to supply data covering the entire period analysed, failed to do so.

16. (a) Could the parties comment on the following argument made by China in its oral statement (page 5):

"Given that both Article 5.2 and Article 6.1.3 use the same wording "known exporter", the "known exporters" under Article 6.1.3 refer to "each known exporter" under Article 5.2. Therefore, the AD Agreement suggests that investigating authorities shall rely on the petitioners to identify "known" exporters in their petition(s)".

Answer:

Mexico agrees with China's interpretation that the investigating authorities should rely on known exporters identified by the petitioners in an investigation.

(b) Is it Mexico's view that the term "known" exporters in Article 6.1.3 AD Agreement, only relates to the exporters that are "made known" to it by the petitioner?

Answer:

In the specific case of the notification under Article 6.1.3 of the AD Agreement, only exporters notified by the petitioner are deemed to be known exporters.

(c) UNITED STATES

17. The US argues that all the Mexican investigating authority had to do was to look into the "pedimentos" to find out who the other US exporters were.

(a) Could Mexico indicate whether this assertion is correct, do the "pedimentos" identify all the exporters ?

Answer:

The IA does not have the *pedimentos*, which are in the hands of the Ministry of Finance and Public Credit. To request and await reception of these documents would significantly delay the initiation of the investigation. Instead, the IA has an electronic list of the documents, which does not contain all the information set out in the *pedimentos*.

(b) Could Mexico clarify whether the investigating authority attempted to obtain the "pedimentos"? If so, what was the reason why such information was not obtained, or could not be used?

Answer:

For the purposes of initiating an investigation, Mexico sees no requirement in the AD Agreement to obtain the *pedimentos* or to identify all of the exporters. The IA therefore did not attempt to obtain them, because it considered that it was under no obligation to do so. To have sought to obtain them would have considerably delayed the initiation of the investigation (by approximately 40 days), because as many as 1,183 transactions were conducted in 1997, 1,088 in 1998 and 1,207 in 1999. As stated in the preceding reply, the IA relied on the list of *pedimentos* to initiate the investigation.

(c) Could Mexico explain whether the Mexican investigating authority in its normal practice verifies the information provided by the petitioners concerning the exporters mentioned in the petition? If so, how does the authority go about checking this information ?

Answer:

The IA verifies the information provided in the petition using the list of *pedimentos* to check the value and volume of exports. It cannot, however, determine the number of exporters that performed the transactions.

18. UNITED STATES

19. UNITED STATES

Questions concerning Article 5.8 AD Agreement

20. In Mexico's view, does it suffice for one exporter to have been found to be dumping above *de minimis* levels for all other exporters to be included in the application of the measure under Article 5.8 AD Agreement or does Mexico consider that some sort of country-wide rate needs to be established and that, only if that country-wide rate is above *de minimis*, will all exporters from that country be covered by the measure? Could Mexico clarify whether an exporter for which a below *de minimis*, but more than zero margin of dumping was found, would receive a 0 per cent duty or would a duty be imposed on such an exporter equal to the *de minimis* margin?

Answer:

Mexico considers that it does suffice for one exporter to have found to be dumping above the *de minimis* level for all exporters to be included in the application of the measure. Each enterprise will be assigned the anti-dumping duty corresponding to its individual margin, provided that the total volume of imports from the country in question is above the *de minimis* level.

Any exporter for which the IA finds a more than zero and below *de minimis* margin of dumping would receive a zero per cent duty.

21. Could Mexico clarify whether this is a correct understanding of the way in which the Mexican system operates: if an exporter was not dumping during the POI, but a dumping margin was found for other exporters of the product, this non-dumping exporter will be included in the measure, but a 0 per cent duty will be imposed. If later the review shows that the exporter had since engaged in dumping, a duty will be imposed on him equivalent to the new margin of dumping.

(a) Is this a correct understanding of the system?

Answer:

Yes. If the IA determines that an exporter has not been engaged in dumping, the exporter will be assigned a zero per cent duty, which de facto does not constitute an anti-dumping duty. If a later review shows that the exporter is engaged in dumping and its volume of exports exceeds the *de minimis* level, the exporter will indeed be imposed a duty equivalent to the new margin of dumping.

(b) Will a new injury analysis be required before such duties may be imposed?

Answer:

Mexico has not conducted any reviews of exporters with a zero per cent margin of dumping. Were it to do so, however, a new injury analysis would probably be carried out before an anti-dumping duty was imposed.

22. UNITED STATES

Questions concerning the use of facts available and the all others rate

23. In para. 176 of its submission, and para. 61. (c) of its oral statement, Mexico argues that para. 6 of Annex II was complied with as the information of the non-shipping exporter, Producers Rice, was "accepted".

(a) Could Mexico clarify what information this company provided which was accepted by the authority?

Answer:

Paragraph 176 of Mexico's first written submission states that paragraph 6 of Annex II to the AD Agreement addresses the case where the IA does not accept information or evidence from an interested party. In the specific case of *Producers Rice Mill, Inc.*, the circumstances are different because the IA did accept the information submitted by that company. In its various submissions, *Producers Rice Mill, Inc.* explained that it had had no exports of the subject product during the period of investigation and presented arguments in respect of the injury alleged by the CMA.

As mentioned earlier, the IA thus took account in its investigation of the company's assertion that it had had no exports of the subject product during the period of investigation. Moreover, the IA examined the information and evidence submitted by *Producers Rice Mill, Inc.* in the light of the allegations of injury made by the petitioner, as stated in paragraphs 62, 138, 157 and 226 of the Final Determination.

(b) Is Mexico of the view that para. 6 does not apply to situations in which the information is not provided, or is not provided within a reasonable period of time, but only to situation in which information which *was* provided is rejected?

Answer:

Mexico considers that paragraph 6 of Annex II to the AD Agreement does not apply to situations in which information is not provided. On the other hand, it notes that the paragraph does apply where the information provided has been rejected.

24. Article 68 of the Foreign Trade Act mentions three categories of exporters to which the highest margin shall be applied. One of these categories seems to cover the situation provided for in Article 6.8 AD Agreement.

(a) Does Mexico consider that the two other categories (non-appearing exporters and non-shipping exporters) are not covered by the situation described in Article 6.8 AD Agreement?

Answer:

Mexico considers it necessary to clarify that Article 68 of the Foreign Trade Act (FTA) does not address the three situations referred to in the question. In any event, the relevant provision is Article 64 of the FTA.

The cases covered by Article 64 concern the situation where exporters or foreign producers fail to provide the information needed to determine margins of dumping, if any. This corresponds to the second situation described in Article 6.8 of the AD Agreement.

(b) What is the view of the US on the relevance, if any, of the fact that Article 68 of the Foreign Trade Act provides for these three separate categories?

(c) Is Mexico of the view that the AD Agreement does not provide any rules on how to calculate an all others rate for non-appearing parties and non-shipping exporters, or is Mexico arguing that the maximum duty that can be imposed on such exporters under the Agreement is a facts available margin?

Answer:

Indeed, Mexico considers that the AD Agreement does not regulate how the anti-dumping duty should be calculated for exporters that did not appear in the investigation and had no exports during the period of investigation.

25. In Mexico's view, does para. 7 of Annex II allow for unfavourable results only in case of non-cooperative parties or in all cases in which the necessary information is not provided?

Answer:

In the case of the long-grain white rice anti-dumping investigation, the fact that *Producers Rice Mill, Inc.* did or did not cooperate bears no relationship to the fact that the Mexican IA calculated a facts-available dumping margin for that company, since Article 6.8 of the AD Agreement stipulates – as mentioned earlier – that its provisions apply when an interested party does not provide the necessary information. The IA therefore did not apply paragraph 7 of Annex II to the AD Agreement. Instead, it applied paragraph 1 of the Annex, which clearly establishes that if a party does not provide the information requested by the IA, the authority will be free to make determinations on the basis of the facts available, including those contained in the application for initiation.

Questions concerning the challenge of the law as such

26. According to the parties, to what extent is the distinction mandatory/discretionary legislation still applicable in WTO law after the Appellate Body statement in para. 93 of its decision in the *US – Corrosion Resistant Steel* case (DS 244)?

Answer:

We note that in paragraph 93 of its report in *US – Corrosion-Resistant Steel Sunset Review* (WT/DS244/AB/R), the Appellate Body recognizes the importance of distinguishing between the mandatory and the discretionary nature of legislation. It emphasizes that the distinction varies from case to case and should not be applied in a mechanistic fashion. This is why we believe that when a petitioner and a respondent argue over the mandatory or discretionary nature of challenged provisions, it is crucial for the Panel to analyse and, if need be, distinguish between the mandatory and the discretionary nature of a law or of its various provisions in the light of the particular circumstances of each case.

Mexico notes that in this dispute all of the United States' complaints concerning the alleged inconsistency of a number of FTA Articles as such are premised on the fact that the provisions are mandatory. Hence, the United States tacitly recognizes that if those provisions were not mandatory there would be no inconsistency whatsoever. In view of the foregoing, Mexico considers it essential to determine the discretionary or mandatory nature of the FTA provisions challenged by the United States. This will have to be done in the light of the particular circumstances of the case, as explained in Mexico's first written submission and Mexico's oral statement to the Panel.

27. UNITED STATES

28. Could Mexico explain whether, in case the DSB were to adopt a panel report finding an inconsistency of a Mexican law with the WTO Agreements, it considers that it would be obliged to amend the law to bring the law into conformity with the WTO Agreement?

Answer:

If the DSB were to adopt a final Panel report finding inconsistencies between the FTA and the WTO Agreements, Mexico would be obliged to remedy those inconsistencies.

29. Could Mexico clarify whether private parties may be successful when they file a suit against the administration before the domestic courts of Mexico in case the administration failed to comply with a statutory obligation, even if this obligation is inconsistent with the WTO Agreement, requiring the administration to comply with such obligations?

Answer:

It is our understanding that this question of the Panel concerns a hypothetical case which in no way prejudges the consistency of the FTA provisions challenged by the United States. Mexico therefore requests that its reply be considered in that light.

No. In proceedings before the domestic courts, the Mexican administration would in its defence argue the application of Mexican law in a manner consistent with the country's international commitments, such as the WTO Agreement. Consequently the Mexican courts, basing their interpretation on the structure and characteristics of the Mexican legal system, would be under the obligation to rule in favour of the administration. This would be the case if the country investigated were a WTO Member; if not, domestic legislation prevails.

30. Is it Mexico's view that *if* a certain provision is somehow found to be inconsistent with the WTO Agreements, that is, in case a conflict is found between the Foreign Trade Act and the WTO Agreements, then the WTO Agreements would prevail by virtue of Article 133 of the Political Constitution and Article 2 of the Foreign Trade Act?

Answer:

Yes.

31. In para. 263 – 266 of its submission, Mexico argues that the "representativeness" requirement in Article 68 of the Foreign Trade Act is only a tool, and that the US is wrong in suggesting that it is a condition *sine qua non* for the initiation of a review.

(a) Could Mexico clarify whether a review may be initiated if the party concerned cannot demonstrate that its sales volume for the period was representative?

Answer:

As indicated on previous occasions, a demonstration that trade operations were made in representative volumes is not a *sine qua non* requirement for initiating a review. Nevertheless, the interested party will be required in the course of the review to demonstrate such representativeness so that it can be assigned a margin of dumping.

(b) What in the Mexican practice is considered to be a "representative" volume ?

Answer:

For the purposes of determining the representativeness of volumes of exports to Mexico, the Ministry does not use restrictive criteria but analyses information provided by the exporters which demonstrates that their volumes of exports are regular and representative of their sales policies.

It is important to emphasize that exporters are required to demonstrate that their export sales have not been intermittent during the period of analysis and that the volumes involved are consistent with their trade practices.

In order that the foregoing should not be not interpreted as the only means for enterprises to demonstrate the representativeness of their volumes of export sales, the following are cited as further examples:

- A comparison between the volumes of their export sales to Mexico during the period of investigation and during the period under review;
- a comparison between the volumes of their domestic sales and export sales to Mexico during the period under review;
- a comparison between the volumes of their export sales to Mexico and sales to other markets during the period under review.

32. Is it the view of Mexico that, with regard to new shippers (Article 89 D of the Foreign Trade Act), the representativeness requirement is not inconsistent with the AD Agreement or the Subsidies and Countervailing Measures ("SCM") Agreement because it is the only logical and sensible way of ensuring that the Authority can make a proper price comparison for the establishment of an individual margin (as Mexico seems to be saying in para. 270 of its written submission) or is Mexico's argument simply that it is not a condition *sine qua non*, and is this "requirement" for that reason not inconsistent with the AD and SCM Agreements (as paras. 263 – 266 of the written submission seem to suggest with regard to the similar requirement in Article 68 of the Foreign Trade Act)?

Answer:

Mexico supports both arguments cited by the Panel in its question regarding new shippers.

33. In its submission and oral statement, Mexico does not directly reply to the US argument in para. 261 of the US submission that Article 89 D of the Foreign Trade Act only applies to producers, but clearly asserts that it will apply its laws in accordance with the Agreement. Could Mexico clarify whether Article 89 D of the Foreign Trade Act also applies to exporters?

Answer:

In the case of new shippers, Mexico applies Article 89.D of the FTA concurrently with Article 47 of the FTA Regulations, as duly notified to the WTO and circulated to Members on 18 May 1995 in document G/ADP/N/1/MEX/1, for reviews of exporters or traders that so request.

34. Could Mexico clarify whether, pending a judicial review, no definitive duties will be imposed or collected as it seems to be arguing in paras. 301 - 302 of its written submission?

Answer:

As stated in paragraph 302 of Mexico's first written submission and pursuant to Article 98.III of the FTA, interested parties are not required to pay anti-dumping duties and may provide a guarantee of payment while the challenge procedure is under way.

35. Could Mexico clarify whether the importation of "identical or like goods" on which fines may be imposed under certain circumstances in Article 93 V of the Foreign Trade Act also refers to imports of the products from third countries, i.e. from countries other than the one investigated in the anti-dumping investigation?

Answer:

The fine provided for in Article 93.V of the FTA would apply, where appropriate, to imports of identical or like goods from the country under investigation, regardless of the country of provenance. It would not apply to imports from third countries.

ANNEX B-3

RESPONSES OF THE EUROPEAN COMMUNITIES

2 June 2004

1. Question (a)

Could the EC provide a detailed reasoning on why it considers that the "investigation" in Article 5.8 AD Agreement unambiguously refers to a country-wide investigation?

1. A country-wide approach to an anti-dumping investigation can be deduced from a number of both substantial and procedural provisions of the *Anti-Dumping Agreement.*

2. Article 2 *Anti-Dumping Agreement* defines dumping. Article 2.1 *Anti-Dumping Agreement* refers to the word "country" three times – and specifically to the product exported "from one country to another". The word "country" is used a further five times in Article 2.2 and footnote 2 *Anti-Dumping Agreement.* These provisions reflect the language of Article VI GATT 1994, which also repeatedly refers to imports from one country to another. They indicate that the concept of dumping involves a strong connotation of a country-wide assessment, which will inevitably have an impact on the scope of the investigation. Thus, absent particular provisions requiring a company specific approach, a country-wide approach will reflect a permissible interpretation of the *Agreement.*

3. Article 5.2(ii) *Anti-Dumping Agreement* requires the provision of the "names of the country or countries of origin or export in question". This is the primary obligation, in the sense that it is mentioned first in this provision, and is not qualified in any way – a complainant cannot state that it does not know the country or countries of origin. There is a secondary obligation – to describe known exporters or producers and importers. This obligation is, however, subject to the important qualification of the word "known" – if the names of the exporters or producers are not known, they do not need to be indicated in the complaint. It would be a permissible interpretation of the *Anti-Dumping Agreement* to initiate an original investigation even in circumstances where only the country of origin would be known – even if there were no known exporters or producers. Thus, the country-wide nature of the investigation is also reflected in the complaint, right from the start, that being the very basis of a possible subsequent investigation.

4. Such an approach is confirmed by Article 12.1.1 *Anti-Dumping Agreement*, which requires that the public notice of the initiation of an original investigation states the name of the exporting country or countries. There is no obligation to state the names of known exporters or producers. Thus, what is clear from both Article 5.2 (ii) and Article 12.1.1. *Anti-Dumping Agreement* is that the investigating authority is not obliged to pick-out particular exporters from a given

country of origin for the purposes of the initiation of an investigation. The initiation of an anti-dumping investigation may thus lawfully be country-specific.

5. In addition to these strong textual arguments, one may observe that the country-wide approach to the initiation of an original investigation is common sense. The primary objective of an anti-dumping proceeding is to address the economic problem (injury) caused by dumped imports from a particular source. The legal structures of exporters and producers in the exporting country are, in terms of the scope of the investigation, incidental and may be difficult or impossible to ascertain. If the investigation were initiated in the first place only in relation to known exporters and producers, then each time a further exporter or producer became known, it would presumably be necessary to extend the investigation. An investigating authority has no real means of ascertaining with complete certainty the full list of exporters or producers in the exporting country, and the *Anti-Dumping Agreement* imposes no obligation on an investigating authority to actively seek out that information.

6. The first part of the first sentence of Article 5.8 *Anti-Dumping Agreement* refers to the rejection of an application under paragraph 1, an application which, we have just observed, could lawfully be country-wide only – and indeed is likely to be so. In order for this sentence to be interpreted in an internally consistent manner, it necessarily follows that the ensuing obligation to terminate the investigation contained in the second part of the first sentence of Article 5.8 *Anti-Dumping Agreement* refers to the same types of investigation as those referred to in the first part of the sentence, that is, including an investigation with a country-wide scope. Members may go further, by considering such matters on a company specific basis, but they are not obliged to do so by the terms of Article 5.8 *Anti-Dumping Agreement.*

2. Question (b)

What, if any, is the significance of the wording used in the second sentence of Article 5.8 that there shall be immediate termination "in cases" where the authorities determine that the margin of dumping is *de minimis*? In the view of the EC, would one not expect the Agreement to have used the singular "in such a case" in the second sentence of Article 5.8 as well, if, as the EC argues, the investigation in the first sentence was a reference to a country-wide investigation?

7. The European Communities understands the final words "the case" in the first sentence of Article 5.8 *Anti-Dumping Agreement* to refer to the case as reflected in the application – which may lawfully be country-wide, as explained above. Furthermore, the European Communities understands the words "the cases" in the second sentence of Article 5.8 *Anti-Dumping Agreement* to have the same meaning (except that the plural is used) as the words "the case" in the first sentence of Article 5.8. The European Communities agrees that the text might have read : "in a case". However, the European Communities does not attach any significance to the use of the plural in the second sentence of Article 5.8. It is common when drafting an abstract and normative piece of legislation to have in

mind its future application in concrete terms to many individual cases (plural), and that may often be reflected in the drafting.

8. The European Communities would find it unpersuasive to suggest that by using the plural "the cases" the drafters intended to refer to several company specific cases or investigations, as opposed to "the case" referred to in the first sentence of Article 5.8 *Anti-Dumping Agreement* – that being a country-wide case. It seems to the European Communities that had the drafters wished to write such a distinction into this provision, they would have done so more clearly – choosing, for example, a difference abstract noun, rather than relying on an over-subtle distinction between the singular and the plural.

9. The European Communities finds further support for this view in the fact that the French language version of the first sentence of Article 5.8 *Anti-Dumping Agreement* does not use the word "cas". That strongly militates in favour of rejecting the notion that the drafters intended to build on a distinction between the singular and the plural – had they so intended they would surely have ensured that the text had the same meaning in all the language versions.

10. Finally, the European Communities would observe that the second sentence of Article 5.8 *Anti-Dumping Agreement* refers both to *de minimis* dumping margins and to a negligible volume of imports. Both of these are linked to the words "in cases where". The import threshold factor is clearly country-wide, as reflected, for example, in the fourth sentence of Article 5.8. It follows that the words "in cases where" cannot, in themselves, lead to the conclusion that the investigating authority must conduct a company specific assessment.

Question (c)

Is the EC of the view that its interpretation requires an authority to calculate a country-wide margin to examine whether this country-wide margin is above *de minimis*? If not, why not?

11. The European Communities considers that Article 5.8 *Anti-Dumping Agreement* imposes an obligation on an investigating authority to calculate a country-wide dumping margin when the investigating authority has reasons to believe that such a margin could be *de minimis* and the case would thus have to be terminated (even though individual exporters might have dumping margins above *de minimis*). Where it is obvious from the company specific dumping margin calculations that the country-wide dumping margin is well above *de minimis*, no precise calculation is required.

Question (d)

Is it the EC practice to calculate such a country-wide margin?

12. The answer to question (c) reflects the practice of the European Communities.

ANNEX C

PARTIES' RESPONSES TO QUESTIONS POSED IN THE CONTEXT OF THE SECOND SUBSTANTIVE MEETING OF THE PANEL

ANNEX C-1

RESPONSES OF THE UNITED STATES

Questions concerning the period of investigation (the "POI")

1. In its answer to question number 2 (b) of Panel's questions in relation to the first substantive meeting with the parties (the "Panel's questions"), Mexico replies that "the petitioners in an investigation suggest a POI in their application for initiation; the investigating authority analyses the information and evidence contained in the application and decides what POI it will use, which is reflected in the determination concerning the initiation of the investigation". Could Mexico further explain what the criteria are for reviewing the POI suggested by the petitioners? In other words, in which case would Mexico consider the POI as suggested by the petitioner to be inappropriate?

Answer:

1. During the second Panel meeting, Mexico stated that Economía examines whether the petitioner has provided export price ("EP") and normal value ("NV") information, as well as injury information for at least a six month period. Mexico also stated that Economía ensures that the petitioner has provided the dumping information for a period that overlaps with ("corresponds to") the injury information. Mexico stated that the AD Agreement requires a petitioner to provide evidence of dumping and injury, but it disclaimed any obligation to obtain updated data.

2. Mexico's response demonstrates that Economía's analysis is with respect to the adequacy of the information that the petitioners submit *within* the suggested period of investigation ("POI"); it does not analyze whether the particular POI itself – *i.e.*, the suggested time period – is proper, or whether it includes the most recent available information. This conclusion is further illustrated by Mex-

ico's response to question 5 from the Panel, where Mexico said "in principle the period of investigation proposed by a petitioner is adequate in terms of performing a dumping analysis and that it can serve as a basis for the injury analysis." The United States discusses this issue further in response to question 2 below.

2. In its answer to question 5 of the Panel's questions, Mexico is saying that "in principle the period of investigation proposed by a petitioner is adequate in terms of performing a dumping analysis and that it can serve as a basis for the injury analysis", but that "the IA has the authority to modify the initial period of investigation provided that it receives relevant arguments, accompanied by pertinent evidence, which lead it to consider that the period is not adequate".

(a) Could Mexico explain this apparent contradiction between the process as explained in its answer to question 2(b) in which it stated that it is the IA which analyses and decides whether the POI is appropriate and its answer to question 5 (i.e. petitioners suggest a POI which is accepted unless the other interested parties come up with convincing arguments supported by pertinent evidence that this POI is inappropriate)?

(b) Could Mexico explain how this process of changing the POI after initiation works in practice (e.g. will new questionnaires have to be sent to interested parties in light of the changed POI?)? Has this ever happened in Mexican practice?

Answer:

3. Mexico stated during the second Panel meeting that Economía can "extend" the POI if the importers provide sufficient evidence to justify such a change. It also stated that the types of evidence that might lead to a modification of the POI would include economic factors that might have had an effect on prices, or cyclical problems.

4. Mexico's response illustrates again that Economía accepts the POI that the petitioners propose, and it places the burden on the importers and foreign producers and exporters to demonstrate that an alternative POI should be used instead. Economía does not appear to place any burden on the petitioners to justify the use of a period that is not as close to the initiation date as practicable. In addition, the idea that Economía would merely "extend" the POI suggests that it would still use the petitioners' selected POI, even if it also included some more recent data.

5. Mexico also stated at the second Panel meeting that it has extended the POI that the petitioners requested in very few cases. The United States is not aware of any such cases. The United States is also unaware of any cases where Economía has used a POI different than the one the petitioners requested. As the United States noted in its response to question 2 in the first set of Panel questions, Economía accepted the POI suggested by the petitioners in all of the antidumping investigations initiated against US products in 2004. Moreover, the

lengths of the POIs varied widely, and the gap between the end of the POI and the date of initiation was as long as 20 months.[1]

3. The United States argues on various occasions that the purpose of an anti-dumping investigation is to determine whether a domestic industry is *presently* injured by dumping that is *presently* occurring (see e.g. United States answer to question 1 of the Panel's questions), and refers in support of this argument to the use of the present tense in *inter alia* Article 2 and 3.4, 3.5, and 5.8 Anti-Dumping Agreement (the "AD Agreement"). What would be the United States view on the argument that it is the definitional nature of these provisions which explains the use of the present tense and that this use of the present tense in such definitional provisions is thus uninformative of the alleged requirement of the closeness in time between the application of a measure and the conditions for application of the measure?

Answer:

6. The United States does not agree with the above-referenced argument. Article 1 of the AD Agreement states that an anti-dumping measure "shall be applied only under the circumstances provided for in Article VI of GATT 1994...." Article VI:2 of the GATT 1994 states, in turn, that "[i]n order to offset or prevent dumping, a contracting party may levy on any dumped product an anti-dumping duty not greater in amount than the margin of dumping in respect of such product." The ordinary meaning of the term "offset" is "set off as an equivalent *against*; cancel out by, balance by something on the other side or of contrary nature; counterbalance, compensate."[2] The ordinary meaning of the term "prevent" is "[a]ct or do in advance... Act before, in anticipation of, or in preparation for (a future event, a point in time)."[3] An investigating authority will only be in a position to "cancel out" or "balance" or "act in preparation for" dumping if it imposes a measure with respect to activity that is *presently* occurring or that has not yet occurred.

7. Similarly, Article VI:1 of the GATT 1994 states that dumping is to be condemned if it "causes or threatens" material injury to a domestic industry. The term "causes" indicates that the dumping and injury is occurring in the present, and the term "threatens" indicates that the injury may occur in the future. If the drafters had intended instead to permit the imposition of anti-dumping measures when the conditions for doing so only existed in the past, they could have used the terms "caused or threatened" material injury. They did not.

8. An investigating authority may impose an anti-dumping measure on another Member's exports only if it is able to make an objective determination, based on positive evidence, that the conditions for doing so are present at the time it imposes the measure. Although this determination will inevitably have to consider information that pertains to the past, simply because there is a lag in the

1 See US Response to First Panel Question 2.
2 New Shorter Oxford English Dictionary, 1985 (1993) (emphasis in original).
3 *New Shorter Oxford English Dictionary*, 2348 (1993).

availability of current information, this "past" information is serving as a proxy for the present. Therefore, the investigating authority must collect and examine a data set that includes the most recent available information.

9. In the rice investigation, there was a nine month gap between the end of the petitioners' suggested POI and the date the petition was filed. The gap stretched to 15 months by the time Economía initiated its investigation. By the time of the final determination, the injury information that Economía was using for its determination was three to five years old. Economía's failure to collect or examine recent data, and its failure to update its injury information over the course of its investigation, left it with no basis for an objective evaluation of present dumping and injury.

4. In paragraph 23 of its second submission, Mexico asserts that it is *desirable* that the POI ends as closely as possible to the date of initiation of the investigation, but that no such obligation exists. Could Mexico explain why it considers that this closeness in time is desirable in light of its argument that the purpose of an anti-dumping investigation is not to offset or prevent dumping presently causing injury, but to offset dumping that caused injury *in the past* or threatened to cause injury in the past (as argued e.g. in Mexico's second oral statement, para. 18)?

Answer:

10. At the second Panel meeting, Mexico stated that, while it is desirable to have the POI end as closely to the initiation date as practicable, its industries are not always sufficiently organized to provide more recent data. The United States is confused by Mexico's statement. Once an investigating authority initiates an investigation, it sends its own questionnaires to the foreign producers and exporters, and to the domestic producers and importers. Given this fact, the organization of the domestic industry when it prepares the petition would not seem relevant to the selection of a proper POI, and it would not seem to justify using a stale POI when the exporters and producers are able to supply more recent data.

11. Furthermore, while it is to be expected that the dumping POI would end prior to the initiation of the investigation (otherwise, the foreign exporters and producers could avoid the imposition of an anti-dumping order by temporarily raising their export prices or lowering their home market prices), an objective investigating authority should collect updated *injury* information *during* the investigation, to ensure that the data used includes the most recent available data.

12. In its second written submission, Mexico stated that it would be "preposterous" for a Member to base its findings on information that is ten years old.[4] In the rice investigation, however, Economía based its findings on data that was three to five years old. The United States fails to see why, if it would be "preposterous" to use data that was ten years old, it is acceptable to use information that is three to five years old. In either case, an investigating authority that failed to

[4] Mexico's Second Written Submission, para. 21.

collect recent information would have no idea whether dumped imports were causing injury to the domestic industry as of the date that it *initiated* its investigation, much less on the date that it published its final determination.

Questions concerning the use of facts available and the all others rate

5. In its answer to question 17 (b) of the Panel's questions, Mexico argues that it was under no obligation to obtain the pedimentos to identify all of the exporters. At the same time, it argues that "to have sought to obtain them would have considerably delayed the initiation of the investigation". Can Mexico explain whether the investigating authority considered obtaining the pedimentos but decided in the end not to do so because of the delay it would cause ? If so, would it not have been possible for the authority to consult a small number of pedimentos, simply to check whether such a sample would lead to more exporters being identified, without unnecessarily delaying the investigation?

Answer:

13. Mexico confirmed at the second Panel meeting that the *listados* name the volume and value of each shipment, the *pedimento* number, and the name of the importer of record. Therefore, if Economía had so chosen, it could have used the *listados* to identify a sample of shipments from a sample of importers (such as the largest percentage of the volume of exports that it could reasonably investigate), requested just those *pedimentos*, and in that way could have obtained the contact information for those known exporters and producers.

14. Mexico also stated at the second Panel meeting that there is a 40-day lag between the date of entry of a particular shipment and the date that the shipment appears in the *listados*. If this is true, then in June 2000, when the petitioners filed the petition, Economía would have had information as current as April, 2000. Similarly, by the December 2000 initiation of the investigation, Economía would have had information current to October 2000. In either case, it would have had access to data that was substantially more current than August 1999, which is the final month of its dumping and injury POIs.

6. Could Mexico explain what happens if the petitioners do not mention any known exporters in their petition (a possibility envisaged by the US in its second submission, para 66): will no questionnaires be sent and no individual margin of dumping be calculated for anyone? Does the authority verify whether an exporter mentioned by the petitioner in the application actually exists?

Answer:

15. At the second Panel meeting, Mexico stated that it would not initiate an investigation if the petitioners identified no known exporters, because the AD

Agreement requires petitioners to identify the known exporters. Mexico's answer does not explain, however, what it would do if the petitioners claimed not to know the identity of any of the exporters, or if Economía would take any steps to verify such an assertion. For example, there is no evidence in the record of the rice investigation suggesting that Economía took any steps at all to verify the petitioners' identification of only two "known" exporters in the petition (or to question their failure to identify the Rice Company as a known exporter). The record does, however, show that Economía is perfectly willing to apply the facts available in setting dumping margins for exporters and producers that the petitioners do not identify, and that are never sent the questionnaire. Mexico has not satisfactorily explained why it is willing to take this approach when the petitioners identify only two exporters, but would not do the same if the petitioners identified none.

7. The United States on various occasions mentions the fact that apart from the two exporters listed as "known exporters" by the petitioner in the application, the application also contained information and referred for example in Annex H to another exporter, the Rice Corporation, which later appeared and took part in the investigation out of its own initiative. (See e.g. para. 13 United States first submission.) According to the United States, did the application contain any other names of United States exporters, in addition to these three?

Answer:

16. In addition to the numerous references to The Rice Company in the petition, petition annex M contains contact information for the USA Rice Council and the Rice Millers' Association. The description of the Rice Millers' Association states that its members represent 97 per cent of all US milled rice production.[5] Therefore, Economía had contact information for US industry associations that could have provided it with a virtually complete listing of US exporters and producers of long-grain white rice.

17. Petition Annex M (as well as the petition itself) also notes that long-grain white rice is grown in Arkansas, Mississippi, Missouri, Texas, and Louisiana.[6] Rice millers are located in each of those states.[7] Nevertheless, the petitioners limited their listing of the "known" exporters to Producers Rice and Riceland, two Arkansas corporations.[8]

8. Could Mexico indicate whether the "Official form for exporting companies investigated for price discrimination" (MEX-5) is the same as the actual questionnaire that was sent to the known exporters or is it a form which exporting companies who have not been identified by the petitioners

5 Petition Annex M at 4 (Exhibit US-17).

6 Petition Annex M at 2 (Exhibit US-17); Petition at 10 (Exhibit US-8).

7 See Exhibits US-18&19 (excerpts from *Rice Journal*).

8 See Petition at 17 (Exhibit US-8).

need to return to the authority in order to be sent the questionnaire and to be examined individually?

9. The United States notes in its first submission with regard to the listados that "These abstracts are known as "listings" ("listados"), and they provide import values and import volumes, along with the identity of the importer of record. Even these abstracts were apparently considered to be confidential information, and they were not placed on the public record of the investigation." (United States first written submission, para. 15.) Could Mexico confirm that this is all the information contained in the listados? In Mexico, are these listados as well as the pedimentos themselves considered as confidential information?

Answer:

18. Mexico stated during the second Panel meeting that the *listados* as well as the *pedimentos* are confidential information. It also stated, wrongly, that it did not disclose the *listados* to the domestic industry. As the United States noted during the second Panel meeting, the petitioners explicitly state in their petition that they obtained the export price that they used for the petition margin from the *listados*.[9] Therefore, contrary to Mexico's suggestion, Mexico did in fact provide confidential customs valuation information to its domestic industry for use in the anti-dumping case.

19. Furthermore, in its second submission, Mexico made the remarkable admission that the Mexican Customs Service enters into agreements with certain Mexican industry associations to provide *pedimentos* to them.[10] The United States does not understand how Mexico can possibly justify its practice of sharing this customs valuation information with its domestic industries, in light of its admission that the information is confidential.

10. In its answer to question 17 (b) of the Panel's questions, Mexico stated that "For the purposes of initiating an investigation, Mexico sees no requirement in the AD Agreement to obtain the *pedimentos* or to identify all of the exporters. The IA therefore did not attempt to obtain them, because it considered that it was under no obligation to do so. To have sought to obtain them would have considerably delayed the initiation of the investigation (by approximately 40 days), because as many as 1,183 transactions were conducted in 1997, 1,088 in 1998 and 1,207 in 1999. As stated in the preceding reply, the IA relied on the list of *pedimentos* to initiate the investigation."

(a) Could Mexico clarify that the 40 days delay referred to in this answer relates to the time it would have taken to obtain the information from the Ministry actually holding the *pedimentos*? Or does this delay include the time it would have taken to go through the pedimentos to find *e.g.* the names of exporters?

9 See, *e.g.*, Petition at 21 (final sentence), 23, 44 (referencing Annex F) (Exhibit US-8).

10 Mexico's Second Written Submission, para. 57.

Answer:

20. Mexico has previously stated that obtaining the *pedimentos* would delay initiation of the investigation by approximately 40 days. If this period did not include the time needed to examine the *pedimentos*, Mexico would have stated a period longer than 40 days.

21. Moreover, as the United States noted in its second written submission, Mexico's "40-day" estimate is almost certainly overstated, because the dumping POI only covered the period March – August 1999.[11] Therefore, Economía would not have needed to obtain the *pedimentos* for 1997 and 1998 for purposes of identifying the contact information for the "known" exporters.

22. In any event, if Mexico's position is that it would have taken 40 days to *obtain* the *pedimentos*, then there is no basis for its assertion that obtaining them would have delayed the initiation of the investigation. Although the petitioner filed its petition in June 2000, Economía did not initiate the investigation until December 2000.[12] Therefore, if Economía had requested the *pedimentos* in June after the petition was filed, it would have received them almost five months prior to the date of initiation. Even if it had waited to request them until October, Economía still would have received the *pedimentos* well in advance of the initiation date.

23. On the other hand, Mexico also stated during the second Panel meeting that there is a 40-day lag between the date of entry of a particular shipment and the date that the shipment appears in the *listados*. If Mexico's response to this question 10(a) abandons its previous explanations and asserts instead that the 40-day delay only refers to the alleged time lag, then the United States refers the Panel to its response to question 5 above.

(b) Could Mexico indicate whether the only two relevant documents in this respect are (i) the pedimentos in which all of the information including the identity of the exporter is included, and (ii) the listados, an abstract of the pedimentos containing only limited information, or does there exist a third type of document which is also called a listado and which is actually an electronic version of the pedimentos?

Answer:

24. The United States noted in response to question 17(b) in the first set of Panel questions that the petitioners in the *Crystal Polystyrene* case used *pedimentos* that they obtained from the Mexican Government to separate out imports of the subject product from other, non-subject merchandise imported under the same tariff heading.[13] The reason for the US comment was to illustrate that the

11 See US Second Written Submission, para. 58 and n.43.

12 See US First Written Submission, paras. 12, 18.

13 See US Reply to First Panel Question 17(b), para. 52 and accompanying footnotes.

pedimentos could in fact be used to obtain accurate volume and value data that Economía could have used in its investigation.

25. On 30 July 2004, Economía published its preliminary determination in the *Crystal Polystyrene* case. The foreign respondents in that case challenged the anti-dumping margin in the petition on the grounds that the export price component of the petition margin was based on imports of both subject and non-subject merchandise. Economía rejected the respondents' argument on the grounds that the petitioners had obtained detailed information from the *pedimentos*.[14] Thus, the *Crystal Polystyrene* preliminary determination demonstrates again that, contrary to Mexico's arguments, it is possible to use the *pedimentos* to obtain detailed volume and value data.

26. Furthermore, in its response to question 15 in the first set of Panel questions, Mexico justified its refusal to examine the *pedimentos* by arguing that it would not have been possible to identify with precision the precise amount of imports of long-grain white rice. But in *Crystal Polystyrene*, Economía accepted the use of *pedimentos*, when they accounted for 73.6 per cent of total imports of the subject merchandise during the POI.[15] Thus, Economía is clearly willing to use information from *pedimentos* that represent less than 100 percent of total imports during the POI, when it suits the interests of its domestic industry.

27. As the United States has previously stated, we are noting Mexico's use of *pedimentos* that it supplied to its petitioners as a way of illustrating Mexico's willingness to use them in a way that favours the interests of its domestic industries. The United States does not mean to suggest, however, that releasing the *pedimentos* to private industry is appropriate.

Questions concerning the non-shipping exporter

11. (a) What is the view of the parties concerning the reference in the last sentence of Article 9.5 AD Agreement to the term "guarantees" rather than anti-dumping "duties"?

---

[14] The preliminary determination states in pertinent part:

> The Ministry considers invalid the argument of Atofina Petrochemicals [one of the foreign respondents] given that the sample of the import *pedimentos* [*pedimentos fisicos de importacion*] provided by the petitioners accounted for 73.6 percent of the total volume imported during the period of investigation under headings 3903.19.02 and 3903.19.99 of Mexico's Tariff Schedule, and for this reason [this sample] was considered representative. On the basis of this information, petitioners were capable of identifying the type of product bought by each purchaser, *the terms of sale*, the means of transportation, the way in which the product was packed (bags or bulk) *as well as the value and volume of the imports....*"

See Preliminary Determination of the Antidumping Investigation on Imports of Crystal Polystyrene, Currently Classifiable under Headings 3903.19.02 and 3903.19.99 of the Schedule of the Law on the General Tax on Import and Exports, Originating from the United States of America, Independently of the Country of Export, paras 75-76 (emphasis added) (Exhibit US-27).

[15] See *Ibid.*

Answer:

28. The third sentence of Article 9.5 prohibits an investigating authority from levying anti-dumping duties on the entries of an exporter or producer seeking an expedited review while the review is underway. The fourth sentence of Article 9.5 permits the authority to withhold appraisement of those entries, or request a guarantee, to preserve the possibility of retroactively levying duties on the entries if the authority reaches an affirmative finding of dumping. The guarantees might take the form of bonds or cash deposits, for example.

(b) In the view of the parties, is the appropriate level of the guarantee that may be requested from a new shipper under Article 9.5 AD Agreement in any way limited by the AD Agreement, and, if so, where in the AD Agreement is this limit to be found ?

Answer:

29. Article 9.4 of the AD Agreement states that "the antidumping duty applied to imports from exporters or producers not included in the examination shall not exceed:

> (i) the weighted average margin of dumping established with respect to the selected exporters or producers or,
>
> (ii) where the liability for payment of antidumping duties is calculated on the basis of a prospective normal value, the difference between the weighted average normal value of the selected exporters or producers and the export prices of the exporters or producers not individually examined."

30. Thus, for example, if an authority were to investigate the largest volume of exports that could reasonably be investigated under Article 6.10, it would be under an obligation to apply a duty rate calculated in accordance with Article 9.4 to *any* exporter or producer not included in the examination. The text does not distinguish between firms that were known and firms that were unknown, or firms that had shipments during the POI and firms that did not. On the contrary, Article 9.4 creates an across-the-board ceiling on the permissible margin that may be assigned to *any* exporter or producer that "is not included" in the initial investigation.

31. Article 9.5 of the AD Agreement provides a basis for an exporter or producer that did not export during the POI to obtain an individual margin. Nothing in Article 9.5 *requires* an exporter or producer to seek an individual margin, however. The producer or exporter may choose instead to accept the imposition of anti-dumping duties on its exports at the "all others" rate established in accordance with Article 9.4. Inasmuch as the neutral "all others" margin would apply to the exporter's or producer's exports in the absence of an expedited review, there is no logical basis to interpret Article 9.5 as allowing an authority to require guarantees during the expedited review at a level higher than the all other's margin.

32. Furthermore, Article 9.3 of the AD Agreement states that "[t]he amount of the antidumping duty shall not exceed the margin of dumping as established under Article 2." Although the all other's margin is not directly established under Article 2, it is indirectly established under that article, because it is a weighted average of the calculated margins. Thus, Article 9.3 of the AD Agreement also supports the conclusion that the margin assigned to exporters and producers that did not ship during the POI (and thus the guarantees for those margins) may not exceed the neutral all other's margin.

33. In addition, the chausette in Article 9.4 requires authorities to disregard any margins established under Article 6.8 when calculating the all other's margin. This fact also supports the conclusion that the all other's margin (and thus any guarantee of that margin) is meant to be a neutral number, and not adverse.

34. Finally, Article 7.2 of the AD Agreement limits the cash deposit or bond that an authority may apply as a provisional measure to an amount "not greater than the provisionally estimated measure of dumping." This text provides further support for the conclusion that the appropriate level for an Article 9.5 guarantee would be not greater than the estimated measure of dumping for the company at issue - *i.e.*, the neutral all other's margin from the investigation.

(c) According to the parties, are non-shipping exporters to be considered as an interested party in the sense of Article 6.11 (i) AD Agreement, *i.e.* an exporter or foreign producer or the importer of a product subject to investigation?

Answer:

35. Non-shipping exporters are "exporters or producers" of the product subject to investigation, even if they are not exporting the product *during* the investigation. Therefore, they are interested parties within the meaning of Article 6.11(i) of the AD Agreement. It is important to note, however, that an investigating authority may choose to limit its investigation in accordance with Article 6.10 of the AD Agreement, and not include a particular exporter or producer in its investigation. In that case, it may only apply a neutral "all others" rate, calculated in accordance with Article 9.4 of the AD Agreement, to the unexamined exporters and producers. As the panel stated in *Argentina – Definitive Anti-dumping Measures on Imports of Ceramic Floor Tiles from Italy,* "an investigating authority may not fault an interested party for not providing information it was not clearly requested to submit."[16]

(d) Are the parties of the view that "non-shipping exporters" and "new shippers" are one and the same thing under the AD Agreement? If

---

[16] Report of the Panel, WT/DS189/R, adopted 5 November 2001, para. 6.54 ("*Argentina – Ceramic Tiles*"). The Panel also stated that "the inclusion, in an Annex relating specifically to the use of best information available under Article 6.8, of a requirement to specify in detail the information required, strongly implies that investigating authorities are *not* entitled to resort to best information available in a situation where a party does not provide certain information if the authorities failed to specify in detail the information which was required." *Ibid.*, para. 6.55.

so, why? If not, are they in the parties' view nevertheless entitled to the same treatment? What is the basis for this view in the Agreement?

Answer:

36. The United States has used the term "new shipper" as shorthand for exporters that did not export the subject merchandise to the importing Member during the POI, that subsequently do export the merchandise and then seek an expedited review under Article 9.5 of the AD Agreement. In this sense, "new shippers" are a subset of "non-shipping exporters." As the United States discussed in response to the Panel's question 11(b) above, Article 9.4 of the AD Agreement creates an across-the-board ceiling on the permissible margin that may be assigned to *any* exporter or producer that "is not included" in the initial investigation. The United States is not aware of any basis in the AD Agreement for concluding that "new shippers" should be treated differently than other non-shipping exporters merely because they seek an expedited review under Article 9.5.

Questions concerning the law as such

12. With regard to Article 2 of Mexico's Foreign Trade Act (the "FTA"):

(a) Could Mexico explain whether the administration has the discretion to apply the law in a manner which goes against the clear meaning of the law if it considers that this is what is required in order for Mexico to comply with the AD Agreement?

(b) In the view of Mexico, is it relevant for the application of Article 2 FTA that some of the amendments to the FTA challenged by the United States in the current proceedings were introduced after the end of the Uruguay Round and the entry into force of the Anti-Dumping Agreement?

(c) Is it the view of Mexico that the provisions of the FTA challenged by the United States in the present case are all consistent with the WTO Anti-Dumping Agreement?

Answer:

37. The fact that each of the challenged provisions was introduced after the end of the Uruguay Round is evidence that, in Mexico's view, the provisions are consistent with the AD Agreement, the SCM Agreement, and the GATT 1994. Mexico's repeated insistence before this Panel that the challenged provisions are not contrary to its WTO obligations provides further evidence that Mexico sees no conflict between these provisions and the WTO Agreements. Given Mexico's view that, as a matter of Mexican municipal law, the actions that the challenged laws require are consistent with WTO rules, Mexico does not, as a matter of mu-

nicipal law, have discretion to disregard their mandates. Therefore, Article 2 of the FTA cannot shield Mexico from claims that the challenged provisions of its domestic law are, in fact, in breach of its WTO obligations.

38. Mexico's approach throughout this dispute has been to try to interpret its WTO obligations in a way that is consistent with what its laws require, and not the reverse. The fact that it is taking this approach suggests that Mexico may have been misinterpreting its WTO obligations when it drafted its law. Thus, it is all the more important for the Panel to clarify the WTO provisions at issue in this dispute, and determine whether Mexico's laws are consistent with these WTO provisions as clarified.

13. The Mexican law provides that interested parties shall submit their arguments and evidence within a period of 28 days from the day following the publication of the initiating resolution. (Article 53 FTA). How many days are given to exporters that appear following initiation?

Answer:

39. The panel in the *Argentina Poultry* dispute concluded that Argentina breached Article 6.1.1 of the AD Agreement when it provided only 20 days for a group of respondents to respond to questionnaires that it sent for the first time approximately eight months after initiation.[17] The same panel stressed that the 30-day period provided for in the first sentence of Article 6.1.1 "is an absolute minimum that must be granted to exporters from the outset," and that the extensions provided for in the second sentence of that provision are *in addition to*, not in lieu of, the 30-day period provided for in the first sentence.[18] Article 53 of the FTA, however, when applied to companies not identified as "known" exporters in the petition (and thus not sent the questionnaire immediately following initiation), legally forecloses both the 30-day response period and an opportunity for an extension of that period. Therefore, Article 53 is inconsistent as such with Article 6.1.1 of the AD Agreement and Article 12.1.1 of the SCM Agreement.

14. In its answer to question 31 of the Panel's questions, Mexico replies in the first sentence that "representativeness" is not a requirement for initiating a review. In the second sentence, Mexico adds that the interested party will be required in the course of the review to demonstrate such representativeness so that it can be assigned a margin of dumping. Is it the argument of Mexico that it is not a requirement for *initiating* a review, but it is a requirement in order to be *successful in obtaining* a review? Could Mexico explain to what extent it considers this distinction to be relevant?

---

[17] Report of the Panel, *Argentina–Definitive Anti-Dumping Duties on Poultry from Brazil*, WT/DS241/R, paras. 7.134 (when questionnaires sent), 7.136-7.147.

[18] *Argentina Poultry*, para. 7.140.

Answer:

40. As the United States has previously noted, Mexico's argument is form over substance. Whether one characterizes it as a requirement to initiate a review of the margin, or a requirement to conduct a review of the margin, or a requirement to obtain a new individual margin, the fact remains that Articles 68 and 89D of the FTA require exporters and producers to demonstrate a representative volume of sales in order to change the level of duties levied against them. The AD and SCM Agreements do not permit authorities to impose such a condition.

15. On page 19 of its second submission, the United States argues that an investigating authority may not apply facts available to exporters that were never sent a questionnaire and asked to respond. Does this imply that in the United States view a facts available duty can be applied only to known exporters? Or would the United States argue that a residual rate based on the facts available for unknown exporters is possible?

Answer:

41. Articles 6.10 and 9.4 of the AD Agreement establish two approaches for calculating anti-dumping margins: either the authority examines and calculates an individual margin for every exporter or producer of the subject merchandise in the country under investigation, or it examines fewer than all exporters and producers. In the latter case, the maximum permissible margin that may be applied to the unexamined exporters or producers is the neutral all other's margin calculated in accordance with Article 9.4 of the AD Agreement. This limitation applies regardless of whether the exporter or producer is known or unknown, and whether it had exports during the POI or not. Although the all other's margin would apply to the unknown exporters, it would not be a facts available margin, because it would be calculated under Article 9.4, and not under Article 6.8.

42. The obligations of Articles 6.1, 6.8, and Annex II of the AD Agreement apply to those individual exporters and producers that an investigating authority includes in its investigation. If an investigating authority fails to provide an exporter or producer the individual notice that those provisions require, then the authority cannot claim to be including the exporter or producer "in the investigation," and it will not have the ability to apply a margin based on the facts available to that exporter or producer. Nothing in Articles 6.1 or 6.8, or Annex II, suggests that the applicability of the facts available rules varies depending on whether a particular exporter is "known" to the investigating authority.

43. Therefore, it would not normally be permissible for an authority to apply a margin based on the facts available to an unknown exporter. Rather, that firm would be entitled to the neutral all other's margin calculated in accordance with Article 9.4 of the AD Agreement. If the domestic industry would prefer instead that the exporter receive an individual margin, it could simply do a better job of identifying the known exporters in the first place.

44. It is possible to imagine a situation where every investigated exporter is assigned a margin based on the facts available. In that case, an investigating authority would not be able to apply one of the methods listed in Article 9.4(i) and (ii) in determining the all other's rate.[19] The present case does not involve such a scenario, however.

[19] See Appellate Body Report, *United States – Hot-Rolled Steel from Japan*, WT/DS184/AB/R, adopted 23 August 2001, paras. 125-126.

ANNEX C-2

RESPONSES OF MEXICO

Questions concerning the period of investigation (the "POI")

1. In its answer to question number 2(b) of Panel's questions in relation to the first substantive meeting with the parties (the "Panel's questions"), Mexico replies that "the petitioners in an investigation suggest a POI in their application for initiation; the investigating authority analyses the information and evidence contained in the application and decides what POI it will use, which is reflected in the determination concerning the initiation of the investigation". Could Mexico further explain what the criteria are for reviewing the POI suggested by the petitioners? In other words, in which case would Mexico consider the POI as suggested by the petitioner to be inappropriate?

Answer:

With regard to the first question, in examining the POI suggested by the petitioner, the investigating authority checks that: (a) the period suggested by the domestic producers is at least six months; (b) together with their application the petitioners submit information and evidence pertaining to the period they suggest; (c) the petitioner's information and evidence concerning normal value and export price correspond to the suggested POI.

With regard to the second question, a POI would be deemed inappropriate in the event of failure to meet all the conditions set out above.

2. In its answer to question 5 of the Panel's questions, Mexico is saying that "in principle the period of investigation proposed by a petitioner is adequate in terms of performing a dumping analysis and that it can serve as a basis for the injury analysis", but that "the IA has the authority to modify the initial period of investigation provided that it receives relevant arguments, accompanied by pertinent evidence, which lead it to consider that the period is not adequate".

(a) Could Mexico explain this apparent contradiction between the process as explained in its answer to question 2(b) in which it stated that it is the IA which analyses and decides whether the POI is appropriate and its answer to question 5 (i.e. petitioners suggest a POI which is accepted unless the other interested parties come up with convincing arguments supported by pertinent evidence that this POI is inappropriate)?

Answer:

In our view there is no contradiction. When the investigating authority receives an application for initiation of an anti-dumping investigation, it checks compliance with the requirements listed in the answer to question 1. If the information submitted by the petitioners is adequate, then – as stated in the answer to question 5 of the Panel's questions in relation to the first substantive meeting – the POI proposed by the petitioners is deemed adequate for initiation of an investigation. However, in the course of the investigation importers and exporters may propose changing the period of investigation provided they submit relevant arguments and supporting evidence. In other words, Mexico's point is that an assertion alone without any evidence (as was submitted by the exporters in the investigation concerning long-grain white rice) will not suffice for the POI to be changed.

(b) Could Mexico explain how this process of changing the POI after initiation works in practice (e.g. will new questionnaires have to be sent to interested parties in light of the changed POI?)? Has this ever happened in Mexican practice?

Answer:

In Mexican administrative practice there have been no cases of importers and exporters showing a need for a change of POI.

3. The United States argues on various occasions that the purpose of an anti-dumping investigation is to determine whether a domestic industry is *presently* injured by dumping that is *presently* occurring (see e.g. United States answer to question 1 of the Panel's questions), and refers in support of this argument to the use of the present tense in *inter alia* Article 2 and 3.4, 3.5, and 5.8 Anti-Dumping Agreement (the "AD Agreement"). What would be the United States view on the argument that it is the definitional nature of these provisions which explains the use of the present tense and that this use of the present tense in such definitional provisions is thus uninformative of the alleged requirement of the closeness in time between the application of a measure and the conditions for application of the measure?

Answer:

It is important to bear in mind that so far the United States has made only bald assertions and has not explained how it is possible in an anti-dumping investigation to determine whether a domestic industry is being presently injured by *dumping that is presently occurring*.

Mexico further observes that Articles 2, 3.4, 3.5 and 5.8 of the AD Agreement make use of the present tense because of the nature of the concepts they set forth. The same Articles also make use of the future, without this necessarily implying that the tense of the verb is to be read in the narrow and literal sense, as the following examples illustrate:

(a) The Spanish and French versions of Article 2.2.1 of the AD Agreement state:

> " ... Si los precios inferiores a los costos unitarios ... son superiores ... *se considerará* [English version: "shall be considered"] que esos precios permiten recuperar los costos dentro de un plazo razonable." (Emphasis added.)
>
> " ... Si les prix qui sont inférieurs aux coûts unitaires ... sont supérieurs ... *il sera considéré* que ces prix permettent de couvrir les frais dans un délai raisonnable." (Emphasis added.)

(b) The Spanish and French versions of 3.4 of the AD Agreement read as follows:

> "El examen de la repercusión de las importaciones objeto de dumping sobre la rama de producción nacional de que se trate *incluirá* [English version: "shall include"] una evaluación de todos los factores e índices económicos ... Esta enumeración no es exhaustiva, y ninguno de estos factores aisladamente ni varios de ellos juntos *bastarán* [English version: "can … necessarily give"] necesariamente para obtener una orientación decisiva..". (Emphasis added.)
>
> "L'examen de l'incidence des importations faisant l'objet d'un dumping sur la branche de production nationale concernée *comportera* une évaluation de tous les facteurs et indices économiques ... Cette liste n'est pas exhaustive, et un seul ni même plusieurs de ces facteurs *ne constitueront* pas nécessairement une base de jugement déterminante." (Emphasis added.)

(c) The Spanish and French versions of Article 3.5 of the AD Agreement state:

> "*Habrá de demostrarse* [English version: "It must be demonstrated"] que, por los efectos del dumping ... Estas examinarán también cualesquiera otros factores de que tengan conocimiento, distintos de las importaciones objeto de dumping ... y los daños causados por esos otros *factores no se habrán de atribuir* [English: "must not be attributed] a las importaciones objeto de dumping." (Emphasis added.)
>
> "*Il devra être démontré* que les importations faisant l'objet d'un dumping ... Celles-ci *examineront* aussi tous les facteurs connus autres que les importations faisant l'objet d'un dumping ... et les dommages causés par ces autres *facteurs ne devront pas être imputés* aux importations faisant l'objet d'un dumping." (Emphasis added.)

(d) The Spanish and French versions of Article 5.8 of the AD Agreement read:

> "La autoridad competente rechazará [English version: "shall be rejected"] la solicitud presentada con arreglo al párrafo 1 y pondrá fin [English version: "shall be terminated"] a la investigación sin demora ... " (Emphasis added.)
>
> "Une demande présentée au titre du paragraphe 1 *sera rejetée* et une enquête *sera close* dans les moindres délais ... ". (Emphasis added.)

Consequently, the United States' arguments based on the use of the present tense in the above Articles are without merit since, as shown above, the same Articles also use verbs in the future tense which are not necessarily to be construed in a narrow and literal sense.

4. In paragraph 23 of its second submission, Mexico asserts that it is *desirable* that the POI ends as closely as possible to the date of initiation of the investigation, but that no such obligation exists. Could Mexico explain why it considers that this closeness in time is desirable in light of its argument that the purpose of an anti-dumping investigation is not to offset or prevent dumping presently causing injury, but to offset dumping that caused injury *in the past* or threatened to cause injury in the past (as argued e.g. in Mexico's second oral statement, paragraph 18)?

Answer:

First, it should be made clear that in paragraph 18 of its second oral statement, Mexico did not assert that the purpose of an anti-dumping investigation is to offset dumping that caused or threatened to cause injury in the past. What Mexico said is that the purpose of such investigations is to offset or prevent dumping – which does not necessarily have to occur in the present – that causes or threatens to cause injury to the domestic industry.

Secondly, in Mexico's view the very nature of investigations precludes any finding of present dumping because the period set for investigation is bound to be a period that has already elapsed and that precedes the initiation of the investigation. For example, no investigating authority in fact asks importers and exporters to provide information on transactions they carry out between the initiation of the investigation and the date of the final determination with a view to basing the latter on the present. In other words, it is impossible to set a POI to be updated over time so that at the end of the investigation the authority is in a position to determine the existence of present dumping. Indeed, recognizing this to be the case, the AD Agreement provides for the possibility of yearly reviews of anti-dumping duties which determine the new margin of dumping to be applied to a period subsequent to the one considered in the investigation.

Thus, for injury to be determined it must be found that dumping causes or threatens to cause injury to the domestic industry in the period in which it occurs and not necessarily afterwards. In the case of threat of injury, it must be found that a threat exists at the time when the dumping occurs. On this basis the authority in the investigation concerning long-grain white rice found dumping to be the cause of the injury to the domestic industry. In other words, it was determined that dumping caused injury in the period in which the United States exporters carried out their transactions and that the injury was caused by the dumped exports.

It is desirable for the POI to be as close as practicable to the initiation of the investigation because that period having already elapsed, the closer it is to the date of initiation the greater the likelihood that the circumstances prevailing during the POI will still obtain. But Mexico maintains that this is not mandatory, since no rule in the AD Agreement so provides.

Questions concerning the use of facts available and the all other rate

5. In its answer to question 17(b) of the Panel's questions, Mexico argues that it was under no obligation to obtain the pedimentos to identify all of the exporters. At the same time, it argues that "to have sought to obtain them would have considerably delayed the initiation of the investigation". Can Mexico explain whether the investigating authority considered obtaining the pedimentos but decided in the end not to do so because of the delay it would cause? If so, would it not have been possible for the authority to consult a small number of pedimentos, simply to check whether such a sample would lead to more exporters being identified, without unnecessarily delaying the investigation?

Answer:

It must first be pointed out that in its reply to question 17(b) of the Panel, Mexico did not state that it was under no obligation to obtain the pedimentos to identify all of the exporters. What Mexico said is *that it was not required under the AD Agreement to identify all the exporters or to obtain the pedimentos*; in other words, the Agreement lays down no such obligation. Consequently, the United States cannot plead breach of the Agreement on the basis of a non-existent obligation. And there is no point in taking up the United States' arguments as to whether Mexico planned to consult them and decided in the end not to because of the delay it would cause, since the AD Agreement does not require Mexico to do so.

As to consulting a small number of pedimentos without unnecessarily delaying the investigation, the time it takes to obtain the pedimentos is what largely causes the delay. As occurs with many WTO Members, import declarations are in the hands of the customs authority, not the investigating authority. In Mexico, they therefore have to be obtained through the Ministry of Finance and Public Credit, which can take several weeks or perhaps months, even if only a sample is requested, in addition to the time needed to examine them. As explained in the reply to question 17(b), it would have taken more than 40 days to obtain the pedimentos, for the sake of complying with the United States' wishes and not out of any obligation under the AD Agreement.

6. Could Mexico explain what happens if the petitioners do not mention any known exporters in their petition (a possibility envisaged by the US in its second submission, paragraph 66): will no questionnaires be sent and no individual margin of dumping be calculated for anyone? Does the authority verify whether an exporter mentioned by the petitioner in the application actually exists?

Answer:

It must first be pointed out that a petition that does not specify the identity of the exporters has never been submitted to the Mexican authority. In the 200 or more cases dealt with by the Ministry there has never been such a petition; and this holds good for the investigations concerning long-grain white rice and beef.

Failure to mention any exporters in a petition would be treated as inconsistent with Article 5.2(ii) of the AD Agreement and Article 75(X) of the Regulations of the Foreign Trade Act, and the investigating authority would advise the petitioner under Article 78 of the Regulations that it had 20 days within which to notify known exporters. The question is purely hypothetical and we confirm that the Mexican authority has never been faced with such a situation, including in investigations concerning exports from the United States. It is our view, generally speaking, that it is virtually impossible for a domestic producer not to know its foreign competitors.

As to the question whether the authority verifies the existence of exporters mentioned by the petitioner, Mexico is of the view that this is not part of the requirement laid down in Article 5.3 of the AD Agreement. That provision requires the examination of the accuracy and adequacy of the evidence to ascertain whether it is sufficient to justify initiation, and covers not the identity of exporters known to the petitioner but the information and evidence on dumping, injury and causal link submitted to justify initiation of an investigation.

7. The United States on various occasions mentions the fact that apart from the two exporters listed as "known exporters" by the petitioner in the application, the application also contained information and referred for example in Annex H to another exporter, the Rice Corporation, which later appeared and took part in the investigation out of its own initiative. (See e.g. paragraph 13 United States first submission). According to the United States, did the application contain any other names of United States exporters, in addition to these three?

Answer:

Apart from the exporters listed as known exporters and the company mentioned in "Annex H" of the application for initiation of an investigation, the application mentions no other United States companies that can be deemed to be exporters.

8. Could Mexico indicate whether the "Official form for exporting companies investigated for price discrimination" (MEX-5) is the same as the actual questionnaire that was sent to the known exporters or is it a form which exporting companies who have not been identified by the petitioners need to return to the authority in order to be sent the questionnaire and to be examined individually?

Answer:

Mexico confirms that exhibit MEX-5 is a questionnaire like the one sent to the known exporters and the United States Embassy in Mexico. It should also be noted that when unknown exporters request the questionnaire for exporters from the Mexican authority, it is sent to them with no prior formalities and they are allowed to participate in the investigation with no restrictions.

9. The United States notes in its first submission with regard to the listados that "These abstracts are known as "listings" ("listados"), and they provide import values and import volumes, along with the identity of the importer of record. Even these abstracts were apparently considered to be confidential information, and they were not placed on the public record of the investigation." (United States first written submission, paragraph 15). Could Mexico confirm that this is all the information contained in the listados? In Mexico, are these listados as well as the pedimentos themselves considered as confidential information?

Answer:

We confirm that the listings of pedimentos contain information on the value and volume of the imports. They also contain data on the tariff heading, country of origin, country of consignment, freight, gross weight, exchange rate, identity of the importers (name and federal taxpayers' registration), *inter alia.*

In Mexico, both the listings of pedimentos and the pedimentos themselves are treated as confidential information under Mexican law.

10. In its answer to question 17(b) of the Panel's questions, Mexico stated that "For the purposes of initiating an investigation, Mexico sees no requirement in the AD Agreement to obtain the *pedimentos* or to identify all of the exporters. The IA therefore did not attempt to obtain them, because it considered that it was under no obligation to do so. To have sought to obtain them would have considerably delayed the initiation of the investigation (by approximately 40 days), because as many as 1,183 transactions were conducted in 1997, 1,088 in 1998 and 1,207 in 1999. As stated in the preceding reply, the IA relied on the list of *pedimentos* to initiate the investigation."

(a) Could Mexico clarify that the 40 days' delay referred to in this answer relates to the time it would have taken to obtain the information from the Ministry actually holding the pedimentos? Or does this delay include the time it would have taken to go through the pedimentos to find e.g. the names of exporters?

Answer:

Mexico confirms that the 40 days referred to in its reply to question 17(b) of the Panel correspond to the time it would have taken just to obtain the pedimentos from the Ministry of Finance and Public Credit.

(b) Could Mexico indicate whether the only two relevant documents in this respect are (i) the pedimentos in which all of the information including the identity of the exporter is included, and (ii) the listados, an abstract of the pedimentos containing only limited information, or does there exist a third type of document which is also called a listado and which is actually an electronic version of the pedimentos?

Answer:

The only relevant documents are the pedimentos and the listings of pedimentos. The investigating authority has electronic access to the latter. There is no electronic version of the pedimentos, which Customs handles only in paper form.

Questions concerning the non-shipping exporter

11. (a) What is the view of the parties concerning the reference in the last sentence of Article 9.5 AD Agreement to the term "guarantees" rather than anti-dumping "duties"?

Answer:

It is our understanding that under Article 9.5 of the AD Agreement, during the new shipper procedure petitioners are not bound to pay anti-dumping duties and may instead provide guarantees. Thus, the term "guarantees" implies that the authorities of the importing Member may ask the exporter to provide for the duration of the above-mentioned procedure guarantees sufficient to cover any anti-dumping duties the new shipper may have to pay as a result of the review.

We further observe that the term "guarantees" is not limited to the cash deposits or bonds referred to in Articles 7.2, 10.3, 10.4 and 10.5 of the AD Agreement, but allows that there may be other forms of guaranteeing the payment of anti-dumping duties.

It should nonetheless be noted that although the English version of the AD Agreement makes a distinction between "security" (Article 7.2) and "guarantees" (Article 9.5), in the Spanish and French versions there is no such difference. The Spanish version uses "garantías" and the French version, "garantie", in both those Articles (7.2 and 9.5) and in Articles 10.3, 10.4 and 10.5 as well. Thus, for the purpose of the grant of guarantees under Article 9.5 of the Agreement, cash deposits and bonds will be allowed.

(b) In the view of the parties, is the appropriate level of the guarantee that may be requested from a new shipper under Article 9.5 of the AD Agreement in any way limited by the AD Agreement, and, if so, where in the AD Agreement is this limit to be found?

Answer:

Mexico is of the view that the AD Agreement sets no guidelines for determining the amount of the guarantee that may be requested of a new shipper and that this will be dealt with on case-by-case basis.

(c) According to the parties, are non-shipping exporters to be considered as an interested party in the sense of Article 6.11(i) of the AD Agreement, i.e. an exporter or foreign producer or the importer of a product subject to investigation?

Answer:

In Mexico's view, a non-shipping exporter is an interested party in the sense of Article 6.11(i) of the AD Agreement, since in establishing that interested parties are to include exporters or foreign producers, this provision does not exclude or limit participation by any exporter in the investigation.

(d) Are the parties of the view that "non-shipping exporters" and "new shippers" are one and the same thing under the AD Agreement? If so, why? If not, are they in the parties' view nevertheless entitled to the same treatment? What is the basis for this view in the Agreement?

Answer:

Mexico believes that, from a purely conceptual standpoint, a non-shipping exporter is not the same thing as a new shipper. A non-shipping exporter is an exporter that did not export during the POI to the WTO Member conducting the anti-dumping investigation. A new shipper is an exporter that did not export during the POI but has exported since the POI, which may be before the end of the investigation or once the anti-dumping duties have been imposed. Thus, a non-shipping exporter may become a new shipper if it exports after the POI.

Under Article 6.11(i) of the AD Agreement, both are interested parties in that both are exporters of the product subject to investigation and therefore have the same rights under the Agreement. However, for the purposes of levying anti-dumping duties the Agreement does not require the investigating authority to afford them different treatment. Mexico accordingly takes the view that if a non-shipping exporter and a new shipper fail to provide adequate information for the determination of their individual margins of dumping, the investigating authority will base its preliminary or final determination on Article 6.8 of the Agreement.

Questions concerning the law as such

12. With regard to Article 2 of Mexico's Foreign Trade Act (the "FTA"):

(a) Could Mexico explain whether the administration has the discretion to apply the law in a manner which goes against the clear meaning of the law if it considers that this is what is required in order for Mexico to comply with the AD Agreement?

Answer:

In Mexico federal laws are general in nature and mandatory, being acts of parliament. Federal laws – including the FTA – accordingly apply nationwide. If Mexico has undertaken through an international treaty to fulfil certain obligations, the provisions of the FTA must obviously apply to the country with which the treaty was signed, in accordance with what is stipulated in that treaty. Consequently, for WTO Members the FTA must be applied – as its Article 2 provides – consistently with the provisions of the Marrakesh Agreement and the Agreements it encompasses. In other words it must not go against them, which on no account means that the investigating authority may breach the FTA at its discretion.

Accordingly, Mexico emphasises that in the case of the FTA, Article 2 of the latter serves as the guide for interpreting all other articles of the Act. Consequently, since the FTA establishes that *all* its articles must be applied in accordance with international treaties to which Mexico is a party, there is *no possibility whatever* of the authority going against the meaning of the FTA at its discretion.

(b) In the view of Mexico, is it relevant for the application of Article 2 of the FTA that some of the amendments to the FTA challenged by the United States in the current proceedings were introduced after the end of the Uruguay Round and the entry into force of the AD Agreement?

Answer:

No. This has no relevance for the application of Article 2 of the FTA.

(c) Is it the view of Mexico that the provisions of the FTA challenged by the United States in the present case are all consistent with the WTO AD Agreement?

Answer:

Yes. Mexico considers that the provisions of the FTA impugned by the United States are consistent with the WTO Agreements as demonstrated by the claims and arguments, both oral and written, that Mexico has submitted to the Panel.

13. The Mexican law provides that interested parties shall submit their arguments and evidence within a period of 28 days from the day following the publication of the initiating resolution (Article 53 FTA). How many days are given to exporters that appear following initiation?

Answer:

Article 53 of the FTA must be read in conjunction with the last paragraph of Article 3 of the FTA, which states: "Where this Act refers to time-limits in days, these shall be understood to mean working days and where it refers to months or years, these shall be understood to mean calendar months or years".

Thus, calculated in calendar days the period of 28 working days is longer than the period of 30 days prescribed in Article 6.1.1 of the AD Agreement, even including the week specified in footnote 15 of the Agreement. Mexican practice thus allows all exporters, known and unknown alike, a period of 28 working days after the initiation of the investigation in which to submit a duly completed exporters' questionnaire. This does not impair their right to apply for an extension of the deadline.[1]

Article 6.1.1 of the AD Agreement and Article 12.1.1 of the SCM Agreement, on the other hand, are very emphatic: "Exporters or foreign producers (or interested Members) *receiving questionnaires used in an ... investigation* shall be given at least 30 days for reply ... ". (Emphasis added).

Consequently, according to the rules of interpretation of international treaties and agreements described by Mexico in earlier submissions, *there is no requirement to grant the 30 days to exporters that are not sent a questionnaire.*

This is borne out by the report of the Appellate Body in *Argentina – Poultry Anti-Dumping Duties*, which said:

> "7.145 ... We read the first sentence of Article 6.1.1 to mean that *if questionnaires are sent* to exporters or foreign producers, they shall be given at least 30 days for reply."

Besides, it would be illogical to grant this period to every newly arrived exporter or foreign producer of which the investigating authority was unaware. To do so would undoubtedly hold up the investigation and the ensuing delay

---

[1] In addition, Article 164 of the FTA Regulations allows unknown exporters that appear after initiation of the investigation to submit their replies to the questionnaire even after the preliminary determination, at which stage they are given a new period of thirty working days. Exporters' information, arguments and evidence will be taken into account for the final determination.

would entail failure to observe the time-limits set in Article 5.10 of the AD Agreement and Article 11.11 of the SCM Agreement.

Along the same lines, the Appellate Body in *United States – Hot-Rolled Steel* said in its report:

> "73. Indeed, in the absence of time-limits, authorities would effectively cede control of investigations to the interested parties, and could find themselves unable to complete their investigations within the time-limits mandated under the *Anti-Dumping Agreement.*"

14. In its answer to question 31 of the Panel's questions, Mexico replies in the first sentence that "representativeness" is not a requirement for initiating a review. In the second sentence, Mexico adds that the interested party will be required in the course of the review to demonstrate such representativeness so that it can be assigned a margin of dumping. Is it the argument of Mexico that it *is not* a requirement for *initiating* a review, but it *is* a requirement in order to be *successful in obtaining* a review? Could Mexico explain to what extent it considers this distinction to be relevant?

Answer:

What Mexico wishes to emphasize is that representativeness is a requirement not for initiating a new shipper review or a review of anti-dumping duties, *but for determining, at the end of the procedure, an individual dumping margin or subsidy* for the company applying for the review. It is natural and logical that an applicant's export volume during the period under review should be representative. In other words, it is not enough to export one unit of the product under investigation for the purpose of obtaining a lower or zero margin. Otherwise, the investigating authority would *not* conduct a proper price comparison and would therefore fail in its obligation to determine a fair individual margin of dumping.

15. On page 19 of its second submission, the United States argues that an investigating authority may not apply facts available to exporters that were never sent a questionnaire and asked to respond. Does this imply that in the United States view a facts available duty can be applied only to known exporters? Or would the United States argue that a residual rate based on the facts available for unknown exporters is possible?

Answer:

Mexico believes that the following should be borne in mind:

First, Article 6.11(i) of the AD Agreement says that exporters of products subject to investigation must be treated as "interested parties", but does not determine whether only known exporters are to be regarded as interested parties. Since it makes no such distinction, the AD Agreement considers both known exporters and unknown exporters to be interested parties. Accordingly, all exporters of the product under investigation are subject to the relevant provisions of the AD Agreement.

Article 6.8 of the AD Agreement states: "In cases in which *any interested party* refuses access to, or otherwise does not provide, necessary information … or significantly impedes the investigation, preliminary and final *determinations*, affirmative or negative, *may be made on the basis of the facts available*." (Emphasis added).

On the basis of the foregoing, we observe that according to the AD Agreement, the provisions of Article 6.8 of the Agreement (facts available) may apply both to known and to unknown exporters, since both are interested parties.

Secondly, we note that in this dispute arguments have been adduced about the use of Articles 9.4 or 6.8 of the AD Agreement for the purpose of calculating the margin of dumping for unknown exporters.

Article 9.4 of the Agreement applies only to known exporters, as can be seen from the following:

(a) Article 6.10 of the Anti-Dumping Agreement states: "The Authorities shall, as a rule, determine an individual margin of dumping for *each known exporter or producer concerned* … In cases where the number of exporters … *is so large* as to make *such a determination impracticable*, the authorities may limit their examination … by using samples which are statistically valid … " (Emphasis added).

Thus, according to Article 6.10 of the AD Agreement, investigating authorities must as a rule calculate the individual margin of dumping for each known exporter except where the number of *known exporters* is so large as to make such a determination impracticable, in which case they may limit their examination using statistical samples. In other words, Article 6.10 of the AD Agreement allows statistically valid sampling only among the exporters known to the authority. This is perfectly logical since it is impossible to select a sample from among a set of unknown elements.

Furthermore, Article 9.4 of the AD Agreement provides that the calculation method it sets out shall apply only "[w]hen the authorities have limited their examination in accordance with … paragraph 10 of Article 6 … ", in other words, where the investigating authority has limited its examination by using statistically valid samples.

Since – as already stated – statistical samples may be used only for known exporters, the calculation method set forth in Article 9.4 of the Agreement may be used only for known exporters and provided a sample has been selected.

Accordingly, because Article 6.8 of the AD Agreement can be applied both to known and to unknown exporters and because Article 9.4 of the Agreement cannot be applied to unknown exporters, we conclude that it is consistent with the Agreement to calculate the residual margin of dumping on the basis of Article 6.8 (facts available). Likewise, since it does not apply to unknown exporters the calculation method described in Article 9.4 of the AD Agreement cannot properly be used to calculate a "residual" margin of dumping.

ANNEX D

REQUEST FOR CONSULTATIONS AND REQUEST FOR THE ESTABLISHMENT OF A PANEL

ANNEX D-1

REQUEST FOR CONSULTATIONS BY THE UNITED STATES

WORLD TRADE ORGANIZATION

WT/DS295/1
G/L/631
G/ADP/D50/1
G/SCM/D54/1
23 June 2003
(03-3349)

Original: English

MEXICO – DEFINITIVE ANTI-DUMPING MEASURES ON BEEF AND RICE

Request for Consultations by the United States

The following communication, dated 16 June 2003, from the Permanent Mission of the United States to the Permanent Mission of Mexico and to the Chairman of the Dispute Settlement Body, is circulated in accordance with Article 4.4 of the DSU.

My authorities have instructed me to request consultations with the Government of Mexico pursuant to Article 4 of the *Understanding on Rules and Procedures Governing the Settlement of Disputes*, Article XXII:1 of the *General*

Agreement on Tariffs and Trade 1994 ("GATT 1994"), Article 17.3 of the *Agreement on Implementation of Article VI of the General Agreement on Tariffs and Trade 1994* ("AD Agreement"), and Article 30 of the *Agreement on Subsidies and Countervailing Measures* ("SCM Agreement"), with respect to Mexico's definitive anti-dumping measures on beef and long grain white rice, published in the *Diario Oficial* on 28 April 2000[1] and 5 June 2002[2] respectively, as well as any amendments thereto or extensions thereof[3] and any related measures[4] and also with respect to certain provisions of Mexico's Foreign Trade Act and its Federal Code of Civil Procedure. These measures appear to be inconsistent with Mexico's obligations under the provisions of GATT 1994, the AD Agreement, and the SCM Agreement.

In particular, the United States believes that the anti-dumping measures on beef and rice are inconsistent with at least the following provisions:

- Article 3 of the AD Agreement, because Mexico, *inter alia*, based its injury (or threat) and causation analyses on only six months of data for each of the years examined; failed to collect or examine recent data; failed in the beef investigation to evaluate all relevant economic factors and indices having a bearing on the state of the industry; and failed to base its injury determinations on positive evidence or to conduct objective examinations of the volume of dumped imports, the effect of those imports on prices in the domestic market of like products, and the impact of the imports on domestic producers of those products;
- Article 5.8 of the AD Agreement, because Mexico failed to terminate the rice investigation after a negative preliminary determination of injury, and Articles 5.8 and 11.1 of the AD Agreement because Mexico failed to exclude certain respondent US exporters from the beef and rice measures after negative final determinations of dumping;
- Article 6 of the AD Agreement, because Mexico, *inter alia*, failed to provide respondent US exporters with ample opportunity to pre-

1 *Resolución final de la investigación antidumping sobre las importaciones de carne y despojos comestibles de bovino, mercancía clasificada en las fracciones arancelarias 0201.10.01, 0202.10.01, 0201.20.99, 0202.20.99, 0201.30.01, 0202.30.01, 0206.21.01, 0206.22.01 y 0206.29.99 de la Tarifa de la Ley del Impuesto General de Importación, originarias de los Estados Unidos de América, independientemente del país de procedencia, Diario Oficial, Segunda Sección 8 (28 de Abril de 2000).*

2 *Resolución final de la investigación antidumping sobre las importaciones de arroz blanco grano largo, mercancía clasificada en la fracción arancelaria 1006.30.01 de la Tarifa de la Ley de los Impuestos Generales de Importación y de Exportación, originarias de los Estados Unidos de América, independientemente del país de procedencia, Diario Oficial, Segunda Sección 1 (5 de Junio de 2002).*

3 Including any further determinations made pursuant to court order or remand.

4 These include, for example, the *Resolución final de la investigación sobre elusión del pago de cuotas compensatorias impuestas a las importaciones de carne de bovino en cortes deshuesada y sin deshuesar, mercancía clasificada en las fracciones arancelarias 0201.20.99, 0202.20.99, 0201.30.01, 0202.30.01 de la Tarifa de la Ley del Impuesto General de Importación, originarias de los Estados Unidos de América, independientemente del país de procedencia, Diario Oficial, Primera Sección 1 (22 de Mayo 2001).*

sent in writing all evidence which they considered relevant in respect of the anti-dumping investigations and failed to give all interested parties a full opportunity for the defense of their interests, and Article 6 and Annex II of the AD Agreement by improperly applying the facts available to a US respondent rice exporter that was investigated and found to have no shipments during the period of investigation;

- Article 9 of the AD Agreement, in conjunction with Article 6, because of the manner in which Mexico determined anti-dumping margins for US exporters that were not individually investigated;
- Article 6 and 9 of the AD Agreement and Article VI of GATT 1994, because Mexico, *inter alia*, limited the application of the respondent-specific margins that it calculated in the beef investigation to selected grades of meat imported within 30 days of slaughter (applying "facts available" margins to the respondents' other shipments) and limited the application of a particular US respondent exporter's margin after conducting an "anti-circumvention review" that found the respondent was not engaged in circumvention;
- Articles 9 and 11 of the AD Agreement, because Mexico rejected requests by certain US respondent exporters to conduct reviews of the beef anti-dumping order; and
- Article 12 of the AD Agreement, because Mexico failed in its final determinations in both investigations to set forth in sufficient detail the findings and conclusions reached on all issues of fact and law considered material or to provide all relevant information on the matters of fact and law and reasons which led to the imposition of final measures.

In addition, the following provisions of Mexico's Foreign Trade Act appear to be inconsistent with Mexico's obligations under the provisions of the AD Agreement and the SCM Agreement:

- Article 53, which requires interested parties to present arguments, information, and evidence to the investigating authorities within 28 days of the day after publication of the initiation notice. This provision appears to be inconsistent with Articles 6.1.1 and 12.1.1 of the AD and SCM Agreements, respectively, which specify that exporters/foreign producers shall be given at least 30 days to respond to questionnaires, and that, as a general rule, the 30 days are to be counted from the date of receipt of the questionnaire;
- Article 64, which codifies the "facts available" approach that Mexico applied in the rice and beef investigations, as described in the fourth bullet above. This provision appears to be inconsistent with Article 9 of the AD Agreement, in conjunction with Article 6; and with Article 6.8 of the AD Agreement and Article 12.7 of the SCM Agreement to the extent that it requires the application of facts

available rates to exporters with no shipments during the period of investigation;

- Article 68, which appears to require reviews of respondent exporters that were not assigned a positive margin in an investigation, and appears to require that respondent exporters seeking reviews demonstrate that their volume of exports during the period of review was "representative." This provision appears to be inconsistent with Articles 5.8 and 11.1 of the AD Agreement (as described in the second bullet above), with Article 9 of the AD Agreement, and with Articles 11.9 and 21.1 of the SCM Agreement;
- Article 89D, which appears to require that "new shippers" requesting expedited reviews demonstrate that their volume of exports during the period of review was "representative." This provision appears to be inconsistent with Article 9.5 of the AD Agreement and Article 19.3 of the SCM Agreement, which require authorities to conduct reviews without regard to such a condition; and
- Article 93V, which appears to provide for the application of definitive anti-dumping or countervailing duties on products entered prior to the date of application of provisional measures (1) for longer than allowed under the AD and SCM Agreements, and (2) even if not all AD or SCM Agreement requirements for applying such duties are met. This provision appears to be inconsistent with Articles 7 and 10.6 of the AD Agreement and Articles 17 and 20.6 of the SCM Agreement.

Finally, Article 366 of Mexico's Federal Code of Civil Procedure, in conjunction with Article 68 of the Foreign Trade Act, appears to be inconsistent with Articles 9 and 11 of the AD Agreement and Articles 19 and 21 of the SCM Agreement to the extent that the provisions prevent Mexico from conducting reviews of anti-dumping or countervailing duty orders while a judicial review of the order is ongoing, including a "binational panel" review pursuant to Chapter Nineteen of the *North American Free Trade Agreement.*

Mexico's measures also appear to nullify or impair benefits accruing to the United States directly or indirectly under the cited agreements.

We look forward to receiving your reply to the present request and to fixing a mutually convenient date for consultations.

ANNEX D-2

REQUEST FOR THE ESTABLISHMENT OF A PANEL
BY THE UNITED STATES

WORLD TRADE ORGANIZATION

WT/DS295/2
22 September 2003

(03-5043)

Original: English

MEXICO – DEFINITIVE ANTI-DUMPING MEASURES
ON BEEF AND RICE

Request for the Establishment of a Panel by the United States

The following communication, dated 19 September 2003, from the Permanent Mission of the United States to the Chairman of the Dispute Settlement Body, is circulated pursuant to Article 6.2 of the DSU.

The United States considers that certain measures of the Government of Mexico are inconsistent with Mexico's commitments and obligations under the *General Agreement on Tariffs and Trade 1994* ("GATT 1994"), the *Agreement on Implementation of Article VI of the General Agreement on Tariffs and Trade 1994* ("AD Agreement"), and the *Agreement on Subsidies and Countervailing Measures* ("SCM Agreement"). In particular:

(1) On 5 June 2002, Mexico published in the *Diario Oficial* its definitive antidumping measure on long-grain white rice.[1] This measure appears to be inconsistent with the following provisions of the AD Agreement and the GATT 1994:

(a) Article VI of the GATT 1994 and Articles 1, 3.1, 3.2, 3.4, 3.5, and 4.1 of the AD Agreement because Mexico based its injury and causation analyses on only six months of data for each of the years

[1] Resolución final de la investigación antidumping sobre las importaciones de arroz blanco grano largo, mercancía clasificada en la fracción arancelaria 1006.30.01 de la Tarifa de la Ley de los Impuestos Generales de Importación y de Exportación, originarias de los Estados Unidos de América, independientemente del país de procedencia, Diario Oficial, Segunda Sección 1 (5 de Junio de 2002).

examined; failed to collect or examine recent data; failed to properly evaluate the relevant economic factors; failed to base its determination on a demonstration that the dumped imports are, through the effects of dumping, causing injury within the meaning of the AD Agreement; and failed to base its injury determinations on positive evidence or to conduct objective examinations of the volume of dumped imports, the effect of those imports on prices in the domestic market of like products, and the impact of the imports on domestic producers of those products;

(b) Article 5.8 of the AD Agreement, because Mexico failed to terminate the antidumping investigation after a negative preliminary determination of injury, and Articles 5.8 and 11.1 of the AD Agreement because Mexico failed to exclude certain respondent US exporters from the measure after negative final determinations of dumping;

(c) Articles 6.1, 6.2, and 6.4 of the AD Agreement, because Mexico, *inter alia*, failed to give all of the interested parties in the investigation notice of the information that the authorities required or ample opportunity to present in writing all evidence which they considered relevant in respect of the antidumping investigation, failed to give all interested parties a full opportunity for the defense of their interests, and failed to provide timely opportunities for the respondent US exporters to see all information that was relevant to presentation of their cases, that was not confidential as defined in Article 6.5, and that the authorities used in their investigation;

(d) Article 6.8 of the AD Agreement, and paragraphs 1, 3, 5, 6, and 7 of Annex II of the AD Agreement, by improperly rejecting information submitted by US exporters and applying the facts available in the evaluation of injury;

(e) Article 6.9 of the AD Agreement, because the investigating authorities, before the final determination was made, failed to inform the respondent US exporters of the essential facts under consideration which formed the basis for the decision to apply a definitive measure;

(f) Articles 6.6, 6.8, 6.10, 9.3, 9.4, and 9.5 of the AD Agreement, and paragraphs 1, 3, 5, 6, and 7 of Annex II of the AD Agreement, by applying the facts available to a US respondent rice exporter that was investigated and found to have no shipments during the period of investigation;

(g) Articles 1, 6.1, 6.6, 6.8, 6.10, 9.3, 9.4, 9.5, 12.1, and 12.2 of the AD Agreement, and paragraphs 1, 3, 5, 6, and 7 of Annex II of the AD Agreement, by applying the facts available in establishing the antidumping margins that it assigned to US exporters that were not individually investigated, and by doing so in an improper manner;

(h) Article 12.2 of the AD Agreement, because Mexico failed in its final determination in the rice investigation to set forth in sufficient detail the findings and conclusions reached on all issues of fact and law considered material or to provide all relevant information on the matters of fact and law and reasons which led to the imposition of final measures; and

(i) Article VI:2 of the GATT 1994, because Mexico levied an anti-dumping duty greater in amount than the margin of dumping.

(2) Certain provisions of Mexico's Foreign Trade Act also appear to be inconsistent with Mexico's obligations under various provisions of the AD Agreement and the SCM Agreement. Specifically:

(a) Article 53 of the Foreign Trade Act requires interested parties to present arguments, information, and evidence to the investigating authorities within 28 days of the day after publication of the initiation notice. This provision does not appear to permit the investigating authorities to grant extensions of the 28-day deadline. Accordingly, the provision appears to be inconsistent with Articles 6.1.1 and 12.1.1 of the AD and SCM Agreements, respectively, which specify that due consideration should be granted to extension requests and that such requests should, upon cause shown, be granted whenever practicable;

(b) Article 64 of the Foreign Trade Act codifies the "facts available" approach that Mexico applied in the rice investigation, as described in subparagraphs (f) and (g) of section (1) above. This provision appears to be inconsistent with Articles 6.1, 6.6, 6.8, 6.10, 9.3, 9.4, and 9.5 of the AD Agreement, and paragraphs 1, 3, 5, 6, and 7 of Annex II of the AD Agreement; and with Articles 6.6, 6.8, 6.10, 9.3, 9.4, and 9.5 of the AD Agreement, paragraphs 1, 3, 5, 6, and 7 of Annex II of the AD Agreement, and Articles 12.5, 12.7, and 19.3 of the SCM Agreement, to the extent that it requires the application of facts available rates to exporters with no shipments during the period of investigation;

(c) Article 68 of the Foreign Trade Act appears to require reviews of respondent exporters that were not assigned a positive margin in an investigation, and appears to require that respondent exporters seeking reviews demonstrate that their volume of exports during the period of review was "representative." This provision appears to be inconsistent with Articles 5.8 and 11.1 of the AD Agreement (as described in subparagraph (b) of section (1) above), with Articles 9.3 and 11.2 of the AD Agreement, and with Articles 11.9, 21.1, and 21.2 of the SCM Agreement;

(d) Article 89D of the Foreign Trade Act appears to require that "new shippers" requesting expedited reviews demonstrate that their exports were subsequent to the period of investigation and that the volume of exports during the period of review was "representative." This provision appears to be inconsistent with Article 9.5 of the AD Agreement and Article 19.3 of the SCM Agreement;

(e) Article 93V of the Foreign Trade Act appears to provide for the application of fines on importers that enter products subject to antidumping and countervailing duty investigations while such investigations are underway. This provision appears to be inconsistent with Article 18.1 of the AD Agreement and Article 32.1 of the SCM Agreement.

(3) Mexican officials have asserted that Article 366 of Mexico's Federal Code of Civil Procedure and Articles 68 and 97 of the Foreign Trade Act prevent Mexico from conducting reviews of antidumping or countervailing duty orders while a judicial review of the order is ongoing, including a "binational panel" review pursuant to Chapter Nineteen of the *North American Free Trade Agreement*. These provisions appear to be inconsistent with Articles 9.3, 9.5, and 11.2 of the AD Agreement, and Articles 19.3 and 21.2 of the SCM Agreement.

On 16 June 2003, the United States Government requested consultations with the Government of Mexico pursuant to Article 4 of the *Understanding on Rules and Procedures Governing the Settlement of Disputes* ("DSU"), Article XXII:1 of the GATT 1994, Article 17.3 of the AD Agreement, and Article 30 of the SCM Agreement. The United States and Mexico held such consultations on 31 July and 1 August 2003. These consultations provided some helpful clarifications but unfortunately did not resolve the dispute.

Accordingly, the United States respectfully requests, pursuant to Article 6 of the DSU, Article 17.4 of the AD Agreement, and Article 30 of the SCM Agreement, that the Dispute Settlement Body establish a panel to examine this matter, with the standard terms of reference as set out in Article 7.1 of the DSU. The United States further asks that this request for a panel be placed on the agenda for the next meeting of the Dispute Settlement Body to be held on 2 October 2003.

UNITED STATES – FINAL COUNTERVAILING DUTY DETERMINATION WITH RESPECT TO CERTAIN SOFTWOOD LUMBER FROM CANADA

Recourse By Canada to Article 21.5 of the Understanding on Rules and Procedures Governing the Settlement of Disputes

Report of the Appellate Body

WT/DS257/AB/RW

Adopted by the Dispute Settlement Body on 20 December 2005

United States, *Appellant*	Present:
Canada, *Appellee*	Janow, Presiding Member
China, *Third Participant*	Baptista, Member
European Communities, *Third Participant*	Sacerdoti, Member

TABLE OF CONTENTS

TABLE OF CASES CITED IN THIS REPORT

Short Title	Full Case Title and Citation
Australia – Automotive Leather II (Article 21.5 – US)	Panel Report, *Australia – Subsidies Provided to Producers and Exporters of Automotive Leather – Recourse to Article 21.5 of the DSU by the United States*, WT/DS126/RW and Corr.1, adopted 11 February 2000, DSR 2000:III, 1189
Australia – Salmon(Article 21.5 – Canada)	Panel Report, *Australia – Measures Affecting Importation of Salmon – Recourse to Article 21.5 of the DSU by Canada*, WT/DS18/RW, adopted 20 March 2000, DSR 2000:IV, 2031
Canada – Aircraft (Article 21.5 – Brazil)	Appellate Body Report, *Canada – Measures Affecting the Export of Civilian Aircraft – Recourse by Brazil to Article 21.5 of the DSU*, WT/DS70/AB/RW, adopted 4 August 2000, DSR 2000:IX, 4299
EC – Bed Linen (Article 21.5 – India)	Appellate Body Report, *European Communities – Anti-Dumping Duties on Imports of Cotton-Type Bed Linen from India – Recourse to Article 21.5 of the DSU by India*, WT/DS141/AB/RW, adopted 24 April 2003
EC – Bed Linen (Article 21.5 – India)	Panel Report, *European Communities – Anti-Dumping Duties on Imports of Cotton-Type Bed Linen from India – Recourse to Article 21.5 of the DSU by India*, WT/DS141/RW, adopted 24 April 2003, as modified by Appellate Body Report, WT/DS141/AB/RW

Short Title	Full Case Title and Citation
Mexico – Corn Syrup (Article 21.5 – US)	Appellate Body Report, *Mexico – Anti-Dumping Investigation of High Fructose Corn Syrup (HFCS) from the United States – Recourse to Article 21.5 of the DSU by the United States*, WT/DS132/AB/RW, adopted 21 November 2001, DSR 2001:XIII, 6675
US – Shrimp (Article 21.5 – Malaysia)	Appellate Body Report, *United States – Import Prohibition of Certain Shrimp and Shrimp Products – Recourse to Article 21.5 of the DSU by Malaysia*, WT/DS58/AB/RW, adopted 21 November 2001, DSR 2001:XIII, 6481
US – Softwood Lumber IV	Appellate Body Report, *United States – Final Countervailing Duty Determination with Respect to Certain Softwood Lumber from Canada*, WT/DS257/AB/R, adopted 17 February 2004
US – Softwood Lumber IV	Panel Report, *United States – Final Countervailing Duty Determination with Respect to Certain Softwood Lumber from Canada*, WT/DS257/R and Corr.1, adopted 17 February 2004, as modified by Appellate Body Report, WT/DS257/AB/R
US – Softwood Lumber IV (Article 21.5 – Canada)	Panel Report, *United States – Final Countervailing Duty Determination with Respect to Certain Softwood Lumber from Canada, Recourse by Canada to Article 21.5*, WT/DS257/RW, 1 August 2005

TABLE OF ABBREVIATIONS USED IN THIS REPORT

Abbreviation	Description
DSB	Dispute Settlement Body
DSU	*Understanding on Rules and Procedures Governing the Settlement of Disputes*
Final Countervailing Duty Determination	"Notice of Final Affirmative Countervailing Duty Determination and Final Negative Critical Circumstances Determination: Certain Softwood Lumber Products from Canada", *United States Federal Register*, Vol. 67, No. 63 (2 April 2002), p. 15545, as amended, Vol. 67, No. 99 (22 May 2002), p. 36070 (Exhibit US-1 submitted by the United States to the Panel)

Abbreviation	Description
First Assessment Review	"Notice of Final Results of Countervailing Duty Administrative Review and Rescission of Certain Company-Specific Reviews: Certain Softwood Lumber Products from Canada", *United States Federal Register*, Vol. 69, No. 243 (20 December 2004), p. 75917 (Exhibit CDA-8 submitted by Canada to the Panel)
GATT 1994	*General Agreement on Tariffs and Trade 1994*
Original Appellate Body Report	Report of the Appellate Body in the original *US – Softwood Lumber IV* proceedings
Original panel	Panel in the original *US – Softwood Lumber IV* proceedings
Original panel report	Report of the Panel in the original *US – Softwood Lumber IV* proceedings
Panel	Panel in these *US – Softwood Lumber IV (Article 21.5 – Canada)* proceedings
Panel Report	Report of the Panel in these *US – Softwood Lumber IV (Article 21.5 – Canada)* proceedings
SAA	"Statement of Administrative Action" in *Message from the President of the United States Transmitting the Uruguay Round Trade Agreements, Texts of Agreements Implementing Bill, Statement of Administrative Action and Required Supporting Statements*, H.R. Doc. No. 103-316, Vol. 1, p. 656 (Exhibit CDA-1 submitted by Canada to the Panel)
SCM Agreement	*Agreement on Subsidies and Countervailing Measures*
Section 129	Section 129 of the Uruguay Round Agreements Act, Pub. L. No. 103-465, § 129, 108 Stat. 4838, codified at 19 USC § 3538 (2000) pp. 720-721 (Exhibit CDA-2 submitted by Canada to the Panel)
Section 129 Determination	"Notice of Implementation Under Section 129 of the Uruguay Round Agreements Act; Countervailing Measures Concerning Certain Softwood Lumber Products from Canada", *United States Federal Register*, Vol. 69, No. 241 (16 December 2004), p. 75305 (Exhibit CDA-7 submitted by Canada to the Panel)

Abbreviation	Description
USDOC	United States Department of Commerce
Working Procedures	*Working Procedures for Appellate Review*, WT/AB/WP/5, 4 January 2005
WTO	World Trade Organization

I. INTRODUCTION

1. The United States appeals certain issues of law and legal interpretations developed in the Panel Report, *United States – Final Countervailing Duty Determination with Respect to Certain Softwood Lumber from Canada, Recourse by Canada to Article 21.5* (the "Panel Report").[1] The Panel was established to consider a complaint by Canada with respect to the consistency with the *Agreement on Subsidies and Countervailing Measures* (the "*SCM Agreement*") and the *General Agreement on Tariffs and Trade 1994* (the "GATT 1994") of measures claimed by Canada to have been taken by the United States to comply with the recommendations and rulings of the Dispute Settlement Body (the "DSB") in the *US – Softwood Lumber IV* proceedings.[2]

2. In the proceedings before the original panel, Canada challenged a number of aspects of the final determination by the United States Department of Commerce (the "USDOC") that led to the imposition of countervailing duties on softwood lumber from Canada (the "Final Countervailing Duty Determination").[3] The original panel found that the failure of the USDOC to conduct a pass-through analysis[4] in respect of certain categories of log and lumber sales was inconsistent with Articles 10 and 32.1 of the *SCM Agreement* and Article

---

[1] WT/DS257/RW, 1 August 2005.

[2] The recommendations and rulings of the DSB resulted from the adoption on 17 February 2004, by the DSB, of the Original Appellate Body Report, WT/DS257/AB/R, and the Original Panel Report, WT/DS257/R and Corr.1, in *US – Softwood Lumber IV*.

[3] "Notice of Final Affirmative Countervailing Duty Determination and Final Negative Critical Circumstances Determination: Certain Softwood Lumber Products from Canada", *United States Federal Register*, Vol. 67, No. 63 (2 April 2002), p. 15545, as amended, Vol. 67, No. 99 (22 May 2002), p. 36070 (Exhibit US-1 submitted by the United States to the Panel).

[4] The claims made by Canada included claims that the United States had acted inconsistently with its obligations under the *SCM Agreement* because "the USDOC erred in not conducting a pass-through analysis in determining subsidization of softwood lumber in the case of certain upstream transactions for inputs." (Original Panel Report, *US – Softwood Lumber IV*, para. 7.66) In general, a "pass-through" analysis involves an examination of whether subsidies paid to the producers of primary or upstream products (that do not fall within the scope of a countervailing duty investigation) "pass through" the production chain to downstream products (that are covered by the countervailing duty investigation). In this dispute, Canada claimed that the USDOC was required to conduct an analysis of the degree to which subsidies paid on the production of the input products, such as logs or primary lumber, passed through the production process to the downstream softwood lumber products covered by the investigation and the Final Countervailing Duty Determination (that is, to the products upon which countervailing duties were imposed). See *infra*, paras. 49-50.

VI:3 of the GATT 1994.[5] With regard to the pass-through issue, the Appellate Body upheld the original panel's finding that the "USDOC's failure to conduct a pass-through analysis in respect of arm's length sales of *logs* by tenured harvesters/sawmills to unrelated sawmills is inconsistent with Articles 10 and 32.1 of the *SCM Agreement* and Article VI:3 of the GATT 1994", and reversed the original panel's finding that the "USDOC's failure to conduct a pass-through analysis in respect of arm's length sales of *lumber* by tenured harvesters/sawmills to unrelated remanufacturers is inconsistent with Articles 10 and 32.1 of the *SCM Agreement* and Article VI:3 of the GATT 1994."[6]

3. On 17 February 2004, the DSB adopted the Appellate Body Report and the original panel report, as modified by the Appellate Body Report.[7] The parties to the dispute agreed that the United States would have until 17 December 2004 to implement the recommendations and rulings of the DSB.[8] On 16 December 2004, the USDOC published a determination pursuant to Section 129 of the Uruguay Round Agreements Act ("Section 129").[9] In the determination made pursuant to Section 129 (the "Section 129 Determination")[10], the United States performed a pass-through analysis in respect of certain transactions. The rate of subsidization established in the Section 129 Determination became the estimated countervailing duty rate (referred to as a cash deposit rate) applicable to imports of softwood lumber from Canada entering the United States on or after 10 December 2004.[11]

4. On 20 December 2004, the USDOC published the final results of the first administrative review of the countervailing duties on imports of softwood lum-

---

[5] Original Panel Report, *US – Softwood Lumber IV*, para. 8.1(c). The original panel also addressed claims by Canada in respect of the USDOC's determination regarding the existence of a "financial contribution", the existence and amount of a "benefit", and the existence of "specific" subsidies.

[6] Original Appellate Body Report, *US – Softwood Lumber IV*, para. 167. (original emphasis) In addition to its findings with respect to the pass-through issue, the Appellate Body: upheld the original panel's finding that the USDOC's determination regarding the existence of a "financial contribution" was not inconsistent with Article 1.1(a)(1)(iii) of the *SCM Agreement*; reversed the panel's finding with respect to the interpretation of Article 14 of the *SCM Agreement*, as well as the panel's consequential finding that the United States acted inconsistently with Articles 10, 14, 14(d), and 32.1 of the *SCM Agreement* in its determination of the existence and amount of benefit in the underlying countervailing duty investigation; but found, however, that there were insufficient facts for it to complete the legal analysis with respect to Canada's claims regarding the calculation of the benefit. (*Ibid.*)

[7] WT/DS257/11.

[8] WT/DS257/13.

[9] Pub. L. No. 103-465, § 129, 108 Stat. 4838, codified at 19 USC § 3538 (2000) pp. 720-721 (Exhibit CDA-2 submitted by Canada to the Panel). Section 129 is entitled "Administrative action following WTO panel reports" and establishes a procedure that, amongst other things, allows the USDOC to issue a revised determination in a countervailing duty proceeding following relevant recommendations and rulings by the DSB. Excerpts from the text of Section 129 are set out *infra*, footnotes 79 and 82.

[10] "Notice of Implementation Under Section 129 of the Uruguay Round Agreements Act; Countervailing Measures Concerning Certain Softwood Lumber Products from Canada", *United States Federal Register*, Vol. 69, No. 241 (16 December 2004), p. 75305 (Exhibit CDA-7 submitted by Canada to the Panel). See also USDOC Memorandum from B. Tillman to J. Jochum, "Section 129 Determination: Final Countervailing Duty Determination, Certain Softwood Lumber from Canada" (6 December 2004) (Exhibit CDA-5 submitted by Canada to the Panel).

[11] Section 129 Determination, *supra*, footnote 10, p. 75306.

ber from Canada that had been initiated in July 2003 (the "First Assessment Review").[12] In that review, the USDOC adopted the same pass-through methodology as it had used in the Section 129 Determination.[13] However, the USDOC's application of this methodology in the First Assessment Review did not, in the light of the evidence before it, result in any reduction to its calculated rate of subsidization.[14] The First Assessment Review established the final countervailing duty liability for imports of softwood lumber that entered the United States during the period 22 May 2002 to 31 March 2003. The results of the First Assessment Review also fixed the estimated countervailing duty rate (the cash deposit rate) for imports entering the United States on or after 20 December 2004.

5. Additional details regarding the Section 129 Determination and the First Assessment Review are set out in Section IV.A of this Report.

6. At the DSB meeting held 17 December 2004, the United States informed the DSB that it had complied with its recommendations and rulings in the original *US – Softwood Lumber IV* dispute.[15] Canada was of the view that the United States had failed to comply with the recommendations and rulings. On 30 December 2004, Canada requested that the matter of compliance be referred to a panel pursuant to Article 21.5 of the *Understanding on Rules and Procedures Governing the Settlement of Disputes* (the "DSU").[16] On 14 January 2005, the DSB referred the matter to the original panel.[17] A member of the original panel was unable to participate in the proceedings and the parties, therefore, on 7 February 2005, agreed on a new panelist.[18] Before the Article 21.5 Panel (the "Panel"), Canada claimed that the United States had failed to comply with the recommendations and rulings of the DSB in both the Section 129 Determination and the First Assessment Review.[19] Canada claimed that the United States thereby continued to violate its obligations under Article VI:3 of the GATT 1994 and Articles 10 and 32.1 of the *SCM Agreement*.[20]

---

[12] "Notice of Final Results of Countervailing Duty Administrative Review and Rescission of Certain Company-Specific Reviews: Certain Softwood Lumber Products from Canada", *United States Federal Register*, Vol. 69, No. 243 (20 December 2004), p. 75917 (Exhibit CDA-8 submitted by Canada to the Panel). See also USDOC Memorandum from B. Tillman to J. Jochum, "Issues and Decisions Memorandum: Final Results of Administrative Review: Certain Softwood Lumber Products from Canada" (13 December 2004) (Exhibit CDA-11 submitted by Canada to the Panel), section II.F. In the parlance of the United States, reviews intended to assess final duty liability are usually referred to as "administrative reviews". (United States' additional written memorandum, para. 2) In these proceedings, however, both participants, and the Panel, used the term "assessment review" to describe this type of review. We adopt the same approach in this Report.

[13] Panel Report, footnote 50 to para. 4.58. See also United States' additional written memorandum, para. 12.

[14] See *infra*, footnote 86.

[15] WT/DSB/M/180, paras. 22-25.

[16] WT/DS257/15.

[17] WT/DSB/M/181.

[18] WT/DS257/19.

[19] Canada's first written submission to the Panel, para. 35; Panel Report, p. A-13. See also Panel Report, para. 4.51.

[20] Canada's first written submission to the Panel, para. 37; Panel Report, p. A-13.

7. In its first written submission to the Panel, the United States requested a preliminary ruling that the First Assessment Review fell outside of the mandate of the Panel under Article 21.5 of the DSU. The Panel instructed the parties to "assume" in making their submissions "that the first assessment review *does* fall within the scope of these proceedings", but added that such assumption was "without prejudice to the Panel's eventual ruling on this issue".[21]

8. The Panel Report was circulated to the Members of the World Trade Organization (the "WTO") on 1 August 2005. The Panel rejected:

> - the US request for a preliminary ruling that the First Assessment Review falls outside the scope of the present DSU Article 21.5 proceeding, insofar as the pass-through analysis is concerned[.][22]

9. The Panel upheld Canada's claims that:

> - in the Section 129 Determination, and in the treatment of pass-through in the First Assessment Review, the United States failed to properly implement the recommendations and rulings of the DSB in this dispute by failing to conduct a pass-through analysis in respect of sales, found by [the] USDOC not to be at arm's length, of logs by tenured timber harvesters, whether or not they also produce lumber, to unrelated lumber producers, whether or not they hold a stumpage contract; and
> - in the Section 129 Determination, and in the First Assessment Review, the USDOC therefore included in its subsidy numerator transactions for which it had not demonstrated that the benefit of subsidized log inputs had passed through to the processed product.[23]

10. The Panel accordingly concluded that the United States remained in violation of Articles 10 and 32.1 of the *SCM Agreement* and Article VI:3 of the GATT 1994.[24] On this basis, and in the light of Article 3.8 of the DSU, the Panel concluded that, to the extent the United States acted inconsistently with the provisions of the *SCM Agreement* and the GATT 1994, and failed to implement properly the relevant recommendations and rulings of the DSB, it nullified or impaired benefits accruing to Canada under those Agreements.[25] Pursuant to

---

[21] Statement by the Chairman of the Panel at the Substantive Meeting of the Panel with the Parties, 21 April 2005. (original underlining)

[22] Panel Report, para. 5.1. See also para. 4.50.

[23] Panel Report, para. 5.2. The Panel rejected a claim by Canada that the USDOC improperly disregarded all aggregate transaction and pricing data submitted by the Canadian respondents. The Panel also rejected Canada's claim against the benchmarks used by the USDOC in its pass-through analysis. (*Ibid.*, para. 5.1)

[24] *Ibid.*, para. 5.4.

[25] *Ibid.*, para. 5.5.

Article 19.1 of the DSU, the Panel recommended that the United States bring its Section 129 Determination and First Assessment Review into conformity with such provisions.[26]

11. On 6 September 2005, the United States notified the DSB of its intention to appeal certain issues of law covered in the Panel Report and certain legal interpretations developed by the Panel, pursuant to Articles 16.4 and 17 of the DSU, and filed a Notice of Appeal[27], pursuant to Rule 20(1) of the *Working Procedures for Appellate Review* (the "*Working Procedures*"). On 13 September 2005, the United States filed an appellant's submission.[28] On 3 October 2005, Canada filed an appellee's submission.[29] On the same day, China and the European Communities each filed a third participant's submission.[30]

12. On 26 September 2005, pursuant to Rule 28(1) of the *Working Procedures*, the Appellate Body Division hearing this appeal requested the United States to submit an additional written memorandum explaining certain aspects of relevant United States laws and procedures. The United States filed an additional written memorandum on 5 October 2005. On 10 October 2005, Canada submitted a written response to the United States' additional written memorandum.[31] The Division allowed the third participants additional time during the presentation of their oral statements at the hearing to respond to these additional memoranda.[32]

13. The oral hearing in this appeal was held on 12 October 2005. The participants and third participants presented oral arguments and responded to questions posed by the Members of the Division hearing the appeal.

II. ARGUMENTS OF THE PARTICIPANTS AND THE THIRD PARTICIPANTS

A. Claims of Error by the United States – Appellant

14. The United States appeals the Panel's conclusion that the First Assessment Review fell within the scope of review under Article 21.5 of the DSU. The United States considers this conclusion to be based on erroneous findings on issues of law and an incorrect interpretation of Article 21.5 of the DSU.

15. The United States submits that the Panel's jurisdiction under Article 21.5 is limited to those measures taken to comply with the recommendations and rulings of the DSB in the original *US – Softwood Lumber IV* proceedings. Although the United States acknowledges that a panel has the authority to decide whether a

---

26 *Ibid.* The Panel declined to make a further recommendation under Article 19.1 of the DSU, as requested by Canada, and left it to the United States to determine the modalities of the implementation of its recommendation. (*Ibid.*, para. 5.7)

27 WT/DS257/22 (attached as Annex I to this Report).

28 Pursuant to Rule 21(1) of the *Working Procedures*.

29 Pursuant to Rule 22(1) of the *Working Procedures*.

30 Pursuant to Rule 24(1) of the *Working Procedures*.

31 Pursuant to Rule 28(2) of the *Working Procedures*.

32 Pursuant to Rule 28(3) of the *Working Procedures*.

measure is one "taken to comply", it emphasizes that "measures taken to comply" within the meaning of Article 21.5 of the DSU are limited to those that have been, or must be, taken to address WTO-inconsistencies identified in the recommendations and rulings of the DSB. According to the Unites States, the relevant recommendations and rulings related solely to the USDOC's approach to the "pass-through" issue in the Final Countervailing Duty Determination. This was the measure identified in Canada's request for the establishment of the original panel; it was also the measure addressed in the relevant recommendations and rulings adopted by the DSB. The United States implemented those recommendations and rulings by means of a revision to the Final Countervailing Duty Determination through the Section 129 Determination. The relevant recommendations and rulings did not relate to any assessment review. The United States was, therefore, under no compliance obligation in regard to the First Assessment Review. Thus, the United States did not conduct the First Assessment Review with the intention of complying with the DSB's recommendations and rulings. Nonetheless, "in view of the original WTO findings", the USDOC applied the same pass-through methodology in the First Assessment Review as it had applied in the Section 129 Determination.[33]

16. The United States argues that the Panel erred in overlooking the "fundamental" and "qualitative" differences between countervailing duty investigations and assessment reviews.[34] Instead, the Panel focused solely upon the fact that both procedures involved duties on softwood lumber. According to the United States, the *SCM Agreement* distinguishes between investigations—the purpose of which is "to determine the existence, degree, and effect of any alleged subsidy"—and assessment reviews—the purpose of which is to levy the duty. That the *SCM Agreement* recognizes assessment reviews—which are only used in retrospective duty assessment systems—as well as the fact that such reviews are distinct from investigations is, in the view of the United States, made clear by footnote 52 of the *SCM Agreement*. This footnote provides for different consequences to flow from a finding of no subsidies during the review period (no requirement to terminate the duty) than must flow from a finding of no subsidies during the period of investigation (no duty may be levied).

17. The United States explains that, under its system of retrospective duty assessment, even though liability for the payment of duties attaches at the moment the merchandise subject to a countervailing duty measure enters the United States, the actual amount of countervailing duties to be paid will not be calculated until an assessment review has been conducted, or until the time to request an assessment review has passed without any such request. In the course of a review, the USDOC determines the assessment rate based on the examination of previous imports; this rate also establishes the estimated countervailing duty (cash deposit) rate to be applied to future imports. After concluding the review, the USDOC instructs the customs administration to assess the definitive rate of countervailing duties to be levied. The DSB recommendations and rulings in the

[33] United States' additional written memorandum, para. 12.

[34] Unites States' appellant's submission, paras. 4 and 17, and p. 8, sub-heading II.B.1.

original proceedings encompassed only the Final Countervailing Duty Determination establishing the existence and amount of the subsidy under Article 18 of the *SCM Agreement*. These recommendations and rulings did not, asserts the United States, extend to duty assessment proceedings.

18. The United States notes that, as part of the reasoning that led the Panel to refuse to exclude the First Assessment Review from the scope of the present Article 21.5 proceedings, the Panel claimed that "US law allows DSB rulings and recommendations to be implemented through administrative reviews in certain circumstances" and that this "undermines the US argument that assessment reviews should be excluded from the scope of DSU Article 21.5 proceedings."[35] The United States submits that the Panel's reasoning in this regard is based on a misinterpretation of a provision of the Statement of Administrative Action to the Uruguay Round Agreements Act (the "SAA").[36] The United States adds that the SAA is, in any event, irrelevant in the present case because implementation was carried out through the Section 129 Determination and *not* through an administrative review.

19. The United States argues that the timing of the initiation of the First Assessment Review—*before* the adoption of the DSB recommendations and rulings—underlines that it was not a measure taken to comply with those recommendations and rulings. The United States argues that a "measure taken to comply with recommendations and rulings" presupposes the existence of adopted recommendations and rulings. The United States emphasizes that the word "'comply' when followed by the preposition 'with' is defined as 'accommodate oneself to (a person, circumstances, customs, etc.) ... Act in accordance with or *with* a request, command, etc. ... Consent or agree *to, to do*".[37] The USDOC initiated the First Assessment Review on 1 July 2003, eight months *before* the adoption of the DSB recommendations and rulings on 17 February 2004. The First Assessment Review, therefore, could not have been taken in order *to comply* with those recommendations and rulings.

20. The United States considers that the standard applied by the Panel to determine the scope of Article 21.5 proceedings is so broad as to render the jurisdictional limitations of Article 21.5 "nearly meaningless".[38] The United States claims that the interpretation by the Panel was guided by dispute settlement panel reports, and not by the customary rules of interpretation of public international law. For the United States, the Panel's interpretation of Article 21.5 had "no basis in the text or context of Article 21.5 itself, and ... is inconsistent with the object and purpose of the DSU."[39]

---

[35] *Ibid.*, para. 24 (quoting Panel Report, footnote 42 to para. 4.45).

[36] "Statement of Administrative Action" in *Message from the President of the United States Transmitting the Uruguay Round Trade Agreements, Texts of Agreements Implementing Bill, Statement of Administrative Action and Required Supporting Statements*, H.R. Doc. No. 103-316, Vol. 1, p. 656 (Exhibit CDA-1 submitted by Canada to the Panel).

[37] United States' appellant's submission, para. 30 (quoting *The New Shorter Oxford English Dictionary*, L. Brown (ed.) (Clarendon Press, 1993), Vol. 1, p. 461 (original italics)).

[38] *Ibid.*, paras. 5 and 32.

[39] *Ibid.*, para. 5.

21. The United States emphasizes that the Section 129 Determination serves as the basis for the imposition of the countervailing duty and that it still applies. Contrary to Canada's arguments, "the 'existence' and 'consistency' of the Section 129 Determination is undisturbed. It has not been superseded, replaced, undone or rendered non-existent by the First Assessment Review."[40] The Panel, however, concluded that the First Assessment Review fell within the scope of the Article 21.5 proceedings because it "'could have an impact on' or could 'possibly undermine'" the Section 129 Determination.[41] The United States contests this conclusion. The Section 129 Determination confirmed the existence of a subsidy that justified the imposition of countervailing duties. The First Assessment Review did not have, nor could it have had, any impact on that determination. The United States also emphasizes that the Section 129 Determination (and the Final Countervailing Duty Determination that it revised) considered the existence and amount of subsidization in the original period of investigation; the First Assessment Review, by contrast, was concerned with the amount of subsidization in a different period of review.

22. The United States argues that Section 129 proceedings and assessment reviews have different legal consequences and "wholly different" administrative records.[42] They are neither "inextricably linked" nor "clearly connected" proceedings.[43] Indeed, the Panel's erroneous finding to the contrary hinges on two aspects of an ancillary relationship between the Final Countervailing Duty Determination, the Section 129 Determination, and the First Assessment Review. The first is the fact that some imports, which were subject to the cash deposit rate determined in the Final Countervailing Duty Determination and revised in the Section 129 Determination, were also subject to final assessed duties determined in the First Assessment Review. The second aspect is that the cash deposit rate set in the Final Countervailing Duty Determination and amended by the Section 129 Determination was also affected, prospectively, by the First Assessment Review. On these bases, the Panel concluded that there was "considerable overlap in the effect of these various measures".[44]

23. Furthermore, according to the United States, the "effects" of a measure cannot be the appropriate standard to determine the scope of jurisdiction in Article 21.5 proceedings. This standard has no basis in the text of Article 21.5: the "effect" of a measure does not indicate whether that measure was "taken to comply".[45] Indeed, the United States argues, any alleged "overlap" in the effect of the three distinct measures was simply a "natural consequence" of the United States' system of retrospective duty assessment. That some imports initially subject to a cash deposit rate set by the Final Countervailing Duty Determination were later assessed based on the First Assessment Review is simply the logical consequence of having two separate sets of proceedings. Similarly, with respect to the

---

[40] United States' statement at the oral hearing.

[41] United States' appellant's submission, paras. 32-33 (quoting Panel Report, para. 4.41).

[42] *Ibid.*, para. 6.

[43] *Ibid.*, para. 34 (referring to Panel Report, para. 4.41).

[44] *Ibid.*, para. 36 (quoting Panel Report, para. 4.41).

[45] *Ibid.*, para. 40.

fact that the cash deposit rate set by the Final Countervailing Duty Determination was also affected (prospectively) by the First Assessment Review, the United States submits that changes to the cash deposit rate are a natural result of taking into account information pertaining to a more recent period in an assessment proceeding. The United States underlines that the cash deposit rate is always subject to change for subsequent imports if an assessment review is requested, irrespective of any WTO or Section 129 proceedings.

24. The United States claims that the Panel's interpretation of Article 21.5 treats WTO Members with a retrospective duty assessment system differently from Members with a prospective duty assessment system. The overlap in effect identified by the Panel simply would not exist in a prospective duty assessment system. Nevertheless, the Panel itself stated that "interpretation and application of Article 21.5 must accommodate both prospective and retrospective duty assessment systems."[46]

25. The United States submits that the Panel's only reference to customary rules of interpretation was its reference to the object and purpose of the DSU. The Panel asserted that a decision declining to examine the First Assessment Review in Article 21.5 proceedings would fail to ensure the "prompt settlement" of the dispute. Yet, the objective of promptly settling disputes does not, in itself, "justify sweeping into the limited expedited Article 21.5 procedures measures that are not 'taken to comply'"[47] with recommendations and rulings of the DSB. If a Member has a complaint regarding the *assessment* of countervailing duties in an assessment review, the regular dispute settlement procedures are available to address the dispute, consistent with the object and purpose of the DSU. In this context, the United States argues that the Panel's reference to the Appellate Body Report in *EC – Bed Linen (Article 21.5 – India)* was misplaced because, in that case, the Appellate Body used the notion of prompt settlement as an argument *against* including a new claim in Article 21.5 proceedings.

26. According to the United States, the Panel not only unduly relied on the reports by previous panels that dealt with Article 21.5 of the DSU, it also misapplied those panel reports. The United States considers that the situation before the panel in *Australia – Automotive Leather II (Article 21.5 – US)* can be distinguished from the present case. In that dispute, the repayment of a WTO-inconsistent subsidy and the payment of a new non-commercial loan were announced on the same day, with the loan being contingent upon repayment of the subsidy. The loan was therefore clearly within the scope of Article 21.5 as a "measure taken to comply". In this case, by contrast, the two proceedings at issue are separate and distinct both in timing and in nature. The United States also considers that the panel in *Australia – Salmon (Article 21.5 – Canada)* dealt with a matter quite distinct from that in the present dispute. The panel in that dispute used a "clearly connected" standard to include in the Article 21.5 proceedings a ban on salmon imports by the Australian state of Tasmania that had been implemented shortly after the removal of a ban on salmon imports by the Australian

46 United States' appellant's submission, para. 39 (quoting Panel Report, para. 4.49).

47 *Ibid.*, para. 42.

federal government. The United States submits that the Tasmanian ban in that proceeding was, by its timing and its nature, an "obvious" and "specific" response to the removal of the ban by the Australian federal government.[48] By contrast, an assessment review is a procedure that occurs upon request of a party regardless of any compliance obligation resulting from WTO dispute settlement. The United States emphasizes that, in the present case, the First Assessment Review was requested eight months before the adoption of the *US – Softwood Lumber IV* original panel and Appellate Body reports.

27. Although the Panel in the present case made a distinction between the facts in this case and those in *EC – Bed Linen (Article 21.5 – India)*, the United States argues that there are obvious parallels between the facts in both cases, such that there should be a similar outcome in both disputes. In *EC – Bed Linen (Article 21.5 – India)*, the panel found that its jurisdiction did not extend to a measure that, according to the United States, was far more closely related to the measure taken to comply with the relevant recommendations and rulings of the DSB in that case than was the First Assessment Review to the measure taken to comply in this case. The United States adds that, like the measure considered in *EC – Bed Linen (Article 21.5 – India)*, the First Assessment Review was a result of "events subsequent to"[49] the Final Countervailing Duty Determination, namely, the request by Canada and others for a review of the sales and subsidies in a subsequent period.

28. Finally, although it admits that this argument is not relevant to the legal analysis, the United States considers the Panel's inclusion of the First Assessment Review in these Article 21.5 proceedings to be "unfairly prejudicial".[50] After having implemented the recommendations and rulings of the DSB, the United States considers it should not have been expected to defend its actions in a separate assessment proceeding for the first time under the expedited timeframes of Article 21.5 proceedings.

29. In addition to its appeal of the Panel's refusal of its request for a preliminary ruling excluding the First Assessment Review from the Article 21.5 proceedings, the United States requests the Appellate Body to reverse all of the Panel's consequential findings of inconsistency with respect to the First Assessment Review on the grounds that the First Assessment Review was not within the jurisdiction of the Panel under Article 21.5 of the DSU.[51]

B. Arguments of Canada – Appellee

30. Canada requests the Appellate Body to reject the United States' appeal and uphold the relevant findings and conclusions of the Panel with respect to the First Assessment Review. Canada observes that the USDOC, in its Section 129 Determination, completed a limited pass-through analysis but "refused to exam-

---

48 United States' appellant's submission, para. 52.

49 *Ibid.*, para. 59.

50 *Ibid.*, para. 6.

51 United States' Notice of Appeal, WT/DS257/22 (attached as Annex I to this Report), paras. 2-5.

ine the vast majority of [the] transactions" between unrelated parties, "claiming they were not 'arm's length' transactions".[52] Canada alleges that, in the First Assessment Review, the USDOC completed no pass-through analysis and, therefore, no adjustment was made to the countervailing duty rate, notwithstanding the recommendations and rulings of the DSB and the limited pass-through analysis in the Section 129 Determination issued one week earlier. Canada emphasizes that the final countervailing duty rate established in the First Assessment Review applied *retrospectively* to import entries that were initially subject to the original countervailing duty rate established in the Final Countervailing Duty Determination. At the same time, the rate resulting from the First Assessment Review replaced *prospectively* the duty rate that had been revised by the Section 129 Determination. The First Assessment Review thus established a countervailing duty rate in the form of a cash deposit rate that reflected no pass-through analysis, but which superseded and replaced the rate determined in the Section 129 Determination. In this way, the First Assessment Review "effectively undid" any compliance purportedly achieved through the Section 129 Determination.[53]

31. Canada agrees with the Panel's interpretation and application of Article 21.5 of the DSU. In Canada's view, an Article 21.5 panel has jurisdiction to examine all measures that a WTO Member declares to be "measures taken to comply", but adds that this jurisdiction also extends to other measures taken by the Member that affect its compliance with the recommendations and rulings of the DSB. Measures affect compliance—and are, therefore, "measures taken to comply" under Article 21.5 of the DSU—if they affect the "existence" or "consistency" of measures that are declared to be taken to comply, that is, if they undermine or nullify the purported compliance. Canada asserts that an Article 21.5 panel cannot properly assess the effect of measures that are declared to be "measures taken to comply" unless it also reviews other measures that affect those expressly taken to comply. Canada submits that accepting the United States' arguments in this appeal would mean that in examining compliance under Article 21.5 of the DSU, the Panel could have reviewed only a measure that no longer applies—the Section 129 Determination—but could not have considered the First Assessment Review, which replaced and effectively undid the measure that had been taken to comply.

32. According to Canada, an Article 21.5 panel must examine fully the application and effect of all relevant measures, including the legal and factual setting in which they operate, in order to make findings on the "existence" of a measure taken to comply, or its "consistency with a covered agreement". This interpretation is consistent with the context in which the term "measures taken to comply" is used. Furthermore, the object and purpose of the DSU, as reflected in Articles 3.3, 3.7, and 21.1 of that Agreement, may be achieved only through a comprehensive review of measures that affect the "existence" or "consistency" of measures declared to be taken to comply.

---

52 Canada's appellee's submission, para. 17.

53 *Ibid.*, para. 2.

33. Canada argues that the United States' appeal ignores the overlapping effects of its measures. Canada asserts that the First Assessment Review affects the "existence" and "consistency" of the Section 129 Determination for two reasons: first, because the subject-matter of the dispute—that is, the obligation to examine "pass-through" of alleged stumpage subsidies—arises in both the Section 129 Determination and the First Assessment Review; and, secondly, because the Final Countervailing Duty Determination, the Section 129 Determination, and the First Assessment Review have significantly overlapping effects, particularly in respect of the cash deposit rate. Canada emphasizes that the application and the effect of the First Assessment Review undid any compliance that might have resulted from the Section 129 Determination. Thus, after a limited pass-through analysis, the Section 129 Determination replaced the cash deposit rate under the Final Countervailing Duty Determination, which was based on no pass-through analysis at all. However, this revised cash deposit rate of the Section 129 Determination was then replaced, a mere ten days later, by the results of the First Assessment Review, which—like the original measure—contained no pass-through analysis at all.

34. Canada supports the Panel's finding that the First Assessment Review "was 'clearly connected to the panel and Appellate Body reports concerning the Final [Countervailing Duty] Determination' and 'inextricably linked to the treatment of pass-through in the Section 129 Determination.'"[54] In this context, Canada believes that the Panel relied on and correctly applied earlier jurisprudence on Article 21.5 of the DSU. Both the *Australia – Salmon (Article 21.5 – Canada)* and the *EC – Bed Linen (Article 21.5 – India)* panels found that barring an Article 21.5 panel from examining measures that have a clear connection to the original panel and Appellate Body reports would lead to "unreasonable or absurd results".[55] Furthermore, Canada understands the Appellate Body in *Canada – Aircraft (Article 21.5 – Brazil)* to have emphasized that an Article 21.5 panel may examine not only how the measures of a Member purport to achieve compliance, but also how they "*ought to have achieved* compliance".[56]

35. According to Canada, much of the United States' argument hinges on the distinction it draws between original investigations and assessment reviews within the United States' retrospective duty assessment system. However, the United States' description of its regime omits important points. In the view of the United States, an original determination establishes the basis for a countervailing duty, and an assessment review establishes the actual amount of duties to be levied. Canada points out, however, that the final results of an assessment review both replace the estimated duties collected for entries that occurred during the review period and establish the new estimated countervailing duty rate in the form of cash deposits. Furthermore, both the original investigation and the assessment review entail a substantive and "essentially the same"[57] analysis to de-

---

[54] Canada's appellee's submission, para. 38 (quoting Panel Report, para. 4.41).

[55] *Ibid.*, para. 26.

[56] Canada's appellee's submission, para. 28 (original emphasis) (referring to Appellate Body Report, *Canada – Aircraft (Article 21.5 – Brazil)*, para. 36).

[57] Comments of Canada on United States' additional written memorandum, para. 3.

termine whether, and to what extent, the imports were subsidized. This includes at each stage the legal obligation to examine whether a benefit was passed through. Canada notes that it is "routine practice" for the USDOC to incorporate into the administrative record of an assessment review "much, and sometimes all", of the record of the original investigation in the same proceedings.[58]

36. Canada dismisses as irrelevant the United States' argument that the recommendations and rulings of the DSB did not require the United States to conduct an assessment review because, had the First Assessment Review not been conducted, the Section 129 Determination would still be in effect and duties would be collected at the rate established in that determination. Canada further supports the finding of the Panel that it is not the timing of the *initiation* of an assessment review that is important, but, rather, the application and effects of the *results* of this review. The results of the First Assessment Review in the present case were issued about ten months after the adoption of the recommendations and rulings of the DSB.

37. Canada also considers "disingenuous" the United States' arguments with respect to the Panel's "misinterpretation" of the SAA.[59] As evidence of the linkage between assessment reviews and original countervailing duty investigations, the Panel noted that United States law allows DSB recommendations and rulings to be implemented through assessment reviews in certain circumstances. That the circumstances described in the SAA may be limited to cases where a USDOC methodology is at issue, rather than where the basis for the underlying definitive countervailing duty order is at issue, does not mean that implementation in an assessment review is restricted to cases not involving investigation final determinations, as the United States suggests. Nor does the Panel's observation mean, as the United States intimates, that all DSB recommendations and rulings arising from final countervailing duty determinations could be implemented in an assessment review. Indeed, the SAA makes clear that, DSB recommendations and rulings that can only be implemented by revocation of the order would have to be implemented through a Section 129 determination rather than an assessment review. Accordingly, none of the United States' arguments discounts the Panel's observations with respect to the SAA.

38. Canada rejects the United States' argument that the overlapping effects identified by the Panel "are nothing more than the natural consequence of the U.S. system of retrospective assessment".[60] Canada believes that such overlapping effects can also occur in prospective duty systems because a Member's compliance obligations must be factored into subsequent proceedings affecting the countervailing duties (such as reviews or duty refund procedures) when such proceedings come within the scope of Article 21.5 of the DSU. In any event, a potential distinction between a retrospective duty assessment system and a pro-

---

58 *Ibid.*, para. 5.

59 Canada's appellee's submission, para. 51.

60 Canada's appellee's submission, para. 44 (quoting United States' appellant's submission, para. 37).

spective duty system is irrelevant to the United States' obligation to comply with the recommendations and rulings of the DSB.

39. Canada disagrees with the United States regarding the significance of qualitative differences between final determinations and assessment reviews. Such differences do not require the exclusion of the First Assessment Review from the mandate of the Panel in this dispute. Canada maintains that the United States ignores the fact that a final countervailing duty determination involves both the "imposition" and the "levying" of definitive duties. The United States does not deny that the "collection" of definitive countervailing duties includes the collection of cash deposits following a final countervailing duty determination. However, the United States mischaracterizes the meaning of "levy" under the relevant provisions of the GATT 1994 and the *SCM Agreement*. According to Canada, footnote 51 to Article 19 of the *SCM Agreement* confirms that the term "levy" encompasses both the assessment and the "collection" of countervailing duties. Furthermore, Article 10 and footnote 36 thereto of the *SCM Agreement* define the term "countervailing duty" to mean "a special duty *levied* for the purpose of offsetting any subsidy". (emphasis added) Canada asserts that even if the United States is correct in arguing that the "levying" of definitive duties occurs only pursuant to an assessment review, this would not mean that the First Assessment Review would be excluded from the Article 21.5 proceedings in this case. Canada adds that the assessment of definitive duties is a "specific action" contemplated under Article 32.1 of the *SCM Agreement* and, therefore, is encompassed by the recommendations and rulings of the DSB that apply to "specific actions" under Article 32.1 of that Agreement.

40. Finally, Canada submits that the United States' position as to the scope of Article 21.5 proceedings is inconsistent with the object and purpose of the DSU—that is, the prompt settlement of disputes. Canada argues that, if the United States' position in the appeal were upheld, Canada would be forced to initiate new proceedings in respect of each annual assessment review and could never secure compliance with the recommendations and rulings of the DSB before the measure at issue would be superseded by the results of a new assessment review. To avoid these "absurd consequences"[61], the jurisdiction of an Article 21.5 panel must be interpreted to allow for a comprehensive review of all measures affecting the "existence" or "consistency" of measures declared to be taken to comply.

C. Arguments of the Third Participants

1. China

41. China supports the position of the Panel that the First Assessment Review fell within the scope of review under Article 21.5 of the DSU. China submits that the word "existence" in Article 21.5 suggests that a "measure taken to comply" must remain in place and in effect, and must not be nullified, invalidated, or ren-

[61] Canada's statement at the oral hearing.

dered non-existent by other measures. Existence requires a lasting effect of the measure in place, which is more than the simple adoption of a single measure. In China's view, the adoption of additional measures, where these could invalidate the first measure, must be taken into account by an Article 21.5 panel in determining the existence of "measures taken to comply". On this basis, China believes that the Panel had jurisdiction to examine the First Assessment Review, which effectively invalidated the Section 129 Determination by establishing a new cash deposit rate. China asserts that acceptance of the United States' view—according to which a new case would have to be brought against new measures, because such measures may not be included in Article 21.5 proceedings—would run counter to the object and purpose of the DSU, which is the prompt settlement of disputes. If Members were allowed to replace, at their discretion and convenience, measures taken to comply, the object and purpose of the DSU could not be achieved.

42. Like the Panel, China believes that the First Assessment Review is "clearly connected" to the recommendations and rulings of the DSB and is "inextricably linked" to, and has an important effect on, the "existence" of the "measure taken to comply"—that is, the Section 129 Determination.[62] Unlike the United States, China does not see "qualitative differences" between the original investigation and the First Assessment Review: both proceedings calculated the amount of the subsidy that, in turn, was the basis for fixing the amount of the countervailing duties to be levied.[63] China also supports the Panel's findings with regard to the "considerable overlap" in the prospective effects of the Section 129 Determination and the First Assessment Review regarding the determination of the cash deposit rate for future imports.

43. China does not support the argument of the United States that the First Assessment Review cannot be a "measure taken to comply" because it was initiated before the recommendations and rulings of the DSB. China asserts that what should be taken into consideration is the time when the First Assessment Review came into effect, not when it was initiated. China also disagrees with the view of the United States that the present situation may be distinguished from *Australia – Automotive Leather II (Article 21.5 – US)* on the grounds that, in that case, the loan was contingent upon repayment of the subsidy identified in the original proceedings. The test in that case was not one of "contingency"; rather, the panel considered whether the measures were "inextricably linked". In this case, the Panel was correct to find an "inextricable link" between the Section 129 Determination and the First Assessment Review. Nor does China support the United States' view that the facts outlined in the panel report in *EC – Bed Linen (Article 21.5 – India)* are parallel to the present case, because the First Assessment Review was not a result of events subsequent to the adoption of a compliance measure, as was the case in that dispute.

[62] China's third participant's submission, para. 12.
[63] China's third participant's submission, paras. 21-22.

2. *European Communities*

44. Although the European Communities supports generally the conclusions of the Panel, it "regrets" the limited reasoning of the Panel.[64] The European Communities requests the Appellate Body to dismiss the United States' appeal, and also to modify the Panel's reasoning, taking account of the following observations made by the European Communities.

45. The European Communities asserts that the United States' arguments in this appeal are "entirely misconceived" and that "(if accepted) [they] would not only be contrary to Article 21.5 of the DSU, but also turn the US system of countervailing duty assessment into a moving target that escapes the WTO disciplines."[65] In the view of the European Communities, the role of an Article 21.5 panel is different from the role of an original panel. Whilst the task of an original panel is to solve a dispute relating to a particular specified measure, an Article 21.5 panel has the task of assessing whether or not the original dispute has been resolved. For that reason, an Article 21.5 panel has a broad mandate to determine whether a WTO Member has implemented fully its compliance obligations. These compliance obligations endure until full compliance is achieved.

46. The European Communities argues that Article 21.5 panels, in principle, have jurisdiction with respect to all factual and legal matters relating to the resolution of the original dispute. Measures initiated before the recommendations and rulings of the DSB do not necessarily fall outside the jurisdiction of the Article 21.5 panel. Indeed, the mandate of an Article 21.5 panel is not confined to the examination of only those measures that explicitly or deliberately relate to the measures found to be WTO-inconsistent in the original proceedings. A broad mandate to determine whether a Member has fully implemented its compliance obligations is consistent with the special rules for Article 21.5 proceedings, notably, recourse in most cases to the original panel as well as expedited timeframes. The purpose of Article 21.5 proceedings is to deal with any further dispute that relates to the original dispute with a view to delivering "swift justice".[66] This view is further corroborated by the terms "existence" of "measures taken to comply" in Article 21.5 of the DSU, which imply that situations of a complete failure of compliance also fall within the mandate of an Article 21.5 panel.

47. The European Communities argues that the existence of the requisite relationship between original measures and measures taken to comply must be decided on a substantive, rather than a formal, basis. The European Communities argues that the United States errs in its view regarding the delineation of measures challenged in countervailing duty cases. The measure to be reviewed by this Article 21.5 Panel is not a discrete determination, but, rather, the "continued application of a *countervailing duty* on the basis of the administrative review (superseding both the original determination and the Section 129 review)".[67] This is because it is the duty itself that interferes with trade and is the measure of con-

---

64 European Communities' third participant's submission, para. 8.

65 *Ibid.*

66 European Communities' third participant's submission, para. 23.

67 *Ibid.* para. 9. (original emphasis)

cern. It is not, as the United States argues, the determination made by an investigating authority. Therefore, independently of the retrospective or prospective nature of the duty assessment system at issue, the question should be whether an interim or changed circumstances review relates to the same countervailing duty imposed on the same product for the same purpose. It must be assessed on a case-by-case basis whether a particular countervailing duty based on, or concerning the same product and purpose as, the original countervailing duty continues to exist. If so, a complaining Member may have recourse to an Article 21.5 panel. The European Communities argues that, otherwise, Members could escape their WTO obligations by formally terminating a measure and then re-adopting it.

III. ISSUES RAISED IN THIS APPEAL

48. The following issues are raised in this appeal:

(a) whether the Panel erred in finding that the First Assessment Review falls within the scope of the present Article 21.5 proceedings, insofar as the pass-through analysis is concerned[68]; and

(b) whether, as a result of the above legal finding, the Panel also erred in making the following findings regarding the pass-through analysis in the First Assessment Review[69]:

(i) that, in the treatment of pass-through in the First Assessment Review, the United States failed to implement properly the recommendations and rulings of the Dispute Settlement Body (the "DSB") by failing to conduct a pass-through analysis in respect of sales, found by the United States Department of Commerce (the "USDOC") not to be at arm's length, of logs by tenured timber harvesters, whether or not they also produce lumber, to unrelated timber producers, whether or not they hold a stumpage contract[70];

(ii) that, in the First Assessment Review, the United States included in its subsidy numerator transactions for which it had not demonstrated that the benefit of subsidized log inputs had passed through to the processed product[71];

(iii) that, with respect to the First Assessment Review, the United States remains in violation of Articles 10 and 32.1 of the *Agreement on Subsidies and Countervailing Meas-*

---

68 Panel Report, paras. 4.41, 4.50 and 5.1.

69 We understand that the United States challenges all of the Panel findings identified in its Notice of Appeal on the same basis, namely, that the First Assessment Review could not be examined by a panel acting pursuant to Article 21.5 of the DSU. (See *infra* para. 94)

70 Panel Report, para. 5.2.

71 *Ibid.*

ures (the "*SCM Agreement*") and Article VI:3 of the *General Agreement on Tariffs and Trade 1994* (the "GATT 1994")[72]; and

(iv) that, with respect to the First Assessment Review, the United States has nullified or impaired benefits accruing to Canada under the *SCM Agreement* and the GATT 1994.[73]

IV. SCOPE OF ARTICLE 21.5 OF THE DSU

A. Background and Procedural History

49. In the original *US – Softwood Lumber IV* proceedings, Canada challenged the final determination by the USDOC that led to the imposition of countervailing duties on softwood lumber from Canada (the "Final Countervailing Duty Determination").[74] Canada made a number of claims in respect of the USDOC's findings as to the existence and amount of the "benefit" element of the relevant subsidies, including that the USDOC had failed to conduct a "pass-through" analysis. The original panel described the pass-through issue as follows:

> The heart of the pass-through issue is whether, where a subsidy is received by someone other than the producer or exporter of the product under investigation, the subsidy nevertheless can be said to have conferred benefits in respect of that product.[75]

50. In the original proceedings, Canada argued that, because the imported softwood lumber products subject to investigation were not the same as the upstream product (standing timber) in respect of which the alleged subsidies[76] were paid, the USDOC was required to establish, rather than presume, that any benefit

---

[72] *Ibid.*, para. 5.4.

[73] Panel Report, para. 5.5.

[74] "Notice of Final Affirmative Countervailing Duty Determination and Final Negative Critical Circumstances Determination: Certain Softwood Lumber Products from Canada", *United States Federal Register*, Vol. 67, No. 63 (2 April 2002), p. 15545, as amended, Vol. 67, No. 99 (22 May 2002), p. 36070 (Exhibit US-1 submitted by the United States to the Panel). The period of investigation for purposes of this proceeding was 1 April 2000 to 31 March 2001.

[75] Original Panel Report, para. 7.91. See also Panel Report, para. 4.65.

[76] Most notably, the so-called "stumpage" programmes. In Canada, "stumpage contracts" are the mechanism through which provincial governments provide timber harvesters with the right to harvest standing timber on Crown land. The original panel described certain characteristics of the various stumpage programmes run by the Canadian provincial governments as follows:

> [T]he provinces own the forests and the trees that grow in them. The only way for harvesters to obtain the trees standing on government-owned Crown land for harvesting and processing is by concluding stumpage agreements (tenures or licences) with the governments concerning these trees. The only way for the government to provide the standing timber that it owns to the harvesters and the mills for processing is by allowing the harvesters to come on the land and harvest the trees. Such legal rights and obligations are transferred through the stumpage agreements. It is thus through the stumpage agreements that the governments provide the standing timber to the harvesters.

(Original Panel Report, para. 7.15) (footnotes omitted)

received by the harvesters of standing timber passed through to the producers of the downstream softwood lumber products subject to investigation. Ultimately, the original panel and the Appellate Body found that the USDOC's calculation of the benefit was inconsistent with the United States' obligations under the covered agreements, due to the failure of the USDOC to complete a pass-through analysis with respect to two categories of transactions.[77]

51. Following the DSB's adoption on 17 February 2004 of the original panel and Appellate Body reports, the United States and Canada agreed on a reasonable period of time for implementation that would expire on 17 December 2004.[78] In response to the DSB's recommendations and rulings, the United States initiated a proceeding pursuant to Section 129 of the Uruguay Round Agreements Act ("Section 129")[79] and, on 16 December 2004, the USDOC published a determination pursuant to that provision (the "Section 129 Determination").[80] In this determination, the USDOC sought to bring the Final Countervailing Duty Determination into conformity with the recommendations and rulings of the DSB by completing a pass-through analysis in respect of certain transactions. This pass-through analysis resulted in a small reduction of the countervailing duty rate that had been calculated in the Final Countervailing Duty Determina-

---

77 The first such category was where a harvester of subsidized logs, that did not itself own a sawmill, sold logs to a producer of softwood lumber. The second was where a harvester of subsidized logs, that did own a sawmill, sold logs to a different producer of softwood lumber. (See also the summary of the findings of the original panel and the Appellate Body at para. 4.59 of the Panel Report.)

78 WT/DS257/13.

79 Section 129 (*supra*, footnote 9) is entitled "Administrative action following WTO panel reports" and provides, in relevant part:

> (b) Action by Administering Authority.—
>
> (1) Consultations with Administering Authority and Congressional Committees— Promptly after a report by a dispute settlement panel or the Appellate Body is issued that contains findings that an action by the administering authority in a proceeding under title VII of the Tariff Act of 1930 is not in conformity with the obligations of the United States under the Antidumping Agreement or the Agreement on Subsidies and Countervailing Measures, the Trade Representative shall consult with the administering authority and the congressional committees on the matter.
>
> (2) Determination by Administering Authority— Notwithstanding any provision of the Tariff Act of 1930, the administering authority shall, within 180 days after receipt of a written request from the Trade Representative, issue a determination in connection with the particular proceeding that would render the administering authority's action described in paragraph (1) not inconsistent with the findings of the panel or the Appellate Body.
>
> (3) Consultations before Implementation— Before the administering authority implements any determination under paragraph (2), the Trade Representative shall consult with the administering authority and the congressional committees with respect to such determination.
>
> (4) Implementation of Determination— The Trade Representative may, after consulting with the administering authority and the congressional committees under paragraph (3), direct the administering authority to implement, in whole or in part, the determination made under paragraph (2).

80 *Supra*, footnote 10.

tion.[81] The rate of subsidization established in the Section 129 Determination became the cash deposit rate (estimated duty rate) applied to softwood lumber entries as from 10 December 2004.[82] At the DSB meeting held on 17 December 2004, the United States informed the DSB that it had complied with the recommendations and rulings of the DSB in the *US – Softwood Lumber IV* dispute.[83]

52. Three days later, on 20 December 2004, the USDOC published the final results of the first administrative review on imports of softwood lumber from Canada (the "First Assessment Review")[84], which established final countervailing duty liability for imports of softwood lumber that entered the United States during the period 22 May 2002 to 31 March 2003. In that review, the USDOC adopted the same pass-through methodology as it had used in the Section 129 Determination.[85] However, the USDOC's application of this methodology in the First Assessment Review did not, in the light of the evidence before it, result in any reduction to its calculated rate of subsidization.[86] In addition to establishing final duty liability for imports that entered the United States during the period of review, the results of the First Assessment Review also fixed the estimated countervailing duty rate (the cash deposit rate) for imports entering the United States as from 20 December 2004.

---

[81] The final countervailing duty rate that resulted from the Final Countervailing Duty Determination was 18.79 per cent, once corrected for ministerial errors. The Section 129 Determination reduced the rate to 18.62 per cent.

[82] Section 129(c) (*supra*, footnote 9) establishes the effective date for determinations made pursuant to that provision as follows:

> (c) Effects of Determinations; Notice of Implementation—
>
> (1) Effects of Determinations— Determinations concerning title VII of the Tariff Act of 1930 that are implemented under this section shall apply with respect to unliquidated entries of the subject merchandise (as defined in section 771 of that Act) that are entered, or withdrawn from warehouse, for consumption on or after—
>
> ...
>
> (B) in the case of a determination by the administering authority under subsection (b)(2), the date on which the Trade Representative directs the administering authority under subsection (b)(4) to implement that determination.

[83] WT/DSB/M/180, paras. 22-25.

[84] *Supra*, footnote 12.

[85] Panel Report, footnote 50 to para. 4.58. See also United States' additional written memorandum, para. 12.

[86] The USDOC determined in the First Assessment Review that the five Canadian provinces claiming that it was necessary to conduct a pass-through analysis in respect of transactions occurring during the relevant period of review had "each failed to substantiate its claim that logs entering sawmills during the [period of review] included logs purchased in arm's length transactions." (USDOC Memorandum from B. Tillman to J. Jochum "Issues and Decision Memorandum: Final Results of Administrative Review: Certain Softwood Lumber Products from Canada" (13 December 2004) (Exhibit CDA-11 submitted by Canada to the Panel), section II.F) In the First Assessment Review, the USDOC calculated a rate of subsidization of 17.18 per cent *ad valorem* based on data from the period of review of 22 May 2002 to 31 March 2003. At the oral hearing in this appeal, the United States explained that this rate was subsequently reduced to 16.37 per cent to correct ministerial errors. (See "Notice of Amended Final Results of Countervailing Duty Administrative Review: Certain Softwood Lumber Products from Canada", *United States Federal Register*, Vol. 70, No. 36 (24 February 2005), p. 9046)

53. For ease of reference, we set out the relevant sequence of events in the following chart:

22 May 2002	The USDOC publishes the Final Countervailing Duty Determination in respect of softwood lumber from Canada.*
17 February 2004	The DSB adopts the reports of the panel and the Appellate Body in *US – Softwood Lumber IV*.
16 December 2004	The USDOC publishes the notice of implementation of the Section 129 Determination.† The Section 129 Determination applies to softwood lumber entries on or after 10 December 2004.
17 December 2004	The agreed "reasonable period of time" to implement the DSB's recommendations and rulings in *US – Softwood Lumber IV* expires.
20 December 2004	The USDOC publishes the final results of the First Assessment Review.± The cash deposit rate that resulted from the First Assessment Review applies to softwood lumber entries on or after 20 December 2004.

* *The period of investigation preceding the imposition of countervailing duties was 1 April 2000–31 March 2001.*

† *Because the Section 129 Determination revised the Final Countervailing Duty Determination, it examined data relating to the original period of investigation from 1 April 2000–31 March 2001.*

± *The period of review for purposes of the First Assessment Review was 22 May 2002–31 March 2003.*

54. In its request for recourse to a panel under Article 21.5 of the *Understanding on Rules and Procedures Governing the Settlement of Disputes* (the "DSU"), Canada made claims that both the Section 129 Determination and the First Assessment Review were inconsistent with the United States' obligations under the covered agreements.[87] In the proceedings before the Panel, the United States argued that the pass-through analysis conducted in the Section 129 Determination was consistent with its obligations under the covered agreements. The United States also argued that the First Assessment Review was not a measure taken to comply with the recommendations and rulings of the DSB in this dispute and did not, therefore, fall within the scope of the Panel's jurisdiction under Article 21.5 of the DSU. The United States did not, in its arguments to the Panel, respond to Canada's claims regarding the consistency of the First Assessment Review; in particular, it did not engage in a substantive defence of the pass-through analysis conducted by the USDOC in the First Assessment Review.[88] Instead, the essence of the United States' argument was that the Panel lacked jurisdiction to consider those claims.

55. The Panel found that it could examine the pass-through analysis in the First Assessment Review, and that, due to deficiencies in both pass-through analyses conducted by the USDOC, the United States had failed, in both the Section 129 Determination and the First Assessment Review, to demonstrate that

[87] WT/DS257/15.

[88] Panel Report, paras. 4.96, 4.105-4.106, and footnote 50 to para. 4.58.

"the benefit of subsidized log inputs had passed through to the processed product".[89] The United States does not appeal the Panel's findings with respect to the Section 129 Determination. Nor does the United States ask us to review the *substance* of the Panel's findings with respect to the First Assessment Review. Instead, as explained below, the principal issue on appeal is whether the Panel had jurisdiction to review the results of the First Assessment Review in these proceedings under Article 21.5 of the DSU.

B. Introduction to the Principal Issue on Appeal

56. On 10 March 2005, the United States submitted a request for a preliminary ruling to the Panel, along with its first written submission. The United States claimed that the results of the First Assessment Review fell "outside the scope of Article 21.5, and this Panel lack[ed] jurisdiction to review them".[90] Accordingly, the United States asked the Panel to make a preliminary ruling that:

> ... the final results of the first assessment review of the countervailing duty order on softwood lumber from Canada, cited by Canada in its request for the establishment of a panel in this dispute, are not "measures taken to comply" with the recommendations and rulings of the DSB under Article 21.5 of the DSU.[91] (footnote omitted)

57. On 16 March 2005, the Panel invited Canada to comment on this request in its second written submission to the Panel, due on 31 March 2005.[92] In its second written submission, Canada asked the Panel to reject the United States' request for a preliminary ruling, and argued that the First Assessment Review was within the jurisdiction of the Panel under Article 21.5 of the DSU.[93] At the substantive meeting of the parties with the Panel, held on 21 April 2005, the Chairman of the Panel informed the parties that, for purposes of their submissions at that meeting, they "should assume that the first assessment review *does* fall within the scope of these proceedings", but added that such assumption was "without prejudice to the Panel's eventual ruling on this issue".[94]

58. In its Report, the Panel declined to make the ruling sought by the United States, and said as follows:

> [W]e reject the US request for a preliminary ruling that the First Assessment Review falls outside the scope of these DSU Article 21.5 proceedings, in so far as the pass-through analysis is concerned.[95]

---

89 *Ibid.*, para. 5.2.

90 United States' first written submission to the Panel, para. 12; Panel Report, p. B-4.

91 *Ibid.*

92 Letter from the Secretary to the Panel (on behalf of the Chairman of the Panel) to Canada, 16 March 2005.

93 Canada's second written submission to the Panel, paras. 3-5; Panel Report, p. A-35.

94 Statement by the Chairman of the Panel at the Substantive Meeting of the Panel with the Parties, 21 April 2005. (original emphasis)

95 Panel Report, para. 4.50. See also para. 5.1.

59. The United States appeals this ruling and requests the Appellate Body to find that the Panel erred in concluding that the First Assessment Review fell within the scope of its mandate, insofar as the pass-through analysis is concerned. For the same reasons, the United States also requests the Appellate Body to reverse the Panel's findings of inconsistency with respect to the First Assessment Review.[96]

60. The United States alleges that, in its interpretation of Article 21.5, the Panel adopted an unduly broad standard that is not supported by a proper analysis of text, context, and object and purpose of Article 21.5, and that is not consistent with previous panel and Appellate Body reports. The United States points out that the recommendations and rulings of the DSB in the original dispute related solely to the USDOC's failure to analyze pass-through in the original countervailing duty investigation, and that these recommendations and rulings were implemented in the Section 129 Determination, *not* the First Assessment Review. The United States points out the fundamental differences between investigations and assessment reviews, emphasizing that these differences, along with the distinct nature and purpose of assessment reviews, make clear that such reviews cannot be "measures taken to comply" with recommendations and rulings relating to an original countervailing duty determination. The United States further contends that the Panel's ruling is "unfairly prejudicial" because it compelled the United States to defend its actions in an assessment review—an "entirely separate" proceeding from the original countervailing duty investigation, with a "wholly different" administrative record—for the first time under the expedited time-frames of an Article 21.5 review.[97]

C. The Scope of Proceedings under Article 21.5 of the DSU

61. The principal issue in this appeal concerns the scope of proceedings under Article 21.5 of the DSU. Specifically, we must consider whether and to what extent a panel acting pursuant to Article 21.5 of the DSU may assess a measure that the implementing Member maintains is *not* "taken to comply", when the complaining Member nevertheless identifies that measure in its request for recourse to an Article 21.5 panel and raises claims against it.

62. The United States points to the express limitation on the category of measures that may be subject to review in Article 21.5 proceedings, namely "measures taken to comply with the recommendations and rulings of the DSB". The United States emphasizes that Article 21.5 neither directs nor authorizes panels to examine any "connected" measures that "could have an impact on", or "possibly undermine", the measures taken to comply.[98] Canada asserts that even measures not declared by Members as "taken to comply" may nevertheless be reviewed by an Article 21.5 panel when they affect the "existence" or "consistency" of measures that *are* declared to be "taken to comply". For Canada, such

96 See *supra*, para. 48(b).
97 United States' appellant's submission, para. 6.
98 *Ibid.*, para. 33 (referring to Panel Report, para. 4.41).

"undeclared measures are also 'measures taken to comply' for purposes of Article 21.5", in particular, when they "undermine or undo purported compliance with DSB recommendations and rulings."[99]

1. Text, Context, Object and Purpose

63. We begin by setting out the full text of Article 21.5:

> Where there is disagreement as to the existence or consistency with a covered agreement of measures taken to comply with the recommendations and rulings such dispute shall be decided through recourse to these dispute settlement procedures, including wherever possible resort to the original panel. The panel shall circulate its report within 90 days after the date of referral of the matter to it. When the panel considers that it cannot provide its report within this time frame, it shall inform the DSB in writing of the reasons for the delay together with an estimate of the period within which it will submit its report.

64. The first sentence of Article 21.5 is of most relevance to the question before us. It identifies the types of disputes ("disagreement as to the existence or consistency with a covered agreement of measures") covered by that provision, and the procedures that are to be employed ("these dispute settlement procedures") in resolving them. With respect to the subject matter of Article 21.5 proceedings, "the 'matter' in Article 21.5 proceedings consists of two elements: the specific *measures* at issue and the legal basis of the complaint (that is, the *claims*)."[100] As we have stated, we are called upon in this appeal to consider the *measures* that may be evaluated by a panel acting pursuant to Article 21.5.

65. The words of Article 21.5 themselves delimit a particular category of measures that fall within the scope of proceedings conducted pursuant to that provision, as was recognized by the Appellate Body in *Canada – Aircraft (Article 21.5 – Brazil)*:

> Proceedings under Article 21.5 do not concern just *any* measure of a Member of the WTO; rather, Article 21.5 proceedings are limited to those "measures *taken to comply* with the recommendations and rulings" of the DSB.[101] (original emphasis)

66. In examining the meaning of "measures taken to comply" in Article 21.5, we begin with the word "taken". There is a wide range of dictionary meanings of the word "taken", which is the past participle of the verb "take". The meanings of "take" include, for example, "[b]ring into a specified position or relation";

---

[99] Canada's appellee's submission, para. 5.

[100] Appellate Body Report, *EC – Bed Linen (Article 21.5 – India)*, para. 78. (original emphasis)

[101] Appellate Body Report, *Canada – Aircraft (Article 21.5 – Brazil)*, para. 36.

"[s]elect or use for a particular purpose."[102] The preposition "to" is "[u]sed in verbs ... in the sense of 'motion, direction, or addition to', or as the mark of the infinitive."[103] As the United States points out, the word "comply" is defined as "accommodate oneself to (a person, circumstances, customs, etc.) ... Act in accordance with or *with* a request, command, etc."[104] The French and, in particular, Spanish versions of this phrase ("mesures prises pour se conformer" and "medidas destinadas a cumplir", respectively) also imply that relevant measures are associated with the objective of complying. On its face, therefore, the phrase "measures taken to comply" seems to refer to measures taken *in the direction of*, or *for the purpose of achieving*, compliance.

67. By virtue of the remainder of its first sentence, it is also clear that the scope of Article 21.5 encompasses any "disagreement as to the existence or consistency with a covered agreement of measures taken to comply". Canada, as well as the third participants, assert that the words "existence or consistency" are key to understanding the scope of a panel's jurisdiction under Article 21.5.[105] In order to make an assessment of the "existence or consistency" of "measures taken to comply", it seems to us that a panel must be able to assess measures taken to comply in their full context, including how such measures are introduced into, and how they function within, the particular system of the implementing Member. The word "existence" suggests that measures falling within the scope of Article 21.5 encompass not only positive acts, but also *omissions*. It also suggests that, as part of its assessment of whether a measure taken to comply *exists*, a panel may need to take account of facts and circumstances that impact or affect such existence. The word "consistency" implies that panels acting pursuant to Article 21.5 must objectively assess whether new measures are, in fact, consistent with relevant obligations under the covered agreements. As the Appellate Body has already stated, such an evaluation involves consideration of "that new measure in its totality" and the "fulfilment of this task requires that a panel consider both the measure itself and the measure's application."[106] The fact that Article 21.5 mandates a panel to assess "existence" and "consistency"

---

[102] *Shorter Oxford English Dictionary*, 5th edn, W.R. Trumble, A. Stevenson (eds) (Oxford University Press, 2002), Vol. 2, p. 3170.

[103] *Ibid.*, Vol. 2, p. 3284.

[104] United States' appellant's submission, para. 30 (quoting *The New Shorter Oxford English Dictionary*, *supra*, footnote 37, p. 461 (original italics) (Exhibit US-15 submitted by the United States to the Panel)).

[105] Canada argues that "[o]nly through a comprehensive review of measures that affect the 'existence' or 'consistency' of measures declared to be taken to comply can an Article 21.5 proceeding contribute to the prompt settlement of disputes and fulfil the aim of the dispute settlement mechanism." (Canada's appellee's submission, para. 31) China, for its part, argues that "the existence of a measure requires the state of being or continuance in being of the subject measure, and to maintain such a state of being, there should not be any other measure that would in effect nullify or invalidate such measure." (China's third participant's submission, para. 7) The European Communities submits that "[t]he term 'existence' envisages a situation of failure to comply with the DSB's rulings and recommendations" and argues that it is "of fundamental importance that Article 21.5 panels have a broad mandate to determine whether or not the 'situation' after the expiry of the reasonable period of time for implementation is such that the Member concerned has fully implemented its compliance obligations." (European Communities' third participant's submission, paras. 18 and 20)

[106] Appellate Body Report, *US – Shrimp, (Article 21.5 – Malaysia)*, para. 87.

tends to weigh against an interpretation of Article 21.5 that would confine the scope of a panel's jurisdiction to measures that *move in the direction of*, or *have the objective of achieving*, compliance. These words also suggest that an examination of the effects of a measure may also be relevant to the determination of whether it constitutes, or forms part of, a "measure[] taken to comply".[107]

68. A further feature of the first sentence of Article 21.5 is the express link between the "measures taken to comply" and the recommendations and rulings of the DSB. Accordingly, determining the scope of "measures taken to comply" in any given case must also involve examination of the recommendations and rulings contained in the original report(s) adopted by the DSB. Because such recommendations and rulings are directed at the measures found to be inconsistent in the original proceedings[108], such an examination necessarily involves consideration of those original measures. Lastly, the end of the first sentence of Article 21.5 indicates that where there is disagreement regarding measures taken to comply, there should be recourse to the original panel "wherever possible", thus expressing a preference for dealing with these "disagreements" before the original panel that made the original recommendations and rulings in the dispute, rather than starting over again in new proceedings before a new panel.

69. Having thus considered the first sentence of Article 21.5, we note first that the phrase "measures taken to comply" does place some limits on the scope of proceedings under that provision—an issue that is not disputed. At the same time, in order to fulfil its mandate under Article 21.5, a panel must be able to take full account of the factual and legal background against which relevant measures are taken, so as to determine the existence, or consistency with the covered agreements, of measures taken to comply.

70. Article 21.5 is one paragraph within an Article entitled "Surveillance of Implementation of Recommendations and Rulings". As a whole, Article 21 deals with events *subsequent* to the DSB's adoption of recommendations and rulings in a particular dispute. The various paragraphs of Article 21 make clear that following such recommendations and rulings, further relevant developments and disagreements are to be dealt with through the reporting and surveillance modalities set out therein, and in such a way as to achieve "prompt resolution". Article 21 obliges an implementing Member to keep the DSB apprised of its intentions (paragraph 3) and ongoing efforts (paragraph 6) regarding implementation. At the same time, Article 21 sets out a number of mechanisms to ensure collective oversight of that Member's implementation. With respect to the determination of the reasonable period of time, these are found in Article 21.3, and with respect to measures taken to comply, they are found in Article 21.5. Thus, within Article 21

---

[107] Both participants agree that the effects of measures taken by an implementing Member can be relevant to determining whether or not that measure may be examined in proceedings under Article 21.5 of the DSU. (Participants' responses to questioning at the oral hearing)

[108] Article 19.1 of the DSU mandates the recommendations that panels and the Appellate Body are to make in the event of a finding that a measure is inconsistent with a covered agreement: they "shall recommend that the Member concerned bring the measure into conformity with that agreement." (footnotes omitted) Thus, the text of Article 19.1 confirms the link between the measure taken to comply and the inconsistent measure that was the subject of the original proceedings.

as a whole, the declarations of the implementing Member form an integral part of the surveillance of implementation, but they do not stand alone. Rather, they are complemented by, and subject to, multilateral review within the World Trade Organization (the "WTO").

71. Turning to the role played by Article 21.5 within the broader framework of the DSU, we note that there are key differences between proceedings under Article 21.5 of the DSU and "regular" panel proceedings. First, the composition of an Article 21.5 panel is, in principle, already determined—wherever possible, it is the original panel. These individuals will be familiar with the contours of the dispute, and the experience gained from the original proceedings should enable them to deal more efficiently with matters arising in an Article 21.5 proceeding "against the background of the original proceedings".[109] Secondly, the time-frames are shorter—an Article 21.5 panel has, in principle, 90 days in which to issue its report, as compared to the six to nine months afforded original panels. Thirdly, there are some limits on the claims that can be raised in Article 21.5 proceedings.[110] Yet, these limits should not allow circumvention by Members by allowing them to comply through one measure, while, at the same time, negating compliance through another.

72. Taken together, these observations underscore the balance that Article 21.5 strikes between competing considerations. On the one hand, it seeks to promote the prompt resolution of disputes, to avoid a complaining Member having to initiate dispute settlement proceedings afresh when an original measure found to be inconsistent has not been brought into conformity with the recommendations and rulings of the DSB, and to make efficient use of the original panel and its relevant experience. On the other hand, the applicable time-limits are shorter than those in original proceedings, and there are limitations on the types of claims that may be raised in Article 21.5 proceedings. This confirms that the scope of Article 21.5 proceedings logically must be narrower than the scope of original dispute settlement proceedings. This balance should be borne in mind in interpreting Article 21.5 and, in particular, in determining the measures that may be evaluated in proceedings pursuant to that provision.

---

[109] Appellate Body Report, *Mexico – Corn Syrup (Article 21.5 – US)*, para. 121.

[110] The Appellate Body has confirmed the existence of such limits in several cases. For example, in *US – Shrimp (Article 21.5 – Malaysia)*, the Appellate Body found that the panel had committed no error in refusing to "re-examine, for WTO-consistency, even those aspects of a new measure that were part of a previous measure that was the subject of a dispute, and were found by the Appellate Body to be *WTO-consistent* ... and that remain unchanged as part of the new measure." (Appellate Body Report, *US – Shrimp (Article 21.5 – Malaysia)*, para. 89 (original emphasis)) The Appellate Body has also found that a complaining party may not ask an Article 21.5 panel to re-examine certain matters ("the *particular* claim and the *specific* component of a measure that is the subject of that claim") when the original panel made findings in respect of these matters and those findings were not appealed. (Appellate Body Report, *EC – Bed Linen (Article 21.5 – India)*, para. 92-93) See also Appellate Body Report, *Mexico – Corn Syrup (Article 21.5 – US)*, paras. 121-122) However, when the measure taken to comply is a new measure, different from the measure at issue in the original proceedings, "a panel is not confined to examining the 'measures taken to comply' from the perspective of the claims, arguments and factual circumstances that related to the original measure". (Appellate Body Report, *Canada – Aircraft (Article 21.5 – Brazil)*, para. 41) See also the discussion in Appellate Body Report, *EC – Bed Linen (Article 21.5 – India)*, paras. 88-89.

2. *Examination of Previous Cases*

73. A number of previous proceedings have raised the issue of what measures fall within the scope of jurisdiction of a panel acting pursuant to Article 21.5. Panels and the Appellate Body alike have found that what is a "measure taken to comply" in a given case is not determined exclusively by the implementing Member. A Member's designation of a measure as one taken "to comply", or not, is relevant to this inquiry, but it cannot be conclusive.[111] Conversely, nor is it up to the complaining Member alone to determine what constitutes the measure taken to comply. It is rather for the Panel itself to determine the ambit of its jurisdiction.[112]

74. To be sure, characterizing an act by a Member as a measure taken to comply when that Member maintains otherwise is not something that should be done lightly by a panel. Yet, a panel, in examining the factual and legal circumstances within which the implementing Member takes action, may properly reach just such a finding in some cases. We regard the cases of *Australia – Salmon (Article 21.5 – Canada)* and *Australia – Automotive Leather II (Article 21.5 – US)* as useful illustrations of when such a finding is appropriate. In each of these cases, the panel examined a measure that the implementing Member maintained was not a measure taken to comply. At issue in *Australia – Salmon (Article 21.5 – Canada)* was whether the Article 21.5 panel could examine an import ban on salmon that had been adopted by the Australian state of Tasmania shortly after the Australian federal government had notified a number of steps that it had taken in order to remove the inconsistencies identified by the original panel regarding its treatment of imported salmon.[113] In reaching the conclusion that it could examine this ban, the panel looked at the *timing* of the ban, in particular, the fact that it was introduced "subsequent to the adoption on 6 November 1998 of DSB recommendations and rulings in the original dispute—and within a more or less limited period of time thereafter"[114]; as well as the *nature* of the ban, which was,

---

[111] In response to questioning at the oral hearing, both parties agreed that a Member's designation of the relevant measure taken to comply is relevant, but it is not dispositive of the issue of what measures may be considered by a panel acting pursuant to Article 21.5 of the DSU. If this were otherwise, an implementing Member would be able to avoid proceedings under Article 21.5 simply by deciding what measures to notify, or not to notify, to the DSB. (See Panel Report, *Australia – Automotive Leather II (Article 21.5 – US)*, para. 6.4)

[112] Appellate Body Report, *EC – Bed Linen (Article 21.5 – India)*, para. 78. See also Panel Report, *Australia – Automotive Leather II (Article 21.5 – US)*, para. 6.4; and Panel Report, *Australia – Salmon (Article 21.5 – Canada)*, para. 7.10, sub-para. 22.

[113] That panel observed that it could not merely allow an implementing Member to identify the relevant measure to be assessed in Article 21.5 proceedings because:

> ... an implementing Member could simply avoid any scrutiny of certain measures by a compliance panel, even where such measures would be *so clearly connected* to the panel and Appellate Body reports concerned, both in time and in respect of the subject-matter, that any impartial observer would consider them to be measures "taken to comply".

(Panel Report, *Australia – Salmon (Article 21.5 – Canada)*, para. 7.10, sub-para. 22) (emphasis added)

[114] *Ibid.*

like the measures challenged in the original proceedings, "a quarantine measure ... that applies to imports of fresh chilled or frozen salmon from Canada".[115]

75. In *Australia – Automotive Leather II (Article 21.5 – US)*, Australia withdrew from a company a grant that had been found to be a prohibited subsidy. At the same time, Australia granted a loan on non-commercial terms to a related company. The loan was specifically conditioned on repayment of the original subsidy. Although Australia argued that the loan was "not part of the implementation of the DSB's ruling and recommendation" and did not, therefore, fall within the scope of the Article 21.5 proceedings[116], the panel disagreed. It found that the loan fell within the scope of its terms of reference because, *inter alia*, the loan at issue was "inextricably linked" to the measure that Australia itself stated it had taken to comply, "in view of both its timing and its nature".[117]

76. The panel in *Australia – Automotive Leather II (Article 21.5 – US)* also explained that, to have excluded the new loan offered by Australia from its mandate, would have "severely limit[ed its] ability to judge, on the basis of the United States' request, whether Australia ha[d] taken measures to comply with the DSB's ruling."[118] Finally, we recall that, in *EC – Bed Linen (Article 21.5 – India)*, the Appellate Body upheld the panel's finding that certain parts of a measure may fall within the scope of Article 21.5 proceedings when other, separate elements of the same measure do not, and recognized that the ways in which distinct elements of a measure interact with and affect each other may be relevant to the determination of which of them falls within the scope of Article 21.5 proceedings.[119]

3. *Summary*

77. Taking account of all of the above, our interpretation of Article 21.5 of the DSU confirms that a panel's mandate under Article 21.5 of the DSU is not necessarily limited to an examination of an implementing Member's measure declared to be "taken to comply". Such a declaration will always be relevant, but there are additional criteria, identified above, that should be applied by a panel to determine whether or not it may also examine other measures. Some measures with a particularly close relationship to the declared "measure taken to comply", and to the recommendations and rulings of the DSB, may also be susceptible to review by a panel acting under Article 21.5. Determining whether this is the case requires a panel to scrutinize these relationships, which may, depending on the particular facts, call for an examination of the timing, nature, and effects of the various measures. This also requires an Article 21.5 panel to examine the factual and legal background against which a declared "measure taken to comply" is adopted. Only then is a panel in a position to take a view as to whether there are sufficiently close links for it to characterize such an other measure as one "taken

---

115 *Ibid.*

116 Panel Report, *Australia – Automotive Leather II (Article 21.5 – US)*, para. 6.1.

117 *Ibid.*, para. 6.5.

118 *Ibid.*

119 Appellate Body Report, *EC – Bed Linen (Article 21.5 – India)*, para. 86.

to comply" and, consequently, to assess its consistency with the covered agreements in an Article 21.5 proceeding.

4. *Review of the Panel's Approach*

78. Turning to examine the legal standard articulated by the Article 21.5 Panel in this case, we note that the Panel stated, first, that it would be "guided by dispute settlement decisions regarding the scope of DSU Article 21.5".[120] The Panel observed that "Article 21.5 proceedings are not restricted to measures formally, or explicitly, taken by Members to implement DSB rulings and recommendations."[121] The Panel then went on to examine the panel reports in *Australia – Salmon (Article 21.5 – Canada)* and *Australia – Automotive Leather II (Article 21.5 – US)*. The Panel observed that, in this case, there was no dispute that the Section 129 Determination fell within the scope of the Article 21.5 proceedings.[122] With respect to the First Assessment Review, the Panel's reasoning reveals that it employed the following two tests:

> [Whether] the USDOC's treatment of pass-through in the First Assessment Review is also covered by these proceedings, because it is *clearly connected* to the panel and Appellate Body reports concerning the Final [Countervailing Duty] Determination, and because it is *inextricably linked* to the treatment of pass-through in the Section 129 Determination.[123] (emphasis added)

and

> [Whether there was] sufficient overlap in the timing, or temporal effect, and nature of the Final [Countervailing Duty] Determination, Section 129 Determination and First Assessment Review for the latter to fall within the scope of the present DSU Article 21.5 proceedings.[124]

79. Accordingly, it is clear from the previous panel reports the Panel cited, and from the language it used ("clearly connected" and "inextricably linked"), that the Panel employed a nexus-based test similar to the ones articulated in *Australia – Automotive Leather II (Article 21.5 – US)* and *Australia – Salmon (Article 21.5 – Canada)* to determine whether the First Assessment Review fell within the scope of its jurisdiction. We see no error in the Panel's adoption of such a standard, which accords with our own interpretation of Article 21.5. Accordingly, in the next section, we consider whether the Panel erred in its *application* of this legal standard.

---

[120] Panel Report, para. 4.38.
[121] *Ibid.*
[122] *Ibid.*, para. 4.41.
[123] *Ibid.*
[124] *Ibid.*, para. 4.42.

D. The Panel's Application of Article 21.5 in this Case

80. In examining whether the Panel erred in finding that it had authority to review the pass-through analysis in the First Assessment Review, we recall the United States' arguments that the DSB recommendations and rulings were implemented in the Section 129 Determination, *not* the First Assessment Review, and that there are fundamental differences between investigations and assessment reviews. Further, the United States stresses that the First Assessment Review was initiated eight months before the recommendations and rulings of the DSB in this case and was governed by statutory provisions, timelines, and procedures that have nothing to do with those recommendations and rulings. Hence, according to the United States, the Panel erred in finding the First Assessment Review to be a "measure taken to comply" with the DSB recommendations and rulings in this dispute.

81. Turning to the Panel's application of Article 21.5 to the facts of this case, we observe, first, that the United States appears to cast the Panel's refusal to grant its request for a preliminary ruling as a finding that the First Assessment Review *per se* is a "measure taken to comply" within the meaning of Article 21.5 of the DSU. Our examination of the Panel's reasoning, however, indicates that the Panel took a more nuanced approach. The Panel determined that the Section 129 Determination was a "measure taken to comply". At the same time, it found that *the pass-through analysis* in the First Assessment Review was so "inextricably linked" and "clearly connected" to both the Section 129 Determination and the Final Countervailing Duty Determination as to fall within the scope of the Panel's authority under Article 21.5.[125] We understand the Panel, therefore, to have found that a specific component of the First Assessment Review—rather than the First Assessment Review in its entirety—fell within the scope of its jurisdiction under Article 21.5. Indeed, the Panel itself expressly so stated, albeit in a footnote:

> [W]e are only finding that part of the First Assessment Review (i.e., the pass-through analysis) is covered by these DSU Article 21.5 proceedings. We are not finding that the entirety of the First Assessment Review is covered by these proceedings.[126]

82. We also observe that the United States emphasizes the separate nature of original countervailing duty investigations and duty assessment proceedings, and cites, *inter alia*, to its domestic law in this regard. Although such references may be useful, the Appellate Body has already observed that municipal law classifications are not determinative of issues raised in WTO dispute settlement proceedings.[127] We also note the argument of the United States that the *SCM Agreement* recognizes that original countervailing duty investigations are proceedings dis-

---

[125] Panel Report, para. 4.41.

[126] *Ibid.*, footnote 42 to para. 4.45.

[127] Appellate Body Report, *US – Softwood Lumber IV*, para. 56.

tinct from duty assessment reviews.[128] This does not, in our view, answer the question of whether the Panel was entitled, in these proceedings under Article 21.5 of the DSU, to examine the pass-through analysis conducted by the USDOC in the First Assessment Review.

83. To answer that question, we turn to the specific circumstances of this case and examine them in the light of our interpretation of Article 21.5.[129] As regards *subject matter*, we note that the Final Countervailing Duty Determination, the Section 129 Determination, and the First Assessment Review are all countervailing duty proceedings that were conducted by the USDOC. Each of these proceedings involved a determination of the rate of subsidization of softwood lumber from Canada. Moreover, in each of these proceedings, the USDOC calculated the rate of subsidization of *softwood lumber* based on financial contributions made to, and benefit received by, *timber harvesters*. In other words, the product that was subject to the three countervailing duty proceedings was the same, and in each proceeding the issue of whether the subsidy had "passed through" was raised by Canadian interested parties and considered by the USDOC. Moreover, the "pass-through" methodology adopted by the USDOC was the same in the Section 129 Determination and the First Assessment Review.[130] Looking to the scope of coverage of the three relevant measures, we note that the Section 129 Determination revised the Final Countervailing Duty Determination and confirmed the continued existence of the conditions for the imposition of a countervailing duty. To the extent that the Section 129 Determination revised or replaced the Final Countervailing Duty Determination, and thereby became the basis for the continued imposition of countervailing duties, then the Section 129 Determination must be deemed to have the same relationship to the First Assessment Review that the Final Countervailing Duty Determination has with the First Assessment Review. In this connection, we observe that the softwood lumber imports that entered during the period 22 May 2002 to 31 March 2003 were, upon entry, subjected to the cash deposit rate determined in the Final Countervailing Duty Determination, and, subsequently, to the final duty liability determined in the First Assessment Review.[131]

84. An additional link between the Section 129 Determination and the First Assessment Review relates to *timing*. The publication and effective dates of both

---

[128] United States' appellant's submission, para. 20. The United States refers in footnotes 22 and 23 to Article 11.1 and footnote 52 of the *SCM Agreement*.

[129] *Supra*, para. 77.

[130] The Panel also noted that "the USDOC adopted the same approach to pass-through in the First Assessment Review as in the Section 129 Determination." (Panel Report, footnote 50 to para. 4.58)

[131] Having made a similar observation, the Panel added that:

> [i]mport entries subject to the Section 129 Determination cash deposit would be assessed pursuant to a subsequent assessment review, if requested. We do not attach importance to the fact that import entries subject to the Section 129 Determination cash deposit were not formally subject to the First Assessment Review, since the Section 129 Determination amended and replaced the Final Determination, such that there is no need to distinguish between the coverage of these two measures for present purposes.

(Panel Report, footnote 38 to para. 4.41)

proceedings coincided in time, with each also corresponding closely to the time of the expiration of the reasonable period of time for implementation. In fact, the First Assessment Review took effect a mere 10 days after the effective date of the Section 129 Determination. Although, as regards timing, the United States emphasizes that the First Assessment Review was initiated eight months before the DSB's recommendations and rulings, we do not consider the date of initiation to be determinative in this case for two reasons. First, the results of the First Assessment Review were published 10 months after adoption of the recommendations and rulings of the DSB. Secondly, in acknowledging that the pass-through methodology used by the USDOC in the First Assessment Review was adopted "in view of"[132] the recommendations and rulings of the DSB in *US – Softwood Lumber IV*, the United States appears also to acknowledge that the USDOC had time to take account of those recommendations and rulings.

85. The First Assessment Review also directly affected the Section 129 Determination because the cash deposit rate resulting from the Section 129 Determination (which reflected a small reduction due to pass-through analysis contained therein) was "updated"[133], or "superseded"[134], by the cash deposit rate resulting from the First Assessment Review (which reflected no reduction from the pass-through analysis contained therein).[135] Even if, as the United States argues, modification of the cash deposit rate was not the *purpose* of the First Assessment Review[136], it was undeniably *an effect.*

86. Turning to the evaluation by the Panel of the various links between these measures, we note that the Panel observed that the pass-through analysis in the First Assessment Review was "clearly connected to the panel and Appellate Body reports concerning the Final [Countervailing Duty] Determination".[137] The Panel also characterized the pass-through analysis in the First Assessment Review as "inextricably linked to the treatment of pass-through in the Section 129 Determination".[138] The Panel made these observations based on the following explanation:

---

132 United States' additional written memorandum, para. 12.

133 In response to questioning at the oral hearing, the United States explained that one of the consequences of an assessment review is that it updates the amount of the deposits that are required from importers.

134 Canada's appellee's submission, para. 19.

135 From the date of imposition of the countervailing duties until 10 December 2004 (the effective date of the Section 129 Determination), softwood lumber imports from Canada were subject to the cash deposit rate established as a result of the Final Countervailing Duty Determination; from 10 December 2004 to 19 December 2004, such lumber imports were subject to the cash deposit rate established as a result of the Section 129 Determination; and as from 20 December 2004, softwood lumber imports were subject to the cash deposit rate established as a result of the First Assessment Review.

136 The United States submitted that "the purpose of an assessment review ... is to levy the duty, *i.e.*, to determine the definitive or final legal assessment of duties." (United States' appellant's submission, para. 20) (footnote omitted)

137 Panel Report, para. 4.41.

138 *Ibid.*

> [C]ertain import entries subject to the prospective effect of the Final Determination are also subject to the retrospective effect of the First Assessment Review. Thus, while the First Assessment Review resulted in an assessment rate for import entries during the period 22 May 2002–31 March 2003, those entries had initially been subject to the cash deposit rate determined in the Final Determination. Furthermore, the prospective effect of the Section 129 Determination was superseded by the prospective effect of the First Assessment Review, in the sense that import entries that would have been subject to the cash deposit rate fixed by the Section 129 Determination became subject to the cash deposit rate fixed by the First Assessment Review, once the latter took effect. Thus, ... there is in fact considerable overlap in the effect of these various measures.[139] (footnote omitted)

87. In the sentence immediately following this excerpt, the Panel added that "[s]ince the pass-through analysis in the First Assessment Review could, therefore, have an impact on, and possibly undermine" implementation by the Section 129 Determination with respect to pass-through, "we consider that the pass-through analysis in the First Assessment Review should also fall within the scope of these DSU Article 21.5 proceedings."[140] The United States takes issue with this statement, and argues that the Panel's finding must be reversed because the "universe of measures that have some connection with measures taken to comply and that 'could have an impact on' or could 'possibly undermine' those measures is so broad as to render meaningless the strict requirement of the text of Article 21.5".[141] We do not read this statement by the Panel as a separate or independent test of when measures may be considered in Article 21.5 proceedings, or even as the primary reason for the Panel's finding. The statement is, rather, an additional reason, which follows the Panel's detailed review of the multiple points of convergence, both in terms of subject matter and time, that exist among the relevant measures. We do not, therefore, understand the Panel to have found, as the United States argues[142], that *every* measure that has "some connection" with and that "could have an impact on" or could "possibly undermine" a measure taken to comply may be scrutinized in proceedings under Article 21.5 of the DSU. Indeed, such an approach would be too sweeping.[143]

---

[139] *Ibid.*

[140] *Ibid.* (footnote omitted)

[141] United States' appellant's submission, para. 33 (referring to Panel Report, para. 4.41).

[142] *Ibid.*

[143] Furthermore, we observe that, in these proceedings, Canada did not challenge the First Assessment Review *per se*. Rather, in raising claims against the pass-through analysis, Canada challenged a single element among the many different issues presented to, and analyzed by, the USDOC in the context of the First Assessment Review. The pass-through analysis that was the subject of Canada's claims was, for purposes of these Article 21.5 proceedings, a discrete component of the First Assessment Review, and could be assessed as such.

88. We recognize that the First Assessment Review was not initiated in order to comply with the recommendations and rulings of the DSB, and that it operated under its own timelines and procedures, which were independent of the Section 129 Determination. Nevertheless, these considerations are not sufficient to overcome the multiple and specific links between the Final Countervailing Duty Determination, the Section 129 Determination, and the pass-through analysis in the First Assessment Review.

89. Lastly, we note that the United States refers to the "prejudice" that it suffered by virtue of the fact that the Panel's failure to grant the request for a preliminary ruling meant that it was forced to defend its actions in an assessment review—an "entirely separate" proceeding, with a "wholly different" administrative record—for the first time under the expedited time-frames of an Article 21.5 proceeding.[144] We observe, in this connection, that the measure at issue in proceedings under Article 21.5 will, in principle, be a different measure than the measure at issue in the original proceedings.[145] Thus, a Member cannot be said to suffer prejudice solely by virtue of the fact that it must defend a *new* or *different* measure in Article 21.5 proceedings. Moreover, the arguments made by the United States do not identify any prejudice suffered to the conduct of its *defence* in these Article 21.5 proceedings. The United States was invited by the Panel to submit arguments in defence of the pass-through analysis in the First Assessment Review as an alternative argument, in the event that the Panel did not grant its request for a preliminary ruling, but it elected not to do so. For these reasons, the United States has not established that it suffered any prejudice by virtue of the fact that the Panel's approach forced it to defend the pass-through analysis in the First Assessment Review in Article 21.5 proceedings.

90. In view of the above, we conclude that the Panel properly included the pass-through analysis in the First Assessment Review in its examination of the "measures taken to comply" because of the close connection that the Panel found to exist between that pass-through analysis and both the Final Countervailing Duty Determination and the Section 129 Determination.

91. We therefore see no error on the facts of this case in the Panel's finding that:

> ... there is sufficient overlap in the timing, or temporal effect, and nature of the Final Determination, Section 129 Determination and First Assessment Review for the latter to fall within the scope of the present DSU Article 21.5 proceedings.[146]

92. Accordingly, we *uphold* the Panel's finding, in paragraphs 4.41, 4.50, and 5.1 of the Panel Report, that the First Assessment Review falls within the scope

---

[144] United States' appellant's submission, para. 6. See also para. 43.

[145] Appellate Body Report, *Canada – Aircraft (Article 21.5 – Brazil)*, para. 36.

[146] Panel Report, para. 4.42.

of the present Article 21.5 proceedings, insofar as the pass-through analysis is concerned.[147]

93. In upholding the Panel's finding with respect to the scope of Article 21.5, we wish to make clear that the Panel's approach is not, in our view, so "broad [as] to render the jurisdictional limits of Article 21.5 nearly meaningless"[148], as the United States contends. In particular, the Panel's reasoning—which we have upheld—should not be read to mean that every assessment review will necessarily fall within the jurisdiction of an Article 21.5 panel.[149]

E. Disposition of the Remaining Issues on Appeal

94. We understand, and the United States confirmed at the oral hearing, that the sole basis for its appeal of the remaining Panel findings identified in its Notice of Appeal is the same as the basis for its principal ground of appeal: that the First Assessment Review could not be examined by the Panel in these Article 21.5 proceedings. Because we have upheld the Panel's finding that it could examine the pass-through analysis in the First Assessment Review, and because the United States did not appeal the substance of the remaining findings that the Panel made with respect to the pass-through analysis in the First Assessment Review, we have no basis for disturbing those remaining findings.[150]

V. FINDINGS AND CONCLUSIONS

95. For the reasons set forth in this Report, the Appellate Body *upholds* the Panel's finding, in paragraphs 4.41, 4.50, and 5.1 of the Panel Report, that the First Assessment Review falls within the scope of the present Article 21.5 proceedings, insofar as the pass-through analysis is concerned.

96. Having so held, and in the absence of a request by the United States that we review the Panel's examination of the substance of the pass-through analysis in the First Assessment Review[151], the Appellate Body *finds* that the Panel acted within the scope of its authority in reaching the following legal conclusions:

(a) in paragraph 5.2 of the Panel Report, that the United States failed, in the treatment of pass-through in the First Assessment Review, to implement properly the recommendations and rulings of the DSB by not conducting a pass-through analysis with respect to sales, found not to be at arm's length, of logs by tenured timber harvest-

---

[147] *Ibid.*, paras. 4.50 and 5.1.

[148] United States' appellant's submission, para. 32.

[149] This dispute does not raise the issue of whether or to what extent the obligations that apply in the context of an assessment review are the same as the obligations that apply in an original countervailing duty investigation. The United States did not argue before the Panel, or before us, that it had no obligation, under the covered agreements, to conduct the same pass-through analysis in an assessment review as it must conduct in an original countervailing duty investigation.

[150] United States' Notice of Appeal, WT/DS257/22 (attached as Annex I to this Report), paras. 2-5 (referring to Panel Report, paras. 5.2 and 5.4-5.5).

[151] *Supra*, para. 94.

ers, whether or not they also produce lumber, to unrelated timber producers, whether or not they hold a stumpage contract;

(b) in paragraph 5.2 of the Panel Report, that, in the First Assessment Review, the United States included in its subsidy numerator transactions for which it had not demonstrated that the benefit of subsidized log inputs had passed through to the processed product;

(c) in paragraph 5.4 of the Panel Report, that, with respect to the First Assessment Review, the United States remains in violation of Articles 10 and 32.1 of the *SCM Agreement* and Article VI:3 of the GATT 1994; and

(d) in paragraph 5.5 of the Panel Report, that, with respect to the First Assessment Review, the United States has nullified or impaired benefits accruing to Canada under the *SCM Agreement* and the GATT 1994.

97. The Panel recommended, in paragraph 5.5 of the Panel Report, that the United States bring its measures, found to be inconsistent with the *SCM Agreement* and the GATT 1994, into conformity with its obligations under those Agreements. Having found that the Panel acted within the scope of its jurisdiction in making such findings of inconsistency, it is not for us to make any additional recommendation, under Article 19.1 of the DSU.

ANNEX I

WORLD TRADE ORGANIZATION

WT/DS257/22
12 September 2005

(05-3950)

Original: English

UNITED STATES – FINAL COUNTERVAILING DUTY DETERMINATION WITH RESPECT TO CERTAIN SOFTWOOD LUMBER FROM CANADA

Recourse by Canada to Article 21.5 of the DSU

Notification of an Appeal by the United States under Article 16.4 and Article 17 of the Understanding on Rules and Procedures Governing the Settlement of Disputes (DSU), and under Rule 20(1) of the *Working Procedures for Appellate Review*

The following notification, dated 6 September 2005, from the Delegation of the United States, is being circulated to Members.

Pursuant to Article 16 of the *Understanding on Rules and Procedures Governing the Settlement of Disputes* ("DSU") and Rule 20 of the Working Procedures for Appellate Review, the United States hereby notifies its decision to appeal to the Appellate Body certain issues of law covered in the Report of the Panel on *United States – Final Countervailing Duty Determination with Respect to Certain Softwood Lumber from Canada: Recourse to Article 21.5 of the DSU by Canada* (WT/DS257/RW) ("Panel Report") and certain legal interpretations developed by the Panel in this dispute.

1. The United States seeks review by the Appellate Body of the Panel's legal conclusion that the First Assessment Review does not fall outside the scope of the present DSU Article 21.5 proceeding, insofar as the pass-through analysis is

concerned.[1] This conclusion is in error and is based on erroneous findings on issues of law and related legal interpretations of DSU Article 21.5.

2. The United States seeks review by the Appellate Body of the Panel's legal conclusion that the United States failed, in the treatment of pass-through in the First Assessment Review, to properly implement the recommendations and rulings of the Dispute Settlement Body by not conducting a pass-through analysis with respect to sales, found not to be at arm's length, of logs by tenured timber harvesters, whether or not they also produce lumber, to unrelated timber producers, whether or not they hold a stumpage contract.[2] This erroneous conclusion is based on the Panel's erroneous legal conclusion, described in paragraph 1, above, that the First Assessment Review does not fall outside the scope of the DSU Article 21.5 proceeding.

3. The United States seeks review by the Appellate Body of the Panel's legal conclusion that, in the First Assessment Review, the United States included in its subsidy numerator transactions for which it had not demonstrated that the benefit of subsidized log inputs had passed through to the processed product.[3] This erroneous conclusion is based on the Panel's erroneous legal conclusion, described in paragraph 1, above, that the First Assessment Review does not fall outside the scope of the DSU Article 21.5 proceeding.

4. The United States seeks review by the Appellate Body of the Panel's legal conclusion that, with respect to the First Assessment Review, the United States remains in violation of Articles 10 and 32.1 of the *Agreement on Subsidies and Countervailing Measures* ("SCM Agreement") and Article VI:3 of the *General Agreement on Tariffs and Trade 1994* ("GATT 1994").[4] This erroneous conclusion is based on the Panel's erroneous legal conclusion, described in paragraph 1, above, that the First Assessment Review does not fall outside the scope of the DSU Article 21.5 proceeding.

5. The United States seeks review by the Appellate Body of the Panel's legal conclusion that, with respect to the First Assessment Review, the United States has nullified or impaired benefits accruing to Canada under the SCM Agreement and the GATT 1994.[5] This erroneous conclusion is based on the Panel's erroneous legal conclusion, described in paragraph 1, above, that the First Assessment Review does not fall outside the scope of the DSU Article 21.5 proceeding.

---

1 Panel Report, paras. 4.36-4.50, and 5.1, first subparagraph.

2 Panel Report, paras. 4.58-4.82, 4.104-4.106, and 5.2, first subparagraph.

3 Panel Report, paras. 4.114-4.115, and 5.2, second subparagraph.

4 Panel Report, paras. 4.114-4.115 and 5.4.

5 Panel Report, para. 5.5.

UNITED STATES – FINAL COUNTERVAILING DUTY DETERMINATION WITH RESPECT TO CERTAIN SOFTWOOD LUMBER FROM CANADA

Recourse by Canada to Article 21.5 of the Understanding on Rules and Procedures Governing the Settlement of Disputes

Report of the Panel
WT/DS257/RW

Adopted by the Dispute Settlement Body on 20 December 2005 as Upheld by Appellate Body Report

TABLE OF CONTENTS

TABLE OF ANNEXES

ANNEX A

SUBMISSIONS OF CANADA

ANNEX B

SUBMISSIONS OF THE UNITED STATES

ANNEX C

SUBMISSIONS OF THIRD PARTIES

ANNEX D

REQUEST FOR ESTABLISHMENT OF A PANEL

Contents	

TABLE OF CASES CITED IN THIS REPORT

Short Title	Full Case Title and Citation of Case
Australia – Automotive Leather II (Article 21.5 – US)	Panel Report, *Australia – Subsidies Provided to Producers and Exporters of Automotive Leather – Recourse to Article 21.5 of the DSU by the United States*, WT/DS126/RW and Corr.1, adopted 11 February 2000, DSR 2000:III, 1189
Australia – Salmon (Article 21.5 – Canada)	Panel Report, *Australia – Measures Affecting Importation of Salmon – Recourse to Article 21.5 of the DSU by Canada*, WT/DS18/RW, adopted 20 March 2000, DSR 2000:IV, 2031
Brazil – Aircraft	Appellate Body Report, *Brazil – Export Financing Programme for Aircraft*, WT/DS46/AB/R, adopted 20 August 1999, DSR 1999:III, 1161
Canada – Aircraft	Panel Report, *Canada – Measures Affecting the Export of Civilian Aircraft*, WT/DS70/R, adopted 20 August 1999, as upheld by the Appellate Body report, WT/DS70/AB/R, DSR 1999:IV, 1443
Dominican Republic – Import and Sale of Cigarettes	Appellate Body Report, *Dominican Republic – Measures Affecting the Importation and Internal Sale of Cigarettes*, WT/DS302/AB/R, 25 April 2005, adopted 19 May 2005.
Dominican Republic – Import and Sale of Cigarettes	Panel Report, *Dominican Republic – Measures Affecting the Importation and Internal Sale of Cigarettes*, WT/DS302/R, 26 November 2004, adopted 19 May 2005.

Short Title	Full Case Title and Citation of Case
EC – Bed Linen (Article 21.5 – India)	Appellate Body Report, *European Communities – Anti-Dumping Duties on Imports of Cotton-Type Bed Linen from India – Recourse to Article 21.5 of the DSU by India*, WT/DS141/AB/RW, adopted 24 April 2003 Panel Report, *European Communities – Anti-Dumping Duties on Imports of Cotton-Type Bed Linen from India – Recourse to Article 21.5 of the DSU by India*, WT/DS141/RW, adopted 24 April 2003, as modified by the Appellate Body Report, WT/DS141/AB/RW
US – Line Pipe	Appellate Body Report, *United States – Definitive Safeguard Measures on Imports of Circular Welded Carbon Quality Line Pipe from Korea*, WT/DS202/AB/R, adopted 8 March 2002
US – Shrimp (Article 21.5 – Malaysia)	Appellate Body Report, *United States – Import Prohibition of Certain Shrimp and Shrimp Products – Recourse to Article 21.5 of the DSU by Malaysia*, WT/DS58/AB/RW, adopted 21 November 2001, DSR 2001:XIII, 6481
US – Softwood Lumber III	Panel Report, *United States – Preliminary Determinations with Respect to Certain Softwood Lumber from Canada*, WT/DS236/R, adopted 1 November 2002
US – Softwood Lumber IV	Appellate Body Report, *United States – Final Countervailing Duty Determination with Respect to Certain Softwood Lumber from Canada*, WT/DS257/AB/R, adopted 17 February 2004 Panel Report, *United States – Final Countervailing Duty Determination with Respect to Certain Softwood Lumber from Canada*, WT/DS257/R and Corr.1, adopted 17 February 2004, as modified by the Appellate Body Report, WT/DS257/AB/R

I. PROCEDURAL BACKGROUND

1.1 On 17 February 2004, the Dispute Settlement Body ("DSB") adopted the recommendations and rulings in the reports of the original panel and the Appellate Body in *US – Softwood Lumber IV*.

1.2 In respect of pass-through, the original panel concluded that:

"the USDOC's[1] failure to conduct a pass-through analysis in respect of upstream transactions for log and lumber inputs between unrelated entities was inconsistent with Article 10 SCM Agreement and Article VI:3 of GATT 1994."[2]

1.3 More specifically, the original panel found that:

"the USDOC's failure to conduct a pass-through analysis in respect of logs sold by tenure-holding timber harvesters (whether or not also lumber producers) to unrelated sawmills producing subject softwood lumber; and in respect of lumber sold by tenure-holding harvester/sawmills to unrelated lumber re-manufacturers was inconsistent with Article 10 and thus Article 32.1 SCM Agreement, and with Article VI:3 of GATT 1994."[3]

1.4 The original panel therefore upheld Canada's claim that the United States' imposition of countervailing duties in respect of such transactions was inconsistent with Articles 10 and 32.1 SCM Agreement and Article VI:3 of GATT 1994.[4]

1.5 The United States appealed from the original panel's pass-through conclusion. The Appellate Body stated that the United States "contend[ed] that the [original panel] erred in finding that a pass-through analysis is required in respect of sales of *logs* from tenure-holding sawmills producing softwood lumber to unrelated sawmills, and for sales of lumber by tenure-holding sawmills to unrelated lumber remanufacturers."[5] According to the Appellate Body, the United States "[did] not appeal the [original panel's] finding that, where a subsidy is received by an independent timber harvester[[6]], a pass-through analysis is required in respect of sales to unrelated sawmills or unrelated remanufacturers".[7]

1.6 In respect of pass-through, the Appellate Body stated that it upheld the original panel's finding that:

"USDOC's failure to conduct a pass-through analysis in respect of arm's length sales of *logs* by tenured harvesters/sawmills to unrelated sawmills is inconsistent with Articles 10 and 32.1 of the *SCM Agreement* and Article VI:3 of the GATT 1994."[8]

---

1 We shall continue the original panel's practice of referring to the US Department of Commerce as "USDOC".

2 Panel Report, *US – Softwood Lumber* IV (hereinafter "Panel Report"), para. 8.1(c).

3 Panel Report, para. 7.99.

4 Panel Report, para. 8.1(c).

5 Appellate Body Report, *US – Softwood Lumber* IV, (hereinafter "Appellate Body Report"), para. 16, emphasis in original.

6 Before the Appellate Body, the United States used the term "independent harvester" in the same way as it had in the original dispute, namely, "'entities that do *not* produce [softwood lumber] product[s] under investigation'". Appellate Body Report at para. 127. In the Section 129 Determination, the USDOC used the term "independent harvester" to refer to "tenured independent harvesters/sawmills" (see note 52 *infra*).

7 Appellate Body Report, para. 16, footnote omitted.

8 Appellate Body Report, para. 167 (c), emphasis in original.

1.7 The Appellate Body stated that it reversed the original panel's finding that:

> "USDOC's failure to conduct a pass-through analysis in respect of arm's length sales of *lumber* by tenured harvesters/sawmills to unrelated remanufacturers is inconsistent with Articles 10 and 32.1 of the *SCM Agreement* and Article VI:3 of the GATT 1994."[9]

1.8 At the DSB meeting of 17 December 2004, the United States informed the DSB that it had complied with the DSB's recommendations and rulings.

1.9 On 30 December 2004, Canada requested the establishment of a panel pursuant to Article 21.5 of the *Understanding on Rules and Procedures Governing the Settlement of Disputes* ("DSU").[10] At the same time, Canada also requested authorization from the DSB to suspend the application to the United States of certain concessions or other obligations, pursuant to DSU Article 22.2.

1.10 At its meeting of 14 January 2005, the DSB decided, in accordance with DSU Article 21.5, to refer to the original panel the matter raised by Canada in document WT/DS257/15. At that meeting, it also was agreed that the Panel should have standard terms of reference as follows:

> "To examine, in the light of the relevant provisions of the covered agreements cited by Canada in document WT/DS257/15, the matter referred to the DSB by Canada in that document, and to make such findings as will assist the DSB in making the recommendations or in giving the rulings provided for in those agreements".[11]

1.11 The Panel was composed as follows:

Chairman: Mr Elbio O. Rosselli

Members: Ms Marta Calmon Lemme

Mr Remo Moretta

1.12 On 14 January 2005, the DSB also referred the matter of suspension of concessions to the Panel for arbitration pursuant to DSU Article 22.6.[12]

1.13 China and the European Communities reserved their rights to participate in the Panel proceedings as third parties.

1.14 The Panel met with the parties and third parties on 21 April 2005.

1.15 The Panel submitted its interim report to the parties on 20 May 2005. The Panel submitted its final report to the parties on 3 June 2005.

II. FACTUAL ASPECTS

2.1 With a view to implementing the rulings and recommendations of the DSB in respect of this dispute, on 19 November 2004, the United States issued a

---

9 Appellate Body Report, para. 167 (f), emphasis in original.
10 WT/DS257/15.
11 WT/DS257/19.
12 WT/DS257/20.

draft determination pursuant to Section 129 of the *Uruguay Round Agreements Act*. The United States issued its final Section 129 Determination on 6 December 2004 (the "Section 129 Determination").

2.2 On 20 December 2004, the United States published the final results of the first assessment review of the countervailing duties on imports of softwood lumber from Canada (the "First Assessment Review"). Pursuant to the US retrospective system of duty assessment, the First Assessment Review provided for retrospective final assessment of the countervailing duties to be levied on import entries of softwood lumber from Canada between 22 May 2002 and 31 March 2003. The First Assessment Review also determined the cash deposit rate to be levied on imports of softwood lumber from Canada as of 20 December 2004. The First Assessment Review was initiated in July 2003, pursuant to a request in May 2003 from Canada and other interested parties.

2.3 The arguments of the parties and third parties as presented to the Panel are contained in their written and oral submissions, the texts of which are appended to this report.

III. INTERIM REVIEW

3.1 The Panel issued its interim report to the parties on 20 May 2005. On 24 May 2005, both parties submitted written requests to the Panel to review precise aspects of the interim report but neither party requested an interim review meeting. On 26 May 2005, both parties commented in writing on the other party's requests for review of the interim report. This section summarizes the parties' requests and comments, and contains the Panel's responses thereto, and forms part of the Panel's findings.

A. Request by Canada for review of precise aspects of the Panel report

1. Request of Canada

3.2 Canada asks the Panel to introduce changes into paragraphs 4.71-4.73, 4.82, 4.83, 4.88, and 4.89.

3.3 Canada asks the Panel to make findings, in paragraph 4.73, concerning the USDOC's exclusion of certain transaction-specific data on log sales (submitted by Tembec (Manitoba)). Canada notes that although the USDOC excluded these data from pass-through analysis for reasons other than not being at arm's length[13], these reasons were "equally inconsistent" with the United States' obligations pursuant to the DSB's recommendations and rulings. Canada asserts that the parties would "benefit" from findings by the Panel on the Tembec (Manitoba) data.

[13] According to both parties, USDOC did not conduct a pass-through analysis in respect of these log sales because the sales were made after the end of the period of investigation.

3.4 Canada also asks the Panel to expand the description of Canada's arguments in paragraph 4.83, concerning the USDOC's treatment of aggregate data submitted by Canadian respondents. The suggested amendments would expand on the description of Canada's arguments that the sample data submitted by Canadian respondents were representative, that it was impossible for respondents to provide the full data requested by the USDOC, or more data than they did provide, and that USDOC was obliged to use the data provided by the respondents as the basis of the pass-through analysis.

3.5 Concerning paragraph 4.88, Canada takes issue with the Panel's statement that Canada "has not disputed that the USDOC needed" company-specific and/or transaction-specific data for the purpose of determining affiliation of parties to the log sales transactions, which according to Canada is inaccurate in the light of the totality of Canada's arguments, as reflected in Canada's suggested redraft of paragraph 4.83. Canada also asks the Panel to insert a statement that the USDOC accepted that aggregate data could, and did, control for affiliation.

3.6 In paragraph 4.89, Canada asks the Panel to insert a statement that "investigating authorities nevertheless have an obligation to perform analyses, on the basis of available data, in a manner that is consistent with the obligation under Article VI:3 of GATT 1994 and Articles 10 and 32.1 of the SCM Agreement not to presume that the subsidy passed through to an unrelated purchaser of the input product".

3.7 Canada states that the Panel finds in paragraphs 4.71-4.73, and 4.82 that the USDOC was required to conduct a pass-through analysis irrespective of any considerations as to whether or not sales were at "arm's length". Canada requests that the Panel insert a statement in this context that "even if the U.S. arguments on 'arm's length' were accepted, the five 'factors' identified by USDOC in this case, including who pays the stumpage and the presence of non-cash components to a transaction, do not transform an arm's-length transaction into one that is not at arm's length".

2. *Comments of the United States*

3.8 The United States submits that the Panel should reject all of the amendments proposed by Canada. Concerning paragraph 4.73, the United States argues that the issue concerning Tembec (Manitoba) raised by Canada in its request for interim review is outside the Panel's terms of reference, as Canada's claim on pass-through was concerned with the appropriateness of USDOC's arm's length analysis. The United States further argues that in any case, as acknowledged by Canada, Tembec (Manitoba) submitted no data to the USDOC concerning log sales during the period of investigation.

3.9 The United States objects to Canada's request to expand the description of Canada's arguments in paragraph 4.83, stating that the original summary is sufficient, and that if Canada's request were accepted, without an equivalent expansion of the description of the US arguments, this would create an appearance of imbalance. Furthermore, given that the submissions of the parties are appended to the report, the United States considers a full recitation of detailed arguments unnecessary.

3.10 Concerning paragraph 4.88, the United States disagrees as a factual matter that Canada disputed the USDOC's need for company-specific and/or transaction-specific for purposes of determining affiliation. The United States asserts that Canada is confusing the question of whether the USDOC needed certain data with whether the USDOC should have accepted whatever data Canada offered.

3.11 The United States also disagrees with Canada's suggested amendment to paragraph 4.89, stating that the suggestion is inappropriate, and would directly contradict the Panel's immediately preceding statement that the Panel is reluctant to instruct investigating authorities concerning data issues in pass-through analysis.

3.12 Finally, the United States takes issue with Canada's suggested amendment to paragraphs 4.71-4.73 and 4.82 to "clarify" certain points in respect of the USDOC's arm's length factors. According to the United States, given that the Panel found that the USDOC should have conducted a pass-through analysis regardless of the issue of arm's length, Canada's suggestion is irrelevant and would call on the Panel to make substantial new findings that would then need to be subjected to additional interim review.

B. Request by the United States for review of precise aspects of the Panel report

1. Request of the United States

3.13 The United States requests the Panel to make certain technical drafting corrections and clarifications to paragraphs 2.2, 4.20, 4.21, and 4.48, and to footnote 45 of the interim report (footnote 47 of the final report). The United States also requests substantive changes to paragraphs 4.38, 4.41, 4.47, 4.48 and 4.49.

3.14 First, the United States requests that in paragraphs 4.38, 4.41 and 4.49, we change the references to "dispute settlement decisions" to "dispute settlement reports", to avoid potential confusion with "decisions" that might be made, for example, pursuant to Article IX of the Marrakesh Agreement.

3.15 Second, the United States asserts that at paragraph 4.47, the Panel mischaracterizes the United States' argument concerning the *EC – Bed Linen (Article 21.5)* dispute. The United States indicates that its argument on that point is correctly summarized at paragraph 4.45.

3.16 Third, the United States contends that paragraph 4.48 is factually incorrect in stating that the Final Determination and the First Assessment Review involve "'pass-through of the subsidy benefit, in respect of **the same import entries** ... '"

2. Comments of Canada

3.17 Canada only comments on the last of the United States' comments, concerning the factual accuracy of the reference to "the same import entries" in paragraph 4.48. According to Canada, this statement is factually accurate, and the issue is correctly described at paragraph 4.41, the accuracy of which the United States does not contest.

C. Evaluation by the Panel

1. Request of Canada

3.18 Concerning Canada's request in respect of paragraph 4.73, we have not made any findings in respect of the issue concerning Tembec (Manitoba)'s sales of logs. We consider that this issue falls outside our terms of reference, as set by the request for establishment of the Panel, as it does not correspond to any of the legal claims set forth in the first four "tirets" on page two of the request (WT/DS257/15).

3.19 In response to Canada's requests concerning the summary of its arguments in paragraph 4.83, we have slightly modified the text of that paragraph, and have inserted footnote 65.

3.20 Concerning paragraph 4.88, we do not consider that Canada has disputed the USDOC's need for company-specific and/or transaction-specific data to determine affiliation of parties to log transactions. We have introduced footnote 66 to clarify our understanding of the nature of, and the USDOC's use of, the aggregate data that the USDOC accepted for purposes of determining affiliation.

3.21 We have not introduced in paragraph 4.89 the statement requested by Canada, but have introduced a final sentence to that paragraph, as well as footnote 67, to clarify our view in respect of the issues raised by Canada's comment.

3.22 We have not introduced in paragraphs 4.71-4.73 and 4.82 the statement requested by Canada concerning certain of the arm's length factors applied by the USDOC. Such a statement would be inappropriate in view of our findings that pass-through analysis should have been conducted in respect of log sales between unrelated parties, irrespective of any considerations as to whether or not such sales were "arm's length".

2. Request of the United States

3.23 We have accepted the United States' suggested changes to paragraphs 2.2, 4.20, 4.21, and 4.48, and to footnote 45 of the interim report (footnote 47 of the final report). We also have made other technical corrections to the report, as necessary.

3.24 We have not accepted the United States' suggestion in respect of paragraphs 4.38, 4.41 and 4.49, because we believe that it is clear from the context that the word "decisions" refers to the findings cited in that section of the report, and is not used in a generic sense that could potentially sweep in other kinds of actions.

3.25 In the light of the US comments, we have amended paragraph 4.47 slightly, to refer to what we see as the implication of the US argument, rather than to refer to the US argument as such.

3.26 We have added footnote 44, to clarify to which import entries the phrase in paragraph 4.48 "the same import entries" refers. Footnote 44 contains a cross-reference to paragraph 4.41, cited by Canada in its comments on the US suggestion concerning this paragraph.

IV. FINDINGS

4.1 This case concerns Canada's claim that the USDOC failed to properly implement the rulings and recommendations of the DSB in respect of the *US – Softwood Lumber IV* proceeding. In particular, Canada claims that, in the Section 129 Determination and First Assessment Review, the USDOC continued to presume pass-through of subsidy benefit in respect of various categories of sales of logs to unrelated purchasers. Before examining Canada's claims, we shall first rule on a preliminary ruling requested by the United States.

A. US request for preliminary ruling

1. Arguments of the parties

4.2 The United States requests a preliminary ruling that the final results of the First Assessment Review of the countervailing duty order on softwood lumber from Canada are not "measures taken to comply" with the recommendations and rulings of the DSB under Article 21.5 of the DSU. According to the United States, these results fall outside the scope of Article 21.5, and this Panel lacks jurisdiction to review them.

4.3 The United States submits that the First Assessment Review was a proceeding: separate from both the original countervailing duty investigation determination challenged by Canada and the Section 129 Determination at issue here; initiated prior to the DSB's adoption of recommendations and rulings in this dispute; that had nothing to do with complying with the recommendations and rulings of the DSB.

4.4 The United States notes that the *EC – Bed Linen (Article 21.5 – India)* panel granted the European Communities' preliminary ruling request to exclude from consideration certain antidumping duty measures taken by the European Communities that were cited by India, but that the panel found were not "taken to comply." The United States asserts that, in that dispute, in which the European Communities was found to have incorrectly calculated anti-dumping duties in an investigation of bed linens from India, the European Communities voluntarily applied the revised calculation method to anti-dumping duties imposed on Pakistan and Egypt. The United States asserts that, after concluding that no duties should be imposed on bed linen from those sources (as a result of the recalculation), the European Communities re-examined whether imports from India, considered alone, caused injury to the domestic industry. According to the United

States, the European Communities concluded that they did, and therefore affirmed the imposition of anti-dumping duties on bed linen from India. The United States asserts that India challenged this finding of injury and the resulting imposition of duties on bed linen from India as a WTO-inconsistent measure "taken to comply" under Article 21.5.

4.5 The United States notes that the panel, in deciding not to review the latter measure, stated that

> "[T]he fact that the EC, subsequent to its re-examination of the dumping determinations with respect to imports from Egypt and Pakistan, and in the context of a review initiated on the request of Eurocoton, carried out an analysis of whether injury was caused by imports from India alone does not, *ipso facto*, establish that Regulation 696/2002 is a measure "taken to comply". Rather the opposite would seem to be the case – that Regulation would seem to be an entirely new determination, reached as a result of events subsequent to the EC having adopted a measure to comply with the DSB's recommendation."[14]

4.6 The United States submits that the final results of the First Assessment Review are not "measures taken to comply". The United States asserts that, before the original panel, Canada challenged the USDOC's Final Determination in the countervailing duty investigation on softwood lumber from Canada.[15] After the DSB adopted its recommendations and rulings, and within the agreed "reasonable period of time", the United States made the Section 129 Determination, in which it conducted a "pass through" analysis and recalculated the countervailing duty rate.[16] The new reduced rate was applicable to entries of subject merchandise on or after 10 December 2004. The United States submits that original investigations and assessment reviews are different processes which serve distinct purposes. The purpose of an investigation is to determine the existence, degree, and effect of any alleged subsidy; the purpose of an assessment review is to determine the amount of duty to be assessed on previous imports of subject merchandise and the estimated countervailing duty rate to be applied to future imports. The United States argues that the distinction between countervailing duty investigations and assessment procedures is explicitly recognized in the Agreement on Subsidies and Countervailing Measures ("SCM Agreement").[17]

4.7 The United States submits that the First Assessment Review was not a measure taken to comply with the recommendations and rulings of the DSB. Rather, it resulted from a separate affirmative request by Canada, among others, that USDOC review new sales and subsidies data for the purposes of assessing countervailing duties for imports during the review period and of setting a new estimated countervailing duty rate for subsequent imports.

---

14 *EC – Bed Linen (Article 21.5 – India)* (Panel), para. 6.20.

15 Panel Report, paras 2.1 - 2.4.

16 Section 129 Determination. Exhibit CDA-5.

17 The US refers in this regard to SCM Agreement, fn. 52.

4.8 The United States also argues that the First Assessment Review was initiated on 1 July 2003, eight months before the DSB's recommendations and rulings in this dispute were adopted. The United States asserts that the First Assessment Review, therefore, had nothing whatsoever to do with "implementing" the DSB's recommendations and rulings. The United States submits that, for obvious temporal reasons, the results of this assessment review – which was initiated before the DSB issued its recommendations and rulings – cannot be considered "measures taken to comply". By contrast, the United States asserts that the USDOC initiated the Section 129 proceeding for the specific purpose of addressing the DSB's recommendations and rulings. The United States further asserts that the agreement of the parties on the "reasonable period of time" to implement the recommendations and rulings in this dispute was negotiated in the light of, and specifically refers to, the US procedures for implementing WTO reports[18] – that is, the Section 129 procedures.

4.9 The United States submits that Article 21.5 proceedings are by their nature more focused and limited than other panel proceedings under Article 6.2 of the DSU. The United States argues that it is beyond the scope of such a limited 90-day inquiry to fully examine an entirely new set of assessment review results based on a wholly new administrative record, consisting of new sales, new imports, potentially new respondents and potentially new subsidy programmes.

4.10 Canada submits that the final results of the First Assessment Review rendered non-existent the pass-through analysis and adjustment under the Section 129 Determination, and that the final results of the First Assessment Review are therefore an integral part of the Panel's determination "as to the *existence* ... of measures taken to comply" under Article 21.5 of the DSU. Canada also argues that upholding the US preliminary objection would be contrary to the purpose of Article 21.5 proceedings.

4.11 Regarding the Section 129 Determination being rendered non-existent by the First Assessment Review, Canada argues that in *Australia – Leather II (Article 21.5 - US)*, the United States itself argued that measures that undo measures taken to comply appropriately fall within the scope of Article 21.5 of the DSU:

> Under Article 21.5, this panel is to consider "the existence or consistency with a covered agreement of measures taken to comply with the recommendations and rulings." Plainly, if this Panel can determine the "existence" of measures taken to comply with the recommendations, it can consider whether the measures purportedly taken to comply were effectively rendered non-existent.

4.12 Furthermore, Canada asserts that, in declining to include certain EC measures in its compliance review, the abovementioned *EC – Bed Linen (Article*

[18] WT/DS257/13.

21.5 - India) panel specifically noted that India "does not argue that the subsequent two measures undo the compliance effectuated by the first measure."[19]

4.13 Canada also submits that the final results of the First Assessment Review are properly before the Panel because they are inextricably linked to the recommendations and rulings of the DSB and to what the United States claims as being its "measures taken to comply". Canada asserts that the treatment by USDOC of the pass-through issue in the final results of its First Assessment Review is nearly identical to its treatment of pass-through in the Section 129 Determination. Canada also notes that USDOC published preliminary results for the First Assessment Review containing a "pass-through" section nearly four months after the DSB made its recommendations and rulings, and issued final results nearly ten months after those recommendations and rulings. Canada asserts that the Section 129 Determination and the First Assessment Review are inextricably linked to the DSB recommendations because they both address the obligations of the United States to conduct pass-through analyses with respect to independent harvester and sawmill-to-sawmill log transactions for the same exports for the same period of time.

4.14 Regarding the US argument that assessment reviews and original investigations are different proceedings, and that the review was initiated prior to the recommendations and rulings of the DSB, Canada submits that the United States ignores the fact that, under US law, the USDOC may implement the recommendations and rulings of the DSB concerning an original investigation through a subsequent administrative review.[20]

4.15 Canada asserts that Article 21.5 of the DSU requires a compliance panel to examine the substance of a Member's measures notwithstanding any argument that the form of the measures could preclude compliance review. Canada notes that in *Australia – Automotive Leather II (Article 21.5 - US)*, for example, the panel found that the subsequent loan was within its jurisdiction to examine under Article 21.5 of the DSU because it was "inextricably linked to the steps taken by Australia in response to the DSB's ruling in this dispute, in view of both its timing and its nature."[21] Canada also notes the finding of the panel in *Australia – Salmon (Article 21.5 - Canada)* that:

---

[19] *EC – Bed Linen (Article 21.5)*, Panel Report, at para. 6.21. Canada also refers to the Third Party Submission of the European Communities (Annex C-3), at para. 26, citing *Dominican Republic – Import and Sale of Cigarettes*, at paras. 7.11-7.21.

[20] Canada refers in this regard to the "Statement of Administrative Action" in *Message from the President of the United States Transmitting the Uruguay Round Agreements, Texts of Agreements Implementing Bill, Statement of Administrative Action and Required Supporting Statements*, H.R. Doc. No. 103-316, vol. 1 at 656 (Exhibit CDA-1), at 356-357. ("Furthermore, while subsection 129(b) [of the Uruguay Round Agreements Act] creates a mechanism for making new determinations in response to a WTO report, new determinations may not be necessary in all situations. In many instances, such as those in which a WTO report merely implicates the size of a dumping margin or countervailable subsidy rate (as opposed to whether a determination is affirmative or negative), it may be possible to implement the WTO report recommendations in a future administrative review under section 751 of the Tariff Act.")

[21] Panel Report, *Australia – Automotive Leather II (Article 21.5 – US)*, para. 6.5.

> ... an Article 21.5 panel cannot leave it to the full discretion of the implementing Member to decide whether or not a measure is one "taken to comply". If one were to allow that, an implementing Member could simply avoid any scrutiny of certain measures by a compliance panel, *even where such measures would be so clearly connected to the panel and Appellate Body reports concerned, both in time and in respect of the subject-matter, that any impartial observer would consider them to be measures "taken to comply".*[22]

4.16 Canada submits that the US reliance on *EC – Bed Linen (Article 21.5 - India)* is misplaced, as the panel in that dispute found that the EC measures in question were not "taken to comply" within the meaning of Article 21.5 of the DSU because they did not deal with the subject matter upon which the DSB had made recommendations and rulings. Canada submits that the panel expressly noted that "[t]he situation might be different had there been a claim in the original dispute challenging the cumulative assessment of the effects of imports from India, Egypt, and Pakistan."[23]

4.17 Canada asserts that the US argument that an Article 21.5 panel does not have jurisdiction to evaluate USDOC's treatment of additional record evidence concerning exports subject to a US definitive countervailing duty misses the point entirely, as a panel's assessment "as to the existence or consistency with a covered agreement of measures taken to comply" under Article 21.5 of the DSU necessarily involves an examination of new factual information. Canada notes in this regard that the Appellate Body stated in *EC – Bed Linen (Article 21.5 - India)* that:

> [A]n Article 21.5 panel is not confined to examining the "measures taken to comply" from the perspective of the claims, arguments, and factual circumstances relating to the measure that was the subject of the *original* proceedings. Moreover, the relevant facts bearing upon the "measure taken to comply" may be different from the facts relevant to the measure at issue in the original proceedings. It is to be expected, therefore, that the claims, arguments, and factual circumstances relating to the "measure taken to comply" will not, necessarily, be the same as those relating to the measure in the original dispute. Indeed, a complainant in Article 21.5 proceedings may well raise *new* claims, arguments, and factual circumstances different from those raised in the original proceedings, because a "measure taken to comply" may be *inconsistent* with WTO obligations in ways different from the original measure.[24]

---

[22] *Australia – Salmon (Article 21.5 - Canada)*, at para. 7.10(22) [emphasis added]. Canada also refers to *EC – Bed Linen (Article 21.5)*, Panel Report, at para. 6.17.

[23] *EC – Bed Linen (Article 21.5)*, Panel Report, at para. 6.18, fn. 36.

[24] *EC – Bed Linen (Article 21.5)*, Appellate Body Report, at para. 79 [emphasis in original]. Canada also refers to the EC Third Party Submission (Exhibit C-3), at para. 28, referring in addition to the Appellate Body's report in *US – Shrimp (Article 21.5 – Malaysia)*, at para. 86.

4.18 Canada also submits that the US request for a preliminary ruling runs contrary to the very purpose of an Article 21.5 panel in its review of the imposition of countervailing measures, since the US obligation to demonstrate whether, and to what extent, alleged subsidies to log production pass through arm's length log purchases before imposing duties on softwood lumber products would remain in dispute for each annual assessment review under Article 21 of the SCM Agreement during the potential five-year life (or longer) of the US definitive countervailing measure. Canada asserts that such a result would leave the DSB in the absurd situation of having made numerous identical recommendations and rulings concerning a definitive countervailing duty for which compliance may never be secured. In this regard, Canada notes that the United States argued in *Australia – Salmon (Article 21.5 - Canada)* that:

> [W]e also wish to express the agreement of the United States with the broad and inclusive approach the Panel has taken thus far in defining the scope of this proceeding. The Panel's approach is the only one consistent with the purpose of the WTO dispute settlement system as reflected in Articles 3 and 21 of the Dispute Settlement Understanding: the prompt settlement of disputes. Disputes could not be settled "promptly" if a defending party were permitted to thwart a thorough review of its WTO compliance by staging the introduction of details of new measures over a period of time, and then arguing that they must escape WTO scrutiny for a further period of time.[25]

4.19 The United States denies that the results of the First Assessment Review rendered the Section 129 Determination non-existent. The United States submits that the Section 129 Determination, in implementing the recommendations and rulings of the DSB with respect to the final investigation determination, confirmed that the resulting imposition of countervailing duties on May 22, 2002, was consistent with the SCM Agreement. According to the United States, the very fact that Canada is, itself, challenging the Section 129 Determination shows that Canada believes that it is of ongoing effect and relevant to the issue of compliance.

4.20 The United States asserts that the present case is not a situation like that presented in *Australia – Automotive Leather II (Article 21.5 - US)*, in which a WTO-inconsistent subsidy was both withdrawn and "regranted" in another form on the same day, in "inextricably linked elements of a single transaction."[26] The United States asserts that first, in *Australia – Leather II (Article 21.5 - US)*, the United States was arguing that the panel should review whether a prohibited subsidy had actually been withdrawn, as specifically required by Article 4.7 of the SCM Agreement, when the repayment of a grant had been contingent on the simultaneous grant of a loan on non-commercial terms. The United States submits

[25] *Australia – Salmon (Article 21.5 - Canada)*, Third Participant Submission of the United States, 9 December 1999, at para. 5. (Exhibit CDA-54)

[26] Panel Report, *Australia Leather II (Article 21.5 - US)*, para. 6.50.

that, in contrast, this proceeding involves the question of whether a measure has been brought into conformity with a WTO agreement.

4.21 The United States submits that second, the *Australia – Leather II (Article 21.5 - US)* panel concluded that the subsidy had not been withdrawn at all, because the supposed repayment and the non-commercial loan were, in effect, a single transaction in which the subsidy simply shifted form. The United States asserts that, in this dispute, the Section 129 Determination and the First Assessment Review results are separate and independent actions. The United States asserts that the Section 129 Determination was made to bring the measure in dispute into conformity with the SCM Agreement as recommended by the DSB, whereas the First Assessment Review was conducted for a completely unrelated reason. According to the United States, therefore, the First Assessment Review in no way affects that result of the Section 129 Determination.

4.22 The United States also submits that the results of the First Assessment Review are not inextricably linked, either to the Section 129 Determination, or to the recommendations and rulings of the DSB. The United States notes Canada's reliance on *Australia – Leather II (Article 21.5 - US)*, and that panel's finding that the relevant subsidy had not been withdrawn, because the supposed repayment and the non-commercial loan were "inextricably linked elements of a single transaction."[27] The United States asserts that that situation is very different from this one. In particular, the United States notes that the Section 129 Determination and the First Assessment Review results were not in any sense contingent on one another, nor were they in any sense part of a single transaction. The United States submits that the First Assessment Review would have taken place regardless of whether there was a Section 129 proceeding under way, and, indeed, regardless of whether there even was a WTO dispute.

4.23 The United States notes that Canada also relies on *Australia – Salmon (Article 21.5 - Canada)*. The United States asserts that the imposition of a ban by Tasmania, one of Australia's sub-federal units, was obviously a response to the modification of the ban. The United States asserts that the Tasmanian ban did not arise from a proceeding initiated as a matter of domestic law requirements, irrespective of any WTO challenge, but was rather an *ad hoc* action taken after the DSB had made recommendations and rulings against an Australian import ban and after Australia had taken action to modify the ban. By contrast, the United States asserts that the assessment review was initiated:

- upon request of the parties (including Canada), eight months before the DSB's recommendations and rulings were even adopted;
- pursuant to a US statutory provision that requires initiation upon request on a specific schedule and under specific deadlines; and
- for the purpose of assessing countervailing duties on entries not previously examined – not for the purpose of implementing any recommendations or rulings.

---

27 *Australia –Leather II (Article 21.5 - US)*, para. 6.50.

4.24 Regarding Canada's argument that the facts of *EC – Bed Linen (Article 21.5 - India)* should be distinguished from the present case, the United States submits that the *EC – Bed Linen (Article 21.5 - India)* dispute demonstrates that a new determination that was made in a subsequent segment of an antidumping or countervailing duty proceeding – and *not* made to implement recommendations and rulings of the DSB – falls outside the jurisdiction of Article 21.5 panels.

4.25 The United States further submits that properly applying DSU Article 21.5 does not "ignore the purpose of compliance proceedings". The United States asserts that, contrary to Canada's arguments, a review under Article 21.5 of the Section 129 Determination permits the prompt settlement of disputes: Canada complained about an inconsistency in the final investigation determination, and this Panel will review whether that inconsistency has been corrected. The United States argues that Canada appears to suggest that the US system of retrospective duty assessments somehow compels the Panel, in the special case of the United States, to sweep the assessment review into this Article 21. 5 proceeding.[28] The United States submits, however, that there is nothing in Article 21.5 or in the SCM Agreement that requires a different interpretation of "measures taken to comply" for those Members that employ a retrospective duty assessment system, rather than a prospective one.

2. *Arguments of the third parties*

4.26 The European Communities considers that the US view (if accepted) would turn the US system of countervailing duty assessment into a moving target that escapes the WTO disciplines. The European Communities submits that the phrase "taken to comply" cannot be read to limit the 21.5 proceeding to those measures that were explicitly taken to replace the measure at issue in the original proceedings, but must be read together with its immediate and broader context as well as the purpose of the DSU to reach a prompt solution of a dispute. The European Communities asserts that because the phrase is preceded by the term "existence" and followed by the expression "with the recommendations and rulings of the DSB", an Article 21.5 panel is tasked to assess whether or not there is a failure to comply and whether or not the original dispute has been resolved (as opposed to assessing the conformity of a particular measure with a particular provision of the *Agreement Establishing the World Trade Organization* ("WTO Agreement"), as panels are required to do in initial proceedings).

4.27 The European Communities submits that the broader purpose of Article 21.5 of the DSU is to secure the solution of a dispute between two WTO Members relating to the measures brought before the original Panel. The European Communities asserts that this was explicitly recognised by the panel in *Australia – Salmon (Article 21.5 - Canada)*, which even considered a measure taken during the Article 21.5 proceeding since "to do otherwise would, in our view, go

[28] The United States refers in this regard to Canada's Second Written Submission, para. 27 (Annex A-2).

against the principle of prompt settlement of disputes and could hamper implementation of both DSB recommendations in the original dispute and our findings in this case."[29]

4.28 The European Communities submits that the US view is based on the assumption that the measures to be attacked in countervailing duty cases are the determinations made by the investigating authorities. The European Communities asserts that this is false, since Article 10 of the SCM Agreement clarifies that the measure of concern is the "imposition of a countervailing duty", defined as a "special duty levied" for the purpose of offsetting a subsidy. The European Communities submits that it is the duty itself that interferes with trade and is the measure of concern. The European Communities asserts that the assessment review at hand in this case is a hybrid instrument. It fixes the final duty rate for the assessment period with retrospective effect, but is not a fully-fledged review of both the subsidy and injury within the meaning of Article 21 of the SCM Agreement.[30] The European Communities notes that the assessment review does not change the date of the expiry of the measure under Article 21.3. The European Communities does not accept the US argument that footnote 52 of the SCM Agreement recognises that these types of assessment review are separate from the original determination (and / or a Section 129 determination). The European Communities also notes that the United States has not disputed Canada's characterisation of the First Assessment Review as superseding both the original countervailing duty determination and the Section 129 Determination. The European Communities asserts that, at the date of the establishment of the Panel (14 January 2005), only the First Assessment Review was effectively in place. The European Communities submits that, according to WTO jurisprudence, a measure that essentially replaces an earlier measure remains within the terms of reference of an original Panel.[31] The European Communities submits that, *a fortiori*, an Article 21.5 Panel must be in a position to assess whether an annual administrative review determination that confirms and supersedes the original determination relating to the same countervailing duty constitutes a "continuing violation".

4.29 The European Communities also rejects the US argument that *EC – Bed Linen (Article 21.5 - India)* stands for a general proposition that any review measure is outside the scope of a 21.5 proceeding. The European Communities asserts that the review measures at issue in that case were entirely different in nature. In particular, those measures were either specific reviews of antidumping duties imposed on exporters from other Members (Egypt and Pakistan) or entirely new determinations in a review based on results of an event subsequent to the European Communities having adopted the implementing measure in *EC – Bed Linen (Article 21.5 - India)*. In other words, they were dismissed because they did not relate to the original dispute between the European Communities and India.

---

[29] Panel Report, *Australia – Salmon (Article 21.5 - Canada)*, para. 7.21.

[30] Panel Report *US – Softwood Lumber III*, para 7.151.

[31] The European Communities refers to the Panel Report in *Dominican Republic – Import and Sale of Cigarettes*, paras. 7.11-7.21

4.30 According to the European Communities, accepting the US view that the First Assessment Review is not subject to a DSU 21.5 panel review would turn the US system of duty assessment into a moving target that escapes from countervailing duty disciplines. Each assessment review would have to be subject to a new panel request, and by the time the panel, Appellate Body and implementation procedure was completed, another assessment review would have overtaken the results of any Section 129 determination. A new panel would have to be started against this review, creating a "Groundhog Day" situation.

4.31 China asserts that, on the one hand, the First Assessment Review was made in a totally separate investigation procedure and based on the import data that is irrelevant to that of the original investigation. On the other hand, China asserts that the two determinations at issue were made under the framework of the same set of proceedings which effectively affects import of softwood lumber from Canada and the First Assessment Review supersedes the Section 129 Determination. In China's view, the first argument relates to the question of whether the First Assessment Review is a "measure[] taken to comply", while the second argument concerns the matter whether the Section 129 Determination is rendered non-existent.

4.32 Although China acknowledges that the First Assessment Review may not be properly categorized as a "measure[] taken to comply", China argues that this consideration does not lead to a decisive answer to the question of whether this measure is properly before this panel. China recalls that, on the basis of the plain language of Article 21.5, the purpose of the proceedings under this provision is to review and solve the dispute on "the *existence* or *consistency* with a covered agreement of measures taken to comply with the recommendations and rulings" of the DSB. China believes that "existence" and "consistency" are two distinct aspects of the subject measure. The latter involves review that is not only "limited to 'the issue of whether or not [a Member] has implemented the DSB recommendation'" [32], but also "in the light of any provision of any of the covered agreements."[33] On the other hand, the former relates to the status of the revised new measure. According to China, both aspects are equally important though the "existence" matter is crucial in solving the threshold issue in these proceedings.

4.33 China asserts that the dispute of *Australia – Automotive Leather II (Article 21.5 - US)* demonstrates a similar fact pattern that should be referenced by this Panel. China notes that, in that case, the Article 21.5 panel said:

> The 1999 loan is inextricably linked to the steps taken by Australia in response to the DSB's ruling in this dispute, in view of both its timing and its nature. In our view, the 1999 loan cannot be excluded from our consideration without severely limiting our ability to judge, on the basis of the United States' request, whether Australia has taken measures to comply with the DSB's ruling. In the absence of any compelling reason to do so, we decline to conclude

32 *Canada - Aircraft (Article 21.5)*, Appellate Body Report, para.40.

33 *Australia - Salmon (Article 21.5 - Canada)*, para.7.10.

> that a measure specifically identified in the request for establishment is not within our terms of reference. [34]

4.34 In China's view, in an Article 25.1 procedure, if the complaining party submits that a "measure[] taken to comply" is invalidated by a subsequent measure, the compliance panel should at least assess this claim that relates to the "measure[] taken to comply" on the basis of relevant facts – the subsequent measure. China asserts that to exclude the second measure would put the panel at the risk of failing to make a comprehensive and well-founded judgement on the existence of a measure taken to comply with DSB recommendations and rulings. China believes that, as a result of the countervailing duty assessment system adopted by the US, the results of an assessment review may, at least in form, replace the original final determination. In particular, China notes that the results of the First Assessment Review were announced ten days after the Section 129 Determination took effect. Thus, the First Assessment Review established a new rate for cash deposit for the goods from Canada and replaced the rate in the Section 129 Determination. According to China, such changes in the applicable duty rate deserve further consideration on whether the First Assessment Review, in substance, rendered the Section 129 Determination non-existent. China therefore submits that the facts presented by Canada in these proceedings, at least, have demonstrated that there is likelihood that the First Assessment Review may nullify the Section 129 Determination.

4.35 In summary, China is of the opinion that, although the First Assessment Review may not be a measure taken to comply, it is closely linked to and may have an important effect on the existence of the purported measure taken to comply – the Section 129 Determination. On such basis, China believes it is the mandate of this Panel to consider the First Assessment Review in these proceedings.

3. *Evaluation by the Panel*

4.36 The US request for a preliminary ruling concerns the scope of Article 21.5 of the DSU, which provides in relevant part:

> Where there is disagreement as to the existence or consistency with a covered agreement of measures taken to comply with the recommendations and rulings such dispute shall be decided through recourse to these dispute settlement procedures, including wherever possible resort to the original panel.

4.37 In particular, the US request requires us to determine whether or not the First Assessment Review, or at least the treatment of pass-through contained therein, constitutes a "measure[] taken to comply" with the rulings and recommendations of the DSB in respect of the Final Determination.

4.38 In addressing this issue, we are guided by dispute settlement decisions regarding the scope of DSU Article 21.5. These decisions indicate that Article

---

[34] *Australia – Automotive Leather II (Article 21.5 - US)*, para. 6.5.

21.5 proceedings are not restricted to measures formally, or explicitly, taken by Members to implement DSB rulings and recommendations. In this regard , we note that the panel in *Australia – Salmon II (Article 21.5 – Canada)* found that:

> an Article 21.5 panel cannot leave it to the full discretion of the implementing Member to decide whether or not a measure is one "taken to comply". If one were to allow that, an implementing Member could simply avoid any scrutiny of certain measures by a compliance panel, even where such measures would be so clearly connected to the panel and Appellate Body reports concerned, both in time and in respect of the subject-matter, that any impartial observer would consider them to be measures "taken to comply".[35]

4.39 That case concerned Australia's implementation of DSB rulings and recommendations regarding import restrictions on untreated fresh, chilled or frozen salmon from Canada. Australia stated that it implemented the DSB's rulings and recommendations through a series of import risk analyses that entered into force on 19 July 1999. On 20 October 1999, during the course of the Article 21.5 proceedings concerning the measures adopted by Australia in July 1999, the Government of Tasmania adopted measures restricting all imports of salmonids. The panel employed the following terms in finding that the October 1999 measure fell within the terms of its DSU Article 21.5 review:

> "Without attempting to give a precise definition of "measures taken to comply" that should apply in *all* cases, we are of the view that in the context of this dispute at least any quarantine measure introduced by Australia subsequent to the adoption on 6 November 1998 of DSB recommendations and rulings in the original dispute – and within a more or less limited period of time thereafter - that applies to imports of fresh chilled or frozen salmon from Canada, is a "measure taken to comply". The Tasmanian ban, introduced on 20 October 1999, imposes an import prohibition on all imports of salmonids into part of Australia on quarantine grounds. We thus find that it is a measure taken to comply in the sense of Article 21.5."[36]

4.40 The scope of DSU Article 21.5 proceedings was also addressed by the panel in *Australia – Leather II (Article 21.5 - US)*. That case concerned Australia's implementation of DSB's rulings and recommendations regarding the withdrawal of a prohibited export subsidy. In September 1999, the subsidy recipient repaid the prospective element of the subsidy. Simultaneously, the Government of Australia provided a loan to the original subsidy recipient. In finding that both the repayment of the original subsidy, and the new loan, fell within the scope of its DSU Article 21.5 review, the panel stated:

> The 1999 loan is inextricably linked to the steps taken by Australia in response to the DSB's ruling in this dispute, in view of both its

35 *Australia – Salmon (Article 21.5 – Canada)*, page 106.

36 *Australia – Salmon (Article 21.5 – Canada)*, page 106 (footnote deleted).

> timing and its nature. In our view, the 1999 loan cannot be excluded from our consideration without severely limiting our ability to judge, on the basis of the United States' request, whether Australia has taken measures to comply with the DSB's ruling. In the absence of any compelling reason to do so, we decline to conclude that a measure specifically identified in the request for establishment is not within our terms of reference.[37]

4.41 The parties agree that the Section 129 Determination falls within the scope of these DSU Article 21.5 proceedings. In our view, and taking into account previous dispute settlement decisions regarding DSU Article 21.5, the USDOC's treatment of pass-through in the First Assessment Review is also covered by these proceedings, because it is clearly connected to the panel and Appellate Body reports concerning the Final Determination, and because it is inextricably linked to the treatment of pass-through in the Section 129 Determination. In particular, we note that certain import entries subject to the prospective effect of the Final Determination are also subject to the retrospective effect of the First Assessment Review. Thus, while the First Assessment Review resulted in an assessment rate for import entries during the period 22 May 2002 – 31 March 2003, those entries had initially been subject to the cash deposit rate determined in the Final Determination.[38] Furthermore, the prospective effect of the Section 129 Determination was superseded by the prospective effect of the First Assessment Review, in the sense that import entries that would have been subject to the cash deposit rate fixed by the Section 129 Determination became subject to the cash deposit rate fixed by the First Assessment Review, once the latter took effect. Thus, even though the period of investigation of the Final Determination and Section 129 Determination may differ from the period of review of the First Assessment Review, and even though the latter was initiated before the DSB adopted any rulings or recommendations regarding this matter, there is in fact considerable overlap in the effect of these various measures. Since the pass-through analysis in the First Assessment Review could, therefore, have an impact on, and possibly undermine, any implementation of the DSB rulings and recommendations regarding pass-through by the Section 129 Determination, we consider that the pass-through analysis in the First Assessment Review should also fall within the scope of these DSU Article 21.5 proceedings.[39]

---

37 *Australia – Leather II (Article 21.5 - US)*, para. 6.5.

38 Import entries subject to the Section 129 Determination cash deposit would be assessed pursuant to a subsequent assessment review, if requested. We do not attach importance to the fact that import entries subject to the Section 129 Determination cash deposit were not formally subject to the First Assessment Review, since the Section 129 Determination amended and replaced the Final Determination, such that there is no need to distinguish between the coverage of these two measures for present purposes.

39 We do not here mean to imply that, on the basis of our interpretation and analysis of the scope of DSU Article 21.5, other elements of the First Assessment Review, dealing with issues unrelated to the scope of the DSB's adopted recommendations and rulings in the original dispute between the parties, could be treated as part of a "measure[] taken to comply" and thereby challenged through an Article 21.5 proceeding.

4.42 The United States argues that the findings of the *Australia – Leather II (Article 21.5 - US)* panel should be distinguished, because the Section 129 Determination and First Assessment Review were not contingent on one another. We acknowledge that the First Assessment Review was not contingent on the Section 129 Determination, and note that the First Assessment Review might very well have been initiated even if the Section 129 Determination had not been undertaken. However, the degree of contingency between the relevant measures was clearly not the sole, or determining factor, in the reasoning of the *Australia – Leather II (Article 21.5 - US)* panel regarding the inclusion of the loan in the DSU Article 21.5 proceeding.[40] That panel was concerned more generally with the "timing and nature" of the subsequent loan. As noted above, we consider that there is sufficient overlap in the timing, or temporal effect, and nature of the Final Determination, Section 129 Determination and First Assessment Review for the latter to fall within the scope of the present DSU Article 21.5 proceedings.

4.43 The United States also argues that the findings of the panel in *Australia – Salmon (Article 21.5 - Canada)* should be distinguished because that case concerned an *ad hoc* action taken after the DSB adopted its rulings and recommendations, whereas the First Assessment Review was initiated pursuant to domestic law requirements, eight months before, and independent of any consideration of, the rulings and recommendations of the DSB in *US – Softwood Lumber IV*. We note, however, that the *Australia – Salmon (Article 21.5 - Canada)* panel made no reference to the *ad hoc* nature of the Tasmanian import ban in its findings. Accordingly, since the *ad hoc* nature of that import ban did not influence that panel's findings, this is no basis on which to distinguish those findings from the present case. In any event, we consider that the *Australia – Salmon (Article 21.5 - Canada)* panel was concerned primarily with the timing and subject-matter of the Tasmanian import restriction, and its subsequent impact on the July 1999 implementing measures adopted by the Government of Australia, just as we are concerned primarily with the potential impact of the results of the First Assessment Review on the Final Determination and Section 129 Determination.

4.44 The United States also argues that the First Assessment Review is a new determination, separate from the Final Determination and Section 129 Determination, and initiated prior to the DSB's adoption of recommendations and rulings in this dispute. The United States relies on the following findings of the panel in *EC – Bed Linen (Article 21.5 - India)*:

> [T]he fact that the EC, subsequent to its re-examination of the dumping determinations with respect to imports from Egypt and Pakistan, and in the context of a review initiated on the request of

[40] In its comments on Canada's reply to Question 21 from the Panel, the US asserts that "the fact that the grant repayment was conditioned on the provision of the new non-commercial loan was central to the panel's finding that the two actions were 'inextricably linked elements of a single transaction'". We note that the US refers in this regard to para. 6.50 of the *Australia – Leather II (Article 21.5 - US)* report, where the panel was addressing the substantive issue of whether or not Australia had withdrawn its prohibited subsidies. Contingency between the subsidy repayment and new loan was not mentioned explicitly by that panel at para. 6.5 of its report, where it was determining whether or not to include the new loan in the scope of its DSU Article 21.5 proceeding.

> Eurocoton, carried out an analysis of whether injury was caused by imports from India alone does not, *ipso facto*, establish that Regulation 696/2002 is a measure "taken to comply". Rather the opposite would seem to be the case – that Regulation would seem to be an **entirely new determination**, reached as a result of **events subsequent** to the EC having adopted a measure to comply with the DSB's recommendation.[41]

4.45 According to the United States, the *EC – Bed Linen (Article 21.5 - India)* dispute demonstrates that a new determination that was made in a subsequent segment of an anti-dumping or countervailing duty proceeding – and not made to implement recommendations and rulings of the DSB – falls outside the jurisdiction of DSU Article 21.5 panels.[42]

4.46 In *EC – Bed Linen (Article 21.5 - India)*, the European Communities imposed anti-dumping duties on imports of bed linen from Egypt, India and Pakistan. The European Communities made a cumulative injury assessment. The European Communities was found to have incorrectly calculated anti-dumping duties on imports from India. The European Communities amended its calculation in respect of such imports from India. The parties agreed that the re-determination of dumping in respect of imports from India fell within the scope of DSU Article 21.5. The European Communities also applied the revised calculation method to other anti-dumping duties imposed on imports from Egypt and Pakistan. As a result, the European Communities found that anti-dumping duties should not be imposed on such imports. Consequently, the European Communities conducted a separate injury analysis in respect of imports from India, to determine whether such imports alone caused injury to the domestic industry. The European Communities found that they did, and therefore affirmed the imposition of anti-dumping duties on imports of bed linen from India. India claimed that the determinations in respect of Egypt and Pakistan, and the finding of injury and the resulting imposition of anti-dumping duties on bed linen from India,

---

[41] *EC – Bed Linen (Article 21.5)*, para. 6.20 (bold emphasis added).

[42] The US also argues that Article 21.5 proceedings are by their nature more focused and limited than other panel proceedings under Article 6.2 of the DSU, and that it is beyond the scope of such a limited 90-day inquiry to fully examine an entirely new set of assessment review results based on a wholly new administrative record, consisting of new sales, new imports, potentially new respondents and potentially new subsidy programmes. We note, however, that US law allows DSB rulings and recommendations to be implemented through administrative reviews in certain circumstances (see "Statement of Administrative Action" in *Message from the President of the United States Transmitting the Uruguay Round Agreements, Texts of Agreements Implementing Bill, Statement of Administrative Action and Required Supporting Statements*, H.R. Doc. No. 103-316, vol. 1 at 656 (Exhibit CDA-1), at 356-357). This undermines the US argument that assessment reviews should be excluded from the scope of DSU Article 21.5 proceedings. Furthermore, we note that measures taken to comply with the rulings and recommendations of the DSB may be every bit as complex, if not more so, than the original measure in dispute. DSU Article 21.5 does not provide for accelerated procedures because implementation measures are necessarily simple, or straightforward. It does so in order to ensure that justice is delivered swiftly. In any event, we note that we are only finding that part of the First Assessment Review (i.e., the pass-through analysis) is covered by these DSU Article 21.5 proceedings. We are not finding that the entirety of the First Assessment Review is covered by these proceedings.

were measures "taken to comply" under DSU Article 21.5. The above panel finding relied on by the United States concerns the Panel's exclusion of the India-specific injury determination from the scope of the DSU Article 21.5 proceedings.

4.47 While we acknowledge that the First Assessment Review is a new determination made in a subsequent segment of a countervailing duty proceeding, we disagree with what we see as the implication of the United States argument, i.e., that *EC – Bed Linen (Article 21.5 – India)* stands for the principle that a measure taken in a subsequent segment of a proceeding could never constitute a "measure[] taken to comply" in the meaning of DSU Article 21.5, if it is not explicitly so identified. Rather, we understand the panel in *EC – Bed Linen (Article 21.5 – India)* to have ruled that, in the particular circumstances of that case, the measure taken in a subsequent segment of a proceeding did not constitute a "measure[] taken to comply". In our view, the above finding of the *EC – Bed Linen (Article 21.5)* panel can be distinguished from the present case, as the First Assessment Review does not concern "events subsequent" to the Final Determination and Section 129 Determination. The relevant measure in *EC – Bed Linen (Article 21.5 - India)* concerned an injury determination initiated as a result of a re-determination of dumping in respect of imports that were not covered by the relevant rulings and recommendations of the DSB. Thus, not even the re-determination of dumping in respect of those imports was a "measure[] taken to comply", let alone the new injury determination prompted by that re-determination of dumping. By contrast, the First Assessment Review is far more closely connected to what the United States considers is the "measure[] taken to comply", i.e., the Section 129 Determination. In particular, the First Assessment Review is concerned with the same substantive issue as the Section 129 Determination, i.e., pass-through. In addition, the First Assessment Review applies to import entries that were initially subject to the cash deposit rate fixed by the measure subsequently replaced by the Section 129 Determination. Furthermore, the panel in *EC – Bed Linen (Article 21.5 - India)* explicitly noted that India "[did] not argue that the subsequent two measures und[id] the compliance effectuated by the first measure".[43] We can only assume that the panel would have reached a different conclusion if India had argued that the subsequent measures undid the compliance effectuated by the first measure, as Canada has done in the present case.

4.48 We further note that in addressing the scope of the Article 21.5 proceedings in *EC – Bed Linen (Article 21.5 - India)*, the Appellate Body had regard to "the object and purpose of the DSU". In this regard, the Appellate Body noted that, by virtue of Article 3.3 of the DSU, "the prompt settlement of disputes" is "essential to the effective functioning of the WTO". Given the overlap in effect of the Final Determination, Section 129 Determination, and the First Assessment Review, we are very conscious that if we exclude the pass-through analysis in the First Assessment Review from these proceedings, Canada and the United States will still dispute the same issue, i.e., pass-through of subsidy benefit, in

---

43 *EC – Bed Linen (Article 21.5)*, para. 6.21.

respect of the same import entries[44], as they did in the original proceedings concerning the Final Determination. In our view, this would be wholly inconsistent with the object and purpose of the DSU which, as noted above, is to ensure the prompt settlement of disputes.

4.49 Before concluding, we note that Canada, China and the European Communities have made a number of arguments that might suggest that DSU Article 21.5 should be interpreted broadly in the present case because of the peculiarities of the system of retrospective duty assessment applied by the United States. We do not consider it appropriate to base our findings on such arguments, because the interpretation and application of DSU Article 21.5 must accommodate both prospective and retrospective duty assessment systems. As a consequence, we have considered carefully the operation of DSU Article 21.5 in the context of both prospective and retrospective duty assessment systems, in light of the abovementioned dispute settlement decisions.

4.50 For the foregoing reasons, we reject the US request for a preliminary ruling that the First Assessment Review falls outside the scope of these DSU Article 21.5 proceedings, in so far as the pass-through analysis is concerned.

B. Scope of USDOC's pass-through analysis

4.51 Canada's main argument in this proceeding is that USDOC, in implementing the rulings and recommendations of the DSB, continued to presume a pass-through of subsidy benefits, rather than conducting the required analysis. Canada claims that this resulted in the imposition of countervailing duties in a manner inconsistent with Articles 10 and 32.1 of the SCM Agreement, and Article VI:3 of the GATT 1994. In particular, Canada argues that USDOC completely excluded entire groups of transactions, on the basis that these were not arm's length sales, and in addition erred by rejecting the aggregate data and information provided by Canada in support of its pass-through claim, requiring instead company-specific data[45], and also by applying "inappropriate"[46] benchmark prices for those transactions that were individually examined for pass-through. Canada also claims that, in the Section 129 Determination and the First Assessment Review, the USDOC continued to presume pass-through in respect of purchases of logs from sawmills by unrelated tenure-holding sawmills. Furthermore, Canada claims that the USDOC presumed pass-through in respect of all sawmill-to-sawmill transactions in the context of the First Assessment Review. Canada claims that, as a result of all the above, the United States impermissibly inflated

---

[44] We refer to those import entries for which the Final Determination set the cash deposit rate, and the First Assessment Review finalized the duty assessment. See, para. 4.41, *supra*.

[45] We recall here that the United States objected (at our substantive meeting with the parties) to Canada's assertion that the USDOC had "rejected" any data submitted by Canada in the Section 129 proceeding (Canada's first written submission, para. 32). In commenting on this argument, Canada clarified that it was not claiming that the United States had outright rejected the information in question, but instead that the USDOC had failed to analyse various record data when any of the five factors existed (Canada's reply to Question 27 from the Panel).

[46] Canada's first written submission, page 22, heading 2 (Annex A – 1).

the amount of countervailing duties levied on imports of softwood lumber from Canada. We shall examine each of these claims in turn.[47]

1. Arm's length transactions

(a) Arguments of the parties

4.52 Canada asserts that pass-through should be investigated whenever there is a transaction between unrelated parties. In both the Section 129 Determination and the First Assessment Review, however, USDOC only investigated pass-through in respect of a narrower category of transactions, namely those that were found by USDOC to be at arm's length. Canada states that the USDOC found that transactions between unrelated parties were not at arm's length if any one of the following factors existed in the province: (1) limitations on log sales in Crown tenure contracts; (2) wood supply commitment letters; (3) payment of the stumpage fees by the downstream log purchaser; (4) log purchase agreements of a certain structure; or (5) fibre exchange agreements between tenured sawmills.

4.53 Canada disputes the application of what Canada refers to as USDOC's "external factor" test. According to Canada, a transaction between unrelated parties is by definition an arm's length transaction. Canada asserts that, because the external factors identified by the USDOC do not transform an arm's length transaction into one that is not at arm's length, the existence of any such factors cannot excuse the United States from its obligation to conduct the required benefit pass-through analysis. According to Canada, none of the factors identified by USDOC alters the fact that sellers of logs attempt to obtain the best price available in transactions with unrelated purchasers.

4.54 The United States asserts that the DSB's recommendations and rulings concerned only (1) arm's length sales (2) between unrelated parties. According to the United States, both of these conditions must be fulfilled before a pass-through analysis becomes necessary. In particular, the United States argues that sales between formally unrelated parties are not necessarily arm's length. The United States asserts that the DSB's recommendations and rulings themselves recognize a distinction between arm's length and affiliation, presenting arm's length sales as a subset of sales between unrelated entities, since the DSB (by virtue of para. 167(e) of the Appellate Body's report) ruled that USDOC should have conducted "a pass-through analysis in respect of arm's length sales of *logs*...to unrelated sawmills." (emphasis in original) The United States argues

[47] Canada's request for establishment of a panel also refers to a claim concerning the USDOC "applying the results of the 'pass-through' analysis to a countervailing duty cash deposit rate invalidated as a result of judicial review proceedings conducted in accordance with US law, and failing to apply the results to a valid rate" (WT/DS257/15, page 2). Although this claim was alluded to in the introduction to Canada's first written submission (para. 10) (see Annex A – 1), Canada did not revert to this claim in the substantive part of that submission. Nor did Canada pursue this claim in its subsequent oral or written submissions to the Panel. We therefore consider that Canada has effectively abandoned this claim. In any event, we find that the very brief reference to this issue at para. 10 of Canada's first written submission is insufficient to establish a *prima facie* case in support of Canada's claim.

that whether the entities operate "at arm's length" involves more than just a question of formal affiliation; it involves an analysis of whether one party effectively "controls" the other or whether the parties have roughly equal bargaining power. The United States argues that its five factor test addresses this issue of control, since many of the circumstances of sales of lumber in Canada are controlled by government mandates and other government-imposed conditions.

4.55 The United States asserts that USDOC identified two categories of government-mandated restrictions whereby log sellers are not free to act in their best interests to choose and negotiate among potential buyers: (1) limitations on log sales that are contained in Crown tenure contracts, such as appurtenancy and local processing requirements, and (2) wood supply agreements. The United States asserts that USDOC also determined that many of the Canadian log sales could not be considered to be at arm's length because the actual structure of certain log purchase agreements empowered the purchasing sawmill to control many aspects of the transaction. Specifically, with respect to certain log purchase agreements, the sawmill actively manages all aspects of harvest and delivery. With respect to others, the sawmill finances or provides other goods or services as part of the transaction.

4.56 The United States asserts that USDOC also considered that it was not required to conduct a pass-through analysis when two other factors were present: (i) payment of the stumpage fees by the downstream lumber producers and (ii) fibre exchange agreements between Crown tenure holders. Although the United States submits that these factors are "not exclusively arm's-length issues",[48] it is clear that the USDOC found that transactions were not arm's length when these factors existed.[49]

4.57 The United States argues that its approach to implementing the DSB's recommendations and rulings is based on the explicit language of the Appellate Body's ruling.

(b) Evaluation by the Panel

4.58 The United States has emphasized before us throughout this Article 21.5 proceeding that it based its approach to pass-through, in the Section 129 Determination[50], on the language of the Appellate Body's report, and specifically on the Appellate Body's use of the phrase "arm's length" in its ruling. We recall that the exact wording of the Appellate Body's ruling is:

> "the Appellate Body ... *upholds* the Panel's finding ... that USDOC's failure to contact a pass-through analysis in respect of

---

[48] US second written submission, para. 23 (see Annex B – 2).

[49] See, for example, page 4 of Section 129 Determination (Exhibit CDA-5) ("where we determined that any of the sales reported by the Canadian parties were affected by one or several of the five factors listed above, we concluded that the transactions were not conducted at arm's length").

[50] The US arguments in this proceeding did not cover USDOC's conduct of the Final Assessment Review. We note, however, that the USDOC adopted the same approach to pass-through in the First Assessment Review as in the Section 129 Determination.

arm's length sales of *logs* by tenured harvesters/sawmills to unrelated sawmills is inconsistent..."[51]

We further recall that our finding being upheld by the Appellate Body makes no reference to the term "arm's length".

(i) Scope of original panel findings compared with scope of appeal and scope of Appellate Body rulings

4.59 Before entering into the details of the Appellate Body's ruling, and its potential implications for the parties, we first recall that in the original dispute there were three broad categories of transactions in respect of which we found that the United States' failure to conduct a pass-through analysis was inconsistent with various provisions of the covered Agreements. Specifically, these categories were: (1) sales of logs by tenured timber harvesters that do not produce lumber to unrelated lumber producers; (2) sales of logs by tenured harvester-sawmills to unrelated sawmills; and (3) sales of lumber by tenured harvester-sawmills to unrelated lumber re-manufacturers. The United States did not appeal our finding in respect of the first of these categories of transactions. It did appeal our findings in respect of the second and third categories of transactions. The Appellate Body, in turn, upheld our finding in respect of the second category, and reversed our finding in respect of the third category.

4.60 Given both the scope and the outcome of the US appeal, the DSB's recommendations and rulings which the United States was obliged to implement in respect of the first category of transactions consist exclusively of our findings. In respect of the second category, these recommendations and rulings consist of our findings and the relevant findings of the Appellate Body. In respect of the third category, in view of the reversal on appeal of our findings, there were no DSB recommendations and rulings for the United States to implement. We take up the first and second categories separately.[52]

---

[51] Appellate Body Report, para. 167(e) (italic emphasis in original, bold emphasis supplied).

[52] We note that Canada's arguments concerning the USDOC pass-through analysis refer to transactions between "independent harvesters" and sawmills. This could mean that Canada's claim is limited to the first category of transactions identified above. However, since note 2 of the USDOC's Section 129 Determination provides that "[f]or purposes of this determination, the referenced log sales by tenured independent harvesters/sawmills will be referred to as sales by independent harvesters", we understand Canada's claim concerning "independent harvester" transactions to include both of categories of transactions. Furthermore, we understand that both categories of transactions were covered by the Section 129 Determination, whereas only the first category of transaction was covered by the First Assessment Review. If the USDOC were to have applied its five factor approach in respect of the second category of transactions in the First Assessment Review, our evaluation would have been the same as for the USDOC's treatment of that category of transactions in the Section 129 Determination.

(ii) Sales of logs by tenured timber harvesters that do not produce lumber to unrelated lumber producers

4.61 Canada objects to USDOC's application of the five factors in all situations in order to identify for further pass-through analysis log sale transactions that were made at "arm's length". Canada argues that, instead, a pass-through analysis is required in respect of all log sales between unrelated entities. The United States did not appeal our findings in respect of sales of logs by tenured timber harvesters that do not produce lumber to unrelated lumber producers. Thus, as noted, our findings alone constitute the substance of the DSB's recommendations and rulings in respect of this category of transactions. We therefore start by recalling the details of our analysis and findings on the pass-through issue in general, along with our specific pass-through findings on this category of transactions.

4.62 We recall that, as a general matter, the primary focus of our discussion and findings on pass-through in our Panel Report centred on affiliation. Thus, we described the "basic question" presented by Canada's pass-through claim as

> "whether USDOC was obligated to conduct a pass-through analysis in respect of the input transactions between timber harvesters (both those that produce lumber and those that do not) and **unrelated** sawmills, and between sawmills and unrelated re-manufacturers ...".[53]

4.63 We then explained that we understood Canada's claim to be

> "that where upstream transactions between **unrelated** entities exist for inputs, any subsidies to the producers of those inputs cannot be assumed also to be subsidies to the downstream product under investigation."[54]

4.64 We noted that

> "[w]here the subsidies at issue are received by **someone other than** the producer of the investigated product, the question arises whether there is subsidization in respect of that product."[55]

4.65 We then stated that

> "[t]he heart of the pass-through issue is whether, where a subsidy is received by **someone other than** the producer or exporter of the product under investigation, the subsidy nevertheless can be said to have conferred benefits in respect of that product."[56]

4.66 Finally, we concluded, at paragraph 7.99 of our report, that

> the USDOC's failure to conduct a pass-through analysis in respect of logs sold by tenure-holding timber harvesters (whether or not

---

[53] Panel Report, para. 7.81 (emphasis supplied).
[54] Panel Report, para. 7.85 (emphasis supplied).
[55] *Ibid.*
[56] Panel Report, para. 7.91 (emphasis supplied).

> also lumber producers) to **unrelated** sawmills producing subject softwood lumber ... was inconsistent with Article 10 and thus Article 32.1 SCM Agreement, and with Article VI:3 of GATT 1994.[57]

4.67 This conclusion was repeated in similar terms in the final section of the Panel Report, where we held that:

> "the USDOC's failure to conduct a pass-through analysis in respect of upstream transactions for log and lumber inputs between **unrelated** entities was inconsistent with Article 10 SCM Agreement and Article VI:3 of GATT 1994".[58]

4.68 At most places in our analysis and conclusions, therefore, we did not use the term "arm's length" in discussing the pass-through issue, but instead addressed the potential obligation to conduct a pass-through analysis as pertaining to transactions between *unrelated* parties.

4.69 We acknowledge, however, that we did make some limited references to the term "arm's length" in our findings, although we did not define that term. Footnote 163 of our Panel Report, which was included in a sentence describing the "basic question presented by [Canada's] claim" as concerning the need to conduct a pass-through analysis in respect of transactions between *unrelated* entities, states, in relevant part:

> "We note that this claim only concerns such alleged **arms'-length** transactions between unrelated entities ..."[59]

4.70 We also used the term "arm's length" at paragraphs 7.94 and 7.95 of our report, in the context of the first category of transactions, namely log sales to lumber producers by timber harvesters that do not produce lumber. In particular, in paragraph 7.94 we identified such sales as the first type of "arms' length" transaction that we needed to address. We then summarized the US position as being that no pass-through analysis was needed for such transactions because of their small volume and because they might not be at "arms' length". This latter was a reference back to the US argument, summarized at paragraph 7.76 of our report, that "the many restrictions imposed on tenure holders, including requirements to process timber locally, 'suggests that all or most of the sales by independent loggers may not be at arms'-length'". We noted, at paragraph 7.95 of our report, that the United States neither cited to any record evidence establishing "the volume of the possible arms'-length sales at issue", nor argued that USDOC had made efforts to collect such information. We went on to say that the United States had not conducted the required pass-through analysis for these transactions, and had "point[ed] to no factual basis in the record for its conclusion that such an analysis was not necessary".

4.71 As noted above, however, our overall conclusion in respect of all categories of log sales (including by timber harvesters not owning sawmills to sawmills) was clear in stating that pass-through analysis was required where the par-

---

[57] Panel Report, para. 7.99 (emphasis supplied).

[58] Panel Report, para. 8.1(c) (emphasis supplied).

[59] Panel Report, note 163 (emphasis supplied).

ties to such transactions were *unrelated.* In short, based on the language of our conclusion and the underlying language of our analysis, in the original dispute before us, our primary focus in respect of the pass-through issue was in fact transactions between *unrelated* parties.

4.72 Indeed, in the present Article 21.5 proceeding, even the United States explicitly acknowledges that our findings were *not* premised on or restricted by any concept of "arm's length" transactions. In particular, in response to one of our questions, the United States notes that

> "as evident in paragraph 7.95, however, the original panel's findings did not depend upon whether or not the sales claimed by Canada were, in fact, arm's length sales."[60]

4.73 We thus conclude that, in respect of log sales by tenure-holding timber harvesters that do not own sawmills to unrelated sawmills, the USDOC's exclusion from pass-through analysis of certain such sales on the grounds that they were not at "arm's length" was inconsistent with the United States' obligations pursuant to the DSB's recommendations and rulings.

(iii) Sales of logs by tenured harvester-sawmills to unrelated sawmills

4.74 We now turn to the second broad category of log sales at issue in this Article 21.5 proceeding, in respect of which the United States appealed our finding that a pass-through analysis was required. For this category – log sales by tenured harvester/sawmills to unrelated sawmills – the Appellate Body upheld our finding but in doing so introduced the term "arm's length", which does not appear in our finding. We recall that in the original dispute and before the Appellate Body, both parties used the term "arm's length" at various points in their arguments, apparently with considerably different meanings. They presented no arguments concerning the issue of "arm's length" as such, however. As noted above, in the Panel Report we did make some limited references to the term "arm's length", although not in the context of the second category of log sales, and we did not ascribe any particular definition to this term. In addition, and most significantly for this Article 21.5 proceeding, the term arm's length appears in numerous places in the Appellate Body's analysis (although without being defined), especially in its ruling at paragraph 167(e) upholding our finding in respect of this category of log sales.

4.75 We understand the United States to argue in the present proceeding that it based its implementation of the DSB's recommendations and rulings on the explicit wording used by the Appellate Body, which according to the United States upheld our finding to the extent of "arm's length" sales of logs by tenured harvester/sawmills to unrelated sawmills. In other words, the United States views the Appellate Body (and thus the DSB) as having modified, albeit implicitly, our conclusions concerning the pass-though issue in respect of this category of log sales. On this basis, a primary focus of the USDOC's analysis in the Section 129

[60] US Answers to Panel's questions, 29 April 2005 (Article 21.5 proceeding), at paragraph 9.

Determination in respect of log sales by tenured harvester/sawmills to unrelated sawmills was to identify which transactions in the universe of such sales were and were not at arm's length. For Canada, however, the term "arm's length" has to do exclusively with corporate affiliation – any transaction between unaffiliated parties is, by definition, an arm's length transaction. Thus, for Canada, the Appellate Body used the term "arm's length" synonymously with "unrelated".[61] Canada argues that therefore, the USDOC, by not conducting a competitive benefit analysis in respect of the sales between unrelated parties that it found not to be at "arm's length", failed to comply with the DSB's recommendations and rulings.

4.76 We thus find ourselves confronted with significant ambiguity surrounding the issue of pass-through in the DSB's recommendations and rulings in respect of log sales by tenured harvester/sawmills to unrelated sawmills, which ambiguity seems to have arisen from the inclusion of the term "arm's length" in the conclusion set forth at para. 167(e) of the Appellate Body Report.[62] It is not clear to us why the Appellate Body chose to include this term in its ruling. This ambiguity is compounded by the fact that the participants in the appellate proceedings were each relying on separate meanings of that term. In this regard, while we can understand that the United States sought to give meaning to the Appellate Body's use of the term "arm's length", we disagree with the United States' reasoning.

4.77 There are several important factors in respect of which we are in no doubt. First, the scope of the DSB recommendations and rulings to be implemented by the United States is not based exclusively on the adopted findings of the Appellate Body. The findings of the original panel adopted by the DSB are also relevant in this regard.

4.78 Second, as noted above and as acknowledged by the United States, *our* overall conclusion in respect of all categories of log sales (whether or not the tenured log seller owns a sawmill) was clear in stating that pass-through analysis was required where the parties to such transactions were unrelated.

4.79 Third, the explicit language used by the Appellate Body at para. 167(e) of its report was to "uphold" our conclusion in respect of log sales by tenured harvester/sawmills to unrelated sawmills, as set forth in the relevant part of the first sentence of para. 7.99 of the Panel Report. That is, para. 167(e) of the Appellate Body Report contains no explicit modification of the finding at para. 7.99 of the Panel Report in respect of log sales by tenured harvester/sawmills to unrelated sawmills.

4.80 Nor does the United States argue that there is such an *explicit* modification. Rather, the United States' argument is that the Appellate Body, in introducing the word "arm's length" into its ruling, *implicitly modified* our conclusion. In this context we recall that Article 17.13 of the DSU permits the Appellate Body to "uphold, modify or reverse" the findings of a panel. We would expect, however, that any such action would be explicit. In particular, if the Appellate Body

61 See, for example, para. 10 of Comments of Canada on the Responses by the United States Following the Substantive Meeting of the Panel.

62 We recall here that the United States does not consider that our findings in the original dispute were conditioned on any concept of "arms' length". See para. 4.72, *supra*.

intended to modify a finding that it was explicitly upholding, such modification presumably likewise would be made explicitly. Indeed, in other cases, the Appellate Body has been very explicit when modifying a panel's findings, identifying precisely which finding (or which part of a finding) was being modified.[63] In this case, however, the Appellate Body Report contains no discussion of the meaning of the term "arm's length", nor any explanation of how it may have intended to distinguish that term from the word "unrelated". We consider that for an Article 21.5 panel to accept, in such circumstances, that the Appellate Body had *implicitly* modified the underlying panel findings could have serious systemic implications, since it could result in significant uncertainty regarding the import of Appellate Body reports, and the resultant DSB rulings and recommendations. For these reasons, it would not be appropriate for us to proceed on the basis that the Appellate Body may have intended to modify our findings in respect of sales by tenured harvester/sawmills to unrelated sawmills but refrained from saying so explicitly.

4.81 In any event, while acknowledging the existence of a certain ambiguity, on balance we are not persuaded that the Appellate Body's finding that a pass-through analysis was required in respect of "arm's length sales of *logs* by tenured harvesters/sawmills to unrelated sawmills" is necessarily different from (in the sense that it would modify) our finding that a pass-through analysis was required in respect of "logs sold by tenure-holding timber harvesters (whether or not also lumber producers) to unrelated sawmills". In particular, we note that the Appellate Body used a virtually identical formulation – also including a reference to "arm's length sales" - at para. 123 of its Report. Footnote 147 to para. 123 confirms that, in para. 123, the Appellate Body was indeed referring to para. 7.99 of the Panel Report. Since para. 123 of the Appellate Body report marks the beginning of the Appellate Body's introduction to the pass-through issue, we do not understand the Appellate Body to be substantively modifying para. 7.99 of the Panel Report at that juncture. Instead, it would seem much more reasonable to conclude that the Appellate Body was merely paraphrasing the relevant finding set forth at para. 7.99 of the Panel Report. Equally, we do not agree that a modification should necessarily be implied from the use of virtually identical language later in the Appellate Body Report. Instead, one could again understand the Appellate Body to be merely paraphrasing the relevant finding of the original panel.

4.82 In light of all of the foregoing considerations, and notwithstanding our acknowledgement of a certain ambiguity in respect of the term "arm's length", we do not accept the US argument, based on para. 167(e) of the Appellate Body Report, that the rulings and recommendations of the DSB only required a pass-through analysis in respect of "arm's length" log sales by tenured har-

---

[63] See, for example, para. 196(d) of the Appellate Body Report in *Brazil –Aircraft.* See also paras. 199 and 263(f) of the Appellate Body Report in *US – Line Pipe*. Although para. 168 of the Appellate Body Report refers to modification of the Panel Report, there is no indication precisely which part of the Panel Report is being modified. In such circumstances, there is no reason to believe that the Appellate Body was referring to anything other than the modification resulting from the Appellate Body's explicit reversal of certain of the original panel's findings.

vester/sawmills to unrelated sawmills. Instead, given that the Appellate Body upheld, without explicit modification, the relevant finding at para. 7.99 of the Panel Report, we consider that the United States was required to implement the recommendations and rulings of the DSB by conducting a pass-through analysis in respect of all log sales by tenured harvester/sawmills to unrelated sawmills - covered by the finding at para. 7.99 of the Panel Report regarding sales of logs by "tenure-holding harvesters (whether or not also lumber producers) to unrelated sawmills producing softwood lumber" - irrespective of any considerations as to whether or not such sales were "arm's length".

2. *Rejection of aggregate data*

(a) Arguments of the parties

4.83 Canada claims that in its Section 129 Determination, USDOC considered only company-specific, transaction-by-transaction data for the pass-through analysis, disregarding all aggregate transaction and pricing data submitted as an alternative by the Canadian respondents[64,65]. Canada asserts that the specific data requested by USDOC was impossible to collect as it involved hundreds of thousands of transactions by thousands of companies in Canada. Canada claims that USDOC nevertheless refused to provide reasonable alternatives for data submission, even though its CVD investigation was undertaken on an aggregate basis. Canada claims that the Panel already made it clear that company-specific data are not necessarily required to conduct a pass-through analysis. Canada refers in this regard to para. 7.98 of the Panel Report, where the Panel stated that it was "not convinced that the need to conduct a pass-through analysis for these transactions would necessarily or inevitably convert every aggregate case into a company-specific case." Canada also refers to footnote 170 of the Panel Report, where the Panel stated "[f]or example, inquiry into possible relationships between the entities concerned, and the use of sampling or other statistical techniques in respect of the relevant transaction at issue, might offer possible approaches to be explored."

4.84 The United States asserts that, to conduct its pass-through analysis, the USDOC first had to obtain data from Canada supporting Canada's claim that a portion of the total volume of Crown logs processed into lumber – as reported by Canada – should be reduced to account for arm's length log sales between unrelated parties in which no benefit passed through. The United States submits that, because the USDOC had conducted the original investigation on an aggregate basis and not on a company-specific basis and had not previously conducted

---

[64] As noted above, however, Canada clarified in response to questioning by the Panel that it did not claim that USDOC outright rejected the data. Rather, Canada challenged how the USDOC did and did not use them. See para. 4.51 and footnote 45, *supra*.

[65] Concerning these alternative data, Canada asserts that in many instances, Canadian respondents provided data from a representative sample of Canadian companies. According to Canada, the data provided were as much as were practicably available, and could and should have been used by the USDOC to complete its pass-through analysis.

such a pass-through analysis, the administrative record did not contain evidence supporting Canada's claims.

4.85 The United States asserts that the USDOC therefore asked Canada, through questionnaires, to identify the volume of log sales subject to its pass-through claims, and to provide specific information necessary to determine whether during the period of investigation there were arm's length sales of logs by independent harvesters to unrelated sawmills and by tenured harvesters/sawmills to unrelated sawmills. According to the United States, this would allow the USDOC to identify transactions that were eligible for the last phase of the analysis (competitive benefit). The requested information related to, *inter alia*, the relationship between the parties to the specific transactions (such as whether the parties were affiliated) and the circumstances surrounding the subject sales.

4.86 The United States further submits that the DSB's recommendations and rulings treated pass-through as a company-specific issue. In particular, the United States notes that the Appellate Body referred to the need to determine whether a benefit conferred "on the input *producer*" passed through to the "*producer* of the processed product" (emphasis supplied).

4.87 The United States rejects Canada's argument that the Panel already indicated that company-specific data are not necessarily required to conduct pass-through analyses. The United States argues that, in response to US arguments to the effect that there is a mismatch between an investigation conducted on an aggregate basis and the company-specific nature of the pass-through issue, the Panel simply found that pass-through can indeed be examined during an aggregate investigation. According to the United States, the Panel did not suggest that company-specific information should not be used to analyze whether there was a pass-through of subsidies.

(b) Evaluation by the Panel

4.88 First, we note the US argument that the USDOC needed company-specific and / or transaction-specific data in order to determine whether or not the parties to the transactions were related. Canada has not disputed that the USDOC needed such data for this purpose. Since the question of affiliation is central to the threshold issue of whether or not a pass-through analysis is required, we see no reason why the USDOC should be prevented from collecting company-specific and /or transaction-specific data for this purpose.[66]

4.89 Second, Canada has not argued that a company-specific and/or transaction-specific analysis is inconsistent with any particular provision of the SCM Agreement. In the absence of specific provisions, we are reluctant to instruct

[66] We note that the USDOC did accept some aggregate data for purposes of determining affiliation in respect of parties to log transactions in certain provinces. The Section 129 Draft Decision Memorandum (Exh. CDA-6 at pp. 9, 10, 13, 14) indicates that the basis for doing so was certifications provided with the data to the effect that the individual companies included in the aggregate figures were unaffiliated. Thus, our understanding is that it was these certifications, which necessarily concerned only the *specific* companies involved, that were accepted by the USDOC.

investigating authorities what data they should collect, and how they should use those data, in the context of their pass-through analyses. Nor do we consider that investigating authorities have an obligation simply to accept such alternative data as may be volunteered to them by respondents based on the respondents' assessment that the authorities' information requests are too burdensome.[67]

4.90 Third, Canada has not established that a company-specific and/or transaction-specific analysis is precluded by the rulings and recommendations of the DSB. Although we stated in our Panel Report that we were "not convinced that the need to conduct a pass-through analysis for these transactions would necessarily or inevitably convert every aggregate case into a company-specific case",[68] we certainly did not state that the USDOC should be precluded from proceeding on a company-specific basis if it chose to do so.

4.91 Finally, we recall that Canada has acknowledged that it does not assert that the USDOC rejected outright all of the aggregate information submitted by Canadian respondents.[69]

4.92 For the above reasons, we reject Canada's claim that the USDOC improperly disregarded all aggregate transaction and pricing data submitted by the Canadian respondents.

3. *Sawmill-to-sawmill transactions*

(a) Arguments of the parties

4.93 Canada claims that in the Section 129 Determination, the USDOC continued to presume pass-through in respect of all log transactions between tenured sawmills. Canada's claim is based on its assertion that, in the Section 129 Determination, the USDOC did not investigate sales of logs between tenured sawmills. Canada asserts that the original Panel and Appellate Body findings provide no basis for refusing to conduct a pass-through analysis simply because the purchasing sawmill holds tenure.

4.94 Canada also claims that in the First Assessment Review, USDOC presumed pass-through in respect of all sawmill-to-sawmill transactions since it failed to request information on any purchases of logs by sawmills from other sawmills.

4.95 Regarding the USDOC's Section 129 Determination, the United States asserts that the scope of the Appellate Body's ruling was limited – by footnote 151 of the Appellate Body's report – to sales of logs to sawmills that "do[] not hold a stumpage contract", i.e., to sawmills that do not hold tenure. According to the United States, the Appellate Body therefore only upheld the original panel's finding that the USDOC should have conducted a pass-through analysis with respect to transactions between tenured timber harvester/sawmills and unrelated,

---

67 In this regard, we consider that the accuracy of certain aggregate data in respect of affiliation is not informative of whether the substance of the aggregate data in terms of volume and price is either representative or accurate. These are entirely separate issues.

68 Panel Report, para. 7.98.

69 See footnote 45 *supra*.

non-tenure holding sawmills. The United States submits that the USDOC properly implemented the rulings and recommendations of the DSB by following the specific direction issued by the Appellate Body.

4.96 The United States does not respond to Canada's claim concerning the scope of the information requested by USDOC in the First Assessment Review.

(b) Evaluation by the Panel

4.97 We shall first address Canada's claim regarding the scope of the information requested by the USDOC in its Section 129 Determination. We shall then examine Canada's claim regarding the First Assessment Review.

(i) Section 129 Determination

4.98 As a preliminary matter, we note that Canada's claim does not cover purchases of logs by sawmills from tenured timber harvesters that do not themselves produce lumber. Canada's claim concerning the scope of the USDOC's investigation is restricted to sawmill-to-sawmill transactions.[70]

4.99 On substance, we note that the United States' defence to this claim is based on the definition of "sawmill" found at footnote 151 of the Appellate Body Report. That definition explicitly restricts the term "sawmill" as used in the Appellate Body Report to "an enterprise that processes logs into softwood lumber and does not hold a stumpage contract". Our Panel Report, however, does not adopt the same definition of "sawmill" as employed by the Appellate Body. Rather, our findings regarding inter-sawmill transactions concerned purchases by all sawmills, whether or not they hold a stumpage contract. [71] Furthermore, in the panel proceedings, neither party suggested that the definition of "sawmill" should be restricted in any way.

4.100 Second, we recall that the Appellate Body did not explicitly modify our finding at para. 7.99 of the Panel Report concerning inter-sawmill transactions. Rather, our finding was explicitly upheld by the Appellate Body. The United States submits that, because of the definition of "sawmill" set forth at footnote 151 of the Appellate Body Report, our finding regarding inter-sawmill transactions (as set forth at para. 7.99 of the Panel Report) was only upheld by the Appellate Body in so far as it concerned log purchases by sawmills that did not hold a stumpage contract. We disagree.

4.101 The considerations that we highlight at para. 4.80, *supra,* in respect of the issue of *implicit modification* of a panel's findings are equally pertinent here, to the extent that the US argues that the Appellate Body made such an implicit modification. We do acknowledge the possibility that the Appellate Body's use

---

[70] Thus, at para. 55 of its first written submission (see Annex A – 1), Canada accuses the United States of ignoring the findings of the original panel and Appellate body concerning "sawmill-to-sawmill transactions" . Canada does not complain, in the context of this claim, that the USDOC failed to investigate sales by tenured timber harvesters that do not produce lumber.

[71] In order to avoid any uncertainty, in these proceedings we continue to use the term "sawmill" to refer to an enterprise that processes logs into softwood lumber, whether or not it holds a stumpage contract.

of a different, narrower definition of "sawmill" in its report than we did in the Panel Report may have led to a certain ambiguity as to the scope of the Appellate Body's, and thus the DSB's rulings, and it is not clear to us why the Appellate Body introduced this narrower definition. That said, however, the practical effect of the definition set forth at footnote 151 of the Appellate Body Report is that the Appellate Body's findings regarding inter-sawmill transactions were restricted to transactions involving purchases by sawmills that did not hold a stumpage contract. In other words, the Appellate Body made no findings regarding our conclusion concerning inter-sawmill transactions involving purchases by sawmills that did hold a stumpage contract. In the absence of any findings by the Appellate Body regarding this latter category of transactions, our findings regarding such transactions stand, and form the sole basis for the DSB's recommendations and rulings in respect of these transactions.

4.102 We note the US argument in this regard that in its notice of appeal, the United States challenged "the entirety of the findings of the original panel that Commerce had to conduct a pass-through analysis with respect to transactions between producers of subject merchandise"[72]. We understand the United States to argue that the scope of its appeal therefore covered the Panel's findings regarding purchases by all sawmills, whether or not they hold a stumpage contract, and that the Appellate Body's findings should therefore reflect the scope of the US appeal. This would mean that our conclusion regarding log purchases by sawmills that do hold a stumpage contract would somehow be subject to the findings of the Appellate Body. While we see merit in such an argument (in the sense that the scope of the Appellate Body's findings should normally reflect the scope of the appellant's appeal), we note that the Appellate Body's "sawmill" definition would appear to apply to the entirety of the Appellate Body Report, including the section entitled "Claims of Error by the United States – Appellant". In that section, the Appellate Body states that the United States "contends that the Panel erred in finding that a pass-through analysis is required in respect of sales of *logs* from tenure-holding sawmills producing softwood lumber to unrelated **sawmills**".[73] Furthermore, in describing the "Scope of the Issue Appealed", the Appellate Body states that "[t]his appeal thus concerns the situations where: (i) a tenured timber harvester owns a sawmill and processes some of the logs it harvests into softwood lumber, but at the same time sells at arm's length some of the logs it harvests to unrelated **sawmills** for processing into lumber ...".[74] Notwithstanding the terms of the US Notice of Appeal, therefore, the issue addressed by the Appellate Body, and therefore the scope of the Appellate Body's findings, was explicitly restricted (as a result of footnote 151 of the Appellate Body's Report) to inter-sawmill transactions involving log purchases by sawmills not holding a stumpage contract. Inter-sawmill transactions involving log purchases by sawmills holding a stumpage contract were therefore not covered by the Appel-

72 See US Response to Question 1 from the Panel.

73 Appellate Body Report, para. 16 (italic emphasis in original, bold emphasis supplied).

74 Appellate Body Report, para. 128 (emphasis supplied).

late Body's findings.[75] Accordingly, our finding regarding such transactions could not have been reversed or otherwise modified by the Appellate Body.

4.103 Since our finding at para. 7.99 of the Panel Report regarding inter-sawmill transactions involving log purchase by sawmills holding a stumpage contract could not have been reversed or otherwise modified by the Appellate Body, that finding must be reflected in the scope of the rulings and recommendations of the DSB. Thus, by failing in the Section 129 Determination to analyse pass-through in respect of inter-sawmill transactions involving purchases by (unrelated) sawmills that hold a stumpage contract, the United States failed to properly implement the rulings and recommendations of the DSB regarding such transactions.

(ii) First Assessment Review

4.104 Canada submits that, in its administrative review, the USDOC failed to request information on any sawmill-to-sawmill transactions. Canada asserts that, in its only request for information on arm's length log transactions, the USDOC restricted its request in its initial questionnaire to the volume and value of Crown logs sold by independent harvesters (i.e., "by any person or company that did not own or operate a sawmill" or "by non-mill-owning tenure holders") to softwood lumber producers. Canada refers in this regard to the questionnaires sent by the USDOC to various Canadian provinces (Exhibit CDA-9), and the USDOC's Preliminary Assessment Review Determination Exhibit CDA-10).

4.105 The United States did not respond to Canada's claim, which concerns the conduct of the First Assessment Review. When asked a question regarding this claim, the United States responded on the basis of the information requested by the USDOC in the Section 129 Determination, rather than the First Assessment Review.[76] We presume that the United States declined to respond in respect of the First Assessment Review because of its view that the latter measure falls outside the scope of the present proceedings. We recall, however, our finding that the First Assessment Review does fall within the scope of these proceedings insofar as the pass-through issue is concerned. We also recall that we warned the parties at our substantive meeting with them in the present proceeding that, in the absence of any ruling on the US preliminary request at that time, the parties should assume in their arguments and submissions that the First Assessment Review falls within these proceedings.

4.106 We find that Canada has *prima facie* established, on the basis of the abovementioned Exhibits, that the USDOC failed in the First Assessment Review to investigate pass-through in respect of any sawmill-to-sawmill transactions. Given the original panel and Appellate Body findings regarding sawmill-

[75] The scope of the appeal is described in the penultimate sentence of para. 124 of the Appellate Body Report. That sentence refers to certain sales of logs and lumber "to sawmills". Since the word "sawmills" is qualified by the abovementioned footnote 151, it is clear that the scope of the appeal was restricted to certain sales of logs and lumber to "enterprise[s] that process[] logs into softwood lumber and do[] not hold a stumpage contract".

[76] See US Response to Question 4 from the Panel.

to-sawmill transactions, we do not see how the USDOC could have properly implemented the rulings and recommendations of the DSB in this case without also analysing pass-through in respect of sales of logs between sawmills in the First Assessment Review. In the absence of any argumentation concerning this matter by the United States, we find on the basis of the above that Canada has established a *prima facie* case that the United States has failed to properly implement the rulings and recommendations of the DSB by excluding sawmill-to-sawmill transactions from the pass-through analysis in the First Assessment Review.

C. The benchmarks used in the USDOC's pass-through analysis

1. Arguments of the parties

4.107 In its first submission, Canada challenges the benchmarks used by the USDOC in determining whether subsidy benefits passed through in certain log sales between unrelated parties. In particular, Canada challenges the import price data used by the USDOC (in conjunction with price data for logs purchased from private holders of forested land) in constructing the market price benchmarks for determination of benefit.

4.108 The United States disputes this challenge on two grounds. First, the United States asserts that this issue is outside the Panel's terms of reference as it is not referred to in Canada's request for establishment of a panel. Second, the United States argues that even if the issue were properly before the Panel, it has no substantive merit, as the import data used by USDOC were reasonable, and Canada has pointed to no provision of any covered agreement that has been violated by the use of these data.

2. Evaluation by the Panel

4.109 Turning to whether this challenge is outside our terms of reference, we recall that Canada's request for establishment refers to four specific alleged failures by the United States to comply with the DSB's recommendations and rulings, which can be summarized as (1) excluding certain categories of transactions from pass-through analysis; (2) presuming that certain transactions were not at arm's length and thus that benefits passed through; (3) applying the results of the pass-through analysis to a countervailing duty cash deposit rate that had been invalidated in judicial review procedures under US law[77]; (4) failing to conduct a pass-through analysis in the first administrative review of the lumber CVD measure.

4.110 None of these four alleged failures refers to or has any evident connection with either the methodology or the data that USDOC used in its *calculations* of pass-through of benefits in respect of those transactions where it performed such calculations. Rather, this issue is distinct from and independent of the four listed

[77] We have already expressed our view that Canada has effectively abandoned this claim, or at least failed to establish a *prima facie* case in support thereof. See note 47 above.

allegations. While Canada, in response to a question from us, asserts that "Canada identified its challenge to the pass-through benchmarks in its panel request", it points to no specific language in the request in this regard, and we find no such reference. Canada's argument seems to be, rather, that the statement in the request that the United States' measure(s) taken to comply are "inconsistent with Articles 10 and 32.1 of the SCM Agreement and Article VI:3 of the GATT 1994" is sufficient to bring this challenge within our terms of reference. We disagree. Canada's request describes the four specific alleged violations (legal claims), none of which has to do with the benchmarks used, and then identifies the various measures which in Canada's view are inconsistent by virtue of these alleged violations. Thus, we find that the issue of the market benchmarks used by USDOC represents a separate challenge, not referred to in the request for establishment. It therefore falls outside our terms of reference.

4.111 In light of the above, we reject Canada's claim regarding the benchmarks used by the USDOC in its pass-through analysis.

D. Countervailing duty amount

1. Arguments of the parties

4.112 Canada submits that the effect of the failure by the United States to comply with the recommendations and rulings of the DSB is an impermissible inflation of the amount of its countervailing duties. Canada submits that the United States is now required to do one of two things: either (1) conduct an appropriate pass-through analysis for all Crown log transactions involving unrelated parties, including through the use of aggregate data; or (2) exclude from the calculation of the overall *ad valorem* subsidy rate amounts of subsidy that have been presumed to pass through such transactions.

4.113 The United States submits that the USDOC properly calculated the revised countervailing duty rate by reducing the numerator of the *ad valorem* subsidy rate by C$ 28,344,121.

2. Evaluation by the Panel

4.114 We have identified a number of deficiencies in the USDOC's implementation of the rulings and recommendations of the DSB regarding *US – Softwood Lumber IV*, in particular in respect of the pass-through issue in both the Section 129 Determination and the First Assessment Review.

4.115 As a result of such failures to properly implement the rulings and recommendations of the DSB, the USDOC included in its numerator transactions for which it had not demonstrated that the benefit of subsidized log inputs had passed through to the processed product. As in the original proceeding, we find that this results in the imposition of countervailing duties in a manner inconsistent with Articles 10 and 32.1 of the SCM Agreement, and Article VI:3 of the GATT 1994.

V. CONCLUSIONS AND RECOMMENDATIONS

5.1 In light of the above, we reject:

- the US request for a preliminary ruling that the First Assessment Review falls outside the scope of the present DSU Article 21.5 proceeding, insofar as the pass-through analysis is concerned;
- Canada's claim that the USDOC improperly disregarded all aggregate transaction and pricing data submitted by the Canadian respondents;
- Canada's claim against the benchmarks used by the USDOC in its pass-through analysis;

5.2 We uphold Canada's claims that:

- in the Section 129 Determination, and in the treatment of pass-through in the First Assessment Review, the United States failed to properly implement the recommendations and rulings of the DSB in this dispute by failing to conduct a pass-through analysis in respect of sales, found by USDOC not to be at arm's length, of logs by tenured timber harvesters, whether or not they also produce lumber, to unrelated lumber producers, whether or not they hold a stumpage contract; and
- in the Section 129 Determination, and in the First Assessment Review, the USDOC therefore included in its subsidy numerator transactions for which it had not demonstrated that the benefit of subsidized log inputs had passed through to the processed product.

5.3 We do not consider it necessary to make any conclusion regarding the claim identified in Canada's Request for Establishment of a panel regarding USDOC "applying the results of the 'pass-through' analysis to a countervailing duty cash deposit rate invalidated as a result of judicial review proceedings conducted in accordance with US law, and failing to apply the results to a valid rate".

5.4 We therefore conclude that the United States remains in violation of Article 10 and 32.1 of the SCM Agreement, and Article VI:3 of the GATT 1994.

5.5 Under Article 3.8 of the DSU, in cases where there is infringement of the obligations assumed under a covered agreement, the action is considered *prima facie* to constitute a case of nullification or impairment of benefits under that agreement. Accordingly, we conclude that, to the extent the United States has acted inconsistently with the provisions of the SCM Agreement and of GATT 1994, and failed to properly implement the recommendations and rulings of the DSB in this dispute, it has nullified or impaired benefits accruing to Canada under that Agreement. Pursuant to Article 19.1 of the DSU, therefore, we recommend that the United States bring its Section 129 Determination and First Assessment Review into conformity with these provisions.

5.6 Pursuant to DSU Article 19.1, Canada has requested that we suggest ways in which the United States could implement our recommendation. In particular, Canada suggests[78] that the United States do one of the following two things:

- It should refund the amount of the countervailing duties it imposed to offset alleged subsidy amounts impermissibly presumed to pass through;

or

- It should revise its measures to meet its WTO obligations and refund the amount of the countervailing duties it imposed to the extent that they exceeded the amount of the alleged subsidy demonstrated to have passed through to the production of softwood lumber.

5.7 Given the complexities of the issue at hand, we consider that in the first instance the modalities of the implementation of our recommendation are for the United States to determine. We therefore decline to make the suggestions proposed by Canada.

[78] Canada's suggestion is made at para. 58 of its oral statement (see Annex A – 3). That paragraph also contains a request for a recommendation which differs from the request set forth at para. 72 of Canada's first written submission (see Annex A – 1). We understand that para. 58 of Canada's oral statement is intended to amend and replace para. 72 of Canada's first written submission. This was certainly the understanding expressed by the United States at our meeting with the parties, to which Canada did not object.

ANNEX A

SUBMISSIONS OF CANADA

Contents		Page
Annex A-1	First Written Submission of Canada – 24 February 2005	11447
Annex A-2	Second Written Submission of Canada: Response of Canada to the Request by the United States for Preliminary Rulings and Rebuttal Submission of Canada – 31 March 2005	11483
Annex A-3	Oral Statement of Canada – 21 April 2005	11499

ANNEX A-1

FIRST WRITTEN SUBMISSION OF CANADA
24 February 2005

TABLE OF CONTENTS

Appellate Body Report	*United States - Final Countervailing Duty Determination with Respect to Certain Softwood Lumber from Canada*, Report of the Appellate Body, WT/DS257/AB/R, adopted 17 February 2004.
Panel Report	*United States – Final Countervailing Duty Determination with Respect to Certain Softwood Lumber from Canada*, Report of the Panel, WT/DS257/R, adopted 17 February 2004.
Canada – Aircraft	*Canada – Measures Affecting the Export of Civilian Aircraft*, Report of the Appellate Body, WT/DS70/AB/R, adopted 20 August 1999.
US – Canadian Pork	*United States – Countervailing Duties on Fresh, Chilled and Frozen Pork from Canada*, Report of the Panel, adopted 11 July 1991, BISD 38S/30.
US – Countervailing Measures on Certain EC Products	*United States – Countervailing Measures Concerning Certain Products from the European Communities*, Report of the Panel, WT/DS212/R, adopted 8 January 2003.
US – Countervailing Measures on Certain EC Products	*United States – Countervailing Measures Concerning Certain Products from the European Communities*, Report of the Appellate Body, WT/DS212/AB/R, adopted 8 January 2003.

US – Lead and Bismuth II	*United States – Imposition of Countervailing Duties on Certain Hot-Rolled Lead and Bismuth Carbon Steel Products Originating in the United Kingdom*, Report of the Panel, WT/DS138/R and Corr.2, adopted 7 June 2000.
US – Lead and Bismuth II	*United States – Imposition of Countervailing Duties on Certain Hot-Rolled Lead and Bismuth Carbon Steel Products Originating in the United Kingdom*, Report of the Appellate Body, WT/DS138/AB/R, adopted 7 June 2000.
US – Softwood Lumber III	*US – Preliminary Determinations with Respect to Softwood Lumber*, Report of the Panel, WT/DS236/R, adopted 2 November 2002.

TABLE OF ABBREVIATIONS USED IN THIS SUBMISSION

Alberta 21 May 2004 Pass-Through Questionnaire Response	Response of the Government of Alberta to the Department's 14 April 2004 Questionnaire Concerning Pass Through of Alleged Benefits (May 21, 2004) (Exhibit CDA-13).
Alberta 15 September 2004 Supp.Pass-Through Questionnaire Response	Response of the Government of Alberta to the Department's 17 August 2004 Supplemental Questionnaire Concerning Pass Through of Alleged Benefits (15 September 2004) (Exhibit CDA-14).
Alberta 12 November 2003 AR Questionnaire Response	Response of the Government of Alberta to the Department's 12 September 2003 Questionnaire (12 November 2003) (Exhibit CDA-38).
B.C. 15 September 2004 Supp. Pass-Through Questionnaire Response	Response of the Government of British Columbia to the Department's 17 August 2004 Supplemental Questionnaire Concerning Pass Through of Alleged Benefits (15 September 2004) (Exhibit CDA-32).
B.C. 12 November 2003 AR Questionnaire Response	Response of the Government of British Columbia to the Department's 12 September 2003 Questionnaire 12 (November 2003) (Exhibit CDA-33).

Draft Section 129 Determination	USDOC Memorandum from J. Jochum to J. May, *Draft Decision Memorandum, 129 Proceeding for the WTO Appellate Body finding in the Final Countervailing Duty Determination, Certain Softwood Lumber from Canada* (19 November 2004) (Exhibit CDA-6).
DSB	Dispute Settlement Body
DSU	*Understanding on Rules and Procedures Governing the Settlement of Disputes*
Final AR Determination	*Issues and Decision Memorandum: Final Results of Administrative Review: Certain Softwood Lumber from Canada*, C-122-839 (13 December 2004) (Exhibit CDA-11).
Final AR Determination Notice	*Notice of Final Results of Countervailing Duty Administrative Review and Rescission of Certain Company-Specific Reviews: Certain Softwood Lumber Products from Canada*, 69 Fed. Reg. 75,917 (Dep't Commerce, 20 December 2004) (Exhibit CDA-8).
Final Section 129 Determination	USDOC Memorandum from J. Jochum to B. Tillman, *Section 129 Determination: Final Countervailing Duty Determination, Certain Softwood Lumber from Canada* (6 December 2004) (Exhibit CDA-5).
GATT 1994	*General Agreement on Tariffs and Trade 1994*
Kalt 2004a	J.P. Kalt and D. Reishus, *Statement for the First Administrative Review*, Attachment 1 to Letter from British Columbia Lumber Trade Council to USDOC (15 March 2004) (Exhibit CDA-21).
Kalt 2004d	J.P. Kalt and D. Reishus, *Economics of Arms's Length Transactions and Subsidy Pass-Through*, submitted as Response of the Government of British Columbia to the Department's 17 August 2004 Supplemental Questionnaire Concerning Pass Through of Alleged Benefits (15 September 2004), Exhibit BC-PT-39 (Exhibit CDA-20).
Manitoba 21 May 2004 Pass-Through Questionnaire Response	Response of the Government of Manitoba to the Department's 14 April 2004 Questionnaire Concerning Pass Through of Alleged Benefits (May 21, 2004) (Exhibit CDA-43).

Manitoba 12 November 2003 AR Questionnaire Response	Response of the Government of Manitoba to the Department's 12 September 2003 Questionnaire (12 November 2003) (Exhibit CDA-47).
Norcon A	Response of the Government of British Columbia to the Department's April 14, 2004 Questionnaire Concerning Pass Through of Alleged Benefits (21 May 2004), Exhibit BC-PT-18 (Letter from Steptoe & Johnson to Akin, Gump, Strauss, Hauer & Feld (20 May 2004) attaching *Survey of Primary Sawmills' Arm's Length Log Purchases In the Province of British Columbia* (21 December 2001), filed with Letter from Steptoe & Johnson to USDOC (21 December 2001)) (Exhibit CDA-30).
Norcon B	Response of the Government of British Columbia to the Department's 17 August 2004 Supplemental Questionnaire Concerning Pass Through of Alleged Benefits (15 September 2004), Exhibit BC-PT-40 (*Supplemental Report on Survey of Primary Sawmills' Arm's Length Log Purchases In the Province of British Columbia* (14 September 2004)) (Exhibit CDA-15).
Norcon C	Norcon Forestry Ltd., *Survey of Primary Sawmills' Arm's Length Log Purchases in British Columbia* (15 March 2004), submitted with Letter from Steptoe & Johnson to USDOC (15 March 2004) (Exhibit CDA-31).
OFIA/OLMA 15 September 2004 Supp. Questionnaire Response	Response of the Ontario Forest Industries Association and the Ontario Lumber Manufacturers Association on behalf of their members to the Department's 17 August 2004 Questionnaire Concerning Pass Through of Alleged Benefits (16 September 2004) (Exhibit CDA-49).
OFIA/OLMA 25 October 2004 Supp. Questionnaire Response	Response of the Ontario Forest Industries Association and the Ontario Lumber Manufacturers Association on behalf of their members to the Department's 5 October 2004 2nd Supplemental Questionnaire Concerning Pass Through of Alleged Benefits (26 October 2004) (Exhibit CDA-50).

Ontario 21 May 2004 Pass-Through Questionnaire Response	Response of the Government of Ontario to the Department's 14 April 2004 Questionnaire Concerning Pass Through of Alleged Benefits (21 May 2004) (Exhibit CDA-48).
Preliminary AR Determination	*Notice of Preliminary Results of Countervailing Duty Administrative Review: Certain Softwood Lumber from Canada*, 69 Fed. Reg. 33,204 (Dep't Commerce, 14 June 2004) (Exhibit CDA-10).
SAA	"Statement of Administrative Action" in *Message from the President of the United States Transmitting the Uruguay Round Agreements, Texts of Agreements Implementing Bill, Statement of Administrative Action and Required Supporting Statements*, H.R. Doc. No. 103-316, vol. 1 at 656 (Exhibit CDA-1).
Saskatchewan 21 May 2004 Pass-Through Questionnaire Response	Response of the Government of Saskatchewan to the Department's 14 April 2004 Questionnaire Concerning Pass Through of Alleged Benefits (May 21, 2004) (Exhibit CDA-39).
Saskatchewan 12 November 2003 AR Questionnaire Response	Response of the Government of Saskatchwan to the Department's 12 September 2003 Questionnaire (12 November 2003) (Exhibit CDA-42).
SCM Agreement	*Agreement on Subsidies and Countervailing Measures*
USDOC	United States Department of Commerce
Weyerhaeuser 16 September 2004 Supp. Pass-Through Questionnaire Response	Response of Weyerhaeuser Company to the Department's 14 April 2004 Questionnaire Concerning Pass Through of Alleged Benefits (September 16, 2004) (Exhibit CDA-40).
Weyerhaeuser 26 October 2004 Supp. Pass-Through Questionnaire Response	Response of Weyerhaeuser Company to the Department's Second WTO Supplemental Pass-Through Questionnaire (26 October 2004) (Exhibit CDA-41).

I. INTRODUCTION

1. This case is about the failure of the United States to implement the recommendations and rulings of the DSB in respect of its obligation to demonstrate whether, and to what extent, an input subsidy passes through arm's-length sales

of input products. Article VI:3 of the GATT 1994 and Articles 10 and 32.1 of the SCM Agreement require the United States to demonstrate such a "pass through" as a precondition to imposing countervailing duties on downstream products produced from those inputs. The original panel and the Appellate Body in this dispute found that where the United States presumes, rather than demonstrates, a pass-through, it impermissibly imposes countervailing duties where no subsidy has been determined to exist.

2. On the facts of this dispute, the alleged input subsidy is the provision of goods – standing timber – by Canadian provincial governments for less than adequate remuneration. The input product is a log, which is produced from standing timber harvested from public lands (Crown logs). The downstream processed product is softwood lumber, which is produced from Crown logs.

3. The United States is imposing countervailing duties on imports of Canadian softwood lumber products. Accordingly, it must demonstrate how, and to what extent, any subsidy to Crown logs is *also* an indirect subsidy to softwood lumber in every instance where, on the facts of this dispute, the producer of the Crown log and the producer of the softwood lumber are unrelated.

4. The USDOC has failed to make any such demonstration. Despite the recommendations and rulings of the DSB requiring a demonstration of pass-through, the USDOC continues to presume that pass-through occurred for virtually all arm's-length transactions. Based on this presumption, the USDOC included the subsidy amount attributable to the production of the *log* in its calculation of the amount of the subsidy attributable to the production of *softwood lumber*, thereby significantly inflating the overall amount of the countervailing duty imposed on softwood lumber.

5. A pass-through analysis in this dispute would involve comparisons of log input sale prices to a market benchmark price, to establish whether, and to what extent, a benefit within the meaning of Article 1.1(b) of the SCM Agreement is conferred upon the recipients that used the inputs in the production of softwood lumber. Because the USDOC failed to consider virtually all of the arm's-length log transactions at issue, it did not make such comparisons. The USDOC therefore presumed that log producers lowered the price of logs by the full amount of the alleged input subsidy in their sales to unrelated softwood lumber producers.

6. The USDOC failed to consider arm's-length log transactions for three reasons.

7. First, it refused to collect or analyze record evidence pertaining to log transactions between tenured sawmills.

8. Second, the USDOC ignored record evidence concerning pricing submitted by the Canadian respondents because the information was in aggregate form. Although the USDOC used aggregate data to conduct the softwood lumber investigation, and consistently refused throughout the investigation to consider company-specific information, it nevertheless deemed aggregate data inappropriate for a pass-through analysis. No exception exists in the GATT 1994 or in the SCM Agreement allowing the USDOC to refuse to conduct the required pass-through analysis on the grounds that available data are in aggregate form.

9. Third, with respect to the evidence of log transactions that the USDOC did consider, it deemed there to have been a full pass-through of the alleged log subsidy if any of five factors it identified existed. Nothing in the original panel or Appellate Body reports suggests that these factors are relevant to a pass-through analysis. Those reports confirm that an investigating authority must establish the existence and amount of a benefit pass-through where a subsidy is received by someone other than the producer or exporter of the investigated product; this obligation is without further qualification. The USDOC reliance on such factors to reject log transactions as being not at arm's length also is contrary to generally accepted economic principles.

10. The USDOC applied the results of the limited pass-through analysis that it did conduct to the countervailing duty rate established in the original investigation, which long before had been invalidated as a result of judicial review proceedings conducted in accordance with US law. A few days later, the USDOC imposed a new countervailing duty rate based on the results of its administrative review, in which it conducted no pass-through analysis at all.

11. In order to bring its imposition of duties into conformity with US obligations under the GATT 1994 and the SCM Agreement, the USDOC must establish, and not presume, whether and to what extent the benefit from the alleged log subsidy flows through to the production of softwood lumber where the parties to the log transaction are unrelated. The USDOC has not done so. Instead, it has claimed that for the vast majority of transactions no such analysis was required. This claim of compliance has no basis, and Canada asks the Panel to so determine.

12. Canada begins this submission with a description of the relevant facts underlying the dispute. Canada then addresses the US obligations at issue, the violation of these obligations, and the consequential effect on the US countervailing duties that continue to be imposed.

II. FACTUAL BACKGROUND

A. *Procedural History*

13. On 17 February 2004, the DSB adopted the recommendations and rulings in the reports of the original panel and the Appellate Body in *United States – Final Countervailing Duty Determination with Respect to Certain Softwood Lumber from Canada.*[1]

14. On 5 March 2004, the United States notified the DSB, pursuant to Article 21.3 of the DSU, of its intention to implement these recommendations and rulings.[2] Canada and the United States agreed shortly afterward on a ten-month

[1] DSB, *Minutes of Meeting (17 February and 19 March, 2004)*, WT/DSB/M/165, 30 March 2004, at 4(a), para. 49. See also Appellate Body Report and Panel Report.

[2] United States – Final Countervailing Duty Determination with Respect to Certain Softwood Lumber from Canada, Communication from the United States, WT/DS257/12, 9 March 2004.

"reasonable period of time", beginning 17 February 2004, for the United States to implement the recommendations and rulings of the DSB.[3]

15. At the DSB meeting of 17 December 2004, the United States informed the DSB that it had complied with its recommendations and rulings. Canada subsequently requested the establishment of an Article 21.5 compliance panel.[4]

16. The DSB established this Panel at its meeting of 14 January 2005, and referred the matter of suspension of concessions to Article 22.6 arbitration.[5]

B. DSB Recommendations and Rulings Concerning the US Failure to Demonstrate Pass-Through

17. The United States imposes countervailing duties on imports of certain Canadian softwood lumber products based on the USDOC determination that Canadian provincial stumpage programmes subsidize the production of softwood lumber. Stumpage programmes impose obligations such as the payment of fees, road construction and maintenance requirements, and fire protection and insect and disease control, in exchange for rights to harvest standing timber on public lands. Standing timber is harvested and processed into logs.[6] Logs may then serve as inputs for further processing in, *inter alia*, sawmills and pulp mills to produce a wide variety of forest products, including softwood lumber. These facts, as confirmed by the original panel and the Appellate Body, as well as by the panel in *US – Softwood Lumber III*, have not changed since the initiation of the US countervailing duty investigation.[7]

18. On the basis of these facts, the original panel found that the USDOC was required to conduct subsidy "pass-through" analysis where:

---

[3] United States – Final Countervailing Duty Determination with Respect to Certain Softwood Lumber from Canada, Agreement under Article 21.3(b) of the DSU, WT/DS257/13, 30 April 2004.

[4] United States – Final Countervailing Duty Determination With Respect to Certain Softwood Lumber from Canada, Recourse to Article 21.5 of the DSU by Canada, Request for Establishment of a Panel, WT/DS257/15, 4 January 2005; and United States – Final Countervailing Duty Determination With Respect to Certain Softwood Lumber from Canada, Recourse to Article 22.2 of the DSU by Canada, WT/DS257/16, 4 January 2005.

[5] United States – Final Countervailing Duty Determination With Respect to Certain Softwood Lumber from Canada, Recourse by Canada to Article 21.5 of the DSU, Constitution of the Panel, WT/DS257/19, 14 February 2005; and United States – Final Countervailing Duty Determination With Respect to Certain Softwood Lumber from Canada, Recourse by the United States to Article 22.6 of the DSU, Constitution of the Arbitrator, WT/DS257/20, 14 February 2005.

[6] These obligations are imposed through complex tenure and licensing agreements.

[7] Panel Report, at para. 7.84 ("In considering Canada's pass-through claim in detail, we recall that countervailing measures are applied to imports of certain products (the subject merchandise), which in the countervailing duty investigation in dispute before us comprises softwood lumber products produced by sawmills from logs, and re-manufactured softwood lumber products produced by re-manufacturers from lumber obtained from sawmills."); Appellate Body Report, at para. 124 ("We found above that the stumpage programmes of Canadian provinces at the heart of this case provide standing timber to timber harvesters, allegedly conferring a benefit. The standing timber eventually becomes felled trees or logs, which are processed into softwood lumber as well as remanufactured lumber products. USDOC defined the product subject to the investigation at issue as 'certain softwood lumber', which includes 'primary' lumber and 'remanufactured' lumber. The United States imposed countervailing duties on imports of these softwood lumber products from Canada."). See also *US – Softwood Lumber III*, at paras. 7.68-7.69.

- tenured timber harvesters who do not produce softwood lumber provide logs to unrelated downstream lumber producers ("independent harvester" transactions);
- tenured timber harvester/lumber producers provide logs to other unrelated lumber producers ("sawmill-to-sawmill" transactions); and
- tenured timber harvester/lumber producers sell lumber to unrelated downstream lumber re-manufacturers ("re-manufacturer" transactions).[8]

19. The panel concluded:

> that the USDOC's failure to conduct a pass-through analysis in respect of upstream transactions for log and lumber inputs between unrelated entities was inconsistent with Article 10 SCM Agreement and Article VI:3 of GATT 1994, and we therefore *uphold* Canada's claim that the United States' imposition of countervailing duties in respect of such transactions was inconsistent with Articles 10 and 32.1 SCM Agreement and Article VI:3 of GATT 1994 (…).[9]

20. On appeal, the United States accepted these findings and conclusions, as applied to independent harvester transactions.[10] However, the United States asked the Appellate Body to reverse the panel's findings regarding sawmill-to-sawmill transactions and re-manufacturer transactions. The Appellate Body reversed the panel's findings on re-manufacturer transactions[11], but upheld the panel's findings on sawmill-to-sawmill transactions:

> [T]he Appellate Body… *upholds* the Panel's finding, in paragraph 7.99 of the Panel Report, that USDOC's failure to conduct a pass-through analysis in respect of arm's length sales of *logs* by tenured harvesters/sawmills to unrelated sawmills is inconsistent with Articles 10 and 32.1 of the *SCM Agreement* and Article VI:3 of the GATT 1994.[12]

21. The DSB subsequently adopted the Appellate Body report and the panel report and recommended that the United States bring its measure into conformity with its obligations under the SCM Agreement and the GATT 1994.[13]

---

[8] Panel Report, at para. 7.99.

[9] Panel Report, at para. 8.1(c) [emphasis in original].

[10] Appellate Body Report, at para. 127, and footnote 154. ("The United States notes that it 'does *not appeal* the Panel's finding that, where the subsidy is received by independent harvesters, *i.e.*, entities that do *not* produce [softwood lumber] product[s] under investigation and operate at arm's length, a pass through analysis would be required to determine if the subsidy received by the independent harvesters was indirectly bestowed on production of softwood lumber'."[emphasis in original])

[11] Appellate Body Report, at paras. 165, 167(f).

[12] Appellate Body Report, at para. 167(e) [emphasis in original].

[13] DSB, *Minutes of Meeting (17 February and 19 March, 2004)*, WT/DSB/M/165, 30 March 2004, at 4(a), para. 49.

C. US Action Taken to Address Pass-Through Subsequent to the Recommendations and Rulings of the DSB

1. Section 129 Determination

22. The United States has enacted legislation that provides for proceedings to address DSB recommendations and rulings concerning a US countervailing duty measure. Section 129(b) of the *Uruguay Round Agreements Act* authorizes the USDOC to "issue a second determination ... to respond to the recommendations in a WTO panel or Appellate Body report."[14] Section 129 proceedings may involve the issuance of new questionnaires and application of new methodologies. The section 129 process represents one way in which the United States may bring the imposition of its countervailing duties into conformity with its obligations.

23. As a result of the DSB recommendations and rulings concerning the US failure to demonstrate a pass-through for independent harvester and sawmill-to-sawmill transactions, the USDOC initiated section 129 proceedings.

24. In questionnaires issued by the USDOC, the Canadian respondents were requested to identify the volume of Crown timber purchased by sawmills in independent harvester transactions. With respect to sawmill-to-sawmill transactions, the USDOC request for information was limited to only a small subset of such transactions.[15] The Canadian respondents replied to these questionnaires, providing a detailed breakdown of the volume of independent harvester transactions and, in many cases, comprehensive data on sawmill-to-sawmill transaction volumes.[16] Annex I contains a detailed explanation of the volumes of record evidence submitted by Canadian provinces and industry associations. For example, British Columbia provided the USDOC with a survey demonstrating that 11.6 per cent of Crown logs consumed in B.C. sawmills were purchased from unrelated non-lumber-producing tenure holders.[17] The survey also demonstrated that an additional 6.2 per cent of Crown logs consumed in B.C. sawmills were purchased in arm's-length transactions from unrelated lumber-producing tenure holders.[18]

25. The USDOC also requested company- or transaction-specific information for each individual log transaction, such as copies of the applicable log purchase agreements and confirmation of which party paid the stumpage fee.[19] In many

[14] SAA, at 1022 (Exhibit CDA-1). See also *Uruguay Round Agreements Act*, Pub. L. No. 103-465, § 129(b), 108 Stat. 4838, *codified at* 19 U.S.C. § 3538(b) (2000) (Exhibit CDA-2).

[15] Letter from USDOC to Embassy of Canada, *Certain Softwood Lumber Products from Canada*: WTO "Pass-Through" Questionnaire (14 April 2004), Question 2, at 11 (Exhibit CDA-3). ("Of the total volume of Crown timber entering sawmills reported by the province, what portion does the province claim was sold in arm's length transactions by tenured timber sawmills to sawmills that do not have a tenure and, therefore, requires an analysis to determine if the purchaser received a subsidy benefit?")

[16] The "Canadian respondents" comprise the Government of Canada, the Canadian provincial governments, the industry associations and certain Canadian lumber producers.

[17] See Annex I, at para. 79.

[18] *Ibid.*

[19] *Ibid.*, at para. 75.

instances, the Canadian respondents provided sample data, explaining that much of the information was impossible to collect as it involved hundreds of thousands of arm's-length transactions by thousands of companies in Canada. The USDOC nevertheless refused to provide reasonable alternatives even after Canadian respondents explained the impossibility of the USDOC request both in writing and in meetings with USDOC officials, and rejected all information provided in aggregate form.[20]

26. The USDOC then eliminated from consideration most of the transactions for which individual company data were provided on a transaction-by-transaction basis, claiming that "... a significant portion of the transactions included in the claims by Alberta, British Columbia, Manitoba, Ontario and Saskatchewan are not arm's-length sales."[21] The USDOC found that transactions between unrelated parties were not at "arm's length" if any of the following factors existed in the province: (1) limitations on log sales in Crown tenure contracts; (2) wood supply commitment letters; (3) the payment of stumpage fees by the downstream log purchaser; (4) log purchase agreements of a certain structure; or (5) fibre exchange agreements between tenured sawmills. Where any of these "factors" existed, the USDOC did not undertake any price comparisons to establish the pass-through of the log subsidy benefit or its amount.[22] These factors eliminated the vast majority of log transactions remaining after the USDOC had already excluded all aggregate data reported on the record, including all transactions in British Columbia and roughly 90 per cent of the transactions in Alberta.

27. The USDOC maintained that a pass-through analysis was therefore required for only a small fraction of the log transactions occurring between unrelated parties.[23] This analysis led to a reduction in the amount of the countervail-

---

[20] See Letter from Weil, Gotshal & Manges to USDOC (16 September 2004), at 2 (Exhibit CDA-4). See also Final Section 129 Determination, at 3-4 (Exhibit CDA-5) ("For sales not conducted at arm's length or for which respondents failed to provide sufficient data to determine whether they were conducted at arm's length, we did not conduct any further pass-through analysis and the volume of these sales was not removed from the numerator of the subsidy calculations."); and Comment 8, at 12-13 ("Although the surveys and sample data provided by the Canadian parties are sufficient for certain analyses undertaken in the context of the aggregate case, such data is not sufficient for the purposes of our pass-through analysis.").

[21] Final Section 129 Determination, at 6 (Exhibit CDA-5). See also Draft Section 129 Determination, at 7 (Exhibit CDA-6).

[22] Final Section 129 Determination, at 4 (Exhibit CDA-5) ("[W]here we determined that any of the sales reported by the Canadian parties were affected by one or several of the five factors listed above, we concluded that transactions were not conducted at arm's length."); and at 6-7 ("If, based on the evidence on the record, we were unable to ascertain that the amount qualified as an arm's-length transaction or that the stumpage for the log was paid by the harvester, we did not compare the price per cubic meter with the benchmark input price and the numerator was not reduced by that volume."). See also Draft Section 129 Determination, at 5, 7-8 (Exhibit CDA-6).

[23] Final Section 129 Determination at 7 (Exhibit CDA-5). ("We determine that the evidence on the record sufficiently demonstrates that, during the POI, there were some arm's-length log sales between sawmills and tenured harvesters/sawmills in Alberta, Manitoba, Ontario and Saskatchewan. ... The result of these calculations is that only a small portion of the Crown harvest volume originally included in the numerator is excluded from the numerator of our revised subsidy calculations.")

ing duty imposed by 0.17 percentage points (*i.e.*, from 18.79 per cent to 18.62 per cent), which came into force on 10 December 2004.[24]

28. On 13 December 2004, the USDOC released the final results of its administrative review, which contained no pass-through analysis despite arguments and evidence supplied by Canadian respondents that would have enabled the USDOC to conduct one. The revised countervailing duty amount resulting from the administrative review came into force on 20 December 2004.[25] Accordingly, ten days after the final section 129 determination came into force, subsequent action of the USDOC rendered moot the minor pass-through adjustment resulting from it.

2. *The Administrative Review*

29. The United States uses a "retrospective" duty assessment system to periodically review the amount of any countervailing duty imposed as a result of an original final countervailing duty determination. Where no administrative review is requested by an "interested party", final assessment occurs at the amount of the countervailing duty established in the original determination. Where an administrative review is conducted, the USDOC reviews data for a period of approximately one year from the date of first imposition of final duties (the "period of review"). The revised amount of the countervailing duty established through an administrative review applies, for final assessment purposes, to imports made during that period of review.[26] The revised amount also serves as the amount of duties imposed on imports made after the results of the review come into force, and takes the form of a cash deposit required pending final assessment.

30. As they did for the section 129 proceeding, the Canadian respondents provided the USDOC with all the information necessary to conduct a pass-through analysis in the administrative review. Annex I contains a detailed explanation of this record evidence, which confirmed that a significant volume of log transactions required a pass-through analysis. Here, the USDOC's request for information was limited exclusively to independent harvester transactions.[27]

31. On 14 June 2004, nearly four months after the adoption of the recommendations and rulings of the DSB, the USDOC published the preliminary results of its administrative review.[28]

---

[24] *Notice of Implementation under Section 129 of the Uruguay Round Agreements Act; Countervailing Measures concerning Certain Softwood Lumber Products from Canada*, 69 Fed. Reg. 75,305, at 75,306 (Dept. Commerce, 16 December 2004) (Exhibit CDA-7).

[25] Final AR Determination Notice, 69 Fed. Reg. at 75,919-75,920 (Exhibit CDA-8).

[26] The amount of duty applies only to those imports that represent merchandise entered or withdrawn from warehouse for consumption during this period. See, *e.g.*, Final AR Determination Notice, 69 Fed. Reg. at 75,919-75,920 (Exhibit CDA-8).

[27] See Annex I at para. 77. See *e.g.*, Letter from USDOC to Embassy of Canada, *Countervailing Duty Administrative Review: Certain Softwood Lumber Products from Canada* (12 September 2003), Questionnaire for the Province of Alberta, Question III (J) at III-6 (Exhibit CDA-9) ("Did the Government of Alberta (GOA) permit any person or company that did not own or operate a sawmill and was not affiliated with a sawmill to harvest Crown timber during the [period of review]?").

[28] Preliminary AR Determination, 69 Fed. Reg. 33,204 (Exhibit CDA-10).

32. The USDOC's preliminary results did not contain a pass-through analysis for any of the log volumes in question. Instead, the USDOC rejected all record evidence provided by the Canadian respondents for reasons similar to those in its section 129 determination. For example, the USDOC rejected record evidence from Alberta, British Columbia and Ontario because, in some log transactions, the purchasing sawmill paid the government stumpage charge rather than the independent harvester.[29]

33. The USDOC issued the final results of its administrative review on 13 December 2004.[30] In its final results, the USDOC mirrored the approach it took in its final section 129 determination and reproduced its discussion of the same five "factors" as the basis for not conducting a pass-through analysis for any of the transactions in question.[31] It applied these factors to reject all record evidence provided by the Canadian respondents, and determined that each province "failed to substantiate its claim that logs entering sawmills during the [period of review] included logs purchased in arm's-length transactions."[32]

34. As mentioned, the amount of the countervailing duty established in the administrative review superseded the amount adjusted as a result of its section 129 determination ten days after the latter came into force, thereby rendering any purported "prompt compliance with recommendations or rulings of the DSB" under Article 21.1 of the DSU of no effect.

III. LEGAL ARGUMENT

35. The United States continues to violate its obligations under Article VI:3 of the GATT 1994 and Articles 10 and 32.1 of the SCM Agreement on three fronts.

36. First, the USDOC failed in both the 129 determination and the final results of the administrative review to collect or analyze record evidence pertaining to log transactions between tenured sawmills. It offered no explanation in its determinations or questionnaires for its disregard of the DSB recommendations and rulings in this respect.

37. Second, in its section 129 determination, the USDOC failed to analyze whether, and to what extent, a subsidy pass-through occurred for the vast majority of independent harvester transactions identified in the record evidence, and failed to do so for all such transactions in its administrative review. To justify this failure in its section 129 determination, the USDOC claimed that such analysis may only be done on a company-specific, transaction-by-transaction basis. This claim is without basis, and fails to take into account the efforts of the Canadian respondents to provide the necessary information in the context of an aggregate case.

---

[29] *Ibid.*, at 33,208-33,209.

[30] Final AR Determination (Exhibit CDA-11).

[31] Compare Final Section 129 Determination, at 5-7 (Exhibit CDA-5) with Final AR Determination, at 46-47 (Exhibit CDA-11).

[32] Final AR Determination, at 7.

38. The USDOC also justified its failure to conduct a pass-through analysis in both its section 129 and administrative review determinations by claiming that unrelated parties do not operate at "arm's length" from each other if any one of five factors external to the transaction exists. There is no basis for the USDOC position under the GATT 1994 and the SCM Agreement, or in the findings of either the original panel or the Appellate Body. Its position also contradicts fundamental principles of economics. The USDOC is required to conduct a pass-through analysis, which involves comparisons to market benchmarks, where the direct recipient of an alleged benefit – the producer of the input product (in this case, logs) – is not the same entity as the indirect recipient of the benefit – the producer of the further processed product (in this case, softwood lumber). The United States may not now evade this obligation by disregarding transactions as being not at "arm's length" on the basis of an unfounded standard.

39. Third, even in the few instances in its section 129 determination where the USDOC considered log transactions, it nevertheless failed to conduct a proper analysis under Article 1.1(b) of the SCM Agreement because most of the benchmarks it used did not reflect prevailing market conditions for logs in Canada.

40. Thus, for the vast majority of transactions in its section 129 determination and for all transactions in its administrative review, the USDOC conducted no pass-through analysis, and where it purported to conduct such analysis, it did so incorrectly. As a result, the USDOC continues impermissibly to presume a pass-through of the alleged input subsidy. In this dispute, the original panel and the Appellate Body have already confirmed that such a presumption is a violation of WTO obligations.

A. GATT 1994 and the SCM Agreement Prohibit the United States From Imposing Countervailing Duties To Offset Subsidization That Has Not Been Demonstrated To Exist

41. In this section, Canada sets out the basic WTO obligations requiring the United States to demonstrate, rather than presume, the existence and amount of a subsidy. Canada also sets out how these obligations have already been interpreted in this dispute as applying in a pass-through context.

42. A Member must establish that a subsidy exists before it may impose countervailing duties, and it may not impose such duties in an amount greater than the amount of the subsidy demonstrated to exist. Article VI:3 of the GATT 1994 sets out this fundamental obligation:

> No countervailing duty shall be levied on any product of the territory of any contracting party imported into the territory of another contracting party *in excess* of an amount equal to the estimated bounty or subsidy determined to have been granted, directly or indirectly, on the manufacture, production or export of such product ... The term "countervailing duty" shall be understood to mean a special duty levied for the purpose of *offsetting* any bounty or sub-

> sidy bestowed, directly, or indirectly, upon the manufacture, production or export of any merchandise. [emphasis added]

43. Under this provision, any countervailing duty levied on a product that has not been determined to have been subsidized is necessarily, and fully, "in excess" and there is no lawful "offset".[33] The obligation is reaffirmed in Article 10 of the SCM Agreement:

> Members shall take all necessary steps to ensure that the imposition of a countervailing duty[36] on any product of the territory of any Member imported into the territory of another Member is in accordance with the provisions of Article VI of GATT 1994 and the terms of this Agreement. Countervailing duties may only be imposed pursuant to investigations initiated [footnote omitted] and conducted in accordance with the provisions of this Agreement and the Agreement on Agriculture.
>
> ----------------------
>
> [36] The term "countervailing duty" shall be understood to mean a special duty levied for the purpose of offsetting any subsidy bestowed directly or indirectly upon the manufacture, production or export of any merchandise, as provided for in paragraph 3 of Article VI of GATT 1994.

44. Finally, Article 32.1 of the SCM Agreement confirms that the imposition of duties is unlawful where a Member fails in this obligation. It provides that "[n]o specific action against a subsidy of another Member can be taken except in accordance with the provisions of GATT 1994, as interpreted by this Agreement."

45. Nothing in the context or object and purpose of these provisions alters the fundamental obligation to demonstrate the existence and the amount of a subsidy with respect to a product before imposing countervailing duties on that product.[34]

46. Article 1.1 of the SCM Agreement sets out an exhaustive definition of "subsidy" that applies to this obligation.[35] Under this provision, there is no "sub-

---

[33] The ordinary meaning of the verb "offset" is "[s]et off as an *equivalent* against; cancel out by, *balance* by something on the other side or of contrary nature; *counterbalance*, *compensate*". See *New Shorter Oxford English Dictionary* (Oxford: Clarendon Press, 1993), at 1985 (Exhibit CDA-12) [emphasis added].

[34] See Panel Report, at paras. 7.90-7.91 ("[B]oth of these provisions make explicit that there must be direct or indirect *subsidization* in relation to the manufacture, production or export of a *product* for a 'countervailing duty' in the sense of the [SCM] Agreement and GATT Article VI to be imposed on that product." [emphasis in original]. See also *US – Softwood Lumber III*, at paras. 7.75, 8.1(c), and *US – Countervailing Measures on Certain EC Products*, Panel Report, at paras. 7.41-7.44, *as upheld in US – Countervailing Measures on Certain EC Products*, Appellate Body Report, at paras. 139 and 161(a), and *US – Lead and Bismuth II*, Panel Report, at para. 6.56, *as upheld in US – Lead and Bismuth II*, Appellate Body Report, at para. 63.

[35] The relationship between the definition in Article 1.1 of the SCM Agreement and the obligations under Article VI:3 of the GATT 1994 and Articles 10 and 32.1 of the SCM Agreement has been explained by the original panel. See Panel Report, at para. 7.88 ("[Footnote 36 to Article 10 of the SCM Agreement] defines what a countervailing duty is, and in so doing makes explicit the link between a 'subsidy' to a recipient in the sense of Article 1.1 and the manufacture, production or export

sidy" when a "benefit" has not been conferred upon a recipient.[36] The original panel, referring to the findings of the Appellate Body in *Canada – Aircraft*, found that the term "benefit" "implies some kind of comparison" and that the "marketplace" provides a basis for this comparison.[37]

47. In a pass-through context, the obligation on Members is to compare the transactions in question to the marketplace to determine whether, and to what extent, a benefit under Article 1.1(b) of the SCM Agreement is conferred.[38] As explained by the original panel, the results of such analysis may not be presumed:

> The heart of the pass-through issue is whether, where a subsidy is received by someone other than the producer or exporter of the product under investigation, the subsidy nevertheless can be said to have conferred benefits in respect of that product. If it is not demonstrated that there has been such a pass-through of subsidies from the subsidy recipient to the producer or exporter of the product, then it cannot be said that subsidization in respect of that product, in the sense of Article 10, footnote 36, and Article VI:3 of GATT 1994, has been found. Thus, we find that a pass-through analysis is required by these provisions ... where there are such upstream transactions.[39]

48. Accordingly, where a subsidy is received by "someone other than the producer or exporter of the product under investigation", a Member must establish whether and to what extent the benefit to an upstream recipient passes to a downstream entity through the purchase of an input product.

---

of a *product* that is the subject of a CVD investigation and ultimately a countervailing duty. [emphasis in original]").

36 Panel Report, at para. 7.53; *Canada – Aircraft*, at para. 154.

37 The original panel considered this issue in detail in the context of other claims in this dispute. See *e.g.*, Panel Report, at paras. 7.53-54. See also *Canada – Aircraft*, at para. 157.

38 That pass-through analysis required pricing analysis had been established as far back as the *US – Canadian Pork* dispute. This GATT panel determined that:

> [G]iven the existence of separate industries for swine and pork production in Canada operating at arm's length, the subsidies granted to swine producers could be considered to be bestowed on the production of pork only if they had led to a decrease in the level of prices for Canadian swine paid by Canadian pork producers below the level they have to pay for swine from other commercially available sources of supply.

US – Canadian Pork, at para. 4.9.

39 Panel Report, at para. 7.91. The original panel also explained that a Member may not simply presume whether and to what extent any subsequent "benefit" passed through an input transaction where the transacting parties are unrelated. In agreeing with the findings of the GATT panel in *US – Canadian Pork*, the panel stated:

> That panel found, as we do, that investigating authorities had the affirmative obligation to make a determination of subsidization in respect of *a product*, and could not simply assume such subsidization where the subsidies were bestowed in respect of a product (the input product) that was different from the *product subject to countervailing duty*, and where the input producers were unrelated to the producers of that subject merchandise. [emphasis in original]
>
> [at para. 7.92]

49. The Appellate Body agreed. Drawing on the text of Article VI:3 of the GATT 1994, it found that a Member may not presume that a subsidy passes through transactions where "the producer of the input is not the same entity as the producer of the processed product".[40] The Appellate Body also explained in no uncertain terms that analysis under Article 1.1(b) of the SCM Agreement is required:

> Where a subsidy is conferred on input products, and the countervailing duty is imposed on processed products, the initial recipient of the subsidy and the producer of the eventually countervailed product, may not be the same. In such a case, there is a *direct recipient* of the benefit – the producer of the *input* product. When the input is subsequently processed, the producer of the *processed product* is an *indirect recipient* of the benefit – provided it can be established that the benefit flowing from the input subsidy is passed through, at least in part, to the processed product. Where the input producers and producers of the processed products operate at *arm's length*, the pass-through of input subsidy benefits from the direct recipients to the indirect recipients downstream cannot simply be presumed; it must be established by the investigating authority. In the absence of such analysis, it cannot be shown that the essential elements of the subsidy definition in Article 1 are present in respect of the *processed product.*[41]

50. Despite the clarity of these findings, the United States, in purporting to bring the imposition of its countervailing duties into conformity with this obligation, ignored this obligation entirely with respect to some transactions and unilaterally re-defined the circumstances under which this obligation arises with respect to all other transactions.

B. The United States Continues to Impose Countervailing Duties Based On an Impermissible Presumption of Subsidization

51. Applied to the two factual situations at issue in this dispute, both the original panel and the Appellate Body have made abundantly clear to the United States that it is required under Article VI:3 of the GATT 1994 and under Articles 10 and 32.1 of the SCM Agreement to perform a benefit analysis under Article

---

[40] Appellate Body Report, at paras. 140-141. See also *US – Softwood Lumber III*, at paras. 7.74-7.75.

[41] Appellate Body Report, at para. 143 [emphasis in original]. See also Panel Report, at para. 7.92. The United States had even agreed with the original panel. As noted by the Appellate Body:

> [T]he United States accepts that a pass-through analysis is required where a subsidy is bestowed *indirectly* on producers of products subject to the investigation ("subject products"). Thus, if a subsidy is received directly by an entity *other* than a producer of subject products, and that entity subsequently sells inputs to producers of subject products, the investigating authority is required to determine whether at least some of that subsidy is passed through in the sale to the producers of such products.

Appellate Body Report, at para. 129 [emphasis in original], *US – Softwood Lumber III*, at para. 7.70.

1.1(b) for both independent harvester and sawmill-to-sawmill transactions. It has not done so.

52. Instead, the United States has attempted at every turn to avoid its obligations to perform the required analysis and make the required demonstration. This non-compliance with the recommendations and rulings of the DSB has allowed the United States to continue to illegally inflate the amount of its countervailing duties on softwood lumber.

1. The United States Failed to Conduct Pass-Through Analysis for Log Transactions Between Unrelated Parties

53. The USDOC failed to conduct the required pass-through analysis for three reasons.

54. First, it presumed a full pass-through of the alleged input subsidy for all log transactions between tenured sawmills. In its section 129 determination, the USDOC restricted its request to the following information:

> Of the total volume of Crown timber entering sawmills reported by the province, what portion does the province claim was sold in arm's length transactions *by tenured timber sawmills to sawmills that do not have a tenure* and, therefore, requires an analysis to determine if the purchaser received a subsidy benefit?[42]

55. By restricting its request to log purchases by "sawmills that do not have a tenure", the USDOC inexplicably excluded information on transactions in which the purchasing sawmill had tenure – transactions that constitute the vast majority of sawmill-to-sawmill transactions in Canada. Nowhere did the USDOC make any request for information relating to purchases by sawmill owners that *did* hold tenure. It simply ignored the findings of the original panel and the Appellate Body with respect to such sawmill-to-sawmill transactions, which provide no basis for refusing to conduct a pass-through analysis simply because the purchasing sawmill holds tenure.[43]

56. The transaction volumes between tenured sawmills were excluded by the USDOC despite explicit calls for their inclusion. For example, Alberta noted at the outset of an initial questionnaire response that it believed "that the Department also should be requesting data on arm's length sales of logs between tenureholders where both the buyer and seller are sawmillers" and that it "stands ready to collect and supply this additional information on an expedited basis".[44] These calls went unanswered.

---

42 Letter from USDOC to Embassy of Canada, Certain Softwood Lumber Products from Canada: WTO "Pass-Through" Questionnaire (April 14, 2004), Question 2 (Exhibit CDA-3) [emphasis added].

43 Appellate Body Report, at para. 167(e); Panel Report, at paras. 7.99 and 8.1(c).

44 Alberta 21 May 2004 Pass-Through Questionnaire Response, at AB-1 (Exhibit CDA-13); See also Alberta 15 September 2004 Supp. Pass-Through Questionnaire Response, at 1 (Exhibit CDA-14). ("At the outset, Alberta wishes to note that Alberta's response to the original questionnaire of 14

57. In its administrative review, the USDOC failed to request information on any sawmill-to-sawmill transactions. In its only request for information on arm's-length log transactions, the USDOC restricted its request in its initial questionnaire to the volume and value of Crown logs sold by independent harvesters to softwood lumber producers ("by any person or company that did not own or operate a sawmill" or "by non-mill-owning tenure holders").[45]

58. Second, in its section 129 determination, the USDOC disregarded all aggregate transaction and pricing data submitted by the Canadian respondents. The USDOC considered only information on a company-specific, transaction-by-transaction basis knowing that there were hundreds of thousands of eligible transactions made by thousands of companies.[46] The USDOC disregarded such evidence even though its investigation was undertaken on an aggregate basis precisely because there are thousands of companies involved.[47] The USDOC thus ignored entirely the original panel's views that company-specific data are not necessarily required to conduct pass-through analysis.[48] The USDOC stated only that, while the aggregate information provided by the Canadian parties is sufficient for certain analyses undertaken in the context of its aggregate case, "such data is not sufficient for the purposes of our pass-through analysis." [49]

April 2004 did not provide all the relevant data on arm's length sellers of Crown logs, due to the constraints imposed by the Department's narrow questions. Specifically, in the original questionnaire on this subject, the Department told Alberta to limit our responses to those sellers of softwood logs harvested from provincial lands who did not own sawmills themselves.")

[45] Letter from USDOC to Embassy of Canada, *Countervailing Duty Administrative Review: Certain Softwood Lumber Products from Canada* (September 12, 2003), attaching Questionnaire for the Province of Alberta, Questions III (J), (K), and (L), at III-6; Questionnaire for the Province of British Columbia, Questions III (K), (L), and (M), at IV-7; Questionnaire for the Province of Manitoba, Questions III, (D), (E) and (F), at V-5; Questionnaire for the Province of Ontario, Questions III, (K) and (L), at VI-6; and Questionnaire for the Province of Saskatchewan, Questions III, (D), (E) and (F), at VIII-4 (Exhibit CDA-9). See also Preliminary AR Determination, 69 Fed. Reg., at 33,208 (Exhibit CDA-10).

[46] See *e.g.,* B.C. September 15, 2004 Supp. Questionnaire Response, Narrative, at 5 and Norcon B, at 4 (Exhibit CDA-15).

[47] USDOC Memorandum from B.T. Carreau to F. Shirzad, *Issues and Decision Memorandum: Final Results of the Countervailing Duty Investigation of Certain Softwood Lumber Products from Canada* (21 March 2001), at 15 (Exhibit CDA-16) ("In the *Initiation Notice*, we stated that, due to the extraordinarily large number of Canadian producers, we anticipated that we would conduct this investigation on an aggregate basis consistent with section 777A(e)(2)(B) of the Act. No parties objected to this. [footnote omitted] For the purposes of this final determination, we have aggregated the subsidy information on an industry-wide basis. Specifically, we used the information provided by the [Government of Canada] and the Provincial governments and calculated one subsidy rate for the Canadian softwood lumber industry for exports of softwood lumber to the United States.").

See also Final AR Determination, at 47 (Exhibit CDA-11) ("In this proceeding we are examining subsidies that directly benefit the lumber manufacturing process in Canada *on an aggregate basis*" [emphasis added]).

[48] Panel Report, at para. 7.98 ("[W]e are not convinced that the need to conduct a pass-through analysis for these transactions would necessarily or inevitably convert every aggregate case into a company-specific case.") and footnote 170 ("For example, inquiry into possible relationships between the entities concerned, and the use of sampling or other statistical techniques in respect of the relevant transactions at issue, might offer possible approaches to be explored.").

[49] Final Section 129 Determination, Comment 8, at 12 (Exhibit CDA-5).

59. Third, in both its section 129 and administrative review determinations, the USDOC applied a contrived standard to limit the number of Crown log transactions requiring analysis. In the USDOC view, a log transaction requires analysis only if it is at arm's length, and a transaction is at arm's length only where:

- the transacting parties are unrelated; *and*
- none of the external factors identified by the USDOC exists.[50]

60. While the USDOC did not contest that the Crown log volumes identified by the Canadian respondents satisfy this first condition, it nevertheless rejected nearly all remaining transactions in its section 129 determination and did reject all transactions in its administrative review based on the second condition.[51]

61. The second condition in the USDOC test has no foundation under the GATT 1994 or the SCM Agreement, nor does it accord with basic economics. Under this condition, the USDOC excluded from examination any reported independent harvester and sawmill-to-sawmill transactions that included any of the following five "factors", chosen arbitrarily as exclusive criteria: (1) limitations on log sales in Crown tenure contracts; (2) wood supply commitment letters; (3) payment of the stumpage fees by the downstream lumber producers; (4) the structure of certain log purchase agreements; or (5) fibre exchange agreements between Crown tenure holders.[52] The USDOC concluded, without any demonstrative analysis, that these factors "affect" the outcome of these transactions.[53] The USDOC conclusion has no basis and should be rejected.

---

[50] *Ibid.*, at 2 ("[T]o determine whether transactions are at arm's-length requires information about the relationship between the parties to the transaction (*e.g.* affiliations) *and the circumstances surrounding the transactions.*"[emphasis added]). See also Draft Section 129 Determination, at 3 (Exhibit CDA-6).

Final Section 129 Determination, at 4 (Exhibit CDA-5) ("We first examined whether any of the log sale transactions at issue were between affiliated parties, as defined by section 771(33) of the Tariff Act of 1930, as amended. If any of the log sales reported by the Canadian parties were determined to have been between affiliated parties, we concluded that these were not arm's-length transactions and no further pass-through analysis was conducted"). See also Draft Section 129 Determination, at 5 (Exhibit CDA-6).

[51] See *e.g.*, Draft Section 129 Determination, at 9 ("The Department accepted the certifications that the transactions listed in the PWC's survey results submitted by the [Government of Alberta] were transactions between unaffiliated parties.") and at 10 ("In its 25 October 2004 questionnaire response, the [Government of British Columbia] explained that the Norcon survey controlled for affiliation between the 74 participating mills and independent harvesters based on the Department's statutory test, which we accepted."). The US law standard that the USDOC directed the Canadian respondents to rely on to certify that transactions occurred between unrelated parties was section 771(33) of the *Tariff Act of 1930* (19 U.S.C. § 1677(33)). See Exhibit CDA-17.

[52] The United States relied on the same factors in both its section 129 determination and its administrative review determination.

[53] Final Section 129 Determination, at 4 (Exhibit CDA-5) ("Evidence on the record indicates that government-mandated restrictions affect many of the log transactions that Canada reported as arm's-length sales."). See also Final AR Determination, at 47 (Exhibit CDA-11), where the USDOC states, in the absence of any prior demonstration, that "[t]he government mandates at issue here are conditions that are placed on the tenure licenses that have a direct impact on the disposition of Crown logs sold by independent harvesters."

62. A transaction between unrelated parties is by definition an arm's-length transaction.[54] Because the external factors identified by the USDOC do not transform an arm's-length transaction into one that is not at arm's length, the existence of any such factors cannot excuse the United States from its obligation to conduct the required benefit pass-through analysis. As the original panel and the Appellate Body confirmed, such analysis is required in every instance where the subsidized input producer is unrelated to the producer of the subject merchandise.[55] The creation of this new definition of "arm's length" by the USDOC is nothing more than an attempt to resurrect US arguments that failed before the panel in *Canada – Softwood Lumber III*.[56]

63. The USDOC refusal to conduct a pass-through analysis on the basis of these factors is also inconsistent with basic economics. Extensive economic evidence placed on the record demonstrated that none of the factors identified by the USDOC alters the fact that sellers of Crown logs attempt to obtain the best price available in transactions with unrelated purchasers.[57] These factors do not make the transacting parties act in accordance with interests other than their own, nor do they align the parties' otherwise opposing objectives regarding the outcome of the transaction.[58] Accordingly, they do not obviate the need to demonstrate and quantify any alleged log subsidy pass-through.

64. In particular, record economic evidence demonstrated that the government regulations identified by the USDOC do not change the fact that transactions between unrelated parties occur in a market setting, and that a market absent of any form of government intervention is not a *sine qua non* for an arm's-length transaction.[59] Requirements by the government to supply, for example, say nothing about the subsequent negotiations and whether the transaction outcome is a market price. The evidence also demonstrated that the question of who remits the government stumpage fee is irrelevant; the mere payment of the fee by a downstream purchaser does not mean the upstream seller reduced the market value of its log by the amount of the stumpage subsidy.[60] This typical business arrangement, merely guaranteeing payment of base fees, logically has nothing to

---

[54] See *e.g.*, *New Shorter Oxford English Dictionary* (Oxford University Press: New York, 1993) at 114 (Exhibit CDA-18) ("at arm's length… (of dealings) with neither party controlled by the other"); *Black's Law Dictionary*, 6th ed. (St. Paul, Minn.: West, 1990), at 109 (Exhibit CDA-19) ("Arm's-length transaction… [one that is] negotiated by unrelated parties, each acting in his or her own self interest; the basis for a fair market value determination."). The SAA also defines an arm's length transaction as a transaction between unrelated parties "or between related parties such that the terms of the transaction are those that would exist if the transaction had been negotiated between unrelated parties." See SAA, at 928 (Exhibit CDA-1).

[55] Panel Report, at para. 7.92 ("…where the input producers were unrelated to the producers of that subject merchandise"); Appellate Body Report, at para. 140 ("Where the producer of the input is not the same entity as the producer of the processed product..."). See also *US – Softwood Lumber III*, at para. 7.74 ("… here a downstream producer of subject merchandise is unrelated to the allegedly subsidized upstream producer of the input ...").

[56] See *Ibid.*, at paras. 4.289-4.291, and 7.79.

[57] See Kalt 2004d (Exhibit CDA-20). See also Kalt 2004a, at 43-48 (Exhibit CDA-21).

[58] See *e.g.*, Kalt 2004a, at 43-46.

[59] *Ibid.*, at 48-51; Kalt 2004d, at 9-10 (Exhibit CDA-20).

[60] Kalt 2004d, at 4-7.

do with whether a transaction is at arm's length. Nor does the presence of non-cash components in a transaction (*e.g.*, payment through exchange of goods or services) imply that the harvester has accepted anything less than the market value of the log.[61]

65. As a result of its refusal to analyze log transactions as required by the findings of the original panel and the Appellate Body and by basic principles of economics, the USDOC impermissibly presumed that the alleged log input subsidy fully passed through all such transactions.

2. *In the Few Instances Where the United States Did Perform Pass-Through Analysis, It Used Inappropriate Benchmarks That Produced Results That Were Subsequently Nullified*

66. Even in the few instances in its section 129 determination where the USDOC considered log transactions, it nevertheless failed to conduct proper analyses under Article 1.1(b) of the SCM Agreement.

67. In conducting pass-through analyses in its section 129 determination, the USDOC relied on benchmarks that do not reflect a comparison to the "marketplace".[62] The USDOC, for example, derived its benchmark, in part, from log imports that were: (1) extremely small and highly variable in volume; (2) largely unrepresentative of the species harvested in each province; and (3) extraordinarily high in value and unrepresentative of prices paid in each province for logs used in softwood lumber production. Accordingly, these prices did not reflect market conditions in Canada during the period of investigation. The Canadian respondents urged the USDOC to correct its use of benchmarks, but these comments were disregarded.[63]

68. The marginal decrease the USDOC made to the amount of its countervailing duties as a result of this flawed benefit analysis in its section 129 determination was in any event overtaken ten days later, and after the end of the reasonable period of time to implement, by full re-inflation of the countervailing duty amount as a result of its administrative review determination. As explained above, the United States undertook no pass-through analysis for any of the log transactions identified in the administrative review. Accordingly, in both its determinations, occurring within days of each other, the United States failed to conform to its obligations concerning the imposition of countervailing duties.

---

[61] *Ibid.*, at 8-9.

[62] See *e.g.*, Panel Report, at para. 7.53-54. See also *Canada – Aircraft*, at para. 157. The USDOC used as a benchmark company-specific prices that individual purchasing sawmills paid for other logs it obtained from private lands or for logs it imported. Where actual company-specific purchase data were not available, the USDOC used a weighted-average of private log prices and imported log prices. See Final Section 129 Determination, at 6 (Exhibit CDA-5).

[63] See Letter from Weil, Gotshal & Manges to USDOC (26 November 2004), at 5 (Exhibit CDA-22).

3. *As a Result of Its Failure to Conduct the Required Pass-Through Analysis, the United States Continues Impermissibly to Inflate the Amount of Countervailing Duties*

69. The effect of the failure by the United States to comply with the recommendations and rulings of the DSB is an impermissible inflation of the amount of its countervailing duties. Because the USDOC calculated the amount of the subsidy going to the production of softwood lumber based on the entire volume of the Crown harvest that entered sawmills, *either directly or indirectly*, it is now required to do one of two things: either (1) conduct an appropriate pass-through analysis for all Crown log transactions involving unrelated parties, including through the use of aggregate data; or (2) exclude from the calculation of the overall *ad valorem* subsidy rate amounts of subsidy that have been presumed to pass through such transactions.

70. More particularly, should the USDOC choose not to conduct the required pass-through analysis, it must exclude from the numerator of the subsidy rate calculation benefit amounts derived from the following transaction volumes:

- Crown logs purchased in independent harvester transactions; and
- Crown logs purchased in sawmill-to-sawmill transactions.

71. Only by taking these steps will the United States comply with the recommendations and rulings of the DSB.

IV. REQUEST FOR FINDINGS AND RECOMMENDATIONS

72. The United States failed to implement the recommendations and rulings of the DSB in respect of its obligation to demonstrate whether, and to what extent, a subsidy to the production of Crown logs passes through transactions between unrelated parties. As such, Canada requests that the Panel:

- Find that the US imposition of countervailing duties in respect of the Crown log transactions identified in this dispute is inconsistent with Article VI:3 of GATT 1994 and Articles 10 and 32.1 of the SCM Agreement;
- Recommend in accordance with Article 19.1 of the DSU that the United States: (1) refund the amount of the countervailing duties imposed to offset alleged subsidy amounts presumed to pass through; or, (2) revise its measures to meet the requirements of Article VI:3 GATT 1994 and Articles 10 and 32.1 of the SCM Agreement and refund the duties to the extent that they exceed the amount of the alleged subsidy demonstrated to have passed through to the production of softwood lumber; [64] and
- Recommend that the United States bring its measures into conformity with its WTO obligations.

ANNEX I: RECORD EVIDENCE

73. The Canadian respondents provided the USDOC with detailed evidence that could have been used to properly establish and calculate the amount of any benefit pass-through in both the section 129 proceedings and the administrative review. As explained, the United States rejected nearly all of the record evidence and instead simply presumed a full pass-through.

74. After initiating implementation proceedings under section 129, the USDOC issued a first questionnaire on 14 April 2004.[65] The Canadian respondents provided responses in accordance with the USDOC's directions on 21 May 2004. In providing their responses, the provinces relied on the definition of "affiliated person" under US law to certify whether the transacting parties were unrelated and the USDOC accepted all such certifications.[66]

75. After receiving responses to its first questionnaire, the USDOC issued two supplemental "pass-through" questionnaires on 17 August and 5 October 2004, requesting the provinces to collect large amounts of company-specific data.[67] The USDOC asked the provinces to collect the government tenure agreements applying to every independent harvester and sawmill involved in arm's-length log transactions.[68] The USDOC also requested information on all parties related to (*i.e.*, affiliated with) both the independent harvester and the purchasing

---

64 See *US – Canadian Pork*, at para. 4.11.

65 Letter from USDOC to Embassy of Canada, Certain Softwood Lumber Products from Canada: WTO "Pass-Through" Questionnaire (April 14, 2004) (Exhibit CDA-3).

66 See *e.g.*, Final 129 Determination, at 9 (Exhibit CDA-5) ("Based on the certifications and information provided by the relevant companies and the [Government of Alberta], the Department accepted the data reported to be from unaffiliated parties."). See also Draft 129 Determination, at 9 (Exhibit CDA-6) ("The Department accepted the certifications that the transactions listed in the PWC's survey results submitted by the [Government of Alberta] were transactions between unaffiliated parties"); at 10 ("In its October 25, 2004 questionnaire response, the [Government of British Columbia] explained that the Norcon survey controlled for affiliation between the 74 participating mills and independent harvesters based on the Department's statutory test, which we accepted."); at 12 ("The Department accepts the [Government of Manitoba]'s claim that the transactions were conducted between unaffiliated parties"); at 13 ("The Department accepts the certifications that the transactions listed in the [Government of Ontario]'s breakdowns [are between unaffiliated parties]"); and at 15 ("The Department accepts the [Government of Saskatchewan]'s claim that the transactions were conducted between unaffiliated parties.").

67 Letter from USDOC to Embassy of Canada, Certain Softwood Lumber Products from Canada: WTO Supplemental "Pass-Through" Questionnaire (17 August 2004) (Exhibit CDA-23); Letter from USDOC to Embassy of Canada, Certain Softwood Lumber Products from Canada: WTO Second Supplemental "Pass-Through" Questionnaire (5 October 2004) (Exhibit CDA-24).

68 See Letter from USDOC to Embassy of Canada, Certain Softwood Lumber Products from Canada: WTO "Pass-Through" Questionnaire (April 14, 2004), Question 1(c), Question 2(c), at 10-11 (Exhibit CDA-3); Letter from USDOC to Embassy of Canada, Certain Softwood Lumber Products from Canada: WTO Supplemental "Pass-Through" Questionnaire (August 17, 2004), British Columbia, Questions 3, 9(b), at 3-4; Alberta, Question 1, at 8; Manitoba, Question 2, at 10; and Saskatchewan, Question 3, at 12 (Exhibit CDA-23); and Letter from USDOC to Embassy of Canada, Certain Softwood Lumber Products from Canada: WTO Second Supplemental "Pass-Through" Questionnaire (October 5, 2004), British Columbia, Questions 3, 4, at 3-5; Alberta, Question 1, at 8 (Exhibit CDA-24).

sawmill, on who paid the stumpage fee related to the log in question, and on the contractual terms and pricing of each individual transaction that required a pass-through analysis.[69]

76. The Canadian respondents provided as much information as was practicably available to them and emphasized that the USDOC could complete its pass-through analysis with the aggregate provincial data.[70] For example, in meetings and written submissions to the USDOC, British Columbia noted that the documentation relating to all log purchase agreements and tenure agreements would involve several truckloads of paper, and offered several alternative approaches, all of which were rejected. British Columbia nevertheless provided hundreds of pages of sample agreements, and offered to provide any additional samples requested by the USDOC. As outlined above, the USDOC rejected almost all record evidence submitted in the section 129 proceeding.

77. In relation to the administrative review, the USDOC initiated this segment of this proceeding on 1 July 2003, for the period from 22 May 2002–31 March 2003.[71] In its initial questionnaire issued on 12 September 2003, the USDOC requested the Canadian provinces to report the volume and value of Crown logs sold by independent harvesters to unrelated lumber producers, but solicited no information on sawmill-to-sawmill transactions.[72] The Canadian respondents

[69] See Letter from USDOC to Embassy of Canada, Certain Softwood Lumber Products from Canada: WTO "Pass-Through" Questionnaire (April 14, 2004), Question 1(b), Question 2(b), at 10-11 (Exhibit CDA-3); Letter from USDOC to Embassy of Canada, Certain Softwood Lumber Products from Canada: WTO Supplemental "Pass-Through" Questionnaire (August 17, 2004), British Columbia, Questions 2, 4, 6-7, 9, at 3-5; Ontario, Questions 1-4, at 6; Alberta, Questions 2-3, 6-7, at 8-9; Manitoba, Question 3, at 10; and Saskatchewan, Questions 4, 6, at 12-13; and Pass-Through Appendix, at 9-17 (Exhibit CDA-23); and Letter from USDOC to Embassy of Canada, Certain Softwood Lumber Products from Canada: WTO Second Supplemental "Pass-Through" Questionnaire (October 5, 2004), British Columbia, Questions 1, 6-7, 9, at 3-5; Ontario, Question 1, at 7; Alberta, Questions 5, 8, 10, at 9-10; Manitoba, Question 1, at 11; Saskatchewan, Question 1, at 13, Second Pass-Through Appendix, at 22-23 (Exhibit CDA-24).

[70] See *e.g.*, B.C. 15 September 2004 Supp. Questionnaire Response, Narrative, at 5 and Norcon B, at 4 (Exhibit CDA-15); B.C. 5 October 2004 Supp. Questionnaire Response, at BC-PT-22, Exhibit BC-PT-55 (Exhibit CDA-25). The public version of Exhibit BC-PT-55, which supplements the information provided in Norcon B, excludes business proprietary information as it is not susceptible to public summarization.

[71] *Initiation of Antidumping and Countervailing Duty Administrative Reviews and Request for Revocation in Part*, 68 Fed. Reg. 39,055 (Dep't Commerce 1 July 2003) (Exhibit CDA-26). On 16 January 2004, the USDOC extended the time for completion of the preliminary results. See *Certain Softwood Lumber Products from Canada: Extension of Time Limit for Preliminary Results of Countervailing Duty Administrative Review*, 69 Fed. Reg. 2,568 (Dep't Commerce 16 January 2004) (Exhibit CDA-27). Similarly, in the preliminary results the USDOC extended the amount of time available for the final results of the administrative review. See Preliminary AR Determination, 69 Fed. Reg. at 33,205 (Exhibit CDA-10).

[72] See Letter from USDOC to Embassy of Canada, *Countervailing Duty Administrative Review: Certain Softwood Lumber Products from Canada* (12 September 2003), attaching Questionnaire for the Province of Alberta, Questions III (J), (K), and (L), at III-6; Questionnaire for the Province of British Columbia, Questions III (K), (L), and (M), at IV-7; Questionnaire for the Province of Manitoba, Questions III, (D), (E) and (F), at V-5; Questionnaire for the Province of Ontario, Questions III, (K) and (L), at VI-6; and Questionnaire for the Province of Saskatchewan, Questions III, (D), (E) and (F), at VIII-4 (Exhibit CDA-9); and Preliminary AR Determination, 69 Fed. Reg. at 33, 208 (Exhibit CDA-10) ("During the underlying investigation, the Canadian parties claimed that a portion of the

provided the USDOC with evidence that confirmed that there was a significant volume of logs sold in such transactions and which therefore required a pass-through analysis.[73] The Canadian parties also provided additional information throughout the proceedings and during verification. The USDOC collected no additional information and issued no new questionnaires concerning pass-through. In the preliminary and final results of the administrative review, the USDOC refused to conduct a pass-through analysis using any of the information provided by the Canadian respondents.[74]

78. What follows is a brief summary of the record evidence for each province in both the section 129 proceedings and the administrative review.

A. *British Columbia*

79. In the section 129 proceeding, British Columbia provided the USDOC with a study by Norcon Forestry Ltd. and the accounting firm Pricewaterhouse-Coopers ("Norcon A") of 74 sawmills representing approximately 53 per cent of the total volume of the Crown timber harvest, which reviewed thousands of log purchase transactions with unrelated parties. Norcon A was supplemented by a further study by Norcon Forestry Ltd. ("Norcon B"). Norcon B demonstrated that 11.6 per cent of Crown logs consumed in B.C. sawmills were purchased from independent harvesters that held tenure.[75] These surveys also demonstrated that an additional 6.2 per cent of Crown logs consumed in B.C. sawmills were purchased in arm's-length sawmill-to-sawmill transactions.[76] The USDOC accepted that the surveys controlled for affiliation based on the affiliation standard under section 771(33) of the *Tariff Act of 1930*.[77] In addition to providing the aggregate results of these surveys, British Columbia provided detailed transaction-specific information on the thousands of transactions included in the surveys, including information on volume, value, the types of logs sold, the purchaser and the seller, for both private and Crown log purchases. The company-specific evidence provided in these surveys was equivalent to the information the USDOC requested

---

Crown logs processed by sawmills were purchased by the mills in arm's-length transactions with independent harvesters. Canada further claimed that such logs must be excluded from the subsidy calculation unless the Department determines that the benefit to the independent harvester passed through to the lumber producers. In anticipation of a similar claim in this administrative review, we requested in the original questionnaire that each of the Canadian provinces report the volume and value of Crown logs sold by independent harvesters to unrelated parties during the [period of review].").

[73] See Letter from Weil Gotshal & Manges to USDOC, *Certain Softwood Lumber from Canada: First Administrative Review, Pass Through of Benefit to Arm's Length Purchasers of Logs and Lumber Inputs* (24 May 2004) (Exhibit CDA-28). See also Norcon C (Exhibit CDA-29), as revised in Letter from Steptoe & Johnson to USDOC (April 26, 2004) (Exhibit CDA-30); and Kalt 2004a, at 43-50 (Exhibit CDA-21).

[74] Preliminary AR Determination, 69 Fed. Reg., at 33,208-33,209 (Exhibit CDA-10); Final AR Determination, at 45-48 (Exhibit CDA-11).

[75] Norcon A (Exhibit CDA-31), as revised in B.C. 15 September 2004 Supp. Pass-Through Questionnaire Response, at 2, note 1 (Exhibit CDA-32) and Norcon B, at 2 (Exhibit CDA-15).

[76] Norcon A, at Appendix III (Exhibit CDA-31); Norcon B (Exhibit CDA-15). Purchases under fibre exchange agreements were not within the scope of the surveys.

[77] Draft 129 Determination, at 10 (Exhibit CDA-6).

in its supplemental questionnaires and could have been used to calculate pass-through using the USDOC's price-to-price comparison methodology.[78] British Columbia also provided hundreds of pages of sample log purchase agreements and tenure agreements, as well as three economic studies demonstrating that the factors identified by USDOC do not alter the arm's-length nature of the transactions at issue.

80. British Columbia also commissioned Norcon Forestry Ltd. to conduct an additional, larger survey of sawmills for the administrative review ("Norcon C"). Norcon C surveyed 132 sawmills, receiving responses that accounted for 87 per cent of the logs consumed by sawmills in 2002.[79] Norcon C demonstrated that 20 per cent of logs consumed in sawmills were harvested from Crown lands and purchased from independent harvesters.[80] In addition, British Columbia also provided evidence that 5.7 per cent of logs consumed in sawmills were purchased in sawmill-to-sawmill transactions.[81] In total, British Columbia demonstrated that a minimum of 25.7 per cent of logs harvested from Crown lands and consumed in sawmills were purchased from unrelated parties during the period of review.[82] The USDOC subsequently verified the evidence contained in Norcon C.[83]

B. Alberta

81. Alberta used a computer database for the section 129 proceedings to identify the volume of softwood logs sold by: (1) harvesters who did not own sawmills; and (2) harvesters that did own sawmills but that did not supply these sawmills with Crown logs from their own tenure. Alberta provided this data to PricewaterhouseCoopers, who conducted a confidential survey of the recipients of these logs.[84] The confidential survey requested that the recipient sawmills identify whether each transaction was a purchase and whether the transaction

---

[78] Norcon B (Exhibit CDA-15); and B.C. October 25, 2004 Supp. Pass-Through Questionnaire Response, Narrative, at BC-PT-22 and Exhibit BC-PT-55 (Exhibit CDA-25). The public versions of Norcon B and Exhibit BC-PT-55 do not contain the company-specific evidence referred to, as it is business proprietary information that is not susceptible to public summarization.

[79] Norcon C (Exhibit CDA-29).

[80] *Ibid.*; as amended in Letter from Steptoe & Johnson to USDOC (April 26, 2004) (Exhibit CDA-30).

[81] *Ibid.*

[82] *Ibid.* As further corroboration of the substantial percentage of the B.C. harvest yielding logs traded in arm's-length transactions, the record of the administrative review also establishes that, over the past three years, between 26 and 30 per cent of the logs from timber harvested on the B.C. Coast was sold through the Vancouver Log Market. Similarly, in the B.C. Interior, logs accounting for about 26 per cent of the total harvest were sold domestically rather than internally consumed by integrated companies. See B.C. 12 November 2003 AR Questionnaire Response, Log Export Response at BC-LER-8, Exhibit BC-LER-1 (Exhibit CDA-33).

[83] USDOC Memorandum from S. Moore to File, *Countervailing Duty Administrative Review of Certain Softwood Lumber from Canada: Verification of the Norcon Forestry Survey and the British Columbia Lumber Trade Council (BCLTC) Survey* (June 2, 2004) at 9-12 (Exhibit CDA-34).

[84] Alberta September 15, 2004 Supp. Pass-Through Questionnaire Response, Exhibit AB-S-78; revising Alberta 21 May 2004 Pass-Through Questionnaire Response, Narrative at AB-2, Exhibit AB-S-75, and Exhibit AB-S-76 (Exhibit CDA-35). The public versions of Exhibit AB-S-76 and Exhibit AB-S-78 do not contain the cited business proprietary information as it is not susceptible to public summarization.

involved an unrelated vendor using the definition of "affiliated" found in section 771(33) of the *Tariff Act of 1930*. PricewaterhouseCoopers then used the survey results to determine the volume of logs sold between unrelated parties.[85] The report contained confidential company-specific data on the total qualifying transactions for each company broken down by vendors without sawmills and vendors who were not selling from sawmill-related tenures.[86] Alberta demonstrated on this basis that there were some 730,618 cubic metres of arm's-length transactions between unrelated entities.[87]

82. Alberta also provided the USDOC in the administrative review with evidence that 2,399,893 cubic metres of logs were transferred to sawmills from unrelated parties in the period of review.[88] Furthermore, Alberta demonstrated that some 1,724,826 cubic metres of logs moved from unrelated parties to the 15 largest lumber-producing mills.[89] Alberta indicated that these data likely represented both cash sales and other forms of transactions (*e.g.*, log swaps). Alberta also provided evidence showing that a total of 1,513,171 cubic metres of logs were purchased in "cash transactions" by mills from unrelated entities, from both Crown and private sources.[90]

C. *Saskatchewan*

83. In the section 129 proceeding, Saskatchewan provided evidence that Forest Product Permit ("FPP") licensees that did not own sawmills sold some 81,403 cubic metres of logs, which represented approximately 4.9 per cent of the Crown harvest in the period of investigation.[91] Saskatchewan collected this evidence through "woodflow reports" maintained in six sawmills as a condition of their tenure.[92] These "woodflow reports" listed the source of all logs processed in these sawmills. Saskatchewan also requested that sawmills identify whether they were related to these FPP licensees. Saskatchewan and Weyerhaeuser also pro-

---

85 As Alberta does not have a category for "sawlogs", Alberta's submissions use "Section 80/81" logs as a basket category of coniferous volume used to produce either lumber products, pulp or roundwood.

86 Alberta 15 September 2004 Supp. Pass-Through Questionnaire Response, AB-S-78; revising Alberta 21 May 2004 Pass-Through Questionnaire Response, at Exhibit AB-S-76 (Exhibit CDA-35). The public versions of Exhibit AB-S-76 and Exhibit AB-S-78 do not contain the cited information as it is business proprietary and not susceptible to public summarization.

87 *Ibid.*

88 See Government of Alberta Verification Exhibit GOA-6, Amended Table 50 (18 April2004) (Exhibit CDA-36).

89 Government of Alberta Verification Exhibit GOA-7, Amended Table 59 (Exhibit CDA-37).

90 See Bearing Point, *Timber Damage Assessment (TDA) Table – 2003 Update* (17 October 2003), at 9, submitted in Alberta 12 November 2003 AR Questionnaire Response, Exhibit AB-S-69 (Exhibit CDA-38).

91 Saskatchewan 21 May 2004 Pass-Through Questionnaire Response, at SK-1, Exhibit SK-S-29 (Exhibit CDA-39). The public version of Exhibit SK-S-29 does not contain the cited business proprietary information as it is not susceptible to public summarization.

92 Saskatchewan May 21, 2004 Pass-Through Questionnaire Response, at SK-3-4 (Exhibit CDA-39).

vided additional company-specific evidence to the USDOC in response to the supplemental questionnaires.[93]

84. Saskatchewan provided evidence concerning transactions between independent harvesters and unrelated sawmills in the administrative review. In particular, this evidence demonstrated that licensees that did not hold a license to operate sawmills harvested 173,766 cubic metres of Crown timber during the period of review.[94] Saskatchewan also submitted business proprietary evidence that demonstrated that at least 3.8 per cent of the softwood logs were sold by independent harvesters to unrelated sawmills.

D. *Manitoba*

85. Manitoba provided evidence during the section 129 proceeding that some 48,100 cubic metres or 8.7 per cent of timber harvested from Crown land was sold by Timber Sales Agreement ("TSA") licensees that did not own sawmills.[95] Manitoba requested that these TSA licensees provide certification of: (1) the volume of their Crown harvest; (2) the identity of the purchasing sawmills; and (3) whether they were related to the purchasing sawmills.[96]

86. In the administrative review, Manitoba demonstrated that "independent loggers," *i.e.*, those TSA licensees and Quota holders that did not own sawmills, harvested 61,583 cubic metres or 4.45 per cent of the total Crown harvest of logs in the period of review.[97]

E. *Ontario*

87. Ontario provided the USDOC with the requested pass-through data for the total value and volume of Crown timber entering the 25 largest sawmills from independent harvesters that accounted for 91.3 per cent of all Crown softwood timber in the section 129 proceeding.[98] Furthermore, these sawmills certi-

---

[93] Weyerhaeuser 16 September 2004 Supp. Pass-Through Questionnaire Response (Exhibit CDA-40); and Weyerhaeuser26 October 2004 Supp. Pass-Through Questionnaire Response (Exhibit CDA-41).

[94] Saskatchewan 12 November 2003 AR Questionnaire Response, at SK-34-35 (Exhibit CDA-42).

[95] Manitoba 21 May 2004 Pass-Through Questionnaire Response, Exhibit MB-S-38 (Exhibit CDA-43); as revised in Manitoba September 15, 2004 Supp. Pass-Through Questionnaire Response, Revised Exhibit MB-S-38 (Exhibit CDA-44).

[96] Manitoba 21 May 2004 Pass-Through Questionnaire Response, at MB-1 (Exhibit CDA-43). Tembec (Manitoba) the largest of the independent harvesters accounting for 51 per cent of this volume also completed the USDOC Pass-Through Appendix. See Response of Tembec (Manitoba) to the US Department of Commerce 17 August 2004 Supplemental Questionnaire "Pass-Through Appendix" (16 September 2004) (Exhibit CDA-45); and Response of Tembec (Manitoba) to the US Department of Commerce 5 October 2004 Second Supplemental Questionnaire "Supplemental Pass-Through Appendix" (25 October 2004) (Exhibit CDA-46). In its final section 129 determination, the USDOC wrongly excluded all of these transactions on the basis that they occurred outside the period of investigation. See Draft Section 129 Determination, at 12 (Exhibit CDA-6).

[97] Manitoba 12 November 2003 AR Questionnaire Response, Narrative at MB-16, Exhibits MB-S-2 and MB-S-4b (Exhibit CDA-47).

[98] See Ontario 21 May 2004 Pass-Through Questionnaire Response, Narrative at ON-2, Exhibit ON-PASS-1, Exhibit ON-PASS-3 (Exhibit CDA-48). The data provided to the USDOC were drawn

fied that these transactions occurred with unrelated tenure holders and provided the USDOC with the relevant certifications for specific sales. On this basis, Ontario determined that 17.75 per cent of Crown logs were sold at arm's length.[99] The Ontario Forest Industries Association and the Ontario Lumber Manufacturers Association also provided extensive transaction specific evidence, sales documentation, and other documents supporting the absence of pass-through of benefit in the data supplied by the Government of Ontario.[100]

88. In the first administrative review, Ontario provided evidence demonstrating that approximately 6,465,085 cubic metres (or 42 per cent of the total timber harvested from Crown land) was harvested by independent harvesters.[101] In addition, in response to the USDOC's request at verification, Ontario provided detailed evidence concerning the largest 25 sawmills in Ontario log purchases from unrelated tenure holders during the period of review.[102] As the USDOC verified, those 25 sawmills purchased 31 per cent or 4,391,708 cubic metres of Crown softwood logs from unrelated tenure holders.[103] The 4,391,708 cubic metres of Crown softwood logs from unrelated tenure holders equal 29 per cent of the total Crown softwood volume harvested during the period of review.

---

directly from the TREES database maintained by the Ontario Ministry of Natural Resources ("MNR"). This MNR database was carefully examined and verified by the USDOC during the period of investigation, as it contains all the needed independent harvester and sawmill-specific sales data for this timeframe.

[99] *Ibid.* The 17.75 per cent is a subsequent revision to the 18.12 per cent referred to in the Ontario 21 May 2004 Pass-Through Questionnaire Response.

[100] OFIA/OLMA 16 September 2004 Supp. Questionnaire Response (Exhibit CDA-49) and OFIA/OLMA 25 October 2004 Supp. Questionnaire Response (Exhibit CDA-50).

[101] See Letter from Hogan & Hartson to USDOC, *Certain Softwood Lumber Products from Canada*: Service of Government of Ontario Verification Exhibits on Petitioner's Counsel (6 April 2004), Minor Corrections, at 16-127 (Exhibit CDA-51). The "Minor Corrections" verification exhibit is not included in Exhibit CDA-51 as it contains business proprietary information that is not susceptible to public summarization. See also Letter from Hogan & Hartson to USDOC, *Certain Softwood Lumber Products from Canada*: Factual Submission (15 March 2004), Exhibit 9 (final version of Exhibit ON-STATS-1) (Exhibit CDA-52).

[102] See Letter from Hogan & Hartson to USDOC, *Certain Softwood Lumber Products from Canada*: Service of Government of Ontario Verification Exhibits on Petitioner's Counsel (6 April 2004), Ownership Interest Data, at 4750-4760 (Exhibit CDA-51). The "Ownership Interest Data" verification exhibit is not included in Exhibit CDA-51 as it contains business proprietary information that is not susceptible to public summarization. See also *ibid.*, Minor Corrections, at 16-127 and Letter from Hogan & Hartson to USDOC, *Certain Softwood Lumber Products from Canada*: Factual Submission (March 15, 2004), Exhibit 9 (final version of Exhibit ON-STATS-1) (Exhibit CDA-52).

[103] See Letter from Hogan & Hartson to USDOC, *Certain Softwood Lumber Products from Canada*: Service of Government of Ontario Verification Exhibits on Petitioner's Counsel (6 April 2004), Ownership Interest Data, at 4756 (Exhibit CDA-51).

TABLE OF EXHIBITS

CDA-1	"Statement of Administrative Action" in *Message from the President of the United States Transmitting the Uruguay Round Agreements, Texts of Agreements Implementing Bill, Statement of Administrative Action and Required Supporting Statements*, H.R. Doc. No. 103-316, vol. 1 at 656, 928, 1022-1027.
CDA-2	*Uruguay Round Agreements Act*, Pub. L. No. 103-465, § 129, 108 Stat. 4838, *codified at* 19 U.S.C. § 3538 (2000).
CDA-3	Letter from USDOC to Embassy of Canada, Certain Softwood Lumber Products from Canada: WTO "Pass-Through" Questionnaire (14 April 2004).
CDA-4	Letter from Weil, Gotshal & Manges to USDOC, *Certain Softwood Lumber from Canada*: WTO Implementation Questionnaire Response Concerning Pass-Through of Alleged Benefit (16 September 2004).
CDA-5	USDOC Memorandum from J. Jochum to B. Tillman, *Section 129 Determination: Final Countervailing Duty Determination, Certain Softwood Lumber from Canada* (6 December 2004).
CDA-6	USDOC Memorandum from J. Jochum to J. May, *Draft Decision Memorandum, 129 Proceeding for the WTO Appellate Body finding in the Final Countervailing Duty Determination, Certain Softwood Lumber from Canada* (19 November 2004).
CDA-7	*Notice of Implementation under Section 129 of the Uruguay Round Agreements Act: Countervailing Measures concerning Certain Softwood Lumber Products from Canada*, 69 Fed. Reg. 75,305 (Dep't. Commerce 16 December 2004).
CDA-8	*Notice of Final Results of Countervailing Duty Administrative Review and Recission of Certain Company-Specific Reviews: Certain Softwood Lumber Products from Canada*, 69 Fed. Reg. 75,917 (Dep't Commerce 20 December 2004).
CDA-9	Letter from USDOC to Embassy of Canada, *Countervailing Duty Administrative Review: Certain Softwood Lumber Products from Canada* (12 September 2003), attaching Questionnaire for the Province of Alberta, Questions III (J), (K), and (L), at III-6; Questionnaire for the Province of British Columbia, Questions III (K), (L), and (M), at IV-7; Questionnaire for the Province of Manitoba, Questions III, (D), (E) and (F), at V-5; Questionnaire for the Province of Ontario, Questions III, (K) and (L), at VI-6; and Questionnaire for the Province of Saskatchewan, Questions III, (D), (E) and (F), at VIII-4-5.

CDA-10	*Notice of Preliminary Results of Countervailing Duty Administrative Review: Certain Softwood Lumber from Canada*, 69 Fed. Reg. 33,204 (Dep't Commerce 14 June 2004)
CDA-11	USDOC Memorandum from B.E. Tillman to J.J. Jochum, *Issues and Decision Memorandum: Final Results of Administrative Review: Certain Softwood Lumber from Canada*, C-122-839 (13 December 2004).
CDA-12	*New Shorter Oxford English Dictionary* (Oxford: Clarendon Press, 1993) at 1985 ("offset").
CDA-13	Response of the Government of Alberta to the Department's 14 April 2004 Questionnaire Concerning Pass Through of Alleged Benefits (21 May 2004), Narrative at AB-1 – AB-7.
CDA-14	Response of the Government of Alberta to the Department's 17 August 2004 Supplemental Questionnaire Concerning Pass Through of Alleged Benefits (15 September 2004), Narrative at 1.
CDA-15	Response of the Government of British Columbia to the Department's 17 August 2004 Supplemental Questionnaire Concerning Pass Through of Alleged Benefits (15 September 2004), Narrative at 5 and Exhibit BC-PT-40.
CDA-16	USDOC Memorandum from B.T. Carreau to F. Shirzad, *Issues and Decision Memorandum: Final Results of the Countervailing Duty Investigation of Certain Softwood Lumber Products from Canada*, (21 March 2001) at 15.
CDA-17	*Tariff Act of 1930,* § 771(33), *codified at* 19 U.S.C § 1677(33) (2000).
CDA-18	*New Shorter Oxford English Dictionary* (Oxford: Clarendon Press, 1993) at 114 ("at arm's length… (of dealings) with neither party controlled by the other")
CDA-19	*Black's Law Dictionary*, 6th ed. (St. Paul, Minn.: West, 1990) at 109 ("arm's-length transaction").
CDA-20	J.P. Kalt and D. Reishus, *Economics of Arms's Length Transactions and Subsidy Pass-Through,* submitted as Response of the Government of British Columbia to the Department's 17 August 2004 Supplemental Questionnaire Concerning Pass Through of Alleged Benefits (15 September 2004), Exhibit BC-PT-39.
CDA-21	J.P. Kalt and D. Reishus, *Statement for the First Administrative Review*, Attachment 1 to Letter from British Columbia Lumber Trade Council to USDOC (15 March 2004).
CDA-22	Letter from Weil, Gotshal & Manges to USDOC, *Certain Softwood Lumber from Canada: Comments on Draft Section 129 Determination* (26 November 2004).

CDA-23 Letter from USDOC to Embassy of Canada, *Certain Softwood Lumber Products from Canada: WTO Supplemental "Pass-Through" Questionnaire* (17 August 2004).

CDA-24 Letter from USDOC to Embassy of Canada, *Certain Softwood Lumber Products from Canada: Second WTO Supplemental "Pass-Through" Questionnaire* (5 October 2004).

CDA-25 Response of the Government of British Columbia to the Department's 5 October 2004 Supplemental Questionnaire Concerning Pass Through of Alleged Benefits (25 October 2004), Narrative at BC-PT-22 and Exhibit BC-PT-55.

CDA-26 *Initiation of Antidumping and Countervailing Duty Administrative Reviews and Request for Revocation in Part*, 68 Fed. Reg. 39,055 (Dep't Commerce 1 July 2003).

CDA-27 *Certain Softwood Lumber Products from Canada: Extension of Time Limit for Preliminary Results of Countervailing Duty Administrative Review*, 69 Fed. Reg. 2,568 (Dep't Commerce 16 January 2004).

CDA-28 Letter from Weil, Gotshal & Manges to USDOC, *Certain Softwood Lumber from Canada*: First Administrative Review, Pass-Through of Benefit to Arm's-Length Purchasers of Log and Lumber Inputs (24 May 2004).

CDA-29 Norcon Forestry Ltd., *Survey of Primary Sawmills' Arm's Length Log Purchases in British Columbia* (15 March 2004), submitted with Letter from Steptoe & Johnson to USDOC (15 March 2004).

CDA-30 Letter from Steptoe & Johnson to USDOC (26 April 2004), recording minor corrections to the *Norcon Arm's Length Log Survey.*

CDA-31 Response of the Government of British Columbia to the Department's 14 April 2004 Questionnaire Concerning Pass Through of Alleged Benefits (21 May 2004), Exhibit BC-PT-18 (Letter from Steptoe & Johnson to Akin, Gump, Strauss, Hauer & Feld (20 May 2004) attaching *Survey of Primary Sawmills' Arm's Length Log Purchases In the Province of British Columbia* filed with Letter from Steptoe & Johnson to US Department of Commerce (21 December 2001)).

CDA-32 Response of the Government of British Columbia to the Department's 17 August 2004 Supplemental Questionnaire Concerning Pass Through of Alleged Benefits (15 September 2004), Narrative at 2, note 1.

CDA-33 Response of the Government of British Columbia to the Department's 12 September 2003 Questionnaire (12 November 2003), Log Export Response Narrative at BC-LER-7 – BC-LER-9 and Exhibit BC-LER-1.

CDA-34 USDOC Memorandum from S. Moore to File, *Countervailing Duty Administrative Review of Certain Softwood Lumber from*

	Canada: Verification of the Norcon Forestry Survey and the British Columbia Lumber Trade Council (BCLTC) Survey (2 June 2004) at 9-12.
CDA-35	Response of the Government of Alberta to the Department's 14 April 2004 Questionnaire Concerning Pass Through of Alleged Benefits (21 May 2004) at AB-2-3, Exhibit AB-S-75, Exhibit AB-S-76, and Exhibit AB-S-78.
CDA-36	Government of Alberta Verification Exhibit GOA-6, Amended Table 50 (18 April 2004).
CDA-37	Government of Alberta Verification Exhibit GOA-7, Amended Table 59.
CDA-38	Bearing Point, *Timber Damage Assessment (TDA) Table – 2003 Update* (17 October 2003), submitted in Response of the Government of Alberta to the Department's 12 September 2003 Questionnaire (12 November 2003), Exhibit AB-S-69.
CDA-39	Response of the Government of Saskatchewan to the Department's 14 April 2004 Questionnaire Concerning Pass Through of Alleged Benefits (21 May 2004), Narrative at SK-1 – SK-5 and Exhibit SK-S-29.
CDA-40	Response of Weyerhaeuser Company to the Department's 14 April 2004 Questionnaire Concerning Pass Through of Alleged Benefits (16 September 2004).
CDA-41	Response of Weyerhaeuser Company to the Department's Second WTO Supplemental Pass-Through Questionnaire (26 October 2004).
CDA-42	Response of the Government of Saskatchewan to the Department's 12 September 2003 Questionnaire (12 November 2003), Narrative at SK-34 – SK-35.
CDA-43	Response of the Government of Manitoba to the Department's 14 April 2004 Questionnaire Concerning Pass Through of Alleged Benefits (21 May 2004), Narrative at MB-1, Exhibit MB-S-38.
CDA-44	Response of the Government of Manitoba to the Department's 17 August 2004 Supplemental Questionnaire Concerning Pass Through of Alleged Benefits (15 September 2004), Revised Exhibit MB-S-38.
CDA-45	Response of Tembec Inc. (Manitoba) to the Department's 17 August 2004 Questionnaire Concerning Pass Through of Alleged Benefits (16 September 2004), at 1-7.
CDA-46	Response of Tembec Inc. (Manitoba) to the Department's 5 October 2004 Second Supplemental Questionnaire Concerning Pass-Through of Alleged Benefits (25 October 2004), Narrative, at 1-2 and Attachments A and B.

CDA-47	Response of the Government of Manitoba to the Department's 12 September 2003 Questionnaire (12 November 2003), Narrative at MB-14 – MB-16, Exhibit MB-S-2 and Exhibit MB-S-4b.
CDA-48	Response of the Government of Ontario to the Department's 14 April 2004 Questionnaire Concerning Pass Through of Alleged Benefits (21 May 2004), Narrative at ON-1 - ON-2, Exhibit ON-PASS-1 and Exhibit ON-PASS-3.
CDA-49	Response of the Ontario Forest Industries Association and the Ontario Lumber Manufacturers Association on behalf of their members to the Department's August 17, 2004 Questionnaire Concerning Pass Through of Alleged Benefits (16 September 2004).
CDA-50	Response of the Ontario Forest Industries Association and the Ontario Lumber Manufacturers Association on behalf of their members to the Department's 5 October 2004 2nd Supplemental Questionnaire Concerning Pass Through of Alleged Benefits (26 October 2004).
CDA-51	Letter from Hogan & Hartson to USDOC, Certain Softwood Lumber Products from Canada: Service of Government of Ontario Verification Exhibits on Petitioner's Counsel (6 April 2004).
CDA-52	Letter from Hogan & Hartson to USDOC, *Certain Softwood Lumber Products from Canada*: Factual Submission (15 March 2004), Exhibit 9 (final version of Exhibit ON-STATS-1).

ANNEX A-2

RESPONSE OF CANADA TO THE REQUEST BY THE UNITED STATES FOR PRELIMINARY RULINGS AND REBUTTAL SUBMISSION OF CANADA

31 March 2005

TABLE OF CONTENTS

TABLE OF CASES CITED IN THIS SUBMISSION

Panel Report	*United States – Final Countervailing Duty Determination With Respect to Certain Softwood Lumber from Canada*, Report of the Panel, WT/DS257/R, adopted 17 February 2004.
Appellate Body Report	*United States – Final Countervailing Duty Determination With Respect to Certain Softwood Lumber from Canada*, Report of the Appellate Body, WT/DS257/AB/R, adopted 17 February 2004.
Australia – Automotive Leather II *(Article 21.5 – US)*	*Australia – Subsidies Provided to Producers and Exporters of Automotive Leather – Recourse to Article 21.5 of the DSU by the United States*, Report of the Panel, WT/DS126/RW and Corr. 1, adopted 11 February 2000.
Australia – Salmon *(Article 21.5 – Canada)*	*Australia – Measures Affecting the Importation of Salmon – Recourse to Article 21.5 of the DSU by Canada*, Report of the Panel, WT/DS18/RW, adopted 20 March 2000.
Canada – Aircraft (Article 21.5 – Brazil)	*Canada – Measures Affecting the Export of Civilian Aircraft – Recourse by Brazil to Article 21.5 of the DSU*, Report of the Appellate Body, WT/DS70/AB/RW, adopted 4 August 2000.
Chile – Price Band System	*Chile – Price Band System and Safeguard Measures Relating to Certain Agricultural Products*, Report of the Appellate Body, WT/DS207/AB/R, adopted 23 October 2002.
Dominican Republic – Cigarettes	*Dominican Republic – Measures Affecting the Importation and Internal Sale of Cigarettes,* Report of the Panel, WT/DS302, issued 26 November 2004 (under appeal).
EC – Bed Linen (Article 21.5 – India), Panel Report	*European Communities – Anti-Dumping Duties on Imports of Cotton-Type Bed Linen from India – Recourse to Article 21.5 of the DSU by India*, Report of the Panel, WT/DS141/RW, adopted 24 April 2003.
EC – Bed Linen (Article 21.5 – India), Appellate Body Report	*European Communities – Anti-Dumping Duties on Imports of Cotton-Type Bed Linen from India – Recourse to Article 21.5 of the DSU by India*, Report of the Appellate Body, WT/DS141/AB/RW, adopted 24 April 2003.

US – Shrimp (Article 21.5 – Malaysia	*United States – Import Prohibition of Certain Shrimp and Shrimp Products – Recourse to Article 21.5 of the DSU by Malaysia*, Report of the Appellate Body, WT/DS58/AB/RW, adopted 21 November 2001.

I. INTRODUCTION

1. In this submission, Canada addresses the arguments made by the United States in two parts. First, Canada responds to the request by the United States for a preliminary ruling that the final results of the administrative review fall outside the jurisdiction of the Panel in this dispute. Second, Canada rebuts the few assertions the United States makes in its first written submission.

2. For the reasons set out in this submission, Canada requests that the Panel reject the US request as being without merit, and determine that the final results of the administrative review are properly reviewable under Article 21.5 of the *Understanding on Rules and Procedures Governing the Settlement of Disputes* ("DSU"). Canada also requests that the Panel reject the US assertion that the US Department of Commerce ("USDOC") conducted proper pass-through analyses.

II. RESPONSE OF CANADA TO THE REQUEST BY THE UNITED STATES FOR PRELIMINARY RULINGS

3. The request by the United States for a preliminarily ruling in this dispute is a request that the Panel insulate the US imposition of countervailing measures on softwood lumber from compliance under the WTO Agreement. The Panel should reject this request as being without legal basis, and as running contrary to the very purpose of the dispute settlement system.

4. First, the final results of the administrative review are properly before the Panel because they rendered the pass-through analyses and resulting adjustment provided in the section 129 determination non-existent. There is no support in the DSU for the US contention that a panel may not review, under Article 21.5, measures that undo claimed "measures taken to comply". Article 21.5 requires the Panel in this case to determine the "existence" of any measure taken by the United States to bring the imposition of its countervailing duty into compliance with the recommendations and rulings of the Dispute Settlement Body ("DSB") on pass-through.

5. Second, the administrative review results are within the jurisdiction of the Panel under Article 21.5 of the DSU because, like the section 129 determination, these results are inextricably linked to the recommendations and rulings of the DSB in this case. In both measures, the USDOC purports to bring its countervailing duty on softwood lumber into conformity with its obligations to conduct pass-through analyses; in both measures, its treatment of the pass-through issue and record evidence is nearly identical.

6. Third, the US request runs contrary to the very purpose of Article 21.5 compliance proceedings. If the US position were to prevail, Canada would be required to bring an absurd multiplicity of "new" dispute settlement cases on the same issue, involving the same claims, to secure the same recommendations and rulings from the DSB. Acceding to the request would preclude any "prompt settlement of situations" under Article 3.3, "positive solution to a dispute" under Article 3.7, or "prompt compliance" under Article 21.1 of the DSU. Acceptance of the US position would allow the United States to evade compliance with DSB rulings in perpetuity, frustrating the very purpose of the DSU.

A. Article 21.5 of the DSU Establishes a Broad Scope for Review

7. Article 21.5 of the DSU provides for expedited dispute settlement procedures to ensure full implementation of recommendations and rulings of the DSB:

> Where there is disagreement as to the existence or consistency with a covered agreement of measures taken to comply with the recommendations and rulings such dispute shall be decided through recourse to these dispute settlement procedures, including wherever possible resort to the original panel...

8. The ordinary meaning of the phrase "measures taken to comply," read in context and in light of the object and purpose of Article 21 and of the DSU as a whole, provides the Panel with wide discretion to examine whether a Member has complied with the recommendations and rulings of the DSB. The Appellate Body in *Canada – Aircraft (Article 21.5 – Brazil)* confirmed that the scope of Article 21.5 is to be interpreted broadly:

> [T]he phrase "measures taken to comply" refers to measures which have been, *or which should be*, adopted by a Member to bring about compliance with the recommendations and rulings of the DSB.[1]

9. An Article 21.5 panel is therefore not limited to examining only those measures that an implementing Member claims to have been "taken to comply". As the United States itself has recognized, it is for the Panel alone to determine the "measures taken to comply".[2] It is also for the Panel to determine whether such measures exist and, if so, whether they are consistent with the implementing Member's WTO obligations.

---

[1] *Canada – Aircraft (Article 21.5 – Brazil)*, at para. 36 [emphasis added]. ("[I]n principle, there would be two separate and distinct measures: the original measure which *gave rise* to the recommendations and rulings of the DSB, and the 'measures taken to comply' which are – or should be – adopted to *implement* those recommendations and rulings.") [emphasis in original]

[2] US First Submission and Request for Preliminary Rulings, at para. 14. See also *EC – Bed Linen (Article 21.5 – India)* Appellate Body Report, at para. 78 ("We agree with the Panel that it is, ultimately, for an Article 21.5 panel – and not for the complainant or the respondent – to determine which of the measures listed in the request for its establishment are 'measures taken to comply'.").

B. The Final Results of the Administrative Review Are within the Panel's Jurisdiction of the Panel under Article 21.5 Because They Rendered Non-Existent Any Purported Compliance Achieved in the Section 129 Determination

10. In its request for a preliminary ruling, the United States fails to address the fact that the final results of the administrative review rendered non-existent, the limited pass-through analysis and resulting adjustment provided in the section 129 determination.

11. As explained in Canada's first written submission, the USDOC failed to perform appropriate pass-through analysis for the log transactions identified in the administrative review.[3] The USDOC therefore presumed, rather than demonstrated, the full pass-through of a benefit in arm's-length transactions.[4] Accordingly, on 20 December 2004, the date on which the final results of the administrative review came into force, the USDOC nullified the pass-through analysis and resulting adjustment it provided in the section 129 determination.[5]

12. It is an uncontested fact that the final results of the administrative review rendered ineffective the pass-through analysis and adjustment under the section 129 determination. Consequently, the final results of the administrative review are an integral part of the Panel's determination "as to the *existence* ... of measures taken to comply" under Article 21.5 of the DSU.[6]

13. The Appellate Body in *EC – Bed Linen (Article 21.5 – India)* explained that the mandate of a compliance panel under Article 21.5 includes examining the existence of "measures taken to comply" and that such an examination is not limited to the factual circumstances or legal issues addressed in the original panel proceedings:

> We addressed the function and scope of Article 21.5 proceedings for the first time in *Canada – Aircraft (Article 21.5 – Brazil)*. (...) We explained there that the mandate of Article 21.5 panels is to examine either the "existence" of "measures taken to comply" or, more frequently, the "*consistency with a covered agreement*" of implementing measures. This implies that an Article 21.5 panel is not confined to examining the "measures taken to comply" from the perspective of the claims, arguments, and factual circumstances relating to the measure that was the subject of the *original* proceedings.[7]

---

3 First Written Submission of Canada, at paras. 53-60.

4 *Ibid.*, at paras. 3-5.

5 *Ibid.*, at paras. 28, 68.

6 An examination of the "existence" of something, according to the ordinary meaning of that term, includes assessing "Reality, as [opposed] to appearance" and establishing "[t]he fact or state of existing". *The New Shorter Oxford English Dictionary* (Oxford: The Clarendon Press, 1993), at 882. (Exhibit CDA-53)

7 *EC – Bed Linen (Article 21.5 – India)*, Appellate Body Report, at para. 79 [italics in original].

14. In *Australia – Leather II (Article 21.5 – US)*, the United States itself argued that measures that undo implementation appropriately fall within the scope of Article 21.5 of the DSU:

> Under Article 21.5, this panel is to consider "the existence or consistency with a covered agreement of measures taken to comply with the recommendations and rulings." Plainly, if this Panel can determine the "existence" of measures taken to comply with the recommendations, it can consider whether the measures purportedly taken to comply were effectively rendered non-existent.[8]

15. As discussed, the compliance panel in that case found the government replacement loan at issue was within their terms of reference under Article 21.5 of the DSU.

16. The panel in *EC – Bed Linen (Article 21.5 – India)* shared the view that the scope of Article 21.5 is wide. In declining to include certain EC measures in its compliance review, that panel specifically noted that India "does not argue that the subsequent two measures undo the compliance effectuated by the first measure."[9]

17. Because the final results of the administrative review undo the pass-through analysis and resulting adjustment provided in the section 129 determination, the final results are properly before the Panel.

C. *The Final Results of the Administrative Review Are Inextricably Linked to the Recommendations and Rulings of the DSB and Are Therefore "Measures Taken to Comply"*

18. The final results of the administrative review are properly before the Panel also because they are inextricably linked to the recommendations and rulings of the DSB and to what the United States claims as being its "measures taken to comply".

19. As explained in Canada's first written submission, the treatment by USDOC of the pass-through issue in the final results of its administrative review is nearly identical to its section 129 pass-through determination.[10] The USDOC reproduced in the former the discussion of the five "factors" from the latter nearly word for word.[11] Moreover, these discussions apply to the same Canadian

---

[8] *Australia – Automotive Leather II (Article 21.5 – US)*, Annex 1-2, at para. 30. See also Third Party Submission of China, at paras. 12-18.

[9] *EC – Bed Linen (Article 21.5 – India)*, Panel Report, at para. 6.21. See also Third Party Submission of the European Communities, at para. 26, citing *Dominican Republic – Cigarettes*, at paras. 7.11-7.21 ("The Panel also considers it necessary to examine Law 2-04 to secure a positive solution to the matter mandated to this Panel since Decree 636-03 has been replaced by Law 2-04."); and, *e.g.*, *Chile – Price Band System*, at para. 144. ("[A] complaining party should not have to adjust its pleadings throughout dispute settlement proceedings in order to deal with a disputed measure as a 'moving target'.")

[10] First Written Submission of Canada, at para. 33.

[11] Compare USDOC Memorandum from J. Jochum to B. Tillman, *Section 129 Determination: Final Countervailing Duty Determination, Certain Softwood Lumber from Canada* (6 December 2004), at 5-7 (Exhibit CDA-5) with *Issues and Decision Memorandum: Final Results of Administra-*

exports over the same period. In addition, the USDOC published preliminary results for the administrative review containing a "pass-through" section nearly four months after the DSB made its recommendations and rulings, and issued final results nearly ten months after those recommendations and rulings.[12]

20. The United States, recognizing the complete identity of issues in both determinations and the relevance of their timing, is left with arguing before the Panel that form ought to prevail over substance. The United States argues that assessment reviews and original investigations are different proceedings, and that while the administrative review attempted to address the pass-through issue, the review itself was initiated prior to the recommendations and rulings of the DSB.[13] In doing so, the United States ignores the fact that, under US law, the USDOC may implement the recommendations and rulings of the DSB concerning an original investigation through a subsequent administrative review.[14]

21. Article 21.5 of the DSU requires a compliance panel to examine the substance of a Member's measures notwithstanding any argument that the form of the measures could preclude compliance review. In *Australia – Automotive Leather II (Article 21.5 – US)*, for example, the panel rejected Australian claims that a government loan issued to an automotive leather producer as a replacement measure for a previous grant, which the DSB had recommended be withdrawn, was not a measure "taken to comply". The panel confirmed that the subsequent loan was within its jurisdiction to examine under Article 21.5 of the DSU because it was "inextricably linked to the steps taken by Australia in response to the DSB's ruling in this dispute, in view of both its timing and its nature."[15]

---

tive Review: Certain Softwood Lumber from Canada, C-122-839 (13 December 2004), at 46-47 (Exhibit CDA-11).

[12] First Written Submission of Canada, at paras. 31, 33-34. The USDOC also recognized that arguments from the Canadian respondents regarding the need to conduct pass-through analyses were based on the recommendations and rulings of the DSB in this respect. See *Issues and Decision Memorandum: Final Results of Administrative Review: Certain Softwood Lumber from Canada*, C-122-839 (13 December 2004), at 43 (Exhibit CDA-11). ("They argue that, in accordance with recent WTO Appellate Body and Panel findings, the Department should conduct a pass-through analysis of logs purchased at arm's length by lumber producers to determine whether the alleged subsidy to timber harvesters from provincial stumpage benefited those lumber producers.")

[13] US First Submission and Request for Preliminary Rulings, at paras. 21-23.

[14] See "Statement of Administrative Action" in *Message from the President of the United States Transmitting the Uruguay Round Agreements, Texts of Agreements Implementing Bill, Statement of Administrative Action and Required Supporting Statements*, H.R. Doc. No. 103-316, vol. 1 at 656 (Exhibit CDA-1), at 356-357. ("Furthermore, while subsection 129(b) [of the Uruguay Round Agreements Act] creates a mechanism for making new determinations in response to a WTO report, new determinations may not be necessary in all situations. In many instances, such as those in which a WTO report merely implicates the size of a dumping margin or countervailable subsidy rate (as opposed to whether a determination is affirmative or negative), it may be possible to implement the WTO report recommendations in a future administrative review under section 751 of the Tariff Act.")

[15] *Australia – Automotive Leather II (Article 21.5 –US)*, at para. 6.5. ("In our view, the [new] loan cannot be excluded from our consideration without severely limiting our ability to judge, on the basis of the United States' request, whether Australia has taken measures to comply with the DSB's ruling.")

22. In *Australia – Salmon (Article 21.5 – Canada)*, the panel was faced with a sub-national ban on certain imported Canadian salmon products, which was introduced subsequent to national measures that Australia declared were taken to comply. Australia argued that the sub-national ban was not a measure "taken to comply" within the meaning of Article 21.5 of the DSU. The panel rejected the Australian argument, reasoning that:

> … an Article 21.5 panel cannot leave it to the full discretion of the implementing Member to decide whether or not a measure is one "taken to comply". If one were to allow that, an implementing Member could simply avoid any scrutiny of certain measures by a compliance panel, *even where such measures would be so clearly connected to the panel and Appellate Body reports concerned, both in time and in respect of the subject-matter, that any impartial observer would consider them to be measures "taken to comply".*[16]

23. The United States avoids such rationale and attempts to shield its administrative review results from examination by the Panel by selectively quoting from the panel findings in *EC – Bed Linen (Article 21.5 – India)*.[17] The US reliance on *EC – Bed Linen (Article 21.5 – India)*, however, is misplaced. As the EC notes in its third party submission, the panel in that dispute found that the EC measures in question were not "taken to comply" within the meaning of Article 21.5 of the DSU because they did not deal with the subject matter upon which the DSB had made recommendations and rulings.[18] Indeed, the panel expressly noted that "[t]he situation might be different had there been a claim in the original dispute challenging the cumulative assessment of the effects of imports from India, Egypt, and Pakistan."[19]

24. The United States also attempts to confuse the issue by claiming that an Article 21.5 panel does not have jurisdiction to evaluate USDOC treatment of additional record evidence concerning exports subject to a US definitive countervailing duty.[20] This assertion misses the point entirely. The Panel's assessment "as to the existence or consistency with a covered agreement of measures taken to comply" under Article 21.5 of the DSU necessarily involves an examination of new factual information. As stated by the Appellate Body in *EC – Bed Linen (Article 21.5 – India)*:

> [A]n Article 21.5 panel is not confined to examining the "measures taken to comply" from the perspective of the claims, arguments, and factual circumstances relating to the measure that was the sub-

---

[16] *Australia – Salmon (Article 21.5 – Canada)*, at para. 7.10(22) [emphasis added]. See also *EC – Bed Linen (Article 21.5 – India)*, Panel Report, at para. 6.17.

[17] US First Submission and Request for Preliminary Rulings, at paras. 15-16.

[18] Third Party Submission of the European Communities, at para. 17 ("It is important to note that the two measures in *EC – Bed linen* were not dismissed from the scope of that 21.5 proceeding because they were 'review measures'. They were dismissed because they did not relate to the original dispute between the EC and India.").

[19] *EC – Bed Linen (Article 21.5 – India)*, Panel Report, at para. 6.18, fn. 36.

[20] US First Submission and Request for Preliminary Rulings, at para. 24.

> ject of the *original* proceedings. Moreover, the relevant facts bearing upon the "measure taken to comply" may be different from the facts relevant to the measure at issue in the original proceedings. It is to be expected, therefore, that the claims, arguments, and factual circumstances relating to the "measure taken to comply" will not, necessarily, be the same as those relating to the measure in the original dispute. Indeed, a complainant in Article 21.5 proceedings may well raise *new* claims, arguments, and factual circumstances different from those raised in the original proceedings, because a "measure taken to comply" may be *inconsistent* with WTO obligations in ways different from the original measure.[21]

25. The section 129 determination and the final results of the administrative review are inextricably linked to the DSB recommendations and rulings in this dispute because they both address the obligations of the United States to conduct pass-through analyses with respect to independent harvester and sawmill-to-sawmill log transactions for the same exports for the same period of time.[22] The mere fact that the administrative review might have been initiated under a distinct provision of US law does not excuse the failure by the USDOC, for example under Article 10 of the *Agreement on Subsidies and Countervailing Measures* ("SCM Agreement"), to "take all necessary steps to ensure that the imposition" of the US countervailing duty on softwood lumber "was in accordance with" the requirement to conduct pass-through analyses under "the provisions of Article VI of GATT 1994 and the terms of this Agreement".

D. *The US Request to Exclude the Final Results of the Administrative Review from the Panel's Jurisdiction Ignores the Purpose of Compliance Proceedings*

26. As a broader systemic matter, the US request for a preliminary ruling runs contrary to the very purpose of an Article 21.5 panel in its review of the imposition of countervailing measures.

27. The US request, taken to its logical conclusion, would require Canada to make a series of identical claims to address an unchanging issue under Article VI:3 of the *General Agreement on Tariffs and Trade 1994* ("GATT 1994") and Articles 10 and 32.1 of the SCM Agreement. The US obligation to demonstrate whether, and to what extent, alleged subsidies to log production pass through arm's-length log purchases *before* imposing duties on softwood lumber products would remain in dispute for each annual assessment review under Article 21 of the SCM Agreement during the potential five-year life (or longer) of the US definitive countervailing measure. Such a result would leave the DSB in the absurd situation of having made numerous identical recommendations and rulings concerning a definitive countervailing duty for which compliance may never be se-

---

[21] *EC – Bed Linen (Article 21.5 – India)*, Appellate Body Report, at para. 79 [italics in original]. See also EC Third Party Submission, at para. 28, referring in addition to the Appellate Body's report in *US – Shrimp (Article 21.5 – Malaysia)*, at para. 86.

[22] Third Party Submission of China, at paras. 14-15.

cured. Were the Panel to allow the US request in this case, it would effectively insulate US countervailing measures from compliance with the recommendations and rulings of the DSB concerning pass-through.

28. The EC has noted the absurdity of the US request in this respect in its third party submission:

> Accepting the US view that the administrative review is not subject to a DSU 21.5 Panel review would turn the US system of duty assessment into a moving target that escapes from countervailing duty disciplines. Each administrative review would have to be subject to a new panel request, and by the time the panel, Appellate Body and implementation procedure was completed, another administrative review would have overtaken the results of any Section 129 determination.[23]

29. Acceding to the US request would therefore preclude any "prompt settlement of situations" under Article 3.3, "positive solution to a dispute" under Article 3.7, or "prompt compliance" under Article 21.1 of the DSU. In *Australia – Salmon (Article 21.5 – Canada)*, the United States paradoxically took the following position:

> [W]e also wish to express the agreement of the United States with the broad and inclusive approach the Panel has taken thus far in defining the scope of this proceeding. The Panel's approach is the only one consistent with the purpose of the WTO dispute settlement system as reflected in Articles 3 and 21 of the Dispute Settlement Understanding: the prompt settlement of disputes. Disputes could not be settled "promptly" if a defending party were permitted to thwart a thorough review of its WTO compliance by staging the introduction of details of new measures over a period of time, and then arguing that they must escape WTO scrutiny for a further period of time.[24]

30. In this dispute, the DSB ruled that the United States must demonstrate, rather than presume, that a subsidy passes through arm's-length log transactions. The United States defies this ruling when, in an administrative review of the amount of the countervailing duty that gave rise to the matter before the DSB, it performs none of the required analysis and continues to presume pass-through. The Panel should therefore reject the U.S. preliminary ruling request and find that the results of the first administrative review are properly before it in this proceeding.

---

[23] Third Party Submission of the European Communities, at para. 29.

[24] *Australia – Salmon (Article 21.5 – Canada)*, Third Participant Submission of the United States, 9 December 1999, at para. 5. (Exhibit CDA-54)

III. REBUTTAL SUBMISSION OF CANADA

31. Canada established in its first written submission that in both the section 129 determination and in the administrative review, the USDOC continued to presume, rather than demonstrate, a pass-through of a subsidy in arm's-length purchases of logs by sawmills in violation of US obligations under Article VI:3 of the GATT 1994 and Articles 10 and 32.1 of the SCM Agreement.

32. The United States responds to the entirety of Canada's claims in only two paragraphs.[25] In these paragraphs, the United States contends that the USDOC properly determined that the overwhelming majority of log purchase transactions were not at arm's length and properly rejected significant volumes of record evidence. It also claims that the "recommended analysis" was performed for transactions that were found to be at arm's length, using "appropriate log prices as benchmarks". Finally, the United States claims that the recommendations and rulings of the DSB concerned only those sawmill-to-sawmill transactions in which the purchaser did not hold tenure.

33. Canada addresses each of these US assertions in turn.

34. First, the reliance by the USDOC on the five "factors" as a pretense to reject arm's-length log transactions is not supported by the GATT 1994, or the SCM Agreement, nor does it accord with basic economics. As a matter of well-established economic principles, transactions do not have to take place in a regulatory vacuum, if such a marketplace even exists, to be "at arm's length".

35. Second, where the USDOC accepted that transactions were at arm's length, it failed to perform proper market comparisons.

36. Third, neither the original panel nor the Appellate Body restricted the requirement for a pass-through analysis to log transactions where the purchasing sawmills did not hold tenure, and nowhere in the original proceeding or appeal did Canada or the United States argue that a pass-through analysis should be restricted to such transactions.

A. The Five "Factors" Used by the USDOC to Disregard Arm's-Length Transactions Are Irrelevant to Whether Entities Operate at Arm's Length

37. Both the original panel and the Appellate Body confirmed that a Member may not presume that a subsidy passes through transactions where a subsidy is received by "someone other than the producer or exporter of the product under investigation" or where "the producer of the input is not the same entity as the producer of the processed product".[26]

38. Canada has demonstrated that the US softwood lumber subsidy calculations include amounts attributable to log purchases by sawmills from unrelated

---

[25] US First Submission and Request for Preliminary Rulings, at paras. 33-34.

[26] First Written Submission of Canada, at paras. 47-50.

parties.[27] The Canadian respondents provided substantial record evidence concerning such purchases, which the USDOC rejected without having demonstrated that a pass-through occurred. The United States can point to no record evidence or analysis demonstrating that alleged stumpage subsidies passed through to the purchasing lumber producers; instead, it asserts only that "Commerce did not 'presume' pass-through".[28] Nevertheless, the USDOC continued to include that alleged stumpage subsidy amount in its softwood lumber subsidy calculations.

39. The reliance by the USDOC on its five "factors" to dismiss, without analysis, the majority of the transactions as non-arm's-length is not supported by the GATT 1994, the SCM Agreement, or basic economics. None of the "factors" identified by the USDOC as having "an impact on the disposition of the Crown logs sold by independent harvesters"[29] transform an arm's-length transaction into one that is not at arm's length. Nor can these "factors" otherwise be used to avoid conducting an analysis of log transactions.[30]

40. Basic economic principles dictate that domestic processing requirements do not affect the arm's-length nature of a transaction, as such regulations do not alter the opposition of economic interest between sawmill and harvester.[31] Indeed, if anything, such a requirement may provide the harvester greater market power because it would limit where a sawmill may acquire its inputs.[32] Thus, there is no basis to disregard transactions due to the presence of domestic processing requirements.

41. The USDOC's assertion that a transaction is not at "arm's length" where a log purchaser is responsible for the payment of stumpage fees is equally without support. An independent harvester will extract from a sawmill the *full market value* of what it provides to the sawmill (*i.e.*, the log), regardless of who "writes the check".[33] This fundamental economic principle is commonly found in introductory economic texts. Although the party writing the check may affect the observed log price, it will never affect the *value paid* by the sawmill for the logs.[34] Moreover, a contractual provision specifying the party responsible for remitting stumpage is no different than a provision specifying which party is responsible for satisfying outstanding liens or governmental obligations that might affect a transaction.

---

27 Canada First Submission, at paras. 3-5, 26.

28 US First Submission and Request for Preliminary Rulings, at para. 33.

29 Final Section 129 Determination, at 9 (Exhibit CDA-5).

30 First Written Submission of Canada, at paras. 62-64.

31 J.P. Kalt and D. Reishus, *Statement for the First Administrative Review*, Attachment 1 to Letter from British Columbia Lumber Trade Council to USDOC (15 March 2004), at 42-43, 48-51, 55 (Exhibit CDA-21); J.P. Kalt and D. Reishus, *Economics of Arms's Length Transactions and Subsidy Pass-Through*, submitted as Response of the Government of British Columbia to the Department's 17 August 2004 Supplemental Questionnaire Concerning Pass Through of Alleged Benefits (September 15, 2004), Exhibit BC-PT-39, at 9-10 ["Kalt 2004d"] (Exhibit CDA-20).

32 Kalt 2004d, at 10.

33 *Ibid.*, at 4-5.

34 *Ibid.*, at 6-7.

42. Finally, in an industrial context it is common for a buyer of goods or services to provide equipment, expertise or materials as part of a transaction. The essence of an arm's-length transaction is that the seller is able to extract from the buyer the value of what the seller provides. Accordingly, these transactions remain at arm's length even if the buyer provides goods or services used by the seller – whether cash, material, credit extended or other consideration.[35]

43. Moreover, the United States cannot be excused from its obligation to conduct the required pass-through analysis on the pretense that transaction-specific information, which was not reasonably required to perform the analysis, was not available. Given that the investigation and review were conducted on an aggregate basis, it is particularly incongruous for the United States to refuse to consider such information with respect to its pass-through analysis. The Canadian respondents provided all information that was reasonably available, including aggregate information sufficient to conduct the analysis.[36]

B. The USDOC Improperly Relied on Log Import Transactions in Performing Its Pass-Through Analysis

44. In the few instances where the USDOC purported to perform a pass-through analysis, it used benchmarks derived from log import transactions that did not reflect "market" conditions.[37] As the Appellate Body and the original panel made clear, the USDOC was required to establish whether the alleged stumpage subsidy conferred on timber harvesters was passed through the arm's-length log transaction. The section 129 determination benchmarks, however, which included prices for imported logs, were unrepresentative of the timber and market conditions in these provinces for which they were being used.

45. Specifically, the USDOC used extremely small and highly variable log imports relied on to calculate the benchmark for Saskatchewan. For all provinces other than Québec, log import volumes are extremely low, representing only 22.85 per cent of imports into Canada.[38] Accordingly, the use of import prices in benchmarks for Saskatchewan (which accounted for only 0.00175 per cent of imports during the period of investigation) necessarily resulted in the introduction of unrepresentative values. The USDOC did not investigate whether this small volume of imported logs was representative of the Crown harvest, and should not have assumed that it was.

---

35 Kalt 2004d, at 8-9.

36 First Written Submission of Canada, at paras. 76, 79.

37 USDOC Memorandum from Robert Copyak to James Terpstra, *"Pass-Through" Analysis Calculations for the Province of Saskatchewan, 129 Proceeding for the WTO Appellate Body Finding in the Final Countervailing Duty Determination, Certain Softwood Lumber from Canada* (6 December 2004) (Exhibit CDA-59); USDOC Memorandum from Robert Copyak to James Terpstra, *"Pass-Through" Analysis Calculations for the Province of Ontario, 129 Proceeding for the WTO Appellate Body Finding in the Final Countervailing Duty Determination, Certain Softwood Lumber from Canada* (6 December 2004) (Exhibit CDA-60).

38 Response of the Government of Canada to USDOC's November 24, 2003 Supplemental Remand Questionnaire Response (3 December 2003), at GOC-2 and Exh. GOC-GEN-59 (Exhibit CDA-55).

46. Additionally, log import prices are extraordinarily high in value because they typically involve special purchases. The prices are unrepresentative of prices paid for logs used in softwood lumber production. The tariff categories that apply to logs are overly inclusive and capture products used as inputs for high-end applications. Tariff item 4403 of the Canadian *Customs Tariff*, "wood in the rough" is a catch-all category for rough wood items not otherwise specified. Subheading 4403.20 – "other coniferous" – refers to a broad category – coniferous wood in the rough that is untreated. While the category may include untreated logs, it can also include logs that have been debarked, sawn logs such as roughly squared logs, house logs, pulp logs, round logs for veneer production, tree stumps and roots of special woods, and 'certain growths' for making special furniture veneers or smoking pipes. Many of these products are of higher value and are of a higher price than untreated logs destined, for example, for housing construction and many are not used for lumber production at all.[39] As a result, these import prices did not reflect a "market" price for logs used in softwood lumber production and should not have been used to derive benchmarks.

47. Accordingly, the use by the USDOC of these unrepresentative log import prices in the section 129 determination distorted the results of its limited pass-through analysis.

C. US Arguments Concerning Sawmill-to-Sawmill Transactions Have No Basis in the Findings of Either the Original Panel or the Appellate Body

48. Finally, the United States contends that the recommendations and rulings of the DSB were limited to a particular category of sawmill-to-sawmill transactions, even though no such argument was made by either Canada or the United States during the original proceedings, and neither the original panel nor the Appellate Body made any such distinction.[40] The United States seeks to place tenured sawmills on one side of the transaction, but non-tenured sawmills on the other.[41] The United States, through this limitation, is attempting in yet another creative way to avoid its obligation to conduct the pass-through analysis identi-

---

39 See also Response of the Government of Alberta to the USDOC's 25 September 2003 Questionnaire (14 October 2003), at AB-17 ("To repeat, it is critical to note that the statistics [used by the Department] ...are for 'wood in the rough,' which would include roughly squared timbers, untreated telephone poles and other such processed wood products and may not include any logs in the round, with bark attached.") (Exhibit CDA-56)l Response of the Government of British Columbia to the USDOC's September 25, 2003 Questionnaire (14 October 2003), at BC-19 (Exhibit CDA-57); and Response of the Gouvernement du Québec to the USDOC's 25 September 2003 Questionnaire (October 14, 2003), at 14 (Exhibit CDA-58).

40 In footnote 151 of its report, the Appellate Body indicates that the term "sawmill" refers to "an enterprise that processes logs into softwood lumber and does not hold a stumpage contract." Appellate Body Report, at para. 124, fn. 151. The Appellate Body also cites to record evidence on independent harvester transactions Canada provided before the original panel as confirming the existence of arm's-length sales of logs by "... tenured timber harvesters/sawmills to unrelated sawmills not holding stumpage rights ...", Appellate Body Report, at para. 150.

41 First Submission and Request for Preliminary Ruling of the United States, at para. 34.

fied by both the original panel and the Appellate Body under Article VI:3 of the GATT 1994 and Articles 10 and 32.1 of the SCM Agreement.

49. The original panel concluded that a pass-through analysis is required for all arm's-length log transactions between unrelated sawmills:

> [T]he USDOC's failure to conduct a pass-through analysis in respect of logs sold by tenure-holding timber harvesters (whether or not also lumber producers) to unrelated sawmills producing subject softwood lumber ... was inconsistent with Article 10 and thus Article 32.1 SCM Agreement, and with Article VI:3 of GATT 1994.[42]

50. The Appellate Body agreed and upheld:

> ... the Panel's finding, in paragraph 7.99 of the Panel Report that USDOC's failure to conduct a pass-through analysis in respect of arm's length sales of *logs* by tenured harvesters/sawmills to unrelated sawmills is inconsistent with Articles 10 and 32.1 of the *SCM Agreement* and Article VI:3 of the GATT 1994.[43]

51. The Appellate Body, therefore, upheld the conclusions of the original panel that a pass-through analysis was required for all arm's-length log transactions between sawmills. There is no qualifier in the Appellate Body's decision that purchasing sawmills must be "non-tenured", and there is no such qualifier in the original panel decision that it upheld. There would be no legal or economic reason to restrict the requirement to conduct a pass-through analysis to purchasing sawmills without tenure, and had the Appellate Body intended to restrict the scope of its ruling in this manner, it would have done so explicitly.

52. Whether the purchasing sawmill holds or does not hold stumpage rights is irrelevant to the Appellate Body's reasoning. The crux of the Appellate Body's reasoning relates to the fact that the transaction concerns an input product (*i.e.*, a log). Where a lumber producer sources its log input other than from its own timber harvesting and *log production*, the receipt of an alleged stumpage subsidy is necessarily indirect and requires pass-through analysis before it may be countervailed as an alleged subsidy to *lumber production.*[44] The Appellate Body did not condition its conclusion on circumstances concerning the purchasing sawmills.

IV. CONCLUSION

53. Canada requests that the Panel determine the final results of the first administrative review are within the jurisdiction of the Panel under Article 21.5 of the DSU. Canada also requests the Panel to reject as unfounded the claims made by the United States in its first written submission.

---

[42] Panel Report, at para. 7.99.

[43] Appellate Body Report, at para. 167(e) [italics in original].

[44] Appellate Body Report, at paras. 146-47, 156-59.

TABLE OF EXHIBITS

CDA-53	*The New Shorter Oxford English Dictionary*, (Oxford: The Clarendon Press, 1993), at 882.
CDA-54	*Australia – Salmon (Article 21.5 - Canada)*, Third Participant Submission of the United States, 9 December 1999, at para. 5.
CDA-55	Response of the Government of Canada to USDOC's November 24, 2003 Supplemental Remand Questionnaire Response (3 December 2003), at GOC-2 and Exh. GOC-GEN-59.
CDA-56	Response of the Government of Alberta to the USDOC's 25 September 2003 Questionnaire (14 October 2003), at AB-17.
CDA-57	Response of the Government of British Columbia to the USDOC's 25 September 2003 Questionnaire (14 October 2003), at BC-19.
CDA-58	Response of the Gouvernment du Québec to the USDOC's 25 September 2003 Questionnaire (14 October 2003), at 14.
CDA-59	USDOC Memorandum from Robert Copyak to James Terpstra, *"Pass-Through" Analysis Calculations for the Province of Saskatchewan, 129 Proceeding for the WTO Appellate Body Finding in the Final Countervailing Duty Determination, Certain Softwood Lumber from Canada* (6 December 2004).
CDA-60	USDOC Memorandum from Robert Copyak to James Terpstra, *"Pass-Through" Analysis Calculations for the Province of Ontario, 129 Proceeding for the WTO Appellate Body Finding in the Final Countervailing Duty Determination, Certain Softwood Lumber from Canada* (6 December 2004).

ANNEX A-3

ORAL STATEMENT OF CANADA
21 April 2005

I. INTRODUCTION

1. We are here today because the Dispute Settlement Body has ruled that a subsidy on harvested timber – that is, logs – does not necessarily pass-through to the softwood lumber manufactured from those logs. This is so where the producer sells the logs to an unrelated entity who turns the logs into lumber. In these circumstances, before the United States may apply countervailing duties to the softwood lumber manufactured from those logs, it has an obligation under Article VI:3 of the GATT and Articles 10 and 32.1 of the SCM Agreement to establish that the benefit of the subsidy has passed-through from the producer of the logs to the producer of the lumber.

2. The United States' compliance obligations in this case were uncomplicated. Before it applied countervailing duties to lumber made from logs acquired in such arm's-length transactions, it had an obligation to conduct a pass-though analysis to determine whether the benefit of any subsidies on those logs passed through to the lumber. By agreement with Canada, the United States had ten months in which to conduct that analysis.

3. Instead of complying, the United States has gone to great lengths to avoid the obligations flowing from the DSB's ruling. At the end of the ten months the United States issued a revised countervailing duty determination under section 129 of its *Uruguay Round Implementation Act*. The United States did conduct a pass-through analysis for a small fraction of the transactions that were the subject of the DSB's ruling, but for the overwhelming majority of transactions it did no pass-through analysis. Instead, it invented an elaborate threshold test which it used to exclude most arm's-length transactions from any pass-through analysis. The test the United States invented to exclude arm's-length transactions from pass-through analysis has no basis in WTO law. It defies basic principles of economics and is even contrary to the criteria for arm's-length transactions under the United States' own law.

4. On the basis of its flawed threshold test, the United States has also sought to evade its obligations by claiming that it lacked the necessary information to do a pass-through analysis. As Canada will show, it supplied the United States with all the information it needed and went to great lengths to comply with its requests. The United States' onerous additional demands involved information that was irrelevant to a pass-through analysis, did not come until most of its reasonable period of time to comply had expired, and would have imposed an impossible evidentiary burden on Canadian respondents in the process.

5. The United States also failed to perform any pass-through analysis for other sales of logs, those to companies that produced both logs and lumber. Nothing in the adopted findings of the panel or the Appellate Body licensed the exclusion of these transactions.

6. In all of these instances, the United States simply assumed that the entire benefit passed through from the logs to the softwood lumber and included the full amount of that benefit in its duty calculations on the lumber. In the original case, the DSB ruled that the United States' presumption of pass-through was inconsistent with its obligations under the GATT and the SCM Agreement. The United States has repeated its presumption of pass-through in the determinations challenged here and they are similarly inconsistent with its WTO obligations.

7. The United States' purported compliance measure took effect on 10 December 2004. But then, three days later, the United States issued another determination covering the same products over the same period. In this new determination, which was made pursuant to the United States' administrative review process, the United States definitively set the countervailing duties for the softwood lumber covered by the DSB's ruling using the same flawed that it used reasoning in its section 129 determination. Yet this time it conducted no pass-through analysis at all, not even the extremely circumscribed analysis of the section 129 determination.

8. This administrative review determination took effect on December 20, 2004 and superseded the section 129 determination. That is, the section 129 determination ceased to be effective after just ten days, and just three days after the United States informed the DSB that it had complied with its recommendations and rulings by properly conducting a pass-through analysis.

9. In sum, the United States' section 129 determination did not redress its non-compliance with its obligations under the GATT and the SCM Agreement. Moreover, to the extent that it even partially complied with these obligations, it rendered that limited compliance non-existent by the administrative review.

10. Despite this, the United States continues to insist that it has complied with the recommendations and rulings of the DSB. It insists, as well, that its administrative review determination is not properly before this panel, regardless of how that determination has undone even the United States' purported compliance measure in this case, the section 129 determination.

11. Canada's response to the United States' request for a preliminary ruling has addressed why the administrative review determination is properly within the scope of your review. The third party submission of the European Communities reaches the same conclusion. So too does the third party submission of China, although it takes a different path to get there. In Canada's view, this issue is crucial, as it goes directly to the ability of the United States to impose a non-compliant measure while relying on its domestic anti-dumping and countervail regime to evade its WTO obligations. Canada will be pleased to take questions on this matter, but because it has been thoroughly canvassed in previous submissions and in the third party submissions, Canada will not take up time today with further affirmative argument on it.

12. Canada will focus today on the assertions made by the United States in its second written submission. First, Mr. Cochlin will explain why the US presumption of pass-through is contrary to its obligations under the GATT and the SCM Agreement and why the threshold test the United States has devised is both incorrect and unfounded. Then, Mr. Owen will explain that the United States had all the available information it required to perform the pass-through analysis mandated by the DSB's ruling, and how Canada nevertheless made considerable efforts to comply with the unreasonable and irrelevant US demands for additional information.

II. COMMERCE CONTINUED TO PRESUME, RATHER THAN DEMONSTRATE, INDIRECT SUBSIDIZATION

13. Mr. Chairman, Members of the Panel, the central question in dispute before you is this: did the United States continue to *presume* the pass-through of alleged stumpage subsidies in violation of Article VI:3 of the GATT and Articles 10 and 32.1 of the SCM Agreement?

14. Contrary to the numerous, repeated assertions by the United States, a presumption of pass-through is exactly what the United States Department of Commerce ("Commerce") applied where it, first, rejected transactions based on its contrived "arm's-length" threshold test; second, refused to consider in any way certain sawmill-to-sawmill transactions; and finally, claimed that information necessary to conduct pass-through analyses was otherwise deficient.

15. The issue of "pass-through" arises in this case because, in many instances, sawmills could have only received the alleged stumpage subsidy *indirectly* – through purchases of Crown log inputs from unrelated harvesters or other sawmills. Indirect subsidization of softwood lumber production therefore would occur only if the input subsidy "passed through" from the log seller to the purchasing sawmill.

16. Both the original panel and the Appellate Body made clear that Commerce is required to demonstrate – and not presume – such alleged indirect subsidization before it could lawfully impose countervailing duties under Article VI:3 of the GATT and Articles 10 and 32.1 of the SCM Agreement.[1] Commerce must demonstrate that the alleged direct subsidy to *log* production passes through and becomes an indirect subsidy to *lumber* production. Such analysis involves demonstrating, by making appropriate market comparisons, that the purchasing sawmills received a "benefit" within the meaning of Article 1.1(b) of the SCM Agreement.

17. The United States does not contest that it has an obligation to conduct a pass-through analysis in this case.[2] Indeed, for a small fraction of the log transactions identified in its section 129 determination, Commerce compared log prices

---

1 First Written Submission of Canada, at paras. 41-50.

2 Second Written Submission of the United States, at para. 35-36.

to market benchmarks to demonstrate the existence and amount of a pass-through.[3] In most respects, Canada does not contest this limited analysis.

18. However, for the vast majority of log transactions covered by its section 129 determination, and for all transactions covered by its administrative review results, Commerce performed no such analysis. Instead, it attempted at every turn to avoid the obligation to demonstrate a pass-through.

19. For all log volumes rejected by Commerce, it presumed, rather than demonstrated, a pass-through. It deemed – without proof or analysis – that the alleged subsidy to the upstream log producer *automatically* becomes a subsidy to the unrelated downstream purchasing sawmill.

20. The United States goes to great lengths to divert the Panel's attention from Commerce's presumption of a pass-through.[4] It wants the Panel to believe that it is operating within its discretion, and that it is aggressively trying to meet its pass-through obligations. The fact remains, however, that without having done pass-through analyses and without having employed a presumption, Commerce would have been required to limit its numerator to only Crown timber going *directly* to softwood lumber production. As the United States explains, however, Commerce instead established the numerator of its subsidy calculation by requesting and using the total volume of all harvested Crown timber entering sawmills either directly *or indirectly*.[5]

III. COMMERCE APPLIED A CONTRIVED "ARM'S LENGTH" TEST TO AVOID PERFORMING THE REQUIRED PASS-THROUGH ANALYSES

21. The primary way in which Commerce avoided having to perform a pass-through analysis was by devising a novel test for determining whether a transaction was at arm's length. The United States no longer claims that it had no obligation to conduct any pass-through analysis at all, as it did in the original proceedings. It now claims, instead, that the obligation only arises where Canada can demonstrate that a transaction has occurred not only between unrelated parties, but also outside any possible influence of "government-mandated restrictions and other factors".[6] The United States maintains that an "arm's length" transaction is defined by more than "mere affiliation".[7] In so doing, it ignores even the arm's length standard set out in its own law, and which it has routinely used.[8]

22. Through an exercise in *ex post facto* rationalization, the United States argues that Commerce's so-called factors are justified by a three-pronged test,

3 *Ibid.*, at para. 39.
4 *Ibid.*, at paras. 15, 40-42.
5 *Ibid.*, at paras. 7 and 9, footnote 12.
6 *Ibid.*, at para. 20.
7 *Ibid.*, at paras. 16-17.
8 First Written Submission of Canada, at para. 62, footnote 54 (citing SAA at 928; Exhibit CDA-1).

custom-tailored for this dispute.[9] First, a transaction must be between unrelated parties. Second, one party to the transaction must not "effectively control" the other. Third, both parties must have "roughly equal bargaining power".

23. Canada does not contest the first of these requirements. It is the only part of Commerce's arm's length test that is warranted, based on the findings and conclusions of the original panel, as upheld by the Appellate Body.[10]

24. The second requirement of the US test is no different than the first. "Effective control" is already covered in the US statutory definition of "affiliated parties", which Commerce incorporated in its questionnaires. The only transactions for which Canadian respondents claimed that Commerce should do a pass-through analysis were those between parties that were not "affiliated". That statutory definition covers a wide range of relationships between parties to a transaction, ranging from family relationships, to direct or indirect ownership of an organization, and expressly includes any situation where one person "controls" any other person. According to the statute, the term "control" refers to situations in which a person "is legally or operationally in a position to exercise restraint or direction over the other person".[11] Commerce did not contest, but rather confirmed, that the definition of "affiliated parties" was applied properly in this case.[12]

25. The third requirement – "roughly equal bargaining power" – is pure fabrication, tailored for this case to justify Commerce's use of so-called factors to reject transactions. Nowhere is it found in the analysis of the original panel or the Appellate Body. Moreover, were "roughly equal bargaining power" a requirement for arm's-length transactions, almost any transaction anywhere could be rejected by investigating authorities on that basis alone. One party to a transaction will often have greater bargaining power than the other, but this does not mean that the terms of the transaction do not reflect a market outcome.

26. Fundamentally, by rejecting transactions on the hypothesis that their outcome might somehow be "affected" by market conditions, Commerce conflates the obligation to conduct a pass-through analysis, which would demonstrate the existence and amount of a pass-through, with the task of identifying transactions to which that obligation applies.[13]

27. Moving to the five factors themselves, we have detailed in our written submissions why they are irrelevant to whether a pass-through analysis is required. I therefore propose to make just three points today.

28. First, the United States makes the telling concession that its "additional factors" are not "exclusively arm's-length issues".[14] The factors in question here

---

9 Second Written Submission of the United States, at para. 16.

10 First Written Submission of Canada, at paras. 47-49.

11 *Ibid.*, at para. 60, footnote 51, citing to section 771(33) of the *Tariff Act of 1930* (19 U.S.C. § 1677(33)) (Exhibit CDA-17).

12 First Written Submission of Canada, at paras. 60, 74; Second Written Submission of the United States, at para. 15, footnote 18.

13 See, *e.g.*, Third Party Submission of China, at paras. 26-27.

14 Second Written Submission of the United States, at para. 22, footnote 29, and at para. 23.

regard who paid the stumpage fees, and whether transactions involved a fibre exchange agreement.

29. As a matter of basic economics, neither factor is an "arm's length" issue at all. The issue of who remits the government stumpage fee says nothing about whether the alleged input subsidy passed through to the purchaser. A contractual provision assigning to the buyer the obligation to pay a debt owed by the seller does not affect the value of the good sold. The value of a log is determined by the supply and demand for that log.[15] Moreover, what the United States calls the "vehicle by which the Crown bestows the subsidy"[16] has been found in this case to be the provision by government of standing timber to timber harvesters. Therefore, the US argument that the government provided the alleged stumpage subsidy directly to sawmills, where they paid the stumpage fee on behalf of the harvester, is not supported by the facts. Standing timber is provided to the upstream timber harvester, not the downstream sawmill. These facts do not suddenly change simply because the purchasing sawmill might remit the government stumpage on behalf of the upstream stumpage holder.

30. Similarly, a barter arrangement in the form of a fibre exchange agreement merely provides that the buyer is paying the consideration owed to the seller in goods rather than in cash. Indeed, barter is perhaps the oldest form of market transaction. This factor is irrelevant to determining whether the seller is able to extract from the buyer the value of what the seller provides, and hence whether any subsidy has passed through.

31. Second, with respect to Commerce's "log purchase agreement" factor, the United States in its rebuttal submission cites various possible contractual arrangements to explain Commerce's failure to conduct a pass-through analysis.[17] These contractual terms are part of the agreed structure of a transaction between unrelated parties, and as Canada has explained, simply reflect the results of the bargain reached.[18]

32. Finally, Canada explained that provincial regulations imposing "limitations on log sales" and "wood supply agreements"[19] do not dictate the material terms of the log sale agreement, such as price, delivery arrangements, or timing. A regulatory vacuum is not a prerequisite for arm's-length transactions.[20] Were it so, no sale could ever be found to be at arm's-length.

33. By way of conclusion to this section, we note that the United States to date has offered no justification regarding Commerce's presumption of a pass-through for all transactions in the administrative review; it argues only that the measure is not properly before the Panel.[21] Accordingly, up to this point, the United States here has essentially conceded that the failure by Commerce to per-

---

15 First Written Submission of Canada, para. at 64; Rebuttal Submission of Canada, at para. 41.

16 Second Written Submission of the United States, at para. 23.

17 *Ibid.*, at para. 22.

18 First Written Submission of Canada, at paras. 64; Rebuttal Submission of Canada, at para. 42.

19 Second Written Submission of the United States, at para. 21.

20 First Written Submission of Canada, at paras. 64; Rebuttal Submission of Canada, at para. 40.

21 Second Written Submission of the United States, at paras. 46-47.

form a pass-through analysis in the administrative review was inconsistent with US obligations.

IV. COMMERCE FAILED TO CONDUCT ANY ANALYSIS WHERE THE PURCHASING SAWMILL HELD A STUMPAGE CONTRACT

34. I turn now to address another instance in which Commerce impermissibly presumed a pass-through.

35. Commerce limited its questionnaires to only a select subset of sawmill-to-sawmill transactions, denying a pass-through analysis where the purchasing sawmills held tenure.

36. As justification here, the United States claims that the Appellate Body reversed, rather than upheld, the original panel's conclusion in paragraph 7.99 of its report.[22] Allow me to quote directly from paragraph 7.99:

> "[T]he USDOC's failure to conduct a pass-through analysis in respect of logs sold by tenure-holding timber harvesters (whether or not also lumber producers) to unrelated sawmills producing subject softwood lumber... was inconsistent with Article 10 and thus Article 32.1 SCM Agreement, and with Article VI:3 of GATT 1994."

37. The original panel's conclusion covers transactions where the purchasing sawmills held tenure. There is no reversal of this conclusion in the Appellate Body's report; to the contrary, there are pages of reasoning in support.[23]

38. In an attempt to explain Commerce's exclusion of these transactions, the United States offers only that, "tenure-holding sawmills are direct subsidy recipients".[24] This statement fails entirely to explain how the alleged stumpage subsidy passes from upstream timber harvesters to downstream purchasing sawmills. Commerce simply presumed the pass-through.

39. The only other reason the United States offers for Commerce's refusal to conduct the required analysis is that the Canadian respondents failed to provide necessary data. As my colleague Mr. Owen will now explain, the US claims in this respect are false, and the Canadian respondents provided more than sufficient evidence to allow Commerce to conduct a pass-through analysis in both determinations.

---

22 *Ibid.*, at para. 44.

23 Rebuttal Submission of Canada, at paras. 51-52.

24 Second Written Submission of the United States, at para. 44.

V. THE RECORD EVIDENCE WAS SUFFICIENT TO PERFORM A PROPER PASS-THROUGH ANALYSIS

A. The Canadian Respondents Provided All Available Evidence Necessary for Commerce to Perform a Pass-Through Analysis

40. Mr. Chairman, Members of the Panel, the United States complains that Canada failed to provide the necessary data to allow Commerce to conduct a pass-through analysis and is, in fact, "attempting to restrict" its ability to conduct such an analysis.[25]

41. These assertions are patently false. Commerce had everything it needed and more to conduct a pass-through analysis.[26] The Canadian respondents provided pricing data that was representative of the arm's-length transactions in these provinces and was more than sufficient to conduct a pass-through analysis. Commerce should have used this information to calculate the amount of pass-through applicable to the entire volume of arm's-length transactions for each province.

42. Allow me to briefly outline this information.

43. British Columbia provided Commerce with the name of the seller, volume, value, and species information for each of the more than 3,000 arm's-length purchases by sawmills that accounted for 53 per cent of the Crown harvest in that province.[27] In addition, for these same sawmills, British Columbia provided equally detailed information on more than 2,500 arm's-length transactions involving logs harvested from private lands.[28] These data could have been used to calculate the amount of pass-through for these transactions and an average amount of pass-through for the remaining arm's-length volumes in this province. Instead, Commerce ignored all of these data.

44. Alberta had PricewaterhouseCoopers compile transaction-specific pricing data for approximately 80 per cent of arm's-length transactions for which it claimed a pass-through analysis.[29] Commerce relied on these transaction-specific data to calculate its pass-through adjustment. It failed, however, to use these pricing data to calculate the average pass-through of subsidies – if any – for the remaining volumes of arm's-length transactions.

45. Saskatchewan and Manitoba both provided extensive transaction-specific pricing data. More specifically, Saskatchewan requested Weyerhaeuser – its largest softwood lumber producer – to provide their data. Weyerhaeuser was involved in approximately 40 per cent of independent harvester transactions in this province.[30] Similarly, Manitoba provided Commerce with transaction-

[25] *Ibid.*, at paras. 14, 32.
[26] See First Written Submission of Canada, at para. 58.
[27] First Written Submission of Canada, at para. 80.
[28] *Ibid.*
[29] *Ibid.*, at para. 81.
[30] *Ibid.*, at para. 83.

specific information from Tembec, an independent harvester which was involved in 51 per cent of the arm's-length transactions in that province.[31]

46. Ontario provided company-specific data relating to sawmills responsible for 91.3 per cent of the Crown harvest.[32] The Ontario industry associations also provided Commerce with transaction-specific information for two of the largest independent harvesters and 23 of the largest sawmills in that province. In fact, Commerce received transaction-specific pricing data from companies accounting for over 90 per cent of the Crown harvest entering sawmills during the period of investigation.[33]

47. In short, Canadian respondents provided Commerce with transaction-specific information for the majority of transactions between independent harvesters and sawmills in most provinces. In addition, Ontario provided company- or sawmill-specific data. Commerce, therefore, had more than enough information to conduct pass-through analyses.

48. No pricing data was requested by Commerce in the administrative review.[34] Moreover, the Canadian respondents had no opportunity to present this information, as Commerce did not request this evidence in the section 129 proceeding until after closure of the factual record in the administrative review. Commerce is now requesting this transaction-specific information in its second administrative review.

49. Given Commerce's failure to request transaction-specific evidence, it should have either removed the arm's-length volumes that had been identified from the numerator or used the sawmill-specific information submitted by some provinces to conduct pass-through analyses. Instead, Commerce chose to rely on its "factors" to once again impermissibly presume a full pass-through of the alleged stumpage subsidy.

B. Commerce's Accusation that Canada Withheld Evidence is Without Merit

50. So, as I have outlined, the United States had everything it needed to conduct its analysis. It now accuses Canada, however, of being unprepared to support its pass-though claims with evidence. Why? Because Canada did not provide transaction-specific information for each of the five "factors" in response to supplemental questionnaires issued six to eight months into the reasonable period of time. This information was unnecessary and irrelevant to a pass-through analysis. Given the timing of the questionnaire and the type of information sought, this information was also impossible to provide.

51. A large portion of the evidence Commerce complains it did not receive was irrelevant and unnecessary for conducting a pass-through analysis.[35] As Mr.

31 *Ibid.*, at fn 96.
32 *Ibid.*, at para. 87.
33 *Ibid.*
34 *Ibid.*, at para. 77.
35 *Ibid.*, at paras. 75-76.

Cochlin has explained, tenure agreements, wood supply commitment letters, payment of stumpage fees by the log purchaser, log purchase agreements and fibre exchange agreements are not relevant to whether a transaction is conducted at arm's length.

52. In many instances, the amount of information requested by Commerce was impossible to provide. For example, British Columbia was expected to retrieve, copy and submit more than 3,000 tenure agreements that were scattered over dozens of district forestry offices.[36] This would have amounted to upwards of 60,000 pages of documents. Canada notified Commerce on multiple occasions of the impossibility of complying with this request, offered numerous sample agreements, and otherwise sought a reasonable alternative. Only after nearly five months did Commerce agree to modify its demands, requesting "excerpts" from all agreements in the province containing certain specified provisions. Commerce's "compromise" would have required British Columbia to locate and manually review all tenure agreements in the province to identify the relevant excerpts, and submit reams of complete tenure agreements, in a little over two weeks.

53. Further, Commerce solicited none of the transaction-specific pricing data that it now asserts are so "essential" for a pass-through analysis in its first questionnaire. Instead, Commerce waited until more than half of the reasonable period of time had elapsed before requesting these data in its supplemental questionnaires and pass-through appendices.[37] Commerce also waited until this time to request information on three of its five "factors", including copies of log purchase agreements and fibre exchange agreements for every arm's-length transaction in the provinces during the period of investigation.[38] In addition, Commerce demanded that the Canadian respondents identify every transaction where a sawmill paid stumpage on behalf of an independent harvester.

54. The pass-though appendices used to collect information from companies on affiliation, pricing data and the "factors" contained more than twenty-four pages of questions and attachments. The supplemental questionnaires directed the provinces to distribute the appendices to *all independent harvesters and sawmills* that were involved in arm's-length transactions. In the case of British Columbia, this would have required the distribution of the appendices to 3,000 independent harvesters and 175 sawmills operating in that province. If British Columbia had provided Commerce with the required nine copies and produced the other twenty copies required for the service list, *without responses*, this would have amounted to *almost two million, two hundred and ten thousand pages of information*. If the independent harvesters and sawmills had filled out the questionnaires, Commerce would have received *millions more pages of documentation*. As I am sure you will agree, it is hardly reasonable to expect

---

[36] *Ibid.*, at para. 76 (citing to BC September 15, 2004 Supp. Questionnaire Response, Narrative, at 5 and Norcon B, at 4 (Exhibit CDA-15)).

[37] *Ibid.*, at para. 75.

[38] *Ibid.*

British Columbia to manage the printing and submission of millions of pages of documents in under two months; in fact, it borders on the absurd.

55. Finally, as we explained earlier, Commerce was given more than enough data to conduct a pass-through analysis. The United States has not offered a single valid reason for refusing to use most of this information.

VI. CONCLUSION

56. In conclusion, the United States presumed a pass-through in violation of its WTO obligations. Commerce's presumption of a pass-through covers the vast majority of log transaction volumes identified in the section 129 proceedings, and all transaction volumes identified in the administrative review. Canada has explained that Commerce was not justified in rejecting the log transactions that it did, whether by: first, applying a new "arm's length" threshold test; second, claiming that the Appellate Body reversed the original panel findings and conclusions with respect to certain sawmill-to-sawmill transactions; or third, claiming that information was missing or deficient.

57. In both its section 129 determination and its administrative review, Commerce once again necessarily and impermissibly presumed pass-through.

58. Canada therefore requests that the Panel:

- *Find* that the US imposition of countervailing duties in respect of the Crown log transactions identified in this dispute is inconsistent with Article VI:3 of the GATT and Articles 10 and 32.1 of the SCM Agreement;
- *Recommend* that the United States bring its measures into conformity with its obligations under those provisions; and
- *Suggest*, in accordance with Article 19.1 of the DSU, that the United States do one of the following two things:
  - It should refund the amount of the countervailing duties it imposed to offset alleged subsidy amounts impermissibly presumed to pass through;

    or

  - It should revise its measures to meet its WTO obligations *and* refund the amount of the countervailing duties it imposed to the extent that they exceeded the amount of the alleged subsidy demonstrated to have passed through to the production of softwood lumber.

ANNEX B

SUBMISSIONS OF THE UNITED STATES

Contents		Page

ANNEX B-1

FIRST SUBMISSION AND REQUEST FOR PRELIMINARY RULING OF THE UNITED STATES
10 March 2005

I. INTRODUCTION

1. On 6 December 2004, the US Department of Commerce ("Commerce") issued a revised determination ("Section 129 Determination")[1] that implemented the recommendations and rulings of the Dispute Settlement Body ("DSB") in *United States – Final Countervailing Duty Determination With Respect to Certain Softwood Lumber From Canada.*[2] The recommendations and rulings of the DSB at issue relate to Commerce's decision not to conduct a pass-through analysis with respect to certain arm's-length sales of logs in its Final Determination.[3]

2. As discussed further below, Commerce's Section 129 Determination fully implements the recommendations and rulings of the DSB, and is consistent with the *Agreement on Subsidies and Countervailing Measures* ("SCM Agreement")

---

[1] *Section 129 Determination: Final Countervailing Duty Determination, Certain Softwood Lumber from Canada*, December 6, 2004 ("Section 129 Determination") (Exhibit CDA-5). "Section 129" refers to the provision of the Uruguay Round Agreements Act that provides procedures for implementing certain DSB recommendations and rulings with respect to countervailing duty investigations.

[2] Appellate Body Report, WT/DS257/AB/R, adopted 17 February 2004, ("Appellate Body Report"); Panel Report, WT/DS257/R, adopted 17 February 2004 ("Panel Report").

[3] *Notice of Final Affirmative Countervailing Duty Determination and Final Negative Critical Circumstances Determination: Certain Softwood Lumber Products from Canada*, 67 Fed. Reg. 15545 (2 April 2002), as amended, 67 Fed. Reg. 36070 (May 22, 2002) ("Final Determination"). Exhibit US-1.

and the *General Agreement on Tariffs and Trade 1994* ("GATT 1994"). The Panel should find, therefore, that Canada's claims are unfounded.

3. In addition, as set out below, the United States requests a preliminary ruling that the final results of the first assessment review[4] of the countervailing duty order on softwood lumber from Canada, cited by Canada in its request for the establishment of a panel[5], are not "measures taken to comply" with the recommendations and rulings of the DSB under Article 21.5 of the *Understanding on Rules and Procedures Governing the Settlement of Disputes* ("DSU"). Therefore, these results fall outside the scope of Article 21.5, and this Panel lacks jurisdiction to review them.

4. As provided for in the Panel's working procedures, the United States will be providing a rebuttal submission on 31 March 2005.

II. PROCEDURAL HISTORY

5. On 2 April 2002, Commerce published the Final Determination, finding that provincial stumpage programmes in Canada provided a countervailable subsidy to Canadian lumber producers and that certain non-stumpage programmes provided countervailable subsidies.[6] Commerce did not conduct a pass-through analysis in the Final Determination.

6. On 3 May 2002, Canada requested consultations with the United States and thereafter the DSB established a panel pursuant to Article 6 of the DSU ("original panel").

7. On 29 August 2003, the original panel found that Commerce's failure to conduct a pass-through analysis in the Final Determination with respect to arm's-length sales to unrelated sawmills and lumber remanufacturers was inconsistent with Articles 10 and 32.1of the SCM Agreement and Article VI:3 of the GATT 1994[7] However, the Appellate Body in its 19 January 2004, report reversed that aspect of the original panel report relating to Commerce's decision in its investigation not to conduct a pass-through analysis in respect of arm's-length sales of lumber by tenured harvesters/sawmills to remanufacturers[8]

8. The Appellate Body upheld, however, the original panel's finding that Commerce acted inconsistently with the SCM Agreement and GATT 1994 by failing in the Final Determination to conduct a pass-through analysis in respect

[4] An "administrative review", in US parlance.

[5] WT/DS257/15, citing *Notice of Final Results of Countervailing Duty Administrative Review and Recission of Certain Company-Specific Reviews: Certain Softwood Lumber Products from Canada*, 69 Fed. Reg. 75,917 (Dep't Commerce December 20, 2004) (Exhibit CDA-8) and *Issues and Decision Memorandum: Final Results of Administrative Review: Certain Softwood Lumber Products from Canada*, December 13, 2004.

[6] The Final Determination subsequently was amended on May 22, 2002.

[7] Panel Report, para. 7.99.

[8] Appellate Body Report, para. 167(f). The United States did not appeal the Panel's findings with respect to arm's-length log sales between tenured timber harvesters not owning sawmills and sawmills. Appellate Body Report, fn. 157.

of arm's-length sales of logs by tenured harvesters/sawmills to unrelated sawmills.[9] On 17 February 2004, the DSB adopted its recommendations and rulings.[10]

9. On 5 March 2004, the United States notified the DSB of its intention to implement the recommendations and rulings of the DSB.[11] Thereafter, the United States and Canada established a ten-month "reasonable period of time" ending 17 December 2004, within which the United States agreed to implement the recommendations and rulings of the DSB.[12]

10. On 19 November 2004, Commerce issued a draft Section 129 Determination and provided an opportunity for parties to comment. On 6 December 2004, Commerce issued the Section 129 Determination, which revised the original countervailing duty investigation determination and implemented the DSB's recommendations and rulings, effective for imports on or after 10 December 2004. On 16 December 2004, the notice of implementation was published in the Federal Register.[13]

11. On 17 December 2004, the United States informed the DSB that it had complied with the DSB's recommendations and rulings by properly conducting its pass-through analyses of certain arm's-length log sales occurring during the period of investigation ("POI").

III. PRELIMINARY RULING REQUEST WITH RESPECT TO THE FINAL RESULTS OF THE FIRST ASSESSMENT REVIEW

12. The United States requests a preliminary ruling that the final results of the first assessment review of the countervailing duty order on softwood lumber from Canada, cited by Canada in its request for the establishment of a panel in this dispute[14], are not "measures taken to comply" with the recommendations and rulings of the DSB under Article 21.5 of the DSU. Therefore, these results fall outside the scope of Article 21.5, and this Panel lacks jurisdiction to review them.

---

[9] The other issues either appealed by the United States or Canada were decided in favor of the United States. Appellate Body Report, para. 167.

[10] DSB, Minutes of Meeting (17 February and 19 March, 2004), WT/DSB/M/165, 30 March 2004, at 4(a), para. 49.

[11] WT/DS257/12, 9 March 2004.

[12] WT/DS257/13, 30 April 2004.

[13] *Notice of Implementation Under Section 129 of the Uruguay Round Agreements Act; Countervailing Measures Concerning Certain Softwood Lumber Products From Canada*, 69 FR 75305 (16 December 2004). Exhibit CDA-7.

[14] WT/DS257/15, citing *Notice of Final Results of Countervailing Duty Administrative Review and Recission of Certain Company-Specific Reviews: Certain Softwood Lumber Products from Canada*, 69 Fed. Reg. 75,917 (Dep't Commerce 20 December 2004) (Exhibit CDA-8) and *Issues and Decision Memorandum: Final Results of Administrative Review: Certain Softwood Lumber Products from Canada*, 13 December 2004.

A. Article 21.5 Proceedings are Limited to "Measures Taken to Comply" With the DSB's Recommendations and Rulings

13. The subject matter of these proceedings is determined by the Panel's terms of reference and by Article 21.5 of the DSU, which provides that recourse be had to dispute settlement procedures "[w]here there is disagreement as to the existence or consistency with a covered agreement *of measures taken to comply with the recommendations and rulings*." (emphasis added). Therefore, as the Appellate Body has stated, "[p]roceedings under Article 21.5 do not concern just *any* measure of a Member of the WTO; rather Article 21.5 proceedings are limited to those 'measures *taken to comply* with the recommendations and rulings' of the DSB.[15]

14. Although the complaining party in an Article 21.5 proceeding decides the scope of its request for panel establishment, including the measures it wishes to challenge, it is the responsibility of the Article 21.5 panel to determine whether the measure identified is or is not a "measure[ ] taken to comply".[16] If it is not, the measure falls outside of Article 21.5, and the panel lacks jurisdiction to review the measure. As the panel in *EC – Bed Linens* stated, it is neither the complaining nor the responding party that decides which measures are taken to comply: "Rather", said the panel, "this is an issue which must be considered and decided by an Article 21.5 panel".[17] That panel concluded that "[t]o the extent a party may have challenged, in a request for establishment of an Article 21.5 panel, measures which were *not* 'taken to comply' by the implementing Member, it is our view that a Panel may decline to address claims concerning such measures".[18]

15. And, indeed, in the *EC – Bed Linens* dispute, the panel granted the EC's preliminary ruling request to exclude from consideration certain antidumping duty measures taken by the EC that were cited by India, but that the panel found were not "taken to comply". In that dispute, in which the EC was found to have incorrectly calculated dumping duties in an investigation of bed linens from India, the EC voluntarily applied the revised calculation method to antidumping duties imposed on Pakistan and Egypt. After concluding that no duties should be imposed on bed linens from those sources (as a result of the recalculation), the EC re-examined whether imports from India, considered alone, caused injury to the domestic industry. The EC concluded that they did, and therefore affirmed the imposition of dumping duties on bed linen from India. India challenged this finding of injury and the resulting imposition of duties on bed linen from India as a WTO-inconsistent measure "taken to comply" under Article 21.5.

16. The panel, in deciding not to review the latter measure, stated that

---

[15] Appellate Body Report, *Canada – Measures Affecting the Export of Civilian Aircraft*, WT/DS70/AB/R, adopted 20 August 1999, para. 36.

[16] See, *e.g.*, Panel Report, *European Communities - Anti-Dumping Duties on Imports of Cotton-Type Bed Linen from India - Recourse to Article 21.5 of the DSU by India*, WT/DS141/RW, adopted 24 April 2003, as modified by the Appellate Body Report, WT/DS141/AB/RW, ("*EC – Bed Linens (Panel)*"), para. 6.15.

[17] *EC – Bed Linens* (Panel), para. 6.15.

[18] *EC – Bed Linens* (Panel), para. 6.17 (emphasis in original).

> [T]he fact that the EC, subsequent to its re-examination of the dumping determinations with respect to imports from Egypt and Pakistan, *and in the context of a review initiated on the request of Eurocoton*, carried out an analysis of whether injury was caused by imports from India alone does not, *ipso facto*, establish that Regulation 696/2002 is a measure "taken to comply". Rather the opposite would seem to be the case – *that Regulation would seem to be an entirely new determination*, reached as a result of events subsequent to the EC having adopted a measure to comply with the DSB's recommendation.[19]

17. In sum, Article 21.5 proceedings are limited to "measures taken to comply" with the DSB's recommendations and rulings. As discussed below, the final results of the first assessment review are not "measures taken to comply" and therefore this Panel should decline to review those results.

B. The Final Results of the First Assessment Review Are Not "Measures Taken to Comply"

18. As discussed above, before the original panel, Canada challenged Commerce's Final Determination in the countervailing duty *investigation* on softwood lumber from Canada.[20] After the DSB adopted its recommendations and rulings, and within the agreed "reasonable period of time", the United States made a redetermination – the Section 129 Determination – in which it conducted a "pass through" analysis and recalculated the countervailing duty rate.[21] The new reduced rate was applicable to entries of subject merchandise on or after 10 December 2004.[22]

19. In this Article 21.5 dispute, Canada states that the Section 129 Determination is a "measure[ ] taken to comply with the recommendations and rulings" of the DSB and alleges that it fails to implement the recommendations and rulings of the DSB.

20. But Canada also includes, without explanation, a completely separate Commerce determination, *i.e.*, the results of an *assessment review,* among the "measures taken to comply" which it asks the Panel to examine under Article 21.5. The results of this assessment review are, in no sense, "measures taken to comply" with the recommendations and rulings of the DSB concerning the Final Determination in the original countervailing duty investigation.

21. As an initial matter, original investigations and assessment reviews are different processes which serve distinct purposes. The purpose of an investigation is to determine the existence, degree, and effect of any alleged subsidy; the

---

19 *EC – Bed Linens* (Panel), para. 6.20 (emphasis added).

20 Panel Report, paras 2.1-2.4.

21 Section 129 Determination. Exhibit CDA-5.

22 *Notice of Implementation under Section 129 of the Uruguay Round Agreements Act: Countervailing Measures concerning Certain Softwood Lumber from Canada*, 69 Fed. Reg. 75,917 (Dep't Commerce 16 December 2004). Exhibit CDA-7.

purpose of an assessment review is to determine the amount of duty to be assessed on previous imports of subject merchandise and the estimated countervailing duty rate to be applied to future imports. Indeed, the distinction between countervailing duty investigations and assessment procedures is explicitly recognized in the SCM Agreement.[23]

22. In May 2003, Canada (among other interested parties) requested such an assessment review, covering entries of subject merchandise during the period 22 May 2002, through 31 March 2003. The resulting assessment review was not taken to comply with the recommendations and rulings of the DSB. Rather, it resulted from a *separate* affirmative request by Canada, among others, that Commerce review *new* sales and subsidies data for the purposes of assessing countervailing duties for imports during the review period and of setting a new estimated countervailing duty rate for subsequent imports. US law required Commerce to conduct this assessment review once Canada, among others, requested it.[24]

23. Indeed, the assessment review was initiated on 1 July 2003, *eight months* before the recommendations and rulings in this dispute were adopted. This review proceeding, therefore, had nothing whatsoever to do with "implementing" the DSB's recommendations and rulings. For obvious temporal reasons, the results of this assessment review – which was initiated before the DSB issued its recommendations and rulings – cannot be considered "measures taken to comply".

24. Article 21.5 proceedings are by their nature more focused and limited than other panel proceedings under Article 6.2 of the DSU. Notably, instead of six months, the DSU anticipates that Article 21.5 proceedings will normally take no more than 90 days.[25] Canada, for its part, has underscored this aspect of these proceedings by systematically opposing any extensions of time in this proceeding.[26] For this reason, Article 21.5 proceedings are intended to focus, not on *any* measure cited by the complaining Member – as is the case for other dispute settlement proceedings – but only on *measures taken to comply* with DSB recommendations and rulings. It is beyond the scope of such a limited 90-day inquiry to fully examine an entirely new set of assessment review results based on a wholly new administrative record, consisting of new sales, new imports, potentially new respondents and potentially new subsidy programmes.

25. In sum, in this Article 21.5 proceeding, the Panel lacks jurisdiction to review the final results of the assessment review cited by Canada because these results are not "measures taken to comply" with the DSB's recommendations and rulings, adopted on 17 February 2004, related to Commerce's Final Determination in the original countervailing duty investigation.

---

23 See, *e.g.*, SCM Agreement, fn. 52.

24 See 19 USC 1675(a). Exhibit US-2.

25 *Compare* Articles 12.8 and 21.5 of the DSU.

26 Recall, *e.g.*, statements by the Canadian representative during the Panel organization meeting of 14 February 2005, as well as paragraph 2 of Canada's letter of 15 February 2005, to the Panel regarding its draft working procedures and timetable.

IV. CANADA BEARS THE BURDEN OF PROVING ITS CLAIMS

26. It is well-established that the complaining party in a WTO dispute bears the burden of coming forward with argument and evidence that establish a *prima facie* case of a WTO inconsistency.[27] If the balance of evidence and argument is inconclusive with respect to a particular claim, Canada, as the complaining party, must be found to have failed to establish that claim.[28] Canada has not met its burden in this proceeding.

27. With respect to the standard of review, Article 11 of the DSU sets forth the standard of review for this Panel. Article 11 calls for panels to "make an objective assessment of the matter before it, including an objective assessment of the facts of the case and the applicability of and conformity with the relevant covered agreements ... ."

28. With respect to disputes involving a determination made by a domestic authority based upon an administrative record, the Appellate Body, in *Cotton Yarn*, summarized the role of a panel under Article 11 as follows:

> [P]anels must examine whether the competent authority has evaluated all relevant factors; they must assess whether the competent authority has examined all the pertinent facts and assess whether an adequate explanation has been provided as to how those facts support the determination; and they must also consider whether the competent authority's explanation addresses fully the nature and complexities of the data and responds to other plausible interpretations of the data. However, panels must not conduct a *de novo* review of the evidence nor substitute their judgement for that of the competent authority.[29]

29. Thus, the Panel's task is to determine whether a reasonable, unbiased person, looking at the same evidentiary record as Commerce, could have – not would have – reached the same conclusions.

---

[27] See, *e.g.*, Appellate Body Report, *United States – Measures Affecting Imports of Woven Shirts and Blouses from India*, WT/DS33/AB/R, adopted 23 May 1997, page 14; Appellate Body Report, *European Communities – Measures Concerning Meat and Meat Products (Hormones)*, WT/DS26/AB/R, WT/DS48/AB/R, adopted 13 February 1998, para. 104; and Panel Report, *Korea – Definitive Safeguard Measure on Imports of Certain Dairy Products*, WT/DS98/R, as modified by the Appellate Body, adopted 12 January 2000, para. 7.24.

[28] See, *e.g.*, Panel Report, *India – Quantitative Restrictions on Imports of Agricultural, Textile and Industrial Products*, WT/DS90/R, as affirmed by the Appellate Body, adopted 22 September 1999, para. 5.120.

[29] Appellate Body Report, *United States – Transitional Safeguard Measure on Combed Cotton Yarn from Pakistan*, WT/DS192/AB/R, adopted 5 November 2001, para. 74.

V. COMMERCE CONDUCTED A PASS-THROUGH ANALYSIS CONSISTENT WITH THE SCM AGREEMENT, THE GATT 1994, AND THE DSB'S RECOMMENDATIONS AND RULINGS

30. As described in detail in the Section 129 Determination, Commerce responded to the DSB's recommendations and rulings by conducting a pass-through analysis, first issuing questionnaires seeking record evidence to determine whether during the period of investigation there were arm's-length sales of logs by independent harvesters to unrelated sawmills and by tenured harvesters/sawmills to unrelated sawmills. Based upon its analysis of the record evidence, Commerce determined that there were such arm's-length log sales. For those arm's-length sales, Commerce then determined whether a benefit was passed through to the purchasing sawmills, using appropriate benchmarks, and removed from the numerator of the aggregate subsidy calculation any benefit that it found did not pass through to the purchasing sawmills.

31. Other sales, however, were determined not to be at arm's length, either because the record facts demonstrated that they were not or because Canada failed to provide sufficient record evidence that would have enabled Commerce to analyze those sales. Ultimately, Commerce's analysis of log sales demonstrated to be at arm's length resulted in a C$28,344,121 reduction in the numerator of the *ad valorem* subsidy rate, which had the effect of reducing the country-wide subsidy rate from 18.79 per cent *ad valorem* to 18.62 per cent *ad valorem.*[30]

32. Canada now challenges Commerce's Section 129 Determination under Article 21.5 of the DSU. This challenge, however, has no basis in the SCM Agreement, the GATT 1994, or the recommendations and rulings of the DSB. Commerce's pass-through analysis was conducted in accordance with the recommendations and rulings of the DSB and is WTO-consistent, and Canada's claims must therefore fail.

33. First, Commerce did not "presume" pass-through. To implement the DSB's recommendations and rulings, Commerce sought data from Canada substantiating its claims that subsidies were not passed through. In some instances, the Canadian respondents provided the requested data and Commerce conducted the recommended analysis, using appropriate log prices as benchmarks. In other instances, however, despite repeated requests by Commerce, Canada failed to provide the necessary data. Lacking sufficient data, Commerce was not able to conduct its analysis for all of the log sales for which Canada requested such an analysis.[31]

34. Second, Commerce properly investigated and made a determination concerning whether particular sales were at "arm' s length." Contrary to Canada's arguments[32], nothing in the SCM Agreement, the GATT 1994, or the DSB's recommendations and rulings supports Canada's argument that an arm's-length

---

30 *Section 129 Determination, at 1. Exhibit CDA-5.*

31 *E.g.,* Section 129 Determination, at 3 and 13 (comment 8).

32 *E.g.,* First Written Submission of Canada, paras. 59 -65.

analysis should be restricted to, in essence, a *per se* test based on affiliation alone. Further, part of the DSB's recommendations and rulings related only to a particular category of arm's-length log sales: those between tenured harvester/sawmills and unrelated, non-tenured sawmills.[33] The scope of the DSB' s recommendations and rulings should therefore not be broadened to include entities that were not part of those recommendations and rulings.

35. Finally, the results of Commerce's recalculation were applied to the only rate that was before the original panel and Appellate Body, *i.e.*, the 18.79 per cent *ad valorem* rate calculated in the Final Determination. Therefore, Canada's argument that Commerce applied the results of its pass-through analysis to a rate "which long before had been invalidated as a result of judicial review proceedings"[34] is without basis.

VI. CONCLUSION

36. For the reasons stated above, Canada's claims against US implementation of the DSB's recommendations and rulings have no basis in the SCM Agreement, the GATT 1994, or the recommendations and rulings of the DSB. The United States therefore requests that the Panel find that the United States properly implemented the recommendations and rulings of the DSB and that the Panel reject Canada's claims in their entirety. Further, the United States requests that this Panel find that the results of the first assessment review fall outside the Panel's jurisdiction in this Article 21.5 dispute.

---

[33] *E.g.*, Appellate Body Report, para. 167(e).
[34] First Written Submission of Canada, para. 10.

ANNEX B-2

SECOND WRITTEN SUBMISSION OF THE UNITED STATES
31 March 2005

I. INTRODUCTION

1. On 10 March 2005, the United States filed its First Submission and Request for Preliminary Ruling. Pursuant to the Panel's working procedures, the United States is now filing its rebuttal submission.

2. To implement the recommendations and rulings of the Dispute Settlement Body ("DSB") in *United States – Final Countervailing Duty Determination With Respect to Certain Softwood Lumber From Canada*[1],, on 6 December 2004, the US Department of Commerce ("Commerce") issued a revised determination ("Section 129 Determination").[2] In accordance with those recommendations and rulings, in the context of its Final Determination[3], Commerce determined the amount of the subsidy that passed through the purchase transaction with respect to certain arm's-length log sales between unrelated parties. Ultimately, Commerce's analysis of log sales demonstrated to be at arm's length resulted in a C$28,344,121 reduction in the numerator of the *ad valorem* subsidy rate, which had the effect of reducing the country-wide subsidy rate from 18.79 per cent *ad valorem* to 18.62 per cent *ad valorem.*[4] Commerce's Section 129 Determination is consistent with the DSB's recommendations and rulings, the *Agreement on Subsidies and Countervailing Measures* ("SCM Agreement") and the *General Agreement on Tariffs and Trade 1994* ("GATT 1994"), and the Panel should so find.

---

[1] Appellate Body Report, WT/DS257/AB/R, adopted 17 February 2004, ("Appellate Body Report"); Panel Report, WT/DS257/R, adopted 17 February 2004 ("Panel Report").

[2] *Section 129 Determination: Final Countervailing Duty Determination, Certain Softwood Lumber from Canada*, 6 December 2004 ("Section 129 Determination") (Exhibit CDA-5). The Section 129 Determination was implemented on 10 December 2005, at the request of the Office of the United States Trade Representative. See *Notice of Implementation Under Section 129 of the Uruguay Round Agreements Act; Countervailing Measures Concerning Certain Softwood Lumber Products From Canada*, 69 FR 75305 (16 ecember 2004). Exhibit CDA-7. For summaries of provincial claims and the results of Commerce's pass-through determination, see "Draft Decision Memorandum" In the Matter of the Section 129 Determination on the Final Countervailing Duty Determination with Respect to Certain Softwood Lumber from Canada ("Draft Section 129 Determination"), 19 November 2005, at 8-15 (Exhibit CDA-6). Any modifications to Commerce's analysis are discussed in the Comment section of the Section 129 Determination. "Section 129" refers to the provision of the Uruguay Round Agreements Act that provides procedures for implementing certain DSB recommendations and rulings with respect to countervailing duty investigations.

[3] *Notice of Final Affirmative Countervailing Duty Determination and Final Negative Critical Circumstances Determination: Certain Softwood Lumber Products from Canada*, 67 Fed. Reg. 15545 (2 April 2002), as amended, 67 Fed. Reg. 36070 (May 22, 2002) ("Final Determination"). Exhibit US-1.

[4] Section 129 Determination, at 1. Exhibit CDA-5.

3. In this proceeding, however, Canada is asking the Panel to find that the United States is subject to conditions and restrictions that are nowhere to be found in the SCM Agreement or GATT 1994, that were not part of the DSB's recommendations and rulings, and that are entirely otherwise unwarranted. In so doing, Canada attempts to deflect attention away from its own failure in many instances to provide Commerce with the data necessary to conduct the analysis recommended by the DSB. Neither Canada' s attempt to prevent Commerce from conducting a meaningful pass-through analysis, nor its failure to provide the requested data, however, translates into a failure by the United States to comply with the DSB's recommendations and rulings or results in a measure that is inconsistent with the SCM Agreement or the GATT 1994.

4. As described below, and contrary to Canada's arguments, Commerce conducted its pass-through analysis consistently with the DSB's recommendations and rulings, and the resulting measure at issue is consistent with the SCM Agreement and the GATT 1994.

II. COMMERCE CONDUCTED A PASS-THROUGH ANALYSIS THAT IS CONSISTENT WITH THE DSB'S RECOMMENDATIONS AND RULINGS AND WITH THE SCM AGREEMENT AND GATT 1994

5. Canada does not challenge Commerce's general approach of reducing the numerator of the *ad valorem* subsidy rate calculation to eliminate subsidies attributed to arm's-length sales in which no benefit was passed through. Instead, Canada complains that Commerce, rather than conducting a pass-through analysis, "presumed" pass through. A foundation of Canada's "presumption" argument is its assertion that Commerce must adopt an unreasonable definition of the term "arm's length"[5] that would prevent Commerce from conducting a meaningful analysis of whether, in fact, sales are at arm's length. Consequently, whenever Commerce determined that a transaction was not at arm's length, according to Canada's unreasonable definition of arm's length, Commerce improperly "presumed" pass-through of the subsidy. Additionally, Canada argues that Commerce "presumed" pass-through by disregarding aggregate data submitted by Canada[6] and excluding from its analysis sales between tenure-holding sawmills.[7] In making its arguments Canada ignores the necessarily company-specific nature of the analysis undertaken by Commerce and the actual findings of the DSB, including the specific definitions of the categories of companies for which a pass-through analysis had to be performed. As set forth below, Commerce properly conducted its pass-through analysis.

---

5 First Written Submission of Canada, February 24, 2005 ("First Written Submission of Canada"), paras. 38, 59-65.

6 First Written Submission of Canada, para. 58.

7 First Written Submission of Canada, para. 54-55.

A. Commerce Issued Questionnaires to Obtain Data Necessary to its Analysis

6. To conduct its pass-through analysis, Commerce first had to obtain data from Canada[8] supporting Canada's claim that a portion of the total volume of Crown logs processed into lumber – as reported by Canada – should be reduced to account for arm's-length log sales between unrelated parties in which no benefit passed through. Because Commerce had conducted the original investigation on an aggregate basis and not on a company-specific basis and had not previously conducted such a pass-through analysis, the administrative record did not contain evidence supporting Canada's claims.

7. In the original investigation, Commerce calculated the subsidy benefit from Provincial Crown timber programmes by assessing the extent to which each Province sold timber for less than adequate remuneration. This subsidy benefit is the numerator, which is divided over the relevant sales of lumber and by-products that benefit from the subsidy, the denominator, to determine the countervailable *ad valorem* subsidy rate. Commerce needed specific information and data to calculate any adjustment to this subsidy benefit numerator to account for potentially arm's-length sales of Crown logs between unrelated parties in which the subsidy did not pass through. Specifically, Commerce needed the volume of the log sales in Canada during the period of investigation ("POI") for which Canada sought a pass-through analysis. Additionally, to determine whether the reported log transactions were between unrelated parties, Commerce required information concerning any affiliation between the buyer and seller of the logs. Further, Commerce required information concerning government-mandated restrictions and other factors that could limit or control the terms of the sale, and thus undermine the arm's-length nature of the sale. Finally, to conduct the "competitive benefit" analysis, through which Commerce measured whether and to what extent any subsidy passes through, Commerce required specific data on prices, species, size, grade, quality, discounts delivery terms, and payment terms.

8. Therefore, Commerce asked Canada, through questionnaires, to identify the volume of log sales subject to its pass-through claims, and to provide specific information necessary to determine whether log sales were between unrelated parties and at arm's length. This would allow Commerce to identify transactions that were eligible for the last phase of the analysis (competitive benefit). The requested information related to, *inter alia*, the relationship between the parties to the specific transactions (such as whether the parties were affiliated) and the circumstances surrounding the subject sales.

---

[8] First Written Submission of Canada, para. 6. As acknowledged by Canada, "Section 129 proceedings may involve the issuance of new questionnaires...."

9. On 14 April[9], 17 August[10] and 5 October 2004[11] Commerce issued questionnaires and supplemental questionnaires to Canada with respect to this issue. Commerce notified Canada in its initial questionnaire that if a province was claiming that any portion of the volume of Crown logs reported in the numerator[12] was sold in arm's-length transactions and was between unrelated parties and required an analysis to determine if the purchasing sawmill received a subsidy benefit, the province was required to provide an explanation of how the volume was calculated and documentation supporting its claims.[13] The Canadian provincial governments provided questionnaire responses on 21 May 2004. Although the provincial governments provided certain information that had been requested, the responses were incomplete.

10. Therefore, on 17 August 2004, Commerce issued a supplemental "pass-through" questionnaire in which it informed Canada that its 21 May 2004, responses were deficient in a number of respects and that the "information provided in the questionnaire response is insufficient for the Department to complete its 'pass-through' analysis.[14] In that supplemental questionnaire, Commerce requested additional and clarifying information from the provincial governments and from independent harvesters and mills with respect to log sales that they claimed were at arm's length. Responding to Canada's complaint that certain of its requests could not be answered because the provincial governments lacked access to certain data, Commerce modified its requests for information.

11. Notably, Commerce attached a pass-through appendix to the supplemental pass-through questionnaire and requested that the provincial governments provide the appendix to the independent harvesters and sawmills involved in the log sales for which a pass-through analysis was requested. In the pass-through appendix Commerce requested information directly from the sawmills and independent harvesters concerning affiliations and corporate relationships, as well as information relating to the terms of the sales, including log sales data and purchase contracts.[15]

---

9 See, Letter from Department of Commerce to Embassy of Canada, 14 April 2004, Pass-Through Questionnaire. Exhibit CDA-3.

10 See, Letter from Department of Commerce to Embassy of Canada, 17 August 2004, Supplemental Pass-Through Questionnaire. Exhibit CDA-23.

11 See, Letter from Department of Commerce to Embassy of Canada, 5 October 2004, Second Supplemental Pass-Through Questionnaire. Exhibit CDA-24.

12 The numerator of Commerce's final subsidy calculation consisted of the total benefit received, which was calculated based on the total volume of Crown timber harvested during the POI that actually entered and was processed by sawmills, as reported by each of the provinces.

13 In accordance with the DSB's recommendations and rulings (Panel Report, at para. 7.99; Appellate Body Report, at para. 167(e)), Commerce specifically requested information relating to the portion of the total volume of Crown timber entering sawmills reported by the provinces claimed to be "sold in arm's length transactions by tenure holders that did not own a sawmill . . ." and "sold in arm's- length transactions by tenured timber sawmills to sawmills that do not have tenure . . ." Exhibit CDA-3, at 10, 11 (questions 1 and 2).

14 Exhibit CDA-23.

15 Exhibit CDA-23, at 1 and Pass-Through Appendix - 1.

12. On 15 September 2004, the Canadian parties submitted their responses to this supplemental questionnaire. Certain sawmills and independent harvesters submitted responses to the pass-through appendix. However, notwithstanding Commerce's earlier notice to Canada that in the absence of the requested data Commerce might not have sufficient data to complete its pass-through analysis, Canada once again provided incomplete responses to Commerce's data requests. Canada posited two reasons for its failure to respond properly to Commerce's requests: first, it claimed that certain of the requests were voluminous and that it was burdensome for it to collect the data; second, it claimed that certain information requested by Commerce was not relevant.[16]

13. On 5 October 2004, Commerce issued a second supplemental pass-through questionnaire and a supplemental pass-through appendix. Because the provincial governments failed to respond adequately to Commerce's earlier questionnaires, Commerce again requested clarifying and additional information. As noted in its second supplemental pass-through questionnaire, Commerce modified certain of its requests, where practicable, in response to Canada's claim that to provide the information was burdensome.[17] With respect to Canada's claim that certain information was not relevant, Commerce reiterated to Canada that it needed the data to conduct the DSB's recommended analysis. The Canadian parties submitted a response to the second supplemental questionnaire on 25 October 2004.

14. By refusing to provide certain of the data requested by Commerce, Canada was and is attempting to restrict Commerce's ability to conduct a meaningful pass-through analysis. Canada contends that Commerce's arm's-length analysis should be nothing more than a simple determination of whether the parties to the transaction are unrelated. Indeed, Canada argues that Commerce erred in not relying upon Canada's "aggregate" data – data that (although limited to sales between unrelated parties) fails to address factors other than affiliation that could render the transactions something other than arm 's length. As discussed below, Commerce's arm's-length analysis properly included examination of issues beyond mere affiliation.

---

[16] See, *e.g.*, CDA-23, at 6 (Ontario question 1); Response of the Government of Ontario to the Department's 17 August 2004 Supplemental Pass-Through Questionnaire (15 September 2004), at ON-PASS-2, -3 ("Ontario September 15 Pass-Through Response"). Exhibit US-3. See *also*, Response of the Government of British Columbia to the Department's 17 August 2004 Supplemental Questionnaire Concerning Pass Through of the Alleged Benefits (15 September 2004), at 10 ("British Columbia September 15 Pass-Through Response"). Exhibit US-4.

[17] In the second supplemental questionnaire, Commerce further modified its requests. By way of example, in response to the Government of British Columbia's ("GBC") statement that it did not have access to log purchase agreements for the transactions claimed to be at arm's length, Commerce limited its request to those sawmills that participated in the Norcon Survey that was prepared at the GBC's request. Exhibit CDA-24, page 5 at 6. With respect to a the Government of Alberta's ("GOA") concern that it could not provide all copies of tenure agreements relating to commercial timber permits ("CTPs"), Commerce limited its request to tenure agreements associated with coniferous timber quotas ("CTQs") and certain CTPs that were identified by Commerce. Exhibit CDA-24, page 8 at 1. Similarly, Commerce modified its requests for timber return data from the GOA to those portions containing the text relating to the payment of the stumpage dues. Exhibit CDA-24, page 9 at 7.

B. *Commerce Properly Conducted Its Arm's-Length Analysis as Part of Its Pass-Through Analysis*

15. Commerce first analyzed the information provided by Canada to determine whether the sales were between related parties. If they were, no further analysis was conducted, because the DSB's recommendations and rulings concerned only sales between unrelated parties.[18] Commerce next analyzed the sales between unrelated parties to determine if they were at arm's length. Canada challenges this necessary step in its entirety, in the apparent and mistaken belief that all sales between formally unrelated parties are necessarily at arm's length. Therefore, according to Canada, by even analyzing whether such sales are, in fact, at arm's length, and then eliminating sales that fail the arm's-length test from the pass-through analysis, Commerce is somehow illegally "presuming" pass-through. This is incorrect. Indeed, it is Canada that is "presuming" no pass through for all sales between unrelated parties. Further, there is nothing in the SCM Agreement, the GATT 1994, or the DSB's recommendations and rulings that suggests that Commerce' s analysis of whether sales are at arm's length should be so severely limited, or indeed, eliminated.

1. *Commerce's Approach to Determining Whether Sales are at "Arm's Length" – Involving Factors Other Than Mere Affiliation – is Consistent with the DSB's Recommendations and Rulings, the SCM Agreement, and the GATT 1994*

16. Canada claims that Commerce "applied a contrived standard"[19] in determining whether its claimed log sales were at arm's length. However, the term "arm's length" is not used or defined in the text of the SCM Agreement; thus, it is unclear on what basis Canada makes its claim that the standard Commerce applied is "contrived". The Appellate Body concluded in this dispute that both the SCM Agreement and the GATT 1994 require that, where subsidies are bestowed directly on producers of an *input* product, while countervailing duties are to be imposed on *processed* products, "*and where input producers and downstream processors operate at arm 's length*," Commerce must establish that the benefit is passed through to the downstream processor.[20] Therefore, where the two producers do not operate at "arm's length", no determination of the amount of the subsidy passing through the transaction is required because the subsidy bestowed on the input producer benefits the producer of the processed product. Whether the entities operate "at arm's length" involves more than just a question of formal affiliation; it involves an analysis of whether one party effectively "controls" the other or whether the parties have roughly equal bargaining power.[21] In other

---

[18] Canada has not challenged Commerce's affiliation determinations. First Written Submission of Canada, para. 74, fn. 66.

[19] First Written Submission of Canada, para. 59.

[20] Appellate Body Report, para. 146 (emphasis on "arm's length" in original).

[21] See BLACK'S LAW DICTIONARY, Seventh Edition (West Group 1999) at 103 ("Of or relating to dealings between two parties who are not related or not on close terms and who are presumed to

words, if one of the parties controls the other or their dealings are not between entities of equal bargaining power, neither the SCM Agreement nor the GATT 1994 require that the amount of the subsidy passing through the transaction be determined; rather, the investigating authority may regard the subsidy bestowed on the input as benefiting the processed product.[22]

17. Thus, the issue is not merely one of affiliation. In this regard, the DSB's recommendations and rulings themselves recognize a distinction between arm's length and affiliation presenting arm's-length sales as a subset of sales between unrelated entities. Specifically, the DSB ruled that Commerce should have conducted "a pass-through analysis in respect of *arm's length sales* of *logs*...to *unrelated* sawmills".[23] This is completely inconsistent with Canada's contention that an arm's-length analysis requires nothing more than a determination of affiliation.[24]

18. Commerce properly examined, in its pass-through analysis, whether the parties to the log sales were related through common ownership and also whether any of the circumstances surrounding the log sales affected the nature of the sales to such an extent that they could not be considered arm's length. Initially, and as discussed above, Commerce examined whether any of the log sales at issue were between affiliated parties. Consistent with the DSB's recommendations and rulings, when Commerce found that sales were between affiliated parties, it performed no further pass-through analysis.[25] If the sales were between unaffiliated parties, Commerce examined the circumstances surrounding the transactions as part of its "arm's length" analysis.

19. Commerce properly examined the circumstances surrounding the sales Canada reported as occurring between unrelated parties. Although Canada objects to Commerce's approach, Canada can point to no language in the SCM

---

have roughly equal bargaining power; not involving a confidential relationship...."). Exhibit US-5. See *also*, THE NEW SHORTER OXFORD ENGLISH DICTIONARY, Thumb Index Edition (Oxford University Press 1993) at 114 ("without undue familiarity; (of dealings) with neither party controlled by the other"). Exhibit CDA-18.

In the specific context of a dispute concerning countervailing duties, see Panel Report, *Korea - Measures Affecting Trade in Commercial Vessels*, WT/DS273 (7 March 2005), para. 7.135 . (European Communities' challenged certain Korean subsidies as prohibited subsidies under Articles. 3.1 and 3.2 of the SCM Agreement). In determining the appropriateness of a market benchmark, the panel considered whether purchasing negotiations were at arm's length when the buyer was able to dictate the source from which a shipyard was to procure an advanced payment refund guarantee (APRG). According to the panel, "[i]n such cases, the designation of the APRG-provider by the buyer means that there is a risk that the APRG is not negotiated at arm's length, since the shipyard is a captive buyer. The rate paid by the shipyard might therefore be higher than it would if the shipyard were able to shop around and compare offers from alternative suppliers."

[22] See Appellate Body Report, para. 143 ("*Where the input producers and producers of the processed products operate at arm's length*, the pass-through of input subsidy benefits from the direct recipients to the indirect recipients downstream cannot simply be presumed; . ..") (underscored emphasis added).

[23] Appellate Body Report, para. 176(e) (emphasis added, except that emphasis on "logs" is in original.)

[24] Appellate Body Report, para. 124. (emphasis added).

[25] Section 129 Determination, at 4. Exhibit CDA-5.

Agreement, the GATT 1994, or the DSB's recommendations and rulings that establishes the *per se* affiliation analysis advanced by Canada. Indeed, the record evidence demonstrates that many of the sales that Canada claims are arm's-length sales are affected by government mandates and other conditions that render those sales not at arm's length or otherwise ineligible for the pass-through analysis. These will be discussed in the following section.

2. The Record Demonstrates that Under the Canadian Stumpage System, Many of the Circumstances of the Sales are Controlled by Government Mandates and Other Conditions

20. Canada's simplistic *per se* approach is divorced from the reality of the Canadian stumpage system. With respect to many transactions, record information demonstrates that certain government-mandated restrictions and other factors controlled, limited, or otherwise affected the log sales, warranting Commerce's determination that they were not conducted at arm's length or, in some instances, were not sales at all.

21. Specifically, record evidence demonstrates that the provincial governments impose restrictions upon log sales that affect many of the transactions that Canada reported as arm's-length sales. Commerce identified two such categories of government-mandated restrictions: (1) limitations on log sales that are contained in Crown tenure contracts, such as appurtenancy and local processing requirements, and (2) wood supply agreements.[26] Canada does not suggest that such governmental mandates do not exist, but instead submits that such mandates do not affect the arm's-length nature of the transaction between the parties.[27] According to Canada, the fact that the government dictates the disposition of Crown timber by dictating to whom a seller must sell has no bearing on the actual terms of sale – so long as parties are not formally affiliated, any transaction between them must be considered at arm's length. Despite Canada's protestations to the contrary, under both categories of government-mandated restrictions, log sellers are not free to act in their best interests to choose and negotiate among potential buyers. Where the provincial governments limit the ability of a seller to sell freely and instead dictate to whom the seller must sell, Commerce reasonably determined, consistent with any reasonable reading of the term "arm's length," that the affected sales were not at arm's length.[28]

22. Further, based on the record, Commerce determined that there was an additional factor[29] – other than the above government-mandated restrictions – that affected many of the Canadian log sales such that they could not be considered to be at arm's length. The actual structure of certain log purchase agree-

[26] *Ibid.*

[27] First Written Submission of Canada, paras. 62-64.

[28] See, *e.g.*, Panel Report, *Korea - Measures Affecting Trade in Commercial Vessels*, WT/DS273 (7 March 2005), para. 7.135 ("captive buyer" creates risk that the transaction is not at arm's length.).

[29] Commerce identified three additional factors affecting its pass-through analysis. However, as discussed above, two of the three factors are not exclusively arm's-length issues.

ments[30] empowered the purchasing sawmill to control so many aspects of the transaction that Commerce determined that transactions covered by such purchase agreements could not be considered to be arm's length. Specifically, with respect to certain log purchase agreements, the sawmill actively manages all aspects of harvest and delivery. With respect to others, the sawmill finances or provides other goods or services as part of the transaction.[31] To enable Commerce to distinguish log purchase agreements that do represent arm's-length log sales from those that do not, it was necessary for Commerce to review the purchase agreements themselves.

23. Although not exclusively arm's-length issues, Commerce identified two additional factors affecting its pass-through analysis – factors that Canada contends should have had no bearing upon Commerce's analysis. Specifically, Commerce determined that in certain transactions the purchasing sawmills pay the Crown stumpage fees directly to the government for logs obtained from independent harvesters. Because the vehicle by which the Crown bestows the subsidy is through the administered stumpage programmes, when the purchasing sawmill pays the Crown directly for the stumpage, the purchasing sawmill directly receives the benefit and "pass-through" is not at issue.[32] Additionally, excluded from Commerce's analysis were fibre exchanges between Crown tenure holders, which often involved simple exchanges of, for instance, logs for chips, to meet appurtenancy and other harvesting requirements. These exchange agreements are a mechanism for tenured sawmills to deal with various government restrictions concerning the disposition of the harvested timber and are not log sales.[33]

24. The record was replete with evidence that demonstrated that certain government-mandated restrictions and other factors controlled, limited, or otherwise affected the log sales (in fact rendering some of them not sales at all), supporting Commerce's determination to examine more than simple affiliation in analyzing whether sales were at arm's length for the purpose of its pass-through analysis.

C. Commerce Appropriately Required That Canada Provide Company-Specific Information to Determine Whether the Transactions for Which a Pass-Through Analysis Was Requested Were Eligible for Such Analysis

25. Canada contends that Commerce improperly disregarded "aggregate" data that it submitted containing sales information from the provinces that generally identified the purchasers and sellers and the volume and value of sales that Can-

[30] Section 129 Determination, at 5. Exhibit CDA-5. The log purchase agreements that were provided to Commerce are proprietary documents. However, Commerce can state generally that these agreements contained vastly differing conditions and terms of sale. As evidenced by Commerce's reduction in the numerators of Alberta, Ontario and Saskatchewan, there were log purchase agreements that did satisfy Commerce's pass-through analysis.

[31] Section 129 Determination, at 5. Exhibit CDA-5.

[32] *Ibid.*

[33] Section 129 Determination, at 5-6. Exhibit CDA-5.

ada identified using its *per se* test as arm's-length transactions.[34] Canada also complains that Commerce refused to rely upon certain "sample" data. As discussed above, however, Commerce correctly determined that the arm's-length component of its pass-through analysis required more than just a determination concerning whether parties were affiliated. Additionally, Commerce correctly determined that other factors affected the pass-through analysis. Thus, Commerce required specific information on each transaction for which Canada requested a pass-through analysis, which necessitated that Canada provide more than just its aggregate data and, in some cases, more than its self-selected sample data.[35] This follows not only from the very nature of the enquiry, but also from the DSB's recommendations and rulings themselves.

26. The DSB's recommendations and rulings required that Commerce determine whether transactions between independent harvesters and sawmills, as well as between tenured harvesters/sawmills and sawmills, "passed through" the benefit from subsidies provided to the independent harvesters or tenured harvesters/sawmills. This is a company-specific issue, *i.e.*, an issue that is specific to each combination of log buyer and log seller, and the DSB recognized it as such.

27. Specifically, for instance, the Appellate Body referred to "the producer of the input" and "the producer of the product processed from the input", finding that, "it would not be possible to determine whether countervailing duties levied on the processed product are *in excess* of the amount of the total subsidy accruing to that product, without establishing whether, and in what amount, subsidies bestowed upon the producer of the input flowed through, downstream, to the producer of the product processed from that input".[36] While noting that the United States, in accordance with Article 19.3 of the SCM Agreement, had conducted an aggregate countervailing duty investigation, both the original panel and the Appellate Body found that this did not excuse Commerce from examining whether the *individual transaction* between the input supplier and the producer passed through the subsidy benefit. Thus, "before being entitled to impose countervailing duties on a processed product, for the purpose of offsetting an input subsidy, a Member must first determine, in accordance with Article 1.1, that a financial contribution exists, and that the benefit conferred directly on *the*

---

[34] First Written Submission of Canada, paras. 8, 76.

[35] Commerce did not disregard "sample" data provided by Canada. To the contrary, in response to certain concerns expressed by Canada, Commerce permitted Canada to submit subsets of data responding to its questionnaires. As noted previously, for example, with respect to British Columbia, Commerce limited its request for log purchase agreements to the 74 sawmills that participated in the Norcon Survey that was prepared at the GBC's request. Exhibit CDA-24, page 5 at 6. With respect to the Government of Alberta's ("GOA") concern that it could not provide all copies of tenure agreements relating to commercial timber permits ("CTPs"), Commerce limited its request to tenure agreements associated with coniferous timber quotas ("CTQs") and certain CTPs that were identified by Commerce. Exhibit CDA-24, page 8 at 1. Similarly, Commerce modified its requests for timber return data from the GOA to those portions containing the text relating to the payment of the stumpage dues. Exhibit CDA-24, page 9 at 7.

[36] Report of the Appellate Body, para. 141 (emphasis in original).

input producer has been passed through, at least in part, to *the producer* of the processed product."[37]

28. Finally, the Appellate Body was unequivocal that, where the input transaction is *not* at arm's length, there is no need for the investigating authority to analyze whether the subsidy passed through:

> Where countervailing duties are used to offset subsidies granted to producers of input products, while the duties are to be imposed on *processed* products, and where input producers and downstream producers operate at *arm's length*, the investigating authority must establish that the benefit conferred by a financial contribution directly on input producers is passed through, at least in part, to producers of the processed product subject to the investigation.[38]

Commerce implemented these findings by requesting the data necessary to establish whether each independent harvester or tenured harvester/sawmill sold logs at arm's length to each sawmill. Such company-specific information was necessary for Commerce's analysis of whether, in any particular transaction, the subsidy was passed through from the input producer to the producer of the subject merchandise. Indeed, the Appellate Body acknowledges this fact when it reasoned that the administering authority should determine "whether, and in what amount, subsidies bestowed upon the *producer of the input* flowed through, downstream, to the *producer of the product* processed from that input".[39]

29. Canada errs when it states that Commerce "ignored entirely the original panel's view that company-specific data are not necessarily required to conduct [sic] pass-through analysis".[40] The original panel said nothing of the sort. In response to US arguments to the effect that there is a mismatch between an investigation conducted on an aggregate basis and the company-specific nature of the pass-through issue, the panel simply found that pass through can indeed be examined during an aggregate investigation.[41] The panel did not suggest that company-specific information should not be used to analyze whether there was a pass-through of subsidies.

30. Where parties provided the requisite information, Commerce was able to conduct its pass-through analysis.[42] For instance, although the Government of Ontario did not identify all transactions in which the stumpage was paid by the purchasing sawmills rather than the harvesting tenure holders, eight Ontario harvesters and mills did provide such company-specific information in response to

---

37 Report of the Appellate Body, para. 154 (emphasis added).

38 Report of the Appellate Body, para. 147 (emphasis in original).

39 Report of the Appellate Body, para. 141 (emphasis added).

40 First Written Submission of Canada, para. 58 (citing Panel Report, at para. 7.98).

41 Report of the Panel, para. 7.98.

42 By way of example, at the request of Commerce, Ontario identified the quantity of sales that were sold to the purchasing mill subject to wood supply agreements. Exhibit CDA-23, at question 2; Ontario 15 September Pass-Through Response, at On-PASS-4, question 2 referring to ON-PASS-6, ON-PASS-7. Exhibit US-3. Because Commerce determined that volume of sales not to be at arm's length, no further analysis was conducted with respect to those sales.

Commerce's questionnaires.[43] Using the data provided by those companies, Commerce was able to conduct its pass-through analysis for those sales found, in light of the factors identified in the section above, to be at arm's length.[44] Similarly, with respect to Alberta, eight companies provided Commerce with company-specific data, including sample purchase contracts, information identifying those transactions for which the mill paid the stumpage directly to the Crown, and information concerning purchases from private lands.[45] Just as it did for Ontario, using the company-specific data provided by the Alberta companies, Commerce was able to conduct its pass-through analysis for those sales found to be at arm's length. Commerce was able to conduct its analysis as well with respect to certain company-specific data that it received in response to the pass-through appendices provided to Saskatchewan.[46]

31. In many instances, however, Canada failed to provide the requisite information despite repeated requests that it do so. For example, although Commerce limited its request for tenure agreements containing domestic processing or other mandated requirements to those companies that participated in the Norcon Survey, British Columbia failed to provide the copies that Commerce requested.[47] British Columbia did, however, provide *samples* of such tenure agreements, but the domestic processing requirements included in the samples that British Columbia submitted varied widely.[48] Although British Columbia argued that the domestic processing requirements contained in the tenure agreements were outdated, standardized, or otherwise inapplicable during the POI, it failed to provide any record evidence demonstrating that the requirements were not in force during the POI.[49] As a consequence, Commerce was not able to rely upon the sample agreements provided by British Columbia to support its pass-through claim. Additionally, British Columbia failed to identify that portion of the sales subject to its pass-through claim in which the sawmills pay the Crown stumpage fee directly to the government rather than paying the independent harvester from whom they obtained the logs.[50] Finally, although British Columbia did provide certain log purchase agreements it failed to provide the underlying tenure agree-

---

[43] 6 December 2004, "Pass-Through" Analysis Calculations for the Province of Ontario, at 2-4. Exhibit US-6.

[44] Section 129 Determination, at Comment 8. Exhibit CDA-5.

[45] 6 December 2004, "Pass-Through" Analysis Calculations for the Province of Alberta, at 2-5. Exhibit US-7.

[46] 6 December 2004, "Pass-Through" Analysis Calculations for the Province of Saskatchewan, at 2. Exhibit US-8.

[47] Exhibit CDA-24, at 3.

[48] Exhibit CDA-6, at 10.

[49] See Exhibit CDA-24, at 5, question 5; Response of the Government of British Columbia to the Department's 5 October 2004 Supplemental Questionnaire Concerning Pass Through of Alleged Benefits (25 October 2004), at BC-PT-3, -4, -15. ("British Columbia October 25 Pass-Through Response"). Exhibit US- 9.

[50] British Columbia September 15 Questionnaire Response, at 10 (Exhibit US-4); British Columbia 25 October Pass-Through Response, at BC-PT-17 -19 (Exhibit US-9). See *also* , Draft Section 129 Determination, at 10-11(Commerce summarizes the data that British Columbia failed to provide). Exhibit CDA-6.

ments.[51] There were similar deficiencies with respect to Manitoba[52], and to lesser degrees with respect to Alberta, Ontario and Saskatchewan.[53] Where Canada failed to provide the information requested, Canada prevented Commerce from completing its pass-through analysis.[54]

32. The truth is that, although Canada prevailed before both the original panel and the Appellate Body in arguing that Commerce was required to conduct this pass-through analysis, Canada apparently was unprepared to support many of its claims of no pass through with necessary evidence. Instead, Canada seeks to undermine Commerce's ability to conduct a full examination of the pass-through issue. Commerce – reasonably and in accordance with the DSB's recommendations and rulings – found that the subsidy benefit passed through where the evidence indicated that the input transaction was not at arm's-length or where the transaction otherwise was ineligible for a pass-through analysis because it was not a sale or because the purchasing sawmill paid the stumpage to the Crown. Where Commerce found the input transaction to be a sale at arm's length, Commerce completed the pass-through analysis required by the recommendations and rulings.

33. As demonstrated by the Section 129 Determination, when Canada properly supported its claims, Commerce was able to, and did, conduct its analysis. Commerce did not improperly "presume" pass-through – to the contrary, as set

51 Draft Section 129 Determination, at 11. Exhibit CDA-6.

52 Manitoba failed to substantiate its claim that 8.70 per cent of the Crown log harvest did not result in a pass-through of subsidies because its data deficiencies precluded Commerce from conducting its pass-through analysis. Draft Section 129 Determination, at 11-12. Exhibit CDA-6. Although one company did respond to Commerce's pass-through appendix, the sales data provided by that company were for sales arising after the POI so Commerce determined that it was not appropriate to include those sales in its analysis. Draft Section 129 Determination, at 12. Exhibit CDA-6. Canada now argues – but has offered no evidence support its assertion – that those sales were not outside the POI. First Written Submission of Canada, para. 85, fn. 96.

53 As evidenced by the Section 129 Determination, although there were some data issues with respect to Alberta, Saskatchewan, and Ontario that precluded Commerce from conducting its pass-through analysis with respect to the entire volumes for which these provinces claimed no pass through, Commerce was able to use data that had been provided and determined that a certain benefit did not pass through.

54 Contrary to Canada's argument, Commerce was in fact precluded from conducting its pass-through analysis with respect to the log sales contained in the Norcon Survey – a survey that Canada contends demonstrates that 11.6 per cent of Crown logs consumed in British Columbia mills were purchased from independent harvesters that held tenure. First Written Submission of Canada, para. 79. Although Canada submits that it provided transaction-specific data, it continually failed to provide necessary information concerning government-mandated restrictions and other conditions that Commerce required to complete its analysis. The Norcon Survey and the data that Canada refers to in Annex I of its first written submission obscure the fact that the data could be relied upon for little more than information about *affiliation* between parties to the log transactions. Indeed, as explained in the Norcon Survey itself, "[f]or purposes of this survey, arm's length log purchases were defined as logs purchased by a lumber manufacturer from a person with which it is not affiliated applying the definition of 'affiliated persons' contained in" US law. Exhibit CDA- 31, at 2. As the United States demonstrates above, however, affiliation is only one component of the pass-through analysis. The remaining 6.2 per cent referenced by Canada apparently represent transactions between tenure-holding sawmills. First Written Submission of Canada, para. 79. As discussed below, such transactions were not part of the DSB's recommendations and rulings.

forth above, Commerce conducted a pass-through analysis in compliance with the SCM Agreement, the GATT 1994, and the recommendations and rulings of the DSB.

D. Commerce Used Appropriate Benchmarks in its Pass-Through Analysis

34. Canada criticizes Commerce benchmarks but fails to allege any inconsistency with a provision of the SCM Agreement, the GATT 1994, or the DSB's recommendations and rulings. Thus, the Panel should reject Canada's argument on this basis alone.

35. In any event, Commerce selected appropriate benchmarks. Where Commerce – upon examining record evidence – determined that the input transaction was at arm's length, it proceeded to determine whether there was a competitive benefit: *i.e.*, whether the benefit "passed through". As previously explained, a subsidy provided to the producer of an input product confers a competitive benefit on a downstream purchaser of the input when the price paid for the subsidized input is lower than the a market determined benchmark price for the same product. In selecting a market determined benchmark, Commerce used, where possible, the actual company-specific prices that the purchasing mill paid for logs harvested from private lands and for imported logs.[55] Where those data were not available, Commerce relied on publicly available prices for logs harvested from private lands and logs imported into the province.[56]

36. Commerce's competitive benefit analysis demonstrated that many of the arm's-length log sales during the POI in Alberta, Ontario, and Saskatchewan, were made at prices below the benchmark prices, and therefore conferred a competitive benefit to the purchasing sawmills. As a result of Commerce's competitive benefit calculations, therefore, only some portion of the Crown harvest volume originally included in the numerator is excluded from the numerator of the revised subsidy calculations.

37. Canada now contends that Commerce relied on benchmarks that do not reflect "a comparison to the marketplace"[57] because they were unrepresentative of both the species harvested and of the prices paid in each province for logs used in lumber production. Canada is incorrect. The benchmark prices Commerce used were observable market-determined prices for logs that were sold in Canada. These prices corresponded to the same species of logs sold in each province for which a competitive benefit analysis was conducted and were otherwise representative of market prices.

38. For Alberta, Commerce used company-specific prices the mills paid for logs harvested from private lands in the province and logs they imported into the province. Where those company-specific prices were not available, Commerce

[55] See, e.g., Exhibit CDA-23, at 3, 6, 8, 10, 12 and pass-through appendix; Exhibit CDA-24, at 3, 6, 8, 11, 13 and supplemental pass-through appendix.

[56] Final Section 129 Determination, at 6. Exhibit CDA-5.

[57] First Written Submission of Canada, para. 67.

used the weighted-average price published in the annual 2000 Timber Damage Assessment (TDA) survey conducted by KPMG.[58] For Ontario, Commerce used a weighted-average price of transactions for timber harvested from private lands, as reported in the KPMG the "Delivered wood costs" schedule of the KPMG Report on Ontario Softwood Timber Costs and Sources, 1 April 2000 to 31 March 2001, dated 22 June 2001.[59] For Saskatchewan, which did not provide any company-specific or published provincial log prices, Commerce used a weighted-average price of the domestic and import prices for spruce-pine-fir (SPF), as reported by Alberta, Manitoba, Ontario, and Quebec.[60]

39. In sum, Commerce used as benchmarks observable market-determined prices for logs that were sold in Canada from unsubsidized sources to determine whether and to what extent a subsidy passed through in arm's length sales of logs between unrelated parties. For the reasons described above, the benchmark prices Commerce used to conduct its competitive benefit analysis properly reflected market conditions in Canada during the POI.

E. Commerce Did Not "Presume" Pass-Through

40. As demonstrated above, Commerce thoroughly investigated Canada's claims that no subsidy passed through as a consequence of certain transactions. As a result of its analysis, Commerce removed from the numerator of its *ad valorem* subsidy calculation any subsidy benefits it determined did not pass through in arm's length log sales between independent harvesters and sawmills and between unrelated tenured timber harvesters/sawmills and sawmills. Commerce thus ensured that its Section 129 Determination provided for a countervailing duty only with respect to the benefit from countervailable subsidies demonstrated to exist. Canada's attempt to characterize Commerce's analysis as a "presumption" of pass through is not supported by the record.

41. Indeed, as noted earlier, it is Canada that is "presuming". Under Canada's theory, when it comes to pass-through, responding parties can control the analysis. If the country under investigation chooses to provide proper evidence supporting its pass-through claim, authorities are able to conduct their analysis and, depending upon the determination, reduce the *ad valorem* rate. However, if the country chooses not to provide necessary information, according to Canada, the authorities are precluded from conducting their analysis and must presume no pass-through – *i.e.*, presume that no subsidy is bestowed on the subject merchandise. Consequently, under Canada's theory, once a country under investigation raises a pass-through issue, it would be in a position simply to refuse to provide any evidence supporting its claim, because the authorities would be prohibited from including any of the claimed volume in their calculations.

---

[58] See, *e.g.*, 6 December 2004, "Pass-Through" Analysis Calculations for the Province of Alberta, at 2. Exhibit US-7.

[59] 6 December 2004, "Pass-Through" Analysis Calculations for the Province of Ontario, at 1-4. Exhibit US-6.

[60] 6 December 2004, "Pass-Through" Analysis Calculations for the Province of Saskatchewan, at 2. Exhibit US-8.

42. From Canada's perspective, there is a certain simplicity in its argument – Commerce should simply accept Canada's unsubstantiated assertions. For instance, because British Columbia informed Commerce that 11.6%[61] of the log sales were between unrelated parties, according to Canada, Commerce must automatically find that the benefit for that associated volume of log sales did not pass through and must be removed from the numerator. However, nothing in the DSB 's recommendations and rulings, the SCM Agreement, or the GATT 1994 requires that the investigating authority simply accept assertions of the country under investigation. To the contrary, the DSB recommended that Commerce *conduct* a pass-through analysis. Commerce did so and based its determination upon what the record evidence *demonstrated* the facts to be and not upon what Canada *presumed* the result should be for sales between all unrelated parties.

F. Commerce Properly Investigated Categories of Sales Identified by the DSB

43. According to the DSB's recommendations and rulings, Commerce should investigate transactions between independent harvesters and sawmills[62], as well as between tenured harvesters/sawmills and unrelated sawmills.[63] Although Canada claims that Commerce "inexplicably excluded information of transactions in which the purchasing sawmill had tenure"[64] there is nothing inexplicable about it, as these transactions were not part of the DSB's recommendations and rulings. In this respect, there was a specific definition of both "tenured timber harvester/sawmill" and "sawmill". "Tenured timber harvester/sawmill" was defined as "an enterprise holding a stumpage contract that fells trees and produces logs, and also processes logs into softwood lumber."[65] "Sawmill" was defined as "an enterprise that processes logs into softwood lumber and *does not hold a stumpage contract*"..[66]

44. Given these precise definitions that bear directly upon the DSB recommendations and rulings with respect to pass-through, Commerce properly limited this aspect of its pass-through analysis to arm's-length log sales by an enterprise holding a stumpage contract that fells trees and produces logs, and also processes logs into softwood lumber, to an enterprise that processes logs into softwood lumber and does not hold a stumpage contract, *i.e.*, tenured timber harvester/sawmills to unrelated, non-tenured sawmills. As the DSB recommendations and rulings recognized, tenure-holding sawmills are direct subsidy recipients. It is entirely appropriate therefore to include the volume of logs processed by those sawmills in the total subsidy calculation.

---

[61] First Written Submission of Canada, para. 79.

[62] The United States did not appeal the Panel's findings with respect to arm's-length log sales between tenured timber harvesters not owning sawmills and sawmills. Appellate Body Report, fn. 157.

[63] Appellate Body Report, para. 167(e); see CDA-3, at questions 1 and 2.

[64] First Written Submission of Canada, para. 55.

[65] Appellate Body Report, fn. 150.

[66] Appellate Body Report, fn. 151 (emphasis added).

G. *Commerce Properly Calculated the Revised Rate*

45. Contrary to Canada's arguments that Commerce somehow applied its results to an "invalidated" countervailing duty rate[67], Commerce properly calculated the revised rate by removing from the numerator of the *ad valorem subsidy* rate calculation the volume of log sales determined not to have passed through[68]68 The numerator of the *ad valorem* subsidy rate was reduced by C$28,344,121. The revision reduced the only rate that was before the original panel and Appellate Body, *i.e.*, the 18.79 per cent *ad valorem* rate calculated in the Final Determination, to 18.62 per cent *ad valorem.*[69] With the exception of this limited pass-through analysis, there are no outstanding DSB recommendations or rulings that would have required further modification of the *ad valorem* rate calculation.

III. THE RESULTS OF THE FIRST ASSESSMENT REVIEW ARE NOT WITHIN THE PANEL' S JURISDICTION

46. The United States reiterates its request, set out in its submission of 10 March 2005, that the Panel preliminarily rule that the results of the first assessment review are not "measures taken to comply" and therefore are outside Panel's jurisdiction in this proceeding. In particular, the United States noted in its preliminary ruling request that original investigations and assessment reviews are different processes with different administrative records that serve distinct purposes.[70] In this case, the assessment review was initiated at the behest of Canada, among others, eight months before the recommendations and rulings in this dispute were adopted.

47. This is not a situation like that presented in *Australia – Automotive Leather*, in which a WTO-inconsistent subsidy was both withdrawn and "regranted" in another form on the same day, in "inextricably linked elements of a

---

[67] First Written Submission of Canada, para. 10.

[68] See 6 December 2004, Country-wide Rate Calculations Net of Subsidy Benefits That Did Not Pass-Through - Revised as a Result of Comments Submitted by Parties to the Proceeding, at 2-8. Exhibit US-10.

[69] See *Notice of Implementation Under Section 129 of the Uruguay Round Agreements Act; Countervailing Measures Concerning Certain Softwood Lumber Products From Canada*, 69 FR 75305 (16 December 2004). Exhibit CDA-7.

[70] See Appellate Body Report, *European Communities - Anti-Dumping Duties on Imports of Cotton-Type Bed Linen from India - Recourse to Article 21.5 of the DSU by India*, WT/DS141/AB/RW, adopted 24 April 2003, para 123. "(the imposition and collection of anti-dumping duties under Article 9 is a separate and distinct phase of an anti-dumping action that necessarily occurs after the determination of dumping, injury, and causation under Articles 2 and 3 has been made.") Footnotes omitted. Although there is no specific corollary to Article 9 of the Anti-Dumping Agreement in the SCM Agreement, the SCM Agreement recognizes that Members may conduct assessment proceedings to determine the final amount of countervailing duty to be assessed. See Footnote 52 of the SCM Agreement.

single transaction".[71] Rather, the assessment review is a completely separate proceeding, based on a different record, designed to assess countervailing duties – a proceeding, moreover, that can be requested by Canada at regular intervals well into the future. Finally, it cannot be seriously asserted that, where there have been DSB recommendations and rulings with respect to the imposition of supplemental duties on a product, any subsequent proceedings related to those duties are "measures taken to comply". A previous panel has already found this not to be the case, in *EC – Bed Linens (Panel).*[72] In sum, the United States reiterates that the results of the first assessment review are neither "measures taken to comply" with recommendations and rulings, nor do they render actual measures taken to comply "non-existent".

IV. THE PANEL SHOULD NOT MAKE THE SPECIFIC RECOMMENDATIONS SOUGHT BY CANADA

48. In its first submission, Canada has asked the Panel to make certain findings and recommendations in the event that it agrees with Canada. Specifically, Canada asks that the DSB find that the imposition of duties by the United States is inconsistent with the SCM Agreement and the GATT 1994 and recommend either that the United States refund the duties collected to offset the amounts determined to pass through or revise its measure to be consistent with the relevant agreements and refund the duties to the extent they exceed the amount of the subsidy determined to have passed-through.[73]

49. The Panel should decline to make such recommendations. The text of DSU Article 19.1 is unequivocal regarding the recommendation that a panel is to make in such a case: "Where a panel or the Appellate Body concludes that a measure is inconsistent with a covered agreement, it *shall* recommend that the Member concerned bring the measure into conformity with that agreement." (Emphasis added). In short, the recommendations that Canada seeks here are not authorized by the DSU.

V. CONCLUSION

50. For the reasons stated above, Canada's claims against the measure taken to comply with the DSB's recommendations and rulings have no basis in the SCM Agreement, the GATT 1994, or the recommendations and rulings of the DSB. Thus, the United States requests that the Panel find that the United States

---

[71] Panel Report, *Australia – Subsidies Provided to Producers and Exporters of Automotive Leather – Recourse to Article 21.5 of the DSU by the United States*, WT/DS126/RW and Corr.1, adopted 11 February 2000, para. 6.50.

[72] See Panel Report, *European Communities - Anti-Dumping Duties on Imports of Cotton-Type Bed Linen from India - Recourse to Article 21.5 of the DSU by India*, WT/DS141/RW, adopted 24 April 2003, as modified by the Appellate Body Report, WT/DS141/AB/RW, para. 6.15.

[73] First Written Submission of Canada, para. 72.

properly implemented the recommendations and rulings of the DSB and that the Panel reject Canada's claims in their entirety.

EXHIBIT LIST

Number	Name
US-3	Response of the Government of Ontario to the Department's 17 August 2004 Supplemental Pass-Through Questionnaire (15 September 2004) (relevant pages).
US-4	Response of the Government of British Columbia to the Department's 17 August 2004 Supplemental Questionnaire Concerning Pass Through of the Alleged Benefits (September 15, 2004) (relevant pages).
US-5	BLACK'S LAW DICTIONARY, Seventh Edition (West Group 1999) at 103 (definition "arm' s length").
US-6	6 December 2004, "Pass-Through" Analysis Calculations for the Province of Ontario
US-7	6 December 2004, "Pass-Through" Analysis Calculations for the Province of Alberta
US-8	6 December 2004, "Pass-Through" Analysis Calculations for the Province of Saskatchewan
US-9	Response of the Government of British Columbia to the Department's 5 October 2004 Supplemental Questionnaire Concerning Pass Through of Alleged Benefits (October 25, 2004)(relevant pages).
US-10	6 December 2004, Country-wide Rate Calculations Net of Subsidy Benefits That Did Not Pass-Through - Revised as a Result of Comments Submitted by Parties to the Proceeding

ANNEX B-3

ORAL STATEMENT OF THE UNITED STATES
21 April 2005

INTRODUCTION

1. Good morning, Mr. Chairman and members of the Panel. Thank you for agreeing to serve as panelists in this proceeding and for the opportunity to appear before you today.

2. We recognize that our statement is lengthy, which flows from the fact that this is our first opportunity to respond to Canada's second submission. We were disappointed that Canada opposed our request for sequential second submissions in this proceeding, which would have helped to avoid this situation. We thank you in advance for your time and attention as we deliver our statement.

3. We will begin this morning by addressing Canada's response to our preliminary ruling request. Then we will explain how the United States properly implemented the recommendations and rulings of the DSB by conducting the appropriate pass-through analysis.

PRELIMINARY RULING REQUEST

4. As you know, the United States has requested a preliminary ruling that the results of the assessment review are not "measures taken to comply" pursuant to DSU Article 21.5, and are therefore outside this Panel's jurisdiction. As our request notes, the assessment review was a proceeding separate from both the original countervailing duty investigation determination challenged by Canada and the Section 129 Determination at issue here, was initiated prior to the DSB's adoption of recommendations and rulings in this dispute, and had nothing to do with complying with the recommendations and rulings of the DSB.

5. In an attempt to justify sweeping the separate assessment review results into its Article 21.5 panel request, Canada has resorted to relying on the supposed "broad" scope of Article 21.5 and "wide discretion" of the Panel to review measures under Article 21.5.[1] Canada also argues that a failure to include the assessment review results in this compliance proceeding would be contrary to the overall "purpose" of Article 21.5 proceedings.[2]

6. But the issue is simpler than Canada would have us believe. Either a measure *is* taken to comply – and falls within the terms of Article 21.5 – or it is not, and is thus not within this Panel's jurisdiction. As the Appellate Body stated in *Canada – Aircraft* – and none of the reports cited by Canada are to the con-

[1] E.g., Canada Second Written Submission, paras. 7 - 8.
[2] Canada Second Written Submission, paras. 6, 26 - 30.

trary – Article 21.5 proceedings "do not concern just *any* measure of a Member of the WTO; rather Article 21.5 proceedings are limited to those 'measures *taken to comply* with the recommendations and rulings' of the DSB."[3]

7. Let us review the facts. Canada's original request for consultations concerned the *final countervailing duty investigation determination* published on 2 April 2002, and its panel request alleged errors in that final investigation determination.[4] The original panel's findings with respect to pass-through related solely to that final investigation determination. The Appellate Body stated that "[b]efore the Panel, Canada challenged a number of aspects of the final determination by [the Commerce Department] that led to the imposition of duties"[5] and the Appellate Body's findings and conclusions – including those with respect to the need for a "pass-through" analysis – thus related only to that final investigation determination.

8. Therefore, to implement the DSB's recommendations and rulings, Commerce issued a new determination – the Section 129 Determination – that revised the original final investigation determination by conducting the recommended pass-through analysis. By correcting the only "inconsistency" identified by the DSB with respect to the final investigation determination, the United States fully implemented the recommendations and rulings of the DSB to bring the measure into compliance with the SCM Agreement.

9. Long before there were any DSB recommendations and rulings to implement, and pursuant to long-standing, standard procedures, Commerce initiated the first assessment review, at the request of Canada, among others. The purpose of the assessment review was to determine the precise countervailing duties that would be levied on particular entries of merchandise entering the United States after the United States had already imposed the countervailing duty measure (in US parlance, after the publication of the countervailing duty order). This assessment review would have been conducted regardless of the existence of any dispute challenging the original investigation determination and it was nearly half over when the recommendations and rulings in this dispute were adopted.

10. Thus, Canada's repeated assertions that Commerce itself "purported" or "alleged" that it conducted the assessment review to implement the DSB's recommendations and rulings are inaccurate and have no basis.

11. Canada cannot deny that – in contrast to the assessment review – Commerce initiated the Section 129 proceeding for the specific purpose of addressing the DSB's recommendations and rulings. Indeed, the agreement of the parties on the "reasonable period of time" to implement the recommendations and rulings

---

3 Appellate Body Report, *Canada – Measures Affecting the Export of Civilian Aircraft*, WT/DS70/AB/R, adopted 20 August 1999, para. 36.

4 WT/DS257/3, 19 August 2002.

5 Appellate Body Report, *United States – Final Countervailing Duty Determination with Respect to Certain Softwood Lumber from Canada*, WT/DS257/AB/R, adopted 12 February 2004, para. 1 ("Appellate Body Report").

in this dispute was negotiated in the light of, and specifically refers to, the US procedures for implementing WTO reports[6] – that is, the Section 129 procedures.

12. Faced with the undeniable fact that the assessment review results were *not* taken to comply with the DSB's recommendations and rulings, Canada instead argues that the Panel should nonetheless consider them in this proceeding, because the assessment review results either (a) somehow rendered the Section 129 Determination "non-existent" or (b) were "inextricably linked" to the recommendations and rulings of the DSB.

13. Neither of these assertions is true.

The assessment review results did not render the Section 129 Determination "non-existent"

14. First, in no way did the assessment results render the Section 129 Determination non-existent. The final investigation determination challenged by Canada – a determination of the existence and the amount of the subsidy – established one of the prerequisites under Article 19.1 of the SCM Agreement for the imposition of a countervailing duty. That investigation determination did not establish the amount of duties that would be levied, or assessed, on the imports; that task is undertaken as part of the separate assessment review. The final investigation determination simply established one of the bases for imposing countervailing duties. The Panel should recall in this connection that the remedy Canada sought in the dispute before the original panel was the revocation of the countervailing duty order, which was based in part on the final investigation determination.

15. The Section 129 Determination, in implementing the recommendations and rulings of the DSB with respect to the final investigation determination, confirmed that the resulting imposition of countervailing duties on 22 May 2002, was consistent with the SCM Agreement. The assessment review could not, and did not, render that Section 129 Determination non-existent. Indeed, the very fact that Canada is, itself, challenging the Section 129 Determination shows that Canada believes that it is of ongoing effect and relevant to the issue of compliance.

16. Further, the Section 129 Determination was fully implemented, and revised the original final investigation determination in every respect necessary to implement the recommendations and rulings of the DSB. For instance, the Section 129 Determination revised the cash deposit rate established by the final investigation determination – a cash deposit rate that, under US law, stays in effect unless and until a party requests an assessment review. If no assessment review is requested, countervailing duties are assessed at the cash deposit rate.

17. Canada's allegation that the Section 129 Determination was "rendered non-existent" appears to be an allusion to the argument that the United States made in the dispute *Australia – Leather*, where *withdrawal of the subsidy* was

[6] WT/DS257/13.

non-existent. The situation there, however, is not at all analogous to the facts of this dispute.

18. First, in *Australia – Leather*, the United States was arguing that the panel should review whether a prohibited subsidy had actually been withdrawn, as specifically required by Article 4.7 of the SCM Agreement, when the repayment of a grant had been contingent on the simultaneous grant of a loan on non-commercial terms. In contrast, this proceeding involves the question of whether a measure has been brought into conformity with a WTO agreement.

19. Second, the *Australia – Leather* panel concluded that the subsidy had not been withdrawn at all, because the supposed repayment and the non-commercial loan were, in effect, a single transaction in which the subsidy simply shifted form. By contrast, in this dispute, the Section 129 Determination and the assessment review results are separate and independent actions. The simple fact is, the Section 129 Determination was made to bring the measure in dispute into conformity with the SCM Agreement as recommended by the DSB, whereas the assessment review was conducted for a completely unrelated reason. As such, the assessment review in no way affects that result of the Section 129 Determination, and Canada has not shown otherwise.

The Results of the Assessment Review are not "Inextricably Linked", either to the Section 129 Determination, or to the Recommendations and Rulings of the DSB.

20. In the alternative, Canada uses three WTO reports to argue that the assessment results are "inextricably linked" to the recommendations and rulings of the DSB, and therefore should be considered "measures taken to comply". These reports, however, only demonstrate further how the assessment review is not within the scope of this Article 21.5 proceeding.

21. We've just discussed one of those disputes, *Australia – Leather*, in which the panel reviewed both the measure that Australia claimed was taken to comply – the repayment of a subsidy grant – and another measure that Australia claimed was *not* taken to comply – the new non-commercial loan. The panel in that dispute concluded that the subsidy had not been withdrawn, because the supposed repayment and the non-commercial loan were, as Canada quotes the panel, "inextricably linked elements of a single transaction."[7]

22. But, as we mentioned, that situation is very different from this one. In *Australia – Leather*, the repayment of the grant by the grant recipient was specifically and directly conditioned on the grant recipient receiving the non-commercial loan – there would have been no repayment at all if there had been no loan. It was on that basis that the panel found that the loan was "inextricably linked to the steps taken by Australia in response to the DSB's rulings in [that] dispute, in view of both its timing and nature."[8]

---

[7] Panel Report, *Australia – Subsidies Provided to Producers and Exporters of Automotive Leather – Recourse to Article 21.5 of the DSU by the United States*, WT/DS126/RW, adopted 11 February 2000, para. 6.50 ("*Australia – Leather*").

[8] *Australia – Leather*, para. 6.5.

23. In this dispute, by contrast, there is no such connection between the Section 129 Determination and the assessment review results: they were not in any sense contingent on one another, nor were they in any sense part of a single transaction. The assessment review would have taken place regardless of whether there was a Section 129 proceeding under way, and, indeed, regardless of whether there even was a WTO dispute.

24. Canada similarly cites to the dispute *Australia – Salmon*, in which, in response to DSB recommendations and rulings, Australia modified its ban on salmon imports to permit imports that satisfied certain criteria. In what was obviously a response to the modification of the ban, Tasmania, one of Australia's sub-federal units, imposed its own ban. The Tasmanian ban did not arise from a proceeding initiated as a matter of domestic law requirements, irrespective of any WTO challenge. Rather, it was an ad hoc action taken after the DSB had made recommendations and rulings against an Australian import ban and after Australia had taken action to modify the ban. All of the evidence – both in terms of timing and subject matter – pointed to these bans being truly "inextricably linked". Therefore, that panel properly found that the Tasmanian ban was a measure taken to comply.

25. By contrast, in this case, the assessment review was initiated

- upon request of the parties (including Canada), *eight months before* the DSB's recommendations and rulings were even adopted,
- pursuant to a US statutory provision that requires initiation upon request on a specific schedule and under specific deadlines, and
- for the purpose of assessing countervailing duties on entries not previously examined – not for the purpose of implementing any recommendations or rulings.

Unlike the obvious "close connection" in *Australia – Salmon*, there is nothing that links the assessment review to the recommendations and rulings of the DSB in this dispute.

26. Finally, Canada tries to distinguish the findings in *EC – Bed Linens* from this dispute, claiming that the panel excluded the results of a review from that Article 21.5 proceeding because that review did not deal with the same "subject matter" as the original determination. Canada also cites *EC – Bed Linens* as establishing that it is appropriate for this Panel to review Commerce's actions with regard to a subsequent time period characterized by new data, including completely different import entries.

27. To the contrary, however, the *EC – Bed Linens* dispute demonstrates that a new determination that was made in a subsequent segment of an antidumping or countervailing duty proceeding – and not made to implement recommendations and rulings of the DSB – falls outside the jurisdiction of Article 21.5 panels. For instance, the fact that measures taken to comply might involve new facts does not justify expanding Article 21.5 proceedings to encompass measures not taken to comply. Indeed, this Appellate Body discussion cited by Canada has nothing to do with the question of what constitutes "measures taken to comply",

but rather the question of whether those measures are "consisten[t] with a covered agreement".

28. In sum, the assessment review that Canada has attempted to sweep into this Article 21.5 proceeding has nothing in common with those measures considered to be "inextricably linked" or "closely connected" in other disputes. To the contrary, the assessment review results have no relation at all to either the Section 129 Determination or the recommendations and rulings. They are simply not measures taken to comply and are therefore outside this Panel's jurisdiction.

Contrary to Canada's arguments, respecting the jurisdictional mandate of Article 21.5 does not "ignore the purpose of compliance proceedings".

29. Canada has failed to show that the assessment review is a measure taken to comply in that it is "inextricably linked" to the recommendations and rulings of the DSB. Nor has Canada shown that measures taken to comply do not exist because the assessment review rendered the Section 129 Determination non-existent.

30. Canada therefore resorts to the argument that limiting the Panel's review only to the measures taken to comply – that is, not sweeping the separate assessment review into the Article 21.5 basket – somehow ignores the "purpose of compliance proceedings". The United States disagrees, for reasons which we will discuss shortly. But regardless, a baseless reference to the general "purpose of compliance proceedings" cannot direct a result that is not supported by a good faith reading of the text, in its context and in light of the object and purpose of the DSU.

31. Further, the United States does not understand how properly applying DSU Article 21.5 can result in "ignor[ing] the purpose of compliance proceedings". Contrary to Canada's arguments, with respect to the only claim found to be WTO-inconsistent – the pass-through analysis conducted in the final investigation determination – a review under Article 21.5 of the Section 129 Determination permits the prompt settlement of disputes: Canada complained about an inconsistency in the final investigation determination, and this Panel will review whether that inconsistency has been corrected.

32. What Canada appears to be seeking is to avoid the need to bring a separate WTO dispute against the United States on the separate assessment proceeding. Canada instead hopes to "kill two birds with one stone" – albeit improperly – by sweeping a review of the separate assessment proceeding into this Article 21.5 proceeding. Canada complains that having to initiate a separate dispute settlement proceeding with respect to an assessment review somehow ignores the purpose of compliance proceedings. However, in negotiating the DSU, Members agreed that the expedited procedures of Article 21.5 would only be available for two very specific questions: (1) the existence or (2) the consistency of *measures taken to comply*. Members did not agree that the special procedures under Article 21.5 would be available for any claim for which the complaining party felt it would be more convenient to use Article 21.5.

33. If Canada believes that an assessment review is conducted inconsistently with the SCM Agreement, it is within its WTO rights to request consultations with respect to that assessment review and, if appropriate, request a panel. Indeed, assessment reviews can present different legal issues and entail different obligations from final investigation determinations – in addition to involving completely different administrative records – that make a separate set of consultations entirely appropriate.

34. Moreover, Canada appears to suggest that the US system of retrospective duty assessments somehow compels the Panel, in the special case of the United States, to sweep the assessment review into this Article 21. 5 proceeding.[9] But there is nothing in Article 21.5 or in the SCM Agreement that requires a different interpretation of "measures taken to comply" for those Members that employ a retrospective duty assessment system, rather than a prospective one.

35. Canada suggested this morning, in paragraph 33 of its oral statement, that the United States had somehow conceded that the assessment review was inconsistent with US WTO obligations. Canada bases this suggestion on the absence of an explanation in the US submissions or oral statement of the pass-through analysis in the first assessment review. This is untrue. The United States has not discussed the assessment review because it falls outside of this Panel's jurisdiction. The United States does not in any sense concede that the pass-through analysis in the assessment review is inconsistent with WTO obligations.

Conclusion

36. In sum, Mr. Chairman and members of the Panel, the results of the first assessment review are not "measures taken to comply" and therefore fall outside the Panel's jurisdiction in this Article 21.5 dispute. Therefore, we reaffirm our request that the Panel so rule.

PASS-THROUGH ANALYSIS

Canada Bears the Burden of Proof

37. It is important to recall that Canada bears the burden of establishing a prima facie case of a WTO inconsistency. In its panel request, Canada specifically refers to three separate provisions: Articles 10 and 32.1 of the SCM Agreement and Article VI:3 of the GATT 1994.[10] Although Canada concludes that the United States has acted inconsistently with these provisions, it has failed to demonstrate any such inconsistency or to describe why any of the specific actions that form the bases of its arguments are inconsistent with these provisions. For instance, Canada challenges Commerce's arm's-length analysis yet fails to identify how that analysis is inconsistent with any of the cited provisions. Similarly, Canada challenges the pass-through benchmarks Commerce relied

9 Canada Second Written Submission, para. 27.
10 WT/DS257/15.

upon yet once again fails to identify any way in which these benchmarks are inconsistent with the cited provisions. Consequently, Canada has failed to make its prima facie case and for that reason alone the Panel should reject Canada's claims.

The United States Properly Implemented the DSB's Recommendations and Rulings

38. The substantive issue facing this Panel is whether the United States properly implemented the recommendations and rulings of the DSB in conducting its pass-through analysis with respect to the final investigation determination. The answer is clearly "yes". The positions of the United States with respect to its Section 129 Determination are more fully contained in our written submissions. This morning, we will not repeat all of the points made in those submissions but rather will briefly highlight what we consider to be significant issues as well as respond to the issues raised in Canada's second written submission. As to those issues not raised in this oral statement, we refer the Panel to our written submissions.

39. Initially, we will briefly outline Commerce's pass-through methodology. Next, we will discuss the nature of Commerce's arm's-length analysis and Canada's attempt to truncate that analysis. Then we will focus upon Canada's improper challenge to the benchmarks Commerce relied upon in conducting its pass-through analysis. Finally, we will address Canada's peculiar claim that US compliance with the express terms of the Appellate Body Report, was an effort by the United States to avoid its WTO obligations.

Pass-Through Methodology

40. The DSB determined that the United States acted inconsistently with certain of its WTO obligations when it failed in its final investigation determination to conduct a pass-through analysis with respect to two categories of arm's-length log sales between unrelated parties. To implement those recommendations and rulings Commerce was first required to obtain additional information from Canada relating to the POI. That information was requested through a series of questionnaires. Specifically, Commerce requested information relating to those log sales for which Canada was claiming that the subsidy did not pass through to the purchasing sawmill.

41. As a threshold matter, Commerce examined the data provided by Canada to determine whether the sales were between affiliated, that is, related, parties. Consistent with the DSB's recommendations and rulings, when Commerce found that the sales were between affiliated parties, it performed no further pass-through analysis. If the sales were identified as being between unaffiliated parties, Commerce examined the circumstances surrounding the transactions to determine whether the parties operated at arm's length. Where Commerce determined that the transaction was at arm's length, it next determined whether there was a competitive benefit, that is, whether the benefit "passed through" to the

purchasing mill using market-determined benchmarks. Ultimately Commerce's analysis of arm's-length log sales between unaffiliated parties resulted in a reduction in the numerator of the *ad valorem* subsidy rate which in turn, had the effect of reducing the country-wide subsidy rate.

42. Consistent with the DSB's recommendations and rulings, Commerce conducted a pass-through analysis and based its determination upon what the record evidence demonstrated the facts to be.

Commerce Properly Conducted its Arm's-Length Analysis

43. There is no dispute between the parties that for a transaction to be eligible for consideration in Commerce's pass-through analysis, the DSB determined that the transaction must be between unrelated parties and be at arm's length.[11] Canada does not challenge Commerce's affiliation determinations, so we will not discuss those threshold determinations. Rather, the dispute between the parties concerns the interpretation of the term "arm's length" – a term that is not defined in the text of the SCM Agreement.

44. The Appellate Body found that both the SCM Agreement and the GATT 1994 require that Commerce establish that the benefit is passed through to the downstream processor where subsidies are bestowed directly on producers of an input product while the countervailing duties are to be imposed on processed products, "and where the input producers and downstream processors operate at *arm's length*".[12] Thus, where the two producers do not operate at arm's length, no pass-through analysis is required because the subsidy bestowed on the input producer benefits the producer of the processed product. The United States properly determined that whether entities operate at "arm's length" involves more than simply an examination of formal affiliation – rather, it involves analysis of whether one party effectively controls the other or whether the parties have roughly equal bargaining power.

45. Canada, however, conflates the issues of affiliation and arm's length arguing that an arm's-length determination requires nothing more than a determination of affiliation. Indeed, Canada's *per se* approach to arm's length is set forth in paragraph 62 of its first written submission when it states "that a transaction between unrelated parties is by definition an arm's-length transaction". Because Canada treats these disparate concepts as one, Canada contends that by analyzing whether such sales are, in fact, at arm's length, and then eliminating sales that are not at arm's-length from the pass-through analysis, Commerce somehow "presumed" pass-through. To the contrary, it is Canada that is presuming no pass through whenever there are sales between unaffiliated parties.

46. By contrast, the DSB recognized a distinction between arm's length and affiliation in its recommendations and rulings, noting that Commerce should have conducted a "pass-through analysis in respect of *arm's length* sales of

---

[11] Appellate Body Report, para 176(e).

[12] Appellate Body Report, para. 146 (emphasis in original).

logs...to unrelated sawmills".[13] Canada's approach which would end the analysis once affiliation is determined is thus inconsistent with the DSB's recommendations and rulings.

47. In contrast, and consistent with the DSB's recommendations and rulings, Commerce properly examined the circumstances surrounding the sales that Canada reported as occurring between unrelated parties to determine whether those transactions were at arm's length. Where parties to a transaction are not free to bargain with whomever they choose or to bargain on terms not encumbered by government mandates and restrictions that were imposed as a condition of obtaining the logs in the first place, Commerce properly determined that such transactions were not at arm's length.

48. The SCM Agreement, the GATT 1994 and the DSB's recommendations and rulings do not require that Commerce's arm's-length analysis be constrained in the fashion proposed by Canada. Indeed, as previously noted, although Canada generally alleges that Commerce's arm's-length analysis is inconsistent with WTO obligations, it fails to cite to any specific WTO provision that supports its position that an arm's-length analysis can be nothing more than an examination of affiliation.

49. As we will discuss next, the facts presented to Commerce demonstrate that under the Canadian stumpage system, many of the circumstances of the log sales are controlled by government mandates and other conditions that rendered those sales not at arm's length or otherwise ineligible for the pass-through analysis.

Commerce Properly Considered the Circumstances of the Sales in its Arm's Length Analysis

50. In our second written submission we detailed the government mandates and other conditions that Commerce identified in its Section 129 Determination as controlling, limiting or otherwise affecting the subject log sales. Briefly, the government-mandated restrictions include appurtenancy, local processing requirements, and wood supply agreements which dictate to the harvester those entities to which it must sell. These government mandates restrict the ability of a seller to act in its best interests when selecting from among potential buyers. Where parties are not able to negotiate freely, such sales could not be considered to be at arm's length.

51. Additionally, certain log purchase agreements were such that the purchasing mill controls significant aspects of the transaction or provided other goods or services as part of the transaction so that sales under these agreements could not be arm's-length sales. Canada does not deny the existence of these conditions (although the Government of British Columbia does contend, with no support, that it does not enforce the appurtenancy requirements contained in its tenure

[13] Appellate Body Report, para 176(e)(emphasis added, except that emphasis on "logs" is in original.)

agreements). Rather, Canada argues that it is basic economics that these restrictions do not affect the arm's-length nature of the transactions between the parties.

52. Canada's view of introductory economics does not amount to a WTO obligation. **Canada's argument glosses over the reality of the system created by these mandates and conditions.** By way of example, where a subsidy is provided to an input producer who can only sell to a particular purchaser, the purchaser is in a position substantially to dictate the price. Consequently, such a sale would not be at arm's length. The same result obtains where local processing requirements exist.

53. As noted above, these government mandates and other conditions are imposed as a condition of the tenures. Consequently, they go to the very heart of the issue Commerce is investigating. Contrary to Canada's assertion, as evidenced by the fact that Commerce has found arm's-length transactions in Canada's regulated market, Commerce is not requiring a marketplace free from regulation as a prerequisite for finding transactions to be at arm's length. However, because these mandates and conditions substantially control timber transactions in Canada, they were fundamental to Commerce's arm's-length analysis.

54. Finally, Commerce identified two additional factors – that are not exclusively arm's-length issues – that affected its pass-through analysis. Notably, for those transactions in which the purchasing mill paid the Crown stumpage fees directly to the government for logs obtained from the independent harvester, Commerce determined that no pass-through issue arose. Because the stumpage fee is the vehicle through which the Crown bestows the subsidy the purchasing sawmill *directly receives the benefit*. Canada misses the point when it argues that "[a]lthough the party writing the check may affect the observed log price, it will never affect the *value paid* by the sawmill for the logs."[14] Unlike the transactions identified by the DSB, in these transactions the sawmill is the direct recipient of the subsidy and thus there is no need to examine whether the benefit passed through to the purchasing mill. Moreover, because the very essence of the pass-through analysis is determining with whom the benefit resides, Canada's analogy to a situation in which a party generally satisfies an outstanding lien on behalf of another is irrelevant.[15]

55. Additionally, Commerce properly excluded from its analysis fiber exchange agreements between Crown tenure holders, which often involved, by way of example, exchanges of logs for chips, to meet appurtenancy and other harvesting requirements. These exchange agreements are not log sales but rather are tools by which tenured sawmills satisfy their appurtenancy and local processing requirements. Because such exchanges are not "sales" at all, there was no need for Commerce to conduct an arm's-length analysis of the transactions.

56. In sum, Canada has not established that Commerce's arm's-length analysis is in any way contrary to the SCM Agreement, the GATT 1994 or the DSB's recommendations and rulings.

---

[14] Canada Second Written Submission, para. 41 (emphasis in original).

[15] Canada Second Written Submission, para. 41.

The Panel Should Decline to Consider Canada's Challenge to Commerce's Benchmarks and in Any Event, Commerce Used Appropriate Market-Determined Benchmarks

57. Canada criticizes Commerce's benchmarks as not reflecting "market" conditions, but has thus far failed in its written submissions to specify in what way the benchmarks were inconsistent with the SCM Agreement, the GATT 1994, or the DSB's recommendations and rulings. More significantly, Canada failed to even identify its challenge to the pass-through benchmarks in its panel request. Consequently, not only has Canada failed to make a *prima facie* case that there is a WTO inconsistency, this claim is outside the Panel's terms of reference.

58. In terms of the substance, and as explained in the second written submission of the United States, a subsidy provided to the producer of an input product confers a competitive benefit on a downstream purchaser of the input when the price paid for the subsidized input is lower than a market-determined benchmark price for the same product. Thus, to determine whether a benefit "passed through" to the purchasing mill, that is, whether there was a competitive benefit to the purchasing mill, Commerce required market-determined benchmarks. Canada does not dispute the necessity for such benchmarks but rather, argues that because Commerce's benchmarks include import prices, the benchmarks are not representative of market conditions in Canada.

59. In selecting market-determined benchmarks, Commerce used, where possible, the actual company-specific prices that the purchasing mill paid for logs harvested from private lands and for imported logs. Commerce requested in its supplemental pass-through questionnaires and accompanying pass-through appendices that Canada provide such data to assist Commerce in developing market benchmarks. As evidenced by Commerce's calculations, where those company-specific purchase data were available, Commerce used them. Where such data were not available, Commerce used publicly available prices for logs harvested from private lands and for imported logs.

60. Canada raises two separate challenges to the US benchmarks in its second submission. The first challenge relates solely to the benchmark developed for Saskatchewan. The second challenge relates to Commerce's inclusion of import prices in its benchmarks generally. We will discuss Canada's general challenge to the inclusion of import prices in the benchmarks before discussing Canada's specific challenge relating solely to Saskatchewan.

61. In developing its benchmarks, Commerce determined to use prices based on market conditions in Canada. Import log prices, like domestic log prices, reflect prices that purchasers in Canada paid for logs during the POI. Consequently, Commerce included import prices in its benchmarks. Despite the fact that these import prices are actual Canadian transaction prices, Canada argues that Commerce must ignore these prices. There is no basis, however, for doing so.

62. Moreover, Canada's claim that the import data are taken from an excessively broad tariff classification is misplaced. Canada collects data on several

categories of imports of "wood in the rough...Other, coniferous" - "Poles," "Piles and fence posts," "Logs for pulping," and "Other," (the "Other" category is broken down by species).[16] Logs used for lumber production thus fall into this last category, which was the *only* category Commerce included in its benchmarks. **Although Canada speculates that other higher value products may also have been included in this last category, the evidence is to the contrary. For example, Canada states that imports of high-value veneer logs would also fall into this category. But Quebec - the province with by far the largest value of log imports - reported that veneer mills in Quebec used zero imported softwood logs during the period of investigation.[17] Additionally, contrary to Canada's statement in paragraph 46 of its second submission, pulp log imports were reported separately by Statistics Canada and were not included in Commerce's calculation.**

63. With respect to Saskatchewan, Canada provided no data regarding prices of private log sales in the province, and – as Canada notes – only very limited data on log imports. Accordingly, there was insufficient data on prices for logs purchased by sawmills in Saskatchewan. Commerce therefore developed a proxy based on prices paid by mills in Canada for logs of the same species as found in Saskatchewan. As elsewhere, Commerce treated all log purchases consistently, irrespective of whether they were purchased from domestic or imported sources.

64. In sum, the United States developed market-determined benchmarks which included import prices, where available, for use in its pass-through analysis. As previously noted, Canada has failed to allege any WTO inconsistency in Commerce's development of the benchmark.

65. As a final point, there is an error in paragraph 39 of the second written submission of the United States. Specifically, the word "unsubsidized" should be deleted from the first sentence of that paragraph.

Commerce Properly Investigated Categories of Sales Identified by the DSB

66. As discussed in both our first and second written submissions, the two transaction categories subject to Commerce's pass-through analysis were the transactions identified in the DSB's recommendations and rulings. Consistent with those recommendations and rulings, Commerce properly conducted a pass-through analysis with respect to transactions between unrelated (i) independent harvesters and sawmills, and (ii) tenured timber harvesters/sawmills and non-tenured sawmills. Canada alleges that Commerce's investigation of the second of these categories was nothing more than a "creative way" for the United States to avoid its obligation to conduct the pass-through analysis contained in the DSB's recommendations and rulings.

---

[16] GOC 17 October 2003, Questionnaire Response at Exh. GOC-GEN-51 (relevant pages). Exhibit US – 11.

[17] GOC 28 June 2001, Questionnaire Response, Exhibit QC-S-5, at QC-11, and Quebec Exhibit 5. Exhibit US – 12.

67. Canada is wrong. The Appellate Body specifically defined the second category of transactions for which it recommended a pass-through analysis. The term "sawmill", the purchasing mill in the second category, was defined as "an enterprise that processes logs into softwood lumber *and does not hold a stumpage contract*".[18] The seller in the second category was specifically identified as a "tenured timber harvester/sawmill".[19]

68. Canada, in effect, asks this Panel to find that in evaluating whether there is compliance with the DSB's recommendations and rulings, the Panel should ignore the express language used in those recommendations and rulings. Canada's approach makes no sense. Instead, consistent with the DSB's recommendations and rulings, Commerce accorded those terms the definitions established by the DSB. This Panel should do the same.

CONCLUSION

69. In conclusion, we want to thank the Panel again for this opportunity to respond to Canada's arguments in its written submissions, and we look forward to responding to any questions that the Panel may have.

[18] Appellate Body Report, fn. 151 (emphasis added).
[19] Appellate Body Report, fn. 150 (emphasis added).

ANNEX C

SUBMISSIONS OF THIRD PARTIES

ANNEX C-1

THIRD PARTY SUBMISSION OF CHINA

17 March 2005

TABLE OF CONTENTS

Page

I. INTRODUCTION

1. China welcomes this opportunity to present its views in these proceedings involving the United States' compliance with the DSB recommendations and rulings in *United States – Final Countervailing Duty Determination With Respect to Certain Softwood Lumber from Canada*. China believes these proceedings relate to the correct understanding of Article 21.5 of the DSU and Article VI:3 of GATT 1994 as well as the rulings by the original Panel and the Appellate Body in the original dispute in which China has systemic interests.

2. In this third party submission, China will focus on the following two key issues:

(i) the threshold issue of whether the USDOC administrative review determination is properly before this Panel;

(ii) whether the five external factors identified by the USDOC can be used to exempt the US from conducting pass-through analysis as required by the rulings of the original panel and the Appellate Body with respect to sales of logs between tenured harvesters/sawmills and unrelated sawmills.

II. WHETHER THE USDOC ADMINISTRATIVE REVIEW DETERMINATION IS PROPERLY BEFORE THIS COMPLIANCE PANEL

A. The Threshold Issue Presented in These Proceedings

3. In the *Request for Establishment of A Panel*, Canada refers to the following measures by the US: (i) the Section 129 Determination[1]; and (ii) the First Administrative Review Determination (the "Review Determination")[2]. In its First Written Submission, Canada argues that the US, by adopting these "measures taken to comply", "continues to violate its obligations under Article VI:3 of the GATT 1994 and Articles 10 and 32.1 of the SCM Agreements"[3] and failed to implement the recommendations and rulings of the DSB. The US, in turn, request a preliminary ruling that the Review Determination is not a "measure[]

---

[1] *Notice of Implementation Under Section 129 of the Uruguay Round Agreements Act; Countervailing Measures Concerning Certain Softwood Lumber Products from Canada*, 69 Fed. Reg. 75,305; *Section 129 Determination: Final Countervailing Duty Determination, Certain Softwood Lumber from Canada*; *Notice of Amended Final Affirmative Countervailing Duty Determination and Notice of Countervailing Duty Order: Certain Softwood Lumber Products from Canada*, 67 Fed. Reg. 36,070.

[2] *Notice of Final Results of Countervailing Duty Administrative Review and Rescission of Certain Company-Specific Reviews: Certain Softwood Lumber Products from Canada*, 69 Fed. Reg. 75,917; and *Issues and Decision Memorandum*: *Final Results of Administrative Review: Certain Softwood Lumber Products from Canada*.

[3] First Written Submission of Canada, paras. 35~40.

taken to comply" and thus falls outside the scope of these Article 21.5 proceedings[4].

4. Thus, a threshold issue presented in this dispute is whether the Review Determination is properly before this compliance panel.

B. *Terms of Reference of An Article 21.5 Panel*

5. In China's view, WTO jurisprudence establishes that the mandate of an Article 21.5 panel is subject to two limitations.

6. First, the mandate of a compliance panel shall be confined by the coverage of the measures referred to by the complaining party in its panel request. If the parties to a dispute do not agree otherwise, a compliance panel, as an ordinary panel, shall have the standard terms of reference set forth in Article 7.1 of the DSU. Specifically, the outer edge of the terms of reference of a compliance panel shall be the scope of the panel request by the complaining party at a given dispute. This has been confirmed by many compliance panels.[5]

7. Second, the mandate of a compliance panel shall be limited by the scope of "measures taken to comply" with DSB recommendations and rulings. The Appellate Body in *Canada – Aircraft (Article 21.5 – Brazil)* held that,

> Proceedings under Article 21.5 do not concern just *any* measure of a Member of the WTO; rather, Article 21.5 proceedings are limited to those "measures *taken to comply* with the recommendations and rulings" of the DSB[6]. (original emphasis)

In *EC - Bed Linen (21.5)*, the Appellate Body explicitly stated that "[i]f a *claim* challenges a *measure* which is not a 'measure taken to comply', that *claim* cannot properly be raised in Article 21.5 proceedings."[7] (Original Emphasis)

8. Practically, there may be fewer disputes over whether a measure is cited by the complaining party in its panel request. Rather, many of the disputes rest with whether a particular measure, although cited by the complaining party, is a "measure[] taken to comply". This is exactly the case in this dispute.

C. *China's Views on The Threshold Issue*

9. In these proceedings, both parties seem to have no dispute on whether the Review Determination was cited by Canada in its panel request. As noted on the document WT/DS257/19, the parties to this dispute agreed that the Panel should have standard terms of reference. As a result, the Panel's terms of reference shall be defined by Canada's Request for Establishment of a Panel (WT/DS257/15). In that document, Canada manifestly referred to the Review Determination issued

---

[4] First Submission and Request for Preliminary Ruling of the United States (the "First Submission of the US"), para. 12.

[5] *EC - Bananas (21.5)*, WT/DS27/RW/ECU, para.6.5; *Australia - Leather (21.5)*, WT/DS126/RW, para.6.3.

[6] *Canada – Aircraft (Article 21.5 – Brazil)*, WT/DS70/AB/RW, para 36.

[7] *EC - Bed Linen (21.5)*, WT/DS141/AB/RW, para.78.

by the USDOC. However, "Article 21.5 proceedings are limited to those 'measures *taken to comply* with the recommendations and rulings' of the DSB"[8] and "it is, ultimately, for an Article 21.5 panel — and not for the complainant or the respondent — to determine which of the measures listed in the request for its establishment are "measures taken to comply"[9]. Therefore, the threshold issue in this dispute is whether the Review Determination cited by Canada in its panel request is properly before this panel.

10. In this dispute, it may be argued, on the one hand, that the Review Determination was made in a totally separate investigation procedure and based on the import data that is irrelevant to that of the original investigation. On the other hand, it is arguable that the two determinations at issue were made under the framework of the same set of proceedings which effectively affects import of softwood lumber from Canada and the Review Determination supersedes the Section 129 Determination. In China's view, the first argument relates to the question of whether the Review Determination is a "measure[] taken to comply" while the second argument concerns the matter whether the Section 129 Determination is rendered non-existent.

11. Initially, the Review Determination may not be properly categorized as a "measure[] taken to comply". This point has been elaborated by the US in its First Submission. The date of commencement of the review process was well before the date when the DSB adopted the panel and Appellate Body report. The Review Determination was not issued under the US domestic proceedings that are specifically enacted to address its violation of WTO rules concerning a countervailing duty measure (Section 129(b) of the *Uruguay Round Agreements Act*).

12. However, in China's view, the fact that the Review Determination is not a "measure[] taken to comply" does not lead to a decisive answer to the question of whether this measure is properly before this panel. China recalls that, on the basis of the plain language of Article 21.5, the purpose of the proceedings under this provision is to review and solve the dispute on "the *existence* or *consistency* with a covered agreement of measures taken to comply with the recommendations and rulings" of the DSB. China believes that "existence" and "consistency" are two distinct aspects of the subject measure. The latter involves review that is not only "limited to 'the issue of whether or not [a Member] has implemented the DSB recommendation'"[10], but also "in the light of any provision of any of the covered agreements."[11] On the other hand, the former relates to the status of the revised new measure. Both aspects are equally important though the "existence" matter is crucial in solving the threshold issue in these proceedings.

13. The dispute of *Australia – Automotive Leather (21.5 – US)* demonstrates similar fact pattern that deserves the reference by this Panel. In that dispute, Australia, subsequent to the DSB recommendations and rulings, ordered the repayment of the grants of A$8.065 million from Howe on 14 September 1999 and

---

8 *Canada – Aircraft (Article 21.5 – Brazil)*, WT/DS70/AB/RW, para 36.

9 *EC Bed Linen (Article 21.5 – India)*, WT/DS141/AB/RW, para 78.

10 *Canada - Aircraft (21.5)*, WT/DS70/AB/RW, para.40.

11 *Australia - Salmon (21.5)*, WT/DS18/RW, para.7.10.

reported to the DSB that it had carried out the recommendations and rulings of the DSB. However, on the same date, Australia provided a loan of A$13.65 million on non-commercial terms to Howe's parent company, ALH. The U.S. requested an Article 21.5 panel and submitted that "it is clear that if the Panel can determine the "existence" of measures taken to comply with the ruling, it can consider whether the measures purportedly taken to comply were effectively rendered non-existent".[12] Australia maintained that the loan of A$13.65 was not part of the implementation of the DSB's rulings and recommendations which was not even notified to the DSB.[13] In considering this issue, the compliance panel said,

> The 1999 loan is inextricably linked to the steps taken by Australia in response to the DSB's ruling in this dispute, in view of both its timing and its nature. In our view, the 1999 loan cannot be excluded from our consideration without **severely limiting** our ability to judge, on the basis of the United States' request, whether Australia has taken measures to comply with the DSB's ruling. In the absence of any compelling reason to do so, we decline to conclude that a measure specifically identified in the request for establishment is not within our terms of reference. [14].

In China's view, in an Article 25.1 procedure, if the complaining party submits that a "measure[] taken to comply" is invalidated by a subsequent measure, the compliance panel should at least assess this claim that relates to the "measure[] taken to comply" on the basis of relevant facts – the subsequent measure. To exclude the second measure would put the panel at the risk of failing to make a comprehensive and well-founded judgement on the **existence** of a measure taken to comply with DSB recommendations and rulings.

14. As China understands, the US applies a retrospective countervailing duty assessment system. Under such a system, the results of a review (if conducted), not only determine the duty that shall be assessed on the goods imported during the period of review, but also establish the amount of cash deposit for future imports of the subject product following the review. In this sense, the results of a review may be deemed to replace the original determination except in certain extraordinary cases (e.g., in case where the amount of subsidization found to be zero in a review the result of which will not lead to the termination of the original determination). Thus, China believes, due to the countervailing duty assessment system adopted by the US, the results of an administrative review may, at least in form, replace the original final determination.

15. In the particular factual circumstance of this dispute, the Review Determination was announced ten days after the Section 129 Determination took effect. Thus, the Review Determination established a new rate for cash deposit for the goods from Canada and replaced the rate in the Section 129 Determination. Such changes in the applicable duty rate deserve further consideration on

---

[12] *Australia – Automotive Leather (21.5 – US)*, WT/DS126/RW, para. 6.2.

[13] *Australia – Automotive Leather (21.5 – US)*, WT/DS126/RW, para. 6.1.

[14] *Australia – Automotive Leather (21.5 – US)*, WT/DS126/RW, paras. 6.5.

whether the Review Determination, **in substance**, rendered the non-existence of the Section 129 Determination. Therefore, China is of the view that the facts presented by Canada in these proceedings, at least, have demonstrated that there is likelihood that the Review Determination may nullify the Section 129 Determination.

16. On the basis of the above, it follows that if the Review Determination is found not to be a "measure[] taken to comply", it is still of importance to establish whether, as a matter of fact, the Section 129 Determination is nullified by the Review Determination and therefore, no "measure[] taken to comply" exists. In China's opinion, in order to perform the duty of "mak[ing] an objective assessment of the matter before it" as required by Article 11 of the DSU, it is advisable for the Panel to keep the Review Determination within its terms of reference instead of disregarding it at the very beginning of the procedure. In the meantime, however, China wishes to emphasize that, if the Review Determination is held not to be a measure taken to comply, the panel need only review the Review Determination to the extent that it can make a ruling on whether the Section 129 Determination was rendered non-existent and it is not the task of this Panel to review the Review Determination as a "measure[] taken to comply" in parallel with the Section 129 Determination.

17. Furthermore, it has been consistently ruled by compliance panels that it may be appropriate to consider events occurring until the date of panel request.[15] Such a view supports the position that this Panel should consider the Review Determination, as relevant facts, which happened prior to the panel request.

18. In summary, China is of the opinion that, although the Review Determination may not be a measure taken to comply, it is closely linked to and may have an important effect on the existences of the purported measure taken to comply – the Section 129 determination. On such basis, China believes it is the mandate of this Panel to consider the Review Determination in these proceedings. China suggests that the Panel may assess: (i) whether Section 129 Determination fully implements the DSB recommendations and rulings and is consistent with the covered agreements; and (ii) if it does, whether the Review Determination invalidates the Section 129 Determination and consequently renders the non-existence of the latter.

III. WHETHER "ARM'S-LENGTH TRANSACTION" AND "NON-AFFILIATION" ARE ONE AND THE SAME CONDITION OR TWO SEPARATE CONDITIONS TO NECESSITATE A PASS-THROUGH ANALYSIS

19. In its First Written Submission, Canada argues that the US failed to conduct pass-through analysis for three reasons, one of which is the USDOC imposed two conditions to limit the number of log transactions requiring analysis.

[15] See, *e.g.*, *EC – Bed Linen (21.5)*, WT/DS141/RW, para. 6.28; *US – Shrimp (21.5)*, WT/DS58/RW, paras. 5.12~5.13.

These two conditions are: (i) the transacting parties are unrelated; and (ii) none of the external factors identified by the USDOC exists.[16] The US, in its First Submission, does not deny its application of these two conditions.[17]

20. In the following, China would like to share with the parties to this dispute as well as this Panel its views on this disputed issue.

A. The Analysis of the Appellate Body

21. In the course of reaching its conclusion, the Appellate Body largely relied on the interpretation of Article VI:3 of the GATT 1994. In its report, the Appellate Body stated that,

> The phrase "subsid[ies] bestowed ... indirectly", as used in Article VI:3, implies that financial contributions by the government to the production of inputs used in manufacturing products subject to an investigation are not, in principle, excluded from the amount of subsidies that may be offset through the imposition of countervailing duties on the processed product. Where the producer of the input is **not the same entity** as the producer of the processed product, it cannot be presumed, however, that the subsidy bestowed on the input passes through to the processed product. In such case, it is necessary to analyze to what extent subsidies on inputs may be included in the determination of the total amount of subsidies bestowed upon processed products. For it is only the subsidies determined to have been granted upon the processed products that may be offset by levying countervailing duties on those products.[18] (original emphasis in italic and added emphasis in bold)

The Appellate Body seemed to be of the view that if subsidies are bestowed on an entity different from the producer of the subject product, pass-through of subsidies cannot be presumed. In this respect, the Appellate Body did not emphasize that the transactions between the two entities shall be free of interference by any external factor. In addition, the Appellate Body found further supports from the definition of subsidy in Article 1 of the SCM Agreement as well as its interpretation of "benefit" in Canada – Aircraft.[19] In such analysis, the Appellate Body also focused on whether the cumulative condition in Article 1 of the SCM Agreement are met for the producer of the subject products and whether the producer of the subject product is an indirect recipient. All such legal analysis, in China's view, relies on the presumption that the two entities, producer of the input and producer of the subject product, are not the same entity.

---

[16] First Written Submission of Canada, paras. 53 and 59.

[17] See the First Submission of the US, para. 34. The US argues that "[c]ontrary to Canada's arguments, nothing in the SCM Agreement, the GATT 1994, or the DSB's recommendations and rulings supports Canada's argument that an arm's-length analysis should be restricted to, in essence, a per se test based on affiliation alone".

[18] *US – Lumber CVDs Final*, WT/DS257/AB/R, Para. 140.

[19] *US – Lumber CVDs Final*, WT/DS257/AB/R, Paras. 142~143

22. The Appellate Body, in its analysis, did mention from time to time the term "arm's-length transactions". However, it did not put forward the implication of this term. Neither did it base its analysis on the presumption that the transactions at issue are free from influence by any external factors.

B. The Rulings of the Original Panel and the Appellate Body

23. Paragraph 167(e) of the Appellate Body Report is as follows,

> *upholds* the Panel's finding, in paragraph 7.99 of the Panel Report, that USDOC's failure to conduct a pass-through analysis in respect of arm's length sales of logs by tenured harvesters/sawmills to unrelated sawmills is inconsistent with Articles 10 and 32.1 of the SCM Agreement and Article VI:3 of the GATT 1994;

This ruling does mention the terms "arm's length sales" and "unrelated" in parallel. However, referring to paragraph 7.99 of the original Panel Report would easily exclude any potential confusion that may be caused by the use of these two terms, which reads,

> We therefore conclude that, for the reasons set forth above, the USDOC's failure to conduct a pass-through analysis in respect of logs sold by tenure-holding timber harvesters (whether or not also lumber producers) to **unrelated** sawmills producing subject softwood lumber; (emphasis added)

The above ruling does not refer to "arm's-length transactions" as an extra condition to necessitate pass-through analysis. The condition is only that the tenure-holding timber harvesters are unrelated to sawmills. If the Appellate Body intended to insert "arm's-length transaction" as an addition condition, it should have said so and should have partially reversed the original panel's ruling on this matter. Therefore, the term "arm's-length transactions" in the ruling of the Appellate Body can be understood to bear the same meaning as that of "unrelated".

C. China's View on the Issue of Pass-through

24. In China's view, under the particular factual circumstances of this dispute and the countervailing duty investigation on softwood lumber, it is not necessary to satisfy the test of five external factors identified by the USDOC in order to require for a pass-through analysis.

25. First, China agrees with the analysis by the Appellate Body that an instance that require for pass-through analysis is one where the direct recipient of the subsidies at issue is not the same entity as the producer of the countervailed subject product. In this respect, the meaning of the so-called "same entity" is obvious – both entities are not related to or affiliated with each other in any other way so that they cannot be treated as one and the same. Such an instance does not imply that the transactions at issue should be free of interference by any of the five external factors identified by the USDOC.

26. Second, it is possible that the five external factors may affect the transactions between the separate entities and thereby influence the pass-through of the direct subsidies on the production of logs. For example, due to limitations on log sales in Crown tenure contracts, the tenured harvester may not sell its products to the sawmills at fair market value. As a result, the transaction price may be lower than fair market value through which, subsidies on logs pass through to the production of the subject products. In China's view, it is the external factors and, potentially, other unknown factors that cause the transaction price to be below fair market value and thereby, result in pass-through of subsidies.

27. China further submits that the influence by any external factor can be fully taken into account if a proper pass-through test is carried out. By choosing a permissible market benchmark, the investigating authorities could precisely calculate the part of benefits that are passed through to the purchasers of logs. Conversely, if the investigating authorities rule that, due to the existence of external factors, pass-through of subsidies need not be analyzed and can be presumed in its totality, the calculated subsidy amount would not reflect the actual amount of benefits that are actually bestowed indirectly on the production of the subject product. Such an approach would most likely lead to imposition of countervailing duty in excess of subsidies bestowed "directly, or indirectly" on the subject product in violation of Article VI:3 of the GATT 1994.

28. On the basis of the above, China is of the view that the five external factors identified by the USDOC could not exempt the US from conducting pass-through analysis with respect to sales of logs between unrelated harvesters/sawmills and sawmills.

IV. CONCLUSION

29. In conclusion, China is of the following views:

(i) Although the Review Determination may not be a measure taken to comply with the DSB recommendations and rulings at issue, it is closely linked to and may have an important effect on the existences of the purported "measure[] taken to comply" – the Section 129 determination; it is the mandate of this Panel to consider the Review Determination in these proceedings from the perspective of whether it invalidates the Section 129 Determination;

(ii) The five external factors identified and applied by the USDOC in the Section 129 Determination could not exempt the U.S. from conducting pass-through analysis as required by the rulings of the original panel and the Appellate Body with respect to sales of logs between unrelated harvesters/sawmills and sawmills.

ANNEX C-2

ORAL STATEMENT OF CHINA

21 April 2005

INTRODUCTION

1. Mr. Chairman, members of the Panel, it is our great honor to appear before you today to present the views of China as a third-party to these proceedings. As the Panel already has our written submission, we do not intend to restate all the comments contained in that document. Rather, we seek to offer the Panel a concise synopsis of the views of China in regards to the current dispute between Canada and the United States. In short, the issues we will focus on today pertain to (1) whether the administrative Review Determination of the US Department of Commerce is properly within the mandate of this Panel and (2) whether the five external factors identified by the US Department of Commerce exempt the US from conducting a pass through analysis as required by the original Panel and the Appellate Body in their rulings.

USDOC ADMINISTRATIVE REVIEW DETERMINATION

2. China is of the opinion that the mandate of an Article 21.5 panel is subject to two limitations. First, the mandate of a compliance panel shall be confined by the coverage of the measures referred to by the complaining party in its panel request. Second, as held by the Appellate Body in *Canada - Aircraft (Article 21.5 – Brazil)*, "Article 21.5 proceedings are limited to those 'measures taken to comply with the recommendations and rulings of' the DSB."[1]

3. Applying the first limitation to this dispute, it seems indisputable that Canada specifically and explicitly refers to the DOC's Administrative Review Determination in its panel request and therefore, this measure passes the test of the first limitation. However, to reiterate what was said above, the mandate of this Panel shall be limited to those "measures taken to comply with the recommendations and rulings" of the DSB.

4. In this regard, given the facts of this dispute, China tends to agree with the US that the Review Determination may not be properly categorized as a "measure taken to comply". However, while China does not consider the Review Determination to be a "measure taken to comply," it also does not believe that a decisive answer has yet been reached in regards to whether the Review Determination is properly before this Panel. The underlying purpose of these proceedings is to review and to resolve this particular dispute as to "the existence or consistency with a covered agreement of measures taken to comply with the recom-

[1] *Canada – Aircraft (Article 21.5 – Brazil),* WT/DS70/AB/RW, para.36.

mendations and rulings" of the DSB. Although the words "existence" and "consistency" are of equal importance, in this particular dispute, China surmises that the correct interpretation of "existence" will be crucial to the resolution of whether the Review Determination is properly before the Panel.

5. The dispute of *Australia – Automotive Leather (21.5 – US)* offers pertinent insight concerning such interpretation and deserves the attention of this Panel. In a similar fact pattern to the current dispute, Australia, on the one hand, ordered the repayment of a grant, a move that was purported to withdraw the illegal subsidy; while on the other hand, it provided a non-commercial loan to the parent company of the subsidy recipient. The United States requested an Article 21.5 panel. That compliance panel stated that the loan in dispute was "inextricably linked to the steps taken by Australia in response to the DSB's ruling...in view of both its timing and its nature".[2] The panel determined that the "loan cannot be excluded from our consideration without severely limiting our ability of judge, on the basis of the United State's request, whether Australia has taken measures to comply with the DSB's ruling".[3] Consequently, believing there to be no presence of a compelling reason to act otherwise, the panel declined "to conclude that a measure specifically identified in the request for establishment . . ."[4] was not in the panel's terms of reference.

6. Consequently, in China's view, because Canada has submitted that a "measure taken to comply" has been invalidated by a subsequent measure, this Panel should at least be allowed to assess the relationship between the Section 129 Determination and the Review Determination. To exclude such an assessment would put this Panel at the risk of failing to make a comprehensive and well-founded judgment as to the "existence" of a measure taken to comply with the relevant DSB recommendations and rulings.

7. Looking at the particular facts of this dispute, the Review Determination was announced ten days after the Section 129 determination took effect which resulted in the establishment of a new rate for the cash deposit for Canadian goods and replaced the rate in the Section 129 determination. Such facts warrant further consideration on whether these changes rendered the non-existence of the Section 129 determination.

8. For all the reasons above, China believes that while the Review Determination itself may not be classified as a "measure taken to comply," it is inextricably linked to the steps taken by the US in response to the DSB's ruling in both its timing and its nature. Because excluding the Review Determination would severely limit the Panel's ability to judge, upon Canada's request, whether the US has taken measures to comply with the DSB's rulings and recommendations, China concludes the Review Determination to be within this Panel's mandate.

---

2 *Australia – Automotive Leather (21.5 – US)*, WT/DS126,RW, para.6.5.

3 *Ibid.*

4 *Ibid.*

THE PASS-THROUGH ANALYSIS

9. We now turn briefly to the second issue of the dispute, namely that of the pass-through analysis conducted by the US. Specifically, the issue revolves around the DOC imposing two conditions that in effect limited the number of log transactions that were subjected to a pass-through analysis.

10. The DOC effectively required that relevant log transactions (1) be conducted between unrelated parties; and (2) satisfy an "arm's length transaction" test before a pass-through analysis was necessitated. As a result, the question ultimately becomes whether the phrases "arm's length transaction" and "unrelated" are one and the same or rather distinctive terminology.

11. In its report, the Appellate Body seemed to be of the view that if subsidies are bestowed on an entity different from the producer of the subject product, then a pass-through of subsidies cannot be presumed. However, the Appellate Body did not intimate that the transactions between the two entities had to be free of interference by external factors. Neither did it base its analysis on such a premise.

12. Referring specifically to paragraph 167(e) of the Appellate Body Report, in which the Appellate Body affirms the original Panel's finding with respect to sales of logs by tenured harvesters/sawmills to sawmills, the phrases "arm's length sales" and "unrelated" are mentioned in parallel. However, looking at paragraph 7.99 of the original Panel Report, which the Appellate Body has purportedly affirmed, there is no mention of the phrase "arm's length transactions" or "arm's length sales"; rather the only condition referenced is that the parties be unrelated. If the Appellate Body had intended to impose an extra condition, as the US actually did, it should have said so and partially reversed the original Panel's rulings. Therefore, China believes that the phrase "arm's length transactions" in the ruling of the Appellate Body should be construed to bear the same meaning as that of "unrelated".

13. Finally, China would like to present its own views on the five external factors identified by the US DOC. China believes that it is not necessary to satisfy this test of five external factors in order to require a pass-through analysis. China submits that an instance requiring a pass-through analysis is one where the direct recipient of the subsidies at issue is not the same entity as the producer of the countervailed subject product. Such an instance does not require the transactions to be free of influence by any external factors.

14. In addition, China believes that the five external factors may themselves be responsible for resulting in the pass-through of subsidies. However, to skip a pass-through analysis would presume that the subsidies are passed through in its entirety. Such an approach would most likely exaggerate the actual benefit indirectly bestowed on the subject product producers. China believes, by using an appropriate pass-through analysis, the effects of the five external factors can be fully accounted for without incorrectly calculating the actual amount of benefit on the subject product producers.

CONCLUSION

15. Mr. Chairman, that concludes the third-party statement of China. Thank you very much for the attention.

ANNEX C-3

THIRD PARTY SUBMISSION BY THE EUROPEAN COMMUNITIES
17 March 2005

TABLE OF CONTENTS

I. INTRODUCTION

1. The European Communities (EC) welcomes this opportunity to present its views in this DSU Article 21.5 proceeding. Canada claims that the United States has failed to implement the recommendations and rulings of the DSB in *United States –Lumber CVD Final*. The Appellate Body found that the countervailing duty imposed on softwood lumber was not based on a pass-through-analysis ensuring that the numerator is not artificially inflated through non-subsidised arm's length sales.[1]

2. The United States informed the DSB on 17 December that it had implemented its recommendations and rulings through a determination pursuant to Section 129(b) of the *Uruguay Round Agreements Act* ("Section 129 determination"). The Section 129 determination reduced the original rate of 18.79% to a rate of 18.62% (because of no pass-through in some cases) and was effective on 10 December 2004.[2] However, ten days later, the first administrative review[3] of the countervailing duty order kicked in, establishing a definitive countervailing duty rate for the period of review and replacing the amended Section 129 countervailing duty cash deposit rate with a new cash deposit rate (17.18%, not containing any reduction resulting from a lack of pass-through).[4]

---

1 Appellate Body Report, *United States – Lumber CVD Final*, adopted on 17 February 2004.

2 19 U.S.C. § 3538(b). *Final Countervailing Duty Determination, Certain Softwood Lumber from Canada*, 6 December 2004; *Notice of Implementation Under Section 129 of the Uruguay Round Agreements Act; Countervailing Measures Concerning Certain Softwood Lumber Products From Canada*, 69 Fed. Reg. 75,305 (Dep't Commerce 16 December 2004).

3 Referred to as the "assessment review" in the US First Written submission.

4 *Notice of Final Results of Countervailing Duty Administrative Review and Rescission of Certain Company-Specific Reviews: Certain Softwood Lumber Products from Canada*, 69 Fed. Reg. 75,917

3. Canada claims that the United States failed to implement the recommendations and rulings of the DSB because neither the Section 129 determination nor the administrative review carry out the pass-through analysis required by Articles VI:3 of the GATT 1994 and Articles 10 and 32.1 of the *SCM Agreement.*[5]

4. The United States has raised a preliminary objection contending that the administrative review is not a measure "taken to comply" within the meaning of Article 21.5 of the DSU and therefore not within the jurisdiction of this 21.5 Panel.[6] According to the United States, the administrative review is legally separate from the original investigation/ Section 129 determination and concerns new factual data.[7] The United States relies on *EC – Bed linen 21.5*, to argue that annual administrative review measures are entirely new determinations and therefore not a measure "taken to comply" within the scope of Article 21.5 proceeding.[8]

5. The EC considers that the US arguments are entirely misconceived. The US view (if accepted) would turn the US system of countervailing duty assessment into a moving target that escapes the WTO disciplines. Given that WTO jurisprudence is limited, the EC will confine this third party brief to this important jurisdictional question. As will be detailed below:

- Article 21.5 panels, in principle, have jurisdiction on all factual and legal matters relating to the resolution of the original dispute (as defined by that panel's terms of reference);

- The measure to be reviewed by this DSU Article 21.5 Panel is the continued application of a countervailing duty on the basis of the administrative review (superseding both the original determination and the Section 129 review).

6. This submission concludes that the Panel should dismiss the preliminary objection made by the United States. However, the EC wishes to clarify that it does not take a position on whether or not the administrative review complies with the recommendations and rulings of the DSB. The EC expects to provide its views on this substantive issue at the oral hearing (after having received the parties' rebuttal submissions).

II. THE SCOPE OF DSU ARTICLE 21.5 PROCEEDINGS

7. The scope of DSU Article 21.5 proceedings has several aspects that have not yet been fully clarified in WTO jurisprudence. Some jurisdictional issues relate to the claims that can be made in a DSU Article 21.5 proceeding. Here, the

---

(Dep't Commerce 20 December 2004); and *Issues and Decision Memorandum: Final Results of Administrative Review: Certain Softwood Lumber Products from Canada*, December 13, 2004.

[5] panel Request (WTDS257/15), Canada's First Written Submission, para. 72.

[6] US First Written Submission, para. 12.

[7] US First Written Submission, paras. 21-24.

[8] US First Written Submission, paras. 15-16.

Appellate Body has already clarified that panels are to review the "totality" of claims relating to the consistency of that measure with the covered agreements[9] (continuing violations, new violations and consequential violations of the covered agreements). The precise issue before this Panel is whether the phrase "taken to comply" limits the 21.5 Panel's jurisdiction to reviewing only a measure explicitly taken to comply (here the Section 129 review) as opposed to an administrative review.

8. Article 21.5 of the DSU provides in relevant part:

> Where there is disagreement as to the existence or consistency with a covered agreement of measures taken to comply with the recommendations and rulings such dispute shall be decided through recourse to these dispute settlement procedures, including wherever possible resort to the original panel. The panel shall circulate its report within 90 days after the date of referral of the matter to it. When the panel considers that it cannot provide its report within this time frame, it shall inform the DSB in writing of the reasons for the delay together with an estimate of the period within which it will submit its report.

9. Contrary to what the US argues, the phrase "taken to comply" cannot be read to limit the 21.5 proceeding to those measures that were explicitly taken to replace the measure at issue in the original proceedings. The phrase "taken to comply" must be read together with its immediate and broader context as well as the purpose of the DSU to reach a prompt solution of a dispute.

10. Most importantly, it is preceded by the term "existence" and followed by the expression "with the recommendations and rulings of the DSB". This suggests that the role of a 21.5 Panel is different from the task of an original Panel. While the original Panel is faced with a dispute relating to a precise measure, the 21.5 Panel is tasked to assess whether or not there is a failure to comply and whether or not the original dispute has been resolved.

11. Indeed, the broader purpose of Article 21.5 of the DSU is to secure the solution of a dispute between two WTO Members relating to the measures brought before the original Panel. This purpose is reflected in Article 3.3 of the DSU which reads;

> The prompt settlement of situations in which a Member considers that any benefits accruing to it directly or indirectly under the covered agreements are being impaired by measures taken by another Member is essential to the effective functioning of the WTO and the maintenance of a proper balance between the rights and obligations of Members.

12. Moreover, Article 3.7 of the DSU clarifies that Article 21.5 proceedings form part of the adjudication of an initial dispute by determining whether the

---

9 Appellate Body Report, *United States – Shrimp (21.5)* , para. 87.

defendant has withdrawn the measure or otherwise complied. Article 3.7 of the DSU reads:

> In the absence of a mutually agreed solution, the first objective of the dispute settlement mechanism is usually to secure the withdrawal of the measures concerned if these are found to be inconsistent with the provisions of any of the covered agreements. The provision of compensation should be resorted to only if the immediate withdrawal of the measure is impracticable and as a temporary measure pending the withdrawal of the measure which is inconsistent with a covered agreement. The last resort which this Understanding provides to the Member invoking the dispute settlement procedures is the possibility of suspending the application of concessions or other obligations under the covered agreements on a discriminatory basis vis-à-vis the other Member, subject to authorization by the DSB of such measures.

13. This particular nature of the DSU Article 21.5 proceeding was explicitly recognised by the Panel in *Australia – Salmon (21.5)* which even considered a measure taken during the Article 21.5 proceeding on the basis of the following consideration:

> To do otherwise would, in our view, go against the principle of prompt settlement of disputes and could hamper implementation of both DSB recommendations in the original dispute and our findings in this case.[10]

14. Although the Appellate Body has not yet been faced with the precise point at issue here, it has already confirmed the above principle in *Canada – Aircraft 21.5:*

> In our view, the phrase "measures taken to comply" refers to measures which have been, or which should be, adopted by a Member to bring about compliance with the recommendations and rulings of the DSB. In principle, a measure which has been "taken to comply with the recommendations and rulings" of the DSB will *not* be the same measure as the measure which was the subject of the original dispute, so that, in principle, there would be two separate and distinct measures34: the original measure which *gave rise* to the recommendations and rulings of the DSB, and the "measures taken to comply" which are – or should be – adopted to *implement* those recommendations and rulings.[11]

15. Moreover, the Appellate Body clarified in the accompanying footnote 34:

> We recognize that, where it is alleged that there exist *no* "measures taken to comply", a panel may find that there is *no* new measure.

---

[10] Panel Report, *Australia – Salmon (21.5)*, para. 7.21.

[11] Appellate Body Report, *Canada – Aircraft 21.5,* para. 36 (footnote omitted).

16. The Panel in *EC – Bed linen*, on which the United States relies, based itself explicitly on the *Australia – Salmon 21.5* case law and only discarded later review measures adopted by the EC as they were:

> not so clearly connected to the panel and Appellate Body reports concerned, both in time and in respect of the subject-matter, that any impartial observer would consider them to be measures "taken to comply".[12]

17. It is important to note that the two measures in *EC – Bed linen* were not dismissed from the scope of that 21.5 proceeding because they were "review measures". They were dismissed because they did not relate to the original dispute between the EC and India.

18. The EC submits that the case-by-case test applied by the Panel in *EC – Bed linen* should be further interpreted in line with the above considerations. In particular, it is the EC's submission that the scope of the 21.5 proceeding is determined by all aspects of the measure giving rise to the initial dispute. The purpose of the 21.5 proceeding is to determine whether or not the defendant has complied by either withdrawing that measure or bringing it otherwise in full compliance with the covered agreements. Whether a measure is taken to comply must then be decided on a case-to-case basis having regard to the original dispute (as defined by the terms of reference of the Panel) and the particular obligations of the covered agreement at issue.

19. As already confirmed by the DSU Article 21.5 Panel in *EC – Bed linen*, it is for the Panel alone to determine which measures it reviews when determining whether or not there is compliance.[13] Moreover, the appropriate date for assessing the compliance of a Member with the recommendations of the DSB is the date of establishment of the Article 21.5 panel.[14]

III. IS THE ADMINISTRATIVE REVIEW WITHIN THE SCOPE OF THIS PROCEEDING?

20. Canada claims that the United States failed to comply with the rulings and recommendations of the DSB (pass-through analysis) because none of the measures taken by the United States carries out such pass-through analysis.

21. The United States defends itself legally by arguing that the administrative review is a separate measure from the (i) original determination and (ii) Section 129 determination and, hence, not before the Panel.

22. The US view is based on the assumption that the measures to be attacked in countervailing duty cases are the determinations made by the investigating authorities. This is false. As is clarified in Article 10 of the *SCM Agreement*, the measure of concern is the "imposition of a countervailing duty", defined as a

---

[12] Panel Report, *EC – Bed linen 21.5*, para. 6.17.

[13] Panel Report, *EC – Bed linen 21.5*, para. 6.15.

[14] Panel Report, *United States – Shrimp 21.5*, paras. 5.12-5.13.

"special duty levied" for the purpose of offsetting a subsidy. The WTO Member imposing the countervailing duty is under the obligation to demonstrate through an investigation and determination that such duty is not "in excess of the ... subsidy" as required by Article VI:3 of the GATT 1994. Therefore, the accompanying determinations play a significant role in assessing whether the duty is in excess of a subsidy. However, it is the duty itself that interferes with trade and is the measure of concern. To the extent a countervailing duty is not imposed on the basis of a proper determination, it is incompatible with WTO law.[15]

23. The United States has a retrospective system of imposing countervailing duties. The administrative review at hand in this case is a hybrid instrument. It fixes the final duty rate for the assessment period with retrospective effect. It is similar to a retrospective assessment within the meaning of Article 9.3 of the *Anti-Dumping Agreement* and it certainly is not a fully-fledged review of both the subsidy and injury within the meaning of Article 21 of the *SCM Agreement*.[16] Significantly, the administrative review does not change the date of the expiry of the measure under Article 21.3. The administrative review happens to change the cash deposit rate provisionally for future imports, but only subject to a further annual review in the future.

24. While footnote 52 of the *SCM Agreement* recognises the existence of such annual reviews used in a retrospective system, it does not, as suggested by the United States[17], recognise that these types of administrative review are separate from the original determination (and or a Section 129 determination).

25. The United States has not disputed Canada's characterisation of the administrative review as *superseding* both the original countervailing duty determination and the Section 129 determination.[18] As explained by the United States, the Section 129 determination exclusively focused on the original investigation and partially redid it. However, that Section 129 determination was only in place for 10 days. It was then superseded by the administrative review which definitively fixed the duties for the relevant period. At the date of the establishment of the Panel (14 January 2005) only the administrative review was effectively in place.

26. According to WTO jurisprudence, a measure that essentially replaces an earlier measure remains within the terms of reference of an original Panel.[19] *A fortiori*, a 21.5 Panel must be in a position to assess whether an annual administrative review determination that confirms and supersedes the original determination relating to the same countervailing duty constitutes a "continuing violation".

27. Contrary to what the US attempts to argue, the Panel in *EC – Bed linen 21.5* does not stand for a general proposition that any review measure is outside the scope of a 21.5 proceeding. As noted already under point 17 above, the re-

---

[15] See description of the measure in Appellate Body Report, *United States – Lumber CVD Final*, para. 2.

[16] Panel Report *US – Softwood Lumber (Preliminary)*, para 7.151.

[17] US First Written Submission, para. 21 and footnote 23.

[18] Canada's First Written Submission.

[19] See most recently, Panel Report *Dominican Republic – Cigarettes*, paras. 7.11-7.21

view measures at issue in that case were entirely different in nature. The EC applies a prospective system of assessing duties and therefore does not carry out such annual administrative reviews. The measures at hand in *EC – Bed linen* were either specific reviews of anti-dumping duties imposed on exporters from other Members (Egypt and Pakistan) or entirely new determinations in a review based on results of an event subsequent to the EC having adopted the implementing measure in *EC – Bed linen.*

28. Also the final US argument that it would not be possible to fully assess a new set of facts relating to an assessment review, based on a wholly new administrative record, within the 90 day period prescribed by Article 21.5 and that therefore administrative reviews must be subject to a different proceeding[20], is without merit. The Appellate Body already recognised that the examination of an Article 21.5 measure can require assessment of a new set of facts.[21] The 90 day period reflects the right of the complaining Member to a prompt resolution of the original dispute by determining whether or not compliance exist before he may resort to suspension of concessions.

29. Accepting the US view that the administrative review is not subject to a DSU 21.5 Panel review would turn the US system of duty assessment into a moving target that escapes from countervailing duty disciplines. Each administrative review would have to be subject to a new panel request, and by the time the panel, Appellate Body and implementation procedure was completed, another administrative review would have overtaken the results of any Section 129 determination. A new panel would have to be started against this review, creating a "Groundhog Day" situation.

IV. CONCLUSION

30. For the above reasons, the EC considers that the Panel has full jurisdiction over the administrative review measure in this case and that the US preliminary objection should therefore be dismissed.

---

20 US First Written Submission, para. 90.

21 Appellate Body Report, *Canada – Aircraft 21.5*, para. 41. See also, Appellate Body Report, *United States – Shrimp 21.5*, para. 86.

ANNEX C-4

ORAL STATEMENT BY THE EUROPEAN COMMUNITIES
21 April 2005

TABLE OF CONTENTS

I. INTRODUCTION

Mr. Chairman, Members of the Panel, good afternoon, and thank you for providing the European Communities (EC) with an opportunity to present its views before you today.

1. The EC intervenes in this proceeding because of its systemic interest in the correct interpretation of the *SCM Agreement*, the GATT 1994 and the DSU. This dispute raises two key issues:

> What is a "measure taken to comply" within the meaning of Article 21.5 of the DSU?

> What are the substantive and procedural requirements for ensuring a proper analysis of pass-through?

II. MEASURE TAKEN TO COMPLY

2. The US continues to argue in its rebuttal submission that the administrative review is not a measure taken to comply.[1] Indeed, the US does nothing to defend the administrative review, but only focuses on the determination under Section 129. The EC regrets that it has not received Canada's rebuttal submission on the due date (although this is a right of third parties under Article 10 of the DSU).[2] The EC obtained Canada's rebuttal submission only this Tuesday after close of business, and had, therefore, only one working day to consider it.

3. From a first reading of Canada's submission, the EC can confirm that overall, it fully supports Canada's request to dismiss the US objection. Yet, the EC notes that there are some differences in the legal concepts on how to determine the scope of a DSU Article 21.5 proceeding.

---

1 US rebuttal submission, paras. 2 and 46.
2 Appellate Body, *US – FSC 21.5*, para. 251.

4. The EC refers to all its arguments made in its third party submission, which it will not repeat today. As detailed therein, the broad mandate of DSU Article 21.5 panels stems directly from the term "existence" of a measure taken to comply read in the light of the broader purpose of DSU Article 21.5 to secure a prompt solution of a dispute between WTO Members.[3] Canada also explicitly agreed with the EC's basic proposition that the jurisdiction of DSU Article 21.5 Panels must, therefore, be determined in a way that prevents implementation measures from becoming "moving targets".

5. There are different legal concepts on how to do this. Canada and China put much emphasis on the fact that the administrative review while not being the "measure taken to comply" undid the Section 129 determination and, therefore, falls (as a successor measure) under the Panel's purview.[4] While the EC agrees with this characterisation of the relationship between the administrative review and the Section 129 determination[5], it considers that this general procedural criterion (Panel's terms of reference also cover successor acts) is not exclusively determinative for the jurisdiction of this DSU 21.5 Panel.

6. Given the major systemic importance of this issue, in particular for the EC, the EC respectfully requests the Panel to give the third parties further opportunity to comment in detail on Canada's arguments on how to define the scope of an Article 21.5 proceeding through written questions.

7. Let me close today's observations on this point by noting that, ironically, the US, through its preliminary objection, brings itself into a catch-22 situation. If it rejects the consideration by the Panel of the administrative review as compliance measure, no measure taken to comply existed (because the Section 129 determination had expired before the establishment of the 21.5 Panel). The Panel's report could therefore be quite short.

III. PASS-THROUGH

8. Turning now to the key substantive issue in this dispute: pass-through. The US and Canada disagree whether the US investigating authorities have done enough in terms of procedure and substance to demonstrate that subsidies received by certain upstream producers were passed-through to the down-stream producer of lumber products.

9. The need to ensure a pass-through analysis is not written explicitly into the *SCM Agreement* but stems directly from the obligation of a WTO Member imposing a countervailing duty to comply with Article VI:3 of the GATT 1994, and Article 10 of the *SCM Agreement* which require that investigating authorities:

---

[3] EC Third Party Submission, paras. 10-18.

[4] Canada's rebuttal submission, para. 4, China's Third Party submission, para 12.

[5] EC Third Party Submission, paras. 2.and 25.

> before imposing countervailing duties, must ascertain the precise amount of a subsidy attributed to the imported products under investigation.[6]

10. There are different situations in which the need for a pass-through analysis may arise, e.g., whether a subsidy was extinguished following a transfer of ownership. This Panel is tasked to assess whether the US investigating authorities established that subsidies to input producers benefited the downstream producers of the processed product subject to the investigation.[7] The key question is whether the US investigating authorities established that benefits received by the input producers

> have been passed through, at least in part, from producers of logs to producers of softwood lumber (and remanufactured lumber) which are the products subject to the investigation.[8]

11. The US and Canada disagree on whether the approach taken by the US investigating authorities suffices to establish the correct amount of subsidisation.

12. The EC as a third party is not in a position to comment in detail on this fact-intensive issue before the Panel. However, it wishes to offer a few general comments:

13. As regards the test for pass-through, the main parties appear to disagree on the meaning of "arm's length", in particular, whether it refers exclusively to a "related person" test. The EC notes that neither of these two notions are set out anywhere in the *SCM Agreement*. The obligation of an investigating authority is to establish the precise amount of subsidisation benefiting the product on which a CVD is imposed in accordance with Article VI:3 of the GATT 1994.

14. The Appellate Body referred for contextual guidance to Article 19.3 of the *SCM Agreement* whereby countervailing duties "shall be levied, in the appropriate amounts in each case, on a non-discriminatory basis on imports of such product from all sources found to be subsidised and causing injury". The Appellate Body recognised that this provision gives investigating authorities broad discretion to choose between different means of demonstrating and calculating the amount of the subsidisation, in particular whether they resort to sampling, aggregate or company specific investigations.[9]

15. The precise methodological approach to determine pass-through (or better: the amount of benefit received by the producer of the target product) inevitably varies from case-to case. The pass-through is likely to be somewhere between 0 and 100% depending, amongst other things, on the relationship between the input supplier and the processor as well as the economic context. Where the producers of the input and the processed product form part of the same *economic entity*, it may be presumed that 100% of the subsidy passed through.[10] By con-

---

6 Appellate Body Report, US – Countervailing Measures on Certain EC Products, para. 139.

7 Appellate Body Report, US – Lumber, para. 146.

8 *Ibid.*, para. 147.

9 Appellate Body Report, US – Lumber, paras. 152-153.

10 *Ibid.* para. 142.

trast, where the input product was sold on a functioning market at arm's length and for fair market value, there is a presumption of 0% pass-through.[11]

16. The existence and amount of pass-through must be established on a case-by-case basis. While a number of different factors may be relevant, the EC considers that the price charged by the input supplier to the producers of the product (in comparison to some relevant benchmark) plays a key role in measuring to which extent (if at all) the subsidy benefited the producer of the processed product.

17. The discretion of investigating authorities on how to establish pass-through is (as always) limited by the general obligation of investigating authorities to carry out an objective and unbiased examination, and the need to ensure that the countervailing duties are imposed in "appropriate" amounts "in each case" and on a "non-discriminatory basis" from "all sources found to be subsidised".

18. Procedurally, the investigating authority must do its best to facilitate the pass-through examination, e.g., by preparing a questionnaire and offering a company-specific approach unless the number of respondents is too high to allow a meaningful individual examination to take place. In such cases sampling or similar techniques may be required.

19. The investigating authority must then provide an adequate and reasoned explanation why, on the basis of the information received, the amount of pass-through calculated in the individual case is appropriate and that its assessment of the facts on the record is objective and unbiased.

IV. CONCLUSION

20. Mr. Chairman, Members of the Panel, this concludes our oral statement. I thank you for your attention and stand ready to respond to any questions you may have.

[11] Appellate Body Report, US – CVD on Certain EC Products, WT/DS212, para. 126.

ANNEX D

REQUEST FOR ESTABLISHMENT OF A PANEL

Contents	Page

ANNEX D-1

REQUEST FOR ESTABLISHMENT OF A PANEL

WORLD TRADE ORGANIZATION

WT/DS257/15
4 January 2005

(05-0008)

Original: English

UNITED STATES – FINAL COUNTERVAILING DUTY DETERMINATION WITH RESPECT TO CERTAIN SOFTWOOD LUMBER FROM CANADA

Recourse to Article 21.5 of the DSU by Canada

Request for the Establishment of a Panel

The following communication, dated 30 December 2004, from the delegation of Canada to the Chairperson of the Dispute Settlement Body, is circulated pursuant to Article 21.5 of the DSU.

On 17 February 2004, the Dispute Settlement Body (DSB) adopted the Panel and Appellate Body reports in *United States – Final Countervailing Duty*

Determination with Respect to Certain Softwood Lumber from Canada.[1] The Panel and Appellate Body found that the US Department of Commerce (Commerce) was required to conduct a "pass-through" analysis in respect of arm's length sales of logs by tenured harvesters/sawmills[2] and independent harvesters to unrelated sawmills pursuant to the *General Agreement on Tariffs and Trade, 1994* (*GATT 1994*) and the *Agreement on Subsidies and Countervailing Measures* (*SCM Agreement*).

On 28 April 2004, Canada and the United States reached an agreement on a "reasonable period of time" pursuant to Article 21.3(b) of the *Understanding on Rules and Procedures Governing the Settlement of Disputes* (*DSU*).[3] The United States confirmed in this agreement that it would complete implementation no later than 17 December 2004.

Shortly after adoption of the Panel and Appellate Body reports, the United States commenced implementation proceedings pursuant to section 129(b) of the *Uruguay Round Agreements Act* (*URAA*).[4] On 6 December 2004, Commerce released a countervailing duty determination pursuant to section 129 that announced results of its purported "pass-through" analysis. On 10 December 2004, in accordance with an instruction of that date from the US Trade Representative to implement the determination, Commerce issued a notice of implementation of its section 129 determination, in which it announced that the countervailing duty cash deposit rate would be reduced, effective 10 December 2004, by 0.17 (*i.e.*, from 18.79 per cent to 18.62 per cent).[5] On 20 December 2004, with the publication of the final results of the first administrative review of the countervailing duty order, Commerce established a definitive countervailing duty rate for the period of review and replaced the amended section 129 countervailing duty cash deposit rate with a new cash deposit rate without any "pass-through" analysis.[6] At the DSB meeting of 17 December 2004, the United States informed the DSB that it had complied with its rulings and recommendations.

---

[1] Dispute Settlement Body, *Minutes of Meeting (17 February and 19 March, 2004)*, WT/DSB/M/165, 30 March 2004, at para. 49. Also See *United States – Final Countervailing Duty Determination with Respect to Certain Softwood Lumber from Canada*, Report of the Appellate Body, WT/DS257/AB/R, adopted 17 February 2004 ["Appellate Body Report"]; and *United States – Final Countervailing Duty Determination with Respect to Certain Softwood Lumber from Canada*, Report of the Panel, WT/DS257/R, adopted 17 February 2004.

[2] The Appellate Body used the term "tenured harvester/sawmill" to refer to an enterprise holding a stumpage contract that fells trees and produces logs, and also processes logs into softwood lumber. See Appellate Body Report, at fn. 150.

[3] *United States – Final Countervailing Duty Determination with Respect to Certain Softwood Lumber from Canada, Agreement under Article 21.3(b) of the DSU*, WT/DS257/13, 30 April 2004.

[4] 19 U.S.C. § 3538(b).

[5] *Section 129 Determination: Final Countervailing Duty Determination, Certain Softwood Lumber from Canada*, 6 December 2004; *Notice of Implementation Under Section 129 of the Uruguay Round Agreements Act; Countervailing Measures Concerning Certain Softwood Lumber Products From Canada*, 69 Fed. Reg. 75,305 (Dep't Commerce 16 December 2004).

[6] *Notice of Final Results of Countervailing Duty Administrative Review and Rescission of Certain Company-Specific Reviews: Certain Softwood Lumber Products from Canada*, 69 Fed. Reg. 75,917 (Dep't Commerce 20 December 2004); and *Issues and Decision Memorandum*: *Final Results of Administrative Review: Certain Softwood Lumber Products from Canada*, December 13, 2004.

Canada considers that the United States has failed to comply with the DSB's recommendations and rulings by incorrectly:

- limiting the category of transactions reviewed in the "pass-through" analysis to sales of logs by independent harvesters to unrelated sawmills, excluding transactions between harvesters/sawmills and unrelated sawmills, contrary to the DSB's recommendations and rulings;
- presuming, without an appropriate "pass-through" analysis, that certain transactions between independent harvesters and unrelated sawmills were not at arm's-length and that a "pass-through" of the alleged benefit occurred;
- applying the results of the "pass-through" analysis to a countervailing duty cash deposit rate invalidated as a result of judicial review proceedings conducted in accordance with US law, and failing to apply the results to a valid rate;[7] and
- failing to conduct a "pass-through" analysis in the final results of the first administrative review.[8]

Canada considers that the following measures allegedly taken by the United States to comply with the DSB's recommendations and rulings were inconsistent with US obligations under Articles 10 and 32.1 of the *SCM Agreement* and Article VI:3 of the *GATT 1994*:

- *Notice of Implementation Under Section 129 of the Uruguay Round Agreements Act; Countervailing Measures Concerning Certain Softwood Lumber Products from Canada*,[9] and *Section 129 Determination: Final Countervailing Duty Determination, Certain Softwood Lumber from Canada*;[10]
- *Notice of Amended Final Affirmative Countervailing Duty Determination and Notice of Countervailing Duty Order: Certain Softwood Lumber Products from Canada*;[11] and
- *Notice of Final Results of Countervailing Duty Administrative Review and Rescission of Certain Company-Specific Reviews: Certain Softwood Lumber Products from Canada*,[12] and *Issues and Decision Memorandum: Final Results of Administrative Review: Certain Softwood Lumber Products from Canada*.[13]

Accordingly, as there is a disagreement as to the existence or consistency with a covered agreement of the measures taken to comply with the rulings and

---

[7] *Section 129 Determination: Final Countervailing Duty Determination, Certain Softwood Lumber from Canada*, 6 December 2004, Comment 6, at 11.

[8] See e.g., *Issues and Decision Memorandum: Final Results of Administrative Review: Certain Softwood Lumber Products from Canada*, 13 December 2004, at 43-48.

[9] 69 Fed. Reg. 75,305 (Dep't Commerce December 16, 2004)

[10] 6 December 2004.

[11] 67 Fed. Reg. 36,070 (Dep't Commerce 22 May 2002).

[12] 69 Fed. Reg. 75,917 (Dep't Commerce 20 December 2004).

[13] 13 December 2004.

recommendations of the DSB, Canada seeks recourse to Article 21.5 of the DSU in this matter. Accordingly, Canada requests that a special meeting of the DSB be held on 14 January 2005 to consider the following agenda item:

> *United States – Final Countervailing Duty Determination with Respect to Certain Softwood Lumber from Canada*
>
> *Recourse by Canada to Article 21.5 of the Understanding on Rules and Procedures Governing the Settlement of Disputes.*

Canada requests that the DSB refer the matter to the original panel, if possible, pursuant to Article 21.5 of the DSU.

EUROPEAN COMMUNITIES – EXPORT SUBSIDIES ON SUGAR

Arbitration Under Article 21.3(c) of the Understanding on Rules and Procedures Governing the Settlement of Disputes

Award of the Arbitrator

WT/DS265/33, WT/DS266/33, WT/DS283/14

Circulated to Members on 28 October 2005

Parties:	Arbitrator:
Australia	A.V. Ganesan
Brazil	
European Communities	
Thailand	

TABLE OF CONTENTS

TABLE OF CASES CITED IN THIS AWARD

Short Title	Full Case Title and Citation
Argentina – Hides and Leather	Award of the Arbitrator, *Argentina – Measures Affecting the Export of Bovine Hides and Import of Finished Leather – Arbitration under Article 21.3(c) of the DSU*, WT/DS155/10, 31 August 2001, DSR 2001:XII, 6013
Canada – Patent Term	Award of the Arbitrator, *Canada – Term of Patent Protection – Arbitration under Article 21.3(c) of the DSU*, WT/DS170/10, 28 February 2001, DSR 2001:V, 2031
Canada – Pharmaceutical Patents	Award of the Arbitrator, *Canada – Patent Protection of Pharmaceutical Products – Arbitration under Article 21.3(c) of the DSU*, WT/DS114/13, 18 August 2000, DSR 2002:I, 3
Chile – Alcoholic Beverages	Award of the Arbitrator, *Chile – Taxes on Alcoholic Beverages – Arbitration under Article 21.3(c) of the DSU*, WT/DS87/15, WT/DS110/14, 23 May 2000, DSR 2000:V, 2583
Chile – Price Band System	Award of the Arbitrator, *Chile – Price Band System and Safeguard Measures Relating to Certain Agricultural Products – Arbitration under Article 21.3(c) of the DSU*, WT/DS207/13, 17 March 2003
EC – Bananas III	Award of the Arbitrator, *European Communities – Regime for the Importation, Sale and Distribution of Bananas – Arbitration under Article 21.3(c) of the DSU*, WT/DS27/15, 7 January 1998, DSR 1998:I, 3
EC – Export Subsidies on Sugar	Appellate Body Report, *European Communities – Export Subsidies on Sugar*, WT/DS265/AB/R, WT/DS266/AB/R, WT/DS283/AB/R, adopted 19 May 2005
EC – Export Subsidies on Sugar	Panel Reports, *European Communities – Export Subsidies on Sugar*, WT/DS265/R (*Australia*), WT/DS266/R (*Brazil*), WT/DS283/R (*Thailand*), adopted 19 May 2005, as modified by Appellate Body Report, WT/DS265/AB/R, WT/DS266/AB/R, WTDS283/AB/R

Short Title	Full Case Title and Citation
EC – Hormones	Award of the Arbitrator, *EC Measures Concerning Meat and Meat Products (Hormones) – Arbitration under Article 21.3(c) of the DSU,* WT/DS26/15, WT/DS48/13, 29 May 1998, DSR 1998:V, 1833
EC – Tariff Preferences	Award of the Arbitrator, *European Communities – Conditions for the Granting of Tariff Preferences to Developing Countries – Arbitration under Article 21.3(c) of the DSU*, WT/DS246/14, 20 September 2004
Indonesia – Autos	Award of the Arbitrator, *Indonesia – Certain Measures Affecting the Automobile Industry – Arbitration under Article 21.3(c) of the DSU,* WT/DS54/15, WT/DS55/14, WT/DS59/13, WT/DS64/12, 7 December 1998, DSR 1998:IX, 4029
Korea – Alcoholic Beverages	Award of the Arbitrator, *Korea – Taxes on Alcoholic Beverages – Arbitration under Article 21.3(c) of the DSU*, WT/DS75/16, WT/DS84/14, 4 June 1999, DSR 1999:II, 937
US – 1916 Act	Award of the Arbitrator, *United States – Anti-Dumping Act of 1916 – Arbitration under Article 21.3(c) of the DSU*, WT/DS136/11, WT/DS162/14, 28 February 2001, DSR 2001:V, 2017
US – Gambling	Award of the Arbitrator, *United States – Measures Affecting the Cross-Border Supply of Gambling and Betting Services – Arbitration under Article 21.3(c) of the DSU*, WT/DS285/13, 19 August 2005
US – Offset Act(Byrd Amendment)	Award of the Arbitrator, *United States – Continued Dumping and Subsidy Offset Act of 2000 – Arbitration under Article 21.3(c) of the DSU*, WT/DS217/14, WT/DS234/22, 13 June 2003
US – Oil Country Tubular Goods Sunset Reviews	Award of the Arbitrator, *United States – Sunset Reviews of Anti-Dumping Measures on Oil Country Tubular Goods from Argentina – Arbitration under Article 21.3(c) of the DSU*, WT/DS268/12, 7 June 2005
US – Section 110(5) Copyright Act	Award of the Arbitrator, *United States – Section 110(5) of the US Copyright Act – Arbitration under Article 21.3(c) of the DSU*, WT/DS160/12, 15 January 2001, DSR 2001:II, 657

I. INTRODUCTION

1. On 19 May 2005, the Dispute Settlement Body (the "DSB") adopted the Appellate Body Report[1] and the Panel Report[2], as modified by the Appellate Body Report, in *European Communities – Export Subsidies on Sugar*.[3] At the meeting of the DSB held on 13 June 2005, the European Communities stated that it intended to comply with the recommendations and rulings of the DSB in this dispute, and that it would need a reasonable period of time in which to do so.[4]

2. On 9 August 2005, Australia, Brazil and Thailand (the "Complaining Parties") informed the DSB that consultations with the European Communities had not resulted in an agreement on the reasonable period of time for implementation. The Complaining Parties therefore requested that such period be determined through binding arbitration, pursuant to Article 21.3(c) of the *Understanding on Rules and Procedures Governing the Settlement of Disputes* (the "DSU").[5]

3. On 30 August 2005, the Complaining Parties and the European Communities requested me to act as Arbitrator, pursuant to Article 21.3(c) of the DSU, to determine the reasonable period of time for implementation of the recommendations and rulings of the DSB in this dispute. I accepted the appointment on 5 September 2005[6], and undertook to issue my award no later than 1 November 2005, the period of time that had been agreed between the parties.

4. In a letter to me dated 6 September 2005, the European Communities made certain requests concerning the sequencing in the filing of submissions by the parties; allocation of time for the opening statement of the European Communities at the oral hearing; and the date of circulation of the arbitral award. By a letter dated 7 September 2005[7], Australia, Brazil and Thailand were invited to submit their views on the European Communities' requests, which views I received on 12 September 2005.[8] I responded to these requests in a letter dated 13 September 2005, in which I undertook to issue my award no later than 28 October 2005.

5. The 90 day period following adoption of the Panel and Appellate Body Reports has expired on 17 August 2005. The parties have confirmed that my award, circulated no later than 28 October 2005, shall be deemed to be the award of the arbitrator for the purpose of Article 21.3(c) of the DSU, notwithstanding the expiry of the 90 day period stipulated in Article 21.3(c).

6. The European Communities filed its written submission on 21 September 2005; the Complaining Parties each filed its written submission on 28 September 2005. By a letter dated 4 October 2005, Thailand requested authorization to

---

[1] Appellate Body Report, WT/DS265/AB/R, WT/DS266/AB/R, WT/DS283/AB/R.

[2] Panel Report, WT/DS265/R, WT/DS266/R, WT/DS283/R.

[3] WT/DS265/29, WT/DS266/29, WT/DS283/10.

[4] WT/DSB/M/191, para. 19.

[5] WT/DS265/30, WT/DS266/30, WT/DS283/11.

[6] WT/DS265/31, WT/DS266/31, WT/DS283/12.

[7] Letter from the Director of the Appellate Body Secretariat to the Parties, dated 7 September 2005.

[8] Joint letter from Australia, Brazil, and Thailand, dated 12 September 2005.

make a "typographical correction" to its submission, such that it would add the word "related" to the fifth sentence of paragraph 77 on page 23 of its submission, so that it would read "... 1.5 million farmers' and sugar-*related* workers' households" (underlining added). By a letter dated 5 October 2005, I invited the other parties to comment on Thailand's request. None of the other parties objected to Thailand's request. By a letter dated 7 October 2005, I authorized Thailand to make the requested correction to its submission.

7. An oral hearing was held on 10 October 2005. The parties presented oral arguments and responded to the questions posed by me. During the hearing, Brazil presented an additional exhibit, and the European Communities presented two additional exhibits. Australia requested that I disregard the European Communities' additional exhibits. I provided the parties the opportunity to submit their written comments on the exhibits at issue, if they so wished. Brazil and the European Communities submitted their comments the day following the hearing, serving a copy to the other parties.

II. ARGUMENTS OF THE PARTIES

A. European Communities

8. The European Communities requests that I determine the "reasonable period of time" for implementation of the recommendations and rulings of the DSB in this dispute to be 19 months and 12 days from 19 May 2005, the date of adoption by the DSB of the Panel and Appellate Body Reports, that is to say, a period of time expiring on 1 January 2007.[9]

9. As a fundamental general principle, the European Communities emphasizes that "it is the prerogative of the implementing Member to select the means of implementation [of the recommendations and rulings of the DSB] which it deems most appropriate"[10], that "the implementing Member is entitled to choose the method which it deems most appropriate"[11], and that "an Arbitrator cannot prescribe any particular implementation method"[12], as "the selection of the implementing measure ... is the prerogative of the implementing Member".[13]

10. The European Communities' assessment of the "reasonable period of time" required for implementation is based on the following seven sets of "particular circumstances" of the case.

11. First, the European Communities submits that "[t]he measures in the underlying panel proceedings were contained in Council Regulation 1260/2001 and implementing and related instruments"[14], and that, therefore, implementation in the present case requires the adoption of a regulation by the Council of the Euro-

---

9 European Communities' written submission, para. 95.

10 *Ibid.*, paras. 22 and 36.

11 European Communities' statement at the oral hearing.

12 *Ibid.*

13 *Ibid.*

14 European Communities' written submission, para. 30.

pean Union (the "Council"), followed by the adoption of implementing regulations by the European Commission (the "Commission"). Under the present Council Regulation 1260/2001, the Commission has no legal authority to "limit the exports of C sugar on the ground that such exports exceed the reduction commitments."[15] As a result, according to the European Communities, "to the extent that the Commission has no control over the exports of C sugar, it cannot ensure compliance with the recommendations and rulings of the DSB."[16] The European Communities also argues that if it refuses to grant export licences for exporting C sugar, it would act inconsistently with Article XI of the *General Agreement on Tariffs and Trade 1994*.[17]

12. The European Communities contends that even if the Commission had the authority to limit export of C sugar, this circumstance would not be dispositive for the purpose of establishing the "reasonable period of time" in the present dispute. This is because the European Communities, as the implementing Member, is entitled to choose the means of implementation which it deems most appropriate. Among "many different ways" available to the European Communities to ensure compliance with its reduction commitments, the European Communities may legitimately choose a method that acts "upon the underlying factors which, under the current regime, cause the subsidized exports, such as the level of domestic prices, the volume of production quotas, or the availability of alternative uses for sugar, rather than by placing restrictions on the exports themselves".[18]

13. The second set of particular circumstances, according to the European Communities, is that, as its sugar regime is "complex" and "all its components are ... closely connected and interdependent"[19], it considers that "[a]n implementation method which addresses the structural causes of the subsidized exports of sugar would serve best the objectives of the *Agreement on Agriculture* ..."[20], even if it may require a longer implementation period. Keeping this in view, after a careful assessment of all the options available, the Commission has submitted a proposal to the Council on 22 June 2005 for a new Council regulation, based on an approach that aims at "preserving some level of support for the beet farmers and sugar producers while at the same time minimising the production of export-

---

[15] European Communities' written submission, para. 33. (footnote omitted) The European Communities' sugar regime provides for quota sugar and non-quota sugar. Quota sugar is composed of A quota sugar and B quota sugar. Quota sugar is the maximum quantity of sugar eligible for domestic price support and direct export subsidies. Quotas are allocated on an annual basis to individual European Communities Member States who, in turn, allocate shares of their national quotas to individual undertakings. Sugar produced over and above the A and B quota is referred to as C sugar; such sugar may not be sold on the domestic market and must be exported. However, an undertaking may decide to "carry forward" C sugar into the next marketing year. In that event, the undertaking need not export C sugar and may sell that C sugar in the next marketing year on the domestic market as quota sugar. However, such carry forward of C sugar is subject to a quantitative limit; this limit is currently set at 20 per cent of the A quota.

[16] European Communities' written submission, para. 35.

[17] *Ibid.*, para. 33; European Communities' statement at the oral hearing.

[18] European Communities' written submission, para. 36.

[19] *Ibid.*, para. 40.

[20] *Ibid.*, para. 41.

able surpluses."[21] According to the European Communities, a "comprehensive and coherent legal system" will have to be devised by the European Communities' legislator[22], but, regardless of which specific option is ultimately chosen, the implementing measures are "likely to be technically complex".[23]

14. Thirdly, the European Communities submits that a Council regulation repealing, amending or replacing the current Council Regulation 1260/2001 would have to be based on Articles 36 and 37 of the Treaty Establishing the European Community (the "EC Treaty"). Consequently, the following procedural steps are necessary: submission of a Commission proposal to the Council; opinions of the European Parliament and of the Economic and Social Committee of the European Community (the "EESC") to the Council; consultations with the African, Caribbean and Pacific ("ACP") countries; and, finally, the adoption of a regulation by the Council.

15. Following the normal procedure, the Commission proposal of 22 June 2005 will be examined by several committees of the European Parliament[24], and their reports will be debated in one or more plenary sessions of the Parliament. The European Communities estimates that the European Parliament will require at least six months from the reception of the proposal to deliver its opinion, that is, until January 2006. In addition, although Articles 36 and 37 of the EC Treaty do not require the consultation of the EESC, the EESC nevertheless will be consulted pursuant to a 2001 Co-operation Protocol agreed between the Commission and the EESC, as the routine practice in such matters. The European Communities estimates that the EESC will require six months to deliver its opinion, that is, until January 2006.

16. Furthermore, the European Communities is obligated, by Article 12 of the Cotonou Agreement between itself and the ACP countries, to consult ACP countries when it intends to take measures "which may affect the interests of the ACP states".[25] Accordingly, the European Communities has informed the ACP countries of the Commission proposal to the Council and has engaged in an "extensive consultation process".[26] This process will "add to the complexity of the debate by the different [European Communities'] institutions involved and require additional time."[27]

17. As regards the adoption of the regulation by the Council, the European Communities maintains that, although the Council may start deliberating on a Commission proposal while it is being considered by the European Parliament and the EESC, the Council will require additional time to take into account the opinions issued by those bodies. Referring to the "potential complexity of the

---

21 European Communities' written submission, para. 43.

22 *Ibid.*, para. 45.

23 *Ibid.*

24 The Committee on Agriculture and Rural Development (COMAGRI); the Committee on Budgets (BUDG); the Committee on International Trade (INTA), and the Committee on Development (DEVE).

25 European Communities' written submission, para. 61.

26 European Communities' written submission, para. 63.

27 *Ibid.*

implementing measures" and to "recent precedents concerning similar agricultural legislation", the European Communities estimates that the Council will require nine months to adopt formally the relevant regulation, that is, until the end of March 2006.[28]

18. As regards the implementing regulations, the European Communities emphasizes that the Commission will have to enact "a comprehensive set of detailed" implementing regulations. [29] In so doing, the Commission must follow a "comitology procedure[]", under which the Commission is assisted by a "management committee" composed of representatives of the Member States and chaired by a Commission representative.[30] Under that procedure, the Commission presents its proposals to the management committee, which in turn provides its opinion; if a favourable or no opinion is issued by the management committee, the Commission adopts the proposed regulation. If the management committee issues an unfavourable opinion, the Commission nevertheless adopts the regulation, but the Council may take a different decision from the Commission within a specified time period.

19. The European Communities submits that, although Commission staff may start preparing the implementing legislation before adoption of the Council regulation, they cannot finalize the texts and launch the "comitology procedure" until the Council has taken a definitive decision. The Commission will, according to the European Communities, need three months in order to enact the implementing regulations, that is, until the end of June 2006.[31]

20. The fourth set of "particular circumstances" in the present dispute, according to the European Communities, are requirements concerning the publication and entry into force of the regulations at issue. All regulations must be published in the Official Journal of the European Union. Although not explicitly required by the EC Treaty, it is an "established legislative practice" that regulations which must be implemented by the customs authorities are published "at least six weeks before their entry into force and take effect from 1 January or, exceptionally, from 1 July".[32] This practice is based on a Council Resolution of 27 June 1974. The European Communities argues that previous arbitration awards have acknowledged the relevance of this practice for the determination of the reasonable period of time.[33] Moreover, it is also a "well-established legislative practice" that "significant changes to the rules of a common market organization" take effect from the start of the following marketing year, "so as to take account of production in course and avoid disrupting the market".[34] The marketing year 2005/2006 of the European Communities runs from 1 July 2005 to 30 June 2006.

---

[28] *Ibid.*, para. 68.

[29] *Ibid.*, para. 69.

[30] *Ibid.*, paras. 71–72.

[31] *Ibid.*, para. 75.

[32] European Communities' written submission, para. 77.

[33] *Ibid.*, para. 77, referring to Award of the Arbitrator, *EC – Bananas III*, para. 3 and Award of the Arbitrator, *EC – Tariff Preferences*, paras. 50–51.

[34] European Communities' written submission, para. 78.

21. As the fifth set of "particular circumstances", the European Communities argues that the European Communities' sugar regime is of a "longstanding nature", because it has been in place since the early 1970s, and is "essentially integrated" in the European Communities' policies.[35] As a result, the implementation of the recommendations and rulings of the DSB will have "a major impact" on the European society and not just on the sugar industry. [36] It is therefore "unavoidable" for the European Communities to consider the "continued viability" of the sugar regime as a whole.[37] In this context, the European Communities refers to the "numerous and very different implementation options"[38] available to it, the significance of sugar as an "essential component of the diet of the European population"[39], energy and environmental policies, as well as the relationship between the European Communities and the ACP countries. These varied factors will show that the implementation of the recommendations and rulings of the DSB necessitates a "serious debate", both within and outside the European Communities' legislature.[40]

22. As the sixth set of "particular circumstances", the European Communities refers to sugar beet production already undertaken before the present dispute was decided by the Appellate Body in April 2005. In Europe, beets are sown in February and March and harvested in the autumn. As a result, decisions concerning the volume of beet and sugar to be produced in the marketing year 2005/2006 had been agreed upon between farmers and sugar producers before the DSB made its recommendations and rulings. Reversing their production decisions would be "very costly and often materially impossible".[41] The European Communities points out that the Commission proposal of 22 June 2005 provides for levies to be imposed on the production of "surplus sugar", designed to avoid the accumulation of sugar; however, it would be inappropriate to apply those levies to sugar produced from beet sown before the present dispute was decided.[42] In any event, even if such exports were not allowed after 31 July 2006, its consequence might be that the European producers "would be forced to make all their exports within a shorter period of time", thereby "exacerbat[ing] the effects of those exports", to the detriment of all sugar exporting countries.[43]

23. As the seventh, and final, set of "particular circumstances", the European Communities argues that the reasonable period of time it suggests is "broadly in line" with the time periods granted to the European Communities in previous arbitration awards concerning "similar" legislative measures.[44] The European Communities refers to the awards in *EC – Bananas III* and *EC – Tariff Preferences*, in which the reasonable period of time was 15 months and 6 days, and 14

---

35 *Ibid.*, para. 81.
36 *Ibid.*
37 *Ibid.*, para. 82.
38 *Ibid.*, para. 83.
39 *Ibid.*, para. 84.
40 *Ibid.*, para. 87.
41 European Communities' written submission, para. 88.
42 *Ibid.*, para. 90.
43 *Ibid.*, para. 91.
44 *Ibid.*, para. 92.

months and 11 days, respectively. The longer reasonable period of time in the present case is necessary so as "not to penalise production already undertaken" prior to the decision of the Appellate Body in April 2005.[45]

B. Complaining Parties

1. Australia

24. Australia disagrees with the reasonable period of time proposed by the European Communities. Australia provides three distinct scenarios to decide how the European Communities could bring itself into compliance with its obligations under World Trade Organization ("WTO") law and the recommendations and rulings of the DSB in the "shortest period possible within the legal system" of the implementing Member. Under the first scenario, the European Communities can implement the DSB's recommendations and rulings by doing three things: by adopting a Commission regulation that limits export licences such that the relevant commitment levels are not exceeded; by adopting a second Commission regulation increasing the permitted carry forward of C sugar; and by adopting a third Commission regulation to reduce the level of export availability of sugar. Under this scenario, the required reasonable period of time is no more than six months and six days from the date of adoption of the Appellate Body Report and the Panel Report by the DSB, that is to say, it would expire on 25 November 2005.[46]

25. Under the second scenario, should the Arbitrator find that, contrary to Australia's assertions, Commission regulations can be used to *regulate*, but not to *limit* the export of C sugar through export licences, then the European Communities can adopt and implement a different set of Commission regulations, spreading C sugar exports over the 2005/2006 and 2006/2007 quantity commitment marketing years; limiting export licences for quota sugar; increasing the permitted carry forward of C sugar; and reducing the level of export availability of sugar.[47] The reasonable period of time under this scenario is no more than six months and six days, that is to say, it would expire on 25 November 2005.[48]

26. The third scenario put forward by Australia is applicable "[i]f the Arbitrator finds ... that a Commission Regulation cannot be used to control the export of C sugar at all"[49]; under this scenario, the European Communities can implement by adopting a Commission regulation limiting export licences for quota sugar and adopting a Council regulation granting the Commission the authority to control the export of C sugar; the Commission could subsequently adopt an implementing Commission regulation to impose such controls.[50] Under this third sce-

---

45 *Ibid.*, para. 94.
46 Australia's written submission, para. 201.
47 *Ibid.*, para. 166.
48 *Ibid.*, para. 203.
49 *Ibid.*, para. 163.
50 Australia's written submission., paras. 165–167.

nario, the reasonable period of time is no more than 220 days and it would expire on 27 December 2005.[51]

27. Finally, in addition to the three scenarios put forward by it, Australia argues that, even on the basis of the European Communities' submission that a Council regulation on a new common market organization ("CMO") in the sugar sector is required—which basis Australia considers "incorrect"[52]—the reasonable period of time should be shorter than that requested by the European Communities; it should be no more than 11 months and 2 days and should expire on 21 April 2006.

28. Turning to Australia's specific arguments under these various scenarios, Australia argues that the European Communities does not substantiate why a date "significantly in excess" of the Article 21.3(c) guideline of 15 months is justifiable.[53] Australia emphasizes that the reasonable period of time in this dispute must be determined by reference to the action needed to comply with the recommendations and rulings in question, and not by reference to "any wider reform" that the European Communities may choose to undertake in response to a WTO ruling.[54]

29. Australia argues that the European Communities has "full legal authority" under its existing regime to regulate the levels of refunds, to determine the quantity of "export availability of ... C sugar" and to regulate such exports.[55] Contrary to the assertions of the European Communities, the Commission has the authority, under the existing sugar regime, to suspend the granting of export licences for exports of any sugar, *including C sugar*. The requirement in Article 13 of Council Regulation 1260/2001 that C sugar must be exported is not an impediment to this authority, because the relevant provision does not apply to all C sugar, but rather only to C sugar that is not carried forward to the following marketing year. The current limit on such carry forward, amounting to 20 per cent of the A quota[56], has been established by the Commission and could either be increased or "abolished entirely", without requiring a change to Council Regulation 1260/2001.[57]

30. Should the Arbitrator find that, contrary to Australia's assertions, the current authority of the Commission cannot be used to prevent or limit the export of C sugar, Australia argues that this "would not serve as a barrier" to compliance by the European Communities by means of Commission regulations.[58] Commission authority under the existing regime can still be used to regulate such exports. Although C sugar not carried forward must be exported within a defined time period, there is no requirement to export C sugar *within the year of its pro-*

---

51 *Ibid.*, para. 205. The reasonable period of time would expire on 25 December; the next working day is 27 December 2005.

52 Australia's written submission, para. 206.

53 *Ibid.*, para. 11.

54 *Ibid.*, para. 174.

55 *Ibid.*, para. 21.

56 For a description of A, B, and C sugar, see *supra*, footnote 15.

57 Australia's written submission, para. 122.

58 Australia's written submission, para. 125.

duction. Under the existing regime, producers have a period between the end of the marketing year and 31 December to export C sugar not carried forward; in the event that C sugar production in any one year were to exceed the European Communities' quantity commitment level, the European Communities has the legal authority to limit export licences to that quantity commitment level; the balance of C sugar production not carried forward could then be exported in the period 1 October to 31 December in the following marketing year.

31. According to Australia, all of the above-referred measures can be adopted by the Commission under the "management committee procedure". The time period for the Commission to adopt measures in the sugar sector under this procedure in the past has been "very short".[59] Under that procedure, the Commission presents proposals to the management committee, which in turn provides an opinion; if a favourable or no opinion is issued by the management committee, the Commission adopts the proposed regulation. If the management committee issues an unfavourable opinion, the Commission nevertheless adopts the regulation, but the Council may take a different decision from the Commission within a specified time period. Australia argues that, for a range of regulations adopted by the Commission in the sugar sector under the "management committee procedure", the average and median duration of the procedure has been 23 days. Although the European Communities could have, therefore, already implemented the recommendations and rulings of the DSB, Australia proposes that, "exceptionally and as a gesture to the [European Communities]", the reasonable period of time should end four weeks from the date of the circulation of the arbitration award.[60] Thus, the reasonable period of time would expire on 25 November 2005. This reasonable period of time is applicable for both the first and second scenarios for implementation set out in Australia's written submission.

32. In the event that the Arbitrator were to consider "necessary to calculate ... periods"[61] for the adoption of a new Council regulation amending the CMOs in the sugar sector, as well as for the subsequent adoption of implementing Commission regulations, Australia refers to a "study of Council [r]egulations adopted by the [European Communities] between 1 January 1998 and 31 July 2005 which amended existing common market organizations for agricultural products".[62] On the basis of "median figure[s]" derived from this sample, Australia argues that the adoption of a new Council regulation should occur by 27 November 2005, and the entry into force of this regulation on 2 December 2005.[63] Subsequently, when adopting implementing regulations, the Commission should be granted an additional 23 days to complete the management committee procedure. The reasonable period of time for this scenario should therefore expire on 27 December 2005.[64]

---

[59] *Ibid.*, para. 142.
[60] *Ibid.*, para. 144.
[61] Australia's written submission, para. 146.
[62] *Ibid.*, para. 147.
[63] *Ibid.*, para. 149.
[64] *Ibid.*, para. 205. The reasonable period of time would expire on 25 December; the next working day is 27 December 2005.

33. As stated above, in Australia's view, contrary to the European Communities' arguments, it is not necessary, for purposes of implementation, to adopt a Council regulation *creating* an entire *new* CMO for sugar; rather, according to Australia, it is sufficient to adopt a Council regulation *amending* the *existing* CMO. Nevertheless, even if the reasonable period of time were calculated on the basis of adopting a Council regulation *creating* a *new* CMO, the reasonable period of time should be shorter than that suggested by the European Communities. Using a median figure from a sample of previous Council regulations that created new CMOs, Australia argues that a new Council regulation could be adopted by 7 March 2006 and it could enter into force by 29 March 2006. Subsequently, for adopting implementing regulations, the Commission should need no more than 23 days to complete the "management committee procedure". The reasonable period of time under this scenario should therefore expire on 21 April 2006.

34. Australia, moreover, disputes that certain factors invoked by the European Communities constitute "particular circumstances" within the meaning of Article 21.3(c) of the DSU, justifying a longer reasonable period of time. Australia points out that arguments related to the likely impact on the domestic industry have been rejected in previous arbitrations. The correction of possible "structural market imbalances" should similarly not be taken into account in the determination of the reasonable period of time.[65] Moreover, the present dispute does not present circumstances comparable to those in *Chile – Price Band System*; this is because export subsidies under the European Communities' sugar regime do not have a "unique role and impact" on society, they do not serve as a "cornerstone" of the European Communities' agricultural policy, and they are not "fundamentally integrated" into the "central agricultural policies" of the European Communities.[66] Finally, the implementation period proposed by the European Communities is not, as claimed by the European Communities, "broadly in line"[67] with previous awards under Article 21.3(c) concerning legislative measures of the European Communities; the reasonable periods of time granted in *EC – Bananas III* and *EC – Tariff Preferences* were "only, at the most, around half as long" as the "effective reasonable period of time" sought by the European Communities in this arbitration.[68]

2. *Brazil*

35. Brazil requests that the Arbitrator determine the reasonable period of time to be six months and six days, that is, until 25 November 2005, if implementation is brought about by administrative action. Alternatively, if implementation requires legislative measures, Brazil requests that the Arbitrator determine the

---

[65] Australia's written submission, para. 185, referring to the European Communities' written submission, para. 41.

[66] Australia's written submission, para. 192, referring to Award of the Arbitrator, *Chile – Price Band System*, paras. 46 and 48.

[67] Australia's written submission, para. 197, referring to the European Communities' written submission, para. 92.

[68] Australia's written submission, para. 197.

reasonable period of time to be seven months and eight days, that is, until 27 December 2005.

36. Brazil recalls that the European Communities is required to comply "in the shortest time legally possible"[69] and rejects the European Communities' argument that the implementation period should be the period that it will take for the European Communities to reform its overall sugar regime. Rather, implementation requires only the adoption of measures that will ensure that the European Communities respects its export subsidy reduction commitment levels.

37. Brazil submits that the existing legal framework of the European Communities' sugar regime permits the European Communities to comply within four weeks. Three principles of European Communities' law are relevant in this respect: first, international agreements are binding on the institutions of the European Communities and on its Member States; secondly, secondary legislation of the European Communities must, as far as possible, be interpreted in a manner consistent with these agreements; and thirdly, the management of agricultural policy is left "very largely" to the Commission, acting under the implementing authority delegated to it by the Council.[70] In this respect, Brazil argues that the Commission enjoys the authority to suspend the grant of export licences for sugar, "for the express reason of ensuring compliance with the [European Communities'] obligations under the *Agreement on Agriculture*"[71]; the Commission also enjoys the authority to amend the existing rules to enable producers to carry forward, to the following marketing year, any C sugar that cannot be exported in a given year.

38. With respect to export licences, Brazil argues that Article 22 of current Council Regulation 1260/2001 "subjects all exports of sugar ... to an export licence and draws no distinctions between A, B and C sugar".[72] Furthermore, the Commission is authorized to lay down detailed implementing rules governing the conditions for granting export licences for all exports of sugar, including C sugar. In 1995, the Commission adopted rules to govern import and export licences "among other reasons, to enable the [European Communities] to control the level of its exports of subsidized sugar".[73] These rules are still in force and contain rules regulating the grant of export licences for A, B and C sugar. The Commission does not require express authorization to control exports of C sugar, provided that such controls are not prohibited by Council Regulation 1260/2001 or implementing regulations, which is not the case. In this respect, Brazil also rejects the European Communities' argument that Council Regulation 1260/2001 *requires* that C sugar be exported; rather, C sugar can also be carried forward into the following marketing year.

---

[69] Brazil's written submission, heading IV.A.

[70] Brazil's written submission, para. 28.

[71] *Ibid.*, para. 33. (original italics)

[72] Brazil's written submission, para. 34. (For a description of A, B, and C sugar, see *supra*, footnote 15.)

[73] Brazil's written submission, para. 38.

39. With respect to the rules governing the carry forward of C sugar into the next marketing year, Brazil argues that under Council Regulation 1260/2001 *all* C sugar could be carried forward. The implementing rules concerning this provision are contained in a Commission regulation that limits the carry forward to 20 per cent of the A quota; however, if it wishes, the Commission can "increase the quantity of C sugar that can be carried forward from the current 20 [per cent] limit [or] eliminate *entirely* the current ... restriction on carry-forward."[74] Indeed, previously, the relevant implementing rules permitted producers to carry forward 100 per cent of their sugar production. If the Commission permitted full carry forward of C sugar, it could, in conjunction with a suspension of export licences, ensure that subsidized sugar in excess of its quantity commitment levels is not passed onto the world market; rather, this sugar would remain within the Community and would "be[] absorbed internally in the next marketing year".[75]

40. Neither of these two measures—suspending the grant of export licences for A, B and C sugar, as well as raising or eliminating the 20 per cent restriction on the carry forward of C sugar—is, in Brazil's view, particularly complex, and both are similar to measures that have been adopted previously by the Commission. Both measures could be adopted under the "management committee procedure" and could be adopted in "just four weeks".[76] Brazil notes that, for a range of 27 regulations adopted by the Commission in the sugar sector under this procedure, the length of the procedure has varied between 14 and 43 days, with an average and median length of 23 days.

41. Brazil concludes that, on the basis of the Commission's existing authority, the European Communities could secure compliance within a period of 28 days, to be counted from the date of the adoption by the DSB of the Appellate Body Report and the Panel Report. Brazil notes that, in fact, the European Communities "did not take the necessary steps to implement within the shortest possible period".[77] Brazil therefore proposes, "exceptionally and as a gesture" to the European Communities, that the reasonable period of time should end 28 days from the date of circulation of the arbitration award, that is, on 25 November 2005.[78]

42. In the event that the Arbitrator decides that the Commission's existing authority under Council Regulation 1260/2001 does not permit the European Communities to secure implementation, Brazil argues, alternatively, that a limited amendment to Council Regulation 1260/2001 would permit the European Communities to comply in seven months. Under this scenario, the European Communities would have to "extend the existing [control] system to apply expressly to C sugar", and this involves "no more than a straightforward amendment of ... Regulation [1260/2001]".[79]

---

74 *Ibid.*, para. 62. (original italics)

75 Brazil's written submission, para. 64.

76 *Ibid.*, para. 68.

77 *Ibid.*, para. 78.

78 *Ibid.*

79 *Ibid.*, para. 79.

43. Although Brazil "generally agrees" with the procedural steps for the adoption of a Council regulation, as explained by the European Communities, it disagrees with the asserted duration of this procedure.[80] In providing its estimate on the basis of previous legislative procedures, the European Communities refers only to the duration of procedures for the adoption of *new* CMOs, rather than *amendments* to *existing* CMOs. The median period for the adoption of a new CMO is 9.2 months, while it is 5.4 months for the adoption of an amendment to an existing CMO. Thus, the adoption of an amending regulation is "considerably quicker" than the adoption of a new CMO.[81] Although the reasonable period of time should be the shortest possible period within which a Member can implement in its domestic law, Brazil states that it does not object if the Arbitrator uses this median figure for purposes of determining the reasonable period of time. This median period runs from the date of the Commission proposal to the entry into force of the Council regulation and, consequently, it should expire on 2 December 2005.

44. Furthermore, Brazil rejects the European Communities' arguments on publication and entry into force of the regulation. The alleged European Communities' practice of publishing regulations to be implemented by customs authorities six weeks before their entry into force, and implementing them only from 1 January or 1 July, is "not as widespread" as the European Communities claims[82]; Brazil lists 33 European Communities' regulations whose implementation did not follow that practice. Moreover, Brazil contends that the Council document setting out this alleged practice does not indicate that it applies to measures regulating import and export licences. Brazil also rejects the argument that "significant changes to the rules of a common market organization should take effect, at the earliest, from the start of the following marketing year, so as to take account of production in course and avoid disrupting the market."[83] Brazil refers to ten Council amendments to existing CMOs that did not take effect at the commencement of the marketing year. In any event, the changes that implementation would entail are not "significant", as the European Communities suggests, because the Commission already has significant authority to control sugar exports.[84]

45. Brazil acknowledges that, when the Council amends Council Regulation 1260/2001, the Commission "will likely have to adopt" an implementing regulation.[85] The Commission could, as the European Communities admits, "start preparing the implementing regulations before the adoption of the Council regulation", such that this regulation enters into force eight days after the Council

80 Brazil's written submission, para. 83.
81 *Ibid.*, para. 88.
82 *Ibid.*, para. 94.
83 *Ibid.*, para. 98, referring to the European Communities' written submission, para. 78.
84 Brazil's written submission, para. 102, referring to the European Communities' written submission, para. 78.
85 Brazil's written submission, para. 104.

amending the regulation.[86] However, "exceptionally and as a gesture to the [European Communities]", Brazil requests that the Arbitrator grant the European Communities the "full average or median period" of 23 days for the completion of the management committee procedure, such that the reasonable period of time expires on 27 December 2005.[87]

46. Brazil rejects that four additional factors invoked by the European Communities constitute "particular circumstances" relevant to the determination of the reasonable period of time in this case. First, concerning the need for consultations with the ACP countries, Brazil argues that the European Communities fails to substantiate how the ACP countries will be affected by implementation. This is because the European Communities' obligations to the ACP countries are to *import* certain quantities of ACP sugar, whereas the European Communities' obligations in the present dispute relate to *exports* of the European Communities' own subsidized sugar. Secondly, with respect to the alleged need for debate within European society, Brazil argues that previous arbitrators have declined to accept that domestic "contentiousness" and "political sensitivity" are a particular circumstance relevant under Article 21.3(c).[88] Thirdly, there is "no justification" for additional time for structural adjustment for the [European Communities'] domestic industry.[89] Brazil submits that no arbitrator to date has granted a Member additional time to enable its domestic industry to make structural adjustments facilitating the transition to a WTO-consistent regime; a right to such a transition period does not exist even under European Communities law. Fourthly, the duration of reasonable periods of time in previous cases in which the European Communities was the implementing Member is "irrelevant".[90]

47. Finally, Brazil requests that, Brazil being a developing country Member, the Arbitrator pay particular attention to the significance of prompt compliance for Brazil's development objectives, pursuant to Article 21.2 of the DSU. Brazil's sugar industry is an important part of its economy; the European Communities' WTO-inconsistent subsidized sugar exports "cost Brazil USD $ 494 million annually".[91]

3. *Thailand*

48. Thailand requests that the reasonable period of time for implementation of the recommendations and rulings of the DSB in this case be set at six months and six days, that is, until 25 November 2005, if implementation is effected by administrative action. Alternatively, should legislative action be required, Thai-

---

[86] Brazil's written submission, para. 106, referring to the European Communities' written submission, para. 74.

[87] Brazil's written submission, para. 110. The reasonable period of time would expire on 25 December; the next working day is 27 December 2005.

[88] Brazil's written submission, para. 118, referring to Award of the Arbitrator, *Canada – Pharmaceutical Patents*, para. 60; Award of the Arbitrator, *Canada – Patent Term*, para. 58; and Award of the Arbitrator, *US – Offset Act (Byrd Amendment)*, para. 61.

[89] Brazil's written submission, heading IV.D(3).

[90] *Ibid.*, heading IV.D(4).

[91] Brazil's written submission, para. 140, referring to a study by Oxfam International.

land argues that the reasonable period of time be set at seven months and eight days, that is, until 27 December 2005.

49. Thailand argues that the European Communities bears the burden of proof of demonstrating that the duration of its proposed implementation period constitutes a reasonable period of time and that it has not discharged this burden. The European Communities is required to implement within the "shortest period possible within [its] legal system" by making changes to those aspects of its sugar regime that were subject to the recommendations and rulings of the DSB.[92] The European Communities "must not delay its immediate obligation to implement ... to facilitate any broader review of its agricultural policy".[93] According to Thailand, the relevant circumstances in this case "all [militate] in favour of speedy implementation by the [European Communities]."[94]

50. Thailand argues further that the European Communities needs no additional time to consider its implementation options. Thailand also takes issue with the European Communities' argument that, due to the complexity of the sugar regime, there are many different options available to it to implement the recommendations and rulings of the DSB. The fact that the European Communities has already decided upon a proposed means of implementation "suggests" that it has already engaged in consultations with its domestic industry, the ACP countries and other interested parties, so that there is no reason to permit further consideration of alternative options.[95] Similarly, the fact that implementation may engender political debate is not a factor that can affect the determination of the reasonable period of time. In addition, unlike in *Chile – Price Band System*, the European Communities' measure is not one of "horizontal application affecting a number of agricultural products and their pricing", but rather it relates only to the European Communities' sugar policy and does not require any changes to policy regarding other agricultural products.[96]

51. Thailand emphasizes that the European Communities' implementation obligations relate only to the measure that was found inconsistent with WTO law and can be fulfilled promptly by administrative means. Thailand argues that the only point of disagreement between the parties is "whether the [European Communities] can control exports of C sugar by administrative means".[97] By "suspending export licences and enabling producers to carry-over [C sugar] that cannot be exported in a given year to the next", the European Communities could secure "rapid and prompt compliance".[98]

52. Thailand argues that, contrary to the European Communities' assertions, the Commission does have the authority under existing regulations to control the export of C sugar in a manner that would enable it to comply with its reduction commitments. Council Regulation 1260/2001 permits all C sugar to be carried

---

[92] Thailand's written submission, heading IV.A.2.
[93] *Ibid.*, para. 24.
[94] *Ibid.*, para. 28.
[95] *Ibid.*, para. 34.
[96] Thailand's written submission., para. 36.
[97] *Ibid.*, para. 39.
[98] *Ibid.*

forward; decisions on limits on the carry forward of C sugar—like the current limit of 20 per cent of the A quota—lie with the Commission, are "purely discretionary"[99], and are currently found in a separate Commission regulation.[100] This shows that the Commission enjoys "full authority" under Council Regulation 1260/2001 either not to restrict the carry forward of C sugar or to increase the quantity of C sugar that can be carried forward above the current limit of 20 per cent of the A quota.[101] According to Thailand, the Commission can accomplish this by following the management committee procedure under Council Regulation 1260/2001. Similarly, according to Thailand, the Commission could control exports by suspending the issuance of export licences for A, B, and C sugar. There is no legal basis to the European Communities' assertion that the Commissions' authority to suspend licences with respect to A and B sugar does not extend to C sugar. Requiring C sugar to be carried forward and suspending export licences "together constitute the most flexible and efficient means by which the [European Communities] can reduce the level of its subsidised exports".[102]

53. In Thailand's view, the shortest period possible for the aforementioned administrative action is the period required for the "management committee procedure" under Council Regulation 1260/2001, namely, one month. Under this procedure, the Commission submits a proposal for a Commission regulation to the management committee that must render an opinion within a time-limit fixed by the Chairman of that committee. If the committee renders a favourable opinion, the Commission regulation is adopted immediately; if the opinion is unfavourable, the Commission nevertheless adopts the regulation, but the regulation is also referred to the Council, which may take a different decision within one month. There have been no unfavourable opinions delivered in the management committee procedure, and the average as well as median period for completion of the procedure has been 23 days. Thailand considers that the management committee procedure could "certainly" be completed within 28 days.[103] As a result, Thailand takes the view that the European Communities could have implemented the recommendations and rulings of the DSB even before commencement of the present arbitration. However, "[a]s a practical matter", given that the European Communities has not taken these steps, Thailand proposes that the reasonable period of time end 28 days from the date of circulation of the arbitration award, that is, on 25 November 2005.[104]

54. In Thailand's view, the European Communities has failed to prove that a legislative measure to implement would take 12 months to enact. However, in the event that the Arbitrator considers that the European Communities needs to take legislative action to allow a greater proportion of C sugar to be carried forward, Thailand submits that this can be achieved by a simple amendment to the existing Council Regulation 1260/2001. An implementing Member's decision to

[99] *Ibid.*, para. 43.
[100] Commission Regulation (EEC) No. 65/82 of 13 January 1982.
[101] Thailand's written submission, para. 44.
[102] *Ibid.*, para. 49.
[103] Thailand's written submission, para. 58.
[104] *Ibid.*, para. 60.

"undertake broad systemic reforms" does not justify a longer implementation period.[105] Moreover, Thailand argues that the European Communities has overstated "significantly" the time required to implement by legislative means.[106] Thailand refers to a table submitted as an exhibit to the submissions of Australia, Brazil and Thailand and argues that regulations amending existing CMOs can be adopted in periods considerably shorter than the median figure of 5.4 months. Nevertheless, Thailand states that it would not object if the Arbitrator were to use this median figure as the basis for assessing the duration of the reasonable period of time.

55. In Thailand's view, applying the period of 5.4 months to the date of the Commission proposal, that is, 22 June 2005, the Council amendment could enter into force on 2 December 2005. Allowing another 23 days for the Commission to adopt implementing regulations, the reasonable period of time should expire on 27 December.[107] Thailand also points out that a number of regulations to be implemented by customs authorities have in the past entered into force on dates other than 1 January or 1 July, and that therefore this plea of the European Communities has no validity.

56. Finally, Thailand argues that the particular circumstances in this case favour prompt implementation. Referring to the special provisions of Articles 21.2 and 21.8 of the DSU for developing country Members, Thailand submits that the implementation of the rulings in this dispute is "crucial" to Thailand's development objectives.[108] Thailand argues that the WTO-inconsistent sugar export subsidies maintained by the European Communities impose an annual loss of USD 151 million on Thailand, affect approximately 1.5 million farmers' and sugar-related workers' households and have "very serious consequences for the Thai sugar industry".[109] Concerning the ACP countries' interests, Thailand submits that the European Communities should fully respect its commitments with respect to these countries, but argues that these countries' interests "cannot take priority over the obligation of the [European Communities] to ensure prompt implementation."[110] Thailand also notes that it has not "in any way" contested the preferential access enjoyed by the ACP countries and India to the European Communities' market.[111] Furthermore, the European Communities should not be permitted to use the alleged effects of its sugar regime reform on the ACP countries for "doing nothing"[112]; the European Communities must be deemed to have taken into account the interests of the ACP countries in announcing its proposal on 22 June 2005; as a result, no additional time need be considered to permit further consultations with the ACP countries.

---

[105] *Ibid.*, para. 63.
[106] *Ibid.*, para. 64.
[107] Thailand's written submission., para. 68. The reasonable period of time would expire on 25 December; the next working day is 27 December 2005.
[108] Thailand's written submission, heading IV.E.1.
[109] *Ibid.*, para. 77.
[110] *Ibid.*, para. 81.
[111] *Ibid.*, para. 80.
[112] *Ibid.*, para. 82.

57. Thailand also argues that the reasonable period of time should not include a phase-in period, during which European Communities sugar producers would be permitted to export out of quota until 1 January 2007. Previous arbitral awards under Article 21.3(c) have established that the fact that implementation may require some structural adjustments on the part of a domestic industry does not constitute a "particular circumstance[]" within the meaning of that provision. Moreover, the European Court of Justice has held that recipients of a subsidy are not entitled to a transition period on the elimination of that subsidy; thus, even under the European Communities' own law, there is no requirement to build in a transition period before changes to a subsidy programme take effect. Thailand submits that, by requesting a phase-in period, the European Communities is effectively requesting a waiver for its obligations, pursuant to Article IX of the *Marrakesh Agreement Establishing the World Trade Organization* (the "*WTO Agreement*").

III. REASONABLE PERIOD OF TIME

58. Pursuant to Article 21.3(c) of the DSU, my task as arbitrator in this case is to determine the "reasonable period of time" for the European Communities to implement the recommendations and rulings of the Dispute Settlement Body (the "DSB") in *EC – Export Subsidies on Sugar*.[113] The "reasonable period of time" will be calculated as from 19 May 2005, the date on which the Panel and Appellate Body Reports relating to this dispute were adopted.

59. Article 21.3(c) of the DSU provides that, when the "reasonable period of time" is determined through arbitration:

> ... a guideline for the arbitrator should be that the reasonable period of time to implement panel or Appellate Body recommendations should not exceed 15 months from the date of adoption of a panel or Appellate Body report. However, that time may be shorter or longer, depending upon the particular circumstances. (footnote omitted)

In this regard, I would observe, as have other arbitrators before me, that, in arbitrations conducted pursuant to Article 21.3(c), the implementing Member bears the burden of proof to demonstrate that the period of time it seeks is a reasonable period of time within the meaning of Article 21.3 of the DSU.

60. Before I proceed to determine the reasonable period of time for the European Communities to implement the recommendations and rulings of the DSB in this dispute, I set out the views of the parties on certain general principles applicable to the determination of the reasonable period of time under Article 21.3(c) of the DSU, as articulated in previous arbitration awards.

61. These governing principles at issue are:

---

[113] See WT/DS265/29, WT/DS266/29, WT/DS283/10.

- the reasonable period of time should be the shortest period of time possible within the legal system of the implementing Member[114];
- the implementing Member must utilize all the flexibility and discretion available within its legal and administrative system in order to implement within the shortest period of time possible; and
- the "particular circumstances" of the case must be taken into account in determining the reasonable period of time.

62. While the parties agree with the first principle, they differ sharply on the implementing measure with respect to which the "shortest period of time" is to be determined. The European Communities places considerable emphasis on the proposition that "it is the *prerogative* of the implementing Member to select the means of implementation which it deems most appropriate"[115], and that, therefore, the "shortest period of time possible" must be determined with respect to the implementation method chosen by the implementing Member. The European Communities submits that it is not for the arbitrator, or the complaining parties, to impose any particular method on the implementing Member on the ground that it would result in the fastest implementation of the recommendations and rulings of the DSB. According to the European Communities, "[w]hen previous Arbitrators have said that the 'reasonable period of time' is the 'shortest period of time' within the legal system of the implementing Member, they referred to the procedure for the adoption of the implementing measure, and not to the selection of the implementing measure, which is the prerogative of the implementing Member."[116] Thus, in the view of the European Communities, it is not for the arbitrator to select a particular method of implementation and determine the reasonable period of time on the basis of that selection. Rather, the task of the arbitrator under Article 21.3(c) is to determine the "shortest period [of time] possible"[117] within which the Member can implement through the method it has chosen, taking into account the time required to adopt the necessary legislative, regulatory, and administrative measures.

63. In contrast, Australia, Brazil, and Thailand (the "Complaining Parties") argue that "prompt compliance" with the recommendations and rulings of the

---

[114] Award of the Arbitrator, *Chile – Price Band System*, para. 34 (quoting Award of the Arbitrator, *US – 1916 Act*, para. 32). See also Award of the Arbitrator, *EC – Hormones*, para. 26; Award of the Arbitrator, *Canada – Pharmaceutical Patents*, para. 47; Award of the Arbitrator, *EC – Tariff Preferences*, para. 26; and Award of the Arbitrator, *US – Oil Country Tubular Goods Sunset Reviews*, para. 25.

[115] European Communities' written submission, para. 22, referring to Award of the Arbitrator, *Korea – Alcoholic Beverages*, para. 45; Award of the Arbitrator, *Canada – Pharmaceutical Patents*, para. 43; Award of the Arbitrator, *Chile – Price Band System*, para. 32; Award of the Arbitrator, *US – Offset Act (Byrd Amendment)*, paras. 48 and 53; Award of the Arbitrator, *EC – Tariff Preferences*, para. 30; and Award of the Arbitrator, *US – Oil Country Tubular Goods Sunset Reviews*, para. 26. (emphasis added)

[116] European Communities' statement at the oral hearing.

[117] Award of the Arbitrator, *Chile – Price Band System*, para. 34 (quoting Award of the Arbitrator, *US – 1916 Act*, para. 32). See also Award of the Arbitrator, *EC – Hormones*, para. 26; Award of the Arbitrator, *Canada – Pharmaceutical Patents*, para. 47; Award of the Arbitrator, *EC – Tariff Preferences*, para. 26; and Award of the Arbitrator, *US – Oil Country Tubular Goods Sunset Reviews*, para. 25.

DSB, as required by Article 21.1 of the DSU, is fundamental to the functioning of the dispute settlement system[118]; therefore, it is only when "prompt compliance" is "impracticable" that the implementing Member is entitled to a "reasonable period of time" for implementation under Article 21.3 of the DSU. The shortest possible period of time for implementation—the standard articulated by previous arbitrators, which flows from the fundamental requirement in Article 21.1 of "prompt compliance"—must, therefore, be determined on the basis of a method available to the implementing Member that is consistent with its legal system and that would result in implementation within the shortest period of time possible. Furthermore, the scope of the implementation method must be confined to that required to implement the recommendations and rulings of the DSB, and it must not extend to extraneous objectives that the implementing Member may seek to include in it. In the view of the Complaining Parties, the right of a Member to choose the means of implementation is not unlimited, and should not be allowed to be used by the implementing Member as a means to obtain a longer period of time for implementation.

64. As regards the second principle governing the determination of the reasonable period of time pursuant to Article 21.3(c), the European Communities contends that the requirement that a Member use all flexibility available to it within its legal system should not be interpreted to mean that an implementing Member is required "to utilize an *extraordinary* procedure rather than the *normal* procedure"[119]. The European Communities points out, furthermore, that, as previous arbitrators have held, the reasonable period of time must include the time required, not only for procedural steps that are explicitly mandated by legal instruments, but also for procedural steps that constitute the normal and "routine[]" legislative or administrative practices of the implementing Member.[120]

65. In contrast, the Complaining Parties argue that, even where legislative and regulatory steps are required for implementation, it is incumbent upon the implementing Member to utilize all the discretion and flexibility available within its system to ensure fast implementation of its international obligations.

66. As regards the third principle relating to the "particular circumstances" of the case within the meaning of Article 21.3(c) of the DSU, the European Communities and the Complaining Parties agree that "particular circumstances" are a relevant factor to be taken into account by the arbitrator in determining the reasonable period of time. However, the parties differ on what constitutes such "particular circumstances" for the purposes of the present dispute. The European Communities requests that I take into account seven "particular circumstances"[121]; the Complaining Parties disagree. Furthermore, Brazil and Thailand

---

[118] Australia's written submission, para. 4; Brazil's written submission, para. 13; Thailand's written submission, para. 20.

[119] European Communities' written submission, para. 23. (original emphasis)

[120] *Ibid.*, paras. 58–59. The European Communities relies on the statement of the Arbitrator in *EC – Tariff Preferences*, para. 42.

[121] The European Communities' seven "particular circumstances" are: (i) implementation requires the adoption of a Council regulation and of implementing Commission regulations; (ii) the implementing measures are complex; (iii) the implementation process involves a number of procedural

argue that the arbitrator should pay "particular attention" to their respective development interests, pursuant to Article 21.2 of the DSU. The divergence in views is particularly acute with respect to three issues: first, the scope of the means of implementation proposed by the European Commission (the "Commission"), as contained in its proposal to the Council of the European Union (the "Council") dated 22 June 2005; secondly, the need for "serious debate" within European Communities society concerning the implementing measures as well as the need to consult the African, Caribbean, and Pacific ("ACP") countries[122]; and, thirdly, the need for a transition period with respect to domestic production already undertaken.

67. The parties disagree sharply with respect to the scope of the implementing measure needed in this dispute. The essence of this disagreement is that, according to the Complaining Parties, the sole obligation to be implemented by the European Communities in this dispute is to limit the budgetary outlay on export subsidies on sugar to € 499.1 million, and the quantity of subsidized exports of sugar to 1,273,500 tonnes in any marketing year. This being so, the European Communities can simply use an export licensing system to limit the quantity of exports in any marketing year to 1,273,500 tonnes. The Complaining Parties argue that the Commission has the necessary legal and delegated authority to do this under existing Council Regulation 1260/2001. Moreover, even if the Commission does not already have the legal authority to control the export of C sugar, the Commission can simply acquire such authority by means of an amendment to Council Regulation 1260/2001.[123]

68. The European Communities observes that there are two "extreme[]" options available to it as means of implementation, namely, "plac[ing] direct restrictions on the exports of sugar"[124], while "leav[ing] the level of [domestic] support unmodified"[125], as propounded by the Complaining Parties on the one extreme, and "dismantling the system of support for sugar or ... liberalising completely the imports of sugar into the [European Communities'] market" on the other extreme.[126] Between these two extremes, after a "careful assessment of all the options available"[127], the European Communities, in its proposal of 22 June 2005, has chosen an intermediate option which "aim[s] at preserving some level of support for the beet farmers and sugar producers while at the same time minimising the production of exportable surpluses".[128] According to the Euro-

---

steps that are mandated by legal documents or by constitutional practice; (iv) there are requirements concerning the publication and entry into force of the regulations at issue; (v) the impact of the measures on European society requires serious debate; (vi) account must be taken of production undertaken or planned prior to the decision in the underlying dispute; and, finally, (vii) reasonable periods of time awarded in previous awards concerning legislative measures of the European Communities.

122 European Communities' written submission, paras. 28 and 80.

123 The parties to this proceeding agree that the Commission has the authority to control exports of A and B sugar.

124 European Communities' written submission, para. 41.

125 *Ibid.*, para. 41.

126 *Ibid.*, para. 42.

127 *Ibid.*, para. 44.

128 *Ibid.*, para. 43.

pean Communities, unless the "structural causes of the subsidized exports of sugar"[129] are addressed by modifying the level of support given for beet farmers and sugar producers, surplus production of sugar in the European Communities cannot be avoided or controlled. Therefore, the European Communities considers that the means of implementation set out in its proposal of 22 June 2005 is the most appropriate means for implementation from the long-term point of view. In this connection, the European Communities contends that, as recognized by both the Panel and the Appellate Body in the underlying dispute, the European Communities' sugar regime is "very complex"[130] and its various components are "closely connected and interdependent".[131] More importantly, the Panel and the Appellate Body had found that it is the operation of the European Communities' sugar regime as a whole that has led to the subsidization of C sugar exports within the meaning of Article 9.1(c) of the *Agreement on Agriculture*. The European Communities is, therefore, of the view that the means of implementation it has chosen flows logically from the Panel and Appellate Body Reports.[132]

69. Having considered the arguments of the parties on the general principle of "shortest period of time possible" for implementation, I set out my views in this regard. I am in agreement with previous arbitrators that it is not "the role of the arbitrator under Article 21.3(c) to identify [or select] a particular method of implementation and to determine the 'reasonable period of time on the basis of that method'".[133] Rather, the choice of the method of implementation rests with the implementing Member. However, the implementing Member does not have an unfettered right to choose any method of implementation. Besides being consistent with the Member's WTO obligations, the chosen method must be such that it could be implemented within a reasonable period of time in accordance with the guidelines contained in Article 21.3(c). Objectives that are extraneous to the recommendations and rulings of the DSB in the dispute concerned may not be included in the method if such inclusion were to prolong the implementation period. Above all, it is assumed that the implementing Member will act in "good faith" in the selection of the method that it deems most appropriate for implementation of the recommendations and rulings of the DSB.

70. Turning to the dispute underlying this arbitration, I note that the Appellate Body upheld "as a result of its findings ... the Panel's finding ... that the European Communities, through its sugar regime, acted inconsistently with its obligations under Articles 3.3 and 8 of the *Agreement on Agriculture*".[134] Under Articles 3.3 of the *Agreement on Agriculture*, the European Communities has the obligation,

[129] *Ibid.*, para. 41.

[130] *Ibid.*, para. 37.

[131] *Ibid.*, para. 40.

[132] European Communities' response to questioning at the oral hearing.

[133] Award of the Arbitrator, *US – Gambling*, para. 33. See also Award of the Arbitrator, *Korea – Alcoholic Beverages*, para. 45. In this regard, I also note, as the parties agree, that the question whether a measure taken to comply by the implementing Member is in conformity with the obligations of the implementing Member is a matter that falls under Article 21.5 of the DSU. I also note that under Article 21.3(a), it is the implementing Member that proposes the reasonable period of time required by it to implement through the measure it chooses to take.

[134] Appellate Body Report, *EC – Export Subsidies on Sugar*, para. 346(f).

inter alia, "not [to] provide export subsidies ... in excess of the budgetary outlay and quantity commitment levels specified [in its Schedule]."[135] With respect to C sugar, as noted earlier, the export subsidy that was found to exist was a subsidy falling within the meaning of Article 9.1(c) of the *Agreement on Agriculture*, the source of which was the domestic support given, under the complex and integrated sugar regime of the European Communities, for beet farmers and sugar producers.

71. I turn first to the argument of the Complaining Parties that limiting or prohibiting exports of sugar, or of C sugar more specifically[136], by means of suspending the grant of export licences, is the only option available to the European Communities to comply with the recommendations and rulings of the DSB in this dispute. The Complaining Parties have not succeeded in rebutting the arguments of the European Communities that the latter could, besides limiting its exports of sugar, choose to comply with the recommendations and rulings of the DSB by "withdrawing or reducing the subsidies"; "by repealing the requirements that make the subsidies export contingent"; or "by taking measures to offset the subsidies (e.g. in the form of export duties)".[137] I do not therefore agree that limiting or prohibiting the exports of sugar, or of C sugar more specifically, is the only option available, or the most effective, for implementation in this dispute.

72. Given this conclusion, I need not decide here whether it is within the legal authority of the Commission, as a matter of European Communities law under existing Council Regulation 1260/2001, to suspend the granting of export licences with respect to C sugar. Similarly, I need not address the European Communities' argument that, by suspending export licences with respect to C sugar, the European Communities would be acting inconsistently with Article XI of the *General Agreement on Tariffs and Trade 1994*.

73. As I held earlier with respect to the governing principle, the choice of the method of implementation rests with the implementing Member. Given the facts of the dispute underlining this arbitration, I am satisfied that the European Communities is not pursuing extraneous objectives in addressing "the structural causes of the subsidized exports of sugar".[138] I therefore proceed to determine the reasonable period of time required by the European Communities with respect to its proposal of 22 June 2005.

74. I address first the arguments of the parties concerning the steps involved in the European legislative process. The Complaining Parties agree, in principle, with the European Communities on the basic steps involved in the legislative process under Articles 36 and 37 of the Treaty Establishing the European Community (the "EC Treaty"), namely: preparation of a proposal by the Commission and its presentation to the Council; obtaining the opinions of the European Par-

[135] Article 8 of the *Agreement on Agriculture* provides that "[e]ach Member undertakes not to provide export subsidies other than in conformity with this Agreement and with the commitments as specified in that Member's Schedule."

[136] Under the European Communities' existing sugar regime, C sugar is exported without the benefit of export refunds.

[137] European Communities' statement at the oral hearing.

[138] European Communities' written submission, para. 41.

liament and the Economic and Social Committee of the European Community (EESC); adoption of a regulation by the Council; and, finally, adoption of implementing regulations by the Commission.[139] The adoption of the implementing regulations by the Commission is governed by the so-called "management committee procedure".[140]

75. However, a disagreement exists as to whether, under the so-called "management committee procedure", the Commission may start preparing the implementing regulations before the adoption of the Council regulation. The European Communities acknowledges that the Commission can start preparing such regulations before the Council has formally adopted the Council regulation; however, the Commission "cannot finalise the texts and launch the formal inter-service procedure and the comitology procedure until the Council has taken a definitive decision".[141] In contrast, Brazil argues that a Commission proposal can be finalized by the Commission, and approved by the management committee, before adoption of the Council regulation.[142]

76. The European Communities' legislative system is characterized by "considerable flexibility", in the sense that no mandatory minimum time periods are imposed for any particular step in the legislative process as outlined by the European Communities.[143] Furthermore, as acknowledged by the European Communities, it is possible that certain steps of the legislative process may proceed in parallel. Thus, for instance, the European Communities agrees that the Council may start deliberating a Commission proposal, which is still being considered by the European Parliament and the EESC. However, the European Communities argues, in this regard, that the Council will "in any event require additional time in order to take due account of the opinions issued by those bodies".[144]

77. I take note of the "flexibility" available that the Council could begin its examination of the Commission proposal of 22 June 2005 before it receives the opinions of the European Parliament and the EESC.[145] This could save some time as compared with the Council examining the Commission proposal only

[139] Australia's written submission, paras. 145–156; Brazil's written submission, para. 82; Thailand's written submission, paras. 61–70. The Complaining Parties do not agree with the European Communities' arguments that additional time is required for purposes of consulting ACP countries. I address this point in paragraphs 80–81, *infra*.

[140] Under the "management committee procedure" or "comitology procedure", the Commission is assisted by a "management committee" composed of representatives of the Member States and chaired by a Commission representative. Under that procedure, the Commission presents its proposals to the management committee, which in turn provides its opinion on the proposal. In the event that a favourable or no opinion is issued by the management committee, the Commission adopts the proposed regulation. In the event that the management committee issues an unfavourable opinion, the Commission nevertheless adopts the regulation, but the Council may take a different decision from the Commission within a specified time period.

[141] European Communities' written submission, para. 74.

[142] Brazil's written submission, para. 108.

[143] The same observation was made by the Arbitrator in *EC – Tariff Preferences*, para. 36.

[144] European Communities' written submission, para. 67.

[145] This flexibility was also noted by the Arbitrator in *EC – Tariff Preferences*, para. 43.

after receiving the opinion of the European Parliament and the EESC.[146] I agree, however, with the European Communities that, even if the Council has begun examination of the Commission proposal prior to receiving the opinions of the European Parliament and the EESC, it will still require time to consider these opinions after it has received them. As the Arbitrator in *EC – Tariff Preferences* noted, "[i]f no such time were provided for this, it would defeat the purpose of seeking the opinions."[147]

78. I also note that the European Communities agrees that, under the "management committee procedure", the Commission could begin preparing its implementing regulations prior to the adoption of a Council regulation.[148] The European Communities points out that the staff of the Commission "may start preparing the implementing regulations before the adoption of the Council regulation"[149]; however, the Commission cannot finalize the text and present it to the management committee, for purposes of obtaining the opinion of that committee, "until the Council has taken a definitive decision".[150] In this respect, the Complaining Parties submitted an exhibit indicating three instances where the management committee delivered its opinion *before* the Council adopted the relevant regulation. The European Communities responds that, although the management committee may be invited by the Commission to deliver its opinion before the Council regulation has been adopted, this, nevertheless, remains an extraordinary procedure in the practice of the European Communities' institutions.[151]

79. I agree with previous arbitrators that an implementing Member is not required to adopt "extraordinary legislative procedures" in every case.[152] In this respect, I am not persuaded by the argument of the Complaining Parties that, although the instances cited by them are few, the flexibility suggested by them should not be regarded as "extraordinary". In this respect, I take note of the requirement that the opinion of the management committee would have to be sought again in the event that the Council, in adopting the regulation, modified the original Commission proposal.[153]

80. Another aspect of the European Communities' legislative procedure on which the parties disagree concerns the need to consult ACP countries. The European Communities argues that it is obliged, under the Cotonou Agreement between itself and the ACP countries, to consult ACP countries on measures that

---

[146] I note that, according to the time limit proposed by the European Communities, both these opinions will be available to the Council at about the same time, namely, January 2006.

[147] Award of the Arbitrator, *EC – Tariff Preferences*, para. 43.

[148] European Communities' written submission, para. 74.

[149] *Ibid.*

[150] *Ibid.*

[151] European Communities' response to questioning at the oral hearing.

[152] Award of the Arbitrator, *US – Section 110(5) Copyright Act,* para. 32; Award of the Arbitrator, *US – Offset Act (Byrd Amendment)*, para. 74. Award of the Arbitrator, *EC – Tariff Preferences*, para. 42.

[153] At the oral hearing, the European Communities stated that the opinion rendered by the management committee before the adoption of a Council regulation would be "conditional" on the Council adopting the Commission proposal without modifications.

may "affect the interests" of those countries.[154] This requirement to consult the ACP countries "throughout the legislative process", as well as the need "to consider and respond to their submissions", will, according to the European Communities, "add to the complexity of the debate ... and require additional time".[155]

81. I do not question the need for the European Communities to consult the ACP countries under the Cotonou Agreement on "measures which may affect the interests of the ACP states".[156] However, the European Communities has not demonstrated why this should have an impact so as to require additional time for the European Communities to implement the recommendations and rulings of the DSB. I observe, first, that implementation by the European Communities in this dispute relates to its *export subsidy commitments* under the *Agreement on Agriculture*, whereas the ACP countries enjoy preferential *market access* to the European Communities' market. Secondly, the European Communities did not provide sufficient information on what consultations have taken place with the ACP countries, nor on past experience on how consultations with ACP countries had an impact on the European Communities' legislative process. The European Communities has not provided me with information sufficient to substantiate its assertion that consultations with the ACP Countries will necessitate additional time for implementation of the recommendations and rulings of the DSB.[157]

82. I now turn to the disagreement between the parties concerning the time needed for the legislative procedure in this case. In this respect, I note that the European Communities estimates that the Council will adopt a Council regulation at the end of March 2006 and that, thereafter, the Commission will need three months to enact the necessary implementing regulations, that is, until the end of June 2006.[158] In contrast, the Complaining Parties argue that the Council could adopt a regulation by 2 December 2005 and that the Commission could adopt implementing regulations by 27 December 2005. The Complaining Parties base their estimate on the adoption of a "narrow"[159] and "straightforward ... amend[ment]"[160] to the existing European Communities' sugar regime[161], rather than on a broader reform of that regime, as propounded by the European Communities. Australia[162] and Brazil[163] have also argued that, even on the basis of a broader reform of the European Communities, the Council should adopt a regu-

[154] European Communities' written submission, para. 61. The Cotonou Agreement is a partnership agreement between, on the one hand, the European Communities and, on the other hand, the ACP countries; it relates to political, trade, and development issues.

[155] European Communities' written submission, para. 63.

[156] *Ibid.*, para. 61.

[157] I discuss the relevance, under Article 21.2 of the DSU, of the interests of ACP countries in para. 102, *infra*.

[158] The period of time between the date of the adoption of the Panel and Appellate Body Reports—that is, 19 May 2005—and 30 June 2006 is 13 months and 11 days.

[159] Brazil's written submission, para. 81.

[160] Thailand's written submission, para. 65.

[161] This amendment, according to the Complaining Parties, should be limited to granting the Commission the legal authority to limit exports of C sugar by means of suspending the granting of export licences.

[162] Australia's written submission, para. 206.

[163] At the oral hearing, Brazil stated that it agreed with Australia in this respect.

lation by 29 March 2006 and the Commission should adopt implementing regulations by 21 April 2006.

83. The Complaining Parties have presented several tables containing information about the duration of prior legislative procedures of the European Communities based on Articles 36 and 37 of the EC Treaty. On the basis of a sample of previous regulations *amending* an *existing* common market organization ("CMO") for agricultural products, and on the basis of another sample of previous regulations *adopting* a *new* CMO for agricultural products, the Complaining Parties argue that the relevant median periods are 5.4 months for the adoption of an *amendment* to an *existing* CMO, and 9.2 months for the *adoption* of a *new* CMO.

84. As I have stated earlier, limiting or prohibiting exports of C sugar by means of suspending the grant of export licences is not the only option available to the European Communities to comply with the recommendations and rulings of the DSB in this dispute. Accordingly, I do not base my determination of the reasonable period of time exclusively on the procedure for adopting such an *amending* regulation as suggested by the Complaining Parties, or on the basis of the evidence concerning the duration of the adoption process for such amending regulations.

85. At the same time, I note that the information submitted by the Complaining Parties shows that the average time for the adoption of a Council regulation and of implementing Commission regulations establishing a new CMO for agricultural products is 11.4 months, and the median figure is 9.2 months. The European Communities has not contested the validity of this data, but emphasizes the complexity and sensitivity of the present dispute. I note that these time periods are shorter than those suggested by the European Communities in this arbitration proceeding for the completion of its legislative process.[164] I also agree with Thailand that an average or median figure "inherently represent[s] more than the shortest possible period of time necessary within [an implementing Member's] legal system".[165] Even granting that the circumstances of adoption of previous Council regulations may have been different and that the proposal at issue here may involve a different degree of complexity, it would appear that the European Communities can use the flexibility and discretion in its legal system to ensure that the relevant Council regulation, as well as the Commission implementing regulations, are enacted more speedily than the proposed timeline it has suggested. Indeed, the fact that the legislative process at hand is intended to bring the European Communities into compliance with its international obligations reinforces the need for the European Communities to use all flexibility and discretion that may be available to it within its legal system.

---

[164] The period between 22 June 2005, the date on which the Commission presented its proposal to the Council, and 30 June 2006, the date suggested by the European Communities as the end point of its legislative process, is 12 months and 8 days. Moreover, a legislative process ending on 30 June 2006 represents a period of 13 months and 11 days from the date of adoption of the Panel and Appellate Body Reports in this dispute, that is, 19 May 2005.

[165] Thailand's written submission, para. 70.

86. I now turn to the *other* "particular circumstances"[166] alleged by the European Communities: first, the alleged complexity of the implementing measures; secondly, the need for a serious debate in European society; thirdly, that it would be "appropriate" to permit European Communities sugar producers to export C sugar until 1 January 2007; fourthly, the requirements concerning the publication and entry into force of regulations; and, fifthly, the reasonable periods of time determined in previous arbitration awards concerning legislative measures of the European Communities.

87. The European Communities contends that the reasonable period of time must be determined taking into account that the implementing measures are "complex".[167] The European Communities submits that its sugar regime is "a very complex regulatory regime, consisting of many different support mechanisms"[168] that are "closely connected and interdependent"[169]; as a result, the European Communities has "many different options in order to implement the recommendations and rulings of the DSB".[170] Regardless of which specific option is ultimately chosen, "the content of the implementing measures is likely to be technically complex".[171]

88. As previous arbitrators have noted, the complex nature of implementing measures can be a relevant factor for the determination of the reasonable period of time under Article 21.3(c) of the DSU.[172] But the degree of complexity of an implementing measure depends on the facts of the case. I am not persuaded that the standard of "complexity" is, as the European Communities appears to suggest, reached every time that implementation of the recommendations and rulings of the DSB requires more than "simply ... rewrit[ing] an isolated legal provision or ... repeal[ing] without more the whole measure at issue".[173] As an example of "complexity" of an implementing measure, I refer to the one given by the arbitrator in *Canada – Pharmaceutical Patents*, namely where "implementation is accomplished through extensive new regulations affecting many sectors of activity".[174] Although I acknowledge that the sugar regime of the European Communities has many components that are interrelated, I am not convinced that the Commission proposal of 22 June 2005 possesses such a level of "complexity" as to warrant the granting of any additional time for implementation.

89. The next argument of the European Communities is that the impact of the implementation measures on European society requires a "serious debate" because the European Communities' sugar regime is of a "long-standing nature", is "essentially integrated" in the European Communities' policies and, in some

---

[166] See *supra*, footnote 121.

[167] European Communities' written submission, para. 45.

[168] *Ibid.*, para. 37.

[169] *Ibid.*, para. 40.

[170] European Communities' written submission, para. 40.

[171] *bid.*, para. 45.

[172] Award of the Arbitrator, *Canada – Pharmaceutical Patents*, para. 50; Award of the Arbitrator, *US – Offset Act (Byrd Amendment)*, para. 60.

[173] European Communities' written submission, para. 45.

[174] Award of the Arbitrator, *Canada – Pharmaceutical Patents*, para. 50; see also Award of the Arbitrator, *US – Offset Act (Byrd Amendment)*, footnote 67 to para. 60.

cases, "go[es] back ... to the Napoleonic wars of the early XIX century".[175] The European Communities relies on a finding of the arbitrator in *Chile – Price Band System* in contending that this "particular circumstance[]" should have a bearing on the determination of the reasonable period of time. The Complaining Parties respond that the need for "serious debate" or the "political sensitivity" of the subject matter cannot be regarded as a "particular circumstance[]" for extending the reasonable period of time required for implementation[176]; this is all the more so, according to the Complaining Parties, as implementation required in this dispute consists only in the prevention of subsidized exports taking place beyond the European Communities' reduction commitments.

90. Previous arbitrators have consistently held that the "contentiousness" or "political sensitivity" of the measure to be implemented is not a "particular circumstance[]" that is relevant under Article 21.3(c).[177] In any event, I am not persuaded that the European Communities' export subsidies on sugar are characterized by a degree of political contentiousness that would fundamentally distinguish these measures from any other measure that is likely to be the subject of a WTO dispute. I do not consider that the measures at issue in this dispute raise concerns comparable to those recognized by the arbitrator in *Chile – Price Band System*. Thus, in my view, the European Communities' reliance on the award of the arbitrator in *Chile – Price Band System* is misplaced; the measure in that dispute had a "unique role and impact on Chilean society", was "fundamental[ly] integrat[ed] into the central agricultural policies of Chile", and had a "price-determinative regulatory position in Chile's agricultural policy".[178]

91. I turn now to the European Communities' contention that production already undertaken before the dispute in *EC – Export Subsidies on Sugar* was decided should be given consideration as a "particular circumstance[]". More specifically, the European Communities argues that "it would be appropriate to allow the European Communities' exporters to continue to export out of quota sugar until 1 January 2007 without being subject to the payment of the 'surplus' levies provided [for] in the Commission proposal."[179] The Complaining Parties consider it unwarranted to grant an additional six months as a transition period to enable the domestic industry to export the sugar it has already produced. The Complaining Parties submit that previous arbitrators have rejected arguments that additional time should be granted for "structural adjustment" of the domestic industry.[180] Brazil and Thailand also argue that, even under the European Com-

---

[175] European Communities' written submission, para. 81.

[176] Australia's written submission, para. 196; Brazil's written submission, paras. 118 and 122; Thailand's written submission, para. 33.

[177] See Award of the Arbitrator, *Canada – Patent Term*, para. 58; and Award of the Arbitrator, *US – Offset Act (Byrd Amendment)*, para. 61.

[178] Award of the Arbitrator, *Chile – Price Band System*, para. 48.

[179] European Communities' written submission, para. 90.

[180] Australia's written submission, paras. 181–191; Brazil's written submission, para. 124; Thailand's written submission, paras. 87–88.

munities' own law, subsidies may be discontinued without advance notice to the affected industry.[181]

92. I agree with the views put forth by the Complaining Parties. In my view, the European Communities effectively requests a transitional period *following* the withdrawal or modification of a WTO-inconsistent measure, so that the domestic industry may adjust to such withdrawal or modification. As previous arbitrators have held, the perceived need for such "structural adjustment" or phase-in periods for the domestic producers does not constitute a "particular circumstance[]" within the meaning of Article 21.3(c) and, as such, cannot have an impact on the determination of the reasonable period of time under that provision.[182] In my view, allowing such a transitional period would have the effect of including in the reasonable period of time action that is extraneous to implementation of the recommendations and rulings of the DSB.

93. I turn next to the European Communities' argument concerning the entry into force of its implementing measures. The European Communities argues that the Council regulation under discussion must enter into force on 1 July 2006 because "it is an established legislative practice that regulations which must be implemented by the customs authorities should be published at least six weeks before their entry into force and take effect from 1 January, or exceptionally, from 1 July".[183] This practice is based on a Council resolution from 1974. In addition, the European Communities also argues that it is a "well-established legislative practice" that significant changes to the rules of a CMO should take effect from the start of the following marketing year.[184]

94. In response, the Complaining Parties have submitted two tables showing 33 Council and Commission regulations that, according to the Complaining Parties, "appear to fall within the [European Communities'] description of the Council's long-standing practice"[185]; however, in the case of these regulations, the alleged European Communities' practice was not followed, in that the relevant regulations did not enter into force on 1 January or 1 July, and were not published six weeks prior to their entry into force. The European Communities does not dispute the data submitted by the Complaining Parties; however, it argues that this practice has been in place since 1974 and that, as a result, a long list of exceptions can be expected to exist.[186]

95. In my view, the statistical information submitted by the Complaining Parties suggests that a degree of flexibility exists with respect to the practice alleged by the European Communities. I am aware that the arbitrator in *EC – Tariff Preferences* regarded this administrative practice of the European Communities as a

---

[181] For this proposition, Brazil and Thailand rely on the judgment of the European Court of Justice in Case C-14/01, *Molkerei Wagenfeld Karl Niemann*. (See Brazil's written submission, para. 99; Thailand's written submission, para. 89.)

[182] Award of the Arbitrator, *Indonesia – Autos*, para. 23; Award of the Arbitrator, *Argentina – Hides and Leather*, para. 41.

[183] European Communities' written submission, para. 77.

[184] *Ibid.*, para. 78.

[185] Brazil's written submission, para. 96.

[186] European Communities' response to questioning at the oral hearing.

relevant factor in determining the reasonable period of time for implementation.[187] However, unlike in that case, the Complaining Parties have presented clear evidence that the practice has not been followed in a number of instances. The European Communities has not explained why, in this particular case, the European Communities cannot make use of the flexibility it appears to have with respect to this particular administrative practice.

96. With respect to the European Communities' argument that there is a "well established legislative practice"[188] that significant changes to the rules of a CMO should take effect from the start of the following marketing year, I note that the European Communities has not directed my attention to any factual evidence in support of this claim. In contrast, the Complaining Parties have submitted evidence that casts doubt on the existence of the "legislative practice" in the form of a table with ten Council amendments to existing CMOs that, according to the Complaining Parties, did not take effect at the start of the marketing year. I am therefore of the view that the European Communities has not discharged its burden of proof with respect to this issue. Therefore, the alleged "legislative practice" that "significant changes to the rules of a common market organization should take effect ... from the start of the following marketing year"[189] is not a "particular circumstance[]" that I propose to take into account in determining the reasonable period of time.

97. I now turn to the fifth "particular circumstance[]" suggested by the European Communities as affecting the determination of the reasonable period of time to comply, namely, the periods of time awarded in previous arbitration awards concerning legislative measures of the European Communities. In my view, Article 21.3(c) requires an arbitrator to take into account the "particular circumstances" of the case before the arbitrator. Although an arbitrator could derive some useful guidance from previous arbitration awards in this regard, the facts and circumstances of implementation in one dispute may, and in most instances will, differ from the facts and circumstances of implementation in another dispute. As a result, I decline to consider as a "particular circumstance[]" here the reasonable periods of time awarded in previous arbitration awards concerning legislative measures of the European Communities, exclusively on the ground that the present arbitration also involves implementation by the European Communities by means of a legislative measure.

98. Finally, I turn to the parties' arguments concerning Article 21.2 of the DSU. Brazil and Thailand argue that I should pay "[p]articular attention", within the meaning of that provision, to their respective interests as developing WTO Members, and have submitted extensive evidence with a view to demonstrating those interests. The European Communities agrees that the scope of Article 21.2 of the DSU is not limited to developing country Members as *implementing*, rather than as *complaining*, parties to a dispute. Rather, the European Communities argues that Article 21.2 is also applicable to developing country Members

---

187 Award of the Arbitrator, *EC – Tariff Preferences*, para. 50.
188 European Communities' written submission, para. 96.
189 *Ibid.*, para. 78.

who are *not* parties to a dispute.[190] The European Communities does not appear to dispute the development interests of Brazil and Thailand, nor the evidence submitted by Brazil and Thailand. Instead, the European Communities argues that a consequence of a shorter implementation period, combined with the suspension of export C sugar as advocated by the Complaining Parties, "could be" an increase in the world market price of sugar[191], and that would adversely affect the interests of sugar importing developing countries. The European Communities also argues that these interests, as well as the interests of ACP countries, are also interests within the meaning of Article 21.2 to which I should pay "[p]articular attention".

99. I find that previous arbitrators have not explicitly resolved the question whether the phrase "developing country Members" in Article 21.2 refers exclusively to the *implementing* Member, or whether it also applies to developing country Members *other* than the implementing Member such as, for instance, the complaining Member, third parties to the dispute, or any developing country Member of the WTO.[192] I consider that Article 21.2 is to be interpreted as directing an arbitrator to pay "[p]articular attention" to "matters affecting the interests" of both an *implementing* and *complaining* developing country Member or Members.[193] I note that Brazil, the European Communities and Thailand explicitly agree on this point.[194] In arriving at this conclusion, I agree with the arbitrator in *US – Gambling* that the text of Article 21.2 does not limit its scope of application to an implementing developing country Member.[195] I also note that Articles 21.7 and 21.8 refer to circumstances in which a "matter ... has been raised by a developing country Member" or "the case is one brought by a developing country Member"; this suggests that, where the drafters of the DSU wished to limit the

---

[190] European Communities' statement at the oral hearing and response to questioning at the oral hearing.

[191] The European Communities has submitted a study according to which the Complaining Parties do not have the necessary production capacity to replace the European Communities as a supplier of sugar to the world market by December 2005, in the event that the European Communities were to suspend its exports of C sugar. According to the European Communities, this circumstance would lead to a higher world market price for sugar, which in turn would adversely affect the developing countries that are importers of sugar. (European Communities' statement at the oral hearing and response to questioning at the oral hearing.)

[192] Previous arbitrators have considered that the interests of an *implementing* developing country Member of the WTO fall within the scope of Article 21.2. (Award of the Arbitrator, *Indonesia – Autos*, para. 24; Award of the Arbitrator, *Chile – Alcoholic Beverages*, para. 45; and Award of the Arbitrator, *Argentina – Hides and Leather*, para. 51.) The Arbitrator in *EC – Tariff Preferences* stated explicitly that he was not required to resolve the question whether Article 21.2 also applied to interests of developing Member countries not parties to the arbitration. (Award of the Arbitrator, *EC – Tariff Preferences*, para. 59.) The Arbitrator in *US – Gambling* stated explicitly that he was not required to resolve the question whether Article 21.2 applied to a *complaining* developing country Member. (Award of the Arbitrator, *US – Gambling*, para. 62.)

[193] As noted in paragraph 104, *infra*, it is not necessary for me to decide whether Article 21.2 is applicable to developing countries that are *not* parties to the arbitration proceedings.

[194] Brazil's written submission, para. 137; European Communities statement at the oral hearing and response to questioning at the oral hearing; Thailand's written submission, para. 74.

[195] Award of the Arbitrator, *US – Gambling*, para. 59.

scope of a provision to a particular category or group of developing country Members, they did so expressly.[196]

100. Having concluded that I am enjoined by Article 21.2 to pay "[p]articular attention" to matters affecting the interests of Brazil and Thailand as complaining parties in this dispute, I turn to consider the specific arguments of Brazil and Thailand in this respect. Brazil argues that its sugar industry constitutes more than a fifth of its total agribusiness gross domestic product; that a study in 1997 concluded that the sugar industry was "responsible for creating more than 654,000 direct and 937,000 indirect jobs in Brazil" and directly employed 764,593 persons in Brazil[197]; that the sugar industry has added importance because it is often located in rural areas and has a tradition of socially responsible employment; and that the European Communities' exports of subsidized sugar have a "detrimental effect on prices in the export market".[198] Thailand argues that the European Communities' sugar exports have a "depressive effect ... on the world market price for sugar".[199] Thailand also refers to adverse consequences flowing from continued subsidized exports from the European Communities on "1.5 million farmers' and sugar-related workers' households".[200] Thailand also argues that a large portion of its sugar-producing areas are located in parts of Thailand with annual incomes below the average annual income of Thailand. Both Brazil and Thailand submit evidence in support of their respective arguments.

101. Upon perusal of the evidence, I am satisfied, overall, that Brazil and Thailand have demonstrated their interests as developing country Members for purposes of Article 21.2 and that these interests are relevant for my determination of the reasonable period of time in this arbitration.

102. With respect to the development interests of the ACP countries[201], I am aware of the preferential market access to the European Communities' market that the ACP countries enjoy under the Cotonou Agreement. However, the rather limited evidence before me does not enable me to glean in which specific manner the ACP countries will be affected by implementation of the recommenda-

---

[196] For instance, Article 3.12 also explicitly refers to a situation in which "a complaint based on any of the covered agreements is brought by a developing country Member against a developed country Member". Article 12.10 refers to "consultations involving a measure taken by a developing country Member" and a "complaint against a developing country Member".

[197] Brazil's written submission, para. 138.

[198] *Ibid.*, para. 140.

[199] Thailand's written submission, para. 75.

[200] *Ibid.*, para. 77.

[201] With respect to ACP countries that were involved in the dispute as third parties with enhanced rights and that are least-developed countries, the European Communities refers to Article 24.1 of the DSU. Article 24.1 provides that, "[a]t all stages of ... dispute settlement procedures involving a least-developed country Member, particular consideration shall be given to the special situation of least-developed country Members." Specifically, Members are to exercise "due restraint" in raising matters under dispute settlement procedures involving a least-developed country Member; where nullification or impairment is found to result from a measure taken by a least-developed country Member, complaining parties "shall exercise due restraint in asking for compensation or seeking authorization to suspend the application of concessions or other obligations pursuant to [dispute settlement] procedures".

tions and rulings of the DSB in this dispute. Therefore, I have no precise basis on which to rely in order to pay "[p]articular attention" to the interests of the ACP countries in determining the reasonable period of time in this arbitration.

103. Likewise, there is insufficient evidence before me that would demonstrate whether or how the interests of other developing country Members who are exporters or importers of sugar would be affected by the implementation of the recommendations and rulings of the DSB. The European Communities has not specifically identified such other developing country Members in its submission or at the oral hearing.

104. Accordingly, it is not necessary for me, in the specific circumstances of this arbitration, to decide whether Article 21.2 is also applicable to developing country Members that are *not* parties to the arbitration proceedings under Article 21.3(c).

105. Finally, I note that the parties expressed various views on a question raised by me during the oral hearing: if the reasonable period of time expires in the course of a marketing year, how would this circumstance affect budgetary and quantity limitation commitments of the implementing Member for that marketing year, assuming that these commitments under the *Agreement on Agriculture* apply to a marketing year as a whole? Brazil and the European Communities stated expressly that the resolution of this issue does not fall within the mandate of an arbitrator under Article 21.3(c) of the DSU and that it is not of relevance for determining the reasonable period of time under that Article. I do not consider it necessary to address this issue.

106. On the basis of the above considerations, I determine that the "reasonable period of time" for the European Communities to implement the recommendations and rulings of the DSB in this dispute is 12 months and 3 days from 19 May 2005, which was the date on which the DSB adopted the Panel and Appellate Body Reports. The reasonable period of time will therefore expire on 22 May 2006.

UNITED STATES – SUNSET REVIEWS OF ANTI-DUMPING MEASURES ON OIL COUNTRY TUBULAR GOODS FROM ARGENTINA

Arbitration under Article 21.3(c) of the Understanding on Rules and Procedures Governing the Settlement of Disputes

Award of the Arbitrator

WT/DS268/12

Circulated to Members on 7 June 2005

Parties:	Arbitrator:
Argentina	A.V. Ganesan
United States	

TABLE OF CONTENTS

TABLE OF ARBITRATIONS CITED IN THIS AWARD

Short Title	Full Title and Citation of Arbitration
Australia – Salmon	Award of the Arbitrator, *Australia – Measures Affecting Importation of Salmon – Arbitration under Article 21.3(c) of the DSU*, WT/DS18/9, 23 February 1999, DSR 1999:I, 267
Canada – Autos	Award of the Arbitrator, *Canada – Certain Measures Affecting the Automotive Industry – Arbitration under Article 21.3(c) of the DSU*, WT/DS139/12, WT/DS142/12, 4 October 2000, DSR 2000:X, 5079
Canada – Patent Term	Award of the Arbitrator, *Canada – Term of Patent Protection – Arbitration under Article 21.3(c) of the DSU*, WT/DS170/10, 28 February 2001, DSR 2001:V, 2031
Canada – Pharmaceutical Patents	Award of the Arbitrator, *Canada – Patent Protection of Pharmaceutical Products – Arbitration under Article 21.3(c) of the DSU*, WT/DS114/13, 18 August 2000, DSR 2002:I, 3
Chile – Price Band System	Award of the Arbitrator, *Chile – Price Band System and Safeguard Measures Relating to Certain Agricultural Products – Arbitration under Article 21.3(c) of the DSU*, WT/DS207/13, 17 March 2003
EC – Hormones	Award of the Arbitrator, *EC Measures Concerning Meat and Meat Products (Hormones) – Arbitration under Article 21.3(c) of the DSU*, WT/DS26/15, WT/DS48/13, 29 May 1998, DSR 1998:V, 1833
EC – Tariff Preferences	Award of the Arbitrator, *European Communities – Conditions for the Granting of Tariff Preferences to Developing Countries – Arbitration under Article 21.3(c) of the DSU*, WT/DS246/14, 20 September 2004
Japan – Alcoholic Beverages II	Award of the Arbitrator, *Japan – Taxes on Alcoholic Beverages – Arbitration under Article 21.3(c) of the DSU*, WT/DS8/15, WT/DS10/15, WT/DS11/13, 14 February 1997, DSR 1997:I, 3

Short Title	Full Title and Citation of Arbitration
Korea – Alcoholic Beverages	Award of the Arbitrator, *Korea – Taxes on Alcoholic Beverages – Arbitration under Article 21.3(c) of the DSU*, WT/DS75/16, WT/DS84/14, 4 June 1999, DSR 1999:II, 937
US – 1916 Act	Award of the Arbitrator, *United States – Anti-Dumping Act of 1916 – Arbitration under Article 21.3(c) of the DSU*, WT/DS136/11, WT/DS162/14, 28 February 2001, DSR 2001:V, 2017
US – Hot-Rolled Steel	Award of the Arbitrator, *United States – Anti-Dumping Measures on Certain Hot-Rolled Steel Products from Japan – Arbitration under Article 21.3(c) of the DSU*, WT/DS184/13, 19 February 2002
US – Offset Act (Byrd Amendment)	Award of the Arbitrator, *United States – Continued Dumping and Subsidy Offset Act of 2000 – Arbitration under Article 21.3(c) of the DSU*, WT/DS217/14, WT/DS234/22, 13 June 2003
US – Section 110(5) Copyright Act	Award of the Arbitrator, *United States – Section 110(5) of the US Copyright Act – Arbitration under Article 21.3(c) of the DSU*, WT/DS160/12, 15 January 2001, DSR 2001:II, 657

I. INTRODUCTION

1. On 17 December 2004, the Dispute Settlement Body (the "DSB") adopted the Appellate Body Report[1] and the Panel Report[2], as modified by the Appellate Body Report, in *United States – Sunset Reviews of Anti-Dumping Measures on Oil Country Tubular Goods from Argentina* ("*US – Oil Country Tubular Goods Sunset Reviews*").[3] At the DSB meeting of 14 January 2005, the United States indicated its intention to implement the recommendations and rulings of the DSB in this dispute and stated that it would require a reasonable period of time in which to do so.[4]

2. On 11 March 2005, Argentina informed the DSB that consultations with the United States had not resulted in an agreement on the reasonable period of time for implementation. Argentina therefore requested that such period be determined by binding arbitration, pursuant to Article 21.3(c) of the *Understanding*

---

1 Appellate Body Report, WT/DS268/AB/R.
2 Panel Report, WT/DS268/R and Corr. 1.
3 WT/DS268/8.
4 WT/DSB/M/181, para. 10.

on Rules and Procedures Governing the Settlement of Disputes (the "DSU").[5] Subsequently, on 16 March 2005, Argentina and the United States communicated to the DSB their agreement that the award of the arbitrator made within 60 days after the date of appointment of the arbitrator shall be deemed to be an arbitration award under Article 21.3(c) of the DSU, notwithstanding the expiry of the 90-day period stipulated in Article 21.3(c).[6]

3. On 22 March 2005, Argentina advised the Director-General in writing that Argentina and the United States had been unable to agree on an arbitrator. Argentina therefore requested the Director-General to appoint an arbitrator pursuant to footnote 12 to Article 21.3(c) of the DSU, which provides for the Director-General to do so "within 10 days, after consulting the parties". However, before the Director-General had completed consultations with the parties, Argentina and the United States agreed on the selection of an arbitrator and, by a joint letter dated 30 March 2005, Argentina and the United States requested me to act as the arbitrator in this matter. On 8 April 2005, I informed Argentina and the United States in writing of my acceptance of the appointment as the arbitrator[7] and confirmed that I would issue my award no later than 7 June 2005, that is, no later than 60 days after my appointment as the arbitrator on 8 April 2005.

4. The United States and Argentina provided their written submissions to me on 22 April 2005. An oral hearing with them was held on 18 May 2005.

II. ARGUMENTS OF THE PARTIES

A. United States

5. The United States requests that I determine the "reasonable period of time" for implementation of the recommendations and rulings of the DSB in this dispute to be 15 months from the date of adoption by the DSB of the Panel and Appellate Body Reports, ending on 17 March 2006.[8]

6. According to the United States, in order to comply with the relevant recommendations and rulings, the United States Department of Commerce (the "USDOC") would have to first amend the waiver provisions of its regulations. Once these amended regulations have been issued, the USDOC would begin the process of making a new determination of likelihood of continuation or recurrence of dumping in the sunset review regarding oil country tubular goods from Argentina. The USDOC submits that it cannot complete these two phases of implementation in parallel "because of the impact of the WTO-inconsistent waiver provisions on the order-wide likelihood determination".[9] In this regard, the Uni-

---

[5] WT/DS268/9.

[6] WT/DS268/10. The 90-day period following adoption of the Panel and Appellate Body Reports expired on 17 March 2005.

[7] WT/DS268/11.

[8] United States' submission, paras. 3 and 27.

[9] *Ibid.*, para. 9 (referring to Appellate Body Report, *US – Oil Country Tubular Goods Sunset Reviews*, *supra*, footnote 1, paras. 234 and 260; and Panel Report, *US – Oil Country Tubular Goods Sunset Reviews*, *supra*, footnote 2, paras. 7.101 and 7.222). See also *ibid.*, para. 3.

ted States highlights the fact that the Panel in the present dispute "expressly declined" to recommend how the United States should implement the recommendations and rulings of the DSB.[10] In any case, the United States argues that previous arbitration awards confirm that it is for the implementing Member to decide the means of implementation, including the sequence of implementing steps.[11]

7. Beginning with the first phase of implementation, the United States contends that it will take approximately nine months for the USDOC to publish a new rule in the *United States Federal Register* (the "*Federal Register*"). The United States submits that this phase, which is governed by section 123 of the Uruguay Round Agreements Act, comprises the following steps:

(a) the first three months will involve consultations between: the United States Trade Representative (the "USTR") and the USDOC; the USTR and the United States Congress; and the USTR and certain private sector advisory committees. These consultations are already underway: the USTR and the USDOC have consulted; the USTR and Congress have consulted; and the USTR is consulting with the advisory committees. This three-month period will end with the USTR submitting a report to Congress describing the proposed rule, the reasons for the proposed rule and the advice provided by private sector advisory committees. The USTR has already begun to prepare this report;

(b) the USDOC will then need three months to complete the preparatory steps for, and to publish the proposed rule in, the *Federal Register*. Prior to publication, the USDOC must circulate the proposed rule for internal approval, modify it as a result of the USTR consultations with Congress and private sector advisory committees, and seek approval for publication of the proposed rule from the Office of Management and Budget (the agency with oversight for agency rule-making); and

(c) after the publication of the proposed rule, the USDOC will need a further three months to prepare for and publish the final rule in the *Federal Register*. Before publication, the USDOC will need to address public comments on the proposed rule and the USTR will hold final consultations with Congress. The United States explains that the final rule must not go into effect before the end of the 60-day period beginning on the date when consultations with Congress on the final rule began, unless the President determines that an earlier effective date is in the national interest.[12]

---

[10] *Ibid.*, para. 13 (referring to Panel Report, *US – Oil Country Tubular Goods Sunset Reviews*, *supra*, footnote 2, paras. 8.3 and 8.5).

[11] United States' submission, para. 13 (referring to Award of the Arbitrator, *Australia – Salmon*, para. 35; and Award of the Arbitrator, *US – Offset Act (Byrd Amendment)*, para. 52).

[12] *Ibid.*, paras. 4, 8, 15, and 18-20 (referring to section 123 of the Uruguay Round Agreements Act, codified as 19 U.S.C. §3533 (Exhibit US-1 attached to the United States' submission)).

8. As for the second phase of implementation, the United States submits that it will take six months for the USDOC to issue a new likelihood determination in the sunset review at issue. The United States argues that this phase, which is governed by section 129 of the Uruguay Round Agreements Act, involves the following steps:

(a) during the first month, consultations will be held between the USTR and the USDOC, and between the USTR and Congress;

(b) during the following two months, the USDOC will prepare questionnaires for interested parties and review responses before issuing a preliminary redetermination;

(c) interested parties will have one month to submit comments to the USDOC on the preliminary redetermination. This may include a hearing, in appropriate case;

(d) the USDOC will then have one month to address the comments of interested parties before issuing its final redetermination; and

(e) an additional month will be required for the USTR to review the final redetermination and for consultations to be held between the USTR and the USDOC, and between the USTR and Congress. Depending on the circumstances, the USTR may instruct the USDOC to implement the final redetermination and to notify the public of the implementation by publishing it in the *Federal Register*.[13]

9. The United States indicates that, during the course of the second phase of implementation, the USTR will formally request the USDOC to issue a redetermination to "render [its] actions not inconsistent"[14] with the relevant panel or Appellate Body findings. The USDOC will have 180 days from this request to issue a new determination. The United States adds that, "[i]n practice, USTR has sometimes delayed transmitting that request until just before [the USDOC] indicated informally that it was ready to issue a new determination".[15]

10. The United States argues that the time required to carry out these procedural steps in the two phases of implementation demonstrates the need for a 15-month implementation period in this dispute. In particular, the USTR must seek input from various bodies and interested parties throughout the implementation process. The United States indicates that previous arbitrators have recognized the importance of such consultations and have allowed sufficient time for them to take place.[16] In the second phase, the USDOC also needs sufficient time to ensure that it complies with its obligations of transparency and due process under Articles 6 and 12 of the *Agreement on Implementation of Article VI of the Gene-*

---

[13] United States' submission, paras. 4, 16, and 21-26 (referring to section 129 of the Uruguay Round Agreements Act, codified as 19 U.S.C. §3538 (Exhibit US-2 attached to the United States' submission)).

[14] *Ibid.*, para. 16.

[15] *Ibid.*, footnote 29 to para. 16.

[16] United States' submission, para. 10 (referring to Awards of the Arbitrators in *Canada – Autos* and *Canada – Pharmaceutical Patents*).

ral Agreement on Tariffs and Trade 1994 (the "*Anti-Dumping Agreement*"). The United States argues that, in accordance with previous arbitration awards, this should include time to obtain and analyze information from interested parties, even though this is not expressly required by statute or regulation.[17]

11. For these reasons, the United States contends that a period of 15 months, ending on 17 March 2006, is a reasonable period of time for it to implement the recommendations and rulings of the DSB in this dispute.

B. Argentina

12. Argentina requests that I determine the "reasonable period of time" for implementation of the recommendations and rulings of the DSB in this dispute to be seven months from the date of adoption by the DSB of the Panel and Appellate Body Reports, ending on 17 July 2005.[18]

13. Argentina highlights three "particular circumstances" of this dispute that it regards as relevant to the determination of the reasonable period of time pursuant to Article 21.3(c) of the DSU. The first relates to the nature of one of the provisions of the *Anti-Dumping Agreement* with which the United States has been found to have acted inconsistently, namely, Article 11.3 of the *Anti-Dumping Agreement* dealing with "sunset" reviews of anti-dumping duties. Article 11.3 contains a temporal element in that it requires Members to terminate anti-dumping duties not later than five years after they are *imposed*. In this dispute, approximately five years have passed after the date by which the United States was required to *terminate* the duties. According to Argentina, this reinforces the need for "[p]rompt compliance" in accordance with Article 21.1 of the DSU.

14. Secondly, the United States has invoked the exception in Article 11.3, whereby a Member may continue the anti-dumping duty beyond five years if its authorities have made a specific determination in a review that complies with certain "exacting conditions".[19] The DSB has ruled invalid the United States' invocation of the "exception".[20] Therefore, the question in this dispute is simply how much time the United States needs to comply with the "rule"[21] in Article 11.3, namely, the termination of the duties.

15. Thirdly, the primary inconsistency of the United States' measures, *as applied*, in the sunset review at issue is "the lack of positive evidence supporting [the USDOC's] determination that dumping would be likely".[22] This inconsistency is separate from the "as such" violations of the United States law and regulations. Modifying the law and regulations to address the inconsistency of the waiver provisions, and then applying the modified law and regulations to this sunset

---

[17] *Ibid.*, para. 12 (referring to Award of the Arbitrator, *EC – Tariff Preferences*, para. 42).
[18] Argentina's submission, para. 1.
[19] *Ibid.*, para. 4.
[20] Argentina's submission, para. 4.
[21] *Ibid.*
[22] *Ibid.*, para. 5.

review, would not cure this primary "as applied" inconsistency, because "the record evidence developed by [the USDOC] at the time of the Article 11.3 review could not then, and cannot now, support [the USDOC's] likely dumping determination".[23] Argentina therefore argues that I should not determine the reasonable period of time on the basis of this sequence of implementation, which cannot lead to compliance. Rather, in the present case, the amount of time required to implement the recommendations and rulings of the DSB with respect to the USDOC's likelihood determination in the sunset review at issue is simply the amount of time required to withdraw the underlying anti-dumping duty order.[24] The United States need not wait until it has amended its law and regulations before addressing this administrative "as applied" violation. In this regard, Argentina refers to a previous arbitration award that recognized that an implementing Member can take administrative steps towards implementation at the same time as legislative steps.[25]

16. In relation to the sequence of implementation, Argentina refers to the methods of implementation followed by the United States in certain disputes. Argentina points out that in *United States – Anti-Dumping Measures on Certain Hot-Rolled Steel Products from Japan*[26] and *United States – Countervailing Measures Concerning Certain Products from the European Communities*[27], the United States first amended the inconsistent regulations and then applied the new regulations to the specific proceedings at issue. However, "there is no basis in U.S. law for such a position".[28] On the contrary, United States law contemplates the issuance of a new determination that is not inconsistent with the relevant recommendations and rulings of the DSB. Moreover, in those two cases, the "as applied" violation resulted from the application of a law or regulation that was "as such" inconsistent with WTO obligations. This is not the case in this dispute. Instead, "fix[ing] the 'as such' violations first and then apply[ing] the amended waiver provisions would not cure the principal 'as applied' violation" in this dispute, which, according to Argentina, is "the lack of any evidence supporting [the USDOC]'s likelihood determination."[29] Argentina argues that a case more similar to this one is *United States – Countervailing Duties on Certain Corrosion-Resistant Carbon Steel Flat Products from Germany*[30], where the United States simply revoked the inconsistent countervailing duty order under the "changed circumstances" provisions of the United States law.

---

[23] *Ibid.*, para. 53.
[24] *Ibid.*, para. 36.
[25] *Ibid.*, para. 29 (referring to Award of the Arbitrator, *US – Hot-Rolled Steel*, para. 32).
[26] Appellate Body Report, WT/DS184/AB/R, adopted 23 August 2001, DSR 2001:X, 4697; Panel Report, WT/DS184/R, adopted 23 August 2001, as modified by the Appellate Body Report, WT/DS184/AB/R, DSR 2001:X, 4769.
[27] Appellate Body Report, WT/DS212/AB/R, adopted 8 January 2003; Panel Report, WT/DS212/R, adopted 8 January 2003, as modified by the Appellate Body Report, WT/DS212/AB/R.
[28] Argentina's submission, para. 46.
[29] *Ibid.*, para. 47.
[30] Appellate Body Report, WT/DS213/AB/R and Corr.1, adopted 19 December 2002; Panel Report, WT/DS213/R and Corr.1, adopted 19 December 2002, as modified by the Appellate Body Report, WT/DS213/AB/R and Corr.1.

17. Argentina also raises certain general considerations that it regards as relevant in this arbitration proceeding. According to Argentina, the implementing Member bears the burden of demonstrating that the implementation period it proposes is the shortest period possible under the legal system of the implementing Member.[31] In addition, that Member must take steps towards implementation as soon as the DSB adopts the relevant reports. Argentina points out that the United States was aware of the recommendations and rulings of the DSB regarding the "as applied" violations well before their adoption by the DSB on 17 December 2004, because it did not appeal the Panel's findings in this regard. Argentina further submits that if I find that the United States did not begin the compliance process upon adoption of the Panel and Appellate Body reports by the DSB, then I should take this "dilatory conduct" into account in determining the reasonable period of time.[32] Argentina also emphasizes that the United States must use the flexibility and discretion available in its legislative system to comply as quickly as possible.

18. Turning to the implementation process, Argentina maintains that the United States can, simultaneously, over a single seven-month period: revoke the inconsistent USDOC determination in the sunset review at issue; amend the Tariff Act of 1930; and amend the relevant USDOC regulations. Argentina submits that the United States can revoke the anti-dumping order at issue either under the "changed circumstances" provisions of United States law or under section 129(b) of the Uruguay Round Agreements Act.[33] Section 129(b) imposes no specific time frames for implementation, apart from requiring that the USDOC render a new determination within 180 days of a request by the USTR to do so. Argentina contends that the United States should use this flexibility to complete implementation quickly. Argentina also points out that amendments to USDOC regulations are governed by section 123(g) of the Uruguay Round Agreements Act.[34] Under this provision, a 60-day consultation period is required before a final rule goes into effect, unless the President determines that an earlier date is in the national interest. Argentina states that section 123(g) provides the United States with significant flexibility. In sum, Argentina argues that "[t]here are no constitutional or other legal impediments to U.S. implementation" within a short period of time.[35]

19. Argentina also considers that I should take into account, in making my determination, the fact that Argentina is a developing country complainant.[36] In particular, Argentina declares that "Argentina, a developing country Member,

[31] Argentina's submission, paras. 18-20 (referring to Award of the Arbitrator, *EC – Hormones*, para. 26; Award of the Arbitrator, *Canada – Pharmaceutical Patents*, para. 47; and Award of the Arbitrator, *US – Offset Act (Byrd Amendment)*, para. 44).

[32] *Ibid.*, paras. 23 and 56 (quoting Award of the Arbitrator, *Chile – Price Band System*, para. 43).

[33] Argentina's submission, para. 50; 19 U.S.C. §3538(b) (Exhibit ARG-1 attached to Argentina's submission).

[34] Argentina's submission, para. 64; 19 U.S.C. §3533(g) (Exhibit ARG-3 attached to Argentina's submission).

[35] Argentina's submission, para. 71.

[36] *Ibid.*, paras. 31-32 and 78-80 (referring to Award of the Arbitrator, *Chile – Price Band System*, paras. 55-56).

continues to suffer impaired access to the U.S. market because of the WTO-inconsistent U.S. measures".[37] Argentina also points out that, unlike in the arbitration in *Chile – Price Band System*, the implementing Member in this dispute is not a developing country Member.

20. Finally, Argentina identifies some considerations that it regards as irrelevant to the determination of the reasonable period of time, in particular, the internal practices of the United States Congress. Therefore, Argentina argues that I should not take into account the time required for the United States to implement broader legislative changes, such as in an Omnibus Trade Bill combining a large number of trade measures[38], or the fact that Congress usually passes a large number of bills at the end of each legislative session.[39] In addition, Argentina maintains that "extraneous considerations" such as the contentiousness of the compliance process are irrelevant, and additional time should not be granted on that basis for extended consultations with interested parties.[40]

21. For these reasons, Argentina contends that a period of seven months, ending on 17 July 2005, is a reasonable period of time for the United States to implement the recommendations and rulings of the DSB in this dispute.

III. REASONABLE PERIOD OF TIME

A. General Principles

22. Pursuant to Article 21.3(c) of the DSU, my task as arbitrator in this case is to determine the "reasonable period of time" for the United States to implement the recommendations and rulings of the DSB in *US – Oil Country Tubular Goods Sunset Reviews*.[41] As the Panel and Appellate Body Reports relating to this dispute were adopted by the DSB on 17 December 2004, the "reasonable period of time" will be calculated as from that date.

23. Article 21.3(c) of the DSU provides that, when the "reasonable period of time" is determined through arbitration:

> ... a guideline for the arbitrator should be that the reasonable period of time to implement panel or Appellate Body recommendations should not exceed 15 months from the date of adoption of a panel or Appellate Body report. However, that time may be shorter or longer, depending upon the particular circumstances. (footnote omitted)

24. Prior to examining the factual situation in this dispute, I wish to highlight certain general principles that have been followed in previous arbitrations under

---

37 *Ibid.*, para. 78.

38 *Ibid.*, paras. 30 and 73-74 (referring to Award of the Arbitrator, *EC – Tariff Preferences*, para. 31).

39 *Ibid.*, para. 75 (referring to Award of the Arbitrator, *US – 1916 Act*, para. 38).

40 *Ibid.*, paras. 76-77.

41 See WT/DS268/11.

Article 21.3(c) and that are pertinent to the determination of the "reasonable period of time" in this dispute.

25. First, the "reasonable period of time" under Article 21.3(c) should be "the shortest period possible within the legal system of the Member to implement the relevant recommendations and rulings of the DSB", in the light of the "particular circumstances" of the dispute.[42] Both the United States and Argentina are in agreement with this general principle.

26. Secondly, the nature of the steps to be taken for implementation has a bearing on the "reasonable period of time" required to fully implement the recommendations and rulings of the DSB. The implementation may require amendments to laws or regulations that may involve legislative action, or it may require amendments to administrative guidelines or procedures that may not involve such action. Implementation may also involve only the remedying of the deficiencies in a particular determination. Previous arbitration awards under Article 21.3(c) have recognized that when implementation requires legislative action, the "reasonable period of time" required may be longer than in cases where only administrative action is required to amend guidelines or procedures or to remedy the deficiencies in particular determinations.[43] It is, however, not for the arbitrator under Article 21.3(c) to prescribe a particular method of implementation and to determine the "reasonable period of time" on the basis of that method.[44]

27. Thirdly, whatever be the method of implementation chosen by the implementing Member, that Member must take advantage of the flexibility and discretion available within its legal and administrative system to implement the recommendations and rulings of the DSB as speedily as possible.[45]

28. Fourthly, as the text of Article 21.3(c) makes clear, the "particular circumstances" of each case must be taken into account in determining the "reasonable period of time" for implementation. The United States and Argentina are not in agreement, however, as to what constitutes the "particular circumstances" in this dispute within the meaning of Article 21.3(c).

29. Argentina argues that I should take into account, as one of the "particular circumstances", the *nature of the provisions* of the WTO agreement that the United States has been found to have violated in the underlying dispute. That

---

42 Award of the Arbitrator, *Chile – Price Band System*, para. 34 (quoting Award of the Arbitrator, *US – 1916 Act*, para. 32). See also Award of the Arbitrator, *EC – Hormones*, para. 26; and Award of the Arbitrator, *EC – Tariff Preferences*, para. 26.

43 See Award of the Arbitrator, *Canada – Pharmaceutical Patents*, para. 49; Award of the Arbitrator, *Chile – Price Band System*, para. 38; and Award of the Arbitrator, *US – Offset Act (Byrd Amendment)*, para. 57.

44 See, for example, Award of the Arbitrator, *Korea – Alcoholic Beverages*, para. 45; Award of the Arbitrator, *US – 1916 Act*, para. 36; Award of the Arbitrator, *Chile – Price Band System*, para. 32; Award of the Arbitrator, *US – Offset Act (Byrd Amendment)*, para. 48; and Award of the Arbitrator, *EC – Tariff Preferences*, para. 30.

45 See Award of the Arbitrator, *Canada – Patent Term*, paras. 63 and 64; and Award of the Arbitrator, *US – Offset Act (Byrd Amendment)*, para. 64 (referring to Award of the Arbitrator, *US – Section 110(5) Copyright Act*, para. 39 and Award of the Arbitrator, *US – 1916 Act*, para. 39).

violation pertains to a "sunset review" determination as envisaged under Article 11.3 of the *Anti-Dumping Agreement.* Article 11.3 requires Members to terminate anti-dumping duties not later than five years after they are *imposed.* This is the "rule", and the continuation of the anti-dumping duties beyond five years, after a sunset review, is an "exception" that must fulfil "exacting conditions".[46] Argentina observes that, in this case, approximately five years have passed since the date by which the United States was required to *terminate* the duties. Argentina argues that, as the United States' "invocation" of the "exception" to the "rule" of Article 11.3 has been found to be "invalid", the "sole issue ... is the amount of time required under U.S. law to withdraw the antidumping duty order".[47]

30. The United States, in contrast, argues that the relevant "particular circumstances" in this dispute cannot include the nature of the specific provision at issue in the underlying proceeding, namely, Article 11.3 of the *Anti-Dumping Agreement.* Nor can they include the particular method of implementation proposed by Argentina, namely, the revocation of the anti-dumping duty order, or the consideration that the termination of the duty is the "rule" and its continuation is an "exception" under Article 11.3. Rather, "the particular circumstances" that previous arbitrators have taken into account include the legal form of implementation, the technical complexity of the necessary measures to be adopted and implemented, and the period of time in which the implementing Member can achieve the proposed form of implementation within its legal system.[48] Thus, the relevant "particular circumstances" in this dispute are the amount of time the United States needs to complete the domestic procedures that would fully implement the DSB recommendations and rulings, taking into account the fact that the USDOC is required to amend the "waiver provisions" of the USDOC Regulations[49] found to be WTO-inconsistent "as such". The United States emphasizes that the USDOC will not be in a position to begin the process of issuing a redetermination in respect of the "as applied" violation until its modified regulations are effective, because of the Panel and Appellate Body findings on "the impact of the WTO-inconsistent waiver provisions on the order-wide likelihood determination."[50]

31. Lastly, I note that Argentina argues that the implementing Member—in this case, the United States—bears the burden of demonstrating that the period it proposes—in this case, 15 months—is the "shortest period possible" to bring its measures into conformity with the relevant recommendations and rulings of the

46 Argentina's submission, para. 4.

47 *Ibid.*, paras. 4 and 36.

48 United States' statement at the oral hearing; United States' submission, para. 7 (referring to Award of the Arbitrator, *Japan – Alcoholic Beverages II*, para. 12 and Award of the Arbitrator, *Canada – Pharmaceutical Patents*, paras. 49-51).

49 The "USDOC Regulations", as they relate to sunset reviews, are found in Procedures for Conducting Five-year ("Sunset") Reviews of Antidumping and Countervailing Duty Orders, *United States Federal Register*, Vol. 63, No. 54 (20 March 1998), p. 13516 (Exhibit US-3 submitted by the United States to the Panel), codified in Title 19, section 351.218 of the *United States Code of Federal Regulations*.

50 *Supra*, footnote 9.

DSB.[51] The United States responds that it has discharged this burden as it has demonstrated in detail both the specific steps needed to implement the recommendations and rulings of the DSB and the time needed to comply with those steps, emphasizing that, within its legal framework, the amendment of the USDOC Regulations and the application of the amended regulations to the redetermination must be done *in seriatim*.

32. With these considerations in mind, I turn now to an examination of the facts of this case.

B. The Recommendations and Rulings of the DSB to be Implemented

33. In this dispute, the United States is required to bring the following three measures, found in the Panel Report, as modified by the Appellate Body Report, to be inconsistent with the *Anti-Dumping Agreement*, into conformity with its obligations under that Agreement:

(a) the USDOC's determination of likelihood of continuation or recurrence of dumping (the "likelihood-of-dumping determination") made with respect to imports of oil country tubular goods from Argentina, which was found to be inconsistent with Article 11.3 as well as Article 6.2 of the *Anti-Dumping Agreement* (the "as applied" violation);

(b) the "waiver provisions" of section 751(c)(4)(B) of the Tariff Act of 1930 and section 351.218(d)(2)(iii) of the USDOC Regulations, which were found to be inconsistent, as such, with Article 11.3 of the *Anti-Dumping Agreement* ("as such" violation); and

(c) the "deemed waiver provision" of section 351.218(d)(2)(iii) of the USDOC Regulations, which was found to be inconsistent, as such, with Articles 6.1 and 6.2 of the *Anti-Dumping Agreement* with respect to respondents that file incomplete submissions ("as such" violation).

34. With respect to the "as applied" violation mentioned above, both parties agree that the likelihood-of-dumping determination underlying this dispute is the "order-wide likelihood determination" by the USDOC that "revocation of the antidumping duty orders on oil country tubular goods from Argentina ... would likely lead to continuation or recurrence of dumping" that was published in the *Federal Register* on 7 November 2000.[52]

---

[51] Argentina's submission, paras. 19 and 34.

[52] USDOC, Final Results of Expedited Sunset Reviews: Oil Country Tubular Goods from Argentina, Italy, Japan, and Korea, *United States Federal Register*, Vol. 65, No. 216 (7 November 2000) p. 66701 at 66703 (Exhibit ARG-46 submitted by Argentina to the Panel). During the oral hearing, the United States clarified that although the order-wide determination includes countries other than Argentina, it is a combination of the determinations made with respect to each country and, so far as this dispute is concerned, the determination made with respect to Argentina could be dealt with separately.

C. *The Means of Implementation*

35. With respect to the "as such" violations described above[53], it is not in dispute that, in order to implement the relevant recommendations and rulings of the DSB in *US – Oil Country Tubular Goods Sunset Reviews*, the United States is required to amend the USDOC Regulations. At the oral hearing, the United States confirmed that it "intends to address the DSB's recommendations and rulings concerning the waiver provision in the statute (section 751(c)(4)(B) of the Tariff Act of 1930) through modification of its regulations."[54] With respect to the "as applied" violation described above[55], there is, however, a disagreement between the parties as to whether the USDOC can make a "new determination" or a "redetermination"[56] of the likelihood of continuation or recurrence of dumping in the underlying sunset review without first issuing amended regulations that are in conformity with the *Anti-Dumping Agreement*.

36. Argentina argues that the "principal" inconsistency that the Panel found with respect to the underlying likelihood-of-dumping determination was that it "was not based on positive evidence"; that is to say, there was no "evidentiary basis" to support the USDOC's likelihood-of-dumping determination.[57] According to Argentina, amending the waiver provisions and then applying them to a new determination cannot "remedy the absence of positive evidence of likely dumping".[58] Argentina submits, therefore, that a "shorter option" for implementation of the recommendations and rulings of the DSB in this dispute is to "conduct an administrative proceeding *without* applying the waiver provision, or *without* allowing it to affect the country-wide determination based on the facts of this case."[59] In sum, Argentina contends that there is no basis for the United States' assertion that implementation requires an *in seriatim* approach.[60]

37. The United States argues, in contrast, that the Panel's finding that the likelihood-of-dumping determination was inconsistent with Article 11.3 of the *Anti-Dumping Agreement* was based on two grounds: first, one of the factual bases of the USDOC's affirmative determination, namely, that dumping by Argentine exporters continued over the life of the measure, was not proper; and, secondly, in reaching this determination, the USDOC applied to Argentine exporters other than Siderca the waiver provisions of United States law that the Panel found to be inconsistent, as such, with Article 11.3 of the *Anti-Dumping Agreement*. With respect to the first ground, the United States emphasizes that the Panel's conclusion was based not on a finding "that there was a lack of any evidence in support of the affirmative determination", but rather on a finding that the USDOC "did

53 See *supra*, paras. 33(b) and 33(c).

54 United States' submission, footnote 7 to para. 3.

55 See *supra*, para. 33(a).

56 The United States explained at the oral hearing that, in order to make this new determination or redetermination, it would "reassess the evidence" on the record and "seek clarification" from interested parties.

57 Argentina's submission, paras. 5, 9, 47, 48, and 58.

58 Argentina's statement at the oral hearing.

59 *Ibid.* (original emphasis)

60 *Ibid.*

not have sufficient grounds for finding that dumping had continued over the life of the order".[61] With respect to the second ground, the United States points out that the application of WTO-inconsistent waiver provisions in the underlying sunset review determination cannot be remedied without amending the USDOC Regulations. The United States submits that Argentina's arguments are based on its assumption that the only way for the United States to cure the "as applied" violation in this case is by revoking the anti-dumping duty order in its entirety. According to the United States, it is, however, for the implementing Member to decide the most appropriate way of bringing an impugned measure into conformity with its obligations under a covered agreement.

38. In response to questioning at the oral hearing as to why the process of reassessing the evidence on record for a factual determination by the USDOC to remedy the "as applied" violation and the process of amending the USDOC Regulations to remedy the "as such" violations cannot proceed in parallel, the United States argued that it would be "getting into legally murky waters" if it were to make a redetermination based on the existing regulations that were found to be WTO-inconsistent, or if it began the process of making the redetermination based on existing regulations, amended the regulations "mid-stream", and then applied the amended regulations to the final determination. The United States stressed in this regard that both the Panel and the Appellate Body had found that the existing waiver provisions have an "impact ... on the order-wide likelihood determination".[62] When the USDOC issues new questionnaires in order to make a redetermination, there may well be Argentine "non-respondents", unknown to the USDOC now, and if the USDOC applies the existing waiver provisions to them, the redetermination could again be challenged as being inconsistent with Article 11.3 of the *Anti-Dumping Agreement*. Thus, to comply fully with the recommendations and rulings of the DSB and to remedy the "as applied" violation, the United States submits that it must first amend the waiver provisions of the USDOC Regulations and then apply the amended regulations to the redetermination. The United States emphasizes that this does not, however, mean that the USDOC would engage in a *de novo* sunset review determination.[63]

39. In response to questioning at the oral hearing as to how the USDOC could engage in a redetermination without first amending the waiver provisions of the USDOC Regulations (given that the Panel's conclusion rests in part on the application of the waiver provisions to Argentine exporters other than Siderca), Argentina acknowledged that the United States is required to amend the waiver provisions of the USDOC Regulations. However, in this case, because the underlying determination lacked a sufficient factual basis with respect to exports either by Siderca or by other Argentine exporters, it is open to the United States to make its redetermination without taking into account the waiver provisions. Argentina further argued that, under the facts of this case, with respect to "non-respondent" Argentine companies, the United States has a "discretion" not to

61 United States' statement at the oral hearing.

62 *Supra*, footnote 9.

63 United States' response to questioning at the oral hearing.

apply the "automatic assumption" of continuation of dumping, and instead to assign a "zero weight" to such companies. Argentina further observed that the United States has the discretion under its law and regulations to determine, on a case-by-case basis, the amount of weight to assign to company-specific findings and how those findings impact upon a country-wide determination. If the United States chose to exercise such discretion in this case, it would be left only with the factual evidence on record "as it stood at the time the [USDOC] invoked the exception from Article 11.3", and it could make the redetermination on that basis. In Argentina's view, that would lead to a revocation of the anti-dumping duty order. Argentina therefore contended that an *in seriatim* approach was not necessary or required on the facts of this case.

D. *The Implementation Process*

40. I now turn to the arguments advanced by the United States in support of its position that it requires 15 months to complete the implementation process in this case.[64]

41. The United States submits that it requires 15 months because the implementation process needs to be carried out in two phases *in seriatim*. The United States explains the two phases as follows. In the first phase, the USDOC will amend the waiver provisions of its regulations to bring them into conformity with the DSB's recommendations and rulings. The United States has already begun the work in respect of this phase, which, according to the United States, will take nine months to complete. In the second phase, the USDOC will issue a new determination of likelihood of continuation or recurrence of dumping that is consistent with the DSB's recommendations and rulings. According to the United States, this phase will take six months, but the USDOC will not be able to begin this phase until the regulations are first amended and made effective.

42. Explaining the United States statutory framework, the United States submits that "[t]here are two principle U.S. statutory provisions governing implementation in this dispute – section 123 of the Uruguay Round Agreements Act, which governs implementation involving a [USDOC] regulation, and section 129 of the Uruguay Round Agreements Act, which governs implementation involving an action by [the USDOC] in an antidumping (or countervailing duty) proceeding".[65]

43. According to the United States, the first and second phases of the implementation process require the specific procedural steps outlined above.[66] At the oral hearing, the United States explained that it expected to complete the section 123 process by 17 September 2005. Although this was "about a month and a half behind" the schedule for the first phase, the United States expected that it could "still make up the time" during the section 129 process for the second phase.

---

[64] United States' submission, para. 3.

[65] *Ibid.*, para. 14. (footnote omitted)

[66] See *supra*, paras. 7 and 8.

44. Argentina argues that the United States "can adopt a new regulation within four months of a DSB ruling" because "there are no rules that limit the speed at which regulatory amendments could be made in order for the United States to comply with its WTO obligations".[67] According to Argentina, "there is only one provision of section 123(g) that imposes any defined time limit", and this provision merely provides that a "final rule may not go into effect before the end of the 60-day consultation period", but even this is "subject to an exception".[68] In this regard, Argentina cites *United States – Anti-Dumping Duty on Dynamic Random Access Memory Semiconductors (DRAMS) of One Megabit or Above from Korea* ("*US – DRAMS*")[69], in which the United States changed its regulation in six months and seven days, and put in place a new regulation five weeks later, for a total implementation period of seven months and seventeen days.

45. As regards the second phase of the implementation process, Argentina contends that some of the activities outlined by the United States, such as the issuance of original and supplemental questionnaires, verification of information, and issuance of a preliminary determination, are not warranted or required under United States law in a sunset review proceeding. Argentina also submits that some of the other activities, such as determining what information is needed, reviewing and analyzing the comments received, and making a final determination, do not require the long time periods indicated by the United States. Argentina also points out that it is open to the United States to conduct its section 129(b) determination concurrently with the section 123(g) process.[70] Lastly, Argentina submits that the redetermination needed in this case is "akin to the administrative proceeding [that the USDOC] conducts when other tribunals (such as a reviewing court or a [North American Free Trade Agreement ("NAFTA")] panel) find a [USDOC] determination to be unlawful", and that "such tribunals often provide [the USDOC] only *30 or 60 days* to render a redetermination".[71] In sum, Argentina argues that the six-month period proposed by the United States for the second phase cannot possibly be justified, and that a redetermination could be done in this case in three months.[72]

46. Responding to Argentina's citation of previous disputes, the United States submits that the facts in *US – DRAMS* were "very different" from those that are relevant to implementation in this dispute.[73] With respect to implementation of decisions by NAFTA panels, the United States points out that "NAFTA applies US law", that a NAFTA ruling "is subject to US rules", and that this is not the case with WTO proceedings, which have the additional procedural and transpa-

67 Argentina's statement at the oral hearing.
68 *Ibid.*
69 Panel Report, WT/DS99/R, adopted 19 March 1999, DSR 1999:II, 521.
70 Argentina's statement at the oral hearing.
71 *Ibid.* (original emphasis)
72 Argentina notes in this regard that the United States had proposed only a four-month period to issue a new determination in *US – Hot-Rolled Steel*. (Argentina's statement at the oral hearing)
73 United States' statement at the oral hearing.

rency requirements set out in section 129 of the Uruguay Round Agreements Act.[74]

E. Argentina as a Developing Country Member

47. Both in its written submission, and during the oral hearing, Argentina referred to Article 21.2 of the DSU, which provides:

> Particular attention should be paid to matters affecting the interests of developing country Members with respect to measures which have been subject to dispute settlement.

48. Argentina suggests that, in determining the reasonable period of time in this case, I should take "cognizance of Argentina's continuing hardship as a developing country as long as the WTO-inconsistent U.S. measures are maintained."[75] Argentina clarified at the oral hearing that it was not suggesting that I should depart from the basic principle that the "reasonable period of time" be determined on the basis of "the shortest period possible", but rather that Article 21.2 provides "context" for my determination of the "reasonable period of time" in this case.[76]

F. Determination of "Reasonable Period of Time"

49. As noted above, both parties agree with the general principle articulated in previous arbitration awards under Article 21.3(c) of the DSU that the "reasonable period of time" should be determined on the basis of the "shortest period possible within the legal system of the Member to implement the relevant recommendations and rulings of the DSB".[77] Both parties also agree that the implementing Member must take advantage of the flexibility and discretion available within its legal and administrative system to implement the recommendations and rulings of the DSB as speedily as possible.[78] During the oral hearing, Argentina agreed that it is for the implementing Member to choose the most appropriate method of implementation and that it is not for the arbitrator under Article 21.3(c) of the DSU to prescribe a particular method of implementation. But Argentina emphasized that, whatever be the method or process chosen by the implementing Member, the implementation must be carried out within the "shortest period possible" by the implementing Member, utilizing all the flexibility and discretion available to it within its legal and administrative system to do so.

50. The United States considers that the waiver provisions of the USDOC Regulations must first be amended to bring them into conformity with the DSB's recommendations and rulings, and that only after the amended regulations are issued could they be applied to a new determination to remedy the "as applied" violation in this dispute. In this regard, I note two aspects of this dispute: first,

[74] United States' response to questioning at the oral hearing.
[75] Argentina's submission, para. 80.
[76] Argentina's statement and response to questioning at the oral hearing.
[77] See *supra*, para. 25 and footnote 42.
[78] See *supra*, para. 27.

one of the reasons for the Panel finding the "as applied" violation was that WTO-inconsistent waiver provisions were applied to Argentine exporters other than Siderca; and, second, an amendment of the waiver provisions of the USDOC Regulations is in any event required to remedy the "as such" violations in this dispute. The United States has explained why it considers an *in seriatim* approach to be necessary in this case to ensure that the redetermination is in conformity with its own legal system.[79] Argentina does not question what the United States considers to be the requirements of its legal system, but emphasizes that the United States, as the implementing Member, bears the responsibility to exercise all flexibility and discretion available to it to remedy the WTO violations as rapidly as possible.[80]

51. I further note that the United States agrees that some of the steps and the time periods indicated for them in its implementation process are not required by law. But they are needed for the implementation to be carried out in a transparent and efficient manner.[81] I also note that the United States agrees that some of the steps included in the two phases of implementation, such as consultations with Congress, can be carried out in a flexible or concurrent manner to save time, consistent, however, with the legal requirements of sections 123 and 129 of the Uruguay Round Agreements Act.[82]

52. As noted above, for my determination of the reasonable period of time, Argentina requests me to use as "context" the fact that Argentina is a developing country Member.[83] Having regard to the implementation process involved in this dispute, I consider that, beyond the fundamental requirement that the implementation process should be completed in the shortest period possible within the legal and administrative system of the United States, the "reasonable period of time" for implementation is not affected by the fact that Argentina, as the complaining Member, is a developing country.

IV. THE AWARD

53. In the light of what has been stated above, I determine that the "reasonable period of time" for the United States to implement the recommendations and rulings of the DSB in this dispute is 12 months from 17 December 2004, which was the date on which the DSB adopted the Panel and Appellate Body Reports. The reasonable period of time will therefore expire on 17 December 2005.

---

79 See *supra*, para. 38.

80 See *supra*, para. 39.

81 United States' response to questioning at the oral hearing.

82 *Ibid.*

83 See *supra*, para. 48.

UNITED STATES – MEASURES AFFECTING THE CROSS-BORDER SUPPLY OF GAMBLING AND BETTING SERVICES

Arbitration under Article 21.3(c) of the Understanding on Rules and Procedures Governing the Settlement of Disputes

Award of the Arbitrator

WT/DS285/13

Circulated to Members on 19 August 2005

Parties:	Arbitrator:
Antigua and Barbuda	Claus-Dieter Ehlermann
United States	

TABLE OF CONTENTS

TABLE OF CASES CITED IN THIS AWARD

Short Title	Full Title and Citation
Australia – Salmon	Award of the Arbitrator, *Australia – Measures Affecting Importation of Salmon – Arbitration under Article 21.3(c) of the DSU* ("*Australia – Salmon* "), WT/DS18/9, 23 February 1999, DSR 1999:I, 267.
Canada – Patent Term	Award of the Arbitrator, *Canada – Term of Patent Protection – Arbitration under Article 21.3(c) of the DSU*, WT/DS170/10, 28 February 2001, DSR 2001:V, 2031
Canada – Pharmaceutical Patents	Award of the Arbitrator, *Canada – Patent Protection of Pharmaceutical Products – Arbitration under Article 21.3(c) of the DSU* ("*Canada – Pharmaceutical Patents* "), WT/DS114/13, 18 August 2000, DSR 2002:I, 3.
Chile – Price Band System	Award of the Arbitrator, *Chile – Price Band System and Safeguard Measures Relating to Certain Agricultural Products – Arbitration under Article 21.3(c) of the DSU* ("*Chile – Price Band System* "), WT/DS207/13, 17 March 2003.
EC – Bananas III	Award of the Arbitrator, *European Communities – Regime for the Importation, Sale and Distribution of Bananas – Arbitration under Article 21.3(c) of the DSU*, WT/DS27/15, 7 January 1998, DSR 1998:I, 3.
EC – Hormones	Award of the Arbitrator, *EC Measures Concerning Meat and Meat Products (Hormones) – Arbitration under Article 21.3(c) of the DSU*, WT/DS26/15, WT/DS48/13, 29 May 1998, DSR 1998:V, 1833
EC – Tariff Preferences	Award of the Arbitrator, *European Communities – Conditions for the Granting of Tariff Preferences to Developing Countries – Arbitration under Article 21.3(c) of the DSU* ("*EC – Tariff Preferences*"), WT/DS246/14, 20 September 2004.
Guatemala – Cement I	Appellate Body Report, *Guatemala – Anti-Dumping Investigation Regarding Portland Cement from Mexico* ("*Guatemala – Cement I* "), WT/DS60/AB/R, adopted 25 November 1998, DSR 1998:IX, 3767.

Short Title	Full Title and Citation
Japan – Alcoholic Beverages II	Award of the Arbitrator, *Japan – Taxes on Alcoholic Beverages – Arbitration under Article 21.3(c) of the DSU*, WT/DS8/15, WT/DS10/15, WT/DS11/13, 14 February 1997, DSR 1997:I, 3
Korea – Alcoholic Beverages	Award of the Arbitrator, *Korea – Taxes on Alcoholic Beverages – Arbitration under Article 21.3(c) of the DSU* ("*Korea – Alcoholic Beverages* "), WT/DS75/16, WT/DS84/14, 4 June 1999, DSR 1999:II, 937.
US – 1916 Act	Award of the Arbitrator, *United States – Anti-Dumping Act of 1916 – Arbitration under Article 21.3(c) of the DSU* ("*US – 1916 Act* "), WT/DS136/11, WT/DS162/14, 28 February 2001, DSR 2001:V, 2017.
US – Gambling	Appellate Body Report, *United States – Measures Affecting the Cross-Border Supply of Gambling and Betting Services* ("*US – Gambling*"), WT/DS285/AB/R, adopted 20 April 2005.
US – Gambling	Panel Report, *United States – Measures Affecting the Cross-Border Supply of Gambling and Betting Services* ("*US – Gambling*"), WT/DS285/R, adopted 20 April 2005, as modified by Appellate Body Report, WT/DS285/AB/R.
US – Hot-Rolled Steel	Award of the Arbitrator, *United States – Anti-Dumping Measures on Certain Hot-Rolled Steel Products from Japan – Arbitration under Article 21.3(c) of the DSU*, WT/DS184/13, 19 February 2002
US – Hot-Rolled Steel	Appellate Body Report, *United States – Anti-Dumping Measures on Certain Hot-Rolled Steel Products from Japan* ("*US – Hot-Rolled Steel* "), WT/DS184/AB/R, adopted 23 August 2001, DSR 2001:X, 4697.
US – Offset Act (Byrd Amendment)	Award of the Arbitrator, *United States – Continued Dumping and Subsidy Offset Act of 2000 – Arbitration under Article 21.3(c) of the DSU*, WT/DS217/14, WT/DS234/22, 13 June 2003.

Short Title	Full Title and Citation
US – Oil Country Tubular Goods Sunset Reviews	Award of the Arbitrator, *United States – Sunset Reviews of Anti-Dumping Measures on Oil Country Tubular Goods from Argentina – Arbitration under Article 21.3(c) of the DSU*, WT/DS268/12, 7 June 2005.
US – Section 110(5) Copyright Act	Award of the Arbitrator, *United States – Section 110(5) of the US Copyright Act – Arbitration under Article 21.3(c) of the DSU* WT/DS160/12, 15 January 2001, DSR 2001:II, 657.

I. INTRODUCTION

1. On 20 April 2005, the Dispute Settlement Body (the "DSB") adopted the Appellate Body Report[1] and the Panel Report[2], as modified by the Appellate Body Report, in *United States – Measures Affecting the Cross-Border Supply of Gambling and Betting Services.*[3] At the DSB meeting of 19 May 2005, the United States indicated its intention to implement the recommendations and rulings of the DSB in this dispute and stated that it would require a reasonable period of time in which to do so.[4]

2. On 6 June 2005, Antigua and Barbuda ("Antigua") informed the DSB that consultations with the United States had not resulted in an agreement on the reasonable period of time for implementation. Antigua therefore requested that such period be determined by binding arbitration, pursuant to Article 21.3(c) of the *Understanding on Rules and Procedures Governing the Settlement of Disputes* (the "DSU").[5]

3. Antigua and the United States were unable to agree on an arbitrator within 10 days of the matter being referred to arbitration. Therefore, by letter dated 17 June 2005[6], Antigua requested that the Director-General appoint an arbitrator pursuant to footnote 12 to Article 21.3(c) of the DSU. The Director-General appointed me as arbitrator on 30 June 2005, after consulting the parties.[7] I informed the parties of my acceptance of the appointment by letter dated 30 June 2005.

1 Appellate Body Report, WT/DS285/AB/R.
2 Panel Report, WT/DS285/R.
3 WT/DS285/10.
4 WT/DSB/M/189, para. 47.
5 WT/DS285/11.
6 Antigua's letter was received on 20 June 2005.
7 WT/DS285/12.

4. Antigua and the United States have agreed that this award will be deemed to be an arbitration award under Article 21.3(c) of the DSU, notwithstanding the expiry of the 90 day period stipulated in Article 21.3(c).[8]

5. Antigua and the United States provided their written submissions to me on 12 July 2005. On 20 July 2005 I requested the United States, by letter, to provide me with a copy of the 2006 schedules for the House of Representatives and the Senate. An oral hearing was held on 21 July 2005. At the outset of that hearing, the United States informed me that the 2006 schedules for the United States Congress are not yet available, but that the recess periods in 2006 were likely to be similar to those in the 2005 schedules.[9] On 22 July 2005, in response to a question posed at the oral hearing, the United States informed me by letter that there is currently one bill under consideration by the United States Congress related to the subject of internet gambling.[10]

II. ARGUMENTS OF THE PARTIES

A. United States

6. The United States requests that I determine the "reasonable period of time" for implementation of the recommendations and rulings of the DSB in this dispute to be 15 months from the date of adoption by the DSB of the Panel and Appellate Body Reports, until the end of July 2006.[11]

7. The United States asserts that in the particular circumstances of this case, the legal form of implementation and the technical complexity of the measures require a reasonable period of time of at least 15 months. Such a period is consistent with the periods that have been determined in previous arbitrations under Article 21.3(c) of the DSU for implementation by legislative means, which is how the United States intends to implement the recommendations and rulings of the DSB in this case. The United States also explains that, since the date of adoption of the Panel and Appellate Body Reports in this dispute, the executive branch has been consulting internally with Congress and with domestic stakeholders on possible legislative action.

8. The United States contests Antigua's argument that, with respect to "non-sports" betting and gambling, the United States could implement through issuance of a presidential executive order. According to the United States, the issue of executive orders is not relevant to my determination of the reasonable period of time because Antigua accepts that implementation must, in any case, include

---

[8] The 90 day period following adoption of the Panel and Appellate Body Reports expired on 19 July 2005.

[9] The United States included the 2005 schedules of both chambers of Congress as Exhibit US-9 to its submission.

[10] The United States referred to H.R. 1422, the Student Athlete Protection Act. The United States also conveyed its understanding that a Senator is in the process of preparing an internet gambling bill to strengthen penalties for illegal gambling and limit the use of financial instruments in connection with internet gambling.

[11] United States' submission, paras. 5, 8, 9, 14, 19, 35 and 36.

some form of legislative action (if only with respect to "sports-related" betting and gambling). The text of Article 21.3(c) refers to "*a* reasonable period of time" (emphasis added). It follows that an arbitrator is to determine a *single* reasonable period of time, which in this case must be the reasonable period of time necessary for *legislation*. That there is no basis in the DSU for an arbitrator to assign multiple reasonable periods of time for different forms of implementation is confirmed, argues the United States, by the previous arbitral awards that have considered multiple proposed forms of implementation, namely the awards in *US – Hot-Rolled Steel* and *US – Oil Country Tubular Goods Sunset Reviews*.

9. The United States does not, in any event, accept Antigua's proposed distinction between "sports" and "non-sports" gambling and betting. The United States contends that no such distinction exists under any of the three federal statutes at issue in this dispute, namely the Wire Act, the Travel Act and the Illegal Gambling Business Act (the "IGBA"). For the same reason, the United States disputes that an executive order could be used in the manner suggested by Antigua, because an executive order may not contradict an existing statute. In addition, in this specific case, it is extremely unlikely that an executive order could achieve the necessary clarification of the relationship between the Interstate Horseracing Act ("IHA"), on the one hand, and the Wire Act, Travel Act and the IGBA, on the other hand. The United States points, in this regard, to the presidential statement on signing accompanying the bill enacting the December 2000 amendments to the IHA, which expressed the view that nothing in the IHA overrode previously enacted criminal laws. The Panel in this dispute found that this statement was not sufficient to resolve the ambiguity in the relationship, and the Appellate Body did not depart from this view.[12] The United States submits that if a presidential statement accompanying signature of a bill could not achieve the requisite clarity in the relationship between the relevant statutes, then a presidential executive order could not do so either.

10. The United States emphasizes that it will use legislative means to clarify the relationship between the IHA and the three pre-existing federal criminal statutes. Referring to the Appellate Body Report in this dispute, the United States observes that it must demonstrate "that—in the light of the existence of the Interstate Horseracing Act—the Wire Act, the Travel Act, and the Illegal Gambling Business Act are applied consistently with the requirements of the chapeau"[13] to Article XIV of the GATS. Thus, "a reasonable legislative option would have the effect of clarifying that relevant U.S. federal laws entail no discrimination between foreign and domestic service suppliers in the application of measures prohibiting remote supply of gambling and betting services".[14] Taking account of this objective, and in the light of the "multifaceted nature of the obligation in the chapeau of Article XIV", there "will be ample room for reasonable and principled disagreements among legislators as to precisely how to achieve such a clari-

---

12 United States' submission, footnote 6 to para. 9, referring to Panel Report, para. 6.597, and Appellate Body Report, para. 373(D)(v)(c).

13 United States' submission, para. 11, referring to Appellate Body Report, para. 373(D)(v)(c).

14 United States' submission, para. 11.

fication in the context of Internet gambling".[15] The United States contrasts the complexities involved in implementation in this dispute with the simple legislative change—to the length of patent term—that was required in *Canada – Patent Term*, where the arbitrator determined the reasonable period of time for implementation to be 10 months.[16]

11. The United States adds that the legislative exercise will be further complicated by the fact that since 1997, the United States Congress has considered a wide range of legislative proposals aimed at internet gambling, none of which has been adopted. The existence of this complex, and as-yet unresolved legislative debate means that the task of adopting compliance legislation will take longer due to the need to assess the potential impact of each option on a variety of other proposed legislative changes.

12. The United States argues that a 15 month implementation period is consistent with previous arbitration awards under Article 21.3(c) of the DSU that have involved legislative change and refers, in particular, to the awards of the Arbitrators in *Japan – Alcoholic Beverages II*, *EC – Bananas III*, and *EC – Hormones*. Consistent with the approach taken in those arbitrations, the United States underlines that it is not for Antigua to determine what type of legislative option the United States should choose, or that a less complex option could be enacted in less than 15 months.

13. In support of its argument that a 15 month period is necessary in order to implement the recommendations and rulings of the DSB in this dispute, the United States explains the process by which the United States Congress passes legislation. Proposed legislation can only become law after it has been approved in identical form by both chambers of Congress—the House of Representatives and the Senate—and approved by the President of the United States. A bill passes through at least ten steps between the time that it is introduced and the time that it is approved by both chambers. The first step is introduction of the bill in Congress. Generally, bills are referred to a committee, and possibly also to subcommittees, where public hearings will be conducted. Then the bill goes through a "mark-up" process where changes and amendments are made before the subcommittee "reports" the bill to the full committee. The committee may conduct further study and hearings, and another mark-up process follows before the relevant committee votes on whether to "report" the bill to the full House. If so, a detailed, section-by-section committee report is prepared and the bill is "reported back" to the House. The bill is debated and amendments may be offered before the House votes on the bill. The bill may be returned to the committee or, if passed by the House, must be referred to the Senate. The Senate may approve the bill as received, reject it, ignore it or change it. Most bills passed by the Senate are not precisely the same as the bill referred by the House and, in such circumstances, a conference committee is organized to reconcile differences between the House and Senate versions. If the conference committee is able to

---

15 United States' submission, para. 12.

16 United States' submission, para. 12, referring to Award of the Arbitrator, *Canada – Patent Term,* paras. 55-56.

reach agreement on a single bill, a conference report is prepared, and this must be approved by both chambers, in identical form, before it can be sent to the President for approval.

14. The United States stresses that the executive branch has no control over the procedures and timetable followed by Congress. The United States declined, at the oral hearing, to estimate on a disaggregated basis the length of time that would be necessary in this case for each one of the steps in its legislative process, noting that such time periods vary widely and are, in many cases, determined on an *ad hoc* basis by the House of Representatives and/or the Senate. The United States also explained, in response to questioning at the oral hearing, that although the above procedure reflects, in practice, how Congress operates, the only two steps that are explicitly required under the United States Constitution are the approval of a bill by both chambers of Congress and the signature of the President.

15. The United States adds that an important determinant of when a bill becomes law is the Congressional schedule. Each Congress consists of two sessions of one year each, and the United States is currently in the first session of the 109th Congress. Sessions of Congress typically begin in January and end in October, November or December of the calendar year. At present, the first session of the 109th Congress is scheduled to end on 30 September 2005. The United States explains that most bills that become law are acted on only in the last weeks or months of the legislative session, and that a bill introduced in the first session of a Congress may be carried over to the second session. According to the United States, these reasons explain why I should not attach any significance to the 15 measures already passed by Congress in the 109th session, which Antigua cites as illustrative of how quickly the United States Congress can act. These 15 measures will represent only a tiny fraction of all the laws that will be passed in the 109th session. Moreover, of these 15 measures, four dealt with disaster relief or emergencies, three were legislative packages that had been thoroughly considered in a previous Congress or Congresses, four dealt with the renewal of measures previously enacted but due to expire, and four involved the naming of buildings and museum regents.[17] Thus, explains the United States, the rapidity with which these measures were passed in the first half of the 109th session of Congress is not at all representative of the ordinary workings of the United States legislative process.

16. The United States argues that, given the complexity of the legislative task required in this case, the need to consider implementing legislation in a deliberate manner, and the other matters that will be under consideration during the remainder of the first session of the 109th Congress, the legislation implementing the recommendations and rulings of the DSB will not be completed in the first session of the current Congress, but will instead need to be carried over into the second session, in 2006. The United States suggests that, in the same way that Congress is often spurred to pass legislation prior to the end of a legislative

[17] United States' statement at the oral hearing.

session, so too is it prompted to pass legislation prior to a recess. In the light of the fact that Congress will adjourn for its August recess in late July 2006, the United States suggests that this would be an appropriate point at which to conclude the reasonable period of time for implementation in this dispute.

17. As regards the application of Article 21.2 of the DSU in this arbitration, the United States cautions me not to expand the scope of a proceeding under Article 21.3(c) of the DSU by acceding to Antigua's request to resolve any ambiguities in Antigua's favour and to ensure that the proposed method of compliance is consistent with the recommendations and rulings of the DSB and the provisions of the covered agreements. The United States emphasizes that my task is to determine the shortest period possible within the legal system of the United States, and that this determination cannot be affected by the fact that the complaining party in the dispute is a developing country Member.

B. Antigua

18. Antigua requests that I determine the "reasonable period of time" for implementation of the recommendations and rulings of the DSB in this dispute to be: (i) as regards the provision of non-sports related and horseracing gambling and betting services, either immediately or not later than one month following the issuance of this award; and (ii) as regards the provision of other sports-related gambling and betting services, six months from the date of adoption by the DSB of the Panel and Appellate Body Reports, ending on 20 September 2005.[18]

19. With respect to "non-sports related and horse race gambling and betting services", Antigua observes that there is significant doubt that the Wire Act, the Travel Act or the IGBA apply to the provision to United States consumers of such services supplied from a foreign country in which such services are legal. Antigua points to the fact that no court has held any of these laws applicable to non-sports betting services supplied by remote means, and that the opinions of experts on this subject are "decidedly equivocal".[19] Moreover, according to Antigua, prior to March 1998 the United States Department of Justice publicly maintained that the provision of gambling and betting services into the United States from foreign jurisdictions was not subject to federal prosecution. Since this policy was shifted once, argues Antigua, it can be shifted back to the pre-March 1998 position again. Although such a shift could be effected on an informal basis within the Department of Justice and other agencies of the United States government, Antigua argues that it could be *definitively* accomplished

---

18 Antigua's submission, para. 62.

19 Antigua's submission, para. 13, referring in footnote 25 to: United States General Accounting Office, GAO/GCD – 96-28, *Internet Gambling: An Overview of the Issues* (December 2002) (Exhibit AB-17 submitted by Antigua to the Panel), pp. 12-16; J. Rodefer, "Internet Gambling in Nevada: Overview of Federal Law Affecting Assembly Bill 466", published on 18 March 2003 on the website of the Department of Justice of Nevada, <www.ag.state.nv.us> (Exhibit AB-54 submitted by Antigua to the Panel); and J. Kelly, R. Mignin, and S. Saxman, "US Policy" in M. Balestra and A. Cabot (eds.), *Internet Gambling Report: An Evolving Conflict Between Technology and Law*, 8th ed. (River City Group LLC Publisher, 2005), p. 217.

through a presidential "executive order". Executive orders are orders or decrees given by the President of the United States to agencies of the federal government such as the Department of Justice. Antigua observes that the power to issue executive orders forms part of the general executive powers of the President under Article II of the United States Constitution, and that executive orders have been used by every President for a wide variety of subjects. Antigua refers to a study that has defined executive orders as "directives or actions by the President" that have the "force and effect of law" when "founded on the authority of the President derived from the Constitution or a statute."[20]

20. Thus, concludes Antigua, with respect to the provision of non-sports related and horseracing gambling and betting services, the United States should implement the recommendations and rulings of the DSB by issuing an executive order to the agencies of the United States government to the effect that: (i) these services may be lawfully offered by Antiguan operators to consumers in the United States; and (ii) all enforcement and related action to the contrary should immediately cease and desist. Antigua adds that executive orders can be promulgated in a simple and expedient manner, requiring only a matter of weeks, and that once signed by the President, an executive order becomes law in the United States upon its publication in the *Federal Register.* Given that executive orders are short and do not require the consent of anyone other than the President, Antigua submits that the United States should be accorded only the briefest practical period of time to issue the necessary order, namely immediately or in any event no less than one month after the issuance of this award.

21. In response to questioning at the oral hearing on the issue of executive orders, Antigua accepted that, in principle, the United States, as the implementing Member, has discretion to decide how best to effect implementation. Antigua added, however, that if the United States chooses a more complicated and lengthy means of implementation, rather than a shorter one that has been shown to be available, then this choice should have as a consequence that the time period which the United States is afforded in order to pursue its legislative solution is shorter than it would otherwise be.

22. With respect to the application of the Wire Act, the Travel Act and the IGBA to the provision of sports-related gambling and betting services, Antigua accepts that legislative action will be necessary for the United States to implement the recommendations and rulings of the DSB. In this regard, Antigua again recognizes that the implementing Member may choose its method of implementation, but stresses that this choice is subject to the proviso that the means chosen must be consistent with the relevant recommendations and rulings. Antigua submits that an arbitrator under Article 21.3(c) faced with a proposed method of compliance that is not so consistent could take this factor into account in making his award.

[20] Antigua's submission, para. 19, referring in footnote 37 to T.L. Branum, "President or King? The Use and Abuse of Executive Orders in Modern-Day America", *Journal of Legislation*, Vol. 28 (2002), p. 1 at 6, citing Commission on Government Operations, 85th Congress, "Executive Orders and Proclamations: A Study of the Use of Presidential Powers" 14 (Comm. Print 1957).

23. Antigua submits that, in general, the burden of proof is on the implementing Member, and emphasizes that the political sensitivity or contentiousness of a particular course of action is irrelevant to the determination of the reasonable period of time.[21] Equally irrelevant, submits Antigua, are the consideration by the legislature of various legislative options, the volume of legislation considered by the legislature, and the high percentage of bills that do not become law.[22] On the other hand, Antigua urges me to take account of the flexibility that exists within the United States legislative system, as well as of the actions taken by the United States with respect to implementation since adoption by the DSB of the Reports in this dispute.

24. In response to questioning at the oral hearing, Antigua confirmed that it agrees, in principle, with the United States' description of the process by which legislation is enacted by the United States Congress. Antigua stresses, however, that except for obtaining Congressional approval, none of the specific steps identified by the United States is required by law and none is assigned a required time period. It follows that considerable flexibility is built into the United States legislative system. Antigua submits that the flexibility enjoyed by the United States Congress has been recognized by previous arbitrators, and is also illustrated by a survey of legislation adopted during the current, 109th, session of Congress. According to Antigua, of the 15 measures enacted into law through 19 June 2005, two became law within a day of introduction, the longest period from introduction to adoption was 91 days, and the average number of days from introduction to adoption was 43.27 days.[23] Antigua also points out that the amendment to the IHA in 2000 took a mere five months to pass.[24]

25. According to Antigua, legislation to bring the Wire Act, the Travel Act and the IGBA into compliance with the recommendations and rulings of the DSB need not be complicated. Antigua draws a contrast between certain public pronouncements made by the United States to the effect that implementation will be very simple, and its position in this arbitration, namely that implementation will be "technically complex". In Antigua's view, the United States has failed to demonstrate any such complexity. Accordingly, Antigua submits that there are no compelling reasons why the United States would require more than six months to implement the recommendations and rulings of the DSB regarding the Wire Act, the Travel Act and the IGBA.

26. Finally, Antigua invokes Article 21.2 of the DSU, which provides for "particular attention" to be paid to "matters affecting the interests of developing country Members". Antigua underlines the importance of a well-regulated cross-border gambling and betting service industry to the economic health and growth of Antigua, as well as the strain that this dispute has placed on Antigua's limited

---

[21] Antigua's submission, paras. 30 and 31, referring in footnote 53 to Award of the Arbitrator, *US – Section 110(5) Copyright Act* para. 42; and Award of the Arbitrator, *Canada – Patent Term*, para. 58.

[22] Antigua's submission, para. 31, referring in footnotes 57 and 58 to Award of the Arbitrator, *US – Offset Act (Byrd Amendment)*, paras. 53 and 59; and Award of the Arbitrator, *US – 1916 Act,* para. 38.

[23] Antigua's submission, para. 54.

[24] Antigua's submission, para. 54, referring in footnotes 94 and 95 to Sections 3001-3007 of Title 15 of the United States Code, H.R. 4942.

resources. Antigua submits that I should rely on Article 21.2 of the DSU to resolve any ambiguities or uncertainties related to compliance in this case in favour of Antigua, and in this regard asks that I carefully scrutinize the efficacy of the United States' proposed means of implementation. In response to questioning at the oral hearing, Antigua emphasized that the United States legislative process is very flexible and does not include fixed time periods for each step in the process. Accordingly, Antigua submits that in this case it would be proper for me to use Article 21.2 to require the United States to be especially diligent and to use the flexibility inherent in its system to achieve rapid implementation. In other words, Antigua asks me to use Article 21.2 of the DSU in order to determine a shorter reasonable period of time for implementation than I might otherwise do.

III. REASONABLE PERIOD OF TIME

A. Preliminary Matters

1. Mandate

27. The Panel and Appellate Body Reports in this dispute were adopted by the DSB on 20 April 2005 and, pursuant to Article 21.3 of the DSU, the United States informed the DSB of its intentions with respect to implementation shortly thereafter.[25] Article 21.3 of the DSU establishes that, when it is "impracticable" for a Member to comply "immediately" with the recommendations and rulings of the DSB, then that Member "shall have a reasonable period of time in which to do so." The United States informed the DSB that it would require such a reasonable period of time in this dispute.

28. My task as arbitrator in this proceeding is to determine such reasonable period of time, taking due account of the relevant provisions of the DSU, and, specifically, of the following directions set forth in Article 21.3:

> ... The reasonable period of time shall be:
>
> ...
>
> (c) a period of time determined through binding arbitration ... In such arbitration, a guideline for the arbitrator should be that the reasonable period of time to implement panel or Appellate Body recommendations should not exceed 15 months from the date of adoption of a panel or Appellate Body report. However, that time may be shorter or longer, depending upon the particular circumstances. (footnotes omitted)

[25] Minutes of the DSB meeting held on 19 May 2005, WT/DSB/M/189, para. 47.

2. *The Measures to be Brought into Conformity*

29. Both the Panel and Appellate Body Reports in this dispute contained findings that the United States had acted inconsistently with its obligations under the covered agreements. More specifically, the Appellate Body upheld the Panel's finding that, by maintaining the following three measures, the United States acts inconsistently with its obligations under Article XVI:1 and sub-paragraphs (a) and (c) of Article XVI:2 of the GATS:

- Section 1084 of Title 18 of the United States Code (the "Wire Act");
- Section 1952 of Title 18 of the United States Code (the "Travel Act"); and
- Section 1955 of Title 18 of the United States Code (the "Illegal Gambling Business Act", or the "IGBA").[26]

30. The Appellate Body also upheld, albeit for different reasons, the Panel's finding that the United States had not demonstrated that its measures, found to be inconsistent with Article XVI of the GATS, satisfy the requirements of Article XIV of the GATS.[27] Accordingly, the Appellate Body recommended that the DSB request the United States to bring its inconsistent measures into conformity with its obligations under the GATS.

B. *Factors Affecting the Determination of the Reasonable Period of Time under Article 21.3(c)*

1. *Burden of Proof*

31. Both of the parties to this dispute agree that the United States, as the implementing Member, bears the burden of establishing that its proposed implementation period is a "reasonable period of time".[28] I do not disagree with the principle that when an implementing Member seeks a reasonable period of time for implementation, then it is appropriate for that Member to carry the burden of demonstrating the reasonableness of its proposal.[29]

2. *Choice of Method of Implementation*

32. Both the Appellate Body and the Panel found that, due to ambiguity in the relationship between the Wire Act, the Travel Act and the IGBA, on the one hand, and a federal civil statute known as the Interstate Horseracing Act (the "IHA") on the other hand, the United States had not satisfied its burden of justifying the measures at issue under the chapeau to Article XIV of the GATS.[30] Referring to these findings, the United States indicates that it will seek to imple-

---

[26] Appellate Body Report, para. 373(C)(ii); Panel Report, para. 7.2(b)(i).

[27] Appellate Body Report, para. 373(D)(vi); Panel Report, para. 7.2(d).

[28] Antigua's submission, para. 30; United States' response to questioning at the oral hearing.

[29] Award of the Arbitrator, *US – 1916 Act*, para. 33. A similar sentiment was also expressed by the Arbitrator in *EC – Tariff Preferences*, at paragraph 27 of his award.

[30] Appellate Body Report, para. 373(D)(v)(c); Panel Report, paras. 6.599-6.600.

ment the recommendations and rulings of the DSB by further clarifying the relationship between these statutes. Antigua, on the other hand, believes that broader action is necessary. Antigua submits that the United States can properly implement the recommendations and rulings of the DSB only if, consistently with the requirements of the chapeau to Article XIV of the GATS, it removes any discrimination in the treatment of Antiguan suppliers of "remote" gambling and betting services, on the one hand, and the treatment of domestic suppliers of the same services, on the other.[31] To do so, argues Antigua, the United States will have to either grant market access to Antiguan service providers or prohibit the supply of all domestic remote gambling services.

33. It is not the role of an arbitrator under Article 21.3(c) to identify a particular method of implementation and to determine the "reasonable period of time" on the basis of that method. Rather, the implementing Member retains the discretion to choose its preferred method of implementation.[32] Nevertheless, it will be necessary for me to consider certain aspects of the means of implementation proposed by each of the parties, as explained in more detail below.

3. *Particular Circumstances*

34. Article 21.3(c) requires that I determine the "reasonable period of time for implementation", establishes a guideline that this period "should not exceed 15 months", and directs that in fixing the relevant period I should have regard to "the particular circumstances" of this case.

35. It is by now well established that a key determinant of the reasonable period of time for implementation is the nature of the implementing action that is to be taken. Legislative action will, as a general rule, require more time than regulatory rule-making, which in turn will normally need more time than implementation that can be achieved by means of an administrative decision.[33]

---

[31] In this dispute, the Panel used the term "remote" supply to refer to:

> "any situation where the supplier, *whether domestic or foreign*, and the consumer of gambling and betting services are not physically together". In other words, in situations of remote supply, the consumer of a service does not have to go to any type of outlet where the supply is supervised, be it a retail facility, a casino, a vending machine, etc. Instead, the remote supplier offers the service directly to the consumer through some means of distance communication. Hence, cross-border supply is necessarily remote, but remote supply amounts to "cross-border" supply only when the service supplier and the consumer are located in territories of different Members.

(Panel Report, para. 6.32; original emphasis, footnote omitted)

[32] See, for example, Award of the Arbitrator, *EC – Hormones*, para. 38; Award of the Arbitrator, *Australia – Salmon,* para. 35; Award of the Arbitrator, *Korea – Alcoholic Beverages*, para. 45; Award of the Arbitrator, *Chile – Price Band System*, para. 32; Award of the Arbitrator, *US – Offset Act (Byrd Amendment*), para. 48; Award of the Arbitrator, *EC – Tariff Preferences*, para. 30; and Award of the Arbitrator, *US – Oil Country Tubular Goods Sunset Reviews,* para. 26.

[33] See, for example, Award of the Arbitrator, *Australia – Salmon*, para. 38; Award of the Arbitrator, *US – Section 110(5) Copyright Act*, para. 34; Award of the Arbitrator, *Canada – Pharmaceutical Patents*, para. 49; Award of the Arbitrator, *Canada – Patent Term*, para. 41; Award of the Arbitrator, *Chile – Price Band System*, para. 38; Award of the Arbitrator, *US – Offset Act (Byrd Amendment)*, para. 57; and Award of the Arbitrator, *US – Oil Country Tubular Goods Sunset Reviews*, para. 26.

36. In this arbitration, Antigua contends that the United States can implement, in part, through executive action, and in part through legislative action. With respect to what Antigua characterizes as the supply of "non-sports related and horseracing" gambling and betting services, Antigua argues that the United States can, and should, implement the recommendations and rulings of the DSB through the issuance of an executive order by the United States President that would clarify that the supply of such services from Antigua is not prohibited under the Wire Act, the Travel Act or the IGBA.[34] As regards the supply of "other sports-related" gambling and betting services, Antigua accepts that legislative change will be necessary in order to clarify whether and how the Wire Act, the Travel Act and the IGBA apply to these activities.

37. The United States maintains that I need not address Antigua's arguments concerning implementation by executive order for at least three reasons. First, and foremost, it is my role under Article 21.3(c) to determine a *single* reasonable period of time for implementation. Since both parties agree that implementation by legislative means is required in this case, Antigua's argument that partial implementation could be achieved in a shorter period of time is irrelevant. For the United States, the only reasonable period of time that I am to determine is the reasonable period of time for *legislative* implementation. The United States points, in this respect, to two previous arbitrations in which a single reasonable period of time for implementation was determined, notwithstanding that the parties agreed that two different methods of implementation were required.[35] Secondly, the United States rejects Antigua's distinction between the supply of "non-sports related and horseracing" gambling and betting services, on the one hand, and the supply of "other sports-related" gambling and betting services, on the other. In the view of the United States, the three federal statutes at issue apply equally to, and prohibit, the supply of all forms of remote gambling and betting services. Thirdly, the United States contends that it is neither appropriate nor possible to achieve implementation in this dispute by means of a presidential executive order. The order that Antigua contends the United States President should issue could not properly form the subject of an executive order. Furthermore, the United States points out that it argued before the Panel that a presidential statement that accompanied the passage of the amendments to the IHA made clear that nothing in that Act, as amended, overrides the previously enacted

---

[34] Specifically, Antigua argues that:

> ... it is well within the power of the president to issue an executive order to the agencies of the United States government to the effect that (i) these services may be lawfully offered by Antiguan operators to consumers in the United States and (ii) all enforcement and related action to the contrary, including (A) asset forfeitures, (B) restrictions on money transfers and use of financial instruments, (C) threats of federal prosecution by the DOJ against service providers to these industries, including advertisers, banks and credit card companies and processors, and (D) current pending prosecutions against persons operating these businesses, should in each instance immediately cease and desist.

(Antigua's submission, para. 22; footnote omitted)

[35] Award of the Arbitrator, *US – Hot-Rolled Steel*; and Award of the Arbitrator, *US – Oil Country Tubular Goods Sunset Reviews.*

criminal laws relating to gambling. Nevertheless, neither the Panel nor the Appellate Body considered that this presidential statement was sufficient to resolve the ambiguity in the relationship between the IHA, on the one hand, and the Wire Act, the Travel Act, and the IGBA, on the other. Given that the presidential statement was not considered by the Panel or the Appellate Body to provide sufficient clarity regarding this relationship, the United States submits that an executive order issued by the President would not do so either. For this reason, the United States emphasizes that the only means of implementation that will achieve the necessary clarification is legislative means.

38. As I understand it, although there is no express provision creating the power to issue executive orders, it is commonly accepted that the United States President has the authority to issue such orders, and that such authority derives from the general executive powers vested in the President by Article II of the United States Constitution.[36] In practice, United States presidents do issue executive orders. Nevertheless, the scope of the authority to issue such orders, and the types of matters that may be dealt with by executive order, appear to be matters of some debate. At the oral hearing, both parties agreed that the United States President may not issue an executive order that contradicts an existing statute. The parties disagree, however, on the issue of whether the Wire Act, the Travel Act and the IGBA, as they stand, prohibit the supply of "non-sports related and horseracing" gambling and betting services from Antigua to consumers in the United States.

39. Neither the Panel nor the Appellate Body referred to the distinction that Antigua now draws, namely between the United States' regulation of the supply of "non-sports related and horseracing" gambling and betting services, on the one hand, and its regulation of the supply of "other sports-related" gambling and betting services, on the other. In response to a question at the oral hearing, Antigua acknowledged that neither report distinguishes between types of gambling. Moreover, it seems to me that the findings of both the Panel and the Appellate Body are based on the premise that each of the three statutes in question prohibits a broad category of gambling activities.[37]

---

[36] Antigua's submission, para. 17.

[37] The Panel's explanation of the three federal laws is set out in paragraphs 6.360 to 6.380 of the Panel Report, and the Appellate Body's treatment of the three statutes is found in paragraphs 257-265 of the Appellate Body Report. With respect to the Wire Act, the Panel observed that it prohibits "the use of a wire communication facility for, *inter alia*, the transmission in interstate or foreign commerce of bets or wagers". (Panel Report, para. 6.362. See also Appellate Body Report, para. 259) As for the Travel Act, the Panel stated that it prohibits:

> ... gambling activity that entails the supply of gambling and betting services by 'mail or any facility' to the extent that such supply is undertaken by a "business enterprise involving gambling" that is prohibited under state law and provided that the other requirements in subparagraph (a) of the Travel Act have been met.

(Panel Report, para. 6.370. See also Appellate Body Report, para. 261)

Lastly, the Panel explained that the IGBA prohibits:

> ... gambling activity that entails the conduct, finance, management, supervision, direction or ownership of all or part of such a business to the extent that such supply is undertaken by a "gambling business" that is prohibited under state law and pro-

40. In asking me to draw this distinction, therefore, Antigua is effectively asking me to make a ruling concerning the meaning and scope of application of United States municipal law. I do not consider that it forms part of my mandate to do so, given that the findings of the Panel and the Appellate Body make no such distinction.

41. Because I do not rule on whether the distinction asserted by Antigua exists, I need not, in this proceeding, resolve the issue of whether it is permissible for an arbitrator under Article 21.3(c) of the DSU to determine more than one reasonable period of time for implementation. I am not persuaded that the mere use of the indefinite article "a" in the phrase "a reasonable period of time" suffices, as the United States suggests, to establish definitively that an arbitrator is authorized only to determine a *single* reasonable period of time for implementation in a dispute. At the same time, conceptually, I have difficulty accepting that it may be possible to determine, as Antigua seems to request me to do, two separate reasonable periods of time in respect of the *same* measure.[38] I would not, however, want to exclude *a priori,* and without having carried out a thorough interpretative analysis of the relevant provisions of the DSU, the possibility that an arbitrator might be able to fix separate reasonable periods of time for separate measures. It is true that, to date, no arbitrator has done so.[39] Yet it is also true that, to date, no arbitrator has been asked to do so.

42. Having declined to rule on the distinction on which Antigua bases its assertion that the United States could undertake two separate methods of implementation, I need not consider the reasonable period of time that would be necessary for implementation by means of an executive order. I turn, instead, to the question of the reasonable period of time needed for the United States to implement by legislative means.

43. In response to a question at the oral hearing, Antigua suggested that even if I were to consider that the United States enjoys the discretion to decide to implement by legislative means, rather than by means of an executive order, then the United States should be required to "pay the price" for having chosen a "complicated, more lengthy way" of implementing rather than another available method that would be shorter. Thus, submits Antigua, I should reduce the reasonable period of time for legislative implementation. Given that I do not rule on the distinction on which Antigua bases its assertion that two separate means of implementation are possible in this case, I need not decide whether a Member's

---

> vided that the other requirements in sub-paragraph (b)(1) of the Illegal Gambling Business Act have been met.

(Panel Report, para. 6.377. See also Appellate Body Report, para. 263)

[38] Essentially, Antigua is asking me to determine two separate reasonable periods of time for the United States to implement the DSB's recommendations and rulings regarding the Wire Act, two separate reasonable periods of time for the United States to implement the DSB's recommendations and rulings regarding the Travel Act, and two separate reasonable periods of time for the United States to implement the DSB's recommendations and rulings regarding the IGBA.

[39] In Award of the Arbitrator, *US – Hot-Rolled Steel*, the Arbitrator determined a single reasonable period of time of 15 months (para. 40); and in Award of the Arbitrator, *US – Oil Country Tubular Goods Sunset Reviews,* the Arbitrator determined a single reasonable period of time for implementation of 12 months (para. 53).

decision to opt for one means of implementation (legislative) notwithstanding that another, more rapid means of implementation has been demonstrated to be available, could affect the determination of the reasonable period of time for implementation under Article 21.3(c) of the DSU.

44. Antigua and the United States agree that, as previous arbitrators have stated, the "reasonable period of time" under Article 21.3(c) should be "the shortest period possible within the legal system of the Member to implement the relevant recommendations and rulings of the DSB", in the light of the "particular circumstances" of the dispute.[40] Yet, it is useful to recall that the DSU does not refer to the "shortest period possible for implementation within the legal system" of the implementing Member. Rather, this is a convenient phrase that has been used by previous arbitrators to describe their task. I do not, however, view this standard as one that stands in isolation from the text of the DSU. In my view, the determination of the "shortest period possible for implementation" can, and must, also take due account of the two principles that are expressly mentioned in Article 21 of the DSU, namely reasonableness and the need for prompt compliance. Moreover, as differences in previous awards involving legislative implementation by the United States have shown, and as the text of Article 21.3(c) prescribes, each arbitrator must take account of "particular circumstances" relevant to the case at hand. Strict insistence on the "shortest period possible for implementation within the legal system" of the implementing Member would, in my view, tie an arbitrator's hands and prevent him or her from properly identifying and weighing the particular circumstances that are determinative of "reasonableness" in each individual case.[41]

45. The United States raises, as a "particular circumstance" relevant to my determination, the complexity of the legislation that will be necessary in order to implement the recommendations and rulings of the DSB in this case. The United States contrasts the complexity of the task of eliminating discrimination in this

---

[40] Award of the Arbitrator, *Chile – Price Band System*, para. 34 (quoting Award of the Arbitrator, *US – 1916 Act*, para. 32). See also Award of the Arbitrator, *EC – Hormones*, para. 26; Award of the Arbitrator, *Canada – Pharmaceutical Patents*, para. 47; Award of the Arbitrator, *EC – Tariff Preferences*, para. 26; and Award of the Arbitrator, *US – Oil Country Tubular Goods Sunset Reviews*, para. 25.

[41] With respect to the overriding principle of "reasonableness" I find it useful, like the Arbitrator in *US – Hot-Rolled Steel* (para. 25), to refer to the Appellate Body's elaboration of the meaning of the word "reasonable", albeit in another context. In its Report in *US – Hot-Rolled Steel*, the Appellate Body stated that the word "reasonable":

> ... implies a degree of flexibility that involves consideration of all of the circumstances of a particular case. What is "reasonable" in one set of circumstances may prove to be less than "reasonable" in different circumstances. This suggests that what constitutes a reasonable period or a reasonable time under Article 6.8 and Annex II of the *Anti-Dumping Agreement*, should be defined on a case-by-case basis, in the light of the specific circumstances of each investigation.
>
> In sum, a "reasonable period" must be interpreted consistently with the notions of flexibility and balance that are inherent in the concept of "reasonableness", and in a manner that allows for account to be taken of the particular circumstances of each case.

(Appellate Body Report, paras. 84-85)

case with the relative simplicity involved in amending the statutory term of patent protection in *Canada – Patent Term*.[42]

46. I agree with the United States that the legislative task faced by its Congress in this dispute is more complex than the one confronted by the Canadian Parliament in *Canada – Patent Term*. I attach some significance to the fact that, as the United States explained at the oral hearing, the field of internet gambling is one that is highly regulated in the United States. A myriad of interconnected and overlapping laws apply to these activities, including state and federal laws, and criminal and civil statutes. For this reason, a careful examination of how proposed legislation will impact the existing regulatory regime will be a necessary part of the process of adopting implementing legislation in this dispute.

47. I am also conscious of the fact that any legislation adopted by the United States will inevitably, as the Appellate Body Report demonstrates, bear on questions of public morals and public order.[43] It seems to me that, within the field of public morals and public order, only prohibitions are simple. In other words, to the extent that the United States may consider authorizing any form of internet gambling or wagering, this will increase the complexity of any legislative solution. The more such activities are authorized, the greater lengths the legislator will have to go to in order to ensure that sufficient safeguards are in place to make the system consistent with, and acceptable under, prevailing standards of public morals and public order. This is, in my view, separate from the question of contentiousness. However, the United States has not, in this proceeding, explained in any precise manner how it intends to implement the recommendations and rulings of the DSB. The few indications that it has given suggest that it is leaning more in the direction of "confirming" or "clarifying" the prohibitions on the remote supply of gambling and betting services, rather than in the direction of authorizing, even in part, the supply of such services. In the absence of any more specific information from the United States on this issue, I do not consider the fact that the legislative activity called for in this case will inevitably touch on questions of public morals and public order to be a "particular circumstance" affecting my determination of the reasonable period of time.

48. The United States also submits that I should take account of the fact that several previous Congresses have considered bills related to internet gambling, but that none of these bills has passed. The United States did not, however, pro-

---

[42] In paragraph 12 of its submission, the United States quotes the following statement from paragraphs 55 and 56 of my award in *Canada – Patent Term*:

> In prescribing a precise result, that is, the duration of the minimum period of patent protection, Article 33 of the TRIPS Agreement is quite different from provisions which limit only marginally the discretion of the legislator, *such as prohibitions of discrimination between imported and domestic goods or services*. Such discrimination can, of course, be eliminated in several ways, while a violation of Article 33 of the TRIPS Agreement can only be remedied through one action, that is, by providing for the required minimum period of patent protection.
>
> Thus, with respect to the minimum period of patent protection, Article 33 of the TRIPS Agreement *leaves no room for any legislative discretion or legislative choices*. (emphasis added by the United States)

[43] Appellate Body Report, para. 373(D)(iii)(c).

vide me with any explanation as to the reasons why such bills have not been enacted into law. I am, therefore, unable to determine whether Congress' inability to pass previous bills was related to their complexity—a relevant particular circumstance—or to their contentiousness—something that would not constitute a relevant particular circumstance for purposes of my determination.[44]

49. As regards the specific details of the United States legislative process, the United States and Antigua agree on the basic steps involved.[45] They also agree that the only steps that are required by law are the approval of a bill by both chambers of Congress as well as presidential signature. Furthermore, both parties accept that there is no fixed time frame attached to any one of the steps involved in the United States legislative process. Finally, both parties accept that, as previous arbitrators have observed, there is a considerable degree of flexibility inherent in the United States legislative system.[46]

50. In my view, the need for prompt compliance means that it is incumbent upon the United States to use the flexibility available in its legislative process to ensure rapid implementation. The United States is not, however, obliged to have recourse to extraordinary legislative procedures.[47]

51. The United States suggests that another "particular circumstance" that has a strong influence on the passage of legislation within the United States and that should, therefore, influence my determination in this proceeding, is the Congressional schedule. The United States points out that the vast majority of legislation is passed near the end of a Congress. Each Congress lasts for two years and consists of two sessions, each of which runs over one calendar year. The United States Congress is currently in the first session of the 109th Congress. Although the United States submits that it would be impossible to pass the necessary implementing legislation by the end of the first session of the 109th Congress, currently scheduled to end on 30 September 2005, the United States does not request that I fix the reasonable period of time to coincide with the end of the second session of the 109th Congress, at the end of 2006. Rather, the United States argues that, "much as the end of a Congressional session spurs legislative activity, the opportunity to pass legislation may be greater prior to a Congressional recess."[48] Thus, reasons the United States, it would be appropriate for the reasonable period of time for implementation to expire just before Congress begins its August 2006 recess, as this would provide a concrete impetus for passage of the necessary legislation.

---

[44] Award of the Arbitrator, Canada – Pharmaceutical Patents, para. 60; Award of the Arbitrator, US – Section 110(5) Copyright Act, paras. 41-42; Award of the Arbitrator, Canada – Patent Term, para. 58; and Award of the Arbitrator, US – Offset Act (Byrd Amendment), para. 61.

[45] At the oral hearing Antigua indicated that it accepts the description of the process provided by the United States, which is summarized *supra,* para. 13.

[46] Award of the Arbitrator, US – Section 110(5) Copyright Act, para. 45; Award of the Arbitrator, US – 1916 Act, para. 39; Award of the Arbitrator, US – Offset Act (Byrd Amendment), paras. 63-64 and 74.

[47] Award of the Arbitrator, *Korea – Alcoholic Beverages*, para. 42; Award of the Arbitrator, *US – Section 110(5) Copyright Act*, paras. 32 and 45; Award of the Arbitrator, *US – Offset Act (Byrd Amendment)*, para. 43; and Award of the Arbitrator, *EC – Tariff Preferences*, para. 42.

[48] United States' submission, para. 35.

52. I do not take the view that a legislature's schedule is totally irrelevant to the determination of the reasonable period of time for implementation of the recommendations and rulings of the DSB. Rather, it seems to me that this is a circumstance that may or may not be relevant depending on the particular case.[49] Thus, for example, in *Canada – Patent Term* I did not consider Canada's parliamentary schedule to be determinative of the reasonable period of time in the circumstances of that case.[50] In this case, I do not attach much weight to this "particular circumstance", for the reasons that follow. The United States has taken the position that it would be appropriate for the reasonable period of time to expire just before Congress begins its August 2006 recess. In response to a written request that I addressed to the United States prior to the oral hearing, the United States informed me that the tentative 2006 Congressional Schedule is not yet available. The United States nonetheless indicated that in all likelihood the recesses taken by Congress in 2006 will closely resemble those in the 2005 Schedule, which the United States has provided.[51] I note, in this respect, that in addition to its August recess (the "Summer District Work Period"), Congress takes a number of recesses of a week or more throughout the year. In 2005, these include: a "Presidents Day District Work Period" in February; a "Spring District Work Period" in March/April around the time of Easter; a "Memorial Day District Work Period" at the end of May/early June; and an "Independence Day District Work Period" around the time of the 4th of July. In my view, the United States' argument that a recess period spurs legislative action must apply in the same way to these recesses as it does to Congress' August recess and to the end of a session of Congress. Thus, Congress has, throughout the year, a number of breaks that could serve to push forward the legislative process.

53. Antigua emphasizes the speed with which the 109th Congress has passed legislation to date, pointing out that this Congress adopted 15 measures through 19 June 2005.[52] In Antigua's view, this illustrates why the United States needs no more than six months in order to achieve legislative implementation in this case. The United States, however, argues that the rapidity with which these measures were passed in the first half of the 109th session of Congress is not at all representative of the ordinary workings of the United States legislative process. According to the United States, these 15 measures represent only a tiny fraction of all the laws that will be passed in the 109th Congress. Moreover, of these 15 measures, four dealt with disaster relief or emergencies, three were legislative packages that had been thoroughly considered in a previous Congress or Congresses, four dealt with the renewal of measures previously enacted but due to expire, and four involved the naming of buildings and museum regents.[53]

---

[49] Award of the Arbitrator, US – Offset Act (Byrd Amendment), paras. 69-70.

[50] Award of the Arbitrator, *Canada – Patent Term*, paras. 65-66.

[51] Exhibit US-9 to the United States' submission.

[52] According to Antigua, of these 15 measures: "two became law within a day of introduction, the longest period from introduction to adoption was 91 days, and the average number of days from introduction to adoption was 43.27 days." (Antigua's submission, para. 54; footnotes omitted)

[53] United States' statement at the oral hearing.

54. I find the rebuttal arguments of the United States concerning the work of the 109th Congress to be persuasive. Given that the 109th Congress has only been in session for half a year, it follows that any law that it has adopted during that time must have been adopted in less than half a year. Taken in isolation, however, that fact is not probative of the average length of time that it takes to pass legislation, nor of the relationship between the content of specific legislation and the length of time that is required for it to be passed. In the absence of any additional context that would allow me to evaluate the significance of the time taken to pass the 15 measures cited by Antigua, I do not consider this to be a particular circumstance relevant to my determination.

55. Antigua also points to the fact that the United States Congress took just five months to pass the 2000 amendments to the IHA. I take note of this fact. Given that these amendments relate to the same field as the one in which the United States intends to implement in this case, I consider it relevant that Congress was able to act so expeditiously on a prior occasion.

4. *Article 21.2 of the DSU*

56. Antigua requests that, in making my determination, I apply Article 21.2 of the DSU and pay particular attention to Antigua's interests as a developing country Member of the WTO. Antigua underlines the importance of the cross-border gambling and betting service industry to the economic health and growth of Antigua, as well as the strain that this dispute has placed on Antigua's limited resources. Antigua suggests that I should rely upon Article 21.2 of the DSU in two ways. First, I should use Article 21.2 to examine the consistency of the United States' proposed means of implementation with the recommendations and rulings of the DSB and with the covered agreements generally. Secondly, Antigua submits that I should rely on Article 21.2 to require the United States to use the considerable flexibility that exists within its legislative system to achieve implementation in a shorter period of time than I might otherwise do.

57. The United States argues that Article 21.2 is not relevant to my determination in this proceeding. For the United States, Article 21.2 can be relevant in an arbitration to determine the reasonable period of time for implementation only when it is the *implementing* Member that is a developing country. This is because the task of an Article 21.3(c) arbitrator is to determine the shortest possible period of time for implementation within the legal system of the implementing Member. The fact that the *complaining* Member may be a developing country cannot, in the view of the United States, have any impact on such a determination.

58. Article 21.2 provides:

> Particular attention should be paid to matters affecting the interests of developing country Members with respect to measures which have been subject to dispute settlement.

59. On its face, this provision does not contain any limitation of the type suggested by the United States. In other words, the text of Article 21.2 does not ex-

pressly limit its scope of application to developing country Members as *implementing,* rather than as complaining, parties to a dispute. Any such limitation, if it exists, must therefore be found in the context and/or object and purpose of this provision.[54]

60. Before considering relevant context for the interpretation of Article 21.2 of the DSU, however, I consider it useful to examine in further detail the words that are used in this provision. The provision requires that "particular attention" be paid to: (i) matters; (ii) affecting the interests of developing country Members; (iii) with respect to the measures at issue. At first blush, it is not clear whether the word "matters" in Article 21.2 has the same meaning as elsewhere in the DSU[55], or whether it refers simply to the subject matter covered by Article 21. In any event, it seems to me that Article 21.2 contemplates a clear nexus between the interests of the developing country invoking the provision and the measures at issue in the dispute, as well as a demonstration of the adverse affects of such measures on the interests of the developing country Member(s) concerned.

61. Turning briefly to the context in the light of which Article 21.2 must be interpreted, I note that the provision is located within Article 21, which is entitled "*Surveillance of Implementation of Recommendations and Rulings*". The second paragraph of Article 21, like the first[56], sets out a broad principle that guides and informs the more specific paragraphs that follow, including Article 21.3. Given that Article 21 contains a number of additional paragraphs dealing with different aspects of surveillance and implementation, it seems likely that Article 21.2 informs each of the subsequent paragraphs in a different manner. Arguably, for example, Article 21.2 could constitute a legislative expression of a factor that is to constitute a "particular circumstance" to be taken into account under Article 21.3(c). The last two paragraphs of Article 21 are also, as Antigua pointed out at the oral hearing, of potential use in interpreting the scope and role of Article 21.2. Each of those provisions also deals with developing country Members of the WTO at the stage of surveillance and implementation of DSB recommendations and rulings.[57] Yet, contrary to Article 21.2, both Article 21.7

---

[54] I note that the Arbitrator in *EC – Tariff Preferences* identified, but did not decide, the issue of whether Article 21.2 might apply to developing country Members whose interests are affected by measures at issue in the dispute but which are not parties to the arbitration. (Award of the Arbitrator, para. 59) No such issue arises in this arbitration.

[55] The Appellate Body has held, for example, that the "matter" referred to in Article 7 of the DSU "consists of two elements: the specific *measures* at issue and the *legal basis of the complaint* (or the *claims*)." (Appellate Body Report, *Guatemala – Cement I*, para. 72; original emphasis)

[56] Article 21.1 stipulates that "[p]rompt compliance with recommendations or rulings of the DSB is essential in order to ensure effective resolution of disputes to the benefit of all Members."

[57] Paragraphs 7 and 8 of Article 21 provide as follows:

> 7. If the matter is one which has been raised by a developing country Member, the DSB shall consider what further action it might take which would be appropriate to the circumstances.
>
> 8. If the case is one brought by a developing country Member, in considering what appropriate action might be taken, the DSB shall take into account not only the trade coverage of measures complained of, but also their impact on the economy of developing country Members concerned.

and Article 21.8 expressly apply to the developing country Members that brought the case, that is, to developing countries as *complaining* parties.

62. The significance to be attached to this context, and the precise nature of the relationship between Article 21.2 and Article 21.3(c), are not issues that need be resolved in this arbitration. This is because, in my view, Antigua has not satisfied the criteria expressly mentioned in Article 21.2. In its submission, Antigua pointed out that its population, as well as its gross domestic product per capita, are tiny fractions of those of the United States. Antigua also asserted that the "continuation and responsible further development of the well-regulated cross-border gambling and betting service industry in Antigua is critical to the economic health and growth of the country"[58], and that the "prosecution of the Dispute has put considerable stress on the very limited resources available to Antigua."[59] In response to questioning at the oral hearing, Antigua explained that, prior to 1998, the cross-border gambling and betting industry employed a significant percentage of the Antiguan work force, but that the number of active firms and employees now involved in the sector has shrunk significantly. Antigua did not, however, provide specific data in support of these arguments. Nor did Antigua seek to demonstrate any clear relationship between the decline of its industry and the measures which were subject to this dispute, that is, the Wire Act, the Travel Act, and the IGBA.

63. In the absence of any more specific evidence or elaboration of the affected interests of Antigua and their relationship with the measures at issue, I am not persuaded that the criteria referred to in Article 21.2 have been satisfied. For this reason, I need not consider further the issue of the precise relationship between paragraphs 2 and 3 of Article 21, nor how I might apply Article 21.2 so as to pay "particular attention" to the interests of Antigua in fixing the reasonable period of time for implementation by the United States in this dispute.

5. *Summary*

64. The United States, as the implementing Member, bears the burden of persuading me that the 15 month period that it proposes would constitute a "reasonable period of time" within the meaning of Article 21.3(c). I accept as relevant "particular circumstances" the following considerations raised by the United States: (i) implementation will occur by legislative means; (ii) the task of implementing by legislation is complicated both by the objective of eliminating, or clarifying the absence of, discrimination in the treatment of Antiguan and domestic service suppliers, and by the highly regulated nature of the field of internet gambling and betting in which this objective must be achieved. I take note of, but attach little significance to, Congress' likely 2006 schedule. Taken together, these factors do not, in my view, suffice to discharge the United States' burden of persuading me that 15 months would be a reasonable period of time for imple-

---

58 Antigua's submission, para. 58.

59 Antigua's submission, para. 59.

mentation in this dispute, particularly given the acknowledged flexibility in the United States legislative process.

65. I also accept as a relevant "particular circumstance" the fact that, as Antigua points out, the United States Congress passed the 2000 amendments to the IHA in only five months.

66. I am not persuaded that several other factors invoked by the United States (to date, Congress has not been able to pass any of the bills relating to internet gambling that have been proposed) or Antigua (the asserted availability of partial implementation through a presidential executive order, the fact that the 109th Congress has already passed 15 laws in approximately 6 months of work, or Antigua's status as a developing country Member) are properly characterized as particular circumstances relevant to my determination in this case.

67. Lastly, I wish to observe that, in the four previous Arbitrations in which the issue of the reasonable period of time for implementation by *legislative* means within the United States system arose, each arbitrator determined a different reasonable period of time, ranging from 10 to 15 months.[60]

IV. THE AWARD

68. In the light of what has been stated above, I determine that the "reasonable period of time" for the United States to implement the recommendations and rulings of the DSB in this dispute is 11 months and 2 weeks from 20 April 2005, which was the date on which the DSB adopted the Panel and Appellate Body Reports. The reasonable period of time will therefore expire on 3 April 2006.

---

[60] In *US – Section 110(5) Copyright Act,* the Arbitrator determined that 12 months would be a reasonable period of time (para. 47); in *US – 1916 Act*, the Arbitrator determined that 10 months would be a reasonable period of time (para. 45); in *US – Hot-Rolled Steel*, the Arbitrator determined that 15 months would be a reasonable period of time (para. 40); and in *US – Offset Act (Byrd Amendment),* the Arbitrator determined that 11 months would be a reasonable period of time for the United States to implement the recommendations and rulings of the DSB in that dispute (para. 83).

DOMINICAN REPUBLIC – MEASURES AFFECTING THE IMPORTATION AND INTERNAL SALE OF CIGARETTES

Arbitration under Article 21.3(c) of the Understanding on Rules and Procedures Governing the Settlement of Disputes

Report of the Arbitrator

WT/DS302/17

Circulated to Members on 29 August 2005

1. On 19 May 2005, the Dispute Settlement Body (the "DSB") adopted the Appellate Body Report[1] and the Panel Report[2], as modified by the Appellate Body Report, in *Dominican Republic – Measures Affecting the Importation and Internal Sale of Cigarettes*.[3] At the DSB meeting of 13 June 2005, the Dominican Republic confirmed its intention to implement the recommendations and rulings of the DSB in this dispute and stated that it would require a "reasonable period of time" in which to do so, pursuant to Article 21.3 of the *Understanding on Rules and Procedures Governing the Settlement of Disputes* (the "DSU").[4]

2. On 12 July 2005, Honduras informed the DSB that consultations with the Dominican Republic had not resulted in agreement on the reasonable period of time for implementation. Honduras, therefore, requested that such period be determined by binding arbitration, in accordance with Article 21.3(c) of the DSU.[5]

3. In a joint letter dated 14 July 2005, Honduras and the Dominican Republic communicated to the Chairman of the DSB their agreement that, notwithstanding the 90-day period for arbitration described in Article 21.3(c) of the DSU (which would expire on 17 August 2005), an arbitration completed within 60 days after the date of the appointment of the arbitrator would be deemed by the parties to be the award of the arbitrator under Article 21.3(c) of the DSU.[6]

4. On 21 July 2005, the parties requested me to act as Arbitrator, pursuant to Article 21.3(c) of the DSU, to determine the reasonable period of time for implementation of the recommendations and rulings of the DSB in respect of this matter. I accepted the appointment on 22 July 2005[7], and undertook to issue my award no later than 20 September 2005.

---

1 Appellate Body Report, WT/DS302/AB/R.
2 Panel Report, WT/DS302/R.
3 WT/DS302/12.
4 WT/DSB/M191, para. 27.
5 WT/DS302/13.
6 WT/DS302/14.
7 WT/DS302/15.

5. By joint letter to me dated 29 July 2005, Honduras and the Dominican Republic communicated their agreement to suspend the arbitration proceedings, pending agreement on a reasonable period of time for implementation. By letter dated 4 August 2005, I acknowledged receipt of the joint letter and agreed to treat the matter as suspended until further notice.[8]

6. By joint letter to me dated 16 August 2005, the parties informed me that they had reached agreement on the reasonable period of time for compliance in this matter, and requested that I "issue such rulings reflecting this agreement as [I] may deem appropriate in the circumstances". The parties' agreement is set out in the joint letter dated 16 August 2005, attached as Annex 1 to this Report. Under the circumstances, it will not be necessary for me to issue an award in this arbitration.

---

[8] WT/DS302/16.

ANNEX I

Geneva, 16 August 2005

Mr. John Lockhart
World Trade Organization
Centre William Rappard
Rue de Lausanne 154
1211 Geneva 21

Dominican Republic - Measures Affecting the Importation and Internal Sale of Cigarettes

Arbitration under Article 21.3(c) of the DSU

Sir,

The Dominican Republic and Honduras have mutually agreed that the reasonable periods of time for the Dominican Republic to implement the recommendations and rulings of the Dispute Settlement Body (the "DSB") in *Dominican Republic - Measures Affecting the Importation and Internal Sale of Cigarettes* (WT/DS202) are as follows:

1. In respect of the finding of the Panel specified in paragraph 8.1(b) of the Panel Report relative to the transitional surcharge for economic stabilisation, found to be inconsistent with the provisions of Article II:1(b) of the GATT 1994, the Dominican Republic shall immediately bring the measure into conformity with its obligations under the GATT 1994.
2. In respect of the finding of the Panel specified in paragraph 8.1(e) of the Panel Report relative to the requirement that a tax stamp be affixed to all cigarette packets in its territory and under the supervision of the local tax authorities, found to be inconsistent with Article III:4 of the GATT 1994, the Dominican Republic shall immediately bring the measure into conformity with its obligations under the GATT 1994.
3. In respect of the finding of the Panel specified in paragraph 8.1(c) of the Panel Report relative to the foreign exchange fee, found to be inconsistent with the provisions of Article II:1(b) of the GATT 1994, the Dominican Republic shall bring the measure into conformity within twenty four (24) months from 19 May 2005, the date of the adoption of the Panel and Appellate Body Reports.

./.

In respect of the measures that have to be brought into conformity immediately (the measures referred to in paragraphs 8.1(b) and 8.1(e) of the Panel Report, *i.e.*, the transitional surcharge for economic stabilisation and the requirement that a tax stamp be affixed to all cigarette packets in the territory of the Dominican Republic and under the supervision of the local tax authorities), the Dominican Republic and Honduras have likewise agreed that Honduras may, at its discretion, exercice its rights under Article 21.5 or Article 22.6 of the *Understanding on Rules and Procedures Governing the Settlement of Disputes* (the "DSU") at anytime starting sixty (60) days from the date of this notification, without prejudice to the rights of Honduras relative to the bringing into conformity of the measure referred to in paragraph 8.1(c) of the Panel Report, *i.e.*, the foreign exchange fee.

In addition to the foregoing, the Dominican Republic and Honduras have also agreed that the Dominican Republic shall forthwith desist from requiring importers of cigarettes to post the bond referred to in paragraph 8.1(f) of the Panel Report.

The Dominican Republic and Honduras respectfully request the Arbitrator to issue such rulings reflecting this agreement as he may deem appropriate in the circumstances.

Yours sincerely,

Dacio Castillo	Homero Hernandez
Ambassador	Ambassador
Permanent Mission of Honduras	Permanent Mission of the Dominican Republic

cc: H.E. Mr. Eirik Glenne
Chairman, Dispute Settlement Body
World Trade Organization
Rue de Lausanne 154
1211 Geneva 21

EUROPEAN COMMUNITIES – THE ACP-EC PARTNERSHIP AGREEMENT

– RECOURSE TO ARBITRATION PURSUANT TO THE DECISION OF 14 NOVEMBER 2001[1]

Award of the Arbitrator

WT/L/616[*]

Circulated to Members on 1 August 2005

TABLE OF CONTENTS

[1] For previous documents with respect to this arbitration, see WT/L/607 and addenda 1-12.

[*] This arbitration was initiated pursuant to the procedures set out in the Annex to the waiver decision with respect to Article I of the General Agreement on Tariffs and Trade 1994 ("GATT 1994") contained in the document "European Communities - The ACP-EC Partnership Agreement, Decision of 14 November 2001" (the "Doha Waiver" WT/MIN(01)/15).

I. BACKGROUND

1. The present arbitration was initiated pursuant to the procedures set out in the Annex to the waiver decision with respect to Article I of the *General Agreement on Tariffs and Trade 1994* ("GATT 1994") contained in the document "European Communities – The ACP-EC Partnership Agreement, Decision of 14 November 2001" (the "Doha Waiver", attached).[2] This was one of two waivers adopted at the Doha Ministerial Conference, *inter alia*, to facilitate implementation by the European Communities of two understandings (between the European Communities and the United States, and the European Communities and Ecuador[3], respectively) relating to the resolution of the WTO *EC – Bananas III* dispute.

2. As part of those understandings, the European Communities undertook to reform its banana regime so as to replace its then existing WTO-inconsistent measures based on several tariff rate quotas with a "Tariff Only regime for imports of bananas". The tariff-only regime is to be implemented by 1 January 2006, with interim tariff quota arrangements until that date. The *EC - Bananas III* dispute was initiated by Ecuador, Guatemala, Honduras, Mexico and the United States in 1996 and addressed the then EC banana regime. In the context of those proceedings, Ecuador and the United States were authorized by the Dispute Settlement Body (the "DSB") to suspend certain concessions and, in the case of Ecuador, other WTO obligations towards the European Communities. In the context of seeking to resolve outstanding implementation issues, Ecuador and the United States negotiated understandings with the European Communities that included, *inter alia,* suspension (United States) or termination (Ecuador) of the right to suspend concessions or other obligations *vis-à-vis* the European Communities, adjustment of the tariff quota levels and the introduction of a tariff-only regime for imports of bananas as from 1 January 2006 as well as the lifting of these countries' reservation with respect to the banana waiver.

3. On 15 July 2004, the European Communities announced, in a communication to WTO Members, that it intended to modify, in accordance with Article XXVIII, paragraph 5 of GATT 1994, its concessions with respect to tariff item CN 08030019 (bananas) included in the EC Schedule CXL[4].

4. In a communication dated 31 January 2005, the European Communities notified the Members of the WTO that it intended "to replace its concessions on item CN 08030019 (bananas) included in Schedule CXL of the European Communities annexed to the General Agreement with a bound duty of 230€/t." It also indicated that the communication constituted "the announcement under the terms of the Annex to the Decision of the WTO Ministerial Conference of 14 November 2001 concerning the ACP-EC Partnership Agreement (WT/MIN(01)/15)".[5]

---

[2] WT/MIN(01)/15, Attachment 1 to this Award.
[3] WT/DS27/58 and WT/DS27/60.
[4] G/SECRET/22.
[5] G/SECRET/22/Add.1.

5. At the invitation of the Parties to the Cotonou Agreement[6] and in accordance with the procedures of the Annex to the Doha Waiver, consultations were held on 22 February 2005 with WTO Members exporting bananas to the European Communities on an MFN basis, in order to "provide in particular an opportunity to answer any question which interested parties may have concerning the methodology used for the rebinding of the EC tariff on bananas."[7]

6. On 30 March 2005, Colombia, Costa Rica, Ecuador, Guatemala, Honduras and Panama, followed by the Bolivarian Republic of Venezuela and Nicaragua on 31 March 2005 and Brazil[8] in a communication dated 1 April 2005, notified the WTO that they were requesting arbitration pursuant to the procedures in the Annex to the Doha Waiver.[9] According to the Annex, "the arbitrator shall be appointed within ten days following the request ... failing which the arbitrator shall be appointed by the Director-General of the WTO, following consultations with the parties, within 30 days of the arbitration request."

7. On 12 April, the parties notified the Director-General that no agreement had been reached between the parties within the stipulated ten days with respect to the appointment of the arbitrator. After consultations with the parties on 15 and 18 April 2005, the Director-General appointed the Arbitrator on 2 May 2005 as follows:

John Weekes, Chairman
John Lockhart
Yasuhei Taniguchi.

8. The Annex to the Doha Waiver provides, *inter alia,* that the "mandate of the arbitrator shall be to determine, within 90 days of his appointment, whether the envisaged rebinding of the EC tariff on bananas would result in at least maintaining total market access for MFN banana suppliers, taking into account the above-mentioned EC commitments."[10]

9. At the request of certain African, Caribbean and Pacific ("ACP") banana exporting countries, the Arbitrator, after consultations with the parties, invited Saint Lucia, Cameroon, Côte d'Ivoire, Dominica, Dominican Republic, Ghana, Grenada, Jamaica, Kenya, Madagascar, Suriname, Tanzania, Belize and Saint Vincent and the Grenadines (the "relevant ACP Members") to participate, in a limited manner, in this arbitration.

10. The Arbitrator explained its decision in a letter to the parties and the relevant ACP Members. It noted in particular that there was no rule precluding participation by such Members and that the Arbitrator enjoyed the discretion to organize the conduct of the proceedings. The Arbitrator further noted that such participation should have no adverse effect either on the timetable for the pro-

[6] The official title of the Agreement is the "ACP-EC Partnership Agreement". It was signed in Cotonou on 23 June 2000. The parties to the Cotonou Agreement are the EC, on the one hand, and certain African, Caribbean and Pacific ("ACP") countries, on the other.

[7] WT/L/602.

[8] That group of Members is referred to, in this Award, as the "Interested Parties".

[9] WT/L/607/Add.1-9, respectively.

[10] Fourth indent of the Annex to the Doha Waiver.

ceedings, or on the timeframe for the conclusion of the Arbitration, as foreseen in the Annex to the Doha Waiver. Accordingly, the relevant ACP Members were invited to make a written communication to the Arbitrator, in the form of one collective submission. The relevant ACP Members were also invited to attend the meeting with the parties and were given the opportunity to make a single brief statement at that meeting and to answer questions by the Arbitrator. Furthermore, the relevant ACP Members were given access to the submissions made by the parties prior to the hearing with the Arbitrator.

11. In the course of the proceedings, the Arbitrator requested[11] and received information from the Food and Agriculture Organization of the United Nations (the "FAO") with respect to certain price data collected by that organization.[12]

12. The Arbitrator met with the parties and relevant ACP Members on 28, 29 and 30 June 2005. The Arbitrator decided that its Award should be distributed to the parties at 12 noon on 1 August 2005, and notified to the General Council as well as circulated to the Members of the WTO by 5 p.m. on that date.

II. THE EC BANANA REGIME

13. Schedule CXL of the EC-15 records commitments by the European Communities detailing a 2.2 million metric ton tariff quota with a bound in-quota tariff of €75 per metric ton and a final bound out-of-quota tariff of €680 per metric ton. The current EC banana import system is based on three tariff quotas: A, B and C.

14. Since the introduction of the common organization of the EC banana market in 1993, the EC import regime for bananas has changed several times. From 1 January 1995 to 30 June 2001, specific country shares were allocated to some Latin American exporters and to non-traditional ACP banana suppliers, totalling 2.553 million metric tons (of which 2.2 million metric tons was bound (tariff quota A) and the rest was autonomous, unbound, quantities (tariff quota B)). Traditional ACP suppliers enjoyed a duty-free tariff quota of 857,700 metric tons (tariff quota C).

15. On 1 July 2001, country specific allocations within the 2.553 million metric tons tariff quotas A/B were abolished. These tariff quotas were now also available to both traditional and non-traditional ACP suppliers. As a result of the *EC – Bananas III* understandings with Ecuador and the United States, respectively, the European Communities increased, from 1 January 2002, the unbound, autonomous, tariff quota B to 453,000 metric tons and reduced the C tariff quota to 750,000 metric tons. Preferential suppliers continued to have exclusive access to tariff quota C.

---

[11] This request was contained in a letter dated 1 July 2005 from the Secretary to the Arbitrator, copied to the parties and the relevant ACP Members.

[12] The FAO responded by facsimile on 5 July 2005. The FAO's response was distributed to the parties.

16. On 1 May 2004, following the accession of ten Central and Eastern European countries to the European Communities, the European Communities enlarged the autonomous tariff quota adding 300,000 metric tons for the period 1 May 2004-31 December 2004. For the year 2005, the additional quantity was fixed at 460,000 metric tons, increasing the total MFN tariff quotas to 3.113 million metric tons, of which 2.2 million metric tons are bound (tariff quota A).

17. Tariff quotas A and B are open to all suppliers, at a tariff of €75 per metric ton for suppliers other than preferential suppliers, and at a zero duty level for preferential suppliers. The out-of-quota rate for non-preferential suppliers is €680 per metric ton and for preferential suppliers €380 per metric ton.

18. In summary, the existing EC banana import system consists of tariff quotas totalling 3.113 million metric tons open to all suppliers, and a tariff quota of 750,000 metric tons at zero duty open exclusively to preferential suppliers. MFN suppliers are subject to a bound in-quota tariff of €75 per metric ton, whereas all in-quota banana imports from preferential suppliers enter the European Communities at zero duty. In 2004, the EC-25 imported a total of 3.87 million metric tons of bananas.[13] More detailed data on EC imports of bananas is contained in Attachment 2.

III. THE MANDATE OF THE ARBITRATOR

A. Introduction and Arguments of the Parties

19. The mandate of the Arbitrator is set out as follows in the Annex to the Doha Waiver:

> ... to determine, ... whether the envisaged rebinding of the EC tariff on bananas would result in at least maintaining total market access for MFN banana suppliers, taking into account [all EC WTO market-access commitments relating to bananas].[14]

20. The terms of the mandate thus require the Arbitrator to consider whether or not a certain outcome "would result" from a certain action. The text of the mandate may be broken down into three elements. The first is the "envisaged rebinding of the EC tariff on bananas". This language describes the action at the centre of the required analysis. The second element comprises a benchmark against which the envisaged rebinding of the EC tariff on bananas is to be assessed. Thus, this element of the mandate requires the Arbitrator to determine

---

[13] Excluding all intra-EC trade. The enlargement of the EC took place on 1 May 2004. Thus the figure includes imports into the ten new Member States when they were not yet part of the common market on bananas. Source of the data: Eurostat (information extracted or downloaded on 20 July 2005).

[14] The parties agree that "the above-mentioned EC commitments" specified in the fourth tiret of the Annex are "all EC WTO market-access commitments relating to bananas", as referred to in the second indent of the Annex. First Written Submission of the EC, para. 5; and the respective First Written Submissions of Honduras, Nicaragua and Panama, para. 240. All parties confirmed their acceptance of the proposition that "the above-mentioned EC commitments" means "all EC WTO market-access commitments relating to bananas" in response to questions at the oral hearing.

whether the envisaged rebinding "would result in at least maintaining total market access for MFN banana suppliers". The third, and final, element is a direction to the Arbitrator to take into account all EC WTO market-access commitments relating to bananas whilst performing the analysis under its mandate.

21. There is no disagreement as to the meaning and scope of the first element of the mandate. The parties agree that the "envisaged rebinding of the EC tariff on bananas" is reflected in the EC proposal to record a new commitment in its WTO schedule under tariff heading CN 08030019 at €230 per metric ton.[15]

22. The parties differ, however, over the interpretation of the second and third textual elements of the mandate. With respect to the second element, the Interested Parties generally argue that the concept of "at least maintaining" denotes that—at a minimum—the European Communities must keep in existence and must not allow diminution of the relevant market access of MFN suppliers through the rebinding.[16] The European Communities, for its part, submits that the Arbitrators are required to examine "if the proposed new concession would not increase the level of protection (and conversely diminish the market access rights of MFN suppliers) as compared with the level of protection offered by the European Communities' current concession".[17] The Interested Parties add that "maintaining" total market access carries with it a temporal, prospective dimension, such that total market access—appropriately defined—must be preserved in time.[18]

23. The parties offer markedly different interpretations as to the meaning of the phrase "total market access for MFN banana suppliers", and the significance and scope of the EC commitments to be taken into account. The European Communities reads these two textual elements of the mandate together and argues that the level of protection for EC banana producers (or, conversely, the degree of liberalization) accorded by the tariff commitments scheduled in the EC-15 Schedule CXL *alone* comprises the benchmark against which its envis-

---

[15] In "Article XXVIII:5 Negotiations: Schedule CXL – European Communities – Addendum", G/SECRET/22/Add.1 (1 February 2005), the EC notified:

> that it intends to replace its concessions on item 08030019 (bananas) included in Schedule CXL of the European Communities annexed to the General Agreement with a bound duty of 230€/t.

The Interested Parties referred to this announcement in their requests for arbitration: see documents referred to *supra*, footnote 8.

[16] First Written Submission of Brazil, paras. 151-154; First Written Submission of Colombia, Costa Rica, Ecuador and Guatemala, para. 57-58; respective First Written Submissions of Honduras, Nicaragua and Panama, paras. 233-234. The Arbitrator notes that, in a letter dated 24 May 2005, the Bolivarian Republic of Venezuela associated itself with, and endorsed as its own, the First Written Submission of Colombia, Costa Rica, Ecuador and Guatemala. Subsequent references to that submission should be read in that light.

[17] First Written Submission of the EC, para. 8.

[18] First Written Submission of Brazil, para. 154; First Written Submission of Colombia, Costa Rica, Ecuador and Guatemala, para. 57; Honduras, Nicaragua and Panama first submission, para. 234. At the oral hearing, the EC indicated that the rebinding of the EC tariff would lead to a new WTO concession for the EC in respect of bananas and that concession would be maintained in time, in the sense that it would be a bound commitment. *See* also First Written Submission of the EC, para. 8.

aged rebinding is to be compared.[19] Colombia, Costa Rica, Ecuador and Guatemala, as well as Brazil, argue that the concept of "total market access for MFN banana suppliers" requires a broader analysis, including, but not limited to, the European Communities' scheduled commitments, and which would encompass analysis of all relevant conditions affecting competition in the marketplace, including both the level of protection accorded to EC producers and the margin of preference enjoyed by preferential suppliers to the EC banana market.[20] Honduras, Nicaragua and Panama also contend that the position of preferential suppliers is relevant to an assessment of whether the envisaged rebinding "would result in at least maintaining total market access for MFN banana suppliers".[21] In addition, these parties argue that an analysis of "total market access for MFN banana suppliers" must be "quantity-based, exclusive to *MFN* suppliers, and encompasses the full amount of MFN volumes now authorized for MFN entry".[22] Honduras, Nicaragua and Panama submit that the taking into account of "all EC WTO market-access commitments relating to bananas" must go beyond consideration of the European Communities' scheduled commitments, and must include analysis of commitments owed to MFN suppliers in the light of EC enlargement[23]; under the understandings concluded between the European Communities and the United States and Ecuador respectively in the context of the settlement of the *EC – Bananas III* dispute; under the negotiating mandate of the Doha Development Agenda (the "DDA"), as well as under the Doha Waiver itself.[24]

B. Analysis

24. The starting point for the Arbitrator's analysis is the "envisaged rebinding of the EC tariff on bananas". The parties agree that the envisaged rebinding referred to in the mandate is the EC proposal, announced in a communication to WTO Members on 1 February 2005, to rebind its concessions for bananas under tariff heading CN 08030019 at €230 per metric ton. [25]

25. The Arbitrator's task is to determine whether this envisaged rebinding "would result in at least maintaining total market access for MFN banana suppli-

---

[19] Rebuttal Submission of the EC, paras. 28-57. The EC confirmed its submission that the scheduled commitments are the exclusive benchmark against which the proposed tariff is to be assessed in response to questions at the oral hearing.

[20] First Written Submission of Colombia, Costa Rica, Ecuador and Guatemala, para. 53; and First Written Submission of Brazil, para. 160.

[21] Honduras, Nicaragua and Panama accordingly factor the capacity of certain ACP banana suppliers to increase exports into their analysis of the envisaged rebinding: see, for example, respective First Written Submissions of Honduras, Nicaragua and Panama, paras. 266 ff.

[22] Respective First Written Submissions of Honduras, Nicaragua and Panama, para. 235. (Emphasis original.)

[23] Following the enlargement of the EC from 12 to 15 and then to 25 member States, the overall quantities of bananas benefiting from the in-quota tariff rate of €75 per metric ton have been expanded through "autonomous" tariff quotas not recorded in the EC's tariff schedule. *Supra*, paras. 13-18.

[24] Respective First Written Submissions of Honduras, Nicaragua and Panama, paras. 243-244.

[25] G/SECRET/22/Add.1.

ers". In doing so, the Arbitrator must take into account "all EC WTO market-access commitments relating to bananas".

26. The phrase "would result in at least maintaining" centres on the word "maintaining". "Maintaining" is synonymous with "preserving" or "causing to continue" and carries with it the connotation of guarding from loss or deterioration.[26] The "maintaining" of a state of affairs denotes a temporal, prospective element in the sense that the state of affairs must continue. Accordingly, in the context of the Annex, "maintaining" indicates that the "total market access for MFN banana suppliers" enjoyed before the envisaged rebinding must continue following that rebinding.

27. The word "maintaining" is qualified in several ways by the terms that precede it in the phrase "would result in at least maintaining". "Would" is a conditional form of "will". In the current context, the use of "would" with the verb "maintain" denotes both a prospective analysis as well as conditionality: the specified result *will* follow, if the condition (here, the rebinding of the EC banana tariff) comes to pass. "Result" describes a relationship of cause and effect. "At least" underscores the concept of guarding from loss that is inherent in the word "maintaining". The expression "at least maintaining" requires that "total market access for MFN banana suppliers" is the *minimum* level that must be maintained. Read together, therefore, the words in the expression "would result in at least maintaining" denote that the effect of the envisaged rebinding, if it is put in place, will, at a minimum, be the continuation or preservation of "total market access for MFN banana suppliers". The phrase "would result in at least maintaining" describes the relationship that is required between the "envisaged rebinding" and the benchmark of "total market access for MFN banana suppliers".

28. The phrase "total market access for MFN banana suppliers" centres on the expression "market access". The ordinary meaning of the term "access" suggests that it relates to "a way or means to approach or entrance".[27] The ordinary meaning of the term "market", in turn, may be defined as "a locus of competition for sales of a particular commodity".[28] Read together, the meanings of the terms "market" and "access" indicate that "market access" deals with the conditions under which suppliers may enter a product (or service) into an area of economic activity, so as to compete for sales with other suppliers. In other words, market access relates to the conditions of entry of the product into the market. In the context of the current proceeding, the relevant "market" is the market of the European Communities for bananas. Insofar as bananas of different origins are in competition on the market[29], outcomes within the EC market for bananas will be

---

[26] *Shorter Oxford English Dictionary*, 5th edn, W.R. Trumble, A. Stevenson (eds) (Oxford University Press, 2002), Vol. 1, p. 1674.

[27] *Ibid.*, p. 13.

[28] Panel Report, *US – Upland Cotton*, para. 7.1429. This definition, which arose in the context of a discussion of "world market share" in Article 6.3(d) of the *Agreement on Subsidies and Countervailing Measures* (the "*SCM Agreement*"), was not addressed by the Appellate Body.

[29] The panel in *EC – Bananas III* concluded that "bananas are 'like' products, for purposes of Articles I, III, X, and XIII of GATT 1994, irrespective of whether they originate in the EC, in ACP coun-

a function, *inter alia*, of the conditions within which different suppliers are allowed to compete for sales of bananas.

29. This general definition of "market access" is consistent with the use of the term in the context of the *Marrakech Agreement Establishing the World Trade Organization* (the "*WTO Agreement*"), where "market access" (or "market-access") in respect of trade in goods relates to the conditions imposed upon foreign goods by an importing Member on entry into that Member's market. Such measures imposed at the time of entry impact on the competitiveness of foreign suppliers in the market of the Member concerned. In the WTO context, the expression "market access" is generally used in describing tariff concessions, as well as other commitments, such as tariff quota commitments, used in relation to the importation of goods by WTO Members. Indeed, the final element of the mandate—which refers to "all EC WTO market-access commitments relating to bananas"—uses just such a construction. A similar construction is used in Article 4.1 of the *Agreement on Agriculture*, which defines a category of "[m]arket access concessions contained in Schedules". These "relate to bindings and reductions of tariffs, and other market access commitments as specified therein". By referring to bindings in Schedules, Article 4.1 of the *Agreement on Agriculture* evokes Article II of GATT 1994, the provision that provides for the scheduling of tariff concessions and that requires the commerce of WTO Members to be accorded "treatment no less favourable than that provided for in the appropriate part of the appropriate Schedule". The Arbitrator notes, at this point, that the "envisaged rebinding of the EC tariff on bananas"—the proposal to be measured against the benchmark of "total market access for MFN banana suppliers"—is an envisaged tariff binding governed by Article II of GATT 1994. As such, Article II may provide contextual assistance for defining correctly the benchmark level.

30. The essence of a commitment under Article II of GATT 1994 is an undertaking not to apply a tariff above the level specified in the Schedule of the Member concerned. The exercise is therefore fundamentally about guaranteeing certain conditions of entry into the EC market through an undertaking not to apply protective instruments or a level of protection above a bound level. For this reason, it has been stated that tariff bindings under Article II of GATT 1994 represent, generally, "commitments on conditions of competition for trade, not on volumes of trade".[30] Market access *commitments* undertaken in the context of Article II of GATT 1994 have often been described as giving rise to market access *opportunities* for the Members benefiting from the concessions.[31] These

tries, in BFA countries or in other third countries". (Panel Report, *EC – Bananas III*, para 7.63) This finding of the panel was not appealed.

[30] GATT Panel Report, *EC – Oilseeds*, para. 150.

[31] This notion has been referred to in particular in the context of defining the legitimate expectations arising from tariff bindings, in the context of analyses of non-violation claims. The panel on *Japan – Film* thus found that:

> The second required element which must be considered to establish a case of non-violation nullification or impairment under Article XXIII:1(b) is the existence of a benefit accruing to a WTO Member under the relevant agreement (in this case, GATT 1994). In all but one of the past GATT cases dealing with Article XXIII:1(b)

opportunities afforded by the granting of tariff concessions relate to certain legal conditions governing the ability of exporters to enter and compete on the market of another Member. Indeed, as far as market access opportunities provided through tariff concessions are concerned, all that is guaranteed for an exporting Member is an opportunity to enter the market of an importing Member under secure and predictable conditions (but not a guarantee to export certain volumes to that market).

31. In the context of this proceeding, the "envisaged rebinding" referred to in the mandate is a proposed *tariff binding* to be undertaken by the European Communities under Article II of GATT 1994. The benchmark against which it is to be assessed is not the specific concept of tariff bindings, but the more general concept of "*market access*" for the MFN suppliers. Although tariff bindings under Article II of GATT 1994 are an aspect of "market access", the general concept of "market access" may involve other aspects of the conditions under which suppliers enter a market to compete for sales. Moreover, the question to be resolved in this proceeding does not deal with the expression "market access" in isolation. Nor indeed does it deal with "market access commitments", other than to require that such commitments be taken into account. Instead, the term "market access" is qualified in the context of the Annex by two further expressions: the mandate requires analysis of "*total* market access *for MFN banana suppliers*".

32. The phrase "for MFN banana suppliers" indicates that the benchmark against which the European Communities' envisaged rebinding is to be measured is to be determined from the perspective of the opportunities afforded to MFN suppliers by the existing conditions of entry to the EC market.

33. The ordinary meaning of the adjective "total" is "[o]f or pertaining to the whole of something".[32] It denotes completeness or all-inclusiveness and may also indicate an aggregate measurement. The use of the expression "*total* market access" further clarifies that what is to be taken into account is the *entirety* of the opportunity actually afforded to MFN suppliers by the existing conditions of entry to the EC market.

34. In the light of the above, it is difficult to accept the submission of the European Communities that an assessment of "total market access for MFN banana suppliers" in the context of the Annex must be limited *exclusively* to the market access commitments recorded in the European Communities' Schedule CXL. Such commitments may well be an important factor affecting the opportunity afforded by the conditions of entry for MFN banana suppliers, and the mandate clearly requires that such commitments - which are certainly included in the phrase "all EC WTO market-access commitments relating to bananas" - be taken into account during the analysis. Nevertheless, it is clear that the scheduled

> claims, the claimed benefit has been that of legitimate expectations of improved market-access opportunities arising out of relevant tariff concessions.

(Panel Report, *Japan – Film*, para. 8.285)

[32] *Shorter Oxford English Dictionary*, 5th edn, W.R. Trumble, A. Stevenson (eds) (Oxford University Press, 2002), Vol. 2, p. 3305.

commitments of the European Communities relating to bananas do not exhaust the full scope of "total market access for MFN banana suppliers" currently enjoyed. As noted above, the European Communities grants MFN suppliers a greater opportunity to enter the EC banana market than is recorded in its Schedule CXL, through additional "autonomous" tariff quota amounts.[33] They form part of the opportunities enjoyed by the MFN banana suppliers on the EC market and thus part of the "total market access for MFN suppliers" that is to be maintained, or preserved, under the new tariff.

35. The third and final element of the mandate requires that "all EC WTO market-access commitments relating to bananas" be "tak[en] into account". This requires that such commitments be considered in the Arbitrator's analysis. The expression "taking into account" does not, however, in itself require that such factors be the *only* factors to be considered.

36. The parties have expressed differing views as to what is encompassed in the expression "all EC WTO market-access commitments relating to bananas". The parties agree that "all EC WTO market-access commitments relating to bananas" includes the European Communities' scheduled commitments.[34] Honduras, Nicaragua and Panama argue however that other commitments are also captured by this phrase, notably commitments arising out of EC expansion (including under Article XXIV:6 of GATT 1994), the negotiating mandate of the DDA, under the *EC – Bananas III* understandings with the United States and Ecuador, and under the Doha Waiver itself. The Arbitrator finds that "all EC WTO market-access commitments relating to bananas" includes commitments incurred as a result of EC enlargement under Articles XXIV:6 and XXVIII of GATT 1994. The Arbitrator also accepts that the European Communities has commitments under the negotiating mandate of the DDA. However, these commitments consist of a political undertaking to achieve market access improvements, including for bananas. As such, the Arbitrator finds that these commitments are not of a character that would allow them to be factored into the analysis under the mandate. As regards the understandings concluded between the European Communities and the United States and the European Communities and Ecuador, as well as the Doha Waiver itself, these clearly comprise important background to the arbitration and the Arbitrator has taken them into account as well.

37. In summary, the mandate requires a determination as to whether the proposed new EC tariff for bananas would preserve, at a minimum, the effective opportunities to enter the EC banana market afforded to MFN suppliers by the existing conditions of entry. The analysis must factor in, not only bound commitments, but all other aspects of the import regime, *as applied*. The Arbitrator notes that, because it relates to certain opportunities to enter the market, "total market access for MFN banana suppliers" is not a guarantee of any particular level or volume of trade or price. Rather, it relates to the opportunity for MFN suppliers to enter and compete on the EC banana market.

---

33 *Supra*, paras. 13-18.

34 First Written Submission of the EC, para. 8; respective First Written Submission of Honduras, Nicaragua and Panama, Table 11.

IV. CLAIM UNDER PARAGRAPH 1 OF THE DOHA WAIVER

A. Arguments of the Parties

38. Honduras, Nicaragua and Panama argue that the scope of the arbitration is not limited to the consideration of whether the envisaged rebinding of the European Communities' tariff on bananas would result in at least maintaining total market access for MFN banana suppliers, and instead submit that the Arbitrator may also review the EC proposal under the terms of Paragraph 1 of the Doha Waiver.[35] Honduras, Nicaragua and Panama thus call for the Arbitrator to examine whether the proposed EC rebinding is "necessary" within the terms of Paragraph 1, or "required" pursuant to the relevant provisions of the Cotonou Agreement. They submit that an interpretation that did not lead to an examination of Paragraph 1 would render meaningless the term "additional" in Paragraph 3*bis* of the Doha Waiver, because "additional" denotes that the provisions are "extra" rules that apply on top of the general provisions. They argue that such an interpretation is also consistent with the negotiating history and would avoid an absurd result whereby interested parties, in addition to having recourse to arbitration under the Annex to the Doha Waiver, would have to follow ordinary dispute settlement rules in order to bring a claim under Paragraph 1.

39. The European Communities submits that such an examination is outside the specific terms of the mandate of the Arbitrator, which refers only to the determination of whether the envisaged rebinding "would result in at least maintaining total market access for MFN banana suppliers". The European Communities submits that, were the Arbitrator to address this issue, it would deny it (and the ACP countries) important due process rights.[36]

B. Analysis

40. As noted above, the mandate of the Arbitrator in this proceeding is defined in the fourth tiret of the Annex to the Doha Waiver as follows:

> ... to determine, ... whether the envisaged rebinding of the EC tariff on bananas would result in at least maintaining total market access for MFN banana suppliers, taking into account [certain] EC commitments.

41. Paragraph 1 of the Doha Waiver provides as follows:

> Subject to the terms and conditions set out hereunder, Article I, paragraph 1 of the General Agreement shall be waived, until 31 December 2007, to the extent necessary to permit the European Communities to provide preferential tariff treatment for products originating in ACP States as required by Article 36.3, Annex 5 and its Protocols of the ACP-EC Partnership Agreement, without being

[35] Respective First Written Submissions of Honduras, Nicaragua and Panama, paras. 168 ff.

[36] Rebuttal Submission of the EC, paras. 71-85.

> required to extend the same preferential treatment to like products of any other member. (footnote omitted)

42. It is clear, on a plain reading of the fourth tiret of the Annex to the Doha Waiver, that the Arbitrator's mandate does not explicitly require the Arbitrator to assess whether the European Communities' envisaged rebinding is consistent with the conditions set forth in Paragraph 1 of the Doha Waiver. Honduras, Nicaragua and Panama argue, however, that the Arbitrator may consider substantive claims that the European Communities' envisaged rebinding does not comply with the conditions of the Doha Waiver, and request the Arbitrator to review the consistency of the European Communities' proposed rebinding against the terms of Paragraph 1. The European Communities contests this submission, submitting that the Arbitrator's "terms of reference" (or "jurisdiction") are limited to the terms of the mandate.[37]

43. In seeking to show that an examination under Paragraph 1 of the Doha Waiver is within the jurisdiction of the Arbitrator in this proceeding, notwithstanding the lack of any express authority for such jurisdiction within the terms of the Annex to the Doha Waiver, Honduras, Nicaragua and Panama rely, in particular, upon the wording of Paragraph 3bis of the Doha Waiver, which provides that:

> With respect to bananas, the additional provisions in the Annex shall apply.

44. Honduras, Nicaragua and Panama submit that the use of the term "additional" means that both the general requirements of the Waiver, *and* the "additional" provisions of the Annex, apply in respect of bananas. Thus, in the submission of Honduras, Nicaragua and Panama, claims under the general provisions of the Waiver may be brought before the Arbitrator.

45. The Arbitrator agrees with Honduras, Nicaragua and Panama that *both* the "additional" Annex provisions as well as the general provisions of the Doha Waiver apply to bananas. Compliance with the Doha Waiver in respect of bananas does not turn solely upon fulfilment of the standard of "at least maintaining total market access for MFN banana suppliers" reflected in the fourth tiret of the Annex. Instead, it is clear that, in respect of bananas, as well as all other products covered by the Waiver, the European Communities must comply with all of the conditions of the Waiver, including those in Paragraph 1.

46. However, the jurisdiction of the Arbitrator is governed by the terms of the Annex. That mandate is limited, specifically, to determining whether the "envisaged rebinding would result in at least maintaining total market access for MFN banana suppliers". The Arbitrator is not free to expand its mandate. It must find its jurisdiction in the instrument establishing its authority. There is no indication that the Arbitrator may determine other matters, such as the consistency of the European Communities' envisaged rebinding with Paragraph 1 of the Doha Waiver (which, by its nature would also include consideration of the terms of the

[37] Responses to questions at the oral hearing.

Cotonou Agreement to determine what is "required" under that Agreement[38]). The Arbitrator finds, therefore, that this claim by Honduras, Panama and Nicaragua is beyond its jurisdiction.

47. This interpretation does not render the word "additional" in Paragraph 3*bis* meaningless. Pursuant to the "additional" procedure, the task of the Arbitrator is to review the envisaged rebinding of the EC tariff on bananas against the benchmark laid out in the mandate. This procedure is "additional" in the sense that it provides for a *sui generis* process, with its own benchmark, that would not otherwise have existed, were it not for the additional procedures of the Annex. Again, it must be emphasized that this does not mean that the general provisions of the Doha Waiver do not apply or do not have legal effect; it means, rather, that the Arbitrator is not authorized or required to determine the issue. The compliance of the European Communities with the conditions of the Doha Waiver may be the subject of review in the context of dispute settlement, a point expressly confirmed by Paragraph 6 of the Waiver, which states that:

> This Waiver shall not preclude the right of affected members to have recourse to Articles XXII and XXIII of the General Agreement.

Such procedures safeguard, within an overall balance of rights and obligations agreed by WTO Members, not only the rights of a complaining Member to bring disputes in respect of matters covered by the Doha Waiver, but also the due process rights of other WTO Members.

V. ASSESSMENT OF THE EUROPEAN COMMUNITIES' ENVISAGED REBINDING

48. As observed above, the Arbitrator is required to determine whether the European Communities' envisaged rebinding for bananas would result, at a minimum, in the preservation of the effective opportunities to enter the EC banana market afforded to MFN suppliers by the existing conditions of entry prior to the rebinding. In this assessment, the scheduled market access commitments undertaken by the European Communities are to be taken into account, but the appropriate benchmark is the totality of the opportunities afforded by the existing conditions of entry encountered by MFN suppliers.

49. In this light, the Arbitrator will first outline the main elements of the European Communities' envisaged rebinding. Whether that envisaged rebinding meets the requirement described in the mandate for this arbitration will then be analyzed, in light of the arguments of the parties.

A. The envisaged rebinding

50. As noted above, the European Communities has notified its intention to replace its concessions on bananas with a bound duty of €230 per metric ton.

[38] *See* Appellate Body Report, *EC – Bananas III*, para. 167.

This rebinding exercise takes place in the context of the European Communities' move to a tariff-only regime, as described in the Doha Waiver. The proposed rate is to take effect on 1 January 2006.[39]

51. In the course of the proceedings, the European Communities explained that, in arriving at its proposed rate, it had employed the price gap methodology used in the Uruguay Round agriculture negotiations. This methodology has since been incorporated, with minor modifications, into the *WTO Agreement* as the Attachment to Annex 5 of the *Agreement on Agriculture*. The European Communities had "sought a methodology which would ensure that the new tariff would maintain the same level of protection as did the existing concessions."[40] According to the European Communities, the price gap methodology "was devised precisely to measure the level of protection provided by different types of instruments affecting market access and to convert it into a tariff equivalent."[41] "The exercise envisaged in the Waiver Annex, namely the rebinding of the EC tariff on bananas, while maintaining total market access for MFN banana suppliers, is analogous to the type of exercise for which the price-gap methodology has been used."[42] The European Communities also noted that the price gap methodology is familiar to all WTO Members who participated in the Uruguay Round negotiations, that it was simple, and that it was part of the WTO *Agreement on Agriculture*.[43]

52. The price gap methodology as employed by the European Communities involves calculating the difference between internal and external prices of bananas during a reference period. The difference between the two (i.e., the "price gap") provides a measure of the level of protection afforded to domestic producers on the market. In this instance, the European Communities chose 2000-2002 as the reference period.[44]

53. The external price was obtained using Eurostat data with respect to the volume and c.i.f. value of banana imports into the EC-25 from MFN suppliers.[45] To calculate the external price, the c.i.f. value of banana imports from MFN suppliers was divided by the volume of imports. The European Communities arrived at an external price for the EC-25 of €559 per metric ton, averaged over the period 2000-2002. With the exception of the question of the appropriate reference period, the calculation of the external prices based on Eurostat data is not in dispute.

54. To calculate the internal price, the European Communities used price data collected by the FAO and made available through a publicly accessible database. At the time the European Communities carried out the price gap calculation, i.e., in June 2004, the data series was referred to as "Bananas (C. America, f.o.b.

---

39 G/SECRET/22/Add.1, 1 February 2005.

40 First Written Submission of the EC, para. 3.

41 *Ibid.*, para. 9.

42 *Ibid.*, para. 11.

43 *Ibid.*

44 In respect of the choice of the reference period, *See infra*, paras. 80-83.

45 Exhibit EC-4.

Hamburg - EC duty paid)". The description has since been changed to "L. America, f.o.t. Benelux/Hamburg – EC duty paid".

55. The European Communities then applied a series of coefficients to that price data, to adjust for:

- the higher average price of bananas originating in Central America compared to those originating in South America;
- the higher average price of bananas in Germany compared to the rest of EC-15; and
- the higher average price of bananas in the EC-15 compared to the ten new members of the European Communities.

56. After making these adjustments, the European Communities arrived at an internal EC-25 price of €789 per metric ton. The gap between the external price of €559 per metric ton and the internal price calculated by the European Communities for the 25 member States (€789 per metric ton), amounted to €230 per metric ton in the period 2000-2002, proposed by the European Communities as the new tariff.

57. The Interested Parties have challenged the envisaged rebinding both in respect of the methodology and in respect of the price data used to arrive at the envisaged rebinding. In particular, they have argued that:

(a) the price gap methodology used by the European Communities cannot meet the requirements of the mandate. One important reason is that it fails to take into account the impact of the increase in the preference margin that would result from the rebinding;

(b) even assuming that the price gap methodology were appropriate in the circumstances, the reference period and the price data upon which the European Communities has relied in its calculations are flawed.

The Arbitrator will now consider these issues.

B. Appropriateness of the price gap methodology

58. The Interested Parties have questioned the validity of the price gap methodology to calculate the level at which the EC tariff on bananas should be rebound. Most importantly, they have argued that the price gap methodology fails to account for the impact of the increase in preference margin that would result from the envisaged rebinding. The Interested Parties have argued that the proposed tariff would significantly increase the margin of preference between MFN bananas and preferential bananas.[46] This widening of the preference margin would alter the conditions of competition between preferential and MFN banana suppliers to the latter's disadvantage.[47] Honduras, Nicaragua and Panama have

---

[46] The Interested Parties have argued that the proposed tariff would increase the margin of preference from the current €75 per metric ton in respect of in-quota imports to €230 per metric ton.

[47] Brazil notes that the single tariff to be applied on 1 January 2006 will not apply to imports of all origins. The ACP imports will still enjoy duty-free access to the EC market. Brazil states that the

also questioned the applicability of the price gap methodology to calculate the new tariff for the reason that the EC banana regime has already been subjected to tariffication in the Uruguay Round.[48]

59. The European Communities, for its part, submits that the Annex standard requires that the tariff proposed by the European Communities must maintain the level of liberalisation/level of protection provided by its current WTO commitments. Analyzing the level of liberalisation does not imply, according to the European Communities, taking into account any margin of preference granted to bananas originating in the ACP. Accordingly, the European Communities did not address those criticisms in its arguments on the calculations, because they were rendered irrelevant by its interpretation of the Annex to the Doha Waiver.[49]

60. At the outset, the Arbitrator observes that the fact that there was a tariffication exercise for the EC banana regime during the Uruguay Round does not in itself rule out the use of the price gap approach to determine a tariff equivalent to the existing EC banana regime. The Uruguay Round tariffication involved a price gap calculation of a tariff equivalent to measure the effect of various non-tariff measures that existed during the period 1986-1988. Since then, the European Communities has implemented tariff quotas, increased the volumes subject to in-quota tariff rates and/or made the conditions less restrictive, for example, through the removal of country-specific allocations. The current rebinding exercise involves the calculation of a tariff equivalent for bananas that would estimate the protective effect of the conditions of entry during the period 2000-2002, adjusted for the EC-25. Indeed, Colombia, Costa Rica, Ecuador and Guatemala

issue is whether the €230 per metric ton single-tariff will, or will not result in hampering the access of the MFN bananas to the European market to the benefit of the ACP duty-free suppliers. It argues that the EC's envisaged bound duty of €230 per metric ton will distort the market in favour of the ACP countries and that the MFN suppliers will lose significant market shares. The Bolivarian Republic of Venezuela, Colombia, Costa Rica, Ecuador and Guatemala argue that the EC's price gap methodology fails to address the effects of the envisaged tariff on the conditions under which MFN bananas compete with ACP bananas. The EC considers that compliance with the standard that applies under the Annex to the Doha Waiver requires only the maintenance of the conditions under which MFN bananas compete with EC bananas. However, the Bolivarian Republic of Venezuela, Colombia, Costa Rica, Ecuador and Guatemala argue that the phrase "total market access" requires not merely maintenance of the conditions under which MFN bananas compete with EC bananas, but also maintenance of the conditions under which MFN bananas compete with ACP bananas. They submit that increasing the margin of preference between ACP bananas and MFN bananas to any level higher than the current €75 per metric ton would adversely affect total market access for MFN bananas. In the view of Honduras, Panama and Nicaragua, the price gap method fails to take into account a key factor bearing on a proper analysis of the standard under the Annex to the Doha Waiver, namely the extent to which a subset of the ACP countries-Africa, Belize, and the Dominican Republic-will respond to an enlarged tariff preference by increasing their exports to the EC market. Honduras, Panama and Nicaragua submit that these countries have soils, topography, climate, cost structures and other resources that closely resemble, and are competitive with, those in Latin America. They submit that the envisaged tariff of €230 per metric ton will increase the existing margin of preference between MFN bananas and ACP bananas and create incentives for multinational banana marketing and production companies to expand production in Africa. Since tariff quotas would be removed on ACP bananas, it would enable banana suppliers in Africa to gain unlimited, duty-free access to the EC market leading to displacement of MFN banana suppliers.

48 Respective First Written Submissions of Honduras, Nicaragua and Panama, para. 300.

49 Rebuttal Submission of the EC, para. 92.

admit that, in principle, and if applied correctly, the difference between the internal and external prices could be equated to the effects of the existing trade restriction, measured by its equivalent tariff.[50] The Interested Parties themselves have drawn the Arbitrator's attention to studies from the economic literature which provide, despite its practical difficulties, credibility to the use of the price gap method for measuring non-tariff barriers.[51] While the tariff quota commitments constitute, in the WTO context, a variant of a tariff concession, rather than a non-tariff measure *per se*, the economic effect of the EC tariff quotas for bananas is, in an analytical sense, comparable to a quota regime (non-tariff measure), as evidenced by the negligible volume of banana imports entering the European Communities at the out-of-quota tariff.[52]

61. The principal issue in this instance, however, is whether the result of the EC price gap calculation, i.e., the proposed tariff rebinding, meets the standard of preserving, at a minimum, the effective opportunities to enter the EC banana market afforded to MFN suppliers by the existing conditions of entry.

62. As a preliminary matter, the Arbitrator notes that the result of the EC price gap calculation reflects actual access opportunities during the reference period 2000-2002. Contrary to the European Communities' assertion that the exclusive benchmark for the assessment should be the scheduled commitments[53], it has, in fact, implicitly taken into account the effective access conditions prevailing on the EC-25 banana market during the chosen reference period. As noted above in the analysis of the mandate, "total market access for MFN banana suppliers" requires consideration of the effective opportunities to enter the EC banana market afforded to MFN suppliers by the existing conditions of entry. Accordingly, the analysis must factor in not only bound commitments, but all other aspects of the import regime, *as applied*.[54] It was therefore appropriate for the European Communities to take into account the autonomous tariff quotas currently available to MFN suppliers in addition to its scheduled commitments in its calculations.

63. However, the principal question raised by the Interested Parties in respect of the price gap methodology used by the European Communities is its failure-

---

50 First Written Submission of Colombia, Costa Rica, Ecuador and Guatemala, para. 89.

51 For example, "Measuring Nontariff Barriers" by Robert E. Baldwin, referred to in the First Submission of Brazil, paras. 207 and 208. Exhibit EC-10, available on-line at http://www.nber.org/papers/w2978.pdf; Measurement of Non-Tariff Barriers by Alan V. Deardorff and Robert M. Stern (University of Michigan), available on-line at: http://www.oecd.org/dataoecd/34/3/1863859.pdf

52 The EC has indicated that:

> "According to the information received by the European Commission from the EC member States pursuant to Article 22 (4) of Commission Regulation 896/2001 (4), between 10,000 to 20,000 tonnes of bananas are imported out of quota every year. That represents about 0.3% of the total imports and they correspond to marginal imports of residual quantities, consisting for the most part of a few tonnes, in consignments. There is no consolidated information about their origin."

(Written answer by the EC to a question by the Arbitrator)

53 EC statement at the oral hearing in response to a question by the Arbitrator.

54 In practice, the EC has actually granted MFN suppliers more market access than the minimum recorded in its Schedule. *Supra*, paras. 13-18.

and inability, in the submission of the Interested Parties-to take into account the impact of the increase in the preference margin that would result from the rebinding. According to the European Communities, this is not relevant to the assessment. This question was extensively discussed both in the written submissions of the parties and during the oral hearing.

64. The Interested Parties have stressed that the competitive environment they face in entering the EC banana market is affected importantly by the existence of preferential treatment granted to ACP suppliers. These preferences, which would otherwise be contrary to Article I of GATT 1994, are made possible by a waiver of the European Communities' obligations under that Article. This waiver was granted by the WTO Members subject to certain conditions. In particular, it includes the Annex under which this arbitration procedure is foreseen. This arbitration procedure therefore forms an integral part of the agreement reached by WTO Members in granting the waiver. Indeed, the very continuation of the waiver in respect of bananas is also intimately tied to the conclusion of the rebinding exercise.

65. These elements suggest that the rebinding exercise and the procedures under the Annex were considered *in the context of* the preferences that would be granted under the then proposed waiver. They also suggest that the standard by which the rebinding is to be assessed in these proceedings was developed in consideration of these preferences. Indeed, the essence of the preferences is to exempt their beneficiaries from the application of the MFN tariff rate. There is a direct correlation between that MFN rate and the level of the preferences actually granted: the greater the difference between the MFN rate and the preferential rate, the greater the margin of the preference. These elements suggest at a minimum that, while the mandate refers specifically to MFN suppliers, the context in which this arbitration is being carried out bears a close relationship to the preferences authorized in the same legal instrument (the Doha Waiver) in favour of other suppliers: the level of the MFN tariff and the margin of preference are, in a sense, two sides of the same coin.

66. Bearing in mind that context and turning to the specific assessment that is required under the benchmark in the Annex, it can be recalled that, as determined above, "maintaining total market access for MFN banana suppliers" relates to the preservation of the effective opportunities afforded to MFN suppliers by the existing conditions of entry to the EC banana market. Different suppliers—including MFN and preferential suppliers—compete on the EC market. The existing conditions of entry impact upon the relative competitiveness of each of these groups of suppliers, in that they partly define the competitive environment in which the various suppliers operate. Specifically, the conditions of entry for MFN suppliers have an impact on the competitive relationship between MFN and preferential suppliers. To examine the conditions of entry for MFN banana suppliers under the envisaged rebinding—and the opportunity that would be afforded by such conditions—without consideration of the impact of the rebinding on the preferential suppliers would amount to ignoring a key component of the market on which MFN (and preferential) suppliers compete.

67. Furthermore, the fact that the mandate requires a specific focus on the position of the MFN banana suppliers inevitably involves an examination of the supply response by the ACP suppliers as a result of the rebinding.

68. The Arbitrator therefore finds that the potential impact of the preferences granted to ACP banana suppliers on the effective opportunities afforded by the existing conditions of entry to the MFN banana suppliers is a necessary consideration in assessing the European Communities' envisaged rebinding. In reaching this conclusion, the Arbitrator is not suggesting that it is required, or that it would be appropriate, to consider the treatment that will be granted by the European Communities to preferential suppliers *per se*. Rather, the focus of the analysis, as set out in the mandate, is the access to the EC market *for MFN banana suppliers*. The manner in which the European Communities may decide to preserve also market access for ACP suppliers is, as such, beyond the realm of this arbitration.[55]

69. The European Communities has used the price gap methodology that was used in the Uruguay Round agriculture negotiations for the conversion of non-tariff measures to tariff equivalents. Using the correct prices, this methodology would produce an estimate of the tariff equivalent that, all other things being equal, would confer the same level of protection to domestic producers as the border measures being replaced by the tariff equivalent. Correctly applied, the price gap methodology would be broadly neutral in its effects on domestic producers and on total imports. Thus the price gap methodology would accurately reflect the level of protection accorded to domestic or EC growers from foreign competitors. However, the standard price gap formula does not take into account how the competitive relationship may change between imports from different sources, i.e., MFN and preferential banana suppliers. In this instance, the European Communities' proposed tariff equivalent would result in an increase of the margin of preference enjoyed by ACP suppliers from €75 per metric ton in respect of in-quota imports to €230 per metric ton, significantly increasing the advantage they have enjoyed over MFN banana suppliers prior to the rebinding. Given that the use of the price gap methodology means that the rebinding would have neutral effects on *total* imports, any gains achieved by the preferential suppliers in the EC market as a result of this added advantage would, other factors remaining constant, come at the expense of MFN banana suppliers.

70. A positive supply response from preferential banana suppliers to the increased margin of preference can reasonably be expected. Although the Arbitrator makes no finding as to the correct value to be attributed to that supply response, it observes that all available information on this matter provided by the parties suggests that the export supply elasticity of at least some of the ACP suppliers in this instance is in fact significant.[56] In the model presented by Hondu-

[55] It should be noted that any rebinding above €75 per metric ton automatically increases the preference enjoyed by ACP suppliers over MFN suppliers. Under the EC's proposal of €230 metric ton, and using its calculation of the external price of €559 per metric ton, the preference enjoyed by ACP suppliers would rise from 13.4 per cent for in-quota imports to 41.1 per cent.

[56] The elasticity of export supply is a measure of how much additional export volumes can be produced in response to a given increase in price. It is defined as the ratio of the percentage change in

ras, Panama and Nicaragua, an export supply elasticity of between 1 to 6 was assumed for ACP suppliers.[57] The European Communities has also provided information about the values of the export supply elasticities of various ACP suppliers based on a number of studies of the banana market.[58] Out of thirteen such estimates listed, none is lower than 1 while the maximum is 1.1.[59]

71. The Arbitrator is therefore satisfied that, in a tariff quota-free environment, at least some of the preferential suppliers would have the capacity to respond positively to the increase in the margin of preference resulting from the proposed rebinding. That increase would therefore be such as to affect the effective opportunities afforded to MFN suppliers by the existing conditions of entry to the EC banana market. This has not been taken into account in the calculation of the proposed rebinding.[60] This demonstrates that, absent any adjustment to account for the impact of the rebinding on the margin of preference accorded to ACP suppliers, the price gap methodology used by the European Communities to arrive at its envisaged rebinding leads to an outcome that would not result in at least maintaining total market access for MFN banana suppliers.

72. This conclusion is not modified by the European Communities' assertion at the oral hearing that it would limit duty-free/preferential imports from ACP countries by means of a tariff quota once the rebinding would come into force.[61] According to the European Communities, this intention is based on its objective that the whole change of regime should be "neutral in terms of the level of protection offered in respect both of MFN suppliers and in respect of preferential suppliers".[62] The Interested Parties questioned the consistency with the European Communities' WTO obligations of such an approach, and asked for clarification of the details of what was envisaged by the European Communities.[63]

73. The European Communities declined to provide any further indication as to how such a tariff quota might be implemented. In particular, it has not indicated at what level the tariff quota might be set, in other words, what volumes of preferential ACP imports would be granted duty-free access. The European Communities argued that this aspect of the regime is not pertinent to the assess-

---

exports supplied to the percentage change in price. The higher the export supply elasticity, the greater the amount of exports that can be supplied from a given increase in price.

[57] Respective First Submissions of Honduras, Nicaragua and Panama, para. 281.

[58] Exhibit EC-24.

[59] Exhibit EC-24 also contains information on sixteen estimates of domestic supply elasticities of various ACP suppliers. These reflect a wider range in the values of domestic supply elasticities, from a maximum of 1.3 to a low of 0.16. But nine of these sixteen domestic supply elasticities are equal to or greater than 1.

[60] Indeed, in its written submissions, the EC did not suggest that the €230 per metric ton envisaged rebinding would have no effect on the margin of preference to ACP suppliers. Rather, it simply considered that this was not relevant to the assessment.

[61] The EC, in response to a question by the Arbitrator, indicated that it was simply providing this information in order to highlight that the assumptions upon which the Interested Parties were basing their calculations, i.e. an unlimited duty-free access to the EC market for preferential suppliers, were incorrect.

[62] EC statement at the oral hearing, in response to a question.

[63] The Interested Parties have questioned in particular how this would be compatible with the provisions of Article XIII of GATT 1994.

ment because it relates to the ACP preferences rather than to the MFN rebinding. However, as found earlier, the Arbitrator considers that the impact of the margin of preferences for the ACP suppliers on the rebinding *is* a necessary consideration in assessing whether the envisaged rebinding would maintain total market access for MFN suppliers.

74. The Arbitrator is not convinced that a simple cap in the volume of preferential imports would necessarily address the concern of ensuring that the envisaged rebinding would result in at least maintaining total market access for MFN banana suppliers. Indeed, in the absence of any information as to how such a tariff quota might be administered, it is impossible to assess the effects that would be created by the new system. The Arbitrator also notes that least-developed countries benefiting from the European Communities' Everything But Arms initiative ("EBA") are to be granted duty-free access to the EC market as of 1 January 2006. The terms of access to be granted to certain countries under the EBA do not involve tariff quota restrictions and may affect the competitive situation of MFN banana suppliers.[64] Leaving aside the procedural issues related to the late stage at which the argument was put forward by the European Communities, the Arbitrator therefore sees no basis for modifying its earlier conclusion that the envisaged rebinding would not result in at least maintaining total market access for MFN banana suppliers.

75. In making this determination, the Arbitrator is mindful that it is not requested, in this proceeding, to determine any specific appropriate level of rebinding, or even any specific methodology through which such level might be appropriately determined. Rather, the Arbitrator is required to assess specifically whether the European Communities' proposed rebinding would meet the standard defined in the mandate for this Arbitration.

76. The Interested Parties have suggested that only economic simulation models would provide an adequate tool to determine an appropriate level of rebinding for bananas, and they have presented some results of economic modelling to illustrate the effects of the proposed rebinding on competitive opportunities for MFN suppliers.[65] Specifically, Honduras, Nicaragua and Panama used a simulation of a specific model[66] to argue that the proposed EC rebinding using the price gap methodology would not maintain total market access for MFN banana suppliers.

---

[64] First Submission of Honduras, Nicaragua and Panama, paras. 89 and 91.

[65] Honduras, Nicaragua and Panama stress that it is a theoretically consistent tool for analyzing a wide range of potential changes in the world banana market over time (respective First Written Submissions of Honduras, Nicaragua and Panama, paras. 264-265). Brazil states that the use of models would offer more accurate results and that modelling could provide a far better idea about how the market would behave after the adoption of the single-tariff regime (First Written Submission of Brazil, para. 235). The Bolivarian Republic of Venezuela, Colombia, Costa Rica, Ecuador and Guatemala believe that the use of a model will demonstrate the effects of the envisaged tariff on total market access for MFN bananas, taking into account competition between MFN bananas and ACP bananas (First Written Submission of Colombia, Costa Rica, Ecuador and Guatemala, para. 120).

[66] Attachment 2 of the respective First Written Submissions of Honduras, Nicaragua and Panama.

77. The Interested Parties argue in particular that a simulation model can take into account the capacity of certain ACP banana suppliers to increase exports under various tariff scenarios.[67] These models take into account a range of factors and attempt to capture certain future evolutions in the market, based on certain assumptions about the behaviour of the market under the proposed rebinding. The European Communities, however, has questioned the validity of a number of these assumptions as well as their relevance in the context of its tariff rebinding on bananas.

78. The arguments and factual elements presented in the course of this proceeding suggest that economic modelling affords the analyst the possibility of taking into account a range of factors, as well as the ability to conduct simulations in the banana market that may allow one to obtain a range of tariff equivalents corresponding to the scenario that the analyst believes is the most likely to occur.

79. Some of the factors relied upon by the Interested Parties in their arguments appear to reflect in particular an intention to capture future evolutions of the market, including evolutions based on factors extraneous to the imposition of duties and other charges on importation by the European Communities. The Arbitrator sees difficulty in the suggestion that that hypothetical future evolutions not resulting from the rebinding itself should necessarily be part of the assessment. More generally, although the requirement of "maintaining" total market access for MFN suppliers involves some degree of prospective assessment, the Arbitrator is not convinced that this standard necessarily implies a preservation "at all times into the future" as some Interested Parties have argued. It was also apparent from the exchange of arguments between the parties that the choice and assignment of specific values to the various parameters in an economic modelling simulation can in itself be a source of complexities. Simulation models require more data than the price gap methodology, and the choice of parameters as well as the assignment of values to them make the results of such modelling as vulnerable (or as solid) as the assumptions upon which they are based. The Arbitrator does not find it necessary or appropriate, to take a position on the relative merits and adequacy of the various models presented by the Interested Parties as such. It notes that the benefits from their use must be carefully balanced against the technical hurdles and uncertainties posed by the choice of parameters and data.

C. Reference period

80. The use of the reference period 2000-2002 by the European Communities for its price gap calculation has been criticized by some of the Interested Parties. Brazil noted in its submission that over the base period selected by the European Communities, 2000-2002, the EC common market organization for bananas had at least three different regimes. It submits that an aggregation of these regimes

67 Respective First Written Submissions of Honduras, Nicaragua and Panama, para. 266.

into the same base period renders any result of the price gap methodology meaningless.[68]

81. Colombia, Costa Rica, Ecuador, and Guatemala have submitted that the appropriate reference period should commence in 2002. This is because the EC banana regime, as it is currently applied, was implemented on 1 January 2002, in accordance with the understandings between the European Communities and Ecuador, and the European Communities and the United States, in the *EC - Bananas III* dispute. It is this modified regime, which includes tariff quotas for both MFN suppliers and ACP suppliers, that will be converted into a tariff-only regime.[69] But the European Communities contends that the period 2002-2004 is not representative due to abnormally high freight rates in 2003 and 2004.[70] Moreover, it was pointed out by the European Communities that the 2000-2002 period was based on the most recent Eurostat data available at the time when the European Communities notified its intention to modify its concessions regarding bananas (15 July 2004).[71]

82. The Arbitrator notes that the practice to date in the GATT and the WTO suggests that the reference period should normally be the most recent representative three-year period for which data is available. For example, the "Procedures for Negotiations Under Article XXVIII" (adopted on 10 November 1980) foresee that the notification or request for negotiations should by accompanied by statistics of imports of the products involved "for the last three years for which statistics are available".[72] Paragraph 6 of the *Understanding on the Interpretation of Article XXVIII of the General Agreement on Tariffs and Trade 1994* also provides for the use of trade data on "the most recent representative three year period" in the calculation of future trade prospects in the context of compensation to be granted upon replacement of an unlimited tariff concession by a tariff quota.

83. In the light of the foregoing, the Arbitrator's view is that it is important to reflect in the price gap calculation the existing EC banana regime. The use of the most recent representative reference period minimizes the need for *ad hoc* adjustments to be made to the data and corresponds as closely as possible to the trade regime as applied.

---

68 First Written Submission of Brazil, para. 216.

69 Replies of Colombia, Costa Rica, Ecuador, and Guatemala to Questions Posed by the Arbitrator.

70 The EC explained that

> "According to an article published in 'Fruitrop' in January 2005 (Exhibit EC-30) and based on the presentation made by the director of the company Fruta Rica in Guayaquil (Ecuador) in November 2004, full season prices in 2003 were the highest for seven years and spot market prices were 20 to 25 per cent higher than in 2002. The upward trend continued or even increased in 2004."

(Comments of the European Communities on the Responses of the Interested Parties to the Questions from the Arbitrator, para. 3.)

71 Reply to question by the Arbitrator.

72 "Procedures for negotiations under Article XXVIII", Guidelines adopted on 10 November 1980, BISD 27S/26-28, para. 2.

D. *Price data*

84. The Interested Parties also challenged the validity of the European Communities' proposed rebinding on the basis that the data upon which it has relied upon in its calculation of the price gap is flawed. Whereas the data used for the calculation of the external price is not in dispute, the European Communities and the Interested Parties differed significantly on what data was appropriate for calculating the internal price of bananas.

85. The European Communities used price data from the FAO to calculate the internal price.[73] The European Communities indicated that it chose to base its calculations on data from the FAO, an international organization, in an effort to avoid conflicts of interests in the characterization of the internal price.[74] The European Communities also noted that the FAO web site, from which it downloaded the prices, also publishes prices concerning other international markets for bananas, like the United States, Eastern Europe and European Free Trade Area countries. It thus considered FAO prices as "the most reliable actual prices." [75]

86. The Interested Parties challenged the relevance of these prices. In particular, Colombia, Costa Rica, Ecuador and Guatemala submitted that the prices were derived from price quotations obtained from traders, not actual prices. These price quotations in the banana sector are, according to them, typically well above the actual selling prices at wholesale level.[76] Colombia, Costa Rica, Ecuador and Guatemala also produced affidavits from traders to support their argument that the FAO prices were quoted prices and that actual prices were lower than quoted prices.[77] One of these affidavits was from a trader certifying that it regularly transmitted data to the FAO on quoted prices of bananas.[78] The European Communities disputed the validity of the distinction between quoted and actual prices. It has also pointed to the difficulties associated with obtaining actual price data from transactions on the market, as this is information is private.

87. In the light of the questions raised by the parties' arguments in respect of the nature and sources of the FAO data, the Arbitrator wrote to the FAO to obtain further clarification of these issues. In response to a question in the letter in relation to the collection of the relevant data, the FAO confirmed that "... these are price quotations announced by the traders at the ports of entry and probably not the prices paid by purchasers of bananas at the end of the transaction".[79] In reply to the question "Could the FAO provide information as to the precise source ... and an indication as to the number of sources from which data is obtained ...", the FAO replied that though it could not disclose the source of the data, "the data come from one source".[80]

---

73 *Supra*, para. 54.
74 Rebuttal Submission of the EC, para. 136.
75 First Written Submission of the EC, para. 146.
76 Respective First Written Submissions of Honduras, Nicaragua and Panama, para. 316.
77 Exhibits CCEG-13, CCEG-14, CCEG-18 and CCEG-25.
78 Exhibits CCEG-13, CCEG-14 and CCEG-15.
79 *Ibid.*
80 FAO letter addressed to the Secretary of the Arbitrator, dated 5 July 2005.

88. The parties do not appear to differ on the necessity of using data reflecting actual prices in a price gap calculation. The replies provided by the FAO support the proposition put forward by the Interested Parties that the data relied upon by the European Communities reflects offer prices rather than actual prices. The FAO also clarified that the collection of this data was initiated "in the context of a proposal for an international banana agreement."[81] The submissions by Colombia, Costa Rica, Ecuador and Guatemala provide some evidence that actual prices are lower. They include an attachment[82] from Sopisco News[83] which documents "Banana selling prices in Euro at the Hamburg market for deliveries next week". It distinguishes between "actual" and "official" prices of various brands of bananas sold in the EC market, with the "actual" prices being in a range that is generally lower than the "official" prices.

89. On the basis of the evidence provided, the Arbitrator concludes that the data from the FAO does not reflect actual internal prices.[84]

90. The Interested Parties have submitted various alternative calculations of the internal price, based on reports by external auditors, "reconstructed prices", or data obtained from Corbana in Costa Rica.[85] These alternative sources of price data, however, are all criticized by the European Communities.[86] In particular, the

---

81 *Ibid.*

82 Exhibit CCEG-17.

83 Sopisco News is a newsletter dealing with the international banana trade and reefer shipping.

84 The EC has argued that the Attachment to Annex 5 of the *Agreement on Agriculture* provides an appropriate basis for the calculations. The use of the FAO data as such will not produce the "actual difference" between external and internal prices referred to in paragraph 1 of that Attachment.

85 The submissions by Honduras, Nicaragua and Panama provide four alternative calculations of the internal price, progressively widening the coverage of bananas: (i) EC grown; (ii) EC and ACP bananas; (iii) EC, ACP and MFN bananas (using German ZMP[85] and Aldi/Cirad[85] prices); and (iv) EC, ACP and MFN bananas (using audited data provided by the German Fruit and Vegetable Importers Association). Prices for EC-grown bananas are obtained from "compensatory aid" documents. ACP banana prices are taken from CIRAD. The internal price calculated by Honduras, Nicaragua and Panama range from €552 per metric ton to €617 per metric ton. The submission by Colombia, Costa Rica, Ecuador, and Guatemala provides an internal price based on a certified report made by an auditor (Osterloh & Nottbohm GmbH) hired by the association of German banana importers and wholesalers (Deutscher Fruchthandelsverband e. V.) to verify the actual f.o.t. selling price of green bananas in Hamburg. This results in an estimated internal price of €592.09 per metric ton. Brazil calculates an internal price based on weekly market reports issued by Corbana adjusted for discharge and loading costs estimates from Sopisco News. Corbana (National Banana Corporation) is a public non-governmental body in Costa Rica which was created by national law in 1971. It has been designated as the regulatory body of the Costa Rican banana industry, and its mission is to " serve national producers". Sopisco News publishes a weekly newsletter covering information on banana prices, freight rates, reefer vessel schedules, exchange rates, etc. Based on these sources of information Brazil calculates the internal price at €690.37 per metric ton.

86 The EC disputes the calculation of the internal price based on a certified report made by an external auditor submitted by Colombia, Costa Rica, Ecuador and Guatemala on the grounds that the audited companies are directly involved in the banana business and have a strong conflict of interest in this matter. (Rebuttal Submission of the EC, para. 164) It also takes issue with the use by Honduras, Panama and Nicaragua of "reconstructed" price data from specific sources, suggesting that these data were used "to avoid already available German, Swedish, Dutch, and other EC Member States' prices transmitted by the 15 competent authorities, on the basis of a Commission Regulation, for wholesale yellow banana prices." (*Ibid.*, para. 170) With regard to Brazil's use of price data from Corbana, the EC states that it has no access to the information (it does not appear in the website of

European Communities questioned the price gap calculations derived from these alternatives data by the Interested Parties, which lead to price gaps of less than €75 per metric ton. The Arbitrator notes that this is less than the current in-quota tariff rate, and does not appear to reflect any value for the existence of the tariff quota itself.

91. The Arbitrator takes note that some Interested Parties[87] have also claimed that the internal price used by the European Communities constitutes an f.o.t. (free on truck) price and as such is distorted by the inclusion of discharge and handling costs borne by the seller. These costs arise from discharging the bananas from the vessel at the port of entry and loading them onto railway wagons or truck for transport.[88] Costa Rica, Colombia, Ecuador and Guatemala submit that such costs should be deducted because "it is essential that the difference between the external and internal prices reflects only the effects of the trade restriction and is not distorted by other elements affecting prices that are unrelated to the trade restriction, such discharge and loading costs."[89] The European Communities observed that its internal price is a wholesale price that properly includes handling and transport costs, consistent with the guidelines for price gap calculations in the *Agreement on Agriculture*.[90] The Arbitrator notes that how these charges are accounted for could have a significant bearing on the price data calculation.

92. While the Arbitrator does not discount the difficulties associated with the availability and reliability of actual market prices and does not exclude that an estimation or approximation may be required, it is satisfied that the internal price calculated by the European Communities in order to arrive at its envisaged rebinding does not reflect as accurately as possible the actual prices at which bananas are sold on the EC market.

VI. CONCLUDING REMARKS

93. This arbitration raises questions of considerable political, economic and social importance to the Members concerned. The Arbitrator must, of course, decide the issues before it on their merits according to the evidence and submissions before it. Nevertheless, the Arbitrator takes note of the high importance of this matter to the WTO Members involved.

Corbana) and that Brazil does not advance any evidence to prove that this data is reliable (*Ibid.*, para. 175) In addition, some of the Interested Parties themselves have questioned Corbana prices. Honduras makes the point that these prices "are informal, unpublished data that are intended by Corbana only to spot broad pricing trends, not to reflect real prices. Moreover, even if Corbana's tracking mechanisms were more comprehensive, Costa Rican banana volume represents less than 30 per cent of MFN trade into the EC and no more than 17 per cent of total EC banana consumption. That country is among the highest-cost producers in Latin America. Costa Rican industry 'prices,' thus, can in no sense be considered a 'representative wholesale price ruling in the domestic market'." (Responses by Honduras to Written Questions from the Arbitrators, answer to Question 9)

87 Colombia, Costa Rica, Ecuador and Guatemala.

88 First Written Submission of Colombia, Costa Rica, Ecuador and Guatemala paras. 89-92.

89 First Written Submission of Colombia, Costa Rica, Ecuador and Guatemala, para. 89.

90 Rebuttal of the EC, para. 151.

VII. DETERMINATION

94. For the reasons stated above, the Arbitrator determines that the European Communities' envisaged rebinding on bananas would not result in at least maintaining total market access for MFN banana suppliers, taking into account all EC WTO market-access commitments relating to bananas.

ATTACHMENT 1

WORLD TRADE ORGANIZATION

WT/MIN(01)/15
14 November 2001

(01-5786)

MINISTERIAL CONFERENCE
Fourth Session
Doha, 9 - 14 November 2001

EUROPEAN COMMUNITIES – THE ACP-EC PARTNERSHIP AGREEMENT

Decision of 14 November 2001

The Ministerial Conference,

Having regard to paragraphs 1 and 3 of Article IX of the Marrakech Agreement Establishing the World Trade Organisation (the "WTO Agreement"), the Guiding Principles to be followed in considering applications for waivers adopted on 1 November 1956 (BISD 5S/25), the Understanding in Respect to Waivers of Obligations under the General Agreement on Tariffs and Trade 1994, paragraph 3 of Article IX of the WTO Agreement, and Decision-Making Procedures under Articles IX and XII of the WTO Agreement agreed by the General Council (WT/L/93);

Taking note of the request of the European Communities (EC) and of the Governments of the ACP States which are also WTO members (hereinafter also the "Parties to the Agreement") for a waiver from the obligations of the European Communities under paragraph 1 of Article I of the General Agreement with respect to the granting of preferential tariff treatment for products originating in ACP States as required by Article 36.3, Annex V and its Protocols of the ACP-EC Partnership Agreement (hereinafter also referred to as "the Agreement")[1];

Considering that, in the field of trade, the provisions of the ACP-EC Partnership Agreement requires preferential tariff treatment by the EC of exports of products originating in the ACP States;

---

[1] As contained in documents G/C/W/187, G/C/W/204, G/C/W/254 and G/C/W/269).

Considering that the Agreement is aimed at improving the standard of living and economic development of the ACP States, including the least developed among them;

Considering also that the preferential tariff treatment for products originating in ACP States as required by Article 36.3, Annex V and its Protocols of the Agreement is designed to promote the expansion of trade and economic development of beneficiaries in a manner consistent with the objectives of the WTO and with the trade, financial and development needs of the beneficiaries and not to raise undue barriers or to create undue difficulties for the trade of other members;

Considering that the Agreement establishes a preparatory period extending until 31 December 2007, by the end of which new trading arrangements shall be concluded between the Parties to the Agreement;

Considering that the trade provisions of the Agreement have been applied since 1 March 2000 on the basis of transitional measures adopted by the ACP-EC joint institutions;

Noting the assurances given by the Parties to the Agreement that they will, upon request, promptly enter into consultations with any interested member with respect to any difficulty or matter that may arise as a result of the implementation of the preferential tariff treatment for products originating in ACP States as required by Article 36.3, Annex V and its Protocols of the Agreement;

Noting that the tariff applied to bananas imported in the "A" and "B" quotas shall not exceed 75 €/tonne until the entry into force of the new EC tariff-only regime.

Noting that the implementation of the preferential tariff treatment for bananas may be affected as a result of GATT Article XXVIII negotiations;

Noting the assurances from the Parties to the Agreement that any rebinding of the EC tariff on bananas under the relevant GATT Article XXVIII procedures should result in at least maintaining total market access for MFN banana suppliers and their willingness to accept a multilateral control on the implementation of this commitment.

Considering that, in light of the foregoing, the exceptional circumstances justifying a waiver from paragraph 1 of Article I of the General Agreement exist;

Decides as follows:

1. Subject to the terms and conditions set out hereunder, Article I, paragraph 1 of the General Agreement shall be waived, until 31 December 2007, to the extent necessary to permit the European Communities to provide preferential tariff treatment for products originating in ACP States as required by Article 36.3, Annex V and its Protocols of the ACP-EC Part-

nership Agreement,[2] without being required to extend the same preferential treatment to like products of any other member.

2. The Parties to the Agreement shall promptly notify the General Council of any changes in the preferential tariff treatment to products originating in ACP States as required by the relevant provisions of the Agreement covered by this waiver.

3. The Parties to the Agreement will, upon request, promptly enter into consultations with any interested member with respect to any difficulty or matter that may arise as a result of the implementation of the preferential tariff treatment for products originating in ACP States as required by Article 36.3, Annex V and its Protocols of the Agreement; where a member considers that any benefit accruing to it under the General Agreement may be or is being impaired unduly as a result of such implementation, such consultations shall examine the possibility of action for a satisfactory adjustment of the matter.

3bis With respect to bananas, the additional provisions in the Annex shall apply._4. Any member which considers that the preferential tariff treatment for products originating in ACP States as required by Article 36.3, Annex V and its Protocols of the Agreement is being applied inconsistently with this waiver or that any benefit accruing to it under the General Agreement may be or is being impaired unduly as a result of the implementation of the preferential tariff treatment for products originating in ACP States as required by Article 36.3, Annex V and its Protocols of the Agreement and that consultations have proved unsatisfactory, may bring the matter before the General Council, which will examine it promptly and will formulate any recommendations that they judge appropriate.

5. The Parties to the Agreement will submit to the General Council an annual report on the implementation of the preferential tariff treatment for products originating in ACP States as required by Article 36.3, Annex V and its Protocols of the Agreement.

6. This waiver shall not preclude the right of affected members to have recourse to Articles XXII and XXIII of the General Agreement.

[2] Any reference to the Partnership Agreement in this Decision shall also include the period during which the trade provisions of this Agreement are applied on the basis of transitional measures adopted by the ACP-EC joint institutions.

ANNEX

The waiver would apply for ACP products under the Cotonou Agreement until 31 December 2007. In the case of bananas, the waiver will also apply until 31 December 2007, subject to the following, which is without prejudice to rights and obligations under Article XXVIII.

- The parties to the Cotonou Agreement will initiate consultations with Members exporting to the EU on a MFN basis (interested parties) early enough to finalize the process of consultations under the procedures hereby established at least three months before the entry into force of the new EC tariff only regime.
- No later than 10 days after the conclusion of Article XXVIII negotiations, interested parties will be informed of the EC intentions concerning the rebinding of the EC tariff on bananas. In the course of such consultations, the EC will provide information on the methodology used for such rebinding. In this regard, all EC WTO market-access commitments relating to bananas should be taken into account.
- Within 60 days of such an announcement, any such interested party may request arbitration.
- The arbitrator shall be appointed within 10 days, following the request subject to agreement between the two parties, failing which the arbitrator shall be appointed by the Director-General of the WTO, following consultations with the parties, within 30 days of the arbitration request. The mandate of the arbitrator shall be to determine, within 90 days of his appointment, whether the envisaged rebinding of the EC tariff on bananas would result in at least maintaining total market access for MFN banana suppliers, taking into account the above-mentioned EC commitments.
- If the arbitrator determines that the rebinding would not result in at least maintaining total market access for MFN suppliers, the EC shall rectify the matter. Within 10 days of the notification of the arbitration award to the General Council, the EC will enter into consultations with those interested parties that requested the arbitration. In the absence of a mutually satisfactory solution, the same arbitrator will be asked to determine, within 30 days of the new arbitration request, whether the EC has rectified the matter. The second arbitration award will be notified to the General Council. If the EC has failed to rectify the matter, this waiver shall cease to apply to bananas upon entry into force of the new EC tariff regime. The Article XXVIII negotiations and the arbitration procedures shall be concluded before the entry into force of the new EC tariff only regime on 1 January 2006.

ATTACHMENT 2

TABLE 1

EC-15 IMPORTS OF BANANAS (CN 08030019), 2000-2004
(Metric Tons)

YEAR	ACP SUPPLIERS	MFN SUPPLIERS	TOTAL
2000	755,794.3	2,543,130.2	3,298,924.5
2001	728,775.8	2,474,585.8	3,203,361.6
2002	726,871.5	2,561,065.8	3,287,937.3
2003	786,798.4	2,578,827.0	3,365,625.4

For year 2004, the data is for the twenty five member states of the European Communities (also see footnote 12).

2004	785,583.8	3,084,937.4	3,870,521.2

Source: Eurostat (data extracted or downloaded on 20 and 22 July 2005).

EUROPEAN COMMUNITIES – THE ACP-EC PARTNERSHIP AGREEMENT –

SECOND RECOURSE TO ARBITRATION PURSUANT TO THE DECISION OF 14 NOVEMBER 2001

Award of the Arbitrator

WT/L/625*

Circulated to Members on 27 September 2005

TABLE OF CONTENTS

* This arbitration was initiated pursuant to the procedures set out in the Annex to the waiver decision with respect to Article I of the General Agreement on Tariffs and Trade 1994 ("GATT 1994") contained in the document "European Communities - The ACP-EC Partnership Agreement, Decision of 14 November 2001" (the "Doha Waiver" WT/MIN(01)/15).

I. INTRODUCTION

98. This arbitration was initiated pursuant to the procedures set out in the Annex to the Waiver Decision with respect to Article I of GATT 1994 contained in the document "European Communities – The ACP-EC Partnership Agreement, Decision of 14 November 2001" (the "Doha Waiver").[1] This is the second recourse to arbitration initiated pursuant to that decision. The procedural background of this proceeding is described in Section II below.

II. PROCEDURAL BACKGROUND

99. The Arbitrator issued its first award to the parties on 1 August 2005 and notified the award to the General Council later that same day.[2] The mandate of the Arbitrator in the first arbitration was:

> ... to determine, ... whether the envisaged rebinding of the EC tariff on bananas would result in at least maintaining total market access for MFN banana suppliers, taking into account [all EC WTO market-access commitments relating to bananas].

---

[1] WT/MIN(01)/15.

[2] *European Communities – The ACP-EC Partnership Agreement – Recourse to Arbitration Pursuant to the Decision of 14 November 2001, Award of the Arbitrator*, WT/L/616, dated 1 August 2005 (hereinafter "Award of the Arbitrator").

100. In its first award, the Arbitrator determined "that the European Communities' envisaged rebinding on bananas would not result in at least maintaining total market access for MFN banana suppliers, taking into account all EC WTO market-access commitments relating to bananas."[3]

101. In a letter dated 4 August 2005, the Arbitrator observed that the fifth tiret of the Annex to the Doha Waiver contemplated that "in the absence of a mutually satisfactory solution, the same arbitrator will be asked to determine, within 30 days of the new arbitration request, whether the EC has rectified the matter". In the light of the possibility of a second arbitration, the Arbitrator outlined the procedure that it proposed to follow, were a second arbitration to be requested. This procedure included a tentative timetable for the parties' submissions, the hearing and the award. The letter also invited participation by the same African, Caribbean and Pacific ("ACP") countries that participated in the first arbitration (the "relevant ACP Members") on the same terms as in the first arbitration, including the possibility of presenting a collective written submission and a collective statement at the hearing.

102. The Arbitrator received a letter, dated 18 August 2005, from the relevant ACP Members requesting more extensive rights of participation in the second arbitration. Brazil, Colombia, Costa Rica, Ecuador, Guatemala, Honduras, Nicaragua, and Panama[4] (hereafter referred to as "the Interested Parties") objected to the ACP request in a letter dated 14 September 2005.

103. In a letter from the parties, dated 24 August 2005, the Arbitrator was informed that the European Communities had entered into consultations with the Interested Parties within ten days of the notification of the arbitration award to the General Council. It was also informed that the European Communities would "not be in a position before September to present the Interested Parties its proposal to "rectify the matter" or to propose a timetable for constructive consultations upon presentation of that proposal. Furthermore, the letter noted that the parties agreed "that in the absence of a mutually satisfactory solution, the second arbitration may be requested at any time in such a manner as would enable the Arbitrator to issue its award within 30 days after the request for a second arbitration, and "before the entry into force of the EC tariff-only regime for bananas on 1 January 2006".

104. On 13 September 2005, the European Communities notified the Interested Parties that it had revised its proposal to provide as from 1 January 2006 for an MFN tariff for bananas at €187 per metric ton and a tariff quota for ACP countries of 775,000 metric tons per year at zero duty.

105. On 16 September 2005, Costa Rica, Ecuador, Honduras, Nicaragua and Panama requested a preliminary ruling from the Arbitrator that the European Communities "is not entitled under the terms of the Waiver Annex to request the second arbitration." They further requested, in the alternative, a revision of the procedures and deadlines set out in the Arbitrator's letter of 4 August 2005. In a

---

3 Award of the Arbitrator, para. 94.

4 Together with Venezuela hereafter referred to as "the Interested Parties"

separate communication, Brazil, Colombia and Guatemala also requested a revision of the procedures and deadlines. The Arbitrator replied on 21 September 2005 that, in the light of the fact that no second arbitration had been requested at that date, any organizational matters or requests for preliminary rulings arising in the context of request for a second arbitration could be considered at an organizational meeting convened shortly after any such request.

106. In a communication dated 26 September 2005, the European Communities notified the Arbitrator that, after consultations with the Interested Parties, "there is currently no basis for even seeking a mutually satisfactory solution" within a timeframe that would allow for implementation of the new banana regime of the European Communities by 1 January 2006. It therefore requested the matter be referred back to the same arbitrator in accordance with the Annex to the Doha Waiver. In accordance with the procedures outlined by the Arbitrator in its letter of 4 August 2005, the European Communities also filed a written submission on the same day.

107. The Arbitrator held an organizational meeting with the parties on 28 September 2005. At that meeting, Costa Rica, Ecuador, Honduras, Nicaragua and Panama reiterated their request for a preliminary ruling regarding the validity of a request for arbitration by the European Communities. At the invitation of the Arbitrator, the European Communities filed a written response to the arguments made in the request for a preliminary ruling.

108. In a communication dated 29 September 2005, the Arbitrator informed the parties and the relevant ACP Members of its decisions with respect to the timetable for these proceedings and the request for a preliminary ruling presented by certain Interested Parties. In particular, it accorded some additional time to the Interested Parties and the relevant ACP Members for their submissions. The Arbitrator also indicated that it would address the request for a preliminary ruling in its final award.

109. The Interested Parties and the relevant ACP Members filed written submissions on 10 October 2005. The Arbitrator met with the parties and the relevant ACP Members on 19 October 2005. The parties and relevant ACP Members filed final written communications on 21 October 2005.

III. REQUEST FOR A PRELIMINARY RULING BY COSTA RICA, ECUADOR, HONDURAS, NICARAGUA AND PANAMA

110. The Arbitrator begins by addressing the request by Costa Rica, Ecuador, Honduras, Nicaragua and Panama for a preliminary ruling "that the EC is not legally entitled to initiate the second arbitration".

111. Costa Rica, Ecuador, Honduras, Nicaragua and Panama argued that a request by the European Communities would be contrary to the procedures agreed in the Annex to the Doha Waiver. In particular, this group of Interested Parties argued that the structure of the second arbitration is intended to mirror that of the first round of proceedings. Under this process, the European Communities must make a proposal and consult with the Interested Parties. In the event that the In-

terested Parties are dissatisfied with the European Communities' proposal and no mutually satisfactory solution is found, the Interested Parties may then request arbitration. On this basis, these Members argued that the purpose of the second arbitration is to afford rights to the MFN suppliers and not the European Communities. Allowing the European Communities to request a second arbitration would also prejudice the procedural rights of the Interested Parties by depriving them of adequate time to review and analyse the new proposal. The European Communities disagreed with the position adopted by Costa Rica, Ecuador, Honduras, Nicaragua and Panama. It pointed to the absence of any specification in the fifth tiret of the Annex to the Doha Waiver as to which parties may, or may not, request a second arbitration. Rather, requests for a second arbitration may be made by any party in the absence of a mutually satisfactory solution. The European Communities also disagrees that the procedural rights of the Interested Parties would be prejudiced if the European Communities were entitled to request the second arbitration. Indeed, preventing the European Communities from doing so would prejudice its procedural rights.

112. Against that background, the Arbitrator notes that the appointment of the Arbitrator for purposes of the second arbitration is governed by the following sentence in the fifth tiret of the Annex to the Doha Waiver:

> In the absence of a mutually satisfactory solution, the same arbitrator will be asked to determine, within 30 days of the new arbitration request, whether the EC has rectified the matter.

113. The Arbitrator observes that, on a plain reading of this text, there is no express limitation as to which of the parties may request, or "ask[]", it to fulfil the mandate of the second arbitration. This contrasts with the wording of the third tiret to the Annex, which expressly limits the right to request the initial arbitration to certain interested parties.

114. Costa Rica, Ecuador, Honduras, Nicaragua and Panama argue, in essence, that the context of the Annex requires that the conditions for requesting the first arbitration should also be applied to the request for the second arbitration. The Arbitrator acknowledges that interpreting the provisions of the Annex to the Doha Waiver in the light of their context is appropriate. However, this context may not override the explicit provisions being interpreted. As was emphasized in the first award, the explicit provisions of the Waiver Annex govern the mandate of the Arbitrator,[5] and indeed the manner in which the Arbitrator is appointed. The relevant explicit provision here, namely, the fifth tiret governing initiation of the second arbitration, suggests no limitation regarding which parties may request arbitration. If the drafters of the Annex had desired to limit the right to request the second arbitration to the Interested Parties alone, they could easily have adopted language similar to that used in the third tiret. The Arbitrator is not permitted to read into the text of the fifth tiret words that are not there.

115. That any of the parties may request recourse to a second arbitration is confirmed by the manner in which the precondition for such a request is phrased.

---

[5] Award of the Arbitrator, para.46.

That precondition is "the absence of a mutually satisfactory solution". The ordinary meaning of the term "mutually satisfactory" denotes that such a solution is one that is satisfactory to all parties affected. In its request for the second arbitration, the European Communities asserted that no mutually satisfactory solution was in existence at that time.[6] A "mutually satisfactory solution" would, necessarily, be a solution that was satisfactory to the European Communities. Thus the precondition for recourse to a second arbitration was clearly present.

116. For these reasons, the Arbitrator finds no grounds upon which to determine that the European Communities was not legally entitled to initiate the second arbitration. Accordingly, the Arbitrator declines to grant the preliminary ruling requested by Costa Rica, Ecuador, Honduras, Nicaragua and Panama.

IV. MANDATE OF THE ARBITRATOR

A. The mandate under the second arbitration (whether the European Communities has "rectified the matter")

117. Under the terms of the Annex to the Doha Waiver, the mandate of the Arbitrator in the first arbitration was to determine "whether the envisaged rebinding of the EC tariff on bananas would result in at least maintaining total market access for MFN banana suppliers, taking into account [all EC WTO market-access commitments relating to bananas]". In the context of that initial proceeding, the Arbitrator determined that its mandate involved three elements: first, the "envisaged rebinding of the EC tariff on bananas"; secondly, a benchmark against which that envisaged rebinding is to be assessed (namely, whether it "would result in at least maintaining total market access for MFN banana suppliers"); and thirdly, a direction to the Arbitrator to take into account all EC WTO market access commitments relating to bananas.[7]

118. Having analyzed the terms of its mandate, the Arbitrator found, in its first award, that it was required to determine "whether the proposed new EC tariff for bananas would preserve, at a minimum, the effective opportunities to enter the EC banana market afforded to MFN suppliers by the existing conditions of entry". The Arbitrator also found that the analysis must take into account not only bound commitments, but all other aspects of the import regime, as applied.[8]

119. In respect of a second arbitration, the Annex to the Doha Waiver provides that the Arbitrator would be asked to determine "whether the EC has rectified the matter". The European Communities has proposed to rectify the matter through a tariff on MFN imports of bananas of €187 per metric ton, for which it would modify its Schedule, and opening an autonomous tariff quota of 775,000 mt for imports originating in ACP countries with an in-quota duty of zero. The tariff

6 *Supra*, para. 9.
7 Award of the Arbitrator, para. 20.
8 *Ibid.*, para. 37.

quota would be administered on the basis of the historical system of license allocation, as under the current regime.[9]

120. The parties agree, and the Arbitrator finds, that its mandate in this matter is to determine whether the European Communities has "rectified the matter" in the light of the first award, such that the European Communities' new proposed rebinding would result in at least maintaining total market access for MFN suppliers, taking into account all of the European Communities' WTO market access commitments relating to bananas.[10] The Arbitrator determined in its first award that this mandate required "a determination as to whether the proposed new EC tariff for bananas would preserve, at a minimum, the effective opportunities to enter the European Communities' banana market afforded to MFN suppliers by the existing conditions of entry". This is also the pertinent benchmark for the Arbitrator's assessment in this proceeding. As in the initial proceedings, the analysis of the Arbitrator in the context of this second recourse to arbitration must factor in, not only bound commitments, but all other aspects of the European Communities' import regime for bananas, as applied.[11]

121. Although the parties did not differ on the interpretation of the benchmark to be applied to the Arbitrator's assessment in this proceeding, some of the Interested Parties considered that part of the European Communities' proposed rectification of the matter, namely the proposed application of a tariff quota on ACP imports, could not be taken into account in the assessment. The Arbitrator now turns to the European Communities' proposed "rectification of the matter" and the relevance of the proposed tariff quota to its assessment in this proceeding.

B. The European Communities' proposed rectification of the matter

122. As noted above, the European Communities' proposed rectification of the matter includes two elements: a tariff on MFN imports of bananas of €187 per metric ton, for which it would modify its Schedule, and opening an annual tariff quota of 775,000 mt for imports originating in ACP countries, with an in-quota duty of zero.

123. It is not disputed that the first element constitutes an "envisaged rebinding" within the meaning of the Annex to the Doha Waiver. However, certain Interested Parties argued that the tariff quota component of the EC proposal could not be taken into account by the Arbitrator, because it was not an "envisaged rebinding" of the banana tariff. Honduras, Nicaragua and Panama, as well as Colombia, Costa Rica, Ecuador and Guatemala, also asked the Arbitrator to disregard the tariff quota from its analysis because it would be inconsistent with

---

9 See European Communities' submission, paras. 8 and 9.

10 See submission by Colombia, Costa Rica, Ecuador and Guatemala submission, para. 1; submissions of Honduras, Nicaragua and Panama, para. 3; the issue was not specifically addressed in Brazil's submission, but it seems assumed that the revised European Communities' proposal should be assessed against the benchmark developed in the First Award. This view was also confirmed at the oral hearing in response to a question by the Arbitrator.

11 Award of the Arbitrator, para. 37.

the European Communities' WTO obligations and with its commitment to apply a tariff-only regime as of 1 January 2006.[12] These arguments will be addressed in turn.

1. *Relationship between the proposed tariff quota and the "envisaged rebinding" of the European Communities' tariff on bananas*

124. Colombia, Costa Rica, Ecuador and Guatemala contended that, as was highlighted in the Arbitrator's analysis of its mandate in the first award, it was the European Communities' "envisaged rebinding" of its tariff on bananas that is to be the starting point of the analysis. In their view, the proposed tariff quota for ACP suppliers, which was not an envisaged rebinding, fell outside the scope of the Arbitrator's mandate and thus could not be considered by the Arbitrator.[13]

125. In its first award, the Arbitrator described the "envisaged rebinding" of the European Communities' tariff on bananas as the first element of its mandate and as the "starting point" for the analysis to be performed under the mandate.[14] For the purposes of this second arbitration, the Annex to the Doha Waiver does not specifically identify the different elements that should form the basis for the Arbitrator's analysis, beyond the indication that the Arbitrator should determine whether the European Communities has "rectified the matter". In particular, it does not specify in what form the European Communities might seek to rectify the matter.

126. The Arbitrator determined above – and the parties did not dispute – that its mandate for this arbitration should be understood with reference to the mandate in respect of the initial arbitration. The starting point of the Arbitrator's analysis should therefore be, as in the initial proceedings, the European Communities' "envisaged rebinding" of its tariff on bananas. Under the European Communities' proposed rectification of the matter, this "envisaged rebinding" would be at €187 per metric ton.[15] The European Communities did not suggest that the tariff quota would, in itself, be part of this envisaged rebinding, or otherwise be incorporated into its Schedule of commitments. Rather, it described the proposed tariff quota as an additional measure, to be applied in conjunction with the envisaged rebinding.[16] Nonetheless, this does not necessarily imply that the proposed tariff quota may not be taken into account in the Arbitrator's analysis.

---

[12] Submissions by Nicaragua and Panama, paras. 234 and 235; submission by Honduras, paras. 235 and 236; and submission by Colombia, Costa Rica, Ecuador and Guatemala, paras. 43-57 and 73-75.

[13] Submission by Colombia, Costa Rica, Ecuador and Panama, paras. 58-67.

[14] Award of the Arbitrator, paras. 20 and 24.

[15] It might be argued that the expression "rectify the matter" could be read to imply that such rectification could incorporate more than an envisaged rebinding, if this were intended to "rectify the matter" following a determination that the initial proposed rebinding did not meet the requirements of the Annex of the Doha Waiver. However, we do not find it necessary to explore this issue further, in the light of our determination below that the tariff quota need not necessarily constitute an envisaged rebinding in order to be taken into account.

[16] Submission by the European Communities, paras. 8 to 10.

127. As the Arbitrator found in its first award, the total market access for MFN suppliers is affected importantly by the market access for preferential ACP suppliers. The Arbitrator recognized a "direct correlation between the MFN rate and the level of the preferences actually granted ... [and that] the level of the MFN tariff and the margin of preference are, in a sense, two sides of the same coin".[17] The Arbitrator found that "the potential impact of the preferences granted to ACP banana suppliers on the effective opportunities afforded by the existing conditions of entry to the MFN banana suppliers is a necessary consideration in assessing the envisaged rebinding".[18] The Arbitrator also found in its first award that "[t]he benchmark against which the [rebinding of the tariff rate] is to be assessed is not the specific concept of tariff bindings, but the more general concept of 'market access' for MFN suppliers".[19]

128. It follows for this arbitration proceeding that it is relevant to consider not only the European Communities' proposed increase in the extent of the ACP tariff preference from €75 to €187 per metric ton, but also the effect of the proposed "cap" on that preference through the proposed tariff quota for ACP countries, in order to assess whether the European Communities' envisaged rebinding would result in at least maintaining total market access for MFN banana suppliers so as to "rectify the matter". The envisaged rebinding is to be implemented not in isolation but in the broader context of a new EC import regime for bananas. The Arbitrator thus must consider the new proposed market access regime for bananas as a whole to determine whether the proposed rebinding would meet the standard of at least maintaining total market access for MFN banana suppliers.

2. *Consistency of the proposed tariff quota with the European Communities' WTO obligations and commitments vis-à-vis MFN banana suppliers*

129. As noted above, Honduras, Nicaragua and Panama, as well as Colombia, Costa Rica, Ecuador and Guatemala, also asked the Arbitrator to disregard the tariff quota from its analysis because, in the absence of a waiver, it would be inconsistent with the European Communities' WTO obligations under the General Agreement on Tariffs and Trade 1994 (hereafter "GATT 1994") and with the European Communities' commitment to apply a tariff-only regime as of 1 January 2006.[20] Some of the Interested Parties argued that, aside from the proposed ACP tariff quota's inconsistency with the European Communities' WTO obligations, the granting of a GATT Article XIII waiver for the application of such a tariff quota was uncertain, and that the Arbitrator should therefore decline to consider the proposed tariff quota. The same Interested Parties also argued that the European Communities' proposed tariff quota could not be taken into account

---

[17] Award of the Arbitrator, para. 65.

[18] *Ibid.*, para. 68.

[19] *Ibid.*, para. 31.

[20] Submissions by Nicaragua and Panama, paras. 234 and 235; submission by Honduras, paras. 235 and 236; and submission by Colombia, Costa Rica, Ecuador and Guatemala, paras. 43-57 and 73-75.

because it would not be consistent with the European Communities' commitment to apply a tariff-only regime for bananas as of 1 January 2006.

130. In respect of the potential WTO-inconsistency of the proposed tariff quota, it should first be noted that the European Communities indicated, as part of its proposed rectification of the matter, that the application of the tariff quota on ACP imports would be covered by the existing Doha Waiver in respect of Article I of GATT 1994, and that the European Communities also intends to seek a waiver of its obligations under Article XIII of GATT 1994 to implement its proposed tariff quota.[21]

131. In the Arbitrator's view, the fact that the European Communities' proposal includes the proposition that an Article XIII waiver would be sought, and obtained, for the application of the proposed tariff quota is significant in addressing this issue. Even assuming that the establishment of the proposed tariff quota would otherwise be inconsistent with the European Communities' WTO obligations, the European Communities proposed to apply it under circumstances that would no longer involve an unauthorized WTO-inconsistency. The European Communities' proposal incorporates an assumption that the tariff quota would be applied after a collective authorization has been obtained from the WTO Membership, in conformity with the applicable procedures for waiver decisions under the *Marrakech Agreement Establishing the World Trade Organization* (the *WTO Agreement*).[22] In these circumstances, the Arbitrator is not convinced that the alleged inconsistency of the proposed tariff quota with the European Communities' WTO obligations should, in itself, lead it to disregard in its analysis the proposed application of a tariff quota for ACP banana imports. This does not imply any determination, on the part of the Arbitrator, as to the WTO-consistency or otherwise of such a tariff quota, in the absence of a waiver.

132. At the time of this award, the European Communities has requested an Article XIII waiver for the proposed tariff quota, pursuant to Article IX of the *WTO Agreement*. It is not possible, at this point in time, to predict whether or not such a waiver will, in due course, be granted by the WTO Membership. It is, as an abstract matter, possible that such a waiver might be granted, just as it is conceivable that it might not be granted. This is a matter that depends on collective action by the WTO Membership. However, this uncertainty is not an obstacle to the Arbitrator's consideration of the proposed rectification. There is no need to make any assumptions as to the likelihood of an Article XIII waiver being granted to the European Communities for its proposed tariff quota in order to consider whether, *if* it were to be applied as described, the European Communities' proposed rectification would result in at least maintaining total market access for MFN banana suppliers as required by the Annex to the Doha Waiver.

---

[21] The European Communities informed the Arbitrator, in the course of these proceedings, that it had formally presented such a request to the WTO. That request was circulated on 11 October 2005 in document G/C/W/529.

[22] Indeed, while some of the Interested Parties have disputed the WTO-consistency of the proposed tariff quota in the absence of a waiver, they do not appear to have questioned that the granting of an appropriate waiver by the WTO Membership, if obtained, would be such as to allow the imposition of a measure that may otherwise be incompatible with a Member's WTO obligations.

The Arbitrator's determination in these proceedings is premised on the actual application by the European Communities of its proposed rectification of the matter. At the time of the Arbitrator's determination, even the application of the proposed revised tariff, independently of the tariff quota element, remains dependent on a rebinding of the European Communities' tariff on bananas in accordance with the procedures foreseen in Article XXVIII of GATT 1994.

133. Finally, as regards the European Communities' commitment to apply a tariff-only regime for bananas as of 1 January 2006, the Arbitrator notes that the parties disagree as to the interpretation of the notion of "tariff-only" regime, as contained in the Understandings concluded by the European Communities with the United States and Ecuador, and as referred to in the Doha Waiver. However, the Arbitrator does not find it necessary, for the purposes of its assessment of the proposed rectification, to determine this issue. As noted above, the European Communities' proposal to rectify the matter envisages that the tariff quota on ACP imports would be applied with a waiver, so that it would be specifically authorized by collective endorsement, through the appropriate procedures, of the WTO Membership.

134. For these reasons, the Arbitrator is not persuaded that it is prevented from considering the proposed rebinding in the light of the proposed tariff quota on ACP banana imports. This threshold determination is entirely without prejudice to the question of whether this proposal would result in at least maintaining total market access for MFN suppliers as foreseen under the Doha Waiver. This will be addressed below.

3. *Treatment of Beneficiaries of the "Everything But Arms" Initiative*

135. In its first award, the Arbitrator noted that duty-free access for least developed countries ("LDCs") to the European Communities market under the Everything But Arms ("EBA") Initiative might affect the competitive situation of MFN banana suppliers.[23] In this proceeding, the European Communities indicated that ACP suppliers who are also EBA beneficiaries would not be subjected to the proposed tariff quota. The European Communities considered that the EBA Initiative is independent of the trade regime being regulated through the currently applicable Doha Waiver regarding the EC-ACP Partnership Agreement and thus not relevant to this arbitration.

136. The Arbitrator agrees that the legal basis on which the EBA Initiative (i.e. preferential duty-free treatment for all LDC products except arms) is authorized within the WTO legal framework is distinct from the Doha Waiver. Moreover, no participant in this arbitration has suggested that the EBA is WTO-inconsistent. Nonetheless, as was described in the first award, EBA preferences could have an impact on the total market access for MFN suppliers. As the man-

[23] Award of the Arbitrator, para. 74.

date of the Arbitrator is framed by reference to the market access of MFN suppliers, this issue is returned to later in this award.[24]

V. ASSESSMENT OF THE EUROPEAN COMMUNITIES' RECTIFICATION OF THE MATTER

A. The European Communities' rectification of the matter in the light of the Arbitrator's first award

137. Before assessing whether European Communities' proposed rectification of the matter "would result in at least maintaining total market access for MFN banana suppliers" within the meaning of the Doha waiver, this section describes how the European Communities, in revising its proposal, sought to take into account the findings of the Arbitrator in its first award.

138. In its initial proposal for a rebinding of its tariff on bananas, the European Communities had used the price gap methodology reflected in the attachment to Annex 5 of the Agreement on Agriculture because it "was devised precisely to measure the level of protection provided by different types of instruments affecting market access and to convert it into a tariff equivalent."[25] According to the European Communities, the "exercise envisaged in the Waiver Annex, namely the rebinding of the EC tariff on bananas, while at least maintaining total market access for MFN banana suppliers, is analogous to the type of exercise for which the price-gap methodology has been used."[26] In its first award, the Arbitrator noted that, using correct prices, this methodology would produce an estimate of the tariff equivalent that, all other things being equal, would confer the same level of protection to domestic producers as the border measures being replaced by the tariff equivalent.[27] Correctly applied, the price gap methodology would be broadly neutral in its effects on domestic producers and on total imports.[28]

139. The Arbitrator also found in its first award, however, that the standard price gap formula as applied by the European Communities in its initial calculation did not account for the potential impact of the increase in the margin of preferences enjoyed by ACP suppliers on actual market access opportunities for MFN suppliers.[29] It stated that:

> examin[ing] the conditions of entry for MFN banana suppliers under the envisaged rebinding—and the opportunity that would be afforded by such conditions—without consideration of the impact of the rebinding on the preferential suppliers would amount to ig-

---

[24] See infra, para. 115.
[25] Award of the Arbitrator, para. 51.
[26] *Ibid.*, para. 51.
[27] Award of the Arbitrator, para. 69.
[28] Award of the Arbitrator, para. 69. While the Arbitrator recognized that simulation models might offer an alternative way for calculating tariff equivalents, it also highlighted their complexities regarding the choice of parameters and data. Award of the Arbitrator, paras. 78-79.
[29] Award of the Arbitrator, paras. 65-69.

noring a key component of the market on which MFN (and preferential) suppliers compete.[30]

The Arbitrator also noted that the manner in which the European Communities may decide to preserve market access for ACP suppliers was, as such, beyond the scope of its mandate.[31]

140. As mentioned earlier, in its proposed rectification of the matter, the European Communities proposed, in addition to a rebinding of its tariff on bananas at €187 per metric ton, a tariff quota of 775,000 metric tons for ACP imports. In suggesting this combination of measures, the European Communities purports to respond to the Arbitrator's concern about the impact of the ACP supply response on the market access opportunities of MFN suppliers.[32]

141. The Arbitrator makes no determination as to whether the establishment of a tariff quota on preferential imports is the appropriate manner to address the impact of an increased MFN tariff rate on the conditions of competition between MFN and ACP preferential suppliers. The Arbitrator understands that the establishment of an ACP duty-free tariff quota is intended to allow existing conditions of competition between MFN and preferential ACP suppliers to be preserved. At this stage of its analysis, the Arbitrator takes no position as to whether the proposed MFN tariff accurately reflects the restrictiveness of the existing regime, or as to whether the tariff quota for ACP countries is set at a level such that the conditions of competition between MFN and preferential suppliers would be at least maintained.

142. The European Communities' price gap calculation in its initial proposal for a rebinding was based on the difference between internal and external prices of bananas during the *reference period* 2000-2002. The Interested Parties criticized this reference period as inappropriate.[33] The Arbitrator expressed a preference for using the most recent representative reference period because this "minimizes the need for *ad hoc* adjustments to be made to the data and corresponds as closely as possible to the trade regime as applied."[34] The European Communities responded to the Arbitrator's recommendation by calculating its proposed rectification on the basis of an updated reference period, namely, January 2002 to April 2004.

143. To calculate the *internal price* in its initial proposal, the European Communities had used price data collected by the Food and Agriculture Organization of the United Nations (the "FAO") and made available through a publicly accessible database.[35] The Interested Parties had challenged the use of those prices because they were not "actual" prices but were "official" prices derived from price quotations obtained from traders.[36] In the first arbitration, the parties did not

30 Award of the Arbitrator, para. 66.
31 Award of the Arbitrator, para. 68.
32 See Submission by the European Communities, para. 84.
33 Award of the Arbitrator, paras. 80-81.
34 Award of the Arbitrator, para. 83.
35 Award of the Arbitrator, para. 54.
36 Award of the Arbitrator, para. 86.

appear to differ on the need to use data reflecting actual prices in a price gap calculation.[37] The Arbitrator found that the internal price calculated by the European Communities in order to arrive at its initial rebinding proposal did "not reflect as accurately as possible the actual prices at which bananas are sold on the EC market". In its proposed rectification of the matter, the European Communities addressed this finding of the Arbitrator by discarding FAO data as a basis for calculating internal prices. The European Communities turned instead to price data from Sopisco News, a weekly publication used in the shipping and reefer industry. It then calculated the internal price of the EC-25 for purposes of rectifying its price gap calculation.[38] It did so as described below.

144. First, the internal price was derived from weekly price data from Sopisco News for the period January 2002 to April 2004. Secondly, since Sopisco News provides a range of the "actual prices" of bananas, the European Communities took the mid-point of that range. Thirdly, since Sopisco News published actual prices by bananas brands, the European Communities took the simple (weekly) average of the five major brands (Chiquita, Del Monte, Dole, Bonita and Fyffes) and the minor brands taken together. Fourthly, since Sopisco News does not contain "actual prices" for the years 2002 and 2003 for Chiquita bananas, the European Communities reconstructed "actual" prices for Chiquita bananas in 2003 by applying the ratio between the "actual" and "official" prices in 2004 to the "official" prices of Chiquita in 2003. For 2002, prices for Chiquita bananas were not taken into account and the average annual price was calculated on the basis of the prices for the other four major brands and the minor brands taken together.

145. On this basis, the European Communities calculated annual average prices of the Sopisco price data referred to as "EU" and "Non EU" (referred to as "E15" and "E10" as from the enlargement of the European Communities). These separate price series were taken by the European Communities to represent the EC-15, on the one hand, and the ten countries that acceded to the European Communities on 1 May 2004 (the "AC-10"), on the other hand. The annual price data were weighted using the respective annual import volumes into the EC-15 and AC-10, as reported by Eurostat, to arrive at the EC-25 internal prices for 2002 (€745 per metric ton), 2003 (€669 per metric ton) and January to April 2004 (€727 per metric ton).

146. For purposes of its initial price gap calculation, the European Communities had obtained the *external price* by using Eurostat data with respect to the volume and c.i.f. value of banana imports into the EC-25 from MFN suppliers.[39] With the exception of the question of the appropriate reference period, the calculation of the external prices based on Eurostat c.i.f. data was not in dispute;[40] nor did the Arbitrator find fault with the European Communities' reliance on Eurostat c.i.f. data in its initial price gap calculation. Nevertheless, in its revised price gap calculation, the European Communities decided that Eurostat c.i.f. data were

[37] Award of the Arbitrator, para. 88.
[38] Submission by the European Communities, paras. 38ff.
[39] Exhibit EC-4.
[40] Award of the Arbitrator, paras. 53 and 84.

inappropriate. The European Communities thus turned to alternative data for the external price. For the external price in its revised calculation, the European Communities took the average of the "Non EU" prices reported in Sopisco News for 2002 (€567 per metric ton), 2003 (€461 per metric ton), and January to April 2004 (€488 per metric ton).

147. The price gap was calculated by taking the annual difference between EC-25 prices (the internal price) and the corresponding "Non EU" prices (the external price). The price gap for the period January to April 2004 was adjusted by a factor of 1.35 in order take into account that prices during that period tend to be higher than the annual average due to a lack of supplies of competing fruit.[41] The annual price gaps for 2002, 2003 and January to April 2004 (seasonally adjusted) were then averaged to result in the proposed tariff of €187 per metric ton.

148. In addition to the internal price used in the price gap calculation that resulted in the proposed tariff of €187 per metric ton, the European Communities provided a number of alternative estimates of the EC-25 internal price giving a range of internal prices between €658 per metric ton and €685 per metric ton. For the reference period 2002-2004[42], the average internal price was estimated at €658 per metric ton, and when the major banana brands were weighted by the market shares assumed by European Communities, the resulting internal price was €685 per metric ton for the reference period 2002-April 2004.[43] For these alternative price estimates, the European Communities deducted discharge and handling costs of €44 per metric ton. These alternative estimates, however, were ultimately not retained by the European Communities as the basis for its proposed rectification of the matter.

B. The European Communities' price gap calculation

149. As noted above,[44] the European Communities' proposal combining an increased MFN tariff and a duty-free tariff quota for ACP suppliers is intended to ensure that any increase in the margin of preference resulting from the increased MFN tariff will not affect the conditions of competition between MFN and ACP suppliers in a manner such that total market access for MFN suppliers would not be at least maintained. Under such an import regime, the standard price gap methodology can, in principle, be employed to calculate the tariff equivalent.

150. The Interested Parties challenged the adequacy of the European Communities' proposed tariff rate of €187 per metric ton tariff on the grounds that its price gap calculation was flawed in respect of *both* the internal price and the external price. In particular, the Interested Parties claimed that the European Com-

---

41 Submission by the European Communities, para. 58.

42 The reference period covers the full year of 2004 rather than ending in April 2004, namely the reference period used by the EC in the calculation of the proposed tariff of €187 per metric ton.

43 Submission by the European Communities, para. 48. According to the European Communities, its estimate of the internal price of €685 per metric ton would be lower, if the European Communities had applied a seasonal adjustment factor to account for the seasonally higher prices during the first four months of the year.

44 See paragraphs 43 and 44 supra.

munities *overestimated* the internal price of the EC-25 during the relevant reference period. They also submitted that EC *underestimated* the external price during that same period. At the same time, the European Communities considered that it made *conservative* estimates in respect of each of these variables. Accordingly, the Arbitrator considers that it is appropriate to consider both sides of the calculation performed by the European Communities to determine whether, overall, the resulting tariff equivalent would meet the requirement of "at least maintain[ing] total market access for MFN banana suppliers".[45]

1. *Internal price*

151. As a preliminary matter, the Arbitrator notes that, according to the price gap guidelines set out in the Attachment to Annex 5 of the *Agreement on Agriculture*:

> The internal price shall generally be a representative wholesale price ruling in the domestic market or an estimate of that price where adequate data is not available.

Although the price gap guidelines in the *Agreement on Agriculture* are not binding under the Doha Waiver, they nonetheless provide useful guidance for analyzing the price gap calculation underlying the European Communities' proposed rectification of the matter.[46] These guidelines suggest a certain degree of flexibility in the determination of the internal price, based on the adequacy of available data.

152. In this regard, the Arbitrator stated in its first award:

> While the Arbitrator does not discount the difficulties associated with the availability and reliability of actual market prices and does not exclude that an estimation or approximation may be required, it is satisfied that the internal price calculated by the European Communities in order to arrive at its envisaged rebinding does not reflect as accurately as possible the actual prices at which bananas are sold on the EC market.[47]

153. The Interested Parties raised a number of objections to the EC calculations of the internal price. These related to the use of Sopisco News data in general, and also to the appropriateness of the Sopisco News data for the specific purpose to which it is put by the European Communities, namely, calculating the price gap for the EC-25. The objections raised by the Interested Parties will be considered in turn, to determine whether these concerns, individually or collectively, suggest that the European Communities overestimated the internal price.

---

[45] This analysis is premised, *arguendo*, on the tariff quota for ACP suppliers being set at a level such that the conditions of competition between MFN and ACP banana suppliers would not be affected in a manner such that total market access for MFN suppliers would not be at least maintained. This is without prejudice to the question of whether the tariff quota actually proposed by the European Communities would in fact fulfil that condition.

[46] The Arbitrator notes that parties have referred extensively to these guidelines in their arguments.

[47] Award of the Arbitrator, para. 92.

(a) Use of Sopisco News data as a source of "actual prices"

154. The European Communities based its estimate of the internal price for bananas on data published by Sopisco News. Honduras, Nicaragua and Panama characterized Sopisco News as:

> predominately dedicated to shipping information to complement Sopisco's principal business, shipping brokerage. Its readership has been developed almost entirely because of the shipping volume and related information it contains. Only a small fraction of the newsletter's weekly content is dedicated to banana price estimates in various markets around the world.[48]

Further, these Interested Parties pointed to Sopisco's disclaimer that "the collected price estimates are "obtained from [unnamed] sources believed to be reliable, but the publisher is not responsible for errors or omissions contained herein."[49] The European Communities argued that Sopisco News was a subscription-based newsletter and the viability of a subscription-based service in the trade and shipping business is based on its reliability.[50] The European Communities emphasized that Sopisco News was relied upon by the governments of a number of the Interested Parties, international organizations such as the World Bank and International Monetary Fund, and by the insurance industry when assessing costs for maritime losses.[51] At the oral hearing, the relevant ACP Members argued that "Sopisco is the most reputable source of information for prices in the banana trade" and that this source should be used to calculate the price gap.[52]

155. In considering the concerns of Honduras, Nicaragua and Panama in this regard, the Arbitrator notes that there is considerable evidence on the record that Sopisco News is a widely accepted source of price information in the banana trade. Indeed, Sopisco News prices were relied upon by Brazil, Colombia, Costa Rica, Ecuador and Guatemala, and also by the relevant ACP Members, during the course of the first arbitration. Accordingly, the Arbitrator has no reason to doubt the reliability of Sopisco News as a source of price information for the banana market.

156. Beyond their general criticism of Sopisco News price data for bananas, certain Interested Parties also questioned Sopisco News data more specifically as a source of information of *actual* prices on the banana market.

157. In this respect, the parties disagreed over the meaning of the expression "actual prices" in Sopisco News. Colombia, Costa Rica, Ecuador and Guatemala argued that these prices could not possibly represent actual selling prices, which were confidential between buyers and sellers, and might also not reflect terms and conditions, such as rebates, unknown to Sopisco News. In their view,

48 Submissions by Nicaragua and Panama, paras. 77-78; submission by Honduras, paras. 78-79.
49 Submission by Honduras, Nicaragua and Panama, para. 79.
50 Submission by the European Communities, para. 29.
51 Submission by the European Communities, paras. 31-33.
52 Oral Statement by the relevant ACP Members, page 3.

Sopisco "actual" prices were in fact price quotes that did not reflect as accurately as possible the actual selling prices of bananas.[53] The European Communities argued that there was no alternative to Sopisco News price data for green bananas that is publicly available.[54] It emphasized that it had never claimed that these prices were necessarily actual market prices; nevertheless they were an accurate estimation of those prices.[55]

158. Sopisco News itself states: "The "Actual" prices are claims of the green market price range in the northern and southern European market for the week following negotiation of the cargoes. The information received from our sources includes what they claim is the selling price for their fruit if they are traders and what they believe is the level of what other traders are selling for."[56] The Arbitrator understands the Sopisco News data relied upon by the European Communities to be essentially predictions or estimates of "actual", as opposed to "official" prices, on the market the following week. In this regard, the Arbitrator considers it significant that these same Sopisco prices were relied upon by Brazil and Colombia, Costa Rica, Ecuador and Guatemala in their submissions during the course of the first arbitration to substantiate their claim that there is a difference between "official" and "actual" prices.

159. The Interested Parties proposed certain alternative sources of data, that would, in their view, more accurately reflect actual internal prices. Specifically, Colombia, Costa Rica, Ecuador, Guatemala and Panama argued that the European Communities should have relied on audited actual price data from the German Fruit Trade Association instead of Sopisco News. These Interested Parties provided the Arbitrator with an internal price of €703 per metric ton that appears to be based on audited data by the German Fruit Trade Association. This price was described as the verified and certified average price (f.o.t) for green MFN bananas in the northern European ports for sale in the EC-15 in 2002-2004.[57]

160. The European Communities, however, expressed strong reservations against the use of audited data on the grounds that it did not have access to the data to verify the results. The European Communities also questioned the reliability of the audited internal price because it considered the implied weight per box of bananas to be incorrect (18.5 kg rather than 18.14 kg). Adjusting the audited price to account for this issue of box sizing, the European Communities recalculated the price as slightly over €717 per metric ton.[58] Several of the Interested Parties countered that under the tax laws of the European Communities, importers were prohibited from declaring bananas at a weight of 18.14 kg per box.[59]

---

53 Comments by Colombia, Costa Rica, Ecuador and Guatemala to the European Communities' replies to question 2 of the Arbitrator, para 14.

54 Oral Statement by the European Communities, para. 13.

55 Oral Statement by the European Communities' oral statement, para. 10.

56 Exhibit II-15 of Colombia, Costa Rica, Ecuador and Guatemala.

57 Submission by Nicaragua and Panama, para 115; submission by Honduras, para. 116.

58 Oral Statement by the European Communities, para. 14.

59 Comments by Honduras, Nicaragua and Panama to the European Communities' replies to question 12 of the Arbitrator.

161. The European Communities argued in particular that it had sought to use a data source that was publicly available with a high degree of reliability, distribution and recognition in the banana trade and which required a minimum amount of adjustment.[60] The European Communities explained to the Arbitrator why it considered Sopisco News to fulfil all of these criteria.

162. In considering this issue, the Arbitrator is mindful of the challenges inherent in having access to exact and complete price information in respect of actual market prices. In particular, complete information in respect of actual prices is in the hands of the parties to individual transactions themselves. In these circumstances, as noted by the Arbitrator in its first award,[61] a certain degree of estimation or approximation may be required when calculating the internal price for purposes of a price gap calculation.

163. The Arbitrator notes the reservations of the European Communities with respect to the use of the "audited prices" presented by the Interested Parties. In particular, while this type of document may provide useful indications as to actual prices on the market, the Arbitrator acknowledges the European Communities' concern that it has no means of verifying the information. The Arbitrator also notes that the European Communities does not appear to have taken advantage of the suggestion made in the course of the proceedings by some of the Interested Parties to consult the books of certain companies.[62]

164. In respect of its calculations based on Sopisco News data, the European Communities submitted detailed calculations of the price gap leading to the proposed tariff equivalent of €187 per metric ton. The information provided by the European Communities includes the relevant original price data from Sopisco News, the European Communities' worksheets and step-by-step explanations of its calculations. None of the Interested Parties has challenged the European Communities' calculations on the grounds that they were non-transparent or could not be verified. It appears that the Interested Parties, on the basis of the information provided by the European Communities, were in a position to verify the price gap calculation leading to a tariff of €187 per metric ton, albeit with certain reservations by Honduras, Nicaragua and Panama.[63]

165. The Arbitrator also notes that, in the light of the evidence presented, the internal price derived by the European Communities from Sopisco News is not rendered implausible by the "audited internal price" presented by the Interested Parties.

166. The material thus far considered is not, in the view of the Arbitrator, a sufficient basis for dismissing Sopisco News data as a source of estimates of actual market prices for bananas.

---

[60] Submission by the European Communities, para. 26.

[61] Award of the Arbitrator, para. 92.

[62] Statement by Colombia, Costa Rica, Ecuador and Guatemala at the hearing with the Arbitrator, 19 October 2005.

[63] Submissions by Honduras, Nicaragua and Panama, Table 5.

167. Having accepted that it was not, in principle, inappropriate to use Sopisco News data as a source of estimates of actual market prices of bananas, the Arbitrator now turns to an examination of the EC's calculation based on that data.

(b) The EC's calculation of the internal price based on the Sopisco price data

168. The European Communities made certain assumptions and adjustments in respect of the Sopisco News data in order to calculate the internal price for bananas on the EC market. The Interested Parties have questioned some of these assumptions and proposed alternative adjustments that should, in their view, have been made to Sopisco data to reflect actual internal prices accurately.

169. The first issue relates to whether the "EU" and "Non EU" prices from Sopisco News, which are described as prices "in Hamburg", can be equated with EC-15 and AC-10 prices, or whether an adjustment to that data is required to make them more representative of EC-15 and AC-10 prices. Honduras, Nicaragua and Panama drew attention to the fact that in the latter part of 2004, Sopisco News' pricing annotations refer to prices "mostly for the Hamburg market or other relevant EU country".[64] In their view, estimates "mostly for the Hamburg market" cannot reliably be equated with EC-15 and AC-10 prices. These Interested Parties noted that during the first arbitration, the European Communities adjusted downwards the FAO prices (which were also Hamburg prices) to take into account the lower prices in the rest of the European Communities. But this time, no adjustment was made by the European Communities, suggesting that the internal price was overestimated.

170. The European Communities contended that the Sopisco price data should be considered as representative wholesale prices in the EC market and that an adjustment is not necessary since bananas are a homogeneous product traded on a single market. According to the European Communities, the phrase "or other relevant EU country" meant that the reported prices cover markets other than Hamburg. This indicated that Sopisco's prices were representative of the EC market.[65] Sopisco News itself stated that its EU prices reflected the market price range "in the northern and southern European market".[66]

171. In the absence of clear indications by Sopisco News regarding the geographical representativeness of the reported prices, the Arbitrator is concerned that the Sopisco News price data for the years 2002-2004 may not be sufficiently representative of the actual market prices in the EC-15 and the AC-10. However, on the basis of the limited evidence provided, the Arbitrator is not in a position to determine whether or not an adjustment to Sopisco price data would have been warranted.

172. The second issue for the Arbitrator to consider is the objection raised by the Interested Parties with respect to the inclusion of Chiquita (one of the major

---

64 Submission by Honduras, para. 103; submissions by Nicaragua and Panama, para. 102.

65 Written answer by the European Communities to question 3 by the Arbitrator.

66 Exhibit by Colombia, Costa Rica, Ecuador and Guatemala II-15.

brands) prices in the calculation of the internal price. Colombia, Costa Rica, Ecuador and Guatemala provided evidence that Chiquita brands were not discharged at the port of Hamburg in the period under consideration, that Chiquita did not disclose its actual prices, except to its customers, and that, in any event, Chiquita provided prices for yellow but not green bananas.[67] These Interested Parties also provided alternative calculations of the internal price, excluding prices for Chiquita bananas from the calculations, to show that the internal price could be lower than the price calculated by the European Communities by €26 and €21 per metric ton in 2003 and the first quarter of 2004, respectively.[68]

173. In response, the European Communities noted that Sopisco News reported "official" prices for Chiquita bananas throughout the reference period and "actual" prices in 2004. The European Communities argued that, although Chiquita bananas may have been unloaded in ports other than Hamburg, prices were published by Sopisco News to provide a full picture of the market. Without accounting for prices for Chiquita bananas – which held a market share of approximately 30 per cent for MFN bananas, according to the European Communities – the European Communities would not have been able to estimate a representative internal price for the European Communities.[69]

174. The Arbitrator notes that the European Communities included "actual" Chiquita prices for 2004 in its estimate of the internal EC-25 price, where such data were available from Sopisco News.[70] The Arbitrator considers it reasonable for the European Communities to have included original Sopisco price data of the Chiquita brand to ensure that its 2004 estimate was representative. As far as its EC-25 price estimate for 2003 is concerned, the European Communities employed reconstructed data rather than original data for Chiquita.[71] It appears that, on the one hand, this reconstructed price has resulted in an increase of the internal price (and hence an increase in the price gap) because Chiquita is a high-priced brand. On the other hand, inclusion of Chiquita arguably made the EC-25 price estimate for 2003 more representative. On balance, the Arbitrator considers that the European Communities' approach in the treatment of the price data for Chiquita bananas was not unreasonable.

175. Another issue raised by the Interested Parties was the European Communities' treatment of Sopisco price data for the other major banana brands (Dole, Del Monte, Bonita and Fyffes). Honduras, Nicaragua, and Panama argued that the European Communities used "statistically unsound methods" in deriving its banana brand estimates in the face of significant data gaps for these major brands in Sopisco News. In their view, by ignoring the data gaps and the seasonal behaviour of banana prices, the European Communities' calculation of simple aver-

67 A letter from Chiquita addressed to the Arbitration Counsel of Colombia, Costa Rica, Ecuador and Guatemala (Exhibit II-10 by Colombia, Costa Rica, Ecuador and Guatemala).

68 Submissions by Honduras, Nicaragua and Panama, para. 163.

69 Answer by the European Communities to question 5 from the Arbitrator.

70 The European Communities also included "actual" prices for Chiquita, where available, in the average "non EU" price in 2002-2004.

71 See paragraph 47 supra.

ages of prices of the major banana brands was significantly distorted.[72] To demonstrate the impact of the data gaps on the European Communities' price gap calculation, Brazil made several adjustments to the original data from Sopisco News.[73] Although the Arbitrator finds Brazil's method of filling data gaps plausible, the results of Brazil's calculation (€169 per metric ton) are not directly comparable with the results of the European Communities' calculation (€187 per metric ton). The difference in the resulting price gap may, in part, be due to the fact that Brazil excluded data for Chiquita from its calculation and to the use of a different reference period.

176. The Arbitrator notes that the data gaps are inherent in the Sopisco News data itself and finds that the approach of the European Communities to the treatment of the data in respect of Dole, Del Monte, Bonita and Fyffes was not inappropriate in circumstances.

177. Overall, the Arbitrator does not consider that the European Communities' use of Sopisco News data to estimate the internal price of bananas on the EC market was inappropriate.

2. *External price*

(a) Introduction

178. In the first arbitration, the European Communities chose Eurostat c.i.f. prices as the basis for calculating the external price, a choice to which the Interested Parties did not object. The Arbitrator had noted that "the calculation of the external prices based on Eurostat data is not in dispute"[74] and did not direct the European Communities to revise its approach to this issue.

179. In the revised proposal that led to the proposed MFN tariff of €187 per metric ton, the European Communities used a different source of price information for the external price. The European Communities found that Eurostat data was "inappropriate in the sense of paragraph 2 of the Attachment to Annex 5 of the Agreement on Agriculture." The European Communities employed instead "Non EU" green banana prices from Sopisco News as the basis for calculating the external price.

180. The Interested Parties disagreed with the European Communities' characterization of Eurostat c.i.f. data as inappropriate and with the European Communities' use of Sopisco News "Non EU" prices as the new basis for calculating the external price.

---

[72] Submission by Honduras, para. 110; submissions of Nicaragua and Panama, para. 109.

[73] Submission by Brazil, para. 42. In the case of data gaps for the major brands (Dole, Del Monte, Bonita and Fyffes), Brazil filled the information gaps with the average of the other major brands in the relevant weeks. Amongst other adjustments to the data, Brazil excluded the data for Chiquita on the grounds that Chiquita did not discharge in Hamburg in the reference period. It also adjusted the weighting between the major and minor brands, and extended the reference period to December 2004 arguing that the European Communities was wrong in having excluded the months of May to December 2004 from its price gap calculation. The result of the European Communities' price gap calculation, as modified by Brazil, was €169 per metric ton.

[74] Award of the Arbitrator, para. 53.

181. The change in the source of the price data has a significant impact on the calculation of the external price. If one takes the reference period adopted by the European Communities, namely 2002 to April 2004, it means a reduction in the external price from €597 per metric ton (using Eurostat c.i.f. data) to €461 per metric ton (using Sopisco News "Non EU").

182. In view of the fact that the European Communities applied the price gap methodology for calculating a tariff equivalent for its current banana regime, and because the European Communities itself relied upon the price gap guidelines contained in the Agreement on Agriculture, the Arbitrator again considers that the price gap guidelines in the Attachment to Annex 5 of the *Agreement on Agriculture* provide guidance as to how such a price gap calculation should be performed. The Arbitrator observes that according to paragraph 2 of the Attachment, the external prices used in a price gap calculation shall in general be (1) "actual average c.i.f. unit values for the importing country", where average c.i.f. unit values "are not available or appropriate", the external prices shall be (2) "appropriate average c.i.f. unit values of a near country", or (3) "estimated from average f.o.b. unit values of (an) appropriate major exporter(s)" with certain adjustments.[75]

183. The Arbitrator will first examine the parties' arguments on whether or not Eurostat c.i.f. prices were *inappropriate* "actual average c.i.f. unit values for the importing country" during the reference period. The Arbitrator will then discuss the parties' arguments on whether the alternative external price used by the European Communities qualify as "appropriate average c.i.f. unit values of a near country".

(b) Is Eurostat c.i.f. data "inappropriate"?

(i) The European Communities' arguments

184. The European Communities said that it did not question the accuracy of the Eurostat c.i.f. data as such, but rather their appropriateness for a price gap analysis. It identified two problems with the Eurostat c.i.f. data.

185. One problem related to the results that were obtained using the Eurostat c.i.f. data.[76] The European Communities began its price gap analysis by using data from Sopisco News to calculate the internal price and Eurostat data to calculate the external price. The resulting price gaps that the European Communities obtained with these data fell within a range of €53 per metric ton and €88 per metric ton. The European Communities stated that figures below €75 per metric

---

[75] Paragraph 2 of Attachment 5 to the *Agreement on Agriculture* provides:

> External prices shall be, in general, actual average c.i.f. unit values for the importing country. Where average c.i.f. unit values are not available or appropriate, external prices shall be either:
>
> (a) appropriate average c.i.f. unit values of a near country; or
>
> (b) estimated from average f.o.b. unit values of (an) appropriate major exporter(s) adjusted by adding an estimate of insurance, freight and other relevant costs to the importing country.

[76] Oral Statement by the European Communities, para. 18.

ton were "clearly inappropriate". For the €88 per metric ton result, it stated that "the protective effect of the quota cannot be €13 per metric ton – a figure which cannot be considered realistic ...". The European Communities argued that price gaps that were close to or below the in-quota tariff of €75 per metric ton fell foul of the Arbitrator's finding in its award that a price gap of less than €75 per metric ton was "less than the current-in quota tariff rate, and does not appear to reflect any value for the existence of the tariff quota itself."[77]

186. The second problem the European Communities found was that "the EC-15 CIF price is not consistent with any of the available data for comparable steps in the trading chain. Normally, CIF prices of neighbouring countries will be more or less comparable".[78] Yet it found that the Eurostat c.i.f. price of €638 per metric ton was higher than the €441 per metric ton c.i.f. price given by Eurostat for the AC-10. It also attempted to reconstruct c.i.f. prices from f.o.b. prices provided by the central banks of some of the Interested Parties. Adding Sopisco's estimates of freight and insurance costs from these countries to the European Communities, its reconstructed c.i.f. estimate was €399 per metric ton, which was €239 per metric ton lower than the EC-15 c.i.f. price of €638 per metric ton. Finally, the European Communities examined c.i.f. prices of the United States. Even after adding the estimated freight and insurance cost differential of shipping from Latin America to the European Communities instead of the United States, the amount was only €394 per metric ton, representing a differential of €244 per metric ton. According to the European Communities, all of these calculations led to the same conclusion that the Eurostat c.i.f. price for the EC-15 was in the order of €200 per metric ton higher than one would expect.[79] A similar point about the high c.i.f. prices reported by Eurostat had been made by the relevant ACP countries in their submissions in the first and second arbitrations.

187. The European Communities suggested that the cause for these problems "appears to be ...that some of the quota rent/protective effect of the quotas is included in the Eurostat c.i.f. prices."[80]

(ii) Arguments of the Interested Parties

188. Panama, Honduras and Nicaragua pointed out that the European Communities had relied heavily on these Eurostat data throughout its common market organizations. It specifically used Eurostat banana data to create the MFN quota in 1993, to calculate the out-of-quota "tariff equivalent" in the Uruguay Round, to determine enlargement volumes, and, even in this proceeding, to trade-weigh its "EU" and "Non EU" Sopisco News estimates.[81]

189. Colombia, Costa Rica, Ecuador and Guatemala questioned the European Communities' justification for rejecting Eurostat data - that the price gap cannot be less than €75 per metric ton. In the European Communities' calculations, the

77 Award of the Arbitrator, para. 90.
78 Oral Statement by the European Communities, para. 17.
79 Response by the European Communities at the oral hearing.
80 Answers to Questions from the Arbitrator by the European Communities, para. 20.
81 Submission by Honduras, Nicaragua and Panama, para. 155.

price gap fell in a range between €53 per metric ton and €88 per metric ton. Honduras, Nicaragua and Panama pointed out that, because the applied level of protection for bananas in the AC-10 during the period of January 2002 to April 2004 was lower than in the EC-15, the trade-weighted tariff for bananas in the EC-25 was €66 per metric ton.[82] Hence, in their view the European Communities' reason for rejecting the results of these price gap calculations did not hold.

190. The Interested Parties questioned some of the comparisons that the European Communities undertook to support its determination that Eurostat c.i.f. data was "inappropriate". Honduras, Nicaragua and Panama argued against the use of United States c.i.f. prices as a basis for comparison, since the United States was not a near country. Further, the Interested Parties provided other explanations why Eurostat c.i.f. data may be high, reasons that had nothing to do with the presence of quota rents. According to Colombia, Costa Rica, Ecuador and Guatemala, the European Communities had imposed product standards for bananas that prohibited the sale of lower quality, and hence lower-priced, bananas.[83] Exporters may also have an incentive to change the mix of their products towards higher quality ones when exporting to a market with quota restrictions.[84]

(iii) Evaluation by the Arbitrator

191. First, the Arbitrator notes that paragraph 2 of the Attachment to Annex 5 of the *Agreement on Agriculture* provides that "[e]xternal prices shall be, in general, actual average c.i.f. unit values for the importing country" and that the use of the alternatives in subparagraphs (a) and (b) is foreseen only where "average unit values are not available or appropriate." These terms indicate a preference or general rule that average c.i.f. unit values be used. Accordingly, departure from that general rule and recourse to alternative proxies for the external price requires evidence and reasoned explanation showing why c.i.f. unit values are unavailable or shown to be inappropriate.

192. The parties did not disagree that Eurostat c.i.f. data provide a source for "actual average c.i.f. unit values" data for the European Communities within the meaning of the introductory clause of paragraph 2 of the Attachment to Annex 5. This means that the European Communities has to substantiate why Eurostat c.i.f. data is not "appropriate" as "external prices". This is particularly so in the present circumstances because, during the first arbitration, the European Communities itself had used Eurostat c.i.f. data as the basis for calculating the external price. In its first Award, the Arbitrator noted that "the calculation of the external prices based on Eurostat data is not in dispute"[85] and did not direct the European Communities to revise its approach in this respect. The Arbitrator finds the European Communities' position in the second arbitration proceeding that Eurostat c.i.f. data is "inappropriate" for the purpose of a price gap analysis, difficult to reconcile with use by the European Communities of that same data

---

82 Submission by Honduras, Nicaragua and Panama, par. 149.
83 Responses by Colombia, Costa Rica, Ecuador and Guatemala at the oral hearing.
84 *Ibid.*
85 Award of the Arbitrator, para. 53.

precisely for such a purpose during the first arbitration and with the fact that the Interested Parties and the Arbitrator did not object to that data source.

193. There were two main problems with Eurostat c.i.f data identified by the European Communities to substantiate its claim that it is not "appropriate" in the sense of paragraph 2 of the Attachment to Annex 5. The first relates to the results of price gap calculations which were obtained using Eurostat c.i.f. data and Sopisco News prices. The second is a series of comparisons of Eurostat c.i.f. prices with near country c.i.f. prices and f.o.b. prices of major banana exporters. The European Communities suggested that Eurostat data appears to incorporate some element of the quota rent, resulting in an artificially high c.i.f. price.

194. The first problem identified by the European Communities concerns the *results* of price gap calculations made using the Eurostat data and Sopisco News prices. Although the Arbitrator agrees that comparisons of the results of various calculations may provide a useful "reality check", it is not of the view that the results of any particular comparison should be the starting point for the analysis of whether c.i.f. unit values for the importing country are "appropriate" or not. Rather, such an assessment should begin with the data *per se*. Thus, Paragraph 2 of the Attachment to Annex 5 envisages a test based on whether actual average c.i.f. unit values *themselves* are "appropriate" as "external prices", not of whether the *results* derived from price gap calculations based on c.i.f. unit values are "appropriate". Indeed, to do otherwise in the context of a price gap calculation would risk attributing to defects in the external price, problems that in fact occur within the internal price. If one arrives at an "unrealistic" or "inappropriate" price gap result, but one has not considered the quality of each of the data, one cannot discount the possibility that the problem lies with the internal price rather than the external price. The Arbitrator leaves these considerations to one side for a moment and turns instead to a consideration of the data *per se*.

195. Colombia, Costa Rica, Ecuador and Guatemala provided an extensive description of the manner in which statistics on the European Communities' trade with third countries are collected.[86] According to them, Eurostat data are collected systematically, subject to extensive controls, and objectively compiled by the statistics division of the European Commission, which obtains them from the national authorities of the EC Member States. These Interested Parties referred to the EC's *User Guide on the Statistics on the Trading of Goods,* which describes the kind of controls applied to trade statistics. These controls could be basic (e.g. ensuring documents have been fully completed); other checks are more sophisticated and assess the plausibility of the data; and still others involve mirror comparison of trade flows.

196. The European Communities argued that "the EC-15 CIF price is not consistent with any of the available data for comparable steps in the trading chain in neighbouring countries". It pointed out that, normally, "CIF prices of neighbouring countries will be more or less comparable", chose to look at the AC-10 countries, but found out that the Eurostat EC-15 c.i.f. price of €638 per metric ton was

[86] Submission by Colombia, Costa Rica, Ecuador and Guatemala, paras. 137-149.

much higher than the Eurostat AC-10 c.i.f. price during the 2002-2004 period. The Arbitrator accepts the European Communities' conclusions regarding the c.i.f. prices in the AC-10, but notes that there are also other neighbouring countries, such as Norway and Switzerland, whose c.i.f. prices could have been used for the comparison instead of, or in combination with, the prices of AC-10 countries. Unlike the market of the European Communities, the markets for bananas in these countries are not fettered by tariff quotas and thus, by definition, contain no element of quota rent. Moreover, the consumers in these countries are, in terms of per capita income, more similar to the consumers of EC-15 countries than the populations of AC-10 countries. The c.i.f. prices for these markets during the period 2002-2004 are comparable, if not higher, than those calculated from Eurostat data for the EC-15.[87] Evidence from these neighbouring countries therefore does not support the conclusion reached by the European Communities that Eurostat c.i.f. prices are abnormally high and are therefore not "appropriate" for use in a price gap comparison.

197. Moreover, there are other explanations for the prices of EC-15 countries and AC-10 prices not being similar although one would expect, as does the European Communities, price levels in neighbouring countries to be comparable. Colombia, Costa Rica, Ecuador and Guatemala noted that "quotas may cause exporters to change the mix of products they export. The result is that products with higher unit values are exported under quota regimes."[88] For this reason, "one cannot simply assume that unit values correspond to the same product when comparing quota and non-quota regimes. The product mix will include higher priced versions of the commodity in question in the quota regime" and, therefore, "one would expect higher unit values to the EC-15 countries."[89] According to Colombia, Costa Rica, Ecuador and Guatemala, the European Communities had imposed product standards for bananas that prohibited the sale of lower quality, and hence lower-priced, bananas.

198. Returning to the European Communities' arguments based on the *results* of the use of Eurostat c.i.f. data in a price gap calculation, the Arbitrator notes that the European Communities relies upon the Arbitrator's observation that a price gap of less than €75 per metric ton "is less than the current in-quota tariff rate, and does not appear to reflect any value for the existence of the tariff quota itself". In the European Communities' initial price gap calculations using Eurostat c.i.f. data, the price gap fell in a range between €53 per metric ton and €88 per metric ton. The European Communities considered these figures "unrealistic". In response, Honduras, Nicaragua and Panama have pointed out that, be-

---

87 Table 10 of the submissions of Honduras, Nicaragua and Panama show that, during the three-year period 2002-2004, the c.i.f. price of bananas in Norway averaged € 790 per metric ton compared to the EC-15 average of € 638 per metric ton. In para. 29 of their rebuttal of certain arguments raised by the European Communities in its oral statement, Colombia, Costa Rica, Ecuador and Guatemala submit weighted average prices of €781 per metric ton for Norway and of €951 per metric ton for Switzerland.

88 Rebuttal by Colombia, Costa Rica, Ecuador and Guatemala of certain arguments raised in the oral statement of the European Communities, para. 32.

89 *Ibid.*

cause the applied level of protection for bananas in the AC-10 during the period of January 2002 to April 2004 was lower than in the EC-15, the trade-weighted tariff for bananas in the EC-25, taken as a whole, was € 66 per metric ton.[90]

199. The Arbitrator also notes that, in the calculations that led it to discard Eurostat data, the European Communities deducted discharge and handling costs of €44 per metric ton from the internal price. The European Communities has expressed the view that it "does not believe that it is required to deduct ... discharge and handling costs" from the internal price side of its calculation.[91] The Interested Parties have argued that a proper price gap calculation requires deduction of discharge and handling costs. In this respect, the Arbitrator notes that paragraph 4 of the Attachment to Annex 5 defines "internal prices" as "representative *wholesale* prices *in the domestic market*" and that prices in the domestic market for traded goods, especially at the wholesale level, would be expected to include discharge and handling costs.

200. In the light of the foregoing, the Arbitrator considers that reasonable alternative explanations exist for the problems that the European Communities had found with Eurostat data. The Arbitrator does not discount the possibility that some of the quota rents from the European Communities' banana regime may flow to the exporters. But as the European Communities itself made clear during the first arbitration procedure:

> "[it] is not aware of any reliable information on quota rent divided between importers and exporters. Besides, the world banana market is over-supplied and an important quantity of bananas has difficulty in finding a market. In this situation, there are no reasons for the importer to transfer a part of the quota rent to the exporter."[92]

201. The Arbitrator finds it difficult to reconcile this stated position of the European Communities with its argument that the quota rents that flow to the exporters are so large that they make Eurostat c.i.f. data inappropriate for this price gap analysis. Thus, the Arbitrator is not convinced that the problems identified by the European Communities are significant enough to consider Eurostat c.i.f. "inappropriate" in the sense of paragraph 2 of the Attachment to Annex 5 of the Agreement on Agriculture.

202. It follows that the Arbitrator is not persuaded that the problems identified by the European Communities in respect of the Eurostat c.i.f. price were sufficient justification for departing from the "actual average c.i.f. unit values for the importing country" envisaged in paragraph 2 of the Attachment to Annex 5 as the basis for the external price. In addition, even assuming that there might have been valid reasons to discard the Eurostat data, for the reasons that follow, the Arbitrator is not convinced that the Sopisco "Non-EU" prices used by the Euro-

---

90 Submission by Honduras, Nicaragua and Panama, par. 149.

91 Reply of the European Communities to Written Question 20 from the Arbitrator.

92 Replies of the European Communities to the Questions from the Arbitrators, para. 33.

pean Communities as an alternative external price for purposes of its price gap calculation were appropriate in the circumstances.

(c) Alternative source of the external price

203. As noted above, the Attachment to Annex 5 of the *Agreement on Agriculture* provides for two possibilities for determining the external price, where c.i.f. data for the importing country itself is unavailable or inappropriate. These are: (a) appropriate average c.i.f. unit values of a near country; or (b) an estimate from average f.o.b. unit values of (an) appropriate major exporter(s) with certain adjustments. The European Communities explained that, with this framework in mind, after finding that Eurostat c.i.f. data was "inappropriate", it examined both of these alternative options. First, it took the c.i.f. prices of the AC-10 countries using Eurostat data. For the period, 2002-April 2004, this yielded an estimate of the external price of €439 per metric ton.[93] As an alternative to Eurostat c.i.f. data for the AC-10 countries, it took Sopisco News "Non EU" prices. For the period, 2002-April 2004, this yielded an estimate of the external price of €461 per metric ton.[94] The second alternative it considered was the f.o.b. prices for bananas reported by the Central Banks of Ecuador and Costa Rica. Adding estimates of spot freight rates from Sopisco News, it arrived at an estimate of the external price of €399 per metric ton. The European Communities chose the alternative that resulted in the lowest price gap result, namely, the highest estimate of the external price. On this ground, it chose to base its estimate of the external price on "Non-EU" banana prices published by Sopisco News.

204. The Interested Parties put forward a number of reasons why, in their view, Sopisco "Non EU" price was an inappropriate proxy of the external price of the European Communities. In particular, the Interested Parties emphasize that the acceding countries were markets that were unrepresentative and not comparable to the EC-15. There were differences in per capita incomes. The markets were emerging economies, with lower purchasing power compared to the EC-15. Banana exporters treated the markets in EC-15 and AC-10 countries differently. They were the last-resort markets for MFN bananas, where sales were often at marginal cost, and the prices earned were less than full market prices. In 2002-2004, bananas were in over-production, for which the AC-10 markets were chosen to dispose of that surplus. The impending accession of the AC-10 countries to the European Communities created artificial incentives to expand banana exports to the AC-10 markets at less than full market price. This could be justified because licenses for importing bananas would be distributed on the basis of "historical trade flows."[95]

205. The Arbitrator further notes that there remains some uncertainty regarding whether or not the Sopisco News "Non-EU" prices may be equated directly with AC-10 prices. Honduras, Nicaragua and Panama argued that, although the European Communities claims that the countries covered by "Non EU" were the AC-

93 Submission by the European Communities, para. 62.
94 *Ibid.*
95 Submission by Honduras, Nicaragua and Panama, paras. 164-167.

10, "neither [it] nor Sopisco News has anywhere substantiated that assumption".[96] In its response to the question by the Arbitrator on this issue, the European Communities referred to the fact that in week 20 of the year 2004, Sopisco News changed its designation of "Non EU" to "E10" and of "EU" to "E15".[97]

206. The Arbitrator finds that all these factors affect the appropriateness of using AC-10 prices as a proxy for the external price in the European Communities' price gap calculation.

207. The Arbitrator also notes that the Sopisco News "Non EU" is an *internal* price, as is evident from the data supporting the European Communities' calculations.[98] The price gap would therefore be established as the difference between two sets of internal prices. Effectively, what is being compared by the European Communities, is the level of protection from banana imports in the EC-25, on the one hand, with the level of protection in the AC-10, on the other hand. The Arbitrator recognizes that the use of internal price data from the "Non-EU" countries results in a lower price gap. However, the Arbitrator does not see how the Sopisco "Non EU" prices could serve as an "appropriate" proxy for the external price of the EC-25.

208. The Arbitrator considers that the use of Eurostat data for the purposes of the calculation of the external price may not have been free of problems in the context of European Communities' price gap calculation of its current banana import regime. However, the Arbitrator is not convinced, and has not been provided with sufficient evidence, that, effectively, a downward adjustment in the EC's external price that is in the magnitude of €136 per metric ton, was warranted.[99] The Arbitrator concludes that the European Communities underestimated the external price.

3. *Reference Period*

209. In its first award, the Arbitrator expressed the view "that it is important to reflect in the price gap calculation the existing banana regime of the European Communities. The use of the most recent representative reference period minimizes the need for ad hoc adjustments to be made to the data and corresponds as closely as possible to the trade regime as applied.[100]

210. In its revised proposal, the European Communities moved the reference period for its price gap calculation from 2000-2002 to the period 2002 to end-April 2004. It explained the reason for ending in April 2004, instead of taking the whole year 2004, as avoiding "a commingling of the trade regime of the EC-15 and the EC-25."[101] The Arbitrator is not persuaded that this is a sufficient

---

96 Submission by Honduras, Nicaragua and Panama, para. 163.

97 Answers to Questions by the European Communities, para. 13.

98 Calculation 1 in Exhibit EC-39.

99 See paragraph 82. Using the reference period, 2002 to April 2004, the external price using Eurostat c.i.f data is €597 per metric ton while the same calculation using Sopisco Non EU gives an external price of €461 per metric ton. This represents a difference of €136 per metric ton.

100 Award of the Arbitrator, para. 83.

101 Submission by the European Communities, para. 36.

explanation for not taking into account the whole year 2004. The calculations made by the European Communities of either the internal or external prices effectively commingle the regimes because an average is taken of the prices of the EC-15 and the AC 10 countries. In fact, commingling or blending will always be the consequence of taking an average (whether it be weighted or unweighted) of the EC-25. In this connection, Honduras, Nicaragua and Panama submitted that the European Communities chose to end its reference period in April 2004 because, if it had used Sopisco News prices for the full year of 2004, it would have found no external price from May 2004 onwards because the AC-10 countries had then become part of the European Communities.[102]

211. The Arbitrator notes that by using Eurostat c.i.f. data, one would be able to take the whole year of 2004 into account instead of just the first four months. And it appears that using the whole year would lead to a lower estimate of the external price. If one were to do so, the estimate of the external price would be €605 per metric ton instead of €597 per metric ton. These are additional reasons for concluding that Sopisco "Non EU" prices are not "appropriate average c.i.f. unit values of a near country" within the meaning of paragraph 2(a) of the Attachment to Annex 5.

C. *Conclusion Regarding the European Communities' Price Gap Calculation*

212. In the preceding sections, the Arbitrator considered all pertinent aspects of the European Communities' price gap calculation. In respect of the internal price, the Arbitrator examined the Interested Parties' general criticisms of the Sopisco News data[103], including the availability of alternative price data.[104] The Arbitrator also addressed several specific issues in respect of this internal price data, including: whether Sopisco News prices reflect actual prices[105]; whether an adjustment should be made to the extent Sopisco prices are drawn from the Hamburg market[106]; the inclusion of Chiquita prices[107]; and banana brand estimates.[108] In respect of the external price, the Arbitrator addressed whether Eurostat c.i.f. data for the European Communities was not "appropriate" for the European Communities' price gap calculation[109]; and also considered the European Communities' alternative external price data.[110] The Arbitrator also addressed the reference period used by European Communities for its price gap calculation.[111]

213. Based on its consideration of all these factors, and bearing in mind the absence of perfect price data for bananas, the Arbitrator concludes that the Euro-

---

102 Submission by Honduras, Nicaragua and Panama, para. 92.
103 *Supra*, paras. 57-70.
104 *Supra*, paras. 62-63.
105 *Supra*, paras. 59-68.
106 *Supra*, paras. 72-74.
107 *Supra*, paras. 75-77.
108 *Supra*, paras. 78-79.
109 *Supra*, paras. 87-105.
110 *Supra*, paras. 106-110.
111 *Supra*, paras. 112-114.

pean Communities' calculations did not reflect as accurately as possible the actual difference between internal and external prices, such that the results of the price gap calculation *overestimated* the level of the price gap. On this basis, the Arbitrator finds that the proposed tariff rebinding of €187 per metric ton would not result in at least maintaining total market access for MFN banana suppliers, regardless of whether or not a tariff quota of 775,000 mt is applied to banana imports of ACP origin and regardless of what supply response could be expected from EBA beneficiaries to the margin of preference resulting from the proposed tariff.

214. Because the Arbitrator's conclusion holds true regardless of the effect of the proposed tariff quota or EBA supply response, it is unnecessary for the Arbitrator to continue in its analysis to determine the manner in which these two additional factors would affect, or would not affect, the total market access of MFN suppliers. Accordingly, the Arbitrator makes no substantive findings in respect of either of these factors.

215. In reaching these conclusions, the Arbitrator emphasizes that it has considered the issues, and in particular the various price data, on the basis of the European Communities' proposal and the evidence that has been put before it. Although the Arbitrator is not satisfied that the European Communities has rectified the matter in accordance with the Annex to the Doha Waiver, it takes no view, and this award should not be taken to imply a view, as to the tariff level, or other elements, that would result in at least maintaining total market for MFN banana suppliers.

D. The European Communities' Simulation Model

216. The European Communities proposed a simulation model, which was intended to demonstrate that the proposed MFN tariff of €187 per metric ton and the tariff quota on ACP imports would maintain total market access for MFN banana suppliers. The simulation was not used to determine the MFN tariff nor the size of the tariff quota; rather it was used to confirm that the revised European Communities' proposal was consistent with at least maintaining total market access for MFN banana suppliers.

217. Like the model that was proposed by Honduras, Nicaragua and Panama in the first arbitration, the European Communities' model is a dynamic and partial equilibrium model of the global banana market. Where it differs in structure from that model is that it is also a "spatial" model. The European Communities claims this makes it "capable of representing policies which apply different treatment to products of different origin. Since one of the key issues in this Arbitration is the effect of the ACP preference on the market access opportunities for MFN suppliers, only a spatial model is capable of accurately reflecting bilateral trade flows and thus providing a satisfactory simulation of the European Communities' proposed regime."[112]

---

[112] Submission by the European Communities, para. 109.

218. The European Communities simulated the effect of an MFN tariff of €187 per metric ton and a tariff quota on ACP imports of 775,000 mt over the period from 2007 to 2013. The results of the model showed that the European Communities' proposal results in MFN exports increasing in 2007 by 360,100 tonnes over the level in 2002. If the projection to 2013 is taken into account, an increase of 771,200 tonnes over the level in 2002 is predicted.[113]

219. In the first arbitration, the Arbitrator noted that "economic modelling affords the analyst the possibility of taking into account a range of factors",[114] but cautioned that

> the choice and assignment of specific values to the various parameters in an economic modelling simulation can in itself be a source of complexities. Simulation models require more data than the price gap methodology, and the choice of parameters as well as the assignment of values to them make the results of such modelling as vulnerable (or as solid) as the assumptions upon which they are based.[115]

Thus, "the benefits from their use must be carefully balanced against the technical hurdles and uncertainties posed by the choice of parameters and data."[116]

220. The European Communities stated that, so far as possible, assumptions have been avoided by making use of information provided by sources such as FAO and the World Bank. When this was not possible, the assumptions made were conservative, and were systematically biased against the European Communities. In other words, where the modeller had to make assumptions, those assumptions were made against the interests of the European Communities.

221. But the Interested Parties identified a number of assumptions or features of the model that they found erroneous. Honduras, Nicaragua and Panama objected to the European Communities' assumptions about the values of European Communities' demand and ACP supply elasticities. Colombia, Costa Rica, Ecuador and Guatemala pointed to what they considered erroneous assumptions about transport costs in the European Communities' model that were inconsistent with official data.[117] This "anomaly" seems to have come from the bilateral transaction costs table which estimates the cost of moving bananas from exporting to importing country. The European Communities did not provide any reference or official source of the data represented in the table. In fact, it admitted that "[i]nformation on transportation and other costs incurred in international trading [of] bananas for all possible trade flows is non existent."[118]

222. The Arbitrator asked a question regarding the simulation results of the European Communities' model, which predicted that some large MFN suppliers will export zero volumes to the European Communities in some or in all years of

---

113 Submission by the European Communities, para. 117.
114 Award of the Arbitrator, para. 78.
115 Award of the Arbitrator, para 79.
116 *Ibid.*
117 Submission by Colombia, Costa Rica, Ecuador and Guatemala, paras. 214-215.
118 Answers to questions by the European Communities, para. 41.

the simulation. The Arbitrator noted the European Communities' confirmation of these results and its explanation that this was the most well known limitation of this class of models. It could be argued that, since the attraction of the European Communities' model is precisely its presumed ability to analyze bilateral trade flows, doubts are raised about a model that produces simulation results that are at variance with a reasonable expectation of how future banana exports to the EC-25 are likely to evolve.

223. The Arbitrator notes that there has been less debate over the European Communities' simulation model than over the price gap calculations. It recognizes that this reflects both the technical nature of the model and the complementary role it plays in the analysis. Because of the role that the simulation model plays in the European Communities' arguments, the Arbitrator does not believe that it can be treated as a methodology which is independent of the European Communities' price gap calculation. Having determined that the European Communities' price gap calculation would not result in at least maintaining total market access for MFN banana suppliers, the Arbitrator needs not deal with the simulation model as a separate method to confirm that the proposed tariff of €187 per metric ton and the tariff quota of 775,000 mt on ACP imports will maintain total market access for MFN suppliers.

VI. DETERMINATION

224. For the reasons stated in this award, the Arbitrator determines that the European Communities' proposed rectification, consisting of a new MFN tariff rate on bananas of €187 per metric ton and a 775,000 mt tariff quota on imports of bananas of ACP origin, would not result "in at least maintaining total market access for MFN banana suppliers", taking into account "all EC WTO market-access commitments relating to bananas". Consequently, the Arbitrator finds that the European Communities has failed to rectify the matter, in accordance with the fifth tiret of the Annex to the Doha Waiver.

Cumulative List of Published Disputes

www.ingramcontent.com/pod-product-compliance
Lightning Source LLC
Chambersburg PA
CBHW060913090326
40852CB00094B/1101
9780521886031